☑ W9-AFW-966

CANNON FINANCIAL INSTITUTE
CONCEPTS
FOR PROFESSIONALS

A COMPLETE LIBRARY OF ESSENTIAL FINANCIAL CONCEPTS

Content Meets Current FINRA Guidelines

Substantially similar material that meet current FINRA guidelines can be found in the current version of the Back Room Technician software.

CANNON FINANCIAL INSTITUTE

649-4 S. Milledge Avenue
Athens, GA 30605

Phone: 706.353.3346
Fax: 706.353.3994

www.cannonfinancial.com

18th Edition

This publication is designed to provide accurate and authoritative information in regard to the subject matter covered. It is sold with the understanding that the publisher is not engaged in rendering legal, accounting, or other professional services. If legal advice or other expert assistance is required, the services of a competent professional should be sought. – **From a Declaration of Principles jointly adopted by the Committee of the American Bar Association and a Committee of Publishers and Associations.**

Licensed to
Cannon Financial Institute, Inc.
649-4 S. Milledge Ave.
Athens, Georgia 30605
Phone: 706.353.3346 • Fax: 706.353.3994

ISBN 978-0-9826286-9-0
Copyright 2018

Advisys, Inc.
16969 Von Karman Avenue Ste 125
Irvine, CA 92606
Sales 800-777-3162 • FAX 949-250-0794

All right reserved.
No part of this publication may be reproduced, stored in a retrieval system,
or transmitted, in any form or by means, electronic, mechanical, photocopying,
recording, or otherwise, without prior written
permission of the publisher.

Printed in the U.S.A.

Contents

INCOME TAXES

INVESTMENTS

RETIREMENT PLANNING

Retirement Needs Analysis

Individual Retirement Plans

Employer Sponsored Plans

Education Funding Analysis

PROTECTING YOUR FINANCES

Property and Casualty

Life Insurance and Annuities

Survivor Needs Analysis

SOCIAL SECURITY AND OTHER GOVERNMENT PROGRAMS

ESTATE PLANNING

Advanced Estate Planning Tools

Estate Freezing Techniques

Life Insurance and Estate Taxation

Estate Planning Analysis

BUSINESS PLANNING

Basic Business Concepts

Business Continuation

Benefits to Business Owners

CHARITABLE PLANNING

ADVISOR SUPPORT

The Financial Planning Puzzle

Our financial lives often have many scattered pieces.

A coordinated financial plan provides a framework for achieving financial security.

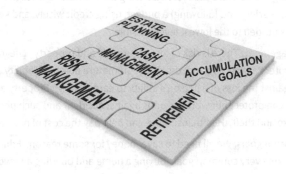

The Need for Financial Planning

Building a successful financial plan can be confusing. As we construct a plan, we find that our financial lives have many scattered pieces.

The Pieces of the Puzzle

Some of the financial issues that each of us can expect to face during life include:

- **Cash management:** More than just balancing the checkbook, cash management includes preparing (and following) a budget, using credit wisely, and keeping the income tax burden to the lowest level possible.

- **Risk management:** There is risk of loss of both life and property. Life insurance can be used to protect a family against the risk of premature death. Disability insurance can protect against the loss of a person's ability to earn a living. Property and casualty insurance can protect our worldly goods against accident and such perils as fire, flood, earthquake and theft. Health insurance can help pay the cost of needed medical care.

- **Accumulation goals:** We all need to save money for some reason. Educating our children is one very common goal. Buying a home and building an investment portfolio are two other typical accumulation goals.

- **Retirement:** Taking action today to insure that the later years are as comfortable and worry-free as possible.

- **Estate planning:** Recognizing that death is inevitable and planning for the ultimate transfer of our assets to our heirs.

The Need for Financial Planning

A coordinated financial plan provides a framework for achieving financial security.

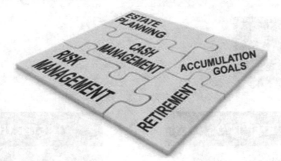

Steps to Achieving Financial Security

Solving financial problems in today's world takes work. Two basic steps are involved:

- **Step 1:** Choose Your Financial Planning Team: In our complex, ever-changing world, expert help is needed. Trained specialists such as your attorney, CPA, IRS enrolled agent, life insurance professional, health insurance agent, securities broker, and financial planner are generally members of your team.

- **Step 2:** Develop Your Plan: With the help of your team, the second step can be taken: the development of a systematic, integrated plan for dealing with each of these issues. This is called developing a financial plan.

You can choose to ignore these problems until it is too late. Or, you can take steps to put the puzzle together and achieve your financial security. The most important step is the first one.

Basic Steps in the Financial Planning Process

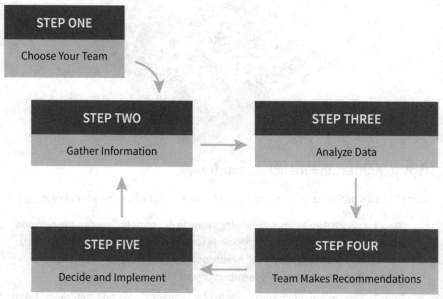

STEP ONE
Choose Your Team

STEP TWO
Gather Information

STEP THREE
Analyze Data

STEP FIVE
Decide and Implement

STEP FOUR
Team Makes Recommendations

The Basic Steps

- **Choose your team:** Choose, as needed, your financial planner, tax advisor, life insurance professional, property & casualty agent, health insurance agent, investment broker, attorney, charitable giving advisor, trust officer, or banker.
- **Gather information:** A completed fact finder serves to list your goals and objectives, shows your assets and liabilities, measures cash flow, and notes the current status of your retirement, estate, and risk management planning.
- **Analyze data:** To determine if current and future needs are met.
- **Team makes recommendations:** Review the suggestions made by your team.
- **Decide and implement:** Select the plan that best fits your needs and goals. As needed, sign essential documents, purchase insurance, and re-allocate investments.
- **Periodic review:** Starting the cycle over. Because the world is constantly changing, many advisors recommend an annual planning review.

Choose the Financial Planning Team

Financial planning is a complex field which covers many areas including investments, education planning, retirement planning, wills, trusts, insurance, accounting, business continuation, and estate, gift, and income taxes.

It would be difficult to find one person who is a trained and licensed expert in all of these areas. Most often, the needed skills and knowledge are available only by bringing together a financial planning team. The various members of your chosen team can then work closely with you to create an estate, to preserve it, and to and pass it on to your heirs with the least amount of expense and aggravation.

Potential members of the team may include the following:

The Captain of the Team

You are the captain of the team. The final decisions must be made by you after carefully reviewing the recommendations of the other members of your financial planning team.

Financial Planner

Often a member of the team will have special training in financial planning. A qualified financial planner should take a very active part in directing the formation of the overall financial plan.

Investment Specialist

Investors face a confusing range of investment tools, each with different characteristics and uses. Professional investment guidance is essential.

Tax Professional

Taxes consume a large part of our income and must be considered in all aspects of a financial plan.

Life Insurance Professional

Life insurance contracts differ greatly and are issued by companies with varying degrees of financial strength. A life insurance professional can help you choose a financially strong company, the correct type of policy for your situation, and the correct amount of insurance.

Property & Casualty Agent

Property & Casualty insurance helps protect the physical assets an individual owns from loss or damage.

Health and Disability Specialist

Health insurance can pay much of the cost of needed medical care. Disability insurance can help replace lost income if you are unable to work for a period of time. Long-term care insurance aids in paying for needed care if a disability or other severe health problem will continue for an extended period of time.

Estate Planning Attorney

Most attorneys can draft a basic will. However, one who specializes in estate planning law will be more familiar with the various tools and techniques available to save you and your heirs thousands of dollars in taxes, probate and administration expenses.

Trust Administrator

If you select a corporate fiduciary (a bank or trust company) as executor of your will or trustee of your trust, you should consider involving them in the development of the estate planning portion of your financial plan.

Planned-Giving Specialist

Charitable organizations often have planned-giving specialists who are well versed in methods of making lifetime gifts or bequests at the time of death, which can benefit you and your heirs.

Planning for the Recently Divorced

Being "suddenly single" can be an emotional and financial roller coaster. It can happen at any age and means that you are in charge of your personal finances. So, it's important to find the right people and resources to help make decisions on financial issues you might not be familiar with. When you have control over your finances, other decisions are easier and the transition to a new life is less stressful.

Create a Plan

For better or worse, we all have a "paper" trail. Following that trail makes creating a plan easier:

- Obtain copies of all key documents such as the divorce decree, bank and brokerage accounts, credit cards, IRS records, and insurance policies.

- Close all joint accounts and open new bank, credit card, and other accounts in your single name.

- Dis-inherit your former spouse. Create a new will and other needed estate planning documents and change the beneficiaries on your life insurance, 401(k), IRA, and pension accounts.

- Create and follow a realistic budget. Keep monthly payments on track so your credit isn't impaired.

If You're a Single Parent – Protect Yourself and the Kids

Be sure you have enough life and disability insurance to protect the children in case something happens to you. As a part of your new estate plan, detail your wishes for the care of your children if you're not around or are no longer able to care for them.

Maximize Your Employee Benefits

Be sure to explore all of the benefits your employer offers – and use the ones that make the most sense for you and those in your household. Employer-sponsored group health insurance, group term life insurance, and qualified retirement plans are valuable employee benefits.

Planning for the Recently Divorced

Reassess Your Long-Term Goals

Take the time to reassess your long-term goals, such as planning for retirement or funding college for the children. Is more education needed to reach your personal and professional goals?

- To reach your retirement goals, make maximum use of employer-provided plans such as a 401(k), 403(b), or pension plans. Consider a traditional or Roth IRA to supplement employer plans.

- Review any existing college funding plans. A reduction in household income may make additional financial aid available. High school counselors can help determine what options are available.

- Don't forget to think of yourself. Where do *you* want to go in life?

And Get the Professional Help You Need

Talk to friends and family for referrals to people they work with and trust. Make a list of your most important concerns and find experienced professionals in those areas.

Planning for Kids Going to College

For many young adults, going off to college is the first time they will be away from the family nest for any extended period of time. And frequently, it's also the first time that they will be required to deal directly with many of the financial issues and problems that characterize modern adult life.

Going to college is not only a half-step *out* of the family home; it's also a half-step *into* the adult world. The goal is not only to gain an education, but also to build the foundation for a successful life – financial and otherwise – in the years after college.

Steps to Financial Success in College

In broad outline, planning for a young adult at college is relatively simple: (1) make the best possible use of available financial resources, and (2) keep the almost inevitable accumulating debt to a minimum. Although debt is an inevitable part of the college experience for many, the less debt accumulated going to school means less debt to pay off afterwards.

- **Budgeting:** For many families, college funds are scarce, so it's essential to make the most of the resources that are available. The self-discipline to create, and then follow, a monthly budget is a key part of meeting this goal.

- **Credit card debt:** The college years are frequently a young person's first introduction to "credit," often in the form of a credit card. Responsible credit card use can build a credit record that will be a valuable asset in future years. Irresponsible credit card usage can do just the opposite.

- **Student debt:** Relatively few students complete their undergraduate studies without at least some student debt. If a graduate degree is involved, student debt levels can become quite high. Matching the earning potential of the degree sought with the amount of debt assumed is a key calculation. Also, making sure that student debt is spent for education, and not for non-essential items, is a good way to keep the debt levels to an absolute minimum.

- **Other financial aid:** School counselors may be able to identify other types of financial aid which don't involve additional debt, such as scholarship or work-study programs.

- **Car loans:** One essential item for many students – particularly those attending schools away from home – is a car. While an expensive sports car might be nice, basic, reliable transportation is more appropriate

- **Self-help:** It doesn't hurt to have the student work, at least part-time, and help pay for college with his or her own labor.

And if Professional Help is Needed?

Many families have existing relationships with financial professionals who will be glad to extend their services to a younger generation. Friends and family are also good sources of referrals to people they work with and trust.

Planning for the Adult Child at Home

An "empty nest" is a term frequently used by those who have finished raising their children. Of late, however, a weak economy, heavy student debt loads, and other personal issues have forced many adult children back to the shelter of the parental home. They're commonly known as "boomerang" children.

When they were first born, these boomerang kids didn't come with an instruction manual. As a parent, you likely followed the basic principles set by your parents, and then improvised when needed. In planning for an adult child at home, this same basic approach still works. Keep a few key principles in mind, and adjust your response to meet individual needs.

Points to Consider

- **Target the basic issue:** What brought the child back to the parental home? Begin by identifying the key problem and then list the steps needed to overcome it. Is there more than one problem? At the same time, move toward re-establishing the child's financial independence from the parents. There should be regular reviews of progress as well as firm deadlines for resolving each issue.

- **Employment:** If the adult child is unemployed, finding a new job should become the child's full-time "job." In an internet age, don't overlook "human" networking. Family, friends, teachers, coaches, and other community leaders are all good sources; frequently they are eager to help. As with all goals, periodically review how things are going.

- **Financial:** The parents and the adult child should create and follow a budget. Set limits on how much you're willing to supplement the cash needs of an adult child. Support is one thing; a free ride is something else. If a child is working, consider having them contribute to the monthly household expenses. Insist on a savings program, to help fund the "re-launch" into the wider world.

- **Living arrangements:** Everybody pitches in on the household chores, including the adult child. Set ground rules to cover how after-hours entrances, parties, and overnight guests will be handled. What about smoking or alcohol use? How and when can they use the family car?

- **Don't be afraid to say "No":** Sometimes saying "no" is the only right answer. At some point, an adult child needs to be able to survive – even if it means struggling - without the help of the parents.

And if Professional Help is Needed?

Many families have existing relationships with financial professionals who will be glad to extend their services to a younger generation. Friends and family are also good sources of referrals to people they work with and trust.

Planning for the "Sandwich" Generation

Even under the best of circumstances, planning your financial life can be complicated. Pursuing a career, raising a family, saving for college, and providing for your own retirement all take time and effort. For an increasing number of individuals, this already challenging situation becomes even more so when an aging parent needs help or an adult child (sometimes with children of their own) returns home.

And, not uncommonly, these events occur at the same time. For those in this situation, the term "sandwich" generation is an apt description.

Basic Planning Steps

Whether a planning problem is simple or complex, the same basic steps apply:

1. Define the goal (or goals). What is it you're trying to accomplish? You may have to prioritize among competing goals.
2. What resources are available? This could be time, money, the personal efforts of you and/or other family members, or governmental resources.
3. Develop a plan. List the steps needed to achieve each goal, and then carry them out.

Individual Points

Although every family and situation is unique, a few general thoughts may help:

- **Aging parents:** As a person ages, health problems can become overwhelming, to the point where the individual is no longer competent. If possible, planning ahead makes any transfer of responsibility (temporary or permanent) from a parent to an adult child much easier. Deciding when to intervene, what needs to be done, and who will be responsible are key issues.

- **College:** Ideally, every family should be able to save enough to pay for college for each child. If this is not possible, consider alternatives such as loans, scholarships, grants, or work/study programs. Consider starting at a local, two-year college and then transferring to a four-year institution.

Planning for the "Sandwich" Generation

- **Adult children:** "Boomerang" kids sometimes temporarily return to the family nest. What problem brought the adult child back to the parental home? Identify the steps needed to solve the problem and work to re-establish the adult child's financial independence from the parents. Don't be afraid to say "no." Loving support is one thing; a free ride is something else.

- **Yourself:** Continue funding your retirement; you can't make up the lost time if you stop or reduce your contributions. Try not to assume additional debt, take a withdrawal from your retirement plan, or dip into personal savings. Consider adult day care for your parent rather than quitting your job. Review your personal financial plan; what may have been appropriate in the past, may no longer be what you need. And, take the time to take care of yourself.

Don't Go It Alone

The advice and guidance of trained, experienced financial professionals can be invaluable. From estate planning and other legal issues, to investments and asset management, insurance, and income tax, get the help you need.

Planning for Women

Whether you are newly married, establishing a career, raising children, running a business, or taking care of aging parents, life can get very, very busy. And it's easy to put off tasks that may not have an immediate, tangible outcome, such as learning about and actively managing your personal finances.

At some point in your life you will likely be responsible for making key decisions that will impact your standard of living far into the future. Thus, it's important to take steps now to make sure you are informed and educated - so you can feel confident about the financial decisions you'll be making.

Plus, planning ahead puts you in the best possible position to deal with the inevitable problems that life brings to everyone.

Actions to Consider

- **Budgeting:** Create a monthly budget by considering all of your expenses, so you don't live beyond your means.

- **Savings:** Identify specific savings goals, such as a new car or a house. Establish an emergency fund with the goal of putting aside enough to cover six months' expenses.

- **Reduce debt:** Chip away at any debt you have by making more than the minimum payment. Start with the highest interest rate debt first.

- **Guard against risk:** Protect yourself and your family with necessary health, life, and disability insurance. Protect your possessions with auto and renter's or homeowner's insurance. Get the most out of your company's employee benefits program by taking advantage of available group coverage.

- **Retirement:** Contribute to your employer's 401(k), 403(b), or other pension plan. If a 401(k) plan is available, contribute at least the minimum percentage needed to qualify for the full employer match. If your employer doesn't offer a retirement plan, open an IRA and set up automatic contributions.

- **College:** If you have children, and once your retirement savings program is established, start saving for college. Explore 529 savings plans or other college saving vehicles while the children are young.

- **Estate plan:** Work with an attorney to develop a will and an estate plan that transfers your assets as efficiently as possible and with the least tax burden. Detail your wishes for the care of your children should something happen to you. Control the health care decisions that directly affect the life of you and your family by working with your attorney to legally document your wishes.

- **Check your progress:** Life is never static. And your plan shouldn't be either. Take time to periodically review your situation and check how you're progressing toward your goals. Are changes needed, or are you on course?

- **Educate the next generation:** The example you set, how you manage your money and the planning steps you take, can serve to instill healthy financial habits in your children.

Get Help When It's Needed

The advice and guidance of trained, experienced financial professionals can be invaluable. From estate planning and other legal issues, to investments, insurance, and income tax, get the help you need.

Planning for the Recent College Graduate

Graduating from college marks an important milestone in the lives of young adults. For many, it's the first time that they will be completely responsible for their own financial lives. And how well, or how poorly, they deal with these new financial responsibilities can have an impact that extends far into the future.

So, what steps should a recent college graduate take to get started on the right financial footing?

Beginning Steps to Financial Security

Graduating from college equips an individual with the intellectual tools necessary for career success. That's not necessarily the case when it comes to understanding money and how to manage it. But the basic steps to get started are usually quite simple:

- **Budgeting:** Create a monthly budget that includes all of your expenses, so you don't live beyond your means. Budgeting can help identify opportunities to make better use of current income.

- **Debt:** Many college graduates start their professional careers with significant student debt. Start with the highest interest rate debt first and pay down your debt as aggressively as you can. Don't add to your debt unnecessarily.

- **Savings:** Pay yourself first! Start by building an emergency fund with the goal of saving enough to cover six months' expenses. Then, target other savings goals such as a down payment on a home.

- **Risk management:** Protect yourself with necessary health, life, and disability insurance. Protect your possessions with auto and renter's or homeowner's insurance. Get the most out of your company's employee benefits program by taking advantage of any available group insurance.

- **Retirement:** Start contributing to your employer's 401(k), 403(b), or other pension plan. If a 401(k) plan is available, contribute at least the minimum percentage to qualify for the full employer match. If your employer doesn't offer a retirement plan, open an IRA and set up automatic contributions.

- **Estate plan:** Work with an attorney to develop a will and an estate plan that transfers your assets as efficiently as possible and with the least tax burden. Control the health care decisions that directly affect the life of you and your family by working with your attorney to legally document your wishes.

- **Get a "financial" education:** Learn how to "use" money. It's important to have a good understanding of investing, insurance, income taxes, and employee benefits.

Get Help When It's Needed

The advice and guidance of trained, experienced financial professionals can be invaluable. Many families have existing relationships with financial professionals who will be glad to extend their services to a younger generation. Friends and co-workers are also good sources of referrals to those they work with and trust.

Life Events Checklist

Change is a constant part of every life. In order to determine how we may best serve you, please complete the form below and return it to us at your earliest convenience.

Common Life Events

- ❑ New child or grandchild
- ❑ New job or promotion
- ❑ Receipt of an inheritance
- ❑ Major investment gain/loss
- ❑ Health concerns

- ❑ Change in marital status
- ❑ Change in estate plan
- ❑ Sale or purchase of home
- ❑ Start/purchase a business
- ❑ Sold or acquired assets

- ❑ Death of family member
- ❑ New investments or insurance
- ❑ Retirement
- ❑ Gain/loss business partner
- ❑ Other: _____

Areas of Interest or Concern

- ❑ Retirement planning
- ❑ Estate planning
- ❑ Major asset purchase/lease
- ❑ Business/exec. benefits
- ❑ Pers. property/liability ins.

- ❑ Education funding
- ❑ Income tax planning
- ❑ Planning for parents
- ❑ Business continuation
- ❑ Disability income

- ❑ Investment review
- ❑ Survivor benefit planning
- ❑ Health/LTC planning
- ❑ Charitable giving
- ❑ Other: _____

Additional Comments and Notes

_____

_____

_____

Contacting You

Name:_____ Address:_____

Telephone:_____

Best time to call:_____

- ❑ Please contact me as soon as possible   Email:_____

Consumer Price Index

The Consumer Price Index is the government's method of measuring the price of goods and services bought by urban wage earners and clerical workers. The graph[1] below charts the overall increase in the cost of living since 1967, as a result of inflation. Over the last 50 years, the average annual inflation rate in the U.S. has been 3.85%.

Consumer Price Index

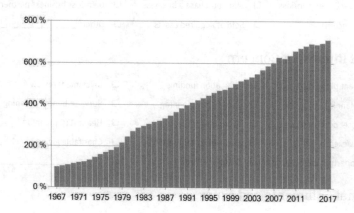

[1] Source: U.S. Bureau of Labor Statistics (CPI-W) (1967 – 2017).

Dealing with Identity Theft

What is Identity Theft?

In an increasingly inter-connected world, the possibility of having private personal and financial information deliberately stolen or accidentally exposed to unauthorized eyes is widely seen as a growing risk. The term "Identity Theft," (ID Theft) is used to describe a situation where such personal information – normally private – is somehow made "public" and then used for an illicit or criminal purpose.

Identity Theft Often Results in Fraud

Common types of ID Theft fraud include:

- **Financial fraud:** Existing account fraud involves essentially "taking over" an existing checking or savings account, draining funds from the account, or running up excess charges on a credit card. New account fraud involves creating new checking, savings, or credit card accounts; the victim is often not aware that these accounts have been opened.

- **Tax identity fraud:** An identity thief can use a stolen Social Security Number (SSN) to file an income tax return, receive a refund, and then disappear before the legitimate owner of the SSN can file his or her own return. A stolen SSN can also be used in schemes involving welfare fraud, unemployment fraud, or Social Security benefit fraud.

- **Child identity fraud:** Some individuals will use a child's identity to obtain credit. With this type of fraud, it may be years before the cime is discovered.

- **Medical identity fraud:** Medical ID fraud is used to illegally obtain medical treatment or supplies.

What to Do If You're a Victim of Identity Theft

Although the specific details will vary from case to case, if you're a victim of ID Theft you'll generally go through these steps:

1. Contact the fraud department of the institution involved. You will need to explain that your identity has been stolen. The affected accounts will need to be closed or frozen so that no new withdrawals or charges may be made. It's also a good idea to change passwords, PINs, and log-in names.

2. Contact one of the three major credit bureaus[1] and set up a "fraud alert." A fraud alert is a warning on your credit file that credit issuers should take extra precautions before granting credit to someone claiming to be you.

- **Equifax:** https://www.equifax.com/

- **Experian:** https://www.Experian.com/

- **TransUnion:** https://www.Transunion.com/

Once you have set up a fraud alert with one of these three credit reporting bureaus, the other two bureaus will be notified. A fraud alert lasts 90 days, is free to set up, and can be renewed as many times as you feel is necessary. Each time a consumer sets up or renews a fraud alert, the consumer is entitled to a free copy of his or her credit report from each credit reporting bureau. If an individual is confirmed to be a victim of ID Theft, he or she can set up an extended fraud alert, for up to seven years.

3. Review your credit report to identify accounts or transactions that you don't recognize. This will help later when making any reports to authorities.

4. Consider setting up a credit "freeze." A credit freeze effectively closes (except for existing accounts and certain government agencies) your credit report until you lift or remove the freeze. There may be a fee involved to set up a credit freeze and you'll need to contact each of the credit reporting bureaus separately.

5. Consider reporting the identity theft to appropriate authorities:

- **Federal Trade Commission (FTC):** The FTC maintains a website dedicated to dealing with ID Theft at https://www.identitytheft.gov/. The website allows you to document what happened and helps to develop a step-by-step plan to recover from the theft. Having reported and documented the theft can help later with getting fraudulent information removed or blocked from your credit report. It can also help in dealing with creditors and debt collectors from reporting and attempting to collect debts you didn't incur.

- **Your local police:** Report the ID theft to your local police or law enforcement. A police report can provide additional support when disputing fraudulent charges.

---

[1] You may also wish to contact a fourth, smaller credit bureau, Innovis, at https://www.innovis.com/.

6. Begin repairing the damage. This may involve a number of steps:

- Closing new accounts fraudulently opened in your name and opening new, valid accounts to replace them.

- Removing fraudulent charges from your accounts.

- Correcting your credit report.

- Defending yourself against debt collectors seeking to recover debts you didn't create.

Preventing Identity Theft

As the foregoing list makes clear, clearing your name after someone steals your identity and uses it fraudulently can involve enormous time and effort. There are things that can be done to prevent – or minimize - the damage from ID Theft. Some basic steps might include:

- **Check your credit report regularly:** Consumers are entitled to one free credit report each year from each of the major credit reporting bureaus.

- **Check your accounts regularly:** Internet access allows an account owner to check an account more frequently than the usual monthly statement. Limiting the number of checking or credit card accounts can facilitate this process.

- **Be safe on the internet:** Always use security software with a firewall and anti-virus protection. Create passwords that are complex and difficult to break. Learn to recognize and avoid "phishing" (pronounced "fishing") e-mails asking you to click on a link and provide personal data. When shopping on the internet, check out companies you buy from to be sure they are legitimate.

- **Protect portable devices:** Portable devices such as cell phones and laptop computers need to be protected. At a minimum, any device with a screen needs a strong password to access the device.

- **Telephone calls and texts:** Be aware that threatening calls and texts can come from identity thieves posing as legitimate organizations such as your bank, credit card, or even the IRS.

Other Resources

There are a number of internet resources available to help individuals learn about and deal with ID Theft:

- **Federal Trade Commission:** https://www.identitytheft.gov/

- **Consumer Financial Protection Bureau:** https://www.consumer.gov/articles/1015-avoiding-identity-theft

- **Internal Revenue Service (IRS):** https://www.irs.gov/identity-theft-fraud-scams/identity-protection

- **Privacy Rights Clearinghouse:** https://www.privacyrights.org/

- **ID Theft Resource Center:** https://www.idtheftcenter.org/

Cash Management Tools

There is a wide range of accounts available to a consumer to control his or her monthly cash flow. Such cash management tools are characterized by easy access to funds, as well as providing for safety of principal.[1] They are typically used for transaction purposes, or as a place to store readily available savings.

Transaction-Oriented Accounts

There are several different types of accounts that are used for transactions such as paying bills:

- **Demand deposits (checking accounts):** Demand deposits in banks and savings and loans are accounts which do not earn interest and which are payable to the owner on demand. Checks or electronic debit cards are used to transfer funds to a third party. Most financial institutions offering checking accounts are protected by federal deposit insurance on account balances up to $250,000.

- **Negotiable order of withdrawal (NOW):** NOW accounts are a type of interest bearing savings account against which checks can be written or electronic debits made. Credit unions offer a similar option in the form of a share-draft account. Most financial institutions offering NOW accounts are protected by federal deposit insurance on account balances up to $250,000.

- **Money market deposit accounts (MMDAs):** Like NOW accounts, MMDAs are a form of savings account against which checks can be written. Unlike NOW accounts, however, MMDAs are limited to six transactions per month. Transfers in excess of these limits can be subject to penalties. Minimum balance requirements for MMDA accounts tend to be larger than for NOW accounts, and MMDA accounts usually pay a slightly higher rate of interest. Most financial institutions offering MMDA accounts are protected by federal deposit insurance, on account balances up to $250,000.[2]

---

[1] Most checking and savings accounts in the U.S. are protected by either the Federal Deposit Insurance Corporation (FDIC) or the National Credit Union Administration (NCUA).

[2] Some mutual funds offer a money market account with a name similar to money market deposit account. These mutual funds are not protected by federal deposit insurance.

Savings Accounts

Savings accounts differ from transaction-oriented accounts in that access to funds in savings accounts may be restricted.

- **Statement savings accounts:** Statement savings accounts, formerly known as "passbook" savings accounts, usually accept small deposits, have no fixed maturity date and pay a relatively low interest rate. Banks and savings and loans that provide this type of account can require a 30-day notice before funds are withdrawn. In practice, however, most institutions do not require advance notice before allowing depositors to withdraw funds. Most financial institutions offering these accounts are protected by federal deposit insurance, on account balances up to $250,000.

- **Certificates of deposit (CDs):** CDs are bank or credit union liabilities which have a fixed maturity date and require certain minimums, for example, $10,000. Some institutions will issue a CD for as little as $500. Interest rates can be either fixed or variable. A substantial penalty[1] generally applies for withdrawals made before the maturity date. Most financial institutions offering these certificates are protected by federal deposit insurance, on account balances up to $250,000.

- **Jumbo CDs:** Jumbo CDs are similar to regular CDs in that they are obligations of the issuing financial institution, have a fixed maturity date, and earn a specified rate of interest. Technically, jumbo CDs are issued only in amounts of $100,000 or more. The interest rate can be either fixed or variable. Penalties apply if funds are withdrawn before the maturity date.[1] Most institutions offering these certificates are protected by federal deposit insurance, on account balances up to $250,000. Amounts in excess of $250,000 are not protected by federal deposit insurance.

Other Options

In addition to the traditional cash management tools available through banks, savings and loans, and credit unions, several other options are available.

---

[1] For certificates with a maturity of less than one year, the penalty is loss of three months' interest; for certificates longer than one year, the penalty is loss of six months' interest.

- **Money market mutual funds (MMMFs):** Money market mutual funds are a specialized type of mutual fund that invests in short term debt such as CDs, high-grade commercial paper, and U.S. Treasury securities. MMMFs are sold by prospectus[1] and usually have minimum balance and transaction limits. Such funds strive to maintain a constant share price of $1.00 per share. There is no guarantee that a fund will be able to maintain a constant share price, nor is there government insurance for such funds. MMMFs typically pay a slightly higher return than do federally insured accounts.

- **U.S. savings bonds:** U.S. savings bonds are both issued and redeemed by the federal government. As an asset class, they are considered to be very safe from default risk and thus earn a relatively low rate of interest. There are three types of savings bonds:

  - **Series EE bonds:** Series EE bonds are considered the "classic" form of U.S. government savings bond:

  - **Paper Series EE bonds:** Effective January 1, 2012, new Series EE bonds may only be purchased in <u>electronic</u> form. Prior to that date, paper EE bonds could be purchased over-the counter at banks and other financial institutions. Such paper EE bonds were sold at 50% of face value, in denominations ranging from $50 to $10,000. "Interest" on existing paper EE bonds is earned by a gradual increase in the value of the bonds.

  - **Electronic Series EE bonds:** Electronic Series EE bonds are purchased at face value, in exact amounts of $25 or more, via the U.S. government's TreasuryDirect website.

  - **Series I bonds:** Series I savings bond strive to provide some protection against inflation. They have a return composed of a (1) fixed-interest rate and (2) an inflation-adjusted rate.

---

[1] The prospectus contains valuable information concerning how an investment works, its goals and risks, and any charges or expenses involved. The prospectus is intended to provide an investor with the facts necessary to make an informed investment decision.

- **Paper Series I bonds:** Like paper Series EE bonds, effective January 1, 2012, new paper Series I bonds were no longer available over-the-counter at banks and other financial institutions. Up to $5,000 in paper Series I bonds per year may still be purchased via TreasuryDirect, but <u>only</u> if paid for with an IRS tax refund. Paper I bonds are issued at face value, in six denominations, $50, $100, $200, $500, $1,000, and $5,000.

- **Electronic Series I bonds:** Electronic Series I bonds are purchased at face value, in exact amounts of $25 or more, via the TreasuryDirect website.

- **Purchase limits:** Specific limits apply to the dollar amount of the various types of savings bonds that may be purchased by a single individual or entity in one calendar year. Savings bonds purchased as gifts are <u>not</u> included in these annual limits.

  - Electronic EE bonds: $10,000.
  - Paper I bonds: $5,000 (only with IRS tax refund).
  - Electronic I bonds: $10,000.

- **Series HH bonds:** Series HH bonds were issued at face value, in $500, $1,000, $5,000, and $10,000 denominations, and pay interest every six months. August 2004 was the last month that the U.S. Treasury issued new HH bonds. Before that date, investors could acquire HH bonds by exchanging matured EE/E bonds, or by reinvesting matured series HH/H bonds.

- **Asset management accounts:** Asset management accounts, available through banks, brokerages and insurance companies, combine a number of different financial tools in one package. Such accounts typically include a brokerage account, bank checking account, and a money market mutual fund. The linked accounts enable excess cash to be automatically swept into the money market fund. Other features such as a credit or debit card, or personal line of credit, may also be included. A consolidated monthly statement covers all accounts.

The various elements of an asset management account may or may not be protected by federal deposit insurance. For example, funds kept in a bank checking account are usually protected by federal deposit insurance. Dollar amounts kept in a money market fund, however, are not protected by government deposit insurance.

FDIC Deposit Insurance

The Federal Deposit Insurance Corporation (FDIC) is an independent agency of the United States government. Established in 1934, in the wake of a disastrous series of bank failures throughout the country, the FDIC's purpose is to protect the depositors of insured banks and savings associations in the United States against the loss of their deposits if the bank or savings association fails. While this "insurance" is funded through premiums paid by the participating banks, the FDIC is ultimately backed by the full faith and credit of the United States government.

How Much Does FDIC Deposit Insurance Cover?

The FDIC covers depositors' accounts at each insured bank, dollar-for-dollar, including principal and any accrued interest, through the date of the insured bank's closing, up to the insurance limits. The standard deposit insurance amount is $250,000 per depositor, per insured bank, for each ownership category.

The FDIC insures deposits that a person holds in one insured bank separately from any deposits that the person may hold in a separately chartered[1] insured bank. The FDIC also provides separate insurance coverage for funds depositors may have in different categories of legal ownership, even if the accounts are with the same insured bank. Thus a customer who has multiple accounts may qualify for more than $250,000 in insurance coverage if the customer's funds are deposited in different ownership categories and the requirements for each ownership category are met.

Ownership Categories

There are a number of "ownership categories" that qualify for FDIC deposit insurance coverage:

Category	Description	Coverage Limit
Single Account	An account owned by one person. May be an individual, a sole proprietorship account, or an individual acting as an agent for someone else.	Up to $250,000 per person, per bank

---

[1] Funds deposited in separate branches of the same insured bank are not separately insured.

FDIC Deposit Insurance

Category	Description	Coverage Limit
Retirement Accounts	A traditional or Roth IRA, a SEP IRA, or a SIMPLE IRA. Also certain self-directed defined contribution plans, or a Sec. 457 deferred compensation plan, whether self-directed or not.	Up to $250,000 per person, per bank.
Joint Account	An account owned by two or more persons. FDIC insurance applies to joint accounts owned in any manner conforming to applicable state law.	Up to $250,000 per co-owner, per bank.[1]
Revocable Trust Account	A deposit account owned by one or more people that identifies one or more beneficiaries who will receive the funds upon the death(s) of the owners. May be informal (Totten Trust, pay-on-death) or formal, as in a living or family trust.	*Five or fewer beneficiaries*: deposits are insured for up to $250,000 per unique beneficiary. *Six or more beneficiaries*: Varies.[2]
Irrevocable Trust Account	A deposit account held in connection with a trust established by statute or written trust agreement in which the owner contributes cash and gives up all power to change or cancel the trust. May also come into being with the death of the owner of a revocable trust.	Generally, insured up to $250,000 per unique beneficiary.
Employee Benefit Plan Account	A deposit of a pension plan, defined benefit plan, or other employee benefit plan that is *not* self-directed. The FDIC insures the deposits, not the plan itself.	Generally, up to $250,000 for each participant's interest in a plan.
Corporation, Partnership, or Unincorporated Association Account	Deposits owned by corporations, partnerships, and unincorporated associations, including for-profit and not-for-profit organizations.	Up to $250,000 per entity.

[1] All co-owners must be living people and have equal withdrawal rights. Other requirements apply.

[2] If all beneficiaries have an equal interest, the trust owner receives up to $250,000 of insurance for each unique beneficiary. If the beneficiaries have *unequal* interests, the owner's deposits are insured for the greater of: (1) the sum of each beneficiary's actual interest in the trust, up to $250,000 per unique beneficiary, or (2) $1,250,000.

FDIC Deposit Insurance

Category	Description	Coverage Limit
Government Accounts	Deposits owned by the United States, including federal agencies; a state, county or municipality, or any subdivision thereof; the District of Columbia, Puerto Rico; other government possessions and territories; and an Indian tribe.	*In-state accounts*: Up to $250,000 for the combined amount of all time and savings accounts, plus up to $250,000 for the combined amount of all demand deposits. *Out-of-state accounts*: Up to $250,000 for the combined amount of all accounts.

An Example

Consider Joe Saver, who has $100,000 in each of three different accounts, all at the same bank. Because all accounts are under the same ownership category, Joe is underinsured by $50,000.

Account	Amount		Totals	Amount
Checking Account	$ 100,000		Total	$ 300,000
Savings Account	$ 100,000		FDIC Limit	$ 250,000
Certificate of Deposit (CD)	$ 100,000		**Uninsured Deposits**	$ 50,000

To cover all of his deposits, Joe could simply move one of his accounts to another bank.

Account	Bank	Amount		Total: All Banks	Amount
Checking Account	Bank A	$ 100,000		Total	$ 300,000
Savings Account	Bank A	$ 100,000		FDIC Limit	$ 500,000
Certificate of Deposit (CD)	Bank B	$ 100,000		**Uninsured Deposits**	$ -

What Types of Accounts Does FDIC Deposit Insurance Cover?

- Checking accounts.
- Negotiable order of withdrawal (NOW) accounts.

- Savings accounts.

- Money market deposit accounts (MMDA).

- Time deposits (such as CDs).

- Official items issued by a bank (cashier's check or money order).

Types of Assets FDIC Deposit Insurance Does NOT Cover

FDIC deposit insurance does not protect the following assets, even if purchased at an insured bank:

- Stocks, bonds, or mutual funds.

- Life insurance policies.

- Annuities.

- Municipal securities.

- U.S. Treasury securities.

- Safe deposit boxes or their contents.

Additional Information

Additional information about FDIC deposit insurance can be obtained by visiting the FDIC website at http://www.fdic.gov/ or by calling 1-877-275-3342.

The Personal Budget

The basic purpose of a personal budget is to plan how an individual's money will be spent. Given limited financial resources, a budget is a method of managing personal cash flow, to meet current needs and save for the future.

Reasons to Prepare a Personal Budget

- **A planning tool:** Correctly used, a personal budget can ensure that income and expenditures match, both in amount and timing. It can both spotlight potential cash-flow problems, and identify opportunities to make better use of current income.

- **A yardstick to measure progress:** By comparing the planned budget against actual results, an individual can see if progress is being made toward meeting specific goals. This measuring process will often highlight areas where changes should be made.

Preparing a Personal Budget

- **Past income and expenditures:** This initial step entails recording information on past cash flow, both income and spending. Ideally, a year's worth of data should be gathered, to even out the effect of seasonal variations. Paycheck stubs, check registers, cancelled checks, copies of paid bills and recent income tax returns are excellent sources of this information. An individual may also want to keep a daily spending diary for a short period of time.

- **Set goals:** Clear goals should be set, with both specific dollar amounts and a realistic time frame for accomplishing each goal. A goal can be as simple and immediate as making ends meet each month, or as complex and long term as planning for retirement.

- **Maintain records:** Perhaps the most difficult part of the budgeting process is consistently keeping adequate monthly records of income and expenditures.

- **Periodic review:** A periodic review, comparing the planned budget with actual results, provides a means of measuring progress toward an individual's goals. The review will usually indicate if changes should be made, either in income, expenditures or both.

National Spending Patterns

How does your spending compare with these broad national budget averages?[1]

	National Spending
Food	12.6%
Clothing and Services	3.1%
Housing	33.0%
Personal	20.6%
Medical	8.0%
Transportation	15.8%
Other	6.9%
Totals	100%

[1] Source: Bureau of Labor Statistics, Consumer Expenditures 2016 August 29, 2017.

The Personal Budget Worksheet

Name: _____

Period covered - From: _____ To: _____

Item	Historical	Current Budget	Current Actual	Difference
Debt, savings and investment				
Credit and charge cards	$_____	$_____	$_____	$_____
Other installment loans	$_____	$_____	$_____	$_____
Education fund	$_____	$_____	$_____	$_____
Retirement	$_____	$_____	$_____	$_____
Other savings goals	$_____	$_____	$_____	$_____
Other	$_____	$_____	$_____	$_____
Total debt, savings, etc.:	$_____	$_____	$_____	$_____
Food				
Home consumption	$_____	$_____	$_____	$_____
Outside the home	$_____	$_____	$_____	$_____
Total food:	$_____	$_____	$_____	$_____
Clothing				
Clothing and shoes	$_____	$_____	$_____	$_____
Cleaning, laundry	$_____	$_____	$_____	$_____
Jewelry, watches, etc.	$_____	$_____	$_____	$_____
Total clothing:	$_____	$_____	$_____	$_____
Housing				
Rent or mortgage	$_____	$_____	$_____	$_____
Real estate taxes	$_____	$_____	$_____	$_____
Insurance	$_____	$_____	$_____	$_____
Furniture and furnishings	$_____	$_____	$_____	$_____
Appliances	$_____	$_____	$_____	$_____
Cleaning, repairs and maint.	$_____	$_____	$_____	$_____
Electricity, gas and heating	$_____	$_____	$_____	$_____
Water and sewer	$_____	$_____	$_____	$_____
Telephone, cable	$_____	$_____	$_____	$_____
Other housing	$_____	$_____	$_____	$_____
Total housing:	$_____	$_____	$_____	$_____
Totals for this page:	$_____	$_____	$_____	$_____

The Personal Budget Worksheet

Name: _____

Period covered - From: _____ To: _____

Item	Historical	Current Budget	Current Actual	Difference
Personal and Legal				
Personal care and toiletries	$_____	$_____	$_____	$_____
Child care	$_____	$_____	$_____	$_____
Legal and accounting	$_____	$_____	$_____	$_____
Life and disability insurance	$_____	$_____	$_____	$_____
Other personal and legal	$_____	$_____	$_____	$_____
Total personal and legal:	$_____	$_____	$_____	$_____
Medical				
Medicines	$_____	$_____	$_____	$_____
Doctors, dentists and hospitals	$_____	$_____	$_____	$_____
Health insurance	$_____	$_____	$_____	$_____
Other medical	$_____	$_____	$_____	$_____
Total medical:	$_____	$_____	$_____	$_____
Transportation				
Auto payments	$_____	$_____	$_____	$_____
Repairs and maintenance	$_____	$_____	$_____	$_____
Insurance	$_____	$_____	$_____	$_____
Gas, oil and tires	$_____	$_____	$_____	$_____
Public transportation	$_____	$_____	$_____	$_____
Other transportation	$_____	$_____	$_____	$_____
Total transportation:	$_____	$_____	$_____	$_____
Miscellaneous				
Books, magazines and newspapers	$_____	$_____	$_____	$_____
Vacations	$_____	$_____	$_____	$_____
Entertainment and clubs	$_____	$_____	$_____	$_____
Charitable	$_____	$_____	$_____	$_____
Education	$_____	$_____	$_____	$_____
Other miscellaneous	$_____	$_____	$_____	$_____
Total miscellaneous:	$_____	$_____	$_____	$_____
Totals for this page:	$_____	$_____	$_____	$_____
Totals from previous page:	$_____	$_____	$_____	$_____
Grand totals:	$_____	$_____	$_____	$_____

Personal Cash Flow Statement

Consumption Item	Your Budget		National Spending[1]
Food	$250	13.0%	12.6%
Clothing and Services	$75	3.9%	3.1%
Housing	$800	41.6%	33.0%
Personal[2]	$200	10.4%	20.6%
Medical	$50	2.6%	8.0%
Transportation	$150	7.8%	15.8%
Other	$400	20.8%	6.9%
Totals	**$1,925**	**100.0%**	100.0%
After-tax income	**$2,250**		
Discretionary income	**$325**		

[1] Source: Bureau of Labor Statistics, Consumer Expenditures 2016, August 29, 2017.
[2] Personal includes personal insurance, pensions, entertainment, and cash contributions.

Debt, Income, Mortgage and Education Analysis (DIME)

Assumptions:

D Total amount of **Debt:** $37,000
- Current Debt: $27,000
- Final Expenses: $10,000

I Current monthly **Income** of $5,000 to be replaced for 12 years: $720,000

M **Mortgage** Balance: $294,000

E **Education** costs of $80,000 for 2 children: $160,000

Total available funds: $800,000
- Available Assets: $300,000
- Life Insurance Proceeds: $500,000

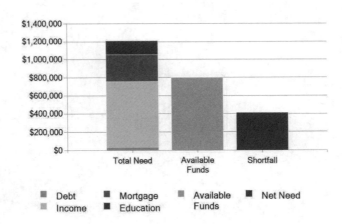

Based upon your current needs, you will need an additional $411,000 in life insurance to meet all your needs.

Personal Finance Data

Personal

Client(s) name	
1) Paul	Johnson
2) Sally	Johnson

Income

Annual employment income

- Client One $ 87,000
- Client Two $ 65,000

Other Income

- Interest and dividends $ 10,770
- Other $ 3,250

Savings & Expenses

Monthly Expenses

Housing	$	3,547	Medical	$	535
Food	$	1,200	Transportation	$	1,556
Clothing	$	525	Entertainment	$	500
Utilities	$	206	Education	$	
Federal Taxes	$		Debt Repayment	$	240
State Taxes	$		Personal	$	359
Other Taxes	$		Other	$	525
Insurance	$	782			

Monthly Savings

Education	$	250	Other	$	1,500
Retirement	$	2,110			

Retirement Plans

Client 1

	Account Name	Balance		Annual Rate of Return
1	My 401(k)	$	106,000	7%
2	My IRA	$	30,000	5%
3		$		%
4		$		%
5		$		%
6		$		%
7		$		%
8		$		%

Client 2

	Account Name	Balance		Annual Rate of Return
1	SEP	$	16,500	6%
2	TSA	$	60,000	4%
3		$		%
4		$		%
5		$		%
6		$		%
7		$		%
8		$		%

Other Assets & Debt

	Asset Name	Balance		Annual Rate of Return	Asset Debt	
1	Savings Account	$	6,000	6%	$	
2		$		%	$	
3		$		%	$	
4		$		%	$	
5		$		%	$	

Other Assets & Debt

Asset Name	Balance	Annual Rate of Return	Asset Debt
6	$	%	$
7	$	%	$
8	$	%	$
9	$	%	$
10	$	%	$
Cash	$ 500	%	
Residence/Mortgage	$ 500,000	%	$ 250,000
Other Debt			$ 25,000

Cash Flow

The basic purpose of a cash flow statement is to determine how your money is being spent. Ideally, a year's worth of data should be gathered, to even out the effect of seasonal variations. Paycheck stubs, check registers, cancelled checks, copies of paid bills and recent income tax returns are excellent sources of this information. If desired, you may want to keep a daily spending diary for a short period of time.

Income

Employment	$152,000	
Interest and dividends	10,770	
Other	3,250	
Total Income		**$166,020**

Expenses and Savings

Household expenses	65,736	
Taxes	0	
Other expenses	53,964	
Savings	46,320	
Total Expenses and Savings		**166,020**
		$0

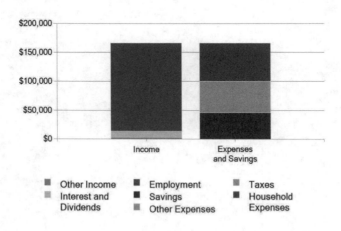

Cash Flow

Cash Flow Detail

The basic purpose of a cash flow statement is to determine how your money is being spent. Ideally, a year's worth of data should be gathered, to even out the effect of seasonal variations. Paycheck stubs, check registers, cancelled checks, copies of paid bills and recent income tax returns are excellent sources of this information. If desired, you may want to keep a daily spending diary for a short period of time.

Income

Employment		$152,000	
Interest and dividends		10,770	
Other		3,250	
	Total Income		$166,020

Expenses

Household			
Housing		42,564	
Food		14,400	
Clothing		6,300	
Utilities		2,472	
	Total Household		65,736
Taxes			
Federal		0	
State		0	
Other		0	
	Total Taxes		0
Other			
Insurance		9,384	
Medical		6,420	
Transportation		18,672	
Entertainment		6,000	
Education		0	
Debt repayment		2,880	
Personal		4,308	
Other		6,300	
	Total Other Expenses		53,964

Savings

Education		3,000	
Retirement		25,320	
Other		18,000	
	Total Savings		46,320
			$0

Net Worth

A personal net worth statement is a snapshot of an individual's financial health, at one particular point in time. It is a summary of what is owned (assets), less what is owed to others (liabilities). The formula used is: assets – liabilities = net worth.

Assets

Paul's retirement plans	$136,000
Sally's retirement plans	76,500
Residence	500,000
Cash	500
Other Assets	6,000
Total Assets	**$719,000**

Liabilities

Mortgage	250,000
Asset Debt	0
Other Debt	25,000
Total Liabilities	**275,000**

Net Worth

Net Worth	**$444,000**

Net Worth

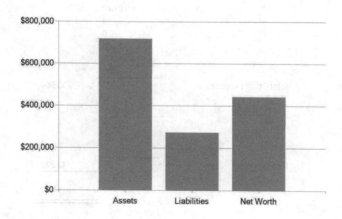

Personal Net Worth

A personal net worth statement is a snapshot of an individual's financial health, at one particular point in time. It is a summary of what is owned (assets), less what is owed to others (liabilities).

The formula used is: assets - liabilities = net worth.

If assets are greater than liabilities, the individual has a positive net worth. If assets are less than liabilities the individual has a negative net worth. Many financial advisors regard having a positive net worth as a primary goal.

Reasons to Prepare a Net Worth Statement

There are a number of reasons why an individual or family should prepare a net worth statement, usually on an annual basis.

- **To keep score:** Preparing an annual net worth statement allows an individual to keep track of progress toward meeting long-term financial goals. Ideally, net worth should increase over time.

- **A planning tool:** The net worth statement also serves as a planning tool. For example, a review of the net worth statement may show that an individual has too few liquid assets (for emergencies) or that investments are too heavily concentrated in one area.

- **Lenders may ask:** An individual's net worth is a common question on many loan applications. College financial aid programs will usually require information on the parents' net worth when a child applies.

- **For certain investments:** Certain types of high-risk investments require prospective investors to have a minimum level of net worth before they are allowed to invest money.

Preparing a Personal Net Worth Statement

The personal net worth worksheet on the following page can be used to prepare a net worth statement.

- **Assets:** For all assets categories (except cash or cash equivalents), a realistic valuation of what a willing, knowledgeable buyer would pay for an asset in an arms-length transaction should be used.

- **Liabilities:** It may be necessary to contact the lender or store to get the current balance on a loan or account.

Worksheet

Date Prepared: _____

Name: _____

Assets		Liabilities	
Liquid Assets		**Current Liabilities**	
Cash and cash equivalents	$ _____	Rent	$ _____
Money owed to you	$ _____	Utilities	$ _____
Life insurance cash value	$ _____	Credit and charge cards	$ _____
Other liquid assets	$ _____	Taxes	$ _____
Total liquid assets	$ _____	Other current liabilities	$ _____
Personal Use Assets		Current portion, LT liabilities	$ _____
Personal residence	$ _____	**Total current liabilities**	$ _____
Home use assets	$ _____	**Long-Term Liabilities**	
Autos or other vehicles	$ _____	Home mortgage	$ _____
Collectibles (art/antiques)	$ _____	Auto or other vehicle loans	$ _____
Other personal use assets	$ _____	Education loans	$ _____
Total personal use assets	$ _____	Margin account loans	$ _____
Investment Assets		Business loan	$ _____
Equity assets	$ _____	Other long-term loans	$ _____
Fixed-income assets	$ _____	**Total long-term liabilities**	$ _____
Investment real estate	$ _____		
Business interests	$ _____		
Commodities	$ _____	**Net Worth Summary**	
Vested portion - Pension plans	$ _____		
IRA or Keogh plans	$ _____	Assets	$ _____
Other investment assets	$ _____		
Total investment assets	$ _____	Less liabilities	$ (_____)
Total Assets	$ _____	**Equals net worth**	$ _____

Explanatory Notes

- **Liquid assets:** Cash or other assets, which can be easily converted into cash.

  - **Cash and cash equivalents:** These include cash in checking or savings accounts and cash equivalents where there is no concern for any loss of principal if the asset is converted into cash. May include CDs, money market funds and short-term (less than one year) Treasury securities.

  - **Money owed to you:** Includes those debts owed to you under a written agreement.

  - **Life insurance cash value:** This is the whole life policy cash surrender value.

- **Personal use assets.**

  - **Home use assets:** Includes furniture, furnishings, household goods, appliances, and sporting and hobby equipment.

  - **Autos or other vehicles:** Includes motorcycles, boats, airplanes and RVs.

  - **Collectibles (art/antiques):** Includes items that have a potential investment value as well as a personal interest value.

- **Investment use assets:** Includes investments with a maturity or a usual holding period of more than one year.

  - **Equity assets:** These include stocks, stock mutual funds or other investments based on stock market investments.

  - **Fixed-income assets:** Includes bonds, bond-based mutual funds, preferred stock or other investments based on bond or bond-type assets.

  - **Investment real estate:** Refers to real estate purchased for investment rather than shelter.

  - **Business interests:** Includes the equity ownership of any business in which you actively participate.

  - **Commodities:** These are gold, silver or other precious metals. Also gems and commodities contracts.

- **Vested portion of pension plans:** Refers to the amount to which you are entitled even if you quit today.

- **IRA or Keogh plans:** Includes the current market value less any taxes payable.

- **Current liabilities:** Refers to bills, which are due today or within thirty days.

  - **Rent and utilities:** Only include those due for the current month.

  - **Credit and charge cards:** Includes the total amount due, even if only minimum payments are made.

  - **Taxes:** Includes income and property taxes due today.

  - **Current portion of long-term liabilities:** Refers to the portion of the total long-term liabilities to be paid within the next 30 days.

- **Long-term liabilities:** These are liabilities, which are typically paid over an extended period of time.

Personal Net Worth Statement

Assets

Liquid assets	$50,000
Personal use assets	25,000
Investment assets	450,000
Total assets	**$525,000**

Liabilities

Current liabilities	$26,000
Long-term liabilities	250,000
Total liabilities	**$276,000**

Net Worth

Total assets	$525,000
Less: Total liabilities	276,000
Net worth	**$249,000**

Lifetime Earnings

Item Description	Client 1	Client 2
Current age	45	42
Age at retirement	66	68
Current annual income	$82,000	$52,000
Estimated annual increase	6.00%	6.50%
Projected earnings	**$3,279,404**	**$3,313,200**
Projected total earnings by retirement		**$6,592,603**

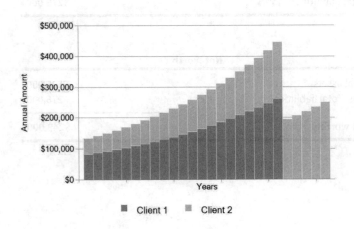

Managing Your Debt

While earlier generations may have followed a "cash only" spending philosophy, most Americans today cannot imagine living without at least some debt. Relatively few of us are able to pay cash for a home or car. The ability to borrow money, when it's needed and on favorable terms, is a privilege earned by carefully managing your debt obligations.

Why Borrow Money?

Many advisors regard borrowing money as a two-edged sword. It can, for example, be used to finance long-term goals such as a home, a business, or an education. Over time, these "investments" tend to increase in value and return far more than the cost to purchase them. Used to excess, or to constantly pay for short-term consumer items, such as clothing, vacations, or a night on the town, debt can become an overwhelming burden.

Managing Your Credit Record

Most lending decisions are made on the basis of your credit record, also known as your credit report. When lenders size you up to determine how much credit, if any, to grant you, they count on the three Cs:

- **Character:** How responsibly will you handle your credit obligations? Lenders will look at how well (or how poorly) you have repaid previous debts.

- **Capacity:** What is your financial ability to assume a certain amount of debt? Do you have enough money coming in the door each month to pay all of your bills?

- **Capital:** What financial assets are at your disposal to pay off debts? If you don't repay the debt as promised, do you have other financial assets that could be used by the lender to pay off the debt?

How well you manage each of these issues is reflected in your credit report. Because your credit report is constantly changing, you should review it at least once a year to check for errors, credit card fraud or identity theft.

What Are My Choices?

Today's consumer has many methods of borrowing money. You could, for example, use your credit card to finance a college education. However, a better choice might be a government-subsidized student loan which typically carries a lower interest rate and defers payments until after the student has finished school. Similarly, you could use part of your home equity line of credit to pay for a car, but do you really want to be making car payments for the next 10 or 20 years?

Whether you do the homework yourself, or seek the help of an advisor, understanding the loan options available, and then appropriately matching the type of loan to the need, is a key part of effective debt management.

Managing the Cost of Your Debt

Interest rates constantly move up and down. Thus, the loan that you took out several years ago at what was then a great rate may not be such a good deal today. Lower interest rates may allow you to refinance an existing loan and lower your monthly payment. Or, if you keep the same monthly payments, a lower interest rate may allow you to pay off the loan sooner.

- **Mortgages and other consumer loans:** As a general rule, the interest saved must be greater than the cost (pre-payment penalties and other closing expenses) of acquiring the new loan before it makes sense to re-finance.

- **Credit cards:** The competition between credit card issuers can be intense. You can sometimes "surf" your credit card balance from one issuer to another to take advantage of issuers' low introductory rates. If you do move your balance from one card to another, be sure that you make at least the minimum payment when due; otherwise, the interest rate can permanently jump from the low single digits to the high 20s.

Seek Professional Guidance

The advice and guidance of a professional financial advisor can be useful in helping sort out the various options for borrowing money. In addition, a qualified advisor can help you understand the impact of any borrowing upon your personal financial and income tax situation.

Other Resources

The federal government makes a number of resources available to the public:

- **Consumer Financial Protection Bureau:** On the internet at http://www.consumerfinance.gov/. Look under *Participate*, then *Know Before You Owe*.

- The **Federal Trade Commission** has a number of free publications available. On the internet, go to http://www.consumer.ftc.gov/topics/credit-and-loans.

- The **Federal Consumer Information Center**, at http://publications.usa.gov/, has a number of free and low-cost publications on a number of topics on interest to consumers.

Up to Your Neck in Debt?

Are you afraid to open your bills? Do you juggle bills, paying Paul one month and Peter the next? Do you make only the required minimum payment? Do you have to pay for basic necessities like food, rent, or gasoline on credit because you're out of cash?

If some or all of these apply to you, it's a good bet you've taken on too much debt.

Initial Steps

Many of us have to deal with a financial crisis at some point in our lives. Whatever the cause, there are ways to overcome these financial problems. Often the first step is to recognize that there is a problem. Then you can begin to take action to solve it.

- **Create a budget:** One key step is to create a realistic budget, a cold, hard look at both your income and your necessary living expenses. Are there ways to increase income, as well as reducing expenses?

- **Talk with your creditors:** Contacting your creditors and explaining why you're having trouble paying your bills on time may lead to a reduced payment plan. Setting up an automatic payment plan from your checking or savings account can help establish how serious you are about paying your bills.

- **Check for mistakes:** Your bills or credit report could contain errors that, once corrected, could provide some partial relief.

Lower the Cost of Debt

Lowering the cost of debt is another way to improve the situation:

Method	Description	Comments
Refinance High-Cost Loans	Lower interest rates may allow you to refinance an existing loan and lower your payment.	Mortgages: Generally, the interest saved must be greater than the cost of acquiring the new loan. Credit cards: You may be able to move balances from one card to another, to take advantage of introductory rates.

Method	Description	Comments
Consolidate Loans	Taking a number of high interest rate debts (often credit card debt) and replacing them with a single loan, often secured by the borrower's home or auto.	If payments are not made on the new loan, the lender often can seize the asset securing the loan.
Reposition Assets	Using existing assets such as cash, jewelry, or securities to pay down or pay off debt. Loans with the highest interest rates should be paid off first.	There may be negative tax implications if an asset with long-term appreciation is sold. Be sure you keep adequate liquid reserves to cover any future emergency.

Outside Help

Many credit counseling agencies are available to help consumers who find themselves in financial trouble. Not all of these agencies work in a consumer's best interest. A reputable credit counseling agency has counselors trained in budgeting, credit, and debt management. A good counselor works closely with you to develop a personalized plan to resolve your individual debt problems.

- **Debt management plan:** A debt management plan, or DMP, may be recommended by a credit counselor. In a DMP, you make monthly payments to the credit counseling agency, which then uses your money to pay your unsecured debts in accordance with an agreement between you and your creditors. DMPs are not for everyone and may have restrictions which are unacceptable to some consumers.

- **Debt negotiation:** For a fee, debt negotiation firms offer to "negotiate" settling a debt with a creditor, often for 10% to 50% of the amount owed. These programs can be highly risky and can have a negative, long-term impact on your credit rating. The IRS may consider any debt forgiven as taxable income.

- **Credit "repair" firms:** Companies or agencies that offer or promise to "repair" your credit record should be regarded as scams. The passage of time and a regular history of repaying your debts are the only way to truly "fix" your credit report.

A Last Resort – Personal Bankruptcy

If your debts are truly overwhelming, personal bankruptcy is a drastic option of last resort. Bankruptcy is a court-supervised process in which a debtor either has his debts eliminated (Chapter 7) or a plan is arranged which allows debt repayment under the supervision of the bankruptcy court (Chapter 13). Certain debts, such as most taxes, child support, and alimony, cannot be "discharged" through bankruptcy. Federal law requires a debtor to undergo credit counseling before filing bankruptcy and to complete debtor education before bankruptcy can be finalized. Competent legal advice is highly recommended.

- **Chapter 7:** Also known as "liquidation", Chapter 7 effectively erases your unsecured debts. With the exception of certain "exempt" property,[1] other assets that you own, such as your home, jewelry, or artwork, may be sold and the proceeds used to pay your debts. Not everyone qualifies for Chapter 7 bankruptcy; if you have a regular income that exceeds certain limits, you may be required to file Chapter 13. A Chapter 7 bankruptcy remains on your credit record for 10 years.

- **Chapter 13:** Also known as "wage earner" bankruptcy, Chapter 13 allows you to propose a plan to repay your debts over a three to five year period. To qualify for Chapter 13, you need a steady source of income and your debts must not exceed certain dollar limits. A Chapter 13 bankruptcy remains on your credit record for 7 years.

- **Online resources:** See the website of the Department of Justice, U.S. Trustee, at www.justice.gov/ust.

---

[1] The amount and type of exempt property can vary with state law.

Checking Your Credit Report

Reasons to Check Your Credit Report

Credit information - an individual's financial history - is an integral part of modern life. Most often used when a consumer applies for a loan, credit reports are also considered when an individual applies for life, auto, or home insurance, rents an apartment, or applies for a job.[1] There are two key reasons an individual's credit report should be periodically reviewed:

- **Errors and mistakes** – Incorrect information can result in being charged a higher rate of interest for a loan, not getting a job, or being denied insurance.

- **Identity theft** – Regularly reviewing a credit report can identify situations where someone else is using an individual's personal information to apply for new credit or to make unauthorized purchases on existing accounts.

Information Found in a Credit Report

Credit-reporting agencies, commonly known as credit bureaus or consumer reporting agencies, collect information on individuals from a variety of sources. Much of the data comes from a credit bureau's business subscribers, such as banks and other lenders. Other information is obtained from public records. A credit bureau's subscribers evaluate the information in a credit report to make their own determination as to whether an individual is a good or a poor lending risk.

A typical credit report usually has the following information:

- **Personal data:** Identifying information such as name, Social Security number, birth date, current address and marital status.

- **Credit history:** Including a list of current and past creditors, credit terms and limits, and how well (or poorly) past debts have been repaid.

- **Inquiries:** A list of requests for credit reports on the individual concerned.

- **Public records:** Information such as bankruptcies or lawsuits.

- **Personal statement:** A limited statement where a consumer can explain his or her position in any dispute with a lender.

---

[1] Federal law prohibits an employer or prospective employer from checking credit records without written permission from the individual involved.

Free Annual Credit Report

Under federal law, a consumer is entitled to one free credit report every 12 months, from each of the three major credit bureaus: Equifax, Experian, and TransUnion. Under Consumer Financial Protection Bureau (CFPB) rules, these credit bureaus must provide a central access point[1], where a consumer may request a copy of his or her credit report, including:

- A website: www.annualcreditreport.com.

- A toll-free telephone number: (877) 322-8228.

- A postal mailing address: Annual Credit Report Request Service, P.O. Box 105281, Atlanta, GA 30348-5281.

Incorrect Negative Information - Correcting Errors

If a review of a credit report reveals incorrect or incomplete information, a consumer should contact the credit bureau in writing, comprehensively detailing the information deemed incorrect. Under the provisions of the Fair Credit-reporting Act, the credit bureau is required to investigate disputed items, usually within 30 days after receiving a written request.

As a part of the investigation, the credit bureau will contact the lender or other information provider. The law also requires the information provider to investigate the claim and report the results to the credit bureau. When the investigation is complete, the credit bureau must give consumers written reports of the results.

If the disputed data is found to be incorrect, resulting in a change in the credit report, the credit bureau will provide a free copy of the corrected report to the consumer. The information provider is also required to correct its own records and provide the corrected information to all national credit bureaus.

---

[1] Specialized bureaus (agencies that specialize in areas such as insurance claims, medical records, and tenant or employment histories) are required to maintain only a toll-free telephone number. A consumer may request one free report from these bureaus every 12 months.

Checking Your Credit Report

The investigation of a disputed item may not result in a change in the credit report. A consumer can ask the credit bureau to include in his or her file a statement concerning the disputed information.

Correct Negative Information

If negative information in your credit report is correct, generally only the passage of time will remove it from the report. Many items, such as charged-off or collected accounts, delinquencies, and child support judgments, remain in the report for seven years. Other types of information can be retained in the report for longer periods, including:

- **Criminal convictions:** These may be reported without any time limit.

- **Bankruptcy:** Under Chapters 7, 11, or 12, bankruptcies can be reported for up to 10 years. Under Chapter 13, they remain in the record for seven years.

- **Job application:** Information reported in conjunction with an application for a position with an annual salary of $75,000 or more may be reported with no time limit.

- **Life insurance:** Information reported in conjunction with an application for credit or life insurance in excess of $150,000 may be reported with no time limit.

- **Lawsuit or unpaid judgment:** These can remain on the report for seven years, or until the statute of limitations expires.

- **Tax liens:** Unpaid liens for federal, state and local taxes can remain in the record indefinitely, while paid liens remain seven years.

Other Useful Resources

- **Consumer Financial Protection Bureau:** http://www.consumerfinance.gov/

- **Federal Trade Commission:** https://www.ftc.gov/

Credit Cards

The use of credit cards has become a widespread and accepted part of modern life. From modest beginnings in the early 1900s, credit card usage has grown to the point where 70.2% of American families have at least one general-purpose credit card, with a median credit balance outstanding of $3,000.[1]

Reasons to Use a Credit Card

There are many reasons individual consumers use a credit card.

- **Safety:** The use of credit cards allows a consumer to purchase goods and services without the need to carry large amounts of cash.

- **Opportunity:** A credit card allows a consumer to deal with short-term situations, such as Christmas or emergency auto repairs, when paying cash might not be possible.

- **Facilitate transactions:** Credit cards allow for payment of goods and services purchased via telephone or the Internet. Some transactions, such as renting a car, purchasing airline tickets, or guaranteeing payment for late arrival at a hotel, would be impossible without the use of a credit card.

- **Leverage:** Paying with a credit card can provide a consumer with additional leverage, in case of disputes with merchants over defective or poor quality merchandise.

- **Identity:** In certain types of transactions, such as cashing a check, credit cards have become a means of personal identification.

Types of Credit Cards

Not all credit cards are alike. They will vary widely in terms of issuer, scope of use and contract terms.

- **Bankcards:** Are issued not only by banks, but also by other financial institutions such as savings and loans or credit unions. These general-purpose credit cards can usually be used to purchase a wide range of goods and services. Credit is usually provided on a revolving basis, under which a borrower is granted a specific amount of credit. Typically, minimum monthly payments are required and any unpaid balance is subject to an interest charge. As borrowed amounts are repaid, the amount of available credit increases, up to the credit limit.

---

[1] Taken from The Statistical Abstract of the United States: 2012. See Report No. 1188 - Usage of General Purpose Credit Cards by Families: 1995 to 2007. Data is from 2007.

- **Charge cards:** Also known as travel and entertainment cards. Unlike bankcards, charge cards typically must be paid in full each month. Balances not paid are subject to heavy penalty fees. Like bankcards, charge cards are usually accepted widely.

- **Retail credit cards:** Retail credit cards are issued by businesses such as department stores, airlines and gasoline companies. Credit is usually provided on a revolving basis and purchases are limited to the goods and services sold by the specific card issuer.

- **Secured credit cards:** Such cards are usually general-purpose bankcards, with a specified (typically lower) credit limit. The card is secured by a deposit in an account with the issuing institution. If a consumer defaults, the card issuer can use the deposited funds to cover the shortage. Such cards are useful for individuals who do not have an established credit history or for those rebuilding their credit rating.

- **Affinity cards:** Affinity cards are issued jointly by a lending institution such as a bank or savings and loan, and some other organization such as an airline, charity or college alumni group. Using an affinity card allows a cardholder to also achieve other goals, such as earning frequent flyer miles or making charitable contributions.

Shopping for a Credit Card

When shopping for a credit card, a consumer should carefully compare the terms under which a card is offered:

- **Interest rate on unpaid balances:** The interest rate on unpaid balances can be either a fixed rate or a variable rate. Card issuers are required to state the interest rate as both an annual percentage rate (APR) and (for each billing cycle) as a periodic interest rate.

- **Unpaid balance computation:** The method by which a card issuer calculates the unpaid balance on an account. The unpaid balance, multiplied by the periodic interest rate, determines the finance charge.

AVERAGE DAILY BALANCE	PREVIOUS BALANCE	ADJUSTED BALANCE
Each day the issuer subtracts any payments from, and adds new purchases to, the account balance. The daily balances for each day in a billing cycle are added together and then divided by the number of days in that cycle.	The issuer charges interest on the balance outstanding at the end of the previous billing cycle.	The issuer starts with the previous balance, subtracts any payments or credits, and charges interest on any remaining unpaid amount.

- **Fees:** Many card issuers will charge an annual fee, just to have the card. Fees may also be charged for such items as cash advances, late payments, charging over the established credit limit and lost card replacement.

- **Grace period:** The amount of time during which no interest is charged, if the entire amount is paid off.

- **Other benefits:** A card may provide other benefits such as cash advances, flight insurance, or discounts on travel or long-distance telephone charges.

- **Acceptance:** Some merchants may not accept a specific type of card.

Using a Credit Card

Many advisors recommend that consumers develop certain habits when using credit cards.

- Keep the number of open credit card accounts to a minimum.

- Understand the terms under which a card is issued.

- Sign all cards as soon as they are received.

- Pay credit card bills promptly to keep interest charges as low as possible and maintain a good credit rating. Authorizing electronic payment of credit card bills from your checking or savings account can automate this process.

- Keep detailed records of credit card account numbers, expiration dates and the telephone number of card issuers. The easiest way to do this is to photocopy the front and back of each card.

- Protect credit card information to avoid unauthorized use.

- Carefully review credit card statements each month. The customer copy of charge slips should be kept, to allow comparison with the monthly statement.

Lost or Stolen Credit Cards

Under federal law, a cardholder can be held liable for charges of up to $50.00 per card, even though the use was unauthorized. Such unauthorized credit card use is often the result of a card being lost, stolen or even counterfeited. If the loss of a card is reported to the issuer before the card is used, however, the issuer cannot hold the consumer liable for any unauthorized use.

- **Notify issuer:** A consumer should report the loss or theft of a credit card to the issuer as soon as possible. Many card issuers have toll-free, 24-hour telephone numbers for this purpose. Written notification should also be sent to the issuer.

- **Check monthly statement:** Review the monthly card statement to be sure that no unauthorized charges were made before it was noticed that the card was missing.

- **Registration service:** A consumer who carries more than one credit card may want to use a credit card registration service. For an annual fee, such services keep a record of all of a consumer's credit cards. In the event of a loss, the consumer makes one call, to the registration service. The registration service notifies all card issuers of the loss and, in many cases, arranges for replacement cards.

Buying a Home

Owning a home has long been a part of the American dream, one that many Americans have already achieved. According to recent statistics from the U. S. Census Bureau, 63.9% of all households in the United States live in owner-occupied housing.[1]

Although the process of buying a home is often complex and confusing, it can be simplified by dividing it into several parts:

Renting vs. Home Ownership

There are advantages and disadvantages to both renting and buying a home:

	Advantages	**Disadvantages**
Renting	**Mobility:** Renter can move without worrying about selling the home or the home's market value at time of sale. **Initial cost:** No need for large down payment. **Monthly cost:** Monthly rent usually less than mortgage payment; in some areas rents are controlled; other opportunities may provide greater investment return. **Maintenance:** Few or no maintenance responsibilities.	**Monthly cost:** Rents can increase over time. **Equity:** Renter builds no equity in home. **Space:** Often less floor space. Personalization: Less freedom to decorate the home. **Taxes:** No deduction for rent payments.[2]
Buying	**Monthly cost:** With a fixed rate mortgage, monthly payments remain level; with a variable rate mortgage, monthly payments can fluctuate. **Equity:** Homeowner can build substantial equity over time. **Space:** Typically larger floor space than with a rented home. **Personalization:** Can usually decorate to make home reflect owner's tastes. **Taxes:** Interest and property taxes may be deductible.[2]	**Mobility:** Ownership limits ability to move; homeowner must be concerned with selling the home as well as the home's market value at time of sale. **Initial cost:** Substantial cash usually needed for down payment and closing costs. **Monthly cost:** Monthly mortgage payment typically higher than monthly rent; other opportunities may provide greater investment return. **Maintenance:** Homeowner is usually responsible for all maintenance and repairs.

---

[1] U.S. Census Bureau News, Residential Vacancies and Homeownership in the Third Quarter 2017, October 31, 2017.

[2] Based on federal income tax law; state or local income tax law may vary.

Financing a Home

- **Qualifying for a mortgage:** Most homebuyers purchase their home by taking out a loan known as a "mortgage." Although the actual standards will vary from one lender to another, the following factors are frequently considered in evaluating a mortgage application:

  - **Credit score:** What is the prospective borrower's credit score? It's a numerical value measuring how well (or how poorly) a loan applicant has dealt with debt in the past.

  - **Down payment:** How much of a down payment is the prospective borrower able to make? 10%? 20%? 30? None?

  - **Loan purpose:** Is the home being purchased as an investment or as a place where the borrower will actually live?

- **How big a monthly payment?** In considering a loan application, a lender may also apply certain financial "tests." One such test limits the monthly housing payment, plus the monthly payments for any other debt, to no more than 36% of a consumer's gross monthly income. For example, if a consumer has gross monthly income of $4,000, the monthly housing payment plus any other debt repayment should not exceed $1,440 ($4,000 x .36).

Given a specified monthly payment limit, the next step is to determine what size mortgage that monthly payment will allow. The answer to this depends on the number of years to repay the loan and the annual interest rate. The table below illustrates the approximate total monthly payments[1] under varying term and interest rate assumptions.

Loan Amount	3.5 % Annual Interest Monthly Payment		4.5 % Annual Interest Monthly Payment		5.5 % Annual Interest Monthly Payment	
	15 Years	30 Years	15 Years	30 Years	15 Years	30 Years
$100,000	$827.00	$562.00	$877.49	$619.19	$929.58	$680.29
$150,000	$1,241.00	$842.00	$1,316.24	$928.78	$1,394.38	$1,020.43
$200,000	$1,655.00	$1,123.00	$1,754.99	$1,238.37	$1,859.17	$1,360.58
$250,000	$2,068.00	$1,404.00	$2,193.73	$1,547.96	$2,323.96	$1,700.72
$300,000	$2,482.00	$1,685.00	$2,632.48	$1,857.56	$2,788.75	$2,040.87

[1] Payment includes principal, interest, and estimated taxes and insurance. Property taxes and insurance are estimated at 1.35% of the loan amount.

- **Down payment and closing costs:** Lenders frequently require a homebuyer to pay a certain portion of the home price in cash. Depending on the lender, this down payment usually ranges from 5% to 20% of the purchase price. With down payments of less than 20%, the lender may require the borrower to apply for private mortgage insurance, which protects the lender in case the buyer defaults. Under some government programs, a buyer may be allowed to purchase a home with no down payment. A buyer will also be required to pay certain "closing costs", fees and charges associated with processing the sale. Closing costs can be 3% to 6% of the purchase price.

- **Tax deductibility of interest and property taxes:** A homebuyer will also want to consider the "after-tax" cost of home ownership. Taxpayers who meet certain requirements may be able to deduct mortgage interest and property taxes from taxable income. For example, assuming a taxpayer pays $10,000 in deductible mortgage interest and property taxes during a year, and is in a 24% marginal tax bracket, the after-tax cost of these expenses is $7,600 ($10,000 x .24 = $2,400; $10,000 - $2,400 = $7,600).[1]

Finding a Home

What type of home? There are three basic forms of home ownership:

	Property Owned	Sell or Rent	Maintenance	Owner Payments	Other Issues
Single-Family Home	The structure and the land	Owner can decide to rent or sell home.	Owner responsible for all repairs and maintenance.	Mortgage, insurance, and real estate taxes. Loan secured by home.	Greater freedom to personalize the home. Generally more responsibility.

---

[1] Under the Tax Cuts and Jobs Act of 2017 (TCJA), for 2018 – 2025, a taxpayer's deduction for property and state and local income or sales taxes, is limited to $10,000 per year ($5,000 MFS). Further, a deduction is allowed only for interest paid on "acquisition debt" (debt used to acquire or substantially improve a home), on a first and second home, of up to $750,000 ($375,000 MFS). TCJA also significantly expanded the standard deduction amounts available to individuals. Many taxpayers will find it more advantageous to use the expanded standard deduction, rather than claiming an itemized deduction for mortgage interest and property taxes.

	Property Owned	Sell or Rent	Maintenance	Owner Payments	Other Issues
Condo	Individual living space. Homeowner's association owns building, land and common areas.	Owner can decide to sell. Restrictions on renting will vary.	Homeowner's association pays for most building maintenance and repair.	Mortgage, insurance, and taxes on individual unit; monthly fee to homeowner's association; mortgage secured by individual unit	Can be more restrictive with regard to issues such as children, pets, outside decoration. Fewer maintenance concerns. May have extra amenities such as swimming pools and tennis courts. Owners may be responsible for additional expenses or charges.
Co-op	Shares in a corporation which owns building. Individual lease with corporation grants exclusive right to use apartment.	Owner can decide to sell. New buyer subject to approval by co-op board. May have restrictions on renting.	Co-op pays for most building maintenance and repair.	Monthly payments to co-op cover insurance, taxes, mortgage on building and operating costs. Loan payments to repay purchase of shares in co-op. Loan secured by shares in co-op.	Can be more restrictive on issues such as children and pets. Fewer maintenance concerns. May have extra amenities (pools, tennis courts, etc.). Owners may be responsible for additional expenses or charges.

Other Factors to Consider

- **Neighborhood:** Real estate agents will often refer to this as "location." In general, the relative attractiveness of an area will usually be reflected in the level of prices in the neighborhood. Personal issues such as good schools, easy access to public transportation, or proximity to features such as shopping, recreation, or work, are important factors in determining what is a "good" location.

- **Home features and characteristics:** Specific home features such as a minimum square footage, number of bedrooms or bathrooms, or a swimming pool. Many shoppers will list the most attractive features in priority order, in case an offered home lacks some of the desirable features. Keeping in mind that the home will one day be sold, many individuals look for features that are attractive and useful both to themselves and to others.

Searching for a Home

- **Real estate agents:** Real estate agents can be quite helpful in locating a home, particularly those who have access to a computerized multiple listings service. A good agent will have extensive real estate experience, as well as detailed knowledge of a specific area or neighborhood.

- **New home developments:** New homes tend to be more expensive than existing homes. New homes also tend to have fewer problems, and often have builder warranties.

- **Classified ads:** Classified ads in newspapers (both in print and online) can be useful sources of information. Such ads can provide a sense of general price levels. They can also provide leads to homes which are being sold directly by their owners, and not through an agent.

Types of Mortgages

Type	Description	Comments
Fixed-rate mortgage	Fixed interest rate. Borrower makes equal monthly payments of principal and interest until debt is fully paid. Loans can range from 10 - 40 years.	Offers payment stability. Interest rates may be higher than other types of financing. New fixed-rate loans are rarely assumable by later owners.
Home equity loan	A mortgage loan secured by the owner's "equity" (market value of home, less any existing mortgage debt) in the home. The loan may be a lump-sum amount or a line of credit (HELOC). Typically have a shorter term, five to 15 years.	Interest rates are frequently lower than those for traditional second mortgages, and can be either fixed or variable. Many home equity loans are interest-only, with a balloon payment due at the end of the loan term.
Adjustable-rate mortgage (ARM)	Interest rate can vary over the life of the loan, resulting in changes in the monthly payments, loan term, and/or principal balance due. Interest rate is based on an "index," such as the prime rate, with interest rate adjustments being made at specified time intervals.	Starting interest rate is typically slightly below market (a "teaser" rate), but payments can increase sharply if index increases. Some loans have interest rate caps that prevent wide fluctuations in payments, but may result in negative amortization.
Renegotiable rate mortgage (rollover)	Interest rate and monthly payments are constant for several years; possible change thereafter. Long-term mortgage.	Less frequent changes in interest rate offer some payment stability.
Balloon mortgage	Monthly payments based on fixed interest rate; usually short-term; payments may cover interest only with principal due in full at term end.	Offers low monthly payments but possibly no equity until loan is fully paid. When due, loan must be paid off or refinanced. Refinancing poses high risk if rates climb.
Graduated payment mortgage	Monthly payments start low and rise gradually (usually over five to 10 years), then level off for duration of loan term. If the loan has an adjustable interest rate, additional payment changes are possible if the underlying index changes.	Generally easier to qualify for. Buyer's income must be able to keep pace with scheduled payment increases. With an adjustable rate mortgage, payment increases beyond the scheduled graduated payments may result in negative amortization.
Shared appreciation mortgage	Below-market interest rate and lower monthly payments, in exchange for a share of profits when property is sold or on a specified date. Many variations.	If home appreciates greatly, total cost of loan jumps. If home fails to appreciate, projected increase in value may still be due, requiring refinancing at possible higher rates.

Types of Mortgages

Type	Description	Comments
Assumable mortgage	Buyer takes over seller's original, below-market rate mortgage.	Lowers monthly payments. May be prohibited if "due on sale" clause is in original mortgage. Not permitted on most new fixed-rate mortgages.
Seller take-back	Seller provides all or part of financing with a first or second mortgage.	May offer a below-market interest rate; may have a balloon payment requiring full payment in a few years or refinancing at market rates, which could sharply increase debt.
Wraparound	Seller keeps original low rate mortgage. Buyer makes payments to seller, who forwards a portion to the lender holding original mortgage. Offers lower effective interest rate on total transaction.	Lender may call in old mortgage and require higher rate. If buyer defaults, seller must take legal action to collect debt.
Growing-equity mortgage (rapid payoff mortgage)	Fixed interest rate but monthly payments may vary according to agreed-upon schedule or index.	Permits rapid payoff of debt because payment increases reduce principal. Buyer's income must be able to keep up with payment increases.
Land contract	Seller retains original mortgage. No transfer of title until loan is fully paid. Equal monthly payments based on below-market interest rate with unpaid principal due at loan end.	May offer no equity until loan is fully paid. Buyer has few protections if conflict arises during loan.
Buy-down	Developer (or another party) provides an interest subsidy which lowers monthly payments during the first few years of the loan. May have a fixed or adjustable interest rate.	Offers a break from higher payments during early years. Enables buyer with lower income to qualify. With adjustable rate mortgage, payments may jump substantially at end of subsidy. Developer may increase selling price to recover loan costs.
Rent with option	Renter pays "option fee" for right to purchase property at specified time and agreed upon price. Rent may or may not be applied to sales price.	Enables renter to buy time to obtain down payment and decide whether to purchase. Locks in price during inflationary times. Failure to take option means loss of option fee and rental payments.

Type	Description	Comments
Reverse mortgage	Borrower owns mortgage-free property and needs income. Loan can be a lump-sum or monthly payments to borrower using property as collateral. Generally, borrower must be at least age 62 and live in the home.	No payments are required as long as borrower lives in the home. The outstanding loan balance is due when the last borrower sells the home, permanently leaves, or dies. Borrower can never owe more than the value of the home at the time loan is repaid.
Interest-only mortgage	Borrower pays only the interest due (no repayment of principal) either for an introductory period or for the life of the loan. At the end of the loan term, the loan must either be refinanced or completely paid off.	Interest-only payments generally allow the homeowner to qualify for a larger loan amount. With little or no equity, a homeowner with an interest-only loan faces higher risk if real estate values decline.

Pay Off the Mortgage or Invest?

Individuals with additional, disposable income can find themselves facing a question. Should I *invest* the extra money? Or, should I use the funds to *pre-pay my mortgage*? The "right" answer to this question is often a highly personal one and frequently involves weighing the pros and cons of a number of different issues. Some of these issues are objective, involving a number-crunching approach, while others are more subjective, reflecting an individual's personality, values, and stage in life.

The Highest Investment Return

From a purely mathematical standpoint, the answer to the question would be: *put the money where you achieve the highest investment return*. In this approach, a comparison is made of the return that could be achieved by paying down the mortgage versus the result of, say, investing in the stock market. In the business world, this is referred to as "Return on Investment," or ROI.

The problem, of course, is that many of the variables used in these calculations are guesses about the future. Although the historical record can provide a rough guide as to how well or how poorly certain investments have done in the past, there's no guarantee that the past will repeat itself. Investing does involve risk, including the possible loss of principal.

Reasons to Pay Off the Mortgage

Even if the mathematical analysis points toward investing, there may be other, more personal reasons why a homeowner would want to pay off the mortgage:

- **You keep the interest:** The interest paid over the life of a loan can amount to a very large sum. Paying a mortgage off early keeps this interest in your pocket and not in someone else's. The investment "return" is equal to the interest rate charged on the mortgage.

- **A sense of security:** A homeowner may rest easier knowing that the home is paid for, in case of unemployment, health problems, or other financial setback.

- **A smaller monthly budget:** For many, the home mortgage is the biggest single expense in the monthly budget. Paying off the mortgage significantly reduces the monthly cost of living. This may be particularly important to those who are near, or already in, retirement.

- **A more stable return:** Financial markets can fluctuate, sometimes wildly. The rental value of a place to live, combined with the savings achieved by not paying interest over a long period of time, can provide a more stable return than that found in other markets.

Reasons Not to Pay Off the Mortgage

There are also a number of very good reasons why someone would not want to pay off the mortgage:

- **Lost income tax deduction:** If an individual itemizes deductions on his or her federal income tax return,[1] home mortgage interest generally reduces taxable income. Paying off a mortgage early eliminates this deduction.

- **Other investments may provide a higher return:** Despite the uncertainties involved (investing does involve risk, including the possible loss of principal), investing the extra money elsewhere may ultimately provide a higher investment return.

- **Loss of diversification:** Paying off a mortgage concentrates a higher proportion of an individual's net worth in one asset, the home. Should something happen to that asset, it could represent a major financial blow. A key tool in fighting investment risk is diversification, spreading your funds over different types of assets.

- **Repay loan with cheaper dollars:** If inflation continues to be a part of our economic lives, then not paying off a mortgage allows an individual to pay for an asset over time with what are effectively "cheaper" dollars.

What Else Could the Money Be Used For?

The additional funds could also be used to meet a number of other personal planning needs, such as:

- **Qualified retirement plans – "free money":** If you're not adequately funding an employer-sponsored, qualified retirement plan, such as a 401(k), you may be walking away from "free money" provided through an employer-matching program.

---

[1] The discussion here concerns federal income tax law. State or local law may vary.

- **IRAs – maximize tax deferral:** Both traditional and Roth IRAs allow an individual to "shelter" savings from income tax. Fully funding an IRA each year maximizes the available tax deferral.

- **Pay off high-interest debt:** The extra funds could be devoted to paying off high-interest debt such as credit cards. As with paying off the mortgage, the investment return equals the interest rate charged on the debt.

- **Build an emergency reserve:** Having extra cash quickly available in case of an emergency is a key part of every individual's financial safety net.

- **Insurance needs:** Do you have enough life insurance? Is your health insurance coverage adequate? Are your home and auto adequately protected?

- **Education needs:** Is there adequate provision for educating your children or grandchildren?

Seek Professional Guidance

The decision to either pay off a mortgage or invest is a personal one. Factors that are important to one individual may not be as important to someone else. The guidance of trained, experienced financial professionals in sorting through the various issues involved is strongly recommended.

The Bi-Weekly Mortgage

By paying one-half of the typical monthly mortgage payment every two weeks rather than one full payment every month, a 30-year mortgage can be paid off in approximately 20 years. The 26 bi-weekly payments are the same as 13 monthly payments during the year; in other words, one "extra monthly payment."

This extra monthly payment, along with the more frequent application of the payments against the loan balance, greatly speeds up the payoff of the loan. Also, since the "extra monthly payment" is spread evenly throughout the year, it generally does not adversely affect the family budget.

Payments on the bi-weekly mortgage are generally made by automatic withdrawal from the homeowner's checking account every two weeks.

Payments on Various Size Loans and Total Interest Saved[1]

Interest Rate / Term in Months[2]	$100,000		$150,000		$200,000	
	Bi-Weekly Payment Amount	Total Interest Savings	Bi-Weekly Payment Amount	Total Interest Savings	Bi-Weekly Payment Amount	Total Interest Savings
4.5% / 308	$253	$14,019	$380	$21,028	$507	$28,037
5.0% / 303	$268	$17,164	$403	$25,750	$537	$34,328
5.5% / 299	$284	$20,755	$426	$31,128	$568	$41,503
6.0% / 294	$300	$24,808	$450	$37,221	$600	$49,624
6.5% / 290	$316	$29,369	$474	$44,061	$632	$58,746
7.0% / 285	$333	$34,464	$499	$51,700	$665	$68,927
7.5% / 280	$350	$40,096	$524	$60,149	$699	$80,203
8.0% / 274	$367	$46,301	$550	$69,452	$734	$92,602
8.5% / 269	$384	$53,079	$577	$79,600	$769	$106,144

[1] The interest savings shown illustrate the difference between the interest paid on a 30-year fixed-rate mortgage making monthly payments vs. bi-weekly payments. All figures are approximate.
[2] The number of months required to fully pay off the loan on a bi-weekly payment schedule.

Payments on Various Size Loans and Total Interest Saved[1]

Interest Rate / Term in Months[2]	$250,000		$300,000		$350,000	
	Bi-Weekly Payment Amount	Total Interest Savings	Bi-Weekly Payment Amount	Total Interest Savings	Bi-Weekly Payment Amount	Total Interest Savings
4.5% / 308	$633	$35,045	$760	$42,050	$887	$49,058
5.0% / 303	$671	$42,907	$805	$51,492	$939	$60,073
5.5% / 299	$710	$51,883	$852	$62,259	$994	$72,632
6.0% / 294	$749	$62,029	$899	$74,440	$1,049	$86,837
6.5% / 290	$790	$73,431	$948	$88,123	$1,106	$102,808
7.0% / 285	$832	$86,155	$998	$103,391	$1,164	$120,619
7.5% / 280	$874	$100,246	$1,049	$120,299	$1,224	$140,352
8.0% / 274	$917	$115,753	$1,101	$138,904	$1,284	$162,042
8.5% / 269	$961	$132,679	$1,153	$159,210	$1,346	$185,743

[1] The interest savings shown illustrate the difference between the interest paid on a 30-year fixed-rate mortgage making monthly payments vs. bi-weekly payments. All figures are approximate.

[2] The number of months required to fully pay off the loan on a bi-weekly payment schedule.

Bi-Weekly Mortgage

Assumptions:

Amount of loan: $285,000
Annual interest rate: 4.5%
Number of monthly payments: 360

	Monthly	Bi-Weekly
Payment Amount	$1,444	$722
Total Interest	$234,859	$194,911
Interest Savings		$39,948
Number of Years to Pay	30.00	25.58

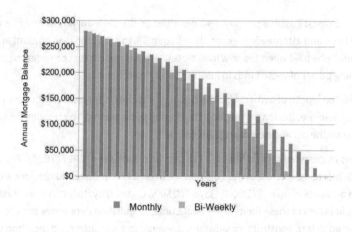

When to Refinance Your Home

There are a number of situations in which refinancing a home mortgage makes sense. For example, you may have purchased a home years ago when interest rates were much higher and now want to take advantage of a decline in mortgage rates. In addition, a homeowner with a volatile variable rate mortgage may want to switch to more predictable fixed-rate loan. You may even want to shorten the term of your loan.

Is Refinancing Worth the Trouble?

Refinancing can be very beneficial, but it is not always the smart thing to do; the costs associated with refinancing must be balanced against any potential savings.

Generally, refinancing a fixed-mortgage makes sense when the interest rate on the current mortgage is at least 2 percentage points higher than the prevailing market rate. In some instances, however, following this "rule" may cost the homeowner a lot of money as a very small percentage point spread may justify refinancing if other factors are present.

Other Factors Which Must Be Considered

There are a number of factors which must be considered in this "cost vs. benefits" calculation, including:

- **Closing costs:** Possible pre-payment penalties on the old loan, points and fees on the new loan, and attorney fees generally will total 3% to 4% of the loan amount and must generally be paid when the new loan closes. The borrower must consider the loss of earning power of these funds in future income projections.

- **Projected length of ownership:** The closing costs can be spread over the period of the loan; therefore, the longer the projected period of ownership, the smaller the spread between the old and new mortgages can be.

- **Loans in excess of certain limits[1] – Tax Cuts and Jobs Act of 2017 (TCJA):** For 2018 – 2025, mortgage interest on "acquisition" debt on a first and second residence, on total loan amounts of up to $750,000 ($375,000 MFS) is generally deductible; interest on debt in excess of these limits is not deductible. Acquisition debt refers to debt incurred to buy, construct, or substantially improve a qualified residence, and which is secured by a qualified home. This dollar limitation applies to debt incurred *after* December 15, 2017.

---

[1] The discussion here concerns federal income tax law; state or local law may vary.

- **Loans in excess of certain limits – before 2018 and after 2025:** Prior to the TCJA, a taxpayer could generally deduct the interest paid on total acquisition debt on two homes of up to $1,000,000 ($500,000 MFS). Additionally, interest on up to $100,000 ($50,000 MFS) of "home equity" debt could also be deducted. Home equity debt is debt which does not qualify as acquisition debt, but which is secured by a qualified home. Under the TCJA, deductibility of interest on up to $1,000,000 of acquisition debt and up to $100,000 of home equity debt is scheduled to return for 2026 and later years.

The New Mortgage - Variable Rate vs. Fixed Rate

VARIABLE RATE	FIXED RATE
- Initially lower interest rate than with a fixed rate loan, but will increase if interest rates go up or decrease if interest rates go down. - Most variable rate mortgages have a limit or a cap on annual rate increases and on lifetime increases.[1] - Usually preferred for short-term ownership of home; e.g., 2 - 3 yrs.	- Rate does not change if interest rates go up or down. - Best for owners with a fixed income or those who plan to stay in their home for several years. - Rates and monthly payments are higher than with a variable loan, at least in the early years. - Fixed rate loans may not be assumable.

[1] Be certain that an annual cap is part of the loan, and carefully examine the index to which the rate is tied.

How Many Months Will It Take to Break Even?

The real cost of refinancing is the closing costs. Determine how many months it will take to make up these costs from the savings under the new loan.

$$\underline{\$\hspace{3cm}} - \underline{\$\hspace{3cm}} = \underline{\$\hspace{3cm}}$$

| Old Payment | New Lower Payment | Monthly Savings |

$$\underline{\$\hspace{3cm}} \div \underline{\$\hspace{3cm}} = \underline{\hspace{3cm}}$$

| Closing Costs | Monthly Savings | Number of Months to Break Even |

Refinancing an old home loan could mean lower monthly payments and perhaps changing from a variable rate mortgage to a fixed rate mortgage. However, if the projected time in the house is short, the closing costs may consume any potential savings.

As an additional alternative, if one plans to sell in a year or two, a variable rate mortgage with an initially lower rate may be advantageous.

Financing an Auto

Once a consumer decides to acquire an automobile, the next step is to decide how to pay for it. There are three methods of financing an auto:

- **Pay cash:** Using already accumulated funds.
- **Borrow the funds:** Taking out a loan and paying for the vehicle over time.
- **Lease:** Allows use of an auto for a specified period of time, in return for regular monthly payments.

The decision as to whether to pay cash, take out a loan, or lease a vehicle is usually made after considering a number of personal and financial issues.

Factors to Consider

The table below compares some of the factors to consider when considering how to finance an auto:

	Pay Cash	Borrow the Funds	Lease
Method of financing	Consumer uses cash to completely pay for the vehicle at the time of purchase.	Consumer borrows the funds to purchase the vehicle, and makes monthly payments to repay the loan.	Consumer obtains the right to use the vehicle for a specified period of time, in return for monthly payments.
Out-of-pocket costs	Entire purchase price.	Down payment and/or trade-in. Special offers may allow zero down.	Down payment and/or trade-in. Often less than for an auto loan. Special offers may allow zero down.
Monthly payments	None.	Payments cover repayment of loan amount, plus interest.	Payments cover estimated depreciation during the lease period, and other costs. Typically less than for an auto loan.
Vehicle ownership	Consumer is the owner.	Consumer is the owner, subject to a lien held by lender. Once loan is repaid, consumer takes title free and clear. Lender may repossess vehicle if payments not made as scheduled.	Leasing firm retains ownership. Consumer usually has the right to purchase the vehicle at the end of the lease.

	Pay Cash	Borrow the Funds	Lease
Excess mileage charges	None.	None.	Typical lease limits consumer to no more than 10,000 – 15,000 miles per year. Miles in excess of lease limits are subject to a per-mile charge.
Excess wear and tear	No additional charges. Excess wear and tear, or high mileage, can reduce a vehicle's resale value.	No additional charges. Excess wear and tear, or high mileage, can reduce a vehicle's resale value.	Additional charges for excess wear and tear usually apply.
Risk of future vehicle resale value	Risk remains with the consumer.	Risk remains with the consumer.	With a closed-end lease, risk of future vehicle resale value remains with leasing firm. With an open-end lease, consumer may be responsible for substantial additional charges.
Early disposal of vehicle	Consumer is free to sell vehicle at any time.	Consumer is free to sell vehicle at any time, subject to repayment of loan balance to lender. Early loan termination fees may apply.	Additional fees for early lease termination normally apply.
Tax issues	Deduction available for business use of vehicle.[1]	Deduction available for business use of vehicle.[1]	Deduction available for business use of vehicle. In certain situations, leasing may provide a larger deduction for business use than an owned vehicle.[1]
Lifestyle issues	Limits consumer to vehicle that he or she can currently afford. Consumer avoids additional debt burden.	Usually allows consumer to purchase more expensive vehicle than if full cash payment is required.	Consumer typically has use of more expensive vehicle than with other financing options. May also allow consumer to drive a new car more frequently. No equity at end of lease.

[1] Based on federal law. State law may vary.

Comparing the Dollar Costs

The following table provides a hypothetical comparison of the costs involved in the three options for financing an auto:

- **Pay cash:** Purchase price of $22,500, sales tax of $1,631, registration and fees of $350. Total purchase price of $24,481.
- **Borrow the funds:** Total purchase price of $24,481, less down payment of $2,250. Financed over a 48-month period at 4.0% annual interest.
- **Lease:** 48-month closed-end lease, with same costs and interest rate as under the "loan" option. $500 down payment and an assumed resale value at the end of the lease of $12,000.

	Pay Cash	Borrow the Funds	Lease
Up-front cash	$24,481	$2,250	$500
Monthly payment	0	502	437
Total payments over 48 months	0	24,096	20,976
Opportunity costs[1]	999	92	20
Total costs after 48 months	25,480	26,438	21,496
Value of vehicle after 48 months	(12,000)	(12,000)	0
Total	$13,480	$14,438	$21,496

[1] The amount of interest the "up-front cash" shown for each option would have earned over the 48 month period, at an assumed 1.0% annual after-tax rate of return.

Loan Amortization Schedule

Assumptions:

Amount of loan: $100,000
Annual interest rate: 8%
Frequency of payments/compounding periods: Monthly
Number of payments: 360
Payment start date: 2/2014
Payment: $734
Total payments: $264,155
Total interest paid: $164,155

Loan Amortization Schedule

The following table shows year-by-year summary of this loan:

Note: The amount of principal vs. interest paid each year as the loan progresses.

Year	Principal Paid This Year	Interest Paid This Year	Total Paid This Year	Balance Remaining
2014	$763	$7,308	$8,071	$99,237
2015	899	7,906	8,805	98,338
2016	973	7,832	8,805	97,365
2017	1,054	7,751	8,805	96,311
2018	1,142	7,664	8,805	95,169
2019	1,236	7,569	8,805	93,933
2020	1,339	7,466	8,805	92,594
2021	1,450	7,355	8,805	91,144
2022	1,570	7,235	8,805	89,573
2023	1,701	7,104	8,805	87,873
2024	1,842	6,963	8,805	86,031
2025	1,995	6,810	8,805	84,036
2026	2,160	6,645	8,805	81,876
2027	2,340	6,465	8,805	79,536
2028	2,534	6,271	8,805	77,002
2029	2,744	6,061	8,805	74,258
2030	2,972	5,833	8,805	71,286

Loan Amortization Schedule

Year	Principal Paid This Year	Interest Paid This Year	Total Paid This Year	Balance Remaining
2031	$3,219	$5,587	$8,805	$68,067
2032	3,486	5,319	8,805	64,581
2033	3,775	5,030	8,805	60,806
2034	4,088	4,717	8,805	56,718
2035	4,428	4,377	8,805	52,290
2036	4,795	4,010	8,805	47,495
2037	5,193	3,612	8,805	42,302
2038	5,624	3,181	8,805	36,677
2039	6,091	2,714	8,805	30,586
2040	6,597	2,209	8,805	23,990
2041	7,144	1,661	8,805	16,845
2042	7,737	1,068	8,805	9,108
2043	8,379	426	8,805	729
2044	729	5	734	0

Rate of Interest for a Loan

Assumptions:

Amount of loan: $30,000
Annual interest rate: 5.843%
Frequency of payments/compounding periods: Monthly
Number of payments: 60
Payment start date: 2/2014
Payment: $575
Total payments: $33,925
Total interest paid: $4,691

Loan Amortization Schedule

The following table shows year-by-year summary of this loan:

Note: The amount of principal vs. interest paid each year as the loan progresses.

Year	Principal Paid This Year	Interest Paid This Year	Total Paid This Year	Balance Remaining
2014	$4,835	$1,490	$6,325	$25,165
2015	5,577	1,323	6,900	19,588
2016	5,912	988	6,900	13,676
2017	6,267	633	6,900	7,409
2018	6,643	257	6,900	766

Payments To Pay Off A Loan

Item Description	Value
Amount of loan	$100,000
Annual interest rate	8.00%
Frequency of payments	Monthly
Number of Monthly payments	360
Monthly payment amount to pay off loan	**$734**

Example

If you borrow $100,000 for 360 months at an annual interest rate of 8.00%, compounded monthly, your monthly payment will be $734.

Making Additional Principal Payments

Assumptions:

Amount of loan: $250,000
Annual interest rate: 4.5%
Number of monthly payments: 300
Additional principal payment: $250

	Monthly Payment	With Additional Payment
Payment Amount	$1,390	$1,640
Total Interest	$166,874	$121,524
Interest Savings		$45,350
Number of Years to Pay	25.00	18.92

Additional Principal Payment

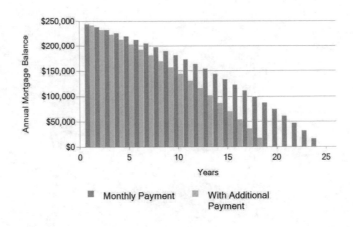

Pay Yourself First

Assumptions:

Beginning balance: $3,000
Beginning monthly savings amount: $700
Years until retirement: 30
Annual rate of return: 6.00%
Expected annual percentage increase in salary: 4.00%
Monthly Income: $7,000

Amount saved by retirement: $1,130,629

Example

If you started with $3,000 and saved 10.00% of your salary for the next 30 years,
while sustaining a 4.00% annual growth in your salary, you would accumulate $1,130,629.

One factor to successfully reaching your financial goal is to save a specific amount every
month.

Pay Yourself First

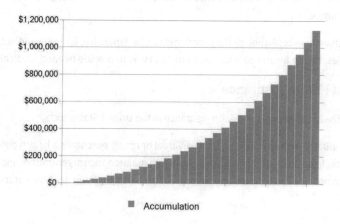

The Need for Health Insurance

Most of us would agree that good health is an extremely valuable attribute. Those in poor health generally have a lower quality of life as well as a reduced ability to work and earn an income. Good health is frequently the result of biology (the genes you inherit), the life style choices you make (exercise, diet, smoking), and appropriate medical care.

And even the healthiest among us need some medical care. Regular physician and dental visits are a normal part of maintaining good health. Accidents, illness, and simply growing older are other reasons medical care is necessary.

Paying For Medical Care

Medical care in the United States is, unquestionably, expensive. According to statistics compiled by the federal government, 6.9% of personal consumption expenditures are directed to medical care.[1] For those needing medical care, there are three basic choices:

- **Don't go:** Not seeking medical care when it is needed can result in small, treatable health problems becoming much bigger ones, with sometimes fatal consequences.

- **Pay out-of-pocket:** Paying for medical care from your own pocket can quickly exhaust your assets. Huge medical bills are one reason cited as a cause of personal bankruptcy.

- **Health insurance:** Although the premiums can be expensive, for many individuals and families, health insurance is the only practical way to provide needed medical care.

Sources of Health Insurance

There are three broad sources of health insurance in the United States today:

- **Individually-owned policies:** The individual or family purchases a health policy directly from an insurance company or health maintenance organization. Individual health policies can be relatively expensive compared to group health insurance.

---

[1] Source: Bureau of Labor Statistics, Consumer Expenditures 2012, September 10, 2013.

- **Group health insurance:** Group health insurance is typically provided through an employer or another related group such as a professional association. The premiums for group health policies tend to be less than those for individually owned policies.

- **American Health Benefit Exchanges:** Beginning in 2014, the Patient Protection and Affordable Care Act (PPACA) provided for the establishment, by either individual states or the federal government, of American Health Benefit Exchanges (AHBE) and Small Business Health Options (SHOP) exchanges. The primary purpose of these exchanges is to create a marketplace where individuals and small businesses can shop for health insurance coverage.

- **Other Government programs:** For those age 65 and older, Medicare provides a base level of health insurance. Medicaid provides health care for the impoverished. The federal government has a number of programs to provide medical care to active duty and former military service members. Some states have individual programs to provide health insurance to low-income individuals and families.

The Choice Is Yours

While health insurance may be expensive, trying to pay medical costs out of your own pocket, or not seeking medical help when needed, can be much more expensive.

Health Insurance Issues

The continuing escalation in health care costs makes a well-designed health insurance program essential to your family's financial security; one or two days in the hospital could equal thousands of dollars in expenses.

When reviewing your health insurance coverage, consider the following:

- **Deductibles:** How much of the initial costs must you absorb in the way of a deductible? Is it charged only once in the calendar year? Is there a limit of two or three deductibles per family or must each member satisfy it?

- **Coinsurance:** Beyond the deductible, what percentage of the expense must you pay, 10%, 20%? Most important - Is there a stop-loss provision that eliminates all coinsurance and pays 100% of the charges after you reach $1,000 (or some specified dollar amount) in out-of-pocket expense?

- **Family benefit maximums:** These should be unlimited or extremely high, e.g., $1,000,000, due to potential costs of a major surgery, hospitalization, a series of family illnesses, etc.

- **Inside limits:** These limits, like $200 for X-rays, etc., should be avoided in favor of comprehensive coverage, i.e., a flat percentage of the cost incurred.

- **Outpatient benefits:** These benefits should be examined carefully since many procedures are now done on an outpatient basis, e.g., preadmission testing, diagnosis, etc., due to the high costs of hospitalization.

- **Preferred providers:** Some medical plans call for the use of a preferred supplier and provide a list of doctors or hospitals from which you must choose.

- **Health maintenance organizations (HMOs):** These medical plans offer a different approach from traditional health insurance, in which you pick the doctor, pay as you go and receive reimbursement from an insurance company. With an HMO, you or your employer pay an annual fee, for which the plan's own doctors handle almost all of your health needs.

Health Insurance Issues

HMOs typically cost less in that there are usually no deductibles and they cover a higher percentage of costs than traditional plans. However, since you are limited to the services of this organization, it is important to ask the following questions:

- Where do I go if I require hospitalization?

- What about emergency treatment out of the local area?

- How substantial is the local staff and are all specialties represented?

- How long must I wait to get an appointment?

- Is the plan facility oversubscribed?

How Employer Provided Health Insurance Works

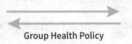

Employer and Employee
Each pays a portion of the premium

EMPLOYER AND EMPLOYEE		HEALTH INSURANCE COMPANY

Group Health Policy

MEDICAL EVENT

(e.g. routine care, accident, illness)

EMPLOYEE	HEALTH INSURANCE COMPANY
Pays deductible, co-insurance amounts and any balance over maximum benefit.	Pays benefits under the terms of the contract, up to policy maximums.

HEALTH CARE PROVIDERS
(E.G., HOSPITALS, DOCTORS)

Business Responsibilities Under the ACA

The Patient Protection and Affordable Care Act (ACA) has several goals, including increasing access to health insurance coverage, expanding federal private health insurance market requirements, and providing for the creation of health insurance exchanges to provide individuals and small employers with access to qualified health insurance.[1]

For employers, ACA includes a requirement (the "employer mandate") for certain "large" employers to provide health insurance to their employees. The law includes a penalty (the "shared responsibility" payment) if a large employer either does not offer health insurance to almost all (95%) of its full-time employees, or offers health insurance that does not meet certain standards. The ACA sets out two elements for determining penalties. First, which firms are considered to be "large" employers, and thus potentially subject to the penalty, and second, for which employees within a firm the penalty is applied.

Who is a "Large" Employer?

In general terms, the ACA defines a "large" employer as an employer who employed an average of at least 50 full-time equivalent employees (FTEs) on business days during the preceding calendar year. For example, an employer will use information (the number of employees and their hours of service) from 2017 to determine whether or not the employer will be considered a "large" employer in 2018. Both full-time and part-time employees are included in this calculation.

- **Full-time employee:** An employee who works on average at least 30 hours per week. 130 hours of service in a calendar month is treated as the monthly equivalent of at least 30 hours per week.

- **Part-time employees:** Part-time employees (less than 30 hours per week) are converted into FTEs. All hours worked by all part-time employees (no more than 120 hours per employee) are added up and the total is divided by 120.

---

[1] The discussion here concerns federal law. State or local law may differ.

Business Responsibilities Under the ACA

Example: Assume a firm has 35 full-time employees (30 or more hours per week) and 20 part-time employees, each of whom works 24 hours per week (96 hours per month). The 20 part-time employees equate to 16 full-time equivalents (FTEs), calculated as follows;

20 employees x 96 hours = 1920 total hours   1920 ÷ 120 = 16 **F**ull-**T**ime **E**quivalent**s**

With 35 full-time employees and 16 FTEs, the employer would be considered a "large" employer because there is a total FTE count of 51.

- **Employee:** The ACA definition of an employee (as contrasted with an "independent contractor") is based on a common law standard under which an employer-employee relationship exists if the employer controls both <u>what</u> and <u>how</u> the work is to be done.

- **Seasonal employees:** Seasonal employees are generally defined as those who work for up to 120 days a year. Full-time seasonal employees who work 120 days per year or less are <u>excluded</u> from the calculation to determine large employer status.

- **Control group rules:** The ACA follows the control group rules of IRC Sec. 414. Thus, if an individual or organization owns all or a substantial part of several other business (for example, a group of fast-food restaurants), all of the business are considered to be one entity. For purposes of the 50-FTE rule, the employees in each business must be aggregated to determine the total.

- **Temporary agency employees:** For purposes of determining who is a large employer, "temp" (or "leased") employees are generally counted as employees of the temporary agency.

Identifying "Full-Time" Employees

The IRS's final regulations provide two methods for determining whether an employee has sufficient hours of service to be considered a "full-time" employee:

- **Monthly measurement method:** Under this approach, an employer simply records an employee's hours of service each month. Once the number of hours of service are known, the rules previously discussed (30 hours per week or 130 hours per calendar month) are applied to determine if an employee is considered to be full-time or not. This method may be used to determine if an employer is a "large" employer as well as for calculating any "shared responsibility" payment.

Business Responsibilities Under the ACA

- **Look-back measurement method:** Under the "look-back" method, an employer determines the status of an employee as full-time during a *future* period (the "stability" period) based upon the hours of service in a *prior* period (the "measurement" period). As with the monthly measurement method, the "30 hours per week or 130 hours per month" rules are applied to determine an employee's status as either full or part-time. The look-back method is available <u>only</u> for computing an employer's "shared responsibility" payment and not for determining if the employer is a "large" employer. The following table outlines this approach:

	Measurement Period	Administrative Period	Stability Period
Description	A period of time during which an employer measures the average hours an employee worked per week.	At the employer's option, a period of time during which full-time employees are identified and enrolled in a health plan.	During the stability period, the employee is treated as full-time regardless of how many hours are worked. This is also the period in which a penalty payment may be due.
On-going employees	From three to 12 months.[1] Uses data from a preceding year.	Up to 90 days.	At least six consecutive calendar months, but cannot be shorter in duration than the measurement period.
New employees, hired as full-time	Not applicable.	Up to 90 days to enroll.	Not applicable.
New variable-hour, part-time, and seasonal employees	From three to 12 months.[2]	Up to 90 days. Measurement period and administrative period cannot exceed 13 months.	Three to 12 months, but cannot be longer than the measurement period.

Minimum Essential Health Insurance

If an employer is determined to be a "large" employer, and, in order to avoid a potential penalty, the employer must offer "minimum essential health coverage" to all full-time employees. The health insurance must also be both <u>affordable</u> and provide <u>adequate coverage</u> to employees and their dependents.

---

[1] For on-going employees, this is referred to as the "standard" measurement period.

[2] For new employees, this is referred to as the "initial" measurement period.

Business Responsibilities Under the ACA

- **Minimum Essential Health Coverage:** The ACA lists the types of services that must be included to be considered "minimum essential health coverage", including ambulatory patient services, emergency services, hospitalization, maternity and newborn care, mental health and substance use disorder services, prescription drugs, rehabilitative and habilitative services, laboratory services, preventive and wellness services, chronic disease management, and pediatric services, including vision and oral care.

- **Coverage must be "affordable":** Coverage under an employer-sponsored plan is "affordable" if the employee's required contribution to the plan does not exceed 9.56% of the employee's household income for the taxable year.[1]

- **Affordability "safe-harbors":** As a practical matter, most employers will not know the family's household income. To overcome this, three, alternative "safe-harbor" tests have been proposed. Under the first safe-harbor, the annualized, required contribution must not exceed 9.56% of the employee's earnings from the employer, as shown in Box 1 of the employee's W-2 Tax and Wage statement. Under the second safe harbor, the 9.56% affordability test is applied to the employee's hourly rate of pay for a month, multiplied by 130. Finally, if the employee's required contribution is less than 9.56% of the federal poverty level for a single individual, the coverage is treated as affordable. A plan can meet any one of these tests to comply with the affordability requirement.

- **"Adequate" coverage:** For ACA purposes, a plan is considered to provide adequate coverage (also called "minimum value") if the plan's actuarial value (i.e. share of the total allowed costs the plan is expected to cover) is at least 60%. Under the ACA, the health insurance plans offered through the health insurance exchanges will generally be available at four "levels" or price points. Each level covers a specified percentage of the actuarial value of the benefits provided by the plan. These levels are: Bronze – 60%; Silver – 70%; Gold – 80%; and Platinum – 90%.

- **Dependent:** Although employers are encouraged to offer health coverage to an employee and all dependents, under IRS regulations, the term "dependent" has a narrow meaning. For ACA purposes, a "dependent" is a child of an employee who has not yet attained age 26. The term does not include a spouse or others (such as parents) that an employee might claim as a dependent on his or her federal income

---

[1] This is the percentage for 2018; for 2017 this value was 9.69%. This percentage is subject to adjustment in future years.

tax return. Thus, in order to meet the letter of the law, an employer must offer health insurance that covers only the employee and his or her children under the age of 26.

What Triggers the Penalty?

Regardless of whether or not a "large" employer offers health coverage, it will be liable for a penalty only if at least one of its full-time employees obtains coverage through a health insurance exchange and receives a premium assistance tax credit or cost-sharing subsidy.

One part of the ACA calls for the creation of health insurance exchanges. These exchanges are intended to provide an online marketplace where individuals and small businesses can shop for qualified health insurance coverage. Individuals who purchase health insurance through a health insurance exchange may receive help in paying for the coverage in several ways:

- **Premium assistance tax credit:** A low-income individual[1] who purchases health insurance through a health insurance exchange may be eligible to receive a refundable "premium assistance" tax credit. The U.S. Treasury pays the premium assistance credit amount directly to the health insurance company, with the individual being responsible for paying any remaining premium.

- **Cost-sharing subsidy:** An individual may also qualify for a "cost-sharing" subsidy, available through the health insurance exchange. The subsidy reduces the dollar amount of "out-of-pocket" expenses (deductibles or co-payments) that the individual might otherwise pay. This subsidy is generally limited to low-income individuals[2] and is only available for those months when the individual qualifies for a premium assistance tax credit.

Calculating the Employer Penalty

Assuming that an employer is a "large" employer, and at least one full-time employee has obtained health insurance coverage through a health insurance exchange, with either a

---

[1] Generally, someone earning from 100% up to 400% of the federal poverty level (FPL) for the family size involved. For 2018, in the continental U.S., 100% of the FPL for a family of one is $12,060; for a family of four it is $24,600; for a family of eight it is $41,320.

[2] Generally, those earning less than 250% of the federal poverty level (FPL), for the family size involved.

premium tax credit or a cost-sharing subsidy, the method used to calculate the employer's "shared responsibility" payment will vary:

- **Large employer not offering health insurance:** For 2018, the monthly penalty assessed to an employer who does not offer health insurance to at least 95% of its full-time employees will be equal to the number of full-time[1] employees minus 30 (the penalty is waived for the first 30 employees), multiplied by one-twelfth of $2,320.[2]

Example: In 2018, Employer X does not offer minimum essential health coverage and has 100 full-time employees, 10 of whom receive a premium assistance tax credit for the year. For each employee over the 30-employee threshold (100 - 30 = 70), the monthly penalty amount for Employer X is $13,533.33, (70 x ($2,320 ÷ 12)) or (70 x $193.33).

- **Large employers offering coverage:** Even though an employer may offer health insurance coverage, the coverage may not be "affordable" or it may not be "adequate." In this situation, for 2018, the monthly penalty assessed to an employer for each full-time employee who receives a premium tax credit or cost-sharing subsidy will be one-twelfth of $3,480.[2] However, the monthly penalty will be capped at an amount equal to the total number of full-time employees during the month (regardless of the number of employees receiving a premium tax credit or cost-sharing reduction) in excess of 30, multiplied by one-twelfth of $2,160.

Example: In 2018, Employer Z offers health coverage and has 100 full-time employees, 20 of whom receive a premium tax credit or cost-sharing subsidy for the year. For these 20 employees, Employer Z employer owes a penalty of $5,800 per month (20 x ($3,480 ÷ 12)) or (20 x $290). The maximum monthly penalty for is capped at the amount that would have been assessed for a failure to provide coverage, or $13,533.33 ((100-30) x ($2,320 ÷12)) or (70 x $193.33). Since the calculated penalty of $5,800 for the 20 employees receiving a premium tax credit or cost-sharing subsidy is less than the maximum amount of $13,533.33, Employer Z will pay the $5,800 monthly penalty.

---

[1] Part-time employees are not included in the penalty calculations. Part-time employees are included in determining whether or not an employer is a "large" employer.

[2] The $2,320 and $3,480 amounts apply to 2018. These values are subject to adjustment for inflation in future years.

Other Requirements

- **Information reporting requirements:** Large employers subject to the employer shared-responsibility requirement are required to report certain health insurance coverage information to both its full-time employees and to the IRS. An employer who fails to comply with these reporting requirements is subject to certain penalties. Additionally, information reporting requirements apply to insurers, self-insuring employers, and certain other providers of minimum essential health coverage.

Seek Professional Guidance

The foregoing is a simplified, high-level summary of a complex piece of legislation. Further, the rules and regulations issued to implement this legislation are subject to change. The guidance of knowledgeable income tax, health insurance, and other financial professionals is highly recommended.

How Individual Health Insurance Works

Individual
Pays premium.

INDIVIDUAL

Individual Health Policy

HEALTH INSURANCE
COMPANY

MEDICAL EVENT

(e.g. routine care, accident, illness)

INDIVIDUAL	HEALTH INSURANCE COMPANY
Pays deductible, co-insurance amounts and any balance over maximum benefit.	Pays benefits under the terms of the contract, up to policy maximums.

HEALTH CARE PROVIDERS
(E.G., HOSPITALS, DOCTORS)

Individual Responsibilities Under the ACA

The Patient Protection and Affordable Care Act (ACA)[1] has several goals, including increasing access to health insurance coverage, expanding federal private health insurance market requirements, and requiring the creation of health insurance exchanges to provide individuals and small employers with access to qualified health insurance.

The ACA includes an individual mandate, applicable to every person in the United States (including children and senior citizens), to either maintain "minimum essential health coverage" for themselves and certain family members[2] or make an additional payment, known as a "shared responsibility payment," with their federal income tax return. Certain classes of individuals may qualify for an exemption to the individual mandate. The requirement to maintain minimum essential health coverage is measured on a <u>monthly</u> basis. Generally, an individual is treated as having minimum essential health coverage if he or she is enrolled and entitled to receive benefits under a qualifying program or plan for at least <u>one day</u> during the month.

The individual requirement to maintain minimum essential health coverage began January 1, 2014.

Exempt Individuals

Some individuals are <u>exempt</u> from the requirement to maintain minimum essential health coverage or the requirement to pay the penalty. An individual's status as exempt or non-exempt is measured on a monthly basis:

- **Members of certain recognized religious sects:** Generally, a group that has established tenets or teachings under which the members are conscientiously opposed to accepting benefits from any private or public insurance that makes payments in the event of death, disability, old age, or retirement, or that pays for or provides medical care.

---

[1] The discussion here concerns federal law. State or local law may differ.

[2] Generally, a spouse and any individual that a taxpayer may claim as a dependent on his or her federal income tax return. The Tax Cuts and Jobs Act of 2017 temporarily suspends the deduction for personal and dependent exemptions for 2018 – 2025.

Individual Responsibilities Under the ACA

- **Members of a health care sharing ministry:** Generally, a health care sharing ministry is an organization, the members of which share a common set of ethical or religious beliefs and share medical expenses among themselves.

- **In jail or prison:** Individuals who are in jail or prison, except those whose cases are pending disposition of charges.

- **Non-citizens:** An exemption applies to an individual who is neither a citizen nor a national of the United States, nor an alien lawfully present in the United States.

- **Minimum essential coverage is not "affordable":** An individual is exempt for a month in which he or she does not have access to "affordable" health coverage. For these purposes, generally, health insurance coverage is affordable if the individual's required contribution (calculated on an annual basis) does not exceed a certain percentage (8.05% in 2018, 8.16% in 2017) of household income.

- **Household Income below filing threshold:** Taxpayers with gross household income below the income tax filing threshold for their filing status are exempt.

- **Hardship:** Individuals who suffer a hardship that makes it impossible to obtain the required minimum essential health coverage are exempt.

- **Member of an Indian tribe:** A taxpayer who is a member of a federally recognized Indian tribe or who is eligible for services through an Indian Health Services provider is exempt.

- **Short coverage gap:** No tax is assessed for an individual who is uninsured for no more than two consecutive months of the year. If there are multiple gaps in coverage during the year, the penalty exemption applies only to the first such gap in coverage.

- **U.S. citizens abroad:** A U.S. citizen who either (1) spent 330 full days abroad during a 12-month period, or (2) who was a bona fide resident of a foreign country (or countries) for a full tax year, is exempt

- **No expanded Medicaid:** A taxpayer, who lived in a state that didn't expand its Medicaid program, but who would have qualified for Medicaid if it had, is exempt.

Individual Responsibilities Under the ACA

Minimum Essential Health Coverage

The following items are included in the minimum essential health package:

- Ambulatory patient services.
- Emergency services.
- Hospitalization.
- Maternity and newborn care.
- Mental health and substance use disorder services, including behavioral health treatment.
- Prescription drugs.
- Rehabilitative and habilitative services.
- Laboratory services.
- Preventive and wellness services and chronic disease management.
- Pediatric services, including oral and vision care.

Health insurance programs which meet these minimum coverage standards include:

- Employer-sponsored health plans, including COBRA and retiree coverage.
- Coverage purchased in the individual market through a state or federal health insurance exchange.
- Medicare coverage, including Medicare Advantage.
- Medicaid coverage.
- Children's Health Insurance Program (CHIP) coverage.
- Certain types of veterans coverage.
- Most TRICARE plans.

Minimum essential coverage does not include specialized coverage, such as coverage only for vision care or dental care, worker's compensation, disability policies, long-term care policies, Medicare supplemental health insurance, or coverage only for a specific disease or condition.

Individual Responsibilities Under the ACA

Acquiring Minimum Essential Health Coverage

Many in the U.S. are already covered by health insurance that qualifies as minimum essential coverage; to comply with the ACA, they need only continue their current policies. For those without health insurance, several options are available:

- **Health insurance exchanges:** The ACA provides for the establishment of state-run health insurance exchanges, where an individual can shop for health insurance. The federal government operates a health insurance exchange (www.healthcare.gov), open to residents of a state which chooses not to establish its own health insurance exchange. All health insurance plans offered through a health insurance exchange must meet certain requirements, including offering the essential health benefits discussed earlier. Through the exchanges, health insurance companies compete on a level playing field, offering consumers a choice of health plans.

- *Premium assistance tax credit*: A low-income individual[1] who purchases a qualified health plan through a health insurance exchange may be eligible to receive a refundable "premium assistance" tax credit. The U.S. Treasury pays the premium assistance credit amount directly to the health insurance company, with the individual being responsible for any remaining premium.

- *Cost-sharing subsidy*: An individual may also qualify for a "cost-sharing" subsidy, available through the insurance exchange. The subsidy reduces the dollar amount of "out-of-pocket" expenses (deductibles or co-payments) that the individual might otherwise pay. This subsidy is generally limited to low-income individuals[2] and is only available for those months when the individual also qualifies for a premium assistance tax credit.

- *Benefit coverage level:* Health insurance plans offered through a health insurance exchange are available at four benefit levels. Each level covers a specified percentage of the actuarial value of the benefits provided by the plan:

---

[1] Generally, someone earning from 100% up to 400% of the federal poverty level (FPL) for the family size involved. For 2018, in the continental U.S., 100% of the FPL for a family of one in the continental U.S. is $12,060; for a family of four it is $24,600; for a family of eight it is $41,320.

[2] Generally, those earning less than 250% of the FPL for the family size involved.

Individual Responsibilities Under the ACA

Plan	% of Actuarial Value Covered
Bronze	60%
Silver	70%
Gold	80%
Platinum	90%

As a general rule, the higher the percentage of benefits covered, the higher the premium. ACA generally eliminated the ability of health insurers to charge higher premiums based on factors other than age, tobacco use, rating area, or family size. An individual's "required contribution" is the premium for the lowest-cost bronze plan that would cover the individual and all non-exempt members of his or her family, reduced by any premium assistance tax credit. The required contribution premium amount is also the standard in determining if a policy is "affordable" or not.

- **Coverage under an employer-sponsored plan:** Many individuals (including individuals covered under COBRA and retirees) will acquire minimum essential health coverage through an employer-sponsored group health plan. An employee's "required contribution" is the portion of the premium for the lowest-cost bronze plan that would cover the individual and all non-exempt members of his or her family.

An employer-sponsored plan will not meet the requirements to be considered minimum essential coverage if the plan fails either of two tests:

- *Coverage must be "affordable"*: In general, coverage under an employer-sponsored plan is "affordable" if the employee's share of the premium for the employer-provided coverage does not exceed 9.56% of the employee's household income for the taxable year in 2018. This value was 9.69% in 2017.

- *"Adequate" coverage*: For ACA purposes, a plan is considered to provide adequate coverage (also called "minimum value") if the plan's actuarial value (i.e. share of the total allowed costs the plan is expected to cover) is at least 60% (i.e. equivalent to a "bronze" plan).

If an employer-sponsored health plan fails to meet either of these requirements, the employee could decline the employer-sponsored health insurance and apply for a policy through a state health insurance exchange, possibly receiving a premium assistance tax credit or a cost-sharing subsidy.

- Other sources of qualified health insurance coverage – Include the following:

  - *"Grandfathered" plans*: An individual may keep an individual or group plan that was in effect on March 23, 2010. Such coverage counts as minimum essential health coverage.

  - *The "open" market*: An individual is free to purchase health coverage through the open market, outside of a state health insurance exchange or employer-sponsored health plan.

The "Penalty" for Not Having Minimum Essential Health Coverage

If a non-exempt individual does not maintain the required minimum essential health coverage, then a penalty, the "shared responsibility payment," will be due with that individual's federal income tax return for that year. The shared responsibility payment for the entire year is the lesser of:

- The annual average cost of a bronze-level plan for the individual and any non-exempt family members purchased from a health insurance exchange ÷ 12 x the number of months without coverage, or
- The sum of the monthly penalty amounts for months when the required coverage was not maintained.

The monthly penalty amount used in this calculation is equal to the greater of:

- A monthly flat dollar amount (the "applicable dollar amount") x the number of uninsured adults in the household, ÷ 12, (limited to the applicable dollar amount x 3), or
- A monthly amount equal to the "applicable percentage" x the amount by which the taxpayer's household income exceeds the taxpayer's income tax filing threshold.

The table below shows the annual percentages and applicable dollar amounts for calendar years 2016-2018.

Year	Applicable Dollar Amount	% of Income
2016	$695	2.5%
2017	695	2.5%
2018	695	2.5%

The flat dollar amount for a child under the age of 18 is one-half of the adult amount.

Example: In 2017, the Smith family, the parents and three children under 18, uses the Married Filing Jointly filing status. The family's household income for the year is $120,000, with an estimated filing threshold of $20,800. They are <u>uninsured for 10 months</u> of the year. The annual cost of a bronze-level plan for the family is $16,320.

(A) Annual average cost for a bronze-level plan: (($16,320 ÷ 12) x 10) = **$13,600.00.**

(B) Monthly flat dollar amount: The <u>lesser</u> of $695 x 3.5 adults (each child counts as one-half) = $2,432.50; (($2,432.50 ÷ 12) x 10) = **$2,027.08**; or $695 x 3 = $2,085; (($2,085 ÷ 12) x 10) = **$1,737.50.**

(C) Monthly percentage of household income: $120,000 - $20,800 = $99,200; $99,200 x 2.5% = $2,480.00; (($2,480.00 ÷ 12) x 10) = **$2,066.67**.

The sum of the monthly penalty amounts is the <u>greater</u> of the flat dollar amount, limited to 3 x the applicable dollar amount, ($1,737.50) or the monthly percentage of household income ($2,066.67).

The 2017 penalty amount for the Smith family is thus $2066.67, the <u>lesser</u> of the average cost of a bronze-level health plan ($13,600.00) or the sum of the monthly penalty amounts ($2,066.67).

The Tax Cuts and Jobs Act of 2017

For years after 2018, the Tax Cuts and Jobs Act of 2017 sets both the flat dollar amount and the percentage of income amount to zero, effectively repealing the penalty.

Seek Professional Guidance

The foregoing is a simplified, high-level review of a complex piece of legislation. Further, the rules and regulations issued to implement this legislation are subject to change. The guidance of knowledgeable income tax, health insurance, and other financial professionals is highly recommended.

Critical Illness Insurance

Critical illness insurance is a relatively new type of insurance coverage designed to help meet the extra, unforeseen financial burdens associated with recovering from a serious, life-threatening illness. While comprehensive health and disability insurance plans cover many expenses, they are not designed to pay all of the costs associated with recovering from a critical illness. If you are diagnosed as having a covered illness, a critical illness policy can provide the extra resources to pay for expenses not covered by other insurance:

- Rehabilitation costs.

- Co-pays and deductibles.

- Experimental and/or alternative medicine.

- Out-of-network expenses.

- Child care costs.

- To supplement or replace lost income.

- Travel, for family members or the insured.

How Does It Work?

Upon being diagnosed with one of the covered illnesses, you will typically receive a lump-sum payment. Some older policies may have a survival period (up to 30 days) that you must live after being diagnosed. Although a policy may cover more than one illness, it will generally only pay benefits on the first one to strike you. With some policies, the payments may be spread out over time.

Types of Illnesses Covered

Coverage will vary from policy to policy and company to company. Typically, however, covered illnesses include: cancer, multiple sclerosis, heart attack, Alzheimer's, stroke, paralysis, renal failure, blindness, deafness, and organ transplant.

Policy Costs

Policy costs vary according to several factors: age; medical condition; and the amount of coverage purchased. If you are a smoker or your family has a history of heart disease, stroke, or cancer, you may be denied coverage – or asked to pay a steep premium. Furthermore, a policy may exclude coverage for a pre-existing condition.

Federal Taxation of Policy Proceeds

The proceeds of a personally owned and paid for critical illness policy are exempt from tax under federal law. In certain situations, the proceeds from an employer-provided policy can be taxable. State and local law can vary. Check with your tax advisor.

As with any insurance purchase, professional guidance is recommended.

Patient Protection and Affordable Care Act

The Patient Protection and Affordable Care Act (PPACA) was signed into law by President Barack Obama on March 23, 2010. A companion package of "fixes" to PPACA, the Health Care and Education Reconciliation Act (HCERA), was signed by the President on March 30, 2010. Taken together, these two bills make the most profound changes to our country's private-market health care system in 50 years.

Many provisions of the new health reform law will impact American employers and private health consumers very soon, while others take effect over the course of the next eight years.[1] For a number of provisions, the actual application and operation of the new law will remain hazy until the federal government creates and issues detailed regulations.

Highlights of Interest to Individuals

Beginning in 2014, federal law required that most U.S. citizens and legal resident aliens, and their dependents, be covered by health insurance, what the law calls "minimum essential coverage." Failure to maintain such coverage will generally result in a monetary penalty, sometimes referred to as a "shared responsibility payment."

- **Minimum Essential Coverage:** Includes government-sponsored programs such as Medicare, Medicaid, Children's Health Insurance Program (CHIP), Tricare for Life, military and veterans' health care, and health care for Peace Corps volunteers. The term embraces employer-sponsored plans such as certain governmental plans, church plans, "grandfathered" plans, and other group health plans offered in the small or large group market within a state. It also includes individual market plans and other plans or programs recognized by the Secretary of Health and Human Services.

---

[1] The discussion here concerns federal law. State and/or local law may differ.

Patient Protection and Affordable Care Act

- **Exempt individuals:** Certain individuals are exempt from the requirement to maintain health insurance coverage. These include prisoners, undocumented aliens, members of a health care sharing ministry,[1] and members of certain recognized religious sects. Individuals living outside the U.S. are deemed to maintain minimum essential coverage.

- **Penalty exemptions:** Some individuals are exempt from any penalty that might apply, including those whose required contribution for self-only employer-sponsored coverage exceeds 8.05% (2018) or 8.16% (2017) of household income, those whose household income is below the threshold for filing a federal income tax return, certain Native Americans, individuals with a "short" (no more than two consecutive months) lapse in coverage,[2] and those whom the Secretary of Health and Human Services determines have suffered a hardship with regard to maintaining health insurance coverage. By definition, dependents are exempt as the penalty is levied on the taxpayer claiming the income tax exemption for the dependent.

- **Penalty amount:** The penalty is calculated on a monthly basis (months when there is no qualifying health insurance coverage) and is equal to the **greater** of (1) a specified percentage of the taxpayer's annual household income over the income tax filing threshold for the taxpayer for the year, or (2) a flat dollar amount per uninsured adult in the household. The fee for an uninsured individual under age 18 is one-half of the adult fee. The table below shows the annual percentages and flat dollar amounts for calendar years 2016-2018.

Shared Responsibility Penalty

Year	Flat Dollar Amount[3]	% of Income
2016	$695	2.5
2017	695	2.5
2018	700	2.5

---

[1] A health care sharing ministry (HCSM), generally, is a nonprofit religious organization in which the members share their medical expenses. An HCSM must meet certain requirements to qualify its members for this exemption.

[2] Only one short-term lapse per calendar year is exempted from the penalty.

[3] Annual amounts are shown. For monthly amounts, divide the annual value by 12.

Patient Protection and Affordable Care Act

Two other limits apply:

- The total annual household penalty may not exceed 300% of the per adult penalty, and

- The total annual household payment may not exceed the nation average annual premium for "bronze" level health coverage offered through the local American Health Benefit Exchange (AHBE).

Tax Cuts and Jobs Act of 2017

For years after 2018, the Tax Cuts and Jobs Act of 2017 sets both the flat dollar amount and the percentage of income amount to zero, effectively repealing the penalty.

The tables on the following pages summarize important changes for individual taxpayers:

Item	Summary
American Health Benefit Exchange (Effective 2014)	By 2014, each state is expected to establish an American Health Benefit Exchange (AHBE) and a Small Business Health Options (SHOP) Exchange. If a state chooses not to establish an AHBE or a SHOP, the federal government will establish health care exchanges that the residents of a state without an exchange may use. A state may create separate exchanges for different regions within the state, or contiguous states can join together to create a single exchange. The primary purpose of these exchanges is to create a marketplace where individuals and small (initially, 100 employees or less) businesses can shop for "qualified" health insurance coverage. Such qualified coverage must include certain categories of benefits and meet specified cost-sharing and level-of-coverage standards, the "essential health benefits package." The scope of essential health benefits must be equal to the scope of benefits provided under a typical employer plan. Qualifying health plans must provide specified levels of coverage, actuarially equivalent to a certain percentage of the full actuarial value of the benefits provided under the plan: Bronze Level = 60%; Silver Level = 70%; Gold Level = 80%; and Platinum Level = 90%. The legislation also provides for "catastrophic" policies (individual market only) for enrollees under age 30 or those who are exempt from the minimum health care coverage requirements because coverage is unaffordable or because of a hardship.

Patient Protection and Affordable Care Act

Item	Summary
Refundable Premium Assistance Credit (Effective 2014)	The premium assistance credit is a refundable tax credit for eligible individuals and their families who purchase health insurance through an AHBE. Under this provision, an eligible individual enrolls in a health plan offered through an AHBE and reports his or her anticipated income to the exchange. The individual then receives a premium assistance credit based on income. The U.S. Treasury pays the premium assistance credit amount directly to the insurance company, with the individual responsible for paying any remaining premium. This credit is available for those with household incomes between 100% and 400% of the Federal Poverty Level (FPL) for the family size involved, and who do not, generally, receive health insurance through an employer-sponsored health plan. The amount that an eligible individual is expected to pay for health insurance ranges from 2.0% for those at 100% of FPL, to 9.5% for those at 400% of FPL. In future years, these percentages will be adjusted to hold steady the share of premiums that enrollees at a given poverty level pay.
Cost-Sharing Subsidy (Effective 2014)	Certain individuals who enroll in a health plan through an AHBE may also qualify for a cost-sharing subsidy. Such a subsidy reduces the dollar amount of out-of-pocket expenses (deductibles, co-payments, or co-insurance) that the eligible individual might otherwise pay for essential health services. The subsidy is generally limited to those whose household income is between 100% and 400% of FPL for the family size involved and is only available for those months when the individual qualifies for a premium assistance credit.
Free Choice Vouchers (Effective 2014)	Employers offering minimum essential health coverage through an eligible employer-sponsored plan, and paying a portion of that coverage, must provide certain employees with a voucher whose value can be used to purchase a health plan through an AHBE. Qualified employees for this purpose are those who do not participate in the employer's health plan and whose required contribution for employer-sponsored minimum essential coverage exceeds 8%, but does not exceed 9.8%, of the employee's household income. Further, the employee's total household income may not exceed 400% of the FPL. The voucher's value is equal to the dollar value of the employer contribution to the employer-offered health plan. If the value of the voucher exceeds the cost of the Exchange plan chosen, the individual keeps (and is taxed on) the excess. **This provision of the PPACA was repealed under the Department of Defense and Full-Year Continuing Appropriations Act, 2011 (H.R.1473).**

Patient Protection and Affordable Care Act

Item	Summary
Health Benefits for Children Under Age 27 (Effective 2010)	Under federal income tax law, a taxpayer, spouse, and "dependents" may receive health care benefits in a tax-advantaged fashion through a number of arrangements, usually by excluding benefits or payments from income or by allowing a deduction for medical expenses or premiums. Under prior law, the definition of "dependent" for these health benefits purposes generally followed the definition of "dependent" for the purposes of claiming an exemption on the income tax return. The new legislation amends the definition of "dependent" for health or medical benefits purposes to specifically include a taxpayer's child (dependent or not) who is under age 27 at the end of the tax year.
Individuals With Pre-Existing Conditions (Effective 2010)	Establishes "high-risk" insurance pools to enable individuals with pre-existing medical conditions to purchase health insurance at rates parallel to those available for individuals without pre-existing conditions. Qualifying individuals will generally be eligible to purchase health coverage if they have not had health insurance for six months.
Children Under Age 19 With Pre-Existing Medical Conditions (Effective 2010)	Group health plans, grandfathered health plans, and health insurance issuers offering group or individual health insurance coverage may not impose any pre-existing condition exclusion on enrollees who are under age 19.
Medicare (Effective 2010-2020)	In 2010, Medicare beneficiaries with Part D (prescription drug) coverage who reach the "donut hole" coverage gap will receive a one-time payment of $250. In 2011, drug manufacturers will be required to provide a 50% discount on name-brand medications, the first step in a gradual reduction in the coverage gap. By 2020, the portion payable by a Medicare enrollee in the coverage gap will shrink from 100% to 25%.
Medicaid Changes (Effective 2014)	Expands eligibility for Medicaid to individuals not currently eligible for Medicare (generally, individuals under age 65), including children, pregnant women, and adults without dependent children, with incomes up to 133% of the federal poverty level (FPL). Coverage will be provided through an essential health benefits package purchased through a state's AHBE.
CLASS Act Long-Term Care Insurance (Effective 2011)	A new, long-term care insurance program, called "CLASS" Act (Community Living Assistance Services and Supports), may begin collecting taxes/premiums as early as 2011. Intended as a voluntary ("opt-out") program offered by employers, premiums will be paid entirely by employees. The program will provide individuals with specified functional limitations a cash benefit of $50 per day or more. There is no lifetime limit on benefits and persons with greater needs in terms of the basic activities of daily living will receive higher benefits. **This provision of the PPACA was repealed as a part of the American Taxpayer Relief Act of 2012.**

Patient Protection and Affordable Care Act

Item	Summary
Health Professional Student Loan Forgiveness Programs (Effective 2009)	Under federal income tax law, gross income generally includes the discharge of a taxpayer's indebtedness. Under one exception to this general rule, gross income does not include amounts from the forgiveness of certain student loans, provided that the forgiveness is contingent on the student's working for a certain period of time in certain professions. The new law expands an existing exception to exclude from gross income any amount received by an individual under any state loan repayment or loan forgiveness program that is intended to provide for the increased availability of health care services in underserved or health-professional shortage areas.
Health Benefits Provided By Indian Tribal Governments (Effective 2010)	This provision allows for an exclusion from gross income for the value of specified Indian tribe health care benefits provided to a member of an Indian tribe, his or her spouse, and dependents. The exclusion does not apply to any amount which may be deducted or excluded from gross income under any other provision of the Internal Revenue Code.
Marketing Reforms and Expanded Benefit Coverage (Various Years)	The new legislation contains significant marketing and coverage reforms, including guaranteeing that coverage will be both available and renewable, regardless of health status, and limiting the range of premiums a health insurer can charge.[1] Health policies must meet comprehensive requirements for coverage and cost-sharing. Generally, no lifetime or annual limits on the dollar amount of benefits per insured are permitted and, except in cases of fraud or misrepresentation, a policy may not be cancelled once issued. Certain preventive health services must be covered without cost-sharing and policies must cover adult children until a child turns age 26.
Health Care Costs Reported on W-2 (Effective for 2011)	An employer must include on an employee's W-2 form the entire cost of the employer-sponsored health coverage. Generally, this refers to the coverage under any group health plan made available to the employee by an employer which is excludable from the employee's gross income. This reporting requirement does not change the tax-free treatment of the employer-provided health coverage. As originally passed, this requirement was applicable to W-2 forms to be issued in early 2012, for tax years beginning in 2011. **The IRS later deferred this requirement for one year, to W-2 forms issued in January 2013 for calendar 2012. For small employers (those issuing less than 250 W-2 forms in the previous calendar year) the health-cost reporting requirement is suspended until "further guidance" from the IRS. See IRS Notice 2012-9 for details.**

---

[1] Factors such as age, geographical area, tobacco use, or family or individual coverage may be considered.

Patient Protection and Affordable Care Act

Highlights of Interest to Business

- **Shared responsibility for employers:** Federal law currently does not require that an employer offer health insurance coverage to employees and dependents. However, beginning in 2014 **(delayed until 2015)**, an applicable large employer (generally defined by having an average of at least 50 full-time employees in the preceding calendar year) who does not offer minimum essential coverage under an employer-sponsored plan for all its full-time employees, offers minimum essential coverage that is unaffordable (with a premium more than 9.5% of an employee's household income), or that offers minimum essential coverage through a plan under which the plan's share of total allowed costs of benefits is less than 60%, may be subject to a non-deductible excise penalty tax.

  The penalty is payable if at least one full-time employee is certified to the employer as having enrolled in health insurance coverage purchased through an AHBE and with respect to which a premium assistance credit or cost-sharing subsidy applies. A similar excise penalty tax also applies to an employer who offers its full-time employees and their dependents the opportunity to enroll in minimum essential coverage under an employer-sponsored plan and any full-time employee is certified as having enrolled in health insurance coverage purchased through an AHBE and with respect to which a premium assistance credit or cost-sharing subsidy applies. Most employers providing minimum essential coverage will be required to report certain health insurance coverage information to both its full-time employees and the IRS. If these reporting requirements are not met, failure to file penalties will apply.

- **Small business tax credit:** Under this provision, which is applicable to premiums paid after December 31, 2009, a tax credit is available to a qualified small employer for nonelective contributions to purchase health insurance for its employees. For this purpose, a qualified small employer is, generally, an employer with no more than 25 full-time equivalent employees (FTEs) during the year, and whose annual full-time equivalent wages average no more than $50,000. Certain employees (2% S Corp. shareholders and more than 5% owners, spouses, and children) are not included in the definition of "full-time" employee. Neither are seasonal employees who work 120 days or less during the year.

The credit is equal to an "applicable tax credit amount" times the <u>lesser</u> of: (1) the amount of contributions the employer made on behalf of employees for qualifying health coverage, or (2) the amount of premiums the employer would have paid had each employee enrolled in coverage with a small business benchmark premium.

The credit is available in two phases. For any taxable year beginning in 2010 – 2013, the applicable tax credit amount is 35% and generally applies to health coverage purchased from an insurance company licensed under local state law. For taxable years beginning after 2013, the applicable tax credit amount is 50% and applies only to health insurance coverage purchased through an AHBE. Additionally, during the second phase, the credit is only available for a maximum period of two consecutive years.

The credit is reduced for employers with more than 10 FTEs. It is also reduced for an employer for whom average wages per employee is between $25,000 and $50,000.

Certain tax-exempt organizations are also eligible to receive the credit. However, for these tax-exempt employers, the applicable credit percentage in the first phase (2010 – 2013) is limited to 25% and the applicable credit percentage in the second phase (after 2013) is limited to 35%.

- **Simple cafeteria plans for small business:** A "cafeteria" plan is an employer-sponsored plan under which participating employees may choose from two or more options, consisting of cash or certain "qualified" benefits, such as health insurance, dependent care, or health flexible spending accounts. If an employer is unable to pay for these fringe benefits, the employee can enter into a salary-reduction agreement with the employer. The employer then uses these funds to pay for the employee's benefits, effectively allowing the employee to pay for his or her own benefits with pre-tax dollars.

  Cafeteria plans are, however, subject to complex nondiscrimination requirements to prevent discrimination in favor of highly compensated individuals. Beginning in 2011, the new law provides eligible small employers (generally with less than 100 employees during any of the two preceding years) with a simplified "safe harbor" method of meeting these nondiscrimination requirements.

Patient Protection and Affordable Care Act

- Early retiree health benefits: Effective in 2010, one provision of the law establishes a temporary reinsurance program for employers that provide retiree health coverage for employees over age 55 and less than age 65. If a plan spends more than $15,000 a year on medical or prescription drug benefits for an early retiree or a dependent, the plan can be reimbursed 80% of the excess, up to a maximum reimbursement of $60,000. Employers may use the reimbursements to reduce retiree cost-sharing. The program will end in 2014 or when $5 billion has been reimbursed, whichever comes first.

Item	Summary
Additional Medicare Hospital Insurance (HI) Tax on High-Income Taxpayers (Effective 2013)	Under current law, an employee is liable for a Medicare Hospital Insurance (HI) tax equal to 1.45% of his or her covered wages. Self-employed individuals are subject to a HI tax of 2.9% of net self-employment income. Beginning in 2013, taxpayers with incomes above certain thresholds will pay an additional HI tax of .9%. For an employee, the additional .9% effectively increases the HI tax from 1.45% to 2.35% on income in excess of the applicable threshold.[1] For self-employed taxpayers, the additional, tax of .9% effectively raises the HI rate to 3.8% of net self-employment income in excess of the applicable threshold. For self-employed individuals, the additional .9% HI tax is not deductible. The thresholds are $250,000 in case of a joint return (the earnings of both spouses are considered) or a surviving spouse, $125,000 in the case of a married individual filing a separate return, and $200,000 for any other taxpayer.

[1] The employer also pays a HI tax of 1.45%, which does not change under the new law.

Patient Protection and Affordable Care Act

Revenue Provisions

Many provisions of the new legislation raise additional tax revenue:

Item	Summary
Unearned Income Medicare Contribution (Effective 2013)	The new legislation imposes a 3.8% unearned income Medicare contribution tax on individuals, estates, and certain trusts. For individuals, the tax is 3.8% of the lesser of net investment income or the excess of modified adjusted gross income over a threshold amount. This threshold is $250,000 in the case of a joint return or a surviving spouse, $125,000 in the case of a married individual filing a separate return, and $200,000 in any other case. In the case of an estate or trust, the tax is 3.8% of the lesser of undistributed net investment income or the excess of adjusted gross income over the dollar amount at which the highest income tax bracket applicable to an estate or trust begins. Investment income, generally, refers to (1) income from interest, dividends, annuities, royalties and rents; (2) gross income from a business to which the tax applies (such as income from "passive" activities); and (3) the net gain from the disposition of certain property. The term does not include distributions from IRAs and other qualified retirement plans.
Itemized Deduction for Medical Expenses Effective 2013)	Under current law, an individual is allowed an itemized deduction for regular tax purposes[1] for unreimbursed medical expenses to the extent that such expenses exceed 7.5% of Adjusted Gross Income (AGI). Beginning in 2013, the new legislation increases the threshold for the itemized deduction for unreimbursed medical expenses from 7.5% of AGI to 10% of AGI. However, for the years 2013, 2014, 2015, and 2016, if either a taxpayer or spouse is age 65 before the end of the taxable year, the threshold remains at 7.5%.
Limitation on Health Flexible Spending Arrangements Under Cafeteria Plans (Effective 2013)	A flexible spending arrangement for medical expenses under a cafeteria plan (Health FSA) is health coverage in the form of an unfunded arrangement under which employees are given the option to reduce their current cash compensation and instead have the amount of the salary reduction made available for use in reimbursing the employee for his or her qualified medical expenses. Such an arrangement effectively allows the employee to pay for his or her own health benefits with pre-tax dollars. Under the new legislation, in order for a Health FSA to be a qualified benefit (and thus be excluded from an employee's income), the maximum amount available for reimbursement of incurred medical expenses must not exceed $2,500 (adjusted for inflation in future years.)

---

[1] For purposes of the Alternative Minimum Tax (AMT), unreimbursed medical expenses are deductible only to the extent that they exceed 10% of AGI. The new law does not change the current AMT treatment of the itemized deduction for unreimbursed medical expenses.

Patient Protection and Affordable Care Act

Item	Summary
Additional Tax on Nonqualified Distributions From HSAs and Archer MSAs (Effective 2011)	Health Savings Accounts (HSAs) and Archer Medical Savings Accounts (MSAs) are similar forms of either a tax-exempt trust or a custodial account to which tax-deductible contributions may be made to benefit individuals with a high-deductible health plan. Distributions from HSAs and MSAs used for qualified medical expenses are excludible from gross income. Under prior law, distributions from HSAs that were not used for qualified medical expenses were subject to an additional 10% tax. Non-qualifying distributions from MSAs were subject to an additional 15% tax. The new legislation increases to 20% the additional tax on non-qualifying distributions from both HSAs and MSAs.
Distributions for Medicines Qualified Only if for Prescribed Drug or Insulin (Effective 2011)	Under prior law, generally, a qualified expense for the purpose of Health Reimbursement Arrangements (HRAs), Archer Medical Savings Accounts (MSAs), Health Savings Accounts (HSAs), and Health Flexible Spending Accounts (Health FSAs) included amounts paid for over-the-counter medications. Under the new legislation, the cost of over-the-counter medications may not be reimbursed with excludible income through an HRA, MSA, HSA, or Health FSA unless prescribed by a physician.
Excise Tax on Tanning Salons (Effective 2010)	This new provision imposes a 10% excise tax on individuals receiving indoor tanning services. If the tax is not paid by the person receiving the services, the person performing the services pays the tax.
Excise Tax on High-Cost Employer-Sponsored Health Coverage[1] (Effective 2018)	This provision imposes an excise tax on health insurers if the aggregate value of employer-sponsored health insurance coverage for an employee exceeds certain limits. The tax is equal to 40% of the aggregate value above a specified threshold amount. For 2018, the threshold amount (subject to adjustment for inflation) is $10,200 annually for individual coverage and $27,500 annually for family coverage. For individuals in high-risk professions, and certain retirees age 55 and older who are not eligible for Medicare, higher thresholds will apply. For these individuals, the threshold in 2018 will be $11,850 annually for individual coverage and $30,950 annually for families. The tax is not paid by the employee, but is imposed pro-rata on issuers of the insurance. **Under the provisions of the Consolidate Appropriations Act, 2016, the effective date of this provision has been delayed until 2020. Additionally, this excise tax will now be deductible for federal income tax purposes. The Savings Act of 2017 further extended the effective date of this provision to 2022.**

[1] Popularly known as "Cadillac" health plans.

Patient Protection and Affordable Care Act

Item	Summary
Retiree Prescription Drug Plans **(Effective 2013)**	Certain sponsors of qualified retiree prescription drug plans are eligible for subsidy payments from the federal government with respect to a portion of each qualified covered retiree's gross covered prescription drug costs. Under prior law, the subsidy payment was not taken into account for the purpose of determining the allowable deduction for retiree prescription drug expenses. Under the new legislation, the amount otherwise allowable as a deduction for retiree prescription drug expenses is reduced by the amount of the excludable subsidy payments received.
Other Fees and Excise Taxes **(Various Years)**	The new legislation imposes a series of aggregate, annual fees on certain organizations involved in the health care industry. For pharmaceutical manufacturers and importers, for example, the 2011 fee is $2.5 billion. The aggregate fee will be apportioned among the covered entitles each year based on an entity's relative share of prescription drug sales. A fee also applies to any covered entity engaged in the business of providing health insurance in the U.S. For 2014, the aggregate annual fee is $8 billion, and will be apportioned among the providers based on a ratio designed to reflect the relative market share of the U. S. health insurance business. Beginning in 2013, an excise tax of 2.3% will be imposed on the sale of any taxable medical device. A taxable medical device is any device, defined in section 201(h) of the Federal Food, Drug, and Cosmetic act, intended for humans. The excise tax does not apply to eyeglasses, contact lenses, hearing aids, and any other medical device determined to be of a type that is generally purchased by the general public at retail for individual use. **The Savings Act of 2017 further extended the effective date of both the annual fee on health insurance providers and the 2.3% tax on medical devices to 2020.**

Other Legislative Changes

A number of other legislative changes – unrelated to health care – were also included:

- **Economic substance doctrine codified:** Federal law provides detailed rules which permit both taxpayers and the government to compute taxable income with reasonable accuracy and predictability. In addition to these statutory provisions, the courts have developed several common-law doctrines which can be applied to deny the tax benefits of a tax-motivated transaction, notwithstanding that the transaction may satisfy the literal requirements of a specific tax provision.

Patient Protection and Affordable Care Act

One common-law doctrine applied over the years is the "economic substance" doctrine. In general, this doctrine denies tax benefits arising from transactions that do not result in a meaningful change in the taxpayer's economic position other than a purported reduction in federal income tax.

Effective on the date of enactment (March 30, 2010), this new legislation codifies this common-law doctrine and provides that in the case of any transaction to which the economic substance doctrine is relevant, such transaction is treated as having economic substance only if (1) the transaction changes in a meaningful way the taxpayer's economic position, and (2) the taxpayer has a substantial purpose (apart from tax reduction) for entering into such transaction. Accuracy related penalties of either 20% or 40% may be imposed, depending on the level of disclosure by the taxpayer.

- **Adoption credit and employer-provided adoption assistance:** For 2010, the new legislation increases the maximum adoption credit by $1,000, to $13,170 per child. This amount, and the phase-out limits applicable to higher-income taxpayers, are subject to adjustment for inflation in 2011. Additionally, the adoption credit is made refundable. Similarly, the maximum income exclusion for benefits received through an employer-sponsored adoption assistance program was increased for 2010 to $13,170 per eligible child, with adjustments for inflation for the dollar amount and phase-out limits in 2011. The EGTRRA[1] sunset provisions for both the adoption credit and the income exclusion for adoption assistance program benefits have been delayed one year, to taxable years beginning after December 31, 2011.

- **Additional information reporting:** Beginning in 2012, a business is generally required to file an information return for all payments aggregating $600 or more in a calendar year to a single payee, other than a payee that is a tax-exempt corporation, for property or services. **Most of the expanded reporting requirements were effectively repealed under The Comprehensive 1099 Taxpayer Protection and Repayment of Exchange Subsidy Overpayments Act of 2011.**

Seek Professional Guidance

The provisions of the PPACA and the HCERA are complex and touch on a wide-range of subjects. To get the maximum benefit from these new laws, the help and guidance of experienced professionals from a number of disciplines is highly recommended.

---

[1] "EGTRRA" refers to the Economic Growth and Tax Relief Reconciliation Act of 2001.

Patient Protection and
Affordable Care Act

Timeline

The Patient Protection and Affordable Care Act (PPACA), was signed into law by President Barack Obama on March 23, 2010. A companion package of "fixes" to PPACA, the Health Care and Education Reconciliation Act (HCERA), was signed by the President on March 30, 2010.

Many provisions of the new law are effective in 2010, while others become law during the years 2011 to 2018.[1] The following pages list the legal effective dates for selected provisions of this new legislation. Note that the actual implementation date may not be the same due to the number of steps required to make a particular provision operational.

In many instances, the legislation is applicable to group plans, "for plan years beginning on or after" a particular date. Since many group plans follow a calendar year, a provision that becomes legally effective in one year may not actually be implemented by a group plan until the following calendar year.

Provisions Effective In 2009

- **January 1, 2009**

  - Expanded exclusion for specified health professionals in certain state student-loan repayment programs.

Provisions Effective In 2010

- **January 1, 2010**

  - $250 one-time payment for a Medicare beneficiary enrolled in Medicare Part D who reaches the coverage gap of $2,830 for the year (2010 only).

  - Small business tax credit for nonelective employer contributions to purchase employee health insurance.

  - Expanded adoption credit and gross income exclusion for employer-provided adoption assistance programs.

---

[1] The discussion here concerns federal law. State and/or local law may differ.

Patient Protection and Affordable Care Act

- March 23, 2010

  - Exclusion from gross income of health benefits provided by Indian tribal governments.

- March 30, 2010

  - Codification of "Economic Substance" doctrine, with associated penalties.

  - Revised definition of "dependent" for purposes of employer-provided health benefits, to include a child (dependent or not) under age 27 at the end of the tax year.

- June 23, 2010

  - High-risk insurance pools for individuals with pre-existing conditions.

  - Temporary reinsurance program for employers that provide early retiree health coverage.

- July 1, 2010

  - 10% excise tax on indoor tanning services.

- September 23, 2010

  - Extension of health coverage to include adult children up to age 26.

  - No pre-existing condition exclusion for children under age 19.

  - No lifetime limit on the dollar value of essential health benefits.

  - Policies may not be cancelled if policyholder becomes sick.

  - Certain preventive health care coverages are required.

Patient Protection and Affordable Care Act

Provisions Effective In 2011

- January 1, 2011

  - Employers required to report the total cost of employer-provided health care on an employee's W-2 form.[1]

  - Increase to 20% of the additional tax on nonqualified distributions from HSAs and Archer MSAs.

  - Distributions from HSAs, Archer MSAs, HRAs, or Health FSAs for over-the counter medicines are considered a "qualified" expense only if prescribed by a physician.

  - Collection of premiums for CLASS Act long-term care program may begin. **(Repealed)**

  - Simple cafeteria plans may be established by small employers.

  - Annual fees levied on branded prescription drug manufacturers and importers.

Provisions Effective in 2012

- January 1, 2012

  - Additional information reporting by a business of payments of $600 or more to a single payee, for property or services. **(Repealed)**

Provisions Effective In 2013

- January 1, 2013

  - 0.9% additional Hospital Insurance (Medicare) tax on high-income taxpayers.

  - 3.8% unearned income Medicare contribution.

  - Threshold for itemized deduction of unreimbursed medical expenses generally increased to 10%.

  - $2,500 reimbursement limitation on Health FSAs under cafeteria plans.

---

[1] This provision was later delayed by the IRS for one year, to W-2 forms issued in January 2013 for calendar 2012. For small employers (less than 250 W-2s) the health-cost reporting requirement is suspended until "further guidance" from the IRS.

- Business deduction for federal subsidies for retiree prescription drug plans repealed.

- 2.3% excise tax on the sale of certain medical devices.[1]

Provisions Effective In 2014

- **January 1, 2014**

  - Minimum essential health coverage required for most U.S. citizens and lawful resident aliens, with monetary penalties for non-compliance.

  - No pre-existing condition exclusion for adults.

  - States required to establish American Health Benefit Exchanges (AHBE) and Small Business Health Options Program (SHOP) Exchanges.

  - Refundable premium tax credit for eligible individuals who purchase health insurance through an AHBE.

  - Cost-sharing subsidies become available to qualified individuals who purchase health insurance through an AHBE.

  - Free Choice vouchers available to qualifying employees to purchase health coverage. **(Repealed)**

  - Expanded Medicaid coverage, to include certain groups with household incomes up to 133% of the federal poverty level.

  - Shared responsibility for employers. Certain employers are required to offer health insurance coverage to employees, with non-deductible excise tax penalty for non-compliance. **(Penalty enforcement delayed until 2015)**

  - Annual fees levied on health insurance providers.

---

[1] Under the provisions of the Protecting Americans From Tax Hikes Act of 2015, the 2.3% medical device tax was suspended for two years, with the suspension effective for sales on or after January 1, 2016 and before January 1, 2018. The Savings Act of 2017 further delayed the effective date of this provision to 2020.

Patient Protection and Affordable Care Act

Provisions Effective in 2019

- **January 1, 2019**

  - For years after 2018, the Tax Cuts and Jobs Act of 2017, with regard to the penalty (Shared Responsibility Payment) for not having minimum essential health coverage, sets both the flat dollar amount and the percentage of income amount to zero, effectively repealing the penalty.

Provisions Effective In 2020

- **January 1, 2020**

  - 40% excise tax on high-cost ("Cadillac") health plans. *Under the provisions of the Consolidated Appropriations Act, 2016, the effective date of this provision has been delayed until January 1, 2020. The Savings Act of 2017 further extended the effective date of this provision to January 1, 2022. As originally passed, the provision had an effective date of January 1, 2018.*

Group Term Life Insurance

An employee is not taxed on premiums paid by an employer under a group term plan meeting the requirements of IRC Sec. 79, unless the amount of coverage exceeds $50,000. If the coverage exceeds $50,000, the employer must compute the cost of the additional protection, and notify the employee of the amount to include in his or her gross income. The

government's Table I is used to determine the tax-reportable cost of the excess insurance protection. See Reg. Sec. 1.79-3(d)(2).

Age	Cost per Thousand per Month
Under Age 25	$0.05
25 through 29	0.06
30 through 34	0.08
35 through 39	0.09
40 through 44	0.10
45 through 49	0.15
50 through 54	0.23
55 through 59	0.43
60 through 64	0.66
65 through 69	1.27
70 and over	2.06

Example: A 44-year-old employee has $150,000 of employer-paid group term:

Total Insurance	$150,000
Less: 1st $50,000	- 50,000 (not reportable)
Taxable Amount	$100,000 X $.10 per thousand

Result: The employee must report as income an extra $10 per month, or $120 per year.

The premiums are tax deductible by the corporation under IRC Sec. 162(a)(1).

If a group term plan is discriminatory with regard to benefits or eligibility to participate, the $50,000 income tax exclusion will not be available to key employees. For discriminatory plans, the amount of imputed income is the greater of actual cost or the IRS Table I cost.

Group Term Life Insurance

See IRC Sec. 79(d). Payments for group term insurance which are included in the employee's income are also subject to FICA taxes. See IRC Sec. 3121(a).

Should an employer not be able to meet these rules, consideration should be given to personally-owned insurance as a supplement or substitute for existing employer plans.

Group Health Insurance

Employer-paid premiums for employee medical insurance are deductible by the company whether the coverage is under a group policy or individual policies. See Reg. Sec. 1.162-10(a).

The employee need not report the amount paid by the employer as current income. See IRC Sec. 106.

When an employee pays the premium and is then reimbursed by the employer, the amount received is not included in the employee's gross income. See Reg. Sec. 1.106-1.

Benefits paid under the insurance plan, which reimburse the employee for payments made for hospital, surgical or other medical expenses, are not included in the employee's gross income.

Group medical plans are an attractive fringe benefit because personally paid medical insurance premiums and qualified medical expenses are only deductible when they *exceed* 7.50% of the taxpayer's adjusted gross income.[1] See IRC Sec. 213.

Self-insured medical reimbursement plans which favor employees who are officers, shareholders or highly-paid employees may not qualify for the above tax benefits.

The Code sets certain eligibility requirements for self-insured plans, similar to those applied in qualified retirement plans, which are designed to discourage discrimination. See IRC Sec. 105(h).

The Health Insurance Portability and Accountability Act of 1996, signed into law on August 21, 1996, expanded the availability of coverage under group health plans. Effective with plan years beginning after June 30, 1997, the Act:

- Limits exclusions for pre-existing conditions.
- Prohibits discrimination in eligibility or premiums solely on the basis of an individual's health situation.
- Guarantees renewability for those employers with group health plans.
- Provides penalties for employers who do not comply with the law.

---

[1] Under current federal law, the 7.5% threshold applies to 2017 and 2018. This threshold is scheduled to increase to 10.0% for 2019 and later years. State or local law may vary.

Health Care Portability

During the summer of 1996, Congress passed the Health Insurance Portability and Accountability Act of 1996. This legislation made it easier for people with existing health insurance to change jobs, and still maintain health insurance coverage. The legislation does nothing to cover those who are currently uninsured, nor does it address the cost of individually owned health policies. Among other points, the Act:

- Restricts exclusions for pre-existing conditions.

- Requires special open enrollment periods.

- Prohibits plans from dropping or denying coverage for employees with medical conditions.

- Guarantees the availability of health insurance to small employers and individuals losing group health coverage, and guarantees renewability for all groups.

Pre-Existing Conditions

The legislation provides that group health plans must reduce any pre-existing conditions exclusion period by the length of time a person had prior coverage. Such prior coverage does not count if there has been a break in coverage longer than 62 days, not counting waiting periods. For example, if someone who had already satisfied a pre-existing condition exclusion, lost his or her group health coverage on June 30, and got a new job September 1, they would not have to satisfy a new pre-existing condition exclusion.

Certain individuals may qualify under federal law to elect COBRA continuation coverage during a special second election period. For these individuals, any days between the initial loss of group health coverage and the first day of the special second election period will not count as a break in coverage.

In order to allow individuals to present evidence of prior creditable coverage, the law requires group health plans to issue a certificate describing the previous coverage, which can include short-term coverage. Employers or insurers must provide this certificate when an individual loses coverage under the plan, or upon request at any time within the following two years.

Under certain circumstances, the law does permit a group health plan to impose a pre-existing condition exclusion. An exclusion is allowed only if related to a condition for which the individual received medical care (or for which medical care was recommended) within the 6-month period ending on the enrollment date. This exclusion period cannot extend more than 12 months after the enrollment date (18 months for a late enrollee), and is reduced by any creditable prior coverage.

Waiting periods must run concurrently with any pre-existing conditions exclusion. Pre-existing conditions exclusions cannot apply to newborn children or children placed for adoption if they are enrolled within 30 days of birth or placement. Pre-existing conditions exclusions cannot apply to pregnancies.

Special Enrollment Periods

The law requires special open enrollment periods for people who lose other coverage, subject to certain conditions. Group health plans offering dependent coverage must allow at least 30 days in which to enroll new dependents following marriage, birth, adoption, or placement for adoption. If the employee is eligible but not enrolled, he or she must also be allowed to enroll at the same time. Plans must now allow eligible spouses to enroll within 30 days of the birth or adoption of a child.

Medical Conditions

Group health plans cannot establish any rules for benefits, premiums, eligibility or continued eligibility based on health-related factors. Insurers can no longer require employees or dependents to complete medical questionnaires in order to prove insurability, although they can require questionnaires as part of the rate–setting process.

This new rule also means that groups cannot single out an individual, based on health status, for denial of a benefit otherwise provided. For example, the plan may not deny prescription drug coverage to a particular person if prescription coverage is available to similarly situated individuals. However, a plan could exclude prescription drug coverage for all beneficiaries. An entire group can be charged higher premiums based on health experience, but a plan cannot single out an individual for higher premiums.

Guaranteed Availability and Renewability

Insurers cannot refuse to cover small groups (2 to 50 employees) based on the health of group members. Larger groups are not guaranteed the availability of coverage, but once they have coverage they are guaranteed renewability. Renewability may be denied for groups that fail to pay premiums, commit fraud, or fail to meet participation or contribution requirements. Employees who lose group coverage can purchase individual health insurance policies without providing evidence of insurability.

Caution

This law is filled with complexities and ambiguities. A complete understanding of the law's impact may require the assistance of a qualified group insurance representative.

COBRA Coverage Continuation

An employer who has 20 or more full-time-equivalent employees on at least 50% of its working days during the prior year must meet the requirements of IRC Sec. 4980B, also known as COBRA.

Failure to comply with COBRA requirements may result in serious penalties.

Under COBRA, an employer must give his covered employees (including spouses and dependent children who are covered) the opportunity to elect continuation coverage under an employer-maintained group health plan (including plans to which the employer does not contribute financially) after any of the following events that would otherwise result in loss of coverage:

- The death of the covered employee.
- The divorce or legal separation of the covered employee.
- The termination of the employee's employment, unless for gross misconduct, or a reduction in hours that results in a loss of coverage.
- The covered employee becomes eligible for Medicare.
- A dependent child ceases to be covered by the plan due to his or her attained age.
- For retired employees, the filing by the employer for Chapter 11 bankruptcy.

Continuation Coverage

The continued coverage offered must be identical to the coverage offered prior to the event causing the continuation.

The plan may require the covered employee (spouse or dependents) to pay a premium, but it generally cannot exceed 102% of the cost to the plan for a person in a similar situation.

Terminated employees and employees with reduced hours must be provided coverage for up to 18 months (up to 29 months if disabled [by Social Security definition] during the first 60 days of COBRA coverage). Widows, divorced spouses, spouses of employees or retirees who lose coverage due to Medicare eligibility and dependent children who become ineligible are given up to 36 months of coverage.

Each health plan must give written notice to each covered employee of his or her continuation coverage rights.

Notice and Election Requirements

COBRA contains detailed rules and timelines specifying when employers, covered employees and health plans/plan administrators must provide notices of certain events or take certain actions. The most important of these is the notice of an individual's right to elect continuation coverage. An individual normally has only 60 days from the date of the COBRA election notice (triggered by a loss of group health coverage due to one of the aforementioned events) in which to elect continuation coverage. If they do not elect continuation coverage during this period, they normally give up their rights under COBRA to choose continuation coverage.

The Department of Labor (DOL) has issued proposed changes to the required employer notices, to include information regarding the availability of health insurance coverage through the Patient Protection and Affordable Care Act (PPACA) established healthcare marketplaces. This PPACA coverage may be less expensive than that provided under COBRA.

Failure to Comply

Employers who fail to comply with the COBRA Rules may incur an excise tax of $100 per qualified beneficiary for each day of noncompliance (with a maximum of $200 per day per covered family). COBRA Administrators who fail to provide the initial COBRA notice or the COBRA election notice when a qualifying event occurs are subject to a penalty of up to $110 per affected beneficiary per day under the Employee Retirement Income Security Act. If the failure to comply is not intentional, but due to reasonable cause, the maximum excise tax is limited to 10% of the prior year's group health plan costs (with a maximum of $500,000).

Cafeteria Plans

IRC Sec. 125

Also called flexible benefit plans, cafeteria plans allow participating employees to choose among two or more benefits consisting of cash and qualified benefits. See IRC Sec. 125(d)(1)(B).

There is no need to change current benefit programs. If the employer is unable to pay for fringe benefits, the employee can enter into a salary-reduction agreement with the employer. The employer then uses these funds to pay for the employee's benefits. This allows the employee to pay for his or her own benefits with pre-tax dollars.

Employee Benefits

Some of the benefits that can be enjoyed by employees include the following:

- Lower FICA and income tax withholding due to lower gross pay.
- Ability to select those benefits most needed.
- Opportunity to refuse benefits already provided by a spouse's employer.
- Option of redirecting tax savings to meet retirement needs, i.e., 401(k) plan.
- Potential qualification for the earned-income credit due to lower gross income.

Employer Benefits

Some of the benefits that can be enjoyed by employers include the following:

- Lower payroll taxes (FICA, FUTA and sometimes worker's compensation insurance) due to lower gross pay.
- Sharing cost of benefits with employee, if desired.
- Help in retaining key employees.
- Improved employee morale due to show of employer concern.
- Potential reduction in fringe benefit costs.

Qualified Benefits May Include

- Accident and health insurance.

- Health Savings Account (HSAs).

- Group term life insurance.

- Dependent care assistance.

- Flexible-spending accounts.

- Cash-or-deferred arrangements (401(k) plans).

- Adoption assistance.

Excluded Benefits

- Scholarships or fellowships described in IRC Sec. 117.

- Educational assistance programs described in IRC Sec. 127.

- Miscellaneous fringe benefits (including transportation and parking) described in IRC Sec. 132.[1]

- Nonqualified deferred compensation plans.

- Qualified retirement plans, except cash or deferred arrangements under IRC Sec. 401(k).

- Long-term care benefits, including long-term care insurance or services.

- Contributions to medical savings accounts described in IRC Sec. 220.

- Health reimbursement arrangements described in Revenue Ruling 2002-41.

Plan Requirements

The plan must be written and include only employees.[2] The plan should include the following items:

---

[1] The Transportation Equity Act of 1998 allows pretax contributions for qualifying transit vouchers or parking, but these cannot be part of a cafeteria plan.

[2] Sole proprietors and partners (or attributed partners) or subchapter S shareholders who own (or who are attributed to own) 2% or more of the business may not participate.

- Description of benefits and coverage periods.

- Eligibility rules for participation.

- How benefit elections are to be made.

- How employer contributions are to be made, i.e., employer funds or salary reduction.

- Maximum amount of employer contributions.

- Plan year.[1]

Discrimination

The plan must be available to employees who qualify under a classification established by the employer and cannot discriminate in favor of highly-compensated or key employees.

One discrimination test that greatly impacts smaller employers is the 25% rule. The statutory, non-taxable benefits provided to key employees may not exceed 25% of the statutory, non-taxable benefits provided to all employees. If nondiscrimination rules are violated, key employees lose the benefit of the cafeteria plan and are taxed on the maximum amount of cash or taxable benefits. There is no effect on rank and file workers.

Key participants are any participants and participants' beneficiaries who, during the determination year,[2]

- are or were an officer of the sponsoring employer and earning more than $175,000[3];

- owned more than 5%[4] of the employer; or

- owned more than 1%[3] of the employer and received more than $150,000 of compensation from the employer.

---

[1] See proposed Regulation Sec. 1.125-1(c)

[2] In-service distributions are subject to a five-year look-back period.

[3] This value applies to 2018.

[4] The family attribution rules of IRC Sec. 318 apply. Any participant is deemed to have the same ownership share as his or her spouse, children, parents and grandparents.

Simple Cafeteria Plans

Beginning in 2011, one provision of the Patient Protection and Affordable Care Act (PPACA) provides qualified small employers with a simplified "safe harbor" method of meeting the nondiscrimination requirements applicable to cafeteria plans. Under this safe harbor, a cafeteria plan is treated as meeting the nondiscrimination rules if the plan satisfies certain minimum eligibility, participation, and contribution requirements. An eligible small employer is, generally, an employer who employed an average of 100 or fewer employees on business days during either of the two preceding years.

2007 Proposed Regulations

On August 6, 2007, the IRS issued proposed regulations (NPRM REG-142695-05) on a number of issues related to cafeteria plans, including nondiscrimination rules. This suggests that the IRS will be paying more attention to this area in the future. These proposed regulations are generally applicable to plan years beginning on or after January 1, 2009.

Flexible Spending Arrangements

Flexible spending arrangements (FSA) are a type of cafeteria plan commonly used by many employers. In an FSA, participating employees generally elect to have their salary reduced each month. The employer then uses these funds to pay for certain benefits with pretax dollars. There are three types of FSAs:

- Medical expenses not otherwise covered.

- Dependent care expenses for both children and parents.

- Adoption expenses.

Tax Benefits

The payment of the benefit is tax deductible for the employer and is non-taxable to the employee. As these dollars are not considered to be wages, they are not subject to either FICA or FUTA tax.[1]

Health Benefits

If an FSA provides health benefits (like medical or dental expenses) to participants, it must be ready to pay the full year's benefits to an employee who qualifies for the benefit.

For example, if the employee has contributed for only one or two months at the time of the claim, the employer must pay for the entire expense up to the amount projected for the full year of contributions by the employee. If the employee then terminates employment before the amounts are deducted from his or her paycheck, the employer must suffer the loss.

In 2018, the maximum amount available to reimburse incurred <u>medical</u> expenses may not exceed $2,650. For 2017 this limit was $2,600. The limit is subject to adjustment for inflation in future years.

"Use-Or-Lose" Rule

Any unused funds remaining in an FSA at the end of the year will be forfeited by the employee. At the beginning of the year, a careful estimate of future expenses is helpful in

---

[1] The discussion here concerns federal income tax law. State or local income tax law may differ.

avoiding this "use-it-or-lose-it" problem. However, employers may (but are not required to) establish a grace period of 2 ½ months after the end of a plan year. During this grace period, any unused funds may be paid or reimbursed to the employee for qualified expenses incurred during the grace period.[1]

In Notice 2013-71, the IRS allowed (but did not require) an employer to amend its plan to provide for the carryover to the immediately following plan year of up to $500 of any amount remaining unused at the end of the plan year in a health FSA. The carryover amount may be used to pay or reimburse medical expenses under the health FSA incurred during the entire plan year to which it is carried over. A plan adopting this carryover provision may not also provide a grace period with respect to a health FSA.

Qualified Reservist Distribution

Under the provisions of the Heroes Earnings Assistance and Tax Relief Act of 2008, for distributions after June 17, 2008, a "qualified reservist distribution," of all or part of any unused balance remaining in a health FSA may be made to an employee who is called to active duty for a period of more than 179 days, or indefinitely. The distribution must be made during the period beginning with the date the individual is called to active duty and ending on the last date that reimbursements could be made under the arrangement for the plan year that includes the date of call to active duty.

Qualified reservist distributions are not required. If a plan sponsor decides to allow them, they must be available to all eligible plan participants and the plan must be amended.

---

[1] See proposed regulation Sec. 1.125-1 (e)

Medical Reimbursement Plans

A plan set up by an employer to reimburse employees for their medical expenses that are not covered by their regular medical insurance is called a medical expense reimbursement plan. Reimbursable expenses might include dental expenses, expenses in excess of policy limits, etc.

Either reimbursement payments to the employee or insurance premiums paid to an insurance company (under an insured plan) are deductible by the corporation.

Payments are generally received by the employee free of income tax, unless he or she is a highly-compensated employee and the plan does not meet the nondiscrimination requirements.

Nondiscrimination Rules

Self-insured plans that discriminate in favor of highly compensated employees will cause the excess reimbursement benefit[1] to be included in the highly-compensated employee's taxable income. To avoid being discriminatory as to who may participate, a plan must meet one of the following tests:

- Benefit 70% or more of all employees.

- Cover 80% of eligible employees where 70% or more of them are eligible.

- Cover a special classification of employees which the IRS determines not to be discriminatory.

To avoid being discriminatory in actual operation, highly-compensated employees must not have greater benefits than the other employees. For example, benefits should not be a percentage of salary.

Highly-Compensated Employees

Those persons who would be classified as highly-compensated employees include:

---

[1] Reimbursement for benefits not available to other plan participants.

- The five highest-paid officers.

- Shareholders owning more than 10% of stock.

- The highest paid 25% of all employees[1].

Uninsured or Insured

Payment from the general funds of the business to reimburse the employee for his or her medical expenses is called an uninsured or self-insured plan. When the corporation pays premiums to an insurance company and thereby shifts the risk to an unrelated third party, it is called an insured plan. The nondiscrimination rules do not apply to insured plans. See Treasury Regs. 1.105-11(b)(1)(ii).

---

[1] See IRC Sec. 105(h)(5).

Health Reimbursement Arrangements

A Health Reimbursement Arrangement (HRA) is an arrangement in which an employer reimburses an employee for certain medical expenses. The employee first pays for the medical expense out of his or her own pocket and is then reimbursed by the employer. If IRS requirements[1] are met, HRA payments are excluded from the employee's income (i.e., they are received income tax-free) and are a deductible business expense for the employer.

At the beginning of the year, the employer will specify the maximum amount that each employee can "spend" under the HRA. Unused HRA balances may be held over to increase the amount available for medical expenses in future years. An employee has no right to any "cash-out," nor is the arrangement portable, upon termination of employment.

In General

Sometimes known as "defined contribution health plans," HRAs can vary in their details, but are designed to provide a financial incentive for employees to make cost-conscious decisions regarding health care. Certain basic requirements apply to all HRAs:

- **Funding:** Only the employer may contribute to an HRA. No employee contributions are permitted, through a salary reduction plan or otherwise. An HRA is typically set up as an unfunded employee benefit program, with reimbursement payments being made from the employer's general assets as medical expenses are incurred.

- **Use of funds:** Generally, HRA funds may only be used to reimburse an employee for qualified, substantiated "medical expenses[2]," as that term is defined in IRC Sec. 213(d).

- **Maximum amount:** There is no IRS limit on the dollar amount that an employer may contribute to an HRA. The employer determines the maximum amount that will be reimbursed during the year.

---

[1] The rules discussed here concern federal income tax law. State or local law may differ.

[2] Including premiums for health or long-term care insurance. See IRS Publication 502, "Medical and Dental Expenses" for a general guide as to what qualifies as a deductible medical expense. Some exceptions apply.

Health Reimbursement Arrangements

Other Key Points

In some instances, an HRA will be combined with an employer-provided health plan, often a high-deductible health plan. In others, HRA reimbursements allow an employee to pay the premiums for the health insurance plan of his or her choice.

- **Eligible individuals:** Include current employees[1], their spouses and dependents, and the spouses and dependents of deceased employees. An HRA may reimburse the medical expenses of retired or terminated employees up to the amount of unused reimbursement left at the time the employee leaves the employer.

- **Non-discrimination:** An HRA may not discriminate in favor of highly compensated employees.

- **COBRA and HIPAA:** An HRA must comply with the requirements of both COBRA and HIPAA.

---

[1] Self-employed individuals, including sole proprietors, partners in a partnership, and more than 2% owners in a S corporation, may not participate in an HRA. See IRC Sec. 105(g) and IRC Sec. 1372.

How a Health Reimbursement Arrangement Works

A Health Reimbursement Arrangement (HRA) is an arrangement in which an employer reimburses an employee for qualifying medical expenses. If IRS requirements are met, the reimbursements are income tax-free to the employee and a deductible expense for the employer.

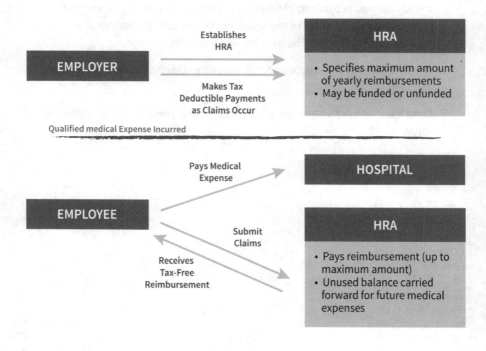

Health Savings Account

A Health Savings Account (HSA) is a tax-favored[1] account set up exclusively to pay certain medical expenses of the account owner, spouse, and dependents. Health insurance coverage must be provided under a high-deductible health plan. Qualified contributions by the account owner are deductible from gross income and growth inside the account is not taxed. Distributions to pay for qualified medical expenses are received income tax-free. Funds not used during one year can be held over and used to pay qualified medical expenses in a later year even if no further contributions are permitted.

Similar in nature to an Individual Retirement Account (IRA) or Archer Medical Savings Account (Archer MSA), an HSA is owned by an individual and is thus portable. If an individual changes employers, the HSA moves with the individual and does not stay with the former employer even though that employer may have contributed to the HSA.

Key Concepts

There are a number of key concepts involved in understanding HSAs:

- **Eligible individual:** Only an "eligible individual" may establish, and then contribute to, an HSA. This is someone who on the first day of any month: (1) is covered by a high-deductible health plan (HDHP); (2) is not also covered by another health plan that is not a HDHP[2]; (3) is not enrolled in Medicare (generally, under age 65); and (4) for 2017 may not be claimed as a dependent on someone else's tax return.

- **High-deductible health plan:** A health plan that meets certain requirements (adjusted annually for inflation) regarding deductibles and out-of-pocket expenses:

Coverage Type	2017 Minimum Deductible	2017 Maximum Out-of-Pocket	2018 Minimum Deductible	2018 Maximum Out-of-Pocket
Self-Only	$1,300	$6,550	$1,350	$6,650
Family	2,600	13,100	2,700	13,300

---

[1] The rules discussed here concern federal income tax law. State or local law may differ.

[2] Certain limited exceptions apply.

As a general rule, the HDHP may not provide benefits (except for certain preventive care) until the minimum deductible for the year has been met.

- **Permitted insurance:** An individual is considered to be "eligible" without regard to any coverage he or she may have under certain "permitted" insurance such as worker's compensation, tort liability, or liability arising from the use or ownership of property (e.g., auto insurance). Also disregarded is insurance for a specific illness or disease or that pays a fixed amount (per day or other period) for hospitalization. Coverage for accidents, disability, dental care, vision care, and long-term care is also disregarded.

- **Flexible Spending Accounts:** FSAs are allowed if they are "limited purpose," covering accidents, disability, dental or vision care, or are a "post-deductible" FSA, providing benefits only after the minimum annual deductible amount under the HDHP is met.

- **A trust or custodial account:** An HSA must be in the form of a trust or custodial account, established with a qualified trustee or custodian, such as an insurance company, bank, or similar financial institution.

Contributions To An HSA

Contributions to an HSA generally must be in cash:

- **Annual contribution limit:** For 2017 and 2018, the maximum deductible contribution to an HSA is as follows:

Coverage Type	2017 Specified Maximum	2018 Specified Maximum
Self-Only	$3,400	$3,450
Family	6,750	6,850

Federal law allows an individual who becomes covered under a high-deductible plan in a month other than January to make a full, deductible HSA contribution for the year; certain restrictions and limitations apply. Individuals age 55 and older may also make "catch-up" contributions of $1,000 per year.

- **Who may contribute:** Contributions may be made by an eligible individual, either directly or through a cafeteria plan, or by the individual's employer. Any person, including family members, may also contribute on behalf of an eligible individual.

- **Deadline for making contributions:** Contributions may be made in one or more payments and must be made no later than the due date for filing the eligible individual's federal income tax return for the year, generally April 15 of the following year. Contributions may not be made before the first day of the year to which they apply.

- **Income tax treatment of contributions:** Qualified contributions to the HSA by an eligible individual (including contributions by family members) are deductible from the eligible individual's gross income, subject to annual limitations. Employer contributions to an HSA are excludable from an employee's gross income and are not subject to withholding for federal income or payroll taxes.[1] Employer contributions to an HSA are not deductible by the eligible employee. Growth or earnings on the contributions are not taxable while held inside the account. Excess contributions may be subject to a 6% excise tax.

- **Full contribution for months preceding becoming an "eligible" individual:** An individual who becomes an "eligible" individual during a month other than January is allowed to make contributions for the months in the year preceding the month he or she enrolls in a HDHP. If an individual makes contributions under this provision, he or she must remain an eligible individual for a "testing period." The testing period is the period beginning with the last month of the taxable year and ending on the 12th month following such month. If an individual makes deductible contributions under this provision and does not remain an eligible individual during the testing period, the amount of contributions made for the months preceding the month the individual became eligible are included in income and a 10% additional tax applies.

- **One time rollovers from IRAs:** This provision allows for a once-in-a-lifetime distribution of amounts from an IRA (either a Traditional IRA or a Roth IRA), in a direct trustee-to-trustee transfer. Amounts distributed under this provision are not includible in income to the extent that they would otherwise be includible in income, and they are not subject to the 10% penalty tax on early distributions. The maximum amount that may be

---

[1] Such as the Federal Insurance Contributions Act (FICA), the Federal Unemployment Tax (FUTA), or the Railroad Retirement Act (RRA).

distributed from the IRA and contributed to the HSA is limited to the otherwise maximum deductible contribution amount to the HSA. No deduction is allowed for the amount contributed from an IRA to an HSA.

An individual who makes such a transfer must remain an eligible individual during a 12-month "testing" period, beginning with the month of the contribution and ending on the last day of the 12th month following that month. If the individual does not remain an eligible individual during this testing period, any amounts transferred are included in income and a 10% additional tax applies.

- **Other:** Rollover contributions from an Archer MSA (or another HSA) to a HSA are permitted and need not be made in cash.

Distributions From a HSA

Distributions from an HSA may be made at any time. Distributions used solely to pay for qualified medical expenses for the account owner, spouse, and dependents are excludable from gross income (i.e., tax-free).

- **Qualified medical expenses:** Qualified medical expenses are expenses (incurred after the HSA has been established) for "medical care" as that term is used in IRC Sec. 213(d). Generally, this includes amounts spent for the diagnosis, cure, mitigation, treatment, or prevention of disease, or for the purpose of affecting any structure or function of the body, to the extent not reimbursed by insurance. Qualified medical expenses do not generally include health insurance premiums.[1]

- **Taxation of amounts not used for qualified medical expenses taxed:** Any distribution from an HSA that is not used for qualified medical expenses is included in the income of the account owner and a 20% penalty is added. The penalty does not apply if a distribution is made because of an account owner's death, disability, or reaching age 65.

- **No longer an eligible individual:** If an account owner is no longer an "eligible individual" (for example, by enrolling in Medicare), the HSA account may continue to be used. No

---

[1] Certain exceptions apply to qualified long-term care insurance, COBRA health continuation coverage, and health insurance premiums paid by an individual while receiving unemployment compensation. For those age 65 and older, premiums paid for Medicare Part A, Part B, Part D, a Medicare HMO, or employee-paid premiums paid under an employer-sponsored health insurance plan also qualify.

- additional contributions may be made, but distributions used solely to pay for qualified medical expenses continue to be received income tax-free.

- **Death of the account owner:** At death, funds in an HSA pass to a named beneficiary. If the beneficiary is a surviving spouse, the account becomes the HSA of the surviving spouse, subject to the normal rules that apply to all HSAs. If the funds in an HSA pass to a non-spousal beneficiary, the account ceases to be an HSA as of the date of death, and the non-spousal beneficiary must include in taxable income the value of HSA assets as of the date of death.[1]

- **Full contribution for months preceding becoming an "eligible" individual:** An individual who becomes an "eligible" individual during a month other than January is allowed to make contributions for the months in the year preceding the month he or she enrolls in a HDHP. If an individual makes contributions under this provision, he or she must remain an eligible individual for a "testing period." The testing period is the period beginning with the last month of the taxable year and ending on the 12th month following such month. If an individual makes deductible contributions under this provision and does not remain an eligible individual during the testing period, the amount of contributions made for the months preceding the month the individual became eligible are included in income and a 10% additional tax applies.

- **One time rollovers from IRAs:** This provision allows for a once-in-a-lifetime distribution of amounts from an IRA (either a Traditional IRA or a Roth IRA), in a direct trustee-to-trustee transfer. Amounts distributed under this provision are not includible in income to the extent that they would otherwise be includible in income, and they are not subject to the 10% penalty tax on early distributions. The maximum amount that may be distributed from the IRA and contributed to the HSA is limited to the otherwise maximum deductible contribution amount to the HSA. No deduction is allowed for the amount contributed from an IRA to an HSA.

  An individual who makes such a transfer must remain an eligible individual during a 12-month "testing" period, beginning with the month of the contribution and ending on the last day of the 12th month following that month. If the individual does not remain an eligible individual during this testing period, any amounts transferred are included in income and a 10% additional tax applies.

---

[1] Less any qualified medical expenses of the deceased account owner, paid within one year after death.

Seek Professional Guidance

Heath Savings Accounts provide a tax favored means to accumulate funds to pay for qualified health care expenses. Because of the complexity of such accounts, the guidance of trained tax and financial professionals is strongly recommended.

How a Health Savings Account Works

A Health Savings Account (HSA) is a tax-favored account established exclusively to pay certain medical expenses of the account owner, spouse, and dependents. Health insurance coverage must be provided under a qualifying high-deductible health plan.

ACCOUNT OWNER

EMPLOYER

HEALTH SAVINGS ACCOUNT

Makes deductible[1] contributions

- Growth in the account is not currently taxed.
- If the account owner changes employers, the HSA moves with him or her, even if the employer contributed to the account.

Optional Contributions (non-taxable to employee and no payroll taxes)

MEDICAL EXPENSES

- Distributions used to pay for "qualified" medical expenses are received income tax-free.
- Qualified medical expenses generally follow the definition used for deductibility as an itemized deduction on form 1040, Schedule "A".

OTHER DISTRIBUTIONS

- Distributions for other purposes are included in the account owner's income and a 20% penalty is added.
- The 20% penalty does not apply if distribution is made because of the account owner's death, disability, or reaching age 65.

---

[1] The discussion here concerns federal income tax law. State or local law may differ.

Medical Savings Accounts

The Health Insurance Portability and Accountability Act of 1996 created a new type of savings account designed to help individual taxpayers meet unreimbursed medical expenses on a tax-favored basis. This saving account, called a medical savings account (MSA), was available only to employees of small businesses and self-employed individuals, and only in conjunction with a high deductible health insurance policy.

MSAs were initially available on a test basis from 1997 through 2000. Subsequent legislation extended this trial period several times, with the last extension ending on December 31, 2007. After 2007, no new MSA accounts could be established. However, for MSAs opened on or before this date, eligible account owners may continue to make contributions. For all MSA accounts, qualified distributions will continue to be received free of federal income tax.

Key Points

- **Contributions:** Employee contributions to an MSA are deductible from gross income in calculating adjusted gross income (AGI). Employer contributions to an MSA are not taxable to the employee but must be reported on the employee's W-2 form. Contributions may be made at any time, up to the due date of the return (not counting filing extensions). Earnings on funds in an MSA are not currently taxable. MSAs cannot be part of an IRC Sec. 125 cafeteria plan, but a high-deductible policy can be.

- **Limit on contributions:** Contributions to an MSA are limited, based on the dollar amount of the health policy's deductible. For single coverage, the annual contribution limit is 65% of the deductible amount. For family coverage, the annual limit is 75% of the deductible amount. The Act sets limits for minimum and maximum deductibles, as well as maximum out-of-pocket expenses. Limits are indexed for inflation annually.

Coverage Type	2018 Minimum Deductible	2018 Maximum Deductible	2018 Maximum Out-of-Pocket
Single	$2,300	$3,450	$4,550
Family	$4,550	$6,850	$8,400

- **Distributions from an MSA:** Funds distributed from an MSA to pay for qualified medical expenses (unreimbursed expenses that would otherwise qualify for the medical expense itemized deduction) are generally tax free. No itemized deduction is allowed for medical expenses paid from an MSA. Funds distributed for other purposes are taxed as ordinary income. A 20% penalty tax would also apply, unless a distribution is made because of death, disability or an MSA owner reaches age 65.

- **Tax savings:** The tax benefits of paying medical expenses through an MSA are significant. The ability to deduct contributions to an MSA above-the-line amounts to a dollar-for-dollar reduction in taxable income. Otherwise, unreimbursed medical expenses are deductible as an itemized deduction only to the extent that they exceed 7.50% of AGI, an amount that many taxpayers never reach.[1]

---

[1] Under current federal law, the 7.5% threshold applies to 2017 and 2018. This threshold is scheduled to increase to 10.0% for 2019 and later years. State or local law may vary.

Long-Term Care

Long-term care (LTC) is the term used to describe a variety of services in the area of health, personal care, and social needs of persons who are chronically disabled, ill or infirm. Depending on the needs of the individual, long-term care may include services such as nursing home care, assisted living, home health care, or adult day care.

Who Needs Long-Term Care?

The need for long-term care is generally defined by an individual's inability to perform the normal activities of daily living (ADL) such as bathing, dressing, eating, toileting, continence, and moving around. Conditions such as AIDS, spinal cord or head injuries, stroke, mental illness, Alzheimer's disease or other forms of dementia, or physical weakness and frailty due to advancing age can all result in the need for long-term care.

While the need for long-term care can occur at any age, older individuals are the typical recipients of such care.

Individuals with Disabilities, by Age[1]

Age Range	No Disability	With a Disability
5-17 Years	95%	5%
18-34 Years	94%	6%
35-64 Years	87%	13%
65-74 Years	75%	25%
75 Years and over	50%	50%

What Is The Cost of Long-Term Care?

Apart from the unpaid services of family and friends, long-term care is expensive. The following table lists national average costs (regional costs can vary widely) for typical long-term care services. One federal government study found that the "average length of time since admission for all current nursing home residents was 835 days."[2]

---

[1] Source: U.S. Census Bureau, 2011-2015 American Community Survey 5-Year Estimates, Sex by Age by Disability Status for the Civilian noninstitutionalized population, male and female.

[2] The National Nursing Home Survey: 2004 Overview. U.S. Department of Health and Human Services, Centers for Disease Control and Prevention, National Center for Health Statistics.

Service	2017[1]
Assisted living facility	$3,750 per month ($45,000 per year)
Nursing home (Private room)	$267 per day ($97,455 per year)
Nursing home (Semi-private room)	$235 per day ($85,775 per year)
Home health aide	$22 per hour
Homemaker/companion	$21 per hour

Paying for Long-Term Care – Personal Resources

Much long-term care is paid for from personal resources:

- Out-of-Pocket: Expenses paid from personal savings and investments.

- Reverse Mortgage: Certain homeowners may qualify for a reverse mortgage, allowing them to tap the equity in the home while retaining ownership.

- Accelerated Death Benefits: Certain life insurance policies provide for "accelerated death benefits" (also known as a living benefit) if the insured becomes terminally or chronically ill.

- Private Health Insurance: Some private health insurance policies cover a limited period of at-home or nursing home care, usually related to a covered illness or injury.

- Long-Term Care Insurance: Private insurance designed to pay for long-term care services, at home or in an institution, either skilled or unskilled. Benefits will vary from policy to policy.

Paying for Long-Term Care – Government Resources

Long-term care that is paid for by government comes from two primary sources:

- Medicare: Medicare is a health insurance program operated by the federal government. Benefits are available to qualifying individuals age 65 and older, certain disabled individuals under age 65, and those suffering from end-stage renal disease. A limited amount of nursing home care is available under Medicare Part A, Hospital

[1] Source: Genworth 2017 Cost of Care Survey.

Insurance. An unlimited amount of home health care is also available, if made under a physician's treatment plan.

- Medicaid: Medicaid is a welfare program funded by both federal and state governments, designed to provide health care for the truly impoverished. Eligibility for benefits under Medicaid is typically based on an individual's income and assets; eligibility rules vary by state.

In the past, some individuals have attempted to artificially qualify themselves for Medicaid by gifting or otherwise disposing of assets for less than fair market value. Sometimes known as "Medicaid spend-down", this strategy has been the subject of legislation such as the Omnibus Budget Reconciliation Act of 1993 (OBRA '93). Among other restrictions, OBRA '93 provided that gifts of assets within 36 months (60 months for certain trusts) before applying for Medicaid could delay benefit eligibility.

The Deficit Reduction Act of 2005 (DRA) further tightened the requirements to qualify for Medicaid by extending the "look-back" period for all gifts from 36 to 60 months. Under this law, the beginning of the ineligibility (or penalty) period was generally changed to the later of: (1) the date of the gift; or, (2) the date the individual would otherwise have qualified to receive Medicaid benefits. This legislation also clarified certain "spousal impoverishment" rules, while making it more difficult to use certain types of annuities as a means of transferring assets for less than fair market value.

Paying for Long-Term Care

Long-term care (LTC) is the term used to describe a variety of services in the areas of health, personal care, and social needs for individuals who are chronically disabled, ill, or infirm. LTC may include services such as skilled nursing home care, assisted living, home health care, or adult day care.

LTC in the United States today is, without doubt, expensive. In 2017, for example, the national median rate (regional costs can vary widely) for a semi-private room in a nursing home was $235 per *day*, just over $85,000 per year. This 2016 figure represents a five-year compound growth rate of 3.28%.[1]

How long do most people need LTC? One federal government study found that the "average length of time since admission for all current nursing home residents was 835 days."[2] Of course, not everyone will need LTC. And, in many cases, LTC will be needed for only a limited period of time. However long the need exists, for many individuals, paying for LTC can be a major challenge. Some resources which have been used to pay for LTC include:

Personal Resources

Method	How It Works	Pros	Cons
Personal assets	Assets that an individual (or a family) has managed to accumulate through work, savings and investment, or inheritance.	• Allows you to choose when, where, and how you receive care. • No concerns about being healthy enough to qualify for LTC insurance or other types of insurance policies. • Funds not needed for LTC can be used for other purposes or left to family or friends at your death.	• Investment returns are variable and subject to both gain and loss. • May need to sell illiquid assets (such as the family home) to free-up the cash needed to pay LTC costs. • LTC expenses may exceed the amount of available assets.

---

[1] Source: The Genworth 2017 Cost of Care Summary, page 2. The five-year compound growth rate is based on surveys conducted from 2012-2017.

[2] The National Nursing Home Survey: 2004 Overview, U.S. Department of Health and Human Services, Centers for Disease Control and Prevention, National Center for Health Statistics.

Personal Resources

Method	How It Works	Pros	Cons
Family caregiving	Family members provide the direct "hands-on" effort needed to care for the individual.	• No need to pay for care provided by family members. • Family support may also be available to meet other needs besides LTC. • To the extent that personal funds are not spent on LTC, they can be left to family or friends at your death.	• Family members may be unwilling or unable to provide the needed care. • Some family members may feel that the burden of providing care is unequally on their shoulders. • You must pay for care that family members cannot or are unable to provide.
Reverse mortgage	A special type of mortgage that allows a homeowner to convert a portion of his or her home equity into cash.[1]	• No income or medical requirements to qualify. • Provides cash needed to pay for LTC. • Cash gives you control over where, when, and how you receive care. • Funds not used to pay for LTC can be used for other purposes or left to family and friends at your death.	• Owner must meet certain requirements to qualify.[2] • Funds from a reverse mortgage are "income" and could affect eligibility for Medicaid or other assistance programs. • LTC costs could exceed the cash received. • A borrower may be forced to sell the home to repay the loan.

---

[1] No loan payments are required as long as at least one borrower lives in the home. The outstanding loan balance, plus accrued interest and loan costs, is due when the last borrower sells the home, permanently leaves, dies, or fails to carry out a contractual obligation such as paying property tax when due.

[2] Generally, to qualify for a reverse mortgage the owner must be at least age 62, the home must be owner-occupied, and it must be the owner's principal residence. Not all types of home qualify. Only first mortgages are permitted; any other debt secured by the home must either be first paid off, or paid off with the proceeds from the reverse mortgage.

Insurance-Based Resources

Method	How It Works	Pros	Cons
Long-term care insurance	Private insurance designed to help pay for many types of LTC services.	• Provides a known benefit for a specified period of time. Benefits paid under a "tax qualified" LTC policy are generally received income tax free.[1] • Gives you more control over where, when, and how you receive care. • Funds not spent on LTC can be used for other purposes or left to family or friends.	• Insured must generally be healthy to qualify for the policy. • Continuing premiums required to keep the policy in force. • Premiums may increase over time, benefits may decrease, or both. • If the insured does not use the policy benefits, there is a sense the money was not well spent. • LTC costs could exceed policy coverage amount.
Life insurance policy surrender	A life insurance policy with accumulated cash values is "surrendered" to the life insurance company.	• Provides cash needed to pay for LTC. • Cash gives you control over where, when, and how you receive care. • Funds not used to pay for LTC can be used for other purposes or left to family and friends at your death	• Cash surrender value is usually less than the policy's death benefit. • A portion of the proceeds from the sale may be taxable. • LTC costs could exceed the cash received.
Life settlement	The healthy owner of a life insurance policy sells it to a third party for a percentage of the death benefit.[2]	• Provides cash needed to pay for LTC. • Policy proceeds give you control over where, when, and how you receive care. • Funds not used to pay for LTC can be used for other purposes or left to family and friends at your death.	• May be difficult to find a buyer. • You generally receive only a portion of the policy's death benefit. • A portion of the proceeds from the sale may be taxable. • LTC costs could exceed the cash received.

[1] The discussion here concerns federal income tax law. State or local income tax law may vary widely.

[2] Generally, a life settlement is considered only when the original purpose of buying the life insurance no longer exists.

Insurance-Based Resources

Method	How It Works	Pros	Cons
Viatical settlement	The owner of a life insurance policy who is either "terminally" or "critically" ill sells the policy to a third party for a percentage of the death benefit.	• Provides cash needed to pay for LTC. • Cash gives you control over where, when, and how you receive care. • If certain requirements are met, proceeds of sale are not taxable. • Funds not used to pay for LTC can be used for other purposes or left to family and friends at your death.	• May be difficult to find a buyer. • You generally receive only a portion of the policy's death benefit. • LTC costs could exceed the cash received.
Accelerated death benefit	Some life insurance policies will pay a portion of the death benefit if the insured becomes "terminally" ill.[1]	• Provides cash needed to pay for LTC. • Cash gives you control over where, when, and how you receive care. • Funds not used to pay for LTC can be used for other purposes or left to family and friends at your death.	• You generally receive only a portion of the policy's death benefit. • LTC costs could exceed the cash received.
Borrow from accumulated cash values	Cash-value life policies typically allow the owner to borrow from the accumulated cash value, often at favorable interest rates.	• Provides cash needed to pay for LTC. • Cash gives you control over where, when, and how you receive care. • Funds not used to pay for LTC can be used for other purposes or left to family and friends at your death.	• When death occurs, outstanding policy loans and interest will be subtracted from the face amount. • LTC costs could exceed the cash received.

[1] If certain requirements are met, the policy proceeds are received income-tax free.

Insurance-Based Resources

Method	How It Works	Pros	Cons
Life insurance-LTC combination policy	A life insurance policy that links a traditional cash-value life policy with a LTC benefit.	• Provides cash needed to pay for LTC. • Cash gives you control over where, when, and how you receive care. • If LTC benefits are not needed, life insurance policy proceeds pass to named beneficiaries at your death.	• Insured may be required to qualify for the underlying life insurance policy. • Typically funded with a large, single premium payment. • Insured must be either "critically" ill or "terminally ill" to qualify for tax-free accelerated death benefit treatment.
Annuity-LTC combination contract	An annuity contract that links a traditional annuity with a LTC benefit.	• Provides cash needed to pay for LTC. • Cash gives you control over where, when, and how you receive care. • If LTC benefits are not needed, annuity can provide additional retirement income or pass to named beneficiaries.	• Typically funded with large, single cash payment. • Accumulated values within the annuity are used first to fund LTC expenses. • Tax-free LTC distributions typically require that an individual be "chronically ill."

Government Resources

Method	How It Works	Pros	Cons
Medicare	A health insurance program operated by the federal government.	• Part A helps pay for a limited amount of skilled-nursing or home health care. • Part B covers doctor's services and certain medical services/supplies. • Part B home health care is available if not covered under Part A. • Part D can help pay for needed medications. • Supplemental (Medigap) policies can help meet some expenses not covered by Medicare.	• Part A skilled nursing facility care is limited to a maximum of 100 days. • Medicare does not pay for custodial care. • Individual is responsible for paying costs not covered by Medicare.
Medicaid	A federal-state program which provides medical care to those with very low resources and income.	• For qualifying individuals, Medicaid pays for LTC services at home, in the community, and in a nursing home.	• Individual must meet Medicaid standards for low income and resources. • Nursing home services usually limited to a Medicaid licensed facility with an available Medicaid bed. • State may seek post-death recovery of amounts paid for LTC.

Seek Professional Guidance

Finding adequate resources to pay for needed LTC services can be difficult. Failing to meet this need can result in essential care being unavailable or, when existing resources are exhausted, in an adverse change in the type or quality of care already being provided. For some individuals, the funds to pay for necessary care will come from multiple sources. The guidance of trained financial professionals can help in creating a program to meet this challenge.

Annuity – LTC
Combination Contracts

Providing for health care is a key part of retirement planning. For most Americans age 65 and over, the federal government's Medicare program, and its various components, provides most of the resources to take care of a typical retiree's health care needs.

One health care need that is only minimally covered by Medicare is that of long-term care (LTC). LTC is the term used to describe a variety of maintenance or "custodial" services required by individuals who are chronically disabled, ill, or infirm. Depending on individual needs, LTC may include nursing home care, assisted living, home health care, or adult day care.

Not everyone will need LTC in retirement. For those that do, LTC is expensive. In 2017, for example, the national median cost for a resident in an assisted living facility was $45,000 per year; the national median cost for a semi-private nursing home room was $85,775 per year.[1] The problem, then, is how to plan for an expensive need that may, or may not, occur.

One answer has been that of a stand-alone, long-term care insurance policy. Should the need arise, a LTC policy can furnish some or all of the resources needed to pay for care. LTC insurance can be expensive, however, and most policies allow for the possibility of future rate increases. Plus, if an individual uses few (or none) of a policy's benefits, there is a sense that the money was not well spent.

Annuity – LTC Combination Contracts

One alternative to a stand-alone LTC insurance policy is a "combination" policy that links an annuity, typically a single-premium, deferred annuity, with a tax-qualified,[2] long-term care benefit. If LTC services are later needed, the accumulated value inside the annuity is withdrawn first to pay LTC expenses. If on-going LTC expenses exhaust the funds inside the annuity, additional, tax-qualified LTC coverage may be provided by the insurance company through a LTC "rider" to the base annuity. If LTC services are not needed, the annuity value can be used to either provide additional income, or, at the owner's death, can pass to named beneficiaries.

---

[1] Source: The Genworth 2017 Cost of Care Summary, page 2.
[2] The discussion here concerns federal income tax law. State or local income tax law may differ.

Annuity – Long-Term Care Combination Contracts

- **The long-term care "rider":** A long-term care "rider" to the annuity adds an insurer-provided layer of LTC benefits to those derived from the cash contributed by the annuity owner. The LTC rider could be paid for by periodic withdrawals from the annuity value. Such withdrawals are tax-free as a reduction in the annuity basis. The additional LTC benefit provided by the insurance company is often measured as a multiple (2x or 3x) of the single premium deposited by the annuity owner.

- **Taxability of LTC benefit:** Annuity-LTC contracts are generally structured to meet the requirements of the Internal Revenue Code (IRC) so that the LTC benefits received (both cash values withdrawn from the annuity and the benefits provided by the insurance company), are received income-tax free.

- **Paying for the contract:** In most cases, the annuity is purchased with a large, single-premium payment, for example a premium of $10,000 - $300,000. A few contracts allow for periodic payments into the annuity. As an alternative, if an individual has an existing cash-value life insurance policy or annuity contract, IRC Sec 1035 allows for the tax-free exchange of the existing policy or contract for a new life insurance policy or annuity contract with LTC benefits.

- **Benefit "triggers":** Tax-free LTC distributions generally require that an individual be "chronically ill." An individual is chronically ill when he or she is either (1) expected to be unable to perform for 90 days two of six activities of daily living (eating, toileting, transferring, bathing, dressing, and maintaining continence), or (2) suffers from a cognitive impairment such as Alzheimer's, dementia, or Parkinson's disease.[1]

- **Deferral period:** Most contracts specify that the LTC benefits cannot be paid from the contract for a specified number of years, known as the "deferral period." Typical deferral periods might range from two to six years.

- **Elimination period:** Once an individual is determined to qualify for LTC benefits (considered to be chronically ill), and assuming that the deferral period has expired, long-term care payments can begin after a waiting, or "elimination" period, which can range from 60-100 days.

---

[1] See IRC. Sec. 7702(b).

Annuity – Long-Term Care Combination Contracts

- **LTC Benefit period:** The annuity owner will select the period of time over which LTC benefits are to be paid, at the time the contract is purchased. Depending on the contract, the benefit period could extend from one to up to nine years. There may be separate benefit periods for benefits paid from the annuity value and the insurer-provided LTC benefits.

- **Monthly LTC benefit amount:** The monthly LTC benefit amount is generally a function of the total dollar amount of benefits available and the period of time selected by the annuity owner. The table below shows hypothetical, sample monthly payment amounts for various scenarios:

Single Premium Paid	Benefit Period	Leverage Factor	Maximum LTC Benefit	Monthly Maximum
$25,000	2 years (24 months)	2x	$50,000	$2,083
$25,000	2 years (24 months)	3x	$75,000	$3,125
$50,000	3 Years (36 months)	2x	$100,000	$2,777
$50,000	3 Years (36 months)	3x	$150,000	$4,166
$100,000	4 Years (48 months)	2x	$200,000	$4,166
$100,000	4 Years (48 months)	3x	$300,000	$6,250

- **Indemnity vs. actual expenses:** Some contracts pay benefits on an *indemnity* or *cash* basis, meaning that once payments begin, the monthly payment is the same regardless of the dollar amount of LTC expenses incurred. Contracts that pay benefits on an *expense* basis pay the <u>lesser</u> of the monthly benefit or the actual expenses incurred. If LTC expenses are less than the normal monthly payment, any unused balance is held over for future use, potentially extending the benefit period.

- **Underwriting:** Generally, annuity-LTC combination contracts, because they are frequently funded with a large, single premium, use a streamlined, simplified underwriting process, involving a telephone interview and a physician's statement.

Annuity – Long-Term Care Combination Contracts

Other Factors to Consider

There are a number of other factors to keep in mind when considering an annuity-LTC combination contract:

- **Not considered state "partnership" LTC policies:** Annuity-LTC combination contracts generally do not qualify as state "partnership" LTC policies. An insured individual with a partnership LTC policy can keep a much larger dollar amount of assets, while still qualifying for Medicaid, once the partnership LTC policy benefits are exhausted. Normally, an individual must be nearly destitute before Medicaid will pay for long-term care.

- **Effect of inflation:** Over time, the cost of LTC, like many other things that we buy, will increase. Since it may be many years in the future before long-term care is needed, consider a combination contract that offers a cost-of-living (COLI) rider. Without such a rider, there is a risk that the contract's LTC benefits will not keep pace with increases in the cost of long-term care.

- **Most funded with a large, single premium:** Most annuity-LTC combination policies are funded with a large, single premium payment. An individual may not have the resources to make such a large payment.

- **Is this the right tool?** An annuity-LTC combination contract may not be the right tool if, for example, the insured already has adequate retirement income. If there is a potential need for additional life insurance, a life insurance-LTC combination policy may be a better fit. For some individuals, a stand-alone LTC policy is more appropriate.

Seek Professional Guidance

One key part of a well-prepared retirement plan is looking ahead to the possible need for long-term care. The advice and guidance of trained financial and insurance professionals, in sorting out the various options for meeting this need, is strongly recommended.

Life Insurance – LTC Combination Policies

Providing for health care is a key part of retirement planning. For most Americans age 65 and over, the federal government's Medicare program, and its various components, provides most of the resources to take care of a typical retiree's health care needs.

One health care need that is only minimally covered by Medicare is that of long-term care (LTC). LTC is the term used to describe a variety of maintenance or "custodial" services required by individuals who are chronically disabled, ill, or infirm. Depending on individual needs, LTC may include nursing home care, assisted living, home health care, or adult day care.

Not everyone will need LTC in retirement. For those that do, LTC is expensive. In 2017, for example, the national median cost for a resident in an assisted living facility was $45,000 per year; the national median cost for a semi-private nursing home room was $85,755 per year.[1] The problem, then, is how to pay for an expensive need that may, or may not, occur.

One answer has been that of a stand-alone, long-term care insurance policy. Should the need arise, a LTC policy can furnish some or all of the resources needed to pay for care. LTC insurance can be expensive, however, and most policies allow for the possibility of future rate increases. Plus, if an individual uses few (or none) of a policy's benefits, there is a sense that the money was not well spent.

Life Insurance – LTC Combination Policies

One alternative to a traditional LTC insurance policy is that of a "combination" policy that links a cash-value life insurance policy with a tax-qualified, long-term care benefit. These combination policies take advantage of federal[2] income tax law which allows for payment of "accelerated death benefits," up to the policy's death benefit, should the insured need long-term care. If LTC services are required, the policy death benefit can be used to help pay these costs. If LTC services are not needed, or only a portion of the death benefit is used to pay LTC expenses, any remaining policy death benefit (less any policy loans) passes to beneficiaries named by the insured. Such a combination policy is most appropriate when there is a need for both life insurance and long-term care protection.

---

[1] Source: The Genworth 2017 Cost of Care Summary, page 2.
[2] The discussion here concerns federal income tax law. State of local income tax law may differ.

Life Insurance – LTC Combination Policies

- **Long-term care "riders":** In return for paying an additional premium, a "rider" can be added to a life insurance policy which allows the insurance carrier to advance the policy's death benefit to the insured, if long-term care is required. With some policies, a second rider can be added to increase the total dollar amount available to pay for LTC services, beyond the policy's original death benefit.

- **Benefit "triggers":** Under federal law, tax-free, accelerated death benefits can be paid from the policy when the insured is considered to be either "terminally ill" (death is expected within 24 months) or "chronically ill." For long-term care purposes,[1] an insured is considered to be chronically ill when he or she is either (1) expected to be unable to perform for 90 days two of six activities of daily living (eating, toileting, transferring, bathing, dressing, and maintaining continence), or (2) suffers from a cognitive impairment such as Alzheimer's, dementia, or Parkinson's disease. With some policies, a more restrictive definition requires the underlying chronic condition to be permanent.

- **Elimination period:** Once the insured is determined to qualify, long-term care payments can begin after a waiting, or "elimination" period, which can range from 60-100 days. The elimination period usually only has to be satisfied one time.

- **Monthly LTC benefit amount:** The monthly LTC benefit is a set percentage of the total death benefit, typically selected by the policy owner when the policy is purchased. The table below shows the payment amount and length of time for a hypothetical policy with a $100,000 death benefit:

Payout Percentage	Exemption Amount	Payout Length
1%	$1,000 per month	100 months
2%	$2,000 per month	50 months
3%	$3,000 per month	33 months
4%	$4,000 per month	25 months
5%	$5,000 per month	20 months

---

[1] See IRC. Sec. 7702(b).

Life Insurance – LTC Combination Policies

- **Effect of LTC payments on policy death benefit:** As LTC benefits are paid out, the policy's death benefit is reduced dollar-for-dollar.

- **Indemnity vs. actual expenses:** Some policies pay benefits on an *indemnity* or *cash* basis, meaning that once payments begin the monthly payment is the same regardless of the dollar amount of LTC expenses incurred. Policies that pay benefits on an *expense* basis pay the lesser of the monthly benefit or the actual LTC expenses incurred. If LTC expenses are less than the normal monthly payment, any unused balance is held over, potentially extending the benefit period.

- **Paying for the policy:** In many cases, a life insurance policy with LTC benefits is funded with a large, single premium. A few policies are paid through periodic premium payments. If appropriate, an existing cash-value life insurance may be exchanged tax-free for a new combination policy.

- **Underwriting:** Some policies, typically those funded with a large, single premium, use a streamlined, simplified underwriting process, with no medical exam. Other policies may require a medical exam and a complete health history.

- **Taxability of benefits:** Depending on the type of policy, long-term care benefits are received income-tax free under either IRC Sec. 101(g) or IRC Sec. 7702B.

- **Rate guarantees:** With many life insurance policies, because the death benefit is a predefined amount, the premiums are often guaranteed not to change. With a few types of life insurance, the premium rates may increase under certain conditions, but normally within a specified range.

- **Guaranteed return of premium:** Certain single-premium policies provide for a return of the premium paid (within a specified period of time) if the insured decides not to keep the policy. Life insurance policies which are paid for through periodic payments typically do not have this feature.

- **Residual death benefit:** In some instance, a policy may include a "residual" death benefit. If this feature is included, even though the policy's death benefits are exhausted through LTC benefit payments, the policy will still pay a small amount (typically 5% - 10% of the initial death benefit) at the insured's death. This benefit allows the survivors to pay for funeral and other final expenses.

Other Factors to Consider

There are a number of other factors to keep in mind when considering a life insurance-LTC combination policy:

- **Not considered state "partnership" LTC policies:** Life-insurance-LTC combination policies generally do not qualify as state "partnership" LTC policies. An insured individual with a partnership LTC policy can keep a much larger dollar amount of assets, while still qualifying for Medicaid, once the partnership LTC policy benefits are exhausted. Normally, an individual must be nearly destitute before Medicaid will pay for long-term care.

- **Effect of inflation:** Over time, the cost of LTC, like many other things that we buy, will increase. Since it may be many years in the future before long-term care is needed, consider a combination policy that offers a cost-of-living (COLI) rider. Without such a rider, there is a risk that a policy's LTC benefits will not keep up with increases in the cost of long-term care. Generally, once a policy is in force, the death benefit does not increase. Certain types of policies (variable life, variable universal life) have a death benefit that may increase, depending on investment results.

- **Most funded with a large, single premium:** Most life insurance-LTC combination policies are funded with a large, single premium payment. In many instances, a minimum of $25,000 - $75,000 is required to purchase a significant LTC benefit amount.

- **Is this the right tool?** A combination life insurance-LTC combination may not be the right tool if, for example, the insured is already covered by adequate life insurance. If there is a potential need for additional retirement income, a deferred annuity-LTC combination may be a better fit. For some individuals, a stand-alone LTC policy is more appropriate.

Seek Professional Guidance

One key part of a well-prepared retirement plan is looking ahead to the possible need for long-term care. The advice and guidance of trained financial and insurance professionals, in sorting out the various options for meeting this need, is strongly recommended.

Long-Term Care Partnership

Private insurance is one of a number of ways that individuals who require long-term care (LTC) are able to pay for the needed help. In 2011, for example, such private coverage provided 8.3% of the funds spent on nursing home care in the U. S. In contrast, Medicaid, the joint federal-state program that provides medical care for the impoverished of our nation, paid for 30.9% of the nation's nursing home care.[1]

Long-Term Care Partnership Program

In a LTC Partnership program, a state government and private health insurers work together to make available to residents of that state LTC insurance policies that are "linked" to Medicaid. If a buyer of a Partnership LTC policy later faces long-term care needs that exceed the policy's limits, he or she may apply for assistance from the state's Medicaid program under more relaxed eligibility rules. In what is termed an "asset disregard," the policy owner may keep a larger amount of assets than would normally be allowed under standard Medicaid rules. In many states, for example, an unmarried Medicaid applicant may keep only $2,000 of assets and his or her estate can be subject to a post-death recovery claim by the state.

These relaxed eligibility rules apply <u>only</u> to the amount of assets that an individual can retain; all other normal Medicaid qualification requirements apply.

Example: Susan, a single woman, purchases a Partnership LTC policy which provides benefits up to lifetime maximum of $100,000. She later receives benefits under the policy, up to the policy's maximum of $100,000. Susan continues to need care and she applies for, and is found to be eligible, for Medicaid. Because she had first received benefits through a Partnership LTC policy, she is allowed to retain $102,000 in assets and her state will not seek to recover that amount after her death. Susan would otherwise have been required to "spend-down" her assets until they totaled only $2,000.

The formula used to determine the amount of assets that a Medicaid beneficiary may keep varies from state to state. In the <u>dollar-for-dollar</u> formula, the amount of assets that may be retained is equal to the dollar amount of benefits received from the Partnership LTC policy.

---

[1] Source: Centers for Medicare & Medicaid Services, Office of the Actuary, National Health Statistics Group; U.S. Bureau of the Census. National Health Expenditures: Selected Calendar Years 1970 – 2011.

In some states, a <u>total asset protection</u> formula is used; a purchaser of a Partnership LTC policy in these states effectively protects all of his or her assets when applying for Medicaid. Generally, Partnership LTC policies in total asset protection states are more comprehensive and cover a longer period of time. In a few states, consumers have a choice of which approach they wish to use.

In an effort to encourage individuals to purchase long-term care insurance, the U.S. Congress included in the Deficit Reduction Act of 2005 (DRA 2005), legislation to expand the long-term care insurance partnership program to all 50 states. Under earlier legislation, LTC Partnership programs had been operating in four states (California, Connecticut, Indiana, and New York) for a number of years. Long-Term Care Partnership

Partnership LTC Policy Qualifications

DRA 2005 established certain standards that all qualifying Partnership LTC policies must meet, including:

- **Insured a state resident:** The insured must be a resident of the state the policy was issued in at the time the coverage is effective. If the policy was received in exchange for a policy issued earlier, the insured must have met the residency requirements at the time the first policy was issued.

- **Tax qualified[1]:** Partnership LTC policies must meet the requirements of IRC Sec. 7702B(b). Under this federal tax code section, premiums paid for LTC policies are considered to be qualifying medical expenses for the Schedule A medical-expense itemized deduction.[2] Policy benefits are treated as "amounts received for personal injury and sickness," excludable from gross income.

- **Consumer Protection:** The policy must meet the requirements specified in the National Association of Insurance Commissioner's (NAIC) Long-Term Care Insurance Model Regulations and Long-Term Care Insurance Model Act (as adopted as of October 2000).

---

[1] The discussion here concerns federal income tax law. State or local law may differ.

[2] For 2017 and 2018, qualified medical expenses are deductible only to the extent they exceed 7.5% of Adjusted Gross Income. Under current law, this threshold will increase to 10.0% for 2019 and later years.

- **Inflation protection:** Partnership policies issued to individuals under age 76 must contain certain benefit inflation protection provisions.

Other Issues To Consider

- **Will you qualify for Medicaid?** Entitlement to Medicaid benefits is not automatic. In addition to certain asset level requirements, a state's Medicaid program will also impose income and functionality limits. Many individuals have too much income or are not "disabled" enough to qualify for Medicaid.
- **Availability:** Partnership LTC policies are available in most (but not all) states as well as the District of Columbia.
- **If you move to a different state:** States that have Partnership LTC programs are automatically considered to have "reciprocity" with each other and to honor the asset disregard earned under a policy purchased in a different state. However, a state can opt out of this requirement at any time.

Seek Professional Guidance

The medical, legal, tax, and investment aspects of planning for long-term care can be complex. The guidance of qualified professionals is highly recommended.

Long-Term Care Tax Issues

Federal law provides generally favorable tax treatment of the expenses connected with long-term care (LTC). However, a number of rules must be carefully followed in order to maximize these tax benefits.[1]

Key Definitions

- **Qualified LTC Services:** The necessary services required by a "chronically ill" individual, provided under a treatment plan prescribed by a licensed health care practitioner.

- **Chronically Ill Individual:** An individual unable to perform at least two of the activities of daily living (ADLs)[2] for at least 90 days, or who requires protective supervision because of severe cognitive impairment. Certification by a licensed health care practitioner within the previous 12 months is required.

- **Qualified LTC Policy:** A LTC policy that meets certain tax-related requirements under federal income tax laws.

Long-Term Care Expenses

Long-term care expenses are medical expenses: Unreimbursed amounts an individual pays for qualified LTC services, as well as premiums paid for qualified LTC policies, are included in the term "medical care." IRC Sec. 213(d)(1), as amended. For individual taxpayers, such expenses thus qualify for the medical expense itemized deduction. Qualifying medical expenses are deductible as an itemized deduction to the extent they exceed 7.50% of adjusted gross income (AGI).[3]

Current law limits the annual amount of LTC premiums that can be deducted, based on the age of the insured.

---

[1] The discussion here concerns federal income tax law; state or local law may vary.

[2] Such as bathing, dressing, eating, toileting, transferring, and continence.

[3] The 7.50% threshold applies to 2017 and 2018. Under current law, the threshold will increase to 10.0% for 2019 and later years.

Long-Term Care Tax Issues

Age Before Close of Tax Year	2017 Limitation	2018 Limitation
40 or less	$410	$420
41 to 50	770	780
51 to 60	1,530	1,560
61 to 70	4,090	4,160
Over 70	5,110	5,200

These annual limitation amounts are subject to adjustment for inflation each year.

Long-Term Care Policy Benefits

Benefits excluded from income: Beginning with policies issued in 1997, benefits received under a "qualified" LTC contract are generally excluded from income as an amount "received for personal injury and sickness." (See IRC Sec. 7702B.) In order for benefits paid under a policy to be excluded from income, the policy must meet strict federal tax requirements to be a qualified contract. Further, benefits must be for services provided to a chronically ill individual. A limited grandfather clause applies to contracts in existence before 1997.

The exclusion from income is limited to the greater of $360 per day (calendar year 2018)[1], or total un-reimbursed LTC expenses actually incurred. The dollar limitation is subject to adjustment for inflation annually.

Other Tax Issues

- **Employees:** Generally, if an employer chooses to purchase tax-qualified long-term care insurance for an employee, neither the coverage provided nor the benefits paid (subject to the limitations described earlier) will be taxable to the employee. If certain requirements are met, self-employed individuals may also include themselves for such coverage.

- **Self-employed individuals:** Self-employed individuals are permitted to deduct qualifying health insurance premiums, including tax-qualified long-term care premiums, as an adjustment to gross income, rather than as an itemized deduction. This deduction is also generally available to general partners in a partnership, limited

---

[1] This amount was also $360 in 2017.

partners in a partnership receiving guaranteed payments, and more than 2% owners of subchapter S corporations who receive wages from the corporation.

- **Combination contracts:** A "combination contract" is an annuity or life insurance contract that also provides qualified LTC coverage. Beginning in 2010, withdrawals from the cash value of either the annuity or life insurance portion of a combination contract to pay for the LTC coverage are generally not includable in income and no medical expense deduction is allowed for such expenditures. The LTC portion of the contract is treated as a separate contract and the amounts received are treated for federal income tax purposes as LTC insurance benefits.

Seek Professional Guidance

Federal, state, and local income tax law can be complex and confusing. The guidance and counsel of a qualified tax or other financial professional is highly recommended.

Long-Term Care Break-Even

Assumptions:

Monthly Premium: $275
Annual Benefit: $54,000
Benefit Inflating Annually by: 3%

Years Premium Paid	Benefits Paid Will Equal Premiums Paid in:
2 years	2 months
5 years	4 months
10 years	6 months
20 years	9 months

Example

If you paid monthly premiums of $275, for five years, your benefits would equal your total outlay in approximately 4 months.

Choosing a Long-Term Care Policy

Assessing the need for long-term care (LTC) insurance is an important part of any risk management program. The heavy economic burden of paying for such care should be measured against your available resources. If you need LTC for even a short period of time, what effect will that have on your estate and any legacy you may wish to leave to your heirs? The decision to purchase LTC insurance, either individually or under a group plan, generally must be made while you are still healthy. Once a disabling condition occurs, it is too late to act.

Common Elements in Long-Term Care Insurance Policies

- **"Qualified" LTC policies:** If a LTC policy meets certain criteria established by the federal government, the premiums for the policy are considered "medical care" and thus qualify for the medical expense itemized deduction. Federal law limits the amount of qualified LTC premiums that may be deducted each year.[1]

- **Amount of the benefit:** A policy will generally specify the maximum dollar benefit payable. A survey of local nursing homes can help determine the amount needed.

- **How benefits are paid:** LTC benefits are generally paid under one of three methods:

  - Reimbursement (expenses-incurred) method – pays the lesser of the actual expenses incurred or the dollar limit specified in the policy.

  - Indemnity (or "per-diem") method – the entire daily benefit is paid as long as the insured requires and is receiving LTC services, regardless of the amount spent.

  - Disability method – once the eligibility criteria have been met, the full daily benefit is paid, even if no LTC services are being provided.

- **Inflation protection:** Since costs inevitably increase, a policy without a provision for inflation may be outdated in a few years. Of course, an additional charge is incurred for this protection.

---

[1] The discussion here concerns federal income tax law; state or local income tax law may vary.

Choosing a Long-Term Care Policy

- **Guaranteed renewability:** Almost all long-term care policies sold today are guaranteed renewable; they cannot be canceled as long as you pay the premiums on time and as long as you have told the truth about your health on the application. The fact that a policy is guaranteed renewable does not mean that the premiums cannot be increased; insurers typically reserve the right to raise premiums for an entire class or group of policyholders. Some policies sold in the past were not guaranteed renewable and a few of these policies may still be in force.

- **Waiver of premium:** Some policies will waive future premiums after you have been in the nursing home for a specified number of days, e.g., 90 days.

- **Prior hospitalization:** This policy provision requires one to be hospitalized (for the same condition) prior to entering the nursing home or no benefits will be paid under the policy. Although prior hospitalization clauses have been prohibited in all states, some older policies still in force may contain this provision. Policies currently sold do not contain prior hospitalization clauses.

- **Place of care:** Does the policy require that the nursing home be licensed or otherwise certified by the state to provide skilled or intermediate nursing care? Must the facility meet certain record keeping requirements?

- **Plan of care:** A plan of care is part of the health care claims process. It is the result of an assessment prepared by the insured's physician, and a multi-disciplinary team, including practical nurses, social workers, and other health care professionals. The plan outlines the appropriate level of care needed to assist the insured in performing the activities of daily living.

- **Level of care:** There are three generally recognized levels of care in an institutional setting:

  - **Skilled care:** Daily nursing and rehabilitation care under the supervision of skilled medical personnel, e.g., registered nurses and based on a physician's orders.

  - **Intermediate care:** The same as skilled care, except it requires only intermittent or occasional nursing and rehabilitative care.

- **Custodial care:** Help in one's daily activities including eating, getting up, bathing, dressing, use of toilet, etc. Persons performing the assistance do not need to be medically skilled, but the care is usually based upon the physician's certification that the care is needed.

- **Pre-existing conditions:** Depending on the state, a policy may limit coverage of pre-existing conditions to discourage persons who are already ill from purchasing a policy. Many policies will provide benefits if the pre-existing condition was overcome six months or more prior to applying for the policy. Also, some policies will not pay benefits if the pre-existing condition re-occurs within six months after the effective date of coverage.

- **Deductible or waiting period:** Most LTC policies require you to "pay your own way" for a specified number of days (generally ranging between zero and 120 days) before the insurance company will begin to pay benefits. Of course, the shorter the waiting period, the higher the cost will be. This is usually referred to as an "elimination period."

- **Alzheimer's disease:** Most policies now include coverage for organic brain disorders like Alzheimer's disease.

- **Home health care (home care):** Many long-term care policies can provide coverage in the insured's home. It is most often offered as a rider (requiring an additional premium) to nursing facility coverage, and reimburses the cost of long-term care received at home.

- **Rating the company:** Companies should be financially sound and have a reputation of treating policyholders fairly.

Seek Professional Guidance

A perfect LTC policy does not exist. Many policy features must be compared and weighed. As a general rule, the more benefits included in a policy, the higher the premium will be. Professional guidance is extremely important in this complicated area.

How Employer Provided LTC Insurance Works

Employer and Employee
Each pays a portion of the premium[1].

EMPLOYER AND EMPLOYEE	Group Long-Term Care Policy	LONG-TERM CARE INSURANCE COMPANY

Long-Term Disability Event

(e.g. stroke, dementia, advancing age)

EMPLOYEE		LONG-TERM CARE INSURANCE COMPANY
Pays any balance over maximum benefit		Pays benefits under the terms of the contract, up to policy maximums.

LONG-TERM CARE PROVIDERS
(E.G.,HOME CARE, NURSING HOME)

---

[1] In some situations, the employer will sponsor a group long-term care insurance plan, but will not pay any portion of the premium.

How Individual LTC Insurance Works

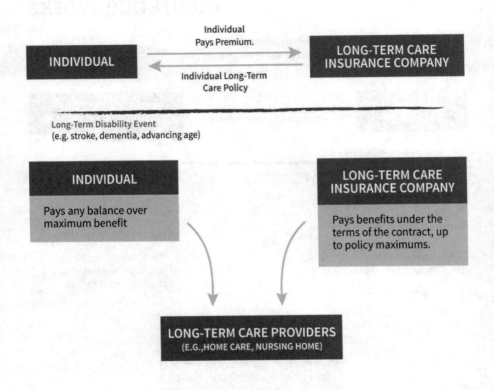

INDIVIDUAL

Individual
Pays Premium.

Individual Long-Term
Care Policy

LONG-TERM CARE
INSURANCE COMPANY

Long-Term Disability Event
(e.g. stroke, dementia, advancing age)

INDIVIDUAL

Pays any balance over
maximum benefit

LONG-TERM CARE
INSURANCE COMPANY

Pays benefits under the
terms of the contract, up
to policy maximums.

LONG-TERM CARE PROVIDERS
(E.G.,HOME CARE, NURSING HOME)

Long-Term Care Analysis Data

Personal

Date   01/01/2018

	Client(s) name	Date of birth	Retirement age
1) Paul	Johnson	01/01/1953	67
2) Sally	Johnson	01/01/1956	65

Long-Term Care Data

Current Insurance

	Paul	Sally
Monthly benefit	$1,000	$0
Annual COLA rate	3%	3%

Long-Term Care Cost

Estimated monthly cost of long-term care today	$4,500

Current Assets

- Market value of assets $950,000
- Assumed rate of return   5%

Assumptions

Age at which long-term care begins	70
Long-term care duration (years)	5
Long-term care cost inflation rate	7%

Long-Term Care Analysis

Can Paul afford to self-insure?

Most people think of long-term care as solely referring to nursing home care, but this kind of specialized assistance can take place at home, in senior centers, assisted living facilities, and community centers as well.

Cost of Long-Term Care

This analysis assumes that long-term care currently costs $4,500 per month, and increases by 7.00% annually to a monthly cost of $6,311 by Paul's age 70.

Current Long-Term Care Insurance

Paul currently has long-term care insurance coverage of $1,000 per month.

Analysis

Your assets of $950,000 are sufficient to fund your potential long-term care needs, however this may significantly impact your retirement.

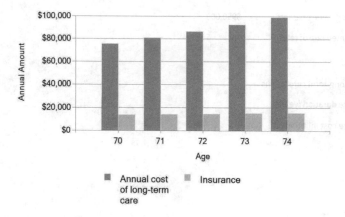

■ Annual cost of long-term care ■ Insurance

The cost to self-insure the total shortfall of $361,691 will be $274,105 at retirement or $248,621 today.

Values shown in this presentation are hypothetical and not a promise of future performance.

Long-Term Care Timeline

If long-term care is needed for Paul

Age	Monthly		
	Need	Benefit	Shortfall
70	$6,311	$1,159	$5,152
71	6,753	1,194	5,559
72	7,226	1,230	5,996
73	7,732	1,267	6,465
74	8,273	1,305	6,968

Odds of Disability

Insurance claims studies indicate that the odds of becoming disabled for 90 days or longer are much greater than dying during one's working years. Studies also suggest that, as the number of business owners or key employees increases, so do the odds that one of them will suffer a long-term disability.

Probability of at Least One Long-Term Disability Prior to Age 65

Age	Number of People in the Age Group					
	1	2	3	4	5	6
25	58%	82%	92%	97%	99%	99%
30	54%	79%	90%	96%	98%	99%
35	50%	75%	88%	94%	97%	98%
40	45%	70%	84%	91%	95%	97%
45	40%	64%	78%	87%	92%	95%
50	33%	55%	70%	80%	86%	91%
55	25%	43%	57%	68%	76%	82%

Note: Based on the 1985 Commissioners Individual Disability Table, most recent available.

Determining Odds of Disability Among People of Different Ages

Use the following table and worksheet to determine the risk of a long-term disability among your business owners or key employees.

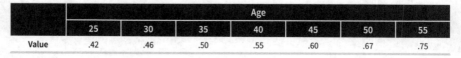

	Age						
	25	30	35	40	45	50	55
Value	.42	.46	.50	.55	.60	.67	.75

Step 1: For each owner or key employee you wish to include in your analysis, choose the value from the table above that corresponds to the age closest to the actual age of the owner or key employee, and include the value in the space below.

Step 2: Multiply all of the values by each other to arrive at a single value.

_____ x _____ x _____ x _____ x _____ = _____

Step 3: Multiply the single value by 100 to convert it to a percent.

100 x _____ **=** _____%

Step 4: Subtract the single value from 100% to determine the odds of long-term disability for any one of the groups of owners or key employees in your company.

100% - _____ **=** _____ %

Note: You can perform this analysis for any number of owners or key employees, not just the five shown in this worksheet.

The Impact of Disability

While most Americans insure their lives and physical possessions such as their homes, cars, etc., many overlook the need to protect their most valuable asset – the ability to earn an income.

How likely is it that someone will become disabled? The table below, developed using data collected by the federal government, shows the number of working-age Americans who have a disability that affects their daily lives.

Individuals with Disabilities by Age[1]

Age Range	No Disability	With a Disability
5-17 Years	95%	5%
18-34 Years	94%	6%
35-64 Years	87%	13%
65-74 Years	74%	26%
75 Years and over	50%	50%

Income Down, Expenses Up

The graph below illustrates the problem typically faced by an individual who becomes disabled for an extended period of time – income decreases while expenses increase.

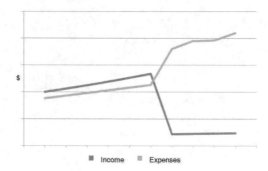

[1] Source: U.S. Census Bureau, 2014 American Community Survey, 1-year estimates. Table B18101, sex by age by disability status for the civilian noninstitutionalized population 5 years and over, male and female.

The Individual Need for Disability Insurance

Many people believe that their biggest asset is their home. For most of us, our biggest asset is the ability to work and earn an income. Not being able to work – due to a job loss or a disability having taken away the ability to work – is often financially devastating.

Everyone who works for a living is familiar with what can happen if they lose their job. On the other hand, the possibility of a serious disability is a risk few seem to consider. How likely is it that you will become seriously disabled? According to one study, 30% of all Americans between the ages of 35 and 65 suffered a disability lasting at least 90 days.[1] The risk is real. The question is, "What to do about it?"

Don't Count on Social Security

A few individuals do manage to qualify for disability benefits from Social Security. However, the Social Security definition of "disability" is so strict that, in 2015, only 35% of initial claims for Social Security disability benefits were accepted.[2] Obviously, something else beyond Social Security is needed.

Group Disability Insurance

Many employers will provide – or make available – disability insurance on a <u>group</u> basis. However, even those who are covered by a group policy can still be at substantial risk. Employer-sponsored disability policies seldom replace more than 60% of your monthly salary. Further, many policies have a monthly maximum benefit that may be far less than what some people earn. Income taxes can also be an issue; if the *employer* is paying the full cost of the coverage, and not including it in the employee's income, disability benefits are fully taxable. If an *employee* pays for disability insurance with after-tax dollars, the benefits are received free of income tax.[3]

---

[1] Based upon the 1985 Commissioners' Individual Disability Table.

[2] Annual Statistical Report on the Social Security Disability Insurance Program, 2016, October 2017. Table 61, Medical decisions at the initial adjudicative level, by year of application and program, all decisions.

[3] The discussion here concerns federal income tax law only. State or local law may vary.

The Individual Need for Disability Insurance

Individual Disability Income Insurance

If group coverage is not available, the solution may be <u>individual</u> disability income insurance. Although individual policies can cost more, as long as you pay the premiums with after-tax dollars, the benefits are not taxable. Plus, an individual policy allows you to tailor its terms to fit your own needs. When shopping for an individual disability policy, consider the following:

- **Company strength:** You need to know if the company is financially sound.

- **Definition of disability:** Look for a policy that defines disability in the broadest terms possible. Some policies will permit you to work in a different occupation and still collect disability benefits.

- **Elimination period:** How long must you wait before disability payments begin?

- **Benefit period:** How long will you need coverage? Both short-term and long-term disability benefits are available.

- **Inflation protection:** Try to find a policy that adjusts benefits for inflation.

Business Need for Disability Insurance

Self-motivated individuals frequently play a crucial role in the success of a business. This is particularly true of small businesses in which one or two talented people possess highly specialized skills or knowledge that other employees do not have. If such a "key" person were to suffer a long-term disability, not only would the individual face substantial financial risk, but the very survival of the company could be in jeopardy.

Although sole-proprietorships and partnerships are generally the most vulnerable, corporations, particularly corporations built around one or two individuals, are also at significant risk. However the business is organized, when you consider the likelihood that you or one of your key employees may become disabled, there is a clear need to protect both your personal income and the financial well-being of the company.

Options to Consider

There is no single strategy or policy to protect your business from the risks posed by a key employee's disability. Like a puzzle, a number of pieces are needed to complete the picture:

- **Adequate cash reserves:** Liquid funds can cover a short-term disability.

- **Key employee disability insurance:** Pays income to a disabled key employee. If the employer pays any portion of the premium, then a proportionate amount of the benefit is taxable income to the employee. If the employer pays the entire premium, the entire benefit is taxable.

- **Business overhead expense insurance:** This type of insurance covers normal operating expenses such as employee salaries, equipment leases, utilities, rent, advertising, maintenance, etc.

- **Qualified sick pay plan:** The federal tax code prohibits a business owner from paying himself (or herself) a salary while disabled, and then deducting the payments as an allowable business expense. A formal, written qualified sick pay plan (also known as a salary continuation plan), established in advance, can provide for funding the disability benefits as well as maximizing the tax benefits.

- **Disability buy-out:** In the event that you or another owner of the business suffers a permanent disability, disability insurance can be used to fund a buy-sell agreement.

Seek Professional Guidance

The guidance of knowledgeable tax and insurance professionals is essential in preparing for the potential impact of disability on a business.

Sources of Disability Insurance

Disability insurance is designed to replace a portion of the income you can lose if you are too sick or injured to work. There are two main sources of disability insurance: private disability insurance programs and government-sponsored disability insurance programs.

Private Disability Insurance Programs

There are two primary sources of private disability insurance:

The individual purchases the policy directly from an insurance company. The terms and benefits of the policy can vary widely.

Group plans are typically purchased through your employer and generally offer a low-cost alternative to individual coverage. The terms and coverage will vary.

Government-Sponsored Disability Insurance Programs

At the federal level, there are a two primary programs offering disability insurance. Both are administered by the Social Security Administration.

Social Security Disability Insurance (SSDI) pays benefits to qualified individuals under the age of 65 regardless of current income. Benefits are based upon your Social Security earnings history.

Social Security Supplemental Security Income (SSI) pays benefits to qualified individuals who are either over 65, blind or disabled, and with limited income. Benefits are not related to the individual's record of Social Security earnings.

The Department of Defense and Veterans Administration offer military service members and veterans disability compensation for service-related health problems. In addition, federal employees covered under the Federal Employees Retirement System (FERS) are eligible for benefits if they have at least 18 months of service, and are unable to perform their job because of injury or disease.

All states and the District of Columbia have workers' compensation laws that provide disability compensation to employed individuals who get sick, become injured, or who are killed on the job. Although most workers are covered, states laws vary dramatically as to who is excluded and to the amount of benefits paid.

A Word of Caution

Neither of these programs offered through Social Security covers partial disability and both have a strict definition of what it means to be disabled. In fact, in 2012, only 35% of initial claims for Social Security disability benefits were accepted.[1]

---

[1] Annual Statistical Report on the Social Security Disability Insurance Program, 2014, November 2015. Table 61, Medical decisions at the initial adjudicative level, by year of application and program, all decisions.

Individual Disability Income Insurance

One approach to the problem of providing income during an extended period of disability is to purchase individual disability income insurance.

What to Look for in a Disability Policy

- **Definition of disability:** Are education, experience, and past earnings taken into account in determining whether the insured is qualified to resume work? Many policies provide for an initial "own occupation"[1] definition of disability, for a specified period of time, after which a different definition of disability applies.

- **Partial or residual benefits:** Partial or residual disability benefits may be paid in some policies when the impairment allows the insured to perform only a portion of his or her duties. This provision may also pay benefits in the event the disability reduces the insured's income by a certain amount (e.g. 20% or more) from pre-disability levels.

- **Cost of living adjustment:** Is there a cost of living adjustment (COLA) which would increase benefit payments after a disability occurs?

- **Cancelability and renewability of policy:** Except for nonpayment of premiums, is the policy noncancelable or guaranteed renewable? Noncancelable generally means the insurer cannot cancel the policy, change the policy provisions or increase policy premiums after issue, as long as premiums are paid on a timely basis. Guaranteed renewable is similar, but allows the insurance company to increase the premium.

- **Waiting and elimination period:** Is the waiting or "elimination" period proper for the insured's circumstances? Commonly available periods may include 30, 60, 90, 180 and 360 days. Naturally, the longer the elimination period one selects, the lower his or her premium payments will be. However, a person's needs, cash reserves and income sources should be the deciding factors in selecting a proper elimination/waiting period.

---

[1] "Own occupation" generally means the insured's current occupation. The own occupation definition of disability may not be available for all occupations or professions.

Individual Disability Income Insurance

- **Benefit period:** What benefit period should be selected? Since a long-term medical disability can be financially devastating, one should elect a long-term benefit where possible. Some companies offer lifetime benefit periods, but periods as short as 24 months to 60 months are also available.

Types of Disability Contracts

Several other specialized disability contracts are available to the businessperson:

- **Business overhead expense:** Covers expenses such as staff salaries, rent, telephone, utilities, malpractice insurance, and other expenses necessary to keep a business open.

- **Key person disability:** Reimburses the business for the loss of a key employee and allows funding of temporary replacement or training of a successor.

- **Disability buyout:** Provides income to fund a buy-sell agreement triggered by the total disability of a shareholder/business owner. Payouts may come in the form of a lump sum, monthly installments, or a combination of the two.

Caution: Highly-compensated employees should be aware of payment caps in many group long-term disability policies. While some programs will provide disability income payments at 60% or 66% of salary, many have a relatively low dollar limitation, such as $3,000 per month.

How Individual Disability Income Insurance Works

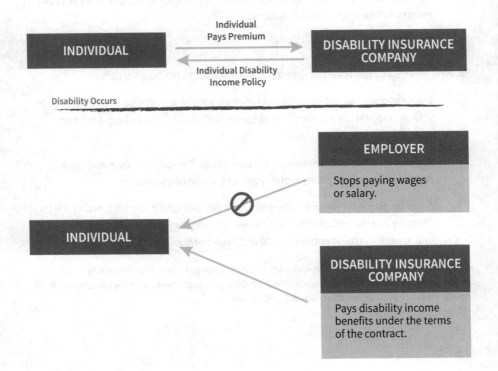

INDIVIDUAL

Individual
Pays Premium

Individual Disability
Income Policy

DISABILITY INSURANCE
COMPANY

Disability Occurs

EMPLOYER

Stops paying wages
or salary.

INDIVIDUAL

DISABILITY INSURANCE
COMPANY

Pays disability income
benefits under the terms
of the contract.

Group Disability Insurance

As the name implies, a "group" disability insurance policy covers a number of people who are linked in some way, such as through an employer, a trade association, or a school. Benefits are paid to replace earnings lost due to accident or sickness. Premiums may be paid for by the individual, the organization, or both. Generally, the cost of group coverage is less expensive than the cost of individual coverage.

Factors to Consider

Group disability policies can vary widely. Factors to keep in mind include:

- **Benefit period:** How long will benefits be paid?

- **Benefit level:** How much (in dollar terms) will the benefit be? Disability income policies usually replace only a portion of an individual's income, typically 60%.

- **Risks covered:** Does the policy cover both occupational (on-the job) and non-occupational (off-the-job) injuries and illnesses, or just one of these?

- **Elimination period:** How long do you have to wait before benefits begin?

Short-Term Disability (STD)

Group STD policies tend to have short elimination periods (1-14 days), typically cover non-occupational illnesses and injuries, and generally pay benefits for six months to one year. Group STD policies are designed to cover temporary situations such as a broken ankle or a pregnancy.

Long-Term Disability (LTD)

There are times when an injury or illness will render an individual unable to perform the essential duties of his or her occupation for an extended period of time. Group LTD policies are designed to meet this type of need. Typically, group LTD covers both occupational and non-occupational illnesses and injuries (24-hour coverage), with longer elimination periods of six months or more. Since some injuries or illnesses are permanent, a group LTD policy may pay benefits for years.

Federal Income Tax Treatment of Disability Income Payments

For federal income tax purposes, if an individual pays for disability insurance with <u>after-tax</u> dollars, the benefits paid under a disability income policy are received free of federal income tax. If, however, the individual pays the premiums with <u>pre-tax</u> dollars, or if the premiums are paid for by someone else (an employer, for example), any benefits received are taxable income to the individual. State or local income tax treatment of disability income benefits can vary widely.

Seek Professional Guidance

In planning for a possible period of disability, the guidance of appropriate financial professionals is strongly recommended.

How Employer Provided Disability Insurance Works

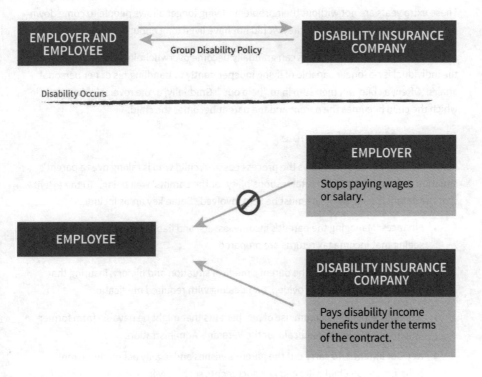

Employer and Employee
Each pays a portion of the premium.[1]

EMPLOYER AND EMPLOYEE ⟶ ⟵ *Group Disability Policy* DISABILITY INSURANCE COMPANY

Disability Occurs

EMPLOYER

Stops paying wages or salary.

EMPLOYEE

DISABILITY INSURANCE COMPANY

Pays disability income benefits under the terms of the contract.

---

[1] In some situations, the employer will sponsor a group disability insurance plan, but will not pay any of the premium.

When the Parent Becomes the Child

Providing Care for Older Individuals

It should come as no surprise to anyone that we're living longer.[1] Over the recent past, medical science has defeated numerous diseases that once shortened the lives of many. These extra years are not without their problems; living longer allows people to come down with illnesses that, in years past, they would not have lived long enough to develop.

As a person ages, health problems can gradually become overwhelming, to the point where the individual is no longer capable of living independently or handling his or her personal affairs. Often, a child will then step in to "help out." Gradually, a role reversal takes place in which the child becomes the parent and the parent becomes the child.

Planning Ahead - If Possible

If possible, planning ahead makes the process easier. A child who is taking over a parent's situation will often be handed total responsibility for the parents' well being. To the extent that the parent is able, he or she must be kept involved. Some key areas include:

- **Finances:** Managing the parent's income, assets, and liabilities, paying the bills, and seeing that income tax returns are prepared.

- **Medical:** Understanding the parent's medical situation and history, insuring that needed medical care is provided, and dealing with required medication.

- **Benefits:** Making maximum use of any benefits that might be payable from former employers, Medicare, Medicaid, or the Veteran's Administration.

- **Key Documents:** To carry out the parent's wishes and legally act on the parent's behalf, an adult child will need key documents such as wills, trust documents, a durable power of attorney for health care, a general power of attorney, and a "living will" or advance health care directive.

---

[1] For example, a child born in the year 1940 had an average life expectancy of 62.9 years. However, for a child born in 2014, average life expectancy had increased to 78.8 years. Source: National Vital Statistics Reports, Volume 65, Number 4, Deaths: Final data for 2014, Table 8. June 30, 2016.

When the Parent Becomes the Child

When to Intervene?

Very few of us want to intrude in our parents' lives. It is only when we begin to notice certain "things" about Mom and Dad that we begin to consider stepping in. Problems such as memory loss, dementia, diminished sight or hearing, incontinence, and falling are signs it's time to intervene. Two initial questions must be answered:

- **What needs to be done?** What is the appropriate level of care and/or type of living arrangement? Often, this question is answered in consultation with the parent's physician or with the help of a geriatric care manager.
- **Who will be in charge?** This task frequently falls to the child who is the closest, geographically, to the area where the parent resides. Sometimes, younger family members may decide to share the responsibilities. In other instances, a child with special skills or aptitudes may be chosen.

Care and Housing Options

Remaining in the family home is often the first choice of many elderly individuals. However, because the home is either unsafe or ill-suited to their needs, other options must be considered. The chart below lists a few of the alternatives:

Facility Type	Description	Advantages	Disadvantages
Senior Adult Condominiums	Similar to home ownership. Usually age restricted.	Living unit can often be matched to the individual's needs. Few maintenance or security concerns.	Individual must arrange for own healthcare and personal service needs. Rules may be restrictive. Costs may be high.
Senior Apartments	Apartment rental units. Often age restricted.	Individual can select a unit to meet needs. May have common services such as transportation, recreation, or meals.	Individual must be able to live safely and independently; must arrange for own healthcare and personal service needs.
Continuing Care Retirement Community	Provide a range of facilities, including independent living, assisted living, and nursing home care.	Different levels of services and living arrangements are available to meet an individual's needs as those needs change over time.	Usually expensive. Require a large initial entrance fee as well as monthly charges. If care provider is not financially strong, monies paid may be lost.

When the Parent Becomes the Child

Facility Type	Description	Advantages	Disadvantages
Assisted Living	Rental of private rooms or apartments, with many services.	A wide range of personal services are provided, including laundry, meals, housekeeping, and 24 hour monitoring.	Individual must be able to move about and handle most of their own physical needs.
Nursing Home	Skilled nursing facility	Provide care for individuals who cannot live independently because of physical or mental impairments.	Can be quite expensive. Quality of care can vary.

Preparing for the End

Even longer lives eventually end. The caregiver's responsibilities in this final stage of life are just as important as in any other. One key goal is to honor the terms of the elderly individual's advance health care directive. A "Do Not Resuscitate" order may be required, when even heroic medical efforts serve no real purpose. You may have to arrange for hospice care when death is near. Allowing the elderly the opportunity for a death with dignity is as important as caring for them when they are alive.

Disability Break-Even

Assumptions:

Monthly Premium: $200
Annual Benefit: $48,000
Benefit Inflating Annually by: 0%

Years Premium Paid	Benefits Paid Will Equal Premiums Paid in:
2 years	2 months
5 years	3 months
10 years	6 months
20 years	1 year

Example

If you paid monthly premiums of $200, for 5 years, your benefits would equal your total outlay in approximately 3 months.

Disability Income Analysis Data

Personal

Client(s) name		Date of birth
1) Paul	Johnson	01/01/1969
2) Sally	Johnson	01/01/1971

Disability Data

Income Needs

	Paul	Sally
Current annual salary	$87,000	$65,000
Percent to replace	60%	60%

Client 1 current disability insurance

	Monthly benefit	Elimination period	Benefit period	COLA rate
Policy #1	$2,400	1 month	6 months	3%
Policy #2	$3,600	2 months	5 years	3%

Client 2 current disability insurance

	Monthly benefit	Elimination period	Benefit period	COLA rate
Policy #1				3%
Policy #2				3%

Assumptions

Annual inflation rate   4%

Disability Income Analysis

In the event of Paul's or Sally's disability.

A disability can cause a significant reduction in income while causing a significant increase in expenses. New funds are required to pay medical and other related costs, as well as to replace existing income necessary to provide for ongoing living expenses for the family. Medical insurance is available to help pay for medical expenses. Disability income protection insurance is available to replace a part of the disabled person's income.

Income Needs and Insurance

This analysis illustrates the need to replace 60.00% of Paul's current monthly income of $7,250 and 60.00% of Sally's current monthly income of $5,417.

Analysis

After 90 days, Paul's current disability income insurance benefits of $6,000 per month are sufficient to meet your needs of $4,350 per month.

After 90 days, Sally's current disability income insurance benefits of $0 per month are not sufficient to meet your needs of $3,250 per month.

Disability Income Needs

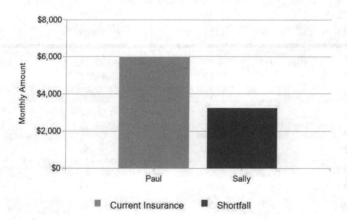

Sally needs additional income of $3,250 per month.

Disability Timeline

In the event of a disability of Paul

Period	Monthly		
	Need	Benefit	Shortfall
Month 1	$4,350	$0	$4,350
Month 2	$4,350	$2,400	$1,950
Month 3	$4,350	$4,350	$0
Month 4	$4,350	$4,350	$0
Month 5	$4,350	$4,350	$0
Month 6	$4,350	$4,350	$0
Month 7	$4,350	$4,350	$0
Month 8	$4,350	$3,600	$750
Month 9	$4,350	$3,600	$750
Month 10	$4,350	$3,600	$750
Month 11	$4,350	$3,600	$750
Month 12	$4,350	$3,600	$750
Year 2	$4,524	$3,708	$816
Year 3	$4,705	$3,819	$886
Year 4	$4,893	$3,934	$959
Year 5	$5,089	$4,052	$1,037
Year 6	$5,292	$0	$5,292
Year 7	$5,504	$0	$5,504
Year 8	$5,724	$0	$5,724
Year 9	$5,953	$0	$5,953
Year 10	$6,191	$0	$6,191
Year 11	$6,439	$0	$6,439
Year 12	$6,697	$0	$6,697
Year 13	$6,964	$0	$6,964
Age 65	$8,147	$0	$8,147

Income Taxes Generally

Three Kinds of Income

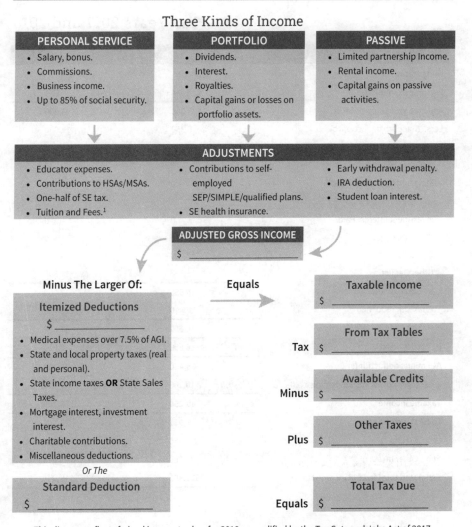

PERSONAL SERVICE	PORTFOLIO	PASSIVE
• Salary, bonus. • Commissions. • Business income. • Up to 85% of social security.	• Dividends. • Interest. • Royalties. • Capital gains or losses on portfolio assets.	• Limited partnership Income. • Rental income. • Capital gains on passive activities.

ADJUSTMENTS

- Educator expenses.
- Contributions to HSAs/MSAs.
- One-half of SE tax.
- Tuition and Fees.[1]
- Contributions to self-employed SEP/SIMPLE/qualified plans.
- SE health insurance.
- Early withdrawal penalty.
- IRA deduction.
- Student loan interest.

ADJUSTED GROSS INCOME

$ _____

Minus The Larger Of: **Equals**

Itemized Deductions

$ _____

- Medical expenses over 7.5% of AGI.
- State and local property taxes (real and personal).
- State income taxes **OR** State Sales Taxes.
- Mortgage interest, investment interest.
- Charitable contributions.
- Miscellaneous deductions.

Or The

Standard Deduction

$ _____

Taxable Income

$ _____

From Tax Tables

Tax $ _____

Available Credits

Minus $ _____

Other Taxes

Plus $ _____

Total Tax Due

Equals $ _____

This diagram reflects federal income tax law for 2018 as modified by the Tax Cuts and Jobs Act of 2017

---

[1] Through December 31, 2017.

Federal Income Tax Approximator

Tax Years 2017 and 2018

Item Description	2017	2018
Filing status	Single	Single
Personal exemptions	4	N/A
Adjusted gross income (AGI)	$82,000	$94,000
Less: Standard deduction, or	6,350	12,000
Less: Itemized deductions, if more		
Medical Expenses	0	0
State and Local Taxes Paid[1]	0	0
Mortgage Interest Paid[2]	0	0
Investment Interest Paid	0	0
Charitable Gifts	0	0
Causality Losses	0	0
Other Deductions	16,550	17,800
Total Deductions	16,550	17,800
Phaseout reduction	0	N/A
Net itemized deductions	16,550	17,800
Deduction used	16,550	17,800
AGI minus deduction(s)	65,450	76,200
Less: Exemptions (including phase outs)	16,200	0
Taxable income	49,250	76,200
Federal income tax	8,051	12,704
Less: Credits	250	500
Plus: Other taxes[3]	3,500	3,800
Estimated total federal income tax	$11,301	$16,004

[1] State and local tax deductions are limited to $10,000 in 2018
[2] Starting in 2018 mortgage interest deduction can not include home equity loans.
[3] Other taxes might include AMT, self-employment tax, etc.

Federal Income Tax Tables - 2017

Filing Status	If Taxable Income Is Between			Pay	Plus Percent on Excess Over 1st Column
Single tax payers	$0	-	$9,325	$0.00	10.0%
	9,325	-	37,950	932.50	15.0%
	37,950	-	91,900	5,226.25	25.0%
	91,900	-	191,650	18,713.75	28.0%
	191,650	-	416,700	46,643.75	33.0%
	416,700	-	418,400	120,910.25	35.0%
	418,400	-	Up	121,505.25	39.6%
Married filing jointly	$0	-	$18,650	$0.00	10.0%
	18,650	-	75,900	1,865.00	15.0%
	75,900	-	153,100	10,452.50	25.0%
	153,100	-	233,350	29,752.50	28.0%
	233,350	-	416,700	52,222.50	33.0%
	416,700	-	470,700	112,728.00	35.0%
	470,700	-	Up	131,628.00	39.6%
Married filing separately	$0	-	$9,325	$0.00	10.0%
	9,325	-	37,950	932.50	15.0%
	37,950	-	76,550	5,226.25	25.0%
	76,550	-	116,675	14,876.25	28.0%
	116,675	-	208,350	26,111.25	33.0%
	208,350	-	235,350	56,364.00	35.0%
	235,350	-	Up	65,814.00	39.6%
Head of household	$0	-	$13,350	$0.00	10.0%
	13,350	-	50,800	1,335.00	15.0%
	50,800	-	131,200	6,952.50	25.0%
	131,200	-	212,500	27,052.50	28.0%
	212,500	-	416,700	49,816.50	33.0%
	416,700	-	444,500	117,202.50	35.0%
	444,500	-	Up	126,932.50	39.6%

Federal Income Tax Tables - 2017

Example

Married Filing Jointly			
Taxable income	$80,000		
Tax on the 1st	75,900	is	$10,452.50
Tax on the remaining	4,100	x 25.0% is	1,025.00
Total Tax			**$11,477.50**

Federal Income Tax Tables - 2018

Filing Status	If Taxable Income Is Between			Pay	Plus Percent on Excess Over 1st Column
	$0	-	$9,525	$0.00	10.0%
	9,525	-	38,700	952.50	12.0%
Single tax payers	38,700	-	82,500	4,453.50	22.0%
	82,500	-	157,500	14,089.50	24.0%
	157,500	-	200,000	32,089.50	32.0%
	200,000	-	500,000	45,689.50	35.0%
	500,000	-	Up	150,689.50	37.0%
	$0	-	$19,050	$0.00	10.0%
	19,050	-	77,400	1,905.00	12.0%
Married filing jointly	77,400	-	165,000	8,907.00	22.0%
	165,000	-	315,000	28,179.00	24.0%
	315,000	-	400,000	64,179.00	32.0%
	400,000	-	600,000	91,379.00	35.0%
	600,000	-	Up	161,379.00	37.0%
	$0	-	$9,525	$0.00	10.0%
	9,525	-	38,700	952.50	12.0%
Married filing separately	38,700	-	82,500	4,453.50	22.0%
	82,500	-	157,500	14,089.50	24.0%
	157,500	-	200,000	32,089.50	32.0%
	200,000	-	300,000	45,689.50	35.0%
	300,000	-	Up	80,689.50	37.0%
	$0	-	$13,600	$0.00	10.0%
	13,600	-	51,800	1,360.00	12.0%
Head of household	51,800	-	82,500	5,944.00	22.0%
	82,500	-	157,500	12,698.00	24.0%
	157,500	-	200,000	30,698.00	32.0%
	200,000	-	500,000	44,298.00	35.0%
	500,000	-	Up	149,298.00	37.0%

Example

Married Filing Jointly			
Taxable income	$80,000		
Tax on the 1st	77,400	is	$8,907.00
Tax on the remaining	2,600	22.0%	572.00
Total Tax			**$9,479.00**

Personal and Dependent Exemptions

Year	Amount of Exemption for Each		
	Taxpayer	Spouse	Dependent Child
2015	$4,000	$4,000	$4,000
2016	4,050	4,050	4,050
2017	4,050	4,050	4,050

For tax years before 2018, for higher income taxpayers, the deductibility of personal and dependent exemptions, as well as that of certain itemized deductions, was gradually reduced as adjusted gross income increased. For 2017, the phase-out thresholds for both of these limitations were: Single - $261,500; Married Filing Jointly - $313,800; Married Filing Separately - $156,900; and Head of Household - $287,650.

For 2018 through 2025, the Tax Cuts and Jobs Act of 2017 (TCJA) repealed both the deduction for personal and dependent exemptions as well as the limitation on specified itemized deductions. Unless the law is later changed, both of these deductions will again be allowed beginning in 2026.

Standard Deduction - Persons Who Do Not Itemize Deductions

Year	Amount of Deduction			
	Married Jointly	Married Separate	Heads of Household	Single
2015	$12,600	$6,300	$9,250	$6,300
2016	12,600	6,300	9,300	6,300
2017	12,700	6,350	9,350	6,350
2018	24,000	12,000	18,000	12,000
2019	Adjusted for Inflation			

Year	Additional Standard Deductions (Each Spouse)			
	65 or Older		Blind	
	Married	Single	Married	Single
2015	$1,250	$1,550	$1,250	$1,550
2016	1,250	1,550	1,250	1,550
2017	1,250	1,550	1,250	1,550
2018	1,300	1,600	1,300	1,600
2019	Adjusted for Inflation			

Children: For 2017, children with income who can be claimed as dependents on a parent's return (even if the exemption has no benefit due to the phase-out) cannot take their own personal exemption. A child's standard deduction is up to $1,050 for unearned income or up to $6,350 for earned income.

Income Tax Tables for
Estates – Trusts – Corporations

Estates and Trusts - 2018[1]

If Taxable Income Is Between...			Pay	Plus	Percent on Excess Over 1st Column
$0.00	-	2,550.00	$0.00		10.00%
2,550.00	-	9,150.00	255.00		24.00%
9,150.00	-	12,500.00	1,839.00		35.00%
12,500.00	-	and higher	3,011.50		37.00%

Corporations

The Tax Cuts and Jobs Act of 2017 made major changes to the income tax rates applicable to corporations:

- **Before 2018** – For tax years before 2018, corporate taxable income was subject to a graduated tax schedule, with marginal tax rates ranging from 15.0% to 35.0%. Personal service corporations were subject to a flat 35.0% rate on all income.

- **2018 and later** – For tax years beginning in 2018 and later, corporate taxable income, including that of personal service corporations, will be taxed at a single rate of 21.0%.

[1] Rates are linked to changes in inflation.

Types of Trusts and Their Tax Treatment

Type of Trust	Income Tax	Estate Tax	Gift Tax
Testamentary trust: Created in the trustor's will and takes effect only at his death. Can be used to avoid tax on a portion of the first spouse's share of the estate, e.g., the bypass trust.	Income which is distributed is taxed to the beneficiary; if income is accumulated, it is taxed to the trust until later distributed to the beneficiary.	Trust assets are included in decedent's estate.	No gift tax.
Revocable living trust: Created while the trustor is still living but can be revoked or amended during his or her lifetime. Assets in the trust will avoid probate expenses, delay and publicity.	No income tax savings while trustor lives. After death, same as testamentary trust for income tax purposes.	Trust assets are included in decedent's gross estate.	No gift tax. Trust is revocable.
Irrevocable life insurance trust: Created while the trustor is still living and cannot be revoked by the trustor. Used to reduce the size of the estate. Works best for removing insurance from the estates of both spouses. Some are "funded," and others are "unfunded" or just own a life insurance policy.[1]	Same as testamentary trust above, except if income from a funded trust is accumulated, it is taxable to the trustor.	Usually excluded unless gift of policy was within three years prior to insured's death.	There may be a gift tax liability, but gifts to the trust can usually be made to qualify for the $15,000[2] annual gift tax exclusion.
Sec. 2503(c) minor's trust: A type of irrevocable trust for minors which qualifies for the annual gift tax exclusion even though the gifts to it are "future interest."[3]	Same as testamentary trust above.	Usually excluded unless transfer was within three years prior to death.	There may be a gift tax liability, but gifts to the trust can usually be made to qualify for the $15,000[2] annual gift tax exclusion.

Note: For 2018-2025, if a child subject to the "Kiddie Tax" has unearned income in excess of certain limits ($2,100 for 2018), the excess is taxed according to the brackets applicable to trusts and estates. The remainder of a child's taxable income is taxed at the child's rates. State or local law may vary.

---

[1] Cash contributions may be made to the trust, to be used by the trustee to make premium payments on the life insurance policy. Careful drafting of the trust document is required to qualify the cash gifts for the annual gift tax exclusion.

[2] The annual gift tax exclusion ($15,000 in 2018) is indexed for inflation in increments of $1,000.

[3] Under federal law, the minor must become the owner of the assets no later than age 21.

Personal Income Tax History

Top Marginal Rates 1913 to Present

The chart[1] traces the highest federal personal income tax rates from 1913 to today. The amount of income subject to these varying rates has also changed. In 1965-67, a rate of 70% applied to taxable incomes over $200,000, equal to approximately $1,322,376 in current dollars.

Top Federal Income Tax Rate

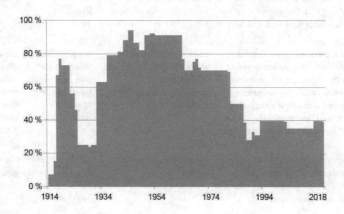

[1] Source: Joseph A. Pechman, "Federal Tax Policy" Fifth Edition, and IRS form 1040.

Capital Gains and Losses

Individuals, Estates, and Trusts[1]

The Internal Revenue Code[2] has long distinguished between income paid due to a person's individual effort (such as wages or self-employment earnings), and income received from the profitable sale of assets known as "capital" assets. Wages and salaries are classified as "ordinary" income. Gain from the sale of a capital asset is termed a "capital" gain. Gains from the sale of capital assets that meet certain requirements are generally accorded more favorable tax treatment than ordinary income.

Basic Terminology

There are several concepts essential to understanding capital gains and losses.

- Capital asset: The law defines the term "capital" asset in a negative sense by first declaring that all types of property are capital assets, and then listing certain exceptions. (See IRC Sec. 1221.) Assets such as stocks, bonds and other securities held by individuals are capital assets. In general terms, assets that are held for investment purposes are capital assets. Some assets are not capital assets by definition, but may be treated as such if used in a trade or business, and sold or exchanged at a gain.

- Holding period: This is the length of time an asset is owned, beginning on the day after it is acquired and ending on the day it is disposed of. The amount of time an asset has been held impacts the tax treatment of any gain or loss when the asset is sold. The law currently provides for two holding periods: short-term and long-term. Short-term assets are those held exactly 12 months or less. Long-term assets are those held more than 12 months.

Capital Losses

At the end of a tax year, a taxpayer's capital gains and losses are totaled and compared. If losses exceed gains, a taxpayer may use up to $3,000 of losses to offset other ordinary income ($1,500 if married filing separately). See IRC Sec. 1211(b). Losses that exceed the $3,000 limit may be carried to future tax years until used up. If a taxpayer dies, any un-used capital loss is gone forever; it may not be carried over to future tax years.

---

[1] Corporate taxpayers are subject to different rules regarding capital gains.

[2] The discussion here concerns federal income tax law; state or local income tax law may differ.

Capital Gains and Losses

Capital Gains

Ordinary income such as wages and salaries can be taxed at marginal federal income tax rates as high as 37.0% Short-term capital gains are treated as ordinary income, taxable at the taxpayer's highest rate. Long-term capital gains are taxed at rates which are capped, and which may be less than a taxpayer's regular rate.

Long-Term Capital Gains Tax Rates

Prior to the Tax Cuts and Jobs Act of 2017, the tax rate applied to individual long-term capital gains was linked to two factors:

- **Taxpayer's income tax bracket** -Those with a marginal tax bracket of less than 15.0% paid tax on capital gains at a 0.0% rate. Taxpayers with a marginal tax bracket between 15.0% and 39.6% paid tax on capital gains at a 15.0% rate. Finally, those with a marginal tax rate of 39.6% paid tax on capital gains at a 20% rate.

- **Type of capital gain** – By statute, real estate depreciation treated as capital gain was taxed at a 25.0% rate and gain from the sale of collectibles was taxed at a 28.0% rate.

The Tax Cuts and Jobs Act of 2017 (JCTA), effective for 2018 – 2025, changed the individual income tax rate structure[1]. Under prior law, individuals paid tax at marginal rates that included 10.0%, 15.0%, 25.0%, 28.0%, 33.0%, 35.0%, and 39.6%. TCJA introduced a tax rate structure that included marginal rates of 10.0%, 12.0%, 22.0%, 24.0%, 32.0%, 35.0%, and 37.0%.

TCJA generally retained the prior-law maximum rates on long-term capital gains. However, rather than linking the capital gains tax rates to the new tax rate structure, TCJA retained the 2017 dollar breakpoints for the 15.0% bracket and the 20.0% bracket and, for 2018, indexed them for inflation.[2] The table on the following page shows the capital gains tax rates applicable at various levels of taxable income in 2017 and 2018.

---

[1] Under the TCJA, the individual income tax rate structure applicable in 2017 will return for tax years after 2025.

[2] The breakpoints are subject to adjustment for inflation in future years.

Capital Gains and Losses

Item	2017 Breakpoint	2018 Breakpoint	Capital Gains Rate
Tax Bracket is less than 15%	15.0% bracket is reached when taxable income reaches: Single: $37,950 HoH: $50,800; MFJ: $75,900; MFS: $37,950	Taxable income less than: Single: $38,600; HoH: $51,700; MFJ: $77,200; MFS: $38,600	0%
Tax bracket is equal to or more than 15.0% and less than 39.6%	39.6% bracket is reached when taxable income reaches: Single: $418,400; HoH: $444,550; MFJ: $470,700; MFS: $235,350.	Taxable income less than: Single: $425,800; HoH: $452,400; MFJ: $479,000; MFS: $239,500.	15%
Tax bracket is 39.6%	39.6% bracket is reached when taxable income reaches: Single: $418,400; HoH: $444,550; MFJ: $470,700; MFS: $235,350.	Taxable income equal to or more than: Single: $425,800; HoH: $452,400; MFJ: $479,000; MFS: $239,500.	20%
Real estate depreciation treated as capital gain[1]	N/A	N/A	25%
Sale of Collectibles	N/A	N/A	28%

Special Rules for Personal Residence

Under current law, a taxpayer may exclude from income up to $250,000 of gain from the sale of a principal residence, if the taxpayer has owned and used the property as his or her principal residence for at least two years of the five-year period ending on the date of the sale or exchange. Only one such exclusion is permitted every two years.

For married couples filing a joint return, the maximum exclusion amount is increased to $500,000 if (a) either spouse meets the ownership requirement; (b) both spouses meet the use requirements, and (c) neither spouse is ineligible because of the one sale every two years rule. If a married couple does not meet the requirements for the $500,000 exclusion, the amount of gain eligible for exclusion is the sum of the amounts to which each spouse would be entitled if they had not been married.

---

[1] Gain in excess of recaptured depreciation is taxed at the taxpayers's regular capital gains rate.

The surviving spouse of a couple who had jointly owned and occupied a residence and who met the general requirements discussed above immediately before the deceased spouse's death, may exclude up to $500,000 of gain as long as the sale of the residence takes place within two years of the date of the deceased spouse's death.

The law also provides for a reduced maximum exclusion for taxpayers who do not meet the requirements to qualify for the full $250,000 ($500,000 if married) exclusion, and who sell or exchange a principal residence because of changes in place of employment, health, or unforeseen circumstances.

Beginning with sales or exchanges after January 1, 2009, gain from the disposition of a principal residence attributable to periods of "nonqualified use" is not excluded from gross income. Nonqualified use, generally, is a period of time (beginning on or after January 1, 2009) when the property is not used by the taxpayer or the taxpayer's spouse (or former spouse) as a principal residence. Common examples of such nonqualified use include use of the property as a rental or vacation home.

A member of the U.S. armed forces, U.S. Foreign Service, Peace Corps volunteers, or specified members of the intelligence community serving on qualified extended duty may choose to suspend the five-year period of use and ownership for up to 10 years.

An individual who acquires his or her principal residence in an IRC Sec. 1031 "like-kind-exchange" must own the property for five years before the exclusion applies.

Timing of Capital Gains Transactions

Note that a taxpayer generally controls when a capital asset will be sold and can, therefore, choose the year in which a gain or loss is to be included in his or her taxable income.

Seek Professional Guidance:

The income tax treatment of capital gains and losses is complex and often confusing. Individuals facing decisions concerning the tax implications of the sale or exchange of a capital asset are strongly advised to first consult with a CPA, IRS enrolled agent, or other competent professional.

Utilizing Passive Losses

Since the Tax Reform Act of 1986, losses flowing through limited partnership investment interests to individuals are generally classified as "passive activity" losses. Federal income tax law[1] mandates that such losses cannot be used to offset or reduce earned (wages, salaries, or self-employment) income or portfolio (dividends, interest, etc.) income. Thus, persons with existing limited partnership interests, many in multiple-year funding commitments, may be unable to fully utilize these tax losses.

The Solution – Passive Income

While passive activity losses may not be used to offset earned or portfolio income, they may be used to offset income from passive sources. An investors can acquired limited partnership programs producing substantial taxable income in order to utilize existing passive losses. Typical partnerships producing high levels of taxable income include oil and gas income programs, unleveraged equipment leasing, and unleveraged rental real estate.

Passive losses in excess of passive income are not "lost." Rather, any unused passive losses are "suspended" and are carried forward until they are either used to offset passive income or until the year the investor disposes of his or her interest in the passive activity.

Limited Exceptions to the Rule

The following are exceptions to the passive loss limitation rules.

- Rental real estate

  - Taxpayers considered to be real estate "professionals" are allowed to deduct their passive losses against income. Real estate professions include brokerage, construction, rental, development, management, or leasing. To qualify for this exception, a taxpayer must "materially participate" in such real estate activities, spend over 750 hours per year working in them, and devote more than one-half of his or her personal services to such businesses. The "material participation" standard requires an individual to participate on a regular, continuous, and substantial basis. Service as an employee is not considered part of a real estate profession, unless the individual is a more than 5% owner. See IRC Sec. 469(c)(7).

---

[1] The discussion here concerns federal income tax law; state or local law may differ

- Taxpayers who actively participate in rental real estate activities may deduct up to $25,000 from nonpassive income.[1] This exception is phased out by 50% of the amount by which their adjusted gross income exceeds $100,000 (no deduction at $150,000 of AGI or above). The "active participation" exception may be easier to qualify for than the "material participation" exception for real estate professionals. Active participation could include approving leases, tenants, capital improvements, etc. See IRC Sec. 469(i).

However, a merely formal or nominal participation in management, without a genuine exercise of independent discretion and judgment, is insufficient.

- **Low-income housing and historic rehabilitation credits**

  - Credits from low-income housing or historic rehabilitation projects may be applied against the tax on up to $25,000 of non-passive income, even if the taxpayer was not personally active.

  - Low-income housing credits may reach up to 9.0% of qualified expenditures annually, depending on the type of building and whether or not it is federally subsidized. However, for 2018 and later years, the Tax Cuts and Jobs Act of 2017 (TCJA) permanently repealed the low-income housing credit.

  - Historic rehabilitation credits are 20.0% for costs on certified historic structures and 10.0% of costs on pre-1936 buildings. For 2017 and earlier, the historic rehabilitation credit was generally claimed in its entirety in the year a project was placed into service. Under the TCJA, for 2018 and later years, a historic rehabilitation credit is claimed ratably over a five-year period, beginning with the year the rehabilitated project is placed into service.

  - Any credit not completely used in a year is "suspended" and carried forward to future tax years. Un-used, suspended credits are lost when a passive activity is disposed of.

---

[1] This amount is reduced to $12,500 for married persons filing separately and who lived apart the entire year. The amount is zero if a married couple files married filing separately and lived together for any part of the year.

Personal Alternative Minimum Tax

The alternative minimum tax (AMT) is designed to prevent taxpayers with substantial income from avoiding or deferring all tax liability through the use of deductions, exemptions and credits. The rules add substantial complexity to the tax system. (See IRC Sec. 55 and IRS Form 6251 and its instructions.)

Adjusted gross income is adjusted to reflect different treatment of certain items by the AMT rules.

Steps in Computing the AMT

1. Adjusted Gross Income (AGI)[1] $ _____

2. Plus or Minus: Certain adjustments   _____

3. Plus: AMT preferences   _____

4. Equals: AMT Income (AMTI)   _____

5. Less: AMT Exemption Amount (see last page)   (_____)

6. Equals: Net AMTI   _____

7. Times: Tax rate
   (26% of 1st $191,100 and 28% of amounts over $191,100.
   For married filing separate, the breakpoint is $95,550.)[2]
   ($ _____ x 0.26) + ($ _____ x 0.28) =   _____

8. Tentative AMT before credits   _____

9. Less: AMT foreign tax credit [3]   (_____)

10. Equals: Tentative minimum tax   _____

11. Less: Regular tax   (_____)

12. Alternative minimum tax due[4] $ _____

---

[1] If the return includes Schedule A, use AGI less the allowable itemized deductions from Schedule A.

[2] The breakpoints values shown are for 2018. These values are subject to adjustment for inflation in future years. For 2017, the breakpoints were: $93,900 (Married Filing Separately); and $187,800 (all other taxpayers).

[3] Any part of the AMT foreign tax credit that is not used in a tax year may be carried back one year and forward 10 years.

[4] The AMT only applies to the extent it is larger than the regular tax liability. Once a taxpayer is subject to the AMT, he or she may be entitled to a credit that can reduce future tax liability. In 2012 and later years, a taxpayer's nonrefundable personal credits are allowed against both the AMT and regular tax liability.

Adjustments

Certain items are treated differently for AMT purposes than for the regular tax and must therefore be adjusted. A partial list includes the following:

- Generally, no deduction is allowed for state and local taxes or for miscellaneous itemized deductions.[1]

- Medical expenses are deductible only to the extent that they exceed 7.50% of adjusted gross income.

- Accelerated depreciation under the cost-recovery rules of the AMT will more closely approximate the investment's useful life.

- Passive investments that offset taxable income generally will not reduce AMTI (alternative minimum taxable income). Therefore, deductions for passive losses may be claimed only against passive income.

- Certain interest on a home mortgage not used to build, buy, or improve a house, is not deductible for AMT purposes.

- Investment interest is deductible for AMT purposes only to the extent of net investment income.

- Incentive stock options: The excess of the fair market value of the stock at the time of exercise, over the price paid for the stock, including any amount paid for the option.

Preferences

Taxable income for AMT purposes must be increased by the following preferences:

- Tax-exempt interest from certain private purpose bonds issued by state and local governments.

- The excess of the deduction for depletion over the adjusted basis of the property at the end of the taxable year.

- Certain expensing of intangible drilling costs to the extent they exceed 65% of net oil and gas income.

---

[1] The Tax Cuts and Jobs Act of 2017, for 2018 – 2025, repealed all current-law miscellaneous itemized deductions subject to the 2.0% of AGI limitation.

Personal Alternative Minimum Tax

Exemption Amounts - 2017

Varies with filing status and is phased out for persons with high income. The exemption amounts for 2017 are:

Filing Status	Exemption Amount	Less 25% of AMTI Over	No Exemption if AMTI is Over
Married Joint/Surviving Spouse	$84,500	$160,900	$498,900
Married Filing Separately	42,250	80,450	249,450
Single or Head of Household	54,300	120,700	337,900

Exemption Amounts - 2018[1]

The AMT exemption amounts for 2018 are as follows:

Filing Status	Exemption Amount	Less 25% of AMTI Over	No Exemption if AMTI is Over
Married Joint/Surviving Spouse	$109,400	$1,000,000	$1,437,600
Married Filing Separately	54,700	500,000	718,800
Single or Head of Household	70,300	500,000	781,200

Note: This summary is not intended to cover all of the details of the alternative minimum tax. It is a very complicated set of rules and will require careful planning to avoid or reduce its potential impact on a taxpayer's overall income tax liability.

---

[1] The AMT exemption amounts, as well as the breakpoints at which the exemption begins to be phased-out, are subject to adjustment for inflation.

Accumulation of Trust Income for Minors

Often, trusts for children grant the trustee the discretion of either accumulating income or distributing it as the trustee determines, to meet the needs of the beneficiaries. Under current federal law,[1] however, income accumulated inside a trust is taxed at relatively high marginal income tax rates.

Potential Problem

In 2018, estates and trusts with taxable income in excess of $12,500 are subject to the highest federal marginal income tax rate of 37.0%. A married couple, however, does not reach this 37.0% marginal bracket until their taxable income reaches $600,000.

As an example, a trust containing $300,000 of assets invested at 5.0% would earn $15,000 per year. Any amount in excess of $12,500 would need to be distributed to avoid taxation at the top 37.0% federal income tax rate. Even if the trustee wants to distribute all or part of the earnings, how can he or she do so if the beneficiaries are minors?

Possible Solutions

If the trust document allows the trustee to make distributions "to or for the benefit of" the beneficiary, the trustee might consider making transfers to the beneficiary under the Uniform Transfer to Minors Act. The person named as custodian can invest these funds and use them for the minor's benefit until he or she is an adult. The advantage of the custodial arrangement is that all of its earnings are taxed at the beneficiary's rate even though they are not distributed. A single person does not reach the 37.0% bracket until his or her taxable income reaches $500,000.[2] For certain children, unearned income in excess of $2,100[2] is subject to taxation at the income tax rates applicable to estates and trusts.

If it is not desirable (or permitted by trust language) to use the custodial arrangement, the trustee should look for other methods of reducing taxable income. One approach would be to switch from income producing assets to more growth-oriented investments.

---

[1] The issues discussed here concern federal income tax law; state and local law may vary.
[2] These values apply to 2018 and are subject to adjustment for inflation in future years.

Accumulation of Trust Income for Minors

Tax-exempt investments are another possible alternative. The yield on a tax-exempt investment can be lower than that of a taxable investment and still enjoy the same net return. For example, to match a tax-free return of 5.00%, an investor in the 37.0% marginal bracket would have to earn a taxable return of 7.94%.

The high marginal income tax rates applicable to trusts apply also to estates. Caution should be used in choosing the executor of one's estate. An unwise executor may allow the income tax burden to be higher than necessary.

Income Tax Basis

Basis is a value used to determine the amount of gain or loss on the sale of an asset and will vary, depending upon how it was acquired:

Cost Basis	=	The amount paid for an asset
Adjusted Basis	=	Cost basis plus improvements less depreciation
Capital Gain	=	Sales price is higher than adjusted basis
Capital Loss	=	Sales price is less than adjusted basis
FMV	=	Fair market value

Basic Rules as They Apply to Various Transfers

Assume owner paid $5,000 for a lot (his cost basis).

Method of Transfer	Basis in Hands of New Owner	Assume at Time of Transfer Lot Had		
		Declined in Value to $3,000	Retained Same Value of $5,000	Increased in Value to $8,000
Sale	Purchaser receives a new basis (the amount he pays for the asset).	$3,000	$5,000	$8,000
Lifetime gift	**For computing gain:** Donee takes donor's basis.	–	$5,000	$5,000[1]
	For computing loss: Donee's basis is FMV at time of gift, or the donor's basis, whichever is lower.	$3,000	–	–
Transfer at death	Beneficiary's basis is equal to value at decedent's death or six months thereafter.[2]	$3,000	$5,000	$8,000
Like kind exchange IRC Sec. 1031	Basis in newly acquired property will be the same as basis in the transferred property, plus any recognized gain and less any cash received.	$5,000	$5,000	$5,000

Note: Transfers of appreciated property to a spouse or former spouse who is a non-resident alien will trigger tax on the gain. See IRC Sec. 1041(d).

---

[1] This amount plus gift tax paid, if any, at time of gift attributable to the appreciation.

[2] IRC 1014(b), unless the beneficiary or his or her spouse had transferred the specific piece of property to the decedent within one year prior to his demise, in which case the beneficiary must carry over the decedent's basis. See IRC Sec. 1014(e).

Taxation of Disability Insurance Premiums and Benefits

Personally-Owned Policies

Premiums for a non-medical benefit such as disability insurance are not deductible when purchased by an individual. See IRC Sec. 213(d)(1).

The benefits from a personally owned disability insurance policy are exempt from income taxation. See IRC Sec. 104(a)(3). State disability compensation is nontaxable if the benefits paid are in the nature of workmen's compensation. However, unemployment compensation from federal and state programs is fully includable in gross income.[1]

Business-Owned Policies

If the premium is paid by the employer for its employee, the results are different.

- The premium is deductible by the employer whether the insurance is a group policy or individual policies, so long as the benefits are payable to the employees or their beneficiaries. See Reg. Sec. 1.162-10(a).

- The amount paid by the employer for disability insurance premiums is not taxable to the employee. See IRC Sec. 106, Reg. Sec. 1.106-1 and Reg. Sec. 1.79-3(f)(3).

- When a benefit is collected, it is fully includable in gross income of the employee. If the employee paid part of the premium, that portion of the benefit will be tax-free.[2] See Reg. Sec. 1.105-1(c).

- If the policy pays for accidental death, the proceeds are generally tax-exempt to the beneficiary under IRC Secs. 106 and 101(a).

---

[1] Based on federal law. State law may vary.

[2] In Revenue Ruling 2004-55, IRB 2004-26, 6/9/04, the IRS reviewed an employer-sponsored disability plan in which an employee could choose to have the employer-paid premium included in current wages, thus treating the premiums as having been made by the employee on an after-tax basis. Any disability benefits received under this arrangement would be excluded from the employee's gross income.

Taxation of Disability Insurance Premiums and Benefits

Key Person Disability Insurance

If the policy is payable to the business to protect it from the loss of services of a key employee, the premium is not tax deductible. See IRC Sec. 265(a)(1), and Rev. Rul. 66-262 and 1966-2 CB 105.

On the other hand, benefits collected by the company are received income tax free. See IRC Sec. 104(a)(3) and Rev. Rul. 66-262.

Deductibility of Interest

Under the current income tax law, not all interest is deductible on your tax return.[1]

Nondeductible Interest

Personal interest is not deductible and includes all interest, except those types listed below. Examples of nondeductible personal interest would include interest on credit card purchases, auto loans, unpaid income taxes and deferral of federal estate taxes made at the government's discretion for "reasonable cause" under IRC Sec. 6161.

Deductible Interest

A partial list of types of deductible interest includes:

- **Interest on loans used to purchase investment properties:** This interest is deductible to the extent there is net investment income. Interest paid on money borrowed to purchase or carry tax-exempt securities is not deductible. Any unused deduction is carried over to future years until used.

  - **Interest incurred in the conduct of your trade or business:** Prior to 2018, interest incurred in the conduct of a trade or business was generally deductible without limit. Under the Tax Cuts and Jobs Act of 2017 (TCJA), for 2018 and later years, the deduction for business interest paid is limited to the sum of business interest income plus 30% of the taxpayer's adjusted taxable income. Some exceptions from this limitation are provided and unused interest deductions may generally be carried forward indefinitely.

  - **Qualified residence interest:** A "qualified residence" is your principal residence and one other property, such as vacation home, a boat you live on, or a motor home. "Acquisition" debt refers to debt incurred to buy, construct, or substantially improve a qualified residence and which is secured by a qualified home.[2]

---

[1] The discussion here concerns federal income tax law; state or local law may vary.

[2] Under recent federal income tax law (state law may differ), premiums paid for qualified mortgage insurance in connection with acquisition indebtedness on a taxpayer's qualified residence are treated as deductible mortgage interest. This provision applies only to mortgage insurance contracts issued after December 31, 2006, and only for premium amounts paid, accrued, or allocable to 2007 through 2017. The deduction phases out for taxpayers with an AGI in excess of certain limits.

Deductibility of Interest

- **Deductibility of mortgage interest – Tax Cuts and Jobs Act of 2017:** Under the TCJA, for 2018 – 2025, mortgage interest on acquisition debt on a first and second residence, on total loan amounts of up to $750,000 ($375,000 MFS), is generally deductible; interest on debt in excess of these limits is not deductible. This dollar limitation applies to debt incurred after December 15, 2017.

- **Deductibility of mortgage interest – before 2018 and after 2025:** Prior to the TCJA, a taxpayer could generally deduct the interest paid on two homes on total acquisition debt of up to $1,000,000 ($500,000 MFS). Additionally, interest on up to $100,000 ($50,000 MFS) of "home equity" debt could also be deducted. Home equity debt is debt which does not qualify as acquisition debt, but which is secured by a qualified home. Under the TCJA, deductibility of interest on up to $1,000,000 of acquisition debt and up to $100,000 of home equity debt is scheduled to return for 2026 and later years.

- **Interest on educational loans:** Taxpayers may deduct up to $2,500 of interest paid on "qualified" education loans. The deduction is taken as an "above-the-line adjustment," directly reducing adjusted gross income (AGI).

The deduction is phased out for taxpayers with a modified AGI in excess of certain limits.

Filing Status	2017	2018	2019
Married Filing Jointly	$135,000 - $165,000	$135,000 - $165,000	Adjusted for inflation
Single, Head of Household, Widow	$65,000 - $80,000	$65,000 - $80,000	Adjusted for inflation

3.8% Tax on Net Investment Income

Beginning in 2013, a new 3.8% tax on net investment income applied to individual taxpayers, estates, and certain trusts. This tax is in addition to any other federal income tax, including the Alternative Minimum Tax (AMT).[1]

Individual Taxpayers

For individual taxpayers, the tax applies to the lesser of (1) net investment income or (2) the excess of modified adjusted gross income (MAGI) over a specified threshold amount.[2] The threshold amounts vary with taxpayer filing status:

Taxpayer Filing Status	Threshold Amount
Married Filing Jointly, Surviving Spouse	$250,000
Married Filing Separately	$125,000
Single, Head of Household	$200,000

For these purposes, MAGI is a taxpayer's regular adjusted gross income (AGI) increased by certain foreign earned income. Those with a MAGI below these thresholds, or with no net investment income, will not be subject to the 3.8% tax.

Estates and Trusts

In the case of an estate or trust, the tax is 3.8% of the lesser of (1) undistributed net investment income, or (2) the excess of adjusted gross income over the dollar amount at which the highest income tax bracket applicable to an estate or trust begins. For 2018, the highest income tax bracket applicable to an estate or trust begins at $12,500; for 2017, it was also $12,500.

The tax does not apply to a trust in which all the unexpired interests are devoted to charitable purposes. The tax also does not apply to a trust that is exempt from tax under IRC Sec. 501 or a charitable remainder trust (CRT) exempt from tax under IRC Sec. 664. Also excluded are "grantor trusts" under IRC Sections 671-679, real estate investment trusts, and common trust funds.

---

[1] The discussion here concerns federal income tax law. State or local income tax law may differ.
[2] The threshold amounts are not subject to adjustment for inflation in future years.

3.8% Tax on Net Investment Income

Net Investment Income

"Net" investment income is "investment income" less allowable "investment expenses." Investment income includes:

- Interest and dividends.

- Non-qualified annuities, including amounts received under IRC Sec. 72(a), 72(b), and 72(e).

- Royalties, including mineral, oil, and gas royalties, as well as amounts received for the use of patents, copyrights, formulas, goodwill, and similar types of property.

- Rents: amounts paid for the use of tangible property.[1]

- Gross income from a trade or business that is considered a "passive activity" with respect to the taxpayer.

- Gross income from a trade or business of trading in financial instruments or commodities.

- Net gain from the disposition of property: Generally, investment income includes the "net" (but not below zero) <u>recognized</u> gain on the disposition of property. It does not include gain deferred or excluded from regular income tax under various code sections such as IRC Sec. 121 (principal residence sale exclusion), IRC 1031 (like-kind exchanges), IRC Sec. 1033 (involuntary conversions), IRC Sec. 1035 (exchanges of life insurance or annuity contracts), or IRC Sec. 453 (installment sales). It also does not include gain from property held in a trade or business to which the tax does not apply.

- Disposition of a partnership interest or S corporation stock: In general, a "deemed sale" rule applies. Gain or loss is included in investment income only to the extent that net gain or loss would be taken into account by the transferor if all property of the partnership or S corporation were sold for fair market value immediately before the disposition of the interest.

---

[1] The first four items are not included in investment income if they are derived from any trade or business to which the tax does not apply.

3.8% Tax on Net Investment Income

- Working capital: Income, gain, or loss from an investment in working capital is included in investment income.
- Investments in foreign corporations: Generally, income with respect to investments in foreign corporations is included in investment income.

Note: Investment capital income does not include any income subject to self-employment tax.

Allowable investment expenses include:

- Investment interest expense.
- Investment advisory and brokerage fees.
- Expenses related to rental and royalty income.
- State and local income taxes properly allocable to items included in investment income.

Income NOT Included in Net Investment Income

A number of income items are not considered investment income, including:

- Operating income from a business in which the taxpayer is an <u>active participant</u>, such as a sole proprietor, partnership, or S corporation.
- Social Security and veterans' benefits.
- Alimony.
- Tax-exempt interest income.
- Distributions from certain qualified retirement plans.
- Alaska Permanent Fund Dividends.

Other Issues

There are a number of other issues surrounding the 3.8% Tax on Net Investment Income that taxpayers should keep in mind:

- Kiddie Tax: For 2017, if a dependent child has unearned income (such as interest, dividends, or capital gains) which the taxpayer chooses to include on his or her income tax return through Form 8814 (Parent's Election to Report Child's Interest and Dividends), the <u>net</u> amounts of this unearned income are included in calculating whether or not the parents' income is subject to this tax.

- Estimated tax provisions: For taxpayers potentially subject to this tax, the estimated tax provisions apply; either salary withholding should be increased, or estimated quarterly payments made.

- How reported and paid: The tax is calculated and reported on Form 8960. For individuals, Form 8960 will be attached to Form 1040. For estates and trusts, Form 8960 will be attached to Form 1041.

- Taxpayers subject to the tax: The tax generally applies to all U.S. citizens and resident aliens. If a U.S. citizen is married to a non-resident alien, the U. S. citizen will be treated, for the purposes of the tax, as if they were using the "married-filing-separately" filing status, with a $125,000 threshold. A special election can be made to treat the non-resident alien spouse as a resident alien, subjecting the couple's world-wide income to U. S. tax and increasing the threshold for the Unearned Income Medicare Contribution Tax to $250,000. Residents of Guam, the Northern Mariana Islands, the U.S. Virgin Island, American Samoa, and Puerto Rico are subject to special rules.

Seek Professional Guidance

The foregoing is a summary of a complex set of tax rules. The advice and guidance of knowledgeable income tax and other financial professionals is strongly recommended.

Federal Taxation of Common Investments

When it comes to deciding where and how to invest[1] money, there are a number of issues that an individual should consider. A clearly defined investment goal, the need for liquidity, an investor's risk tolerance, and the general economic outlook are just a few of the points to think about.

An additional and significant concern is how an investment - and any income derived from it - will be taxed, particularly at the federal level, [2] both now and when the investment is sold or disposed of.

3.8% Tax on Net Investment Income

Certain individuals, estates, and trusts may be subject to the 3.8% surtax on "Net Investment Income" (NII). This surtax is in addition to any other federal tax, including the Alternative Minimum Tax (AMT) or the 0.9% Additional Medicare Tax.

For individuals, the tax applies to the *lesser* of (1) net investment income, or (2) the excess of modified adjusted gross income (MAGI)[3] over a specified "threshold" amount, which varies with taxpayer status:

Taxpayer Filing Status	Threshold Amount
Married Filing Jointly, Surviving Spouse	$250,000
Married Filing Separately	$125,000
Single, Head of Household	$200,000

For estates and trusts, the 3.8% tax applies to the *lesser* of (1) undistributed net income, or (2) the excess of adjusted gross income (AGI) over the dollar amount at which the highest income tax bracket begins. For 2018, the highest income tax bracket applicable to an estate or trust begins at $12,500; for 2017 it was $12,500.

"Net" investment income = investment income - allowable investment expenses

---

[1] Investing involves risk, including the possible loss of principal.

[2] The discussion here concerns federal income tax law. State or local law may vary widely.

[3] For these purposes, MAGI is a taxpayer's regular adjusted gross income (AGI) increased by certain exclusions for foreign earned income. For most taxpayers, MAGI and AGI will be the same. The threshold amounts are not subject to adjustment for inflation.

Federal Taxation of Common Investments

In general, *investment income* includes interest and dividends, non-qualified annuities, royalties, amounts received for the use of patents, rent (tangible property), passive activity income, net gain from the disposition of property, and a number of other, more esoteric types of income.

Investment income does *not* include items such as income from a business in which the taxpayer is an active participant, Social Security or Veteran's benefits, alimony, tax-exempt (municipal bond) interest, distributions from certain qualified retirement plans, and Alaska Permanent Fund dividends.

Investment expenses include investment interest expense, advisory and brokerage fees, expenses related to rental and royalty income, and state and local income taxes allocable to items included in investment income.

Capital Gains

Federal income tax law distinguishes between "earned income" (wages or self-employment income) and income from the profitable sale of "capital" assets. Earned income is termed "ordinary" income and is taxable at marginal rates up to 37.0%.[1] Gain from the sale of capital assets is called "capital" gain and is treated for federal income tax purposes more favorably than ordinary income. A taxpayer is generally not required to include the gain or loss realized from the sale of an asset on his or her income tax return until the asset is actually sold or otherwise disposed of.

- **Capital asset:** The Internal Revenue Code (IRC) defines the term "capital asset" in a negative sense by first declaring that all assets are capital assets and then listing certain exceptions. Assets such as stocks, bonds, and other securities held by individuals are capital assets. In broad, general terms, all assets held for investment purposes are "capital" assets.

- **Holding period:** This is the length of time an asset is owned, beginning on the day after it is acquired and ending on the day it is disposed of. The amount of time an asset is held affects the tax treatment of any gain or loss when the asset is sold. *Short-term* assets are those held 12 months or less. *Long-term* assets are those held more than 12 months.

---

[1] Some high-earning taxpayers may also be subject to the 0.9% Additional Hospital Insurance (HI) Tax on earned income.

Federal Taxation of Common Investments

- **Adjusted basis:** *Basis* is the dollar amount of your investment in property, usually what you paid for it.[1] Basis is used to measure gain or loss when you sell or dispose of an investment. For assets such as stock or bonds, basis is *increased* by costs such as commissions or transfer and recording fees. Basis may also be *decreased* by non-taxable stock dividends, stock splits, or non-dividend distributions. *Adjusted basis* is the term used to describe an asset's basis after any adjustments.

- **Amount realized:** When an asset is sold, the value in money or other property received, less any sales expenses such as commissions or other fees.

Capital gain/loss formula: Amount realized – adjusted basis = gain (or loss)

At the end of a tax year, an individual's short-term (ST) gains are combined with ST losses to determine a net ST gain or loss position for the year.[2] Separately, long-term (LT) gains are combined with LT losses to determine a net LT gain or loss for the year.[3] Finally, the net ST result is combined with the net LT result, to determine an individual's overall capital gain or loss for the year.

Example 1: Sally has the following gains and losses at the end of her tax year:
$4,100 ST capital loss and a $100 ST capital gain = $4,000 ST capital loss.
$1,500 LT capital loss and a $1,000 LT capital gain = $500 LT capital loss.

Sally's net result for the year is a $4,500 capital loss. She can use this loss to offset up to $3,000 of ordinary income from other sources.[3] The remaining $1,500 ST loss is carried forward to future tax years. If a taxpayer dies with un-used capital losses, these losses expire with the taxpayer.

Example 2: Assume Roger has the following gains and losses at the end of his tax year:
$200 ST capital loss and a $10,000 ST capital gain = $9,800 ST capital gain.
$1,000 LT capital loss and a $2,200 LT capital gain = $1,200 LT capital gain.

Roger's net capital gain for the year is $11,000. This amount is included in his income on his form 1040.

---

[1] Special rules apply to the basis of property acquired as a gift, inheritance, or in other types of transactions.
[2] These calculations also include any ST or LT losses carried over from earlier years.
[3] The offset is limited to $1,500 if Sally is using the Married Filing Separately filing status.

Federal Taxation of Common Investments

The following table summarizes the capital gains rates under current federal income tax law:

Item	2017 Breakpoint	2018 Breakpoint	Capital Gains Rate
Tax Bracket is less than 15%	15.0% bracket is reached when taxable income reaches: Single: $37,950 HoH: $50,800; MFJ: $75,900; MFS: $37,950	Taxable income less than: Single: $38,600; HoH: $51,700; MFJ: $77,200; MFS: $38,600	0%
Tax bracket is equal to or more than 15.0% and less than 39.6%	39.6% bracket is reached when taxable income reaches: Single: $418,400; HoH: $444,550; MFJ: $470,700; MFS: $235,350.	Taxable income less than: Single: $425,800; HoH: $452,400; MFJ: $479,000; MFS: $239,500.	15%
Tax bracket is 39.6%	39.6% bracket is reached when taxable income reaches: Single: $418,400; HoH: $444,550; MFJ: $470,700; MFS: $235,350.	Taxable income equal to or more than: Single: $425,800; HoH: $452,400; MFJ: $479,000; MFS: $239,500.	20%
Real estate depreciation treated as capital gain[1]	N/A	N/A	25%
Sale of Collectibles	N/A	N/A	28%

Wash Sales

If an individual sells an investment at a loss, and within the 61-day period beginning 30 days before and ending 30 days after the sale date, acquires "substantially identical" stock or securities, a "wash sale" is created. In this situation the federal income tax code denies a deduction for the loss. The law is intended to discourage "tax-loss harvesting," (to artificially offset gains or other income) without a substantial change in the individual's economic position.

If the wash sale rules are violated, any loss is *disallowed*. Instead, the law requires the investor to add the amount of the loss to the basis of the substantially identical securities. Further, the holding period of the investment sold at a loss is added to the holding period of the replacement stock or securities.

---

[1] Gain in excess of recaptured depreciation is taxed at the taxpayers's regular capital gains rate.

Federal Taxation of Common Investments

Interest Income

- **Savings accounts:** Savings and other interest-bearing accounts generate interest income. The income is typically fully taxable at the federal and state or local level as ordinary income.

- **Money market mutual funds:** Although the income from a money market mutual fund is termed a "dividend," the income is treated as "interest" income and is taxed at all levels as ordinary income.

- **Municipal bonds:** These are debt instruments issued by states, counties, cities, and local government authorities such as a school or water district. With a few exceptions, interest income from municipal bonds is exempt from federal income tax.[1] Generally, municipal bond interest is also exempt from state and local income tax *if* the bond holder resides in the same jurisdiction where the bond was issued.[2]

- **"Private activity" municipal bonds:** Private activity municipal bonds are bonds which serve mixed public and private purposes. Unless such bonds meet certain requirements, the interest income from them is *not* exempt from federal income tax. State and local taxability can vary. In some instances, interest income from private activity bonds is a preference item for the individual alternative minimum tax.[3]

- **Corporate bonds:** Interest from corporate bonds is generally taxable as ordinary income at all levels.

- **U.S. government bonds:** The U.S. government issues a wide range of debt securities, backed by the "full faith and credit" of the federal government. Interest income from these U.S. government bonds is taxable to the federal government, but not taxable for state or local income taxes.

---

[1] Tax-exempt municipal bond income may increase the *taxable* portion of an individual's Social Security benefits.

[2] For example, assume a resident of California owns a municipal bond issued in New York. Interest income from this bond would be exempt from federal income tax, but taxable to the state of California. If the California resident owned a municipal bond issued in California, the interest income would generally be exempt from both federal and California state income tax.

[3] Prior to purchase, an investor should verify the taxability of interest income from these securities.

- **Other "government" securities:** There are a number of debt securities which are commonly regarded as being "federal government" bonds, but which are not backed by the "full faith and credit" of the U.S. government. Examples would include securities issued by the Government National Mortgage Association (GNMA) or the Federal National Mortgage Association (FNMA). Interest income from these securities is taxable at the federal level and may, or may not, be exempt from state or local income tax.[1]

- **Original Issue Discount (OID):** OID exists when a bond is first issued at a price that is *less* than its stated redemption price at maturity. The amount of OID is the difference between the issue price and the stated redemption price at maturity. OID is a form of interest which is generally included in income as it accrues over the life of the debt instrument, whether or not any payments are received from the issuer.

- **Bonds purchased at a discount:** If a bond is purchased at a *discount* (generally, less than face value at maturity), this market discount is considered interest income. A taxpayer can choose to recognize the market discount over the period owned, and include it in current income, or, at maturity or when the bond is disposed of, any gain is considered interest income up to the amount of the market discount.

- **Bonds purchased at a premium:** If a bond is purchased at a *premium*, (generally, for more than face value at maturity), the premium paid is part of the basis in the bond. If a bond yields <u>taxable</u> income, the owner can *choose* to amortize the premium[2] over the remaining life of the bond or recover the premium paid when the bond is sold or redeemed. If a bond yields <u>tax-exempt</u> income, the owner *must* reduce the basis in the bond by amortizing the premium over the remaining bond life. Generally, any amortized bond premium reduces the amount of interest (taxable or tax-exempt) reportable on Form 1040.

Dividends

The term "dividend" generally refers to distributions of money, stock, or other property paid by a corporation. Typically, dividends are paid to shareholders out of the earnings and profits of a corporation.

---

[1] Prior to purchase, an investor should verify the taxability of interest income from these securities.
[2] Each year the basis of the bond is reduced, with taxable interest income being reduced by an equal amount.

Federal Taxation of Common Investments

- **Ordinary dividends:** Ordinary dividends are taxable as ordinary income, at marginal tax rates up to 37.0%.[1] Mutual fund distributions of short-term capital gains are treated as ordinary dividends.

- **"Qualified" dividends:** Qualified dividends are dividends that meet certain requirements of the IRC. Qualified dividends receive favorable income tax treatment compared with that given to ordinary dividends. Prior to the Tax Cuts and Jobs Act of 2017 (TCJA), the tax rate applied to qualified dividends was linked to the taxpayer's marginal income tax rate. The table below shows the tax rates applicable to qualified dividends in years before 2018.

Taxpayer Marginal Tax Bracket	"Qualified" Dividends Taxed At[2]
10% or 15%	0%
25%, 28%, 33% or 35%	15%
39.6%	20%

For 2018 – 2025, TCJA changed the individual income tax rate structure. Under prior law, individuals paid tax at marginal rates that included 10.0%, 15.0%, 25.0%, 28.0%, 33.0%, 35.0%, and 39.6%. TCJA introduced a tax rate structure that included marginal rates of 10.0%, 12.0%, 22.0%, 24.0%, 32.0%, 35.0%, and 37.0%.

TCJA generally retained the prior-law maximum rates on qualified dividends. However, rather than linking the qualified dividend tax rates to the new tax rate structure, TCJA retained the specific 2017 dollar breakpoints for the 15.0% bracket and the 20.0% bracket and, for 2018, indexed them for inflation.[3] The table below shows the income tax rates applicable to qualified dividends at various levels of taxable income in 2018.

2018 Breakpoint	"Qualified" Dividends Taxed At[2]
Taxable income less than: Single: $38,600; HoH: $51,700; MFJ: $77,200; MFS: $38,600	0%
Taxable income less than: Single: $425,800; HoH: $452,400; MFJ: $479,000; MFS: $239,500.	15%
Taxable income equal to or more than: Single: $425,800; HoH: $452,400; MFJ: $479,000; MFS: $239,500.	20%

---

[1] Ordinary dividends are subject to the 3.8% Net Investment Income Tax.
[2] Qualified dividends are not subject to the 3.8% Net Investment Income Tax.
[3] The breakpoints are subject to adjustment for inflation in future years.

- **Dividend reinvestment plans:** Some corporations and mutual funds allow an investor to choose to buy more shares of the same stock or mutual fund, rather than taking the dividend in cash. You must generally report the dividends as ordinary income, fully taxable at the federal and state or local level.

- **Capital gain distributions:** Mutual funds, other regulated investment companies, and real estate investment trusts (REITs) may pay (or credit to your account) capital gain distributions. Capital gain distributions are taxed as long-term gains, regardless of how long you have owned the shares of the mutual fund, regulated investment company, or REIT.

- **Undistributed capital gains:** Some mutual funds and REITS keep their long-term capital gains and pay tax on them. Shareholders must include these gains on their personal income tax returns, even though they did not actually receive a distribution. A taxpayer can claim a credit (or a refund) of any tax paid.

- **Non-dividend distributions:** A "non-dividend" distribution is a distribution that is *not* paid out of the earnings or profits of a corporation. A non-dividend distribution (also known as a "return of capital") is not taxed, but rather reduces your basis in the stock you own. When the basis of your stock has been reduced to zero, any additional non-dividend distributions are reported as capital gain, either long-term or short-term, depending on how long the stock has been owned.

- **Stock dividends and stock rights:** Distributions by a corporation of its own stock are known as stock "dividends." Stock "rights" are distributions by a corporation of the right to acquire the corporation's stock. In most cases, stock dividends and stock rights are not taxable and are not reported on an investor's income tax return. The per-share basis of all shares owned is reduced by dividing the prior basis by the new number of shares owned. If a distribution of stock or stock rights is currently taxable, the basis in the stock or stock rights received is their fair market value when received.

Passive Activities

A number of different types of investments are classified under federal income tax law as "passive" activities. Generally speaking, passive activities are those in which the investor does not materially participate on a regular, continuous, and substantial basis. For example, a limited partner in a partnership would be considered to be a "passive" investor.

Federal income tax law mandates that losses from passive activities cannot be used to offset or reduce "earned" income, such as wages or self-employment income, nor can they be used to offset or reduce "portfolio" income such as dividends or interest. Losses from passive activities can *only* be used to offset income from other passive activities.

Passive losses in excess of passive income are not "lost." Rather, any unused passive losses are "suspended" and are carried to future tax years until they are either used to offset passive income, or until the year the investor completely disposes of his or her interest in the passive activity.

Foreign Tax Credit

If an investor paid or accrued taxes to a foreign country on foreign source income (such as interest or dividends) and is also subject to U.S. tax on the same income, he or she may be able to take a credit for the foreign tax paid. The foreign tax credit is intended to relieve an investor of what is effectively a double tax burden when the foreign source income is taxed by both the U.S. and the foreign country.

As an alternative, a taxpayer can choose to deduct the foreign taxes paid or accrued on foreign source income as an itemized deduction on Schedule A, subject to certain dollar limitations.

Seek Professional Guidance

The foregoing is a brief, high-level overview of some of the federal income tax laws applicable to commonly encountered investments. The advice and guidance of trained, experienced investment and tax professionals is strongly recommended.

0.9% Additional Hospital Insurance Tax

The Federal Insurance Contributions Act (FICA)[1] imposes certain payroll taxes on both employers and employees. The tax levied on the employer and the employee is each composed of two parts: (1) Social Security, or "Old Age, Survivors, and Disability Insurance" (OASDI), of 6.2% of covered wages up to the taxable "wage base," $128,700 in 2018;[2] and (2) the Medicare or "Hospital Insurance" (HI) tax equal to 1.45% of all covered wages. Similar payroll taxes are levied on railroad employers and employees, under the Railroad Retirement Tax Act (RRTA).

Self-employed individuals are also subject to payroll taxes. The "Self-Employed Contributions Act" (SECA), imposes a 12.4% OASDI tax on self-employment income, up to the FICA taxable wage base (reduced by FICA wages, if any), and a 2.9% HI tax, applicable to all self-employment income.

Beginning in 2013, a 0.9% additional HI tax applied to taxpayers with earned income in excess of specified threshold amounts. These threshold amounts are not subject to adjustment for inflation:

Taxpayer Filing Status	Threshold Amount
Married Filing Jointly, Surviving Spouse	$250,000
Married Filing Separately	$125,000
Single, Head of Household	$200,000

Employers are required to withhold the additional HI tax from an employee's wages or compensation once the employee's earned income exceeds $200,000.[3] The employer's obligation to withhold the additional HI tax is not related to the employee's ultimate tax liability. For example, if an employee and spouse filing a joint return each have wages of $175,000 (for a total of $350,000), their employers are not required to withhold the additional HI tax. However, the couple will be liable for the additional HI tax on $100,000 ($350,000 total wages minus the $250,000 threshold amount). If an employee's ultimate liability is less than the amount withheld, the employee may claim a refund.

---

[1] The discussion here concerns federal income tax law. State or local income tax law may differ.

[2] The wage base in 2017 was $127,200.

[3] There is no employer match for the additional 0.9% HI tax.

0.9% Additional Hospital Insurance Tax

The additional HI tax also applies to self-employment income in excess of the same threshold amounts. The threshold amount is first reduced (but not below zero) by any amount of wages taken into account in determining the individual's additional FICA HI tax, if any. Thus, only a single threshold applies for an individual (or individual and spouse) with both FICA wages and self-employment income.

Income Included

All income currently subject to Medicare tax is also subject to the 0.9% HI tax, including:

- Wages, salaries, RRTA compensation, tips, and third-party sick pay.

- Self-employment income.

- Taxable noncash fringe benefits.

- Non-qualified deferred compensation – if included for regular FICA purposes.

- The imputed cost of group-term life insurance in excess of $50,000.

Other Considerations

- **How reported and paid:** The tax is calculated and reported on Form 8959, attached to the taxpayer's Form 1040. Amounts withheld by the employer will be shown on the employee's W-2 form.:

- **Inadequate withholding:** If the employer withholding is insufficient to cover the additional HI tax liability, the taxpayer is responsible for paying any balance due. The employer's withholding, on compensation in excess of $200,000, takes into consideration only the compensation the employer pays to the employee. The employer's withholding does not consider compensation from other sources (wages or self-employment income), nor does it consider a spouse's earnings. To pre-pay any estimated tax liability, a taxpayer can request his or her employer to increase income tax withholding or the taxpayer may make estimated payments directly to the IRS.

- **RRTA income and FICA or SECA income:** Compensation subject to RRTA taxes and wages subject to FICA tax are <u>not</u> combined to determine the additional HI tax liability. The threshold applicable to an individual's filing status is applied separately to each of these categories of income. Similarly, if an individual has compensation subject to RRTA taxes and self-employment income, the threshold limits are also applied separately.

- **Aggregation of certain income:** For purposes of the employer's required withholding, on compensation in excess of $200,000, certain income items are aggregated to determine if the $200,000 threshold has been reached. For example, if an individual is concurrently employed by two or more related employers, the wages and other compensation paid to the employee are added together only if there is a common paymaster for all employers. Similarly, wages paid by an employer and third-party sick pay are also aggregated.

Seek Professional Guidance

The foregoing is a summary of a complex set of tax rules. The advice and guidance of knowledgeable income tax and other financial professionals is strongly recommended.

Tax Cuts and Jobs Act of 2017

On December 22, 2017, President Donald Trump signed into law H.R. 1, the Tax Cuts and Jobs Act of 2017 (TCJA). This new tax legislation, 185 pages in length, is the most significant revision to U.S. federal tax law since the Tax Reform Act of 1986. To some degree, almost every individual and business in the United States will be affected by it.

What follows is a *very* brief summary of some of the more notable individual and small business provisions contained in the TCJA. You can use this summary to begin talking with your clients about the changes in the new law and to review with each client how this legislation may affect his or her (or their) situation.

Because many clients will be impacted by the changes made to itemized deductions, we have attached at the end of this report a "guesstimate" of what Schedule A may look like for 2018. Please pay careful attention to the "Notes" at the end of the form.

Provisions Affecting Individual Taxpayers

Except where noted, all provisions are effective January 1, 2018 and "sunset" on December 31, 2025, when prior law will apply.

- **Pass-through income:** An individual taxpayer generally may deduct 20% of qualified business income from a partnership, S corporation, or sole proprietorship, as well as 20% of aggregate qualified REIT dividends, qualified cooperative dividends, and qualified publicly traded partnership income.

- **Alimony:** Generally, effective for any divorce or separation instrument executed after December 31, 2018, alimony will no longer be deductible by the payor, and alimony payments will no longer be includable in income by the recipient. This change is permanent.

- **Standard deduction:** TCJA temporarily increases the size of the standard deduction. For 2018, the standard deduction will be $24,000 for joint filers, $18,000 for heads of household, and $12,000 for all other taxpayers. The additional standard deduction for the elderly and blind remains the same.

- **"Chained" inflation adjustments:** The new Act specifies that inflation adjustments to a number of income tax items be made using a "chained" CPI-U, or C-CPI-U. The CPI-U is the Consumer Price Index for All Urban Consumers, a standard measure of inflation calculated by the Bureau of Labor Statistics. Historically, the C-CPI-U has resulted in a smaller amount of calculated inflation than the CPI-U. This is a permanent change.

- **Personal Exemptions:** The Act suspends the deduction for personal and dependent exemptions.

- **Medical expense deduction floor:** For 2017 and 2018, the medical expense deduction floor is set at 7.5% of adjusted gross income (AGI) for all taxpayers. This 7.5% threshold also applies for purposes of the individual alternative minimum tax (AMT).

- **State and local taxes:** Generally, a taxpayer (individuals and married couples) may claim an itemized deduction of up to $10,000 ($5,000 for married filing separately - MFS) for the aggregate of personal state and local property taxes, state and local income taxes, war profits, and excess profits taxes. In place of state and local income taxes, a taxpayer may deduct state and local sales tax.

- **Home mortgage interest:** Under the TCJA, a taxpayer may treat as "acquisition indebtedness," and thus deduct the interest on, up to $750,000 ($375,000 for MFS), on up to two homes. For acquisition indebtedness incurred before December 15, 2017, a taxpayer may treat up to $1,000,000 ($500,000 MFS) as acquisition indebtedness. For tax years beginning after December 31, 2025, a taxpayer may treat up to $1,000,000 ($500,000 for MFS) of debt as acquisition debt, regardless of when acquired. Further, the Act suspends the deduction for interest paid on home equity debt.

- **Itemized deduction subject to the 2.0% of AGI floor:** The Act suspends all current-law deductions subject to the 2.0% of AGI floor. Such deductions include expenses for the production or collection of income, tax preparation expenses, investment interest expense, and unreimbursed employee expenses.

- **Overall limit on itemized deductions:** The overall limitation on itemized deductions (the "Pease" limitation) is suspended.

- **Individual alternative minimum tax (AMT):** TCJA modifies the individual AMT by increasing the AMT exemption amount for 2018 to $109,400 for taxpayers filing jointly, $54,700 for MFS, and $70,300 single and head of household (HOH). The Act also increases the exemption phase-out threshold to $1,000,000 for MFJ, and $500,000 for MFS, HOH, and single. These amounts are indexed for inflation in future years.

- **Patient Protection and Affordable Care Act (PPACA) – individual mandate:** The Act reduces the penalty for not having minimum essential coverage as required under the PPACA to zero. This provision is permanent and is effective with respect to health coverage status for months beginning after December 31, 2018.

- **Individual tax rates and brackets:** TCJA provides a new individual tax rate structure, of 10%, 12%, 22%, 24%, 32%, 35%, and 37%. For estates and trusts, the new structure will be 10%, 24%, 35%, and 37%.

- **Child tax credit:** The new law temporarily increases the child tax credit to $2,000 per child and also provides for a $500 nonrefundable credit for qualifying dependents other than qualifying children. Any refundable credit is limited to $1,400 per qualifying child. The credit phase-out limits are increased to $400,000 (MFJ) and $200,000 for all other taxpayers.

- **Estate and gift tax exemption:** TCJA doubles the estate and gift tax exemption for estates of decedents dying and gifts made after December 31, 2017 and before January 1, 2026. This is achieved by doubling the basic exclusion amount specified in IRC Sec. 2010(c)(3) from $5,000,000 to $10,000,000, with the $10,000,000 amount being adjusted for inflation for years after 2011. Following the guidance provided in Rev. Proc 2017-58, this would set the basic, individual estate and gift tax exemption amount at $11,180,000 for 2018. For a married couple, this would be equal to $22,360,000.

Provisions Affecting Business Taxpayers

- **Reduction in corporate tax rate:** The new law eliminates the graduated corporate income tax rate structure and instead taxes corporate taxable income at 21%. The provision is permanent and applies to tax years beginning after December 31, 2017.

- **Repeal of corporate AMT:** TCJA repeals the corporate alternative minimum tax. The provision is permanent and applies to tax years beginning after December 31, 2017.

- **Bonus depreciation:** The new Act allows for 100% first-year "bonus" depreciation for specified new and used business property. The 100% deduction allowance applies to property (including specified plants) acquired and placed in service after September 27, 2017 and before January 1, 2023 (January 1, 2024 for certain, longer-lived property). The 100% allowance is phased down by 20% per calendar year for property placed in service in tax years beginning after 2022 (2023 for certain longer-lived property).

- **Section 179 Expensing:** TCJA increases the maximum amount a taxpayer may expense under IRC Section 179 to $1,000,000, and increases the phase-out threshold amount to $2,500,000. The provision expands the definition of Section 179 property and provides that the $1,000,000 and $2,500,000 amounts be indexed for inflation for tax years after 2018. The provision is permanent and applies to property placed in service in tax years after December 31, 2017.

- **Net Operating Loss (NOL) Deduction:** A net operating loss (NOL) generally means the amount by which a taxpayer's business deductions exceed its gross income. The new Act limits the deduction for an NOL to 80% of taxable income (determined without regard to the deduction), eliminates the current two-year carryback, and allows for an indefinite carryforward. The provision is permanent and applies to tax years beginning after December 31, 2017.

- **Deduction of business interest paid:** TCJA generally limits the deduction for business interest paid to the sum of business interest income plus 30% of the taxpayer's adjusted taxable income. Exceptions are provided for "small" businesses (average gross receipts less than $25 million in three prior tax years), a real property trade or business, "floor plan" financing (such as for a car dealer), and certain regulated public utilities. Unused interest deductions may generally be carried forward indefinitely. The provision is permanent and applies to tax years beginning after December 31, 2017.

- **Domestic Activities Production Deduction:** The Act repeals the deduction for income attributable to domestic production activities. The provision is permanent and applies to tax years beginning after December 31, 2017.

- **Research and Experimentation Expenditures:** Under the TCJA, research and experimental expenditures are required to be amortized ratably over a 5-year period. Expenditures attributable to research and experimentation performed outside the U.S. must be amortized over a 15-year period. The provision is permanent and applies to expenditures made after December 31, 2021.

Tax Cuts and Jobs Act of 2017

2018 Itemized Deductions under the TCJA of 2017

This is NOT an official IRS Worksheet.
It should be used only to estimate allowable itemized deductions for 2018.

MEDICAL EXPENSES

1	Medical and Dental Expenses	$	
2	Adjusted Gross Income:	$	
3	Multiply Line 2 by 7.5% (0.075)	$	
4	Subtract Line 3 from Line 1		$

TAXES YOU PAID

5	State & Local Income or Sales Taxes	$	
6	Real Estate Taxes	$	
7	Personal Property Taxes	$	
8	Other Taxes	$	
9	Add Lines 5 -8		$

INTEREST YOU PAID

10	Home Mortgage Interest	$	
11	Investment Interest	$	
12	Add Lines 10 - 11		$

GIFTS TO CHARITY

13	Gifts by Cash or Check	$	
14	Gifts Other Than by Cash or Check	$	
15	Carryover from Prior Year	$	
16	Add Lines 13 - 15		$

CASUALTY AND THEFT LOSSES

17	Casualty & Theft Losses		$

OTHER MISCELLANEOUS DEDUCTIONS

18	Other Miscellaneous Deductions		$

TOTAL ITEMIZED DEDUCTIONS

19	Add lines 4, 9, 12, 16, 17, and 18		$

Notes

Line 5   You may include either state and local income taxes or state and local sales taxes, but not both.

Notes	
Line 9	Limited to no more than $10,000 ($5,000 if filing Married Filing Separately).
Line 10	Under the TCJA, a taxpayer may treat as "acquisition indebtedness," and thus deduct the interest on, up to $750,000 ($375,000 for Married Filing Separately - MFS) on up to two homes. For loans incurred before December 15, 2017, a taxpayer may treat up to $1,000,000 ($500,000 for MFS) of debt as acquisition debt.
Line 17	A taxpayer may claim a personal casualty loss only if such loss was attributable to a disaster declared by the President under Section 401 of the Robert T. Stafford Disaster Relief and Emergency Assistance Act.
Line 19	There is no overall limitation on the dollar amount of itemized deductions that may be claimed.

Individual Highlights of the Tax Cuts and Jobs Act of 2017

On December 22, 2017, President Donald Trump signed into law H.R. 1, the Tax Cuts and Jobs Act of 2017 (TCJA). This new tax legislation, 185 pages in length, is the most significant revision to the U.S. federal tax code since the Tax Reform Act of 1986. To some degree, almost every individual and business in the U. S. will be affected by it.

What follows is a brief summary of some of the *individual* provisions contained in the TCJA Because of the size and complexity of the legislation, provisions primarily affecting *businesses* are discussed separately.

One notable feature of this legislation is that the majority of the individual tax provisions "sunset" after eight years, while many business provisions are permanent. Unless noted otherwise, the individual changes discussed here are effective for tax years beginning after December 31, 2017 and expire on December 31, 2025, when prior law will apply.

Income Items

Item	Prior Law	TCJA 2017
Deduction for qualified business income	No comparable provision	An individual taxpayer generally may deduct 20% of qualified business income from a partnership, S corporation, or sole proprietorship, as well as 20% of aggregate qualified REIT dividends, qualified cooperative dividends, and qualified publicly traded partnership income. A limitation based on W-2 wages paid applies above a certain threshold. The deduction is disallowed to specified trades and businesses with taxable income above a threshold amount.

Individual Highlights of the Tax Cuts and Jobs Act of 2017

Item	Prior Law	TCJA 2017
Unearned income of children – "kiddie" tax	The net unearned income (for 2017 unearned income in excess of $2,100) of a child is taxed at the parent's rates if the parent's rates are higher than those of the child. The remainder of a child's taxable income is taxed at the child's rates.	Taxable income attributable to net unearned income ($2,100 for 2018) is taxed according to the brackets applicable to trusts and estates. The remainder of a child's taxable income is taxed at the child's rates.
Capital gains and qualified dividends	Prior law generally taxed most capital gains and all qualified dividends at either 0.0% (taxpayer's regular marginal bracket less than 15.0%), at 15.0% (taxpayers regular marginal bracket between 15.0% and 39.6%) or at 20.0% (taxpayer's regular marginal bracket equal to 39.6%).	The new Act retains the 0.0%, 15.0%, and 20.0% tax rate structure applicable to most capital gains and all qualified dividends. To determine which rate applies (0.0%, 15.0%, or 20.0%), the Act retained the specific dollar breakpoints applicable in 2017, and, for 2018, indexed them for inflation using a "chained" CPI-U, or C-CPIU. These 2017 base amounts will continue to be indexed for inflation (through 2025) using the C-CPIU.

Adjustments to Gross Income

Item	Prior Law	TCJA 2017
Moving expenses	Prior law allowed an above-the-line deduction for moving expenses incurred in connection with the start of work at a new location. Also allowed was an exclusion from income for employer-reimbursement of moving expenses. Special rules applied to members of the U.S. armed forces.	Suspends the deduction for moving expenses. The Act also repeals the exclusion from gross income for employer-reimbursement of moving expenses. The special rules applicable to member of the U.S. armed forces remain the same.

Individual Highlights of the Tax Cuts and Jobs Act of 2017

Item	Prior Law	TCJA 2017
Alimony	Alimony and separate maintenance payments are deductible by the payor spouse and included in income of the recipient spouse.	Alimony and separate maintenance payments are not deductible by the payor spouse and are not included in the gross income of the recipient spouse. This change is permanent and is generally effective for any divorce or separation agreement executed after December 31, 2018.

Itemized Deductions

Item	Prior Law	TCJA 2017
Medical expense deduction	For 2017 and 2018, unreimbursed medical expenses were deductible to the extent they exceeded 10% of adjusted gross income (AGI). The 10% limit also applied for individual AMT purposes.	For 2017 and 2018, unreimbursed medical expenses are deductible to the extent they exceed 7.5% of AGI. The 7.5% limit also applies for individual AMT purposes.
State and local taxes	Individuals were permitted an unlimited deduction for certain state and local real and foreign property taxes, state and local personal property taxes, or state, local, and foreign income, war profits, and excess profits taxes.	TCJA limits the individual deduction for state and local real and foreign property taxes, state and local personal property taxes, and state, local, and foreign income, war profits, and excess profits taxes to no more than $10,000 ($5,000 if MFS) per year. These limits are not inflation indexed.
Home mortgage interest deduction	Prior law allowed a deduction for interest paid on "acquisition indebtedness," of up to $1,000,000 ($500,000 for a taxpayer filing married filing separately – MFS), on up to two homes. Prior law also allowed a deduction for up to	The new law limits a taxpayer's deduction to interest paid on no more than $750,000 ($375,000 – MFS) of acquisition indebtedness on two homes. The bill suspends the deduction for interest paid on home equity debt. For debt incurred before December 15,

Item	Prior Law	TCJA 2017
	$100,000 ($50,000 for MFS) of "home equity" debt.	2017, the $1,000,000-$500,000 limits apply.
Charitable contribution deduction	The deduction for cash contributions to specified charities was limited to 50% of AGI. Prior law also allowed a deduction of 80% of a donation to an institution of higher education in return for the right to purchase seating or tickets to athletic events.	The Act increases the AGI limitation for cash contribution to 60% of AGI. It also permanently repeals the deduction for donations to institutions of higher education in return for the right to purchase seating or tickets to athletic events.
Casualty and theft losses	Unreimbursed personal casualty and theft losses were deductible only if they exceeded $100 per casualty or theft and only to the extent that the loss exceeded 10% of the taxpayer's AGI.	For 2018-2025, the Act modifies the law so that a taxpayer may claim a deduction for a casualty or loss (subject to the $100 and 10% of AGI limits) only if the loss was attributable to a federally declared disaster. For 2016 and 2017, for casualty losses arising from a federally declared disaster, the loss may be deducted to the extent that it exceeds $500; the 10% of AGI limitation does not apply. For 2016 and 2017, for a taxpayer who does not itemize deductions, a deductible loss may be added to his or her standard deduction.
Itemized deductions subject to the 2.0% of AGI floor	Allowed a deduction for certain items such as expenses for the production or collection of income, tax preparation expenses, and unreimbursed employee expenses to the extent they exceed 2.0% of the taxpayer's AGI.	The new Act suspends all current-law deductions subject to the 2.0% of AGI floor.

Individual Highlights of the Tax Cuts and Jobs Act of 2017

Item	Prior Law	TCJA 2017
Overall limitation on itemized deductions	Limited the amount of otherwise allowable itemized deductions (except for medical expenses, investment interest, casualty, theft, or gambling losses) by 3% of the amount by which a taxpayer's AGI exceeded a specified threshold amount. The otherwise allowable deductions could not be reduced by more than 80.0%.	TCJA 2017 temporarily suspends the overall limitation on itemized deductions.

Calculating the Tax Due

Item	Prior Law	TCJA 2017
Standard deduction	Allowed a taxpayer who did not itemize deductions to reduce AGI by a standard deduction amount to arrive at taxable income. For 2017 these amounts were $6,350 (single, MFS), $9,350 (HoH), and $12,700 (MFJ). An additional standard deduction was allowed for an individual who was elderly or blind.	TCJA 2017 temporarily increases the size of the standard deduction. For 2018, the standard deduction will be $24,000 for MFJ, $18,000 for HoH, and $12,000 for all others. The additional standard deduction for the elderly or blind is not changed.
Personal and dependent exemptions	A taxpayer was allowed to reduce AGI by any personal or dependent exemption deductions. In 2017, the amount deductible for each personal exemption was $4,050. Certain high-income taxpayers faced a phase-out of their personal exemptions when AGI exceeded certain limits.	The Act temporarily repeals the deduction for personal exemptions.
Individual tax rates and brackets	The tax due for each filing status was determined using a tax table with marginal rates of 10%, 15%, 25%, 28%, 33%, 35%, and 39.6%.	A new tax rate structure will apply, with marginal rates of 10%, 12%, 22%, 24%, 32%, 35%, and 37%.

Individual Highlights of the Tax Cuts and Jobs Act of 2017

Item	Prior Law	TCJA 2017
Child Tax Credit	Prior law allowed a tax credit of $1,000 for each qualifying child under age 17. The aggregate amount of the child credit was phased out for taxpayers with modified AGI in excess of specified amounts. For 2017 these limits were: $75,000 (single or HoH); $110,000 (MFJ); and $55,00o (MFS). For certain taxpayers, a portion of the credit, up to $1,000, was refundable, subject to an earned income limitation of $3,000.	The new law temporarily increases the child tax credit to $2,000 per qualifying child. The credit phases out for taxpayers with modified AGI in excess of $400,000 (MFJ) and $200,000 (all others). The credit also provides for a $500 nonrefundable credit for qualifying dependents other than children. The maximum refundable credit may not exceed $1,400[1] per qualifying child, subject to an earned income limitation of $2,500.
Individual Alternative Minimum Tax (AMT)	The alternative minimum tax (AMT) is a parallel tax system that re-calculates a taxpayer's taxable income in a manner that negates the regular tax treatment of certain deductions and preferences. There is a base amount of income that is exempt from this calculation. In 2017, the exemption amount was $84,500, (MFJ), $54,300 (single, HoH), $42,250 (MFS), and $24,100 (estates and trusts). The exemption was phased-out for income in excess of certain limits: $160,900 (MFJ), $120,700 (single), and $80,450 (MFS, estates and trusts).	For 2018, the AMT exemption amount is increased to $109,400 (MFJ), $54,700 (MFS), and $70,300 (all other taxpayers). The phase-out thresholds are increased to $1,000,000 for married taxpayers filing a joint return, and $500,000 for all other taxpayers. The exemption amount and phase-out thresholds for estates and trust are not affected by the TCJA.

[1] The $1,400 limit is subject to adjustment for inflation using the C-CPI-U.

Individual Highlights of the Tax Cuts and Jobs Act of 2017

Other Provisions to Note

Item	Prior Law	TCJA 2017
Alternative Inflation Calculation	The CPI-U was used to calculate inflation adjustments to a number of income tax items, such as contribution amounts to retirement plans, the amount of income in various income tax brackets, and phase-out limits. The CPI-U is the Consumer Price Index for All Urban Consumers, a standard measure of inflation calculated by the Bureau of Labor Statistics.	Requires use of a "chained" CPI-U, or C-CPI-U. The C-CPI-U is a variation of the CPI-U.[1] This change is permanent and is generally effective for tax years beginning after December 31, 2017.
Patient Protection and Affordable Care Act (PPACA) – shared responsibility payment (Individual Mandate).	Under the PPACA, individuals were required to be covered by a health plan that provided minimum essential health insurance, or be subject to a penalty for failure to maintain such coverage. Generally, the penalty was equal to a flat dollar amount or an excess income amount.	TCJA effectively repeals the individual mandate by setting the penalty for failure to maintain essential health coverage to zero. This change is permanent and is effective with respect to health coverage status for months beginning after December 31, 2018.
Expanded use of IRC Section 529 plans	IRC Section 529 provides for tax-advantaged higher education savings and pre-paid tuition programs. Tax exempt distributions from such plans were only allowed for post-secondary (college or post-graduate) education. Allowable expenses included tuition and fees, books and supplies, computers and related software, expenses for special needs beneficiaries, and room and board for students enrolled at least half-time.	The Act permanently modifies IRC Section 529 plans to allow such plans to distribute no more than $10,000 in expenses for tuition incurred during a taxable year in connection with the enrollment or attendance of the designated beneficiary at a public, private, or religious elementary or secondary school. The $10,000 limitation applies on a per-student basis. The limitation does not apply to post-secondary expenses.

[1] Using the C-CPI-U in place of the CPI-U will result in smaller changes in measured inflation and thus smaller adjustments to the tax items affected by it.

Individual Highlights of the Tax Cuts and Jobs Act of 2017

Item	Prior Law	TCJA 2017
Estate, Gift Tax, and Generation-Skipping Tax exemption amount	Provided for an individual exemption from gift, estate, and generation-skipping taxes of $5,000,000, in 2011. Adjusted for inflation, this amount would have been $5,600,000 per person in 2018.	Increases the base exemption amount to $10,000,000. Adjusted for inflation, this equals $11,180,000 per person in 2018.

Seek Professional Guidance

The foregoing is a simplified overview of some of the more notable provisions of the Tax Cuts and Jobs Act of 2017 affecting individual taxpayers. To receive maximum benefit from the new legislation, the advice and guidance of trained income tax and legal professionals is highly recommended.

Business Highlights of the Tax Cuts and Jobs Act of 2017

On December 22, 2017, President Donald Trump signed into law H.R. 1, the Tax Cuts and Jobs Act of 2017 (TCJA). This new tax legislation, 185 pages in length, is the most significant revision to the U.S. federal tax code since the Tax Reform Act of 1986.

TCJA impacts a wide range of business taxpayers, from street vendors to multi-national corporations with world-wide operations. To some degree, almost every individual and business in the U.S. will be affected by it.

What follows is a brief, high-level summary of a few of the *business* provisions contained in the TCJA. Provisions affecting *individuals* are discussed separately.

One notable feature of this legislation is that most of the provisions affecting businesses are permanent. The majority of the individual tax provisions, however, "sunset" after eight years. Unless noted otherwise, the business provisions discussed here are effective for tax years beginning after December 31, 2017 and are permanent.

Item	Prior Law	TCJA 2017
Reduction in corporate tax rate	Generally, corporate income was taxable under a graduated, four-bracket rate structure, with taxable income in excess of $10,000,000 taxed at a top marginal rate of 35.0%. Personal service corporations paid tax on all taxable income at the 35.0% rate.	Corporate taxable income (including for personal service corporations) is taxed at a flat 21.0% rate.
Dividends received deduction	Prior law allowed a deduction for dividends received from another taxable domestic corporation. The deduction was generally equal to 70.0% of the dividends received. For 20.0% owned corporations, the deduction was 80.0% of the dividends received.	The provision reduces the 70.0% dividends received deduction to 50.0% and the 80.0% dividends received deduction to 65.0%.
Repeal of corporate alternative minimum tax	The corporate alternative minimum tax was a parallel tax system that re-calculated a corporation's income in a manner that negated the regular tax treatment of certain deductions and preferences. If the AMT re-calculation resulted in a higher tax, the corporation paid the higher amount.	The new Act repeals the corporate alternative minimum tax.

Business Highlights of the Tax Cuts and Jobs Act of 2017

Item	Prior Law	TCJA 2017
Enhanced expensing – "Bonus" depreciation	Prior law generally allowed an additional depreciation deduction equal to 50.0% of the adjusted basis of qualified new business property acquired and placed into service before January 1, 2020 (January 21, 2021 for certain long-lived property). The allowable depreciation percentage was gradually reduced for years 2018-2020.	The new Act allows for 100.0% first-year bonus depreciation for specified new and used business property. The 100.0% deduction allowance applies to property (including specified plants) acquired and placed in service after September 27, 2017 and before January 1, 2023 (January 1, 2024 for certain, longer-lived property). The 100% allowance is phased down by 20% per calendar year for property placed in service in tax years beginning after 2022 (2023 for certain longer-lived property).
Enhanced expensing – IRC Section 179	Under IRC Section 179 a taxpayer could elect to "expense" up to $500,000 of qualifying property placed into service for a taxable year. The $500,000 was reduced by the amount by which the qualifying property place in service exceeded $2,000,000.	TCJA increases the maximum amount a taxpayer may expense under IRC Section 179 to $1,000,000, and increases the phase-out threshold amount to $2,500,000. The provision also expands the definition of IRC Section 179 property.
Luxury auto and personal use property	Prior law limited the depreciation deduction for certain "luxury" automobiles. For 2017, the maximum allowable amount of depreciation was generally[1] $3,160 for the year the vehicle is placed in service, $5,100 for the second year, $3,050 for the third year, and $1,875 for the fourth and later years. Computers and peripheral equipment were considered "listed" property, subject to certain depreciation limitations.	The maximum allowable amount of depreciation is generally[1] $10,000 for the year in which the vehicle is placed in service, $16,000 for the second year, $9,600 for the third year, and $5,760 for the fourth and later years. Computers and peripheral equipment are no longer treated as "listed" property.
Net Operating Loss (NOL)	A net operating loss (NOL) generally means the amount by which a taxpayer's business deductions exceed its gross income. Under	Generally, for NOLs arising from tax years after 2017, the TCJA limits the deduction for a NOL to

[1] Assuming no first-year "bonus" depreciation is added.

Business Highlights of the Tax Cuts and Jobs Act of 2017

Item	Prior Law	TCJA 2017
	prior law, an NOL deduction could generally be carried back two years (five years for farming losses) and carried forward 20 years.	80.0% of taxable income, eliminates the two-year carryback (except for farms), and allows for an indefinite carryforward.
Excess business losses	No comparable provision.	For taxpayers other than corporations, an "excess business loss" is, generally, the excess of aggregate deductions of the taxpayer attributable to trades or businesses of the taxpayer, over the sum of aggregate gross income or gain of the taxpayer plus a threshold amount. Any excess business loss is not allowed as a deduction in the current year, but must be carried forward as a NOL. For 2018 the threshold amounts are $500,000 (MFS) and $250,000 for all others.[1]
Like-kind exchanges	Allowed for like-kind exchanges (and deferral of recognized gain) on both personal and real property.	The new law limits the application of the like-kind exchange rules to real property that is not held primarily for sale.
Orphan drug credit	Provided a 50.0% business tax credit for qualified clinical testing expenses incurred in testing of certain drugs for rare diseases or conditions, generally referred to as "orphan drugs."	TCJA reduces the credit to 25.0% of qualified clinical testing expenses.
Small business cash accounting	A C corporation, a partnership that had a C corporation as a partner, or a tax-exempt trust, or corporation with unrelated business income, generally could not use the cash method of accounting. An exception was made for businesses which had less than $5,000,000 in gross receipts based on three prior years.	The new law allows taxpayers with annual average gross receipts that do not exceed $25,000,000 for the three prior taxable years to use the cash method of accounting.

[1] This provision is effective for tax years beginning after December 31, 2017 and before January 1, 2026. The provision applies after the application of the passive loss rules.

Business Highlights of the Tax Cuts and Jobs Act of 2017

Item	Prior Law	TCJA 2017
Deduction of business interest	Business interest was generally deductible as it was paid or incurred.	TCJA limits the deduction for business interest paid to the sum of business interest income plus 30.0% of the taxpayer's adjusted taxable income. Exceptions apply for "small" businesses (average gross receipts less than $25,000,000 in three prior tax years), a real property trade or business, or "floor plan" financing (such as a car dealer). Unused interest deductions may generally be carried forward indefinitely.
Domestic production activities deduction	Prior law allowed a deduction from taxable income equal to 9.0% (6.0% for oil and gas) of the lesser of the taxpayer's qualified domestic qualified production income, or taxable income. Qualified domestic production income, generally, included income derived from goods manufactured, produced, grown, or extracted within the United States.	Repeals the deduction for tax years beginning after December 31, 2017.
Amortization of research and experimentation expenses	Under prior law a taxpayer could generally choose to account for research and experimentation expenses in one of three ways: (1) deduct the expenses when paid; (2) amortize them over a 60-month period; or (3) amortize the expenses over a 10-year period. Software development costs were deductible in the year paid or incurred.	The new Act repeals method 1 (current deduction) and method 2 (60 month amortization) on December 3, 2021. For tax years after 2021, TCJA generally requires that research and experimentation expenditures be amortized ratably over a five-year period (15 years for foreign research). Software development expenses will be required to be amortized over the appropriate period, either five or 15 years.
Certain employer fringe benefits	Prior law generally allowed a taxpayer to deduct as a business expense 50.0 % of expenditures for business-related entertainment. A business taxpayer could	TCJA generally repeals the deduction for 50.0% of expenditures for business-related entertainment. The Act also

Item	Prior Law	TCJA 2017
	also deduct certain qualified transportation fringe benefits provided to employees.	repeals the deduction for qualified transportation fringe benefits.
Excessive employee compensation	Prohibited a publicly-held corporation from deducting employee compensation of more than $1,000,000 paid to certain "covered" employees. The definition of "compensation" for this limit excluded performance-based compensation as well as commission-based compensation.	TCJA expands the number of employees who are considered "covered" employees. The Act also repeals the exclusion for commission-based and performance-based compensation from the definition of compensation subject to the $1,000,000 limit.
Carried interest	In some situations, a general partner of a partnership may receive an interest in the partnership as compensation for services rendered to the partnership. Gain on the sale of the partnership interest was accorded long-term capital gain treatment if sold by the taxpayer after being held more than one year.	The new law generally provides that a partnership interest received as compensation for services rendered must be held for three years in order for any gain realized on the sale of the interest to receive long-term capital gain treatment.

Seek Professional Guidance

Many of the provisions of the Tax Cuts and Jobs Act of 2017 involve complex areas of law. Further, the Internal Revenue Service (IRS) will need to create and issue guidance explaining how the various sections of this new act are to be applied. To receive maximum benefit from the new legislation, the advice and guidance of trained, experienced income tax and legal professionals is highly recommended.

Highlights of 2017 Disaster Tax Relief

Late summer and early fall of 2017 were marked by a series of natural disasters that swept through many parts of the United States. Beginning in August 2017, and within a span of just a few weeks, Hurricane Harvey, Hurricane Irma, and Hurricane Maria struck parts of the United States, Puerto Rico, and the U.S. Virgin Islands. In October 2017, a series of wildfires devastated areas of Northern California. Each of these catastrophes left individuals and businesses struggling to recover from the destruction left behind.

To help with the recovery, the federal government has taken a number of steps to ease the tax burden for victims of these disasters. This tax help has come in two forms: (1) administrative relief provided by the Internal Revenue Service (IRS) and the Department of the Treasury, under existing law, and (2) new legislation passed specifically to aid disaster victims.[1]

IRS Administrative Relief

Administrative relief from the IRS has come in several forms:

- **Extensions of time to complete certain tasks:** The service will allow hurricane and wildfire victims, individuals and businesses, an automatic extension of time, until January 31, 2018, to file returns or pay taxes originally due during the period these disasters took place.

- **Leave based donation programs:** The IRS has issued guidance for employers who have adopted, or who are considering adopting, a leave-based donation program. Under these programs, employees can choose to forego vacation, sick, or personal leave in exchange for cash payments that employer makes to specified charitable organizations. Payments must be made for the relief of disaster victims and must be made by January 1, 2019.

- **Qualified plan loans and hardship distributions:** The IRS relaxed some of the regulations to permit hurricane victims easier access to amounts in their qualified plan (401(k) 403(b), and 457(b)) accounts through plan loans or hardship distributions.

Legislative Tax Relief- Congress and the President Act

On September 28, 2017, both houses of Congress passed the Disaster Tax Relief and Airport and Airway Extension Act of 2017. This legislation was signed into law the following day by President Trump. With regard to hurricane victims, the Act provides:

---

[1] The discussion here concerns federal income tax law. State or local income tax law may differ.

Highlights of 2017 Disaster Tax Relief

- **Withdrawals from IRAs and qualified plans:** The legislation allows individuals affected by the three hurricanes, and who suffered an economic loss, to withdraw up to $100,000 in "qualified hurricane distributions" from an IRA or other qualified retirement plan. While such distributions are subject to normal income tax, they are not subject to the 10% early withdrawal penalty, nor are they subject to the 20% mandatory withholding requirements. These distributions must be made before January 1, 2019, and on or after August 23, 2017 for victims of Hurricane Harvey, on or after September 4, 2017 for Hurricane Irma victims, and on or after September 16, 2017 for victims of Hurricane Maria.

- **Three-year income inclusion:** Any portion of a qualified hurricane distribution that must be included in gross income may be recognized ratably over three years, unless the taxpayer chooses to recognize the income over a shorter period of time.

- **Repaying IRA and qualified plan withdrawals:** If a taxpayer repays a qualified hurricane distribution from an IRA or qualified plan within three years, the initial distribution will be treated as a non-taxable rollover. The taxpayer should file an amended return to claim a refund of tax paid on amounts previously included in income.

- **Loans from qualified plans:** The hurricane relief legislation expands from $50,000 to $100,000 the maximum amount that a qualifying hurricane victim may borrow from his or her pension plan without having the loan being treated as a taxable distribution. In certain situations, the law also allows a one year extension of time to repay a loan.

- **Casualty losses:** Generally, under 2017 federal tax law, individuals may deduct personal casualty or theft losses to the extent that they (1) exceed $100 per casualty or theft, and (2) to the extent they exceed 10% of the taxpayer's adjusted gross income (AGI). On Form 1040, the deduction is taken as an itemized deduction on Schedule A. The new legislation modifies existing law to allow hurricane victims to deduct losses to the extent they exceed $500, and eliminates completely the 10% of AGI limitation. For those taxpayers who do not itemize deductions, an allowable loss may be added to the taxpayer's standard deduction. This provision applies to hurricane losses incurred on or after August 23, 2017 for Hurricane Harvey, on or after September 4, 2017 for Hurricane Irma, and on or after September 16, 2017 for Hurricane Maria.

Highlights of 2017 Disaster Tax Relief

- **Expanded charitable deduction for cash donations:** The legislation expands the deduction available to both individuals and corporations for qualified contributions of cash made between August 23, 2017 and December 31 2017 to qualified organizations for hurricane relief. For individuals, a charitable contribution in excess of the expanded limits may generally be carried forwarded for up to five tax years.

- **Earned Income and child tax credits:** The new legislation permits qualified low-income taxpayers displaced by the hurricanes to use either their 2016 earned income or 2017 earned income to calculate for 2017 any earned income tax credit or refundable child credit. For residents of Puerto Rico, social security taxes are used to determine the credit.

- **Employer retention credit:** Provides for a business credit of 40% of qualified wages, up to $6,000 per employee (40% x $6,000 = $2,400), paid to an eligible employee by an eligible employer in areas impacted by the hurricanes. Qualifying wages include those paid or incurred before January 1, 2018, and after August 23, 2017 for Hurricane Harvey, after September 4, 2017 for Hurricane Irma, and after September 16, 2017 for Hurricane Maria.

California Wildfire Tax Relief

Initially, tax relief for victims of the California wildfires came through administrative action. However, in the Bipartisan Budget Act of 2018 (BBA), signed into law by President Trump on February 9, 2018, the federal government extended to wildfire victims many of the same tax relief measures earlier afforded to hurricane victims. Among these are:

- **Withdrawals from IRAs and qualified plans:** The legislation allows individuals affected by the California wildfires, and who suffered an economic loss, to withdraw up to $100,000 in "qualified wildfire distributions" from an IRA or other qualified retirement plan. While such distributions are subject to normal income tax, they are not subject to the 10% early withdrawal penalty, nor are they subject to the 20% mandatory withholding requirements. These distributions must be made on or after October 8, 2017 and before January 1, 2019.

- **Three-year income inclusion:** Any portion of a qualified wildfire distribution that must be included in gross income may be recognized ratably over three years, unless the taxpayer chooses to recognize the income over a shorter period of time.

Highlights of 2017 Disaster Tax Relief

- **Repaying IRA and qualified plan withdrawals:** If a taxpayer repays a qualified wildfire distribution from an IRA or qualified plan within three years, the initial distribution will be treated as a non-taxable rollover. The taxpayer should file an amended return to claim a refund of tax paid on amounts previously included in income.

- **Loans from qualified plans:** The wildfire relief legislation expands from $50,000 to $100,000 the maximum amount that a qualifying wildfire victim may borrow from his or her pension plan without having the loan being treated as a taxable distribution. In certain situations, the law also allows a one-year extension of time to repay a loan.

- **Casualty losses:** Generally, under 2017 federal tax law, individuals may deduct personal casualty or theft losses to the extent that they (1) exceed $100 per casualty or theft, and (2) to the extent they exceed 10% of the taxpayer's adjusted gross income (AGI). On Form 1040, the deduction is taken as an itemized deduction on Schedule A. The BBA modifies existing law to allow wildfire victims to deduct losses to the extent they exceed $500, and eliminates completely the 10% of AGI limitation. For those taxpayers who do not itemize deductions, an allowable loss may be added to the taxpayer's standard deduction. This provision applies to wildfire losses incurred on or after October 8, 2017.

- **Expanded charitable deduction for cash donations:** BBA expands the deduction available to both individuals and corporations for qualified contributions of cash made between October 8, 2017 and December 31 2018 to qualified organizations for wildfire relief. For individuals, a charitable contribution in excess of the expanded limits may generally be carried forwarded for up to five tax years.

- **Earned Income and child tax credits:** The new legislation permits qualified low-income taxpayers displaced by the wildfires to use either their 2016 earned income or 2017 earned income to calculate for 2017 any earned income tax credit or refundable child credit.

- **Employer retention credit:** Provides for a business credit of 40% of qualified wages, up to $6,000 per employee (40% x $6,000 = $2,400), paid to an eligible employee by an eligible employer in areas impacted by the wildfires. Qualifying wages include those paid or incurred after October 8, 2017 and before January 1, 2018.

Highlights of 2017 Disaster Tax Relief

Seek Professional Guidance

The federal government has provided many types of legislative and administrative relief to those impacted by the 2017 hurricanes and wildfires. To take maximum advantage of these relief measures, the advice and guidance of trained, experienced tax professionals is strongly recommended.

The American Taxpayer Relief Act of 2012

Highlights

In a successful last-minute effort, President Obama and Congressional leaders hammered out an agreement that averted many of the tax increases that were a significant part of what had been popularly termed the "Fiscal Cliff." The American Taxpayer Relief Act of 2012 (ATRA 2012), signed into law by the President on January 2, 2013, makes permanent many of the income and estate tax changes contained in the Economic Growth and Tax Relief Reconciliation Act of 2001, (EGTRRA), and subsequent legislation, as well as providing ongoing tax relief to a slowly-recovering economy.

ATRA 2012 did not address the across-the-board budget cuts that had been required under the Budget Control Act of 2011. Instead, these mandatory spending reductions were delayed until March 1, 2013.

The following is a brief summary of a few of the many provisions of ATRA 2012.[1] Except where noted, the changes are generally effective for tax years beginning after 2012.

Individual Income Taxes

Item	Prior Law	ATRA 2012
Individual Income Tax Rates	Under EGRTRRA, the individual tax rates were 10%, 15%, 25%, 28%, 33% and 35%. These marginal rates were scheduled to revert to 15%, 28%, 31%, 36%, and 39.6% in 2013.	The 10%, 15%, 25%, 28%, 33%, and 35% brackets are made permanent. A 39.6% rate will apply to taxable incomes above $450,000 (MFJ); $425,000 (HoH); $400,000 (Single); and $225,000 (MFS).

---

[1] The discussion here concerns federal income tax law. State or local income tax law may vary.

Individual Income Taxes (continued)

Item	Prior Law	ATRA 2012
Marriage Penalty Relief	The basic standard deduction for a married couple was scheduled to decline to 167% (from 200%) of that for an unmarried person filing a single return. The top of the MFJ 15% marginal bracket was also scheduled to decrease to 167% (from 200%) of the size of the corresponding bracket for an unmarried person filing Single.	The standard deduction and the top of the 15% marginal tax bracket for married taxpayers will permanently remain at 200% of that for Single taxpayers.
Capital Gains and Qualified Dividends	Generally, taxed at a 0% for taxpayers in the 10% and 15% marginal brackets. Taxed at a 15% for all other taxpayers.	For taxpayers in the 39.6% bracket, a 20% tax rate will apply to long-term capital gains and qualified dividends. For those in the 25%, 28%, 33%, or 35% brackets, a 15% rate will apply. For those in the 10% or 15% brackets a 0% rate is applicable.
Alternative Minimum Tax (AMT)	In 2012, AMT exemption amounts were scheduled to drop to $45,000 for MFJ, $33,750 for Single, and $22,500 for MFS. Most nonrefundable personal credits were no longer allowed against the AMT.	Retroactively increases the AMT exemption amounts for 2012 to $78,750 for MFJ; $50,600 for Single; and $39,375 for MFS. These increases are permanent and will be subject to adjustment for inflation in future years. Nonrefundable personal credits are allowed in full against the AMT.
Personal and Dependent Exemption Phase-Out	The phase-out of personal and dependent exemptions was suspended.	Requires taxpayers whose income exceeds certain limits to phase-out their personal and dependent exemptions. For 2013 these limits are: $300,000 for MFJ; $275,000 for HoH; $250,000 for Single; and $150,000 for MFS. The thresholds are subject to adjustment for inflation.

The American Taxpayer Relief Act of 2012

Individual Income Taxes (continued)

Item	Prior Law	ATRA 2012
Itemized Deduction Phase-Out	The phase-out of Schedule A itemized deductions was suspended.	Taxpayers whose incomes exceed specified limits must reduce certain, otherwise deductible, items on Schedule A. The same threshold amounts applicable to the personal exemption phase-out (see above) apply to the itemized deduction phase-out. These threshold amounts will be subject to adjustment for inflation in future years.
Child and Dependent Care Credit	In 2013, the credit was scheduled to decline to 30% of the first $2,400 of eligible expenses for one qualifying individual or $4,800 for two qualifying individuals. The credit was reduced for those with an AGI above $10,000.	Makes permanent the amount of allowable expenses ($3,000 for one qualifying dependent, $6,000 for two qualifying dependents) and a maximum rate of 35%. The credit is phased-out when AGI reaches $15,000.
Child Tax Credit	In 2013, the Child Tax Credit was scheduled to decline to $500 per qualifying child and, for most families, would be non-refundable.	Permanently extends the EGTRRA enhancements to the Child Tax Credit, including a maximum credit of up to $1,000 per child. The reduced threshold ($3,000) for the refundable portion of the credit is extended through 2017.
Earned Income Tax Credit (EITC)	The EITC is a refundable credit available to low-income workers who meet certain requirements. EGTRRA significantly liberalized the availability of this credit.	The new law makes permanent many of the EGTRRA changes to the EITC. ATRA 2012 extends through 2017 some of the EGTRRA provisions.
Unreimbursed Educator Expenses	An above-the-line deduction of up to $250 was allowed to qualifying educators for unreimbursed classroom expenses. The deduction expired at the end of 2011.	Retroactively reinstates the deduction for 2012 and extends it to 2013.

The American Taxpayer Relief Act of 2012

Individual Income Taxes (continued)

Item	Prior Law	ATRA 2012
Mortgage Debt Relief	For 2007-2012, qualifying taxpayers were allowed to exclude from income "cancellation of debt" income arising from forgiven indebtedness on a principal residence.	ATRA 2012 extends this provision for one year, through 2013.
Private Mortgage Insurance as Qualified Residence Interest	During 2007-2011, prior law allowed a taxpayer to deduct as qualified mortgage interest certain private mortgage insurance payments.	The new law extends this provision to amounts paid or accrued in 2012 and 2013.
Deduction for State and Local Sales Taxes	During 2004 – 2011 a taxpayer could deduct the larger of state and local income taxes or state and local sales taxes.	Extends this provision to 2012 and 2013.

Estate, Gift, and Generation-Skipping Taxes

Item	Prior Law	ATRA 2012
Transfer Tax Rates	For 2013, prior law provided for a return to the pre-EGTRRA transfer tax rates of up to 55%, with a 5% surcharge on taxable estates between $10,000,000 and $17,184,000.	In 2013, the new law applies a 40% marginal rate on taxable estates in excess of $1,000,000.
Applicable Exclusion Amount	For 2013, a $1,000,000 applicable exclusion amount, as adjusted for inflation.	A $5,000,000 applicable exclusion amount, as adjusted for inflation. In 2013 this is equivalent to $5,250,000.
Unused Spousal Exemption	For 2011 and 2012, the unused portion of a deceased spouse's applicable exclusion amount could be carried over for use by the surviving spouse.	Provision made permanent.

The American Taxpayer Relief Act of 2012

Estate, Gift, and Generation-Skipping Taxes (continued)

Item	Prior Law	ATRA 2012
State Death Tax Deduction	For 2005 – 2012, provided for a deduction from the gross estate of state and local death taxes.	Provision made permanent.
State Death Tax Credit	Prior to 2005, provided for a credit against the estate tax for state and local death taxes. This provision was scheduled to return in 2013.	Provision permanently repealed.
Qualified Family-Owned Business Exclusion	Prior to 2004, this code section provided for a deduction from the gross estate of Qualified Family-owned Business Interest Property. The provision was repealed for 2004-2012, but was scheduled to return in 2013.	Provision permanently repealed.

Charitable Tax Provisions

Item	Prior Law	ATRA 2012
Tax-Free IRA Distributions to Charity	For 2006 – 2011, provided for an exclusion from gross income for qualified charitable distributions up to $100,000 from an IRA for taxpayers age 70½ and older.	The provision was extended retroactively to 2012 and forward to 2013. Special provisions allow contributions made by January 31, 2013 to be treated as having been made in 2012.
Contributions of Capital Gain Real Property for Conservation Purposes	For 2006 – 2011, allowed an enhanced income tax deduction for the charitable contribution of a qualified conservation easement.	The provision was extended retroactively to 2012 and forward to 2013.

The American Taxpayer Relief Act of 2012

Tax Benefits for Education

Item	Prior Law	ATRA 2012
Coverdell Education Savings Accounts (ESA)	For 2013, pre-EGTRRA law would apply: (1) Maximum annual contribution limited to $500; (2) qualified expenses limited to higher education only; (3) reduced donor contribution phase-out range; (4) no age-limitation wavier for special needs students; (5) 6% excise penalty if contributions for the same beneficiary were made to a 529 and a Coverdell in the same year.	The EGTRRA enhancements to ESAs are made permanent: (1) Maximum annual contribution is $2,000; (2) qualified expenses include those for elementary and secondary schools as well as higher education; (3) higher donor contribution phase-out range; (4) age limitations are waived for special needs student; (5) contributions allowed to an ESA and a 529 for the same beneficiary the same year.
American Opportunity Tax Credit	Through 2012, allowed for a credit of up to $2,500 per student, per year, for tuition and fees paid during the first four calendar years of college.	Extends the credit for five years, 2013 – 2017.
Student Loan Interest Deduction	Pre-EGTRRA law allowed an above-the-line deduction of up to $2,500 during the first 60 months that interest payments were required. The deduction was phased out for high-income taxpayers.	Permanently repeals the 60-month deductibility limitation. Also makes permanent the EGTRRA increased phase-out limitations for high-income taxpayers.
Tuition and Fees Deduction	Under EGTRRA, a taxpayer was allowed an above-the-line deduction for up to $4,000 in tuition and higher-education expenses. The deduction was phased-out for taxpayers with an AGI in excess of certain limits. The deduction expired at the end of 2011.	The provision was extended retroactively to 2012 and forward to 2013.

The American Taxpayer Relief Act of 2012

Tax Benefits for Education (continued)

Item	Prior Law	ATRA 2012
Employer-Provided Educational Assistance	EGTRRA temporarily expanded to $5,250 per year, an employee's exclusion from gross income of employer-provided educational assistance.	Provision made permanent.

Business Tax Changes

Item	Prior Law	ATRA 2012
IRC Section 179 Expensing	In 2012, a business could expense up to $139,000 of tangible personal property, subject to an investment limitation of $560,000. In 2013, the cap was scheduled to drop to $25,000, with an investment limit of $200,000.	Increases the expensing cap to $500,000 with an investment limit of $2,000,000. These increases are applied retroactively to 2012 and forward to 2013.
Bonus Depreciation	During 2012, a business could take an additional 50% "bonus" depreciation on qualifying new business property placed in service during the year.	Extends this provision for one year, to 2013.
Increased Research Tax Credit	A credit allowed to businesses for increasing qualified research activities. Credit previously expired at the end of 2011.	Retroactively reinstates the credit for 2012 and extends it to 2013.

Seek Professional Guidance

Because federal tax law can be complex, the advice and guidance of experienced financial and tax professionals is strongly recommended.

Highlights of the 2010 Tax Relief Act

On December 17, 2010, President Barack Obama signed into law H.R. 4853, the Tax Relief, Unemployment Insurance Reauthorization, and Job Creation Act of 2010 (the 2010 Tax Relief Act). This massive bill affects almost every American taxpayer and has an estimated cost to the U.S. Treasury of $858 billion.[1]

Many of the bill's provisions are designed to provide relief to the unemployed, stimulate job growth, and protect what many observers see as a still-fragile economic recovery.[2] Significant provisions in the legislation include:

- **Unemployment benefits:** Extends federal unemployment benefits at their current levels for an additional 13 months, through the end of 2011.

- **Extend expiring tax provisions:** Many provisions of the Economic Growth and Tax Relief Reconciliation Act of 2001 (EGTRRA), and subsequent legislation, were slated to expire at the end of 2010. If this prior law had ended as scheduled, most taxpayers would have faced a significant increase in their tax burden, beginning in 2011. The 2010 Tax Relief Act has extended many of these provisions for an additional two years.

- **Payroll tax cut:** For one year, 2011, the legislation reduces the OASDI part of the Social Security payroll tax for both employees and the self-employed by 2.0%.

- **Estate tax modification:** EGTRRA included a phased-in reduction in the federal estate tax, which, like EGTRRA's individual income tax provisions, was also scheduled to end after 2010. The 2010 Tax Relief Act sets a 35% tax rate on taxable estates in excess of $5,000,000, with this new estate tax law expiring after 2012.

- **Business tax incentives:** A large number of the provisions are targeted at business with the intention of spurring business investment and economic growth.

---

[1] See JCX-54-10, prepared by the Joint Committee on Taxation, for the estimated budget effects of this legislation.
[2] The discussion here concerns federal income tax law; state or local income tax law may be different.

Highlights of the 2010 Tax Relief Act

The following is a brief, summary description of a few of the provisions in this act.

Provisions Affecting Individual Taxpayers Generally

Item	Prior Law	2010 Legislation
Individual marginal income tax rates	EGTRRA created a 10% income tax bracket for a portion of taxable income that previously was taxed at 15%. All other income tax brackets (except the 15% bracket) were gradually reduced over a period of years. The former brackets were scheduled to reappear after December 31, 2010.	Extends the 10%, 15%, 25%, 28%, 33%, and 35% brackets for an additional two years, 2011 and 2012.

Individual Marginal Tax Rate Comparison

Year	%	%	%	%	%	%
Before EGTRRA	N/A	15.0	28.0	31.0	36.0	39.6
2010 under EGTRRA	10.0	15.0	25.0	28.0	33.0	35.0
2011-2012	10.0	15.0	25.0	28.0	33.0	35.0

Item	Prior Law	2010 Legislation
Marriage penalty relief (A "marriage penalty" exists when the combined tax bill of a married couple is greater than the tax bill that would be due if each files a separate, unmarried return. A "marriage bonus" exists when the combined tax liability is less than the separate unmarried tax liabilities would be.)	EGTRRA increased the basic standard deduction for a married couple filing a joint return to twice that for an unmarried person filing a single return. It also increased the top of the 15% marginal bracket to twice the size of the corresponding bracket for an unmarried person filing a single return. Both provisions were due to expire after 2010.	Extends both provisions for two years, 2011 and 2012.

Highlights of the 2010 Tax Relief Act

Item	Prior Law	2010 Legislation
Employee payroll tax cut	An employee is required to pay 6.2% of covered wages, up to a wage base ($106,800 in 2010 and 2011) for the OASDI portion of Social Security payroll taxes.[1] Medicare hospital insurance (HI) tax is levied at a rate of 1.45% on all of an employee's covered wages. Similarly, a self-employed individual pays 12.4% of self-employment (SE) income, for OASDI payroll taxes, up to the wage base, and 2.9% of SE income for HI tax. A self-employed individual is allowed to deduct 7.65% of SE income in calculating the amount of income subject to payroll taxes. A self-employed taxpayer is also allowed to deduct 50% of the amount of OASDI and HI paid, in determining taxable income.	For 2011 only, the employee portion[2] of the OASDI payroll taxes is reduced to 4.2% of covered wages, up to the wage base.1 For self-employed individuals, the OASDI rate is reduced to 10.4% of SE income, up to the wage base. For self-employed individuals, the 2.0% rate reduction is ignored in determining the amount of SE income subject to OASDI and HI tax and also in calculating the deduction for payroll taxes paid in determining taxable income.[3]
Phase out of itemized deductions for high-income taxpayers	Prior to EGTRRA, certain itemized deductions of taxpayers with adjusted gross income (AGI) in excess of specified limits were reduced by 3% of AGI in excess of those limits. EGTRRA gradually phased out this limitation for high-income taxpayers, completely repealing it in 2010.	Extends the repeal of the limitation on the amount of allowable itemized deductions for higher-income taxpayers for two years, 2011 and 2012.

[1] The provision is equally applicable to Tier 1 payroll taxes under the Railroad Retirement System.

[2] The employer portion of the OASDI tax, also 6.2%, is <u>not</u> reduced.

[3] In 2011, the deduction used to determine the amount of SE income subject to OASDI and HI taxes remains at 7.65%. A self-employed individual will be allowed to deduct the sum of 59.6% of the OASDI portion of payroll taxes and 50% of HI taxes paid, in determining taxable income.

Highlights of the 2010 Tax Relief Act

Item	Prior Law	2010 Legislation
Long-Term Capital gains[1]	Under EGTRRA and subsequent legislation, in 2010, generally, individual capital gain was taxed at a maximum rate of 15% (0% for those in the 10% or 15% marginal brackets); gain on collectibles was taxed at 28%; real estate depreciation treated as capital gain was taxed at 25%.	Extends this capital gain tax treatment for an additional two years, 2011 and 2012.
Dividends[2]	Under EGTRRA and subsequent legislation, in 2010, "qualified" dividends (generally, dividends received from domestic corporations and certain, qualified foreign corporations) were taxed at preferential rates. These rates were either 0% (for those in the 10% or 15% marginal brackets) or 15% for those in a marginal tax bracket above 15%.	Extends this preferential treatment of qualified dividends for an additional two years, 2011 and 2012.
Alternative Minimum Tax (AMT) exemption amount	Under prior law, for 2010, the exemption amounts for the AMT were as follows: Married filing joint - $45,000 Married filing separate - $22,500 Single - $33,750	For 2010, the exemption amounts for the AMT are increased to: Married filling joint - $72,450 Married filing separate - $36,225 Single - $47,450 For 2011, the exemption amounts for the AMT will be: Married filling joint - $74,450 Married filing separate - $37,225 Single - $48,450

---

[1] "Long-term" capital gains are gains on certain property held <u>more than one year</u>. "Short-term" capital gains are gains on certain property held <u>one year or less</u>. Short-term capital gains under both old and new law are treated as ordinary income, taxable at the taxpayer's regular marginal rate.

[2] The discussion here concerns the federal tax treatment of dividends received by individuals and estates and trusts.

Highlights of the 2010 Tax Relief Act

Incentives for Families and Children

- **Child tax credit:** An individual is allowed a tax credit for each qualifying child under the age of 17. This credit is phased out for individuals with income in excess of certain limits. For some taxpayers, a portion of the credit is refundable. Under prior law, the credit was $1,000 per child through 2010, and $500 per child thereafter. The new law extends the maximum $1,000 tax credit amount for two years, 2011 and 2012.

- **Earned income tax credit:** Low- and moderate-income taxpayers may be eligible for a refundable "Earned Income Tax Credit" (EITC), based on earned income and a number of other factors. In general, the credit is calculated by multiplying a specified percentage times a taxpayer's earned income, up to a certain limit (the "cut-off amount"), with the credit completely phased out for higher-income taxpayers. A temporary provision enacted in 2009[1] increased the percentage for taxpayers with three or more children to 45% and expanded the phase-out threshold for couples using the married filing jointly status to $500 above that for other filers. The 2010 Tax Relief Act extends these provisions for two additional years, 2011 and 2012.

- **Child and dependent care tax credit:** Under federal income tax law, a credit is available for expenses paid to care for a dependent (a qualifying child or adult) in order to allow the taxpayer to work. Under EGTRRA, a taxpayer could claim a credit of up to $1,050 (35% x $3,000) for one qualifying dependent or $2,100 (35% x $6,000) for two qualifying dependents. The credit percentage is gradually reduced, but not below 20%, for taxpayers with an AGI more than $15,000. The 2010 Tax Relief Act extends this expanded credit for two additional years, 2011 and 2012.

---

[1] See the American Recovery and Reinvestment Act of 2009.

Highlights of the 2010 Tax Relief Act

- **Adoption credit and employer-provided adoption assistance:** Present law (effective through 2011) provides in 2010 for (1) a maximum adoption credit of $13,170 per eligible child, and (2) a maximum exclusion from income for employer-provided adoption assistance of $13,170 per eligible child. The dollar amounts are adjusted annually for inflation, and the credits are phased out for taxpayers with income in excess of certain levels. The 2010 act extends these two benefits for one year, 2012.

Provisions Affecting Educational Incentives

Item	Prior Law	2010 Legislation
Coverdell Education Savings Account (ESA)	Under EGTRRA, Coverdell ESAs received an increased annual contribution limit of $2,000 (up from $500). EGTRRA also extended the contribution and use periods for special needs beneficiaries, allowed the use of funds for qualified elementary and secondary education expenses, and provided for an increased contribution phase-out range for high-income taxpayers.	The 2010 legislation extends the provisions of EGTRRA affecting Coverdell ESAs for two years, 2011 and 2012.
American Opportunity Tax Credit	ARRA 2009[1] renamed the Hope Credit as the American Opportunity Tax Credit, raised the maximum credit from $1,800 to $2,500 per eligible student per year for qualified tuition and related expenses for each of the student's first four (up from two) years of post-secondary education, increased the credit phase-out range for high-income taxpayers, allowed the credit to be used against the AMT, and made a portion of the credit refundable.	Extends the provisions of ARRA 2009 with regard to the American Opportunity Tax Credit for two years, 2011 and 2012.

---

[1] The American Recovery and Reinvestment Act of 2009 modified the Hope Credit for two tax years, 2009 and 2010.

Highlights of the 2010 Tax Relief Act

Item	Prior Law	2010 Legislation
Deduction for student loan interest	Allows for an above-the-line deduction for qualified student loan interest of up to $2,500 per year. EGTRRA raised the deduction phase-out ranges for high-income tax payers and extended deductibility of interest beyond the first 60 months that payments are required.	Extends the EGTRRA provisions for two years, 2011 and 2012.
Deduction for tuition and related expenses	Allows for an above-the-line deduction for qualified tuition and related expenses for higher education. The deduction is either $4,000 or $2,000 depending on AGI, and a number of restrictions and limitations apply.	This deduction previously expired at the end of 2009. The 2010 legislation extends it for two tax years, 2010 and 2011.

Other Provisions Affecting Individual Taxpayers

- **Deduction for certain expenses of elementary and secondary school teachers:** An above-the-line deduction is allowed for up to $250 of unreimbursed classroom expenses (certain books, equipment, and supplies) for qualifying elementary and secondary school teachers. Under prior law the deduction expired at the end of 2009. The 2010 legislation extends this deduction for an additional two years, to 2010 and 2011.

- **Deduction of state and local sales taxes:** For tax years 2004 – 2009, a taxpayer could choose to deduct as an itemized deduction state and local general sales taxes in lieu of the deduction for state and local income taxes. This provision expired at the end of 2009. The 2010 Tax Relief Act extends this option for two years, to 2010 and 2011.

- **Tax-free distributions from IRAs for charitable purposes:** Through December 31, 2009, federal income tax law provided for an exclusion from gross income for up to $100,000 for distributions made from a Roth or traditional IRA directly to a qualified charitable organization. The IRA owner (or beneficiary of an inherited IRA) must have been at least age 70½ when the distribution was made and no charitable deduction was allowed for such qualified charitable distribution. The 2010 legislation extends this provision for two additional tax years, 2010 and 2011. Further, a taxpayer may elect to have a qualified charitable distribution made in January 2011 treated as having been made on December 31, 2010.

- **Contributions of capital gain real property made for conservation purposes:** In general, a deduction is permitted for charitable contributions, subject to certain limitations that depend on the type of taxpayer, the property contributed, and the donee organization. For 2006 – 2009, federal income tax law allowed an expanded deduction for the charitable contribution of a qualified conservation easement. For individual taxpayers, the deduction was limited to 50% of the donor's AGI, with any unused deduction carried forward for up to 15 years. For "qualified farmers and ranchers," the deduction was generally 100% of AGI, with a 15-year carry-forward of any unused deduction. The 2010 Tax Relief Act extends this expanded deduction of charitable contributions of qualified conservation easements for two years, 2010 and 2011.

Provisions Affecting the Federal Estate, Gift, and Generation-Skipping Taxes

Under EGTRRA, beginning in 2002, the federal estate tax was gradually reduced until it was completely repealed for one year, 2010. If Congress had not acted, the EGTRRA legislation would have "sunset" after 2010, with pre-EGTRRA law returning in 2011.

The 2010 Tax Relief Act reversed the one year repeal of the federal estate tax, raised the applicable exclusion amount to $5,000,000, lowered the top marginal rate to 35%, and pushed the "sunset" of most of the remaining EGTRRA estate tax provisions two years into the future, to December 31, 2012. Estates of decedents dying in 2010 may choose to be taxed under the "repealed" law (no estate tax, but a modified carryover basis adjustment) or under the new legislation, ($5,000,000 applicable exclusion amount, 35% top bracket, full step-up in basis).

Item	Prior Law	2010 Legislation
Gift tax	Before 2004, the estate and gift taxes were fully unified, with a single, graduated rate schedule and a single, effective exemption amount of $1,000,000. Between 2004 - 2009, the applicable exclusion amount for estate tax purposes increased to $3,500,000, while the gift tax applicable exclusion amount remained at $1,000,000. Under EGTRRA, the applicable exclusion amount for both estate and gift taxes was scheduled to be $1,000,000 in 2011.	For gifts made in 2010, the applicable exclusion amount is $1,000,000 and the top gift tax rate is 35%. For gifts made in 2011 and 2012, the gift tax is re-unified with the estate tax with an applicable exclusion amount of $5,000,000 and a top estate and gift tax rate of 35%.
Basis of property	Before 2010, property passing from a decedent generally received a "stepped-up" (or "stepped-down) basis to its fair market value on the date of death (or alternate valuation date). Under EGTRRA, for decedents dying in 2010, a "modified carryover" basis applied. An executor could "step-up" to fair market value the basis of up to $1.3 million in property, or up to $4.3 million for property passing to a surviving spouse.	For decedents dying in 2010, the new law generally repeals the modified carryover basis rules that had applied under EGTRRA and replaces them with a "stepped-up" basis regime, unless an executor chooses to have the estate taxed under the EGTRRA rules. The stepped-up basis rules will apply to decedents dying in 2011 and 2012.

Highlights of the 2010 Tax Relief Act

Item	Prior Law	2010 Legislation
State death tax credit	Before 2005, a credit was allowed against the federal estate tax for death taxes paid to a state or the District of Columbia. Under EGTRRA, the allowable amount of the state death tax credit was gradually reduced from 2002 – 2004. For decedents dying after 2004, the credit was repealed and was replaced with a deduction for state death taxes paid.	For 2010, 2011, and 2012, amounts paid for state death taxes will be allowed as a deduction rather than a credit.
Generation-skipping transfer tax (GSTT)	Under EGTRRA, for 2001-2003, the GSTT exemption was $1,000,000, adjusted for inflation. For 2004-2009, the GSTT exemption amount was tied to the estate tax applicable exclusion amount, reaching $3,500,000 in 2009, with no GSTT in 2010. Assets subject to the GSTT were taxed at a rate linked to the maximum estate tax rate. In addition, EGTRAA also made certain mechanical rules regarding the allocation of the GSTT.	For 2010, the new law exempts up to $5,000,000 (the applicable exclusion amount) in assets from the GSTT.[1] Any amount in excess of $5,000,000 is taxed at a 0% rate, effectively eliminating the GSTT for decedents dying in 2010. For 2011 and 2012, the amount of assets exempt from the GSTT is the same as the estate tax applicable exclusion amount, taxed at the highest estate and gift tax rate in effect in each year, 35%. The 2010 legislation also extends through 2012 the mechanical rules regarding the allocation of the GSTT.

Other Provisions Affecting Estate Planning

- **Portability of unused exemption between spouses:** Beginning with 2011, any applicable exclusion amount that remains unused at the death of a spouse (the "deceased spouse unused exclusion amount") is generally available for use by the surviving spouse, as an addition to the surviving spouse's own applicable exclusion amount.

---

[1] The $5,000,000 GSTT exemption is available regardless of whether the executor of an estate of a decedent who dies in 2010 decides to apply the EGTRRA 2010 estate tax and basis rules.

Highlights of the 2010 Tax Relief Act

- **Extension of filing deadlines:** The 2010 Tax Relief Act provides an extension of nine months for filing certain transfer tax returns, such as estate or GSTT returns. This filing deadline extension applies to decedents dying after December 31, 2009 and before the date of enactment, December 17, 2010.

- **Conservation easements:** Under EGTRRA, an executor could elect to exclude from the taxable estate up to 40% of the post-easement value of any land subject to a qualified conservation easement, up to a maximum of $500,000. The exclusion percentage was reduced by formula if the value of the easement was less than 30% of the land. The new legislation extends this section of the code for two additional years, 2011 and 2012.

- **Qualified family-owned business interests (QFOBI):** Prior to 2004, a deduction from the gross estate was permitted for the adjusted value of a qualified family-owned business of a decedent, up to $675,000. Under EGTRRA, the QFOBI deduction was repealed for decedents dying in 2004 – 2010. The Tax Relief Act of 2010 extends the repeal of the QFOBI deduction for an additional two years, 2011 and 2012.

- **Installment payment of estate tax for closely-held businesses:** Estate tax is generally due within nine months of a decedent's death. However, an executor may elect to pay estate tax attributable to an interest in a closely-held business in two or more installments, up to a maximum of 10. EGTRRA made certain changes to the installment payment provisions of the law, including increasing from 15 to 45 the maximum number of partners in a partnership or shareholders in a corporation that may be treated as a closely-held business interest, and expanding the availability of the installment payment provisions to include an interest in a qualifying lending and financing business. The new legislation extends the EGTRRA modifications of the installment payment provisions for two additional years, 2011 and 2012.

Provisions of Interest to Business

A number of the provisions in the 2010 Tax Relief Act were targeted at business, with the intention of spurring business investment and economic and job growth:

- **100-Percent Bonus depreciation:** The new law boosts 50-percent bonus depreciation to 100-percent for qualified investments made after September 8, 2010 and before January 1, 2012. 50-percent bonus depreciation is available for qualified property placed in service after December 31, 2011 and before January 1, 2013.

- **Code Sec. 179 Expensing:** For 2012, a taxpayer may choose to "expense" up to $125,000 (adjusted for inflation) of qualifying property. The $125,000 limit is reduced by the amount of qualifying property placed into service which exceeds $500,000 (adjusted for inflation). In 2013 and later, a taxpayer may choose to expense up to $25,000 of qualifying property, reduced by the amount of qualifying property placed into service which exceeds $200,000. Off-the-shelf computer software is considered qualifying property for Sec. 179 purposes if placed into service before 2013.

- **Research Tax Credit:** The research tax credit, which expired at the end of 2009, is renewed for two years through December 31, 2011 and is effective for amounts paid or incurred after December 31, 2009.

- **Sale of Small Business Stock:** The act enhanced the exclusion of gain from qualified small business stock to non-corporate taxpayers. For stock acquired after September 27, 2010 and before January 1, 2011, and held for at least 5 years, the 100-percent exclusion is extended for one more year, for stock acquired after January 1, 2012. The excluded gain is not subject to AMT.

- **Energy Tax Incentives:** The act extends for one or two years a number of energy tax incentives, primarily targeted to businesses.

- **Work Opportunity Credit:** The credit is extended for individuals who begin employment after August 31, 2011 (when it was set to expire) and before January 1, 2012, but with some modifications.

Seek Professional Guidance

Because federal tax law can be complex, the advice and guidance of experienced financial and tax professionals is strongly recommended.

American Recovery and Reinvestment Act of 2009

Summary and Highlights

On February 17, 2009, President Barack Obama signed into law H.R.-1, the American Recovery and Reinvestment Act of 2009 (ARRA 2009). Known popularly as the "economic stimulus" bill, ARRA 2009 represents a massive legislative effort to both restart the American economy and lay a foundation for future national economic growth. Running some 407 pages in length, the Act uses a combination of targeted federal spending, new income tax breaks, and major enhancements to many existing credits and deductions to achieve its goals.[1] The Congressional Budget Office estimates that the total 10-year (2009 - 2019) cost of the bill will be approximately $787 billion.

Tax Benefits for Individual Taxpayers

Many of the tax benefits contained in ARRA 2009 are targeted at individual taxpayers. The table below summarizes a few of the more notable individual tax provisions.

Item	Prior Law	ARRA 2009
Making Work Pay Tax Credit **Estimated 10-Year Cost:** $116,199,000,000[2]	No comparable provision.	For tax years 2009 and 2010, provides a refundable tax credit to eligible individuals equal to the lesser of 6.2% of an individual's earned income or $400 ($800 in the case of a joint return). The credit is phased out at a rate of 2% of modified adjusted gross income (MAGI) in excess of $75,000 ($150,000 in case of a joint return).

---

[1] The tax benefits discussed in this report concern federal income tax law; state or local tax law may vary.

[2] The estimated cost for each tax provision shown in this report is taken from the Full Summary of the Act, as prepared by the Senate Finance Committee and the House Ways & Means Committee.

American Recovery and Reinvestment Act of 2009

Item	Prior Law	ARRA 2009
AMT Relief for 2009 Estimated 10-Year Cost: $69,759,000,000	For 2009, the AMT exemption amounts are: Married Filing Jointly and Surviving Spouse = $45,000; Single and Head of Household = $33,750; Married Filing Separately = $22,500.	For 2009, the AMT exemption amounts are: Married Filing Jointly and Surviving Spouse = $70,950; Single and Head of Household = $46,700; Married Filing Separately = $35,475.
Refundable Portion of the Child Credit Estimated 10-Year Cost: $14,830,000,000	To the extent that the Child Credit exceeds a taxpayer's tax liability, the refundable portion of the Child Credit is equal to 15% of earned income in excess of a threshold amount of $8,500.[1]	For 2009 and 2010, redefines the formula to be 15% of earned income in excess of $3,000.
Earned Income Tax Credit (EITC) Estimated 10-Year Cost: $4,663,000,000	For 2009, taxpayers with two or more qualifying children may claim a credit of 40% of earnings up to $12,570. For taxpayers filing jointly, the credit begins to decrease when earnings exceed a phase-out threshold that is $3,120 higher than that for singles, surviving spouses, and heads of household.	For tax years 2009 and 2010, increases the EITC percentage for families with three or more children to 45%. Increases the threshold phase-out amount for taxpayers filing jointly to $5,000 above that for singles, surviving spouses, and heads of household. The $5,000 amount is indexed for inflation beginning in 2010.
American Opportunity Tax Credit Estimated 10-Year Cost: $13,907,000,000	Known as the Hope Credit, a non-refundable credit of up to $1,800 (for 2009) per eligible student per year, for qualified tuition and expenses for the student's first two years of post-secondary education in a degree or certificate program. The credit is phased out ratably for taxpayers with modified adjusted gross income (MAGI) between $50,000 and $60,000 ($100,000 and $120,000 for married taxpayers filing jointly). The credit is not allowable against the AMT for tax years after 2008.	For 2009 and 2010, renames the Hope Credit to be the "American Opportunity Tax Credit." Allows for a credit of up to $2,500 per eligible student per year for qualified tuition and related expenses for each of the student's first four years of post-secondary education in a degree or certificate program. Ratably phases out the credit for taxpayers with MAGI between $80,000 and $90,000 ($160,000 and $180,000 for married taxpayers filing jointly). The credit may be claimed against the AMT and up to 40% of the credit may be refundable.

[1] This formula is termed the "earned income" formula. For taxpayers with three or more children, an "alternative formula" may be used if a larger refundable credit results. Under current law the dollar threshold is adjusted for inflation.

American Recovery and Reinvestment Act of 2009

Item	Prior Law	ARRA 2009
First Time Homebuyer Credit **Estimated 10-Year Cost:** **$6,638,000,000**	Provides for a refundable credit equal to the lesser of $7,500 ($3,750 for married filing separately) or 10% of the purchase price of a principal residence. The home must be purchased on or after April 9, 2008 and before July 1, 2009. The credit is phased out for taxpayers with modified adjusted gross income between $75,000 and $95,000 ($150,000 and $170,000 for married filing joint). The credit is recaptured ratably over a 15 year period beginning two years after the year of purchase.	Extends the existing time period to qualify for the credit to homes purchased before December 1, 2009. Increases the maximum credit to $8,000 ($4,000 for married filing separately) and waives the recapture of the credit for homes purchased after December 31, 2008 and before December 1, 2009. Generally, the home must remain the principal residence for 36 months; otherwise the present rules on the credit recapture apply.
Sales and Excise Tax Deduction for Purchase of New Motor Vehicles **Estimated 10-Year Cost:** **$1,684,000,000**	No comparable provision.	Provides for an above-the-line deduction for state or local sales or excise taxes imposed on the sale of a new (original use starts with the taxpayer) motor vehicle. A qualified motor vehicle includes autos, light trucks, or motorcycles with a gross vehicle weight rating of 8,500 pounds or less, or a motor home. The deduction is limited to the tax imposed on the first $49,500 of the purchase price and is phased out for taxpayers with a modified adjusted gross income between $125,000 and $135,000 ($250,000 and $260,000 for married filing jointly). The vehicle must be purchased on or after the date of enactment (February 17, 2009) and before January 1, 2010. The deduction is not available if a taxpayer chooses to deduct state and local sales taxes on Schedule A.

American Recovery and Reinvestment Act of 2009

Item	Prior Law	ARRA 2009
529 Plans and Computer Technology **Estimated 10-Year Cost:** **$6,000,000**	No comparable provision.	For expenses paid or incurred in 2009 and 2010, expands the definition of "qualified higher education expenses" to include expenditures for computer equipment and technology, including internet access. Applies to both prepaid tuition plans and higher education savings plans.

Tax Benefits For Business

ARRA 2009 also contains a wide range of tax incentives for business taxpayers:

- **IRC Sec. 382 changes:** In 2008, the Treasury Department issued Notice 2008-83, which liberalized rules in the tax code intended to prevent taxpayers that acquire companies from claiming losses that were incurred by the acquired company prior to the taxpayer's ownership of the company. ARRA 2009 repeals this Notice prospectively. The Act also clarifies the application of IRC Sec. 382 to certain companies restructuring pursuant to the Emergency Economic Stabilization Act of 2008. Estimated 10-year cost: $10,141,000,000.

- **Extension of bonus depreciation:** In 2008, federal income tax law was amended to allow businesses to recover the cost of capital expenditures faster than under normal depreciation schedules by allowing businesses to immediately "write-off" 50% of the cost of depreciable property purchased in 2008 for use in the U.S. This "bonus" depreciation is in addition to regular depreciation. ARRA 2009 extends this temporary benefit to capital expenditures incurred in 2009. Estimated 10-year cost: $5,074,000,000.

- **Delayed recognition of certain cancellation of debt income (CODI):** Generally, under current law, a taxpayer has income where the taxpayer cancels or repurchases its debt for an amount less than its adjusted issue price. Under ARRA 2009, certain businesses will be allowed to recognize CODI over a 10-year period, deferring tax on CODI for the first four or five years and then recognizing the income ratably over the following five taxable years. The provision applies to specified types of business debt repurchased by the business after December 31, 2008 and before January 1, 2011. Estimated 10-year cost: $1,622,000,000.

American Recovery and Reinvestment Act of 2009

- **5-Year Carry back of NOLs for small business:** Under existing law, a "net operating loss" (NOL) may be carried back to the two taxable years before the year the loss arises and carried forward to each of the succeeding twenty taxable years after the year that the loss arises. For tax years ending or starting in 2008, the Act extends the maximum NOL carry back period from two to five years for small businesses with gross receipts of $15,000,000 or less. Estimated 10-year cost: $947,000,000.

- **Small business capital gains:** Current federal income tax law provides individuals with a 50% exclusion for gain from the sale of certain small business stock held for more than five years. The non-excluded portion of the gain is taxed at the lesser of ordinary income rates or 28%, instead of the individual capital gains rates. Limits apply to the amount of gain that may be excluded from a taxpayer's income. ARRA 2009 allows for a 75% exclusion for individuals on the gain from the sale of such small business stock held for more than five years, applicable to stock issued after the date of enactment (February 17, 2009) and before January 1, 2011. Estimated 10-year cost: $829,000,000.

- **IRC Sec. 179 Expensing:** IRC Sec. 179 allows small businesses to choose to write-off the cost of certain capital expenditures in the year of acquisition, rather than recovering the costs over time through depreciation. Through 2010, small business taxpayers are allowed to write-off up to $125,000 (indexed for inflation) of capital expenditures, subject to a phase-out once these expenditures exceed $500,000 (also indexed for inflation). In 2008, federal income tax law was amended to allow for a temporary increase in the amount that a small business could write-off to $250,000, with the phase-out threshold increased to $800,000. ARRA 2009 extends these temporary increases to capital expenditures incurred in 2009. Estimated 10-year cost: $41,000,000.

American Recovery and Reinvestment Act of 2009

Provisions Benefiting the Unemployed And Those On Fixed Incomes

In recognition of the financial hardship experienced by those who are unemployed or living on fixed incomes, the Act contains a number of provisions designed to "assist those most impacted by the recession."[1] A few of the more notable provisions include:

- **Extension of emergency unemployment compensation:** Through December 31, 2009, the Act continues the Emergency Unemployment Compensation Program, which provides up to 33 weeks of extended unemployment benefits to workers exhausting their regular benefits. Estimated 10-year cost: $26,960,000,000.

- **Increase in unemployment compensation benefits:** The legislation increases unemployment weekly benefits by an additional $25 through 2009. Estimated 10-year cost: $8,800,000,000.

- **Partial taxation of unemployment benefits:** For 2009, the Act excludes the first $2,400 of unemployment compensation from federal gross income. Under prior law, unemployment income is generally 100% includable in federal gross income. Estimated 10-year cost: $4,740,000,000.

- **COBRA continuation coverage:** The Act provides a 65% premium subsidy for COBRA health insurance continuation premiums for workers who have been involuntarily terminated, and for their families, for up to nine months. The premium subsidy applies to involuntary terminations that occur on or after September 1, 2008 and before January 1, 2010. Estimated 10-year cost: $24,700,000,000.

- **Economic Recovery Credit:** In 2009, a one-time refundable tax credit of $250 will be paid to retirees, disabled individuals, and SSI recipients receiving benefits from Social Security, Railroad Retirement beneficiaries, and disabled veterans receiving benefits from the Veterans Administration. This credit will reduce any "Making Work Pay" credit that might otherwise be allowable. Estimated 10-year cost: $218,000,000.

---

[1] ARRA 2009, Section 3.

American Recovery and Reinvestment Act of 2009

Federal Spending

ARRA 2009 also contains over $308 billion in additional federal spending, directed to a wide range of goals and purposes. The table below outlines these expenditures:[1]

Function/Department	Funds Expended For	Estimated 10-Year Outlay
Agriculture, Rural Development, Food and Drug Administration, Related Agencies	Distance learning; Telemedicine; Broadband program; Supplemental Nutrition Assistance Program; Other.	$26,431,000,000
Commerce, Justice, Science, and Related Agencies	Broadband Technology Opportunities; State and Local Law Enforcement Assistance; National Science Foundation; Other.	$15,810,000,000
Defense	Operation and Maintenance; Research, Development, Testing and Evaluation; Other.	$4,531,000,000
Energy and Water Development	Energy Efficiency and Renewable Energy; Innovative Technology Loan Guarantee Program; Other Energy Programs; Corps of Engineers; Other.	$50,775,000,000
Financial Services and General Government	Federal Buildings Fund; Other	$6,707,000,000
Homeland Security	Equipment; Border Security Fencing, Infrastructure, and Technology; Construction of Land Border Ports of Entry; Other.	$2,744,000,000
Interior, Environment, and Related Agencies	Clean Water and Drinking Water State Revolving Funds; Other.	$10,545,000,000

[1] Source: Congressional Budget Office analysis of the conference agreement for H.R. 1, dated February 13, 2009.

American Recovery and Reinvestment Act of 2009

Function/Department	Funds Expended For	Estimated 10-Year Outlay
Labor, Health and Human Services, Education, and Related Agencies	National Institutes of Health; National Coordinator for Health Information Technology; Other Health and Human Services; Employment and Training Administration; Education for the Disadvantaged; Special Education; Student Financial Assistance; Other Education.	$71,271,000,000
Legislative Branch	Government Accountability Office.	$25,000,000
Military, Veterans Affairs, and Related Agencies	Military Construction; Family Housing; VA Medical Facilities; National Cemeteries; Other.	$4,246,000,000
Department of State, Foreign Operations, and Related Programs	Diplomatic and Consular Programs; Capital Investment Fund; Other.	$602,000,000
Transportation and Housing & Urban Development	Highway Construction; Other Transportation; Public Housing Capital Fund; Other Housing Assistance.	$61,051,000,000
State Fiscal Stabilization Fund	Education Fund; State Incentive Grants; Innovation Fund.	$53,600,000,000

ARRA 2009 also includes an increase in the statutory limit on the public debt by $789 billion, from $11.315 trillion to $12.104 trillion.

Highlights of the Pension Protection Act of 2006

The Pension Protection Act of 2006 (PPA 2006) was signed into law by President George W. Bush on August 17, 2006. During the signing ceremony, President Bush described the act as the "most sweeping reform of America's pension laws in over 30 years."

Over 900 pages in length, the new legislation reflects the move by many employers away from traditional defined benefit (DB) pension plans and toward defined contribution (DC) plans. Its provisions also highlight governmental concern over the shaky financial condition of many DB plans and the potential adverse effect that any future defaults by plan sponsors may have on the federal government and the American taxpayer.

Defined contribution plans are also affected, in a myriad of ways. The act makes permanent many of the provisions of EGTRRA 2001, which encouraged individuals to establish and contribute to both IRAs and employer-sponsored DC plans. PPA 2006 also impacts distributions from qualified plans, with both temporary and permanent changes.

Further, PPA 2006 includes many "miscellaneous" provisions, including those affecting employer-owned life insurance, charitable giving, IRC Sec. 529 plans, and long-term care.

The following is a brief summary of a few notable provisions of this new legislation. Individual taxpayers are strongly encouraged to consult with their own financial and tax advisors to review in detail how the act may impact their own personal situations.

Traditional Defined Benefit (DB) Pension Plans

Much of PPA 2006 is devoted to bolstering traditional DB plans, as well as strengthening the government's "safety net," the Pension Benefit Guaranty Corporation (PBGC).

Item	Prior Law	2006 Legislation
Minimum plan funding	Employer generally required to fund up to 90% of plan's liabilities. Current law applies in 2006 and 2007.	Generally requires employers to fund 100% of plan's liabilities. Underfunded plans have seven years to reach 100%. Minimum annual contribution must cover the value of benefits earned during the years. Effective for plan years beginning in 2008.

Highlights of the Pension Protection Act of 2006

Item	Prior Law	2006 Legislation
Employer deduction limits	Contributions deductible up to 100% of current plan liability.	For new plans, in 2006 and 2007, maximum deduction limited to 150% of current liabilities. In 2008 and later, the maximum deduction will generally be the amount necessary to bring the plan assets up to 150% of the applicable funding target. Some restrictions on this 50% "cushion" apply for small plans recently amended to increase benefits.
"At risk" plans	Lump-sum distributions limited for certain highly compensated employees if less than 110% of current liability funded.	Employer generally subject to funding requirements greater than the normal 100%. Restrictions on certain benefits may apply. Extremely underfunded plans would be automatically frozen. Notices are required to participants in certain events. For plan years beginning in 2008 and later.
Valuing plan liabilities	Valued using investment grade corporate bonds. Prior law applies in 2006 and 2007.	Beginning in 2008, a three-segmented yield curve will be used. May include updated mortality tables or tables based on a plan's experience and trends.
Maximum plan benefit	EGTRRA 2001 increased the maximum annual dollar limit to the lesser of $160,000 (indexed for inflation) or100% of compensation (maximum of $200,000). Benefits were reduced if begun before age 62 and increased if begun after age 65. The provision was originally set to "sunset" on 12/31/2010.	Makes permanent the increased benefit allowed under EGTRRA 2001.[1]
Cash balance plans	Prior legislation left employers who switched to a "cash balance" hybrid plan open to lawsuits over age discrimination.	If a plan meets certain requirements, new cash balance plans are not considered discriminatory. Conversions of existing DB plans to cash balance plans will be permissible, subject to certain requirements.[2]

[1] Effective August 17, 2006, the date of enactment.
[2] Generally effective for periods beginning after June 29, 2005.

Highlights of the Pension Protection Act of 2006

Item	Prior Law	2006 Legislation
Fully insured DB plans	Currently described in IRC Sec. 412(i).	Moved to new IRC Sec. 412(e)(3).[1]

IRAs and Defined Contribution (DC) Plans

PPA 2006 includes many provisions designed to encourage individuals to participate in IRAs and employer-sponsored DC plans. The law makes permanent[1] a number of EGTRRA 2001 provisions that originally were to "sunset" after 2010, including:

- **Increased IRA contribution limits:** In 2006 and 2007, $4,000; in 2008, $5,000; adjusted for inflation in later years.

- **Increased limits for defined contribution plans:** In 2006, a total maximum contribution of $44,000; elective deferrals limited to $15,000 (401(k) and 457 plans) and $10,000 for SIMPLE plans; compensation that may be taken into account ($220,000); all adjusted for inflation in later years.

- **"Catch-up" contributions for workers age 50 and older:** For IRAs, in 2006, $1,000. In 2006 for 401(k) plans, $5,000; for SIMPLE plans, $2,500; adjusted for inflation in later years.

- **Vesting of employer contributions:** 100% vesting under either a three-year cliff or six-year graded schedule.

- **Increased employer deduction for qualified plan contributions:** EGTRRA generally increased the deduction limit from 15% to 25% of compensation and modified the definition of compensation for certain types of plans.

- **Roth 401(k) and 403(b) contributions:** Under EGTRRA 2001, Roth contributions to 401(k) and 403(b) plans were allowed only during 2006-2010.

- **"Deemed" IRAs:** Established under an employer plan which provided for separate employee contributions.

- **"Solo" 401(k) plans:** Elective deferrals are not taken into account for purposes of the limit on deductible plan contributions.

---

[1] Effective August 17, 2006, the date of enactment.

Highlights of the Pension Protection Act of 2006

PPA 2006 also included a number of notable new items:

Item	Prior Law	2006 Legislation
Automatic 401(k) plan enrollment	Permitted by IRS and DOL regulations, but restricted by law in many states.	Beginning with enactment, preempts state laws prohibiting automatic enrollment and withholding of employee wages. Employees must opt-out if they do not wish to participate.
Automatic enrollment safe harbor 401(k) plan	No comparable provision.	Beginning in 2008, allows a new safe harbor 401(k) plan with automatic enrollment features. Must meet special employee notice, matching contribution, and vesting requirements.
Custom investment advice for employee-participants	Considered a "prohibited transaction" under prior law.	Beginning in 2007, allows for an "eligible investment advice arrangement." Any fees or commissions must not vary with the investment option chosen or else a computer model meeting certain requirement must be used.
Direct deposit of federal income tax refunds into an IRA	Allows refunds of federal income taxes to be directly deposited into a checking or savings account.	Beginning in 2007, allows refunds of federal income taxes to also be directly deposited into an IRA.
Qualified reservist distribution	No comparable provision. IRC Sec. 72(t) generally applies a 10% tax penalty to withdrawals from IRAs and other qualified retirement plans made by owners or participants under age 59½, unless certain exceptions apply.	Waives the 10% early withdrawal penalty for withdrawals from an IRA or other retirement plan by qualifying military reservists called to active duty between 09/11/2001 and 12/31/2007. Allows for re-contribution of withdrawn amounts during the two years after active duty ends.

Highlights of the Pension Protection Act of 2006

Distributions from IRAs and Qualified Retirement Plans

Item	Prior Law	2006 Legislation
Public safety employees – distributions from defined benefit plans after age 50	No comparable provision. IRC Sec. 72(t) generally applies a 10% tax penalty to withdrawals from IRAs and other qualified retirement plans made by owners and participants under age 59½, unless certain exceptions apply. One exception applies to employees who separate from service after age 55.	The 10% tax penalty for early withdrawals does not apply to distributions from a qualified governmental defined benefit plan to a qualified public safety employee who separates from service after age 50.[1]
Public safety employees – tax-free distributions to pay for health and long-term care insurance	No comparable provision. Distributions from IRAs and qualified retirement plans are generally taxable to the extent the distribution represent a return of before-tax contributions. A 10% penalty tax may also apply to distributions made before the participant reaches age 59½, unless certain exceptions apply.	Beginning in 2007, provides an exclusion from income of up to $3,000 for distributions from qualifying retirement plans for retired public safety officers to pay for qualified accident, health, or long-term care insurance. Premium payments must be made directly from the retirement plan to the insurer.
Rollovers by nonspouse beneficiaries	No comparable provision. Only a surviving spouse could roll over a distribution from a deceased spouse's qualified plan to his or her own IRA.	Beginning in 2007, beneficiaries other than a surviving spouse may roll over benefits received from a qualified retirement plan, a 457 plan, or a tax sheltered annuity to an inherited IRA.
Direct rollover from a qualified plan to a Roth IRA	No comparable provision. Under prior law, a distribution from a qualified retirement plan, 457 plan, or tax-sheltered annuity had to first be rolled over to a traditional IRA before it could be transferred to a Roth IRA.	Beginning in 2008, distributions from qualified retirement plans, 457 plans, and tax-sheltered annuities may be rolled directly into a Roth IRA. These distributions are subject to the same requirements as a Roth conversion.

[1] Effective for distributions made after the date of enactment, August 17, 2006.

Highlights of the Pension Protection Act of 2006

Item	Prior Law	2006 Legislation
Phased retirement	No comparable provision. Prior law generally prohibited a qualified plan from making retirement distributions to a participant who had not reached normal retirement age and who had not separated from service. Proposed regulations would permit plans to pay a portion of benefits to employees who are at least age 59½ and reduce their work time by at least 20%.	Beginning in 2007, allows retirement distributions to employees who are at least age 62 even if they have not separated from employment at the time of the distribution.

Charitable Giving

Although the vast majority of the act concerns pensions and retirement plans, there are a number of provisions affecting charitable giving. Among these are:

Item	Prior Law	2006 Legislation
Qualified charitable distributions from IRAs	No comparable provision. Withdrawals from IRAs are generally subject to tax, to the extent that they represent a return of before-tax contributions. Contributions to charitable organizations are subject to a number of limitations on the deductibility of such contributions.	For 2006 and 2007, provides an exclusion from gross income of up to $100,000 for distributions made from a Roth or Traditional IRA directly to a qualified charitable organization. The IRA owner must be at least age 70½ when the distribution is made. No charitable deduction is allowed for such qualified charitable distributions.
Charitable contributions of clothing and household items	Generally, taxpayers are permitted to deduct the fair market value of tangible personal property donated to charity. Certain substantiation requirements apply.	Prohibits a charitable deduction for contributions of used clothing or household items unless the items donated are in good used condition or better. A deduction may be allowed for donations of property that is not in good used condition or better if the value exceeds $500 and a qualified appraisal accompanies the taxpayer's return.[1]

[1] Effective for contributions made after August 17, 2006.

Highlights of the Pension Protection Act of 2006

Item	Prior Law	2006 Legislation
Cash contributions to charities	Generally requires a donor to substantiate a charitable donation of cash through written records such as a cancelled check, a receipt, or a letter of acknowledgement from the charitable donee showing the donee's name, the amount and date of the contribution, or other reliable written records.	Requires the donor to substantiate a charitable donation of cash through either a bank record or a written communication from the charitable donee showing the donee's name and the amount, and date of the contribution.1
Charitable contributions of food inventory and book inventory	Under the Katrina Emergency Tax Relief Act of 2005 (KETRA), allowed an expanded business charitable deduction for donations of food items from inventory or donations of books to a public school. Applicable to donations made on or after 08/25/05 and before 01/01/06.	Extends the effective date of these provisions for one year to donations made after 12/31/05 and before 01/01/08.
Qualified conservation easement	Generally allows an income tax deduction for the value of a qualified conservation easement. The deduction is limited to 30% of the donor's adjusted gross income in the year the contribution is made; any excess may be carried forward and deducted for up to five years.	For 2006 and 2007, generally increases the allowable deduction to 50% of the donor's adjusted gross income, with any excess being carried forward for up to 15 years. For qualified farmers and ranchers, the allowable deduction is 100% of the donor's adjusted gross income.

Miscellaneous Provisions

As with many major legislative acts, there are always a few "miscellaneous" provisions:

Item	Prior Law	2006 Legislation
IRC Sec. 529 plans	Many of the key provisions concerning qualified tuition plans came into being with the EGTRRA 2001. Under that act, these provisions were originally set to "sunset" on 12/31/10.	Makes the "temporary" provisions of EGTRRA that apply to qualified tuition plans permanent.2

---

[1] Effective for contributions made in tax years beginning after August 17, 2006.

[2] Effective August 17, 2006, the date of enactment.

Highlights of the Pension Protection Act of 2006

Item	Prior Law	2006 Legislation
Saver's credit	Provides for a nonrefundable tax credit for lower-income taxpayers for contributions to IRAs and certain qualified retirement plans. The credit amount varies with the adjusted gross income of the taxpayer. The provision was originally set to "sunset" on 12/31/06.	Makes the credit permanent. Beginning in 2007, indexes for inflation the income limits applicable to the credit, in multiples of $500.[1]
Start-Up tax credit for small employer-sponsored plans	Allowed small employers a credit of up to $500 per year for the costs of establishing a new qualified retirement plan. The provision was originally set to "sunset" on 12/31/10.	Makes the credit permanent.[1]
1035 exchanges and LTC	No comparable provisions.	Expands the scope of IRC Sec. 1035 to include tax-free exchanges of qualified long-term care (LTC) contracts. The provision also covers LTC provided as a part of, or a rider to, a life or annuity contract.[1]
Tax treatment of LTC as a rider to life or annuity contracts	Some provision for LTC coverage as a part of a life insurance contract.	Establishes new, complex tax rules for long-term care insurance (LTC) which is provided by a rider on, or a part of, either a life insurance or annuity contract. A withdrawal from the life or annuity contract used to pay for LTC is generally not includable in income.[2] No itemized medical expense deduction is allowed for charges against the life or annuity contract for LTC coverage.

[1] Applicable to exchanges occurring after December 31, 2009.
[2] Generally effective for contracts issued after December 31, 1996, but only with respect to taxable years beginning after December 31, 2009.

Highlights of the Pension Protection Act of 2006

Miscellaneous Provisions (continued)

Item	Prior Law	2006 Legislation
Employer-owned life insurance	Generally, amounts received under a life insurance contract paid by reason of the death of the insured are excluded from gross income for federal income tax purposes.	Generally provides that in the case of an employer-owned life insurance contract, the amount excluded from the policyholder's income cannot exceed the premiums and other amounts paid for the contract.[1] Death benefit above these payment amounts is included in income. The new law adds certain notice and consent requirements and provides for specified exceptions to the income inclusion rules.
Restrictions on executive deferred compensation	No comparable provisions.	Generally provides that during periods in which a qualified retirement plan is "at-risk," any funds set aside in a nonqualified deferred compensation plan for high-level executives will become taxable in the year of transfer. An underpayment interest penalty and a 20% penalty tax also apply. Further, the employer is denied a deduction for such transfers.[2]

[1] Effective for contracts issued after August 17, 2006 (the date of enactment) except for contracts acquired under an IRC Sec. 1035 exchange.

[2] Effective for funds transferred or set aside after August 17, 2006, the date of enactment.

Highlights of 2005 Hurricane Tax Relief

A Brief Summary of Selected Provisions

In the wake of the destruction left by Hurricane Katrina, Congress and President Bush moved quickly to provide legislative relief to those affected by that storm. The Katrina Emergency Tax Relief Act of 2005 (KETRA) was passed unanimously by Congress on September 21, 2005 and signed into law by the President on September 23, 2005.

In response to Hurricanes Rita and Wilma, KETRA was soon followed by the Gulf Opportunity Zone Act of 2005, (GOZA), passed by Congress on December 16, 2005, and signed into law on December 21, 2005. This second relief act established a Gulf Opportunity (GO) Zone, for Hurricane Katrina victims, a Rita GO Zone, for victims of Hurricane Rita, and a Wilma GO Zone, for victims of Hurricane Wilma. GOZA provided additional tax relief to those impacted by Hurricane Katrina, and extended a number of the KETRA provisions to those living in areas affected by Hurricanes Rita and Wilma.

Although much of this legislation[1] aids those directly affected by the storms, taxpayers living outside the impacted geographical areas also benefit.

Provisions Applicable to Hurricanes Katrina, Rita, and Wilma

A number of relief provisions apply to individuals affected by any of the storms:

- **Withdrawals from IRAs and qualified plans:** The legislation generally allows an individual living in one of the three disaster zones, and who suffered an economic loss as a result of the hurricanes, to withdraw up to $100,000 in "qualified hurricane distributions" penalty-free (the 10% early withdrawal penalty) from an IRA or other qualified retirement plan. While such withdrawals are subject to normal income tax, they are not subject to the 20% mandatory withholding requirements.[2] These distributions must be made before January 1, 2007, and on or after August 25, 2005 (to a Hurricane Katrina individual), on or after September 23, 2005 (to a Hurricane Rita individual), or on or after October, 23, 2005 (to a Hurricane Wilma individual).

---

[1] The discussion here concerns federal income tax law. State or local law may differ.
[2] Separately, the IRS, in Announcement 2005-70, liberalized the rules for hardship distributions from qualified plans for victims of the hurricane as well as for family members who may be living in other parts of the country.

Highlights of 2005 Hurricane Tax Relief

- **Three-year income inclusion:** Amounts withdrawn from an IRA or qualified plan that must be included in gross income can be recognized ratably over three years, unless the taxpayer elects otherwise.

- **Repaying IRA and qualified plan withdrawals:** If a taxpayer repays a qualified distribution from an IRA or qualified plan within three years, the initial distribution is treated as a non-taxable rollover. The taxpayer should file an amended return to claim a refund of tax paid on amounts previously included in income.

- **Loans from qualified plans:** The legislation expands from $50,000 to $100,000 the maximum amount that a qualifying hurricane victim may borrow from his or her pension plan to purchase a principal residence. Such loans must be made before January 1, 2007, and on or after September 24, 2005 (to a Hurricane Katrina individual), or on or after December 21, 2005 (to a Hurricane Rita or Hurricane Wilma individual).

- **Expanded charitable deduction for cash donations:** The legislation generally expands the deduction available to both individuals and corporations for donations of cash made between August 28, 2005 and December 31, 2005 to qualifying organizations. For corporations, donations must be for relief efforts related to Hurricane Katrina, Hurricane Rita, or Hurricane Wilma.

- **Casualty losses:** Individuals generally may deduct personal casualty or theft losses only to the extent that they exceed $100 per casualty or theft, and to the extent they exceed 10% of the taxpayer's adjusted gross income. For personal losses from Hurricane Katrina on or after August 25, 2005, these casualty loss limitations do not apply. GOZA extended this relief to losses arising from Hurricane Rita on or after September 23, 2005, and to losses arising from Hurricane Wilma on or after October 23, 2005.

- **Earned income and child credits:** The legislation permits qualified low-income taxpayers displaced by the hurricanes to use their 2004 earned income to calculate for 2005 any allowable earned income credit (EIC) or refundable child credit.

- **Employee Retention Credit:** Provides for a credit of 40% of qualified wages (up to $6,000 in qualified wages per employee) paid to an eligible employee by an eligible employer in one of the disaster areas. For employers in the Katrina core disaster area, the wages must have been paid between August 28, 2005 and January 1, 2006. For Hurricanes Rita and Wilma, respectively, these dates are September 23, 2005 - January 1, 2006, and October 23, 2005 - January 1, 2006.

- **Mortgage revenue bonds:** These bonds are commonly used by state and local governments to fund low-interest rate mortgages for low-income, first-time homebuyers. The legislation expands eligibility to receive such loans by eliminating the "first-time homebuyer" requirement for residences located in the GO Zone, the Rita GO Zone, or the Wilma GO Zone. The new laws also expand to $150,000 from $15,000 the permitted amount for a home improvement loan used to repair damage caused by the hurricanes. The rules apply to loans made before January 1, 2011.

Provisions Applicable Only to Hurricane Katrina

Certain provisions of the legislation target those affected by Hurricane Katrina, or those working or living in the Gulf Opportunity Zone:

- **Sheltering evacuees:** A special personal exemption deduction is allowed for a taxpayer (anywhere in the country) who uses his or her principal residence to provide free housing to Katrina evacuees (up to four) for at least 60 consecutive days. The deduction, limited to $2,000, may be claimed, for both 2005 or 2006.

- **Discharge of indebtedness:** Cancellation of a debt generally results in taxable income to the taxpayer whose debt was cancelled. If certain requirements are met, KETRA provides an exclusion from income for victims of Katrina for the cancellation of non-business debt on or after August 25, 2005 and before January 1, 2007.

- **Charitable mileage for Hurricane Katrina relief:** KETRA increased the standard charitable mileage rate from its 2005 value of 14 cents per mile to 70% of the standard business mileage rate, rounded to the next highest cent.[1] If a volunteer is reimbursed for charitable use of a passenger automobile, the legislation generally allows the reimbursement to be excluded from income. Both provisions apply for miles driven from August 25, 2005 through December 31, 2006.

---

[1] For the period August 25, 2005 through August 31, 2005, the Hurricane Katrina standard charitable mileage rate is 29 cents per mile. For the period September 1, 2005 through December 31, 2005, this rate is 34 cents per mile. For 2006, this rate is 32 cents per mile. These provisions apply solely for charitable mileage related to Hurricane Katrina relief efforts.

Highlights of 2005 Hurricane Tax Relief

- **Charitable contributions of food and books from inventory:** KETRA expanded the deduction allowed to a business for donations of food items from inventory. For C corporations, the Act also expanded the deduction for donations of books to a public school. Both provisions apply to contributions made on or after August 28, 2005 and before January 1, 2006.[1]

- **Hope Scholarship and Lifetime Learning Credits:** For 2005 and 2006, students attending eligible institutions within the Gulf Opportunity Zone may claim a Hope Scholarship Credit or Lifetime Learning Credit of up to twice the normally applicable dollar limits. Thus, for 2006, a qualified individual may claim a Hope Scholarship Credit of up to $3,300 or a Lifetime Learning Credit of up to $4,000.[2] Additionally, the definition of "qualified tuition and related expenses" has been expanded to match the much broader definition used for IRC Sec. 529 qualified tuition plans.

- **Work Opportunity Tax Credit:** Expands eligibility for the Work Opportunity Tax Credit by including a "Hurricane Katrina employee" as a member of a "targeted group" for purposes of the credit.

Seek Professional Guidance

Many of the provisions of both KETRA and GOZA are complex. As with all tax-related matters, the advice and guidance of an experienced tax professional is highly recommended.

---

[1] The Emergency Economic Stabilization Act of 2008 extended the effective date of these provisions to December 31, 2009.
[2] For 2005, a qualified individual may claim a Hope Scholarship Credit of up to $3,000 or a Lifetime Learning Credit of up to $4,000.

The Perfect Investment

Once an individual or family has reached the stage in life where there is enough income to easily pay the monthly bills, there is often a desire to put the excess monthly cash flow to work. For some, an inheritance, a large bonus, or a distribution from a qualified plan can provide an investable, lump sum of money. For most people, the key question is, "How do I put this money to work?" In a perfect world, the answer would be an investment that has certain, ideal characteristics:

- **High rate of return:** A total return high enough to out perform inflation and taxes, and still meet the investment goal.

- **Complete safety:** There would be no concern that any part of the investment could ever be lost.

- **Always liquid:** An investor would be able to redeem the investment, and receive cash, at any time of day or night, every day of the year without any penalty or loss of principal.

- **No income taxes:** There would never be any income taxes due on the investment's yield or growth. The investor keeps everything earned.

- **No skill or knowledge required:** No special skill or knowledge would be required to manage the investment. One could just forget about the investment and enjoy life.

The Real World

Such a "perfect" investment does not exist, of course. Most notably, investing involves risk, including the possible loss of all or a part of your principal. In the real world, individual investors must choose from a confusing range of investment tools, each with different characteristics and uses. The process of selecting the best investment for a particular need or situation is made easier by clearly answering the following questions:

- **Why are you investing?** Do you need income for current expenses or are you accumulating money for a future need?

- **When will the money be needed?** At any moment? A year from now? At retirement, 25 years from now?

- **How much risk are you willing to undertake?** Can you afford to lose all or a part of the investment, and not have the loss affect how you live?

- **Are income taxes a concern?** If the investment is currently taxable, to what extent will the additional tax reduce investment growth or push you into a higher tax bracket?

- **What is the economic outlook?** Investment opportunities will vary depending on whether the economy is growing or shrinking.

- **Do you have the skill and knowledge needed to manage your investment?** Is professional investment management needed?

- **How much money is there available to invest?** Are smaller amounts available periodically, or is there currently a larger, lump sum of money?

Key Investment Questions

Many individuals and families have both a need and a desire to accumulate wealth. The inevitable question is, "What do I invest the money in?"

The answer to the question usually depends on the needs, temperament, and available resources of each individual or family. The "best" investment for one person is often not the best for someone else. The process of choosing the most appropriate investment can be made easier by carefully considering, and answering, the following questions:

- **What are your investment goals?** In other words, "What do I want the money to do for me?" For example, an investor might need to have additional income, to meet current living expenses. Other common needs include saving for long term goals such as retirement, a child's education or a dream vacation, or for a quickly available source of emergency funds.

- **How liquid does the investment need to be?** The term "liquidity" refers to how quickly an investment can be turned into cash, without losing any of the invested dollars. The question might also read, "When will the money be needed?" For example, investments meeting longer term goals such as retirement generally do not need to be as liquid as those designed to hold emergency funds.

- **What is your risk tolerance?** Can you afford to risk losing a portion, or even all, of your investment without it affecting how you live? What would be the impact of a loss on your investment goals? In general, risk is related to return: the higher the risk, the higher the potential return; the lower the risk, the lower the potential return.

- **What is the impact of income taxes?** Income taxes can have a significant, negative impact on your investment results. For example, many high-income individuals invest in municipal bonds because the interest from such bonds is generally exempt from federal income tax; in some instances the interest is also exempt from state income tax. Qualified retirement plans, life insurance policies and annuity contracts are used to accumulate funds for retirement because of their tax-deferred nature; generally, no taxes are due until the money is withdrawn.

- **What is the economic outlook?** The state of the economy as a whole can change the mix of desirable investments. For example, during periods of high inflation, tangible assets such as real estate, precious metals, and collectibles such as coins and art, have tended to produce good results. During periods of stable or declining inflation, intangible assets such as stocks and bonds have generally done well. Of course, there is no guarantee that history will repeat itself.

- **Is the skill and knowledge needed to manage the investment available?** An investor may not have the specialized skills and knowledge needed to properly select or manage an investment. In such instances professional investment advice, or investments where such advice is available, should be considered.

- **How much money is available to be invested?** The investment tools open to an investor can vary, depending on the amount of money available. For example, direct investment in the stock market can require a relatively large investment. Many mutual funds, however, will accept smaller contributions on a monthly basis.

Begin Now or Wait?

Assumptions:

Amount to contribute each month: $500
Number of years to contribute: 15
Rate of return: 6.00%
Number of years until retirement: 25

15 Year Strategy

Begin contributions of $500 today and stop in 15 years. Your total contributions will be $90,000 and your funds will continue to grow until retirement.

21 Years 7 Months Strategy

Defer contributions for 3 Years 5 Months and contribute $500 per month for 21 Years 7 Months. Your total contributions will be $129,674.

Your Total Contributions

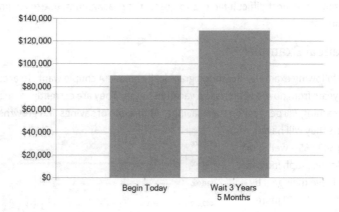

Either way, you can accumulate approximately $266,000 when you are ready to retire.

This is a hypothetical illustration and not a promise of future performance.

Accumulation Goals

Four Key Factors

A savings plan to reach an accumulation goal has four distinct, yet interrelated, factors, each of which contributes to the success or failure of the plan.

- **Contribution amount:** How much is being saved? Should more or less be put aside? Is inflation being considered in future contribution amounts?

- **Rate of return (ROR):** How much is being earned in interest, dividends or capital growth? Can a higher return be earned, without greater risk? How is the growth taxed?

- **Time frame:** How much time remains to reach the goal? Can the time frame be shortened or should it be extended? Compound interest will have its greatest impact in later years. Adding a year or two (or more) can be a tremendous help.

- **Amount of the goal:** Can the goal amount be adjusted? How much is really needed? Sometimes the most difficult factor to adjust is the goal amount, due to an emotional attachment.

A Hypothetical Example[1]

Consider the following example, illustrated graphically below. A couple wants to accumulate $100,000, 20 years from now, to purchase a vacation home. They are currently saving $1,000 per year and earning 7% per year on their savings. At this rate of savings and growth, at the end of 20 years they will have accumulated $43,865 – well short of the goal. As the graph indicates, they could achieve their goal by continuing to save for 10 more years. They don't, however, wish to wait that long.

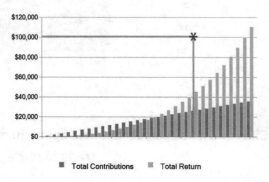

---

[1] The rates of return shown are not indicative of any particular investment and will fluctuate over time.

Small Changes

Now consider how a few coordinated changes can make a difference to the success of the plan. If the couple makes relatively small changes to each of the four factors, the goal can be met. The graph below illustrates the effect of making the following four adjustments:

- Increase their annual contribution to $1,200 – a 20% increase;

- Reallocate their savings to earn an 8% ROR – a 14.3% increase;[1]

- Plan to save for an additional four years – a 20% increase; and

- Reduce the goal from $100,000 to $85,000 – a 15% decrease.

The couple is now on track to meeting their goal. There are, of course, any number of change combinations that can be applied to this example. The right combination will depend on the individuals involved and the importance of the objective.

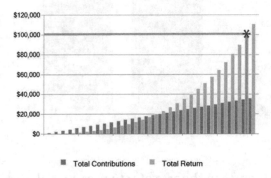

---

[1] A higher rate of return generally involves a greater degree of volatility and risk.

Impact of the Rate of Return

Assumptions:

Initial balance: $25,000

Amount to contribute each month: $10,000

Rate of return: 5.00%

Number of years until retirement: 25

Comparison rate of return: 6.50%

In 25 years at 5.00%, the balance could be $6,066,942, while at 6.50%, the balance could be $7,655,332

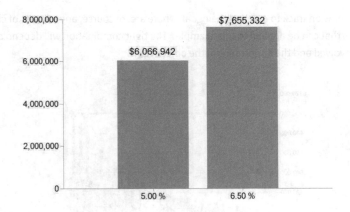

A 1.50% difference in the rate of return can result in an additional 26.18% in value.

This is a hypothetical illustration and not a promise of future performance.
Higher rates of return may imply higher risk.

Cost of Procrastination

Item Description	Value
Desired future sum	$250,000
Annual interest rate[1]	15.00%
Number of years	8

Example

If you wanted to accumulate $250,000 in 8 years, assuming a rate of return of 15.00%, you would need to save $1,361 per month for the next 8 years. If you waited just 5 years, you would need to increase that savings amount to $5,541 per month.

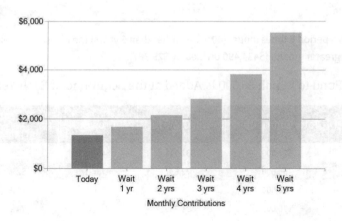

Cost of Procrastination

[1] The rates of return used in this illustration are not indicative of any actual investment and will fluctuate in value. An investment will not provide a consistent rate of return; years with lower (or negative) returns than the hypothetical returns shown may substantially affect the scenario presented.

Time and Growth of Money

Time is a vital factor in accumulating wealth. The following tables illustrate the effect of time and after-tax interest in accumulating funds.

Growth of a Single Lump-Sum Investment

Years of Growth	$20,000 Compounded at	
	5%	8%
5	$25,526	$29,387
10	32,578	43,178
15	41,579	63,443
20	53,066	93,219
25	67,727	136,970
30	86,439	201,253
35	110,320	295,707
40	140,800	434,490

In other words, in a period 8 times longer (40 years rather than 5 years) the investment result at 8% is 15 times greater growth ($434,490 divided by $29,387).

Growth of a Fund to Which $5,500 Is Added at the Beginning of Each Year

$5,500 per Year at 5%	Total Contributed	Will Grow to	Growth	Percent Increase
5	$27,500	$31,911	$4,411	16%
10	55,000	72,637	17,637	32%
15	82,500	124,616	42,116	51%
20	110,000	190,956	80,956	74%
25	137,500	275,624	138,124	100%
30	165,000	383,684	218,684	133%
35	192,500	521,600	329,100	171%
40	220,000	697,619	477,619	217%

These tables assume a 5% rate of return after taxes and that the earnings are reinvested.

Values shown in this presentation are hypothetical and not a promise of future performance.

Future Value of a Single Sum

Item Description	Value
Single sum deposit	$10,000
Annual interest rate[1]	8.00%
How interest is compounded	Monthly
Number of months	360
Amount accumulated at end of period	**$109,357**

Example

If you deposit $10,000 into an account earning an annual return of 8.00%, compounded monthly, then in 360 months your account will grow to $109,357

---

[1] The rates of return used in this illustration are not indicative of any actual investment and will fluctuate in value. An investment will not provide a consistent rate of return; years with lower (or negative) returns than the hypothetical returns shown may substantially affect the scenario presented.

Present Value of a Future Sum

Item Description	Value
Desired future sum	$1,000,000
Annual interest rate[1]	8.00%
How interest is compounded	Monthly
Number of months	360
Present value	**$91,443**

Example

To accumulate $1,000,000 in 360 months earning an annual return of 8.00%, compounded monthly, you will need to deposit a current sum of $91,443.

---

[1] The rates of return used in this illustration are not indicative of any actual investment and will fluctuate in value. An investment will not provide a consistent rate of return; years with lower (or negative) returns than the hypothetical returns shown may substantially affect the scenario presented.

Deposits Needed to Accumulate a Future Sum

Item Description	Value
Current sum (if any)	$10,000
Desired future sum	$1,000,000
Annual interest rate[1]	8.00%
Frequency of deposits	Monthly
Number of months	360
Amount of deposits, if made:	
At the end of each month	$598
At the beginning of each month	$594

Example

To accumulate $1,000,000, with $10,000 to start and earning an annual return of 8.00%, compounded monthly, you will need to deposit $594 at the beginning of each month for 360 months

---

[1] The rates of return used in this illustration are not indicative of any actual investment and will fluctuate in value. An investment will not provide a consistent rate of return; years with lower (or negative) returns than the hypothetical returns shown may substantially affect the scenario presented.

Rate of Return on a Single Sum

Item Description	Value
Value at beginning of period	$100,000
Value at end of period	$125,000
Holding period	36 months
Rate of return[1]	7.46%

Example

If you paid $100,000 for an asset and sold it for $125,000 after owning it for 36 months, your annual rate of return was 7.46% compounded monthly.

---

[1] The rates of return used in this illustration are not indicative of any actual investment and will fluctuate in value. An investment will not provide a consistent rate of return; years with lower (or negative) returns than the hypothetical returns shown may substantially affect the scenario presented.

Future Value of Periodic Deposits

Item Description	Value
Frequency of periodic deposits	Monthly
Monthly deposits	$500
Annual interest rate[1]	8.00%
Number of deposits to make	360

Amount accumulated at end of period if deposits are made:

At the end of each month	**$745,180**
At the beginning of each month	**$750,148**

Example

If you deposit $500 at the beginning of each month into an account earning an annual return of 8.00%, compounded monthly, then in 360 months your account will grow to $750,148

---

[1] The rates of return used in this illustration are not indicative of any actual investment and will fluctuate in value. An investment will not provide a consistent rate of return; years with lower (or negative) returns than the hypothetical returns shown may substantially affect the scenario presented.

Future Value of a Single Sum and Periodic Deposits

Item Description	Value
Single sum deposit	$10,000
Frequency of periodic deposits	Monthly
Monthly deposit	$500
Annual interest rate[1]	8.00%
Number of months to make deposits	360
Future sum, if deposits are made:	
At the end of each month	$854,537
At the beginning of each month	$859,505

Example

If you place $10,000 into an account earning an annual return of 8.00%, compounded monthly, and deposit $500 at the beginning of each month, then in 360 months your account will grow to $859,505

---

[1] The rates of return used in this illustration are not indicative of any actual investment and will fluctuate in value. An investment will not provide a consistent rate of return; years with lower (or negative) returns than the hypothetical returns shown may substantially affect the scenario presented.

Accumulating A Million Dollars

How long does it take to accumulate $1,000,000?

The answer depends on three things.

- How many years are available to accumulate the fund,

- The after-tax rate of return, and

- The method of contribution: One lump sum, or monthly contributions.

The table below shows how long it takes to accumulate $1,000,000 under varying circumstances. The results shown are hypothetical.[1] The actual growth will depend on a number of factors.

Annual Rate of Return (after taxes)

Years	Annual Rate: 2.00%[2]		Annual Rate: 4.00%[2]		Annual Rate: 6.00%[2]		Annual Rate: 8.00%[2]	
	Lump Sum	Monthly	Lump Sum	Monthly	Lump Sum	Monthly	Lump Sum	Monthly
5	$904,913	$15,861	$819,003	$15,083	$741,372	$14,333	$671,210	$13,610
10	818,867	7,535	670,766	6,791	549,633	6,102	450,523	5,466
15	741,003	4,768	549,360	4,064	407,482	3,439	302,396	2,890
20	670,543	3,392	449,927	2,726	302,096	2,164	202,971	1,698
25	606,783	2,572	368,492	1,945	223,966	1,443	136,237	1,051
30	549,086	2,030	301,796	1,441	166,042	996	91,443	671
35	496,875	1,646	247,172	1,094	123,099	702	61,378	436
40	449,628	1,362	202,434	846	91,262	502	41,197	286

Example: If you contribute $2,164 per month to an investment which returns 6% after taxes, you should accumulate $1,000,000 in 20 years. Likewise, if you currently have $302,096 invested at 6% (after-tax) for 20 years, it will grow to $1,000,000 without any additional contribution.

Values shown in this presentation are hypothetical and not a promise of future performance.

---

[1] The calculations shown assume monthly compounding. Monthly contribution amounts are calculated on an end-of-month (ordinary-annuity) basis.

[2] Seeking a higher rate of return generally involves a greater degree of volatility and risk.

The Rule of 72 and the Rule of 115

How Long Will It Take to Double or Triple an Investment?[1]

The rule of 72 is a handy mathematical rule that helps in estimating approximately how many years it will take for an investment to **double** in value at a specified rate of return.

Rule of 72: If 72 is divided by an interest rate, the result is the approximate number of years needed to double the investment. For example, at a 1% rate of return, an investment will double in approximately 72 years; at a 10% rate of return it will take only 7.2 years, etc.

The rule of 115 is similar in that it estimates how long it takes an investment to **triple** in value.

Rule of 115: If 115 is divided by an interest rate, the result is the approximate number of years needed to triple an investment. For example, at a 1% rate of return, an investment will triple in approximately 115 years; at a 10% rate of return it will take only 11.5 years, etc.

Rate of Return	1%	2%	3%	4%	5%	6%	7%	8%	9%	10%	11%
Years to double	72	36	24	18	14.4	12	10.3	9	8	7.2	6.5
Years to triple	115	57.5	38.3	28.8	23	19.2	16.4	14.4	12.8	11.5	10.5

Rate of Return	12%	13%	14%	15%	16%	17%	18%	19%	20%	21%	22%
Years to double	6	5.5	5.1	4.8	4.5	4.2	4	3.8	3.6	3.4	3.3
Years to triple	9.6	8.8	8.2	7.7	7.2	6.8	6.4	6.1	5.8	5.5	5.2

These rules can also tell you how long before a given item will double or triple in price at an estimated average rate of inflation.

For example, at an estimated average inflation rate of 8%, a loaf of bread will double in price every nine years. (72 ÷ 8 = 9).

The examples discussed here are hypothetical illustrations, shown for informational purposes only. They are not intended to represent any specific investment.

---

[1] Investing involves risk, including the possible loss of principal.

Rule of 72

The rule of 72 is a mathematical rule that helps in estimating approximately how many years it will take for an investment to double in value at a specified rate of return.

Item Description	Value
Amount	$100
Interest Rate	5.00%

The approximate number of years to double your funds is 14

Rule of 72

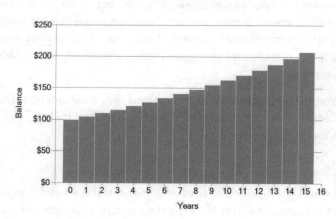

Values shown in this presentation are hypothetical and not a promise of future performance

Types of Investment Risk

Whenever an individual takes cash and puts it to work in any form of investment, he or she does so with the anticipation of receiving a return on the money. At some future point in time, the investor expects to get back both the principal amount and something extra as well. The possibility that an investment will return less than expected is known as "investment risk."

Risk vs. Reward

One of the general truths of the investment world is that risk and reward go hand in hand. The greater the risk an investor is willing to undertake, the greater the potential reward. If an investor is willing to assume only a small amount of risk, the potential reward is also low. In an ideal world, there would be no risk to any investment. Unfortunately, such a risk-free investment does not exist.

There is also more than one type of risk. An investor must understand each type of risk, and use that knowledge to create a portfolio of investments that balances the level of risk assumed, with the desired investment return.

Market Risk

In simple terms, market risk can be defined as the possibility that downward changes in the market price of an investment will result in a loss of principal for an investor. For many, market risk is most closely associated with the ups and downs of the stock market.

Market risk exists for other investments as well. For example, the market price of bonds and other debt investments will move up and down in response to changes in the general level of interest rates. If interest rates rise, bond prices generally fall. If interest rates decline, bond prices generally rise. Tangible assets such as real estate and gold, or collectibles such as art or stamps, also face market risk.

Over time, a number of strategies have been developed to help reduce market risk.

- Invest only dollars that are not required to meet current needs. This helps avoid having to sell an asset when the market may be down.

- Develop a long-term approach. A longer time horizon allows an investor to ride out market ups and downs.

- Diversify your investments over a number of asset categories, such as stocks, bonds, or cash, and tangible investments such as real estate. Holding assets in different investment categories reduces the possibility that all investments will be down at the same time.

Inflation Risk

For many individuals, safety of principal is the primary goal when deciding where to place investment funds. Such investors frequently put much of their money in bank savings accounts, CDs or T-Bills. While such investments can provide protection from market risk, they do not provide much protection from inflation risk. An investor may hold the same number of dollars; over time, however, those dollars buy less and less.

For example, consider a hypothetical investor who places $10,000 in a 10-year certificate of deposit, earning 2.00% per year. The table below summarizes the effect of a 3.00% annual inflation rate on the purchasing power of these dollars.

End of Year	CD Value at End of Year[1] (2%)	Purchasing Power at 3% Inflation Rate[2]	"Real" Value of CD	"Loss" Due to Inflation
1	$10,200	97.09%	$9,903	$297
2	$10,404	94.26%	$9,807	$597
3	$10,612	91.51%	$9,712	$901
4	$10,824	88.85%	$9,617	$1,207
5	$11,041	86.26%	$9,524	$1,517
6	$11,262	83.75%	$9,431	$1,830
7	$11,487	81.31%	$9,340	$2,147
8	$11,717	78.94%	$9,249	$2,467
9	$11,951	76.64%	$9,159	$2,792
10	$12,190	74.41%	$9,070	$3,119

Values shown in this presentation are hypothetical and not a promise of future performance.

---

[1] Assumes a 2.0% annual after-tax return, and that interest is reinvested at the same rate of return.
[2] To calculate, divide previous year's percentage by (1+.03). Example: 1.00 / 1.03 = .9709; .9709 / 1.03 = .9426.

Over the 10-year period, inflation reduces the purchasing power of the investor's dollars by more than 25%. The impact of income taxes, ignored in this example, would further decrease the investor's net return.

While there are ways to potentially shield your portfolio from inflation risk, most involve a higher level of market risk:

- Consider placing a portion of your assets in the stock market.

- Historically, tangible assets such as real estate or gold have tended to do well in periods of high inflation.

Other Common Risk Types

In addition to market and inflation risk, there are a number of other common types of risk that each investor must be aware of:

- **Credit risk:** This is also known as "default risk." The chance that the issuer of a bond or other debt-type instrument will not be able to carry out its contractual obligations. Keeping maturities short, diversifying investments among various companies, and investing in institutions and issues of the highest credit rating are common methods used to help control this type of risk.

- **Liquidity risk:** This risk is the possibility that an investor will not be able to sell or liquidate an asset, without losing a part of the principal, because there is an imbalance between the number of buyers and sellers, or because an asset is not traded very often. Choosing investments traded on an active market, and limiting investments to funds not needed for current expenses are approaches used to help lessen this risk.

- **Interest rate risk:** This is defined as the risk that an increase in the general level of interest rates will cause the market value of existing investments to fall. Generally, this risk applies to bonds and other debt-type instruments, which move opposite to interest rates. As interest rates rise, bond prices tend to fall, and vice versa. One approach to reducing this risk is to stagger or ladder the maturities in the portfolio so that a portion of the portfolio matures periodically, rather than all at the same time. Holding a security until maturity, at which time it is redeemable at full value, is also useful.

- **Tax risk:** This refers to the possibility that a change in tax law, at either the federal, state or local level, will change the tax characteristics of an investment. After such a legislative change, an investment may no longer meet an individual's needs. In some cases, new legislation has included a grandfather clause allowing current investors to continue under the old rules. Making an investment because it's a good investment, rather than focusing on the tax benefits, is an excellent way to help reduce this risk.

Monte Carlo Simulation

Because the future is both uncertain and unknowable, investment planning frequently involves efforts to simulate or "model" the future. Given certain investment decisions, how likely is it that a particular portfolio will succeed in reaching the goals set for it? For example, will a portfolio provide enough retirement income to last the owner's lifetime? Will the expected investment results pay for a child's education?

One way to analyze such questions is through use of a "Monte Carlo" simulation.

What is a Monte Carlo Simulation?

From a theoretical perspective, a Monte Carlo[1] simulation is a method of estimating the probable outcome of an event in which one or more of the variables affecting the outcome are chosen randomly. The essence of the Monte Carlo process is to simulate a process or event many times. During each simulation, the variables which affect the outcome are allowed to fluctuate according to pre-selected criteria. The outcome of each simulation is then ranked according to the likelihood of its occurrence.

As a very simple example, how often would an individual player win at the card game Solitaire? The Monte Carlo approach would have the individual play 100 (or even more) games of Solitaire and then record the results. The number of successful plays is the "probability" of winning the game.

Monte Carlo Simulation and the Investment World

In the investment world, a Monte Carlo simulation is useful in helping an individual investor understand the role that risk plays in portfolio selection and design. Investing does involve risk, including the possible loss of principal.

For example, rates of return for stocks, bonds, and other investments will vary from year to year. Depending on the historical time frame chosen, a particular investment will have good years and bad years. From this historical data, it is possible to calculate the highs, lows, and average rates of return for the investment. The analysis will also determine how widely the annual rates of return varied from the average, resulting in a distribution of probable rates of return around the average.

---

[1] The name "Monte Carlo" derives from a code name given to this type of analysis by scientists working on nuclear weapons projects in the 1940s.

Monte Carlo Simulation

To estimate the return that a particular investment or portfolio could achieve over a future time period, a Monte Carlo simulation randomly generates a rate of return for each year in the analysis, based on the historical distribution of probable rates of return. In more complex simulations, economic data such as inflation, withdrawals and contributions, and income tax rates are also included. This process is repeated numerous times until the simulation is completed; sometimes thousands of simulations are run. The result of each simulation is then ranked by percentiles. In the case of a retirement analysis, "success" would be measured by having enough money to last until the expected mortality. Failure would be running out of money early.

A Monte Carlo simulation is useful in portfolio design in that multiple scenarios can be simulated, with varying portfolio mixes.

What Does a Monte Carlo Simulation Look Like?

The graph below shows the results of a typical Monte Carlo simulation:

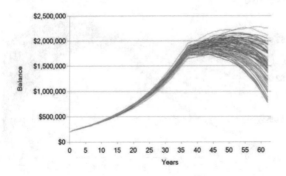

Limitations of the Monte Carlo Simulation Methodology

All hypothetical projections of future investment results, of whatever type, should be regarded as only approximations or a "best guess" as to what the future might bring. Although a carefully constructed Monte Carlo simulation can shed light on the potential risks and rewards of a particular investment or portfolio, it should not be regarded as predictive or a guarantee of future results.

Seek Professional Guidance

When addressing any investment or planning question, the guidance of trained, experienced financial professionals is strongly recommended.

Monte Carlo Simulator

Assumptions:

Current Age: 40
Retirement Age: 65
Mortality Age: 90

Initial Balance: $500,000
Monthly Savings: $1,000
Monthly Income Needs $4,000

Average Rate of Return: 6.00%
Standard Deviation: 2

Randomize Inflation: true

- Average Inflation: 4.00%
- Standard Deviation: 2

Number of Simulations: 500

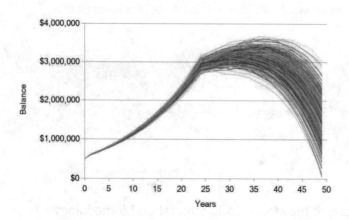

Inflation

Inflation is the annual increase in the price of goods and services as measured by the federal government. The graph[1] below illustrates the annual percentage change every other year since the base year of 1967. Over the last 50 years, the average annual inflation rate in the U.S. has been 3.85%.

Annual Inflation Rates

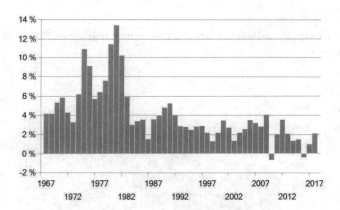

[1] Source: U.S. Bureau of Labor Statistics (CPI-W) (1967 - 2017).

Effect of Inflation

Over the last 50 years, the average annual inflation rate in the U.S. has been 3.85%.[1]

Item Description	Value
Average annual inflation rate	2.00%
Number of years from now	20
Current item cost	$100
Future item cost	**$149**

Example

Assuming an average annual inflation rate of 2.00%, an item which costs $100 today will cost $149 in 20 year(s).

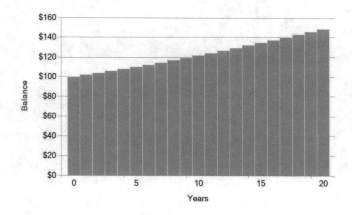

[1] Source: U.S. Bureau of Labor Statistics, Consumer Price Index for Urban Wage Earners and Clerical Workers (CPI-W); U.S. City Average. 1967-2017.

Rate of Inflation

Over the last 50 years, the average annual inflation rate in the U.S. has been 3.85%.[1]

Item Description	Value
Future item cost	$125
Current item cost	$100
Number of years from now	20
Annual inflation rate	**1.12%**

Example

If an item costs $125, 20 year(s) from now and currently costs $100, it will experience an average annual inflation rate of 1.12%.

---

[1] Source: U.S. Bureau of Labor Statistics, Consumer Price Index for Urban Wage Earners and Clerical Workers (CPI-W); U.S. City Average. 1967-2017.

Investment Loss Due to Inflation

Assumptions:

Amount of investment: $50,000
Annual investment return: 6.5%
Annual inflation rate: 4.0%

Even though your investment may be growing,

it may not be growing as fast as you think.

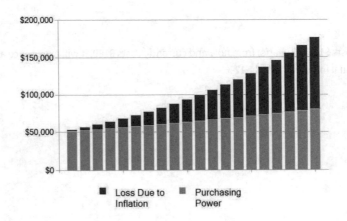

Loss over 20 years due to inflation: $95,775

Wash Sales

As the end of a tax year approaches, individual investors will occasionally enter into tax-oriented transactions.[1] Losing investments are sold, with the losses used to offset income received from selling positions with gains. The net result may be a gain (generally subject to tax at marginal rates up to 20%),[2] a loss (generally limited to a maximum deduction against other income of $3,000 per year), or a situation where gains equal losses. Such transactions are commonly referred to as "tax-loss harvesting."

It is possible for an individual to sell a losing investment and then immediately repurchase the same investment. He or she will have "harvested" the tax loss, but, by quickly re-purchasing identical securities, will have maintained an unchanged economic position. However, using losses from such transactions, known as "wash sales", to offset gains or other income, is prohibited by IRC Sec. 1091.

What is a "Wash Sale"?

For income tax purposes, a wash sale refers to the loss from a sale or other disposition of shares of stock or securities where the seller, within a period beginning <u>30 days before the date of such sale</u> or disposition, and ending <u>30 days after such date</u>, has acquired (by purchase or an exchange on which the entire amount of gain or loss was recognized by law)[3] or has entered into a contract or option to acquire "substantially identical" stock or securities.[4]

> Example #1 – George holds 100 shares of XYZ Corp. purchased two years before for $10 a share, or a total of $1,000. He sells the 100 shares of XYZ Corp. on December 6, for $500, resulting in a loss of $500. Two days later, on December 8, he re-purchases 100 shares of XYZ Corp. for $600. This is considered a "wash sale" as George re-purchased the 100 shares of XYZ Corp. within 30 days of selling his original position. If he wants to avoid the wash sale rules, George will have to wait until at least January 6 (31 days after the sale) of the following year to re-purchase the stock.

---

[1] The discussion here concerns federal income tax law. State or local income tax law may differ.

[2] The 3.8% Tax on Net Investment Income could cause the marginal rate on capital gains to exceed 20%.

[3] For example, an inheritance, a gift, or a tax-free exchange.

[4] IRC Sec.1091 (a) provides a specific exemption for a taxpayer who "is a dealer in stock or securities and the loss is sustained in a transaction made in the ordinary course of such business."

Substantially Identical Stock or Securities

A key factor in determining if the wash sale rules apply to a transaction is whether or not the replacement stock or securities purchased are "substantially identical" to those sold. The code and regulations are vague as to what constitutes substantially identical stock or securities. In general a "facts and circumstances" test applies in making this determination, although a few broad guidelines are available:

- The stocks or securities of one corporation are not ordinarily considered substantially identical to stocks or securities of another corporation.

- In certain situations stocks of two different corporations may be substantially identical. For example, in the case of a corporate re-organization the facts and circumstances may be such that the stocks and securities of predecessor and successor corporations are substantially identical property.

- Bonds or preferred stock of a corporation are not ordinarily considered substantially identical to the common stock of the same corporation. If the bonds or preferred stock are convertible into the common stock of the same corporation, the relative values, price changes, and other circumstances may be such as to make such bonds or preferred stock and the common stock substantially identical.

- The term "stock or securities" generally includes contracts or options to acquire or sell stock or securities.

- In general, bonds are not considered to be substantially identical if they are substantially different in any material feature or because of differences in several material features considered together. Such features could include the interest rate, maturity date, or any differences in the bonds as they existed on the date of sale or purchase.

Basis Adjustment

If a transaction is considered to be a wash sale, the basis of the newly acquired stock or securities is increased to include the disallowed loss from the prior sale:

Example #2 – Recall the facts of example 1. George holds a long-term position of 100 shares of XYZ Corp., with a basis of $1,000. He sells his 100 shares for $500 on

December 6, creating a long-term loss of $500. He then re-purchases 100 shares of XYZ Corp. two days later, on December 8 for $600. Because this is a wash sale (both transactions occurred within the 61 day window), George's basis in the newly acquired shares is $1,100, the $500 disallowed loss added to the $600 paid to acquire the new shares.

Holding Period

The holding period for the replacement substantially identical stock or securities includes the holding period for the original stock or securities.

Example #3 – Recall the facts of examples 1 and 2. George holds a long-term position of 100 shares of XYZ Corp., with a basis of $1,000. He sells his 100 shares for $500 on December 6, creating a long-term loss of $500. He then re-purchases 100 shares of XYZ Corp. two days later, on December 8 for $600. Because this is a wash sale, George's basis in the newly acquired shares is $1,100, a combination of the $500 disallowed loss and the $600 paid to acquire the new shares. George's holding period for the shares purchased on December 8 incudes the holding period of the previous lot, making it long-term. If he then sells the 100 shares of XYZ Corp. for $1,200, on January 8, he will have a long-term capital gain of $100 ($1,200 - $1,100) even though he will have owned the new shares only one month.

Other Points

There are a number of additional points to keep in mind with regard to wash sales:

- **Short sales:** The wash sale rules also apply to short sales. Thus, if a loss is incurred on the *closing* of a short sale, and the investor sells (or enters into another short sale) substantially identical stock or securities in the period 30 days before or 30 days after closing the short sale, the loss will be disallowed.

- **More than one loss:** If there is more than one loss in a tax year, the wash sale rules are applied to the losses in the order in which they occur.

- **More sold than acquired:** If more shares are sold than were later acquired, the loss is disallowed only to the extent that replacement stock or securities are acquired. Any remaining loss is generally deductible.

- **More acquired than sold:** If more shares are acquired than were sold, the entire loss is disallowed.

- **Traditional and Roth IRAs:** In Revenue Ruling 2008-5, the Internal Revenue Service (IRS) reviewed a case in which the taxpayer sold stock at a loss and then caused his IRA to acquire identical securities within the 30 day period after the sale. The IRS determined that the taxpayer's loss was not deductible and that the basis of the acquired securities within the IRA was <u>not</u> increased, as would normally have been the case.

Seek Professional Guidance

Because of the complexities involved, the guidance of income tax, investment, and other financial professionals is strongly recommended.

Purchasing Power of One Dollar

The Consumer Price Index is the government's method of measuring the price of goods and services bought by urban wage earners and clerical workers. The graph[1] below charts the decline in the purchasing power of one dollar since 1967, as a result of inflation. Over the last 50 years, the average annual inflation rate in the U.S. has been 3.85%.

Consumer Price Index

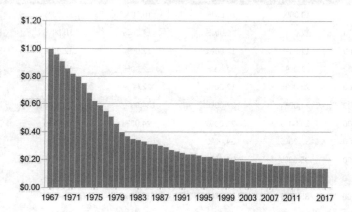

---

[1] Source: U.S. Bureau of Labor Statistics (CPI-W) (1967 – 2017).

The Real Rate of Return Worksheet

To determine the real rate of return on an investment, one must consider the effect of inflation and taxes on the gross return.

Worksheet for 2018

Taxable Income	Single	Married Filing Jointly	Married Filing Separate	Head of Household	Estate or Trust
$6,000	10.00%	10.00%	10.00%	10.00%	24.00%
$10,000	12.00%	10.00%	12.00%	10.00%	35.00%
$25,000	12.00%	12.00%	12.00%	12.00%	37.00%
$50,000	22.00%	12.00%	22.00%	12.00%	37.00%
$75,000	22.00%	12.00%	22.00%	22.00%	37.00%
$100,000	24.00%	22.00%	24.00%	24.00%	37.00%
$125,000	24.00%	22.00%	24.00%	24.00%	37.00%
$175,000	32.00%	24.00%	32.00%	32.00%	37.00%
$200,000	35.00%	24.00%	35.00%	35.00%	37.00%
$300,000	35.00%	24.00%	37.00%	35.00%	37.00%
$400,000	35.00%	35.00%	37.00%	35.00%	37.00%
$500,000	37.00%	35.00%	37.00%	37.00%	37.00%

1. In a perfect world you would be able to keep 100% of your investment return. 1.000

2. Determine your marginal tax bracket from the table above.
   Enter your marginal bracket as a decimal, e.g., 24.00% = .240. _____

3. Subtract line 2 from line 1. This is the percentage left after taxes are paid. _____

4. Enter the before-tax return on the investment as a decimal, e.g., 10% = .10. _____

5. **After-tax return** - Multiply line 3 times line 4. _____

6. Enter an estimated average annual inflation rate, as a decimal _____
   e.g., 5.0% = .05.[1]

7. **Real rate of return** $= \left(\frac{1 + \text{after tax return}}{1 + \text{inflation}} \right) - 1$ _____

---

[1] If line 6 is larger than line 5, there is a negative rate of return on the investment.

The Real Rate of Return Worksheet

Example: Marginal tax bracket = 24% (line 2 = .2400). Line 3 = (1.000-.2400) = .7600. Before-tax return, line 4, = 8.0%, expressed as .0800. The after-tax return, line 5, = (.7600 x .0800) = .0608. Inflation on line 6 is assumed to be 2.0%, expressed as .0200. Line 7 is thus ((1.0608/1.020)-1) = (1.0400-1) = .0400. Multiplied by 100, the "Real Rate of Return" = 4.0%.

How much must you earn on an investment (the gross return) to obtain your desired real rate of return (after taxes and inflation)? The examples shown below are hypothetical.

Assuming 2.0% Inflation

Approx. Tax Bracket	Break Even	Desired Real Rate of Return						
		2.00%	4.00%	6.00%	8.00%	10.00%	12.00%	14.00%
0.00%	2.0%	4.0%	6.0%	8.0%	10.0%	12.0%	14.0%	16.0%
10.00%	2.2%	4.4%	6.7%	8.9%	11.1%	13.3%	15.6%	17.8%
12.00%	2.3%	4.5%	6.8%	9.1%	11.4%	13.6%	15.9%	18.2%
22.00%	2.6%	5.1%	7.7%	10.3%	12.8%	15.4%	17.9%	20.5%
24.00%	2.6%	5.3%	7.9%	10.5%	13.2%	15.8%	18.4%	21.1%
32.00%	2.9%	5.9%	8.8%	11.8%	14.7%	17.6%	20.6%	23.5%
35.00%	3.1%	6.2%	9.2%	12.3%	15.4%	18.5%	21.5%	24.6%
37.00%	3.2%	6.3%	9.5%	12.7%	15.9%	19.0%	22.2%	25.4%

Assuming 4.0% Inflation

Approx. Tax Bracket	Break Even	Desired Real Rate of Return						
		2.00%	4.00%	6.00%	8.00%	10.00%	12.00%	14.00%
0.00%	4.0%	6.0%	8.0%	10.0%	12.0%	14.0%	16.0%	18.0%
10.00%	4.4%	6.7%	8.9%	11.1%	13.3%	15.6%	17.8%	20.0%
12.00%	4.5%	6.8%	9.1%	11.4%	13.6%	15.9%	18.2%	20.5%
22.00%	5.1%	7.7%	10.3%	12.8%	15.4%	17.9%	20.5%	23.1%
24.00%	5.3%	7.9%	10.5%	13.2%	15.8%	18.4%	21.1%	23.7%
32.00%	5.9%	8.8%	11.8%	14.7%	17.6%	20.6%	23.5%	26.5%
35.00%	6.2%	9.2%	12.3%	15.4%	18.5%	21.5%	24.6%	27.7%
37.00%	6.3%	9.5%	12.7%	15.9%	19.0%	22.2%	25.4%	28.6%

The Real Rate of Return Worksheet

Assuming 6.0% Inflation

Approx. Tax Bracket	Break Even	Desired Real Rate of Return						
		2.00%	4.00%	6.00%	8.00%	10.00%	12.00%	14.00%
0.00%	6.0%	8.0%	10.0%	12.0%	14.0%	16.0%	18.0%	20.0%
10.00%	6.7%	8.9%	11.1%	13.3%	15.6%	17.8%	20.0%	22.2%
12.00%	6.8%	9.1%	11.4%	13.6%	15.9%	18.2%	20.5%	22.7%
22.00%	7.7%	10.3%	12.8%	15.4%	17.9%	20.5%	23.1%	25.6%
24.00%	7.9%	10.5%	13.2%	15.8%	18.4%	21.1%	23.7%	26.3%
32.00%	8.8%	11.8%	14.7%	17.6%	20.6%	23.5%	26.5%	29.4%
35.00%	9.2%	12.3%	15.4%	18.5%	21.5%	24.6%	27.7%	30.8%
37.00%	9.5%	12.7%	15.9%	19.0%	22.2%	25.4%	28.6%	31.7%

Values shown in this presentation are hypothetical and not a promise of future performance.

The Real Rate of Return

To determine the real rate of return on an investment, one must consider the effect of inflation and taxes on the gross return.

Assumptions:

Tax year: 2018

Taxable income: $82,000

Filing status: Married filing joint

Marginal income tax bracket: 22.00%

Estimated average inflation rate: 2.00%

Item Description	Value
Before-tax investment return	9.00%
Percentage left after taxes at 22.00%	78.00%
After-tax return	7.02%
Real rate of return at 2.00% inflation rate	**4.92%**

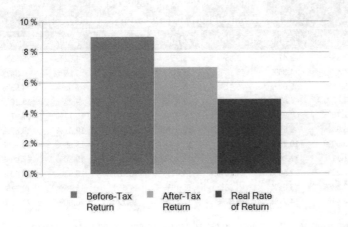

Values shown in this presentation are hypothetical and not a promise of future performance.

Tax-Exempt vs. Taxable Income Tables

The following charts allow you to compare the returns on tax-exempt investments to those that are taxable. After determining your marginal federal income tax bracket on the top chart, locate the taxable or tax-exempt return of interest in the lower tables.

Filing Status	Taxable Income[1] up to:						
	10.00%	12.00%	22.00%	24.00%	32.00%	35.00%	37.00%
Single	$9,525	$38,700	$82,500	$157,500	$200,000	$500,000	$500,000+
Married filing joint	$19,050	$77,400	$165,000	$315,000	$400,000	$600,000	$600,000+
Married filing separate	$9,525	$38,700	$82,500	$157,500	$200,000	$300,000	$300,000+
Head of household	$13,600	$51,800	$82,500	$157,500	$200,000	$500,000	$500,000+
Estates and trusts	$2,550	N/A	N/A	$9,150	N/A	$12,500	$12,500+

Tax-Exempt Return	Taxable Return Required to Equal a Tax-Exempt Return at Various Top Tax Brackets						
	10.00%	12.00%	22.00%	24.00%	32.00%	35.00%	37.00%
3%	3.33%	3.41%	3.85%	3.95%	4.41%	4.62%	5.13%
4%	4.44%	4.55%	5.13%	5.26%	5.88%	6.15%	6.84%
5%	5.56%	5.68%	6.41%	6.58%	7.35%	7.69%	8.55%
6%	6.67%	6.82%	7.69%	7.89%	8.82%	9.23%	10.26%
7%	7.78%	7.95%	8.97%	9.21%	10.29%	10.77%	11.97%
8%	8.89%	9.09%	10.26%	10.53%	11.76%	12.31%	13.68%
9%	10.00%	10.23%	11.54%	11.84%	13.24%	13.85%	15.38%
10%	11.11%	11.36%	12.82%	13.16%	14.71%	15.38%	17.09%
11%	12.22%	12.50%	14.10%	14.47%	16.18%	16.92%	18.80%
12%	13.33%	13.64%	15.38%	15.79%	17.65%	18.46%	20.51%
13%	14.44%	14.77%	16.67%	17.11%	19.12%	20.00%	22.22%

Values shown in this presentation are hypothetical and not a promise of future performance.

---

[1] 2018 federal income tax rates are shown.

Tax-Exempt vs. Taxable Income Tables

Taxable Return	Tax-Exempt Return Required to Equal a Taxable Return at Various Top Tax Brackets						
	10.00%	12.00%	22.00%	24.00%	32.00%	35.00%	37.00%
3%	2.70%	2.64%	2.34%	2.28%	2.04%	1.95%	1.76%
4%	3.60%	3.52%	3.12%	3.04%	2.72%	2.60%	2.34%
5%	4.50%	4.40%	3.90%	3.80%	3.40%	3.25%	2.93%
6%	5.40%	5.28%	4.68%	4.56%	4.08%	3.90%	3.51%
7%	6.30%	6.16%	5.46%	5.32%	4.76%	4.55%	4.10%
8%	7.20%	7.04%	6.24%	6.08%	5.44%	5.20%	4.68%
9%	8.10%	7.92%	7.02%	6.84%	6.12%	5.85%	5.27%
10%	9.00%	8.80%	7.80%	7.60%	6.80%	6.50%	5.85%
11%	9.90%	9.68%	8.58%	8.36%	7.48%	7.15%	6.44%
12%	10.80%	10.56%	9.36%	9.12%	8.16%	7.80%	7.02%
13%	11.70%	11.44%	10.14%	9.88%	8.84%	8.45%	7.61%
14%	12.60%	12.32%	10.92%	10.64%	9.52%	9.10%	8.19%

Values shown in this presentation are hypothetical and not a promise of future performance.

Tax-Exempt vs. Taxable Income

Item Description	Value
Combined federal and state marginal income tax bracket	45.00%
Rate of return on taxable investment	9.00%
Required rate of return on tax-free to match taxable	4.95%
Rate of return on tax-free investment	6.00%
Required rate of return on taxable to match tax-free	10.91%

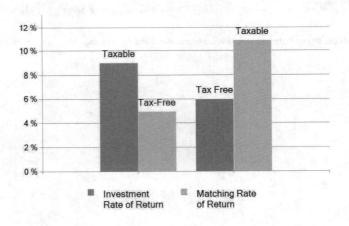

Pyramid of Investments

An investment program should be built like a pyramid - with a strong, broad base. As your potential reward increases so does the potential risk.

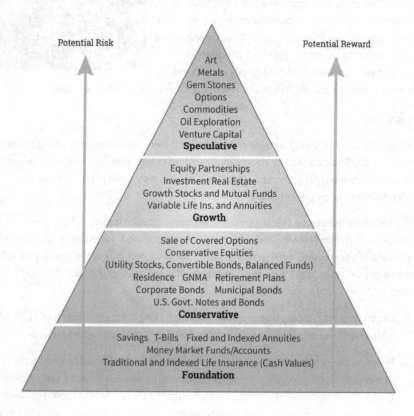

Note: This pyramid is intended solely to illustrate a concept; it is not a promise of investment performance. Investors may differ on the risk level to which a particular asset is assigned. Before making any investment in mutual funds, variable life insurance, or variable annuities, you should be sure to read the appropriate prospectus or offering documents for a complete discussion of the fees and risks involved.

Basic Investment Tools

Individuals with investable funds often have a desire to put those "extra" dollars to work to meet a specific purpose. For some, there may be a desire to accumulate funds for a future purchase, or a need to generate more income to pay current expenses. For others, it may be to put money aside for a "rainy day," or simply to "get rich." Whatever the investment goal, an investor should clearly understand both the role and the potential risks and rewards of each type of investment tool.

Stocks

The terms "stock" and "share" both refer to a fractional ownership interest in a corporation. As "owners," stockholders vote for the company's Board of Directors, and receive information on the firm's activities and business results. Stockholders may share in profits through "dividends" declared by the firm's Board.

When a corporate business is first organized, investors contribute money to fund the enterprise, and in return receive shares of stock representing their ownership in the company. If the business is successful, it will grow and have increasing profits, and the shares generally become more valuable. If the business is not successful, the value of the shares usually declines.

- **Uses:** Investors typically buy and hold stock for its long-term growth potential. Stocks with a history of regular dividends are often held for both income and growth.

- **Risks:** As the long-term growth of a company cannot be predicted, the short-term market value of the company's stock will fluctuate up and down. If the market price of the stock is higher than the purchase price when the stock is sold, a capital gain will result. If the market price of the stock is lower than the purchase price when the stock is sold, the result will be a capital loss.

Bonds

While stocks represent ownership in a business, bonds are debt. Issued by institutions such as the federal government, corporations, and state and local governments, a bond is evidence of money borrowed by the bond issuer. In return, bondholders receive interest and, at "maturity," the principal amount of the bond.

When first issued, a bond will have a specified rate of return, or "yield." For example, a 6.0% bond will pay $60.00 per year for each $1,000 invested. If a bond is traded on a public exchange, the market price will fluctuate, generally with changes in interest rates. Later investors will receive a yield that may be more, or less, than 6.0%, depending on the price paid for the bond in the open market.

- **Uses:** Bonds are typically bought by investors seeking current income. In some instances, bonds are also used for capital growth.

- **Risks:** Like stocks, the market price of bonds will fluctuate up and down. If an investor sells a bond before it matures, a capital gain or loss may result. Unless the issuer defaults, bonds held to maturity will recover the principal amount. Since a bond pays a fixed return, inflation risk can be a problem; over time, the dollars received will buy less and less. Also, the interest income received may be subject to current income taxation.

Savings Accounts

Most investors are familiar with a savings account at a bank, savings and loan, or credit union. For many, the generic term "savings account" includes both the traditional savings account (allowing for deposits and withdrawals of small amounts), as well as fixed-term certificates of deposit (CDs), for larger sums. Savings accounts are usually prized by investors for two primary characteristics: safety of principal, and liquidity. Such accounts are insured (against a failure of the savings institution) by agencies of the Federal government, such as the Federal Deposit Insurance Corporation (FDIC) or the National Credit Union Administration (NCUA), for up to $250,000 per account.

- **Uses:** Savings accounts are often used as a reservoir for emergency funds, or as a "warehouse" for dollars ultimately earmarked for some other purpose. Some investors also use such accounts to generate current income.

- **Risks:** Because there is little risk of principal loss, savings accounts typically have a lower yield than other investments. One "risk" to such accounts is the potential additional interest income foregone in exchange for safety of principal. The relatively low yield can also be heavily impacted by inflation and current income taxes.

Life Insurance

In the last several decades, the life insurance industry has developed a number of products that combine the protection of life insurance death benefits, with a significant cash value element. Policies such as universal life, indexed universal life, variable life, and variable universal life allow an individual to purchase a single financial instrument providing for both life insurance and long-term accumulation goals. Such policies may serve as a form of "forced investment" for those who find it difficult to put funds aside on a regular basis, but who routinely pay their bills. Additionally, life insurance company "annuities," either fixed annuities, variable annuities, or indexed annuities, offer a tax-deferred method of accumulating additional retirement funds.

- **Uses:** While life insurance products are primarily used for death benefit protection, they are commonly used for long-term accumulation goals. Available cash values may also serve as an "emergency reserve," if needed, or a source of loans, since life policies frequently include features permitting borrowing against these cash values.[1]

- **Risks:** Fixed contracts rely on the financial strength of the issuing life insurance company. Inflation may negatively impact a fixed return contract. Variable contracts share the risks of the underlying investments. Loans and withdrawals must be carefully structured to avoid negative income tax results.[1]

Real Estate

Real estate has long been a favored investment for those seeking tax benefits and a hedge against inflation. "Improved" real estate refers to land with apartments, a home, office, store, or other rentable enhancement. Rental income in excess of expenses may provide a "positive" cash flow. Additionally, depreciation may shelter a portion of the cash flow from current income tax. If all goes well, inflation will gradually increase rental income, thus raising the market value of the property.

Real estate investors may also choose to invest in "unimproved" or "raw" land. Typically such land generates no current cash flow, unless rented for agricultural purposes such as animal grazing or farming. Investors in raw land usually try to buy property in the path of expected, long-term growth, with the hope of selling the property at a gain when future demand pushes market prices up.

---

[1] A policy loan or withdrawal will generally reduce cash values and death benefits. If a policy lapses or is surrendered with a loan outstanding, the loan will be treated as taxable income in the current year, to the extent of gain in the policy. Policies considered to be modified endowment contracts (MECs) are subject to special rules.

- **Uses:** Investors in improved real estate typically seek tax-sheltered, current income along with long-term capital growth. Investors in unimproved real estate primarily seek long-term capital gains. Real estate serves as a hedge against inflation.

- **Risks:** An investor may find it difficult to keep a property rented, and thus not receive the expected cash flow. Deflation may decrease both rents and property values. Expected long-term growth in a geographical area may not occur. Real estate can be very illiquid; a quick sale may require a substantial reduction in price. Changes in tax law may reduce or eliminate anticipated tax benefits.

Gold

For centuries gold has served as an enduring store of value during periods of political and social turmoil. It has also functioned to preserve purchasing power during times of high inflation. Demand for gold, for jewelry and industrial purposes, also impacts the price of gold.

There are a number of different ways for an individual to invest in gold. For example, an investor can purchase bars of gold bullion (gold refined to a high level of purity). Gold bullion coins, such as the South African Kruggerand or U.S. Eagle offer a more portable way to own the metal. Risk-oriented speculators can participate in gold markets indirectly via gold futures on commodities exchanges. More conservative individuals may choose to invest in mutual funds which specialize in the stocks of companies mining gold.

- **Uses:** Gold serves as a permanent store of value during periods of economic and political anxiety. It also acts as a hedge against inflation.

- **Risks:** The market value of gold can fluctuate widely. Selling gold when the market is down can result in a capital loss. It can be difficult to own and protect. Direct ownership provides no current income.

Alternative Investments

Most investors are familiar with what can be called "traditional" investments, i.e. stocks, bonds, or cash. However, many will not be familiar with what are termed "alternative" investments.

Categories of Alternative Investments

Although there is no universally accepted definition of an alternative investment, there are a number of broad, general categories which are generally recognized as being alternative investments.

- **Real estate:** Investing in real estate frequently includes rental of residential or commercial property. Real estate investment also embraces raw land, farm land, and may include timberland, although any standing timber is typically not considered real property. Real estate investments may also involve different types of improved real property such as toll roads, airports, or ports which are traditionally owned and/or controlled by government, but which in some situations have been "privatized."

- **Commodities/natural resources:** Commodities are homogenous products that satisfy an economic need or want and which are usually traded in large quantities. Examples include agricultural products such as corn, wheat, or cotton, energy products such as electricity or oil and gas, or metals such as aluminum or copper. Much investing in commodities is through commodity "futures," buying and selling contracts for the purchase or sale (at some *future* time) of the commodity involved. Investing in commodities can also be done through exchange traded funds or natural resource companies.

- **Hedge funds:** In general terms, a hedge fund is a private investment corporation or partnership that provides investors the opportunity to participate in specialized, flexible, and often risky trading strategies, to take advantage of perceived opportunities in the stock, bond, and other markets.

- **Private equity:** Private equity refers to different types of ownership or investment strategies involving privately-held investment companies. Equity financing of new, start-up businesses is referred to as "venture capital." A "leveraged buyout" is used to take a publicly-held company private, typically with a small amount of investor capital supplemented by a large amount of borrowed funds. The term "mezzanine" debt refers to mid-level (in a firm's capital structure) debt such as preferred stock, convertible debt, or debt that may benefit if the company does well financially. Debt of a company that has, or is expected, to file for bankruptcy is called "distressed" debt.

- **Structured products:** Structured products are investments created for specific investment purposes. Collateralized debt obligations (CDO) are a good example of a structured product. In a CDO, debt obligations – such as real estate mortgages or other debt – are pooled together and "tranches" (slices) of the pool are sold to investors who ultimately receive interest and principal payments as the debts are repaid. Certain tranches are senior to others. If some borrowers default, resulting in less cash flow, some junior tranches may not be paid.

- **Speculative:** Speculative assets are assets that do not generate a current return (such as cash), but which are expected to increase in value over time. Gold bullion, fine art, stamps, and other collectibles are common examples of speculative assets. Successful investment in a speculative asset requires that the asset appreciate in value at a rate sufficient to cover any management, storage, insurance, or transaction costs.

Characteristics of Alternative Investments

Alternative investments share certain characteristics that set them apart from traditional investments:

- **Low correlation to traditional assets:** A key concept underlying Modern Portfolio Theory (MPT) is that of building an investment portfolio from various investment types that exhibit low "correlation" to each other. Correlation refers to how a particular asset changes in value in relation to the other assets in the portfolio. According to MPT, a portfolio with a wide variety of investments, exhibiting low correlation to each other, can provide consistent portfolio growth, even if a portion of the portfolio declines in value. Alternative investments tend to have low correlation with traditional investments.

- **Active management:** Many alternative investment strategies require a higher level of hands-on management than more traditional investments. For example, many traditional investors will follow a passive buy-and-hold strategy that attempts to match the return of a particular index or other benchmark. In some alternative investments, a process of actively buying and selling attempts to "beat" the market and achieve a higher rate of return than would theoretically be possible with a buy-and-hold approach.

- **Inefficient markets:** The securities markets that most investors are familiar with, such as the New York Stock Exchange (NYSE), are widely considered to be "efficient" in that all information relevant to an investment's value is easily available and is quickly reflected in the investment's market price. Alternative investments tend to look for opportunities in more "inefficient" markets where relevant information concerning an investment is not easily available. The goal for the manager of an alternative investment is to uncover relevant investment information (for example, the potential value of privately-held timberland) and use this information to realize a higher rate of return.[1]

- **Illiquidity:** The term "liquidity" refers to the ability to quickly buy or sell an investment. Alternative investments tend to "trade" in markets where transactions are infrequent or where no structured market exists. For example, selling a share of stock on the NYSE can usually be done in a fraction of a second. Selling a privately-owned company, however, may take months or years to complete.

Other Points to Consider

There are a number of points to bear in mind when considering an alternative investment:

- **High risk:** By their nature alternative investments carry a high level of risk. Although all investing is risky, including the potential loss of principal, alternative investments are generally seen as carrying a higher level of risk than traditional investments. Of course, the reason for bearing the higher level of risk is to achieve a higher rate of investment return.

---

[1] Not to be confused with "insider" trading. In simple terms, insider trading is the buying or selling of a security while in possession of material, non-public information about the security. Insider trading is criminal activity.

- **Illiquid:** Some alternative investments can be quite illiquid, meaning than an investor must be ready to leave his or her funds in the investment for a long period of time, sometimes years.

- **Higher management costs:** Because many alternative investments have a more active, hands-on management approach, the day-to-day management expenses can be higher than traditional investments. Thus, a higher rate of return is required just to break even.

- **Less regulation:** Because many alternative investments use legal structures that are private in nature, there is frequently less government regulation of alternative investments. If investments are made in foreign countries, or on foreign exchanges, there may be less regulatory protection than in the United States.

- **Not for the small investor:** Although there are investment vehicles which will allow a small investor to participate in alternative investments (real estate investment trusts (REITS) or mutual funds specializing in natural resources are examples), as a general rule alternative investments require a significant dollar investment. Many alternative investments have "suitability" requirements that must be met before accepting an investor. For example, an investor may be required to have a minimum net worth of $2,500,000, an annual income of at least $500,000 and make a minimum initial investment of $250,000. In some instances, suitability requirements limit an investment's availability to institutions and the super wealthy.

Seek Professional Guidance

Because alternative investments are complex, often risky investments, the advice and guidance of experienced investment, tax, and legal professionals is highly recommended.

Modern Portfolio Theory

Everyone with money to invest faces a primary question: what do I invest the funds in? In answering this question, a number of individual factors are typically considered, such as the dollar amount of investable funds, the investment time horizon, the individual's income tax bracket, and his or her ability to tolerate risk. It goes without saying that all investing involves risk, including the possible loss of principle.

Modern Portfolio Theory

Rather than placing all of their funds in one asset type, many individuals will create an investment "portfolio," a collection of many different types of assets. Modern Portfolio Theory (MPT) is a methodology used to construct a diversified portfolio such that the overall risk of the portfolio is less than the risk of any one investment in the portfolio. There are two key concepts involved in MPT:

- **Correlation:** Rather than adding an investment to a portfolio on its individual merits, investments are selected according to how a particular asset changes in value in relation to the other investments in the portfolio.

- **Risk vs. return:** MPT recognizes that there is a relationship between risk and reward; the higher the risk undertaken, the higher the potential reward; the lower the risk, the lower the potential reward. MPT guides an investor in constructing a portfolio that either maximizes return for a given level of risk, or minimizes risk for an expected rate of return.

Correlation

Consider a hypothetical portfolio consisting of 60% domestic corporate stock and 40% government bonds. As a general rule, these two asset classes will respond differently to the same macroeconomic events.

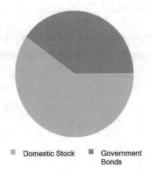

■ Domestic Stock   ■ Government Bonds

A rising stock market will frequently attract investors and decrease demand for "safe" investment such U.S. government bonds, thus driving down bond prices. On the other hand, a declining stock market frequently causes investors to seek "shelter," generally decreasing the price of stocks and increasing the price of government bonds.

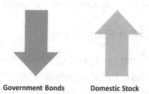

Government Bonds   Domestic Stock

Correlation is the extent to which the investment return of one investment is related to the investment return of a different investment. In the hypothetical example above, U.S. government bonds and domestic corporate stock are considered to be *negatively* correlated. Typically, when one goes up the other goes down and vice versa.

MPT argues that constructing a portfolio from assets that exhibit little correlation to each other is best. Given a long enough time frame, a worthwhile investment will generally appreciate and/or generate income. In the short run, however, the investment will usually experience ups and downs. A portfolio with a wide variety of investments, exhibiting low correlation to each other, can provide consistent portfolio growth, even in the event that a portion of the portfolio declines in value.

Taking the correlation concept one step further, MPT suggests that adding a risky asset to a portfolio can lower total portfolio risk. This risk reduction occurs when this new, "risky" asset has no correlation to the other assets in the portfolio. Continuing with our earlier theoretical example, let's add international stocks:

International stock markets have historically been more volatile (risky) than domestic, US markets. Yet the inclusion of this third class – although by itself risky – lowers the total portfolio risk. This is because each asset in the portfolio shows a low correlation of returns to the other assets in the portfolio.

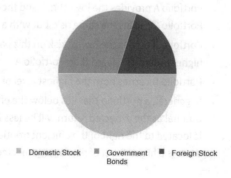

Domestic Stock   Government Bonds   Foreign Stock

Government Bonds   Domestic Stock   Foreign Stock

Risk vs. Return – The Efficient Frontier

MPT assumes that investors are rational and that they seek to maximize investment return with the least possible risk. Using the correlation principles of MPT, it is possible to design a portfolio that, for a given level of risk, maximizes the potential return. Such portfolios are deemed "efficient" as no further diversification will lower an individual portfolio's overall risk. If these risk-return portfolios are plotted on a graph, such as shown below, the line A-B-C-D marks what is termed the "efficient frontier."

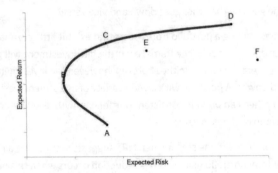

Note the following:

- Portfolio A provides the lowest risk and the lowest possible return. However, Portfolio C carries the same risk, but with a higher potential return.
- Portfolio B carries the lowest risk on this particular risk-reward line, but has a higher potential reward than Portfolio A.
- Portfolio D carries both the highest level of risk and the highest potential return.
- In general, a portfolio that lies below the efficient frontier (Portfolio E) is not optimal as the expected return will be less for a given level of risk. A portfolio that is located to the right of the efficient frontier (Portfolio F) is not a good choice as there is a higher level of risk for an expected rate of return.

Such an efficient frontier assumes that all investments included in the various portfolios carry some degree of risk. According to some, it is theoretically possible to include a "risk-free" asset, such as U.S. government bonds, that could increase the potential return *beyond* a particular efficient frontier. However, not all observers agree that a truly risk-free asset, even U.S. government bonds, actually exists.

Unsystematic vs. Systematic Risk

The diversification and correlation principles that underlie MPT can offset what is known as *unsystematic* risk, i.e. the risk inherent in holding individual stocks and bonds. An individual company or industry could experience significant problems, leading to a decline in the market value of related securities. Under MPT, diversifying the overall portfolio, with assets that are poorly correlated, should result in portfolio growth, even if a portion of the portfolio declines in value.

Systemic risk, on the other hand, affects an entire market or economy, not just individual companies or industries. War, rampant inflation, and major economic crises are examples of systemic risk. During such traumatic events, all asset classes tend to move together (usually downward) and to be much more highly correlated than they might be during "normal" times. MPT makes no claim to provide any protection against such systemic risk.

Criticism of Modern Portfolio Theory

It should be noted that not all observers agree that MPT is the perfect answer to the question of how to construct an investment portfolio. A number of the key assumptions underlying MPT (for example using historical rates of return as a measure of future risk or that the correlations between assets are unchanging) have been challenged by observers as not matching what happens in the real world. All investors should be aware of these controversies and understand the assumptions underlying any recommendations made by a portfolio manager.

Seek Professional Guidance

In constructing and managing an investment portfolio, of whatever size, the guidance of trained, experienced financial professionals is strongly recommended.

Passive vs. Active Investing

One primary question that confronts many individuals is whether to follow a "passive" investment strategy or to be a more "active" investor. Each approach has its adherents.

Passive Investing

Passive investing is based on the concept that an individual should invest in a broad selection of stocks or other securities, rather than trying to pick single issues that will be big winners. Underlying this approach is the assumption that no one individual or group will be able to consistently make investment decisions that will provide a return greater than the market as a whole. The primary goal with passive investing is to earn a market return rather than trying to "beat" the market.

Many passive investors implement this strategy using what are known as "index funds." An index fund is a type of mutual fund, exchange-traded fund, or unit investment trust whose primary investment objective is to mimic the performance of a specific market index such as the S&P500 Index or the Russell 5000 Index. To achieve this goal, an index fund will hold all (or a representative sample) of the securities in the chosen index, in the same proportion as those securities exist in the index itself. For many investors, index funds have significant advantages:

- **Lower management costs:** Without the need to pay for expenses such as investment research and the costs of buying and selling, index funds typically have lower management costs.

- **Lower portfolio turnover:** With a passive investment strategy, there is less portfolio turnover (buying and selling) in an index fund than with an actively managed fund.

- **Risk management:** Using an index fund helps manage the risks inherent in investing by spreading the total risk over a broader, more diversified portfolio. This diversity does not, however, protect against the risk of a general market decline.

Active Investing

Active investing, in comparison, is based on the view that an investor can achieve a return greater than that provided by the overall market by actively buying and selling selected stocks or other securities. In effect, active investors are trying to outguess the market and focus on specific stocks or securities that they believe will change in value. Active investing thus offers the potential for greater rewards, at the price of greater investment risk. Other points that should be noted include:

- **Higher expenses:** Including trading costs, research expenses, and generally higher management fees. Higher costs mean that an actively managed portfolio needs a higher overall rate of return, just to break even.

- **Income tax impact:** Frequent buying and selling can result in short and long term gains and losses, which can complicate tax planning.

- **Concentration increases risk:** By focusing on a limited number of securities or investment sectors, there is less diversification and thus greater investment risk.

- **Luck or skill?** If an active portfolio manager is successful at beating the market, can he or she achieve the same results year after year?

Which is Better?

There are many published studies on whether passive or active investing provides the greatest investment return. Depending on the time frame involved in a particular study, both approaches can be shown to have done well. Ultimately, the question of which approach is "better" often comes down to the facts of an individual's own situation. Personal needs and preferences also play a role in deciding which approach to take. For some investors, a blend of both strategies can be useful.

As a starting point, consider the following key questions:

- **Investment goals:** What do you want your money to do for you? Are you seeking current income, to pay monthly bills? Or, are you accumulating funds to meet a future goal?

- **Risk tolerance:** Investing does involve risk, including the possible loss of principal. In general, risk is related to expected return: the higher the risk, the higher the potential return; the lower the risk, the lower the potential return. Can you afford to lose a portion, or even all, of your investment, without it affecting how you live?

- **Dollar amount of investable assets:** Generally, investors with larger amounts of capital are better equipped to bear a higher level of risk. Also, the investment vehicles open to an investor can vary, depending on the amount of money available.

- **Income taxes:** Income taxes can have a significant impact on your investment results. For high-tax bracket investors, income taxes are a *very* important consideration.

Seek Professional Guidance

The choice of whether to use a passive or active investment approach is an individual one. For many investors, the guidance of trained financial professionals can help in making this decision.

Maintaining Your Asset Mix

Asset Type	Current Amount	% of Total[1]	Assumed Rate of Return	Estimated Amount in 15 Years	% of Total[1]
Cash	$10,000	4.0%	1.000%	$11,610	1.5%
Bonds	$61,000	24.5%	4.000%	$109,858	14.0%
Small Company Stocks	$59,000	23.7%	10.000%	$246,458	31.5%
Large Company Stocks	$65,000	26.1%	6.000%	$155,776	19.9%
International Stocks	$54,000	21.7%	11.000%	$258,368	33.0%
Total	**$249,000**			**$782,069**	

Current Asset Mix

Estimated Asset Mix in 15 Years

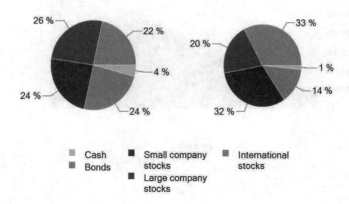

Cash
Bonds
Small company stocks
Large company stocks
International stocks

Values shown in this presentation are hypothetical and not a promise of future performance.

[1] May not total 100% due to rounding.

Value over Time

Item Description	Value
Initial capital	$2,000
Monthly savings	$300
Number of months	36
Future Value	15,000

Assumed annual rate of return, compounded monthly, would be 9.14%

Value Over Time

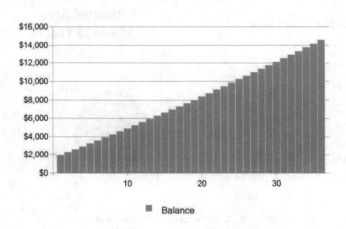

Asset Allocation Data

Personal

Date 01/01/2018

Client(s) name		Date of birth	Retirement age
1) Paul	Johnson	01/01/1963	65
2) Sally	Johnson	01/01/1965	65

☑ Check if clients are married

Assets

	Retirement Plans			
	Client 1	Client 2	Cash	Other Assets
Balance	$ 136,000	$ 86,500	$ 6,000	$ 10,000
US Large/Mid Cap Stocks	40%	25%	%	100%
US Small Cap Stocks	40%	25%	%	%
Aggregate US Bonds	%	25%	%	%
Cash	%	25%	100%	%
International Equity	20%	%	%	%
Total	100%	100%	100%	100%

Risk Profile

Risk Analysis

Risk profile to illustrate in recommending asset allocation

☑ Use profile indicated by score

☐ Use alternative profile

☐ Conservative

☐ Moderately Conservative

☐ Moderate

☐ Moderately Aggressive

☐ Aggressive

Risk Questionnaire

Question	Answer
1	3
2	4
3	4
4	4
5	5
6	3
7	3
8	3

Asset Allocation

Asset allocation is an investment strategy that seeks to reduce investment risk, while maintaining a desired rate of return, by spreading an individual's investments over a number of asset types. It takes advantage of the tendency of different asset types to move in different cycles, and thus smooth out the ups and downs of the entire portfolio. Stocks, bonds, and cash (or cash equivalents) are the investments normally used. Depending on individual needs or preferences, other asset types may also be included.

Asset allocation does not guarantee a profit or protect against a loss in declining markets. There is no guarantee that a diversified portfolio will outperform a non-diversified portfolio or that diversification among asset classes will reduce risk.

A Personal Choice

There is no single asset allocation model to fit every investor, or for every stage of a person's life. The asset allocation decision is a highly individual one, and involves carefully answering a number of key questions:

- **Investment goals:** Why are you investing? Is the primary need for income, to pay current living expenses, or as a source of emergency funds? Or are you accumulating money for a future need?

- **Time horizon:** When will the money be needed? At retirement, or sooner, to send a child to college, for example?

- **Liquidity needs:** How quickly do you need to be able to turn your investment into cash?

- **Risk tolerance:** How comfortable are you with the inevitable ups and downs of the financial markets?

- **Tax impact:** How will the investments affect your tax situation?

- **Economic conditions:** Inflation, interest rates, and the state of the economy are essential factors to consider.

- **International exposure:** How comfortable are you investing in foreign markets?

Although no guarantee of how an investment may perform in the future, an analysis of historical data can provide information about the levels of risk and return for each investment type being considered. These historical values are then used as a guide to structuring a portfolio that matches the investor's individual goals and overall risk tolerance level.

A Changing Choice

Over time, financial markets and an individual's goals and situation will change. Periodically, an investor must review his or her situation to ensure that past investment allocations are still appropriate. If not, adjustments should be made.

Representative Asset Allocation Models

The charts below illustrate three hypothetical asset allocation models, for three age groups, or types of investor. These models are intended to serve only as representative samples of how asset allocation might work, and are not intended to serve as investment or portfolio recommendations.

Asset Allocation Portfolio #1
Younger or Higher Risk Investors

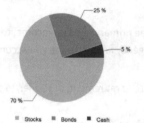

Asset Allocation Portfolio #2
Medium Risk Investors, Those Near Retirement

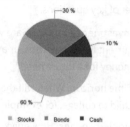

Asset Allocation Portfolio #3
Retired or Low Risk Investors

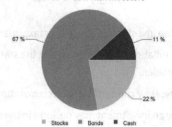

Current Allocation for Assets

Asset Class	Percent of Total Assets	Amount in Each Class
US Large/Mid Cap Stocks	36.07%	$86,025
US Small Cap Stocks	31.88%	76,025
Aggregate US Bonds	9.07%	21,625
Cash	11.58%	27,625
International Equity	11.40%	27,200
Total Assets	100.00%	$238,500

Current Asset Allocation

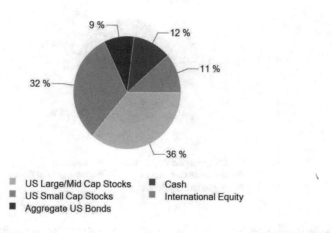

- US Large/Mid Cap Stocks
- US Small Cap Stocks
- Aggregate US Bonds
- Cash
- International Equity

Recommended Allocation for Assets

Portfolio allocation recommended: Moderately Conservative

Asset Class	Percent of Total Assets
US Large/Mid Cap Stocks	23.00%
US Small Cap Stocks	3.00%
Aggregate US Bonds	53.00%
Cash	7.00%
International Equity	14.00%
Total Assets	100.00%

Recommended Asset Allocation

▦ US Large/Mid Cap Stocks	▪ Cash
▪ US Small Cap Stocks	▪ International Equity
▪ Aggregate US Bonds	

Moderately Conservative investors typically have either a moderate time horizon or a slightly higher risk tolerance than the conservative investor and seek both modest capital appreciation and income from their investable assets. The main objective of a moderately conservative investor is still to preserve their capital but they will accept fluctuations in the values of their portfolio from year to year.

©2017 Morningstar Investment Management LLC. Used with permission. All Rights Reserved. Morningstar Investment Management is a registered investment adviser and wholly owned subsidiary of Morningstar, Inc. The Morningstar name and logo are registered marks of Morningstar, Inc. Advisys, Inc. has engaged Morningstar Investment Management LLC to construct asset allocation models for use by financial advisors of Advisys. Morningstar Investment Management LLC is a registered investment adviser and subsidiary of Morningstar. Inc. Morningstar Investment Management is not affiliated with Advisys and its affiliates. The use of an asset allocation model by an Advisys client does not establish an advisory relationship with Morningstar Investment Management, as Morningstar Investment Management is not acting in the capacity of investment advisor to individual investors. Individual investors should ultimately rely on their own judgment and/or the judgment of a financial advisor in making their investment decisions. Morningstar Investment Management makes no warranties, expressed or implied, as to results to be obtained from use of information it provides. Morningstar Investment Management is not responsible for the presentation of performance statistics and other data.

Asset Allocation Comparison

Portfolio allocation recommended: Moderately Conservative

Asset Class	Current Asset Mix			Recommended Asset Mix	
	Percent	Amount	Change	Percent	Amount
US Large/Mid Cap Stocks	36.07%	$86,025	-$31,170	23.00%	$54,855
US Small Cap Stocks	31.88%	76,025	-68,870	3.00%	7,155
Aggregate US Bonds	9.07%	21,625	104,780	53.00%	126,405
Cash	11.58%	27,625	-10,930	7.00%	16,695
International Equity	11.40%	27,200	6,190	14.00%	33,390
Total Assets	100.00%	$238,500		100.00%	$238,500

Current   **Recommended**

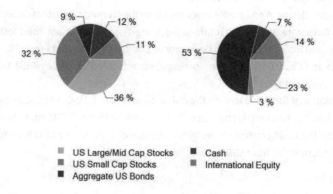

- US Large/Mid Cap Stocks
- US Small Cap Stocks
- Aggregate US Bonds
- Cash
- International Equity

Moderately Conservative investors typically have either a moderate time horizon or a slightly higher risk tolerance than the conservative investor and seek both modest capital appreciation and income from their investable assets. The main objective of a moderately conservative investor is still to preserve their capital but they will accept fluctuations in the values of their portfolio from year to year.

©2017 Morningstar Investment Management LLC. Used with permission. All Rights Reserved. Morningstar Investment Management is a registered investment adviser and wholly owned subsidiary of Morningstar, Inc. The Morningstar name and logo are registered marks of Morningstar, Inc. Advisys, Inc. has engaged Morningstar Investment Management LLC to construct asset allocation models for use by financial advisors of Advisys. Morningstar Investment Management LLC is a registered investment adviser and subsidiary of Morningstar. Inc. Morningstar Investment Management is not affiliated with Advisys and its affiliates. The use of an asset allocation model by an Advisys client does not establish an advisory relationship with Morningstar Investment Management, as Morningstar Investment Management is not acting in the capacity of investment advisor to individual investors. Individual investors should ultimately rely on their own judgment and/or the judgment of a financial advisor in making their investment decisions. Morningstar Investment Management makes no warranties, expressed or implied, as to results to be obtained from use of information it provides. Morningstar Investment Management is not responsible for the presentation of performance statistics and other data.

Asset Allocation
Supplemental Information

Historical Data Sources

The historical rates of return are based on the following data sources:

- **Large Company Stocks:** A composite index derived from the S&P Total Return series and the Cowles Commission total NYSE total return index, with data to 1926. Source: Morningstar Ibbotson *Stocks, Bonds, Bills, Inflation (SBBI) Classic Yearbook*; Large Company Stocks Total Return.
- **Small Company Stocks:** A composite index covering large samples of small company stocks total returns based on data back to 1926. Source: Morningstar Ibbotson *SBBI*; Small Company Stocks Total Return.
- **Domestic Bonds:** A composite index based on the Morningstar Ibbotson *SBBI* Long-Term Corporate Bonds total return series, Long-Term Government Bond total return series, and Intermediate-Term Government Bond series, with data to 1926.
- **T-Bills and Cash:** Derived using Morningstar Ibbotson's *SSBI* 30-Day T-Bill Total Return series, with data to 1926.
- **International Stocks:** Based on the dollar-denominated, MSCI-EAFE (Europe-Americas-Far East) total return stock index. Data extends to 1970, with extrapolation back to 1926 using composite weighted average of large and small U.S. company stock total return series from *SBBI*.

Source Notes

The historical rates of return are calculated by Advisys Inc. using data provided by Morningstar, Inc. © 2015 Morningstar, Inc. All Rights Reserved. The information contained herein: (1) is proprietary to Morningstar and/or its content providers; (2) may not be copied or distributed; and (3) is not warranted to be accurate, complete, or timely. Neither Morningstar nor its content providers are responsible for any damages or losses arising from any use of this information. Past performance is no guarantee of future results.

Data from MSCI may have also been used in the calculations. MSCI has not reviewed this product or report, and does not endorse or express any opinion regarding this or other information contained herein or Advisys and shall have no liability with respect to any data or other information contained herein.

Weighted Average Rate of Return/ Net Worth

A personal net worth statement is a snapshot of an individual's financial health, at one particular point in time. It is a summary of what is owned, less what is owed.

Assets	Market Value	Rate of Return	Weighted Average Rate of Return
Paul's retirement plans			
My 401(k)	$106,000	7.00%	
My IRA	30,000	5.00%	
Total	136,000		6.56%
Sally's retirement plans			
SEP	16,500	6.00%	
TSA	60,000	4.00%	
Total	76,500		4.43%
Other Assets			
Savings Account	6,000	6.00%	
Cash	500	1.00%	
Residence	500,000	7.00%	
Total	506,500		6.98%
Total Assets	**$719,000**		6.63%

Liabilities

Mortgage	250,000
Other Debt	25,000
Total Liabilities	**275,000**

Net Worth

Net Worth	**444,000**
Total Liabilities and Net Worth	**$719,000**

Mutual Funds

Individuals with excess dollars to put to work in some form of investment have an often-bewildering range of choices. An investor may decide to tackle the financial markets alone, and buy and sell investments directly, in his or her own name. A second option is to invest indirectly, using an investment medium known as a mutual fund.

What Is a Mutual Fund?

A mutual fund is an organization designed to pool the assets of many investors, to achieve a common purpose. The money raised is then invested in accordance with pre-defined goals. This mutual effort of a number of investors provides benefits that an individual, working alone, might not be able to receive.

- **Professional management:** Trained, experienced investment professionals provide the research, selection and monitoring skills needed to manage an investment portfolio.

- **Diversification:** Owning shares in a mutual fund allows an investor to participate in a diversified portfolio. Instead of placing all the eggs in one basket, diversification spreads the risk over many different securities.

- **Convenience:** Mutual funds offer many conveniences. Investment programs can be started with relatively small amounts of money. Dividends and other gains can be automatically reinvested. Many funds offer features to automate both contributions and withdrawals. Regular fund statements ease bookkeeping by tracking an investor's purchases, withdrawals and reinvestments, as well as providing tax information.

Types of Mutual Funds

Mutual funds are classified according to their structure and investment objectives:

- **Open-end mutual funds:** Mutual funds that issue as many shares as the public wishes to buy are called open-end mutual funds. When a shareholder wants to sell, open-end funds redeem all shares tendered.

- **Closed-end mutual funds:** Closed-end mutual funds are funds that have a fixed number of shares. Unlike shares in an open-end fund, where the fund itself sells and redeems all shares, the shares in a closed-end fund are traded on public exchanges.

- **Investment objective:** Mutual funds are also classified according to the investment objective of the fund. Examples of mutual fund investment goals include:

  - **Money market funds:** These funds invest in a variety of short-term, money market debt, such as Treasury bills or commercial paper.

  - **Growth funds:** Have an emphasis on long-term capital growth, usually through investment in common stock.

  - **Income funds:** Focus on providing high, current income, using bonds and other income producing securities.

  - **Balanced funds:** Strive to provide income and long-term capital gain. Both stocks and bonds are used.

Key Mutual Fund Concepts

- **Prospectus:** The Securities and Exchange Commission (SEC) requires that every prospective investor in an open-end mutual fund be provided a document called a prospectus. The prospectus contains valuable information concerning how the fund works, the fund's goals and risks, its history, and any expenses or charges involved. The prospectus is intended to provide the facts necessary for an investor to make an informed investment decision and should be reviewed carefully. For closed-end mutual funds, a prospectus is issued only when shares are first offered to the public.

- **Net asset value:** At the end of each business day, the managers of a fund will add up the market value of all securities held by the fund. The total market value is then divided by the number of outstanding shares in the fund. The result is the Net Asset Value (NAV) per share. For open-end funds, NAV is used to calculate the price per share for both purchases and sales. For closed-end funds, NAV measures only the value of the securities in the fund; the market price of shares in the fund can be higher or lower than NAV.

- **Load vs. no-load:** The term "load" traditionally refers to a commission paid to purchase shares in an open-end mutual fund. Funds which are no load do not charge a commission to purchase their shares. Even though a fund is no load, other fees or expenses may apply. Investors are encouraged to consult a fund's prospectus for a discussion of the fees and expenses charged by a fund.

- **Offering price:** This is the price charged to purchase shares in an open-end fund. For a load fund, it is the net asset value (NAV) plus the commission charged. For a no-load fund, offering price and NAV are the same.

Possible Risks

The risks involved in owning shares in a mutual fund are the same as those involved in directly owning the underlying securities. However, these risks are generally "spread" by the fund manager over a range of securities, to help minimize the impact of any one risk on the fund's performance as a whole.

- **Mutual funds holding stock investments.**

  - **Market risk:** The value of stock can fluctuate up and down. If stock purchased at a higher price is sold when the market is down, a loss will result.

- **Mutual funds holding bonds or other debt instruments.**

  - **Market risk:** The value of a bond will fluctuate, usually in response to changes in interest rates. If a bond is sold before it matures, the investor may receive more or less than originally paid.

  - **Default risk:** The possibility that the issuer of a bond or other debt will not pay either principal or interest.

  - **Inflation risk:** As fixed-return investments, bonds are subject to inflation risk; over time, the dollars received have less purchasing power.

Mutual Fund Share Classes – A, B, and C

Mutual funds can be divided into two broad groups, based upon the method by which they are marketed. When you pay a commission to a financial adviser or stock broker to buy mutual fund shares, that charge is called a "load" and the type of fund involved is called a "load fund." With a "no-load" fund, however, there is no commission charged to purchase fund shares. Shares in a no-load fund are purchased directly from the fund itself.

Load or No-Load?

Both load and no-load funds have their role in the marketplace and you must decide which is best for your needs:

- **No-load funds:** The advantage of a no-load fund is that you have all of your money working for you the moment you make your investment. The disadvantage is the lack of professional guidance with regard to your investment; you take direct responsibility for what to buy, when to buy or sell, or when to make changes to your portfolio.

- **Load funds:** The advantage of a load fund is that the broker or adviser can provide professional investment guidance. Your adviser monitors market conditions and can help you select the appropriate fund as well as recommend when to make other portfolio changes. The disadvantage of a load fund is that the commission or fees paid reduce your investment return.

Load Fund Share Classes

Over time the brokerage industry has developed various share "classes," to allow investors a choice as to how to pay the sales charges and service fees associated with load funds. Although the specifics vary from mutual fund to mutual fund, there are three common share classes that generally can be described as follows:

- **Class A Shares:** With the exception of very large purchases, these shares impose a "front-end" sales charge. This means that a sales charge is deducted from your investment each time you purchase shares. For example, if you invest $1,000 with a 4% sales charge, your commission will be $40 and you will receive shares valued at $960. These shares typically have a lower "expense ratio" (total annual operating expenses as a percentage of the fund's assets) compared with other share classes. Most companies will offer discounts for large purchases of Class A shares, termed "breakpoints."

- **Class B shares:** Instead of imposing a sales charge up-front, as with Class A shares, Class B shares levy a "back-end" or "contingent deferred sales charge" (CDSC), which is a sales charge you pay when you redeem your shares. For example, if your mutual fund has a CDSC of 3% and you redeem $1,000 worth of shares, you will receive $970 in cash. $30 is deducted for the CDSC. The percentage amount of the CDSC normally declines over time until it eventually reaches zero. The period of time over which the CDSC is phased out varies, but can range from five to eight years. Once the CDSC is eliminated, Class B shares usually convert to Class A, with the conversion occurring some time (generally one year) after the CDSC reaches zero. Class B shares typically have a higher operating expense ratio than Class A shares.

- **Class C shares:** Class C shares are similar to Class B shares in that they share the same higher operating expenses and both have a CDSC. The CDSC for Class C shares; however, is often lower than that for Class B share and frequently disappears after a relatively short period of time, generally two years or less. Unlike Class B shares, Class C shares generally do not convert to Class A shares once the CDSC is eliminated.

Factors To Consider

There are a number of factors to consider when deciding which share class to use:

- **How much you plan to invest:** If you plan to invest a large amount of money, Class A shares, with their breakpoint discounts and lower operating expenses, may be preferable to Class B or Class C shares.

- **How long you plan to hold your funds:** The length of time you plan to hold your funds is an important factor in deciding whether an up-front sales charge or a back-end sales charge would be more advantageous.

- **Class annual operating expenses:** Annual operating expenses have a direct impact on your investment return. Funds with lower operating expenses are highly desirable.

Mutual Fund Share Classes – A, B, and C

Do Your Homework

Each fund makes available a "prospectus" which explains the investment objectives of the fund and details the expenses and fees the fund charges, as well as the potential risks involved. Investing involves risk, including the possible loss of principal. Read the prospectus carefully before investing.

Crunch The Numbers

The Financial Industry Regulatory Authority (FINRA) makes available on its website a Fund Analyzer which allows you to compare the costs of different mutual funds or share classes and estimate the impact that the various expenses and fees can have over time. This calculator automatically provides the fee and expense data for you. The calculator can be found on the internet at:

http://apps.finra.org/fundanalyzer/1/fa.aspx

Seek Professional Guidance

Your broker or other financial professional is a key source of information and guidance in selecting and managing your investment portfolio.

Mutual Funds – Glossary of Terms

12b-1 Fees: "12b-1" refers to the Securities and Exchange Commission (SEC) rule which permits money to be taken out of a fund's assets to pay the expenses of distributing and marketing the fund. 12b-1 fees (similar to sales charges) may be used to compensate a broker or other financial advisor.

Account Fee: Fee charged by some funds to their shareholders in connection with the maintenance of their accounts.

Account Minimum: Some funds require an investor to make an initial minimum investment, often between $1,000 and $10,000.

Asset-Based Sales Charge: Fees taken out of a mutual fund's assets to pay for marketing and distribution expenses. Asset-based sales charges also include "12b-1" fees.

Average Price Per Share: One of three methods used to determine the cost basis of mutual fund shares. Average price per share is calculated by adding up the total cost of all shares owned and then dividing by the total number of shares owned. (See also "First-In, First-Out (FIFO)" and "Specific Identification.") Also known as "Average Cost."

Back-End Sales Charge: A sales commission paid by mutual fund investors when they redeem shares. These charges typically decline after a certain time period has expired between the purchase and sale of shares and are usually charged in one of two ways: 1) as a percentage of the value of the shareholder's initial investment; or 2) as a percentage of the shareholder's investment upon redemption.

Breakpoint: A mutual fund may offer you a discount ("breakpoint") on the front-end sales charge if any one of the following conditions is met: 1) you make a large purchase; 2) you already hold other mutual funds in the same "fund family"; or 3) you commit to purchasing shares on a regular basis.

Closed-End Fund: A mutual fund with a fixed number of shares. Shares in a closed-end fund are traded on public exchanges.

Contingent Deferred Sales Charge (CDSC): (See "Back-End Sales Charge.")

Dollar Cost Averaging: An investment strategy of buying, at regular intervals, equal dollar amounts of a security such as a mutual fund. When the share price drops, more shares are purchased; when the share price rises, fewer shares are purchased.

Exchange Fee: Fee that some funds impose upon their shareholders if they exchange (transfer) to another fund within the same fund group or "fund family."

Exchange-Traded Fund (ETF): An investment vehicle that is similar in concept to a mutual fund in that it pools the resources of many investors to achieve a pre-determined investment goal. A primary difference is that shares of an ETF are traded on an exchange, rather than being purchased from, or redeemed by, the fund itself.

Expense Ratio: Percentage of assets used to cover all expenses associated with the operation of a mutual fund.

Family Discount: Allows an investor to combine purchases made by related individuals or in related accounts, to reach a higher breakpoint discount.

First In-First Out (FIFO): One of three methods used to determine the cost basis of fund shares. Under FIFO, the shares sold are assumed to be the oldest shares owned. (See also "Average Price Per Share" and "Specific Identification.")

Front-End Sales Charge: A sales commission mutual fund investors pay immediately upon the purchase of shares.

Fund Family: A group of mutual funds offered by the same mutual fund manager. Generally, exchanges are permitted within the fund family for a modest fee.

Investment Advisor: Refers to the company in charge of the person or organization employed by a mutual fund to manage the fund's investment portfolio. The investment advisor is responsible for hiring and monitoring the firm's portfolio manager(s).

Load Fund: A mutual fund which has a sales charge or commission.

Letter of Intent (LOI): A statement signed by an investor that he or she intends to make additional future fund purchases, sufficient to reach a certain discount breakpoint. The LOI allows the investor to obtain a reduced sales charge on all purchases made. If the investor does not invest the amount listed in the LOI, the mutual fund may retroactively levy the higher sales charge.

Management Fees: Fees paid out of the fund's assets to provide compensation to the fund's investment advisor and its affiliates for managing the fund's investment portfolio.

Mutual Fund: An investment vehicle operated by an investment company which pools the assets of many individuals. The money raised is then invested in accordance with pre-defined goals.

Net Asset Value (NAV): The total market value of the securities held by a mutual fund, divided by the number of outstanding fund shares.

No-Load: A fund that does not charge any type of sales charge ("load").

Open-End Fund: A mutual fund that issues as many shares as the public wishes to buy. When an individual wants to sell, an open-end fund redeems all shares tendered.

Operating Expenses: These are the total expenses paid annually by a mutual fund, generally expressed as a percentage of net assets.

Prospectus: A document which explains a mutual fund's goals, risks, history, and any expenses or charges involved in owning shares of the fund. The prospectus is intended to provide the facts necessary for an investor to make an informed investment decision.

Purchase Fee: A type of fee charged by some funds when shareholders purchase their shares. Purchase fees are not considered sales charges ("loads") because they are paid directly to the fund and are not used to compensate outside brokers.

Rebalancing: An investment strategy which requires a periodic adjustment in the investment mix, to maintain a specific asset allocation or risk tolerance.

Redemption Fee: A type of fee that some funds charge their shareholders upon the redemption of shares. Although similar to a back-end or contingent deferred sales charge, redemption fees are not considered sales charges ("loads") because they are paid directly to the fund and not used to compensate outside brokers.

Right of Accumulation (ROA): The right to receive a discounted sales charge on current fund purchases by combining both earlier and current purchases to reach a specific discount breakpoint.

Sales Charge: A sales charge is a commission paid by investors who have purchased shares in a mutual fund. These charges vary from fund to fund and are generally used to provide compensation to outside brokers that distribute fund shares.

Share Class: A mutual fund with one investment advisor may offer more than one share "class" to investors. Each class represents a similar interest in the fund's portfolio. The principal difference between the various share classes is that different fees and expenses apply to each class. The most common share classes are Class A, Class B, and Class C.

Specific Identification: One of three methods used to calculate the cost basis of mutual funds. When you sell or redeem shares, you specifically identify the shares (quantities and dates purchased) to be sold or redeemed. Example: "Sell 300 of the shares of XYZ fund that I purchased on July 5, 1998." (See also "First-In, First Out (FIFO)" and "Average Price Per Share.")

Statement of Additional Information (SAI): A highly detailed version of the prospectus. A SAI is usually written in technical, legal language and can be obtained either from the fund or from the Securities and Exchange Commission (SEC).

Turnover: A measure of the length of time a fund holds the securities it purchases. When a fund purchases or sells securities, it incurs both trading expenses and potential capital gains or losses. Funds with lower turnover typically have lower operating expenses; funds with higher turnover generally have higher operating expenses.

Index Funds

An index fund is a type of mutual fund, exchange-traded fund, or unit investment trust whose primary investment objective is to mimic the performance of a specified market index, such as the S&P 500 Index or the Wilshire 5000 Index. To achieve this, an index fund will hold all (or a representative sample) of the securities in the chosen index, in the same proportions as those securities making up the index.

Investing in an index fund is often referred to as "passive" investing, since changes in the portfolio are generally made only when there is a change in the underlying index. Index funds owners generally believe that it is impossible to "beat" the market; the primary goal is to come as close as possible to a "market" return. Mutual funds that are "actively" managed seek to beat the market, often by frequently trading individual stocks or bonds.

Advantages of Index Funds

For many investors, index funds have several distinct advantages:

- **Lower management costs:** Without the need for expenses such as investment research and the costs of buying and selling, index funds typically have lower management costs.

- **Lower portfolio turnover:** With a passive investment strategy, there is less portfolio turnover in index funds than with actively managed funds. Such trading activity can generate taxable capital gains.

Disadvantages of Index Funds

By their nature and design, index funds will never "beat" the market.

Possible Risks

Shares in an index fund involve the same risks as owning the underlying securities:

- **Funds holding stock investments:** The value of a stock can fluctuate up and down. If shares purchased at a higher price is sold when the market is down, a loss will result.

- Funds holding bonds or other debt instruments:

  - **Market Risk:** the value of a bond will fluctuate, usually in response to changes in interest rates. If a bond is sold before it matures, an investor may receive more or less than originally paid;

  - **Default Risk:** the issuer of a bond may not pay principal or interest when due;

  - **Inflation Risk:** as fixed-return investments, bonds are subject to inflation risk – over time the dollars received have less purchasing power.

Before investing in an index fund, you should carefully read all of the fund's information, including its prospectus and most recent shareholder report.

Exchange-Traded Funds

For many investors, open-end mutual funds serve as a vital component of their investment tool kit. But these funds have limitations, in that they can only be bought from or sold to the issuing mutual fund at the net asset value (NAV) calculated at the end of the trading day. Contrarily, shares in exchange-traded funds (ETFs), may be bought and sold through brokerage firms at the current market price, any time the exchange is open.

How Are Exchange-Traded Funds Structured?

In a traditional open-end mutual fund, individual investors buy shares in the fund directly from the mutual fund itself. The money is then put to work according to the fund's investment mandate. When an investor sells his or her shares, the mutual fund itself redeems those shares. If many shareholders redeem their shares all at once, the fund may need to sell off chunks of its portfolio to repay the departing investors.

Contrarily, an ETF, however, does not deal directly with individual investors. Rather, "creation units", typically representing 50,000 shares, are "sold" to institutional investors like brokerage firms, in exchange for a portfolio of securities that match the ETF's investment goals. The institutional investor, in turn, can then sell the ETF shares to individual investors on the open market. If an individual wishes to sell shares, he or she can do so by selling to other individual investors on the open market. An institutional investor can "sell" a creation unit's worth of ETF shares back to the fund. To complete the redemption, the fund does not have to sell anything; it simply distributes the underlying securities to the institutional investor and then dismantles the creation unit.

Most ETFs are designed to track a particular market index, such as the S&P 500. Other ETFs follow market segments (small-, mid-, or large-cap stocks), individual countries, specific industry sectors, or commodities such as gold or oil.

Advantages of Exchange-Traded Funds

- **Generally lower operating costs:** Because they do not have to deal with a large number of individual investors, many ETFs have very low annual expense ratios. In a mutual fund, the need to provide shareholder services is an additional expense.

- **Tax efficiency:** The low turnover, buy-and-hold approach of many ETFs typically leads to a high degree of tax efficiency. Individual investors will generally realize a gain or loss only when they sell their own ETF shares.

- **Trading flexibility:** Because ETF shares are bought and sold on the open market, an investor can use trading tools such as limit or stop-loss orders, "sell short" the ETF shares, or even trade the shares on margin, using borrowed money.

- **No required minimum purchases:** No minimum purchase requirements are needed to buy shares in an ETF. Many mutual funds have minimum purchase requirements.

Disadvantages of Exchange-Traded Funds

- **Commission charges:** To buy or sell shares in the vast majority of ETFs, an individual investor must pay a commission for each transaction, contrary to many mutual funds, which are no-load and do not charge a fee for purchases or redemptions. Some major ETF purveyors do offer limited non-commission ETF product lines, where the third-party fund providers they contract with actually pay to participate in the programs. But there are caveats to investing in commission-free ETFs. Namely, investors who redeem their positions within 30 days of investing are subject to traditional fees and may consequently be saddled with both buy-side and sell-side commissions. Additionally, commission-free ETFs tend to have fewer sector choices and higher expense ratios.

- **Client services:** Most mutual funds provide client services such as automatic dividend reinvestment or keeping track of average cost basis for tax purposes. For investors in ETFs, these services may be available from the broker, sometimes for an extra fee.

Exchange Traded Funds vs. Index Mutual Funds

ETFs are often seen as an alternative to index mutual funds. Both types of investment typically use a passive, indexing investment approach. ETFs can provide trading flexibility, but at the cost of paying commission charges. Index mutual funds provide many investor services, but have a more limited ability to be bought or sold.

Consider ETFs For....	Consider Index Mutual Funds For....
Investors who buy and hold for long periods of time. ETFs often have very low annual operating expenses.	Those who buy or sell frequently. Investors using dollar cost averaging or who make periodic purchases or sales will incur commission costs with each transaction if ETFs are used.
Those with a single, large, lump-sum to invest. Over time, the lower operating costs of ETFs can outweigh the initial cost to purchase the shares.	Those with a small amount to invest. Regardless of the amount of money invested, a commission must be paid to buy or sell ETF shares.
Those seeking trading flexibility. ETFs can usually be traded with the same ease as can other exchange-listed securities.	Investors who re-balance their portfolios regularly. Commission charges can significantly reduce the benefit of low ETF expense ratios.

Another way to approach this question is to compare the total cost of owning an ETF with the total cost of owning a mutual fund. The Financial Industry Regulatory Authority (FINRA) makes available on its website a Fund and ETF Analyzer which allows you to compare the costs of different funds or share classes and estimate the impact that the various expenses and fees can have over time. This calculator automatically provides the fee and expense data for you. The calculator can be found on the Internet at:

https://tools.finra.org/fund_analyzer/

Seek Professional Guidance

The guidance of trained professionals can be helpful both in selecting the right investment and in monitoring the investment for any needed changes.

Exchange-Traded Funds vs. Index Mutual Funds

Exchange traded funds and index mutual funds have similarities and differences:

Issue	Exchange-Traded Funds	Index Mutual Funds
How structured?	Creation units (typically 50,000 shares) are "sold" to institutional investors in exchange for a basket of securities matching the ETF's investment goals. The institutional investor can then sell the ETF shares to individual investors in the open market. An individual investor wanting to sell shares can do so by selling to other individual investors in the open market. An institutional investor can "sell" a creation unit's worth of ETF shares back to the fund. To complete the transaction, the fund distributes the underlying securities to the institutional investor and then "destroys" the creation unit.	Individual investors buy shares in the fund directly from the mutual fund itself. The money is then invested in accordance with the fund's goals. If many shareholders redeem their shares at one time, the fund may have to sell some of its portfolio to be able to repay the departing investors.
How purchased or sold?	Through a stock broker	Directly with the fund or through a stock broker
Any cost to purchase or sell shares?	Yes. A commission is paid to the broker. There is usually a "spread" between the bid and ask price	For no-load funds, none. A load fund will levy a sales charge.
Trading options?	Trades are executed on the open market. An investor can use a limit or stop order, "sell short," or use a margin account.	Purchases or redemptions are made directly with the fund itself.
What determines the share price?	Market fluctuations in the underling investments, as well as supply and demand for a particular ETF's shares, will cause the market price to rise and fall. Although share prices typically stay near the Net Asset Value (NAV), they can trade above or below NAV.	Net Asset Value, based upon the market prices of the underlying securities at the market close.
Average annual operating expenses	Typically (but not always) lower than that of an index mutual fund.	Low, but generally slightly higher than for an ETF.

Exchange-Traded Funds vs. Index Mutual Funds

Issue	Exchange-Traded Funds	Index Mutual Funds
Tax efficiency	Low portfolio turnover can provide high tax efficiency.	Usually slightly less tax efficient than ETFs.
Automatic dividend reinvestment or average cost statement?	May be available from the broker, sometimes for a fee	Typically provided free of charge by the mutual fund.
Investors who should consider this are:	<ul><li>Investors who buy and hold for long periods of time.</li><li>Those with a single, large, lump-sum to invest.</li><li>Those seeking trading flexibility</li></ul>	<ul><li>Those who buy or sell frequently.</li><li>Those with a small amount of money to invest.</li><li>Investors who rebalance their portfolio regularly.</li></ul>

How a Mutual Fund Works

A large number of people with a common goal purchase shares in a mutual fund.

Investment less fees[1] Investors receive dividends, capital gains or losses[2]

MUTUAL FUND COMPANY

Fund invests according to stated goals Fund receives dividends, capital gains or losses

MONEY MARKET FUNDS	GROWTH FUNDS	INCOME FUNDS	BALANCED FUNDS
Invest in a variety of short-term debt (Treasury Bills, commercial paper, etc.).	Emphasize long-term capital growth. Usually invest in common stock.	Focus on current income using bonds and other income producing securities.	Strive for both income and long-term gain, using both stocks and bonds.

[1] Depending on the fund, sales charges may be deducted at the time an investor purchases shares in the fund, or at a later date. Some mutual funds do not have a sales charge. The Securities and Exchange Commission requires that all prospective mutual fund investors be given a booklet (the prospectus) clearly explaining how a fund works, its goals and risks, and all expenses or charges.

[2] Mutual fund shares will fluctuate in value and investors will receive more or less than their original investment when the shares are redeemed. Investors must include dividends and capital gains in current taxable income even if reinvested in the mutual fund.

Advantages

- **Professional management:** Experienced professionals manage the portfolio.

- **Diversification:** Owning shares in a mutual fund allows an investor to participate in a diversified portfolio, spreading the investment risk over several securities.

- **Convenience:** Many funds offer convenient features, such as consolidated statements, automatic reinvestment of gains and dividends, tax information, etc.

Mutual Fund Families

Mutual funds offer the investor immediate diversification into carefully selected and managed securities. An investment program can be started for a small amount of money (typically $500-$1,000), and subsequent purchases can be as small as $50. Automatic reinvestment of capital gains and dividends[1] is a convenient way to purchase additional shares.

Family of Funds

Many mutual fund families have a broad spectrum of funds to meet the needs and temperaments of various investors. A typical family of funds might include:

MONEY MARKET FUNDS[2]	SECTOR FUNDS
• Invest in short-term money market (debt) instruments.	• Generally invest in stocks and bonds of companies focusing on a particular sector of the economy.
• Yields fluctuate daily.	• Typical areas might include technology, health, energy, utilities, precious metals, etc.
• Taxation of dividends received depends on underlying investments.	• Income and capital gains generally taxable.
• Often used as a liquid, short-term storehouse for funds.	• Usually appeal to investors with a concern or interest in a particular area of the economy.

[1] Federal income tax law taxes qualifying stock dividends at marginal rates, which can be lower than those generally applicable to ordinary income. State and local income tax treatment of such dividends may differ.

[2] Money market mutual funds (MMMFs) are neither insured nor guaranteed by any government agency. There is no assurance that a MMMF will be able to maintain a fixed, net-asset value of $1.00 per share. Such funds should be clearly distinguished from money market deposit accounts (MMDAs) in banks and savings and loans. Most financial institutions offering MMDAs are protected by government deposit insurance.

MUNICIPAL BOND FUNDS

- Invest primarily in municipal bonds, or other short-term municipal debt.
- Federally tax-free dividends.
- Dividends may also be state tax exempt.
- Dividend income may be subject to alternative minimum tax.
- Typically used by high tax-bracket investors seeking current income.

AGGRESSIVE GROWTH FUNDS

- Typically invest in stocks of companies with high potential earnings growth.
- Generally seek capital appreciation.
- Relatively high risk/reward potential; market value can be volatile.

BOND FUNDS

- Invest in bonds and debt-type instruments.
- Taxability of dividends received depends on underlying investments.
- Commonly used as source of current income.

GROWTH FUNDS

- Commonly invest in stocks of companies with relatively stable potential earnings growth.
- Generally seek capital appreciation.
- Typically follow a more conservative investment strategy than aggressive growth funds.

INCOME FUNDS	GROWTH AND INCOME FUNDS
• Invest in bonds and other debt-type instruments such as preferred or high-yield stocks. • Usually seek maximum current income. • Taxation of dividends received depends on underlying investments. • Appeals to investors seeking a relatively high level of current income.	• Often invest in both stocks and bonds or other debt-type instruments. • Commonly seek both capital appreciation and current income. • Taxation of dividends received depends on underlying investments. • Also called balanced funds.

Possible Risks

The risks involved in owning shares in a mutual fund are the same as those involved in directly owning the underlying securities. However, these risks are generally spread by the fund manager over a range of securities, to help minimize the impact of any one risk on a fund's performance as a whole.

- **Mutual funds holding stock investments**
  - **Market risk:** The value of a stock can fluctuate up and down.
- **Mutual funds holding bonds or other debt instruments**
  - **Market risk:** The value of a bond will fluctuate, up and down, usually in response to changes in interest rates.
  - **Default risk:** The possibility that the issuer of a bond or other debt will not pay either interest or principal.
  - **Inflation risk:** As fixed-return investments, bonds are subject to inflation risk; over time, the dollars received may have less purchasing power.

Exchange Privilege

Exchange from one fund to another may be allowed at any time for a nominal fee and no commission charge. There will be tax consequences at the time of exchange if there is a profit or a loss. Purchasing mutual funds from different mutual fund companies may result in paying additional sales loads.

Timing Services

For a fee, these organizations manage funds, typically shifting in and out of the market by switching from growth funds to money market funds through the exchange privilege.

Seek Professional Guidance

All investment decisions should be made only after consultation with a professional advisor and a complete review of the appropriate prospectuses. Investors in mutual funds are subject to a variety of risks; both investment return and market value can fluctuate. When redeemed, an investor's shares may be worth more or less than their original cost.

Dollar Cost Averaging

Many investors look to the stock market for capital growth, investing in individual stocks or mutual funds. Historically, the stock market has charted a long-term upward trend. In the short run, however, daily fluctuations in prices can make it difficult to decide when to buy.

Rather than trying to time the market, and making a single purchase, many investors use a method called dollar cost averaging. Using dollar cost averaging, an investor buys the same stock or mutual fund at regular intervals; e.g., monthly or quarterly, and with a fixed amount of investment dollars; e.g., $100 per month.

When the selected stock or mutual fund declines in value, the investor's $100 will buy a greater number of shares. When the market price increases, the investor's $100 will buy fewer shares. Over a period of time, as market prices fluctuate, the average cost per share to the investor will be less than the average price per share.

For example, assume that a person invests $100 per month for 12 months in XYZ mutual fund.

Month	Dollars Invested	Price per Share	Number of Shares Purchased
Jan	$100	$11.00	9.09
Feb	$100	$13.00	7.69
Mar	$100	$9.00	11.11
Apr	$100	$11.00	9.09
May	$100	$12.00	8.33
Jun	$100	$8.00	12.50
July	$100	$9.00	11.11
Aug	$100	$10.00	10.00
Sept	$100	$12.00	8.33
Oct	$100	$11.00	9.09
Nov	$100	$8.00	12.50
Dec	$100	$11.00	9.09
Total	$1,200	$125.00	117.94

The average price per share: ($125.00 /12) = $10.42

The average cost per share: ($1,200 /117.94) = $10.17

Dollar Cost Averaging

Graphically, the results of dollar cost averaging in our example would look like this.

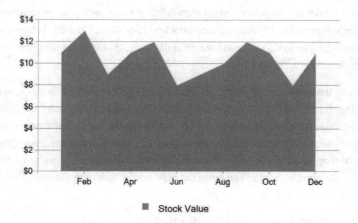

Notes:

- Investments must be regular and the same amount each time. If the investor discontinues the plan when the market value is less than the cost of the shares he or she will obviously lose money.
- The investor must be willing and able to invest during the low price levels.
- Dollar cost averaging cannot assure a profit and does not protect the investor in a steadily declining market.

Securities Investor Protection Corporation (SIPC)

The Securities Investor Protection Corporation (SIPC) is a non-profit, non-government, membership corporation, funded by its member broker-dealers. Most U.S. broker-dealers are required to belong to SIPC. SIPC was created under the authority of the Securities Investor Protection Act of 1970, (SIPA).

The SIPA was the response by Congress to an unexpected surge, in the late 1960s, in the average daily trading volume. This sudden increase in trading activity, combined with a sharp drop in securities prices, overwhelmed the transaction processing systems then in place, leaving many brokerage firms unable to determine their own financial situation. The operational chaos lead to a number of broker-dealers being acquired or merged into other firms or simply being liquidated and going out of business. Public confidence in the financial markets was severely shaken.

What Does SIPC Coverage Actually Do?

The protection offered by SIPC has sometimes been compared to that offered by the Federal Deposit Insurance Corporation, or FDIC, although the comparison is misleading. When a member bank fails, the FDIC insures all depositors at that bank against loss. There are no questions asked and an individual depositor is made whole, dollar-for-dollar, up to a specified dollar limitation.

SIPC, however, is designed to simply *replace* missing stocks and other securities (when possible), even when an investment may have increased or decreased in value. SIPC does not protect investors when the value of their stocks, bonds, or other securities declines in value, whatever the reason.

SIPC protects customers up to $500,000 per insured account for securities and cash, with a $250,000 limit for cash only.

How SIPC Insurance Works

When a brokerage firm fails, the steps SIPC will take to protect investors will vary, depending on the size of the broker-dealer and whether or not the firm's account records are accurate or not. In general, the procedure is as follows:

Securities Investor Protection Corporation (SIPC)

- **Liquidation – first steps:** For larger firms, a court-appointed trustee works with SIPC to liquidate a failed broker-dealer. If the brokerage firm has accurate records, some or all of the accounts may be transferred to other brokerage firms. In other situations, and after reviewing the broker-dealer's account records, the trustee will mail *notices* and *claim forms* to all customers who had accounts with the firm within the previous 12 months. Securities claimed by an investor are valued for purposes of the $500,000/$250,000 limits as of the date the liquidation began, known as the "filing" date.

- **Liquidation – claim form process:** To be eligible for SIPC protection, an investor must submit a completed claim form to SIPC, showing the securities, cash, and other amounts the investor claims are owed to him or her by the failed broker-dealer. The claim form should be accompanied by supporting documentation such as brokerage statements, trade confirmations, and any correspondence with the firm. SIPC will then compare the claim with the books and records of the broker-dealer and determine the investor's "net equity," the difference between what the broker-dealer owes the investor (such as securities and cash) and what the investor owes the broker-dealer, (such as a margin loan).

- **Liquidation – determination letter:** After receiving an investor's claim, SIPC will decide if the claim should be allowed or rejected. A *Determination Letter* is sent to the investor explaining SIPC's decision. If the investor does not agree with the decision in the determination letter, he or she has 30 days to object, in writing, to the court supervising the liquidation.

- **Liquidation – distribution of cash and securities:** If an investor agrees with the determination made by SIPC, the securities and cash that he or she own are returned. The goal is to put customers in the same position – in terms of *what* is owned - they were in before the broker-dealer failed. The *value* of those securities, however, is not guaranteed. In the interim period, market movements may have increased or decreased the value of a customer's securities. In some situations it may not be possible to return all of the securities that were in the account.

- **Direct Payment Procedure:** In situations involving smaller broker-dealers, SIPC may use an out-of-court process known as a *Direct Payment Procedure*. SIPC sends claim forms to customers and publishes notice of the Direct Payment Procedure in one or more newspapers. Securities are valued as of the date the notice is published in the newspaper. Customers have six months to submit their claims to SIPC. Claims submitted are reviewed by SIPC and a determination is made. If a customer disagrees with SIPC's determination, he or she has six months to ask for judicial review of the determination.

Other Points to Keep in Mind

There are several other points to keep in mind:

- **Some "securities" are not protected:** SIPC offers protection to securities as defined in the SIPA. Under the SIPA, some investments commonly thought of as being securities are not protected by SIPC. For example, commodities futures accounts, including cash in a commodities futures account, are generally not protected by SIPC. Similarly, gold and silver coins are not considered to be a security and thus are not protected by SIPC. As the definition of what is – and is not – a security protected by SIPC can be complex, professional guidance is recommended.

- **Multiple accounts:** SIPC account protection is offered on a "separate capacity" basis. Whether or not one account is "separate" from another, and thus benefits from the full $500,000/$250,000 SIPC per-account protection, depends on different ownership. For example, an individual account owned by Mary is separate from the joint account Mary owns with her husband Joe. However, because of the complexities which can occur in securities accounts, professional guidance in this area is strongly suggested.

For Further Information

For additional information concerning the protection provided to investors by SIPC, see your individual broker or visit the SIPC website at http://www.sipc.org/. By telephone, SIPC can be reached at (202) 237-8300.

Types of Securities Orders

Investors in the stock and bond markets should be familiar with the different types of orders that can be used to execute buy and sell orders for stocks and bonds. The table below provides a brief description of some of the more commonly encountered types of securities orders.

Order Type	Considerations
Market Order: A *market* order is an order to buy or sell a stock at the best available price.	The execution price of a market order is not guaranteed. In a fast-moving market, the execution price of a market order is not necessarily the last-traded price. For large orders, parts of the order may be executed at different prices.
Limit Order: A *limit* order is an order to buy or sell a stock at a specific price, or better.	A limit order can only be filled if the stock's market price reaches the limit price. A <u>buy</u> limit order can only be executed at the limit price or lower. A <u>sell</u> limit order can only be executed at the limit price or higher. A limit order does not guarantee execution.
Stop Order: A *stop* order, also known as a *stop-loss* order, is an order to buy or sell a stock once the price of the stock reaches a specified price, the "stop" price.	The stop price is a "trigger" that causes a stop order to become a market order. When the stop price is reached, a stop order becomes a market order; the stop price is not the guaranteed execution price. A <u>buy</u> stop order is entered at a stop price above the current market price. A <u>sell</u> stop order is entered at a stop price below the current market price.[1]
Stop-Limit Order: a *stop-limit* order is an order to buy or sell a stock that combines the features of a stop order and a limit order.	Once the stop price is reached, a stop-limit order becomes a limit order that will be executed at the specified limit price, or better. The stop price and the limit price for a stop-limit order do not have to be the same. A stop-limit order may not be executed if the stock's price moves away from the specified limit price. Short-term fluctuations in a stock's price may activate a stop-limit order.
Day Order: A *day* order is the default time frame for the expiration of a stock order.	Unless an investor specifies a different time frame for the expiration of an order, orders to buy or sell a stock are day orders, good only during that trading day. If not executed, a day order expires at the end of the trading day.
Good-Til-Canceled (GTC) Order: A *GTC* order is an order to buy or sell that lasts until the order is completed or canceled.	Brokerage firms generally limit the length of time that a GTC order can remain open. This time frame may vary from broker to broker.

---

[1] A <u>buy</u> stop order is generally used to limit a loss or protect a profit on a stock which has been sold short. A <u>sell</u> stop order is generally used to limit a loss or protect a profit on a stock already owned.

Order Type	Considerations
Immediate or Cancel (IOC) Order: An *IOC* order is an order that must be executed immediately.	Any portion of the order that cannot be filled immediately will be canceled.
Fill-or Kill Order (FOK): A *Fill-or-Kill* order is an order that must be executed immediately and entirely.	If the entire order cannot be executed immediately, the entire order is canceled; no partial execution of the order is allowed.
All-Or-None Order AON): An *AON* order is an order that must be executed in its entirety or not executed at all.	All-Or-None orders that cannot be executed immediately remain active until they are either executed or cancelled.
Not-Held Order (NH): A *Not-Held* order is a market or limit order in which the customer gives the broker discretion as to time and price.	Typically used for trading in overseas markets, in different time zones. A NH order does not hold the broker responsible for missing the best price.

Check With Your Broker

Not all of the order types and trading instructions discussed above are available through all brokerage firms. Investors are advised to check with their broker to see which types of orders and trading instruction are available. A brokerage may also have specific policies that an investor should be aware of.

Stocks

The terms "stock" and "share of stock" both refer to ownership of a business corporation. When a corporation is first founded, investors provide the capital (money) to get the business going. Those who provide this financing become part owners of the company. A "stock certificate" is then issued, showing the number of "shares" that each investor holds, as evidence of this ownership status.

Common Stock

The most prevalent form of stock is termed "common" stock. As owners of a company, common stockholders have certain rights and privileges:

- **To vote for the board of directors:** The members of the board of directors of a corporation are responsible for the overall direction of the business, and are elected by the stockholders.

- **To receive information about the firm:** Most corporations will hold an "annual meeting" of the stockholders, to conduct necessary corporate business and to publicize the results of the most recent business year. A stockholder unable to attend the meeting may vote by mail or select a "proxy" to act in his or her place. Most corporations publish an "annual report" reviewing the firm's business results.

- **To share in the profits:** Common stockholders may share in the profits of the firm, through payments known as "dividends."[1] Dividends are not guaranteed. Before a dividend is paid, the board of directors must first "declare" a dividend, and decide how large a dividend to pay, and when to pay it. If a firm has no profits, or if the profits are needed by the company for business purposes, the board may decide not to pay a dividend.

Preferred Stock

"Preferred" stock is a hybrid, mixing characteristics of both common stock and bonds. The term "preferred" comes from its status within the financial structure of the firm.

---

[1] Federal law taxes qualifying stock dividends at marginal rates lower than those generally applicable to ordinary income. State and local income tax treatment of such dividends may differ.

- **Dividend preference:** A company which has issued both common and preferred stock generally must first pay a dividend to the preferred stockholders before it can pay a dividend to the common stockholders. Unlike the variable dividend of common stock, preferred stock typically has a fixed dividend amount. Only in dire situations will a firm reduce or eliminate a preferred dividend payment.

- **Preferred position in liquidation:** If a company gets into serious financial trouble, and is forced to sell its assets to pay creditors, there may not be enough money to pay all bills, and also return something to the stockholders. Preferred stockholders have priority over common stockholders in liquidation.

- **Lack of voting control:** Unlike common stockholders, holders of preferred stock generally do not have a right to vote for the members of the board of directors.

Investment Uses

Investors typically buy and hold stocks for long-term capital growth. If a business is successful, over time the value of the business, and the market price of the firm's shares, generally increase. Shareholders who purchased the stock at a lower price can then sell their shares at a profit. If a business is not successful, the value of a firm's shares can fall, sometimes to zero, resulting in an investor loss.

In some instances, investors will purchase stock in companies with a history of paying regular dividends, as a way of generating additional current income. If a firm continues to grow, dividends and stock price can increase, potentially providing both capital gain and increasing current income.

How to Invest

- **Direct ownership:** Working with a stockbroker or other securities licensed professional, investors can own stock by direct purchase, with the shares registered in their own names.

- **Indirect ownership:** Open-end investment companies known as "mutual funds" are an indirect method of stock ownership. Mutual funds pool the resources of many individuals, and offer an investor access to a diversified portfolio of professionally managed securities. Exchange-traded funds, or ETFs, are a variation of the standard mutual fund, and are another way of investing in stocks. Certain life insurance products such as variable life, universal-variable life, and variable annuities, provide another indirect means of stock market participation.[1]

Possible Risks

- **Market risk:** A key risk involved in stock ownership is that of "market risk," the fluctuation of share prices up and down. Stockowners have invested in a business enterprise, and the price of the company's stock will generally follow the firm's business results. Stock prices will also fluctuate in response to general economic and market factors.

---

[1] The Securities and Exchange Commission requires that all prospective ETF and mutual fund investors be given a "prospectus." The prospectus contains valuable information concerning how a fund works, its goals and risks, and any expenses and charges involved. All "variable" life insurance and annuity products also require a prospectus.

Stock Market Indexes and Averages

News reports about the stock market that you see or hear every day on television, on the radio, and in newspapers track the movement of groups of stocks, not individual issues. Citing a specific "index" or "average," these reports give you a general sense of the direction of stock prices. They will not, however, tell you whether the stocks in your own portfolio are up or down. Understanding what these reports mean is important because they are commonly used as benchmarks to measure the performance of individual stocks.

What are Indexes and Averages?

At their most basic, stock indexes and averages are simply ways to measure changes in the market value of certain groups of stocks.

An "average," as the name implies, is the arithmetic average price of a group of stocks. The Dow Jones Industrial Average (DJIA) is such an average. Made up of 30 large industrial stocks, the DJIA was originally calculated by adding up the price of the stocks included in the average and then dividing by 30. This divisor has since been adjusted a number of times to account for mergers, additions, deletions, and other technical factors.

An index, on the other hand, is an average value expressed in relation to a previously determined base number. The Standard & Poors 500 Index (S&P 500), for example, uses a base value of 10, determined during 1941-1943.[1]

These measuring tools can be associated with specific exchanges or industry groups. More specialized indexes are geared toward tracking the performance of specific market sectors, such as high technology, energy, health care, finance, or transportation.

Price-Weighted vs. Market-Value Weighted

An index or average may also be classified according to the method used to determine its price. In a price-weighted index (e.g., the DJIA), the price of each component stock is the only consideration when determining the value of the index. Thus, the price movement of higher-priced stocks influences the average more than that of lower-priced stocks.

In contrast, a market-value weighted index (e.g., the S&P 500) factors in a stock's total market value, equal to the share price times the number of shares outstanding. Therefore, a relatively small shift in the price of a large company can significantly influence the value of the index.

---

[1] It is not possible to directly invest in an index.

Stock Market Indexes and Averages

Commonly Encountered Indexes and Averages

Standard & Poor's 500 Index: The S&P 500 is the benchmark against which many portfolio managers compare themselves. The "S&P" (as it is commonly referred to) is composed of 500 "blue chip" stocks, separated by industry, so that almost all key industries are represented.

Dow Jones Industrial Average (DJIA): This commonly quoted average tracks the movement of 30 of the largest blue chip stocks traded on the New York Stock Exchange (NYSE). When people ask, "How did the market do today?" they are usually referring to this index:

Component Stocks of the Dow Jones Industrial Average[1]			
3M	E.I. DuPont	JPMorgan Chase	UnitedHealth
American Express	Exxon Mobil	McDonald's	United Technologies
AT&T	General Electric	Merck	Verizon
Boeing	Goldman Sachs	Microsoft	Visa Inc.
Caterpillar	Home Depot	Nike Inc.	Wal-Mart
Chevron	IBM	Pfizer	Walt Disney
Cisco	Intel	Procter & Gamble	
Coca-Cola	Johnson & Johnson	Travelers	

Dow Jones and Co., which maintains the DJIA, also tracks utilities (electric and gas) in the Dow Jones Utilities Average and transportation stocks (airlines, railroads, and trucking firms) in the Dow Jones Transportation Average. The combined industrial, utilities, and transportation averages are called the Dow Jones Composite Average.

NASDAQ Composite Index: This index tracks the movement of all companies traded on the NASDAQ National Market System (NMS), which tend to be smaller and more volatile than those in the Dow Jones Industrial Average or the S&P 500. The NASDAQ Composite is market-value weighted, which gives more influence to larger and higher priced stocks.

NYSE Composite Index: This is the index for the trading of all New York Stock Exchange stocks. It is market-value weighted and expressed in dollars and cents. When commentators say, "The average share lost 15 cents on the New York Exchange today," this is the index to which they are usually referring.

---

[1] As of September 23, 2013.

Stock Market Indexes and Averages

NYSE MKT Composite Index: An index which tracks all common stocks listed on the New York Stock Exchange. The index is weighted by the market capitalization of its components, meaning that stocks with a larger number of shares outstanding and with higher stock prices affect the index more than companies with fewer shares outstanding and lower prices.

Wilshire 5,000 Equity Index: The broadest measure of all indexes, the market-value-weighted Wilshire includes all U.S. stocks for which price data are readily available. Thus, it gives a good indication of the overall direction of all stocks, large and small.

Foreign Indexes: A number of indexes follow markets in foreign countries, such as the British FTSE 100, the French CAC 40, the German DAX, and the Japanese Nikkei 225.

Growth vs. Value Investing: Which is Best?

There are two schools of thought within the investment community as to whether higher returns can be achieved by investing for "growth" or by investing for "value."

Value Investing

Those who espouse value investing favor purchasing stocks with higher than average dividend yields and relatively low market value indicators, such as price-to-earnings, price-to-book, and price-to-sales ratios. Value investors rely heavily on their analytical judgment as to whether or not a stock is mispriced; if a stock is underpriced, it's a good buy; if the stock is overpriced, it's time to sell.

Value investors typically buy stocks that have been beaten down in price because the companies they represent, although basically sound, are going through a period of adversity. This strategy calls for selling these shares after they have risen in price as a result of the underlying company having overcome its difficulties. The principal risk in this approach is that the price of the security may not reach its anticipated value.

Growth Investing

By comparison, growth-style investors are more apt to subscribe to the "efficient market" hypothesis, which maintains that the current market price of a stock reflects all the "knowable" information about a company and inherently represents the most reasonable price at that given point in time. In other words, it could be said that "growth investors look for good companies – not good stocks."

Thus, those in the growth camp seek optimum investment performance by investing in quality companies with higher than average earnings growth rates, regardless of the current market valuation of the company's stock.

Which Approach Is Best?

For some time many common stock funds have been divided according to their investment style, either "growth" oriented, "value" oriented, or a "blend" of the two. This has provided

Growth vs. Value Investing: Which is Best?

an opportunity to study the performance records of mutual funds using "growth" or "value" as their primary investment strategies.

As for which strategy achieves the highest returns, most studies show that this largely depends on the specific period over which the two styles are compared. For example, throughout the 1990s the public was deluged with studies extolling the virtues of growth investing over value. With the bursting of the dot.com bubble in 2000, however, until late 2008, the value approach seemed to perform better. As always, the future is never clear.

Because investing involves risk, including the possible loss of principal, an individual investor must understand the strengths and weaknesses of each investment approach and choose that with which he or she is most comfortable. The guidance of financial professionals can be of great help in making this decision.

Coping With Market Volatility

During periods of economic uncertainty, financial markets are often characterized by wide swings in market value. Such "market volatility," with prices sharply rising and falling, is a reflection of changeable investor sentiment as well as more substantive economic or political events. Even during more stable times, financial markets will fluctuate, although price movements tend to be more moderate. By their very nature, financial markets rise and fall constantly, with an ever-present potential for gain or loss.

So, how does an individual cope with constant market volatility?

Avoid an Emotional Response

When markets fall sharply, some investors will panic, sell all or part of their holdings, and shift assets into what are seen as "safer" investments. Such emotion-based selling after a market decline simply turns paper losses into real ones and limits any possible gains should the markets recover. Some individuals will respond emotionally and buy when the markets are "hot" and values are rising. The end result is often an investor who buys high, sells low, and then wonders, "What happened?"

"Timing" the Market

Some investors attempt to "time" the markets, buying when the market is low and then selling when the market is high. The problem is that it's never clear just when the market has reached a trough or a peak. In the classic Wall Street phrase, "No one rings a bell." Market timing is a concept that, in theory at least, seems logical. In practice, however, no one has yet devised a system for consistently and accurately identifying market tops and bottoms.

Diversify Your Portfolio - Asset Allocation

Asset allocation is an investment strategy that seeks to reduce investment risk by spreading an investor's portfolio over a number of different asset types. This approach takes advantage of the tendency of different asset types to move in different cycles, and thus smooth out the ups and downs of the entire portfolio. Stocks, bonds, and cash (or cash equivalents) are the investments normally used. Tangible assets, such as real estate or gold, may also be included.

Coping With Market Volatility

The asset allocation process normally begins with an analysis of the historical levels of risk and return for each asset type being considered.[1] These historical values are then used as a guide to structuring a portfolio that matches the investor's individual goals and overall risk tolerance level.

Regularly Review Your Investment Strategy

An investor's portfolio allocation should reflect factors such as the investment goal, timeframe, need for liquidity, risk tolerance, and income tax bracket. As time passes, and as market and economic conditions change, it is likely that an investor's goals, and the optimal portfolio mix to reach those goals, will also change. Adjusting the asset allocation, known as "rebalancing," is a regular part of good investment management, in both up and down markets.

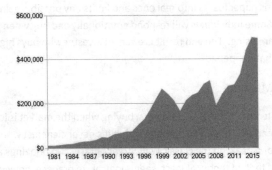

Take a Long-Term View

Historically, the long-term trend in equity markets has been upward, although there have been periods when the markets declined. To illustrate the point, the graph below charts the annual return from a $10,000 investment in the S&P500® Index for the period January 1, 1980, through December 31, 2015.[2]

---

[1] Historical data, while useful as a general guide, cannot be considered an accurate indicator of future results. There is no guarantee that past performance is a predictor of future investment performance.

[2] The chart is for illustrative purposes only and does not represent the actual performance of any investment. It is not possible to directly invest in an index. Past performance is no guarantee of future results. Source: Calculated by Advisys, Inc. using data provided by Morningstar, Inc. © 2015 Morningstar, Inc. All rights reserved. The information contained herein: (1) is proprietary to Morningstar and/or its content providers, (2) may not be copied or distributed, and (3) is not warranted to be accurate, complete, or timely.

Coping With Market Volatility

An investor can more easily ride out periodic economic storms by clearly understanding his or her long-term investment goals and rebalancing the portfolio accordingly. Additionally, a portion of the portfolio can be placed in safer, more liquid assets, which can then be used to meet immediate cash needs. The balance of the portfolio remains invested for the long term.

Automatic Investing

Rather than making a single, lump-sum investment, some investors feel more comfortable investing an equal dollar amount at regular intervals. Also known as "dollar cost averaging," this strategy does not guarantee a profit, nor does it protect against losses in a declining market. It does have the advantage of buying more shares when the price is low and fewer shares when the price is higher.

Seek Professional Guidance

In both bull and bear markets, the guidance of trained financial professionals is strongly advised.

Bonds

When an individual borrows money to purchase a home, a type of debt called a "mortgage" is created. A single organization such as a bank or credit union will loan money to the homeowner, who, in return, makes monthly payments to pay off the loan. Each monthly mortgage payment is part interest and part principal.

When an institution such as a government, a government agency, or a corporation wants to borrow money, it can do so by creating a form of debt called a "bond." Rather than going to a single source for the money, institutional borrowers will sell bonds to many separate investors. In return, investors receive periodic, interest-only payments, with the principal amount of the bond being repaid in a lump sum, no later than a specified future date.

Types of Bonds

There are two basic ways to classify bonds:

- **Bond issuer:** The federal government, state and local governments and agencies, and corporations all issue bonds.

- **Maturity:** Refers to the date when the money borrowed must be repaid. Bond maturities can range from one to 30 years.

The Language of Bonds

There are a number of terms investors use when discussing bonds:

- **Form:** Bonds are issued in many different forms. If a bond is "registered," a bond certificate is issued, listing the name of the owner. The bond issuer sends the interest payment to the owner when due. Some bonds are "bearer" bonds; whoever bears (has possession of) the bond is presumed to be the owner. The "book-entry" form is usually used for very short-term bonds. No certificate is issued; the bond issuer keeps a list of the owners, and sends an informal statement to each to confirm ownership.
- **Denomination:** Refers to the amount to be repaid when the bond matures. The terms "face value," "par," and "par value" are also used. Bonds are most commonly issued in $1,000 denominations.

- **Yield:** The annual return on a bond. For example, an investor who pays $1,000 for a bond paying $60.00 per year has a 6.0% yield. The term "coupon" is also used. Early bonds were issued with a sheet of coupons attached. To receive his interest payment, an investor would clip one of the coupons and return it to the issuer. Zero coupon bonds do not pay interest currently. Instead, such bonds are issued at a discount from face value. The investor receives principal and interest in a lump sum at maturity. Floating rate bonds have a yield that can change under specified circumstances.

- **Credit rating:** Before a bank makes a mortgage loan, it does a credit check to gauge the prospective borrower's ability to repay both principal and interest. The risk that a debt will not be repaid is termed "default" risk. Investors can estimate the probability of default in a particular bond by checking an issuer's credit rating. Moody's Investors Service and Standard and Poor's are two well-known bond-rating agencies. In general, the higher the credit rating, the lower the default risk. A bond issuer's credit rating can change over time.

Bond Prices and Interest Rates

If an investor buys a bond, and holds it to maturity, the issuer is obligated to repay the full face amount. If a bond is sold before it matures, however, the investor may receive more, or less, than originally paid. Bond prices can move up and down, usually in response to changes in the general level of interest rates. If rates rise, the price of existing bonds usually falls; if interest rates decline, the market value of existing bonds generally increases. Other factors may also affect bond prices.

Bonds and Income Taxes

The income tax treatment of bond interest depends primarily on who issued the bond:

- **U.S. government bonds:** Interest from direct obligations of the U.S. government is taxable by the federal government, but is generally exempt from tax at the state and local level.

- **Municipal bonds:** Income from municipal bonds is generally exempt from federal tax. Normally, the interest is also exempt from state and local taxes if the bondholder lives in the same jurisdiction where the bond was issued. In some cases, income from municipal bonds may be subject to the alternative minimum tax (AMT) as well as capital gains taxes.

- **Corporate bonds:** Interest income from corporate bonds is generally taxable by the federal government and state and local governments.

Investment Uses

Bonds are most frequently used as a stable, predictable source of current income. The favorable tax treatment of U.S. government and municipal bond interest is a plus.

How to Invest

- **Direct ownership:** Working with a stockbroker or other securities-licensed professional, investors can buy bonds directly, holding the securities in their own names.
- **Indirect ownership:** Open-end investment companies known as mutual funds are an indirect method of bond ownership. Mutual funds pool the resources of many individuals, and offer an investor access to a diversified, professionally managed portfolio. Exchange-traded funds, or ETFs, are a variation of the standard mutual fund, and are another way of investing in bonds. Unit Investment Trusts (UITs) are a third form of indirect bond ownership. The bond portfolio in a UIT is fixed and not actively managed.[1]

Possible Risks

- **Market risk:** If a bond is sold before maturity, an investor may receive more or less than originally paid.

- **Default risk:** An issuer may default on payment of the principal or interest of a bond.

- **Inflation risk:** As fixed return investments, bonds are subject to inflation risk; over time, the dollars received have less purchasing power.

---

[1] The Securities and Exchange Commission requires that all prospective UIT, ETF, and mutual fund investors be given a prospectus. The prospectus contains valuable information concerning how an investment works, its goals and risks, and any expenses and charges involved.

Corporate Bonds

Corporate bonds are debt instruments issued by large corporations. The proceeds of corporate bond issues are often used to purchase new plant and equipment, or to fund research for future company growth.

Corporate bonds issued today are usually registered in form, and pay interest on a semi-annual basis. Maturities typically range from one to 30 years. By way of contrast, bonds issued in the 19th century were often "bearer" bonds with detachable coupons. The owner of the bond had to clip a coupon every six months and return it to the bond issuer for payment. Maturities could reach up to 100 years.

Types of Corporate Bonds

There are a number of different types of corporate bonds:

- **Mortgage bonds:** Bonds that are secured by identifiable assets such as real estate or equipment.

- **Debentures:** Bonds that are secured only by the faith and credit of the issuer.

- **Convertible bonds:** Bonds that can be converted into a specified number of shares of the common stock of the issuing corporation. An investor who buys a convertible bond usually expects the price of the underlying common stock to rise over time.

- **Commercial paper:** Commercial paper is used to meet very short-term (30-90 days) corporate financing needs. It is essentially an unsecured corporate IOU.

Other Corporate Bond Features

Occasionally, corporate bonds will have additional features.

- **Sinking fund:** Some bonds require the issuing corporation to make regular payments into a special, dedicated fund, designed to ensure that interest and principal payments are made when due.

- **Call feature:** Bonds issued during periods of high interest rates may have a feature which allows the issuer to redeem or "call" the bond prior to maturity. If a bond issue is called, the issuer will normally redeem the bond for full face value, or with a slight premium. Such bonds usually have an initial period of time during which the call feature cannot be used.

- **Put feature:** If a bond has this feature, it allows the investor to force the corporation to redeem the bond and "put" the bond back where it came from, usually at face value.

Bond Prices and Interest Rates

If a corporate bond is held to maturity, the issuer is obligated to repay the full face amount. If the bond is sold before it matures, however, the investor may receive more, or less, than originally paid. Bond prices can fluctuate, most often in response to changes in the general level of interest rates. If rates rise, the price of existing bonds usually falls; if interest rates decline, the market value of existing bonds generally increases. Corporate bond prices may also be affected by general business and economic factors.

Income Tax Treatment

Interest income and capital gain from corporate bonds are fully taxable at the federal, state and local levels.

Investment Uses

Corporate bonds are most frequently used as a stable, predictable source of current income. They typically have a higher yield than either municipal or government bonds due to the tax treatment of the interest income and a generally higher level of default risk. High-quality corporate bonds can be very useful inside a tax-deferred framework such as an IRA or other qualified retirement plan.

How to Invest

- **Direct ownership:** Working with a stockbroker or other securities-licensed professional, investors can buy corporate bonds directly, holding the securities in their own names.

- **Indirect ownership:** Mutual funds (open-end investment companies) are an indirect method of corporate bond ownership. Mutual funds pool the resources of many individuals and offer an investor access to a diversified portfolio of professionally managed securities. Exchange-traded funds, or ETFs, are a variation of the standard mutual fund and are another way of investing in corporate bonds. Unit investment trusts (UITs) are a third form of indirect ownership. The corporate bond portfolio in a UIT is fixed and not actively managed[1].

Possible Risks

- **Market risk:** If a corporate bond is sold before maturity, an investor may receive more or less than originally paid.

- **Default risk:** An issuer may default on payment of a bond's principal or interest.

- **Inflation risk:** As fixed return investments, corporate bonds are subject to inflation risk. Over time, the dollars received have less purchasing power.

---

[1] The Securities and Exchange Commission requires that all prospective UIT, ETF, and mutual fund investors be given a prospectus. The prospectus contains valuable information concerning how an investment works, its goals and risks, and any expenses and charges involved.

U.S. Government Securities

The U.S. federal government issues a wide array of debt securities. Securities which are direct obligations of the federal government are backed by the "full faith and credit" of the government. In terms of default risk, these bonds are widely considered to be the safest debt investment available. Interest income from U.S. government bonds is generally not taxable at the state or local level.

Savings Bonds

The federal government's savings bond program was started in 1935 as a refuge for individual savings, free from market fluctuation. Unlike marketable Treasury securities, savings bonds are not traded on any exchange. The U.S. government is both the issuer and ultimate purchaser of all savings bonds.

- **Series EE bonds:** Series EE bonds are considered the "classic" form of U.S. government savings bond. Bonds issued on or after May 1, 2005 earn a fixed rate of interest.[1] The bonds may be cashed any time after 12 months.[2] Current EE bonds earn interest up to 30 years. EE bond holders can choose to be taxed on the income each year, or to defer taxation until the bonds are cashed or they mature.

  - **Paper Series EE bonds:** Effective January 1, 2012, new Series EE bonds may only be purchased in <u>electronic</u> form, via TreasuryDirect, a secure, web-based system operated by the Bureau of the Public Debt. Prior to that date, paper EE bonds could be purchased over-the-counter at banks and other financial institutions. Such paper EE bonds were sold at 50% of face value, in denominations ranging from $50 to $10,000.[3] "Interest" on existing paper EE bonds is earned by a gradual increase in the value of the bonds. Those holding paper Series EE bonds can continue to redeem them at financial institutions. Paper EE bonds which have not matured, but which are lost, stolen, or destroyed, can be reissued in either paper or electronic form.

---

[1] Series EE bonds issued before May 1, 2005 earn a variable rate of interest which is adjusted every six months.

[2] Series EE bonds issued before February 2003 could be redeemed after being held six months. An EE or I bond redeemed within five years of issuance is subject to a 3-month interest penalty.

[3] For example, the purchaser of a $50 savings bond paid $25.

- **Electronic Series EE bonds:** Electronic Series EE bonds are purchased at face value, in exact amounts of $25 or more, via the TreasuryDirect website.

- **Series I bonds:** Series I bonds are a type of savings bond whose purpose is to provide some protection against loss of purchasing power due to inflation. Series I bonds have a return composed of two parts: (1) a fixed interest rate, and (2) an inflation-adjusted rate. Each May and November the Treasury announces the fixed rate of return (which will never change) that will apply to all Series I savings bonds sold during the following six months. The Treasury also determines an inflation-adjusted rate, based on changes in the consumer price index (CPI-U). The total return for the following six months is the sum of the fixed and inflation-adjusted rates. Interest is credited monthly and compounded on a semiannual basis. Series I bonds earn interest for a maximum of 30 years and may be redeemed any time after 12 months.

- **Paper Series I bonds:** Like paper Series EE bonds, effective January 1, 2012, new paper Series I bonds were no longer available over-the-counter at banks and other financial institutions. Up to $5,000 in paper Series I bonds per year may still be purchased via TreasuryDirect, but only if paid for with an IRS tax refund. Paper I bonds are issued at face value, in seven denominations.[1] Those holding paper Series I bonds can continue to redeem them at financial institutions. Paper I bonds which have not matured, but which are lost, stolen, or destroyed, can be reissued in either paper or electronic form.

- **Electronic Series I bonds:** Electronic Series I bonds are purchased at face value, in exact amounts of $25 or more, via the TreasuryDirect website.

- **Purchase limits:** Specific limits apply to the dollar amount of the various types of savings bonds that may be purchased by a single individual or entity in one calendar year. Savings bonds purchased as gifts are not included in these annual limits.

  - Electronic EE bonds: $10,000.
  - Paper I bonds: $5,000 (only with IRS tax refund).
  - Electronic I bonds: $10,000.

---

[1] The denominations are $50, $75, $100, $200, $500, $1,000, and $5,000.

- **Series HH bonds:** HH bonds pay interest to the bondholder every six months. Yields are fixed, but can change after 10 years. The interest from HH bonds is taxable each year. These bonds were issued in four denominations: $500, $1,000, $5,000, and $10,000, and have a 20-year maturity. August, 2004 was the last month that the Treasury issued new series HH bonds. Before that date, investors could acquire HH bonds by exchanging matured EE/E bonds, or by reinvesting matured series HH/H bonds.[1]

Marketable U.S. Government Securities

There are several types of marketable government debt securities. These bonds are termed "marketable" because they are widely traded in public markets. New issues are in book-entry form. Existing and new marketable U.S. government bonds can be purchased through government securities dealers, usually for a small commission. New issues may be purchased directly from the government without paying commission through the Bureau of Public Debt's Treasury Direct program, at www.treasurydirect.gov.

- **Treasury bills (T-Bills):** T-Bills are short-term debt obligations, with maturities of 13, 26, or 52 weeks. They are sold at a discount from face value; the difference between the purchase price and the face value (or the sales price if sold) is the "interest." The interest is not taxable until the bill is sold, or at maturity. The minimum purchase is $100.

- **Treasury notes:** Treasury notes are medium term debt obligations, with maturities ranging from two to 10 years. Notes have a fixed interest rate and pay interest on a semi-annual basis. The minimum purchase is $100.

- **Treasury bonds:** Treasury bonds are issued for terms of 30 years. Like Treasury notes, T-bonds have a fixed interest rate and pay interest on a semi-annual basis. The minimum purchase is $100.

- **Treasury inflation-protected securities:** With a fixed percentage yield, and paying interest every six months, Treasury Inflation Protected Securities (TIPS) are intended to provide protection from loss of purchasing power due to inflation. At issue, TIPS have a par value or principal amount; the value of the principal amount is adjusted for changes, up or down, in the Consumer Price Index, CPI-U. Each interest payment is calculated by multiplying the adjusted principal amount by the fixed percentage rate. At maturity, the investor receives the greater of the inflation-adjusted principal amount or the face value at original issue. TIPS are issued with maturities of 5, 10, and 20 years.

---

[1] Series E bonds were issued from 1941 to 1980. Series H bonds were issued from 1952 to 1979.

Other Government Securities

There are a number of debt securities available that are widely thought of as being "government" bonds. These debt instruments are normally issued under authority of an act of Congress and usually involve some form of government guarantee or sponsorship. Most are freely traded in public markets. These securities come in different forms and are issued by entities such as the Government National Mortgage Association (GNMA), the Federal National Mortgage Association (FNMA), or the Federal Financing Bank (FFB).

Not all of these securities are backed by the "full faith and credit" of the U.S. government. Further, interest income from these securities may not be exempt from state and local income tax. Investors should check the underlying security for such bonds, as well as the taxability of the interest income.

Marketable Government Bonds and Interest Rates

If an investor buys a marketable government bond and holds it to maturity, the issuer is obligated to repay the full face amount. If such a bond is sold before it matures, however, the investor may receive more, or less, than originally paid. Bond prices can move up and down, most often in response to changes in the general level of interest rates. If rates rise, the price of existing bonds usually falls; if interest rates decline, the market value of existing bonds generally increases. Marketable government bond prices may also be affected by general business and economic factors.

U.S. savings bonds are not subject to fluctuating market values; they are not traded on any market. The U.S. government is both the issuer and ultimate purchaser of savings bonds.

Investment Uses

U.S. government bonds that pay interest currently are frequently used as a stable source of income. Treasury bonds of all types, backed by the full faith and credit of the federal government, are considered highly safe from the risk of default. In a tax-deferred framework such as an IRA or other qualified plan, U.S. government securities are useful investments for retirement purposes. If certain requirements are met, series I or EE Savings Bonds can be a tax-free method of accumulating funds for a child's college education.

How to Invest

- **Direct ownership.**

  - **Savings bonds:** Can only be owned directly and are purchased on the Internet at www.treasurydirect.gov.

  - **Marketable U.S. government securities:** At original issue, can be purchased directly from the Treasury on the Internet at www.treasurydirect.gov. May also be purchased through stockbrokers or other securities-licensed professionals.

- **Indirect ownership.**

  - **Marketable U.S. government securities:** Open-end investment companies known as "mutual funds" are an indirect method of owning marketable U.S. government securities. Mutual funds pool the resources of many individuals and allow an investor to share in a diversified, professionally managed portfolio. Exchange-traded funds, or ETFs, are a variation of the standard mutual fund, and are another way of investing in marketable U.S. government securities. Unit Investment Trusts (UITs) are a third form of indirect ownership. The portfolio in a UIT is fixed and not actively managed.[1]

Possible Risks

- **Savings bonds.**

  - **Inflation risk:** Although yields can vary somewhat, savings bonds are subject to inflation risk; over time, the dollars received have less purchasing power. Series I savings bonds are structured to avoid inflation risk.

- **Marketable U.S. government securities.**

  - **Market risk:** If a bond is sold before maturity, an investor may receive more or less than originally paid.

---

[1] The Securities and Exchange Commission requires that all prospective UIT, ETF, and mutual fund investors be given a prospectus. The prospectus contains valuable information concerning how an investment works, its goals and risks, and any expenses and charges involved.

- **Inflation risk:** As fixed return investments, marketable government securities are subject to inflation risk; over time, the dollars received have less purchasing power. Treasury inflation-protected securities are structured to avoid inflation risk.

- **Default risk:** Some government bonds are not backed by the full faith and credit of the federal government; owners of such bonds face the possibility that interest or principal may not be repaid.

Treasury Inflation-Protected Securities

All bond investors face the risk of inflation. Long-term bond investors in particular can lose a substantial portion of the purchasing power of their invested funds due to a gradual increase in prices. Treasury inflation-protected securities (TIPS) are one answer to the inflation risk problem.

How It Works

TIPS are marketable, book-entry debt securities issued by the U.S. Treasury for 5-year, 10-year, and 30-year maturities. TIPS are sold by the government at a quarterly auction, in minimum amounts of $100. They carry a fixed annual interest rate, and pay interest twice a year. The inflation protection is provided by adjusting the principal amount of the security according to changes in the inflation rate.[1] The semiannual interest payment is then calculated based on the adjusted principal amount. The inflation-adjusted principal amount is paid at maturity.

Example: An investor purchases a $1,000 TIPS bond, paying 3.0% annual interest, in January. By July, when the first interest payment is due, inflation has increased 1.0%. The adjusted principal amount of the bond is now $1,010. The interest payable at that time is $15.15, calculated as ($1,010 x 3.0%) ÷ 2. If by January of the following year, when the second interest payment becomes due, inflation had run at a 3.0% level for the whole year, the principal amount of the bond would be $1,030. The second interest payment would be $15.45, calculated as ($1,030 x 3.0%) ÷ 2.

In a deflationary environment, the principal amount is adjusted downward, resulting in an interest payment that may be less than the stated "coupon" payment. If the adjusted principal amount of the bond at maturity is less than the principal amount at issue, an additional sum will be paid to return to the investor at least the original principal amount.

---

[1] As measured by the change in the inflation rate between the date the bond is issued and the current interest payment date. The index used is the non-seasonally adjusted, U.S. City Average All Items Consumer Price Index for Urban Consumers, the CPI-U. The CPI-U is published every month by the Bureau of Labor Statistics.

Treasury Inflation-Protected Securities

Income Tax Issues[1]

Interest income from treasury inflation-protected securities is treated in the same manner as interest income from other "direct obligations" of the federal government. The interest is taxable by the federal government, but is generally exempt from state and local tax.

A unique characteristic of TIPS is that any adjustment of the principal amount is considered to be currently taxable "interest" income. Thus, in our example above, the investor would have $25.15 of taxable interest income from the bond for the first year; $15.15 of interest actually received as cash, and $10.00 in the form of inflation adjustment to the principal amount.

TIPS - Market Prices and Interest Rates

Although Treasury inflation-protected securities are guaranteed against default by the U.S. government, they are also marketable securities, which means they can be bought and sold in the open market. If an investor buys a TIPS and holds it to maturity, the government is obligated to repay at least the original principal amount. If a bond is sold before it matures, however, the investor may receive more, or less, than originally paid, due to fluctuations in market value. TIPS prices in the open market can move up and down, most often in response to changes in the general level of interest rates. In general, if rates rise, the price of existing bonds will fall; if interest rates decline, the market value of existing bonds will increase.

Investment Uses

Treasury inflation-protected securities can serve as a source of periodic income, for investors seeking to meet current expenses. The inflation adjustment feature of these bonds is expected to be a prime attraction for many fixed-income investors. The currently taxable nature of the inflation adjusted principal amount may be a drawback for some. TIPS can be a useful investment in a tax-deferred IRA or other qualified retirement plan.

---

[1] See Treasury Decision 8830, IRB 1999 – 38, and Treasury Decision 8709, IRB 1997 – 9, for a more detailed discussion of the tax treatment of Treasury Inflation-Protection Securities.

Treasury Inflation-Protected Securities

How to Invest

- **Direct ownership:** Investors can own TIPS directly, in their own names, either through an account with a securities brokerage firm or through an online account with the Treasury Department at www.treasurydirect.gov.

- **Indirect ownership:** Open-end investment companies, known as mutual funds, are an indirect method of owning treasury inflation-protected securities.[1] Mutual funds pool the resources of many individuals, and offer an investor access to a diversified, professionally managed portfolio.

Possible Risks

- **Market risk:** If a bond is sold before maturity, an investor may receive more or less than originally paid.

---

[1] The Securities and Exchange Commission requires that all prospective mutual fund investors be given a prospectus. The prospectus contains valuable information concerning how an investment works, its goals and risks, and any expenses and charges involved.

Municipal Bonds

Municipal bonds are debt instruments issued by states, counties, cities and local government authorities such as a school or water district. The proceeds of municipal bond issues are used for a wide range of public purposes, including building schools, highways or airports, or to fund general government operations.

Perhaps the most notable feature of municipal bonds is the tax treatment of the interest income received. With a few limited exceptions, interest income from municipal bonds is exempt from federal income tax.[1] See IRC Sec. 103(a). Generally, municipal bond interest is also exempt from state and local income tax if the bondholder resides in the same jurisdiction where the bond was issued.

Municipal bonds typically pay interest on a semi-annual basis. On the open market, they normally trade in multiples of $5,000 (par value).

Types of Municipal Bonds

There are two primary categories of municipal bonds:

- **General obligation:** Also known as G.O. bonds, these bonds are secured by the full faith and credit of the issuer. In effect, this means the full taxing power of the issuing government or agency.

- **Revenue bonds:** Revenue bonds are bonds issued by agencies such as a port authority, highway commission or water and sewer district, to build specific public works projects. Such bonds are backed by the revenues generated by these projects for payment of principal and interest.

Other Municipal Bond Concepts

- **Private activity bonds:** Private Activity bonds are municipal bonds which serve mixed public and private purposes. Unless such bonds meet certain requirements (IRC Sec. 103(b)), the interest income from them is not exempt from federal income tax. State and

---

[1] To qualify for the federal income tax exemption, bonds issued after 1982 generally must be in registered form. See IRC Sec. 149(a)(1).

local taxability will vary. Interest income on private activity bonds which do meet the requirements is federally tax-exempt; in certain cases, interest income from tax-exempt private activity bonds is a preference item for the alternative minimum tax (AMT). See IRC Sec. 57(a)(5).

- **Serial and term bonds:** These terms refer to the manner in which a municipal bond issue is redeemed at maturity. A serial bond issue matures over a number of years, with a portion of the issue retired each year. With term bonds, the entire bond issue is retired at one time.

- **Insured municipal bonds:** Municipal bonds described as being "insured" carry an additional protection against the risk of default. A private corporation agrees to pay principal and interest if the issuer of the bond defaults. Investors should check the credit rating of both the bond issuer and the corporation insuring the bond. Such insurance protects only against the risk of default, not the market value of a bond.

Bond Prices and Interest Rates

If an investor buys a municipal bond and holds it to maturity, the issuer is obligated to repay the full face amount. If the bond is sold before it matures, however, the investor may receive more or less than originally paid. Bond prices can move up and down, most often in response to changes in the general level of interest rates. If rates rise, the price of existing bonds usually falls; if interest rates decline, the market value of existing bonds generally increases. Municipal bond prices may also be affected by general business and economic factors.

Income Tax Treatment

The income from municipal bonds is generally exempt from federal income tax and state and local income tax (if the bondholder resides in the same jurisdiction where the bond was issued.) In some cases, income from municipal bonds may be subject to the alternative minimum tax (AMT) as well as capital gains taxes. No federal deduction is allowed for interest or investment expenses attributable to tax-exempt interest. See IRC Secs. 265(a)(1) and (2). Tax-exempt income is added back to a taxpayer's income to determine taxable Social Security. See IRC Sec. 86(b)(2)(B).

Municipal Bonds

Investment Uses

Municipal bonds are attractive to high-tax-bracket individuals seeking a stable source of tax-advantaged income. They can supplement IRAs and other qualified retirement plans when a taxpayer has already made the maximum allowable plan contribution.

How to Invest

- **Direct ownership:** Working with a stockbroker or other securities-licensed professional, investors can buy bonds directly, holding the bonds in their own names.

- **Indirect ownership:** Open-end investment companies known as mutual funds are an indirect method of municipal bond ownership. Mutual funds pool the resources of many individuals and offer access to a diversified, professionally-managed portfolio. Exchange-traded funds, or ETFs, a variation of the standard mutual fund, are another way of investing in municipal bonds. Unit Investment Trusts (UITs) are a third form of indirect ownership. The municipal bond portfolio in a UIT is fixed and not actively managed.[1]

Possible Risks

- **Market risk:** If a municipal bond is sold before maturity, an investor may receive more or less than originally paid.

- **Default risk:** An issuer may default on payment of the principal or interest of a bond.

- **Inflation risk:** As fixed return investments, municipal bonds are subject to inflation risk; over time, the dollars received have less purchasing power.

- **Tax risk:** Federal or local government law concerning the taxability of municipal bond interest income could change.

---

[1] The Securities and Exchange Commission (SEC) requires that all prospective UIT, ETF, and mutual fund investors be given a prospectus. The prospectus contains valuable information concerning how an investment works, its goals and risks, and any expenses and charges involved.

Hedge Funds

Because they can vary considerably, there is no single definition of a "Hedge Fund." In general terms, a hedge fund is a private investment corporation or partnership that provides investors the opportunity to participate in specialized, flexible, and often risky trading strategies, to take advantage of perceived opportunities in the stock, bond, currency, and commodities markets.

Unlike traditional equity fund managers, hedge fund managers typically have far greater flexibility with regard to employing sophisticated investment strategies. In many cases the overall performance of the hedge fund is driven by the unique skill of the portfolio manager(s), rather than general market movements. Also in contrast to most mutual funds, hedge funds are usually set up by principals who typically invest a significant amount of their personal assets in the fund. Most hedge funds have an incentive management fee structure; the higher the investment return, the higher the fee paid to the fund managers.

Hedge Fund Risks

There are a number of risks associated with investing in a hedge fund, including:

- **Speculative in nature:** Hedge funds are generally more speculative in nature than other types of investments, with a higher potential for capital loss.
- **Leverage:** Many hedge funds will employ significant leverage (using borrowed money) to increase potential investment returns. Such leverage also increases the potential for loss.
- **Control:** A single portfolio manager may control most or all of the fund's investments, resulting in a lack of diversification and a higher level of risk.
- **Less regulation:** Hedge funds are typically subject to less governmental regulation than are other investments. If trading is done on a foreign exchange, there may be less regulatory protection than on U.S. exchanges.
- **Illiquid:** It may be difficult to withdraw from a hedge fund; there may be no secondary market for an interest in a fund, there may be time limits on withdrawals, or a fund manager may decide that it would not be in the best interest of the fund to allow an investor to withdraw.
- **Operating expenses:** Many hedge funds are subject to substantial operating expenses that, typically, must be paid from investment returns.

Who Typically Invests In Hedge Funds?

There is no specific profile of a "typical" hedge fund investor. There are "suitability" requirements before a hedge fund will accept an investor, expressed in terms of income and net worth. For example, a fund may require that new investors have a minimum net worth of $1,000,000 and annual income of $200,000. There are also requirements for a minimum investment amount. For example, some hedge funds require a $10,000,000 initial minimum investment, limiting their availability to institutions and the super wealthy. There are other hedge funds that allow one to invest as little as $10,000. In most cases, investors in hedge funds (known as "accredited" investors) tend to be aggressive and willing to sacrifice safety to achieve higher returns.

What Kinds Of Strategies Do Hedge Funds Use?

The investment strategies used will vary from fund to fund. Some hedge funds only invest in a specific asset class (e.g., stocks, bonds, currencies, etc.) or in a combination of asset classes. Others are highly leveraged, while some do not use leverage at all. There are hedge funds with the ability to "sell short," and some that trade only on the "long side" of the market. Relatively few are fully "hedged." In fact, a great many hedge funds are far more speculative than traditional funds.

What Is A "Lock-up" Period?

This is the period of time that a hedge fund requires an accredited investor to hold assets within the fund before they can be removed.

What Should I Know Before Investing?

A hedge fund is a complex investment. Before investing any money, you should be fully aware of the objectives of the fund and the risks involved. When you consider investing in a hedge fund, make sure that you are familiar with the following:

- The track record and investment style of the portfolio manager(s) of the fund.

- The fund's investment strategy and whether or not it is based upon fundamental or technical analysis.

- The fund's decision-making process during the implementation of a strategy.

- The risk-controls and stop-losses employed by the fund.

- The amount of leverage employed by the fund; the greater the leverage the greater the potential for loss.

- The amount and method of calculation for management/performance-based fees.

- The frequency and transparency of the fund's reporting and valuation methods.

- The types of underlying assets the fund invests in and any liquidity constraints (e.g., lock-up periods) imposed by the fund.

- The experience and reputation of all those involved with the management and operation of the fund (brokers, lawyers, custodians, administrators, and portfolio managers).

Seek Professional Guidance

Because hedge funds are complex, risky investments, the advice and counsel of experienced investment advisors is highly recommended.

Limited Partnerships

A "limited" partnership is a form of business organization similar to a "general" partnership, except that in addition to one or more general partners (GPs), there are one or more limited partners (LPs). The general partners have management control, are subject to joint and several liability with regard to the debts of the partnership, and share in the profits of the firm in pre-defined proportions.

The limited partners have a role similar to that of shareholders in a corporation. Typically, limited partners share in the profits of the firm in pre-defined proportions, but have no management authority, and are generally only liable for debts incurred by the partnership to the extent of their individual investment.

When constructing an investment portfolio, limited partnerships are widely seen as being an "Alternative Asset." Common limited partnership programs include real estate (residential, commercial, and raw land), oil, gas, and other energy products (exploration, producing properties, and transportation), equipment leasing, timber, and financial.

Partner Roles Compared

The table below compares the various responsibilities and benefits of limited and general partners:

Topics	Limited Partners	General Partners
Contribution	Cash or assets.	Expertise and time (sometimes money).
Risks	Liability is limited to amount of investment and agreed upon future investments.[1]	Liability is unlimited - creditors can reach the general partner's entire estate.
Management responsibility	None	Provide full management.
Benefits flow through the partnership to the limited partners	Depreciation/depletion, interest deductions, capital growth and periodic distributions.[2]	A percentage of the profits and losses, often after limited partners receive original investment and a specified return.

---

[1] In some instances, a limited partner may be personally liable for partnership loans.

[2] A combination of the benefits may produce tax write-offs in excess of the contribution. However, there are limitations on the use of these excess losses.

Limited Partnerships

General Types of Limited Partnerships

Most limited partnerships will fall into one of several categories:

- Private limited partnerships: Partnerships with no more than 35 limited partners. Because the number of limited partners does not exceed 35, the partnership does not need to be registered with the Securities and Exchange Commission (SEC). "Suitability" requirements (such as net worth and gross income) are generally high, limiting participation to wealthier investors.

- Public limited partnerships: Public limited partnerships are registered with the Securities and Exchange commissions (SEC) and are sold by investment brokers. Suitability requirements are typically less stringent than private limited partnerships, offering opportunities to investors with more modest resources.

- Master limited partnerships: Master limited partnerships (MLPs) are a form of limited partnership that, unlike other types of partnerships, can be easily bought and sold on a public exchange such as the NYSE or NASDAQ. Owners of MLP shares are termed "unit holders."

Use Caution with Limited Partnerships

There are a number of issues to keep in mind when considering an investment in a limited partnership:

- Investment risk: Although the type and level of risk varies from one partnership to another, there is no such thing as a "risk-free" partnership. As with other types of investments, limited partnerships do involve risk, including the possible loss of principal.

- Liquidity: While certain types of limited partnerships, commonly known as "Master Limited Partnerships" can be bought and sold easily, many limited partnerships have no formal secondary market. Thus, these limited partnership investments are very illiquid. Since many partnerships are, be design, long-term investments, it could be years before an individual is able to recover his or her capital.

- Tax complexity: Although some limited partnerships are taxed as corporations, most are taxed as "flow-through" entities, with items of income or loss and expense or credit flowing through to the individual partners. This structure can add considerable tax complexity (and expense) to the preparation of a partner's individual income tax return.

- Economic sense: In the past, individuals would invest in limited partnerships primarily for the tax benefits. Setting aside the tax benefits, however, does an investment in a particular limited partnership make economic sense?

Seek Professional Guidance

Given the tax and investment complexity involved in an investment in a limited partnership, the guidance of trained, experienced income tax and investment professionals is strongly recommended.

Real Estate Investment Trusts

Many individuals are attracted to the benefits of investing in real estate, such as current income or the potential for capital gain. Direct investment in real estate, however, can require large amounts of capital, as well as the time and expertise to properly manage real estate properties. At times, the cyclical nature of real estate can make such investments difficult to sell.

One alternative to direct real estate investment is the real estate investment trust (REIT). REITs allow small investors to share in both the risks and rewards of real estate investing.

What Is a Real Estate Investment Trust?

First authorized by Congress in the 1960s, REITs bring together capital from many individuals specifically to invest in a diversified portfolio of income real estate, or in real estate-related debt (mortgages). A REIT can take the form of a trust, association or corporation. Individuals invest in a REIT by purchasing shares, similar to shares of common stock. The shares of many REITs are publicly traded on major stock exchanges and over-the-counter markets.

Full-time managers conduct the day-to-day operations of a REIT. If a REIT is successful, shareholders can receive dividend income (from rental income and mortgage interest) and capital gain from the profitable sale of real estate assets. Some REITs specialize in a single type of commercial property or region of the country. Other REITs diversify their investments over various types of property or in different geographical areas.

Types of Real Estate Investment Trusts

REITs are usually classified according to their investment focus:

- **Equity REIT:** Equity REITs directly own and operate income properties such as apartment buildings, discount outlet centers, mobile home parks, office buildings, industrial parks, or hotels. Income is generated from property rents. Capital gain income is also possible if properties are sold at a profit.

- **Mortgage REIT:** Mortgage REITs invest their money in various types of mortgages, usually for existing properties. In some cases REIT funds will back mortgages on new construction. Income is generated from the interest received on the mortgages.

- **Hybrid REIT:** As the name suggests, hybrid REITs invest in both direct ownership of real estate as well as mortgage loans.

- **Finite life real estate investment trust (FREIT):** FREITs are a type of equity REIT which have a stated goal of liquidating the real estate portfolio by a specific date. The primary investment goal of a FREIT is to maximize potential capital gain.

Income Tax Issues

The Internal Revenue Code (IRC) contains a number of conditions which a trust must meet to qualify as a Real Estate Investment Trust, including the requirement that a REIT pay out at least 90% of its taxable income.[1] If a REIT meets these conditions, the income paid to the shareholders is not taxed twice (as it would be in a regular corporation), but is taxed only once, in the hands of the shareholders.

- **Ordinary income distributions:** Income from sources such as rents and mortgage interest received is fully taxed to the shareholder as ordinary income.[2]

- **Capital gain distributions:** Capital gain from the profitable sale of real estate investments is long-term gain, regardless of the length of time an individual has owned his or her shares in the REIT.[3]

If a shareholder sells his or her shares in a REIT, the gain or loss for federal income tax purposes generally depends on how long the shares were owned.[4]

---

[1] See IRC Sec. 857(a)(1).

[2] Currently, federal income tax law taxes "qualified" stock dividends at marginal rates lower than those generally applicable to ordinary income. Unless certain, narrow conditions are met, ordinary income distributions from a REIT will <u>not</u> qualify for these lower qualified dividend rates.

[3] Capital gain distributions from a REIT will generally be taxable at the favorable capital gains rates available to taxpayers under the provisions of the American Taxpayer Relief Act of 2012.

[4] State or local law may provide for different tax treatment of income received from a REIT.

Real Estate Investment Trusts

Investment Uses

Many investors are attracted to mortgage REITs because of the relatively high level of current income; REITs in general tend to provide a current yield greater than long-term U.S. Treasury bonds. Equity REITs are often sought for their long-term appreciation potential and as a hedge against inflation. Many investors view real estate as a separate asset class – distinct from other financial assets such as stocks or bonds – and thus value REITs for their diversification benefits.

How to Invest

- **Direct ownership:** Individuals can invest in a publicly traded REIT by purchasing shares through a stockbroker or other securities-licensed professional, holding the shares in their own names.
- **Indirect ownership:** Open-end investment companies, known as mutual funds, are an indirect method of REIT ownership. Mutual funds pool the resources of many individuals and offer an investor access to a diversified portfolio of professionally managed securities. There are many mutual funds that specialize in REITs,[1] including those with a global orientation.

Possible Risks

- **Market risk:** As with all stocks, the value of shares in publicly-traded REITs can fluctuate. An investor who sells shares in a REIT could receive more, or less, than the original purchase price. Factors that can influence market risk include the general level of real estate property values, REIT dividend payouts, management skill, and broad stock market trends.

- **Interest rate risk:** Shares of REITs, especially mortgage REITs, are sensitive to changes in the general level of interest rates. Mortgage REITs respond much like bonds, generally increasing in value as interest rates fall and decreasing in value if interest rates rise.

---

[1] The Securities and Exchange Commission requires that all prospective mutual fund investors be given a prospectus. The prospectus contains valuable information concerning how an investment works, its goals and risks, and any expenses and charges involved.

Accumulation Funding Analysis Data

Date 01/01/2018

The Goals

	Goal 1	Goal 2	Goal 3	Goal 4	Goal 5
Name	Trip to Italy	Wedding	Vacation	Boat	Cruise
Years until start of goal	5	4	3	8	5
Goal duration, in years	1	1	1	1	1
Amount in today's dollars	$10,000	$30,000	$15,000	$50,000	$9,000
Inflate goal amount (Yes/No)	Yes	Yes	Yes	Yes	Yes
Amount currently saved	$2,500	$1,000	$0	$3,000	$0
Planned monthly savings	$90	$400	$300	$400	$100
Assumed rate of return	7%	6%	6%	6%	6%

Assumptions

Annual inflation rate   4.00%

Accumulation Funding Analysis

For Trip to Italy

You want this to take place in 5 years
The total first-year cost will be $12,167
You currently have saved $2,500
You are currently saving $90
This will be worth $10,025

Assumes an annual inflation rate of 4.00% and a rate of return on assets of 7.00%

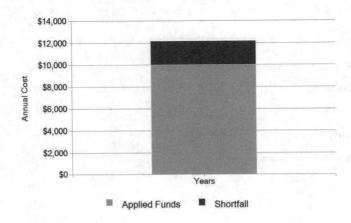

One way to reach your goal would be to increase your monthly savings by $30. Another way to reach your goal would be to increase the rate of return on your savings to 13.00%. Either of these alternatives may not be possible to implement fully. Therefore consider taking steps in both areas.

Values shown in this presentation are hypothetical and not a promise of future performance.

Accumulation Funding Timeline

For Trip to Italy

Year	Cost of Goal	Amount Funded	Annual Shortfall	Funding Contributions	Funding Growth	Funding Balance
					Beg. Balance	$2,500
1	$0	$0	$0	$1,080	$223	$3,803
2	0	0	0	1,080	317	5,199
3	0	0	0	1,080	418	6,697
4	0	0	0	1,080	526	8,303
5	0	0	0	1,080	642	10,025
6	12,167	10,025	2,142	0	0	0

Assumes an annual inflation rate of 4.00% and a rate of return on assets of 7.00%.

Values shown in this presentation are hypothetical and not a promise of future performance.

Do You Desire "Retirement Peace of Mind?"

In December, 2012, a landmark study was launched to determine a national retirement peace of mind.[1] It included more than 6,000 respondents age 45 and older. It found that average Americans have a lot of challenges and a lot of expectations for their retirement years.

Retirement Expectations

Traditionally, many Americans have viewed retirement as a time of leisure. Today, more and more of us expect to work during our retirement years. Seven out of ten of those surveyed in the study said that their ideal plan for balancing work and leisure in retirement would be to include some work.

The reasons are not purely economic. Many Americans see retirement as a time for renewal and accomplishment. When asked if they would seek the same kind of work in retirement or pursue a different career, half of those surveyed said they would seek a different line of work.

A desire for more money and economic security was the most important reason for working in retirement according to a majority of the survey participants, but 48 percent said a desire for stimulation and satisfaction was their top reason for continuing to work during retirement.

When asked about their most important financial goal, 88 percent said they would like to save enough money to have financial peace of mind, versus 12% who said they would like to accumulate as much wealth as possible.

Retirement Challenges

The study also sought information on the greatest concerns facing those nearing retirement. Not surprisingly, in today's complex economic and social climate, they found many complications that could make the task of retirement planning even more challenging.

- **Health problems:** Americans are expected to live longer than ever before. When asked what concerned them about living a long life, 72% of those surveyed said they feared

[1] "Americans' Perspectives on New Retirement Realities and the Longevity Bonus, a 2013 Merrill Lynch Retirement Study, conducted in partnership with Age Wave." © 2013 Bank of America; All rights reserved

serious health problems, making it the top retirement worry. This compares with 47% who said they worried they would run out of the money they need to live a comfortable retirement.

There is good reason for concern. The study found that the top reason for early retirement given by those already retired was due to personal health problems. Fully 57% of study participants who had already retired reported they retired earlier than they had planned.

- **Caring for family members:** More and more Americans today are left caring for others in their families: adult children, grandchildren, parents or in-laws, siblings. These Americans are often referred to as the "Sandwich Generation", finding their own needs for saving and retirement security squeezed by the needs of others they love.

Among study participants aged 45 or older with children, over half said they expected to have to continue to provide support to adult children. More than a third expected to have to support grandchildren. Fewer said they expected to have to support parents (16%) or their siblings (10%).

The types of support they expected to provide included financial support (cash or loans), housing (sharing a home or helping pay for housing), education and healthcare. The study also found a relationship between income and expectations for providing support: participants with higher incomes were two times more likely to say they expected to provide support to their adult children, grandchildren and parents than those with lower incomes.

Do You Have "Retirement Peace of Mind?"

The study tried to determine how close participants were to achieving retirement peace of mind by asking them to respond to these survey questions:

Question
• I feel content and comfortable about how I will spend my retirement years.
• I have many worries about what might happen during my retirement.
• Thinking about my retirement gives me feelings of security and stability.
• I feel anxious and uneasy about how I will support myself and my family during retirement.
• I feel well prepared for whatever may happen during my retirement.

Do You Desire "Retirement Peace of Mind?"

The study found that participants had an average score of 5.3, based on a scale of 1 to 10, or slightly above average. Scores varied, though, by gender, the amount of savings, and if the participant worked with a financial advisor.

- Men were more likely than women to have retirement peace of mind. The average score for male participants was 5.6 while female participants averaged 5.0.

- Participants with $500,000 or more in investable savings averaged a score of 7.5 while those with under $250,000 in investable savings averaged 4.8.

- Participants who worked with a financial advisor at the time of the study had an average score of 6.3, while those who did not work with a financial advisor had a score of 4.7.

How Can You Improve Your Retirement Peace of Mind?

The results of the national study suggest several steps you can take today to improve your peace of mind during retirement:

- **What is your most important financial goal?** Are you like the 88 percent who said they would like to save enough money to have financial peace of mind? Or, are you more like the 12% who said they would like to accumulate as much wealth as possible? The answer may help determine your retirement savings and investment strategy.

- **Do you intend to work during retirement?** Will you stay in the same line of work, or start a new career… maybe even a business of your own? If you do intend to work, it could affect the Social Security benefits for which you qualify. You will want to research the impact carefully.

- **What will you do for personal satisfaction?** While a desire for more income and security was the top reason for working in retirement, almost half of the study participants said they intended to do so for personal stimulation and satisfaction. What will you do for stimulation and satisfaction? Do you wish to travel? Start a new career? Volunteer in your community? Whatever your choices, look carefully to see how they may affect your retirement savings goals. Do you need to save money to start a business? To complete a college education? To travel?

- **Are you prepared for any personal healthcare issues that could arise?** Problems with personal health lead more people to retire earlier than planned more than any other

Do You Desire "Retirement Peace of Mind?"

cause. Do you understand your medical care and long-term care options? Does your employer offer extended healthcare benefits to retirees or will you be required to provide your own? Is disability insurance appropriate for your situation?

- **Do you have any other family obligations to consider?** More and more retirees today find they must continue to provide financial support for their adult children, grandchildren, parents or siblings. Are you supporting family members today? Do you intend to support family members during retirement? How is supporting family today affecting your ability to save for retirement? Are there other strategies you should consider? Is life insurance something you should consider to help care for survivors or heirs?

- **Would you benefit from professional financial advice?** Participants in the nation-wide study reported overall higher levels of retirement peace of mind when they worked with a financial advisor. Would discussing your retirement goals and challenges with a professional help you?

Whatever your expectations for retirement, like all important things in life, it pays to have a plan to achieve them and to regularly measure your progress towards your goals.

Health Care Planning In Retirement

Health care planning is a key part of the overall retirement planning process. Although a healthy life-style and good genes can help, it is a fact of life that as we age we need more medical care. Federal government statistics highlight this reality:

Per-Capita U.S. Personal Health Care Spending[1]

Age Group	2004	2006	2008	2010	2012
0-18	$2,398	$2,747	$3,032	$3,300	$3,552
19-44	3,193	3,576	3,908	4,156	4,458
45-64	7,218	7,922	8,456	9,000	9,513
65-84	13,509	14,623	15,776	16,425	16,872
85+	26,339	28,521	30,827	31,903	32,411

Medicare

There are a number of ways that retired individuals pay for health care. Some are able to pay cash. Others are covered by health insurance plans provided by former employers or under coverage available through a spouse who is still working. For the majority of Americans age 65 and older, however, most health care is provided through the various elements of the federal government's Medicare program:

- **Medicare Part "A" Hospital Insurance:** Provides coverage for inpatient hospital care, post-hospital skilled nursing facility care, home health care, and hospice care.

- **Medicare Part "B" Medical Insurance:** Includes coverage for doctor's services and outpatient care as well as some preventive services to maintain your health or prevent certain illnesses from getting worse.

- **Medicare Part "C" Medicare Advantage Plans:** An alternative to the "classic" Medicare program. Under Medicare Advantage, health care is provided by private companies approved by Medicare. These plans include Part A and Part B and usually provide other coverage, including prescription drugs.

---

[1] Source: Centers for Medicare and Medicaid Services, Office of the Actuary, National Health Statistics Group. Total Personal Health-Care Per-Capita Spending by Gender and Age Group, Calendar Years 2002, 2004, 2006, 2008, 2010, 2012 Level (dollars).

Health Care Planning In Retirement

- **Medicare Part "D" Prescription Drug Coverage:** Helps cover the cost of prescription medications.

Medicare Supplement Insurance (Medigap) Policies

The original Medicare program will pay for many, but not all, health care services and supplies. Many retirees will also consider purchasing a "Medigap" policy, sold by private insurance companies, to help pay some of the health care costs (the "gaps") that the original Medicare program does not cover, including copayments, coinsurance, and deductibles.

Medigap policies provide standardized coverage (in most states identified by the letters A, B, C, D, F, G, K, L, M, and N)[1] and must follow federal and state laws designed to protect the consumer. Each standardized Medigap policy must provide the same basic coverage; cost is frequently the only difference between the same Medigap policy sold by different insurance companies. In some states, another type of Medigap policy, called Medicare SELECT, may be available. Medicare SELECT policies typically require you to use specific hospitals or doctors.

Planning For Incapacity

Retirement health care planning must also consider "incapacity." Major health problems such as a stroke, a heart attack, the onset of Alzheimer's disease or other forms of dementia, or simply becoming weak and frail from advancing age can result in your no longer being able to care for yourself or manage your own affairs. There are two key issues to consider:

- **Paying for "custodial" care:** Medicare and other types of health care insurance are designed to cover "acute" medical conditions. They do not pay for costs associated with "custodial" or "maintenance" care, such as might be needed by an individual whose health problems require nursing home care. With median U.S. nursing home costs for a semi-private room in 2017 of $235 per day ($85,775 per year),[2] the cost of such custodial care for even a short period of time can be enormous.

  Rather than pay these costs "out-of-pocket," many individuals purchase a Long-Term Care (LTC) insurance policy. For individuals without LTC insurance coverage, the jointly-run, federal-state Medicaid program may be able to pay for custodial care, once personal assets are exhausted.

---

[1] In Massachusetts, Minnesota, and Wisconsin, Medigap policies are standardized in a different way.
[2] See the Genworth 2017 Cost of Care Survey, page 2.

- **Managing personal affairs:** If an individual is no longer able to manage his or her personal affairs, someone else will need to step in and take over. In planning for this possibility, three key documents should be considered:

    - **Durable power of attorney:** A written document by which one person (the principal) empowers another person (the agent or attorney-in-fact) to act in his or her behalf; often used for management of financial affairs.

    - **Living Will:** Also known as a "Directive to Physicians", this document provides guidance as to the type of medical treatment to be provided (or withheld) and the general circumstances under which the directive applies.

    - **Durable power of attorney for health care:** Many states have laws allowing a person to appoint someone to make health care decisions for them if they become unable to do so themselves.

Seek Professional Guidance

Planning for health care and incapacity in retirement involves answering a number of complex questions. The guidance of trained professionals in insurance, medical benefits, as well as the counsel of an estate planning attorney, can be invaluable in designing and implementing an effective health care plan.

The Need for Retirement Planning

For much of the 20th century, retirement in America was traditionally defined in terms of its relationship to participation in the active work force. An individual would work full-time until a certain age, and then leave employment to spend a few years quietly rocking on the front porch. Declining health often made retirement short and unpleasant. Retirement planning, as such, typically focused on saving enough to guarantee minimal survival for a relatively brief period of time.

More recently, however, many individuals are beginning to recognize that for a number of reasons, this traditional view of retirement is no longer accurate. Some individuals, for example, are voluntarily choosing to retire early, in their 40s or 50s. Others, because they enjoy working, choose to remain employed well past the traditional retirement age of 65. And, many retirees do more than just rock on the front porch. Retirement is now often defined by activities such as travel, returning to school, volunteer work, or the pursuit of favorite hobbies or sports.

This changed face of retirement, however, with all of its possibilities, does not happen automatically. Many of the issues associated with retirement, such as ill health, and the need to provide income, still exist. With proper planning, however, these needs can be met.

Longer Lives

The single most important factor in this changed retirement picture is the fact that we now live much longer than before. A child born in 1900, for example, had an average life expectancy of 47.3 years. For a child born in 2014, however, average life expectancy had increased to 78.8 years. The following graph[1] illustrates this change.

---

[1] Data for years 1900 – 1965 is taken from National Vital Statistics Reports, Volume 47, Number 28, United States Life Tables, 1997, December 13, 1999. For the years 1966-2014, the data is taken from National Vital Statistics Reports, Volume 65, Number 4, Deaths: Final Data for 2014, June 30, 2016.

The Need for Retirement Planning

Average U.S. Life Expectancy (1900 – 2014)

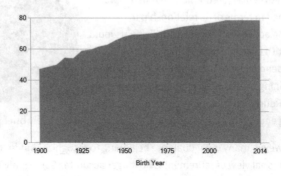

Birth Year

Common Retirement Planning Issues

Planning for a much longer life span involves addressing problems not faced by earlier generations. Some of the key issues include the following:

- **Paying for retirement:** Providing a steady income is often the key problem involved in retirement planning. Longer life spans raise the issue of the impact of inflation on fixed dollar payments, as well as the possibility of outliving accumulated personal savings. Social Security retirement benefits and income from employer-sponsored retirement plans typically provide only a portion of the total income required. If income is insufficient, a retiree may be forced to either continue working, or face a reduced standard of living.

- **Health care:** The health benefits provided through the federal government's Medicare program are generally considered to be only a foundation. Often a supplemental Medigap policy is needed, as is a long-term care policy, to provide needed benefits not available through Medicare. Health care planning should also consider a health care proxy, allowing someone else to make medical decisions when an individual is temporarily incapacitated, as well as a living will that expresses an individual's wishes when no hope of recovery is possible.

- **Estate planning:** Retirement planning inevitably must consider what happens to an individual's assets after retirement is over. Estate planning should ensure not only that assets are transferred to the individuals or organizations chosen by the owner, but also that the transfer is done with the least amount of tax.

- **Housing:** This question involves not only the size and type of home (condo, house, shared housing, assisted living), but also its location. Such factors as climate and proximity to close family members and medical care are often important. Completely paying off a home loan can reduce monthly income needs. A reverse mortgage may provide additional monthly income.

- **Lifestyle:** Some individuals, accustomed to a busy work life, find it difficult to enjoy the freedom offered by retirement. Planning ahead can make this transition easier.

Seek Professional Guidance

Developing a successful retirement plan involves carefully considering a wide range of issues and potential problems. Finding solutions to these questions often requires both personal education and the guidance of knowledgeable individuals, from many professional disciplines. The key is to begin planning as early as possible.

Average Life Expectancy at Age 65

While no one knows how long he or she will live, average life expectancy in the United States has been increasing. The tables and graph below show how the average number of years of life remaining at age 65 has increased since the turn of the 20th century.[1]

Male		Female	
Turned Age 65 In	Average Years of Life Remaining	Turned Age 65 In	Average Years of Life Remaining
1909-1911	11.24	1909-1911	11.96
1919-1921	12.20	1919-1921	12.73
1929-1931	11.72	1929-1931	12.78
1939-1941	12.07	1939-1941	13.57
1949-1951	12.74	1949-1951	14.95
1959-1961	12.95	1959-1961	15.80
1969-1971	12.99	1969-1971	16.83
1979-1981	14.21	1979-1981	18.44
1989-1991	15.12	1989-1991	19.02
1999-2001	16.11	1999-2001	19.12
2012	17.82	2012	20.36

Average Remaining Life Expectancy At Age 65

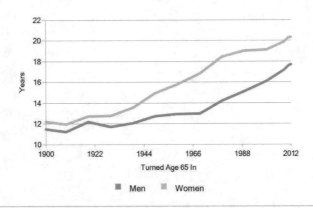

Men   Women

---

[1] Source: National Center for Health Statistics, National Vital Statistics Reports, Volume 65, Number 8. United States Life Tables, 2011. September 22, 2015.

Sources of Retirement Income

Most retirees derive their retirement income from three primary sources: Social Security retirement benefits, qualified retirement plans, and individual savings/investments.

Social Security Retirement Benefits

Social Security retirement benefits are intended to provide only a portion of an individual's retirement income. Traditionally, retirement benefits began at age 65. For those born after 1937, however, full retirement age when full benefits begin, will increase gradually, until it reaches age 67 for those born in 1960 and later. A reduced benefit is available, beginning at age 62. The monthly benefit amount is based on an individual's past earnings record. A worker can earn a larger retirement benefit by continuing to work past full retirement age, up to age 70. Up to 85 percent of a retiree's Social Security retirement benefits may be taxable as ordinary income. Retirement benefits are subject to adjustment for inflation on an annual basis.

Qualified Retirement Plans

A retirement plan is considered to be "qualified" if it meets certain requirements set by federal income tax law. In general, employer or employee contributions to a qualified plan are currently deductible and the earnings are tax deferred until paid out of the plan. Mandatory distribution rules typically apply and taxable withdrawals before age 59½ may be subject to an additional 10% penalty tax.[1]

- **Employer-sponsored qualified plans:** Employer-sponsored plans can generally be classified as either defined benefit or defined contribution. Defined benefit plans specify the benefit amount a participant will receive at retirement; an actuary estimates how much must be contributed each year to fund the anticipated benefit. The investment risk rests on the employer. Benefits are generally taxable. Defined contribution plans, such as 401(k), 403(b) or SEP plans, typically put a percentage of current salaries into the plan each year. The retirement benefit will

---

[1] The rules and regulations surrounding qualified plans are complex. This discussion is intended to be only a brief, general description. State or local law may vary.

depend on the amount contributed, the investment return and the number of years until a participant retires. The investment risk rests on the participant. Benefits are generally taxable.

- **Individual qualified plans:** Include the traditional Individual Retirement Account (IRA) and the Roth IRA. Contributions to a traditional IRA may be deductible and earnings grow tax deferred. Distributions from a traditional IRA are taxable to the extent of deductible contributions and growth. Contributions to a Roth IRA are never deductible and earnings grow tax deferred. If certain requirements are met, retirement distributions from a Roth IRA are tax free.[1]

- **Nonqualified retirement plans:** An employer may set up a plan, often in the form of a deferred compensation plan, which does not meet federal requirements to be considered "qualified." Benefits are generally taxable when received. Such plans are often used as a supplement to qualified retirement plans.

Individual Savings

Individual savings and investments are the third primary source of retirement income. An individual can choose to accumulate funds using a wide range of investment vehicles. The appropriate type of investment will depend on a number of factors such as an individual's investment skill and experience, risk tolerance, tax bracket, and the number of years until retirement. Below are listed some of the more commonly used choices.

- **Savings accounts:** Including regular savings accounts, money market funds and certificates of deposit (CDs) at banks, savings and loans and credit unions.

- **Common stock:** May also include other forms of equity ownership such as preferred stock or convertible bonds. Stock can be owned directly, in a personal portfolio or indirectly through a mutual fund.

- **Bonds:** Includes corporate, government or municipal bonds. Bonds can be directly owned in a personal portfolio or indirectly held in either a mutual fund or unit investment trust.

[1] The discussion here concerns federal income tax law; state or local tax law may vary.

- **Real estate:** Individually owned investment real estate or indirect investment through a real estate investment trust or limited partnership.

- **Precious metals:** Such as gold or silver, in the form of coins, bullion or in the common stock of mining companies.

- **Commercial deferred annuities:** Commercial, deferred annuities are purchased from a life insurance company and can provide tax-deferred growth through a variety of investment choices.

Other Income Sources

Other retirement income sources include the following:

- **Immediate annuity:** An "immediate" annuity is purchased from a life insurance company, typically with a single, lump-sum payment. Within one year after purchase, the annuity begins to make regular, periodic payments to the annuity owner.

- **Continued employment:** On either a full or part-time basis. Wage and salary income is usually taxable and before-full-retirement-age[1] earnings above a certain level may affect the amount of Social Security retirement benefits received.

- **Home equity:** If a home is completely paid for, a reverse mortgage may provide additional income, without giving up home ownership.

---

[1] "Full retirement age" is the age at which an individual is entitled to "full" Social Security retirement benefits – 100% of an individual's Primary Insurance Amount. Under current law, this age will vary from 65 to 67, depending on an individual's year of birth.

When Will Your "Nest Egg" Run Out?

A Hypothetical Look at Retirement

Assumptions:

Inflation rate: 2.00%
Annual pre-tax investment rate: 9.00%

Current Scenario	Amount	Inflate?
Annual pre-tax income desired (in today's dollars)	$100,000	Yes
Years until retirement begins	20	
Desired income in first year of retirement	**$148,595**	
Anticipated annual pension income	-$35,000	Yes
Annual social security estimate	-$25,000	Yes
Other anticipated annual retirement income	-$10,000	Yes
Amount needed from nest egg in first year of retirement	**$78,595**	
Amount currently in nest egg	$100,000	
Annual contribution to nest egg	$10,000	Yes
Amount in nest egg in first year of retirement	**$1,148,793**	

Full years until nest egg runs out: 42

For most, the primary objective of their working lives is to fund a comfortable and secure retirement. The feeling of security comes from the knowledge that their nest egg – accumulated to fund that retirement – is sufficient.

When Will Your "Nest Egg" Run Out?

How to Make the Nest Egg Last Longer

Advance planning is the key to ensuring that there will be enough set aside for a worry-free retirement. If a retirement plan analysis shows that the funds are insufficient, one may change that outcome by several methods. Consider the following:

- **Increase the potential rate of return by reallocating investment assets:** Being sure to get the biggest bang for the buck, while managing investment risk, can have the most dramatic affect on the size of the nest egg;

- **Increase the annual contribution:** Putting more away will certainly help and may require reprioritizing today's spending decisions;

- **Retire later:** Delaying retirement allows more years to accumulate funds while requiring less from the nest egg.

- **Reduce the objective:** Requiring less retirement income, by either living on less or continuing to work after retirement, can help solve the problem.

Values shown in this presentation are hypothetical and not a promise of future performance.

Evaluating Early Retirement Offers

In recent years cost-cutting and restructuring measures have forced a number of companies to offer many of their employees early retirement packages. Although initially attractive, these packages require careful analysis. In deciding to either accept or reject an early retirement offer, several key questions must be answered:

- Do you want to retire?
- If you don't want to retire, what happens if you reject the offer?
- If you do want to retire, can you realistically afford retirement?

Common Elements in Early Retirement Packages

Early retirement offers are carefully structured and may include "sweeteners" such as:

- **Cash:** A cash bonus, either as a lump-sum or periodic payments, may be included. Consider your cash-flow and income tax situation before deciding which to take.

- **Defined benefit pensions:** For companies with defined benefit retirement plans, retirement income is often based on years of service, age at retirement, and a percentage of the highest three years earnings. Any or all of these factors can be adjusted to give an employee a higher pension benefit.

- **Defined contribution pensions:** Employers who sponsor defined contribution plans such as 401(k) or 403(b) plans may allow employees who take early retirement to keep their funds in the company plan.

- **Other fringe benefits:** Some early retirement offers will include valuable benefits such as group health or life insurance, counseling by financial professionals, and education or job placement assistance, if the employee wishes to continue working.

Do You Want to Retire?

Before the offer was made, what were your plans for the future? Were you already considering early retirement or were you planning on working for a few more years? For some, continuing to work is not only enjoyable, but it also helps in reaching goals such as putting a child or grandchild through college or paying off a mortgage. For others, the freedom retirement offers to pursue more personal goals is a life-long dream.

What Happens if You Decide to Reject the Offer?

Sometimes remaining with your current employer is a realistic option, sometimes it isn't. Refusing an early retirement offer may lead to promotions or salary increases that, in the long run, could result in a higher retirement benefit. Also, working longer allows you to save more and reduces the number of retirement years. Alternatively, rejecting an offer may result in being demoted or simply let go when your position is eliminated. Often, you have only a very brief period of time to make this critical decision, typically 60 to 90 days.

Can You Afford to Retire?

For most of us the key question frequently comes down to whether or not we can financially afford to retire. There are a number of issues to consider when answering this question, focusing on how much income you need and where it will come from:

- **A longer retirement:** Early retirement effectively means that your retirement will last longer. With people living longer, some of us may spend as much as 1/3 of our lives in retirement.

- **Taxes and inflation:** When planning your income needs, be sure to keep the impact of both taxes and inflation in mind. What will your marginal tax rate be in retirement? To offset inflation, your income goal cannot remain level, but must increase each year.

- **Lower pension and Social Security income:** Early retirement often results in lower pension income as well as reduced Social Security retirement benefits.

- **Less time to plan and save:** Early retirement leaves you less time to plan for the psychological adjustment needed when you retire. It also leaves less time to save for what will likely be a longer period of retirement.

- **Health care:** Medical care is expensive and as we age we typically need more of it. During our working years, employer provided health insurance is an extremely valuable benefit. After retirement, however, we are much more on our own. Medicare is generally available once you reach age 65, but Medicare has specific limits. Often, additional medical insurance is necessary, but the individual typically has to personally pay for this extra coverage.

- **Continue working:** Some of us, either because we enjoy working, or because we need the income, will want to consider continued employment.

Seek Professional Guidance

Evaluating an early retirement offer from your employer can be a complex and confusing task. The guidance of financial professionals is strongly recommended.

Making the Most of Your Retirement Plan

Defined Contribution Retirement Plans

Many employers offer some form of defined contribution retirement plan. Although the name may vary (401(k), 403(b), 457(b))[1], on a basic level they all function in much the same way. During your working years money is automatically deducted from your paycheck and contributed to the plan. The accumulated funds are ultimately used to help pay for your retirement.

Why Participate?

The answer to this is simple: you'll likely need the money. With people living longer, more money is needed to pay for retirement. And two of the traditional financial pillars of retirement, defined benefit pension plans (providing a known benefit) and Social Security are playing a smaller role in meeting this increased need for retirement income.

- Over the past several decades many employers have changed from defined benefit to defined contribution plans. From 1985 to 2000, for example, the rate of participation in defined benefit plans by full-time employees of medium and large private firms dropped from 80% to 36%.[2] A survey by the Bureau of Labor Statistics, published in 2014, found that only 25% of civilian workers in the U.S. participated in defined benefit pension plans.[3]

  Social Security also faces problems. As the baby boom generation enters retirement (the so-called "silver tsunami"), the number of individuals remaining in the workforce to support these retirees grows smaller. Although politically unpleasant, harsh fiscal realities may force increased payroll taxes, reductions in benefits, or both.

What to Do?

Today, more than ever before, you're on your own. One starting point is to take a more active role in your employer's defined contribution plan:

---

[1] These refer to the sections of the Internal Revenue Code which authorize the different types of retirement plans.
[2] See, "Employee Participation in Defined Benefit and Defined Contribution Plans, 1985-2000." U.S. Bureau of Labor Statistics, updated June 16, 2004.
[3] National Compensation Survey: Employee Benefits in the United States, March 2014, Table 2.

- **Investment options:** Or, where do I invest my money? This will depend on a number of factors, including the plan's available options, the amount of your retirement income goal, the number of years until retirement begins, and your tolerance for risk.

- **Contribution rate:** A 3% rate may be the default, but is that enough to meet your needs? Another factor to consider is whether there is an employer match for part of your contributions. At the least you should contribute to the level which will maximize the employer match. Otherwise, you're walking away from "free money."

- **Annual checkup:** Everyone's situation changes over time. Make sure you thoroughly review your retirement plan at least once a year. Are you saving enough? Are your investments still appropriate?

Seek Professional Guidance

Successful long-term investing requires discipline and patience. The guidance of a financial professional is highly recommended.

Length of Time a Sum Will Last

Item Description	Value
Current sum	$100,000
Assumes annual interest rate[1]	6.00%
Frequency of withdrawals	Monthly
Beginning monthly withdrawal amount:	$2,500
Inflate withdrawal by:	4.00%

Sum will last 3 years and 6 months

Example

If you have $100,000 in your account earning an annual return of 6.00%, compounded monthly, and you withdraw $2,500 monthly, with the withdrawal inflating each year by 4.00%, the account will be exhausted in 3 years and 6 months.

Length of Time a Sum Will Last

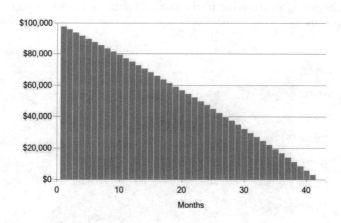

---

[1] The rates of return used in this illustration are not indicative of any actual investment and will fluctuate in value. An investment will not provide a consistent rate of return; years with lower (or negative) returns than the hypothetical returns shown may substantially affect the scenario presented.

Present Value of Future Annuity Payments

Item Description	Value
Frequency of annuity payments	Monthly
Month payment	$1,000
Annual interest rate[1]	8.00%
Number of months to receive payments	360
Total annuity payments received	**$360,000**
Amount of annuity, if payments are:	
At the end of each month	$136,283
At the beginning of each month	$137,192

Example

An annuity of $137,192 earning an annual return of 8.00%, compounded monthly, would pay you $1,000 at the beginning of each month for the next 360 months, at which time your account would be depleted.

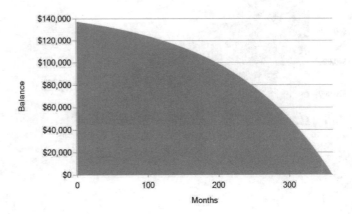

[1] The rates of return used in this illustration are not indicative of any actual investment and will fluctuate in value. An investment will not provide a consistent rate of return; years with lower (or negative) returns than the hypothetical returns shown may substantially affect the scenario presented.

Progress Toward Retirement Goals

On any journey to a goal, it makes sense to check in every now and then to see that you are on the right track. This report shows you the status and expectations as of 1 months ago. This is a good time to make note of where you actually are on your journey. If your progress is not what you desire, perhaps it is time to revisit the particulars of this goal.

Assumptions:

Item Description	Value
Rate of return for Client 1's retirement plan	7.00%
Rate of return for Client 2's retirement plan	7.00%
Rate of return for other assets	6.00%
Annual increase in contributions for Client 1	4.00%
Annual increase in contributions for Client 2	4.00%
Number of months used for projected values	1

Item Description	Original Value	Projected Value	Current Value
Annual employment income for Client 1	$87,000	$87,000	
Annual employment inflation rate for Client 1	4.00%	%	%
Annual employment income for Client 2	$65,000	$65,000	
Annual employment inflation rate for Client 2	4.00%	%	%
Retirement plan amount for Client 1	$136,000	$137,246	
Monthly contributions for Client 1	$450	$450	
Retirement plan amount for Client 2	$86,500	$87,306	
Monthly contributions for Client 2	$300	$300	
Other assets amount	$6,000	$6,080	
Monthly contributions for other assets	$50	$50	

Internal Rate of Return

Internal Rate of Return Defined

The internal rate of return (IRR) is the interest rate at which the present value of expected cash flows equals the value of the initial outlay. Simply put, if all the negative cash flows listed below were placed into an interest-bearing account (in the timeframes indicated) and all the positive cash flows were withdrawn from that same account (in the timeframes indicated), the account would have to earn the rate represented by the IRR in order to have a zero balance after the last cash flow. It can be used to help evaluate the anticipated cash flows of a purchase or investment. If the IRR is positive, then the present value of the positive cash flows outweighs the negative and vice versa.

Assumptions:

Cash Flows

Cash Flow	Amount	Duration in Years
Initial	-$100,000	1
1	$1,000	1
2	$5,000	2
3	$10,000	3
4	$25,000	5

Internal Rate of Return for the assumed cash flows: 6.87%

Social Security Optimizer

Assumptions:

Paul:
- Current age - 42
- Life expectancy = 90
- PIA calculated based on earnings of $87,000

Sally:
- Current age - 40
- Life expectancy = 90
- PIA calculated based on earnings of $65,000

Social Security inflation = 2%

Paul and Sally are married

FILING STRATEGY

Paul files for benefits at 70

Sally files for benefits at 70

Sally files for survivor benefits at 88

Optimal Social Security Filings

Ages	Paul - Own		Sally - Own	Survivor	Total
62/60	$0	$0	$0	$0	$0
63/61	0	0	0	0	0
64/62	0	0	0	0	0
65/63	0	0	0	0	0
66/64	0	0	0	0	0
67/65	0	0	0	0	0
68/66	0	0	0	0	0
69/67	0	0	0	0	0
70/68	51,398	0	0	0	51,398
71/69	52,426	0	0	0	52,426
72/70	53,475	0	40,780	0	94,255
73/71	54,544	0	41,596	0	96,140
74/72	55,635	0	42,427	0	98,063
75/73	56,748	0	43,276	0	100,024
76/74	57,883	0	44,142	0	102,024
77/75	59,041	0	45,024	0	104,065
78/76	60,221	0	45,925	0	106,146
79/77	61,426	0	46,843	0	108,269

Optimal Social Security Filings

Ages	Paul - Own		Sally - Own	Survivor	Total
80/78	$62,654	$0	$47,780	$0	$110,435
81/79	63,907	0	48,736	0	112,643
82/80	65,186	0	49,711	0	114,896
83/81	66,489	0	50,705	0	117,194
84/82	67,819	0	51,719	0	119,538
85/83	69,175	0	52,753	0	121,929
86/84	70,559	0	53,808	0	124,367
87/85	71,970	0	54,884	0	126,855
88/86	73,410	0	55,982	0	129,392
89/87	74,878	0	57,102	0	131,980
90/88	0	0	0	76,375	76,375
91/89	0	0	0	77,903	77,903

Grand Total $2,276,317

Social Security Retirement Claiming Strategies for Married Couples

For many Americans, Social Security benefits are an important source of retirement income. How *much* a retiree receives each month from Social Security is affected by a number of factors, including the retiree's lifetime earnings history, the age at which he or she applies for benefits, and whether more than one type of benefit may be available.

Carefully choosing when and how to claim Social Security retirement benefits can significantly increase the total dollar amount of benefits received. For an unmarried individual, deciding when to claim Social Security retirement benefits is relatively straightforward. For married couples, however, it is a more involved decision.

Basic Ground Rules for Claiming Retirement Benefits

Birth Year	FRA
1943-1954	66
1955	66 + 2 months
1956	66 + 4 months
1957	66 + 6 months
1958	66 + 8 months
1959	66 + 10 months
1960 and Later	67

- Primary Insurance Amount: All Social Security benefits are based on a worker's lifetime earnings record. Higher lifetime earnings generally result in higher benefits. Based on the earnings record, the Social Security Administration calculates an amount, called the "Primary Insurance Amount," (PIA). The PIA is the basic value upon which all of the worker's (and dependent's) benefits are based.

- Full retirement age: For many years, the "full" retirement age (FRA), the age at which "full" benefits -100% of an individual's PIA - are available, was age 65. However, for those born in 1938 or later, FRA has gradually been increasing. It is scheduled to reach age 67 for those born in 1960 or later.

Social Security Retirement Claiming Strategies for Married Couples

- Early retirement = reduced benefits: Age 62 is generally the earliest age that someone can begin to receive Social Security retirement benefits. However, if retirement benefits begin before an individual's FRA is reached, the benefit paid is reduced to reflect the fact that income will be paid over a longer period of time. An individual's PIA is reduced by 5/9 of 1% for each month, up to 36 months, that the individual applies before FRA. If the individual applies for benefits more than 36 months before FRA, an additional reduction of 5/12 of 1% is applied for each month in excess of 36.

- Delayed retirement = a bigger benefit: If an individual delays applying for retirement to FRA or beyond, the benefit is increased. For those born in 1943 or later, delaying retirement increases the benefit by 8% of the full PIA for each full year they wait beyond FRA. The maximum delayed credit is reached at age 70.

- Working and receiving benefits simultaneously: Individuals under FRA, who are both working and receiving Social Security benefits, are subject to certain earnings limitations. Once these limitations are exceeded, a recipient's Social Security benefits are reduced. For 2018, for those under FRA, benefits are reduced by one dollar for every two dollars in excess of $17,040. If the worker reaches FRA in 2018, benefits are reduced by one dollar for every three dollars of earnings in excess of $45,360. At FRA, these "lost" benefits are later partially restored through a benefit re-computation that takes into account the number of months of reduced or no benefits.

- Type of benefit available – unmarried individuals: For single individuals, deciding when to apply for retirement benefits is relatively easy; they have only the retirement benefit itself to consider. Apply early, get a reduced benefit; apply later, get a larger benefit.

A Changing World - Claiming Strategies Available to Married Couples

For married couples, the situation is more complex, for two key reasons: (1) there are several types of benefits that may possibly be claimed by spouses, and (2) the impact of major changes to Social Security law contained in the Bipartisan Budget Act of 2015, signed into law by President Obama on November 2, 2015. These legislative changes effectively ended what

Social Security Retirement Claiming Strategies for Married Couples

Congress saw as an abuse of prior Social Security law, resulting in married beneficiaries receiving more Social Security retirement income than Congress originally intended.[1] Because of this legislation, the Social Security retirement claiming strategies available to married couples have changed. Whether the new law or old law applies will depend on the ages of the spouses and the cutoff dates during a transition period provided for in the new law.

- Types of benefits available to married couples: Through April 29, 2016, there were three types of retirement benefits potentially available to certain married couples:

   1. Retirement benefit: The benefit an individual receives based on his or her own earnings record. If both spouses have worked, each may independently qualify for a retirement benefit.
   2. Spousal benefit: A benefit payable to the spouse of a retired worker. If the spouse has reached FRA, the benefit is generally 50% of the worker's PIA.
   3. Survivor's benefit: A benefit payable to a deceased worker's surviving spouse. If the survivor has reached FRA, the benefit is usually 100% of the worker's PIA.

Under prior law, the optimal Social Security retirement claiming strategy available to a married couple was usually a mix of two basic approaches: (1) File and Suspend, and; (2) Claim Now, Claim More Later. The following examples show how each of these approaches worked.

- File-and-Suspend: In the "File-and-Suspend" approach, a worker, upon reaching FRA, filed for retirement benefits and then immediately suspended their receipt.[2] This had a couple of effects:

   1. The spouse then qualified for "spousal" benefits. Social Security would compute both the spousal benefit (generally 50% of the worker's PIA) and any retirement benefit the spouse may have earned in his or her own right, and, in effect, awarded the *larger* of the two.[3] Except for cost-of-living adjustments, this benefit would continue unchanged until either the spouse or the worker died.

---

[1] The section of the law that changed Social Security benefits, Section 831, is titled, "Closure of Unintended Loopholes."
[2] Under both the old and the new law, the option to file and suspend is not available until an individual reaches FRA.
[3] Benefits taken before FRA are reduced to account for the fact that they will be paid over a longer period of time.

2. The worker, by suspending receipt of benefits, would also have received an increased retirement benefit for each month of delay up to age 70. This would also have provided a larger widow(er)'s benefit (generally 100% of the deceased worker's PIA) to the spouse, assuming that: (a) the worker pre-deceased the spouse, and (b) the worker's retirement benefit was larger than the benefit the spouse was receiving at the time the worker died.

- Claim Now, Claim More Later: If the worker or spouse was at or beyond FRA, they had a choice of collecting either the spousal benefit or their own retirement benefit. Generally, this approach was used by the high-earning spouse:

    1. A low-earning spouse must have claimed his or her own retirement benefit.
    2. The high-earning spouse would do what is known as a "restricted application" where he or she would choose to receive the spousal benefit only while allowing his or her own retirement benefit to grow (via delayed retirement credits) until age 70.
    3. At 70, the high-earning spouse would then switch from spousal benefits to his or her own retirement benefit.

The Impact of the Bipartisan Budget Act of 2015

The Bipartisan Budget Act of 2015 effectively ended both the File-and-Suspend and the Claim Now, Claim More Later strategies. The major impacts of this law on Social Security include:

1. File-and-Suspend: The new legislation, effective for claims filed on or after April 30, 2016, still allows an individual to file-and-suspend, but doing so also suspends all other benefits based on the worker's record. The worker must actually *receive* his or her Social Security benefit in order for a spouse or other qualifying dependents to receive a benefit. The worker's own retirement benefit will still increase due to delayed retirement credits. Families who were already receiving benefits under this strategy, and those who file-and-suspend by April 29, 2016 (i.e. those who reached age 66 by April 29, 2016), were not affected by the new law.

Social Security Retirement Claiming Strategies for Married Couples

2. Claim Now, Claim More Later: Under prior law, the key to this strategy turned on the ability of a spouse, once he or she reached FRA, to file a "Restricted," application for spousal benefits *only*. Under the new legislation, individuals who were *age 62 or older in 2015*[1] will still be able to file a Restricted application in the future, claim spousal benefits, and then later switch to their own (larger because of delayed retirement credits) retirement benefit. However, for those *under age 62 in 2015*, this choice is no longer available. When a spouse who is entitled to both a spousal benefit and a retirement benefit applies for benefits, Social Security will calculate both amounts and award the larger of the two. In essence, the spouse either applies for all possible benefits, or delays all possible benefits. There will no longer be a choice to claim one benefit now and a different benefit later.

3. Key points to remember:

- Those who are already using either the File-and-Suspend or the Claim Now, Claim More Later strategies may continue to do so. The new law does not affect them.

- April 29, 2016 was the last day for those who had reached FRA to request suspension of benefits in order to qualify a spouse or other dependents for Social Security benefits while simultaneously allowing their own retirement benefit grow due to delayed retirement credits.

- Those who were at least age 62 in 2015 will still be able to file a "Restricted" application for spousal benefits only when they reach FRA. The last of these individuals will reach FRA in 2019.

- Those who reach age 62 after 2015 will not be able to file a "Restricted" application, nor will they be entitled to use the File-and-Suspend strategy.

---

[1] Technically, an individual born on January 1, 1954, attained age 62 on December 31, 2015.

Social Security Retirement Claiming Strategies for Married Couples

Choosing Which Approach to Follow

In a shifting legal environment, and with so many variables involved, how does a married couple decide when and how to apply for Social Security retirement benefits? A good first step involves using a specialized software program. This type of computer analysis takes into account factors such as the relative ages of each spouse, their individual earnings history, an anticipated mortality age for each, and whether the old or new Social Security law applies. The end result is a theoretical "optimal" claiming strategy.

This optimal strategy, however, is often affected by real-world difficulties such as poor health (i.e. a shorter life expectancy), a need for income now, a "down" stock market, or other unexpected problems. However, understanding the claiming strategies that are available, and how to best utilize them, can help a married couple coordinate the theoretical with the real- world and maximize, to the greatest extent possible, the retirement and widow(er)'s benefits received from Social Security.

Seek Professional Guidance

The right claiming strategy for Social Security retirement benefits can make an enormous contribution to a retirement that is both secure and comfortable. Because of the complexities involved, the advice and guidance of experienced, trained financial professionals in making these decisions is strongly recommended. Social Security questions can also be answered by directly contacting the Social Security Administration.

Annuities in Retirement Income Planning

For much of the recent past, individuals entering retirement could look to a number of potential sources for the steady income needed to maintain a decent standard of living:

- **Defined benefit (DB) employer pensions:** In these plans the employer promises to pay a specified monthly amount for the life of the retiree and/or spouse.
- **Social Security:** Designed to replace only a part of an individual's working income, Social Security provides a known benefit for the life of a retiree and his or her spouse.
- **Defined contribution (DC) plans:** Such as 401(k), 403(b), or 457[1] plans, which allow for contributions from the employee (in some cases from the employer as well) to a retirement account. The funds in the account, whatever they amount to at retirement, provide retirement income.
- **Individual retirement plans:** Such as Traditional IRAs or Roth IRAs. These are "individual" versions of employer-sponsored DC plans. The funds in the IRA at retirement, whatever the amount, are used to provide retirement income.

The Changing Face of Retirement

The saying that "life is what happens when you're making other plans" is particularly true when it comes to retirement income planning, for several key reasons:

- **Fewer employer pensions:** Over the past several decades, many employers have changed from defined benefit to defined contribution plans. From 1985 to 2000, for example, the rate of participation in defined benefit plans by full-time employees of medium and large private firms dropped from 80% to 36%.[2] A survey by the Bureau of Labor Statistics, published in 2013, found that only 26% of civilian workers in the U.S. participated in defined benefit pension plans.[3]

---

[1] These refer to the sections of the Internal Revenue Code which authorize these different types of retirement plans.

[2] See, "Employee Participation in Defined Benefit and Defined Contribution Plans, 1985-2000." U.S. Bureau of Labor Statistics, updated June 16, 2004.

[3] National Compensation Survey: Employee Benefits in the United States, March 2013, Table 2.

Annuities in Retirement Income Planning

- **Social Security:** Social Security is a "pay-as-you-go" system, with current workers supporting those already receiving benefits. As the baby boom generation begins to retire, the number of individuals remaining in the workforce to support them grows smaller. Although politically unpleasant, fiscal reality may force higher payroll taxes, reductions in benefits, or both.

- **We're living longer:** A child born in 1940 had an average life expectancy of 62.9 years. For a child born in 2010, however, average life expectancy had increased to 78.7 years.[1]

With the stable, lifetime income stream from employer pensions and Social Security playing an ever shrinking role, retirement income planning demands that each individual accept a higher degree of personal responsibility for both accumulating and managing the assets needed to pay for retirement. And managing these assets has to be done in a world where constant inflation, fluctuating interest rates, and sometimes volatile financial markets are a fact of life.

Extended life spans mean that the money has to last longer, although exactly how long is unknown.

One Possible Answer – Immediate Annuities

Life insurance is designed to help solve the problems created when someone dies prematurely. An annuity, on the other hand, is designed to protect against the possibility of living too long. An "immediate" annuity is a contract between an individual and an insurance company. In exchange for a single, lump-sum premium, the insurance company agrees to begin paying a regular income to the purchaser for a period of years or for life. The periodic payment amount depends on a number of factors:

- **Premium paid:** Generally the larger the payment, the larger the income stream.

- **Age:** Older individuals typically receive larger periodic payments.

- **Payout period selected:** A shorter payout period usually results in a larger payment.

- **Underlying investment medium:** Generally, either a fixed or a variable annuity.

---

[1] Source: National Center for Health Statistics: Deaths: National Vital Statistics Reports, Volume 61, Number 4. Deaths: Final Data for 2010. May 8, 2013.

Annuities in Retirement Income Planning

FIXED ANNUITY	VARIABLE ANNUITY
A fixed annuity pays a fixed rate of return. The insurance company invests in a portfolio of debt securities such as mortgages or bonds and pays out a fixed rate of return. Generally, this rate of return is guaranteed for a certain period of time after which a new rate is calculated. Most insurance companies offer a guaranteed minimum rate throughout the life of the contract. Such guarantees are based upon the claims-paying ability of the issuing insurance company.	A variable annuity offers the potential for higher returns in exchange for assuming a higher level of risk. You can choose from among several types of investment portfolios, such as stocks or bonds. The amount of each annuity payment will fluctuate depending on the performance of the underlying investments. Variable annuities are long-term investments designed for retirement purposes. They have certain limitations, exclusions, charges, termination provisions, and terms for keeping them in force, and are sold by prospectus only.[1]

Annuities are not insured by the FDIC or any government agency. Since an annuity may be payable far into the future, dealing with a financially solid insurer is essential. Credit rating companies such as A.M. Best, Standard and Poor's, or Moody's can provide an objective measure of a firm's financial stability.

Seek Professional Guidance

For many individuals, an immediate annuity can form an important part of their retirement income planning. Because an immediate annuity is a complex product, the advice and guidance of a trained financial professional is highly recommended.

---

[1] The prospectus for a variable annuity contains complete information including investment objectives, risk factors, fees, surrender charges, and any other applicable costs.

Deferred Income Annuities

Retirement income planning in today's world needs to deal with several key realities:

- **We're living longer:** A child born in 1940 had an average life expectancy of 62.9 years. For a child born in 2014, however, average life expectancy had increased to 78.8 years.[1]

- **We're on our own, more and more:** Over the past few decades, many employers have changed from defined *benefit* plans, providing predictable, stable lifetime income, to defined *contribution* plans, such as 401(k), 403(b), or 457[2] plans. A worker can also have an individual retirement account, either a traditional IRA or a Roth IRA. In defined contribution plans, the individual contributes (in some cases the employer also contributes) to a tax-deferred retirement account. At retirement, the accumulated cash, whatever it amounts to, is used to generate retirement income.[3] This change from defined benefit to defined contribution plans has effectively shifted the risk involved in managing these retirement assets from the employer to the *employee*.

- **Social Security? Maybe, maybe not:** Social Security is a "pay-as-you-go" system with current workers supporting those already receiving benefits. As the baby boom generation retires (the "Silver Tsunami"), the number of individuals left in the workforce to support them will grow smaller. Although politically unpleasant, fiscal reality may force higher payroll taxes, retirement benefit cuts, or both.

Unless these retirement assets are very carefully managed, it is possible to literally "run out of money." How, then, does a retiree create a stable income stream that will last a lifetime? One possible answer is a type of life insurance annuity contract known as a "Deferred Income Annuity."

What's an Annuity?

The word "annuity" derives from a Latin term meaning "annual" and generally refers to any

---

[1] Source: National Vital Statistics Reports, Volume 65, Number 4. Deaths: Final Data for 2016, Table 8. 6/30/2016

[2] These refer to the section of the Internal Revenue Code which authorizes these different types of retirement plans.

[3] From 1985 to 2000, the rate of participation in defined benefit plans by full-time employees of medium and large private firms dropped from 80% to 36%. (See "Employee Participation in Defined Benefit and Defined Contribution Plans, 1985-2000. U.S. Bureau of Labor Statistics, update June 16, 2004). A survey by the Bureau of Labor Statistics, published in 2014, found that only 23% of workers in the U.S. participated in DB plans. (See "National Compensation Survey: Employee Benefits in the United States, March 2017, Table 2.")

circumstance where principal and interest are liquidated through a series of regular payments. A commercial annuity is a special type of contract issued by a life insurance company. In a typical situation, the contract owner contributes funds to the annuity. In return, the insurance company agrees to make periodic payments over a specified period of time, the life of an individual, or the joint lives of two individuals. In essence, an annuity allows the contract owner to shift the investment risk to the insurance company.

The dollar amount the annuity pays depends on a number of factors, including:

- **Premium paid:** Generally, the larger the payment, the larger the income stream.

- **Age:** Older individuals (with shorter life expectancies) typically receive larger periodic payments.

- **Deferral period:** Waiting a longer period of time before beginning annuity payments usually results in a larger periodic payment.

- **Payout period selected:** A shorter payout period usually results in a larger payment.

Deferred Income Annuities

For many individuals, a "deferred" annuity (one which begins payments at a future date) provides part of their retirement income. In many cases, the annuity contract owner purchases the annuity while relatively young, and then structures the contract so that annuity payments begin at the same time as retirement, receiving payments over his or her remaining lifetime. Since the individual's retirement years may extend over a lengthy period of time, for each dollar invested in the contract, the periodic payments will generally be less than if the contract covered a shorter period of time.

Recently, individuals close to retirement age have begun to utilize a deferred annuity that begins paying not at the beginning of retirement, but at a more advanced age, such as 75, 80, or 85. These annuities are known as "deferred income annuities," or, more popularly, "longevity annuities." When planning for not running out of money in retirement, deferred income annuities have several advantages:

- **Security:** Once the annuity is purchased, the income is guaranteed for the rest of your life, no matter how long that may be. The income amount is fixed and is not subject to change based on market fluctuations.

- **Higher payment amounts:** Monthly income payments are generally higher than those available from traditional deferred annuities.

- **Simplicity:** Once the annuity is purchased, there is nothing more to do or decide. The income will automatically begin on the specified future date.

Until recently, deferred income annuities were paid for exclusively with funds that had already been taxed.

Qualified Retirement Plans and Deferred Income Annuities

An alternative source of funds to purchase a deferred income annuity is the cash saved in individual retirement plans such as a traditional or Roth IRA, or in employer-sponsored qualified[1] retirement plans such as 401(K), 403(b), or 457 plans. In the past, a key roadblock to using these funds was the federal income tax requirement that the money be distributed (generally beginning at age 70½), known as a Required Minimum Distribution, or RMD.[2] However, regulations published in July, 2014[3] by the Internal Revenue Service provide a way to purchase a deferred income annuity with qualified plan funds without tripping over the RMD requirements. These changes reflect an IRS concern that long-lived retirees might exhaust their qualified retirement plan funds too soon, due to the RMD requirements.

Under these regulations, if a deferred income annuity purchased with qualified plan funds meets certain requirements, the funds invested in the contract are *excluded* from the normal RMD requirement calculations prior to the date annuity payments begin, even if the start date is beyond age 70½. Such a contract is referred to a "Qualified Longevity Annuity Contract," or QLAC. In general, these requirements are as follows:

---

[1] These plans are termed "qualified" as they meet certain requirements in the Internal Revenue Code.

[2] The discussion here concerns federal income tax law. State or local income tax law may differ. These RMD distributions can be made either as a lump-sum distribution or periodic payments made over the life or life expectancy of an account owner or an account owner and spouse. Roth IRAs are not subject to the RMD rules during the lifetime of the account owner. There are RMD requirements for *inherited* Roth IRA accounts.

[3] See Treasury Decision 9673, published on July 1, 2014, effective for contracts purchased or exchanged on or after July 2, 2014.

- **Limitations on premiums:** No more than the *lesser* of $130,000 (2018 value) or 25% of the account balance may be used to purchase the deferred income annuity. The $130,000 premium limitation is subject to adjustment for inflation in future years.

- **Maximum age at commencement:** The annuity starting date must be no later than the first day of the month following the month the employee reaches age 85. This maximum age may be adjusted by the IRS for future changes in mortality experience.

- **Return of premium:** A QLAC may provide for a return of premium (ROP) feature. With this provision, if the employee and/or a designated beneficiary die before the entire premium has been returned in the form of annuity payments, a single, lump-sum payment of the un-recovered difference may be made.

- **Underlying investment:** A deferred income annuity will be considered a QLAC <u>only</u> if the earnings under the contract are derived from contractual guarantees. Such an arrangement is commonly referred to as a "fixed" annuity, an annuity which pays a known rate of return. Generally, this rate is guaranteed[1] for a certain period of time after which a new rate is calculated, based on market conditions. Most insurance companies offer a guaranteed[1] minimum rate of return throughout the life of the annuity contract.

- **Other points:** The contract must be identified as a QLAC and the employee must be so notified. Because Roth IRAs are not subject to the RMD requirements during the owner's lifetime, a deferred income annuity purchased within a Roth IRA is not considered to be a QLAC.

Seek Professional Guidance

For many individuals, a deferred income annuity can play an important role in their retirement income planning. However, because annuities are complex products, the advice and guidance of a trained financial professional is highly recommended.

---

[1] Such guarantees are based upon the claims-paying ability of the issuing insurance company.

How a Deferred Income Annuity Works

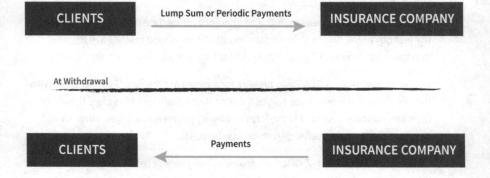

Setting Up a Deferred Income Annuity

- A deferred income annuity (DIA) is typically purchased at or close to retirement age.

- The DIA may be purchased with either a lump-sum payment or periodic payments.

- If the DIA is purchased with qualified plan funds, special requirements apply

Payments

- Payments generally begin at an advanced age, for example 75, 80, or 85.

- Payments can be made over a fixed number of periods, or

- Payments can be made over the lifespan of one or more individuals.

Pension Income Alternative

The Problem

At retirement, married pension plan participants typically must make a choice. They can choose to take:

- The maximum monthly income for the life of the retiring employee only (e.g., $1,000 per month); or

- A substantially reduced pension for the lifetime of both the retiring employee and his/her spouse (e.g., $800 per month).

Many employees and their spouses feel compelled to take the reduced lifetime income.[1] Unfortunately, once selected this option generally may not be changed.

Consider the Potential Costs

- If both spouses die early, no one would receive the pension income.

- If spouse lives but a short time, the surviving retiree generally faces a lifetime of reduced pension benefits.

- If both live a full life and die within a year or so of each other, little benefit is ever realized after 20 years or more of reduced pension.

- In no case do children or other heirs inherit any benefits.

The following examples illustrate the potential lifetime cost of the survivorship benefit:

Example 1 - Full Survivorship Benefit on Pension Plan

	With No Survivorship	With 100% Survivorship
Anticipated monthly income at retirement (age 65)	$1,000	$800
Cost of survivorship election	$200 per month for both spouses' remaining lifetimes	
Joint life expectancy[2] at 65	25 years x $2,400 = $60,000 total potential cost	

---

[1] **Caution:** In some cases, eligibility for continuing the surviving spouse's group health care is dependent on choosing the survivor option.

[2] Based on IRS Annuity Table VI - Ordinary Joint and Last Survivor. Assumes both spouses are the same age.

Pension Income Alternative

Example 2 - 50% Survivorship Benefit on Pension Plan

	With No Survivorship	With 50% Survivorship	
		Retiree	Spouse
Anticipated monthly income at retirement (age 65)	$1,000	$900	$450
Cost of survivorship election	$100 per month for both spouses' remaining lifetimes		
Joint life expectancy[2] at 65	25 years x $1,200 = $30,000 total potential cost		

Conclusion

Pension survivorship options equate to very expensive term life insurance that may never pay a benefit.

A Solution – Alternative Funding

Purchase permanent life insurance prior to retirement in an amount that would provide the survivor or other heirs with a similar monthly income benefit. Then still take the maximum monthly pension benefit.

For example, to provide $800 per month for 25 years (assuming a 5% growth rate on the remaining balance) would require an initial lump sum or life insurance death benefit of approximately $137,000. Of course, the 5% return is not guaranteed, so, if desired, a guaranteed lifetime payout available from the insurance company could be used.

Advantages to Alternative Funding

- Premiums can be paid when income is higher, before retirement, from discretionary income.

- The monthly premium may be more or less than the difference between the Life Only and the Joint & Survivor, depending on the insured's age and health at the time a life insurance policy is issued. However, in general, the overall cost of the life insurance will be less than the total potential cost of lower pension benefits if the insured lives to normal life expectancy.

Pension Income Alternative

- A large part of the death benefit proceeds payable in monthly installments will be income tax free. Normally, pension income is fully taxable.

- If the retiree and spouse die simultaneously or if the spouse dies first, their children or other heirs may receive the insurance death benefits. Typically, no additional benefits would be payable from the pension plan. If the spouse dies first and the retiree does not have any other beneficiaries deserving of the proceeds, the retiree can surrender the policy for its cash surrender value.

Reverse Mortgages

Many retired individuals find themselves living on a fixed income. Many also own a home which is either paid for, or which has a very small mortgage, a situation often described as "house-rich-and-cash-poor." In the past, there were few acceptable ways to take advantage of this home equity, apart from selling the home. Recently, however, a different financial tool – the reverse mortgage – has been growing in popularity. A reverse mortgage

provides qualified individuals access to the equity in their homes, while allowing them to retain ownership of the home.

What Is a Reverse Mortgage?

Most homeowners are familiar with the traditional home mortgage. An individual buys a home, and, over time, as the monthly payments are made, the balance due on the mortgage is gradually reduced. A homeowner's equity – the difference between what is owed and the market value – is also increased if a home's market value increases. In the traditional, *forward* mortgage, as debt decreases, equity increases:

A *reverse* mortgage, as the name implies, works in the other direction. With a reverse mortgage, cash flows from a lender to a borrower. Over time, the balance due increases. In a reverse mortgage, as debt increases, equity decreases.

- **General Requirements:** All borrowers must be at least 62 years of age. The home must be owner-occupied and be the borrower's principal residence. Qualifying residences generally include single-family detached homes, 2-4 unit owner-occupied homes, condominiums, and manufactured homes. Only first mortgages are permitted. Any other debt secured by the home must be first paid off, or paid off with proceeds from the reverse mortgage.

- **Ownership:** During the term of the mortgage, the borrower remains the owner of the home and is responsible for payment of property taxes, insurance, utilities, fuel, maintenance, and other expenses.

- **Repayment:** No payments are required as long as at least one borrower lives in the home. The outstanding loan balance, plus accrued interest and any loan costs, is due when the last borrower sells the home, permanently leaves (an absence of 12 months or more), dies, or fails to carry out an obligation such as paying insurance or property taxes when due. Typically, the loan is repaid by either selling or refinancing the home. Any remaining equity is paid to the borrower, the borrower's estate, or heirs.

- **Maximum loan balance:** A borrower can never owe more than the value of the home at the time the loan is repaid. Reverse mortgages are generally nonrecourse loans, which means the lender can only look to the value of the home for repayment.

The Pros and Cons of Reverse Mortgages

There are a number of reasons why a reverse mortgage may not be appropriate:

- **Not needed:** Some retired individuals will not want to consider a reverse mortgage simply because it is not needed; their financial needs during retirement are already adequately met.

- **Security:** Reflecting long-held attitudes toward savings and debt, some individuals may not be comfortable with the idea of placing any type of mortgage on the home, once it is paid for.

- **Legacy for heirs:** Rather than using the equity in the home for current needs, a homeowner may want the equity to pass to family members or other beneficiaries, such as a charity.

There are also a number of situations where a reverse mortgage can help:

- **Enjoy life:** For some, the extra dollars provided by a reverse mortgage may make it easier to pay routine monthly expenses. For others, it may allow an occasional splurge.

- **Pay off debt:** Funds from a reverse mortgage can be used to pay off other types of personal debt that require monthly payments, such as credit card balances.

- **Maintain independence:** Some may wish to make improvements to the home, or pay for in-home care, to allow them to remain independent as long as possible

- **Provide for the future:** Even though the present financial situation is stable, a reverse mortgage can provide a way to deal with unexpected future problems.

Choosing a Reverse Mortgage

Unlike just a few years ago, a wide range of reverse mortgage programs is available today. Further, the specific details of each program can vary greatly. A standard series of questions can be used to compare and contrast each program:

- **How much cash?** In general, the amount of cash which can be borrowed will generally depend on the lender's policies, the age of the youngest borrower, the value of the home, the home's condition and location, and the interest rate. The amount of available cash can vary greatly from one lender to the next.

- **How will the cash be paid?** The cash from a reverse mortgage is typically available to the borrower in one of three ways. In some cases a combination of payment methods may be available:

  - **Lump sum:** The loan proceeds can be paid with one check, usually at the time the loan is closed.

  - **Periodic advances:** Cash payments of a fixed amount are usually made monthly. Term advances are made for a specified period of time; tenure advances continue as long as at least one borrower lives in the home.

  - **Credit line:** This is a line of credit the borrower can use when needed, up to the loan limit.

- **Cost of the loan:** Federal law requires reverse mortgage lenders to provide prospective borrowers with a loan cost analysis. The total annual loan cost (TALC) analysis looks at the cost of a loan under a specified set of circumstances, over the entire length of the loan. The standardized nature of the TALC makes it easy to compare the cost of loans from different lenders.

- **Remaining equity:** If a borrower decides to sell the home after only a few years, how much equity would be left?

Reverse Mortgage Programs

There are a number of types of reverse mortgage programs, varying by lender, purpose, and security:

- **Single-Purpose Reverse Mortgages:** These are mortgage offered by some state and local government agencies, as well as non-profit organizations. Such loans are typically used to pay for home repairs, improvements, or property taxes.

- **Proprietary Reverse Mortgages:** Reverse mortgages issued by private companies. These loans are usually considered when higher-value homes are involved.

The most widely available reverse mortgage program is operated under the auspices of the federal government:

- **Home Equity Conversion Mortgage (HECM):** The Federal Housing Administration (FHA) part of the U.S. Department of Housing and Urban Development (HUD) insures reverse mortgage loans made by private lenders under its Home Equity Conversion Program. If a lender fails to make the promised payments, the FHA takes over responsibility for fulfilling the lender's obligations. The HECM program has specific loan limits and borrowers under this program can expect to pay origination fees as well as mortgage insurance premiums.

In 2015, HUD put into effect a series of eligibility standards designed to reduce the possibility that a reverse mortgage borrower might default on a loan. These new standards included (1) limiting the amount a borrower could receive at closing as well as the amount a borrower could receive during the first 12 months of a loan; (2) requiring a "financial assessment" of a borrower, including verifying past credit history, current income, other debt owed, and a borrower's record of meeting recurring home obligations such as taxes and insurance, and (3) if needed, setting aside a portion of the loan proceeds to make required insurance and property tax payments if the borrower fails to make them.

- **Home Equity Conversion Mortgage (HECM)for Purchase:** HUD also insures reverse mortgages which allow qualified borrowers to sell their existing (usually larger) home and then use the proceeds from a "HECM for Purchase" to buy a new (usually smaller) home. In effect, this program allowed qualified individuals to "downsize" in a single transaction, with only one set of closing costs.

Additional Resources

The federal government, through several of its agencies such as the FHA, the Consumer Financial Protection Bureau (CFPB), and the Federal Trade Commission (FTC), have freely available information on reverse mortgages. Further, the FHA requires consumer education as a part of the lending process. Reverse mortgage resources on the web include:

- **U.S. Department of Housing and Urban Development (HUD):** http://www.hud.gov/

- **Consumer Financial Protection Bureau:** http://www.consumerfinance.gov/

- **Federal Trade Commission:** http://www.ftc.gov/

- **American Association of Retired Persons (AARP):** The AARP provides publications on reverse mortgages. On the Internet, the AARP maintains a website at: http://www.aarp.org

Seek Professional Guidance

Because they are relatively new, reverse mortgages are unfamiliar to many. Also, those most likely to consider a reverse mortgage are usually at a point in life where long-term commitments must be very carefully considered. Individuals considering a reverse mortgage are strongly advised to seek professional guidance before entering into a loan contract.

How a Reverse Mortgage Works

MORTGAGE LENDER

Loan Amount
(typically as
a series of
payments)

Repayment at sale
of home or death
of last owner

HOME OWNER/BORROWER

Must keep as
primary residence

PERMANENT RESIDENCE

BORROWING

- Must own home free-and-clear or pay-off any existing loan balances with proceeds from reverse mortgage.

- The amount of cash available can vary widely from lender to lender.

- Borrower receives loan as lump sum, line of credit, or periodic payments. Some programs allow for a combination of payment methods.

- Borrower remains owner of home and must continue payments for property taxes, insurance, and repairs.

REPAYMENT

- No repayment required as long as home is borrower's primary residence[1].

- Repayment is due when last borrower sells home, permanently[2] moves away or dies.

- Loan is typically repaid by either selling the home or refinancing the loan.

- A borrower can never owe more than value of home, at the time loan is repaid.

- If proceeds from sale of home exceed loan amount due, borrower or heirs receive the difference.

---

[1] Primary residence is typically defined as where an individual resides at least six months of the year.

[2] Permanently moving away generally means not residing in the home for at least 12 months or more at one time.

Retirement Needs Analysis Data

Personal

Date 01/01/2018

Client(s) name		Date of birth	Retirement age	Social security age
1) Paul	Johnson	01/01/1976	67	67
2) Sally	Johnson	01/01/1978	67	67

☑ Check if clients are married

Income Needs

Beginning at retirement (choose one)

☑ Monthly amount $9,000   or ☐ _____ % of current monthly income

Beginning 10 years after retirement (choose one):

☑ Monthly amount $7,000   or ☐ _____ % of current monthly income

Beginning 15 years after retirement (choose one):

☑ Monthly amount $6,000   or ☐ _____ % of current monthly income

Income Sources

Employment income (Annual)

Paul $87,000   Sally $65,000

Monthly Social Security benefits

Paul	Sally
☐ Spousal Benefits Only ☐ Not Eligible	☐ Spousal Benefits Only ☐ Not Eligible
☑ Based on Current Earnings	☑ Based on Current Earnings
☐ Based on Maximum Earnings	☐ Based on Maximum Earnings
☐ PIA Input (values below required)[1]	☐ PIA Input (values below required)[1]
☐ Monthly Amount Input (values below required)[2]	☐ Monthly Amount Input (values below required)[2]
Retirement $ _____ Survivor $ _____	Retirement $ _____ Survivor $ _____

[1] Use the Social Security benefit at the client's "Full Retirement Age" (FRA).

[2] For retirement input this is the amount to be received at Social Security Age. For survivor input this amount is the PIA

Retirement Needs Analysis Data

Other income sources

Name of income source	Owner	Amount	Start age	Monthly/ lump sum[1]	P/V[2] or F/V	End age	Inflated annually	Available to survivor	Income Type
1)									
2)									
3)									
4)									
5)									

Capital

Retirement plans

Client(s)	Retirement plan balance	Monthly savings	Company match	Annual increase in contributions	Assumed rate of return
1) Paul	$136,000	$300	$150	4%	7%
2) Sally	$86,500	$200	$100	4%	7%

Other assets

Balance	$6,000
Monthly Contributions	$50
Assumed Rate of Return	6%

Assumptions

Paul mortality age	90	Annual employment inflation rate – Sally	4%
Sally mortality age	90	Annual Social Security benefit inflation rate	2%
Annual Inflation rate	4%	Assumed rate of return during retirement	6%
Annual employment inflation rate – Paul	4%	Solution rate of return	6%

---

[1] Enter "M" if paid monthly or "L" if paid as one lump sum.
[2] Enter "P" if amount is present value or "F" if amount is future value.

Retirement Analysis

Income Goals

You have indicated that you would like to have the following monthly retirement income:[1] At Paul's age 67 and Sally's age 65 - 71% of current income, or $9,000. At Paul's age 77 and Sally's age 75 - 55.26% of current income, or $7,000. At Paul's age 82 and Sally's age 80 - 47.37% of current income, or $6,000.

Income Sources

To support your retirement goals you have the following monthly sources:

Earned Income

Sally's employment income from age 65 until age 67

Social Security

Social Security benefits at Paul's age 67 - $3,327

Social Security benefits at Sally's age 67 - $2,631

Other Income

Assets Available at Retirement

Applied Assets

Paul's retirement assets - $1,310,145

Sally's retirement assets - $849,574

Other assets - $61,613

Results

According to the analysis, Your funds will be depleted at Sally's age 78. Your current savings of $550 will need to be increased by $1,557 with the additional monthly savings earning a rate of return of 6.00%.

Retirement Cash Flows

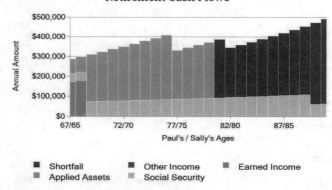

Shortfall   Other Income   Earned Income
Applied Assets   Social Security

An additional $1,084,099 will be required at retirement to meet your goals.

Values shown in this presentation are hypothetical and not a promise of future performance.

---

[1] Monthly amounts shown are in today's dollars.

Capital Available for Retirement

Current Assets

You have indicated that you currently own the following assets that will be used to support your retirement needs:

Paul's retirement plan current value of $136,000 assuming a rate of return of 7.00%
Sally's retirement plan current value of $86,500 assuming a rate of return of 7.00%
Other assets current value of $6,000 assuming a rate of return of 6.00%

Monthly Savings

You are currently, and plan to continue, contributing to the following assets:[1]

Paul's retirement plan - $300 with a company contribution of $150
Sally's retirement plan - $200 with a company contribution of $100
Other assets - $50
Paul's contributions increasing at 4.00% per year; Sally's at 4.00% per year.

Available Assets

You will have accumulated the following at Paul's age 67:
Paul's retirement assets - $1,310,145
Sally's retirement assets - $849,574
Other assets - $61,613

Analysis

You will have accumulated $2,221,332 by Paul's age 67, Sally's age 65.

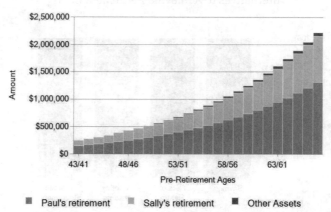

Asset Growth

An additional $1,084,099 will be required at retirement to meet your goals.

Values shown in this presentation are hypothetical and not a promise of future performance.

---

[1] Monthly amounts shown are in today's dollars.

Alternatives to Achieving Retirement Goals

There are several alternatives available which will provide a better chance of meeting your goals.

You Can Save More Until Retirement

Your current savings of $550 will need to be increased by $1,557 with the additional monthly savings earning a rate of return of 6.00%.

You Can Earn More on Your Assets Until Retirement

The rate of return on your existing savings of 6.00% will need to be increased to 20.00%.

You Can Spend Less During Retirement

Your desired retirement spending goals will need to be reduced by 24.00% resulting in $6,840 per month during the first year of retirement.

You Can Retire Later

You can satisfy your spending goals if retirement is postponed until Paul's age 73 and Sally's age 73.

Each of these alternatives may not be possible to implement fully. Therefore you might consider taking some steps in several different areas. Investments with the potential for a higher rate of return also have increased risk of losing principal, and may have increased short-term volatility.

Alternatives to Achieving Retirement Goals

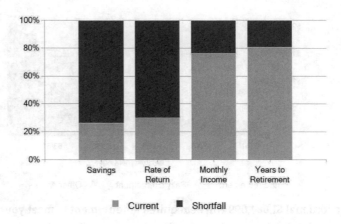

Values shown in this presentation are hypothetical and not a promise of future performance.

Achieving Your Retirement Goals

There are two steps that you can take to provide a better chance of meeting your retirement goals: you can save more or you can earn more. Either of these may not be possible based on your financial situation. Therefore you might consider taking steps in both areas.

You Can Save More Until Retirement

Your current overall portfolio effective rate of return from today until retirement is assumed to be 6.98%. In order to have the additional capital required to meet your retirement goals you will need to save an additional $1,335 per month at this same rate of return.

You Can Earn More on Your Assets Until Retirement

You could also achieve your retirement goals if you were able to increase the rate of return on all assets and contributions to 8.89% from today until retirement. Investments with the potential for a higher rate of return also have increased risk of losing principal and may have increased short-term volatility. This analysis assumes that all of your assets will earn 6.00% during retirement.

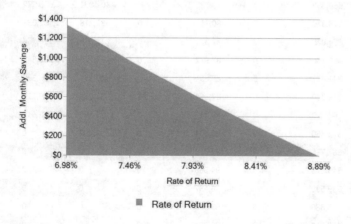

Making no changes will require an additional $1,084,099 at retirement to meet your goals.

Values shown in this presentation are hypothetical and not a promise of future performance.

Retirement Timeline

Assumptions:

Retirement Rate of Return: 6.00%
Rate of Inflation: 4.00%

Analysis Results:

Total of Annual Shortfalls: $3,508,106
Additional Capital Required: $1,084,099

| Age | Need | Sources | | | | Asset Balance | Annual Shortfall |
		Earned Income	Social Security	Other Income	Earnings from Assets		
				Beginning Balance		$2,221,332	
67/65	$287,910	$173,279	$39,920	$0	$134,534	$2,281,154	$0
68/66	299,427	180,211	40,718	0	138,098	2,340,754	0
69/67	311,404	0	73,103	0	136,484	2,238,937	0
70/68	323,860	0	74,565	0	129,840	2,119,482	0
71/69	336,814	0	76,056	0	122,093	1,980,816	0
72/70	350,287	0	77,577	0	113,145	1,821,251	0
73/71	364,298	0	79,129	0	102,891	1,638,972	0
74/72	378,870	0	80,711	0	91,218	1,432,031	0
75/73	394,025	0	82,325	0	78,006	1,198,337	0
76/74	409,786	0	83,972	0	63,125	935,648	0
77/75	331,471	0	85,651	0	49,571	739,399	0
78/76	344,730	0	87,364	0	37,085	519,118	0
79/77	358,520	0	89,112	0	23,100	272,810	0
80/78	372,860	0	90,894	0	7,492	0	1,664
81/79	387,775	0	92,712	0	0	0	295,063
82/80	345,673	0	94,566	0	0	0	251,108
83/81	359,500	0	96,457	0	0	0	263,043
84/82	373,880	0	98,386	0	0	0	275,494
85/83	388,836	0	100,354	0	0	0	288,482

Values shown in this presentation are hypothetical and not a promise of future performance

Retirement Timeline

Age	Need	Sources				Asset Balance	Annual Shortfall
		Earned Income	Social Security	Other Income	Earnings from Assets		
86/84	$404,389	$0	$102,361	$0	$0	$0	$302,028
87/85	420,565	0	104,408	0	0	0	316,156
88/86	437,387	0	106,497	0	0	0	330,891
89/87	454,883	0	108,627	0	0	0	346,256
/88	473,078	0	62,950	0	0	0	410,128
/89	492,001	0	64,209	0	0	0	427,793

Values shown in this presentation are hypothetical and not a promise of future performance

Retirement Analysis Detail

Income Objective

Age of		Income Need	Annual Need (Today's Dollars)	Annual Need (Future Dollars)	Capital Value
Paul	Sally				
67	65	71.05%	$108,000	$287,910	$2,557,721
77	75	55.26%	$84,000	$331,471	850,953
82	80	47.37%	$72,000	$345,673	1,251,327
			Total capital value of income need		**4,660,001**

Income Sources

Income Name	First Year's Payment	From Age	To Age[1]	COLA	Capital Value
Earned Income	$173,279	65	67	4.00%	$333,788
Social Security	$39,920	67 / 67	90 / 90	2.00%	1,020,782
Total capital value of income sources					**1,354,571**
Any shortfall between income objectives and income sources					3,305,431
Any shortfall due to timing of the cash flows					0
Capital required to meet income goals					**3,305,431**

Available Capital

Asset	Current Value	Monthly Contribution	Rate of Return	Value at Retirement
Other assets	$6,000	$50	6.00%	$61,613
Paul's retirement assets	$136,000	$450	7.00%	1,310,145
Sally's retirement assets	$86,500	$300	7.00%	849,574
		Total capital available at retirement		**2,221,332**
		Additional capital needed to meet retirement goals		**$1,084,099**

Assumptions:

Inflation rate: 4.00%
Retirement contribution annual increase:
Paul 4.00%, Sally 4.00%

Annual Social Security benefit inflation rate: 2.00%
Assumed rate of return: 6.00%
Mortality: 90/ 90

Values shown in this presentation are hypothetical and not a promise of future performance.
Investments with the potential for higher rates of return also have an increased risk of loss.

---

[1] The absence of a "To Age" value indicates that this income source is a lump-sum (single payment).

IRAs Compared

There are substantial differences between a traditional (nondeductible) IRA, a traditional (deductible) IRA, and a Roth IRA.

Item	Traditional IRA (Nondeductible)	Traditional IRA (Deductible)	Roth IRA
Basic eligibility requirements	Any person under age 70½ who has compensation.	Any person under age 70½ who has compensation.	Any person of any age who has compensation.[1]
Maximum contribution	Generally, the lesser of $5,500[2] ($11,000[3] for a married couple) or 100% of compensation.[4]		
Is the contribution deductible?	No	Yes, if neither spouse is covered by a qualified plan (QP). If single and covered by a QP, contribution is deductible if modified adjusted gross income (MAGI) is less than $63,000. Deduction phased out for MAGI between $63,000 and $73,000. If MFJ and one spouse is covered by a QP, the nonparticipant spouse may make a deductible contribution if MAGI is $189,000 or less. This deduction is phased out for MAGI between $189,000 and $199,000. The participant spouse may make a deductible contribution if MAGI is $101,000 or less. This deduction is phased out for MAGI between $101,000 and $121,000.[5]	No

[1] For 2018, the maximum contribution to a Roth IRA is phased out for single taxpayers with modified adjusted gross income (MAGI) between $120,000 and $135,000. For married couples filing jointly, the phase-out range is a MAGI of $189,000 to $199,000. For married individuals filing separately, the phase-out range is a MAGI of $0 to $10,000.

[2] This amount applies to 2018. For 2017, the maximum allowable contribution was also $5,500.

[3] This amount applies to 2018. For 2017, the maximum allowable contribution was also $11,000.

[4] If an IRA owner is age 50 or older, he or she may contribute an additional $1,000 ($2,000 if the spouse is also over 50).

[5] These are 2018 limits. For 2017 the phase-out ranges were (1) MFJ - MAGI of $99,000 - $119,000; (2) Single - $62,000 - $72,000. For taxpayers using the MFS filing status, the phase-out range is $0 - $10,000, which does not change.

IRAs Compared

Item	Traditional IRA (Nondeductible)	Traditional IRA (Deductible)	Roth IRA
Are earnings currently taxed?	No	No	No
Taxation of withdrawals at death and disability[1]	Contributions are received tax-free and earnings are taxable.	All distributions are taxable.	No taxation of qualified distributions.
Taxation of $10,000 withdrawn for first-time home purchase[1]	Proportionate part attributable to earnings is taxable.	All $10,000 subject to income tax.	"Qualified" distributions are not subject to tax. The earnings portion of a "non-qualified" distribution is taxable at ordinary rates.[2]
Taxation of withdrawals to pay for deductible medical expenses, e.g., expenses in excess of 7.5% of AGI	Proportionate part attributable to earnings taxed as ordinary income. For those under age 59½, 10% penalty does not apply to amounts that qualify as deductible medical expenses, e.g., amounts in excess of 7.5% of AGI.	Entire withdrawal taxable as ordinary income. For those under age 59½, 10% penalty does not apply to amounts that qualify as deductible medical expenses, e.g., amounts in excess of 7.5% of AGI.	"Qualified" distributions are not subject to tax. The earnings portion of a "non-qualified" distribution is taxable at ordinary rates.[2]
Taxation of withdrawals to pay for qualified higher education expenses[2]	Proportionate part attributable to earnings is taxable.	Entire withdrawal is subject to income tax.	"Qualified" distributions are not subject to tax. The earnings portion of a "non-qualified" distribution is taxable at ordinary rates.[2]

[1] For individuals under age 59½, the 10% penalty tax does not apply in this situation.

[2] Generally, a "qualified" distribution is one made at least five years after a contribution is first made to a Roth IRA and because the owner reaches age 59½, dies, becomes disabled, or uses the funds to pay for first-time homebuyer expenses.

IRAs Compared

Item	Traditional IRA (Nondeductible)	Traditional IRA (Deductible)	Roth IRA
Taxation of distributions not covered above[1]	Nondeductible contributions received tax-free. Earnings are taxed at ordinary rate.	All distributions are taxable at ordinary rates.	"Qualified" distributions are not subject to tax. The earnings portion of a "non-qualified" distribution is taxable at ordinary rates.[2]
Are there required, minimum distributions?	Distributions must start by April 1 of the year following the year the account owner reaches age 70½.	Distributions must start by April 1 of the year following the year the account owner reaches age 70½.	No minimum distribution is required during the life of owner.
Are direct transfers of funds in an IRA to a Health Savings Account allowed?	Yes	Yes	Yes
By when must an IRA be set up and funded?	By the due date for filing the IRA owner's federal income tax return for the year of the contribution, generally April 15 of the following year.		
Federal bankruptcy protection	Federal bankruptcy law protects assets in all IRAs, up to $1,283,025. Funds rolled over from qualified plans are protected without limit.		
May federal income tax refunds be directly deposited into the IRA?	Yes	Yes	Yes
Are tax-free direct transfers of up to $100,000 to a qualified charity by an owner at least age 70½ allowed?[3]	Yes	Yes	Yes

[1] All taxable amounts are subject to penalty tax of 10% if received prior to age 59½, unless an exception applies. For traditional IRAs, the penalty is waived if the distribution is paid out in substantially equal periodic payments over the participant's life or life expectancy.

[2] Generally, a "qualified" distribution is one made at least five years after a contribution is first made to a Roth IRA and because the owner reaches age 59½, dies, becomes disabled, or uses the funds to pay for first-time homebuyer expenses.

[3] Such a distribution is counted towards a taxpayers RMD requirement.

Comparison of Returns from Various Types of IRAs

The table below is a hypothetical illustration of the impact of time and income taxes on the various types of IRAs.[1] The calculations assume that any tax savings from deductible contributions are invested in a separate, annually-taxable fund and that all funds are withdrawn in a lump sum at retirement.

Assumptions:

Desired net annual contribution: $5,500
Marginal income tax bracket – pre-retirement: 28.00%
Marginal income tax bracket – post-retirement: 25.00%
Tax-deferred growth rate: 7.00%
After-tax growth rate: 5.04%
Number of years until retirement: 20

Item		Traditional IRA (Nondeductible)	Traditional IRA (Deductible)	Roth IRA
A.	**Pre-Retirement**			
	1. Contributions are made	After-tax	Before-tax	After-tax
	2. Gross amount	$7,639	$5,500	$7,639
	3. Income taxes payable	2,139	0	2,139
	4. Net annual contribution to IRA	5,500	5,500	5,500
	5. Annual tax savings to taxable account	0	1,540	0
	Total net annual savings	**$5,500**	**$7,040**	**$5,500**
B.	**At Retirement**			
	1. Net accumulation in the IRA[2]	$241,258	$241,258	$241,258
	2. Future value of tax savings	0	53,715	0
	3. Total available before taxes	241,258	294,973	241,258
	4. Income taxes payable	-32,815	-60,315	0
	Net after income taxes	**$208,444**	**$234,659**	**$241,258**

[1] Based on federal law. State or local law may differ.
[2] Assumes annual contributions are made at the beginning of each year.

Tax-deductible Portion of Your IRA Contribution

The annual amount that an individual can contribute to a traditional IRA and then deduct on his or her income tax return depends on the individual's age, income, filing status and whether or not the client or their spouse is participating in a company retirement plan.

Item Description	Value
Age at end of year	59
Contribution year	2014
Contribution	$2,000
Tax-deductible portion	$2,000
Nondeductible portion	$0

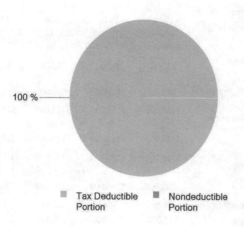

100 %

■ Tax Deductible Portion   ■ Nondeductible Portion

IRA Historical Limits

Traditional and Roth IRAs

Limit[1]	2018	2017	2016	2015	2014
Traditional IRA - Maximum individual contribution	$5,500	$5,500	$5,500	$5,500	$5,500
Traditional IRA - Age 50 and over "catch-up."	$1,000	$1,000	$1,000	$1,000	$1,000
Traditional IRA - Single contribution phase-out range.[2]	$63,000 to $73,000	$62,000 to $72,000	$61,000 to $71,000	$61,000 to $71,000	$60,000 to $70,000
Traditional IRA - Married filing joint contribution phase-out range.[2]	$101,000 to $121,000	$99,000 to $119,000	$98,000 to $118,000	$98,000 to $118,000	$96,000 to $116,000
Traditional IRA - Married filing joint contribution phase-out range, one spouse a qualified plan participant.[3]	$189,000 to $199,000	$186,000 to $196,000	$184,000 to $194,000	$183,000 to $193,000	$181,000 to $191,000
Traditional IRA - Married filing separate contribution phase-out range.[2]	$0 to $10,000	$0 to $10,000	$0 to $10,000	$0 to $10,000	$0 to $10,000
Roth IRA - Maximum individual contribution	$5,500	$5,500	$5,500	$5,500	$5,500
Roth IRA - Age 50 and over "catch-up."	$1,000	$1,000	$1,000	$1,000	$1,000
Roth IRA - Single contribution phase-out range.	$120,000 to $135,000	$118,000 to $133,000	$117,000 to $132,000	$116,000 to $131,000	$114,000 to $129,000
Roth IRA - Married filing joint contribution phase-out range.	$189,000 to $199,000	$186,000 to $196,000	$184,000 to $194,000	$183,000 to $193,000	$181,000 to $191,000
Roth IRA - Married filing separate contribution phase-out range.	$0 to $10,000	$0 to $10,000	$0 to $10,000	$0 to $10,000	$0 to $10,000

Note: The contribution phase-out ranges shown in this table are based on "modified adjusted gross income" (MAGI). MAGI is a taxpayer's normal Adjusted Gross Income (AGI) increased by: (1) the IRA deduction; (2) student loan interest deduction; (3) tuition and fees deduction; (4) domestic production activities deduction; (5) foreign earned income exclusion; (6) foreign housing exclusion or deduction; (7) excluded qualified U.S. savings bond interest; and (8) excluded employer-paid adoption expenses. For most taxpayers, AGI and MAGI will be the same.

[1] The various limits shown in this table reflect federal income tax law; state or local law may vary.
[2] The limits shown apply to a taxpayer who is a qualified plan participant.
[3] The limit shown applies to the spouse who is not a qualified plan participant.

Traditional IRAs

Deadline to Establish and Fund an IRA

An IRA can be established and funded at any time from January 1 of the current year and up to and including the date an individual's income tax return is due (generally, April 15 of the following year), not including extensions.

Can Deduction Be Taken Prior to Investing the Funds?

Yes! This, in effect, permits an individual to file his return early in the year (e.g., January) and use his or her tax refund to make the actual contribution prior to April 15. If desired, refunds of federal income taxes may be directly deposited into an IRA.

Types of Arrangements Permitted

There are currently two types of IRAs:

- **Individual retirement accounts:** These are trusts or custodial accounts with a corporate trustee or custodian.

- **Individual retirement annuities:** These are special annuities issued by an insurance company.

Contribution and Deduction Limits

A wage earner may contribute the lesser of $5,500[1] or 100% of compensation[2] for the year. If the wage earner is married, an additional $5,500 may be contributed on behalf of a lesser earning (or nonworking) spouse, using a spousal IRA. This means the family unit may contribute up to a total of $11,000[3] as long as family compensation is at least that amount. If an IRA owner is age 50 or older, he or she may contribute an additional $1,000 ($2,000 if the spouse is also age 50 or older). If certain requirements are met, the amount contributed may also be deducted from gross income on the federal income tax return.

---

[1] This amount applies to 2018. For 2017, the maximum allowable contribution was also $5,500.

[2] "Compensation" includes taxable wages, salaries, or commissions, or the net income from self-employment.

[3] This amount applies to 2018. For 2017, the maximum allowable contribution was also $11,000.

Participating In Other Retirement Plans May Reduce Deductions

Taxpayers who participate in an employer's plan may make fully-deductible IRA contributions only if their modified adjusted gross income (MAGI)[1] is below $101,000 if married filing jointly, $63,000 if single, and $0 if married filing separately. If MAGI exceeds these amounts, the $11,000 family or $5,500 individual maximum is reduced by a formula that eventually permits no deduction. No IRA deduction is allowed for married couples filing jointly with MAGI over $121,000, single individuals with a MAGI over $73,000, and married couples filing separately with an individual MAGI over $10,000[2].

For 2018, a taxpayer who is not an active participant in an employer plan, but whose spouse is, the maximum deductible IRA contribution is phased out if their combined MAGI is between $189,000 and $199,000.

Employer plans include: regular qualified plans; Keogh plans; Sec. 403(b) tax-sheltered annuity plans; simplified employee pension (SEP) plans; SIMPLE plans; and state, federal and local government plans (except Sec. 457 tax-exempt employer sponsored nonqualified deferred compensation plans).

Individuals with income in excess of the above limits may wish to consider contributing to either a traditional IRA or a Roth IRA, on a nondeductible basis. There are income limits applicable to Roth IRA accounts which may prevent a high-income taxpayer from contributing to a Roth IRA.

Distributions, Withdrawals and Taxation

- **Typical distribution plans.**

    - **Single-sum distribution:** Becomes part of taxable income for that year (less any nondeductible contributions).

    - **Life expectancy:** Each year, participant calculates payout based upon the attained-age life expectancy, using life expectancy tables issued by the federal government.

---

[1] Modified adjusted gross income (MAGI) is a taxpayer's adjusted gross income (AGI) with certain deductions or exclusions added back. For most taxpayers, MAGI and AGI are the same.

[2] These are 2018 limits. For 2017 the phase-out ranges were (1) MFJ - MAGI of $99,000 - $119,000; (2) Single - $62,000 - $72,000. For taxpayers using the MFS filing status, the phase-out range is $0 - $10,000, which does not change.

- **Life annuity:** For individual retirement annuities only, participant/annuitant may elect income for life (and the life of a joint annuitant, if desired).

- **Premature distributions:** Distributions from a traditional IRA prior to age 59½ are generally subject to an additional 10% penalty (plus being subject to current income tax) unless one or more of the following exceptions apply:[1]

    - A distribution is made because of the death or disability of the account owner.

    - A withdrawal is part of a scheduled series of substantially equal periodic payments.

    - A distribution is rolled-over into another IRA.

    - A withdrawal is used to pay for deductible medical expenses.

    - The distribution is used to pay for certain qualified higher-education expenses.

    - Amounts are withdrawn to pay for first-time homebuyer expenses of up to $10,000.

    - In certain situations, to pay health insurance premiums for unemployed individuals.

    - Distributions by certain military reservists called to active duty after 09/11/2001.

    - A distribution is transferred to a Health Savings Account (HSA).

    - In case of an IRS levy on the account.

- **Required minimum distributions (RMDs):** These distributions must begin by April 1 of the calendar year following the year in which the participant reaches age 70½. However, if the distribution is received in the year following attainment of age 70½, two distributions are required in that specific year. Thereafter, the minimum distribution must be made by the end of each calendar year. A 50% excise tax is levied[1] on amounts that should have been distributed, but were not. The dollar amount of each year's required minimum distribution is calculated using one of two life expectancy tables:

---

[1] Based on federal law. State law may vary.

- **Over the life expectancy of the participant:** In general, the required minimum distribution is calculated using the IRA participant's attained age and a minimum distribution factor table prescribed by the IRS, the <u>Uniform Lifetime Table</u>.[1]

- **Spouse more than 10 years younger:** If the participant's spouse is more than 10 years younger than the participant and the spouse is the IRA's sole designated beneficiary for the entire calendar year, the minimum distribution factor used in calculating the required distribution amount is determined in accordance with the <u>Joint and Last Survivor Table</u> specified in Treas. Reg. 1.401(a)(9)-9, Q&A3. The participant's marital status is determined on January 1 of the calendar year.

- Taxation of distributions.

  - **During life:** Distributions are taxable as ordinary income.[2]

  - **At death:** At the participant's demise, the distributions received by a beneficiary are taxed as ordinary income.[3] If the participant dies before payments have begun, distributions must generally be paid out over a five-year period or less, or over the life expectancy of a designated beneficiary, if payments begin by December 31 of the year following the year of the participant's death. If the distributions are paid solely to the surviving spouse, they may be paid out over the life expectancy of the spouse and must begin by the *later* of: (a) the end of the calendar year the participant would have reached age 70½ had he or she lived, or (b) the end of the calendar year after the year of the participant's death. If the surviving spouse elects to treat the IRA as his or her own, distributions must begin by April 1 of the year following the year in which the surviving spouse attains age 70½.

- Federal income tax law provides for an exclusion from gross income of up to $100,000 for distributions made from a Roth or traditional IRA *directly* to a qualified charitable organization. Such a distribution counts towards the taxpayer's RMD requirements. The IRA owner (Or beneficiary of an inherited IRA) must be at least age 70½ when the distribution is made. No charitable deduction is allowed for such a qualified charitable distribution.

---

[1] See Treas. Reg. Sec. 1.401(a)(9)-5, Q&A4(a).
[2] Taxes and penalties do not apply to nondeductible contributions.

- **Transfers to Health Savings Accounts (HSAs):** Federal law allows for a limited, one-time, direct transfer of funds from an IRA to an HSA. If certain requirements are met, any otherwise taxable portion of the distribution is excluded from income and the 10% early distribution penalty will not apply.

Investment Alternatives

- **Banks, savings and loans, credit unions:** Certificates of deposit in Traditional IRAs are generally protected by either the FDIC or the NCUA for amounts up to $250,000. Fixed and variable rates are available. There may be penalties for early withdrawal.

- **Annuities:** Traditional individual retirement annuities issued by insurance companies can guarantee a fixed monthly income at retirement.[1] Variable annuities do not guarantee a fixed monthly income at retirement.

- **Money market:** Yield fluctuates with the economy. Investor cannot lock in the higher interest rates. It is easy to switch to other investments.

- **Mutual funds:** Capital gains, interest and dividends are tax-deferred in an IRA but are taxed as ordinary income at withdrawal.

- **Zero coupon bonds:** Generally purchased at a deep discount from face value, "zeros" are subject to both inflation risk and interest rate risk.

- **Stocks and bonds:** A wide variety of investments and risk is possible. Capital gains are taxed as ordinary income at withdrawal. Losses are generally not deductible.

- **Limited partnerships:** Some limited partnerships are especially designed for qualified plans, specifically in the areas of real estate and mortgage pools.

Prohibited Investments or Transactions for IRAs

- **Life insurance:** IRAs cannot include life insurance contracts.

- **Collectibles:** The purchase of art works, antiques, metals, gems, stamps, etc. will be treated as a taxable distribution. Coins issued under state law and certain U.S. gold, silver, and platinum coins are exceptions; some kinds of bullion may be purchased.

---

[1] Annuity guarantees are based on the claims-paying ability of the issuing insurance company.

- **Loans to IRA taxpayer:** Self-borrowing disqualifies the IRA and triggers a constructive distribution of the fair market value of the entire amount in the IRA as of the first day of the tax year. Amounts so distributed are included in gross income. This is true whether the IRA is an individual retirement account or an individual retirement annuity. If the owner is under age 59½ at the time of a deemed distribution, a 10% tax penalty for early withdrawal will be added, unless an exception applies.

- **IRA as collateral:** If the owner of an individual retirement account pledges any portion of the account as security for a loan, the portion so pledged is deemed distributed, and included in gross income, as of the first day of the tax year in which the loan is made. If the owner of an individual retirement annuity pledges any portion of the contract as security of a loan, the fair market value of the entire amount in the account is deemed distributed, and included in gross income, as of the first day of the tax year. In both situations, if the owner is under age 59½ at the time of a deemed distribution, a 10% tax penalty for early withdrawal will be added, unless an exception applies.

Other Factors to Consider

- Is the interest rate fixed or variable? If interest rates drop, a fixed rate is better, especially if you can make future contributions at the same fixed rate. If interest rates go up, you may be able to roll the current IRA over to another IRA.

- What is the yield? More frequent compounding will produce a higher return.

- How often can you change investments? What is the charge?

- Federal bankruptcy law protects assets in traditional IRA accounts, up to $1,283,025.[1] Funds rolled over from qualified plans, however, are protected without limit

---

[1] Effective April 1, 2016. The limit is indexed for inflation every three years.

How a Traditional IRA Works

Account Owner

- Contribution may be tax deductible.[1]
- Total annual contribution is limited.[2]
- Annual contribution limits are coordinated with any Roth IRA.

IRA ACCOUNT

- May be opened anytime between January 1 of current year until due date of tax return.
- Earnings accumulate tax deferred.
- Account is usually self-directed (owner controls investments)
- A separate spousal IRA may be established for a spouse with little or no earned income.

EARLY WITHDRAWAL

- A 10% penalty applies if withdrawals are made before age 59½.
- Some exceptions to 10% penalty are available.
- Earnings + deductible contributions are taxed as ordinary income in year received.

RETIREMENT

- Distributions must begin by April 1 of year following year owner reaches age 70½.
- Required minimum distribution rules apply.
- Earnings + deductible contributions are taxed as ordinary income in year received.

DEATH

- Value of IRA is included in owner's gross estate.
- Proceeds can pass to surviving spouse, with payments made over survivor's lifetime.
- Income and estate taxes can severely reduce IRA funds left to non-spousal beneficiaries.

---

[1] If an IRA owner (or spouse) is a participant in an employer-sponsored qualified plan, the deductibility of traditional IRA contributions may be limited, based on income level and filing status.

[2] The maximum annual contribution is the lesser of $5,500 ($11,000 for a married couple) or 100% of compensation. For married couples, no more than $5,500 may be contributed for either spouse. If an IRA owner is age 50 or older, he or she may contribute an additional $1,000 ($2,000 if the spouse is also over 50).

Deductible IRA Contributions for Traditional IRAs

The annual amount that an individual can contribute to a traditional IRA and then deduct on his or her income tax return cannot exceed the lesser of $5,500[1] or total compensation for that year. For a married couple filing a joint return, where only one spouse is employed (or where one spouse earns less than $5,500), the annual contribution is limited to the lesser of $11,000[2] (a maximum of $5,500 each to separate accounts) or their combined annual compensation. The contributions on behalf of the non-employed (or lesser earning) spouse are made to an arrangement called a spousal IRA.[3]

The $5,500/$11,000 limits assume no contributions to a Roth IRA. The contribution limits for both a traditional IRA and a Roth IRA are coordinated: a taxpayer may not contribute more than $5,500 ($11,000 spousal) per year into a single IRA or combination of IRAs. Excess contributions are subject to a 6% excise tax.

The maximum limit on the amount that may be deducted is restricted, however, if the individual (or spouse) is a participant in an employer-sponsored retirement plan. If this is the case, and depending on the level of modified adjusted gross income (MAGI), a deduction may be allowed for all, none, or only a portion of an IRA contribution.

The chart below shows the traditional IRA contribution phase-out ranges for tax year 2018.

---

[1] This amount applies to 2018. For 2017, the maximum allowable contribution was also $5,500.
[2] This amount applies to 2018. For 2017, the maximum allowable contribution was also $11,000.
[3] If an IRA owner is age 50 or older, he or she may contribute an additional $1,000 ($2,000 if the spouse is also over 50).

Deductible IRA Contributions for Traditional IRAs

Status	No Participation in a Company Retirement Plan	If Covered by a Company Retirement Plan[1]	
Single	Up to $5,500 is deductible.	**MAGI**	**IRA Deduction**
		Up to $63,000	$5,500
		$63,000 - $73,000	Phased out
		Over $73,000	None
Married filing joint	Up to $5,500 for each is deductible, including spousal IRAs.	**MAGI**	**IRA Deduction**
		Up to $101,000	$5,500 ($11,000 spousal)
		$101,000 - $121,000	Phased out
		Over $121,000	None
Married filing separate	Up to $5,500 for each is deductible, if both spouses are employed.	**MAGI**	**IRA Deduction**
		Up to $10,000	Phased out
		Over $10,000	None

Other Considerations

- Company retirement plans include pension plans, profit sharing plans, 401(k), 403(b) plans, SEP-IRAs, Keogh plans, and SIMPLE plans.

- Generally, compensation includes wages, salaries, professional fees, net self-employment income and other amounts received for performing personal services.

- Compensation also includes alimony received by a divorced spouse which is includable in income.

---

[1] A taxpayer will not be considered an active participant in an employer-sponsored retirement plan merely because the taxpayer's spouse is an active participant. However, in this situation, the taxpayer's deductible IRA contribution will be phased out for couples with a MAGI of $189,000 - $199,000.

Deductible IRA Contributions for Traditional IRAs

Calculating the Maximum Deductible Amount – Single[1] or MFS

For 2018, the following steps may be used to calculate the deductible portion of a contribution to a traditional IRA for a single individual or a married individual using the married filing separately filing status:[2]

1. Modified adjusted gross income (MAGI):[3] $ _____

2. Applicable dollar amount:[4]   (_____)

3. Line 1 minus Line 2:   _____

4. Deduction: _____
    a. If line 3 is greater than $10,000, no deduction allowed.
    b. If line 3 is between $0 and $10,000, subtract line 3 from $10,000.

5. Multiplication factor: .55 (.65 if age 50 or greater)   _____

6. Multiply line 4 x line 5   _____

7. Round line 6 to next highest $10   _____

8. Your compensation for the year: _____

9. Contributions you plan to make   _____
    (Do not enter more than $5,500 [$6,500 if age 50 or older])

10. Maximum deductible IRA amount:[5] $_____
    (Compare the amounts on Lines 7, 8, and 9, and enter the smallest amount.)

---

[1] Including Head of Household.

[2] Married couples where both spouses contribute to an IRA should compute each deduction separately. If an individual receives social security benefits in the same year that a contribution is made to a traditional IRA, a different calculation is involved. See IRS Publication 590, Individual Retirement Arrangements (IRAs) for details.

[3] MAGI = Adjusted Gross Income (AGI) increased by: (1) the IRA deduction; (2) student loan interest deduction; (3) tuition and fees deduction; (4) domestic production activities deduction; (5) foreign earned income exclusion; (6) foreign housing exclusion or deduction; (7) qualified savings bond interest; and (8) excluded employer-paid adoption expenses. For most taxpayers, AGI and MAGI will be the same.

[4] This will vary with filing status. For 2018 these amounts are: Single and Head of Household - $63,000; MFS - $0.

[5] If the deductible portion of the IRA is between $1 and $200, round up to $200. IRC Sec. 219(g)

Deductible IRA Contributions for Traditional IRAs

Calculating the Maximum Deduction – Married Filing Jointly[1]

For 2018, the following steps may be used to calculate the deductible portion of a contribution to a traditional IRA for a married individual using the married filing jointly filing status:[2]

1. Modified adjusted gross income (MAGI):[3] $_____

2. Applicable dollar amount:[4]   ($101,000)

3. Line 1 minus Line 2:   _____

4. Deduction: _____
   a. If line 3 is greater than $20,000, no deduction allowed.
   b. If line 3 is between $0 and $20,000, subtract line 3 from $20,000.

5. Multiplication factor: .275 (.325 if age 50 or greater)   _____

6. Multiply line 4 x line 5   _____

7. Round line 6 to next highest $10   _____

8. Your compensation for the year: _____

9. Contributions you plan to make   _____
   (Do not enter more than $5,500 [$6,500 if age 50 or older])

10. Maximum deductible IRA amount:[5] $_____
    (Compare the amounts on Lines 7, 8, and 9, and enter the smallest amount.)

---

[1] Including a qualified widow(er).

[2] Married couples where both spouses contribute to an IRA should compute each deduction separately. If an individual receives social security benefits in the same year that a contribution is made to a traditional IRA, a different calculation is involved. See IRS Publication 590, Individual Retirement Arrangements (IRAs) for details.

[3] MAGI = Adjusted Gross Income (AGI) increased by: (1) the IRA deduction; (2) student loan interest deduction; (3) tuition and fees deduction; (4) domestic production activities deduction; (5) foreign earned income exclusion; (6) foreign housing exclusion or deduction; (7) qualified savings bond interest; and (8) excluded employer-paid adoption expenses. For most taxpayers, AGI and MAGI will be the same.

[4] The value for 2018. This amount varies with filing status and is subject to change each year.

[5] If the deductible portion of the IRA is between $1 and $200, round up to $200. IRC Sec. 219(g)

Does It Matter When You Contribute to an IRA?

When contributions to an IRA are consistently made at the beginning of the year rather than at the end, the funds have an extra 12 months in which to grow. Over a period of years there may be a substantial difference in the amount accumulated.

Assumptions:

Annual contribution: $2,000

Annual growth rate:[1] 6.00%

Number of Years from the Beginning of the First Year	Contribution Made Jan. 1	Contribution Made Dec. 31	Increase in Amount Accumulated
5	$11,951	$11,274	$676

Does It Matter When You Contribute to an IRA?

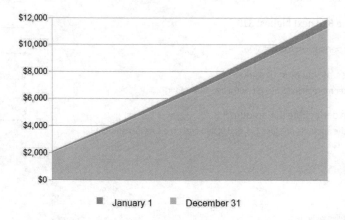

■ January 1   ■ December 31

Values shown in this presentation are hypothetical and not a promise of future performance.

---

[1] Growth is compounded annually. The rates of return used in this illustration are not indicative of any actual investment and will fluctuate in value. An investment will not provide a consistent rate of return; years with lower (or negative) returns than the hypothetical returns shown may substantially affect the scenario presented.

Roth IRA Conversion

Factors to Consider

Before 2010, taxpayers[1] with a modified adjusted gross income (MAGI)[2] in excess of $100,000, or who filed their federal income tax returns using the Married Filing Separately filing status, were prohibited from converting a traditional IRA to a Roth IRA. Beginning in 2010, however, these prohibitions no longer applied. For many individuals, the ability to convert a traditional IRA to a Roth IRA represents a significant tax planning opportunity.[3]

Pay Me Later or Pay Me Now

With a traditional IRA, and assuming certain requirements are met, contributions are deductible in the year they are made. The tax due on the contributions, and the tax due on any earnings or growth, is deferred until funds are distributed from the account, typically at retirement. From an income tax perspective, this is a "pay me **later**" scenario.

With a Roth IRA, contributions are never deductible; they are made with funds that have already been taxed. If certain requirements are met, both the contributions and any earnings or growth are received income-tax free when withdrawn from the account. From an income tax perspective, this is a "pay me **now**" scenario.

A taxpayer who elects to convert a traditional IRA to a Roth IRA has chosen to pay the income tax now rather than waiting until the future to pay it. To justify a conversion, the benefit of not paying taxes tomorrow should be greater than the cost of paying taxes today.

Benefits of Roth IRAs

The benefits of holding assets in a Roth IRA can be considerable:

- **During life – tax-free income:** Assuming that certain requirements are met, including a five-taxable year waiting period after a contribution is first made to a Roth IRA for the owner, "qualified" distributions are received income-tax free.

---

[1] The discussion here concerns federal income tax law. State or local law may differ.

[2] Modified adjusted gross income (MAGI) is a taxpayer's adjusted gross income (AGI) with certain deductions or exclusions added back. For most taxpayers, MAGI and AGI are the same.

[3] Although the discussion here focuses on traditional IRAs, the same rules apply to amounts converted from a SEP IRA or SIMPLE IRA to a Roth IRA. Funds in a SIMPLE IRA that do not meet the two-year period described in IRC Sec. 72(t)(6) may not be converted. Distributions from IRC Sec. 401(a) qualified retirement plans, IRC Sec. 457(b) governmental plans, and IRC Sec. 403(b) plans may also be rolled over into a Roth IRA.

- **At death – income-tax free to beneficiaries:** At death, the value of the Roth IRA is includable in the account owner's estate, subject to federal estate tax. A surviving spouse can treat an inherited Roth IRA as his or her own, with the proceeds being received income-tax free, and with no required minimum distributions. For non-spousal beneficiaries, and assuming that the five-year waiting period requirement has been met, the proceeds are received income-tax free. After the owner's death, however, non-spousal beneficiaries must take certain required minimum distributions.

- **No lifetime required minimum distributions:** Federal income tax law mandates that certain required minimum distributions be made from traditional IRAs, beginning when the account owner reaches age 70½. For Roth IRAs, there are no minimum distribution requirements during the lifetime of the account owner.

- **Contributions after age 70½:** As long as a taxpayer has "compensation" (such as wages or self-employment income), contributions may be made to a Roth IRA regardless of the taxpayer's age, subject to the modified adjusted gross income limitations. No contributions are permitted to a traditional IRA for any year in which the owner is age 70½ or older.

The Cost of Conversion

Converting a traditional IRA to a Roth IRA is a currently **taxable** event. For the year the converted assets are distributed, the taxpayer must include in gross income all previously deducted contributions, plus net earnings (or minus net losses). For individual retirement annuities, gross income is generally increased by the fair market value of the contract on the date of conversion (through a re-designation) or distribution (if held inside an IRA). If a retirement annuity is completely surrendered, the cash received is the amount includable in income. Any 10% penalty tax for early withdrawal is waived.

If a taxpayer has traditional IRA accounts that hold both deductible and non-deductible amounts, he or she may not "cherry-pick" and convert only the non-deductible contributions.[1] Instead, the value of all IRA accounts is added together and a ratio is calculated to determine the tax-free portion of any conversion.[2]

---

[1] Because they have already been taxed, non-deductible contributions are generally not taxable when converted from a traditional IRA to a Roth IRA.

[2] If all of the contributions to the traditional IRA were deductible, a taxpayer may elect to roll over everything, or pick and choose which accounts or portions of an account to convert.

Example: Paul has a traditional IRA to which he has made $20,000 in non-deductible contributions. This year, when he converts the account to a Roth IRA, the balance in this IRA is $30,000. Paul also has a separate IRA containing $70,000 in pre-tax contributions rolled over from a 401(k) plan with a previous employer. The total value of both accounts is $100,000. His "non-deductible" ratio is thus 20%, ($20,000 ÷ $100,000). When Paul converts the $30,000 in his non-deductible IRA, he may exclude only $6,000 (20% x $30,000) from gross income. The remaining $24,000 ($30,000 - $6,000) is includable in his gross income, subject to tax.

Situations Favoring Conversion to A Roth IRA

- **Small account values:** If the dollar amount in the traditional IRA is small, the income-tax cost to convert today would be relatively low.

- **Longer time to retirement:** A longer period of time until retirement allows for greater future growth, necessary to recoup the up-front cost of paying the tax now.

- **Cash to pay the taxes:** Where will the money come from to pay the extra taxes? It's usually better if the account owner has sufficient cash outside of the IRA to pay the tax. Could the funds used to pay the tax today provide a greater return if invested elsewhere?

- **IRA income not needed:** Some individuals have adequate retirement income from other sources, so that IRA monies are not needed to fund retirement. During the lifetime of the account owner, a Roth IRA has no minimum distribution requirements.

- **Higher future tax bracket:** If a taxpayer anticipates being in a higher tax bracket in the future, paying the tax today, at lower rates, is a logical step. Being taxed at a higher marginal rate may be the result of legislative changes, having a higher taxable income, or a change in filing status, such as when a couple divorces or a spouse dies.

Situations NOT Favoring Conversion

In some situations, converting a traditional IRA to a Roth IRA may not be appropriate:

- **Retirement begins soon:** If there is only a short time before retirement begins, there may not be enough time for future growth to offset the cost of paying the tax today.

- **High IRA account values:** If the dollar amount in the traditional IRA is large, the tax bill resulting from the conversion will likely be expensive; the conversion could push a taxpayer into a higher marginal tax bracket or make Social Security benefits taxable.

- **No cash to pay the taxes:** A taxpayer may not have the cash outside the IRA to pay the extra tax that results from the conversion. Taking funds from the IRA to pay the increased tax reduces the amount left in the account to grow into the future. If the account owner is under age 59½ at the time these extra funds are withdrawn from the IRA, a 10% penalty on the amount not converted will likely be added to the tax bill.

- **Lower future tax rates:** If a taxpayer anticipates being in a lower tax bracket in the future, paying the tax today, at higher marginal tax rates, makes no sense.

Recharacterization

Prior to 2018, a taxpayer who converted a traditional IRA to a Roth IRA could "undo" the transaction and "recharacterize" the converted funds, moving them back into a traditional IRA.

However, for tax years beginning in 2018, the Tax Cuts and Jobs Act of 2017 (TCJA), permanently repealed the ability to recharacterize a Roth conversion back to a traditional IRA.

Seek Professional Guidance

The decision to convert all or part of a traditional IRA to a Roth IRA is an individual one. A thorough analysis requires careful consideration of a number of income tax, investment, and estate planning factors, over an extended time horizon. The advice and guidance of appropriate financial, tax, and investment professionals is strongly recommended.

Roth IRA Conversion

Assumptions:

IRA balance: $50,000
Years until withdrawal: 20
Marginal tax rate: 28.00%
Marginal tax rate in retirement: 25.00%
Annual rate of return: 7.00%

Account	After-Tax Amount at Withdrawal
Roth IRA	$193,484
Traditional IRA	$145,113
Separate Account	$37,430

Example

Converting your traditional IRA to a Roth IRA would result in a 2014 tax liability of $14,000. At retirement in 20 years, the Roth IRA would be worth $193,484. If certain requirements are met, all withdrawals from the Roth IRA would be free of federal income tax. Alternatively, you could leave your funds in the traditional IRA and invest the $14,000 that would have gone to taxes, to a separate, taxable account. At retirement, the traditional IRA would be worth $145,113 after paying taxes of $48,371. The separate account would be worth $37,430. The total of these two accounts would be $182,543.

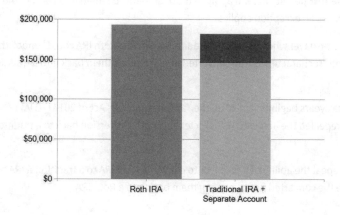

Values shown in this presentation are hypothetical and not a promise of future performance.

Roth IRAs

The Roth IRA differs from the traditional IRA in that contributions are never deductible and, if certain requirements are met, account distributions are free of federal income tax.[1]

Funding a Roth IRA

Annual contributions: A Roth IRA may be established and funded at any time between January 1 of the current year, up to and including the date an individual's federal income tax return is due, (generally April 15 of the following year), not including extensions.

Conversion of a traditional IRA account: A traditional IRA may be converted to a Roth IRA, with the conversion being a taxable event. For the year of conversion, the taxpayer must include in gross income previously deducted contributions plus net earnings (or minus net losses). For individual retirement annuities, gross income is generally increased by the fair market value of the contract on the date of conversion (through a re-designation) or distribution (if held inside an IRA). If a retirement annuity is completely surrendered, the cash received is the amount includable in income. Any 10% penalty tax for early withdrawal is waived. However, if a taxpayer withdraws amounts from the Roth IRA within five years of the conversion, the 10% penalty tax will apply to those amounts deemed to be part of the conversion, unless an exception applies.

Prior to 2018, a taxpayer who converted a traditional IRA to a Roth IRA could "undo" the transaction and "recharacterize" the converted funds, moving them back into a traditional IRA.

However, for tax years beginning in 2018, the Tax Cuts and Jobs Act of 2017 (TCJA), permanently repealed the ability to recharacterize a Roth conversion back to a traditional IRA.

TCJA did *not* repeal the ability of a taxpayer to convert a Roth IRA to a traditional IRA and then recharacterize the converted funds, moving them back into a Roth IRA.

---

[1] Income tax treatment of Roth IRAs at the state or local level may differ.

Rollovers from a qualified plan: Distributions from qualified retirement plans, IRC Sec. 457(b) governmental plans, and IRC Sec. 403(b) plans may also be rolled over to a Roth IRA.

These conversions are taxable events, with gross income for the year of conversion being increased by previously deducted contributions plus net earnings (or minus net losses).

Direct rollover from a designated Roth Account: Funds may be rolled into a regular Roth IRA from a designated Roth account that is part of a 401(k), 403(b), or 457(b) governmental plan. Such a rollover is not a taxable event and the filing status and MAGI limitations normally applicable to regular Roth contributions do not apply.

Military death payments: Under the provisions of the Heroes Earnings Assistance and Relief Tax Act of 2008, an individual who receives a military death gratuity and/or a payment under the Servicemembers' Group Life Insurance (SGLI) program may contribute to a Roth IRA an amount no greater than the sum of any military death gratuity and SGLI payment. Such a contribution is considered a qualified rollover contribution and must be made within one year of receiving the death gratuity or insurance payment. The annual dollar contribution limit and income-based phase-out of the dollar contribution limit do not apply to such contributions.

Type of Arrangements Permitted

There are currently two types of Roth IRAs.

- **Individual retirement accounts:** Trusts or custodial accounts with a corporate trustee or custodian.

- **Individual retirement annuities:** Special annuities issued by a life insurance company.

Contribution Limits

Limits: For 2018, an individual may contribute (but not deduct) the lesser of $5,500 or 100% of compensation[1] for the year. For a married couple, an additional $5,500 may be contributed on behalf of a lesser earning (or nonworking) spouse, using a spousal account.

---

[1] "Compensation" includes taxable wages, salaries, or commissions or the net income from self-employment.

A husband and wife may contribute up to a total of $11,000, as long as their combined compensation is at least that amount.[1] If an IRA owner is age 50 or older, he or she may contribute an additional $1,000 ($2,000 if the spouse is also age 50 or older).

Other IRAs: The contribution limits for a Roth IRA are coordinated with those of a traditional IRA; a taxpayer may not contribute more than the annual limit for that tax year into a single IRA or a combination of traditional and Roth IRAs. Excess contributions to a traditional or Roth IRA are subject to a 6% excise tax.

Contribution phase out: For 2018, the maximum contribution to a Roth IRA is phased out for single taxpayers with MAGI between $120,000 and $135,000. For married couples filing jointly, the phase-out range is a MAGI of $189,000 to $199,000. For married individuals filing separately, the phase-out range is a MAGI of $0 to $10,000.[2]

Taxation of Distributions

A distribution from a Roth IRA that is a "qualified" distribution is excluded from gross income and is not subject to federal income tax. A distribution is qualified if it is made after a five-year waiting period[3] and at least one of the following requirements is met:

- after the taxpayer reaches age 59½; or

- due to the taxpayer's death; or

- because the taxpayer becomes disabled; or

- to pay for first-time-home-buyer expenses up to $10,000.

The **earnings** portion of a "non-qualified" distribution is subject to tax. To determine any taxable distribution, the funds are considered to be withdrawn in a specified order:

- Any withdrawal is considered to come first from nondeductible **contributions**, which are not subject to tax.

---

[1] These amounts apply to 2018. For 2017, the maximum allowable contribution was also $5,500 for a single individual and $11,000 for a married couple.

[2] For 2017, the phase-out ranges were: (1) MFJ – MAGI of $186,000 - $196,000 and (2) Single - $118,000 - $133,000. For those using the MFS filing status, the phase-out range is $0 - $10,000, which does not change.

[3] Generally, five years after a contribution is first made, or amounts are converted to a Roth IRA.

- After all contributions have been withdrawn, any **conversion** amounts are considered next. A distribution of converted funds is not included in gross income, but may be subject to the 10% premature distribution penalty if the funds are withdrawn within five years of being converted.

- Once all contributions and conversions have been withdrawn, any remaining funds are deemed to be **earnings**, and, when distributed, are included in gross income.

Premature Distributions

If a **taxable** distribution is received prior to age 59½, a 10% penalty tax is added to the regular income tax due, unless one or more of the following exceptions apply:

- A distribution is made because of the death or disability of the account owner.

- A withdrawal is part of a scheduled series of substantially equal periodic payments.

- A distribution is rolled-over into another Roth IRA.

- A withdrawal is used to pay for deductible medical expenses.

- The distribution is used to pay for certain qualified higher-education expenses.

- Amounts are withdrawn to pay for first-time homebuyer expenses of up to $10,000.

- In certain situations, to pay health insurance premiums for unemployed individuals.

- Distributions by certain military reservists called to active duty after 09/11/2001.

- A distribution is transferred to a Health Savings Account (HSA).

- In case of an IRS levy on the account.

Other Differences

There are several other significant differences between the traditional and Roth IRAs:

- **Contributions after age 70½**: Contributions to a Roth IRA may be made even after the taxpayer has reached age 70½, as long as the taxpayer has compensation at least equal to the contribution, subject to the phase-out rules.

- **Distribution requirements:** Roth IRAs are not subject to the mandatory required minimum distribution (RMD) rules during the life of the owner (triggered at age 70½) applicable to traditional IRAs. However, there are post-death minimum distribution rules applicable to non-spousal beneficiaries who inherit a Roth account.

Charitable Distributions

Federal income tax law provides for an exclusion from gross income of up to $100,000 for distributions made from a Roth or traditional IRA *directly* to a qualified charitable organization. Such a distribution counts towards the taxpayer's RMD requirements. The IRA owner (Or beneficiary of an inherited IRA) must be at least age 70½ when the distribution is made. No charitable deduction is allowed for such a qualified charitable distribution.

Transfers to Health Savings Accounts (HSAs)

Federal law allows for a limited, one-time, direct transfer of funds from an IRA to an HSA. If certain requirements are met, any otherwise taxable portion of the distribution is excluded from income and the 10% early distribution penalty will not apply.

Investment Alternatives

- **Banks, savings and loans, credit unions:** Certificates of deposit in Roth IRAs are generally insured by either the FDIC or the NCUA for amounts up to $250,000. Fixed and variable rates are available. There may be stiff penalties for early withdrawal.

- **Annuities:** Traditional, fixed individual retirement annuities issued by life insurance companies can guarantee fixed monthly income at retirement and may include a disability-waiver-of-premium provision. Variable annuities do not guarantee a fixed monthly income at retirement.

- **Money market:** Yield fluctuates with the economy. Investor cannot lock in higher interest rates. It is easy to switch to other investments.

- **Mutual funds:** A wide variety of mutual funds with many investment objectives are available.

- **Zero coupon bonds:** Bonds are issued at a deep discount from face value. There are no worries about reinvesting interest payments. Zero coupon bonds are subject to inflation risk and interest rate risk.

- **Stocks:** A wide variety of investments (and risk) is possible. Losses are generally not deductible.

- **Limited partnerships:** Some limited partnerships are especially designed for qualified plans, specifically in the areas of real estate and mortgage pools.

Prohibited Investments or Transactions

- **Life insurance:** Roth IRAs cannot include life insurance contracts.

- **Loans to IRA taxpayer:** Self-borrowing triggers a constructive distribution of the entire amount in an IRA.

- **Collectibles:** Purchase of art works, antiques, metals, gems, stamps, etc., will be treated as a taxable distribution. Coins issued under state law and certain U.S. gold, silver and platinum coins are exceptions. Certain kinds of bullion may be purchased.

Other Factors to Consider

- What is the yield? More frequent compounding will produce a higher return. Is the interest rate fixed or variable? If interest rates drop, a fixed rate may be better, especially if you can make future contributions at the same fixed rate. If interest rates go up, you may be able to roll the account to another Roth IRA.

- How often can you change investments? Is there a charge?

- Refunds of federal income taxes may be directly deposited into an IRA.

- Federal bankruptcy law protects assets in Roth IRA accounts, up to $1,283,025.[1] Funds rolled over from qualified plans are protected without limit.

---

[1] Effective April 1, 2016. The limit is indexed for inflation every three years.

How a Roth IRA Works

Account Owner

- Contributions are not tax deductible.
- Total annual contribution is limited.[1]
- Annual contribution limits are coordinated with any traditional IRA.

ROTH IRA ACCOUNT

- May be opened anytime between January 1 of current year until due date of tax return.
- Traditional IRA can be converted to a Roth IRA.[2]
- Earnings accumulate tax deferred.
- Account is usually self-directed (owner controls investments).
- A separate spousal Roth IRA may be established for a spouse with little or no earned income.

QUALIFIED DISTRIBUTIONS

- Qualified distributions are tax-free if a five-year holding period is met and one of the following applies: the owner is over 59½, dies, becomes disabled, or the distribution is for up to $10,000 of qualified first-time homebuyer expenses.

RETIREMENT

- Assuming compensation, contributions may continue to any age.
- No mandatory age for starting withdrawals.
- No minimum distributions required while owner is alive.
- Qualified distributions are received free of federal income tax.

DEATH

- Value of Roth IRA is included in owner's federal gross estate.
- If five-year holding period is met, beneficiaries receive funds free of federal income tax.
- A surviving spouse may choose to treat an inherited Roth IRA as his or her own.

[1] The maximum annual contribution is the lesser of $5,500 ($11,000 for a married couple) or 100% of compensation. For married couples, no more than $5,500 may be contributed for either spouse. For a Roth IRA owner age 50 or older, an additional $1,000 may be contributed ($2,000 if the spouse is also age 50 or older). The maximum annual contribution to a Roth IRA is phased out for individuals with incomes in excess of certain limits.

[2] The conversion is a taxable event. Gross income for the year of conversion is increased by previously deducted contributions, plus net earnings (or minus net losses). Once completed, a conversion may not be reversed.

Transfers from Employer-Sponsored Retirement Plans to Individual Plans

Back in the era of corporate pensions, US workers didn't have to concern themselves much with account structures and optimizing the tax treatment of their savings. But Americans today face far more onerous and complex choices regarding their retirement strategies.

There are several paths one may take, including retaining assets with an existing employer-savings plan, transferring funds to different company's retirement plan, or opting for a lump-sum distribution. While each of these approaches has its place, decisions must be made regarding conversion of retirement assets from employer-sponsored retirement programs, into traditional and Roth IRAs.

401(k) versus 403(b) Plans

When contemplating transferring assets from an employer-sponsored plan to any type of IRA, the differences between 401(k) plans and the 403(b) counterparts used by governmental organizations, nonprofit groups, school districts and religious groups, are negligible. In fact, there is fundamentally no difference at all between conversion practices, contribution levels, costs or eligibility rules. Therefore, with the same sets of pros and cons in play, the factors investors should consider when weighing their asset transfer options are identical – regardless of the original employer-sponsored plan in question.

Taxing Issues; Pay Now or Pay Later

The chief determining factor between a traditional IRA and a Roth IRA, is the differential tax treatment afforded to each.

Strictly defined, a Roth IRA is an individual retirement account where individuals direct a certain amount of after-tax income into the fund each year, then after reaching the age of 59½, investors may realize earnings and make withdrawals, free of taxation. Roth's contain a special feature letting individuals make a qualified withdrawal up to $10,000 for a first-time home purchase. With Roth IRAs, there are no age restrictions for contributions, which are made with after-tax dollars.

A Traditional IRA is defined as a tax-deferred account where an individual sets aside money each year, where earnings are tax deferred until withdrawals begin at age 59 1/2 or later--

or earlier, but with a 10% penalty. Unlike Roth IRAs, investors cannot make regular contributions to a traditional IRA in the year they reach 70½ and older. Furthermore, IRAs shield wealth from creditors.

For middle market investors – particularly those nearing retirement, transferring money from 401(k) and 403(b) plans into an IRA represents a viable alternative to letting assets sit with a former employer. IRAs offer investors a broader range of investment options than employer-sponsored counterparts, providing access to individual stocks and bonds and a wider spectrum of funds than the narrow slate of choices typically offered by employer saving plans.

Rules of the Roth

As with any governmental tax-advantaged vehicle, Roth IRAs carry certain rules that prospective participants must satisfy in order to meet regulatory requirements.

- Individuals looking to shift assets from a 401(k) to a Roth IRA must have separated from their employer, unless they're already older than 59½.

- Individuals may only make contributions to a Roth IRA with money earned from a job. Therefore, non-working college students with leftover spending money from parents or surplus cash from student loan packages, are prohibited from funneling those extra funds into a Roth IRA.

- Individuals may not invest more than they have made on the job. Therefore, someone who has pocketed $2,000 from a seasonal job may not contribute any more than that amount to a Roth IRA.

Transfer Methodologies

Direct Rollovers

For eligible investors, the most prudent method of transferring 401(k) assets into a Roth account is often believed to be a trustee-to-trustee transfer known as "direct rollover", where

Transfers from Employer-Sponsored Retirement Plans to Individual Plans

money seamlessly shifts from one custodial body to another, and never touches an investor's hands. Parties interested in direct rollovers should begin the process by contacting their chosen IRA provider, which will likely have a rollover specialist on hand to help smoothly facilitate the transfer of assets. Investors would then contact their former employers' plan administrators, to have them initiate the transfer paperwork and send a check with the 401(k)'s account balance directly to the Roth provider. On some occasions, IRA purveyors will accept a wire transfer in lieu of a physical check. But in either case, direct rollovers eliminate potential IRS complications, regarding the amount of the investment transferred and the timeliness of the transaction.

Indirect Rollovers

An investor may opt for an "indirect rollover", which entails he cashing out of his 401(k), and then subsequently giving the money to his IRA provider, within a 60-day period. But be warned: his former employer would systematically withhold 20% of the distribution as a tax safeguard for the IRS, in the event that the investor fails to carry out the transfer in time. Consequently, those choosing an indirect rollover must find that held-over 20% from another source, in order to reliably furnish 100% of the redeemed 401(k) funds to the new IRA custodian, because transferring just 80% of the funds would be viewed as an early distribution, resulting in a 10% tax penalty. But even if an investors has the 20% reserve capital to make up for that portion held back by a former employer, his company wouldn't reimburse him for that 20%, until taxes are filed in April of the following year. And then there's the perilous temptation of an investor to spend *all* of the cash on an impulse purchase, missing the 60-day deadline altogether, in which case the entire amount will be counted as an early distribution, and taxed accordingly. For these reasons, direct trustee-to-trustee rollovers are widely viewed as the most sensible way of shifting assets.

Is a Roth IRA right for you?

Despite their plethora of advantages, Roth IRAs aren't a panacea for everyone. For example, people who leave their long-held jobs in order to start their own businesses, may need start-up capital and the general liquidity essential to running their enterprise. In these situations, the tax consequences from an early Roth IRA could be prohibitively costly.

Transfers from Employer-Sponsored Retirement Plans to Individual Plans

Is a Traditional IRA right for you?

Many believe that the reduction in taxes during the year in which contributions are made is an automatic benefit, given that the unpaid taxes can be invested. But investors should be cognizant of the capital gains taxes that must be made on profitable investments, especially on income-producing stocks, or investments where routine investments are made.

Bottom Line

For those who can hold off until 59½, before cashing in on their Roth IRA benefits, this vehicle can fiscally pave the way towards a healthy and secure retirement. Contrarily, for those in a higher tax bracket, a traditional IRA may be the best bet. Finally, it's important to remember, that those who invest in traditional IRAs always have the option to convert their assets to Roth IRAs. However, Roth IRA assets may not be converted back into a traditional IRA.

Employer Sponsored Plans

Contributing to your employer sponsored plan may be a great way to create a retirement fund.

Item Description	Value
Annual income	$60,000
Anticipated Increase	4.00%
Employee Contribution Percent	6.00%
Company Contribution Percent	3.00%
Years until retirement	25
Rate of Return	7.00%

Your total contributions of $149,925 could result in a total pre-tax account value of $531,488 when you retire

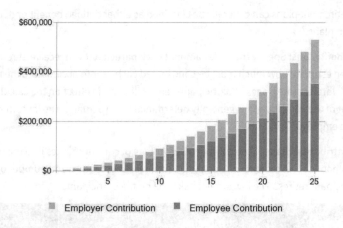

Values shown in this presentation are hypothetical and not a promise of future performance

Qualified Retirement Plans

Qualified retirement plans are Congressionally-approved retirement plans which have several major tax benefits.

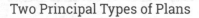

- The employer's contributions can be deducted for income tax purposes.

- The earnings on the plan's investments accumulate on a tax-deferred basis.

- When the funds are distributed at retirement age, they may be eligible for favorable tax treatment.[1]

- Taxpayers may be in a lower income tax bracket after retirement.

Two Principal Types of Plans

Qualified retirement plans can generally be classified as either defined benefit or defined contribution plans.[2]

Defined benefit plans: Specify the dollar amount each participant will receive at retirement age and then estimate how much must be contributed each year to accumulate the necessary future fund. Interest rates, ages of participants, etc., will have an effect on the calculation. The amount of the contribution is generally determined by an actuary. The investment risk rests on the employer.

Defined contribution plans: Generally put a percentage of current salaries into the plan each year. The amount at retirement will depend on the investment return and number of years until a participant retires. The investment risk rests on the participant.

Plan Type	Contributions	Retirement Benefits	Investment Risk
Defined benefit	Vary	Fixed	Employer
Defined contribution	Pension – Fixed Profit sharing – Vary	Vary	Employee

---

[1] Those born before 1936 may be able to elect 10-year averaging or capital gains treatment; these strategies are not available to those born after 1935.

[2] Note that some plans have features of both types.

Qualified Retirement Plans

What Is the Best Type of Plan?

There is no best type of plan. The choice of what type of plan to use is an individual one. The answer depends on factors such as employer goals and available cash flow.

Defined Benefit Plans

The employer contributes an actuarially-determined amount sufficient to pay each participant a fixed or defined dollar amount at his or her retirement. The benefit may be defined as a flat percentage of compensation, a percentage which increases with years of service, or a percentage which changes at certain compensation levels, etc.

This type of plan generally favors older employees, because more of the employer's contributions must go into his or her account to make certain that there will be enough to pay the promised (or defined) benefit at retirement age.

Defined Contribution Plans

There are several variations of defined contribution plans. Some of the more common ones include the following:

- **Money purchase pension:** The employer contributes a specified percentage of the participating employee's salary each year. Whatever that fund grows to is what the retiring employee receives.

- **Profit sharing plan:** Similar to the money purchase pension, except that contributions do not need to be a specific percentage and they do not need to be made every year, as long as they are substantial and recurring.

- **Stock bonus plan:** Similar to the traditional profit sharing plan. The plan may, but is not required to, invest primarily in the employer's stock.

- **ESOP - Employee stock ownership plan:** Like a stock bonus plan, to which the employer can contribute company stock instead of cash. The plan must be primarily invested in company stock.

Qualified Retirement Plans

- **IRC Sec. 401(k) plan:** Also called a cash or deferred plan, this plan is any stock bonus plan or profit sharing plan which meets certain participation requirements of IRC Sec. 401(k). An employee can agree to a salary reduction or to defer a bonus which he or she has coming.

- **SIMPLE plans:** SIMPLE stands for Savings Incentive Match Plan for Employees. SIMPLE plans can be in either an IRA format or a 401(k) format.

- **SEP:** This stands for Simplified Employee Plan. A SEP is a group of individual IRAs established for employees to which the employer and employees may contribute more than an individual employee could contribute to a traditional IRA or Roth IRA.

Life Insurance in Qualified Plans

Legal Limitations

Personal Plans

- **IRAs:** IRAs, IRA rollovers, Roth IRAs, SEPs, and SIMPLE IRA arrangements may not pay the premium for life insurance policies.

- **Tax sheltered annuities:** 403(b) plans may not invest in contracts that provide incidental life insurance protection. See Reg. Sec. 1.403(b)-8(c)(2).[1]

Business Plans

- **Defined contribution plans:** The percentage of the total annual employer contribution that can be allocated to life insurance premiums varies with the type of policy. There is no limit on the face amount.

  - **Term, variable, and universal life insurance:** Less than 25% of the aggregate contributions allocated to the participant.

  - **Ordinary whole life insurance:** Less than 50% of the aggregate contributions allocated to the participant.

  - **Combination:** One-half of the ordinary life premium and all of the term, variable, and/or universal life premium must be less than 25% of the total.

Special rule for profit sharing plans: Allocations that are more than two years old may, in some cases, be totally invested in life insurance.[2] See Rev. Rulings 61-164 1961-2 CB 99.

- **Defined benefit plans**

  - **Basic rule:** The face amount of the insurance may not exceed 100 times the anticipated monthly retirement benefit. For example, if a $5,000 per month retirement benefit were anticipated, the maximum amount of life insurance would be $500,000.

---

[1] Under regulations issued by the Treasury Department on 7/26/07, annuity contracts issued prior to 9/24/07 may provide incidental life insurance protection; contracts issued on or after that date may not provide any life insurance. See Reg. 1.403(b)-11(f).

[2] The IRS has never formally ruled on the taxability of using aged contributions, in excess of the incidental insurance rules, to purchase life insurance. See also Rev. Ruling 60-83 and Rev. Ruling 68-24.

- **Alternative rule:** Total premiums for ordinary life must be less than 66 2/3% (or 33 1/3% for term, variable, and universal life insurance) of the assumed aggregate contributions[1] that have been made for the participant from the beginning of his or her participation in the plan.

- **Fully Insured Plan:** Some plans are funded exclusively with annuities or a combination of annuities and life insurance. These plans are known as 412(e)(3) plans, formerly 412(i). Because of a potential for abuse, special rules apply to these types of plans.

- **Other general rule:** Insurance must be made available or purchased on a uniform and non-discriminatory basis.

Advantages to the Employee

- Because income and estate taxes on the death benefit may be very substantial, the non-income-taxable insurance proceeds may be used to pay the income taxes and/or estate taxes due on the other plan assets or estate assets. Life insurance protects the other non-insurance assets.

- It is an easy way to provide additional protection for one's family if death occurs prior to retirement age.

- It frees up other personal dollars now being spent for life insurance outside the plan.

- For cash-value policies, the majority of the premium is not taxable to the employee. Taxable income to the employee is calculated on the difference between a policy's face value and its cash surrender value at year's end. IRS Table 2001 is generally used to determine the dollar amount included in the employee's income.

- The policy can be moved to another plan if the employee changes employment, providing the new plan will accept it.

- At retirement age, the employee may be able to take a fully paid up policy, rather than face the expense of converting his or her group insurance.

- The pure insurance portion (the face amount less the accumulated cash values) of the death benefit passes to the beneficiaries income tax free, but may be subject to estate tax.

---

[1] The assumed aggregate contribution is a special calculation separate from the funding calculations.

- A waiver of premium may be added which will continue to pay the life insurance premiums should the employee become disabled.

- Uninsurable participants may be able to purchase a limited amount of guaranteed-issue insurance. In larger plans it may be a substantial amount.

- When a participant in a defined benefit plan is rated for insurance risk purposes (usually for poor health or occupational hazards), the plan can pay the higher premium without increasing the cost to the participant.

- Table I costs for group insurance reported as income under group coverage in excess of $50,000 are not recoverable. Economic benefit costs incurred for the pure insurance portion of policies in qualified plans may be recovered at the time of distribution.

- Ordinary, variable, or universal life policies can be used as an annuity at retirement age. The insurer will give the participant the higher of either the rate guaranteed in the contract or the then current rates.

- Traditional financial and estate planning seeks a balanced approach to investment portfolios. Ordinary and universal life insurance policies can represent the fixed side of the program. Variable life and variable universal life policies also offer an equity or stock market option for the cash value portion of the policy.

Advantages to the Employer

- The premiums are deductible as a part of the plan contribution.

- If the employee has a paid-up policy under the qualified plan at retirement age, he or she may not need to convert group insurance to permanent. With larger, experience-rated group life contracts, there is typically a charge (sometimes substantial) to the experience when a policy is converted.

- Under a defined benefit plan, if the insurance proceeds equal the entire preretirement death benefit and a participant dies, all of the other equity assets for that participant can be used to reduce future employer contributions to the plan.

- If participating whole life contracts are used and dividends are used to reduce the premium, the long-term cost in a defined benefit plan may be very favorable.

- In defined benefit plans the employer may be able to make a larger contribution and deduction by including ordinary life insurance in the plan. This is often helpful because of the restrictions on retirement plan benefits and contributions.[1]

- Corporate retained earnings problems may be lessened by increasing the contribution to a defined benefit plan that provides for life insurance. Pension plan assets do not appear on the corporation's balance sheet.

- Younger employees may look at the protection as a current benefit, whereas retirement age may seem to be a long way off.

Disadvantages to the Employee

- If there is an estate tax problem, the life insurance proceeds will increase the size of the gross taxable estate. If the surviving spouse is the beneficiary, there will be no immediate death tax payable, due to the unlimited marital deduction. However, the surviving spouse's estate will be increased, thus increasing the potential estate tax at his or her subsequent death.

  As an alternative, consider having any additional life insurance owned by an irrevocable life insurance trust, designed to keep the proceeds out of the estates of both spouses.

- It is a tax shelter within a tax shelter. Under current law, the buildup of cash values in a life insurance contract are tax deferred and do not need to be in a qualified plan to get this tax advantage.

- If the employee did not recognize the annual imputed income for the insured death benefit per IRS Table 2001, the death benefits paid from the policy are taxable.

- If a contract is distributed from the plan to the employee, the fair market value of the contract (which could be a substantial amount) will generally be included in the employee's income.

---

[1] The Pension Protection Act of 2006 modifies the funding rules for defined benefit plans. Recent comments from IRS officials indicate that life insurance may no longer be funded directly as part of the plan's normal cost. In this case, life insurance may not increase plan contributions significantly in the early years of a plan.

Keogh Plans

H.R. 10

Keogh plans are retirement plans for self-employed individuals, e.g., sole proprietors, partners in a partnership,[1] and employees of either. The differences between Keogh plans and corporate sponsored plans are small and are limited to different tax treatment of life insurance.

The Basics of Keogh Plans

- **Plan type:** A Keogh plan may be either a defined contribution plan or a defined benefit plan[2].

- **Defined contribution plans:** Contributions for individual participants may not exceed the lesser of 100% of includable compensation[3] or $55,000 per year. At the employer level, no more than 25% of the covered compensation of all participants may be deducted. Thus, if the Keogh plan covers only one participant, the effective contribution limit becomes 25% of the includable compensation[2] of the business owner,[4] not to exceed $55,000.

- **Defined benefit plans:** For defined benefit plans, the plan actuary determines the contributions. The deduction for contributions to a defined benefit plan may not exceed net self-employment income. In some circumstances, the required contribution may exceed the allowable deduction. The nondeductible portion of the contribution may be carried over as a deduction in future years.

- **Benefit limits:** Defined benefit Keogh plans are subject to the same percentage of average compensation and dollar limits that apply to all defined benefit plans. For 2018, these figures are 100% and $220,000.

- **Framework:** May use a trust, a custodial account or an insurance company annuity.

---

[1] A partner who owns more than 10% of the capital or profits of the partnership is considered to be an owner-employee. See Reg. Sec. 1.401-10(d).

[2] The term "Keogh" plan is largely obsolete since all entities can sponsor the same plans.

[3] The "net" self-employment income of the owner or partner, less the contribution and the deduction allowed for one-half of the self-employment tax. For 2018, $275,000 is the maximum income that may be considered.

[4] This is the same as 20% of the gross pre-contribution net income.

- **Evidence of plan:** The plan must be in writing and meet certain coverage and non-discrimination requirements for present and future employees.

- **Distributions:** Distributions are generally taxed as ordinary income. Distributions prior to age 59½ may also be subject to a 10% income tax penalty, unless the distribution meets one of the exceptions listed in IRC Sec. 72(t). Except for more-than-5% owners, required minimum distributions (RMDs) must begin by April 1 of the later of (a) the year following the year the participant reaches age 70½, or (b) the year following the year in which the participant retires. More-than-5% owners must begin to receive distributions by April 1 of the year following the year they reach age 70½.

- **Phased retirement:** Federal law allows retirement distributions to employees who are at least age 62 even if they have not separated from employment at the time distributions begin.

- **Available payment plans**

  - Lump-sum distribution.

  - Lifetime of the participant (and spouse if desired).

  - Fixed period of years not to exceed the participant's life expectancy or the joint life expectancy of the participant and a designated beneficiary (see IRC Sec. 401(a)(9)).

- **Other plans:** A participant in a Keogh plan may also have a traditional, deductible IRA (subject to certain income level limitations based on filing status), a traditional, nondeductible IRA, or a Roth IRA.

- **Taxation:** Distributions are generally taxed as ordinary income. Special 10-year income averaging may be available for certain individuals.[1]

- **401(k) feature:** A 401(k) feature may be added, if desired, to a profit sharing plan.

- **Allocation methods:** The same kinds of allocation methods that are available under a corporate-sponsored defined contribution plan are also available under a Keogh plan. These can be age-weighted, tiered, or integrated with Social Security.

---

[1] Those born before 1936 may be able to elect 10-year averaging or capital gain treatment; these strategies are not available to those born after 1935.

- **Participant loans:** Participant loans are permitted without any adverse consequences, provided they follow the regular rules for participant loans.

- **Top-heavy defined contribution plans:** If more than 60% of plan assets are allocated to key employees,[1] non-key employees must receive the same percentage contribution as that received by the key employee with the highest contribution percentage. This requirement applies only to a contribution of up to the first 3% of includable compensation; a higher contribution may be required in some instances, such as when the plan is combined with a defined benefit plan.

- **Top-heavy defined benefit plans:** If more than 60% of the accrued benefits are attributable to key employees,[2] the plan must provide a minimum level of retirement benefits. This is 2% of compensation at retirement for each year of participation, not to exceed 10 years (20%).

- **Federal bankruptcy law:** ERISA and federal bankruptcy law provide significant protection from creditors to participant accounts or accrued benefits in tax-exempt retirement plans.

---

[1] A "key" employee is someone who, at any time during the plan year was: (1) an officer of the employer whose compensation from the employer exceeded $175,000; or (2) a more than 5% owner; or (3) a 1% owner whose compensation from the employer exceeded $150,000.

Traditional Profit Sharing Plan

The basics: Employer contributions to the plan need not be a specific percentage and they need not be made every year, as long as they are "recurring and substantial." Profits are not required in order to make a contribution.

How It Works

- Employer contributions are tax deductible.

- Contributions are not taxed currently to the employee.

- Earnings accumulate income tax-deferred.

- Distributions are generally taxed as ordinary income. Distributions may be eligible for 10-year income averaging,[1] or, at retirement from the current employer, rolled over to a traditional or a Roth IRA, or to another employer plan if that plan will accept such a rollover.

- Except for more than 5% owners, required minimum distributions (RMDs) must begin by April 1 of the later of (a) the year following the year in which the participant reaches age 70½, or (b) the year following the year in which the participant retires. More-than-5% owners must begin to receive distributions by April 1 of the year following the year they reach age 70½.

Additional Considerations

- **Maximum annual deduction:** Up to 25% of covered payroll can be contributed and deducted by the employer.

- **Contribution base:** Plan contributions are normally based on total compensation, e.g., base salary, bonuses, overtime, etc. The maximum compensation recognized in 2018 is $275,000.

---

[1] Those born before 1936 may be able to elect 10-year averaging or capital gain treatment; these strategies are not available to those born after 1935.

- **Individual limits:** The allocation of contributions to a participant's account may not exceed the lesser of 100% of includable compensation[1] or $55,000 per year.

- **Employer contributions:**

  - Most plans are discretionary as to the amount that the employer contributes.

  - If there are profits, the employer is expected to make "recurring and substantial" contributions. See IRS Reg. 1.401-1(b)(2).

- **Excluding persons:** Certain persons can be eliminated on the basis of months of service, age or coverage in a union plan; for example, persons under age 21 can be excluded from the plan.

- **Investment of plan assets:** Investments must be diversified and prudent. Subject to plan provisions, plan assets may be invested in equity products like mutual funds, stocks and debt-free real estate; or debt instruments like T-Bills and CD's. Insurance products like life insurance and annuity policies may also be used.

  - **Social Security integration:** Since the employer already contributes to the employee's Social Security retirement benefit, these contributions can be integrated into the allocation formula of the plan.

  - **Forfeitures:** As participants leave the company and separate from the plan, those less than 100% vested forfeit that part of the account in which they are not vested. The nonvested forfeitures may then be allocated to the remaining participants. Those participants who remain in the plan the longest will share in the most forfeitures, or forfeitures may be used to reduce future employer contributions.

  - **Parties which are favored:** Typically younger participants are favored because they have a longer time for their fund to grow and share in forfeitures.

---

[1] For those self employed, this rate applies to "net" self-employment income of the owner or partner, less the contribution and the deduction allowed for one-half of the self-employment tax.

Traditional Profit Sharing Plan

How Much Will There Be at Retirement?

This will depend upon three factors.

- The frequency and amount of contributions,
- The number of years until retirement, and
- The investment return.

The risk of poor investment returns rests upon the employee. However, if investment results are favorable, the participant will have a larger fund at retirement age.

Years	\multicolumn{4}{c}{An Example of What \$10,000 Per Year Will Grow to Over Several Years at Various Rates of Growth Without Tax[1]}
Years	2.00%	4.00%	6.00%	8.00%
5	$52,040	$54,163	$56,371	$58,666
10	$109,497	$120,061	$131,808	$144,866
15	$172,934	$200,236	$232,760	$271,521
20	$242,974	$297,781	$367,856	$457,620
25	$320,303	$416,459	$548,645	$731,059
30	$405,681	$560,849	$790,582	$1,132,832
35	$499,945	$736,522	$1,114,348	$1,723,168

Top-Heavy Plans

If more than 60% of the plan assets are allocated to "key" employees,[2] then the employer must contribute at least as much for "non-key" participants as it does for key employees. This requirement applies only to a contribution of up to the first 3% of includable compensation (higher in some instances).

---

[1] The rates of return used in this illustration are not indicative of any actual investment and will fluctuate in value. An investment will not provide a consistent rate of return; years with lower (or negative) returns than the hypothetical returns shown may substantially affect the scenario presented.

[2] A "key" employee is someone who, at any time during the plan year was: (1) an officer of the employer whose compensation from the employer exceeded $175,000; or (2) a more than 5% owner; or (3) a 1% owner whose compensation from the employer exceeded $150,000.

Traditional Profit Sharing Plan

Advantages to Employer

- Contributions are tax deductible.

- Contributions and costs are totally flexible.

- The plan is easy to understand by the employees.

- Forfeitures of terminating employees may reduce future costs or be reallocated among the accounts of those in the plan.

- It can provide employees with permanent life insurance benefits that need not expire or require costly conversion at retirement age.

- The employer can direct investments.

- Coordination with Social Security will reduce contributions for rank and file employees.

- If former participants do not provide the plan with distribution instructions, the plan may automatically distribute accounts less than $5,000. In the case of a plan that provides for such mandatory distributions, the plan must automatically roll an eligible distribution amount that exceeds $1,000 to a Rollover IRA in the former participant's name. A plan may allow direct rollovers of less than $1,000.

Advantages to Employees

- Annual employer contributions are not taxed to the participant.

- Earnings on the account are not currently taxed.

- ERISA and federal bankruptcy law provide significant protection from creditors to participant accounts or accrued benefits in tax-exempt retirement plans.

- Participants may be given the right to direct investments. If participants are given the right to "self-direct," plan sponsors are required to provide certain standardized investment fee and performance data. This information is intended to aid participants in making better-informed investment choices.

- Federal law allows a qualified plan to establish an "eligible investment advice arrangement" under which individually tailored investment advice is provided to plan participants. Any fees or commissions charged must not vary with the investment options chosen, or else a computer model meeting certain requirements must be used.

- Participants may also have a traditional, deductible IRA (subject to certain income limitations based on filing status), a traditional, nondeductible IRA, or a Roth IRA.

- If the plan allows, there is the ability to purchase significant permanent life insurance under the plan. Purchase of life insurance will create taxable income to the employee.

- Younger employees can accumulate a larger fund than with a defined benefit plan.

- The forfeited, unvested portion of accounts of former participants may be reallocated to the active participants' accounts; this can have a major impact on future benefits.

- If the plan so provides, vested balances may be withdrawn if the funds have accumulated in the plan for at least two years, if an employee has participated in the plan for at least five years, or if the participant has a "financial hardship." Under IRS regulations, this is defined as "immediate and heavy financial need where funds are not reasonably available from other sources." There are safe harbor rules listing the conditions and requirements for hardship distributions.

- Participants may borrow from the plan within certain guidelines if provided for in the plan documents.

Disadvantages to Employer

- The profit sharing plan will generally not produce as large a contribution and deduction for older employees, as will a defined benefit plan.

- Deductible contribution limits are set at 25% of covered payroll.

- If a plan gives participants the right to direct investments, plan sponsors are obligated to provide participants with standardized investment fee and performance information. Failure to comply with these ERISA requirements may result in a breach of fiduciary duty to plan participants, and the loss of ERISA Section 404(c) protection. In this situation, the plan fiduciaries could be held responsible for the results of the participants' own investment choices.

Disadvantages to Employees

- There is no guarantee as to future benefits.

- Investment risks rest on the participant.

- Older participants may not receive as large a benefit as with a defined benefit plan.

- There is no assurance as to the frequency and amount of employer contributions.

How a Traditional Profit Sharing Plan Works

EMPLOYER

- Employer contributions are discretionary and flexible.
- Employer contributions need not be a specified percentage of compensation, nor made each year, as long as they are recurring and substantial.
- Contributions are tax deductible to the business.[1]

TRADITIONAL PROFIT SHARING PLAN

- Employer contributions are not currently taxable to employee and account growth is tax deferred.
- Investment risk remains on employee.
- The forfeited, unvested portion of former employee's accounts may be reallocated to current participants.

EMPLOYEE

- The allocation of contributions to an employee's account in 2018 may not exceed the lesser of 100% of compensation or $55,000 per year.
- The maximum compensation recognized in 2018 is $275,000.[2]
- Employee may be given right to direct investments.

EARLY WITHDRAWAL

- A 10% penalty generally applies if withdrawals are made before age 59½.
- Some exceptions to 10% penalty are available.
- Employee may borrow from plan within certain guidelines if provided for in plan documents.

RETIREMENT

- Distributions must begin by specified date.[3]
- Funds may be distributed as lump sum or periodic payments.
- Distributions are generally taxed as ordinary income and may be eligible for 10-year income averaging or rolled over into an IRA.

DEATH

- Value of account is included in owner's gross estate.
- Proceeds can pass to beneficiaries with payments made over their lifetimes.
- Income and estate taxes can severely reduce funds left to non-spousal beneficiaries.

---

[1] Up to 25% of covered payroll can be contributed and deducted by the employer.

[2] For those self-employed, compensation is limited to net self-employment income, e.g. gross income less the contribution and the deduction allowed for one-half of the self-employment tax.

[3] Except for 5% owners, distributions must begin by April 1 of the later of (a) the year following the year in which the participant reaches age 70½, or (b) the year following the year in which the participant retires. If the employee is a 5%-or-more owner, withdrawals must begin by April 1 of the year following the year he or she reaches age 70½.

Traditional Money Purchase Plan

The basics: The employer contributes a defined or fixed percentage of the participating employee's compensation each year. The amount to which the fund grows is the amount the employee receives at retirement.

How It Works

- Employer contributes a fixed percentage of the participant's compensation each year to the plan.

- The total employer contribution is then allocated on that basis or on a separately defined basis, such as tiered or integrated with Social Security.

- Employer contributions are tax deductible.

- Contributions are not taxed currently to the employee.

- Earnings accumulate income tax-deferred.

- Distributions are generally taxed as ordinary income. Distributions may be eligible for 10-year income averaging,[1] or, at retirement from the current employer, rolled over to a traditional or a Roth IRA or to another employer plan if that plan will accept such a rollover. Federal law allows retirement distributions to employees who are at least age 62 even if they have not separated from employment at the time distributions begin.

- Except for more-than-5% owners, required minimum distributions (RMDs) must begin by April 1 of the later of (a) the year following the year in which the participant reaches age 70½, or (b) the year following the year in which the participant retires. More-than-5% owners must begin to receive distributions by April 1 of the year following the year they reach age 70½.

---

[1] Those born before 1936 may be able to elect 10-year averaging or capital gain treatment; these strategies are not available to those born after 1935.

Traditional Money Purchase Plan

Additional Considerations

- **Maximum annual contribution:** Up to 25% of covered payroll can be contributed and deducted by the employer.

- **Contribution base:** Plan contributions are normally based on total compensation, e.g., base salary, bonuses, overtime, etc. The maximum compensation recognized in 2018 is $275,000.

- **Individual limits:** The allocation of contributions to a participant's account may not exceed the lesser of 100% of compensation[1] or $55,000 per year.

- **Investment of plan assets:** Investments must be diversified and prudent. Subject to plan provisions, plan assets may be invested in equity products like mutual funds, stocks and debt-free real estate; or debt instruments like T-Bills and CDs. Insurance products like life insurance and annuity policies may also be used.

- **Excluding persons:** Certain persons can be eliminated on the basis of months of service, age or coverage in a union plan; for example, persons under age 21 can be excluded from the plan.

- **Social Security integration:** Since the employer already contributes to the employee's Social Security retirement benefit, these contributions can be integrated into the contribution and/or allocation formulas of the plan.

- **Parties which are favored:** Typically, younger participants are favored because their fund may grow for a longer period and, in some instances, they share in forfeitures that other participants do not.

- **Forfeitures:** As participants leave the company and separate from the plan, those less than 100% vested forfeit that part of the account in which they are not vested. The nonvested forfeitures may then be allocated to the remaining participants. Those participants who remain in the plan the longest will share in the most forfeitures, or forfeitures may be used to reduce future employer contributions.

---

[1] For those self employed, this rate applies to "net" self-employment income of the owner or partner, less the contribution and the deduction allowed for one-half of the self-employment tax.

Traditional Money Purchase Plan

How Much Will There Be at Retirement?

This will depend upon three factors.

- The amount of contributions
- The number of years until retirement
- The investment return

The risk of poor investment returns rests upon the employee; however, if investment results are favorable, the participant will have a larger fund at retirement age.

Years	An Example of What $10,000 Per Year Will Grow to Over Several Years at Various Rates of Growth Without Tax[1]			
	2.00%	4.00%	6.00%	8.00%
5	$52,040	$54,163	$56,371	$58,666
10	$109,497	$120,061	$131,808	$144,866
15	$172,934	$200,236	$232,760	$271,521
20	$242,974	$297,781	$367,856	$457,620
25	$320,303	$416,459	$548,645	$731,059
30	$405,681	$560,849	$790,582	$1,132,832
35	$499,945	$736,522	$1,114,348	$1,723,168

Future Contributions

An employer must make annual contributions to the plan; but to the extent that the future payroll can be forecast, so can the approximate amount of future contributions. Changes may be made prospectively in the level of employer contributions by plan amendment, with advance notice to plan participants.

---

[1] The rates of return used in this illustration are not indicative of any actual investment and will fluctuate in value. An investment will not provide a consistent rate of return; years with lower (or negative) returns than the hypothetical returns shown may substantially affect the scenario presented.

Zero Percent Plans

In some special situations an employer may maintain a money purchase plan that requires no contributions. Creditor protection and self-trusteed asset management are the most common reasons for this.

Top-Heavy Plans

If more than 60% of the plan assets are allocated to "key" employees,[1] the employer must contribute at least as much for "non-key" participants as it does for key employees. This requirement applies only to a contribution of up to the first 3% of includable compensation (higher in some instances).

Advantages to Employer

- Contributions are tax deductible.

- Contributions and costs are known in advance.

- Contributions will rise as compensation rises, but they are controllable both by formula and absolute dollar amounts.

- Forfeitures of terminating employees may reduce future costs or be reallocated among the accounts of those still in the plan.

- The plan is easier to understand by the employees than is a defined benefit plan.

- It can provide employees with permanent life insurance benefits that need not expire nor require costly conversion at retirement age.

- The employer can direct investments.

- If former participants do not provide the plan with distribution instructions, the plan may automatically distribute accounts less than $5,000. In the case of a plan that provides for such mandatory distributions, the plan must automatically roll an eligible distribution amount that exceeds $1,000 to a Rollover IRA in the former participant's name. A plan may allow direct rollovers of less than $1,000.

---

[1] A "key" employee is someone who, at any time during the plan year was: (1) an officer of the employer whose compensation from the employer exceeded $175,000; or (2) a more than 5% owner; or (3) a 1% owner whose compensation from the employer exceeded $150,000.

Traditional Money Purchase Plan

Advantages to Employees

- Annual employer contributions are not taxed to the participant.

- Earnings on the account are not currently taxed.

- Participants may be given the right to direct investments. If participants are given the right to "self-direct," plan sponsors are required to provide certain standardized investment fee and performance data. This information is intended to aid participants in making better-informed investment choices.

- Federal law allows a qualified plan to establish an "eligible investment advice arrangement" under which individually tailored investment advice is provided to plan participants. Any fees or commissions charged must not vary with the investment options chosen, or else a computer model meeting certain requirements must be used.

- Participants may also have a traditional, deductible IRA (subject to certain income limitations based on filing status), a traditional, nondeductible IRA, or a Roth IRA.

- If the plan allows, there is the ability to purchase significant permanent life insurance under the plan. Purchasing life insurance will create taxable income to the employee.

- Younger employees can accumulate a larger fund than with a defined benefit plan.

- Participant may borrow from the plan within certain guidelines if provided for in the plan documents.

- The forfeited, unvested portion of accounts of former participants may be reallocated to the active participants' accounts. This can have a substantial impact on future benefits. Forfeitures may also be used to reduce employer contributions.

- ERISA and federal bankruptcy law provide significant protection from creditors to participant accounts or accrued benefits in tax-exempt retirement plans.

Disadvantages to Employer

- In low profit years, the employer is still obligated to make contributions pursuant to the plan's contribution formula.

- While the plan may be amended to change contribution levels from time to time, this should not be done annually.[1]

- The money purchase plan will generally not produce as large of a contribution and deduction for employees in their late 30's and older, as will a defined benefit plan.

- If a plan gives participants the right to direct investments, plan sponsors are obligated to provide participants with standardized investment fee and performance information. Failure to comply with these ERISA requirements may result in a breach of fiduciary duty to plan participants, and the loss of ERISA Section 404(c) protection. In this situation, the plan fiduciaries could be held responsible for the results of the participants' own investment choices.

Disadvantages to Employees

- There is no guarantee as to future benefits.

- Investment risks rest on the participant.

- Older participants may not receive as great of a benefit as with a defined benefit plan.

---

[1] In 2002, the overall profit sharing plan contribution limit increased to 25% of covered compensation with much greater employer flexibility. However, there are still instances where the employer will want to have a money purchase plan.

How a Traditional
Money Purchase Plan Works

EMPLOYER

- Contributes a fixed percentage of each participant's compensation.
- Total employer contribution is then allocated on that basis or on a separately defined basis.
- Contributions are tax deductible to the business.[1]
- Nondiscrimination rules apply.

MONEY PURCHASE PLAN

- Employer contributions are not currently taxable to employee and account growth is tax deferred.
- Investment risk remains on employee.
- The forfeited, unvested portion of former employee's accounts may be reallocated to current participants.

EMPLOYEE

- The allocation of contributions to an employee's account in 2018 may not exceed the lesser of 100% of compensation or $55,000 per year.
- The maximum compensation recognized in 2018 is $275,000.[2]
- Employee may be given right to direct investments.

EARLY WITHDRAWAL

- A 10% penalty generally applies if withdrawals are made before age 59½.
- Some exceptions to 10% penalty are available.
- Employee may borrow from plan within certain guidelines if provided for in plan documents.

RETIREMENT

- Distributions must begin by specified date.[3]
- Funds may be distributed as lump sum or periodic payments.
- Distributions are generally taxed as ordinary income and may be eligible for 10-year income averaging or rolled over into an IRA.

DEATH

- Value of account is included in owner's gross estate.
- Proceeds can pass to beneficiaries with payments made over their lifetimes.
- Income and estate taxes can severely reduce funds left to nonspousal beneficiaries.

---

[1] Up to 25% of covered payroll can be contributed and deducted by the employer.

[2] For those self-employed, compensation is limited to net self-employment income, e.g. gross income less the contribution and the deduction allowed for one-half of the self-employment tax.

[3] Except for 5% owners, distributions must begin by April 1 of the later of (a) the year following the year in which the participant reaches age 70½, or (b) the year following the year in which the participant retires. If the employee is a 5%-or-more owner, withdrawals must begin by April 1 of the year following the year he or she reaches age 70½.

Nontraditional
Defined Contribution Plan

The basics: These plans are different from traditional money purchase pension and profit sharing plans in that they define different participant groups who will receive different levels of employer contributions. They must comply with very detailed and complicated regulations under IRC Sec. 401(a)(4). They are typically called either cross-tested, tiered, or super-integrated money purchase pension or profit sharing plans.

How It Works

- Employer contributions are tax deductible.
- Contributions are not taxed currently to the employee.
- Earnings accumulate income tax-deferred.
- Distributions are generally taxed as ordinary income. Distributions may be eligible for 10-year income averaging,[1] or, at retirement from the current employer, rolled over to a traditional or a Roth IRA or to another employer plan if that plan will accept such a rollover. Federal law allows pension plans to make retirement distributions to employees who are at least age 62 even if they have not separated from employment at the time distributions begin.
- Except for more than 5% owners, required minimum distributions (RMDs) must begin by April 1 of the later of (a) the year following the year in which the participant reaches age 70½, or (b) the year following the year in which the participant retires. More-than-5% owners must begin to receive distributions by April 1 of the year following the year they reach age 70½.

Additional Considerations

- **Maximum annual deduction:** Up to 25% of covered payroll may be contributed and deducted by the employer.

---

[1] Those born before 1936 may be able to elect 10-year averaging or capital gain treatment; these strategies are not available to those born after 1935.

Nontraditional Defined Contribution Plan

- **Compensation base:** Plan contributions are normally based on total compensation, e.g., base salary, bonuses, overtime, etc. The maximum compensation recognized in 2018 is $275,000.
- **Employer contributions:**

  - For money purchase pension plans, the employer contribution for the specified participant groups is determined by the plan formula and will be fixed unless amended at some future date.

  - Profit sharing plans have a discretionary employer contribution on behalf of the specified participant groups. If there are profits, the employer is expected to make "substantial and recurring" contributions. See IRS Reg. 1.401-1(b)(2).

- **Individual limits:** The allocation of contributions to a participant's account may not exceed the lesser of 100% of compensation[1] or $55,000 per year (2018).
- **Excluding persons:** Certain persons can be eliminated on the basis of months of service, age or coverage in a union plan. For example, persons under age 21 can be excluded from the plan.
- **Investment of plan assets:** Investments must be diversified and prudent. Subject to plan provisions, plan assets can be invested in equity products like mutual funds, stocks and debt-free real estate; debt instruments like T-Bills and CDs. Insurance products like life insurance and annuity policies may also be used.
- **Social Security integration:** While these plans may recognize the impact of Social Security, the differential realized by integrating with Social Security may be minimal.

- **Forfeitures:** As participants leave the company and separate from the plan, those less than 100% vested forfeit that part of the account in which they are not vested. The nonvested forfeitures may then be allocated to the remaining participants. Those participants who remain in the plan the longest will share in the most forfeitures, or forfeitures may be used to reduce future employer contributions.

---

[1] For those self-employed, compensation is limited to "net" self-employment income, e.g., gross income less the contribution and the deduction allowed for one-half of the self-employment tax.

Nontraditional Defined Contribution Plan

- **Parties which are favored:** Cross-tested and super-integrated plans are typically designed to favor the most highly compensated participants in the plan. While these participants will often be the older employees, it is not always the case. In fact, the use of these types of plans is one way in which equity can be achieved between an older owner/professional and a younger owner/professional. At the same time, other participants often receive allocations that are greater than the 3% top-heavy contributions minimum. These types of plans also may aid in allowing owner(s) to reach the maximum $55,000 allocation permitted without having to use a second plan.

How Much Will There Be at Retirement?

This will depend on three factors:

- The frequency and amount of contributions,
- The number of years until retirement, and
- The investment return.

The risk of poor investment returns rests upon the employee. However, if investment results are favorable, the participant will have a larger fund at retirement age.

An Example of What $10,000 Per Year Will Grow to Over Several Years at Various Rates of Growth Without Tax[1]				
Years	2.00%	4.00%	6.00%	8.00%
5	$52,040	$54,163	$56,371	$58,666
10	$109,497	$120,061	$131,808	$144,866
15	$172,934	$200,236	$232,760	$271,521
20	$242,974	$297,781	$367,856	$457,620
25	$320,303	$416,459	$548,645	$731,059
30	$405,681	$560,849	$790,582	$1,132,832
35	$499,945	$736,522	$1,114,348	$1,723,168

[1] The rates of return used in this illustration are not indicative of any actual investment and will fluctuate in value.

Nontraditional Defined Contribution Plan

Top-Heavy Plans

If more than 60% of the plan assets are allocated to "key" employees,[1] the employer must contribute at least as much for "non-key" participants as it does for key employees up to the first 3% of includable compensation (higher in some instances). The plan is typically structured to provide top-heavy benefits for all participants before providing additional allocations to any specified group.

Gateway Contributions

Beginning in 2002 an additional contribution was required on behalf of the nonhighly-compensated participants.[2] The nonhighly-compensated participants must receive a contribution that is the lesser of 5% of compensation or one-third the highest allocation percentage of the highly-compensated participants. Any top-heavy contribution is applied to satisfying this requirement.

Advantages to Employer

- Contributions are tax deductible.
- For profit sharing plans, contributions and costs are totally flexible. For money purchase pension plans, the employer contribution is known in advance.
- The plan is easily understood by employees.
- Forfeitures of terminating employees may reduce future costs or be reallocated among the accounts of those still in the plan.
- It can provide employees with permanent life insurance benefits that need not expire or require costly conversion at retirement age.
- The employer can direct investments.
- If former participants do not provide the plan with distribution instructions, the plan may automatically distribute accounts less than $5,000. In the case of a plan that provides for such mandatory distributions, the plan must automatically roll an eligible distribution amount that exceeds $1,000 to a Rollover IRA in the former participant's name. A plan may allow direct rollovers of less than $1,000.

---

[1] A "key" employee is someone who, at any time during the plan year was: (1) an officer of the employer whose compensation from the employer exceeded $175,000; or (2) a more than 5% owner; or (3) a 1% owner whose compensation from the employer exceeded $150,000.

[2] Highly-compensated employees generally include 5% or more owners and those earning more than $120,000 in the prior year.

Nontraditional Defined Contribution Plan

Allocation of Employer Contributions[1]			
Participant	Age	Annual Compensation	Cross-Tested Allocation
Owner A	55	$275,000	$55,000 [2]
Owner B	50	150,000	$55,000 [2]
Employee 1	40	55,000	$2,750 [3]
Employee 2	35	30,000	$1,500 [3]
Employee 3	30	30,000	$1,500 [3]
Employee 4	25	30,000	$1,500 [3]
Totals		$570,000	$117,250

The cross-tested plan maximizes the contribution for both owners.

Advantages to Employees

- Annual employer contributions are not taxed to the participant.
- Earnings on the account are not currently taxed.
- Participants may be given the right to direct investments. If participants are given the right to "self-direct," plan sponsors are required to provide certain standardized investment fee and performance data. This information is intended to aid participants in making better-informed investment choices.
- Federal law allows a qualified plan to establish an "eligible investment advice arrangement" under which individually tailored investment advice is provided to plan participants. Any fees or commissions charged must not vary with the investment options chosen, or else a computer model meeting certain requirements must be used.
- Participants may also have a traditional, deductible IRA (subject to certain income level limitations based on filing status), a traditional, nondeductible IRA, or a Roth IRA.
- If the plan allows, there is the ability to purchase significant permanent life insurance under the plan. Purchase of life insurance will create taxable income to the employee.

---

[1] Assumes a profit sharing plan
[2] Specified allocation to maximum limits.
[3] Specified allocation of 5.0% of compensation

- The forfeited, unvested portion of accounts of former participants may be reallocated to the accounts of active participants. This can have a substantial impact on future benefits.
- Participant may borrow from the plan within certain guidelines if provided for in the plan documents.
- ERISA and federal bankruptcy law provide significant protection from creditors to participant accounts or accrued benefits in tax-exempt retirement plans.

Disadvantages to Employer

- Money purchase pension plans:

  - In low profit years, the employer is still obligated to make contributions.

  - While the plan may be amended to change contribution levels from time to time, this should not be done annually.

  - Deductible contributions are limited to 25% of covered payroll.

- Profit sharing plans: Deductible contributions are limited to 25% of covered payroll.
- If a plan gives participants the right to direct investments, plan sponsors are obligated to provide participants with standardized investment fee and performance information. Failure to comply with these ERISA requirements may result in a breach of fiduciary duty to plan participants, and the loss of ERISA Section 404(c) protection. In this situation, the plan fiduciaries could be held responsible for the results of the participants' own investment choices.

Disadvantages to Employees

- There is no guarantee as to future benefits.
- Investment risk rests on the participant.

How a Nontraditional Defined Contribution Plan Works

EMPLOYER

- Allows definition of different participant groups who can receive different levels of employer contributions.
- Typically called cross-tested, tiered or super-integrated plans.
- Must comply with detailed and complex regulations under IRC Sec. 401(a)(4).

PROFIT SHARING PLAN

- Employer contributions[1] are not currently taxable to employee and account growth is tax deferred.
- Investment risk remains on employee.
- The forfeited, unvested portion of former employee's accounts may be reallocated to current participants.

EMPLOYEE

- The allocation of contributions to an employee's account in 2018 may not exceed the lesser of 100% of compensation or $55,000 per year.
- The maximum compensation recognized in 2018 is $275,000[2].
- Employee may direct investments.

EARLY WITHDRAWAL

- A 10% penalty generally applies if withdrawals are made before age 59½.
- Some exceptions to 10% penalty are available.
- Employee may borrow from plan within certain guidelines if provided for in plan documents.

RETIREMENT

- Distributions must begin by specified date.[3]
- Funds may be distributed as lump sum or periodic payments.
- Distributions are generally taxed as ordinary income and may be eligible for 10-year income averaging.

DEATH

- Value of account is included in owner's gross estate.
- Proceeds can pass to beneficiaries with payments made over their lifetimes.
- Income and estate taxes can severely reduce funds left to non-spousal beneficiaries.

---

[1] Up to 25% of covered payroll may be contributed and deducted by the employer.

[2] For those self-employed, compensation is limited to net self-employment income, e.g. gross income less the contribution and the deduction allowed for one-half of the self-employment tax.

[3] Except for 5% owners, distributions must begin by April 1 of the later of (a) the year following the year in which the participant reaches age 70 ½, or (b) the year following the year in which the participant retires. If the employee is a 5%-or-more owner, withdrawals must begin by April 1 of the year following the year he or she reaches age 70½.

Traditional Defined Benefit Plan

The basics: Employer contributes an actuarially determined amount sufficient to pay each participant a fixed or defined benefit at his or her retirement.

How It Works

- Employer contributes an actuarially determined amount each year to the plan.

- Employer contributions are tax deductible.

- Contributions are not taxed currently to the employee.

- Earnings accumulate income tax-deferred.

- Distributions are generally taxed as ordinary income. Distributions may be eligible for 10-year income averaging,[1] or at retirement from the current employer, rolled over to a traditional or a Roth IRA, or to another employer plan if that plan will accept such a rollover. Federal law allows retirement distributions to employees who are at least age 62 even if they have not separated from employment at the time distributions begin.

Methods of Defining the Benefit

- **Level percentage plan:** Example - The benefit is equal to 50% of compensation,[2] reduced by 1/25 for each year of participation less than 25 years.

- **Step rate service weighted for prior service:** Example - The benefit is equal to 8% of compensation for the first ten years of service plus 5.2% of compensation for all other years, but not to exceed a total of 33 years.

---

[1] Those born before 1936 may be able to elect 10-year averaging or capital gain treatment; these strategies are not available to those born after 1935.

[2] For those self-employed, compensation is limited to "net" self-employment income, e.g., gross income less the contribution and the deduction allowed for one-half of the self-employment tax. In 2018, $275,000 is the maximum income that may be considered. In unusual circumstances, the required contribution may exceed the allowable deduction, which can trigger an excise tax.

- **Service plan:** Example - The benefit is 2.5% of compensation for each year of service. Younger participants – with a potentially longer working career – may also be favored if the benefit formula is service related.

- **Plan participation:** Example - The benefit is 5% of compensation per year of participation with a maximum of 20 years.

- **Top-heavy plans:** If the present value of the accrued benefits of "key" employees[1] is 60% or more of the total value of all accrued benefits, the plan is top-heavy. In that instance, the plan must provide for a minimum level of benefits for "non-key" participants.

Additional Considerations

- **Investment of plan assets:** Investments must be diversified and prudent. Subject to plan provisions, plan assets can be invested in equity products like mutual funds, stocks and debt-free real estate; or in debt instruments like T-Bills and CDs. Insurance products like life insurance and annuity policies may also be used.

- **Social Security integration:** Since the employer already contributes to the employee's Social Security retirement benefit, these benefits can be integrated into the benefit formula of the plan.

- **Parties which are favored:** Usually favors older employees.

Maximum Benefit

Maximum benefit under a defined benefit plan is measured in two ways:

- **Percentage:** The retirement benefit cannot exceed 100% of the average compensation[2] for the highest three consecutive years of employment. This is reduced by 10% for each year of service less than 10.

---

[1] A "key" employee is someone who, at any time during the plan year was: (1) an officer of the employer whose compensation from the employer exceeded $175,000; or (2) a more than 5% owner; or (3) a 1% owner whose compensation from the employer exceeded $150,000.

[2] For those self-employed, compensation is limited to "net" self-employment income, e.g., gross income less the contribution and one-half of the deduction allowed for the self-employment tax.

Traditional Defined Benefit Plan

- **Dollar amount:** The maximum annual dollar benefit is indexed at $220,000 per year (2018) for retirement at age 62. For retirement prior to age 62, this amount is actuarially reduced. Retirement at age 55 would typically produce a maximum annual benefit of approximately $130,000, depending on the number of years of participation. The dollar amount will also be increased for retirement after age 65, subject to the percentage and dollar limitations. Lastly, if the individual has fewer than 10 years of participation at normal retirement age, the dollar amount is reduced proportionately.

Contributions

The table below illustrates hypothetical first-year contributions for an employee retiring at age 62 with at least 5 years of plan participation. In all instances, the employee's compensation is $220,000 or more. The benefit is 10% of compensation per year of plan participation, which provides the IRS maximum annual benefit per year.[1]

Current Age	1st Year Contributions
30	$57,000
35	73,000
40	94,000
45	120,000
50	155,000
55	198,000
60	255,000

First-Year Contributions

A number of assumptions must be made in determining the amount of current contributions necessary to accumulate the future retirement benefit. The list below includes some of these assumptions:

- Death benefits.

- Retirement age.

---

[1] The Pension Protection Act of 2006 permits a plan sponsor to contribute and deduct an additional amount, generally 50% of the plan's funding target, as advance funding for future plan years.

- Form of annuity.

- IRS Requirements.

- Various government interest rates.

- Annuity rates at retirement.

- Statutory requirements and limits.

- Participants' current ages.

- Compensation.

Annual Contributions

Year-to-year contributions will fluctuate based on the following items:

- Earnings on previous contributions.

- Gains and losses on investments (realized and unrealized).

- Participants' actual compensation.

- Death of participants before retirement.

- Disability retirements.

- Age mix of participants.

- Turnover in participants.

- Cost of annuities at retirement.

- Rate of vesting.

- Timing of contributions.

- Assumptions mandated by IRS.

- Funding limits and requirements of the Internal Revenue Code.

- Legal/actuarial requirements.

Traditional Defined Benefit Plan

Annual funding is done on the assumption that each participant will retire. Accrued benefits are earned each year, and if the participant does not work until scheduled retirement, he or she will not be entitled to the entire benefit.

Advantages to Employer

- Contributions are tax deductible.

- Can reward long-term employees with a substantial retirement benefit even though they are close to retirement age.

- Larger contributions for older employees may reduce corporate tax problem, e.g., excess accumulated earnings, high tax bracket current earnings, etc.

- Forfeitures of terminating employees will reduce future costs.

- It can provide employees with permanent life insurance benefits that need not expire or require costly conversion at retirement age.

- The employer directs investments.

- If former participants do not provide the plan with distribution instructions, the plan may automatically distribute accounts less than $5,000. In the case of a plan that provides for such mandatory distributions, the plan must automatically roll an eligible distribution amount that exceeds $1,000 to a Rollover IRA in the former participant's name. A plan may allow direct rollovers of less than $1,000.

Advantages to Employees

- Annual employer contributions are not taxed to the participant.

- Earnings are not currently taxed.

- Participants may also have a traditional, deductible IRA (subject to certain income level limitations), a traditional, nondeductible IRA, or a Roth IRA.

- There is the ability to purchase significant permanent life insurance, which is not contingent upon the company group insurance program. Purchase of life insurance will generate taxable income to the employee.

- Employee is guaranteed a known retirement benefit.

- Participant may borrow from the plan within certain guidelines if provided for in the plan documents.

- ERISA and federal bankruptcy law provide significant protection from creditors to participant accounts or accrued benefits in tax-exempt retirement plans.

- In most plans, the benefits are guaranteed by the Pension Benefit Guaranty Corporation.

Disadvantages to Employer

- In low profit years, the employer is often still obligated to make contributions.

- Even if profits are low, there is less flexibility with the level of contribution than with some other types of plans.

- Investment risks are on the employer.

- Administration costs are usually higher because an actuary must certify as to the reasonableness of the contribution and deduction (unless it is a fully insured plan).

- Participants often do not understand the defined benefit plan as easily as they do other types of plans.

- If there are rank and file employees and the plan terminates, there may be insufficient assets to pay all accrued benefits. The shortfall must be made up by either the business making a contribution, or by the assets being reallocated from owner-participants to non-highly compensated participants.

- When a plan terminates, it may find that there are surplus assets which may not be distributed to participants. Any such surplus returned to the employer is subject to a 50% (20% in some instances) excise tax.

- An employer with an older work force may find the cost of a defined benefit plan to be prohibitively expensive.

Traditional Defined Benefit Plan

- If a small defined benefit plan terminates with insufficient assets, the rank and file participants receive the full value of their benefits, while the business owners receive the remaining balance. If there are insufficient assets, the Pension Benefit Guaranty Corporation (PBGC) will guarantee some benefits.

- If the employer must prepare audited financial statements (for lenders, bonding, etc.), any unfunded plan liabilities must be reflected on its balance sheet.

Disadvantages to Employees

- Younger employees will generally not receive as great of a benefit as they would under other types of plans.

- The plan concept is more difficult to understand.

How a Traditional Defined Benefit Plan Works

EMPLOYER

- Employer contributes an actuarially-determined amount sufficient to pay each participant a fixed or defined benefit at retirement.
- Employer contributions are tax deductible.

TRADITIONAL DEFINED BENEFIT PLAN

- Employer contributions are not currently taxable to employee and earnings accumulate tax deferred.
- Investment risk remains on employer. Investments must be diversified and prudent. Both equity and debt investments may be used.
- Retirement benefit is typically defined as a percentage of compensation for each year of service or participation.

EMPLOYEE

- Employee has a known retirement benefit.
- Maximum retirement benefit is the lesser of $220,000 per year[1] or 100% of the individual's average compensation for the three highest consecutive years.[2]

EARLY WITHDRAWAL

- A 10% penalty generally applies if withdrawals are made before age 59½.
- Some exceptions to 10% penalty are available.
- Employee may borrow from plan within certain guidelines if provided for in plan documents.

RETIREMENT

- Distributions must begin by specified date.[3]
- Funds may be distributed as lump sum or periodic payments.
- Distributions are generally taxed as ordinary income and may be eligible for 10-year income averaging or rolled over into an IRA.

DEATH

- The PV of the accrued retirement benefit is usually included in owner's gross estate.
- Proceeds can pass to beneficiaries with payments made over their lifetimes.
- Income/estate taxes can severely reduce funds left to nonspousal beneficiaries.

---

[1] These are 2018 limits. This amount is subject to indexing for inflation. Applies when retirement occurs at age 65 or the Social Security full retirement age, if later.

[2] The 100% is reduced by 10% for each year of service less than 10.

[3] Except for more than 5% owners, distributions must begin by the later of (1) April 1 of the year following the year in which the participant reaches age 70½, or (2) the year following the year in which the participant retires. If the employee is a 5%-or-more owner, withdrawals must begin by April 1 of the year following the year he or she reaches age 70½.

Target Benefit Plan

The basics: The target benefit plan has elements of both the defined benefit and defined contribution plans. The contributions are determined as if the plan were a defined benefit plan, while the defined contribution plan annual contribution percentage and dollar amount limitations apply to the actual contributions made on behalf of each participant. Target benefit plans are largely obsolete; a tiered/new-comparability plan would be used instead.

How It Works

- Employer contributes an actuarially determined amount each year subject to percentage and dollar limitations to the plan.

- Employer contributions are tax deductible.

- Contributions not taxed currently to the employee.

- Earnings accumulate income tax-deferred.

- Distributions are generally taxed as ordinary income. Distributions may be eligible for 10-year income averaging,[1] or, at retirement from the current employer, rolled over to a traditional or a Roth IRA, or to another employer plan if that plan will accept such a rollover. Federal law allows retirement distributions to employees who are at least age 62 even if they have not separated from employment at the time distributions begin.

- Except for more than 5% owners, required minimum distributions (RMDs) must begin by April 1 of the later of (a) the year following the year in which the participant reaches age 70½, or (b) the year following the year in which the participant retires. More-than-5% owners must begin to receive distributions by April 1 of the year following the year they reach age 70½.

---

[1] Those born before 1936 may be able to elect 10-year averaging or capital gain treatment; these strategies are not available to those born after 1935.

Methods of Defining the Benefit

- **Level percentage plan:** Example: The benefit is equal to 50% of compensation[1], reduced by 1/25 for each year of participation less than 25.

- **Yearly accrual:** Example: The benefit is equal to 5.0% of compensation for each year of participation.

- **Top-heavy plan:** If more than 60% of the plan assets are allocated to key employees,[2] the employer must contribute at least as much for non-key participants as it does for key employees. This requirement applies only to a contribution of up to the first 3% of includable compensation (higher in some instances).

Additional Considerations

- **Contribution limitations:** The employer contributes an amount actuarially determined but not more than the lesser of 100% of includable compensation or $55,000 annually for each participant.[3] If the plan is top heavy, minimum contributions are required.

- **Deduction limits:** Notwithstanding the individual allocation limits, the maximum employer deduction is limited to 25% of covered compensation.

- **Parties which are favored:** Older employees are favored. A company with principals and key workers older than the rank and file should consider a target plan.

- **Investment of plan assets:** Investments must be diversified and prudent. Subject to plan provisions, plan assets can be invested in equity products like mutual funds, stocks and debt free real estate; or in debt instruments like T-Bills and CDs. Insurance products like life insurance and annuity policies may also be used.

---

[1] For those self-employed, compensation is limited to net self-employment income, e.g., gross income less the contribution and the deduction allowed for one-half of the self-employment tax. For 2018, $275,000 is the maximum income that may be considered

[2] A "key" employee is someone who, at any time during the plan year was: (1) an officer of the employer whose compensation from the employer exceeded $175,000; or (2) a more than 5% owner; or (3) a 1% owner whose compensation from the employer exceeded $150,000.

[3] 2018 values. For those self-employed, compensation is limited to net self-employment income, e.g., gross income less the contribution and the deduction allowed for one-half of the self-employment tax. For 2018, $275,000 is the maximum income that may be considered

- **Social Security integration:** Since the employer already contributes to the employee's Social Security retirement benefit, these contributions can be integrated into the benefit formula of the plan.

How Much Will There Be at Retirement?

This will depend upon three factors:

- The amount of contributions,
- The number of years until retirement, and
- The investment return.

The risk of poor investment returns rests upon the employee. However, if the investment results are favorable, the participant will have a larger fund at retirement age.

An Example of What $10,000 Per Year Will Grow to Over Several Years at Various Rates of Growth Without Tax[1]				
Years	2.00%	4.00%	6.00%	8.00%
5	$52,040	$54,163	$56,371	$58,666
10	$109,497	$120,061	$131,808	$144,866
15	$172,934	$200,236	$232,760	$271,521
20	$242,974	$297,781	$367,856	$457,620
25	$320,303	$416,459	$548,645	$731,059
30	$405,681	$560,849	$790,582	$1,132,832
35	$499,945	$736,522	$1,114,348	$1,723,168

Advantages to Employer

- Contributions are tax deductible.

- Contributions will rise as compensation rises, but they are controllable both by formula and absolute dollar amounts.

- Forfeitures of terminating employees may reduce future costs.

---

[1] The rates of return used in this illustration are not indicative of any actual investment and will fluctuate in value. An investment will not provide a consistent rate of return; years with lower (or negative) returns than the hypothetical returns shown may substantially affect the scenario presented.

- It can provide employees with permanent life insurance benefits that need not expire or require costly conversion at retirement age.

- The employer usually directs investments.

- Often the advantages of a defined benefit plan can be obtained without its problems.

- If former participants do not provide the plan with distribution instructions, the plan may automatically distribute accounts less than $5,000. In the case of a plan that provides for such mandatory distributions, the plan must automatically roll an eligible distribution amount that exceeds $1,000 to a Rollover IRA in the former participant's name. A plan may allow direct rollovers of less than $1,000.

Advantages to Employees

- Annual contributions are not taxed to the participant.

- Earnings on the account are not currently taxed.

- Participants may be given the right to direct investments. If participants are given the right to "self-direct," plan sponsors are required to provide certain standardized investment fee and performance data. This information is intended to aid participants in making better-informed investment choices.

- Federal law allows a qualified plan to establish an "eligible investment advice arrangement" under which individually tailored investment advice is provided to plan participants. Any fees or commissions charged must not vary with the investment options chosen, or else a computer model meeting certain requirements must be used.

- Participants may also have a traditional, deductible IRA (subject to certain income limitations based on filing status), a traditional, nondeductible IRA, or a Roth IRA.

- If the plan allows, there is the ability to purchase significant permanent life insurance under the plan. Purchase of life insurance will generate taxable income to the employee.

- Participant may borrow from the plan within certain guidelines if provided for in the plan documents.

- ERISA and federal bankruptcy law provide significant protection from creditors to participant accounts or accrued benefits in tax-exempt retirement plans.

Disadvantages to Employer

- In low profit years, the employer is still obligated to make contributions.

- There is no flexibility with the level of contributions.

- In some cases, the target benefit plan may not produce as large of a contribution and deduction for older employees as a defined benefit plan might.

- Since these plans are so rare, it may be difficult to find a plan administrator.

- If a plan gives participants the right to direct investments, plan sponsors are obligated to provide participants with standardized investment fee and performance information. Failure to comply with these ERISA requirements may result in a breach of fiduciary duty to plan participants, and the loss of ERISA Section 404(c) protection. In this situation, the plan fiduciaries could be held responsible for the results of the participants' own investment choices.

Disadvantages to Employees

- There is no guarantee as to future benefits.

- Investment risks rest on the participant.

- Older participants may not receive as great of a benefit as with a defined benefit plan.

- Plan is not easily understood by participants.

Employee Stock Ownership Plan (ESOP)

The basics: The ESOP is essentially a stock bonus plan in which employer stock may be used for contributions.

How It Works

- Employer contributes company stock or cash to the plan.

- Employer contributions are tax deductible.

- Contributions are not taxed currently to the employee.

- Earnings accumulate income tax-deferred.

- Distributions are generally taxed as ordinary income. Distributions may be eligible for 10-year income averaging,[1] or, at retirement from the current employer, rolled over to a traditional or a Roth IRA, or to another employer plan if that plan will accept such a rollover.

- Except for more than 5% owners, required minimum distributions (RMDs) must begin by April 1 of the later of (a) the year following the year in which the participant reaches age 70½, or (b) the year following the year in which the participant retires. More-than-5% owners must begin to receive distributions by April 1 of the year following the year they reach age 70½.

- A "KSOP" is an ESOP that allows for employee deferrals and employer matching contributions.

Additional Considerations

- **Maximum annual deduction:** Up to 25% of covered payroll (in some instances up to 50% for a leveraged ESOP) can be contributed and deducted by the firm.

---

[1] Those born before 1936 may be able to elect 10-year averaging or capital gain treatment; these strategies are not available to those born after 1935.

Employee Stock Ownership Plan (ESOP)

- **Individual limits:** For 2018, the annual allocation of contributions to a participant's account may not exceed the lesser of 100% of includable compensation or $55,000 per year. If the plan is a KSOP permitting participant deferrals, participants age 50 and older may also make a $6,000 "catch-up" contribution.

- **Employer contributions:**

  - Most plans are discretionary as to the amount that the employer contributes. If there are profits, the employer is expected to make substantial and recurring contributions.[1]

  - For a "C" corporation, up to an additional 25% of covered compensation may be contributed and deducted if this contribution is used to repay the principal of a loan used by to the plan to acquire employer stock. Contributions used to pay interest on loans used to acquire stock are deductible without limit.

- **Excluding persons:** Certain persons can be eliminated on the basis of months of service, age and coverage in a union plan; for example, persons under age 21 can be excluded from the plan.

- **Investment of plan assets:** Plan assets are required to be invested in employer stock with some exceptions for those participants nearing retirement. In addition, assets may be used to purchase life insurance in some circumstances.

  - **Forfeitures:** As participants leave the company and separate from the plan, those less than 100% vested forfeit that part of the account in which they are not vested. The nonvested forfeitures may then be allocated to the remaining participants. Those participants who remain in the plan the longest will share in the most forfeitures.

  - **Parties which are favored:** Typically, younger participants are favored because they have a longer time for their fund to grow. Also, there may be some special advantages to the major shareholders.

---

[1] See IRS Reg. 1.401-1(b)(2).

Employee Stock Ownership Plan (ESOP)

How Much Will There Be at Retirement

This will depend upon three factors:

- The frequency and amount of contributions,

- The number of years until retirement, and

- The investment return.

The risk of poor investment returns rests upon the employee. However, if the investment results are favorable, the participant will have a larger fund at retirement age.

An Example of What $10,000 Per Year Will Grow to Over Several Years at Various Rates of Growth Without Tax[1]				
Years	2.00%	4.00%	6.00%	8.00%
5	$52,040	$54,163	$56,371	$58,666
10	$109,497	$120,061	$131,808	$144,866
15	$172,934	$200,236	$232,760	$271,521
20	$242,974	$297,781	$367,856	$457,620
25	$320,303	$416,459	$548,645	$731,059
30	$405,681	$560,849	$790,582	$1,132,832
35	$499,945	$736,522	$1,114,348	$1,723,168

Top-Heavy Plans

If more than 60% of the plan assets are allocated to key employees,[2] the employer must contribute at least as much for non-key participants as it does for key employees. This requirement applies only to a contribution of up to the first 3% of includable compensation (higher in some instances).

---

[1] The rates of return used in this illustration are not indicative of any actual investment and will fluctuate in value. An investment will not provide a consistent rate of return; years with lower (or negative) returns than the hypothetical returns shown may substantially affect the scenario presented.

[2] A "key" employee is someone who, at any time during the plan year was: (1) an officer of the employer whose compensation from the employer exceeded $175,000; or (2) a more than 5% owner; or (3) a 1% owner whose compensation from the employer exceeded $150,000.

Employee Stock Ownership Plan (ESOP)

How ESOPs Differ from Stock Bonus Plans

- Under an ESOP, the participants have the absolute right to demand distribution of company stock.

- The plan may repurchase the distributed shares of stock but is not required to do so; only the employer is so required.

- The plan must pass certain voting rights through to the participants. If the stock is not publicly traded or is restricted, the participant or his or her heirs must have the right to offer the stock for sale to the employer.

- The plan may borrow money from a bank to purchase stock, with the employer guaranteeing such loan, without it being considered a prohibited transaction.

- The plan may borrow money from a prohibited person without incurring any penalty.

- The plan may not be integrated with Social Security.

- Whereas a stock bonus plan is not required to invest in employer securities, an ESOP must invest primarily in employer securities, to the extent that employer stock is available.

- The employer can contribute company stock directly to the plan.[1]

- The plan may purchase the securities on the open market for public companies, from the company itself or from the shareholders.

- The employer can contribute and deduct up to 25% of compensation for a leveraged ESOP, which is repaying loan principal. In addition, it can make deductible contributions to pay interest on the loan used to purchase securities.

---

[1] However, it may be better to contribute cash and then have the plan purchase stock from the employer. The valuation of stock directly contributed to the plan may be challenged by the IRS. Contributing cash clearly establishes the value of the contribution.

Employee Stock Ownership Plan (ESOP)

Advantages to Employer

- Contributions are tax deductible.

- Contributions and costs are totally flexible, subject to required loan payments.

- The plan is easy to understand by the employees.

- It can provide employees with permanent life insurance benefits that need not expire or require costly conversion at retirement age.

- Since all or substantially all of the assets may be invested in employer's stock, this is a good method for raising additional capital without going to the market place.

- In effect, the corporation can raise capital with deductible contributions to its plan.

- Stock, rather than cash, can be contributed to the plan.

- An ESOP may be used to facilitate the buyout of a stockholder.

- Dividends paid on stock owned by the ESOP may be deducted if, in accordance with plan language, several requirements are met.

- In effect, both the interest and principal payments of loans are made on a deductible basis.

- If former participants do not provide the plan with distribution instructions, the plan may automatically distribute accounts less than $5,000. In the case of a plan that provides for such mandatory distributions, the plan must automatically roll an eligible distribution amount that exceeds $1,000 to a Rollover IRA in the former participant's name. A plan may allow direct rollovers of less than $1,000.

Advantages to Employees

- Annual employer contributions are not taxed to the participant.

- Earnings on the account are not currently taxed.

- Special treatment of unrealized gains upon the distribution of stock permits significant tax deferral.

Employee Stock Ownership Plan (ESOP)

- Participants may also have a traditional, deductible IRA (subject to certain income limitations based on filing status), a traditional, nondeductible IRA or a Roth IRA.

- There is the ability to purchase significant permanent life insurance, which is not contingent upon the company group insurance program. Purchase of life insurance will generate taxable income to the employee.

- Younger employees can accumulate a larger fund than with a defined benefit plan.

- The forfeited, unvested portion of accounts of former participants is allocated to the active participants' accounts. This can have a major impact on the future benefits.

- Employee participates in employer's growth.

- A potential market is created for deceased owner's stock.

- At distribution, the gain on the stock is not taxed until it is sold.

- The ESOP can provide significant estate planning benefits for shareholders.

- The gain on the sale of employer securities to the ESOP can be deferred under certain situations.

- Participant may borrow from the plan within certain guidelines if provided for in the plan documents.

- ERISA and federal bankruptcy law provide significant protection from creditors to participant accounts or accrued benefits in tax-exempt retirement plans.

- If participants are given the right to direct any investments, plan sponsors are required to provide certain standardized investment fee and performance data. This information is intended to aid participants in making better-informed investment choices.

Disadvantages to Employer

- The ESOP will generally not produce as large of a contribution and deduction for older employees as will a defined benefit plan.

- Deductible contribution limits are set at 25% of covered compensation.

- Certain voting rights must be passed through to the participants.

- An ESOP can be costly to set up. Ongoing administration can also be expensive because of the need to have the stock value appraised each year.

- Future repurchases may not come at a convenient time and must be made with after-tax dollars. This could place a financial strain on the employer.

- If a plan gives participants the right to direct investments, plan sponsors are obligated to provide participants with standardized investment fee and performance information. Failure to comply with these ERISA requirements may result in a breach of fiduciary duty to plan participants, and the loss of ERISA Section 404(c) protection. In this situation, the plan fiduciaries could be held responsible for the results of the participants' own investment choices.

Disadvantages to Employees

- There is no guarantee as to future benefits.

- Investment risks rest on the participant.

- There is no assurance as to the frequency and amount of employer contributions.

- Older participants may not receive as great of a benefit as with a defined benefit plan.

- The value of closely held stock may be difficult to determine at retirement age.

- If the founder or key people die, retire or terminate employment, the company stock may be worth very little.

- The company may not be financially able to repurchase the stock, even though required to do so.

- If the employer's stock is depressed in value at retirement time, there could be a significant loss in the retirement account.

- Both the participant's current livelihood and retirement savings are dependent on the employer's ongoing viability.

Cash or Deferred 401(k) Plan

The Basics

Any profit sharing or stock bonus plan that meets certain participation requirements of IRC Sec. 401(k) can be a cash or deferred plan. An employee can agree to a salary reduction or to defer a bonus which he or she has coming. Tax-exempt entities may also adopt a 401(k) plan.

How It Works

- Employee has the option of taking cash or having it paid to the trust for retirement. This is equivalent to a tax-deductible employee contribution. However, employee deferrals are subject to FICA, medicare and FUTA payroll taxes, with applicable payments from both the employer and employee.

- Any additional employer contributions are tax deductible.

- Employer contributions, if any, are not taxed currently to the employee.

- Earnings accumulate income tax-deferred.

- Distributions are generally taxed as ordinary income; they may be eligible for 10-year income averaging,[1] or, at retirement from the current employer, rolled over to a traditional or a Roth IRA, or to another employer plan if that plan accepts rollovers.

Two Types of Plans

- **Salary reduction:** An employee can agree to a salary reduction, e.g., 10% of compensation, which the employer then pays to the retirement plan trust. It is deductible to the employer but is not included in the employee's gross income.

- **Cash or deferred:** The employer can decide to pay a bonus and give the employees the following choices.

  - Take it as cash.

---

[1] Those born before 1936 may be able to elect 10-year averaging or capital gain treatment.

- Defer it to the trust.

- Take part and defer the rest.

Deposit of 401(k) Salary Deferrals

The Department of Labor (DOL) has conducted many 401(k) plan audits. The deposit rule originally issued by the DOL was that "The employer must deposit the funds as soon as practical, but not later than 15 business days following the close of the calendar month during which the deferrals were made." For years, the DOL enforced the "as soon as practical" portion of this rule and not the "15 business days" part.

In February 2008, the DOL proposed a seven business day "safe harbor" for plans with fewer than 100 participants. If the 401(k) contributions and participant loan payments are remitted to the plan no later than the seventh business day following withholding, the DOL will consider this a timely deposit. While this is still a proposed regulation, the DOL has stated that small employers may rely on this rule.[1]

Plans with more than 100 participants are still subject to the old standard, as-soon-as-practical and not later than 15 business days after the month the deferrals were made. In most situations, however, the DOL expects deposits to be made no later than 2-3 days after the end of the month, regardless of the as-soon-as practical/15 day deadline.

How Much Will There Be at Retirement?

The risk of good or bad investment returns rests upon the employee. The amount available at retirement will depend upon three factors:

- The frequency and amount of contributions.

- The number of years until retirement.

- The investment return.

---

[1] DOL proposed Reg. 2510.3-102(a)(2), of February 21, 2008.

Cash or Deferred 401(k) Plan

| An Example of What $10,000 Per Year Will Grow to Over Several Years at Various Rates of Growth Without Tax[1] | | | |
Years	2.00%	4.00%	6.00%	8.00%
5	$52,040	$54,163	$56,371	$58,666
10	$109,497	$120,061	$131,808	$144,866
15	$172,934	$200,236	$232,760	$271,521
20	$242,974	$297,781	$367,856	$457,620
25	$320,303	$416,459	$548,645	$731,059
30	$405,681	$560,849	$790,582	$1,132,832
35	$499,945	$736,522	$1,114,348	$1,723,168

Additional Considerations

- **Maximum annual allocation:** Employers may deduct contributions of up to 25% of covered payroll. This amount includes employer contributions and account forfeitures.

- **Individual limits:** For 2018, the allocation total of employer contributions and employee deferrals to a participant's account may not exceed the lesser of 100% of compensation or $55,000 per year. An employee's annual elective contributions to the plan are limited to $18,500. For those age 50 and older, additional "catch-up" contributions of $6,000 may be made.

- **Roth 401(k):** A 401(k) plan sponsor may modify plan provisions to allow participants the option to contribute to a Roth account. Contributions to a Roth 401(k) are made with after-tax dollars, subject to the same employee elective deferral limits as the plan.

- **Investment of plan assets:** Plan investments must be diversified and prudent. Subject to plan provisions, plan assets may be invested in equity products such as mutual funds, stocks, or debt-free real estate, or in debt investments such as T-Bills or CDs. Life insurance and annuity policies may also be used. If the plan mandates that employee deferrals must be invested in employer stock (or the trustee can direct such an investment), then the maximum that can be invested in employer stock is generally 10.0%.

---

[1] The rates of return used in this illustration are not indicative of any actual investment and will fluctuate in value.

- **Typically, participants direct the investment of their own deferrals:** They may also direct the investment of employer contributions.

- **Parties which are favored:** The higher paid, younger employee is favored because he or she has a longer time for funds to accumulate tax-deferred.

- **Matching programs:** Some employers choose to match each dollar put in by the employee with some multiple, e.g., 50%, 75%, etc. If the employee does not defer, the employer does not make a match.

- **Fail-safe contribution:** If the non-highly compensated employees do not defer enough relative to what the highly compensated employees want to defer, Treasury Regulations permit the employer to make a contribution sufficient to bring the non-highly compensated employees up to the level necessary to support the highly compensated employee's deferral percentage. This type of contribution must always be fully vested. Highly compensated employees include 5%-or-more owners and those earning more than $120,000[1] in the prior year. If the employer so chooses, the plan may include only those earning more than $120,000 who are also among the top-paid 20% of employees.

- **Salary reductions:** Participants must enter into or be deemed to have entered into a salary-reduction agreement permitting a payroll deduction. This must be done prior to being eligible to receive the compensation.

- **Withdrawal of funds:** Funds can generally be withdrawn in the event of (a) termination of employment; (b) death or disability; or (c) reaching age 59½. If the plan provides, employer contributions may be withdrawn if the funds have accumulated in the plan for at least two years, if an employee has participated in the plan for at least five years.

- **Financial hardship:** Elective contributions can be withdrawn if the participant has a "financial hardship." Treasury regulations define this as "immediate and heavy financial need where funds are not reasonably available from other sources." Safe harbor rules spell out the conditions and requirements for hardship distributions.

---

[1] This limit applies to 2018. This limit was also $120,000 for 2017.

- **Forfeitures:** As participants leave the company and separate from the plan, those less than 100% vested in the employer contribution account forfeit that part of the account in which they are not vested. The nonvested forfeitures may then be allocated to the remaining participants. Those participants who remain in the plan the longest will share in the most forfeitures, or forfeitures may reduce future employer contributions.

- **Automatic enrollment arrangement:** An employer may adopt an arrangement under which a specified percentage of salary will automatically be contributed to the 401(k) plan for each employee unless an employee chooses to "opt-out" of the system.

- **Top-heavy plans:** If 60% or more of plan assets are allocated to key employees,[1] the employer will be required to contribute up to 3% of compensation to all non-key participants if any key participant defers, and/or receives an employer contribution, up to 3% of his or her compensation. In order to meet top-heavy minimum allocation requirements, employee contributions made by non-key employees are not recognized.[2]

- **Discretionary contributions:** In addition to any matching and/or top-heavy contributions, an employer may make discretionary contributions from year to year so long as the allocation among the participants is on a non-discriminatory basis. These contributions may be allocated in several different ways. These contributions can be made to the plan up to the due date of the return plus any extension granted to the employer. Any employer contributions made on a discretionary basis that are not required to maintain the plan qualification may have gradual vesting.

Nondiscrimination Rules

Certain 401(k) plans, generally known as "Safe Harbor" 401(k) plans, automatically pass IRS nondiscrimination tests. 401(k) plans that do not meet one of the IRS safe harbors must use a mathematical test to determine if the plan is discriminatory.

---

[1] A "key" employee is someone who, at any time during the plan year was: (1) an officer of the employer whose compensation from the employer exceeded $175,000; or (2) a more than 5% owner; or (3) a 1% owner whose compensation from the employer exceeded $150,000.

[2] Employer-matching contributions, if any, count toward satisfying the top-heavy requirement. However, if a non-key person does not defer and, hence, not receive a match, the employer would have to make the top-heavy contribution.

First, all employees eligible to participate are divided into two groups according to their compensation and ownership in the employer. The highly compensated[1] may defer up to two times what the non-highly compensated can for the first 2%. If the non-highly compensated on average defer between 2% and 8%, the highly compensated may contribute an additional 2%. (If more than 8%, then up to 125% of the rate.)

In the first year of a 401(k) plan, a 3% deferral rate for non-highly compensated employees may be used if greater than the actual deferral rate.

The amounts contributed by the non-highly compensated employees will set the limit on how much the highly compensated can defer. The deferral percentages must be satisfied for the entire year. An excise tax is assessed if excess deferral amounts are not returned within 2½ months after the close of the plan year. Or, instead of returning deferrals, the employer may make a contribution to the non-highly compensated participants.

If the Nonhighly Compensated Employees Defer (on average)						
.75%	2%	4%	6%	8%	10%	12%
Then the Highly Compensated Employees Can Defer (on average)						
1.5%	4%	6%	8%	10%	12.5%	15%

Average percentages: Highly compensated = 8%; Nonhighly compensated employees = 6%—The test is satisfied.

	Example		Percentage of Compensation		
Employee	Salary and Bonus	Contribution to 401(k) Plan	Individual	Group	Average
HC1	$275,000	$18,500	6.73%		
HC2	150,000	16,190	10.79%	17.52%	8.76%
NHC3	55,000	12,000	21.82%		
NHC4	30,000	1,500	5.00%		
NHC5	30,000	1,200	4.00%		
NHC6	30,000	900	3.00%		
NHC7	25,000	0	0.00%	33.82%	6.76%

[1] In general, a highly compensated participant is one who owns 5% or more of the employer or was paid $120,000 or more (year 2018 limit) in the prior year.

Cash or Deferred 401(k) Plan

IRA vs. 401(k)

Since most 401(k) plans are funded with employee money, the chart below compares the 401(k) plan to an individual retirement arrangement.

Concern	IRA	Sec. 401(k)
Limitations on contributions/allocations	$5,500 or $11,000 (if nonworking spouse is included)[1]	Lesser of 100% or $55,000 of net compensation. Maximum employee elective deferral is $18,500[2] in 2018
Mandatory withdrawal at age 70½	Yes, if traditional IRA No, if Roth IRA	Maybe[3]
Subject to Social Security tax (FICA) and federal unemployment tax (FUTA)	Yes	Yes
Can life insurance be purchased?	No	Yes
Do distributions qualify for 10-year income averaging?	No	Maybe[4]
Can funds be borrowed?	No	Yes, within limits
Anti-discrimination test?	None	Yes - highly compensated/nonhighly compensated employees
Access to funds for financial hardship before age 59½	10% penalty applies, with limited exceptions[5]	Yes, as to elective contributions, but subject to 10% penalty[5]

Advantages to Employer

- Employers are not required to make discretionary contributions.

- If the employer does make a discretionary contribution, it is deductible.

- Any employer discretionary contribution is flexible.

- The plan is easily understood by employees.

---

[1] For those aged 50 and older, additional "catch-up" contributions of $1,000 may be made.

[2] For those age 50 and older, additional "catch-up" contributions of $6,000 may be made.

[3] Except for more-than-5% owners, payments must begin by April 1 of the later of (a) the year following the year in which the participant reaches age 70½, or (b) the year following the year in which the participant retires. If the employee is a 5%-or-more owner, withdrawals must begin by April 1 of the year following the year he or she reaches age 70½.

[4] Those born before 1936 may be able to elect 10-year averaging or capital gain treatment.

[5] See IRC Sec. 72(t).

- An employer matching contribution is a very popular benefit to employees and can be provided at a modest cost.

- The plan can provide employees with permanent life insurance benefits that need not expire nor require costly conversion at retirement age.

- The Plan Trustee can direct plan investments.

- Of all the allocation techniques that can be used for employer discretionary contributions, the one best fitting the employer's objectives can be utilized.

- If former participants do not provide the plan with distribution instructions, the plan may automatically distribute accounts less than $5,000. In the case of a plan that provides for such mandatory distributions, the plan must automatically roll an eligible distribution amount that exceeds $1,000 to a Rollover IRA in the former participant's name. A plan may allow direct rollovers of less than $1,000.

Advantages to Employees

- Participant deferrals are with pre-tax dollars.

- Any employer contributions are not taxable to participant.

- Participants may be given the right to direct investments. If participants are given the right to "self-direct," plan sponsors are required to provide certain standardized investment fee and performance data. This information is intended to aid participants in making better-informed investment choices.

- Federal law allows a qualified plan to establish an "eligible investment advice arrangement" under which individually tailored investment advice is provided to plan participants. Any fees or commissions charged must not vary with the investment options chosen, or else a computer model meeting certain requirements must be used.

- Participants may also have a traditional, deductible IRA (subject to certain income limitations based on filing status), a traditional, nondeductible IRA, or a Roth IRA.

- There is the ability to purchase significant permanent life insurance that is not contingent upon the company group insurance program. Purchase of life insurance will generate taxable income to the employee.

- Younger employees can accumulate a larger fund than with a defined benefit plan.

- The forfeited, unvested portion of any employer-generated accounts may be reallocated to the active participants' accounts.

- Participant may borrow from the plan within certain guidelines if provided for in the plan documents.

- If the plan permits, participants can make hardship withdrawals within the requirements of the plan;[1] these may not be rolled over to any IRA.

- The employer may make matching contributions of some amount.

- The employer may be required to make additional contributions to satisfy top heavy and/or discrimination tests.

- ERISA and federal bankruptcy law provide significant protection from creditors to participant accounts or accrued benefits in tax-exempt retirement plans.

Disadvantages to Employer

- Employers may be required to make a variety of mandated contributions to satisfy top-heavy requirements and/or discrimination requirements.

- The more highly paid participants may not be able to make sufficient contributions to build an adequate retirement. This may bring pressure on the employer to provide additional retirement benefits.

- Since a 401(k) plan can be the most complicated type of plan to have, the administration costs will be greater than with other types of plans.

- If the plan fails the discrimination tests, it may have to make refunds to the highly compensated participants, or make a contribution on behalf of non-highly compensated individuals.

---

[1] See IRC Sec. 402(c)(4) as amended by the IRS Restructuring and Reform Act of 1998.

- Because there are employee contributions made through payroll, a 401(k) plan increases the workload of company staff who handle payroll.

- If a plan gives participants the right to direct investments, plan sponsors are obligated to provide participants with standardized investment fee and performance information. Failure to comply with these ERISA requirements may result in a breach of fiduciary duty to plan participants, and the loss of ERISA Section 404(c) protection. In this situation, the plan fiduciaries could be held responsible for the results of the participants' own investment choices.

Disadvantages to Employees

- There is no guarantee as to future benefits.

- The investment risk rests on the participant.

- The employer may or may not make discretionary contributions.

Safe Harbor 401(k) Plan

Introduction

In general, the Internal Revenue Code (IRC) requires all qualified employer plans to meet certain nondiscrimination requirements. Employer plans established under IRC Sec. 401(k) are subject to one or two additional tests. The first test, applicable to employee deferrals only, is known as the "actual deferral percentage" (ADP) test. The second possible test is the "actual contribution percentage" (ACP) test and is applied only when there are employer-matching contributions.

The Small Business Job Protection Act of 1996 provided 401(k) plans with alternative, simplified methods of meeting these additional nondiscrimination requirements. 401(k) plans that adopt one of these alternative methods are referred to as "safe harbor" 401(k) plans. A safe harbor plan is very similar to a non-safe harbor plan. The primary difference is how a safe harbor plan satisfies the IRC's additional nondiscrimination requirements.

Requirements for a Safe Harbor 401(k) Plan[1]

Effective January 1, 1999, a 401(k) plan which operates as a safe harbor plan must meet one of two employer contribution formulas, as well as a written notice requirement:

- **Employer contributions:** One of two formulas must be followed.

  - **100% vested of 3% of compensation:** The employer may make a 100% vested contribution of 3% of compensation to all non-highly compensated participants. This contribution formula will also satisfy any "top-heavy" requirements, and may be used in the testing for a non-traditional profit sharing plan.[2]

  - **100% vested matching:** As an alternative, the employer may choose to make a 100% vested matching contribution to all non-highly compensated participants who defer under the plan. The match must be 100% of the first 3% of compensation deferred, plus 50% of the next 2% of compensation deferred. The match may also be at the rate of 100% of the first 4% of compensation deferred.

---

[1] See IRS Notices 98-52, 2000-3 and IRS 401(k) regulations effective 1/1/06 for additional detail.

[2] This contribution formula serves triple duty for discrimination, top-heavy, and nontraditional profit sharing testing.

This formula is considered to satisfy the deferral discrimination tests, and can also be used towards satisfying the top-heavy requirements.[1] If the employer is making the matching contributions during the year, the safe harbor rules permit the plan to compute the safe harbor match on a "per pay period" basis, or on an annual basis. If computed annually, the employer may have to true up the match after the plan year end for participants who changed their rate of deferral during the year.

The plan may not have any restrictions on receiving the safe harbor 3% employer or matching contributions, except the minimum age and service requirements needed for plan participation. Neither a 1,000-hour work requirement, nor a requirement that a participant be employed at the end of the plan year, is permitted.

- **Written notice:** To qualify as a safe harbor plan, a 401(k) plan must also provide for written notice to the employees, with both content and timing elements.

  - **Content:** The notice must describe the various conditions concerning the employer's contribution(s), the conditions and methods for employee deferrals, and the employee vesting and withdrawal provisions of the plan.

  - **Timing:** The employer must give notice at least 30 (but not more than 90) days prior to the beginning of the plan year.

If the employer fails to make the required safe harbor contributions, or to meet any other safe harbor requirement, the IRS treats this like any other disqualifying plan failure. The required contributions must be made and any other failures corrected on a timely basis.

The IRS does allow the employer to stop either the safe harbor 3% or matching contributions during a plan year by following specific rules. The employer must provide at least 30 days' advance notice to all eligible employees, ensure employees have a reasonable opportunity to modify their 401(k) contribution elections, and amend the plan accordingly. Furthermore, to stop either safe harbor contribution, it must be due to a substantial business hardship.

---

[1] The match will also satisfy the top-heavy requirements, provided there are no other employer contributions to the plan. If there are other contributions, the plan will have to separately satisfy both top heavy minimum contributions and the discrimination tests on the employer discretionary contributions. The matching contributions made to non-Key employees count toward satisfying the top-heavy minimum.

If the employer stops the safe harbor contributions during the plan year, the plan must meet the regular 401(k) plan non-discrimination requirements and, if applicable, IRS top heavy minimum contributions.

Automatic Enrollment Safe Harbor 401(k) Plan

A 401(k) plan with automatic enrollment will qualify as a safe harbor 401(k) plan if it provides for:

- Automatic enrollment of newly eligible employees, at a contribution rate of at least 3% of compensation, but no more than 10% of compensation.

- Automatic annual increases of 1% per year, such that the employee's 401(k) deferral is at least 6% by their fourth year in the plan.

- Employer matching contributions of 100% on the first 1% of compensation deferred and 50% on the next 5% deferred, or, alternatively, a 3% non-elective employer contribution to all participants.

This automatic enrollment safe harbor 401(k) plan is in addition to other safe harbor 401(k) plans available; it may provide that employer contributions vest 100% after two years of service.

Stacked Matches

In addition to the basic match or the 3% of compensation employer contribution, the plan may provide for two additional types of matches. The plan may have a mandatory employer match, which is based on the first 6% of compensation. There may also be a discretionary match limited to 4% of compensation. The two examples shown on the following page assume the employee's compensation is $275,000.

Safe Harbor 401(k) Plan

Item Description	Value
Maximum compensation for 2018	$275,000
Maximum deferral	18,500
Maximum total allocation	55,000
Matching Approach	
Participant deferral	$18,500
Basic match (4% x $275,000)	11,000
Mandatory match (87.88% x 6.00% x $275,000)	14,500
Discretionary match (4% x $275,000)[1]	11,000
Total	**$55,000**
3.0% Flat Approach	
Participant deferral	$18,500
Flat contribution (3% x $275,000)	8,250
Mandatory match (104.54% x 6.00% x $275,000)[2]	17,250
Discretionary match (4% x $275,000)	11,000
Total	**$55,000**

Top Heavy Plans

Safe harbor 401(k) plans that consist solely of employee 401(k) deferrals and employer contributions that meet the Code Sec. 401(k)(12) safe harbor requirements are exempt from top heavy rules.[3]

Catch-Ups

If a plan participant attains age 50 at any time during 2018 he or she may defer an additional $6,000 to the Safe Harbor 401(k) Plan. This means in the illustrated examples the participant could defer an additional $6,000 for a total allocation of $61,000. The catch-up would not be subject to any of the matches.

---

[1] The actual percentage calculated to satisfy the $55,000 limit.

[2] The actual result rounded down to satisfy the $55,000 limit.

[3] If more than 60% of the plan assets or accrued benefits are allocated to key employees, the plan is top heavy. A "Key" employee is someone who, at any time during the plan year was (1) an officer of the employer whose compensation from the employer exceeded $175,000; or (2) a more than 5% owner; or (3) a 1% owner whose compensation from the employer exceeded $150,000

How a 401(k) Cash or Deferred Plan Works

EMPLOYER

- May provide a voluntary matching fund.
- Contributions are tax deductible to the business.[1]
- May make discretionary contributions any year, so long as allocation is nondiscriminatory.
- Special rules apply for nondiscrimination.

SEC. 401(k) PLAN

- Employer contributions are not currently taxable to employee and earnings accumulate tax deferred.
- Most plans are self-directed (employee controls investments).
- Investment risk remains on employee.

EMPLOYEE

- Employee elects to defer a portion of salary.
- Amounts deferred subject to FICA and FUTA taxes but not current income tax.
- Employee's elective contributions limited to $18,500[2] per year (2018).[3]

EARLY WITHDRAWAL

- A 10% penalty generally applies if withdrawals are made before age 59½.
- Some exceptions to 10% penalty are available.
- Employee elective contributions can be withdrawn for financial hardship.[4]

RETIREMENT

- Distributions must begin by specified date.[5]
- Funds may be distributed as lump sum or periodic payments.
- Earnings + contributions taxed as ordinary income in year received.

DEATH

- Value of account is included in owner's gross estate.
- Proceeds can pass to beneficiaries, with payments over their lifetimes.
- Income/estate taxes can severely reduce funds left to nonspousal beneficiaries.

---

[1] The total deductible employer contribution may not exceed 25% of covered payroll, including employer contributions and account forfeitures.

[2] For those age 50 and older, additional "catch-up" contributions of $6,000 may be made.

[3] For 2018, the allocation total of employer contributions and employee deferrals to a participant's account may not exceed the lesser of 100% of compensation or $55,000 per year.

[4] If provided for by the plan; specific requirements may apply.

[5] Except for more than 5% owners, distributions must begin by April 1 of the later of (a) the year following the year in which the participant reaches age 70½, or (b) the year following the year in which the participant retires. If the employee is a 5%-or-more owner, withdrawals must begin by April 1 of the year following the year he or she reaches age 70-½.

Solo 401(k)

A "Solo 401(k)" is a regular 401(k) plan that covers only a business owner, or the business owner and his or her spouse. In such a plan, the business owner plays two roles, that of employee and that of employer.

How It Works

- As an "employee," the business owner can choose to either receive cash (salary or bonus) or defer the funds into the 401(k) plan. If the 401(k) plan is chosen, these "elective deferrals" are not subject to current income tax, but are subject to FICA and FUTA payroll taxes.[1] For 2018, employee deferrals are limited to $18,500. Additional deferrals of $6,000 may be made if the individual is age 50 or over.

- As the "employer," the business owner may also contribute to the plan. For 2018, the employer's deductible contribution is limited to 25% of the employee's compensation.[2] Employer contributions are not currently taxed to the employee.

- In 2018, total 401(k) contributions (from both employer and employee) are limited to the lesser of 100% of the employee's compensation or $55,000. Assets in the plan grow on a tax-deferred basis. Distributions are generally taxed as ordinary income.

- All 401(k) plans must meet prescribed nondiscrimination tests. Plans in which the business owner, or the business owner and spouse, are the only employees, effectively avoid this issue. Just one additional eligible employee, however, can trigger these nondiscrimination requirements, increasing the administrative complexity and cost.

How Much Can Be Contributed?

A key attraction of a 401(k) plan is the significant amount of money that can be contributed to the plan, as well as being deducted from taxable income. This amount will vary with the level of income and the form of business ownership.

---

[1] The discussion here concerns federal income tax law. State and/or local tax law may differ.
[2] In 2018, a maximum of $275,000 of compensation may be considered in this calculation.

2018 Maximum Deductible Contributions
Under Age 50 – Incorporated Business

Wages & Salary (W-2)	$75,000	$150,000	$200,000	$300,000
401(k)				
Employee Contribution	$18,500	$18,500	$18,500	$18,500
Employer Contribution[1]	18,750	36,500	36,500	36,500
TOTAL	**$37,250**	**$55,000**	**$55,000**	**$55,000**
SEP IRA, Profit Sharing or Money Purchase				
Employer-only Contribution	**$18,750**	**$37,500**	**$50,000**	**$55,000**
SIMPLE IRA				
Employee Contribution	$12,500	$12,500	$12,500	$12,500
Employer Match at 3.0%	2,250	4,500	6,000	9,000
TOTAL	**$14,750**	**$17,000**	**$18,500**	**$21,500**

2018 Maximum Deductible Contributions
Under Age 50 – Unincorporated Business

Self-Employment Income	$75,000	$150,000	$200,000	$300,000
401(k)				
Employee Contribution	$18,500	$18,500	$18,500	$18,500
Employer Contribution[2]	13,940	28,002	36,500	36,500
TOTAL	**$32,440**	**$46,502**	**$55,000**	**$55,000**
SEP IRA, Profit Sharing, or Money Purchase				
Employer Only Contribution	**$13,940**	**$28,002**	**$37,868**	**$55,000**
SIMPLE IRA				
Employee Contribution	$12,500	$12,500	$12,500	$12,500
Employer Match at 3.0%	2,021	4,060	5,491	8,250
TOTAL	**$14,521**	**$16,560**	**$17,991**	**$20,750**

[1] Equals 25% of the employee's W-2 income, subject to the overall $55,000 limitation.

[2] Equals 25% of "net" self-employment income, i.e., gross income less the contribution and one-half the self-employment tax, subject to the overall $55,000 limitation.

Other Points to Consider – Pros and Cons

- Pros

    - **Flexible contributions:** Contribution amounts may vary from year to year.

    - **Loan provisions:** A 401(k) plan may allow for participant loans.

- Cons

    - **Co-ordination with other plans:** If a business owner is also a participant in another 401(k) plan,[1] the overall elective deferral limits apply to deferrals made to both plans.

Seek Professional Guidance

Setting up a qualified plan involves a number of complex issues. The guidance of qualified financial professionals is highly recommended.

---

[1] For example, this would include someone who works full-time for one employer, but who also has a side business from which he or she earns self-employment income.

How a Solo 401(k) Plan Works

INDIVIDUAL AS EMPLOYER

- Makes contributions up to allowable limits.[1]
- Contributions are tax deductible to the business.[2]
- Plan may provide for participant loans.
- Nondiscrimination rules may apply if other employees are hired.[3]

SOLO 401(k) PLAN

- Employer contributions are not currently taxable to employee and earnings accumulate tax deferred.
- Most plans are self-directed (employee controls investments).
- Investment risk remains on employee.

INDIVIDUAL AS EMPLOYEE

- Elects to defer a portion of salary or bonus.
- Employee's elective contributions are limited to $18,500[4] per year (2018).
- Amounts deferred are subject to FICA and FUTA taxes but not current income tax.

EARLY WITHDRAWAL

- A 10% penalty generally applies if withdrawals are made before age 59½.
- Some exceptions to the 10% penalty are available.
- Employee elective contributions can be withdrawn for financial hardship.[5]

RETIREMENT

- Distributions must begin by specified date.
- Funds may be distributed as a lump sum or as periodic payments.
- Earnings + deductible contributions are taxed as ordinary income in the year received.

DEATH

- Value of account is included in owner's gross estate.
- Proceeds can pass to beneficiaries with payments over their lifetimes.
- Income and estate taxes can severely reduce funds left to nonspousal beneficiaries.

---

[1] For 2018, the allocation total of employer contributions, forfeitures and employee deferrals to a participant's account may not exceed the lesser of 100% of compensation or $55,000.

[2] The total deduction is limited to 25% of covered payroll.

[3] Plans covering only the business owner (or the owner and spouse) effectively sidestep the nondiscrimination issue.

[4] In 2018, for those age 50 and older, additional "catch-up" contributions of $6,000 may be made.

[5] If provided for by the plan; specific requirements may apply.

403(b) Salary Deferral Plan

Tax-Sheltered Annuities

Eligible Employers

Religious, charitable, educational, scientific, and literary organizations described in IRC Sec. 501(c)(3), certain governmental employers and public school systems may establish 403(b) plans for their employees.[1]

Who Contributes To The Plan?

While employer contributions are allowed, typically it is the employee who makes the contributions by agreeing to have his or her salary reduced by the contribution amount. If the employer contributes its own funds, the arrangement is subject to many of the same federal tax and labor laws that govern regular qualified plans, such as 401(k) plans. Certain 403(b) plans must satisfy non-discrimination tests. For example, if a non-governmental employer provides a matching contribution, the plan must meet the same Average Contribution Percentage test required of 401(k) plans. The 403(b) plan may be exempt from this test if it provides a "safe harbor" contribution similar to those applicable to 401(k) plans.

Contribution Limits

For 2018, the total of employer contributions and employee deferrals added to a participant's account generally may not exceed the lesser of 100% of compensation[2] (limited to a maximum of $275,000), or $55,000 per year. An employee's elective contributions are generally limited to $18,500 annually. Total elective deferrals for employees of qualifying organizations with 15 years of service may be up to $21,500. For those age 50 or older, additional "catch-up" contributions of $6,000 may be made.

Employer Obligations

In 2007, the IRS issued new 403(b) regulations, generally effective January 1, 2009. These regulations impose specific responsibilities on the employer to ensure the plan operates in accordance with IRS rules. These requirements include:

---

[1] The discussion here concerns federal income tax law. State or local income tax law may vary.

[2] The term "compensation" includes deferrals to 403(b) plans as well as deferrals made to IRC Sec. 125 and IRC Sec. 457 plans.

- **Written plan document:** The plan must have a written plan document adopted by the employer. This document must include eligibility, contribution, distribution, loan and hardship provisions and list the funding vehicles offered. The employer must operate the plan in accordance with these written plan provisions.

- **Ongoing administrative responsibility:** The employer must be responsible for the plan's administrative functions. While many functions may be outsourced to the plan providers, the employer is responsible for the coordination of these functions.

- **Employer as fiduciary:** The employer has a fiduciary duty to ensure the plan operates in the best interests of plan participants by selecting and monitoring service and fund providers and investment options, as well as the fees charged for these services.

- **Expanded Form 5500 reporting and independent plan audit:** The new 403(b) regulations expand the information 403(b) sponsors must report to the federal government, on Form 5500. Further, many non-profit organizations with more than 100 eligible participants will be required to hire an accounting firm to prepare an audit of the plan to accompany Form 5500. These requirements do not apply to sponsors exempt from ERISA, such as governmental organizations and churches.

- **Plan must be universally available to employees:** The plan must be "universally available." If one employee is eligible to make contributions, all employees must be eligible, with limited exceptions.

403(b) plans must meet the same coverage requirements as 401(k) plans. If the employer makes contributions to the plan, these employer contributions must satisfy the same non-discrimination requirements as 401(k) plans. (Governmental entities are exempt from the non-discrimination rules). 403(b) plans are exempt from the Actual Deferral Percentage (ADP) test applicable to 401(k) plans. This is a significant advantage, as highly compensated employees[1] do not have to worry about having excess contributions refunded to them.

The IRS will treat two or more non-profit entities as a single employer if there is at least 80% overlap of directors or trustees (a controlled group). This means that such commonly controlled entities will have to meet the IRS coverage and availability rules for all involved entities. Special rules apply to churches and qualified church-controlled organizations.

---

[1] "Highly compensated" employees generally include 5% or more owners and those earning more than $120,000 (2018 value) in the prior year.

Fee Disclosure Requirements

Effective July 1, 2012, if a plan gives participants the right to direct any investments, plan sponsors must provide participants with expanded, standardized investment fee and performance information. This additional information is intended to aid plan participants in making better-informed investment choices. The failure by a plan sponsor to meet these ERISA requirements may result in a breach of fiduciary duty to plan participants and the loss of ERISA Section 404(c) protection (meaning the plan fiduciaries may be held responsible for the results of the participants' own investment choices).

Other 403(b) Plan Features

- **Roth 403(b) contributions:** If the employer permits, and the written plan so provides, plan participants may choose to have some or all of their salary deferral contributions treated as contributions to a designated Roth account, commonly referred to as a "Roth 403(b)." Unlike normal 403(b) contributions, which are made before-tax, Roth 403(b) contributions are made on an after-tax basis. If certain requirements are met, distributions from the Roth 403(b) are received income tax-free. Contributions to a Roth 403(b) account are subject to the same employee elective deferral limits as the 403(b) plan itself.

- **When to setup a 403(b):** A 403(b) plan may be setup at any time during the year. However, salary-reduction agreements must be entered into before the reduced salary amounts are available to the employee. An employee can later modify the deferral amount, but only with respect to future income.

- **Investment options:** 403(b) plans may offer investments in annuities (fixed or variable and individual or group)[1] or custodial accounts invested in mutual funds.

Withdrawing 403(b) Funds

- **When withdrawals are permitted:** Distributions from 403(b) plans are typically limited and cannot be paid until separation from service, death, disability, termination of the plan, or attainment of age 59½. Some plans may permit hardship distributions. Some 403(b) annuity contracts may have different withdrawal provisions.

---

[1] Under IRS final regulations, life insurance was permitted only if the policy was issued before Sept 24, 2007.

- **Distributions taxed as ordinary income:** Distributions are generally taxed as ordinary income. Distributions may be eligible for 10-year income averaging[1] or, at retirement from the current employer, rolled over to a Traditional or a Roth IRA, or to another employer plan if that plan will accept such a rollover.

- **Early withdrawal penalties:** Taxable distributions from the plan before a participant reaches age 59½ are subject to a 10% federal tax penalty for "early" withdrawal. The 10% penalty may not apply if one of a number of exceptions applies (See IRC Sec. 72(t)). All taxable distributions are included in the participant's gross income in the year of distribution from the plan.

- **Required minimum distributions (RMDs):** Plan assets are usually withdrawn at retirement. To avoid income-tax penalties, distributions must begin by April 1 of the later of (a) the year following the year the participant reaches age 70½, or (b) the year following the year the participant retires.[2]

- **Participant loans:** Participants can borrow funds from their 403(b) and later repay the loan without incurring a tax if certain requirements are met regarding maximum loan amount, amortization requirements, time period for repayments, etc.

- **Financial Hardship:** The salary-reduction amount (but not the earnings) is available for financial hardship; e.g., an immediate and heavy financial need which cannot be met with other sources. Hardship distributions are included in the participant's taxable income in the year of distribution.

The Death of a 403(b) Participant

When a participant dies, 403(b) proceeds become part of his or her taxable estate for federal estate tax purposes. For federal income tax purposes, plan proceeds are generally treated as ordinary income to the beneficiary, except for any "pure" insurance proceeds provided by a 403(b) life insurance contract.[3]

Changing from One 403(b) to Another, Rolling Over to IRA

The transfer of funds from one 403(b) investment to another will not be considered a taxable distribution if the funds remain subject to the same distribution restrictions as on the prior

---

[1] Those born before 1936 may be able to elect 10-year income averaging or capital gain treatment.
[2] If the first distribution is delayed until April 1 of the following year, two distributions will be required in that year.
[3] For insurance policies purchased prior to September 24, 2007.

investment, and the employer has an agreement in place with the new investment provider to permit the new investment. If proceeds from a 403(b) are rolled directly into a traditional IRA, it will defer taxation. A rollover to a Roth IRA is a <u>taxable</u> event. If a distribution is paid directly to the participant first, it will be subject to the mandatory 20% income tax withholding rule.

Federal Bankruptcy Impact

Federal bankruptcy law provides significant protection from creditors to participant accounts or accrued benefits in tax-exempt retirement plans.

Counting Deferred Amounts as Current Compensation

Deferred amounts can be counted as current compensation in computing benefits under a separate qualified pension plan, if the qualified plan so provides.

End Result

Contributing to a 403(b) plan has several significant benefits:

- Except for payroll taxes (e.g., FICA, Medicare), the employee avoids current income taxation on the deferred amount.

- The earnings on the accumulating funds are not taxed until they are distributed, usually at retirement.

Comparison of Federal Income Tax Payable[1]

Without 403(b) Plan		With 403(b) Plan		Benefit
Taxable Income Before $5,000 Salary Reduction	Tax Due Without Annuity	Taxable Income After Reduction	Tax Due with Annuity	Current Income Tax Reduction
$25,000	$2,798	$20,000	$2,048	$750
35,000	4,298	30,000	3,548	750
45,000	5,798	40,000	5,048	750
55,000	7,298	50,000	6,548	750
85,000	12,558	80,000	11,308	1,250

[1] Based on 2018 federal income tax rates and married filing jointly.

How a 403(b) Salary Deferral Plan Works

EMPLOYER[1]

- Contributions are generally tax deductible to the employer.
- May make discretionary contributions[1] from year-to-year so long as allocation is nondiscriminatory.

SEC. 403(b) PLAN

- Employer contributions, if any, are not currently taxable to employee and earnings accumulate tax deferred.
- Plan is self-directed (employee controls investments).
- Investment risk remains on employee.

EMPLOYEE

- Employee elects to defer a portion of salary.
- Amounts deferred subject to FICA and FUTA taxes but not current income tax.
- Employee's elective contributions limited to $18,500 per year (2018).[2]

EARLY WITHDRAWAL

- A 10% penalty generally applies if withdrawals are made before age 59½.
- Some exceptions to 10% penalty are available.
- Employee elective contributions can be withdrawn for financial hardship.[3]

RETIREMENT

- Distributions must begin by specified date.[4]
- Funds may be distributed as lump sum or periodic payments.
- Earnings and contributions taxed as ordinary income in year received.

DEATH

- Value of account is included in owner's gross estate.
- Proceeds can pass to beneficiaries, with payments over their lifetimes.
- Income and estate taxes can severely reduce funds left to nonspousal beneficiaries.

---

[1] If there are employer contributions, the arrangement must generally satisfy the minimum participation requirements as well as the nondiscrimination rules applicable to employer-sponsored qualified plans.

[2] For those age 50 and older, additional "catch-up" contributions of $6,000 may be made.

[3] If provided for by the plan. Under Treasury regulations, financial hardship is defined as "immediate and heavy financial need where funds are not reasonably available from other sources."

[4] Distributions must begin by April 1 of the later of (a) the year following the year in which the participant reaches age 70½, or (b) the year following the year in which the participant retires.

Stock Bonus Plan

The Basics

Employer contributions to the plan are not dependent upon profits, and the plan may, but is not required to, invest primarily in employer stock.

How It Works

- Employer contributes to the plan.

- Employer contributions are tax deductible.

- Contributions are not taxed currently to the employee.

- Earnings accumulate income tax-deferred.

- Distributions are generally taxed as ordinary income. Distributions may be eligible for 10-year income averaging,[1] or, at retirement from the current employer, rolled over to a traditional or a Roth IRA, or to another employer plan if that plan will accept such a rollover.

- Except for more than 5% owners, required minimum distributions (RMDs) must begin by April 1 of the later of (a) the year following the year in which the participant reaches age 70½, or (b) the year following the year in which the participant retires. More than 5% owners must begin to receive distributions by April 1 of the year following the year they reach age 70½.

Additional Considerations

- **Maximum annual deduction:** Up to 25% of covered payroll can be contributed and deducted by the corporation.

- **Individual limits:** The allocation of contributions to a participant's account may not exceed the lesser of 100% of includable compensation or $55,000 per year.

---

[1] Those born before 1936 may be able to elect 10-year averaging or capital gain treatment; these strategies are not available to those born after 1935.

- **Employer contributions:** Most plans are discretionary as to the amount that the employer contributes. If there are profits, the employer is expected to make "substantial and recurring" contributions. See IRS Reg. 1.401-1(b)(2).

- **Excluding persons:** Certain persons can be eliminated on the basis of months of service, age, coverage in a union plan and salary base; for example, persons under age 21 can be excluded from the plan.

- **Investment of plan assets:** Investments must be diversified and prudent. Subject to plan provisions, plan assets can be invested in equity products like mutual funds or stocks; or debt instruments like T-Bills and CDs. Insurance products like life insurance and annuity policies may also be used. Stock bonus plans typically are heavily invested in employer stock. They are not, however, required to invest in employer stock as with an Employee Stock Ownership Program (ESOP).

- **Social Security integration:** Since the employer already contributes to the employee's Social Security retirement benefit, these contributions can be integrated into the contribution formula of the plan.

- **Parties which are favored:** Typically younger participants are favored because they have a longer time for their fund to grow.

- **Forfeitures:** As participants leave the company and separate from the plan, those less than 100% vested forfeit that part of the account in which they are not vested. The nonvested forfeitures may then be allocated to the remaining participants. Those participants who remain in the plan the longest will share in the most forfeitures, or forfeitures may reduce future employer contributions.

How Much Will There Be at Retirement?

This will depend upon three factors:

- The frequency and amount of contributions,
- The number of years until retirement, and
- The investment return.

The risk of poor investment returns rests upon the employee. However, if the investment results are favorable, the participant will have a larger fund at retirement age.

An Example of What $10,000 Per Year Will Grow to Over Several Years at Various Rates of Growth Without Tax[1]				
Years	2.00%	4.00%	6.00%	8.00%
5	$52,040	$54,163	$56,371	$58,666
10	$109,497	$120,061	$131,808	$144,866
15	$172,934	$200,236	$232,760	$271,521
20	$242,974	$297,781	$367,856	$457,620
25	$320,303	$416,459	$548,645	$731,059
30	$405,681	$560,849	$790,582	$1,132,832
35	$499,945	$736,522	$1,114,348	$1,723,168

Top-Heavy Plans

If more than 60% of the plan assets are allocated to key employees,[2] the employer must contribute at least as much for non-key participants as it does for key employees. This requirement applies only to a contribution of up to the first 3% of includible compensation (higher in some instances).

Advantages to Employer

- Contributions are tax deductible.

- Contributions and costs are totally flexible.

- The plan is easy to understand by the employees.

- It can provide employees with permanent life insurance benefits that need not expire or require costly conversion at retirement age.

- Since all or substantially all of the assets are invested in employer's stock, this is a good method for raising additional capital without going to the marketplace.

---

[1] The rates of return used in this illustration are not indicative of any actual investment and will fluctuate in value. An investment will not provide a consistent rate of return; years with lower (or negative) returns than the hypothetical returns shown may substantially affect the scenario presented.

[2] A "key" employee is someone who, at any time during the plan year was: (1) an officer of the employer whose compensation from the employer exceeded $175,000; or (2) a more than 5% owner; or (3) a 1% owner whose compensation from the employer exceeded $150,000.

- In effect, the corporation can raise capital with deductible contributions to its plan.

- If former participants do not provide the plan with distribution instructions, the plan may automatically distribute accounts less than $5,000. In the case of a plan that provides for such mandatory distributions, the plan must automatically roll an eligible distribution amount that exceeds $1,000 to a Rollover IRA in the former participant's name. A plan may allow direct rollovers of less than $1,000.

Advantages to Employees

- Annual employer contributions are not taxed to the participant.

- Earnings on the account are not currently taxed.

- Participants may also have a traditional, deductible IRA (subject to certain income limitations based on filing status), a traditional, nondeductible IRA, or a Roth IRA.

- There is the ability to purchase significant permanent life insurance, which is not contingent upon the company group insurance program. Purchase of life insurance will generate taxable income to the employee.

- Younger employees can accumulate a larger fund than with a Defined Benefit Plan.

- The forfeited, unvested portion of accounts of former participants may be allocated to the active participants' accounts. This can have a major impact on the future benefits.

- Participant may borrow from the plan within certain guidelines if provided for in the plan documents.

- Employee participates in employer's growth.

- A potential market is created for stock of deceased shareholders.

- At distribution, the gain on the stock is not taxed until it is sold.

- ERISA and federal bankruptcy law provide significant protection from creditors to participant accounts or accrued benefits in tax-exempt retirement plans.

- Upon distribution, for stock that is not readily tradable, the participant has the right to require the employer to repurchase the participant's stock.

- If participants are given the right to direct any investments, plan sponsors are required to provide certain standardized investment fee and performance data. This information is intended to aid participants in making better-informed investment choices.

Disadvantages to Employer

- The stock bonus plan will generally not produce as large a contribution and deduction for older employees as will a defined benefit plan or other types of defined contribution plans.

- Deductible contribution limits are set at 25% of covered payroll.

- If a firm's stock is not publicly traded, the voting power of the stock must be passed through to the participants on matters requiring a majority vote of the shareholders.

- The cost of re-valuing closely held stock each year may be expensive.

- Future repurchases required by employee distributions may not come at a convenient time for company cash flow purposes.

- If a plan gives participants the right to direct investments, plan sponsors are obligated to provide participants with standardized investment fee and performance information. Failure to comply with these ERISA requirements may result in a breach of fiduciary duty to plan participants, and the loss of ERISA Section 404(c) protection. In this situation, the plan fiduciaries could be held responsible for the results of the participants' own investment choices.

Disadvantages to Employees

- There is no guarantee as to future benefits.

- Investment risks rest on the participant.

- Older participants will not receive as large a benefit as with a defined benefit plan.

- There is no assurance as to the frequency and amount of employer contributions.

- The value of closely held stock may be difficult to determine at retirement age.

- If the founder or other key people die, retire or terminate employment, the company stock may be worth very little.

- The company may not be financially able to repurchase the stock, even though required to do so.

- If the employer's stock is depressed in value at retirement time, there could be a significant loss in the retirement account.

Age-Weighted Profit Sharing Plan

The Basics

Contributions are totally flexible and at the discretion of the employer, and need not be yearly, so long as they are "substantial and recurring." Employer contributions are allocated to provide an equal assumed retirement benefit as a percentage of compensation at normal retirement age for all participants.

How It Works

- Employer contributions are tax deductible.

- Contributions not taxed currently to the employee.

- Earnings accumulate tax-deferred.

- Distributions are generally taxed as ordinary income. Distributions may be eligible for 10-year income averaging,[1] or, at retirement from the current employer, rolled over to a traditional or a Roth IRA, or to another employer plan if that plan will accept such a rollover.

- Except for more than 5% owners, required minimum distributions (RMDs) must begin by April 1 of the later of (a) the year following the year in which the participant reaches age 70½, or (b) the year following the year in which the participant retires. More-than-5% owners must begin to receive distributions by April 1 of the year following the year they reach age 70½.

Additional Considerations

- **Maximum annual deduction:** Up to 25% of covered payroll can be contributed and can be from current or past profits and deductible by the employer.

---

[1] Those born before 1936 may be able to elect 10-year averaging or capital gain treatment; these strategies are not available to those born after 1935.

Age-Weighted Profit Sharing Plan

- **Individual limits:** The allocation of contributions to a participant's account may not exceed the lesser of 100% of includable compensation[1] or $55,000 per year.

- **Employer contributions:**

  - Plans normally are discretionary as to the amount that the employer contributes.

  - If there are profits, the employer is expected to make "substantial and recurring" contributions. See IRS Reg. 1.401-1(b)(2)

- **Excluding persons:** Certain persons can be eliminated on the basis of months of service, age or coverage in a union plan; for example, persons under age 21 can be excluded from the plan.

- **Investment of plan assets:** Plan assets can be invested in equity products like mutual funds, stocks and real estate; or in debt instruments like T-Bills and CDs; or in insurance products like life insurance and annuity products.

- **Social Security integration:** Since the employer already contributes to the employees' Social Security Retirement, the assumed retirement benefit can be integrated with Social Security, but seldom is.

- **Forfeitures:** As participants leave the company and separate from the plan, those less than 100% vested forfeit that part of the account in which they are not vested. The nonvested forfeitures may then be allocated to the remaining participants. Those participants who remain in the plan the longest will share in the most forfeitures, or forfeitures may be used to reduce future employer contributions.

- **Parties that are favored:** Older participants are favored from a contribution perspective because they are closer to retirement. However, all participants would receive the same projected retirement benefit as a percentage of compensation at age 65.

---

[1] This rate applies to "net" self-employment income of the owner or partner, less the contribution and the deduction allowed for one-half of the self-employment tax.

Age-Weighted Profit Sharing Plan

How Much Will There Be at Retirement?

This will depend upon three factors:

- The frequency and amount of contribution,
- The number of years until retirement, and
- The investment return.

The risk of poor investment return rests on the employee. However, if the investment results are favorable, the participant will have a larger fund at retirement age.

	An Example of What $10,000 Per Year Will Grow to Over Several Years at Various Rates of Growth Without Tax[1]			
Years	2.00%	4.00%	6.00%	8.00%
5	$52,040	$54,163	$56,371	$58,666
10	$109,497	$120,061	$131,808	$144,866
15	$172,934	$200,236	$232,760	$271,521
20	$242,974	$297,781	$367,856	$457,620
25	$320,303	$416,459	$548,645	$731,059
30	$405,681	$560,849	$790,582	$1,132,832
35	$499,945	$736,522	$1,114,348	$1,723,168

Top-Heavy Plans

If more than 60% of the cumulative benefits are going to "key" employees[2], then the employer must contribute at least as much for "non-key" participants as for key employees. This requirement applies only to the first 3%[3] of compensation.

---

[1] The rates of return used in this illustration are not indicative of any actual investment and will fluctuate in value.

[2] A "key" employee is someone who, at any time during the plan year was: (1) an officer of the employer whose compensation from the employer exceeded $175,000; or (2) a more than 5% owner; or (3) a 1% owner whose compensation from the employer exceeded $150,000.

[3] The requirement will be greater than 3% in some instances.

Age-Weighted Profit Sharing Plan

			Traditional		Age-Weighted	Difference Between Age-Weighted and Nonintegrated
			Example – Allocation of Employer Contribution			
Participant	Age	Compensation	Non-integrated	Integrated at 5.7%	Age-Weighted	Difference Between Age-Weighted and Nonintegrated
Owner A	55	$275,000	$39,760	$43,623	$55,000	$15,240
Owner B	50	150,000	21,687	20,460	19,951	-1,736
Employee 1	40	55,000	7,952	7,057	3,236	-4,716
Employee 2	35	30,000	4,337	3,849	1500 [1]	-2,837
Employee 3	30	30,000	4,337	3,849	1500 [1]	-2,837
Employee 4	25	30,000	4,337	3,849	1500 [1]	-2,837
	Totals	$570,000	$82,410	$82,687	$82,687	277

The employer contributions are equal to 14.51% of $570,000 or $82,687. The age-weighted allocation, when accumulated to normal retirement age of 65, would purchase an equivalent retirement benefit as a percent of compensation. The projected retirement is important only to calculate the allocation of the employer contribution.

Advantages to Employer

- Contributions are tax deductible.

- Contributions and costs are totally flexible.

- Forfeitures of terminating employees may reduce future costs or be reallocated among the accounts of those in the plan.

- It can provide employees with permanent life insurance benefits that need not expire nor require costly conversion at retirement age.

- The employer can direct investments.

[1] This is the "gateway" contribution at 5.0%.

- If former participants do not provide the plan with distribution instructions, the plan may automatically distribute accounts less than $5,000. In the case of a plan that provides for such mandatory distributions, the plan must automatically roll an eligible distribution amount that exceeds $1,000 to a Rollover IRA in the former participant's name. A plan may allow direct rollovers of less than $1,000.

- Plan can favor older employees.

Advantages to Employees

- Annual employer contributions are not taxed to the participant.

- Earnings on the account are not currently taxed.

- ERISA and federal bankruptcy law provide significant protection from creditors to participant accounts or accrued benefits in tax-exempt retirement plans.

- Participants may be given the right to direct investments. If participants are given the right to "self-direct," plan sponsors are required to provide certain standardized investment fee and performance data. This information is intended to aid participants in making better-informed investment choices.

- Federal law allows a qualified plan to establish an "eligible investment advice arrangement" under which individually tailored investment advice is provided to plan participants. Any fees or commissions charged must not vary with the investment options chosen, or else a computer model meeting certain requirements must be used.

- Participants may also have a traditional, deductible IRA (subject to certain income limitations based on filing status), a traditional, nondeductible IRA, or a Roth IRA.

- There is the ability to purchase significant permanent life insurance, which is not contingent upon the company group insurance program. Purchase of life insurance will generate taxable income to the employee.

- Older participants will receive a substantially greater allocation of the employer contribution than under traditional type of profit sharing plans.

- The forfeited, unvested portion of accounts of former participants may be allocated to the active participants' accounts. This can have a major impact on future benefits.

- If the plan so provides, vested balances may be withdrawn if the funds have accumulated in the plan for at least two years, if an employee has participated in the plan for at least five years, or if the participant has a "financial hardship." Under Treasury regulations, this is defined as "immediate and heavy financial need where funds are not reasonably available from other sources." Safe harbor rules spell out the conditions and requirements for hardship distributions.

- Participant may borrow from the plan within certain guidelines if provided for in the plan documents.

Disadvantages to Employer

- The maximum deductible employer contribution is 25% of covered payroll.

- If the key employees are younger than the other employees, they will not receive as large a proportion of the employer contribution.

- It is more difficult to explain the plan to employees.

- Administration costs will be higher.

- If a plan gives participants the right to direct investments, plan sponsors are obligated to provide participants with standardized investment fee and performance information. Failure to comply with these ERISA requirements may result in a breach of fiduciary duty to plan participants, and the loss of ERISA Section 404(c) protection. In this situation, the plan fiduciaries could be held responsible for the results of the participants' own investment choices.

Disadvantages to Employees

- There is no guarantee as to future benefits.

- Investment risks rest on the participant.

- There is no assurance as to the frequency and amount of employer contributions.

Fully-Insured Defined Benefit Plan

IRC Sec. 412(e)(3)[1]

Maximum Benefit

The maximum benefit under a defined benefit plan is measured in two ways:

- **Percentage:** The retirement benefit cannot exceed 100% of the average of the highest three consecutive years of compensation.[2] This is reduced by 10% for each year of service less than 10.

- **Dollar amount:** The maximum dollar benefit is indexed at $220,000 per year (2018) for retirement between the ages of 62 and 65.

This amount is actuarially reduced for retirement prior to age 62. Retirement at age 55 would typically produce a maximum annual benefit of about $133,000 in 2017, depending on the assumptions used, cost of living adjustments, and number of years of participation. The dollar amount will also be actuarially increased for retirement after age 65, subject to the percentage and dollar limitations. Lastly, if the individual has fewer than 10 years of participation at normal retirement age, the dollar amount is reduced proportionately.

First- and Subsequent-Year Contributions

The contribution will be the premium for the annuities or combination of annuities and life insurance policies necessary to fund the benefit. This will almost always be higher than in a traditional defined benefit plan when established and then may, or may not, decline as real earnings exceed policy guarantees. The initial contribution for the benefit and future benefit increases are based on the guaranteed rates in the policies. Future premiums will reflect actual investment experience of the policies.

Methods of Defining the Benefit

- **Level percentage plan:** Example - The benefit is equal to 50% of compensation,[2] reduced by 1/25 for each year of participation less than 25 years.

---

[1] The Pension Protection Act of 2006 moved former IRC Section 412 (i) to a new code section, IRC Section 412(e)(3).

[2] For those self-employed, compensation is limited to net self-employment income, e.g., gross income less the contribution and the deduction allowed for one-half of the self-employment tax. In certain unusual circumstances, the required contribution may be more than the allowable deduction.

- **Step rate service weighted for prior service:** Example - The benefit is equal to 8% of compensation for the first ten years of service plus 5.2% of compensation for all other years, but not to exceed a total of 33 years.

- **Service plan:** Example - The benefit is 2.5% of compensation for each year of service. Younger participants may also be favored if the benefit formula is service related.

- **Participation plan:** Example - The benefit is 5% of compensation per year of participation with a maximum of 20 years.

Top-Heavy Plans

If the present value of the accrued benefits of key employees[1] exceeds 60% of the total value of all accrued benefits, the plan is top-heavy. In that instance, the plan must provide for a minimum level of benefits for non-key participants.

Accrued Benefit

Each participant's accrued benefit is measured by the cash value of the policies purchased for each participant.

Special Requirements

For a plan to be considered as "fully insured" under IRC 412(e)(3), certain criteria must be met:

- The total benefits must be provided by one or more annuities or a combination of annuities and life insurance policies.

- The premium on the policies must be level from date of issue until scheduled retirement. Exception: "Dividends" or "excess earnings" may reduce such premium.

- Premiums must not be in default.

- There must be no outstanding policy loans.

---

[1] A "key" employee is someone who, at any time during the plan year was: (1) an officer of the employer whose compensation from the employer exceeded $175,000; or (2) a more than 5% owner; or (3) a 1% owner whose compensation from the employer exceeded $150,000.

Fully-Insured Defined Benefit Plan

Special Considerations

- If a plan qualifies, no actuarial certification is needed.

- If the plan is top-heavy, it may be necessary to fund top-heavy benefits with a separate "side fund." This would require an actuarial certification.

- To convert an existing plan to fully-insured status, several things must happen:

    - All existing assets must first be liquidated.

    - The net proceeds are then used to purchase single premium annuities for each participant based on their accrued benefits at time of conversion.

    - The difference between the projected retirement benefit and the benefit purchased by the single premium annuities is then funded.

    - It may prove difficult to convert from a fully-insured plan to a traditional defined benefit plan.

- In some cases, if care is not taken, the plan may become over funded.

- Because this is a specialized type of plan, someone with experience in this area is necessary to establish a fully-insured plan.

- Converting to fully-insured status may help an "over-funded" defined benefit plan.

- The fully-insured plan is not a universal panacea but may be a useful tool in the right situation.

- In 2004, the IRS issued guidance designed to prohibit certain arrangements that it considers abusive. This guidance prohibits the plan from purchasing life insurance for a participant in excess of the death benefit provided by the plan, requires any policies distributed or purchased from the plan to be done so at full fair market value (not cash surrender value), and requires these plans to provide similar policies in a non-discriminatory manner to all plan participants.[1]

---

[1] See IRS press release IR-2004-21, February 13, 2004.

Fully-Insured Defined Benefit Plan

Advantages to Employer

- Contributions are tax deductible.

- It can reward long-term employees with a substantial retirement benefit even though they are close to retirement age.

- Larger contributions for older employees may reduce corporate tax problem, e.g., excess accumulated earnings, high tax bracket current earnings, etc.

- Forfeitures of terminating employees will reduce future costs.

- It can provide employees with permanent life insurance benefits that need not expire or require costly conversion at retirement age.

- A higher initial contribution will be produced than with a traditional DB plan.

- If former participants do not provide the plan with distribution instructions, the plan may automatically distribute accounts less than $5,000. In the case of a plan that provides for such mandatory distributions, the plan must automatically roll an eligible distribution amount that exceeds $1,000 to a Rollover IRA in the former participant's name. A plan may allow direct rollovers of less than $1,000.

Advantages to Employees

- Annual employer contributions are not taxed to the participant.

- Earnings are not currently taxed.

- Participants may also have a traditional, deductible IRA (subject to certain income limitations based on filing status), a traditional, nondeductible IRA, or a Roth IRA.

- Distributions may be eligible for 10-year income averaging,[1] or, at retirement from the current employer, rolled over to a traditional or a Roth IRA or to another employer plan if that plan will accept such a rollover. Federal law allows retirement distributions to employees who are at least age 62 even if they have not separated from employment at the time distributions begin.

---

[1] Those born before 1936 may be able to elect 10-year averaging or capital gain treatment; these strategies are not available to those born after 1935.

- If the plan allows, there is the ability to purchase significant permanent life insurance under the plan. Purchase of life insurance will generate taxable income to the employee.

- Employee is guaranteed a known retirement benefit.

- ERISA and federal bankruptcy law provide significant protection from creditors to participant accounts or accrued benefits in tax-exempt retirement plans.

Disadvantages to Employer

- In low profit or cash flow years, the employer is still obligated to make contributions, which may be substantial.

- There is far less flexibility with the level of contribution even if profits are low, than with some other types of plans.

- Even though an actuarial certification is not required, other administrative costs arise. The administrative costs will be similar to those in a traditional defined benefit plan.

- Employer contributions may drop dramatically in future years.

- The employer has no control over the investments.

- Participants often do not understand the defined benefit plan as easily as they do other types of plans.

Disadvantages to Employees

- Younger employees may not receive as great a benefit as they would under other plans.

- The plan concept and details are more difficult to understand.

Simplified Employee Pension (SEP)

The basics: A SEP provides an employer with a simplified way to make contributions to an employee's individual retirement account or individual retirement annuity.

- Employer contributions are made directly to SEP-IRAs set up for each employee with a bank, insurance company or other qualified financial institution.

- Employer contributions are generally tax deductible.

- Contributions are not taxed currently to the employee.

- Earnings accumulate income tax-deferred.

How Much Will There Be at Retirement?

This will depend upon three factors:

- The frequency and amount of contributions,

- The number of years until retirement, and

- The investment return.

The risk of poor investment returns rests upon the employee. However, if the investment results are favorable, the participant will have a larger fund at retirement age. The following table illustrates the amount to which annual deposits of $10,000 will accumulate at various growth rates for various periods.

Simplified Employee Pension (SEP)

	An Example of What $10,000 Per Year Will Grow to Over Several Years at Various Rates of Growth Without Tax[1]			
Years	2.00%	4.00%	6.00%	8.00%
5	$52,040	$54,163	$56,371	$58,666
10	$109,497	$120,061	$131,808	$144,866
15	$172,934	$200,236	$232,760	$271,521
20	$242,974	$297,781	$367,856	$457,620
25	$320,303	$416,459	$548,645	$731,059
30	$405,681	$560,849	$790,582	$1,132,832
35	$499,945	$736,522	$1,114,348	$1,723,168

Top-Heavy Plans

If more than 60% of the aggregate contributions have been allocated to key employees[2], then the employer must contribute at least as much as a percentage of compensation for non-key participants as it does for key employees. This requirement applies only to a contribution of up to the first 3% of includable compensation (higher in some instances).

Additional Considerations

- **Annual contribution:** No annual contribution is required. If a contribution is made, and IRS Form 5305-SEP is used as the plan document, the allocation must be the same percentage of compensation for each eligible employee. In calculating the contribution percentage, the compensation must be limited to the maximum amount discussed below. Allocation formulas that favor older employees may not be used. If integration with Social Security is desired, a custom plan or prototype document must be used.

---

[1] The rates of return used in this illustration are not indicative of any actual investment and will fluctuate in value.

[2] A "key" employee is someone who, at any time during the plan year was: (1) an officer of the employer whose compensation from the employer exceeded $175,000; or (2) a more than 5% owner; or (3) a 1% owner whose compensation from the employer exceeded $150,000.

Simplified Employee Pension (SEP)

- **Individual limits:** For 2018, the allocation of excludable employer contributions to a participant's account may not exceed the lesser of 25% of compensation or $55,000. For the self-employed, these maximum values are effectively 20% and $55,000. The maximum amount of compensation that may be considered in this calculation is $275,000.

- **Time of contribution:** Contributions can be made until the due date (plus extensions) of the employer's return.

- **Vesting:** Vesting must always be 100%.

- **Who may participate:** Any employee who is at least 21 years old and has performed service in at least three of the last five calendar years must be permitted to participate under the SEP unless his or her total compensation is less than $600[1] for the year for which the contribution will be made.

- **Investment of contributions:** Each participant directs the investment of the funds contributed on his or her behalf. The funds may be invested in most equity or debt products, but may not be invested in life insurance, "hard" assets, or collectibles, except for U.S. gold and silver coins and certain other coins and precious metals.

- **Withdrawals:** Participants may withdraw or cash out at any time. However, withdrawals are included in taxable income in the year received. Withdrawals prior to age 59½ are subject to an additional 10% penalty tax. Exceptions to the 10% penalty apply if a distribution is made because of the participant's death or disability, or if a distribution is made as a series of substantially-equal periodic payments over the life expectancy of the SEP owner, or joint life expectancies of the owner and a designated beneficiary. Once the periodic payment format is chosen, it generally may not be modified without penalty before the later of five years, or the participant reaches age 59½. Other exceptions to the 10% penalty may apply.[2]

---

[1] This amount applies to 2018. This *de minimis* threshold is subject to change as indexed for inflation.
[2] See IRC Sec. 72(t).

Simplified Employee Pension (SEP)

Advantages to Employer

- Contributions are generally tax deductible.

- Contributions and costs are very flexible.

- Reporting is very minimal—no IRS or Dept. of Labor forms.

- The plan is easy to understand by the employees.

- The plan is easy to set up by merely completing IRS Model Form 5305-SEP,[1] or the funding institution's plan.

- There is little or no administrative expense.

- There is no ongoing fiduciary liability to the employer for plan asset management.

- Plan may be established up until the tax return deadline, including extensions.

Advantages to Employees

- Annual contributions are not taxed currently to the participant.

- Earnings on the account are not currently taxed.

- Participants have the right to direct investments.

- Federal law allows a qualified plan to establish an "eligible investment advice arrangement" under which individually tailored investment advice is provided to plan participants. Any fees or commissions charged must not vary with the investment options chosen, or else a computer model meeting certain requirements must be used.

- Participants may also have a traditional, deductible IRA (subject to certain income limitations based on filing status), a traditional, nondeductible IRA, or a Roth IRA.

---

[1] This model form may not be used if the employer currently maintains any other qualified pension or profit sharing plan.

Simplified Employee Pension (SEP)

- Funds can be withdrawn at any time, e.g., in the event of an emergency such as death or disability. Distributions are includable in taxable income in the year received. A 10% penalty tax may also apply if the participant is under age 59½ when a distribution is received.[1]

- ERISA and federal bankruptcy law provide significant protection from creditors to participant accounts or accrued benefits in tax-exempt retirement plans. In traditional and Roth IRAs, generally, up to $1,283,025[2] is protected. However, funds in a SEP IRA are protected without any dollar limitation.

Disadvantages to Employer

- Contributions must be made for part-time and seasonal employees.

- Employees can withdraw the funds as fast as they are put into the account.

- Employees are always 100% vested—there are no forfeitures to reduce employer contributions.

- Employees control investments.

- Allocation methods that reduce employer costs may not be used; employee costs can be high compared to other types of plans. However, some plan documents used by investment vendors permit integration with social security, which will reduce employer contributions to some extent.

Disadvantages to Employees

- There is no guarantee as to future benefits.

- Investment risks rest on the participant.

- There is no assurance as to the frequency and amount of employer contributions.

- Special lump-sum tax treatment of distributions is not available.

- There are no forfeitures to be reallocated.

---

[1] See "Withdrawals" under "Additional Considerations," above.
[2] Effective April 1, 2016. This limit is indexed for inflation every three years.

Simplified Employee Pension (SEP)

- Life insurance funding is not available.

SEP vs. Profit Sharing Plan

Item	SEP	Profit Sharing
Maximum employer deduction for all plan participants	25% of covered compensation	25% of covered compensation
Maximum amount excludable from current taxation for employee	Lesser of 25% of compensation (limited to $275,000 in 2018) or $55,000	Lesser of 100% of compensation (limited to $275,000 in 2018) or $55,000
Included in employee gross income?	No	No
Eligibility	All categories of employees except union	Some flexibility
Eligibility waiting period	Age 21/any amount of service during 3 of last 5 calendar years	Age 21/1 year service (or 2 years if 100% vested)
Part-time employees	Must be included if they earn more than $600 in the year for which a contribution is made.	Excluded if less than 1,000 hours in plan year
Eligibility for contribution	If eligibility for plan is met, the employee is entitled to contribution whether or not employed on date of contribution	Determined by the plan document
Must annual contributions be made?	No – Discretionary	No – Discretionary
Deadline for making contributions	Tax filing date, including extensions	Tax filing date, including extensions
Reporting and disclosure (employer)	Minimal	Full ERISA requirements
Top-heavy regulations	Apply	Apply
Investments	Decided by employee; no hard assets or collectibles (except certain government coins)	Decided by trustee Plan may allow participants to direct investments

Simplified Employee Pension (SEP)

Item	SEP	Profit Sharing
Allocation of contributions	Pro rata by compensation, but may be integrated with Social Security	Various Most favorable to highly paid and/or older participants
Protects from claims of bankruptcy creditors	Federal bankruptcy law provides significant protection from creditors.	Federal bankruptcy law provides significant protection from creditors.
Who controls withdrawals?	Employee	Terms of the plan trustee/administrator
Vesting requirements	Always 100% vested	May be graded up to six years
Favorable taxation of lump-sum distribution	Not available	Maybe[1]
Employee withdrawals	Anytime, with 10% tax penalty prior to age 59½	Generally, only on death, termination or retirement as provided by plan
Employee loans	No	Yes, provided legal guidelines are observed
Life insurance	Not permitted	Permitted within legal guidelines
Deadline to Establish the Plan	Tax filing date, including extensions	Last day of Employer's fiscal year

[1] Those born before 1936 may be able to elect 10-year averaging or capital gain treatment; these strategies are not available to those born after 1935.

How a SEP-IRA Works

EMPLOYER

- Contributes for all qualified employees.[1]
- Contributions are generally tax deductible.
- Plan is flexible (contributions are not required each year).
- Generally little or no administrative expense.

SEP-IRA

- A separate IRA exists for each participant.
- Employer contributions are not currently taxable.
- Earnings accumulate tax-deferred.
- Plan is self-directed (employee controls investments).
- Investment risk remains on employee.

EMPLOYEE

- Maximum 2018 allocation to a SEP for an employee is $55,000.[2] For a self-employed individual, the limit is also $55,000.[3]

EARLY WITHDRAWLS

- A 10% penalty generally applies if withdrawals are made before age 59½.
- Some exceptions to 10% penalty are available.
- Earnings and contributions taxed as ordinary income in year received.

RETIREMENT

- Distributions must begin by April 1 of year following year owner reaches age 70½.
- Required minimum distribution rules apply.
- Earnings and contributions taxed as ordinary income in year received.

DEATH

- Value of IRA is included in owner's gross estate.
- Proceeds can pass to beneficiaries with payments over their lifetimes.
- Income and estate taxes can severely reduce funds left to nonspousal beneficiaries.

---

[1] Any employee at least 21 years of age who has performed "service" in three of the last five years, and whose total compensation exceeds $600 for the year.

[2] For an employee, contributions may not exceed the lesser of 25% of compensation (maximum of $275,000) or $55,000.

[3] For a self-employed individual, contributions may not exceed the lesser of 20% of compensation (maximum of $275,000) or $55,000.

SIMPLE Retirement Plan

The Small Business Job Protection Act of 1996 created an entirely new type of retirement plan called "SIMPLE," an acronym that stands for Savings Incentive Match Plan for Employees. A SIMPLE plan is essentially a written arrangement providing employer and their employees, with a simplified way to make contributions to provide for retirement income. It is most often set up as a SIMPLE IRA

plan using IRAs, but may also be set up as part of a SIMPLE 401(k) plan. But unlike its traditional 401(k) and 403(b) counterparts, SIMPLE plans are relatively easy to establish and maintain. Furthermore, they have lower administrative costs and lower contribution limits, which currently stand $12,500 per annum. A SIMPLE plan is available for any business which:

- Has 100 or fewer employees (including employees of related entities);

- Does not maintain another tax-qualified retirement plan to which contributions are made; and

- Is either an incorporated or unincorporated entity.

How It Works

- An employer considering offering a SIMPLE plan for a given year, must establish it no later than October 1st of the previous year. Employees must then be given 60 days notice, before the plan takes effect. A SIMPLE plan can be set up through financial service providers such as financial advisors, banks, online brokers and mutual fund purveyors. To launch the plan, the employer plan must execute the paperwork generated by the plan provider, and participants then open SIMPLE accounts at the same place the plan was established.

- Employers must deposit employee contributions to the retirement plan's trust or individual accounts as soon as they can reasonably be segregated from the employer's general assets. And if the plan document explicitly permits, the employer may match contributions for an employee who contributes elective deferrals--for example, 25 cents for each dollar deferred. Employer-matching contributions can be discretionary, meaning they may be made some years, but not others, according to the establishment paperwork.

- Mandatory employer contributions are tax-deductible to the business.

- Employer contributions are not taxed currently to the participants.

- Earnings accumulate income tax deferred.

- The employer must deposit participant contributions within 30 days after the end of the month for which the contribution was made.

- There are two different types of SIMPLE plans that, although similar, do have distinct differences. There is an IRA version and a 401(k) version.

Item	IRA Version	401(k) Version
Plan type	Individual IRA for each participant.	Cash or deferred profit sharing plan.
Participation	Any employee who received $5,000 or more of income during any 2 prior years and is expected to earn $5,000 during the current year must be eligible.	Regular qualified plan rules apply, such as: Minimum age of 21 1 year of service 1000 hours
Do cash or deferred nondiscrimination rules apply? [(401(k), 401(m)]	No	No, unless employer fails to contribute.
Top-heavy rules	They do not apply.	Do not apply unless employer fails to contribute.
ERISA reporting and disclosure rules	Simplified rules apply.	Regular rules apply.
Vesting	Always 100%	Always 100%
Employee contributions	Voluntary up to $12,500[1] (indexed for inflation) per year. May not exceed 100% of compensation. May stop at any time.	Voluntary up to $12,500[1] (indexed for inflation) per year. May not exceed 100% of compensation. May stop at any time.
Minimum participation requirements	There is no minimum number or percentage of eligible employees who must participate.	There is no minimum number or percentage of eligible employees who must participate.

[1] This is the 2018 limit. For those age 50 and older, additional "catch-up" contributions of $3,000 may be made.

SIMPLE Retirement Plan

Item	IRA Version	401(k) Version
Employer contributions	Employer must satisfy one of two alternatives. Election must be made at least 60 days before the start of the plan year.	Employer must satisfy one of two alternatives. Election must be made at least 60 days before the start of the plan year.
Alternative #1 - Matching contributions	Employer matches employee's elective deferral, dollar for dollar, up to 3.0% of compensation.	Employer matches employee's elective deferral, dollar for dollar, up to 3.0% of compensation.
	For any two years out of five, employer may have a lower match, but not less than 1.0%.	Not available.
	The $275,000 compensation limit does not apply.	The $275,000 compensation limit does apply.
	No conditions may be imposed on the right to the employer match such as minimum hours or end of year employment.	No conditions may be imposed on the right to the employer match such as minimum hours or end of year employment.
Alternative #2 - Nonelective contribution	Employer contribution is 2% of compensation to all eligible employees, whether they defer or not.	Employer contribution is 2% of compensation to all eligible employees, whether they defer or not.
	The $275,000 compensation limit does apply.	The $275,000 compensation limit does apply.
Employer contributions are due by:	Due date of employer's income tax return, plus filing extensions.	Due date of employer's income tax return, plus filing extensions.
Employee in-service withdrawals	These are allowed.	Rules are the same as for 401(k) plans. If plan provides for loans or hardship withdrawals, they are allowed.
Taxation of distributions	Generally, treated in the same fashion as withdrawals from a traditional IRA. Ordinary income. Penalty taxes may apply.	Same as 401(k) plans. Distribution is ordinary income. 10-Year averaging[1] may be available.
Additional employer contributions	Are not permitted.	Are not permitted.

[1] Those born before 1936 may be able to elect 10-year income averaging or capital gain treatment; these strategies are not available to those born after 1935.

SIMPLE Retirement Plan

Item	IRA Version	401(k) Version
May employer have another plan to which contributions are made or in which benefits accrue?	No	No
Rollovers	Allowed if to another SIMPLE IRA or, after 2 years of SIMPLE participation, to a traditional IRA.	These are allowed when made to a traditional IRA or qualified plan.
Taxation of premature (before age 59½) distributions within first two years of participation	Taxed as ordinary income, plus a 25% penalty, unless an exception applies.	Taxed as ordinary income, plus a 10% penalty, unless an exception applies.
Taxation of premature (before age 59½) distributions after first two years of participation	Taxed as ordinary income, plus a 10% penalty, unless an exception applies.	Taxed as ordinary income, plus a 10% penalty, unless an exception applies.
Reporting requirements	Plan trustee must provide employer with information on basic plan details.	Regular reporting and disclosure requirements apply. 5500 filing, Summary Plan Description and Summary Annual Report.
	Employer must notify employee of right to defer and provide above information.	
	By January 30, employer must give each participant a statement setting forth account balances as of December 31, and all activity during the calendar year.	401(k)-type of participant reports is required. Time limit is 9 months after the close of the plan year with Summary Annual Report.

Advantages to Employer

- Unlike 401(k) plans, the employer knows in advance approximately what the financial commitment will be.

- Employer contribution is tax deductible.

- The plan is easily understood by employees.

- The 401(k) version of the plan can provide employees with permanent life insurance benefits that need not expire nor require costly conversion at retirement age.

- In the 401(k) version, plan trustee can direct plan investments.

- If former participants do not provide the plan with distribution instructions, the plan may automatically distribute accounts less than $5,000. In the case of a plan that provides for such mandatory distributions, the plan must automatically roll an eligible distribution amount that exceeds $1,000 to a Rollover IRA in the former participant's name. A plan may allow direct rollovers of less than $1,000.

Advantages to Employees

- Participant deferrals are made with pre-tax dollars.

- Employer contributions are not currently taxable to participant.

- In the 401(k) version, distributions may be eligible for 10-year income averaging[1] or, at retirement from the current employer, rolled over to a traditional or a Roth IRA, or to another employer plan if that plan will accept such a rollover.

- Distributions from the IRA version are taxed in the same manner as a traditional IRA, except for a 25% penalty for premature distributions in the first two years.

- In the IRA version, participants have the right to direct investments. In the 401(k) version, participants may have the right to direct investments, depending on plan provisions.

- Federal law allows a qualified plan to establish an "eligible investment advice arrangement" under which individually tailored investment advice is provided to plan participants. Any fees or commissions charged must not vary with the investment options chosen, or else a computer model meeting certain requirements must be used.

- Participants may also have a traditional, deductible IRA, or Roth IRA, subject to certain income limitations based on filing status.

- In the 401(k) version there is the ability to purchase significant permanent life insurance which is not contingent upon the company group insurance program. Purchase of life insurance will generate taxable income to the employee.

---

[1] Those born before 1936 may be able to elect 10-year averaging or capital gains treatment

- Younger employees can accumulate a larger fund than with a defined benefit plan.

- If the 401(k) plan permits, participants can borrow from the plan, within the requirements of the plan and the law.

- In the 401(k) version, if the plan permits, participants can make hardship withdrawals within the requirements of the plan.

- ERISA and federal bankruptcy law provide significant protection from creditors to participant accounts or accrued benefits in tax-exempt retirement plans. In traditional and Roth IRAs, generally, up to $1,283,025[1] is protected. However, funds in either a SIMPLE IRA or SIMPLE 401(k) are protected without any dollar limitation.

Disadvantages to Employer

- The employer is required to contribute.

- The more highly paid participants may not be able to contribute sufficient funds to build an adequate retirement. This may bring pressure on the employer to provide additional retirement benefits.

- While called a "SIMPLE" plan, in operation it is not nearly as simple as often thought.

Disadvantages to Employees

- There is no guarantee as to future benefits.

- Investment risk rests on the participant.

- There are no forfeitures to reallocate as under other types of defined contribution plans.

- For older employees, there may not be sufficient time to accumulate a decent retirement fund. Other types of defined contribution plans can provide a better retirement benefit for older workers.

---

[1] Effective April 1, 2016. This limit is indexed for inflation every three years.

How a SIMPLE IRA Works

EMPLOYER

- SIMPLE plans are only available to firms with 100 or fewer employees and which do not maintain another qualified retirement plan.
- Employer generally must match employee contributions dollar for dollar up to 3%.[1]
- Mandatory contributions are tax deductible to the business.

SIMPLE-IRA

- A separate IRA exists for each participant.
- Employer contributions are not currently taxable to employee and earnings accumulate tax deferred.
- Most plans are self-directed (employee controls investment).
- Investment risk remains on employee.

EMPLOYEE

- Employee may elect to defer a percentage of salary.
- Contributions are pre-tax, thus lowering total taxable income.
- For 2018, elective contributions cannot exceed the lesser of $12,500 or 100% of compensation.[2]

EARLY WITHDRAWAL

- A 25% penalty tax generally applies if withdrawals are made within two years and before age 59½.[3]
- Some exceptions to penalty tax are available.
- Earnings and contributions are taxed as ordinary income in the year received.

RETIREMENT

- Distributions must begin by April 1 of year following year owner reaches age 70½.
- Required minimum distribution rules apply.
- Earnings and contributions are taxed as ordinary income when received.

DEATH

- Value of IRA is included in owner's gross estate.
- Proceeds can pass to beneficiaries with payments over their lifetimes.
- Income and estate taxes can severely reduce IRA funds left to nonspousal beneficiaries.

---

[1] Alternately, employer may choose to contribute 2% of compensation to all eligible employees, whether they defer or not.

[2] For those age 50 and older, additional "catch-up" contributions of $3,000 may be made.

[3] Premature distributions (before age 59½) made after the first two years of participation are generally subject to a 10% penalty tax, unless an exception applies.

Qualified Plans Compared

Plan Type	Defined Benefit	Defined Contribution		
Benefit or Feature	Defined Benefit Plan	Nontraditional Defined Contribution Plan	401(k) Plan	SIMPLE IRA
Employer contributions deductible?	Yes	Yes	Yes	Yes
Employer contributions currently taxable to participant?	No	No	No	No
Earnings accumulate income tax deferred?	Yes	Yes	Yes	Yes
Distributions can be tax favored using 10-year income averaging?	Maybe[1]	Maybe[1]	Maybe[1]	No
Contribution benefit base is total compensation up to $275,000?	Yes	Yes	Yes	Effectively, $416,667[2]
Maximum employer annual contribution/deduction:	Determined by actuary	25% of covered payroll	25% of covered payroll excluding deferral, if plan specifies	Match up to 3% of covered payroll or 2% of covered payroll to all eligible employees
Employer contributions required?	Yes	Money purchase – yes Profit sharing - no	No	Yes at 2% of covered payroll to all eligible employees OR Dollar for dollar match up to 3% of compensation

[1] Those born before 1936 may be able to elect 10-year averaging or capital gain treatment.

[2] The $416,667 amount is based on 3% of the 2018 contribution limit of $12,500 (or $12,500 divided by .03).

Qualified Plans Compared

Plan Type	Defined Benefit	Defined Contribution		
Benefit or Feature	Defined Benefit Plan	Nontraditional Defined Contribution Plan	401(k) Plan	SIMPLE IRA
Employer contributions discretionary?	No	Profit sharing - yes	Yes[1]	No
Voluntary employer matching contributions allowed?	N/A	N/A	Yes	No.[2]
Employer contribution allocation	N/A	1. Age Weighted 2. Cross Tested 3. Super Integrated	1. Prorata by compensation 2. Integrated with Soc. Sec. 3. Age-weighted or 4. Cross tested	Match up to 3% of compensation or 2% of compensation to all eligible employees
Employee contributions Required? Permitted?	No Rarely	No Rarely	Maybe[2] Yes	No Yes
Maximum participant benefits (defined benefit plans only)	Lesser of 100% of compensation or $220,000[3] annually	N/A	N/A	N/A
Maximum participant allocations (employer and employee) (defined contribution plans only)	N/A	Lesser of 100% of compensation or $55,000[3]	Lesser of 100% of compensation or $55,000[3]	Lesser of 100% of compensation or $25,000[4]
Catch-up provisions for those age 50 and older	N/A	No	Yes $6,000[3]	Yes $3,000[3]

[1] Top-heavy minimum employer contribution may be required.

[2] The employer is <u>required</u> to contribute, using one these two methods: (1) at 2% of compensation to all employees, or (2) a dollar-for-dollar match, up to 3.0% of compensation.

[3] Applies to 2018.

[4] For 2018, includes a maximum employee contribution of $12,500, plus a dollar for dollar employer match.

Qualified Plans Compared

Plan Type	Defined Benefit	Defined Contribution		
Benefit or Feature	Defined Benefit Plan	Nontraditional Defined Contribution Plan	401(k) Plan	SIMPLE IRA
Required discrimination tests Coverage?				
Benefits/Contributions?	Yes	Yes	Yes	No
Deferral rates of highly compensated/nonhighly compensated?	Yes	Yes	Yes	No
	N/A	N/A	Yes	No
Can exclude employees from plan participation on basis of age, length of service, or union membership?	Yes	Yes	Yes	No ($5,000 income test applies)
Investments				
Self directed by participants or can be invested at participant discretion (most plans impose some practical considerations) and/or	N/A	Yes	Yes	Yes
Directed by the trustee, must be diversified and prudent	Yes	Yes	Yes	N/A
Self-dealing is prohibited between plan and a number of related persons?	Yes	Yes	Yes	Yes
Plan may recognize employer contributions or benefits of Social Security?	Yes	Yes	Yes	No
Participants who are favored	Older and closer to retirement	Highly compensated and older	Younger	Younger

Plan Type	Defined Benefit	Defined Contribution		
Benefit or Feature	Defined Benefit Plan	Nontraditional Defined Contribution Plan	401(k) Plan	SIMPLE IRA
How much will there be at retirement?				
Benefits specified in plan?	Yes	N/A	N/A	N/A
Investment return affects retirement benefits?	No	Yes	Yes	Yes
Benefits guaranteed at retirement?	Yes	No	No	No
Who bears investment risk?	Employer	Employee	Employee	Employee
Ease of understanding by participants	Difficult	Difficult to Easy	Easy	Easy
Can life insurance be provided?	Yes	Yes	Yes	No
Can participants have a traditional, deductible IRA, or a Roth IRA, subject to income level limitations based on filing status?	Yes	Yes	Yes	Yes
Forfeitures are used to:	Reduce employer contribution	Reduce employer contribution or are reallocated among participants	Reduce employer contribution or are reallocated among participants	N/A
Can participants make loans subject to strict rules?	Yes	Yes	Yes	No
Are hardship withdrawals permitted under well-defined circumstances? (Participant cannot defer for 6 months thereafter.)	N/A	N/A	Yes	N/A

Qualified Plans Compared

Plan Type	Defined Benefit	Defined Contribution		
Benefit or Feature	Defined Benefit Plan	Nontraditional Defined Contribution Plan	401(k) Plan	SIMPLE IRA
Top heavy requirements, if applicable[1]				
Defined benefit plans	Yes - 2% annual benefit for 10 years			
Defined contribution plans		Up to 3% of compensation[2]	Up to 3% of compensation[3]	No

---

[1] If more than 60% of the plan assets or accrued benefits are allocated to key employees, the plan is top heavy. A "Key" employee is someone who, at any time during the plan year was (1) an officer of the employer whose compensation from the employer exceeded $175,000; or (2) a more than 5% owner; or (3) a 1% owner whose compensation from the employer exceeded $150,000

[2] This amount may be greater in some circumstances.

[3] This amount depends on facts and circumstances.

Qualified Plan Historical Limits

Employer-Sponsored Qualified Retirement Plans

Limit[1]	2018	2017	2016	2015	2014
Defined Benefit Plan - Limit on annual benefit	$220,000	$215,000	$210,000	$210,000	$210,000
Defined Contribution Plan - Maximum allocation to individual participant account.	Lesser of $55,000 or 100% of comp.	Lesser of $54,000 or 100% of comp.	Lesser of $53,000 or 100% of comp.	Lesser of $53,000 or 100% of comp.	Lesser of $52,000 or 100% of comp.
Maximum Compensation Amount - Considered in defined contribution plans.	$275,000	$270,000	$265,000	$265,000	$260,000
401(k), 403(b), SAR-SEP - Participant maximum elective deferral.	$18,500	$18,000	$18,000	$18,000	$17,500
401(k), 403(b), SAR-SEP - Age 50 and over "catch-up."	$6,000	$6,000	$6,000	$6,000	$5,500
Simple IRA and Simple 401(k) - Participant maximum elective deferral.	$12,500	$12,500	$12,500	$12,500	$12,000
Simple IRA and Simple 401(k) - Age 50 and over "catch-up."	$3,000	$3,000	$3,000	$3,000	$2,500
457 Plan - Participant maximum elective deferral.	$18,500	$18,000	$18,000	$18,000	$17,500
Simplified Employee Pension (SEP) - Minimum compensation for exclusion.	$600	$600	$600	$600	$550
Key Employee	$175,000	$175,000	$170,000	$170,000	$170,000
Highly Compensated Employee	$120,000	$120,000	$120,000	$120,000	$115,000
Source Document	IR-2017-177	IR-2016-41	IR-2015-118	IR-2014-99	IR-2013-86

Social Security Wage Base

Since employer-sponsored qualified retirement plans are sometimes integrated with Social Security, the Social Security wage base for a particular year is also useful information:

Limit	2018	2017	2016	2015	2014
Social Security Wage Base	$128,400	$127,200	$118,500	$118,500	$117,000

---

[1] The various limits shown in this table reflect federal income tax law; state or local law may vary.

Qualified Roth Contribution Program

Under a regular 401(k), 403(b), or 457(b) governmental plan, a participant chooses to defer a portion of his or her compensation into the plan. Such "elective deferrals" are made on a pre-tax basis, any account growth is tax-deferred, and withdrawals are taxed as ordinary income.[1]

In a qualified Roth contribution program, a participant can choose to have all or part of his or her elective deferrals made to a separate, designated Roth account. Such "designated Roth contributions" are made on an after-tax basis. Growth in the designated Roth account is tax-deferred and qualified distributions are excluded from gross income. Other points:

- Separate accounting and recordkeeping are required for the deferrals under the regular, pre-tax portions of a plan and for those made to the after-tax, designated Roth account.

- Individuals whose adjusted gross income exceeds certain limits may not contribute to a regular Roth IRA. There are no such income limits applicable to a designated Roth account.

- For 401(k) plans, contributions to a designated Roth account are elective deferrals for purposes of the Actual Deferral Percentage (ADP) test.

Contributions

A number of rules apply to contributions to a qualified Roth contribution program:

- **Dollar limitation:** For 2018, a maximum of $18,500 may be contributed. Those who are age 50 and older may make additional contributions of $6,000. A participant may choose to place all of his or her contributions in the regular, pre-tax portion of a plan, all in the designated Roth account, or split the deferrals between the two.

- **Employer contributions:** Employer contributions will be credited only to the regular, pre-tax portion of a plan; they may not be designated as Roth contributions.

---

[1] The discussion here concerns federal income tax law. State or local income tax law may differ.

- **Excess contributions:** Excess deferrals to a designated Roth account must be distributed to the participant no later than April 15 of the year following the year in which the excess deferral was made. Otherwise, the excess deferral will be taxed twice, once in the year of deferral and a second time the year a corrective distribution is made.

Distributions

A distribution from a designated Roth account will be excluded from income if it is made at least five years after a contribution to such an account was first made and at least one of the following applies:

- The participant reaches age 59½;
- The participant dies;
- The participant becomes disabled.

Such distributions are known as "qualified" distributions. Other points:

- **Nonqualified distributions:** If a distribution does not meet the above requirements, it is termed a "nonqualified" distribution. Such distributions are subject to federal income tax, including a 10% premature distribution penalty if the participant is under age 59½ in the year the funds are distributed. Such distributions are taxed under the annuity rules of IRC Sec. 72; any part of a distribution that is attributable to earnings is includable in income; any portion attributable to the original investment (basis) is recovered tax-free. This contrasts sharply with the taxation of nonqualified distributions from a regular Roth IRA account. Nonqualified distributions from a regular Roth IRA are taxed following pre-defined ordering rules under which basis is recovered first, followed by earnings.

- **First-time homebuyer expenses:** In a regular Roth IRA, a qualified distribution may be made to pay for first-time homebuyer expenses. This provision does not apply to distributions from a designated Roth account.

- **Rollovers to designated Roth accounts:** Distributions from the regular, pre-tax portion of a qualified plan may be rolled-over into a designated Roth account. The individual (either the participant or a surviving spouse) must include the distribution in gross income (subject to basis recovery) in the same manner as if the distribution from the pre-tax plan had been rolled over into a Roth IRA.

- **Rollovers <u>from</u> designated Roth accounts:** A distribution from a designated Roth account may only be rolled over into a Roth IRA or another designated Roth account. Such a rollover is not a taxable event.

- **Required minimum distributions:** Generally, amounts in a designated Roth account are subject to the required minimum distribution rules applicable to plan participants when they reach age 70½. However, a participant can avoid the mandated distributions by rolling over amounts in the designated Roth account into a regular Roth IRA.

Which Account To Choose?

The decision as to which type of account should be used will generally be made on factors such as the length of time until retirement (or until the funds are needed), the amount of money available to contribute each year, the participant's current tax situation, and the anticipated marginal tax rate in retirement. An important issue to keep in mind is the overall, lifetime tax burden.

- **Regular 401(k), 403(b), or 457(b) governmental plan:** Generally, individuals with a relatively short period of time until retirement, or who expect that their marginal tax rate will be lower in retirement, will benefit more from a regular, pre-tax qualified retirement plan.

- **Designated Roth account:** Younger individuals with more years until retirement and those who anticipate that their marginal tax rate will rise in retirement will generally benefit more from a designated Roth account. The fact that contributions to a designated Roth account are after-tax may cause current cash-flow problems for some individuals. Higher income participants may find that taxable income will be higher with a designated Roth account than with a regular pre-tax plan, potentially reducing tax breaks such as the child tax credit or AMT exemption.

- **Both:** Some individuals may choose to contribute to both types of plan, to provide flexibility in retirement.

Seek Professional Guidance

Because of the complexities involved, the guidance of tax and financial professionals is strongly recommended.

Defined Contribution Plans Compared

Benefit or Feature	Plan Type			
	SEP	Traditional Defined Contribution Plan	401(k) Plan	SIMPLE IRA
Employer contributions deductible?	Yes	Yes	Yes	Yes
Employer contributions currently taxable to participant?	No	No	No	No
Earnings accumulate income tax deferred?	Yes	Yes	Yes	Yes
Distributions can be tax favored using 10-year income averaging?	No	Maybe[1]	Maybe[1]	No
Contribution benefit base is total compensation up to $275,000?	Yes	Yes	Yes	Effectively $416,667[2]
Maximum plan annual employer deduction	25%[3] of compensation of all covered participants	25% of compensation of all covered participants	25% of compensation of all covered participants	Match deferral up to 3% of compensation or 2% of compensation to all eligible employees
Maximum participant allocation	Lesser of 25% of compensation or $55,000	Lesser of 100% of compensation or $55,000	Lesser of 100% of compensation or $55,000	Lesser of 100% of compensation or $25,000[4]
Catch-up provisions for those age 50 and older?	No	Yes $6,000	Yes $6,000	Yes $3,000

[1] Those born before 1936 may be able to elect 10-year averaging or capital gain treatment; these strategies are not available to those born after 1935.
[2] The $416,667 amount is based on 3% of the 2018 contribution limit of $12,500 (or $12,500 divided by .03).
[3] See the section in IRS Publication 590, Individual Retirement Arrangements (IRAs) on SEPs.
[4] For 2018, includes a maximum employee contribution of $12,500, plus a dollar for dollar employer match.

Defined Contribution Plans Compared

Benefit or Feature	Plan Type			
	SEP	Traditional Defined Contribution Plan	401(k) Plan	SIMPLE IRA
Employer contributions required?	No	Profit sharing Maybe[1] Money purchase Yes	Maybe[1]	Yes, at 2% of compensation to all eligible employees or dollar for dollar up to 3% of compensation
Employer non-matching contributions discretionary?	Yes	Profit sharing = Yes Money purchase = No	Generally, yes[2]	No
Discretionary employer matching contributions allowed?	No	No	Yes	No
How is employer non-matching contribution allocated?	Prorata by compensation	Prorata by compensation or integrated with Social Security	Prorata by compensation, or Integrated with Social Security, or Age-weighted, or Cross tested	Prorata by compensation or up to 3% match on deferrals
Employee contributions Required? Permitted?	No No	No Rarely	No Yes	No Yes
Employee vesting in employer contributions	Always 100%	May be graded over time	May be graded over time	Always 100%

[1] Top-heavy minimum employer contribution may be required.

[2] Employer non-matching contributions may be required to meet nondiscrimination tests, to comply with top heavy minimum requirements, or if the plan is combined with another plan such as a defined benefit plan.

Defined Contribution Plans Compared

Benefit or Feature	Plan Type			
	SEP	Traditional Defined Contribution Plan	401(k) Plan	SIMPLE IRA
Required discrimination test				
Coverage?	Yes	Yes	Yes	No
Contributions?	Yes	Yes	Yes	No
Deferral rates of highly compensated/non-highly compensated?	N/A	N/A	Yes	No
Can exclude employees from plan participation on basis of age or length of service?	Yes[1]	Yes[2]	Yes[3]	No[4]
Can exclude employees from plan participation for union membership or non-resident aliens with no US source income?	Yes	Yes	Yes	Yes
Investments				
Self directed by participants (most plans impose some practical considerations) and/or	Can only be directed by participants	Yes	Yes	Yes
Directed by the trustee, must be diversified and prudent	N/A	Yes	Yes	N/A
Is self-dealing prohibited between the plan and a number of related persons?	Yes	Yes	Yes	Yes
Plan may recognize employer contributions or benefits of Social Security?	Yes, but IRS form 5305 SEP may not be used	Yes	Yes	No

[1] Must allow participation if at least age 21, performed service in 3 of the last 5 years, and earned $600 in the current year.

[2] Must allow participation if at least age 21 and performed 1 or 2 years (1,000 hours per year) of service.

[3] Must allow participation if at least age 21 and has performed 1 year (1,000 hours) of service.

[4] $5,000 income test applies.

Defined Contribution Plans Compared

Benefit or Feature	Plan Type			
	SEP	Traditional Defined Contribution Plan	401(k) Plan	SIMPLE IRA
Participants who are favored	Younger	Younger	Younger	Younger
How much will there be at retirement? Investment return affects retirement benefits?	Yes	Yes	Yes	Yes
Benefits guaranteed at retirement?	No	No	No	No
Who bears investment risk?	Employee	Employee	Employee	Employee
Top heavy requirements, if applicable	Up to 3% of compensation	Up to 3% of compensation[1]	Up to 3% of compensation	No
Ease of understanding by participants	Easy	Easy	Easy	Easy
Can life insurance be provided?	No	Yes	Yes	No
Can participants have a traditional IRA or Roth IRA?[2]	Yes	Yes	Yes	Yes
Forfeitures are used for what purpose	N/A	Reduce employer contribution or are reallocated among participants	Reduce employer contribution or are reallocated among participants	N/A
Can participants make loans subject to strict rules?	No	Yes	Yes	No
Are hardship withdrawals permitted under well-defined circumstances? (Participant cannot defer for 6 months thereafter.)	No	Maybe[3]	Yes	No

[1] This amount may be greater in some circumstances.

[2] Subject to other requirements.

[3] Hardship withdrawals are permitted for profit sharing plans, but not for money purchase plans.

Combinations of Retirement Plans

Can an employer have more than one kind of tax-deductible retirement plan? Under federal law the answer is yes. However, certain limits are imposed at both the individual plan level and at the combined plans level. In combining plans, an employer would not normally adopt more than one plan of the same type.

Individual Plan Limits

At the individual plan level, the maximum annual retirement benefit permitted under a defined benefit plan for a participant is the lesser of 100% of compensation or $220,000.[1] The maximum allocation to a participant under a defined contribution plan is the lesser of 100%[2] of compensation or $55,000.[2] If an employer adopts two plans of the same type, they would be aggregated for the purposes of these limits.

Combined Plan Deduction Limits

If an employer maintains both a defined contribution and a defined benefit plan at the same time, the individual plan limits discussed above apply separately to each type of plan. However, in some situations, there is also an overall limitation to the deduction allowed to an employer for the combined plans.

If the defined benefit plan is subject to coverage by the Pension Benefit Guaranty Corporation (PBGC), there is no combined plan deduction limit, only the individual plan limits discussed above. If the defined benefit plan is not subject to the PBGC coverage, and if any employee participates in both plans, the maximum employer deduction is limited to the greater of 25% of the total compensation of all employees participating in either plan, or the minimum required contribution of the defined benefit plan. This limit applies to employer-paid contributions, including pension, profit sharing, and matching contributions. Employee 401(k) salary deferral contributions are not subject to the 25% deduction limit.

Employer-paid contributions to a defined contribution plan that do not exceed 6% of total compensation of all employees participating in the defined contribution plan do not count toward this 25% deduction limit.

---

[1] These are 2018 limits. In some instances these limits may be reduced.

[2] These are 2018 limits.

Combinations of Retirement Plans

For example, assume an employer maintains both a defined benefit and a defined contribution plan, such as a profit sharing plan. Assume also that the total payroll of covered participants in either plan is $100,000 and that the required defined benefit contribution is $20,000. The most that could be contributed and deducted for the profit sharing plan is $11,000. (25% x $100,000 = $25,000; $25,000-$20,000 = $5,000; 6% x $100,000 = $6,000; $5,000 + $6,000 = $11,000). If the employer in this example were to contribute $13,500 to the profit sharing plan, $2,500 of the contribution would be nondeductible. There would also be a 10% excise tax on the non-deductible $2,500.

If the required defined benefit plan contribution were $35,000, the employer could contribute and deduct the entire $35,000. However, the deductible contribution to the profit sharing plan would be limited to $6,000. If the defined contribution plan has a mandatory contribution (e.g., a target benefit or money purchase plan) a contribution is still required even though it may exceed the deductible limit and incur the 10% excise tax on the non-deductible portion.

Combined Plans with 401(k) Feature

Many different plan combinations are possible. One common arrangement is that of a defined benefit plan paired with a 401(k)/profit sharing plan. Consider what could be contributed and deducted in 2018 for an owner-only business, with the owner over age 50:

Individual	Compensation	Defined Benefit[1]	Profit Sharing	401(k)	Total
Owner	$275,000	$212,000	$16,500	$24,500	$253,000

If there are employees in addition to an owner-employee, the 401(k) might also provide for a safe harbor contribution and a tiered profit sharing contribution. With younger employees, and using a tiered 401(k) safe harbor plan with the defined benefit plan, the amount that could be contributed and deducted in 2018 would be:

---

[1] Normal cost plus 50% funding cushion.

Combinations of Retirement Plans

Individual	Compensation	Defined Benefit[1]	Safe Harbor & Profit Sharing[2]	401(k)[3]	Total
Owner	$275,000	$148,000	$36,500	$24,500	$209,000
Employee 1	$50,000	$830	$4,500	$0	$5,330
Employee 2	$35,000	$460	$3,150	$0	$3,610
TOTAL	$360,000	$149,290	$44,150	$24,500	$217,940

There is a special exception to the 25% deduction limit. If no single employee participates in both plans, the 25% deduction limit does not apply. If this occurs, other discrimination problems may arise unless the plans are designed to work together to satisfy IRS rules.

Sequential Plans

Rather than adopting two different types of plans simultaneously, an employer may choose to use different types of plans, at different points in time. Prior to 2000, a complicated set of rules and limits effectively made it impossible for one employer to have different types of plans, even at different times. For plan years beginning January 1, 2000 and later, however, the former rules and limits no longer applied.

In the mid-1980s, for example, many defined benefit plans were terminated because a change in the law made them fully funded. Under the new rules, an employer who terminated such a plan could now adopt a defined contribution plan, and contribute and deduct the maximum allowable for all eligible participants.

An employer may have chosen a defined contribution plan in the past because the key participants were younger. After many years these same key people could benefit more from a defined benefit plan. With the increased flexibility now available, the employer could switch to a defined benefit plan. Given the deduction limits applicable to combined plans, the employer could adopt a maximum defined benefit plan and either terminate the defined contribution plan or reduce its contribution to no more than 6% of compensation.

---

[1] Plus funding cushion of approximately 50% if desired.

[2] Profit sharing contribution may exceed 6% of pay if the defined benefit plan is subject to Pension Benefit Guaranty Corporation coverage.

[3] The 401(k) deferrals shown are for the owner as part of the owner's contribution. No contribution is shown for the employees as they depend on individual employee elections and are not paid by the employer, but by the employee.

Combinations of Retirement Plans

Allowable Combinations of Employer-Sponsored Plans

The table below lists the allowable combinations of employer-sponsored retirement plans:

Plan Type	Defined Benefit Plan	Defined Contribution Pension[1]	Defined Contribution Profit-Sharing[2]	Simple IRA	Simple 401(k)	SEP
Defined benefit plan	Yes	Yes	Yes	No	No	Maybe[3]
Defined contribution pension[1]	Yes	Yes	Yes	No	No	Yes
Defined contribution profit-sharing[2]	Yes	Yes	Yes	No	No	Yes
Simple IRA	No	No	No	No	No	No
Simple 401(k)	No	No	No	No	No	No
SEP	Maybe[3]	Yes	Yes	No	No	Yes

[1] Defined contribution money purchase or target benefit plans, including tiered or cross-tested varieties.
[2] Profit sharing plans such as 401(k), ESOPs and stock bonus plans, as well as tiered or cross-tested variations.
[3] Depends on whether this is allowed in the SEP plan documents.

Top-Heavy Plans

While large qualified retirement plans are rarely top heavy, most small plans are. In fact, the smaller the plan, the more likely it is to be top heavy.

When Is a Qualified Retirement Plan Top Heavy?[1]

- If the total present value of the accrued benefits for key participants in a defined benefit plan exceeds 60% of the present value of all benefits in the plan, the plan is top heavy.

- If the total account values for key employees in a defined contribution plan exceed 60% of the total value of all accounts, the plan is top heavy.

Key Participants

Key participants are any participants and participants' beneficiaries who, during the determination year:[2]

- are or were an officer of the sponsoring employer and earning more than $175,000[3];

- owned more than 5%[4] of the employer; or

- owned more than 1%[4] of the employer and received more than $150,000 of compensation from the employer.

Special Requirements for Top-Heavy Plans

- Vesting must either provide that a participant is fully vested after three years of service[5] or the vesting schedule must provide for graded vesting over six years of service[5] (0-20-40-60-80-100). More rapid vesting is permitted.

- For defined contribution plans, the employer must contribute and allocate to non-key participants the lesser of 3%[6] of compensation or the highest contribution percent of

---

[1] If there are multiple plans, they are generally aggregated together for determination purposes. Money rolled out or transferred is generally added back to the distributing plan as a key or non-key account for a period of five years (reduced to one year in 2002) and ignored by the receiving plan. In the case of mergers, the opposite is true.

[2] In-service distributions are subject to a five-year look-back period.

[3] This value applies to 2018.

[4] The family attribution rules of IRC Sec. 318 apply. Any participant is deemed to have the same ownership share as his or her spouse, children, parents and grandparents. In community property states spousal attribution may apply.

[5] In some instances, participation may be substituted for service.

[6] This may be higher in some circumstances.

any key employee. Elective deferrals by a key employee under a 401(k) plan are considered to be an employer contribution.[1] The plan may require that a participant be employed at the end of the plan year; it may not require that the participant work a minimum number of hours.

- For defined benefit plans, the employer must contribute and provide for a minimum benefit accrual of 2%[2] of average compensation for a maximum of ten years of participation. The plan may not require that a participant be employed at the end of the plan year; it may require that the participant perform 1,000 (or less) hours of service during the plan year.

- If the employer maintains multiple plans, top-heavy minimum contributions requirements do not have to be satisfied in all plans; special rules apply.

- If a plan is in the process of termination, top-heavy requirements continue to apply. Typically, this will apply only to plans that are not otherwise "frozen" at the time the plan is terminated.

- However, if a defined benefit plan is "frozen", the plan does not need to provide ongoing top-heavy benefit accruals.

- Depending on the plan document, the plan may or may not have to provide top-heavy contributions or benefits to key participants.

- Failure to provide the proper top-heavy benefit accruals or contributions will result in the plan being disqualified.

- If a plan has dual eligibility for different plan contributions, eligibility for any benefit makes a non-key employee eligible to receive a top-heavy benefit, if applicable. Example: A 401(k) plan has no service requirement for employee deferrals but requires one year of service for employer discretionary allocations. A 3% or more deferral by a key employee participant will trigger a 3% top-heavy contribution for all participants including those eligible for employee deferrals only.

---

[1] Beginning in 2002, matching contributions are credited to meeting the top-heavy minimum contribution requirement.
[2] This percentage may be higher in some circumstances.

Fiduciary Standards and Responsibilities

One of the most important functions associated with all qualified retirement plans is the fiduciary role. The definition of fiduciary is a wide ranging one. Section 3 (21) (a) of ERISA[1] defines a fiduciary with respect to a plan to the extent he or she:

"Exercises any discretionary authority or discretionary control respecting management of such plan or exercises any authority or control respecting management of its assets, renders investment advice for a fee or other compensation, direct or indirect, with respect to any moneys or other property of such plan or, has any discretionary authority or discretionary responsibility in the administration of such plan."

Department of Labor (DOL) Regulation 2510.3-21 exempts a securities broker or dealer if that person transacts the purchase or sale of securities on behalf of the plan, in the ordinary course of business as a broker or dealer, if the plan fiduciary is not the broker or dealer and the broker or dealer is operating under instructions from the plan. An insurance agent is similarly exempted if he or she provides the disclosure required in DOL Class Exemption 84-24.[2]

Duties of a Plan Fiduciary

- The fiduciary must follow the prudent man rule, but is held to a higher standard than the normal prudent man rule. ERISA states that the fiduciary is required to discharge his duties "with the care, skill, prudence and diligence under circumstances then prevailing that a prudent man acting in a like capacity and familiar with such matters would use in the conduct of an enterprise of a like character and with like aims."[3]
- A fiduciary has the duty to diversify plan investments so as to minimize the risk of large losses, unless, under the circumstances, it is clearly not prudent to do so.[4] Investment of plan assets in a single bank or other pooled fund, mutual funds, annuity contracts, or life insurance contracts will satisfy the diversification rule if the fund itself is properly diversified.[5]

---

[1] ERISA refers to the Employee Retirement Income Security Act of 1974.
[2] See DOL Reg. 2510.3-21 and DOL Class Exemption 84-24 for more details.
[3] See ERISA Sec. 404(a)(1)
[4] See ERISA Sec. 404(a)(1)(C)
[5] See H Rep. No. 1280, 93rd Cong., 2nd Sess. 305 (1974).

Fiduciary Standards and Responsibilities

- The fiduciary is required to invest plan assets exclusively for the benefit of plan participants and beneficiaries.
- Fiduciaries must act in accordance with the plan documents unless that would violate the law.
- The fiduciary must arrange to purchase the bond required under ERISA. The amount of the bond must be at least 10% of the value of the plan assets.

- Unless given a funding policy by the sponsoring employer or plan trustee, the fiduciary must develop a funding policy for the plan and measure results against such policy on an annual basis.

  - If there are multiple fiduciaries, each fiduciary is responsible for the acts of the other fiduciary(s) unless the fiduciary authority has been delegated in writing to another specific fiduciary(s).

  - If plan assets do not have a readily determinable value, the fiduciary must determine their market value annually. It may be advisable to have an independent appraisal done, depending on the fiduciary's ability to determine the assets' market value.

  - A fiduciary may not engage (directly or indirectly) in the following activities between the fiduciary and the plan:

    - Sale, exchange or lease of property.
    - Lending money or extending credit.
    - Furnishing goods, services or facilities.
    - The transfer of assets to or for the use of the fiduciary.
    - Dealing with the plan assets for his or her own account.
    - Receiving any payment from a party dealing with a transaction involving plan assets.

CPA Audit Requirements

Plans with 100 or more participants at the beginning of the year must obtain an audit by a CPA for that plan year. There is one exception. If the plan in the prior year had less than 100 participants at the beginning of that year, and the current plan year has 120 or fewer participants at the beginning of the year, the CPA audit will not be required.

Fiduciary Standards and Responsibilities

In addition, for plan years beginning on or after April 12, 2001, a CPA audit must be obtained regardless of the number of participants in the plan. If the plan meets either of the two following exceptions a CPA audit will not be required:

- At least 95% of the plan assets as of the end of the prior plan year are "Qualifying Assets." Qualifying Assets are assets held by banks, insurance companies, broker dealers, mutual funds, or for an individually directed account plan, the participant may direct the investment of these assets and receive statements at least annually.

  In addition, the Summary Annual Report given to each must identify the financial institution holding those assets. If there is a bond for non-qualifying assets exceeding 5% of the plan assets, the surety company must be identified. Lastly, the participant must be notified that he or she may examine the bond or the financial reports issued by the qualifying institutions.

- The plan may obtain a bond equal to 100% of the value of the non-qualifying assets as of the end of the prior plan year

It should be stressed that the plan must obtain both bonds if there are non-qualifying assets and the plan does not want to have a full CPA audit.

Failure to satisfy the CPA audit requirement or one of the exceptions for smaller plans means that the annual return is an incomplete filing resulting in penalties for non-filing.

Prohibited Transactions Rules

Certain transactions between the plan and a disqualified person are prohibited.

Prohibited Transactions

- Sale, exchange or lease of property.

- Lending money or extending credit.

- Furnishing goods, services or facilities.

- The transfer of assets to or the use of assets by a disqualified person.

Disqualified Persons

- A plan fiduciary.
- Persons providing services to the plan.
- The employer of plan participants.
- Employee organizations with members in the plan.
- A 50% or more owner of the plan sponsor.
- A spouse, lineal descendant (or spouse) or ancestor of any person described above.
- A partnership, corporation, trust or estate of which 50% or more is owned, directly or indirectly, by a person described in items one through five.
- An officer, director, 10% or more shareholder, employee earning 10% or more of the yearly wages of the employer, or a person described in items three, four, five, and seven.
- A 10% or more partner or joint venturer of a person described in items three, four, five, and seven (IRC Section 4975(e)(2)).

Additional Prohibitions

- A fiduciary is prohibited from dealing with plan assets for his or her own account.

- A fiduciary may not receive any payment from a party dealing with a transaction involving plan assets.

Prohibited Transactions Rules

Penalties for Engaging in a Prohibited Transaction

There is a basic penalty leveled against the party engaging in the transaction equal to 15% of the value of the transaction. In the case of buying property, this would be the sale price. In the case of a loan, the value of the transaction is the interest charged for the use of the money.

Once made, the prohibited transaction is deemed to be a continuing one until corrected by: (a) undoing it; (b) a deficiency notice is delivered; or (c) the penalty tax itself is levied. If, for example, a prohibited transaction occurred in December of year one, in January of year two it is deemed to occur again.

Not only is the 15% penalty levied again in year two but also there is a pyramiding that occurs when the prohibited transaction is not corrected. In year two, there is a 15% tax levied on the prohibited transaction that occurred in year one and that continued in year two. There is also a 15% penalty assessed for the same transaction in year two. Hence, the total penalty for the two years is 15% for the initial year plus another 30% for year two for a total of 45%.

If the prohibited transaction is not reversed by the time the IRS assesses this 15% excise tax, a tax of 100% of the amount involved in the prohibited transaction will be assessed.

Exemptions

There are two types of exemptions.

- **Statutory:** IRC Section 4975(d), ERISA Secs. 407 and 408.

- **Administrative:** This type is granted by the Department of Labor (DOL) either for individual transactions or on a class basis for repetitive or identical transactions. The DOL will not grant an exemption for an act that has already occurred. DOL exemptions are prospective only.

Qualified Plan Participant Loans

Most transactions between a qualified plan and its participants are prohibited transactions. One exception to the prohibited transaction rules concerns the granting of a loan to a plan participant.

Rules for Plan Loans

In order for the exception to apply, certain rules must be followed:

- The maximum loan must not exceed the lesser of 50% of the vested benefit of the participant or $50,000. The largest outstanding balance of any participant loan outstanding during the prior 12 months further reduces this amount.

- The loan must be fully amortized over a period not to exceed five years. In addition, the repayment must be on at least a quarterly basis. More commonly this will be done on a monthly or semi-monthly basis through payroll deduction.[1]

- The loan must bear a reasonable rate of interest. While the government does not give a specific guideline as to what is reasonable, a rule of thumb that has served through the years and has stood the test of time is that reasonable is prime plus 1% or 2%. The plan could also check with local banks for their rates on secured loans.

- If the participant borrowing from the plan is married, then that participant's spouse must also consent to the loan, if the plan or law so requires.

- If the loan is renegotiated during its term, it is considered a new loan. This will often cause additional problems with either the $50,000 maximum limit or the five-year repayment period requirement.

- The plan must have a loan policy and qualification process for granting loans, including a reasonable effort to determine credit worthiness.

---

[1] If the participant goes on active military duty, the loan repayments are suspended.

Qualified Plan Participant Loans

If these rules are not followed, then the participant loan falls outside of the exception and serious results can occur. The outstanding principal and any unpaid interest will be a deemed distribution[1] to the borrower and taxable as ordinary income to that participant in the year during which one or more of the rules are broken. It is entirely possible that the IRS could seek to disqualify the plan in an egregious situation. If this were to occur, the vested benefits of all participants could be immediately taxable to them.

---

[1] While interest will continue to accrue on the defaulted loan, it will not create additional deemed income.

Unrelated Business Taxable Income

UBTI

Under the provisions of IRC Sec. 501(a), a qualified plan trust is treated as a tax-exempt organization. Income and gain from investments held in the trust are not currently taxed.

If, however, the trust operates a trade or business that is not substantially related to the trust's tax-exempt function (funding qualified plan benefits), any income or gain from this activity will be subject to current income taxation.[1] In other words, the trust may not operate an ongoing business, without the income received from the business being taxed to the trust each year.

However, the plan may deduct expenses against income in the year of occurrence. The plan is also entitled to a $1,000 exemption against income. If realized losses and expenses exceed income during the year, these may not be carried forward to future years.

IRC Sec. 514 provides that income earned through the use of debt financing by a tax-exempt organization is taxed currently as unrelated business taxable income (UBTI).

A common transaction that violates this rule is the purchase of securities on margin, using borrowed money. Borrowing the cash value from a life insurance policy to make an investment is another common violation. However, using the cash value to pay premiums on that policy is not a prohibited transaction.

Certain types of real estate transactions are exempt even though a property produces what would normally be considered unrelated business income. However, strict rules[2] must be followed to avoid having the income taxed as UBTI. These rules include:

- At the time of purchase, the sale price must be fixed.

- The timing of the repayment of the debt, or the amount of the debt itself, cannot be pegged to the income derived from the property or the profits arising from the property.

- The real estate cannot be purchased from a disqualified person[3] unless the seller is a fiduciary or provider of services. Furthermore, if such seller provides financing (owner financing), it must be on commercially-reasonable terms.

---

[1] See IRC Secs. 511-513.
[2] See IRC Sec. 514(c)(9).
[3] See IRC Sec. 4975(e)(2).

Unrelated Business Taxable Income

- Some sale/leaseback arrangements will trigger UBTI taxes. A sale/leaseback is permitted to an unrelated[1] party. If the seller is a related party, then the amount of the leaseback may not exceed 25% of the rentable space in the building or complex. The lease must be on commercially reasonable terms.

Calculating UBTI – An Example

After a $1,000 exemption, the income and gain are subject to income tax in the same ratio as the borrowing is to the total value of the asset.

Assume a qualified plan trust buys $100,000 of stock in High Flyer, Inc. To fund the purchase, half of the price, $50,000, is borrowed from the brokerage firm (on margin), with the remaining $50,000 coming from plan funds. The stock is held for two years, and is then sold for a total of $130,000.

The amount of UBTI is calculated as follows.

Value of stock when sold	$130,000
Purchase price	-100,000
Gross profit	**30,000**
Interest expense in year of sale	-5,000
Net taxable income	**25,000**
Percent of total value financed	50%
Amount subject to current tax	12,500
Exemption	-1,000
Net amount subject to income tax[2]	**$11,500**

Reporting and Paying the UBTI

UBTI is reported by the plan separately by filing IRS Form 990-T; it is not reported on the plan's Form 5500 return.

---

[1] See IRC Sec. 267(b).
[2] Capital gains are not relevant to the example.

Retirement Plan Distributions
Before Age 59½

Federal law[1] provides significant income tax benefits to the various types of employer-sponsored and individual retirement plans. Contributions may be tax-deductible and growth inside an account is tax-deferred. The purpose of these tax breaks is to encourage and reward saving for retirement.

If funds are taken out of an account before an owner reaches age 59½, however, the distribution is viewed as being "early" and a 10% penalty[2] is applied to that portion of the distribution which is includable in gross income. The extra 10% penalty, plus the ordinary income tax, can make the total tax burden on such distributions painfully high.

How Bad Is The Tax "Bite"?

Assume that an individual who is in the 25% federal income tax bracket takes a withdrawal of $10,000 from his 401(k) plan. How much will he pay in taxes on that distribution?

Initial amount withdrawn:	$10,000
Less: federal income tax @25%	- 2,500
Less: 10% penalty tax:	- 1,000
= **Net after taxes:**	**$6,500**

Our hypothetical taxpayer must surrender 35% of the amount initially withdrawn just to pay federal income taxes. If state or local law also taxes such distributions, the total cost would be even higher.

What Types Of Retirement Plans Are Subject To The 10% Penalty?

Two types of retirement plans[3] are subject to the 10% penalty for early withdrawal:

- **Qualified plans:** Include "qualified" defined contribution retirement plans such as IRC Sec. 401(k) plans, IRC Sec. 403(b) plans and IRC Sec. 403(b) annuity contracts, IRC Sec.

---

[1] The discussion here concerns federal income tax law. State or local law may differ.

[2] Distributions before age 59½ from SIMPLE IRA plans made within the first two years of participation are subject to a 25% penalty, rather than a 10% penalty, subject to the exceptions discussed here. If a premature distribution from a SIMPLE IRA is made after two years of participation, the 10% penalty applies, subject to the exceptions.

[3] Life insurance policies considered to be "modified endowment contracts" and commercially purchased individual annuities are also subject to a 10% penalty, in certain situations.

Retirement Plan Distributions Before Age 59½

403(a) annuity plans, SIMPLE 401(k) plans, and Profit Sharing and Money Purchase plans. Distributions from IRC Sec. 457 plans are generally not subject to the 10% penalty.

- **Individual retirement plans:** Include traditional IRAs, Roth IRAs, individual retirement annuities, Simplified Employee Pension (SEP) IRAs, and SIMPLE IRA plans.

Possible Exceptions to the 10% Penalty Tax

The table below lists the major exceptions to the 10% penalty tax:

General Description	Applicable To Qualified Plans?	Applicable To IRAs?
Separation from service after age 55. Distributions made to an employee after separating from service after reaching age 55.[1]	Yes	No
Qualified Domestic Relations Order (QDRO). Distributions made to an alternate payee, such as in a divorce.	Yes	No
Death or disability. Distributions made due to the death or disability of the account owner.	Yes	Yes
Substantially equal periodic payments. Distributions that are part of a series of substantially equal periodic payments made over the life (or life expectancy) of the taxpayer or made over the joint life (or joint life expectancies) of the taxpayer and a beneficiary.	Yes	Yes
Medical expenses. Distributions made to pay for deductible medical expenses. Only the portion that <u>exceeds</u> 7.50% of AGI is exempt from the 10% penalty.[2]	Yes	Yes

[1] In the case of certain public safety officials, an exception applies to distributions made after separating from service after age 50.
[2] Under current federal law, the 7.50 % threshold applies to 2017 and 2018. This threshold is scheduled to increase to 10.0% for 2019 and later years. State or local law may vary.

Retirement Plan Distributions Before Age 59½

General Description	Applicable To Qualified Plans?	Applicable To IRAs?
Higher education expenses. Distributions made to pay for "qualified higher education expenses" for the taxpayer, spouse, child, or grandchild. The expenses must be incurred in the year of distribution and generally include tuition, fees, books, supplies and equipment required for attendance at an eligible educational institution.	No	Yes
First-time homebuyer. Distributions of up to $10,000 to buy, build, or rebuild a first home. A "first-time homebuyer" is someone who had no ownership in a principal residence in the two years prior to buying the new home. The funds must be used within 120 days of receipt.	No	Yes
Unemployed health insurance premiums. Distributions made to certain unemployed individuals to pay for health insurance premiums. The individual must have lost a job and generally must have received unemployment compensation for at least 12 weeks because of the job loss.	No	Yes
Qualified reservist. Distributions made to a military reservist called to active duty for more than 179 days (or indefinitely) after September 11, 2001. Such distributions may be repaid within two years after the end of active duty.	Yes	Yes
Transfer to a Health Savings Account (HSA). A once-in-a-lifetime distribution of amounts in a traditional or Roth IRA, in a direct, trustee-to-trustee transfer. The distribution is limited to the maximum amount for the year that could otherwise be contributed to the HSA and deducted.	No	Yes
IRS levy on the account. Distributions made to satisfy an IRS levy on the account.	Yes	Yes
Qualified rollover. Generally, a transfer of funds from one IRA or qualified plan to an eligible recipient IRA or qualified plan are exempt.	Yes	Yes
Correct excess contributions. Generally, distributions made to correct excess contributions, either by the account owner, the employer, or both are exempt.	Yes	Yes

Retirement Plan Distributions Before Age 59½

General Description	Applicable To Qualified Plans?	Applicable To IRAs?
Phased retirement for certain federal employees. An exception applies to pension annuity payments and composite retirement annuity payments paid to certain federal employees participating in a phased retirement program.	Certain federal employees only.	No
2017 Hurricane Victims – Harvey, Irma, and Maria. Individuals affected by the three hurricanes, and who suffered an economic loss, may withdraw up to $100,000 in "qualified hurricane distributions" from an IRA or other qualified retirement plan. Such distributions are not subject to the 10% early withdrawal penalty. Qualifying distributions must be made before January 1, 2019, and on or after August 23, 2017 for victims of Hurricane Harvey, on or after September 4, 2017 for Hurricane Irma victims, and on or after September 16, 2017 for victims of Hurricane Maria.	Yes	Yes
2017 California Wildfire Victims. Individuals affected by the California wildfires, and who suffered an economic loss, may withdraw up to $100,000 in "qualified wildfire distributions" from an IRA or other qualified retirement plan. Such distributions are not subject to the 10% early withdrawal penalty. Qualifying distributions must be made before January 1, 2019, and on or after October 8, 2017.	Yes	Yes

Seek Professional Guidance

The income tax treatment of distributions from employer-sponsored and individual retirement plans is complex and often confusing. Given the potentially heavy cost of such withdrawals, individuals considering taking funds from a retirement plan before reaching age 59½ are strongly advised to first seek the guidance of a Certified Public Accountant (CPA), IRS enrolled agent (EA), or other competent professional.

Substantially Equal Periodic Payments - 72(t)

Item Description	Value
Account Balance	$150,000
Client Age	35
Beneficiary Age	8
Life Expectancy Table	Single Life Expectancy
Interest Rate	6.00%
Fixed Annuitization	**$9,220**
Fixed Amortization	**$9,567**
Minimum Distribution[1]	**$3,093**

Amount to be Withdrawn

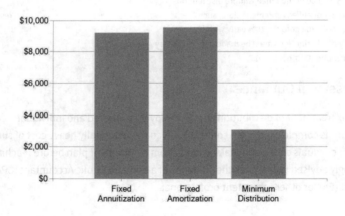

---

[1] The Required Minimum Distribution method must be recalculated each year, as it is based on the account balance at the end of the previous year.

Lump-Sum Distributions Before Age 59½

Qualified Plan Funds when Leaving an Employer

When terminating or changing employment prior to age 59½, a person often has several options as to what to do with the funds in his or her qualified retirement plan:

- Leave funds in current plan: If the current value exceeds $5,000, there may be some benefit to leaving the funds where they are. They will continue to grow tax-deferred and can be transferred at a later date to a rollover IRA or a new employer's eligible recipient plan.

- Take cash in lump sum: This option will require the entire amount (less participant after-tax contributions, if any) to be subject to income taxes in the participant's current tax bracket. There will be an additional 10% penalty tax for a participant under age 59½ unless he or she falls under certain exceptions.[1] The law requires that 20% of the taxable portion of the distribution be withheld for federal income taxes.[2]

- Rollover or transfer within 60 days: Individuals who receive a cash, lump-sum distribution have a 60-day period during which funds may be transferred to either a rollover IRA or a new employer's qualified plan. Because this is a cash distribution, a 20% federal income tax withholding is required. Failure to transfer the funds within the 60-day period will result in the total amount (cash received plus the amount withheld) being added to taxable income for the year. Further, if an individual is under age 59½ at the time of distribution, the total amount will be subject to the 10% penalty tax on early distributions, unless an exception applies.[3]

---

[1] Distributions before age 59½ from SIMPLE IRA plans made within the first two years of participation are subject to a 25% penalty, rather than a 10% penalty subject to the usual exceptions. If a premature distribution from a SIMPLE IRA is made after two years of participation, the 10% penalty applies. See IRC Sec. 72(t)(6). SIMPLE IRAs are not subject to the 20% mandatory withholding requirement.

[2] State law may differ on both the withholding requirements and the penalties for withdrawals prior to age 59½.

[3] Distributions from a Qualified Roth Contribution Program will be subject to the 20% withholding requirement only to the extent of any taxable earnings.

Lump-Sum Distributions Before Age 59½

- Make a direct transfer: The distribution can be transferred directly from the original, employer-sponsored qualified plan to another employer plan or to a rollover IRA. Since the participant does not actually receive the funds, there is no 20% withholding.

Potential Problem

However, if the plan withholds 20% for federal income taxes, which cannot be returned until after the tax returns for that year are filed, the participant may have to come up with additional funds to make a full rollover.

For example, assume a distribution of $100,000 made directly to a terminating employee. The employer would withhold 20%, or $20,000, for income tax purposes and the employee would receive only $80,000 in cash. If the employee decides within the 60-day period to roll the fund over into an IRA or a new employer's qualified plan, then he or she must come up with another $20,000 to make the full transfer.

If the funds are not found to make the full $100,000 transfer, then the $20,000 withheld becomes taxable to the employee as ordinary income. If the employee is under age 59½ when the distribution is made, a 10% penalty tax may also be due, unless certain exceptions apply.

Possible Solutions

To avoid this potential problem, the participant must make some decisions before the plan administrator prepares the check. If the transfer is made directly to a rollover IRA or a new qualified plan, the 20% is not withheld and the entire amount can be transferred.

An alternative might be for the participant to transfer the funds to a rollover IRA, and then elect to receive substantially-equal payments over his or her life expectancy and that of another person, if desired.

IRA Rollover of Qualified Plan Values vs. Lump-Sum Tax Treatment

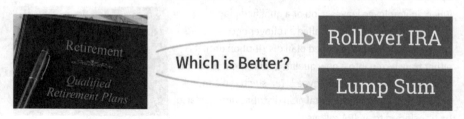

Retirement

Qualified
Retirement Plans

Which is Better?

Rollover IRA

Lump Sum

At retirement, many individuals are faced with the choice of whether to take a lump sum distribution from their qualified plan and pay the income tax or roll the funds into an IRA[1] and pay the tax only as funds are withdrawn.

Consideration	Rollover IRA	Lump-Sum Distribution from Qualified Plan[2]
Generally	Lump sum[3] distributions from qualified plans may be transferred to an arrangement called a "rollover" IRA. To avoid the mandatory 20% federal income tax withholding rule, the payment must be made directly to the rollover IRA.	The taxpayer may choose to take all of a qualified retirement plan distribution outright and pay the tax.[4] There will be a mandatory 20% federal income tax withholding. Some states may also require income tax withholding.
Taxation at distribution	No tax is due at the time of the transfer to the IRA, but later distributions are taxed as ordinary income. The IRA must begin distribution by April 1 following the year in which the individual attains age 70½.	Taxpayers age 50 or more on 1/1/86 will have a choice at retirement age to: (1) Pay tax at capital gains rates (up to 20%) on pre-1974 portion and at ordinary income rates for the post-1973 portion, or (2) Elect 10-year averaging for the post-1973 portion or the entire amount (at 1986 rates).

---

[1] The comments in this report refer to a traditional IRA and not the Roth IRA.

[2] Individuals must be at least age 59½ to avoid the 10% income tax penalty for early withdrawals, subject to certain exceptions.

[3] There are special requirements for lump-sum distributions.

[4] If a lump-sum distribution from a qualified plan includes appreciated employer securities, the tax on the net unrealized appreciation may be deferred until the securities are disposed of in a taxable transaction.

IRA Rollover as a Qualified Plan Conduit

When an employee leaves a job or a qualified plan is terminated, a special IRA – called a rollover or conduit IRA - can be used to hold a qualified plan distribution until it is either transferred into a new qualified retirement plan or is later distributed to the employee.[1] Tax-sheltered annuity and IRC Sec. 457 governmental plan distributions may also be transferred to an IRA rollover.

If the distribution is transferred to an IRA rollover[2] (or another qualified plan) in a direct rollover, no income tax is withheld and the employee avoids current income tax on the distribution.

If the distribution is first paid to the employee before being rolled over (it must be rolled over within 60 days) the plan administrator will withhold 20% of the distribution. In order to roll over the entire distribution and avoid current taxation (and a possible 10% penalty tax on the 20% of the distribution that was withheld), the employee will have to make up the 20% withholding from his or her separate funds.

Distributions from a traditional IRA, Roth IRA, or SIMPLE IRA are not subject to the mandatory 20% tax withholding. However, if the distribution is not rolled to a plan of the same kind within 60 days, the entire distribution is generally taxable.[3]

Two Options

A qualified plan participant has two options when leaving a job:

- Participant may retain funds in an IRA until age 70½ and then begin distributions.

- Participant may roll the funds over from the conduit IRA into another qualified plan (if permitted). This will requalify the funds for 10-year[4] averaging as long as no regular IRA contributions have been made to the conduit IRA.

---

[1] Based on federal law. State or local law may differ.

[2] The IRA referred to here is a traditional IRA, not a Roth IRA.

[3] If a SIMPLE IRA is rolled to any other type of IRA within two years of the SIMPLE IRA being established, a 25% penalty tax is assessed.

[4] Those born before 1936 may be able to elect 10-year income averaging or capital gain treatment; these strategies are not available to those born after 1935.

IRA Rollover as a Qualified Plan Conduit

Other Considerations

- Partial distributions can also qualify as eligible rollover distributions and can be tax deferred.

- Both deductible and nondeductible employee contributions may be rolled to the IRA.

- Noncash assets which are distributed can be sold and the cash proceeds transferred to the rollover IRA without realizing a current tax on any gain.

- Amounts received but not rolled over are generally included in gross income in the year received. If the employee is under age 59½ when the funds are distributed, an additional 10% income tax penalty may apply, unless one of the exceptions in IRC Sec. 72(t) applies. Amounts withheld and remitted as tax withholding are considered to be amounts received.

- Following the decision of the U.S. Tax Court in *Bobrow v. Commissioner*, T.C. Memo. 2014-21, beginning January 1, 2015, the IRS intends to apply the IRC Sec. 408(d)(3)(B) one-rollover-per year limitation for IRAs on an *aggregate* basis, regardless of the number of separate IRA accounts that an individual may hold. Under prior IRS guidance, the one-rollover-per-year limitation applied on a *per-account* basis.

- The IRA conduit rollover should be distinguished from a direct trustee to trustee transfer. In a direct transfer, the funds are transferred directly from one plan to another without going through a conduit rollover or being distributed to the participant.

- Federal bankruptcy law provides significant protection from creditors to participant accounts or accrued benefits in tax-exempt retirement plans. Generally, assets in IRA accounts are protected for amounts up to $1,283,025.[1] However, funds rolled over from qualified plans are protected without limit.

---

[1] Effective April 1, 2016. The limit is indexed for inflation every three years.

Mandatory Withholding
for Plan Distributions

Administrators of qualified plans making distributions which are eligible to be rolled over are required to give a written explanation to participants who are about to receive a plan distribution. This notice must be given at least 30 days (7 days for some plans) and not more than 180 days before the distribution.

This explanation[1] should cover the following:

- Special tax treatment for lump sum distributions, e.g., 10-year[2] averaging (not available for IRAs or TSAs).

- Potential tax penalties for distributions prior to age 59½.

- If the plan is a pension or profit sharing plan subject to the joint-and-survivor rules, an explanation of these rules must also be provided along with various waiver forms. This material allows a participant and spouse the option to elect out of the joint and survivor annuity requirement, if they so desire.

- Regular rollover rules: If the plan distribution is made directly to the participant, he or she has a 60-day period to roll the funds into an IRA[3] to defer the tax. However, the plan administrator is required to withhold 20% of the plan distribution made to individuals, even if the distribution is rolled into an IRA within the 60-day period.[4] The amount withheld is sent to the IRS.

Potential Problem

Assume a hypothetical distribution of $100,000 from a qualified plan to the participant. The administrator is required to withhold 20% (or $20,000) of the distribution. If the participant takes the remaining $80,000 and rolls it into an IRA, he or she will be taxed on the $20,000 which was sent to the IRS because it is considered to be a taxable distribution. There may

---

[1] The IRS has issued sample text for this required explanation. See IRS Notice 2014-74.

[2] Those born before 1936 may be able to elect either 10-year averaging or capital gain treatment.

[3] The comments in this report refer to a traditional IRA and not the Roth IRA. Beginning in 2008, distributions from qualified retirement plans, IRC Sec. 457 plans, and tax-sheltered annuities may be rolled directly into a Roth IRA. These rollover distributions are taxable events, subject to the same requirements as a Roth conversion.

[4] Distributions from a Qualified Roth Contribution Program will be subject to the 20% withholding requirement only to the extent of any taxable earnings.

Mandatory Withholding for Plan Distributions

also be a penalty tax of 10% on the $20,000 if the recipient is less than age 59½, unless certain exceptions apply. To avoid this problem, the distributee could borrow $20,000 and thereby place the full $100,000 into the rollover IRA. The next year, the IRS would generally refund the $20,000 withheld and the loan could then be repaid.

Direct Rollover Option

To avoid the potential problem illustrated above, the administrator must notify plan distributees of the direct rollover option. The participant can elect to have the distribution made directly to the new IRA or a new qualified plan. This defers the tax and avoids the withholding rule.

Net Unrealized Appreciation

Assets distributed from an employer's qualified retirement plan are often transferred directly to a rollover IRA to avoid being currently taxed. However, if the distribution includes employer securities, such as employer stock, automatically moving these securities to a rollover IRA is not always the wise thing to do.

If certain requirements are met, federal income tax law provides preferential treatment to such distributions of employer securities. In effect, this special tax treatment transforms ordinary income into long-term capital gain income. For the right person, this can result in significant income tax savings.[1] Because issues other than income taxes may also be important, a careful analysis is required before deciding to transfer employer securities to a rollover IRA, move them to a taxable securities account, or some mix of the two.

What Is Net Unrealized Appreciation (NUA)?

For income tax purposes, each share of employer stock you receive has two parts:

Part	Description
Appreciation	The value per share when distributed, minus the cost basis.
Cost Basis	How much was paid to purchase the share.

Until the shares are sold, the value represented by the appreciation is "unrealized."

How Is NUA Taxed Under Federal Income Tax Law?

Federal income tax treatment of employer securities, once distributed from the plan, depends on whether they are moved into a taxable securities account or a rollover IRA:

- **Taxable securities account:** The cost basis is taxable in the year of distribution as ordinary income, subject to marginal tax rates of up to 37.0%. Income tax on the appreciation is deferred until the securities are sold, when it is taxable as long-term capital gain, regardless of the holding period. Currently, this type of long-term capital gain is subject to a maximum marginal tax rate of 20%.[2] Any appreciation occurring after the securities are distributed is taxable as capital gain, either short-term or long-term, depending on how long they are held after being distributed.[3] If a distribution of

---

[1] The discussion here concerns federal income tax law. State or local income tax law may vary widely.

[2] The marginal tax rate for this type of capital asset will be 0%, 15%, or 20% depending on the marginal tax rate generally applicable to the taxpayer's ordinary income.

[3] For federal income tax purposes, "long-term" is defined as holding an asset for more than 12 months. Short-term capital gain is taxed in the same manner as ordinary income.

employer securities is subject to the 10% penalty for early withdrawal, the 10% penalty applies only to the cost basis and not to the appreciation.

- **Rollover IRA:** Income tax on the cost basis, the appreciation, and any subsequent appreciation, is deferred until the securities are sold and the proceeds are distributed from the rollover IRA. Once distributed, all funds are taxable as ordinary income, at marginal tax rates of up to 37.0%

A Hypothetical Example

In this hypothetical example, stock was purchased at $25 a share inside the plan. At distribution, the stock had risen in value to $60 per share, giving rise to $35 of net unrealized appreciation. After distribution, the stock is held for a period of time before being sold. When finally sold, the share value had increased to $80 per share.

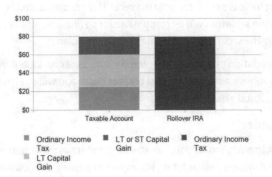

Lump-Sum Distribution Requirement

In order for NUA tax treatment to apply, a distribution from an employer's qualified plan must be a "lump-sum" distribution. A distribution is considered to be a lump-sum distribution if it is a distribution or payment within one taxable year of the recipient of the total balance to the credit of an employee and which becomes payable because of:

- The employee's death, or
- After the employee reaches age 59½, or

- Because the employee separates from service, or
- After the employee becomes disabled.

Without A Lump-Sum Distribution

If a distribution of employer securities is not part of a lump-sum distribution, NUA tax treatment applies only to appreciation attributable to <u>nondeductible employee contributions</u>, if any. If there are no nondeductible employee contributions, both the cost basis and the appreciation are taxable as ordinary income in the year of distribution.[1]

Estate Planning and NUA

Some individuals may simply want to keep any employer securities and pass them on to their children or other heirs, rather than using them to generate retirement income. If the securities are distributed from the qualified plan into a taxable securities account, the income tax due on the cost basis is paid in the year the securities are distributed. Later, the heirs who ultimately receive the securities will be responsible for paying the income tax due on the NUA that occurred while the securities were inside the qualified plan.

However, any appreciation that occurs <u>after</u> the securities are distributed from the employer plan will generally receive a stepped-up cost basis at death and will pass to the heirs free of federal income or capital gains taxes.

Issues to Consider

- **Income tax impact:** You, or your tax advisor, must "crunch the numbers" and calculate the potential income and/or estate tax impact of moving any qualified plan distribution into either a taxable account or a rollover IRA.
- **Need for portfolio diversification:** Is a large part of your retirement assets concentrated in employer stock? Perhaps a portion of the distribution should be transferred to a rollover IRA, with the remainder distributed to a taxable account. The employer securities inside the rollover IRA could then be sold, with no current tax impact, and the proceeds re-invested in a more diversified portfolio.

---

[1] Individuals who were born before January 1, 1936, may be eligible to use either 10-year forward averaging, at 1986 rates, or to pay the tax on any pre-1974 portion at capital gains rates of up to 20%.

- **Time until needed:** Those individuals with a longer period of time before retirement begins will likely benefit more from the NUA approach as any employer securities will have a longer period of time for post-distribution gain.
- **Gifts to individuals:** An individual can gift up to $15,000[1] per year per person to any number of people, without incurring a gift tax. A gift of NUA securities within these limits has no immediate tax consequences to either the donor or the recipient. The gift transfers the donor's basis in the securities to the recipient and removes both the current value, and any future growth, from the donor's estate.
- **Charitable planning:** Highly appreciated employer stock may be a useful asset to contribute to a charitable trust.

Seek Professional Guidance

Because of the complexities involved, the guidance of tax and financial professionals is highly recommended.

---

[1] 2018 value. This amount is subject to adjustment for inflation in future years.

The Basics of
Required Minimum Distributions

Ensuring that Uncle Sam Gets His Due

The benefits of retirement accounts such as a traditional IRA or a 401(k) are two-fold:

- Tax-deductible contributions allow individuals to reduce the size of their current tax burden while they are saving for retirement – which effectively lets them save more.

- Tax-deferred growth inside these accounts allows funds to accumulate without concern for an annual tax bill on that growth.

When It's Time to Pay Taxes

Eventually, however, the government must be paid. The tax benefits of these accounts are provided for one purpose: to help individuals save for retirement. Once an individual reaches retirement age, these same rules now dictate that the funds must be used for retirement purposes and the taxes that have been deferred must be paid.

What does this mean? It means that federal income tax law requires that a minimum amount of money must be withdrawn (distributed) from these accounts each year, starting at a specific age, known as the "required beginning date" (generally age 70½). The amount to be distributed is determined by a special calculation that, in essence, takes the total amount in the account and divides it by the number of years the individual is expected to live. When the required minimum distribution amount is received, it is included as taxable income to the individual and Uncle Sam will, finally, get paid. If an account owner does not make distributions that are large enough, or if distributions are not made at all, a penalty tax of 50% of the amount that should have been distributed is generally due.[1]

But, one bit of good news is that the amount remaining in the account continues to grow tax deferred.

---

[1] This is federal income tax law. State or local income tax law may differ.

The Basics of Required Minimum Distributions

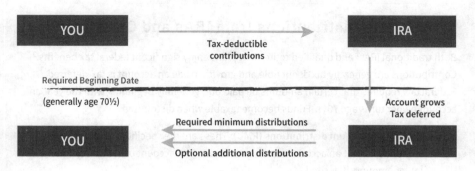

Required Minimum Distributions

Lifetime Distributions from IRAs and Qualified Plans

Both traditional IRAs[1] and qualified retirement plans enjoy significant federal tax benefits.[2] Contributions are generally tax deductible and growth inside an account is tax-deferred. Federal law requires that certain amounts be paid out, generally beginning with the year an account owner turns age 70½. Funds become taxable when distributed.

- **Required minimum distributions (RMD):** These are the specified, minimum withdrawals that an account owner must make. The account owner is free to take larger amounts if desired.

- **Required beginning date:** This is the date by which an account owner must begin to make his or her required minimum distributions.

- **Penalty tax:** If an account owner does not make distributions that are large enough, or if distributions are not made at all, a penalty tax of 50% of the amount that should have been distributed is generally due.

Item	Traditional IRAs	Qualified Plans
Required beginning date	By April 1 of the year following the year you attain age 70½.	By April 1 of the year following the later of (a) the year you reach age 70½, or (b) the year you retire. More than 5% owners must begin to receive distributions by April 1 of the year following the year they reach age 70½.
Initial distributions	If a required first withdrawal for 2018 is made by April 1, 2019, the required distribution for 2019 must be made by December 31, 2019. In effect there are two taxable distributions made in 2019. Each year thereafter, a distribution is required on or before December 31.	

---

[1] For required minimum distribution purposes "traditional IRAs" include SIMPLE IRAs and SEP IRAs. Roth IRAs are subject to different rules.

[2] This discussion concerns federal law only. State or local law may vary.

Required Minimum Distributions

Item	Traditional IRAs	Qualified Plans
More than one IRA or qualified retirement plan	If an individual has more than one IRA, the required minimum distribution must be determined for each IRA. However, the total required distribution may be made from any one or a combination of the IRAs. The IRAs may not be aggregated with employer-sponsored qualified retirement plans.	Generally, each plan must make its own separate required minimum distribution.
Other	The minimum distribution rules do not apply to Roth IRAs during the owner's lifetime.	Qualified plans include TSA 403(b), Keogh, 401(k), SIMPLE 401(k), and pension and profit sharing plans.

Calculating Required Minimum Distributions[1]

The actual amount that must be distributed each year is determined using:

- The balance in the account as of the previous December 31, and;

- The age of the account owner (and spouse, if married) at the end of the year.

The required minimum distribution is calculated by dividing the account balance by a theoretical life span taken from life expectancy tables provided by the Internal Revenue Service (IRS). The life expectancy table used will vary depending on the age of the account owner and, if married, his or her spouse. An individual's marital status is determined as of January 1 of the calendar year.

Single owner/spouse no more than 10 years younger: An IRA owner, age 75, has $100,000 in an IRA as of December 31 of the prior year. The required minimum distribution for the current year would be $4,366.81, ($100,000 divided by 22.9). The divisor of 22.9 is taken from the Uniform Lifetime Table for an individual age 75. The calculation is the same for a single individual or a married individual with a spouse no more than 10 years younger than the IRA owner.

---

[1] The rules reviewed here are those contained in the final regulations issued by the Treasury Department on April 16, 2002, in Treasury Decision 8987. Annuity contracts providing benefits under qualified plans, individual retirement plans, and IRC Sec. 403(b) contracts are subject to special rules. See Treasury Decision 9130.

Required Minimum Distributions

Spouse more than 10 Years Younger[1]: If the participant's spouse is more than 10 years younger than the participant, the minimum distribution factor used in calculating the required minimum distribution is found in the <u>Joint and Last Survivor Table.</u>

An IRA owner, age 75, has $100,000 in the IRA as of December 31 of the prior year. His wife is age 63. The required minimum distribution would be $4,115.23, $100,000 divided by 24.3, the Joint and Last Survivor Table factor for an owner age 75 and a spouse age 63.

Seek Professional Guidance

Given the complex and frequently changing nature of tax law, individuals faced with the need to make required distributions from IRAs or qualified retirement plans should seek the guidance of qualified professionals.

---

[1] The spouse must be the sole beneficiary of the account.

Required Minimum Distributions

Distributions from IRAs and Qualified Plans

Both traditional IRAs and qualified retirement plans enjoy significant federal tax benefits. Contributions are generally tax deductible and growth inside an account is tax deferred. Federal income tax law requires that certain amounts be paid out, generally beginning with the year an account owner turns age 70½.[1] Funds become taxable when distributed.

Assumptions:

Calculation year: 2018   Account owner's age at end of calculation year: 59
Estimated rate of return: 6.00%

Life expectancy determined using the IRS Uniform Lifetime Table

Annual contribution: $3,000, increasing at 3.00%, ending at age 70

Account balance at end of 2017: $200,000

Account Owner's Age	Life Expectancy	Prior Year Account Balance	Required Minimum Distribution
70	27.4	$431,066	$15,732
71	26.5	$441,198	$16,649
72	25.6	$451,021	$17,618
73	24.7	$460,464	$18,642
74	23.8	$469,450	$19,725
75	22.9	$477,892	$20,869
76	22.0	$485,697	$22,077
77	21.2	$492,761	$23,243
78	20.3	$499,083	$24,585
79	19.5	$504,443	$25,869
80	18.7	$508,841	$27,211
81	17.9	$512,161	$28,612
82	17.1	$514,278	$30,075
83	16.3	$515,060	$31,599
84	15.5	$514,365	$33,185
85	14.8	$512,042	$34,597

[1] Except for 5% owners, participants in qualified plans such as 401(k)s or 403(b)s have the option of beginning required minimum distributions (RMDs) at the later of age 70½ or the year they retire.

Required Minimum Distributions

Distributions from IRAs and Qualified Plans

Account Owner's Age	Life Expectancy	Prior Year Account Balance	Required Minimum Distribution
86	14.1	$508,167	$36,040
87	13.4	$502,617	$37,509
88	12.7	$495,265	$38,997
89	12.0	$485,984	$40,499
90	11.4	$474,644	$41,635
91	10.8	$461,487	$42,730
92	10.2	$446,446	$43,769
93	9.6	$429,464	$44,736
94	9.1	$410,496	$45,109
95	8.6	$390,016	$45,351

Required Minimum Distributions

Distributions from Traditional IRAs and Qualified Retirement Plans

Both traditional IRAs and qualified retirement plans enjoy significant federal tax benefits. Contributions are generally tax deductible and growth inside an account is tax deferred. Federal income tax law requires that certain amounts be paid out, generally beginning with the year an account owner turns age 70½.[1] Funds become taxable when distributed.

Assumptions:

Calculation year: 2018

Account owner's age at end of calculation year: 58

Estimated rate of return: 6.00%

Item	Value
Age of Account Owner	70
Life Expectancy	27.4
Prior Year Account Balance	$461,083
RMD	$16,828

Life expectancy determined using the IRS Uniform Lifetime Table Annual contribution: $3,000, increasing at 3.00%, ending at age 70

Account balance at end of 2017: $200,000

First Year's RMD Calculation

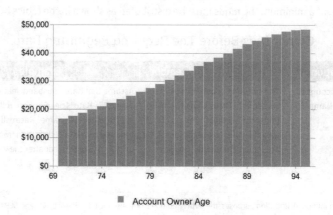

Account Owner Age

Values shown in this presentation are hypothetical and not a promise of future performance.

---

[1] Except for 5% owners, participants in qualified plans such as 401(k)s or 403(b)s have the option of beginning required minimum distributions (RMDs) at the later of age 70½ or the year they retire.

Required Minimum Distributions After Death

Spousal Beneficiary

Funds in both traditional IRAs[1] and qualified retirement plans may not be kept inside these tax-deferred accounts indefinitely. Under federal law the money must eventually be distributed, and then taxed, through yearly "Required Minimum Distributions," or RMDs.[2]

The death of an account owner does not eliminate this requirement. However, the manner in which the assets must be distributed post-death will vary, depending primarily on:

- **Death before or after the required beginning date:** During life, an account owner must generally begin distributions no later than April 1 of the year following the year he or she reaches age 70½. This is known as the "Required Beginning Date," or RBD.[3]

- **Who inherits the assets:** The law mandates different required minimum distribution schedules depending on who inherits the assets in an account.

Surviving Spouse Required Minimum Distributions

If the surviving spouse is the sole designated beneficiary, or if there is no designated beneficiary, at a minimum the funds must be distributed as shown in the tables below:

Owner Dies Before The Required Beginning Date

Situation	Distribution Requirement	Example
Rollover Account to Survivor's Name	The surviving spouse becomes the owner, with RMDs being taken under the normal "during lifetime" rules. No withdrawals are required until the surviving spouse reaches age 70½.	Assume that Kate's husband Jake dies in 2018 at age 67. Kate is age 65. Kate rolls the account over into her own name. Kate will not be required to take a distribution from the account until April 1 of the year after the year she reaches age 70½.

---

[1] For required minimum distribution purposes, the term "traditional IRA" also includes SIMPLE IRAs and SEP IRAs. Roth IRAs are subject to different rules.

[2] This discussion concerns federal income tax law. State or local law may vary.

[3] The RBD for qualified plan participants is April 1 of the year following the later of (a) the year the participant reaches age 70½, or (b) the year he or she retires. More than 5% owners must begin to receive distributions by April 1 of the year following the year they reach age 70½.

Required Minimum Distributions After Death

Situation	Distribution Requirement	Example
Leave Account in Deceased Spouse's Name – Surviving Spouse is Designated Beneficiary	RMDs for the beneficiary-spouse must begin by the later of: (a) 12/31 of the year the owner would have turned age 70½ had he or she lived, or (b) 12/31 of the year after the year the owner dies. Distributions are made over the survivor's life expectancy.	Assume that Jake dies in 2018 at age 67. Kate is then age 65. Also assume that Jake would have reached age 70½ in 2021. Kate must take her first RMD by 12/31/21. This RMD is calculated by dividing the account balance on 12/31/20 by Kate's life expectancy (from the Single Life Table) for her age in 2021. If Kate turns 68 in 2021, this value is 18.6. For later years, her life expectancy is determined using her attained age in each year.
No Designated Beneficiary, the Owner's Estate, a Charity, or a Non-Qualifying Trust	The entire amount must be distributed by the end of the fifth year after the year the owner dies.	Jake dies on 01/01/18, at age 68, leaving his IRA to his estate. The entire IRA balance must be distributed by 12/31/23.

Owner Dies After The Required Beginning Date

Situation	Distribution Requirement	Example
Rollover Account to Survivor's Name	A RMD must be made for the deceased owner for the year of death. The surviving spouse then becomes the owner, with RMDs being taken under the normal "during lifetime" rules. No withdrawals are required until the surviving spouse reaches age 70½.	Assume that Kate's husband Jake dies in 2018 at age 72. Kate is age 65. A distribution must be made for Jake for 2018. Since Kate is not more than 10 years younger than Jake, the life expectancy from the Uniform Lifetime Table is used.[1] The RMD is calculated by dividing the account balance on 12/31/17 by 25.6, the distribution period for a 72 year old account owner. After taking Jake's RMD for 2018, Kate can then roll the account into her own name and delay further distributions until April 1 of the year after the year she reaches 70½.

---

[1] If Kate were more than 10 years younger than Jake, the factor shown on the Joint and Last Survivor Table would be used.

Required Minimum Distributions After Death

Situation	Distribution Requirement	Example
Leave Account in Deceased Spouse's Name – Surviving Spouse is Designated Beneficiary	A RMD must be made for the deceased owner for the year of death. RMDs for the beneficiary-spouse must begin by 12/31 of the year after the year of the owner's death, with distributions made over the survivor's life expectancy.	Assume Jake dies in 2018 at age 72. Kate is age 65. A distribution must be made for Jake for 2018, as discussed above. Distributions for Kate must begin by 12/31/19 based on her attained age in 2019. Assuming that Kate will turn 66 in 2019, the RMD for 2019 would be calculated by dividing the account balance on 12/31/18 by Kate's life expectancy (from the Single Life Table) of 20.2. For 2020, the RMD would be calculated by dividing the account balance as of 12/31/19 by Kate's 2020 life expectancy, at age 67, of 19.4.
No Designated Beneficiary, the Owner's Estate, a Charity, or a Non-Qualifying Trust	A RMD must be made for the deceased owner for the year of death. Thereafter, RMDs are based on the owner's theoretical life expectancy in the year of death.	Jake dies in 2018, at age 75, leaving his IRA entirely to charity. A RMD must be made for him for 2018, using his age 75 life expectancy (from the Uniform Lifetime Table) of 22.9. For later years, Jake's life expectancy in the year of his death (from the Single Life Table), reduced by one for each subsequent year, is used to calculate the RMD. For 2019, Jake's life expectancy would be 12.4, (his 2018 life expectancy at age 75 of 13.4-1). For 2020 the life expectancy used would be 11.4, (12.4-1).

Other Distribution Options

Funds in an inherited IRA or qualified retirement plan may also be distributed as a single lump-sum or as periodic or occasional distributions which withdraw the money at a rate faster than the RMDs required by federal tax law. However, such accelerated distributions will subject the funds to current income tax more quickly than will the RMD withdrawals.

Post-Mortem Distribution Planning

IRAs and qualified plans allow an account owner to name a beneficiary or beneficiaries to receive the account proceeds should the owner die. From this pool of potential inheritors, IRS regulations require that the individual or group of individuals who will ultimately receive the funds, the "designated beneficiaries," be identified by September 30 of the year following the year of death. This time delay allows for a certain amount of post-death estate and income tax planning by "removing" a potential beneficiary through either a qualified

Required Minimum Distributions After Death

disclaimer, a cash distribution, or by dividing the IRA or qualified plan into separate accounts.[1] The life expectancies of those beneficiaries who remain as of September 30 are then used to determine the RMDs for the years after death.

Entities without a measurable life span, such as the owner's estate, a charity, or a trust that does not meet certain IRS requirements, are not considered to be "designated beneficiaries" for RMD purposes. While such beneficiaries may inherit the funds in an account, distributions to these entities are generally made on less favorable terms.

Spousal Rollover

In order to roll the account into the name of the surviving spouse, the survivor must be the sole beneficiary and have an unlimited right to withdraw amounts from the account. If the spouse is not the sole beneficiary of an account at the time of the account owner's death, this requirement can be met by having other beneficiaries disclaim their interests on a timely basis. The surviving spouse could later name those individuals as beneficiaries of his or her own IRA.

The election to roll the account into the surviving spouse's name may be made at any time after the owner's death.

Trusts

In order for the beneficiaries of a trust to qualify as a "designated beneficiaries," the trust must meet certain requirements:

- The trust must be valid under state law;
- The trust must be irrevocable or will, under its terms, become irrevocable upon the death of the account owner;
- The beneficiaries of the trust must be identifiable from the trust document; and
- Certain documents must be provided to the plan administrator.[2]

Distributions to the trust are made over the theoretical life expectancy of the beneficiary. If there is more than one beneficiary, distributions are made over the theoretical life expectancy of the oldest beneficiary.

---

[1] Any separate accounts must generally be established by December 31 of the year following the year of the account owner's death.

[2] Generally, this must occur by October 31 of the year following the year of death.

Required Minimum Distributions After Death

If a trust does not meet these requirements, consideration should be given to reforming the trust, assigning or disclaiming an interest in the trust, cashing-out certain beneficiaries, or separating interests in the trust.

Other Points

- **Marital status:** An account owner's marital status for the entire calendar year is determined as of January 1, even if the account owner and/or spouse die or divorce during the year.

- **Distributions from employer-sponsored qualified plans:** Post-death payments to beneficiaries of qualified plans are typically based on the individual provisions of a particular plan. A lump-sum distribution is perhaps the most frequently encountered option. A surviving spouse who takes a lump-sum distribution from a qualified plan has 60 days to move the funds tax-free into an IRA rollover.

Roth IRAs

Roth IRAs do not have a lifetime distribution requirements. Because of this, a Roth IRA owner is always viewed as having died before the RBD. Post-death distributions from Roth IRAs are thus governed by the "death before RBD" rules.

Seek Professional Guidance

The body of law and regulation surrounding required minimum distributions is complex and often confusing. Further, the failure to correctly distribute the required amounts from an IRA or qualified plan can result in a federal excise tax of 50% of the amount that should have been distributed. Individual state or local law may also provide penalties.

The advice and guidance of qualified professionals is strongly recommended.

Required Minimum Distributions After Death

Non-Spouse Beneficiaries

Funds in both traditional IRAs[1] and qualified retirement plans may not be kept inside these tax-deferred accounts indefinitely. Under federal law the money must eventually be distributed, and then taxed, through yearly "Required Minimum Distributions," or RMDs.[2]

The death of an account owner does not eliminate this requirement. However, the manner in which the assets must be distributed post-death will vary, depending primarily on:

- **Death before or after required beginning date:** During life, an account owner must generally begin distributions no later than April 1 of the year following the year he or she reaches age 70½. This is known as the "required beginning date," or RBD.[3]

- **Who inherits the assets:** The law mandates different required minimum distribution schedules depending on who inherits the assets in an account.

Non-Spouse Beneficiary Required Minimum Distributions

Owner Dies Before The Required Beginning Date

Situation	Distribution Requirement	Example
Individual Beneficiary	RMDs for the beneficiary must begin by 12/31 of the year after the year of death. Distributions are made over the beneficiary's life expectancy.	Paul dies in 2018 at age 67, leaving his IRA to his daughter Paulette, age 42. Paulette must begin to take RMDs by 12/31/19, using her age in 2019 of 43. The RMD for 2019 would be calculated by dividing the account balance on 12/31/18 by Paulette's age-43 life expectancy (from the Single Life Table) of 40.7.[4]

---

[1] For required minimum distribution purposes, the term "traditional IRA" also includes SIMPLE IRAs and SEP IRAs. Roth IRAs are subject to different rules.

[2] This discussion concerns federal income tax law. State or local law may vary.

[3] The RBD for qualified plan participants is April 1 of the year following the later of (a) the year the participant reaches age 70½, or (b) the year he or she retires. More than 5% owners must begin to receive distributions by April 1 of the year following the year they reach age 70½.

[4] The life expectancy factor is reduced by one for each year after the year of the first required distribution.

Required Minimum Distributions After Death

Situation	Distribution Requirement	Example
Multiple Beneficiaries (Assumes that the account is not divided into separate shares.)	RMDs for the beneficiaries must begin by 12/31 of the year after the year of the owner's death. Distributions are made over the <u>oldest</u> beneficiary's life expectancy.	Paul dies in 2018 at age 67, leaving his IRA to his brother Bob, age 76, and his daughter Paulette, age 42. RMDs to them must begin by 12/31/19 and must be made over Bob's life expectancy as of his birthday in the year after Paul's death. The RMD for 2019 would be calculated by dividing the account balance on 12/31/18 by Bob's 2019 (Single Life Table) life expectancy, for age 77, of 12.1.[1]
No Designated Beneficiary, the Estate, a Charity, or a Non-Qualifying Trust	The entire amount must be distributed by the end of the fifth year after the year the owner dies.	Paul dies on 01/01/18, at age 68, leaving his IRA to his estate. The entire IRA balance must be distributed by 12/31/23.

Owner Dies After The Required Beginning Date

Situation	Distribution Requirement	Example
Individual Beneficiary	A RMD must be made for the deceased owner for the year of death. RMDs for the beneficiary must begin by 12/31 of the year after the year of the owner's death. Distributions are made over the <u>longer</u> of the owner's theoretical life expectancy, or the beneficiary's life expectancy.	Paul dies in 2018 at age 72, leaving his IRA to his older brother Bob, age 76. Because Paul has already passed his RBD, a distribution must be made for him for 2018. The RMD for 2018 is determined by dividing the account balance as of 12/31/17 by 25.6, the life expectancy (from the Uniform Lifetime Table) for a 72-year-old account owner. For 2019 and later years, the RMDs are calculated using the longer of the Single Life Table life expectancy for Paul in the year of his death, reduced by one (age 72 =15.5-1=14.5) or Bob's life expectancy in the year after Paul's death (age 77=12.1). In this case, Paul's theoretical life expectancy is greater. The RMD for 2019 is calculated by dividing the account balance as of 12/31/18 by 14.5.[1]

[1] The life expectancy factor is reduced by one for each year after the year of the first required distribution.

Required Minimum Distributions After Death

Situation	Distribution Requirement	Example
Multiple Beneficiaries (Assumes that the account is not divided into separate shares.)	A RMD must be made for the deceased owner for the year of death. RMDs for the beneficiaries must begin by 12/31 of the year after the year of death, with distributions over the <u>longer</u> of the owner's theoretical life expectancy or the oldest beneficiary's life expectancy.	Paul dies in 2018 at age 72, leaving his IRA to his son Peter, age 46, and his daughter Paulette, age 42. Because Paul has already passed his RBD, a distribution for 2018 must be made for him. This distribution is calculated by dividing the account balance as of 12/31/17 by 25.6, the life expectancy (from the Uniform Lifetime Table) for a 72 year old. For 2019 and later years, the RMDs are calculated using the longer of the Single Life Table life expectancy for Paul in the year of his death, reduced by one (age 72=15.5-1=14.5) or Peter's life expectancy (he's older than Paulette) in the year after Paul's death (age 47=37.0). In this case, Peter's life expectancy is the greater. The RMD for 2019 is calculated by dividing the account balance as of 12/31/18 by 37.0.[1]
No Designated Beneficiary, the Estate, a Charity, or a Non-Qualifying Trust	A RMD must be made for the deceased owner for the year of death. Thereafter, RMDs are based on the owner's theoretical life expectancy in the year of death.	Paul dies in 2018, at age 75, leaving his IRA entirely to charity. A RMD must be made for him for 2018, calculated using his age 75 life expectancy (from the Uniform Lifetime Table) of 22.9. For 2019 and later years, Paul's life expectancy in the year of his death (from the Single Life Table), reduced by one for each subsequent year, is used to calculate the RMD. For 2019, Paul's life expectancy would be 12.4, (his 2018 life expectancy at age 75 of 13.4-1).[1]

Other Distribution Options

Funds in an inherited IRA or qualified retirement plan may also be distributed as a single lump-sum or as periodic or occasional distributions which withdraw the money at a rate faster than the RMDs required by federal tax law. However, such accelerated distributions will subject the funds to current income tax more quickly than will the RMD withdrawals.

Post-Mortem Distribution Planning

IRAs and qualified plans allow an account owner to name a beneficiary or beneficiaries to receive the account proceeds should the owner die. From this pool of potential inheritors, IRS regulations require that the individual or group of individuals who will ultimately receive

---

[1] The life expectancy factor is reduced by one for each year after the year of the first required distribution.

the funds, the "designated beneficiaries," be identified by September 30 of the year following the year of death.

This time delay allows for a certain amount of post-death estate and income tax planning by "removing" a potential beneficiary through either a qualified disclaimer, a cash distribution, or by dividing the IRA or qualified plan into separate accounts. Any separate accounts must generally be established by December 31 of the year following the year of the account owner's death. The life expectancies of those beneficiaries who remain on September 30 are then used to determine the RMDs for the years after death.

Entities without a measurable life span, such as the owner's estate, a charity, or a trust that does not meet certain IRS requirements, are not considered to be "designated beneficiaries" for RMD purposes. While such beneficiaries may inherit the funds in the account, distributions to these entities are generally made on less favorable terms.

Trusts

In order for the beneficiaries of a trust to qualify as "designated beneficiaries," the trust must meet certain requirements:

- The trust must be valid under state law;

- The trust must be irrevocable or will, under its terms, become irrevocable upon the death of the account owner;

- The beneficiaries of the trust must be identifiable from the trust document; and

- Certain documents must be provided to the plan administrator.[1]

Distributions to the trust are made over the theoretical life expectancy of the beneficiary. If there is more than one beneficiary, distributions are made over the theoretical life expectancy of the oldest beneficiary.

If a trust does not meet these requirements, consideration should be given to reforming the trust, assigning or disclaiming an interest in the trust, cashing-out certain beneficiaries, or separating interests in the trust.

---

[1] Generally, this must occur by October 31 of the year following the year of death.

Required Minimum Distributions After Death

Other Points

- **Distributions from employer-sponsored qualified plans:** Post-death payments to beneficiaries of qualified plans are typically based on the individual provisions of a particular plan. A lump-sum distribution, with its heavy, immediate taxation, is perhaps the most frequently encountered option.

  The Pension Protection Act of 2006, effective for distributions after December 31, 2006, provides for a direct trustee-to-trustee transfer from a qualified plan to an IRA specifically designed to receive retirement assets inherited by a non-spouse beneficiary. The non-spouse beneficiary is not treated as the owner of the rolled-over assets and the assets may not be rolled-over to another account. Required minimum distributions are made from the "inherited IRA" in accordance with the normal rules applicable to non-spouse beneficiaries.

  Such an after-death transfer has the same result as if the decedent had moved the assets in his or her qualified plan into an IRA rollover prior to death.

Roth IRAs

Roth IRAs do not have a lifetime distribution requirements. Because of this, a Roth IRA owner is always viewed as having died before the RBD. Post-death distributions from Roth IRAs are thus governed by the "death before RBD" rules.

Seek Professional Guidance

The body of law and regulation surrounding required minimum distributions is complex and often confusing. Further, the failure to correctly distribute the required amounts from an IRA or qualified plan can result in a federal excise tax of 50% of the amount that should have been distributed. Individual state or local law may also provide penalties.

The advice and guidance of qualified professionals is strongly recommended.

The Basics of Stretch IRAs

One major benefit of a traditional IRA[1] is that there is no federal[2] tax on growth in the account until the funds are distributed. This deferral of taxes generally allows for faster growth than would be possible if taxes had to be paid each year. Federal law does not allow this tax-deferral to continue forever; certain mandatory distributions (known as Required Minimum Distributions, or RMDs) must be made from these accounts once the owner reaches a specified age.

For traditional IRAs, distributions must begin no later than April 1 of the year following the year the owner reaches age 70½. Funds distributed from the account are generally taxable as ordinary income in the year received. Failure to make the minimum distributions when required can result in a significant income tax penalty.

The Stretch IRA - Extending the Period of Tax-Deferral

The term "stretch IRA" refers to a wealth transfer strategy that seeks to extend the period during which the assets in the IRA continue to grow tax-deferred. The stretch IRA concept is most often of interest to those who do not need extra income or those who wish to leave a legacy to their heirs in an income tax-efficient manner.

To begin, an IRA owner names a spouse or another (usually younger) person such as a child or grandchild, as the account beneficiary. Then, only the legally required, minimum distributions, (the RMDs), are taken from the account each year. Under IRS regulations, the methods used to calculate the RMDs can effectively extend the period over which the assets may be distributed.

The Pros and Cons of Stretch IRAs

Stretch IRAs have potential benefits as well as potential risks:

- **Benefits.**

  - **Income for life:** A stretch IRA has the potential to provide lifetime income to a chosen beneficiary or beneficiaries.

---

[1] The term "traditional IRA" includes SIMPLE IRAs and SEP IRAs.
[2] The discussion here concerns federal income tax law. State and/or local tax law may differ.

- **Minimize tax liability:** The income tax bite may be lessened by taking smaller distributions over a period of years, rather than as a single, large lump sum.

- **Continue tax-deferred growth:** Extending the period over which distributions are made continues the benefits of tax-deferred growth, potentially increasing the wealth that can pass to the beneficiaries.

- Risks.

  - **Beneficiary may die early:** A beneficiary may not live to normal life expectancy.

  - **Tax laws may change:** Tax laws or regulations may change, to the detriment of an IRA owner and/or beneficiaries.

  - **Poor investment returns:** Investment losses and inflation can both erode, or even eliminate, the value of future IRA distributions.

Spousal Beneficiary and a Single Inherited IRA

An IRA owner, age 68, makes his spouse, age 62, the sole beneficiary of his IRA. They have two adult children, ages 35 and 25.

When	What Happens
During the IRA owner's life	Beginning at age 70½, the IRA owner takes his required minimum distributions (RMDs).
IRA owner dies at age 75	The surviving spouse rolls the IRA over into her name. She names her two adult children as joint beneficiaries of her single rollover account.
Surviving spouse reaches age 70½	At age 70½, the surviving spouse begins taking her RMDs.
Surviving spouse dies at age 80	The children inherit the IRA assets. Each child receives RMDs based on the single life expectancy of the oldest child. They may not mix the funds with other IRA assets.

The Basics of Stretch IRAs

Spousal Beneficiary and Separate Inherited IRAs

An IRA owner, age 68, makes his spouse, age 62, the sole beneficiary of his IRA. They have two adult children, ages 35 and 25.

When	What Happens
During the owner's life	Beginning at age 70½, the IRA owner takes his required minimum distributions (RMDs).
IRA owner dies at age 75	The surviving spouse splits the IRA assets into two separate IRA rollover accounts. She names each of her two adult children as the sole beneficiary of one account.
Surviving spouse reaches age 70½	At age 70½, the surviving spouse begins taking her RMDs.
Surviving spouse dies at age 80	Each child inherits a separate IRA. Because there are two separate accounts, each child receives RMDs based on his or her individual life expectancy. They may not mix the funds with other IRA assets.

Nonspousal Beneficiaries and Separate Inherited IRAs

An IRA owner, age 68, has two adult children, ages 35 and 25. He splits his IRA into two separate accounts and names each child as the sole beneficiary of one account.

When	What Happens
During the owner's life	Beginning at age 70½, the IRA owner takes his required minimum distributions (RMDs).
The owner dies at age 75	Each child inherits a separate IRA. Because there are two separate accounts, each child receives RMDs based on his or her individual life expectancy. They may not mix the funds with other IRA assets.

A married IRA owner may need to obtain his or her spouse's written consent before naming someone in place of (or in addition to) the spouse as the primary beneficiary of the IRA.

Post-Death Beneficiary Planning

The stretch IRA examples shown here illustrate situations in which the beneficiary planning takes place **prior** to the account owner's death. However, IRS regulations allow for a certain amount of **post-death** planning. From a pool of potential beneficiaries, those who will ultimately receive the assets must be identified by September 30 of the year following the owner's year of death. This time delay allows for the removal of a potential beneficiary either through a qualified disclaimer, a cash distribution, or by dividing the IRA into separate accounts. The life expectancies of those who remain as of September 30 are then used to determine the RMDs for the years after death.

Any separate accounts must generally be established by December 31 of the year following the year of the account owner's death.

Seek Professional Guidance

Setting up a stretch IRA requires careful consideration of a number of issues:

- Possible changes in tax law.

- The impact of inflation.

- The uncertainty of future investment results.

- The need to integrate the stretch IRA into the overall estate plan.

- The risks inherent in planning for an extended period into the future.

The guidance of appropriate tax, legal, and investment professionals is highly recommended.

Stretch IRA

Both traditional IRAs and qualified retirement plans enjoy significant federal tax benefits. Contributions are generally tax deductible and growth inside an account is tax deferred. The term "stretch IRA" refers to a wealth transfer strategy that seeks to extend the period during which the assets in the IRA continue to grow tax-deferred.

Assumptions:
    Account balance at end of previous year: $120,000
    Estimated rate of return: 12.00%
    Owner's age at death: 85

To begin, an IRA owner names a spouse or another (usually younger) person such as a child or grandchild, as the account beneficiary. Then, only the legally required, minimum distributions, (the RMDs) are taken from the account each year. Under IRS regulations the methods used to calculate the RMDs can effectively extend the period over which the assets may be distributed. Keep in mind that investing involves risk, including the possible loss of principal.

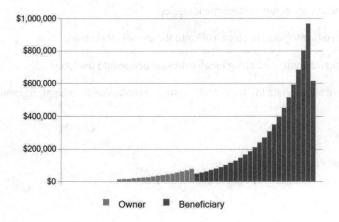

How a Stretch IRA Works

Spousal Beneficiary and a Single Inherited IRA

An IRA owner, age 68, makes his spouse, age 62, the sole beneficiary of his IRA. They have two adult children, ages 35 and 25.

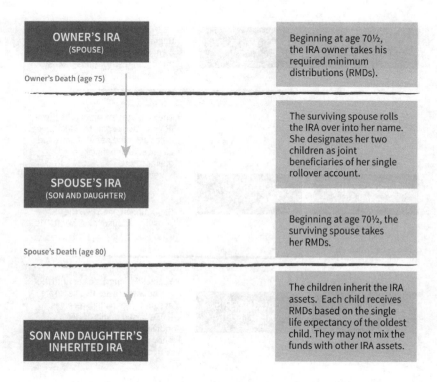

OWNER'S IRA
(SPOUSE)

Owner's Death (age 75)

Beginning at age 70½, the IRA owner takes his required minimum distributions (RMDs).

The surviving spouse rolls the IRA over into her name. She designates her two children as joint beneficiaries of her single rollover account.

SPOUSE'S IRA
(SON AND DAUGHTER)

Beginning at age 70½, the surviving spouse takes her RMDs.

Spouse's Death (age 80)

The children inherit the IRA assets. Each child receives RMDs based on the single life expectancy of the oldest child. They may not mix the funds with other IRA assets.

SON AND DAUGHTER'S INHERITED IRA

Note: This is one example of how a stretch IRA might be structured. Professional tax and legal guidance is strongly recommended.

How a Stretch IRA Works

Spousal Beneficiary and Separate Inherited IRAs

An IRA owner, age 68, makes his spouse, age 62, the sole beneficiary of his IRA. They have two adult children, ages 35 and 25.

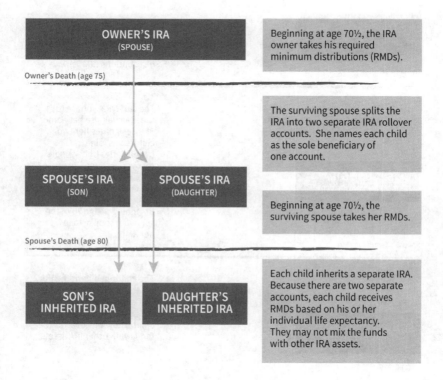

OWNER'S IRA
(SPOUSE)

Beginning at age 70½, the IRA owner takes his required minimum distributions (RMDs).

Owner's Death (age 75)

The surviving spouse splits the IRA into two separate IRA rollover accounts. She names each child as the sole beneficiary of one account.

SPOUSE'S IRA
(SON)

SPOUSE'S IRA
(DAUGHTER)

Beginning at age 70½, the surviving spouse takes her RMDs.

Spouse's Death (age 80)

SON'S INHERITED IRA

DAUGHTER'S INHERITED IRA

Each child inherits a separate IRA. Because there are two separate accounts, each child receives RMDs based on his or her individual life expectancy. They may not mix the funds with other IRA assets.

Note: This is one example of how a stretch IRA might be structured. Post-mortem distribution planning is also possible. Professional tax and legal guidance is strongly recommended.

How a Stretch IRA Works

Non-Spouse Beneficiaries and Separate Inherited IRAs

Assume an IRA owner, age 68, has two adult children, ages 35 and 25.

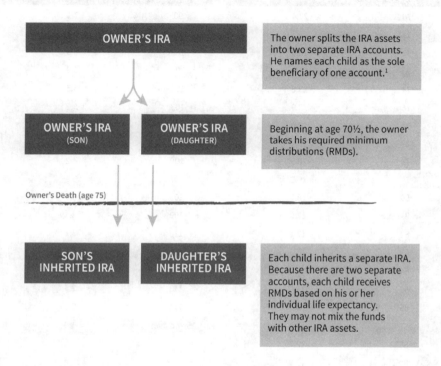

OWNER'S IRA

The owner splits the IRA assets into two separate IRA accounts. He names each child as the sole beneficiary of one account.[1]

OWNER'S IRA (SON) **OWNER'S IRA** (DAUGHTER)

Beginning at age 70½, the owner takes his required minimum distributions (RMDs).

Owner's Death (age 75)

SON'S INHERITED IRA **DAUGHTER'S INHERITED IRA**

Each child inherits a separate IRA. Because there are two separate accounts, each child receives RMDs based on his or her individual life expectancy. They may not mix the funds with other IRA assets.

Note: This is one example of how a stretch IRA might be structured. Post-mortem distribution planning is also possible. Professional tax and legal guidance is strongly recommended.

Uniform Lifetime Table

IRS Reg. 1.401(a)(9)-9, Q+A-2

Age	Distribution Period	Age	Distribution Period
70	27.4	98	7.1
71	26.5	99	6.7
72	25.6	100	6.3
73	24.7	101	5.9
74	23.8	102	5.5
75	22.9	103	5.2
76	22.0	104	4.9
77	21.2	105	4.5
78	20.3	106	4.2
79	19.5	107	3.9
80	18.7	108	3.7
81	17.9	109	3.4
82	17.1	110	3.1
83	16.3	111	2.9
84	15.5	112	2.6
85	14.8	113	2.4
86	14.1	114	2.1
87	13.4	115 and over	1.9
88	12.7		
89	12.0		
90	11.4		
91	10.8		
92	10.2		
93	9.6		
94	9.1		
95	8.6		
96	8.1		
97	7.6		

Joint Life and Last Survivor Table

IRS Reg. 1.401(a)(9)-9, Q+A-3

Ages	20	21	22	23	24	25	26	27	28	29
20	70.1	69.6	69.1	68.7	68.3	67.9	67.5	67.2	66.9	66.6
21	69.6	69.1	68.6	68.2	67.7	67.3	66.9	66.6	66.2	65.9
22	69.1	68.6	68.1	67.6	67.2	66.7	66.3	65.9	65.6	65.2
23	68.7	68.2	67.6	67.1	66.6	66.2	65.7	65.3	64.9	64.6
24	68.3	67.7	67.2	66.6	66.1	65.6	65.2	64.7	64.3	63.9
25	67.9	67.3	66.7	66.2	65.6	65.1	64.6	64.2	63.7	63.3
26	67.5	66.9	66.3	65.7	65.2	64.6	64.1	63.6	63.2	62.8
27	67.2	66.6	65.9	65.3	64.7	64.2	63.6	63.1	62.7	62.2
28	66.9	66.2	65.6	64.9	64.3	63.7	63.2	62.7	62.1	61.7
29	66.6	65.9	65.2	64.6	63.9	63.3	62.8	62.2	61.7	61.2
30	66.3	65.6	64.9	64.2	63.6	62.9	62.3	61.8	61.2	60.7
31	66.1	65.3	64.6	63.9	63.2	62.6	62.0	61.4	60.8	60.2
32	65.8	65.1	64.3	63.6	62.9	62.2	61.6	61.0	60.4	59.8
33	65.6	64.8	64.1	63.3	62.6	61.9	61.3	60.6	60.0	59.4
34	65.4	64.6	63.8	63.1	62.3	61.6	60.9	60.3	59.6	59.0
35	65.2	64.4	63.6	62.8	62.1	61.4	60.6	59.9	59.3	58.6
36	65.0	64.2	63.4	62.6	61.9	61.1	60.4	59.6	59.0	58.3
37	64.9	64.0	63.2	62.4	61.6	60.9	60.1	59.4	58.7	58.0
38	64.7	63.9	63.0	62.2	61.4	60.6	59.9	59.1	58.4	57.7
39	64.6	63.7	62.9	62.1	61.2	60.4	59.6	58.9	58.1	57.4
40	64.4	63.6	62.7	61.9	61.1	60.2	59.4	58.7	57.9	57.1
41	64.3	63.5	62.6	61.7	60.9	60.1	59.3	58.5	57.7	56.9
42	64.2	63.3	62.5	61.6	60.8	59.9	59.1	58.3	57.5	56.7
43	64.1	63.2	62.4	61.5	60.6	59.8	58.9	58.1	57.3	56.5
44	64.0	63.1	62.2	61.4	60.5	59.6	58.8	57.9	57.1	56.3
45	64.0	63.0	62.2	61.3	60.4	59.5	58.6	57.8	56.9	56.1

Joint Life and Last Survivor Table

IRS Reg. 1.401(a)(9)-9, Q+A-3

Ages	20	21	22	23	24	25	26	27	28	29
46	63.9	63.0	62.1	61.2	60.3	59.4	58.5	57.7	56.8	56.0
47	63.8	62.9	62.0	61.1	60.2	59.3	58.4	57.5	56.7	55.8
48	63.7	62.8	61.9	61.0	60.1	59.2	58.3	57.4	56.5	55.7
49	63.7	62.8	61.8	60.9	60.0	59.1	58.2	57.3	56.4	55.6
50	63.6	62.7	61.8	60.8	59.9	59.0	58.1	57.2	56.3	55.4
51	63.6	62.6	61.7	60.8	59.9	58.9	58.0	57.1	56.2	55.3
52	63.5	62.6	61.7	60.7	59.8	58.9	58.0	57.1	56.1	55.2
53	63.5	62.5	61.6	60.7	59.7	58.8	57.9	57.0	56.1	55.2
54	63.5	62.5	61.6	60.6	59.7	58.8	57.8	56.9	56.0	55.1
55	63.4	62.5	61.5	60.6	59.6	58.7	57.8	56.8	55.9	55.0
56	63.4	62.4	61.5	60.5	59.6	58.7	57.7	56.8	55.9	54.9
57	63.4	62.4	61.5	60.5	59.6	58.6	57.7	56.7	55.8	54.9
58	63.3	62.4	61.4	60.5	59.5	58.6	57.6	56.7	55.8	54.8
59	63.3	62.3	61.4	60.4	59.5	58.5	57.6	56.7	55.7	54.8
60	63.3	62.3	61.4	60.4	59.5	58.5	57.6	56.6	55.7	54.7
61	63.3	62.3	61.3	60.4	59.4	58.5	57.5	56.6	55.6	54.7
62	63.2	62.3	61.3	60.4	59.4	58.4	57.5	56.5	55.6	54.7
63	63.2	62.3	61.3	60.3	59.4	58.4	57.5	56.5	55.6	54.6
64	63.2	62.2	61.3	60.3	59.4	58.4	57.4	56.5	55.5	54.6
65	63.2	62.2	61.3	60.3	59.3	58.4	57.4	56.5	55.5	54.6
66	63.2	62.2	61.2	60.3	59.3	58.4	57.4	56.4	55.5	54.5
67	63.2	62.2	61.2	60.3	59.3	58.3	57.4	56.4	55.5	54.5
68	63.1	62.2	61.2	60.2	59.3	58.3	57.4	56.4	55.4	54.5
69	63.1	62.2	61.2	60.2	59.3	58.3	57.3	56.4	55.4	54.5
70	63.1	62.2	61.2	60.2	59.3	58.3	57.3	56.4	55.4	54.4
71	63.1	62.1	61.2	60.2	59.2	58.3	57.3	56.4	55.4	54.4
72	63.1	62.1	61.2	60.2	59.2	58.3	57.3	56.3	55.4	54.4
73	63.1	62.1	61.2	60.2	59.2	58.3	57.3	56.3	55.4	54.4

Joint Life and Last Survivor Table

IRS Reg. 1.401(a)(9)-9, Q+A-3

Ages	20	21	22	23	24	25	26	27	28	29
74	63.1	62.1	61.2	60.2	59.2	58.2	57.3	56.3	55.4	54.4
75	63.1	62.1	61.1	60.2	59.2	58.2	57.3	56.3	55.3	54.4
76	63.1	62.1	61.1	60.2	59.2	58.2	57.3	56.3	55.3	54.4
77	63.1	62.1	61.1	60.2	59.2	58.2	57.3	56.3	55.3	54.4
78	63.1	62.1	61.1	60.2	59.2	58.2	57.3	56.3	55.3	54.4
79	63.1	62.1	61.1	60.2	59.2	58.2	57.2	56.3	55.3	54.3
80	63.1	62.1	61.1	60.1	59.2	58.2	57.2	56.3	55.3	54.3
81	63.1	62.1	61.1	60.1	59.2	58.2	57.2	56.3	55.3	54.3
82	63.1	62.1	61.1	60.1	59.2	58.2	57.2	56.3	55.3	54.3
83	63.1	62.1	61.1	60.1	59.2	58.2	57.2	56.3	55.3	54.3
84	63.0	62.1	61.1	60.1	59.2	58.2	57.2	56.3	55.3	54.3
85	63.0	62.1	61.1	60.1	59.2	58.2	57.2	56.3	55.3	54.3
86	63.0	62.1	61.1	60.1	59.2	58.2	57.2	56.2	55.3	54.3
87	63.0	62.1	61.1	60.1	59.2	58.2	57.2	56.2	55.3	54.3
88	63.0	62.1	61.1	60.1	59.2	58.2	57.2	56.2	55.3	54.3
89	63.0	62.1	61.1	60.1	59.1	58.2	57.2	56.2	55.3	54.3
90	63.0	62.1	61.1	60.1	59.1	58.2	57.2	56.2	55.3	54.3
91	63.0	62.1	61.1	60.1	59.1	58.2	57.2	56.2	55.3	54.3
92	63.0	62.1	61.1	60.1	59.1	58.2	57.2	56.2	55.3	54.3
93	63.0	62.1	61.1	60.1	59.1	58.2	57.2	56.2	55.3	54.3
94	63.0	62.1	61.1	60.1	59.1	58.2	57.2	56.2	55.3	54.3
95	63.0	62.1	61.1	60.1	59.1	58.2	57.2	56.2	55.3	54.3
96	63.0	62.1	61.1	60.1	59.1	58.2	57.2	56.2	55.3	54.3
97	63.0	62.1	61.1	60.1	59.1	58.2	57.2	56.2	55.3	54.3
98	63.0	62.1	61.1	60.1	59.1	58.2	57.2	56.2	55.3	54.3
99	63.0	62.1	61.1	60.1	59.1	58.2	57.2	56.2	55.3	54.3
100	63.0	62.1	61.1	60.1	59.1	58.2	57.2	56.2	55.3	54.3
101	63.0	62.1	61.1	60.1	59.1	58.2	57.2	56.2	55.3	54.3

Joint Life and Last Survivor Table

IRS Reg. 1.401(a)(9)-9, Q+A-3

Ages	20	21	22	23	24	25	26	27	28	29
102	63.0	62.1	61.1	60.1	59.1	58.2	57.2	56.2	55.3	54.3
103	63.0	62.1	61.1	60.1	59.1	58.2	57.2	56.2	55.3	54.3
104	63.0	62.1	61.1	60.1	59.1	58.2	57.2	56.2	55.3	54.3
105	63.0	62.1	61.1	60.1	59.1	58.2	57.2	56.2	55.3	54.3
106	63.0	62.1	61.1	60.1	59.1	58.2	57.2	56.2	55.3	54.3
107	63.0	62.1	61.1	60.1	59.1	58.2	57.2	56.2	55.3	54.3
108	63.0	62.1	61.1	60.1	59.1	58.2	57.2	56.2	55.3	54.3
109	63.0	62.1	61.1	60.1	59.1	58.2	57.2	56.2	55.3	54.3
110	63.0	62.1	61.1	60.1	59.1	58.2	57.2	56.2	55.3	54.3
111	63.0	62.1	61.1	60.1	59.1	58.2	57.2	56.2	55.3	54.3
112	63.0	62.1	61.1	60.1	59.1	58.2	57.2	56.2	55.3	54.3
113	63.0	62.1	61.1	60.1	59.1	58.2	57.2	56.2	55.3	54.3
114	63.0	62.1	61.1	60.1	59.1	58.2	57.2	56.2	55.3	54.3
115+	63.0	62.1	61.1	60.1	59.1	58.2	57.2	56.2	55.3	54.3

Ages	30	31	32	33	34	35	36	37	38	39
30	60.2	59.7	59.2	58.8	58.4	58.0	57.6	57.3	57.0	56.7
31	59.7	59.2	58.7	58.2	57.8	57.4	57.0	56.6	56.3	56.0
32	59.2	58.7	58.2	57.7	57.2	56.8	56.4	56.0	55.6	55.3
33	58.8	58.2	57.7	57.2	56.7	56.2	55.8	55.4	55.0	54.7
34	58.4	57.8	57.2	56.7	56.2	55.7	55.3	54.8	54.4	54.0
35	58.0	57.4	56.8	56.2	55.7	55.2	54.7	54.3	53.8	53.4
36	57.6	57.0	56.4	55.8	55.3	54.7	54.2	53.7	53.3	52.8
37	57.3	56.6	56.0	55.4	54.8	54.3	53.7	53.2	52.7	52.3
38	57.0	56.3	55.6	55.0	54.4	53.8	53.3	52.7	52.2	51.7
39	56.7	56.0	55.3	54.7	54.0	53.4	52.8	52.3	51.7	51.2
40	56.4	55.7	55.0	54.3	53.7	53.0	52.4	51.8	51.3	50.8
41	56.1	55.4	54.7	54.0	53.3	52.7	52.0	51.4	50.9	50.3

Joint Life and Last Survivor Table

IRS Reg. 1.401(a)(9)-9, Q+A-3

Ages	30	31	32	33	34	35	36	37	38	39
42	55.9	55.2	54.4	53.7	53.0	52.3	51.7	51.1	50.4	49.9
43	55.7	54.9	54.2	53.4	52.7	52.0	51.3	50.7	50.1	49.5
44	55.5	54.7	53.9	53.2	52.4	51.7	51.0	50.4	49.7	49.1
45	55.3	54.5	53.7	52.9	52.2	51.5	50.7	50.0	49.4	48.7
46	55.1	54.3	53.5	52.7	52.0	51.2	50.5	49.8	49.1	48.4
47	55.0	54.1	53.3	52.5	51.7	51.0	50.2	49.5	48.8	48.1
48	54.8	54.0	53.2	52.3	51.5	50.8	50.0	49.2	48.5	47.8
49	54.7	53.8	53.0	52.2	51.4	50.6	49.8	49.0	48.2	47.5
50	54.6	53.7	52.9	52.0	51.2	50.4	49.6	48.8	48.0	47.3
51	54.5	53.6	52.7	51.9	51.0	50.2	49.4	48.6	47.8	47.0
52	54.4	53.5	52.6	51.7	50.9	50.0	49.2	48.4	47.6	46.8
53	54.3	53.4	52.5	51.6	50.8	49.9	49.1	48.2	47.4	46.6
54	54.2	53.3	52.4	51.5	50.6	49.8	48.9	48.1	47.2	46.4
55	54.1	53.2	52.3	51.4	50.5	49.7	48.8	47.9	47.1	46.3
56	54.0	53.1	52.2	51.3	50.4	49.5	48.7	47.8	47.0	46.1
57	54.0	53.0	52.1	51.2	50.3	49.4	48.6	47.7	46.8	46.0
58	53.9	53.0	52.1	51.2	50.3	49.4	48.5	47.6	46.7	45.8
59	53.8	52.9	52.0	51.1	50.2	49.3	48.4	47.5	46.6	45.7
60	53.8	52.9	51.9	51.0	50.1	49.2	48.3	47.4	46.5	45.6
61	53.8	52.8	51.9	51.0	50.0	49.1	48.2	47.3	46.4	45.5
62	53.7	52.8	51.8	50.9	50.0	49.1	48.1	47.2	46.3	45.4
63	53.7	52.7	51.8	50.9	49.9	49.0	48.1	47.2	46.3	45.3
64	53.6	52.7	51.8	50.8	49.9	48.9	48.0	47.1	46.2	45.3
65	53.6	52.7	51.7	50.8	49.8	48.9	48.0	47.0	46.1	45.2
66	53.6	52.6	51.7	50.7	49.8	48.9	47.9	47.0	46.1	45.1
67	53.6	52.6	51.7	50.7	49.8	48.8	47.9	46.9	46.0	45.1
68	53.5	52.6	51.6	50.7	49.7	48.8	47.8	46.9	46.0	45.0
69	53.5	52.6	51.6	50.6	49.7	48.7	47.8	46.9	45.9	45.0

Joint Life and Last Survivor Table

IRS Reg. 1.401(a)(9)-9, Q+A-3

Ages	30	31	32	33	34	35	36	37	38	39
70	53.5	52.5	51.6	50.6	49.7	48.7	47.8	46.8	45.9	44.9
71	53.5	52.5	51.6	50.6	49.6	48.7	47.7	46.8	45.9	44.9
72	53.5	52.5	51.5	50.6	49.6	48.7	47.7	46.8	45.8	44.9
73	53.4	52.5	51.5	50.6	49.6	48.6	47.7	46.7	45.8	44.8
74	53.4	52.5	51.5	50.5	49.6	48.6	47.7	46.7	45.8	44.8
75	53.4	52.5	51.5	50.5	49.6	48.6	47.7	46.7	45.7	44.8
76	53.4	52.4	51.5	50.5	49.6	48.6	47.6	46.7	45.7	44.8
77	53.4	52.4	51.5	50.5	49.5	48.6	47.6	46.7	45.7	44.8
78	53.4	52.4	51.5	50.5	49.5	48.6	47.6	46.6	45.7	44.7
79	53.4	52.4	51.5	50.5	49.5	48.6	47.6	46.6	45.7	44.7
80	53.4	52.4	51.4	50.5	49.5	48.5	47.6	46.6	45.7	44.7
81	53.4	52.4	51.4	50.5	49.5	48.5	47.6	46.6	45.7	44.7
82	53.4	52.4	51.4	50.5	49.5	48.5	47.6	46.6	45.6	44.7
83	53.4	52.4	51.4	50.5	49.5	48.5	47.6	46.6	45.6	44.7
84	53.4	52.4	51.4	50.5	49.5	48.5	47.6	46.6	45.6	44.7
85	53.3	52.4	51.4	50.4	49.5	48.5	47.5	46.6	45.6	44.7
86	53.3	52.4	51.4	50.4	49.5	48.5	47.5	46.6	45.6	44.6
87	53.3	52.4	51.4	50.4	49.5	48.5	47.5	46.6	45.6	44.6
88	53.3	52.4	51.4	50.4	49.5	48.5	47.5	46.6	45.6	44.6
89	53.3	52.4	51.4	50.4	49.5	48.5	47.5	46.6	45.6	44.6
90	53.3	52.4	51.4	50.4	49.5	48.5	47.5	46.6	45.6	44.6
91	53.3	52.4	51.4	50.4	49.5	48.5	47.5	46.6	45.6	44.6
92	53.3	52.4	51.4	50.4	49.5	48.5	47.5	46.6	45.6	44.6
93	53.3	52.4	51.4	50.4	49.5	48.5	47.5	46.6	45.6	44.6
94	53.3	52.4	51.4	50.4	49.5	48.5	47.5	46.6	45.6	44.6
95	53.3	52.4	51.4	50.4	49.5	48.5	47.5	46.5	45.6	44.6
96	53.3	52.4	51.4	50.4	49.5	48.5	47.5	46.5	45.6	44.6
97	53.3	52.4	51.4	50.4	49.5	48.5	47.5	46.5	45.6	44.6

Joint Life and Last Survivor Table

IRS Reg. 1.401(a)(9)-9, Q+A-3

Ages	30	31	32	33	34	35	36	37	38	39
98	53.3	52.4	51.4	50.4	49.5	48.5	47.5	46.5	45.6	44.6
99	53.3	52.4	51.4	50.4	49.5	48.5	47.5	46.5	45.6	44.6
100	53.3	52.4	51.4	50.4	49.5	48.5	47.5	46.5	45.6	44.6
101	53.3	52.4	51.4	50.4	49.5	48.5	47.5	46.5	45.6	44.6
102	53.3	52.4	51.4	50.4	49.5	48.5	47.5	46.5	45.6	44.6
103	53.3	52.4	51.4	50.4	49.5	48.5	47.5	46.5	45.6	44.6
104	53.3	52.4	51.4	50.4	49.5	48.5	47.5	46.5	45.6	44.6
105	53.3	52.4	51.4	50.4	49.4	48.5	47.5	46.5	45.6	44.6
106	53.3	52.4	51.4	50.4	49.4	48.5	47.5	46.5	45.6	44.6
107	53.3	52.4	51.4	50.4	49.4	48.5	47.5	46.5	45.6	44.6
108	53.3	52.4	51.4	50.4	49.4	48.5	47.5	46.5	45.6	44.6
109	53.3	52.4	51.4	50.4	49.4	48.5	47.5	46.5	45.6	44.6
110	53.3	52.4	51.4	50.4	49.4	48.5	47.5	46.5	45.6	44.6
111	53.3	52.4	51.4	50.4	49.4	48.5	47.5	46.5	45.6	44.6
112	53.3	52.4	51.4	50.4	49.4	48.5	47.5	46.5	45.6	44.6
113	53.3	52.4	51.4	50.4	49.4	48.5	47.5	46.5	45.6	44.6
114	53.3	52.4	51.4	50.4	49.4	48.5	47.5	46.5	45.6	44.6
115+	53.3	52.4	51.4	50.4	49.4	48.5	47.5	46.5	45.6	44.6

Ages	40	41	42	43	44	45	46	47	48	49
40	50.2	49.8	49.3	48.9	48.5	48.1	47.7	47.4	47.1	46.8
41	49.8	49.3	48.8	48.3	47.9	47.5	47.1	46.7	46.4	46.1
42	49.3	48.8	48.3	47.8	47.3	46.9	46.5	46.1	45.8	45.4
43	48.9	48.3	47.8	47.3	46.8	46.3	45.9	45.5	45.1	44.8
44	48.5	47.9	47.3	46.8	46.3	45.8	45.4	44.9	44.5	44.2
45	48.1	47.5	46.9	46.3	45.8	45.3	44.8	44.4	44.0	43.6
46	47.7	47.1	46.5	45.9	45.4	44.8	44.3	43.9	43.4	43.0
47	47.4	46.7	46.1	45.5	44.9	44.4	43.9	43.4	42.9	42.4

Joint Life and Last Survivor Table

IRS Reg. 1.401(a)(9)-9, Q+A-3

Ages	40	41	42	43	44	45	46	47	48	49
48	47.1	46.4	45.8	45.1	44.5	44.0	43.4	42.9	42.4	41.9
49	46.8	46.1	45.4	44.8	44.2	43.6	43.0	42.4	41.9	41.4
50	46.5	45.8	45.1	44.4	43.8	43.2	42.6	42.0	41.5	40.9
51	46.3	45.5	44.8	44.1	43.5	42.8	42.2	41.6	41.0	40.5
52	46.0	45.3	44.6	43.8	43.2	42.5	41.8	41.2	40.6	40.1
53	45.8	45.1	44.3	43.6	42.9	42.2	41.5	40.9	40.3	39.7
54	45.6	44.8	44.1	43.3	42.6	41.9	41.2	40.5	39.9	39.3
55	45.5	44.7	43.9	43.1	42.4	41.6	40.9	40.2	39.6	38.9
56	45.3	44.5	43.7	42.9	42.1	41.4	40.7	40.0	39.3	38.6
57	45.1	44.3	43.5	42.7	41.9	41.2	40.4	39.7	39.0	38.3
58	45.0	44.2	43.3	42.5	41.7	40.9	40.2	39.4	38.7	38.0
59	44.9	44.0	43.2	42.4	41.5	40.7	40.0	39.2	38.5	37.8
60	44.7	43.9	43.0	42.2	41.4	40.6	39.8	39.0	38.2	37.5
61	44.6	43.8	42.9	42.1	41.2	40.4	39.6	38.8	38.0	37.3
62	44.5	43.7	42.8	41.9	41.1	40.3	39.4	38.6	37.8	37.1
63	44.5	43.6	42.7	41.8	41.0	40.1	39.3	38.5	37.7	36.9
64	44.4	43.5	42.6	41.7	40.8	40.0	39.2	38.3	37.5	36.7
65	44.3	43.4	42.5	41.6	40.7	39.9	39.0	38.2	37.4	36.6
66	44.2	43.3	42.4	41.5	40.6	39.8	38.9	38.1	37.2	36.4
67	44.2	43.3	42.3	41.4	40.6	39.7	38.8	38.0	37.1	36.3
68	44.1	43.2	42.3	41.4	40.5	39.6	38.7	37.9	37.0	36.2
69	44.1	43.1	42.2	41.3	40.4	39.5	38.6	37.8	36.9	36.0
70	44.0	43.1	42.2	41.3	40.3	39.4	38.6	37.7	36.8	35.9
71	44.0	43.0	42.1	41.2	40.3	39.4	38.5	37.6	36.7	35.9
72	43.9	43.0	42.1	41.1	40.2	39.3	38.4	37.5	36.6	35.8
73	43.9	43.0	42.0	41.1	40.2	39.3	38.4	37.5	36.6	35.7
74	43.9	42.9	42.0	41.1	40.1	39.2	38.3	37.4	36.5	35.6
75	43.8	42.9	42.0	41.0	40.1	39.2	38.3	37.4	36.5	35.6
76	43.8	42.9	41.9	41.0	40.1	39.1	38.2	37.3	36.4	35.5
77	43.8	42.9	41.9	41.0	40.0	39.1	38.2	37.3	36.4	35.5

Joint Life and Last Survivor Table

IRS Reg. 1.401(a)(9)-9, Q+A-3

Ages	40	41	42	43	44	45	46	47	48	49
78	43.8	42.8	41.9	40.9	40.0	39.1	38.2	37.2	36.3	35.4
79	43.8	42.8	41.9	40.9	40.0	39.1	38.1	37.2	36.3	35.4
80	43.7	42.8	41.8	40.9	40.0	39.0	38.1	37.2	36.3	35.4
81	43.7	42.8	41.8	40.9	39.9	39.0	38.1	37.2	36.2	35.3
82	43.7	42.8	41.8	40.9	39.9	39.0	38.1	37.1	36.2	35.3
83	43.7	42.8	41.8	40.9	39.9	39.0	38.0	37.1	36.2	35.3
84	43.7	42.7	41.8	40.8	39.9	39.0	38.0	37.1	36.2	35.3
85	43.7	42.7	41.8	40.9	39.9	38.9	38.0	37.1	36.2	35.2
86	43.7	42.7	41.8	40.8	39.9	38.9	38.0	37.1	36.1	35.2
87	43.7	42.7	41.8	40.8	39.9	38.9	38.0	37.0	36.1	35.2
88	43.7	42.7	41.8	40.8	39.9	38.9	38.0	37.0	36.1	35.2
89	43.7	42.7	41.7	40.8	39.8	38.9	38.0	37.0	36.1	35.2
90	43.7	42.7	41.7	40.8	39.8	38.9	38.0	37.0	36.1	35.2
91	43.7	42.7	41.7	40.8	39.8	38.9	37.9	37.0	36.1	35.2
92	43.7	42.7	41.7	40.8	39.8	38.9	37.9	37.0	36.1	35.1
93	43.7	42.7	41.7	40.8	39.8	38.9	37.9	37.0	36.1	35.1
94	43.7	42.7	41.7	40.8	39.8	38.9	37.9	37.0	36.1	35.1
95	43.6	42.7	41.7	40.8	39.8	38.9	37.9	37.0	36.1	35.1
96	43.6	42.7	41.7	40.8	39.8	38.9	37.9	37.0	36.1	35.1
97	43.6	42.7	41.7	40.8	39.8	38.9	37.9	37.0	36.1	35.1
98	43.6	42.7	41.7	40.8	39.8	38.9	37.9	37.0	36.0	35.1
99	43.6	42.7	41.7	40.8	39.8	38.9	37.9	37.0	36.0	35.1
100	43.6	42.7	41.7	40.8	39.8	38.9	37.9	37.0	36.0	35.1
101	43.6	42.7	41.7	40.8	39.8	38.9	37.9	37.0	36.0	35.1
102	43.6	42.7	41.7	40.8	39.8	38.9	37.9	37.0	36.0	35.1
103	43.6	42.7	41.7	40.8	39.8	38.9	37.9	37.0	36.0	35.1
104	43.6	42.7	41.7	40.8	39.8	38.8	37.9	37.0	36.0	35.1
105	43.6	42.7	41.7	40.8	39.8	38.8	37.9	37.0	36.0	35.1

Joint Life and Last Survivor Table

IRS Reg. 1.401(a)(9)-9, Q+A-3

Ages	40	41	42	43	44	45	46	47	48	49
106	43.6	42.7	41.7	40.8	39.8	38.8	37.9	37.0	36.0	35.1
107	43.6	42.7	41.7	40.8	39.8	38.8	37.9	37.0	36.0	35.1
108	43.6	42.7	41.7	40.8	39.8	38.8	37.9	37.0	36.0	35.1
109	43.6	42.7	41.7	40.7	39.8	38.8	37.9	37.0	36.0	35.1
110	43.6	42.7	41.7	40.7	39.8	38.8	37.9	37.0	36.0	35.1
111	43.6	42.7	41.7	40.7	39.8	38.8	37.9	37.0	36.0	35.1
112	43.6	42.7	41.7	40.7	39.8	38.8	37.9	37.0	36.0	35.1
113	43.6	42.7	41.7	40.7	39.8	38.8	37.9	37.0	36.0	35.1
114	43.6	42.7	41.7	40.7	39.8	38.8	37.9	37.0	36.0	35.1
115+	43.6	42.7	41.7	40.7	39.8	38.8	37.9	37.0	36.0	35.1

Ages	50	51	52	53	54	55	56	57	58	59
50	40.4	40.0	39.5	39.1	38.7	38.3	38.0	37.6	37.3	37.1
51	40.0	39.5	39.0	38.5	38.1	37.7	37.4	37.0	36.7	36.4
52	39.5	39.0	38.5	38.0	37.6	37.2	36.8	36.4	36.0	35.7
53	39.1	38.5	38.0	37.5	37.1	36.6	36.2	35.8	35.4	35.1
54	38.7	38.1	37.6	37.1	36.6	36.1	35.7	35.2	34.8	34.5
55	38.3	37.7	37.2	36.6	36.1	35.6	35.1	34.7	34.3	33.9
56	38.0	37.4	36.8	36.2	35.7	35.1	34.7	34.2	33.7	33.3
57	37.6	37.0	36.4	35.8	35.2	34.7	34.2	33.7	33.2	32.8
58	37.3	36.7	36.0	35.4	34.8	34.3	33.7	33.2	32.8	32.3
59	37.1	36.4	35.7	35.1	34.5	33.9	33.3	32.8	32.3	31.8
60	36.8	36.1	35.4	34.8	34.1	33.5	32.9	32.4	31.9	31.3
61	36.6	35.8	35.1	34.5	33.8	33.2	32.6	32.0	31.4	30.9
62	36.3	35.6	34.9	34.2	33.5	32.9	32.2	31.6	31.1	30.5
63	36.1	35.4	34.6	33.9	33.2	32.6	31.9	31.3	30.7	30.1

Joint Life and Last Survivor Table

IRS Reg. 1.401(a)(9)-9, Q+A-3

Ages	50	51	52	53	54	55	56	57	58	59
64	35.9	35.2	34.4	33.7	33.0	32.3	31.6	31.0	30.4	29.8
65	35.8	35.0	34.2	33.5	32.7	32.0	31.4	30.7	30.0	29.4
66	35.6	34.8	34.0	33.3	32.5	31.8	31.1	30.4	29.8	29.1
67	35.5	34.7	33.9	33.1	32.3	31.6	30.9	30.2	29.5	28.8
68	35.3	34.5	33.7	32.9	32.1	31.4	30.7	29.9	29.2	28.6
69	35.2	34.4	33.6	32.8	32.0	31.2	30.5	29.7	29.0	28.3
70	35.1	34.3	33.4	32.6	31.8	31.1	30.3	29.5	28.8	28.1
71	35.0	34.2	33.3	32.5	31.7	30.9	30.1	29.4	28.6	27.9
72	34.9	34.1	33.2	32.4	31.6	30.8	30.0	29.2	28.4	27.7
73	34.8	34.0	33.1	32.3	31.5	30.6	29.8	29.1	28.3	27.5
74	34.8	33.9	33.0	32.2	31.4	30.5	29.7	28.9	28.1	27.4
75	34.7	33.8	33.0	32.1	31.3	30.4	29.6	28.8	28.0	27.2
76	34.6	33.8	32.9	32.0	31.2	30.3	29.5	28.7	27.9	27.1
77	34.6	33.7	32.8	32.0	31.1	30.3	29.4	28.6	27.8	27.0
78	34.5	33.6	32.8	31.9	31.0	30.2	29.3	28.5	27.7	26.9
79	34.5	33.6	32.7	31.8	31.0	30.1	29.3	28.4	27.6	26.8
80	34.5	33.6	32.7	31.8	30.9	30.1	29.2	28.4	27.5	26.7
81	34.4	33.5	32.6	31.8	30.9	30.0	29.2	28.3	27.5	26.6
82	34.4	33.5	32.6	31.7	30.8	30.0	29.1	28.3	27.4	26.6
83	34.4	33.5	32.6	31.7	30.8	29.9	29.1	28.2	27.4	26.5
84	34.3	33.4	32.5	31.7	30.8	29.9	29.0	28.2	27.3	26.5
85	34.3	33.4	32.5	31.6	30.7	29.9	29.0	28.1	27.3	26.4
86	34.3	33.4	32.5	31.6	30.7	29.8	29.0	28.1	27.2	26.4
87	34.3	33.4	32.5	31.6	30.7	29.8	28.9	28.1	27.2	26.4
88	34.3	33.4	32.5	31.6	30.7	29.8	28.9	28.0	27.2	26.3
89	34.3	33.3	32.4	31.5	30.7	29.8	28.9	28.0	27.2	26.3
90	34.2	33.3	32.4	31.5	30.6	29.8	28.9	28.0	27.1	26.3
91	34.2	33.3	32.4	31.5	30.6	29.7	28.9	28.0	27.1	26.3

Joint Life and Last Survivor Table

IRS Reg. 1.401(a)(9)-9, Q+A-3

Ages	50	51	52	53	54	55	56	57	58	59
92	34.2	33.3	32.4	31.5	30.6	29.7	28.8	28.0	27.1	26.2
93	34.2	33.3	32.4	31.5	30.6	29.7	28.8	28.0	27.1	26.2
94	34.2	33.3	32.4	31.5	30.6	29.7	28.8	27.9	27.1	26.2
95	34.2	33.3	32.4	31.5	30.6	29.7	28.8	27.9	27.1	26.2
96	34.2	33.3	32.4	31.5	30.6	29.7	28.8	27.9	27.0	26.2
97	34.2	33.3	32.4	31.5	30.6	29.7	28.8	27.9	27.0	26.2
98	34.2	33.3	32.4	31.5	30.6	29.7	28.8	27.9	27.0	26.2
99	34.2	33.3	32.4	31.5	30.6	29.7	28.8	27.9	27.0	26.2
100	34.2	33.3	32.4	31.5	30.6	29.7	28.8	27.9	27.0	26.1
101	34.2	33.3	32.4	31.5	30.6	29.7	28.8	27.9	27.0	26.1
102	34.2	33.3	32.4	31.4	30.5	29.7	28.8	27.9	27.0	26.1
103	34.2	33.3	32.4	31.4	30.5	29.7	28.8	27.9	27.0	26.1
104	34.2	33.3	32.4	31.4	30.5	29.6	28.8	27.9	27.0	26.1
105	34.2	33.3	32.3	31.4	30.5	29.6	28.8	27.9	27.0	26.1
106	34.2	33.3	32.3	31.4	30.5	29.6	28.8	27.9	27.0	26.1
107	34.2	33.3	32.3	31.4	30.5	29.6	28.8	27.9	27.0	26.1
108	34.2	33.3	32.3	31.4	30.5	29.6	28.8	27.9	27.0	26.1
109	34.2	33.3	32.3	31.4	30.5	29.6	28.7	27.9	27.0	26.1
110	34.2	33.3	32.3	31.4	30.5	29.6	28.7	27.9	27.0	26.1
111	34.2	33.3	32.3	31.4	30.5	29.6	28.7	27.9	27.0	26.1
112	34.2	33.3	32.3	31.4	30.5	29.6	28.7	27.9	27.0	26.1
113	34.2	33.3	32.3	31.4	30.5	29.6	28.7	27.9	27.0	26.1
114	34.2	33.3	32.3	31.4	30.5	29.6	28.7	27.9	27.0	26.1
115+	34.2	33.3	32.3	31.4	30.5	29.6	28.7	27.9	27.0	26.1

Joint Life and Last Survivor Table

IRS Reg. 1.401(a)(9)-9, Q+A-3

Ages	60	61	62	63	64	65	66	67	68	69
60	30.9	30.4	30.0	29.6	29.2	28.8	28.5	28.2	27.9	27.6
61	30.4	29.9	29.5	29.0	28.6	28.3	27.9	27.6	27.3	27.0
62	30.0	29.5	29.0	28.5	28.1	27.7	27.3	27.0	26.7	26.4
63	29.6	29.0	28.5	28.1	27.6	27.2	26.8	26.4	26.1	25.7
64	29.2	28.6	28.1	27.6	27.1	26.7	26.3	25.9	25.5	25.2
65	28.8	28.3	27.7	27.2	26.7	26.2	25.8	25.4	25.0	24.6
66	28.5	27.9	27.3	26.8	26.3	25.8	25.3	24.9	24.5	24.1
67	28.2	27.6	27.0	26.4	25.9	25.4	24.9	24.4	24.0	23.6
68	27.9	27.3	26.7	26.1	25.5	25.0	24.5	24.0	23.5	23.1
69	27.6	27.0	26.4	25.7	25.2	24.6	24.1	23.6	23.1	22.6
70	27.4	26.7	26.1	25.4	24.8	24.3	23.7	23.2	22.7	22.2
71	27.2	26.5	25.8	25.2	24.5	23.9	23.4	22.8	22.3	21.8
72	27.0	26.3	25.6	24.9	24.3	23.7	23.1	22.5	22.0	21.4
73	26.8	26.1	25.4	24.7	24.0	23.4	22.8	22.2	21.6	21.1
74	26.6	25.9	25.2	24.5	23.8	23.1	22.5	21.9	21.3	20.8
75	26.5	25.7	25.0	24.3	23.6	22.9	22.3	21.6	21.0	20.5
76	26.3	25.6	24.8	24.1	23.4	22.7	22	21.4	20.8	20.2
77	26.2	25.4	24.7	23.9	23.2	22.5	21.8	21.2	20.6	19.9
78	26.1	25.3	24.6	23.8	23.1	22.4	21.7	21.0	20.3	19.7
79	26.0	25.2	24.4	23.7	22.9	22.2	21.5	20.8	20.1	19.5
80	25.9	25.1	24.3	23.6	22.8	22.1	21.3	20.6	20	19.3
81	25.8	25.0	24.2	23.4	22.7	21.9	21.2	20.5	19.8	19.1
82	25.8	24.9	24.1	23.4	22.6	21.8	21.1	20.4	19.7	19.0
83	25.7	24.9	24.1	23.3	22.5	21.7	21.0	20.2	19.5	18.8
84	25.6	24.8	24.0	23.2	22.4	21.6	20.9	20.1	19.4	18.7
85	25.6	24.8	23.9	23.1	22.3	21.6	20.8	20.1	19.3	18.6
86	25.5	24.7	23.9	23.1	22.3	21.5	20.7	20.0	19.2	18.5
87	25.5	24.7	23.8	23.0	22.2	21.4	20.7	19.9	19.2	18.4

Joint Life and Last Survivor Table

IRS Reg. 1.401(a)(9)-9, Q+A-3

Ages	60	61	62	63	64	65	66	67	68	69
88	25.5	24.6	23.8	23.0	22.2	21.4	20.6	19.8	19.1	18.3
89	25.4	24.6	23.8	22.9	22.1	21.3	20.5	19.8	19.0	18.3
90	25.4	24.6	23.7	22.9	22.1	21.3	20.5	19.7	19.0	18.2
91	25.4	24.5	23.7	22.9	22.1	21.3	20.5	19.7	18.9	18.2
92	25.4	24.5	23.7	22.9	22.0	21.2	20.4	19.6	18.9	18.1
93	25.4	24.5	23.7	22.8	22.0	21.2	20.4	19.6	18.8	18.1
94	25.3	24.5	23.6	22.8	22.0	21.2	20.4	19.6	18.8	18.0
95	25.3	24.5	23.6	22.8	22.0	21.1	20.3	19.6	18.8	18.0
96	25.3	24.5	23.6	22.8	21.9	21.1	20.3	19.5	18.8	18.0
97	25.3	24.5	23.6	22.8	21.9	21.1	20.3	19.5	18.7	18.0
98	25.3	24.4	23.6	22.8	21.9	21.1	20.3	19.5	18.7	17.9
99	25.3	24.4	23.6	22.7	21.9	21.1	20.3	19.5	18.7	17.9
100	25.3	24.4	23.6	22.7	21.9	21.1	20.3	19.5	18.7	17.9
101	25.3	24.4	23.6	22.7	21.9	21.1	20.2	19.4	18.7	17.9
102	25.3	24.4	23.6	22.7	21.9	21.1	20.2	19.4	18.6	17.9
103	25.3	24.4	23.6	22.7	21.9	21.0	20.2	19.4	18.6	17.9
104	25.3	24.4	23.5	22.7	21.9	21.0	20.2	19.4	18.6	17.8
105	25.3	24.4	23.5	22.7	21.9	21.0	20.2	19.4	18.6	17.8
106	25.3	24.4	23.5	22.7	21.9	21.0	20.2	19.4	18.6	17.8
107	25.2	24.4	23.5	22.7	21.8	21.0	20.2	19.4	18.6	17.8
108	25.2	24.4	23.5	22.7	21.8	21.0	20.2	19.4	18.6	17.8
109	25.2	24.4	23.5	22.7	21.8	21.0	20.2	19.4	18.6	17.8
110	25.2	24.4	23.5	22.7	21.8	21.0	20.2	19.4	18.6	17.8
111	25.2	24.4	23.5	22.7	21.8	21.0	20.2	19.4	18.6	17.8
112	25.2	24.4	23.5	22.7	21.8	21.0	20.2	19.4	18.6	17.8
113	25.2	24.4	23.5	22.7	21.8	21.0	20.2	19.4	18.6	17.8
114	25.2	24.4	23.5	22.7	21.8	21.0	20.2	19.4	18.6	17.8
115+	25.2	24.4	23.5	22.7	21.8	21.0	20.2	19.4	18.6	17.8

Joint Life and Last Survivor Table

IRS Reg. 1.401(a)(9)-9, Q+A-3

Ages	70	71	72	73	74	75	76	77	78	79
70	21.8	21.3	20.9	20.6	20.2	19.9	19.6	19.4	19.1	18.9
71	21.3	20.9	20.5	20.1	19.7	19.4	19.1	18.8	18.5	18.3
72	20.9	20.5	20.0	19.6	19.3	18.9	18.6	18.3	18.0	17.7
73	20.6	20.1	19.6	19.2	18.8	18.4	18.1	17.8	17.5	17.2
74	20.2	19.7	19.3	18.8	18.4	18.0	17.6	17.3	17.0	16.7
75	19.9	19.4	18.9	18.4	18.0	17.6	17.2	16.8	16.5	16.2
76	19.6	19.1	18.6	18.1	17.6	17.2	16.8	16.4	16.0	15.7
77	19.4	18.8	18.3	17.8	17.3	16.8	16.4	16.0	15.6	15.3
78	19.1	18.5	18.0	17.5	17.0	16.5	16.0	15.6	15.2	14.9
79	18.9	18.3	17.7	17.2	16.7	16.2	15.7	15.3	14.9	14.5
80	18.7	18.1	17.5	16.9	16.4	15.9	15.4	15.0	14.5	14.1
81	18.5	17.9	17.3	16.7	16.2	15.6	15.1	14.7	14.2	13.8
82	18.3	17.7	17.1	16.5	15.9	15.4	14.9	14.4	13.9	13.5
83	18.2	17.5	16.9	16.3	15.7	15.2	14.7	14.2	13.7	13.2
84	18.0	17.4	16.7	16.1	15.5	15.0	14.4	13.9	13.4	13.0
85	17.9	17.3	16.6	16.0	15.4	14.8	14.3	13.7	13.2	12.8
86	17.8	17.1	16.5	15.8	15.2	14.6	14.1	13.5	13.0	12.5
87	17.7	17.0	16.4	15.7	15.1	14.5	13.9	13.4	12.9	12.4
88	17.6	16.9	16.3	15.6	15.0	14.4	13.8	13.2	12.7	12.2
89	17.6	16.9	16.2	15.5	14.9	14.3	13.7	13.1	12.6	12.0
90	17.5	16.8	16.1	15.4	14.8	14.2	13.6	13.0	12.4	11.9
91	17.4	16.7	16.0	15.4	14.7	14.1	13.5	12.9	12.3	11.8
92	17.4	16.7	16.0	15.3	14.6	14.0	13.4	12.8	12.2	11.7
93	17.3	16.6	15.9	15.2	14.6	13.9	13.3	12.7	12.1	11.6
94	17.3	16.6	15.9	15.2	14.5	13.9	13.2	12.6	12.0	11.5
95	17.3	16.5	15.8	15.1	14.5	13.8	13.2	12.6	12.0	11.4
96	17.2	16.5	15.8	15.1	14.4	13.8	13.1	12.5	11.9	11.3
97	17.2	16.5	15.8	15.1	14.4	13.7	13.1	12.5	11.9	11.3

Joint Life and Last Survivor Table

IRS Reg. 1.401(a)(9)-9, Q+A-3

Ages	70	71	72	73	74	75	76	77	78	79
98	17.2	16.4	15.7	15.0	14.3	13.7	13.0	12.4	11.8	11.2
99	17.2	16.4	15.7	15.0	14.3	13.6	13.0	12.4	11.8	11.2
100	17.1	16.4	15.7	15.0	14.3	13.6	12.9	12.3	11.7	11.1
101	17.1	16.4	15.6	14.9	14.2	13.6	12.9	12.3	11.7	11.1
102	17.1	16.4	15.6	14.9	14.2	13.5	12.9	12.2	11.6	11.0
103	17.1	16.3	15.6	14.9	14.2	13.5	12.9	12.2	11.6	11.0
104	17.1	16.3	15.6	14.9	14.2	13.5	12.8	12.2	11.6	11.0
105	17.1	16.3	15.6	14.9	14.2	13.5	12.8	12.2	11.5	10.9
106	17.1	16.3	15.6	14.8	14.1	13.5	12.8	12.2	11.5	10.9
107	17.0	16.3	15.6	14.8	14.1	13.4	12.8	12.1	11.5	10.9
109	17.0	16.3	15.5	14.8	14.1	13.4	12.8	12.1	11.5	10.9
110	17.0	16.3	15.5	14.8	14.1	13.4	12.7	12.1	11.5	10.9
111	17.0	16.3	15.5	14.8	14.1	13.4	12.7	12.1	11.5	10.8
112	17.0	16.3	15.5	14.8	14.1	13.4	12.7	12.1	11.5	10.8
113	17.0	16.3	15.5	14.8	14.1	13.4	12.7	12.1	11.4	10.8
114	17.0	16.3	15.5	14.8	14.1	13.4	12.7	12.1	11.4	10.8
115+	17.0	16.3	15.5	14.8	14.1	13.4	12.7	12.1	11.4	10.8

Ages	80	81	82	83	84	85	86	87	88	89
80	13.8	13.4	13.1	12.8	12.6	12.3	12.1	11.9	11.7	11.5
81	13.4	13.1	12.7	12.4	12.2	11.9	11.7	11.4	11.3	11.1
82	13.1	12.7	12.4	12.1	11.8	11.5	11.3	11.0	10.8	10.6
83	12.8	12.4	12.1	11.7	11.4	11.1	10.9	10.6	10.4	10.2
84	12.6	12.2	11.8	11.4	11.1	10.8	10.5	10.3	10.1	9.9
85	12.3	11.9	11.5	11.1	10.8	10.5	10.2	9.9	9.7	9.5
86	12.1	11.7	11.3	10.9	10.5	10.2	9.9	9.6	9.4	9.2
87	11.9	11.4	11.0	10.6	10.3	9.9	9.6	9.4	9.1	8.9

Joint Life and Last Survivor Table

IRS Reg. 1.401(a)(9)-9, Q+A-3

Ages	80	81	82	83	84	85	86	87	88	89
88	11.7	11.3	10.8	10.4	10.1	9.7	9.4	9.1	8.8	8.6
89	11.5	11.1	10.6	10.2	9.9	9.5	9.2	8.9	8.6	8.3
90	11.4	10.9	10.5	10.1	9.7	9.3	9.0	8.6	8.3	8.1
91	11.3	10.8	10.3	9.9	9.5	9.1	8.8	8.4	8.1	7.9
92	11.2	10.7	10.2	9.8	9.3	9.0	8.6	8.3	8.0	7.7
93	11.1	10.6	10.1	9.6	9.2	8.8	8.5	8.1	7.8	7.5
94	11.0	10.5	10.0	9.5	9.1	8.7	8.3	8.0	7.6	7.3
95	10.9	10.4	9.9	9.4	9.0	8.6	8.2	7.8	7.5	7.2
96	10.8	10.3	9.8	9.3	8.9	8.5	8.1	7.7	7.4	7.1
97	10.7	10.2	9.7	9.2	8.8	8.4	8.0	7.6	7.3	6.9
98	10.7	10.1	9.6	9.2	8.7	8.3	7.9	7.5	7.1	6.8
99	10.6	10.1	9.6	9.1	8.6	8.2	7.8	7.4	7.0	6.7
100	10.6	10.0	9.5	9.0	8.5	8.1	7.7	7.3	6.9	6.6
101	10.5	10.0	9.4	9.0	8.5	8.0	7.6	7.2	6.9	6.5
102	10.5	9.9	9.4	8.9	8.4	8.0	7.5	7.1	6.8	6.4
103	10.4	9.9	9.4	8.8	8.4	7.9	7.5	7.1	6.7	6.3
104	10.4	9.8	9.3	8.8	8.3	7.9	7.4	7.0	6.6	6.3
105	10.4	9.8	9.3	8.8	8.3	7.8	7.4	7.0	6.6	6.2
106	10.3	9.8	9.2	8.7	8.2	7.8	7.3	6.9	6.5	6.2
107	10.3	9.8	9.2	8.7	8.2	7.7	7.3	6.9	6.5	6.1
108	10.3	9.7	9.2	8.7	8.2	7.7	7.3	6.8	6.4	6.1
109	10.3	9.7	9.2	8.7	8.2	7.7	7.2	6.8	6.4	6.0
110	10.3	9.7	9.2	8.6	8.1	7.7	7.2	6.8	6.4	6.0
111	10.3	9.7	9.1	8.6	8.1	7.6	7.2	6.8	6.3	6.0
112	10.2	9.7	9.1	8.6	8.1	7.6	7.2	6.7	6.3	5.9
113	10.2	9.7	9.1	8.6	8.1	7.6	7.2	6.7	6.3	5.9
114	10.2	9.7	9.1	8.6	8.1	7.6	7.1	6.7	6.3	5.9
115+	10.2	9.7	9.1	8.6	8.1	7.6	7.1	6.7	6.3	5.9

Joint Life and Last Survivor Table

IRS Reg. 1.401(a)(9)-9, Q+A-3

Ages	90	91	92	93	94	95	96	97	98	99
90	7.8	7.6	7.4	7.2	7.1	6.9	6.8	6.6	6.5	6.4
91	7.6	7.4	7.2	7.0	6.8	6.7	6.5	6.4	6.3	6.1
92	7.4	7.2	7.0	6.8	6.6	6.4	6.3	6.1	6.0	5.9
93	7.2	7.0	6.8	6.6	6.4	6.2	6.1	5.9	5.8	5.6
94	7.1	6.8	6.6	6.4	6.2	6.0	5.9	5.7	5.6	5.4
95	6.9	6.7	6.4	6.2	6.0	5.8	5.7	5.5	5.4	5.2
96	6.8	6.5	6.3	6.1	5.9	5.7	5.5	5.3	5.2	5.0
97	6.6	6.4	6.1	5.9	5.7	5.5	5.3	5.2	5.0	4.9
98	6.5	6.3	6.0	5.8	5.6	5.4	5.2	5.0	4.8	4.7
99	6.4	6.1	5.9	5.6	5.4	5.2	5.0	4.9	4.7	4.5
100	6.3	6.0	5.8	5.5	5.3	5.1	4.9	4.7	4.5	4.4
101	6.2	5.9	5.6	5.4	5.2	5.0	4.8	4.6	4.4	4.2
102	6.1	5.8	5.5	5.3	5.1	4.8	4.6	4.4	4.3	4.1
103	6.0	5.7	5.4	5.2	5.0	4.7	4.5	4.3	4.1	4.0
104	5.9	5.6	5.4	5.1	4.9	4.6	4.4	4.2	4.0	3.8
105	5.9	5.6	5.3	5.0	4.8	4.5	4.3	4.1	3.9	3.7
106	5.8	5.5	5.2	4.9	4.7	4.5	4.2	4.0	3.8	3.6
107	5.8	5.4	5.1	4.9	4.6	4.4	4.2	3.9	3.7	3.5
108	5.7	5.4	5.1	4.8	4.6	4.3	4.1	3.9	3.7	3.5
109	5.7	5.3	5.0	4.8	4.5	4.3	4.0	3.8	3.6	3.4
110	5.6	5.3	5.0	4.7	4.5	4.2	4.0	3.8	3.5	3.3
111	5.6	5.3	5.0	4.7	4.4	4.2	3.9	3.7	3.5	3.3
112	5.6	5.3	4.9	4.7	4.4	4.1	3.9	3.7	3.5	3.2
113	5.6	5.2	4.9	4.6	4.4	4.1	3.9	3.6	3.4	3.2
114	5.6	5.2	4.9	4.6	4.3	4.1	3.9	3.6	3.4	3.2
115+	5.5	5.2	4.9	4.6	4.3	4.1	3.8	3.6	3.4	3.1

Joint Life and Last Survivor Table

IRS Reg. 1.401(a)(9)-9, Q+A-3

Ages	100	101	102	103	104	105	106	107	108	109
100	4.2	4.1	3.9	3.8	3.7	3.5	3.4	3.3	3.3	3.2
101	4.1	3.9	3.7	3.6	3.5	3.4	3.2	3.1	3.1	3.0
102	3.9	3.7	3.6	3.4	3.3	3.2	3.1	3.0	2.9	2.8
103	3.8	3.6	3.4	3.3	3.2	3.0	2.9	2.8	2.7	2.6
104	3.7	3.5	3.3	3.2	3.0	2.9	2.7	2.6	2.5	2.4
105	3.5	3.4	3.2	3.0	2.9	2.7	2.6	2.5	2.4	2.3
106	3.4	3.2	3.1	2.9	2.7	2.6	2.4	2.3	2.2	2.1
107	3.3	3.1	3.0	2.8	2.6	2.5	2.3	2.2	2.1	2
108	3.3	3.1	2.9	2.7	2.5	2.4	2.2	2.1	1.9	1.8
109	3.2	3.0	2.8	2.6	2.4	2.3	2.1	2.0	1.8	1.7
110	3.1	2.9	2.7	2.5	2.3	2.2	2.0	1.9	1.7	1.6
111	3.1	2.9	2.7	2.5	2.3	2.1	1.9	1.8	1.6	1.5
112	3.0	2.8	2.6	2.4	2.2	2.0	1.9	1.7	1.5	1.4
113	3.0	2.8	2.6	2.4	2.2	2.0	1.8	1.6	1.5	1.3
114	3.0	2.7	2.5	2.3	2.1	1.9	1.8	1.6	1.4	1.3
115+	2.9	2.7	2.5	2.3	2.1	1.9	1.7	1.5	1.4	1.2

Ages	110	111	112	113	114	115
110	1.5	1.4	1.3	1.2	1.1	1.1
111	1.4	1.2	1.1	1.1	1.0	1.0
112	1.3	1.1	1.0	1.0	1.0	1.0
113	1.2	1.1	1.0	1.0	1.0	1.0
114	1.1	1.0	1.0	1.0	1.0	1.0
115+	1.1	1.0	1.0	1.0	1.0	1.0

Single Life Table

IRS Reg. 1.401(a)(9)-9, Q+A-1

Age	Life Expectancy	Age	Life Expectancy	Age	Life Expectancy
0	82.4	38	45.6	76	12.7
1	81.6	39	44.6	77	12.1
2	80.6	40	43.6	78	11.4
3	79.7	41	42.7	79	10.8
4	78.7	42	41.7	80	10.2
5	77.7	43	40.7	81	9.7
6	76.7	44	39.8	82	9.1
7	75.8	45	38.8	83	8.6
8	74.8	46	37.9	84	8.1
9	73.8	47	37.0	85	7.6
10	72.8	48	36.0	86	7.1
11	71.8	49	35.1	87	6.7
12	70.8	50	34.2	88	6.3
13	69.9	51	33.3	89	5.9
14	68.9	52	32.3	90	5.5
15	67.9	53	31.4	91	5.2
16	66.9	54	30.5	92	4.9
17	66.0	55	29.6	93	4.6
18	65.0	56	28.7	94	4.3
19	64.0	57	27.9	95	4.1
20	63.0	58	27.0	96	3.8
21	62.1	59	26.1	97	3.6
22	61.1	60	25.2	98	3.4
23	60.1	61	24.4	99	3.1
24	59.1	62	23.5	100	2.9
25	58.2	63	22.7	101	2.7
26	57.2	64	21.8	102	2.5
27	56.2	65	21.0	103	2.3
28	55.3	66	20.2	104	2.1
29	54.3	67	19.4	105	1.9
30	53.3	68	18.6	106	1.7
31	52.4	69	17.8	107	1.5
32	51.4	70	17.0	108	1.4
33	50.4	71	16.3	109	1.2
34	49.4	72	15.5	110	1.1
35	48.5	73	14.8	111+	1.0
36	47.5	74	14.1		
37	46.5	75	13.4		

Substantially Equal Periodic Payments

IRC Sec. 72(t)(2)(A)(iv)

Generally, taxable distributions from employer-sponsored qualified retirement plans, and from traditional and Roth IRAs, made before the account owner reaches age 59½, are subject to a 10% "early" withdrawal penalty.[1] One exception to this 10% penalty is for distributions taken as a series of "substantially equal periodic payments."

This exception applies to distributions made, at least once a year, over the life (or life expectancy) of the participant, or over the joint lives (or joint life expectancies) of the participant and a beneficiary. The payments must continue unchanged (except for death or disability) for the longer of: (a) five years (five years from the date of the first payment), or (b) the participant reaches age 59½. Otherwise, the 10% penalty will be applied retroactively and interest will be charged.

Calculating the Substantially-Equal Periodic Payment

In Notice 89-25, 11989-1, CB 662, Q&A-12 (March 20, 1989), the IRS listed three acceptable methods of calculating such a distribution:

- **Required minimum distribution (RMD):** The annual payment is determined using a method acceptable for calculating the required minimum distribution required under IRC Sec. 401(a)(9). In general, the account balance is divided by a life expectancy factor, resulting in a payment which changes from year to year.

- **Fixed amortization method:** Payment under this method is similar to the annual amount required to pay off a loan (equal to the amount in the plan at the start of distributions), at a reasonable interest rate, over the remainder of one's life. The dollar amount of the payment remains the same in each subsequent year.

- **Fixed annuitization:** An annuity factor is determined from a reasonable mortality table at an interest rate which is then reasonable for the age of the recipient of the distribution. The payment is determined for the first distribution and remains the same in each subsequent year.

---

[1] The discussion here concerns federal income tax law. State or local law may differ. Under federal law, the 10% penalty generally applies to distributions which are includable in gross income.

Substantially Equal Periodic Payments

Revenue Ruling 2002-62

On October 3, 2002, the IRS released Revenue Ruling 2002-62, to address questions raised by taxpayers who had begun to receive distributions under IRC Sec. 72(t)(2)(A)(iv) and who had been adversely affected by a declining stock market. This ruling contained the following key points.

- It expanded the guidance given in Q&A 12 of IRS Notice 89-25 to, among other things, incorporate into the calculation process the new life expectancy tables issued in April, 2002, with regard to required minimum distributions from IRAs and qualified plans.

- Allowed a participant who had been using either the fixed amortization method or the fixed annuitization method to make a one-time change to the RMD method.

- Specified that if a participant who is using an acceptable method to calculate the required substantially equal periodic payments exhausts the assets in an account prior to the required time period, the "cessation of payments will not be treated as a modification of the series of payments."

The guidance provided in Revenue Ruling 2002-62 replaced the guidance of IRS Notice 89-25 for any series of payments beginning on or after January 1, 2003. If distributions began before 2003 under any method that satisfied IRC Sec. 72(t)(2)(A)(iv), a change to the required minimum distribution calculation method may be made at any time.

Comparing the Three Methods[1]

Assumptions:

Plan or IRA account balance on 12/31 of the previous year: $400,000
Age of participant in distribution year: 50
Single life expectancy at age 50: 34.2[2]
Interest rate assumed: 2.98%[3]
Distribution period: Single life only

---

[1] The examples shown are from the IRS web site, www.irs.gov, "Retirement Plans FAQs Regarding Substantially Equal Periodic Payments," August 4, 2017.

[2] Derived from the Single Life Table found in Reg.1.401(a)(9)-9, Q&A-1. The Uniform Lifetime Table found in Appendix A of Revenue Ruling 2002-62 or the Joint and Last Survivor table of Reg.1.401(a)(9)-9, Q&A-3 may also be used.

[3] This rate is equal to 120% of the federal mid-term rate. In these IRS examples, the rate for April 2011 is used. This value will fluctuate and changes monthly.

Substantially Equal Periodic Payments

- **Required minimum distribution method:** For the current year, the annual distribution amount is calculated by dividing account balance by the participant's life expectancy.

$$\$400,000 / 34.2 = \$11,696$$

- **Fixed amortization method:** Distribution amount is calculated by amortizing the account balance over the number of years of the participant's single life expectancy. The calculation is the same as in determining the payment required to pay off a loan.

$$\$400,000 \times (.0298 / (1 - (1 + .0298)^{-34.2})) = \$18,811$$

- **Fixed annuitization method:** The distribution amount is equal to the account balance divided by an annuity factor that for the present value of an annuity of one dollar per year paid over the life of a 50-year-old participant. Such annuity factors are typically calculated by an actuary. In this case, the age-50 annuity factor (21.345) is based on the mortality table in Appendix B of Revenue Ruling 2002-62 and an interest rate of 2.98%.

$$\$400,000 / 21.345 = \$18,740$$

Method	Annual Withdrawal
Required minimum distribution	$11,696
Fixed amortization	18,811
Fixed annuitization	18,740

Rate of Withdrawal in Retirement

When you retire you know how much you own. The question becomes "How much can you spend?"

Item Description	Value
Capital	$500,000
Rate of return	6.00%
Number of years	25
Inflation Rate	4.00%
Annual withdrawal rate	4.98%
First year withdrawal amount	$24,901

Example

You can withdraw 4.98% of your capital, increasing the amount by 4.00%, each year to stay even with inflation.

Capital Balance

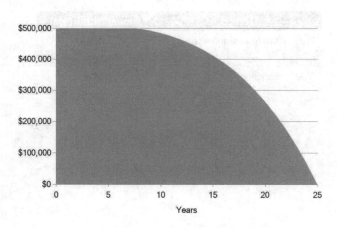

This is a hypothetical example and not a promise of future performance.
This calculator assumes withdrawal at the beginning of the year and interest compounded annually.

The Benefits of a College Education

For many, accumulating funds for the children's education is a savings goal that is often thought about, but seldom acted upon. There are numerous reasons why saving for college is an essential need.

- **Economics:** Statistically, the average worker with a 4-year college education earns far more than the average worker with only a high school diploma.

- **Increasing costs:** In recent years, college costs have increased at a rate greater than the general rate of inflation.[1]

- **Years of study:** Four years of study may not be sufficient. In many professions, six or even eight years of study are required.

What is a College Education Worth?

College educated, full-time workers statistically enjoy a higher median income than those with less education. In a recent report on education and earnings,[2] the Census Bureau found that those with four years of college could expect to have substantially higher annual earnings than high school graduates.

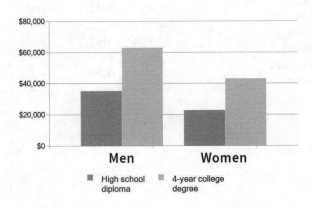

Median Annual Income

---

[1] See "Trends in College Pricing – 2017," published by The College Board, page 3.

[2] Median Earnings in the Past 12 Months (in 2016 Inflation-Adjusted Dollars) of Workers by Sex and Women's Earnings as a Percentage of Men's Earnings by Selected Characteristics. 2016 American Community Survey 1-Year Estimates.

The Benefits of a College Education

Over a lifetime of work, 39 years on average, a four-year college education can increase a man's total income by over $1,086,774. Because of time spent raising children, the average woman spends 28 years in the workforce. A college education could increase her lifetime earnings by over $561,036.[1]

What Does a College Education Cost?

In recent years, college costs have often exceeded the general rate of inflation. The table below projects college costs for a small group of well-known institutions:

Private Institutions	Annual Costs[2] (Assumes inflation is 4.0% per year.)			
	2018	2023	2028	2033
Yale University New Haven, Connecticut	$66,900	$81,394	$99,028	$120,483
Northwestern University Evanston, Illinois	68,725	83,614	101,730	123,770
Stanford University Stanford, California	64,729	78,753	95,815	116,573
Public Institutions	**2018**	**2023**	**2028**	**2033**
State University of New York Stony Brook, New York	$22,704	$27,623	$33,607	$40,889
University of Michigan Ann Arbor, Michigan	26,024	31,662	38,522	46,868
University of Colorado Boulder, Colorado	26,084	31,735	38,611	46,976

[1] Figures do not take inflation into account.

[2] Annual costs are for the 2017-2018 academic year and include tuition, fees, and on-campus room and board. Books, transportation, and personal expenses are additional. Costs for out-of-state students at public institutions are higher.

Saving for College

A college education is generally the largest purchase a family will make, aside from buying a home. And college is expensive. In 2016, for example, the average one-year cost of tuition and fees, and room and board, at four-year public colleges in the U.S. was $19,189.[1] If this annual figure is multiplied for four years of study, the total reaches $76,756. And that's not everything – these figures do not

include books, transportation to and from school, other incidentals, and continuing cost inflation.

Not only is college expensive today, the cost of a college education keeps going up as each year passes. Even worse, higher education costs have been increasing at a rate faster than inflation. The average annual tuition and required fees charged at four-year public colleges in the U.S. in 1985 was $1,228. By 2016 that figure had grown to $8,778[1], a compound annual growth rate of 6.50%. In comparison, inflation, as measured by the Consumer Price Index (CPI-W),[2] increased from 1985 to 2016 by an annual compound rate of only 2.56%. Many expect that college costs will continue to outpace inflation.

Start Planning Early:

With college costs high and rising, a family needs to begin the college planning process as early as possible. Taking key steps now makes it easier to reach the goal:

- **Start a savings program:** Start by estimating the cost of college. Once the cost is known, the needed savings can be calculated. Then compare available cash flow with the savings required. If current cash flow is not enough to save the full amount, at least a partial savings program can be started.

---

[1] Source: U.S. Department of Education, National Center for Education Statistics, Digest of Education Statistics, Table 330.10, Average undergraduate tuition and fees and room and board rates charged for full-time students in degree granting postsecondary institutions, by level and control of institution: 1963-64 through 2015-2016.

[2] The CPI is the Consumer Price Index for Urban Wage Earners and Clerical Workers, CPI-W.

- **Consider tax-advantaged approaches:** 529 Prepaid Tuition Plans, 529 Higher Education Savings Plans,[1] Coverdell Savings Accounts, and cash value life insurance all have important tax advantages.

  - **If there's a shortage:** If personal savings will not be enough, the family can plan for the need to apply for financial aid or begin the search for scholarship.

SAVINGS EXAMPLE

Assume a family has a new born child. College costs are currently estimated to be $15,000 per year, and are expected to increase at 6% per year over the next 18 years. The total amount needed at the start of college for four years will be almost $178,000. If the family can earn 3.5% (after-tax) on their savings, monthly deposits of approximately $590 will be needed to pay for the child's education.

---

[1] Federal law does not allow deductions for contributions to 529 plans, although growth inside a plan is tax deferred and qualified distributions are tax-exempt. The earnings portion of a non-qualified distribution is subject to federal income tax, including a 10% tax penalty. State or local tax law, however, can vary widely. 529 plans involve investment risk, including possible loss of funds, and there is no guarantee a college-funding goal will be met. The fees, expenses, and features of 529 plans vary from state to state.

Ways to Save for College

In accumulating funds for college, one of the first questions a family will face is, "Where do we invest the money?" Many financial professionals will recommend that money for college be placed in relatively low-risk investments. If there is a long enough time frame, the savings may be placed initially in higher risk (and potentially higher return) investments. As the time for college gets closer, the funds can be shifted into more conservative choices.

The ultimate decision will depend on a range of factors such as the number of years until college begins, the amount of money available to invest, a family's income tax bracket, risk tolerance, and investment experience. A few of the more traditional approaches are:

- **Savings accounts:** Including CDs, money market accounts, and regular savings.

- **Tax-free municipal bonds:** Held either directly or through a mutual fund.

- **U.S. Treasury securities:** Such as treasury bills or treasury bonds.

- **Growth stocks/growth mutual funds:** For the long-term investor.

Tax-Advantaged Strategies

Under federal income tax law (state or local income tax law may differ), there are a number of tax-advantaged strategies available to accumulate funds for college expenses. The rules surrounding these strategies can be complicated and they should only be used after careful review with a tax or other financial professional:

- **IRC Sec. 529 qualified tuition program:** These plans allow an individual to either prepay a student's tuition, or contribute to a savings account to pay the student's "qualified higher education expenses." Contributions are not tax deductible, but growth in an account is tax-deferred. If certain requirements are met, distributions to pay qualified higher expenses are excluded from income. 529 plans involve investment risk, including possible loss of funds, and there is no guarantee a college-funding goal will be met. The fees, expenses, and features of 529 plans vary from state to state.

- **Coverdell education savings account:** Up to $2,000 per year may be contributed to a Coverdell ESA for an individual. Contributions are not tax-deductible, but growth is tax-deferred. Distributions are excluded from income if used for qualifying educational expenses. Other restrictions may apply.

- **Cash value life insurance:** Cash value life insurance can be an attractive, tax-favored means of accumulating college funds. If an insured dies before the student starts school, the policy proceeds can be used to pay college expenses.

- **U.S. savings bonds:** Interest on series EE savings bonds issued after 1989, or Series I savings bonds, may (certain limits apply) be excluded from income if qualifying education expenses are paid in the year the bonds are redeemed. The exclusion also applies to savings bond interest contributed to an IRC Sec. 529 qualified tuition program or a Coverdell ESA.

Who Owns the Funds?

A second issue facing families planning for college is the question of "Who will own the funds?" The answer to this question involves issues of control, income and gift taxes, and can impact a future application for financial aid:

- **Parents:** Either in accounts specifically earmarked for college or as a part of a general family portfolio.

- **Child:** Often a custodial account is used, under either the Uniform Gifts to Minors Act (UGMA) or the Uniform Transfers to Minors Act (UTMA).

- **Trust:** In certain situations, usually involving wealthy families, specialized types of trusts may be used, such as a Crummey trust or charitable remainder trust.

Impact On Financial Aid

For need-based financial aid purposes, assets considered to be owned by the **parents** have a relatively small negative impact. Assets considered to be owned by the **child** have a much greater negative impact. Trust assets are often considered to be owned by the child, but this can vary widely. Frequently, trust provisions restrict access to principal, thus forcing inclusion of the trust assets in the eligibility process each year that a student is in school. Non-trust assets can be "spent down" in a year or two, limiting their financial aid impact.

Other Resources

There are a number of excellent references and guides to investments and college planning available in bookstores and public libraries. State and federal agencies involved in higher education also are excellent sources of information. In addition, there are a number of sites on the Internet which can provide information, including the following:

- **The College Board** – https://www.collegeboard.org

- **FinAid! The SmartStudent® Guide To Financial Aid** – http://www.finaid.org

- **College Savings Plan Network** – links to state-run web pages on prepaid tuition or college savings plans, at: http://www.collegesavings.org

- **U.S. Department of Education – student aid website** – https://studentaid.ed.gov/sa/

Begin Early and Seek Professional Guidance

Developing a plan to save for a child's college education can be complicated. Questions can arise involving income tax, estate and gift taxes, investment issues, and the impact of asset ownership on financial aid eligibility. Individuals are strongly advised to begin a savings program as early as possible, and seek professional guidance.

Section 529 Qualified Tuition Plans

To encourage saving for higher education, Congress created Section 529 of the Internal Revenue Code. This law provides for two tax-advantaged programs that parents and others can use to accumulate some or all of the resources needed to pay for education.

- **Prepaid tuition plans:** Cash contributions are made to a qualified trust to "prepay," at today's prices, a beneficiary's future tuition costs. This approach allows you to purchase a number of course units or academic periods that are redeemed when the beneficiary is old enough to attend school.

- **Higher education savings plans:** Cash contributions are made to an account established for a named beneficiary. An investment management firm typically directs the investments. The amount of money available for higher education expenses depends on growth in the account between contribution and withdrawal.

Under federal tax law, contributions are not tax deductible and any growth in an account is tax-deferred. Distributions used solely to pay for qualified higher education expenses are federally tax-exempt. The earnings portion of a "non-qualified" distribution is taxable to the beneficiary and may be subject to a 10% tax penalty. State or local law can vary.

Issues to Consider

- **Investment risk:** Prepaid tuition plans are generally seen as having a lower level of market risk, along with a lower rate of return. Higher education savings plans combine the potential for gain with the possibility of losing money.

- **Home state plans:** Does the plan in your (or the beneficiary's) home state offer any tax or other benefits that are only available to participants in such state's plan?

- **Expenses covered:** Generally, tuition, fees, books, supplies, and equipment required for attendance qualify. Computers, software, peripheral equipment, and internet access also qualify if they are to be used primarily by the beneficiary while the beneficiary is enrolled at an eligible education institution. Reasonable costs of room and board are also included if the student is attending school at least half time. Additionally, qualified expenses include costs incurred to allow a special needs beneficiary to enroll at and attend an eligible institution. Even though the law allows for prepaid tuition plans to include room and board, many plans specifically exclude these expenses.

Beginning in 2018, under the provisions of the Tax Cuts and Jobs Act of 2017 (TCJA), qualified expenses also include expenses for tuition incurred in connection with the enrollment or attendance of the beneficiary at an elementary or secondary public, private, or religious school.

- **Flexibility:** What happens if a beneficiary does not attend school? How easy is it to change the beneficiary, so that the assets may be used for someone else? What expenses or fees are involved if the account owner wants to terminate the plan? Is there a different rate of return if the beneficiary attends school in a different state or if the account owner terminates the plan?

Seek Professional Guidance

Individuals and families considering a qualified tuition plan are faced with a number of complex income, gift, estate, and investment questions. The guidance of appropriate tax, legal, need-based student aid, and financial professionals is highly recommended.

529 Higher Education Savings Plan

Federal tax law allows[1] the states to establish tax-advantaged savings programs to pay for a student's qualified higher education expenses. In these programs, cash contributions are made to an account established for a named beneficiary. An investment management firm typically manages account funds. The amount ultimately available to pay for the beneficiary's education depends

on growth in the account between contribution and withdrawal. Higher education savings accounts are not insured and losses are possible.

Under federal tax law, contributions are not tax deductible and any growth in an account is tax-deferred. Distributions used solely to pay for qualified higher education expenses are federally tax-exempt. State or local law, however, can vary widely; contributions may or may not be tax deductible, and distributions may or may not be tax exempt.

Key Definitions Under IRC Sec. 529

- **Qualified higher education expenses:** For post-secondary education, generally, tuition, fees, books, supplies, and equipment required for attendance qualify. Computers, software, peripheral equipment, and internet access also qualify if they are to be used primarily by the beneficiary while the beneficiary is enrolled at an eligible education institution. Reasonable costs of room and board are also included if the student is attending school at least half time. Additionally, qualified expenses include costs incurred to allow a special needs beneficiary to enroll at and attend an eligible institution.

    Beginning in 2018, under the provisions of the Tax Cuts and Jobs Act of 2017 (TCJA), qualified higher education expenses also include expenses for tuition incurred in connection with the enrollment or attendance of the designated beneficiary at an elementary or secondary public, private, or religious school.

---

[1] "529" refers to Section 529 of the Internal Revenue Code, the section of federal law which authorizes these plans. The discussion here concerns federal income tax law. State or local law may differ.

- **Eligible educational institution:** Generally, accredited post high-school institutions offering associates, bachelors, graduate level, or professional degrees qualify as eligible. Certain vocational schools are also included. Beginning in 2018, under the TCJA, elementary or secondary public, private, or religious schools also qualify.

Contributions

Contributions to a savings plan must be in cash and may not exceed the amount necessary to provide the beneficiary's qualified higher education expenses. While some donors contribute lump-sum amounts, many 529 savings plan accounts are set up with automatic monthly payments. Other considerations include:

- For federal gift tax purposes, contributions are considered completed gifts of a present interest. Generally, no federal gift tax will be payable if a contribution is limited to the annual gift tax exclusion amount. For 2018, this is $15,000. A married couple can elect to "split" gifts for a total annual contribution of $30,000.

- If a contribution for a single beneficiary in one calendar year exceeds the annual exclusion amount, the donor may elect to treat the contribution as having been made ratably over a five-year period.[1] Thus, for 2018, an individual could contribute up to $75,000 for a single beneficiary in one calendar year. If a married couple elects gift splitting, $150,000 could be contributed.

- Contributions may be made to both a savings plan and a Coverdell Education Savings Account (Coverdell ESA) for the same beneficiary in the same year.

Distributions

For federal income tax purposes, distributions used to pay for post-secondary qualified higher education expenses are excluded from gross income if the amount distributed does not exceed the amount of qualified education expenses. If a distribution is greater than the amount of qualified education expenses, a portion of the earnings may be subject to federal income tax and a 10% penalty tax may also apply.

---

[1] If the donor dies before the end of the five years, a pro-rata portion of the contribution is included in his or her estate. Any amounts in a savings plan when the beneficiary dies will generally be includable in the beneficiary's estate.

529 Higher Education Savings Plan

Tax-free distributions in connection with the enrollment or attendance of a designated beneficiary at an elementary or secondary public, private, or religious school are limited to $10,000 per year. This limitation applies on a per-student basis, not a per-account basis. Any distribution in excess of $10,000 is subject to tax.

- **Distributions due to the death or disability of the beneficiary, or the receipt of certain scholarships:** The earnings portion of the distribution is taxable as ordinary income to the recipient of the payment.

- **Rollover distributions:** Federal law allows one tax-free transfer every twelve months, from one savings plan to another, for the same beneficiary. Funds may be rolled from a 529 higher education savings plan to a 529 prepaid tuition plan and vice versa. If there is a change of beneficiary within the same family, the rollover must be completed within 60 days or the earnings portion will be subject to tax. If a new beneficiary is not part of the same family as the original beneficiary, the earnings portion of the transfer is subject to current income tax.

- **ABLE account rollovers:** TCJA, for 2018 – 2025, allows amounts from 529 plans to be rolled over to an ABLE account, provided that the ABLE account is owned by the beneficiary of the 529 account or a member of the beneficiary's family. Such rolled-over amounts count toward the annual limitation ($15,000 in 2018) that can be contributed to an ABLE account. Any amount rolled over in excess of this limit will be included in the beneficiary's gross income.

- **Other distributions:** If a distribution is made from a savings plan for any other reason, the earnings portion of the distribution is included in the taxable income of the recipient. A 10% penalty tax is also applied against the distributed earnings.

- **State and local law:** State and local law can vary widely from federal law with regard to the income tax treatment of contributions and withdrawals.

- **Coordination with other programs:** A beneficiary may generally also claim either the American Opportunity Tax Credit or Lifetime Learning Credit (not both in the same tax year), receive a distribution from a Coverdell ESA, or claim the tuition and the fees deduction, as long as the qualifying educational expenses are not the same.

529 Higher Education Savings Plan

Higher Education Savings Account Characteristics

There are a number of account characteristics that a donor should clearly understand:

- The beneficiary must be identified at the time an account is created.[1] The account owner is usually the primary contributor. However others, such as grandparents, may also contribute.

- The account owner may change the beneficiary. If the new beneficiary is a member of the same family,[2] there is generally no current federal income tax liability.

- Amounts accumulated in a savings plan operated by one state generally may be used at educational institutions in a different state.

- A higher education savings plan involves investment risk, including the potential to lose money. Contributing to a higher education saving plan does not ensure that your education funding goals will be met. Further, there is no guarantee that a beneficiary will be admitted to a particular school or college.

- Under federal law, neither the beneficiary nor the account owner is permitted to direct the investments in the account. Account owners may, however, choose among broad investment strategies established by the program sponsor. A change in investment strategy is generally permitted twice each calendar year, or when a new beneficiary is named.

- Most 529 savings plans require that funds contributed for a beneficiary from a custodial account become the property of the beneficiary when the beneficiary reaches his or her majority. A custodial account is one set up under the Uniform Gifts to Minors Act (UGMA), the Uniform Transfers to Minors Act (UTMA), or the local state version.

Other Issues to Consider

- **Home State Plans:** The fees, expenses, and features of higher education savings plans vary widely from state to state; some states have more than one plan. Consider whether the plan in your (or the beneficiary's) home state offers any tax or other benefits that are only available to participants in that particular state's plan.

---

[1] An exception exists for organizations accumulating funds for future scholarships.

[2] Generally, siblings, children, grandchildren, parents, grandparents, nieces or nephews, uncles or aunts, their spouses, and first cousins are considered members of the same family.

- **Effect on financial aid:** Assets in a 529 savings plan are considered in the "Expected Family contribution" calculations. Tax-free distributions from a 529 savings account (those used to pay for qualified education expenses) are not counted as income to either the parent or student in the financial aid determination process.[1]

Internet Resources

- **The College Board:** https://www.collegeboard.org
- **FinAid! The SmartStudent® Guide To Financial Aid:** http://www.finaid.org
- **College Savings Plan Network:** links to state-run web pages on prepaid tuition or college savings plans, at: http://www.collegesavings.org
- **U.S. Department of Education – student aid website:** https://studentaid.ed.gov/sa/

Seek Professional Guidance

Individuals considering a higher education savings plan are faced with a number of income, gift, estate tax, and investment questions. The guidance of appropriate tax, legal, need-based student aid, and financial professionals is highly recommended.

---

[1] See the U.S. Department of Education "Dear Colleague" letter of January 22, 2004, GEN-04-02.

How a 529 Higher Education Savings Plan Works

A "529" higher education savings plan is a tax-favored program operated by a state designed to help families save for future education costs. While the fees, expenses, and features of these plans will vary from state to state, as long as a plan satisfies the requirements of Section 529 of the Internal Revenue Code,[1] federal tax law provides tax benefits for both the contributor and the beneficiary.

How Does It Work?

HIGHER EDUCATION SAVINGS PLAN

- A tax-advantaged account to save for higher education.
- Earnings accumulate tax deferred.
- Does not guarantee admission.
- If a beneficiary does not use funds, a new beneficiary can be designated.

Tax-Free
Withdrawals

Taxable
Withdrawals

WITHDRAWALS FOR EDUCATION

- Withdrawals for qualified expenses are generally tax-free.

- Qualified expenses generally include tuition, books, fees, supplies, equipment, and room and board.

NON-QUALIFIED

- Any part of a withdrawal that is not applied to a qualified expense is considered non-qualified.

- The earnings portion of non-qualified amounts is taxable and a 10% penalty is generally applied.

---

[1] Federal law does not allow income tax deductions for contributions to 529 plans, although growth inside a plan is tax-deferred and qualified distributions are tax-exempt. State or local tax law can vary widely. 529 plans involve investment risk, including possible loss of funds, and there is no guarantee an education – savings goal will be met.

529 Prepaid Tuition Plan

Federal law[1] allows the states and qualifying private schools and colleges to establish tax-advantaged prepaid tuition plans. Under these plans, contributions are made into a qualified trust to prepay, at today's prices, some or all of a beneficiary's tuition costs. There are two general types of prepaid plans:

- **Contract plans:** Most prepaid plans are contract plans, which commit the account owner to purchase a specified number of years of tuition in exchange for a lump-sum or periodic payments. Generally speaking, contract plans offer lower prices for younger beneficiaries since the state or school will have more time to invest the money.

- **Unit plans:** Unit plans allow the account owner to purchase a fixed percentage of tuition. In a typical unit plan, one unit represents 1% of a year's tuition. All participants in the plan pay the same price for a unit.

Independent 529 Plan

A number of private colleges and universities have joined together to form the Independent 529 Plan. Under this arrangement, an account owner purchases tuition certificates (similar to units in a state-run plan) guaranteeing payment of a specified percentage of future tuition. These certificates can be "redeemed" at a participating college or university when the beneficiary reaches college age.

Key Definitions Under IRC Sec. 529

- **Qualified higher education expenses:** For post-secondary education, generally, tuition, fees, books, supplies, and equipment required for attendance qualify. Computers, software, peripheral equipment, and internet access also qualify if they are to be used primarily by the beneficiary while the beneficiary is enrolled at an eligible education institution. Reasonable costs of room and board are also included if the student is attending school at least half time. Additionally, qualified expenses include costs incurred to allow a special needs beneficiary to enroll at and attend an eligible institution.

---

[1] "529" refers to Section 529 of the Internal Revenue Code, the section of federal law which authorizes these plans.

Beginning in 2018, under the provisions of the Tax Cuts and Jobs Act of 2017 (TCJA), qualified higher education expenses also include expenses for tuition incurred in connection with the enrollment or attendance of the beneficiary at an elementary or secondary public, private, or religious school.

- **Eligible educational institution:** Generally, accredited post high-school institutions offering associates, bachelors, graduate level, or professional degrees qualify as eligible. Certain vocational schools are also included. Beginning in 2018, under the TCJA, elementary or secondary public, private, or religious schools also qualify.

Contributions

Contributions to a prepaid plan must be in cash. Broadly speaking, anyone (parents, grandparents, friends, etc.) can contribute to a plan. Many state plans require that either the account owner or beneficiary be a state resident, either at the time an account is opened, or at the time the beneficiary begins school. Under federal law, contributions are not tax deductible and any growth in an account is tax-deferred:

- Contributions may be made to both a prepaid plan and a Coverdell Education Savings Account (Coverdell ESA) for the same beneficiary in the same year.

- For federal gift tax purposes, contributions are considered completed gifts of a present interest. Generally, no federal gift tax will be payable if a contribution is limited to the annual gift tax exclusion amount. For 2018, this amount is $15,000. A married couple can elect to "split" gifts for a total annual contribution of $30,000.

- If a contribution for a single beneficiary in one calendar year exceeds the annual gift tax exclusion amount, the donor may elect to treat the contribution as having been made ratably over a five-year period.[1] Thus, for 2018, an individual could contribute up to $75,000 for a single beneficiary in one calendar year. If a married couple elects gift splitting, $150,000 could be contributed.

---

[1] If the donor dies before the end of the five years, a pro-rata portion of the contribution is included in his or her estate.

Distributions

For federal income tax purposes, distributions used to pay for post-secondary, qualified higher-education expenses are excluded from gross income if the amount distributed does not exceed the amount of qualified education expenses. If the distribution from a prepaid plan is greater than the amount of qualified education expenses, a portion of the earnings may be subject to federal income tax and a 10% penalty tax may also apply.

Tax-free distributions in connection with the enrollment or attendance of a designated beneficiary at an elementary or secondary public, private, or religious school are limited to $10,000 per year. This limitation applies on a per-student basis, not a per-account basis. Any distribution in excess of $10,000 is subject to tax.

- **Distributions due to the death or disability of the beneficiary, or the receipt of certain scholarships:** The earnings portion of the distribution is taxable as ordinary income to the recipient of the payment.

- **Rollover distributions:** If there is a change of beneficiary within the same family,[1] the rollover must be completed within 60 days or the earnings portion will be subject to tax. If a new beneficiary is not part of the same family as the original beneficiary, the earnings portion of the transfer is subject to current income tax. Funds may be rolled from a 529 prepaid tuition plan to a 529 higher education savings plan and vice versa.

- **ABLE account rollovers:** TCJA, for 2018 – 2025, allows amounts from 529 plans to be rolled over to an ABLE account, provided that the ABLE account is owned by the beneficiary of the 529 account or a member of the beneficiary's family. Such rolled-over amounts count toward the annual limitation $15,000 in 2018) that can be contributed to an ABLE account. Any amount rolled over in excess of this limit will be included in the beneficiary's gross income.

- **Other distributions:** If a distribution is made from a plan for any other reason, the earnings portion of the distribution is included in the taxable income of the recipient. A 10% penalty tax is also applied against the distributed earnings.

---

[1] Generally, siblings, children, grandchildren, parents, grandparents, nieces or nephews, uncles or aunts, their spouses, and first cousins are considered members of the same family.

- **State and local law can vary:** State and local law can vary widely from federal law with regard to the income tax treatment of contributions and withdrawals.

- **Coordination with other programs:** A beneficiary may generally also claim either the American Opportunity Credit or Lifetime Learning Credit (not both in the same tax year), receive a distribution from a Coverdell ESA, or claim the tuition and fees deduction, as long as the qualifying educational expenses are not the same.

Other Issues to Consider

- **Limited use of funds:** Although the federal law governing prepaid plans has a very broad definition of "qualified higher education expenses," most prepaid tuition plans are limited to paying for tuition and required fees for undergraduate study; in a few programs, room and board is also covered. Costs that are not covered by the prepaid tuition plan must be paid for from other resources.

- **Increased tuition costs:** Many prepaid plans agree to cover all future increases in tuition costs. However, some plans limit that promise; if tuition costs increase more than the limit, will you have to contribute more money to the plan?

- **No guarantees:** A prepaid tuition plan does not guarantee that a beneficiary will be admitted to a particular school or college, nor that an educational funding goal will be completely met.

- **Change in plans:** If the beneficiary does not attend school, or does not complete the full course of study, what does it cost to cancel or withdraw from a prepaid plan? Does the plan allow the account owner to "roll over" the funds to another beneficiary? If a beneficiary attends an out-of-state school, what amount of tuition credit is allowed at the out-of-state school?

- **Home state plans:** Prepaid plans will vary widely from state to state. Consider whether the plan in your (or the beneficiary's) home state offers any tax or other benefits that are only available to participants in that particular state's plan.

- **Effect on financial aid eligibility:** Assets in a 529 prepaid tuition plan are considered in the "Expected Family Contribution" calculations. Tax-free distributions from a 529 prepaid tuition plan (those used to pay for qualified educational expenses) are not counted as income to either the parent or student in the financial aid process.[1]

- **Ownership:** The donor is generally the owner of the funds. However, funds in a custodial account (set up under the Uniform Gifts to Minors Act, UGMA, or the Uniform Transfers to Minors Act, UTMA), become the property of the beneficiary when he or she reaches the age of majority, or the age specified in state law.

Internet Resources

- **The College Board** – https://www.collegeboard.org

- **FinAid! The SmartStudent® Guide To Financial Aid** – http://www.finaid.org

- **College Savings Plan Network** – links to state-run web pages on prepaid tuition or college savings plans, at: http://www.collegesavings.org

- **U.S. Department of Education – student aid website** – https://studentaid.ed.gov/sa/

Seek Professional Guidance

Individuals considering a prepaid tuition plan are faced with a number of income tax, gift tax, estate tax, and financial aid issues. The guidance of appropriate tax and financial professionals is highly recommended.

---

[1] See the U.S. Department of Education "Dear Colleague" letter of January 22, 2004, GEN-04-02.

How a 529 Prepaid Tuition Plan Works

A "529" prepaid tuition plan is a tax-favored program operated by a state or eligible private institution designed to help families prepay future educational costs. While the specific details of these plans will vary, as long as a plan satisfies the requirements of Section 529 of the Internal Revenue Code,[1] federal tax law provides tax benefits for both the contributor and the beneficiary.

How Does It Work?

PREPAID TUITION PLAN

Contributor

- A program to prepay tomorrow's tuition at today's prices.
- Earnings accumulate tax deferred.
- Does not guarantee admission.
- If a beneficiary does not use funds, a new beneficiary can be designated.

Tax-Free Withdrawals

Taxable Withdrawals

WITHDRAWALS FOR EDUCATION

- Withdrawals for qualified expenses are generally tax-free.
- Generally covers only tuition and fees. In a few plans, also pays for room and board. Remaining costs must be paid for from other resources.

NON-QUALIFIED

- Any part of a withdrawal that is not applied to a qualified expense is considered non-qualified.
- The earnings portion of non-qualified amounts is taxable and a 10% penalty is generally applied.

---

[1] Federal law does not allow deductions for contributions to 529 plans; growth inside a plan is tax-deferred and qualified distributions are tax-exempt. State or local income tax law can vary widely. The fees, expenses, and features of 529 plans will vary from state to state and from institution to institution and should be carefully considered. 529 plans involve risk, including the possible loss of funds or the need to make additional contributions. There is no guarantee an educational-funding goal will be met.

Coverdell Education Savings Account

The Taxpayer Relief Act of 1997 (TRA '97) created a tax-favored education individual retirement account designed to help certain taxpayers save for a child's education. These plans have been renamed as Coverdell Education Savings Accounts. Money contributed to a Coverdell ESA is nondeductible, but earnings accumulate tax-deferred.

Contributions to a Coverdell ESA are treated as nontaxable gifts to the beneficiary. In general, to the extent that earnings are distributed to pay qualified educational expenses, the earnings are excluded from the beneficiary's income and are received free of federal income tax.[1]

The contributor need not be related to the beneficiary and there is no limit on the number of individual beneficiaries for whom one contributor may set up a Coverdell ESA.

Contributions

Federal income tax law currently limits contributions to a Coverdell ESA to $2,000 per beneficiary per year. Contributions must be in cash and must generally be made before the beneficiary reaches age 18. Other considerations include:

- **Due date for contributions:** Contributions must be made by the due date (not including extensions) of the contributor's return for the tax year of the contribution, generally April 15 of the following year.

- **Special needs beneficiaries:** Contributions to accounts for special needs beneficiaries may be made past the age of 18.[2]

- **Multiple accounts:** May not be used to exceed the $2,000 limit for any one beneficiary.

- **Excess contributions:** Excess contributions are subject to a 6% excise tax paid by the beneficiary for each year that any excess remains in the account.

---

[1] The income tax treatment of Coverdell ESAs discussed here reflects federal law; state or local law may differ.

[2] A special needs beneficiary, generally, is an individual who, because of a physical, mental or emotional condition, needs extra time to complete his or her education.

Coverdell Education Savings Account

- **Contribution phase out:** The $2,000 per year limit is phased out for taxpayers with an adjusted gross income (AGI) above certain levels. For single filers, the contribution phases out when AGI is between $95,000 and $110,000. For married couples filing jointly, the phase-out range is between $190,000 and $220,000.[1]

- **Military death payments:** Under the provisions of the Heroes Earnings Assistance and Relief Tax Act of 2008, an individual who receives a military death gratuity and/or a payment under the Servicemembers' Group Life Insurance (SGLI) program, may contribute to a Coverdell ESA an amount no greater than the sum of any military death gratuity and SGLI payment. Such a contribution, considered a qualified rollover contribution, must be made within one year of receiving the death gratuity or insurance payment. The annual dollar contribution limit and income-based phase-out of the dollar contribution limit do not apply to such contributions.

- **Qualified tuition programs:** Contributions to a Coverdell ESA for a beneficiary are permitted in the same year in which a contribution is made for the same beneficiary to a qualified tuition program (QTP).[2]

- **Contributions by other entities:** Contributions to Coverdell ESA may be made by entities such as corporations or tax-exempt organizations, not subject to the income phase-out rules.

Key Definitions

Coverdell Education Savings Accounts provide a tax-favored framework within which funds may be accumulated to pay for a beneficiary's "qualified education expenses." Depending on the educational level involved, the definition of qualified education expenses will change, as will the allowable educational institutions.

- **Kindergarten - Grade 12:** Qualified elementary and secondary education expenses refers to tuition, fees, academic tutoring, services for special needs individuals, books, supplies, and equipment. The term also includes room and board, uniforms, transportation, and supplemental services such as extended day programs. In specified circumstances, computer equipment and technology, including software and Internet connections, are qualified expenses. Contributions to a Qualified Tuition

---

[1] These phase-out limits are not subject to adjustment for inflation.
[2] See IRC Sec. 529 for more detail.

Plan, under IRC Sec. 529 are considered allowable expenses. The term "school" refers to an institution that provides elementary or secondary education (kindergarten through grade 12), under state law. This may be a public, private, or religious school.

- **Post-secondary:** Qualified higher education expenses include tuition, fees, books, and supplies and equipment needed for attendance. Room and board is included for students attending half time or greater. The term also encompasses the expenses incurred to allow a special needs beneficiary to enroll at and attend an eligible institution. Contributions to a Qualified Tuition Plan, under IRC Sec. 529, are also considered allowable expenses. The term "eligible educational institution" refers, generally, to accredited post-high school educational institutions offering associates, bachelors, graduate level, or professional degrees. Certain vocational schools are also included.

- **Family member:** Certain tax-free transfers of Coverdell ESA assets are permitted between family members. In addition to the spouse, family members include:

Family Members
Son or daughter, or their descendants
Stepson or stepdaughter
Brother, sister, stepbrother, or stepsister
Father or mother or ancestor of either
Stepfather or stepmother
Son or daughter of a brother or sister
Brother or sister of father or mother
Spouse of any person listed above
First cousins

Distributions

Distributions from a Coverdell ESA are considered to be part principal (the original contributions) and part earnings. If qualified education expenses exceed the total amount distributed from the account for the year, all of the distributed earnings are excluded from the beneficiary's income. If qualified education expenses are less than the amount

Coverdell Education Savings Account

distributed, a portion of the distributed earnings will be included in the beneficiary's taxable income for the year. An additional 10% tax may be added to the portion included in taxable income.

- **Additional tax:** Any earnings distributions included in a beneficiary's income because they are not used for qualified educational expenses are subject to an additional 10% tax. Certain exceptions apply, including the death or disability of the beneficiary, or the receipt of certain scholarships.

- **Rollovers/change of beneficiary:** If a beneficiary does not use the funds held for him or her in a Coverdell ESA, the money may be distributed and rolled over into a new account for a different beneficiary. If the rollover occurs within 60 days of the distribution, and if the new beneficiary is a member of the original beneficiary's family[1] and has not yet attained age 30, the distribution is not taxable to the original beneficiary. The same objective may be reached by simply changing the beneficiary of a Coverdell ESA. As long as the new beneficiary is a member of the original beneficiary's family, and has not reached age 30, the change is not treated as a taxable distribution.

- **Beneficiary reaches age 30:** If a beneficiary reaches the age of 30 and there are still funds remaining in the Coverdell ESA, federal tax law deems the remaining funds to be distributed and, therefore, subject to tax for that year. The 10% additional tax also applies to amounts so distributed because of the beneficiary reaching age 30. If a beneficiary dies before age 30, any remaining account balance must be distributed to the beneficiary's estate (and thus become taxable) within 30 days of death.

- **Special needs beneficiaries:** The requirement that any funds left in a Coverdell ESA must be distributed when the beneficiary reaches age 30 does not apply to a special needs beneficiary. Similarly, a special needs individual may be the beneficiary of an account rollover even though he or she is age 30 or older.

- **Coordination with other programs:** A Coverdell ESA beneficiary may generally also claim either the Hope Scholarship Credit or the Lifetime Learning Credit (not both in the same tax year), receive a distribution from a qualified tuition plan, or claim the tuition and fees deduction, as long as the qualifying expenses are not the same.

[1] As defined in IRC Sec. 529 (e)(2)

Coverdell Education Savings Account

Other Issues

- **Effect on financial aid eligibility:** Assets in a Coverdell ESA are considered in the "Expected Family Contribution" calculations. Tax-free distributions from a Coverdell ESA (those used to pay for qualified education expenses) are not counted as income to either the parent or student in the financial aid determination process.[1]

  Private institutions, however, may consider Coverdell ESA assets and income into consideration when awarding school-based financial aid, regardless of who is listed as the account owner.

- **Loss of control:** Ownership of the funds contributed to a Coverdell ESA will eventually pass to the beneficiary. A donor may not simply "take back" the account, as can be done with IRC Sec. 529 qualified tuition plans.

- **Federal bankruptcy impact:** If certain requirements are met, federal bankruptcy law can protect a portion (in some cases all) of the assets in a Coverdell ESA from creditors.

- **Losses:** If certain requirements are met, a complete loss in a Coverdell account may be deducted on your federal income tax return as a miscellaneous itemized deduction, subject to the 2%-of-adjusted-gross-income limit. See IRS Publication 970 for details. State or local law may vary.

Seek Professional Guidance

TRA '97 presented each taxpayer with a wide range of tax-favored tools for funding a child's education. A qualified tax or financial professional can help select the best approach.

---

[1] See the U.S. Department of Education "Dear Colleague" letter of January 22, 2004, GEN-04-02.

How a Coverdell ESA Works

A Coverdell Education Savings Account is a tax-favored account designed to help families accumulate funds for future education costs. While contributions are not deductible, earnings accumulate tax deferred, and qualified withdrawals are tax-free.[1]

How Does It Work?

Contributor

COVERDELL ESA

- Earnings accumulate tax deferred.
- One contributor may benefit any number of beneficiaries.
- If a beneficiary does not use funds, a new beneficiary can be designated.

Tax-Free Withdrawals

Taxable Withdrawals

WITHDRAWALS FOR EDUCATION

- Withdrawals for qualified expenses are generally tax-free.
- Qualified expenses generally include tuition, books, fees, supplies, equipment, and room and board.

NON-QUALIFIED

- Any part of a withdrawal that is not applied to a qualified expense is considered non-qualified.
- The earnings portion of non-qualified amounts is taxable and a 10% penalty is generally applied.

---

[1] The rules discussed here concern federal tax law; state or local law may vary.

Education Savings Plans Compared

Benefit or Feature	"529" Prepaid Tuition Plan[1]	"529" Higher Education Savings Plan[1]	Coverdell Education Savings Account
Basic concept	Buy tomorrow's tuition at today's prices.	Tax-advantaged savings account to accumulate funds for higher education.	Tax-advantaged savings account to accumulate funds for education.
Federal income tax treatment	Contributions are not deductible; growth is tax-deferred; withdrawals for qualified higher education expenses are exempt from tax.	Contributions are not deductible; growth is tax-deferred; withdrawals for qualified higher education expenses are exempt from tax.	Contributions are not deductible; growth is tax-deferred; withdrawals for qualified education expenses are exempt from tax.
State or local income tax treatment	Varies. Some states follow federal income tax law, while others do not.	Varies. Some states follow federal income tax law, while others do not.	Varies. Some states follow federal income tax law, while others do not.
Level of investment risk	Generally a low level of risk. Sponsoring state or organization typically promises to invest funds to match tuition increases. Later contributions may be required.	Varies, depending on the underlying investments. An investment manager typically manages the funds. Both gains and losses are possible.	Varies, depending on the underlying investment. A wide range of self-directed investments is available. Both gains and losses are possible.
Where to purchase	Directly from the state or private institution involved.	Investment brokers, banks, credit unions, insurance companies, or directly from the state involved.	Investment brokers, banks, credit unions, and insurance companies.
Who can contribute?	Generally, anyone. Residency restrictions may apply.	Generally, anyone. Residents in one state can often invest in another state's plan.	Generally, anyone.

[1] "529" refers to Section 529 of the Internal Revenue Code, the section of federal law which authorizes these plans.

Education Savings Plans Compared

Benefit or Feature	"529" Prepaid Tuition Plan	"529" Higher Education Savings Plan	Coverdell Education Savings Account
How much can be contributed?	Contributions must be in cash and may not exceed what is needed to fund the beneficiary's higher education expenses. The program sponsor will specify the maximum amount.	Contributions must be in cash and may not exceed what is needed to fund the beneficiary's higher education expenses. The program sponsor will specify the maximum amount.[1]	Contributions must be in cash and may not exceed $2,000 per beneficiary per year.
Beneficiary age limits for contributions?	None	None	Before age 18 unless a special needs student.
How are payments made?	In a lump-sum or periodic payments.	In a lump-sum or periodic payments.	Typically, in periodic payments.
Do income limitations apply to the donor?	No	No	Yes. Contribution is phased out for donors whose AGI exceeds certain limits.[2]
Who controls the funds?	Generally, the donor.[3] If the account is a custodial account, the beneficiary becomes the owner when he or she reaches age 21 (18 in some states).	Generally, the donor.[2] If the account is a custodial account, the beneficiary becomes the owner when he or she reaches age 21 (18 in some states).	Generally, the donor.[2] If the account is a custodial account, the beneficiary becomes the owner when he or she reaches age 21 (18 in some states).

[1] In some higher education savings programs, more than $250,000 may be contributed for a single beneficiary.

[2] For unmarried individuals, the contribution is phased out when adjusted gross income (AGI) is between $95,000 - $110,000. For married couples filing jointly, the phase-out range is an AGI of $190,000 - $220,000.

[3] With a "529" prepaid tuition plan or a "529" savings plan, if the assets are not used for higher education they may be returned to the donor. In a Coverdell Education Savings Account, if the assets are not used for higher education, they will ultimately become the property of the beneficiary.

Education Savings Plans Compared

Benefit or Feature	"529" Prepaid Tuition Plan	"529" Higher Education Savings Plan	Coverdell Education Savings Account
What expenses are covered?[1]	Tuition and fees for primary, secondary, and post-secondary education are covered. Some plans include a room and board option or allow excess tuition credits to be used for other qualified expenses.	For primary and secondary schools, tuition and fees are covered. For post-secondary education, costs such as tuition, fees, books, supplies, computers, software, and internet access are covered. Reasonable costs for room and board also qualify if the student is attending school at least half time.	A wide range of expenses is allowed, to attend Kindergarten thru 12th grade, as well as post-high school educational institutions. May include tuition, fees, books, supplies, and equipment, as well as reasonable costs for room and board.
What schools may the beneficiary attend?	Prepaid tuition plans typically limit attendance to same-state schools or colleges.	Funds accumulated in the savings plan of one state may usually be used at institutions of higher education throughout the U.S. Some foreign schools also qualify.	For K-12, any school that qualifies under state law, including public, private, or religious schools. For post-high school, most institutions in the U.S. qualify.
Effect on financial aid?	Generally reduces financial aid. Account owned by student penalized more than parent-owned account.	Generally reduces financial aid. Account owned by student penalized more than parent-owned account.	Generally reduces financial aid. Account owned by student penalized more than parent-owned account.
May account be rolled-over to other family members?	Yes	Yes	Yes

[1] Technically, under IRC Sec. 529, the same definition of "qualified higher education expenses" applies to both prepaid tuition plans and higher education savings plans. In practice, however, for prepaid tuition plans, the sponsoring entity will limit the use of the funds to the types of expenses shown above.

Paying for College Today

For many Americans, providing a college education for their children has long been an important family goal. Paying for that education, however, has never been easy. Over the past few years it has become even more of a challenge as college costs continue to rise.[1]

Few families seem able to save enough to fully fund four or more years of higher education. For many students, some type of financial aid, in the form of grants, scholarships, loans, or work-study, is needed to make the dream a reality.

And such financial aid is available. The federal government, through the Department of Education, provides about $120 billion a year[2] in student aid, through a variety of programs. Private organizations and foundations, state governments, as well as the schools and universities themselves, are additional sources of financial aid.

Applying for Financial Aid

The vast majority of financial aid is awarded through a standardized process which, in general, proceeds as follows:

- **Free Application for Federal Student Aid (FAFSA):** The student and his or her family complete the Free Application for Federal Student Aid, the single form used to apply for all types of federal aid; it is also used to apply for state financial aid at many public and private colleges. The FAFSA collects information such as family size and number of family members in college, in addition to financial data such as income and benefits, and net assets.

- **Student Aid Report (SAR):** Using the information supplied on the FAFSA, the government calculates the amount a family is expected to contribute toward a student's education, known as the Expected Family Contribution (EFC). This information is reported on the SAR and is sent to the student. The same information is sent to the financial aid offices of the colleges the student listed on the FAFSA.

- **CSS/Financial Aid PROFILE:** A few schools will require a prospective student to complete an additional standardized financial questionnaire known as PROFILE. The data collected on this form is used to award a college's institutional aid.

---

[1] See "Trends in College Pricing – 2017," published by The College Board, page 3.
[2] Source: Department of Education website: https://studentaid.ed.gov/sa/types, accessed November 2, 2017.

- **Cost of attendance:** To calculate financial aid eligibility, colleges need to first determine the cost of attendance at the institution. The cost of attendance includes, in addition to tuition, fees and books, general living expenses such as rent or dormitory costs, transportation, and personal expenses a student could be expected to incur during the nine-month academic year.

- **Financial aid eligibility or financial need:** Eligibility for need-based financial aid is determined by taking the college's calculated cost of attendance and subtracting the EFC. The difference, if any, is the amount the student may receive in need-based forms of financial aid, including grants, scholarships, and loans.

- **Financial aid package:** Once the need-based eligibility is determined, a college's financial aid office will attempt to provide for that need with a combination or package of financial aid funds that may include grants, loans, scholarships, and work-study funds. The amount and type of financial aid will vary between colleges. In some cases a financial aid package may not cover all costs, leaving a gap that the student and his or her family must cover from other sources.

Federal Financial Aid

A major source of financial aid provided to college students in the U.S. is from programs funded and/or administered by the federal government, with much of the support coming in the form of student loans. The major elements in federal student aid are:

- **Federal Pell Grants:** Pell Grants are designed to assist very low-income undergraduate students and are awarded based on expected family contribution (EFC). Only students with very low EFCs are awarded Pell Grants. Pell Grants do not have to be repaid.

- **Federal Supplemental Educational Opportunity Grant (FSEOG):** Like Pell grants, FSEOGs do not have to be repaid. They are awarded to undergraduate students with exceptional financial need.

- **Teacher Education Assistance for College and Higher Education (TEACH) Grant:** A federal grant to students who agree to teach for four years at an elementary school, secondary school, or educational service agency that serves students. If a grantee does not complete his or her service obligation, the TEACH grant is converted to a Direct Unsubsidized Loan with interest due from the date the TEACH grant was disbursed.

- **Iraq and Afghanistan Service Grant:** A grant awarded to limited group of individuals whose parent or guardian was a member of the U.S. armed forces and who died as a result of military service performed in Iraq or Afghanistan after the events of 9/11. Other requirements apply.

- **The William D. Ford Direct Loan Program:** This program is the Department of Education's main loan program. Direct subsidized loans are made of the basis of financial need. They do not accrue interest nor require repayment until six months after the student ceases to attend college at least half time. Direct unsubsidized loans are not based on need and interest accrues from the date the loan is disbursed. Direct PLUS loans are loans made to graduate or professional students and to parents of dependent undergraduate students to help pay for education expenses not covered by other financial aid. Interest accrues from the date the funds are disbursed, but repayment is not required until six months after the student ceases to attend college at least half time. Direct Consolidation loans allow a student to combine all of his or her eligible federal student loans into a single loan; repayment begins within 60 days of the loan being disbursed.

- **Federal Perkins Loans:** Perkins loans are federal low-interest loans. They are awarded based on need and the availability of funds. No interest accrues while the student is attending school at least half time. Repayment begins nine months after the student ceases to attend school at least half time.

- **Federal Work-Study Program (FWS):** The FWS program provides federally funded employment for qualified students in both on-campus and off-campus positions. The amount a student can earn is limited to the amount of the award.

Other Financial Aid Programs

In addition to the financial aid programs provided through the federal government, there is a wide range of aid available through other organizations.

- **State programs:** Many state governments have their own financial aid programs. Such programs include need-based grants (the family has to show financial aid eligibility), as well as work-study programs, loan-forgiveness programs for targeted careers, and merit-based scholarship programs.

- **Institutional aid programs:** Many schools have additional means of making college affordable. Scholarships, based on either academic or athletic ability, are one example. Some schools have their own student loan programs to replace or supplement federal loan programs. Some institutions offer installment or deferred payment plans for tuition, or a discount may be offered if more than one child from the same family is enrolled, or if the parents are alumni.

- **Military aid programs:** The Armed Forces have available a number of programs to enable prospective, active duty, and former service personnel to attend college. Reserve Officer Training Corps (ROTC) scholarships are available at a number of schools. A ROTC/NROTC Scholarship or an appointment to one of the service academies, West Point, Annapolis, or the Air Force Academy effectively ends any concerns about paying for college. Current active duty personnel can apply for tuition assistance through their education officer. For veterans, the various GI Bills and the Army or Navy college savings funds are additional sources of financing.

- **Private scholarships:** Many private organizations make available scholarships, based on both need and merit. Many scholarships are for relatively small amounts of money or for only a single year and a student may need to apply to many different scholarship programs. Scholarship information is widely available at bookstores and libraries, in high school and college financial aid offices and on the Internet.

Tax Advantaged Strategies

Congress has passed legislation[1] designed to lighten the burden of paying for higher education. Because the rules surrounding these strategies can be complicated, the counsel of a qualified tax or financial professional is recommended.

Education tax credits: Two separate tax credits are available: (1) the American Opportunity Tax Credit, of up to $2,500 per student, per year, for tuition and fees paid during the first four calendar years of college, and (2) the Lifetime Learning Credit, providing a credit of up to $2,000 per return for qualified education expenses. A taxpayer may not take both credits in the same year. Other limitations and restrictions apply.

---

[1] The rules discussed here concern federal income tax law; state or local law may vary.

- Tuition and fees deduction: Through 2017, a taxpayer may deduct, as an adjustment to gross income, up to $4,000 for qualified higher education tuition and related expenses for a qualifying individual at an eligible educational institution. Certain limitations and phase-outs applied to this deduction.

- **Interest deduction on education loans:** A deduction of up to $2,500, taken as an adjustment to gross income, is available for interest paid on student loans. Certain restrictions and requirements apply.

- **Exclusion of U.S. Savings Bond interest:** Interest earned on U.S. Savings Bonds is normally taxable. However, if a taxpayer pays qualified education expenses, the interest earned on qualified U.S. savings bonds may be excluded from income. Certain income level and filing status requirements apply.

- **Withdrawals from Traditional IRAs before age 59½:** Withdrawals from traditional IRAs used to pay qualified education expenses are exempt from the 10% penalty on withdrawals before age 59-1/2. Amounts withdrawn, however, will generally be subject to ordinary income tax.

Other Approaches

A number of other approaches can be used to help pay for college expenses. Consider carefully the pros and cons of each suggestion, including the income tax ramifications, the impact on any possible financial aid, the likelihood that a student might not complete college, and any effect on your long-term financial goals.

- **Home equity loan:** Parents with equity in the family home may want to consider taking out a home equity loan. If certain conditions are met, the interest on such a loan can be tax deductible.

- **Life insurance cash values:** Cash-value life insurance policies can provide another source of low-cost loans.[1]

- **Borrow from qualified plans:** Some types of employer-sponsored qualified plans allow a participant to borrow from the plan. There are generally strict rules regarding the repayment of such loans.

---

[1] Loans from a cash-value life insurance policy will reduce the available death benefit. If a policy lapses or is surrendered with a loan outstanding, the loan will be treated as taxable income in the current year, to the extent of gain in the policy. Also, policies considered to be modified endowment contracts (MECs) are subject to special rules.

- **Skip a year:** Some colleges will admit a student and defer admission allowing the student to live at home, work full-time and save the earnings for college.

- **Live at home and commute:** A family can save several thousand dollars a year by having a student live at home and commute to school.

- **Choose a lower cost school:** State-supported public colleges and universities generally charge a lower tuition for in-state residents. To further save money, some students begin their studies at less expensive community or junior colleges and then transfer to a four-year school to complete their degree.

Other Resources

There are a number of published references and guides to paying for college available in bookstores and public libraries. In addition to providing a wide range of reference materials, many high schools and colleges offer free financial aid seminars presented by professional financial aid administrators. The state and federal agencies involved in higher education are also excellent sources of information.

For those linked to the internet, there are a number of websites which can provide information.

- **The College Board:** https://www.collegeboard.org

- **FinAid! The SmartStudent® Guide To Financial Aid:** http://www.finaid.org

- **U.S. Department of Education – student aid website:** https://studentaid.ed.gov/sa/

- **Free Application For Federal Student Aid (FAFSA):** https://www.fafsa.ed.gov/

- **CSS/Financial Aid Profile®:** https://cssprofile.collegeboard.org

Begin Early and Seek Professional Guidance

The key step in paying for a child's education is to begin the process as early as possible. A great deal of information, as well as counseling, is available from high schools, colleges and the various government agencies involved in higher education, at little or no cost. Questions involving income, gift, or estate taxes should be carefully reviewed with a Certified Public Accountant (CPA), IRS Enrolled Agent (EA), legal counsel or other qualified professionals.

Ways to Pay for College

At Younger Ages

If possible, a college savings program should be started when a child is young:

- **Personal Savings:** Funds put aside by parents or grandparents in taxable investment and savings accounts.

- **Tax advantaged approaches:** IRC Sec. 529 plans,[1] Coverdell Savings Accounts, or U.S. Savings Bonds.

The High School Years

As college draws closer, continue any savings programs begun in the past:

- **Scholarships and grants:** Many college scholarships or grants are awarded to students while they are still in high school.

During College

If savings are inadequate, other resources will be needed. Consider the following:

- **Student aid:** Frequently a "package" which may include grants, loans, scholarships, or work-study programs, with much of the funding coming from the federal government. Individual states, private individuals, and many colleges and universities are also a source of scholarships and grants.

- **Military programs:** The U.S. military has a number of programs to enable prospective, active duty, and former service personnel to attend college.

- **Tax benefits:** Federal income tax law encourages higher education in a variety of ways, including education tax credits and a deduction for student loan interest.[2]

- **Other approaches:** The cost of education can be reduced by living at home or choosing a lower-cost state or community college. A home-equity loan or a loan from an employer-sponsored qualified retirement plan may provide additional funds.

---

[1] Federal income tax law does not allow deductions for contributions to "529" plans, although growth inside a plan is tax-deferred and qualified distributions are tax-exempt. State or local tax law, however, can vary widely. 529 plans involve investment risks, including possible loss of funds, and there is no guarantee a college-funding goal will be met. The fees, expenses, and features of 529 plans vary from state to state.

[2] These comments concern federal income tax law; state or local income tax law may vary widely.

After Graduation

For some students, paying for college extends beyond the college years:

- **Perform any required service:** Some programs require the student to perform a period of service or work after graduation, in return for help in funding college.

- **Repay student loans:** Any outstanding loans should be repaid as quickly as possible.

Choosing a College

With over 4,700[1] degree-granting institutions offering post-high school education in the United States, choosing the right school can be daunting. Although the final choice is an individual one, careful (and early) planning is essential. The following list of key points can help in the decision making process.

Admission

One of the first questions a student faces is whether or not he or she will be accepted for admission to a particular school.

- **Qualifications:** Does the student have the necessary academic and personal qualifications?

- **Ability to pay:** Does the school consider ability to pay as a factor in considering an application? Most colleges evaluate applications on a need-blind basis.

- **Popular schools:** Certain, popular big-name schools may be extremely difficult to enter simply because an overwhelming number of students apply. Lesser-known schools may provide an equal education and have admission standards less difficult to meet.

Cost

With the continually rising cost of a college education, paying for school is often a major concern.

- **Affordability:** How affordable is a school? In general, public schools, partially subsidized by tax dollars, tend to be less expensive than private institutions.

- **Living expenses:** A family may want to weigh the cost of dormitories or off-campus housing versus the cost of having the student live at home and commute to a local school.

---

[1] Source: U.S. Department of Education, National Center for Education Statistics, Digest of Education Statistics, Table 3.17.10, degree-granting postsecondary institutions, by control and level of institution: Selected years, 1949-50 through 2013-14.

- **Cash flow or savings?** Can the education be paid for from current cash flow? If not, has enough money been saved to pay for the entire education or are additional funds needed?

- **Student debt:** Is the student or family willing and/or able to take on the financial burden of student loans?

- **Financial aid:** How much and what type of financial aid can a school make available? Some forms of aid are based on need; others on merit.

- **Scholarships:** Are there scholarships available for which the student may qualify?

Academics

What type and quality of education does the institution provide?

- **Specific programs:** For those individuals with clear ideas of what they want to do in life, does the school have the specific type of education and training needed?

- **Breadth:** For students who are less sure of their career goals, does the institution offer the breadth of courses and majors needed for a good liberal arts education? Can a student be undeclared until a major is chosen or must a major and course of study be decided upon immediately?

- **Academic standards:** Are academic standards rigorous or relaxed?

- **Time to complete:** Can a student complete a course of study in four years? Overcrowding may mean that key required courses are not available when needed.

- **Class size:** Are classes large or small? Do the professors do the teaching or is much of the teaching done by graduate students and/or teaching assistants? How much personal contact is there between professors and students?

- **Special programs:** Are special academic programs available, such as internships or study abroad programs?

Personality

Each college or university has its own personality. Will the student enjoy living and working at a particular school and with a particular student body for four years?

- **Size:** Large institutions can offer greater choice, both academically and in extracurricular activities; however, their large size may be intimidating to some students. Smaller schools can be more personal, with greater opportunities for student involvement.

- **Single sex:** Some students may feel more comfortable and perform better academically at a single-sex, rather than at a co-educational institution.

- **Religious affiliation:** A religious focus to campus life may be an important consideration for a student.

- **Student body diversity:** Is it important that a student body be widely diverse? Or, would a student feel more comfortable at a school where one ethnic or socio-economic group is predominant?

- **Social life:** What is the predominant "flavor" to the social life on campus?

- **Athletics or other extracurricular programs:** Does the student have an interest in a sport or other extracurricular activity that may not be available at certain schools?

Location

Very often the geographic location of a college is a major factor in deciding which school to attend.

- **Locale:** Should the student live at home or move out to attend school?

- **Distance:** How far is a school from home? The cost of round-trip transportation between home and school can affect how often a student is able to return home.

- **Housing type:** What type of housing is available? Do most students live in school dorms or is off-campus housing the preferred choice?

- **Community:** Urban, rural, or suburban? Institutions located in large cities offer diversity, while schools located in rural areas can offer a strong sense of community. Institutions located in suburban areas can offer both.

- **Region:** Which part of the Country? A student from one part of the country may simply want a change and choose to attend a college in a different area. For example, a student raised in a large city may want to attend a school located in a rural area; a student from the Northeast may want to study on the West Coast.

- **Safety:** How safe is the school environment? Federal law requires colleges to make campus crime statistics available to students and applicants.

Additional Resources

There are a number of excellent college guides and handbooks available in bookstores and public libraries. State and federal agencies involved in higher education are also excellent sources of information. In addition, there are a number of sites on the Internet which can provide information, including:

- **University of Texas:** Maintains a useful website with links to the home pages of many schools in the U. S., at: http://www.utexas.edu/world/univ/state/

- **The College Board:** Maintains a searchable database of colleges on their website located at: http://www.collegeboard.org

College and Financial Aid Calendar

As Early as Possible

- Explore college options.
- Research scholarship opportunities via the Internet.

Junior Year/Summer Prior to Senior Year

- Visit campuses and narrow college choices.
- Learn how to apply for scholarships.
- Find out the priority admission application period for the colleges you wish to attend.

Senior Year In High School

NOVEMBER	DECEMBER	JANUARY
• Admission application period for many colleges begins.	• If needed, complete and mail the CSS Profile. • Attend any financial aid nights offered at your school.	• Apply for financial aid every year at this time. • Mail the completed FAFSA. • Apply for scholarships.

College and Financial Aid Calendar

FEBRUARY

- Student aid report received from processor. Review for accuracy.

- Submit required documents to financial aid offices.

MARCH

- Receive and compare financial aid award letters.

APRIL/MAY

- Make final decision regarding college choice. Submit any required deposits.

JUNE/JULY

- Prepare for starting college.

- Work extra hours and save money.

AUGUST/SEPTEMBER

- Start college.

- Look for on-campus employment.

Growth in College Costs

2000-2016

Average Annual Costs[1]

School	Tuition & Fees		Tuition, Fees, Room & Board	
	2000	2016	2000	2016
Public 2 Year	$1,642	$3,520		
Public 4 Year	$3,508	$9,650	$8,439	$20,092
Private 4 Year	$16,072	$33,480	$16,072	$45,365

Tuition and Fees
2000-2016

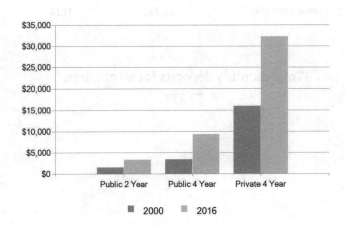

Projected Costs of Education

	Jacob	Jane	John
Name of school	U.C.A.	U.C.B.	U.C.C.
Years until college begins	5	8	11
Years to attend college	6	6	8
Current costs to attend one year	$18,000	$18,000	$22,000
Estimated annual increase in costs	4.00%	4.00%	4.50%
Amount needed at start of college	**$125,354**	**$141,006**	**$271,869**
Amount currently saved	$35,000	$25,000	$10,000
Estimated growth rate	6.00%	6.00%	6.00%
Savings at start of college	**$47,210**	**$40,354**	**$19,316**
Additional amount required	**$78,144**	**$100,653**	**$252,553**
Monthly deposits for each child	**$1,114**	**$815**	**$1,349**

Total monthly deposits for all children
$3,279

Education Funding Analysis Data

Personal

Date 01/01/2018

#	Student(s) name	Date of birth	Portion to fund	Amount currently saved	Planned monthly savings
1)	Robert	01/01/1999	100%	$10,000	$600
2)	Catherine	01/01/2001	100%	8,000	400
3)	Michael	01/01/2008	100%	6,000	300
4)	Rebecca	01/01/2006	100%	3,500	300
5)	Toni	01/01/2006	100%	3,500	300

Education Information

#	School(s) name	Annual cost	Age when school begins	Years in school
1)	University of California: Los Angeles	$24,375	18	4
2)	University of California: Los Angeles	24,375	18	4
3)	University of California: Los Angeles	24,375	18	4
4)	University of California: Los Angeles	12,696	18	4
5)	University of California: Los Angeles	12,696	18	4

Assumptions

Annual education inflation rate	6.00%
Assumed rate of return on assets	6.00%

Education Funding Summary

With education costs increasing at a rate that exceeds the general inflation rate, it is important to prepare as early as possible.

Objective: Your goal is to meet the following education funding needs.

Name	Student Age Today	Student Begin Age	Current Annual Cost	Current Funding Balance	Current Monthly Savings
Robert	19	18	$24,375	$10,000	$600
Catherine	17	18	$24,375	$8,000	$400
Michael	10	18	$24,375	$6,000	$300
Rebecca	12	18	$12,696	$3,500	$300
Toni	12	18	$12,696	$3,500	$300

In order to meet these goals you may need to increase your monthly savings.

For Robert, you will need additional monthly savings of $86,806.

For Catherine, you will need additional monthly savings of $7,232.

For Michael, you will need additional monthly savings of $877.

For Rebecca, you will need additional monthly savings of $470.

For Toni, you will need additional monthly savings of $470.

Assumes college inflation of 6.00% and rate of return on assets of 6.00%.

Current Funding Program

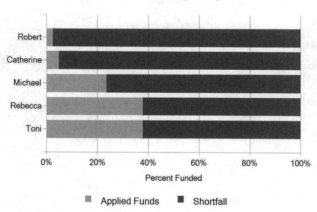

Values shown in this presentation are hypothetical and not a promise of future performance.

Education Funding Analysis

For Robert

You currently have $10,000 saved and you are contributing $600 each month. This could be worth $2,413 when school begins.

Start Age	Number of Years	School Name	Percent to Fund	First Year Amount
18	4	University of California: Los Angeles	100%	$24,375

Current Funding Program

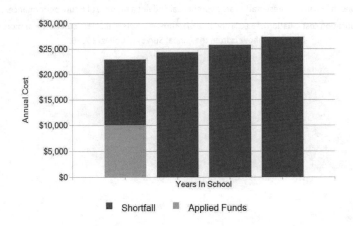

**Your current plan does not provide for a full year of school.
To reach your goal you must set aside an amount of $86,806.
or you must increase your monthly savings by $86,806**

Values shown in this presentation are hypothetical and not a promise of future performance.
Assumes education inflation rate of 6.00% and a rate of return on assets of 6.00%. Source: One or more of the objectives above is from the Annual Survey of Colleges 2016.

Education Funding Timeline

For Robert

Age	School Cost	Amount Funded	Annual Shortfall	Funding Contributions	Funding Growth	Funding Balance
					Beginning Balance	$10,000
18	$22,995	$10,000	$12,995	$0	$0	$0
19	24,375	0	24,375	0	0	0
20	25,838	0	25,838	0	0	0
21	27,388	0	27,388	0	0	0

Values shown in this presentation are hypothetical and not a promise of future performance.

Assumes education cost inflation of 6.00% and rate of return on assets of 6.00%. Source: One or more of the objectives above is from the Annual Survey of Colleges 2016.

Progress Toward Education Goals

On any journey to a goal, it makes sense to check in every now and then to see that you are on the right track. This report shows you the status and expectations as of 18 months ago. This is a good time to make note of where you actually are on your journey. If your progress is not what you desire, perhaps it is time to revisit the particulars of this goal.

Number of months used for projected values   18

Assumes rate of return for education assets   6.00%

Student	Savings	Original Value	Projected Value	Current Value
Robert	Amount currently saved	$10,000	$22,267	
	Planned monthly savings	$600	$600	
Catherine	Amount currently saved	$8,000	$16,303	
	Planned monthly savings	$400	$400	
Michael	Amount currently saved	$6,000	$12,227	
	Planned monthly savings	$300	$300	
Rebecca	Amount currently saved	$3,500	$9,493	
	Planned monthly savings	$300	$300	
Toni	Amount currently saved	$3,500	$9,493	
	Planned monthly savings	$300	$300	

Personal Property and Casualty Insurance

Protecting What You Own

Property and casualty (P&C) is the term commonly used to describe insurance designed to protect an individual from loss or damage to the physical assets he or she owns. For example, a fire may seriously damage or completely destroy a home. Without adequate homeowner's

insurance to provide the funds to repair or rebuild, such a loss could be a financial disaster. Homeowner's policies can also provide protection for the home's contents, such as furniture, appliances, and other personal belongings.

Many P&C policies also provide liability protection. For example, the owner of an automobile who causes an accident may be required by a court (be found "liable") to pay others for repair of property damage, medical expenses, lost wages, or pain and suffering. The dollar amounts of such court decisions can be enormous.

Types of Policies

There is a wide variety of property and casualty policies. A number of additional coverages (endorsements) can be added to a basic policy to provide protection against risks found only in certain geographical areas, to protect specific types of property, or to cover a temporary situation. Some of the most common types of policies and endorsements include:

- **Automobile insurance:** Auto policies typically cover repair of physical damage, payments for medical expenses, and liability protection. A separate policy is often used to cover recreational vehicles such as motor homes, golf carts, snowmobiles, trailers, ATVs, or campers.

- **Homeowner's insurance:** A homeowner's policy can provide protection for both the home and its contents, against a wide range of perils, as well as provide very broad personal liability coverage.

- **Condo unit owner's insurance:** Similar to the homeowner's policy, the condo unit owner's policy differs primarily in that coverage is provided primarily for the contents.

- **Renter's insurance:** Renter's policies provide coverage for the personal property of an individual renting a home, condo, or apartment. A renter's policy can also include personal liability coverage similar to that found in a homeowner's or condo unit owner's policy.

- **Earthquake insurance:** Earthquake insurance is normally offered as an endorsement to a homeowner's, condo unit owner's policy, or renter's policy to provide protection against loss caused by earthquake. It can also be a stand-alone policy.

- **Flood insurance:** Flood insurance is provided through a separate policy. The federal government stands as the ultimate guarantor for flood policies.

- **Watercraft insurance:** Watercraft policies cover loss and liability for the personal use of small watercraft such as boats or jet skis or for larger craft such as ocean-going yachts.

- **Umbrella liability:** Acts as excess or catastrophic protection to the basic liability protection offered with most other P&C policies. The liability coverage offered by an "umbrella" policy begins where the coverage in a basic policy ends and, in some instances, offers broader protection.

Uniform Policy Forms

The Insurance Services Office (ISO) and the American Association of Insurance Services (AAIS) are industry service organizations that provide actuarial and loss information to P&C insurers. These service organizations also provide standardized, uniform policy agreements, called "forms," which are used by many insurers.[1] Such standardized policy forms make it easier for a consumer to understand the terms of the policy and to compare policies offered by different insurance firms.

---

[1] Some insurers have their own forms, which may differ from the standard contracts developed by ISO or AAIS.

Personal Property and Casualty Insurance

Understand the Contract

An insurance policy is a written contract between the insured and the insurance company. The protection provided by P&C policies of all types typically represents a significant part of an individual's overall risk management program. Thus, it's important for an insured individual to read and understand key policy provisions, such as:

- **What perils (or risks) are covered in the policy?** Two basic approaches are involved. In the "named-peril" form, the policy will specify only those perils that are covered. In the "all-risk" form, the policy will list only those perils that are not covered and provide protection for all others.

- **What perils are not covered?** In many cases, perils that are excluded can be covered by endorsement and payment of an additional premium.

- **What are the policy limits?** What is the maximum benefit/coverage payable by the insurance company in the event of a loss? Is a home that would cost $200,000 to rebuild insured for $100,000?

- **What are the deductible amounts?** A policy deductible is the "self-insurance" element in an insurance policy; the term refers to the part of the loss the policy buyer must pay before the insurance company pays its portion. The deductible can be a flat amount or a percentage of the insured value at the time of a loss.

- **Impact of inflation:** A home built 20 years ago can be rebuilt, but at a much higher cost. Most policy forms provide for replacement cost of a home and contents, along with an annual inflation guard of between 2% and 6%.

- **In the event of a loss, what are the duties of the insured?** Each policy will specify certain actions that an insured must take in the event of a loss.

Seek Professional Guidance

Insurance agents and brokers, insurance counselors, and other trained financial consultants can help provide detailed answers to questions about a particular policy. These professionals are also helpful in selecting the right policy and the appropriate amount of coverage.

Automobile Insurance

Why Automobile Insurance?

For most Americans, the automobile is an essential part of modern life. Owning or operating a car, however, can also be a source of serious financial risk. Personal liability arising from losses suffered by others, or the cost of repairing or replacing a damaged or stolen vehicle, can be very high.

Also, most states have auto liability insurance laws, requiring auto owners to maintain liability insurance as a condition of licensing or use on public roadways. Other states require owners to show proof of financial responsibility before and after an accident.

Coverage Under the Policy

Automobile insurance usually covers a number of risks in one package policy. The most frequently used policy is the personal automobile policy (PAP).[1] The PAP is designed primarily for private passenger automobiles, but protection can be extended to cover other types of vehicles. Typical coverage includes the following:

- **Liability:** This coverage protects the owner against losses from legal liability arising from bodily injury or property damage resulting from an auto accident. The coverage can be a split limit, such as $50,000/$100,000/$25,000 (per person/per accident for bodily injury/property damage) or a single limit ($100,000 for each accident).

- **Medical payments:** This provision pays medical and funeral expenses because of bodily injury. Coverage is provided on a "no-fault" basis.

- **Uninsured/underinsured motorist:** Although many states have financial responsibility laws, not all drivers comply. *Uninsured* motorist coverage pays for injuries (in some states property damage is also included) sustained in an accident with an uninsured (or a hit-and-run) driver. *Underinsured* motorist insurance covers the difference between actual losses sustained and what an insured can collect from an at-fault uninsured (or underinsured) driver, up to policy limits.

---

[1] The specific coverage and terms of a policy can vary from company to company, and from state to state.

- **Physical damage:** This section is designed to cover physical damage to the insured auto. *Collision*, as the name implies, covers collision losses. *Comprehensive*, also known as "other than collision," covers losses from non-collision incidents such as theft, fire, or storm damage. Payment is generally based on the lower of actual cash value, or the cost to repair or replace the damaged or stolen vehicle.

Adding Additional Coverage

There are a number of additional coverages that can be added (by endorsement) to a basic policy to provide insurance for unusual situations or to protect other types of vehicles. Two of the most common endorsements include:

- **Extended liability:** Used to cover automobiles that are not legally owned by the insured, such as an auto furnished by an employer for the regular use of the insured and/or the family. Extends the policy coverage to situations involving non-owned vehicles, which standard policy provisions would otherwise exclude.

- **Miscellaneous type vehicle endorsements:** Allows the insured to cover vehicles such as snowmobiles, motorcycles, motor scooters, go-carts, golf carts, antique and classic cars, motor homes, and campers. In some states, a separate policy is used to cover these vehicles.

Understand the Policy

An insurance policy is a written contract between the insured and the insurance company. The protection provided by the policy typically represents a significant part of an individual's overall risk management program. Thus, it is important for an insured individual to read and understand key policy provisions such as:

- **What perils are covered in the policy?** A basic policy may not provide as much protection as is necessary.

- **What perils are not covered?** For an additional premium, coverage for excluded perils or situations can often be added to a policy.

- **What are the limits of coverage?** The maximum dollar amount the insurance company will pay in the event of a covered loss.

- **What are the deductible amounts?** A deductible is a dollar amount the insured must pay before the insurance company pays its portion.

- **In the event of a loss, what are the duties of the insured?** A policy will usually list the steps that must be taken in the event of a loss.

Seek Professional Guidance

Insurance agents and brokers, insurance counselors, and other trained financial consultants can help provide answers to detailed questions about a particular policy. These professionals are also helpful in selecting the right policy and the appropriate amount of coverage.

Homeowner's Insurance

Why Homeowner's Insurance?

A home is the single biggest investment most individuals
will ever make; it is typically the largest asset on the family
"balance sheet." Also, the contents of a typical home, in
the form of furniture, appliances, clothing, family
heirlooms, and other movable personal belongings,
represent a substantial additional investment. The unprotected loss (or partial loss) of a
home and its contents to theft, fire, windstorm, or some other disaster, could be financially
devastating.[1]

Further, everyone faces the risk of personal liability. For example, a visitor to the residence
could slip and fall. Such accidents can result in court decisions awarding large sums to the
injured party for medical expenses, and "pain and suffering."

Coverage Under the Policy

Originally, a standard homeowner's policy covered only the risk of fire. Today's homeowner's
policies provide protection against a number of the "perils" of modern life, in one "package"
policy. A typical[2] homeowner's policy can provide insurance protection for the following:

- **Home:** The physical dwelling structure and other structures attached to it.

- **Other structures:** For example, a detached garage, pool house, guesthouse, green
  house, or tool shed.

- **Personal property:** This covers the contents of the home, such as furniture, appliances
  or clothing. Certain types of property[3] may have specific dollar limits.
- **Loss of use or additional living expense:** If a home is damaged by a covered peril,
  loss-of-use coverage helps meet the costs of hotel bills, apartment or rental home,
  eating out, and other living expenses while the home is being repaired. This policy
  section can also reimburse a homeowner for lost income if a room in the home were
  rented out. This is sometimes insured on an actual-loss-sustained basis.

---

[1] Many mortgage lenders require homeowner's insurance, to protect the dwelling, as a condition of granting the mortgage.

[2] The specific coverage and terms of a policy can vary from company to company, and from state to state.

[3] Jewelry, silverware, securities, cash, and collectibles are examples of personal property subject to these "internal" policy
limits.

- **Personal liability:** Provides protection against legal liability for bodily injury or property damage if a third party is accidentally injured.

- **Medical payments:** Also known as guest-medical payments, this section provides coverage if a third party is accidentally injured and needs medical treatment.

Policy Forms

There are several organizations that work with insurance companies to develop standardized homeowner's policies. While the details of a particular policy can vary, these standardized policies or "forms" are generally very similar.

- **Broad form policy (HO-02):** This policy covers the home, other structures, and personal property on a "named-peril" basis. Only the perils listed are covered.

- **Special form policy HO-03):** Coverage for the home and other structures is written on an "all-risk" basis; damage from any peril is covered, unless specifically excluded. Coverage for personal property is provided on a named-peril basis.

- **Comprehensive form (HO-05):** This policy covers the home, other structures, and personal property on an "all-risk" basis; damage from any peril is covered, unless specifically excluded. This form is typically used for more expensive homes.

- **Modified form coverage (HO-08):** This policy form is generally used with homes where the cost to re-build exceeds the market value of the property. Protection is provided on a named-perils basis. Payment is generally limited to actual cash value.

Policy Exclusions

The standard homeowner's policies specifically exclude a number of perils from coverage. Policy coverage of these excluded perils can generally be added through an endorsement and payment of an additional premium. Typical policy exclusions might include the following:

- **Ordinance or law:** Many homeowner's policies do not cover losses, or have limitations, due to a law or ordinance of the community in which the home is located. For example, if a home is damaged or destroyed, changes in building codes could result in additional, uncovered expense when the home is repaired or rebuilt. Ordinance or law coverage is included in some package policies, often as a percentage of the dwelling coverage (10%, 25%, 50%, etc.). This coverage is required in some states.

- **Earth movement:** Excludes loss caused by events such as earthquake, volcanic eruption, or landslide.

- **Water damage:** Refers to damage from water that backs up from sewers or drains, or water seeping through walls. Many policies contain dollar limits for water damage due to such things as a broken pipe.

- **Flood damage:** Refers to damage from rising water, mudslide, or wave action.

- **Mold Exclusion:** Due to high claims activity for losses caused by mold, many insurance companies are excluding coverage for mold damage.

- **Other exclusions:** Other specific exclusions include war, nuclear hazard, neglect, and intentional loss.

Other Issues

- **Replacement cost condition:** Dwelling and other structures: If a home is damaged or totally destroyed, a homeowner's policy will generally pay (within policy limits) to rebuild or repair on an "actual-cash-value" basis. In simple terms, actual cash value means replacement cost, less a deduction for depreciation or for wear and tear. Reimbursement on this basis could leave a homeowner short of the total funds needed to restore the home.

  Through an endorsement and payment of an additional premium, reimbursement can be on a "replacement-cost" basis. Replacement cost means, simply, restoring the home to its previous condition, using materials and workmanship of similar quality. In some policies, the availability of this feature requires the homeowner to maintain coverage on the home equal to at least 80% of the cost to rebuild or repair. If insurance coverage were not maintained at the 80% level, any loss would be reimbursed at a lesser amount, or on an actual-cash-value or depreciated basis.

- **Replacement cost:** Personal property (contents): Coverage is normally on an actual-cash-value basis. For an additional premium, the policy can usually be endorsed to protect covered personal property on a replacement-cost basis (the cost to buy the item new today) without considering depreciation.

- **Inflation guard rider:** The standard policy forms can usually be endorsed to provide for automatic, periodic increases in policy limits. These increases in policy coverage generally apply to both the dwelling and contents, and help avoid being underinsured due to inflation. Such an endorsement also helps meet the 80%-of-replacement-cost condition to qualify for replacement cost on the home.

Understand the Policy

An insurance policy is a written contract between the insured and the insurance company. The protection provided by the policy typically represents a significant part of an individual's overall risk management program. Thus, it's important for an insured individual to read and understand key policy provisions such as the following.

- **What perils are covered in the policy?** A basic policy may not provide as much protection as is necessary.

- **What perils are not covered?** For an additional premium, perils or situations not covered can often be added to a policy.

- **What are the limits of coverage?** This refers to the maximum dollar amount the insurance company will pay, in the event of a covered loss.

- **What are the deductible amounts?** A deductible is a dollar amount or percentage the insured must pay before the insurance company pays its portion of the loss.

- **In the event of a loss, what are the duties of the insured?** A policy will usually list the steps that must be taken in the event of a loss.

Seek Professional Guidance

Insurance agents and brokers, insurance counselors, and other trained financial consultants can help provide answers to detailed questions about a particular policy. These professionals are also helpful in selecting the right policy and the appropriate amount of coverage.

Renter's Insurance

Why Renter's Insurance?

Many people who rent their home do not consider insurance, usually because they are not making an investment in real property. However, the contents of a home, in the form of furniture, appliances, clothing, family heirlooms and other movable personal belongings, often represent a substantial investment. The unprotected loss

(or partial loss) of a renter's personal property to theft, fire, windstorm or some other incident could be financially devastating.

Further, each individual, whether a renter or homeowner, faces the risk of personal liability. For example, a visitor to the residence could slip and fall. Such accidents can result in court decisions awarding large sums to the injured party for medical expenses and "pain and suffering."

Coverage Under the Policy

Most renter's policies available today are closely related in design to policies created for homeowners, and combine protection against a number of the perils of modern life in a single package policy. The primary difference is that a renter's policy does not provide protection for the building structure. A typical[1] renter's policy can provide insurance protection for the following:

- **Personal property:** Covers the contents of the home, such as furniture, appliances, or clothing. Coverage is generally provided on a broad, named-peril basis. Perils that are not named are excluded from coverage. Certain types of property[2] may have specific dollar limits.

- **Loss of use or additional living expenses:** If a rented home is damaged by a covered peril, loss-of-use coverage helps meet the costs of hotel bills, apartment or rental home, eating out, and other living expenses, while the home is being repaired.

---

[1] The specific coverage and terms of a policy can vary from company to company, and from state to state.
[2] Jewelry, silverware, securities, cash, and collectibles are examples of personal property subject to these "internal" policy limits.

- **Personal liability:** Provides protection against legal liability for bodily injury or property damage if a third party is accidentally injured.

- **Medical payments:** Also known as guest medical payments, this section provides coverage if a third party is accidentally injured and needs medical treatment.

- **Building additions and alterations:** Covers improvements, fixtures or alterations made by a tenant, such as paint, wallpaper, carpets, drapes, and blinds.

Policy Exclusions

A standard renter's policy specifically excludes a number of perils from coverage. Policy coverage of these excluded perils can generally be added through an endorsement and payment of an additional premium. Typical policy exclusions include the following:

- **Earth movement:** Losses caused by earthquake, volcanic eruption, or landslide.

- **Water damage:** Refers to damage from water that backs up from sewers or drains, or water seeping through walls. Many policies contain dollar limits for water damage due to such things as a broken pipe.

- **Flood damage:** Refers to damage from rising water, mudslide, or wave action.

- **Mold exclusion:** Due to high claims activity for losses caused by mold, many insurance companies are excluding coverage for mold damage.

- **Other exclusions:** Such as wear and tear, war, nuclear hazard, neglect, and intentional loss.

Other Issues

- **Personal property (contents):** A standard renter's policy will insure a home's contents for actual cash value, e.g., replacement cost less an allowance for depreciation or wear and tear. For an additional premium, the policy can usually be endorsed to protect covered personal property on a replacement-cost basis (the cost to buy the item new today), without considering depreciation.

- **Inflation guard rider:** The standard policy can usually be endorsed to provide for automatic, periodic increases in policy limits. These automatic increases in policy coverage help avoid being underinsured because items cost more due to inflation.

Understand the Policy

An insurance policy is a written contract between the insured and the insurance company. The protection provided by the policy typically represents a significant part of an individual's overall risk-management program. Thus, it's important for an insured individual to read and understand key policy provisions such as the following:

- **What perils are covered in the policy?** A basic policy may not provide as much protection as is necessary.

- **What perils are not covered?** For an additional premium, excluded perils or situations can often be added to a policy.

- **What are the limits of coverage?** This refers to the maximum dollar amount the insurance company will pay in the event of a covered loss.

- **What are the deductible amounts?** A deductible is a dollar amount or percentage the insured must pay before the insurance company pays its portion of the loss.

- **In the event of a loss, what are the duties of the insured?** A policy will usually list the steps that must be taken in the event of a loss.

Seek Professional Guidance

Insurance agents and brokers, insurance counselors, and other trained financial consultants can help provide answers to detailed questions about a particular policy. These professionals are also helpful in selecting the right policy and the appropriate amount of coverage.

Condominium Unit Owner's Insurance

Why Condo Unit Owner's Insurance?

A home, be it a single-family dwelling or a condominium unit, is usually the biggest investment that most individuals will ever make; it is typically the largest asset on the family balance sheet. Also, the contents of a typical home, in the form of furniture, appliances, clothing, family heirlooms, and other movable personal belongings,

represent a substantial additional investment. The unprotected loss (or partial loss) of a home and its contents, to theft, fire, windstorm, or some other disaster, could be financially devastating.

Further, everyone faces the risk of personal liability. For example, a visitor to the residence could slip and fall. Such accidents can result in court decisions awarding large sums to the injured party for medical expenses, and "pain and suffering."

Condominium Ownership

A condominium is a building divided into separate living spaces (units), owned by individuals, and the common areas, owned jointly by all of the individual unit owners. Overall management of the complex is carried out by a homeowner's or condo unit owner's association. This association makes policy decisions for the community and is responsible for maintaining and insuring the building structure and common areas of the condominium complex. The individual condo unit owner is responsible for the interior of his or her own unit.

Coverage Under the Policy

Most condo unit owner's policies available today are closely related in design to policies created for single-family homeowners, and provide protection against a number of the perils of modern life in a single package policy.

Condominium Unit Owner's Insurance

The protection available under a condo unit owner's policy differs from a typical homeowner's policy primarily in the type of coverage provided for the dwelling. A typical[1] condo unit owner's policy can provide coverage for the following:

- **Condo unit:** This section provides protection for the unit owner's real property, also known as "unit owner's additions and alterations."[2] The items included here will vary with state law, but can include such interior furnishings as wallpaper, paneling, kitchen and bathroom cabinets, carpeting or wet bar. Coverage is generally provided on a broad, named-peril basis. Perils that are not named are excluded. This can be endorsed on an all-risk basis for an additional premium.

- **Other structures:** These might include a detached garage or tool shed, if owned solely by the insured.

- **Personal property:** Covers the contents of the unit, such as furniture, appliances or clothing. Coverage is generally provided on a broad, named-peril basis; perils not named are excluded. Certain types of property[3] may have specific dollar limits.

- **Loss of use or additional living expenses:** If a condo unit is damaged by a covered peril, loss-of-use coverage helps meet the costs of hotel bills, apartment or rental home, eating out, and other living expenses while the home is being repaired.

- **Personal liability:** Provides protection against legal liability for bodily injury or property damage if a third party is accidentally injured.

- **Medical payments:** Also known as guest medical payments, this section provides coverage if a third party is accidentally injured and needs medical treatment.

- **Loss assessment:** If the homeowner's association suffers a loss,[4] it may assess each owner to pay a portion of the loss. If the loss were the result of a covered peril, this policy provision would pay the insured's portion of the assessment, up to the limit specified in the endorsement.

---

[1] The specific coverage and terms of a policy can vary from company to company and from state to state.

[2] In common practice, this has also been described as "from the bare wall in."

[3] Jewelry, silverware, securities, cash, and collectibles are examples of personal property subject to these internal policy limits.

[4] For example, from deductible liability or major, uncovered property damage.

Condominium Unit Owner's Insurance

Policy Exclusions

A standard policy specifically excludes a number of perils from coverage. Policy coverage of these excluded perils can generally be added through an endorsement and payment of an additional premium. Typical policy exclusions include the following:

- **Earth movement:** Losses caused by earthquake, volcanic eruption, or landslide.

- **Water damage:** Refers to damage from water that backs up from sewers or drains, or water seeping through walls. Many policies contain dollar limits for water damage due to such things as a broken pipe.

- **Flood damage:** Refers to damage from rising water, mudslide or wave action.

- **Mold exclusion:** Due to high claims activity for losses caused by mold, many insurance companies are excluding coverage for mold damage.

- **Other exclusions:** Such as wear and tear, war, nuclear hazard, neglect and intentional loss.

Other Issues

- **Personal property (contents):** A standard policy will insure a condominium unit for actual cash value, e.g., replacement cost less an allowance for depreciation or wear and tear. For an additional premium, the policy can usually be endorsed to protect covered property on a replacement cost basis (the cost to buy the item new today), without considering depreciation.

- **Inflation guard rider:** The standard policy can usually be endorsed to provide for automatic, periodic increases in policy limits. These increases in policy coverage generally apply to both the dwelling and contents, and help avoid being underinsured due to inflation.

Condominium Unit Owner's Insurance

Understand the Policy

An insurance policy is a written contract between the insured and the insurance company. The protection provided by the policy typically represents a significant part of an individual's overall risk-management program. Thus, it's important for an insured individual to read and understand key policy provisions such as the following:

- **What perils are covered in the policy?** A basic policy may not provide as much protection as is necessary.

- **What perils are not covered?** For an additional premium, excluded perils or situations can often be added to a policy.

- **What are the limits of coverage?** This refers to the maximum dollar amount the insurance company will pay in the event of a covered loss.

- **What are the deductible amounts?** A deductible is a dollar amount or percentage the insured must pay before the insurance company pays its portion of the loss.

- **In the event of a loss, what are the duties of the insured?** A policy will usually list the steps that must be taken in the event of a loss.

Seek Professional Guidance

Insurance agents and brokers, insurance counselors, and other trained financial consultants can help provide answers to detailed questions about a particular policy. These professionals are also helpful in selecting the right policy and the appropriate amount of coverage.

Earthquake Insurance

Why Earthquake Insurance?

Earthquakes can do a great deal of damage to a home and the personal possessions in it. A severe earthquake can completely destroy a home and its contents. Such a loss, if uninsured, could devastate most individuals and their families.

Excluded from Standard Policies

In most homeowner's, renter's, and condominium unit owner's policies there is a specific exclusion for loss caused by "earth movement," a term that includes earthquakes. To cover this, a basic policy must be endorsed to include earth movement, for which the insured pays an additional premium. As an alternative, a separate earthquake policy may be purchased.

Earth movement is generally defined as "earthquake, including land shockwaves or tremors before, during or after a volcanic eruption; landslide; mine subsidence, mudflow, earth sinking, rising or shifting." The term earthquake generally means a "vibration generating rupture event caused by displacement within the earth's crust through release of strain associated with tectonic processes and includes effects such as ground shaking, liquefaction, seismically-induced land sliding and damaging amplification of ground motion."

Adding Other Coverage

In many locations, an insured can add an earth movement endorsement to a basic policy. The endorsement usually covers only structures and/or personal property, and does not cover damage to the land itself. It usually excludes flood or tidal waves generated by earth movement.

The earth movement endorsement is subject to a percentage deductible (generally 10% to 25% of the value of the property insured), compared with the usual flat dollar deductible amount. To understand this different type of deductible, suppose a person's home is insured for $200,000 and its contents insured for $60,000. If there is a total loss from an earthquake and the policy has a 10% deductible, the individual would face a deductible of $20,000 on the value of the home and $6,000 on the value of the contents.

Seek Professional Guidance

Insurance agents and brokers, insurance counselors, and other trained financial consultants can help provide answers to detailed questions about a particular policy. These professionals are also helpful in selecting the right policy and the appropriate amount of coverage.

Flood Insurance

Why Flood Insurance?

A moderate flood can do a great deal of damage to a home and its personal belongings. A severe flood can completely destroy a home and its contents. Such a loss, if uninsured, could financially devastate most individuals and their families.

In addition to the risk of severe financial loss, individuals purchasing or constructing property in areas subject to severe flooding (a special flood hazard area) may be required to obtain flood insurance as a condition of obtaining a mortgage. Further, the owner of property in a special flood hazard area may be denied federal disaster relief after a flood, unless the owner had previously purchased flood insurance.

Excluded from Standard Policies

In virtually all homeowner's, renter's and condominium unit owner's policies, there is a specific exclusion for loss caused by flood. To cover this peril, a separate flood insurance policy must be purchased.

The term "flood" is generally defined as, "A general and temporary condition of partial or complete inundation of two or more acres of normally dry land area or of two or more properties (at least one of which is your property) from: overflow of inland or tidal waters; or the unusual and rapid accumulation or runoff of surface waters from any source; mudflow; or the collapse or subsidence of land along the shore of a lake or similar body of water as a result of erosion or undermining caused by waves or currents of water exceeding anticipated cyclical levels that result in a flood as defined above."

The National Flood Insurance Program

Because of the catastrophic nature of property losses suffered in floods, flood insurance was, for many years, generally unavailable. In response to this need, the federal government, in 1968, established the National Flood Insurance Program (NFIP). Under this program, managed by the Federal Emergency Management Agency (FEMA), the federal government stands as an insurer of last resort for flood insurance. In exchange for this guarantee, the government requires participating communities to adopt and enforce land use measures that direct future development away from flood prone areas.

Flood Insurance

The availability of flood insurance under the NFIP is conditioned on a community agreeing to follow federal flood planning requirements. The amount of insurance available and the type of structures covered, will vary depending on how far along a community is in meeting all federal conditions:

- **Emergency program:** Basic coverage under the emergency program (EP) is available when a community agrees to adopt federal standards. For example, coverage under the EP for a single-family residence would be limited to $35,000 on the dwelling and $10,000 on personal property.[1]

- **Regular program:** When a community has completed certain federal requirements, it enters the regular program (RP). Under the RP, additional coverage becomes available. For example, coverage under the RP for a single-family residence can be as much as $250,000 on the dwelling and $100,000 for personal property. Excess flood insurance for higher limits outside the program is available.

Policy Forms

There are three Standard Flood Insurance Policy (SFIP) forms:

- **Dwelling Form:** Covers single-family homes, renters, and residential properties of 1-4 units. The insurance may cover the building and/or building contents.

- **General Form:** Covers residential properties with 5 units or more. The insurance may cover the building and/or building contents.

- **Residential Condominium Building Association Form:** Provides coverage for condominium home owners associations. The insurance covers buildings and may cover certain common area contents.

Purchasing Flood Insurance

Flood insurance can be purchased from either the federal government or private insurers and is sold by insurance agents and brokers. The insurance agents receive a commission for policies sold.

---

[1] Under the Emergency Program, higher limits of building coverage are available in Alaska, Hawaii, the U.S. Virgin Islands, and Guam.

With limited exceptions, there is a 30-day waiting period between the time an insured applies for coverage and pays the premium, before the coverage is in effect.

Coverage Under the Policy

A typical residential flood policy provides coverage for "direct physical loss by or from flood," for the following:

- **Dwelling:** Covers damage or loss to the building.

- **Personal property:** Refers to the contents of a home, such as furniture, appliances or clothing. Certain types of property may be excluded or have a specific dollar limit.[1]

- **Other Coverage:** Covers issues such as debris removal after a flood, protective measures such as sandbagging or moving property to a safe location, or a condominium loss assessment.

- **Increased Cost of Compliance:** Provides a limited amount of insurance to help cover the costs of meeting a community's rebuilding requirement to protect an insured property from future flood damage.

Policy Exclusions

The standard flood policy specifically excludes a number of perils from coverage. Policy coverage of these excluded perils can generally be added through an endorsement and payment of an additional premium. Typical policy exclusions include the following:

- **Ordinance or law:** Except for the limited coverage under Increased Cost of Compliance, a standard flood policy does not cover loss due to a law or ordinance of the community in which a building is located. For example, if a building is damaged or destroyed, changes in building codes could result in additional, uncovered expense when the structure is repaired or rebuilt.

- **Earth movement:** Excludes losses from earth movement, even if the earth movement is caused by flood. Other, related exclusions include earthquake, landslide, land subsidence, sinkholes, and gradual erosion.

---

[1] Money, securities, and animals are examples of property usually excluded. Specific dollar limits may apply to items such as paintings, jewelry or furs.

- **Economic losses:** A number of economic losses are excluded from coverage, including loss from interruption of business or production, loss of access to or use of the insured property, and any additional living expenses incurred while the insured building is unavailable for use or is being repaired.

Other Issues

- **Replacement cost condition:** Dwelling: If a home is damaged or totally destroyed, a flood policy will generally pay (within policy limits) to rebuild or repair on an actual-cash-value basis. In simple terms, actual cash value means replacement cost, less a deduction for depreciation or wear and tear. Reimbursement on this basis could leave a homeowner short of the total funds needed to restore the home.

  If coverage under the policy is high enough, however, reimbursement can be on a replacement-cost basis. Replacement cost means, simply, restoring the home to its previous condition using materials and workmanship of similar quality. To qualify for replacement cost coverage, three conditions must be met: (1) the building must be a single-family dwelling; (2) it must be the homeowner's principal residence; and (3) building coverage must be at least 80% of the full replacement cost of the building or is the maximum available for the property under the NFIP.

Understand the Policy

An insurance policy is a written contract between the insured and the insurance company. The protection provided by the policy typically represents a significant part of an individual's overall risk management program. Thus, it is important for an insured individual to read and understand key policy provisions such as the following:

- **What perils are covered in the policy?** A basic policy may not provide as much protection as is necessary.

- **What perils are not covered?** For an additional premium, perils or situations not covered can often be added to a policy.

- **What are the limits of coverage?** This refers to the maximum dollar amount the insurance company will pay, in the event of a covered loss.

- **What are the deductible amounts?** A deductible is a dollar amount or percentage the insured must pay before the insurance company pays its portion of the loss.

- **In the event of a loss, what are the duties of the insured?** A policy will usually list the steps that must be taken in the event of a loss.

Seek Professional Guidance

Insurance agents and brokers, insurance counselors, and other trained financial consultants can help provide answers to detailed questions about a particular policy. These professionals are also helpful in selecting the right policy and the appropriate amount of coverage.

Watercraft Insurance

Why Watercraft Insurance?

A large and increasing number of individuals enjoy the benefits of owning and using a personal watercraft such as a sailboat or motorboat. Owning or operating such watercraft, however, can also be a potential source of serious financial risk. Personal liability arising from losses suffered by others, or the cost of repairing or replacing a damaged, destroyed, or stolen watercraft can be very high.

Further, some states, yacht clubs, marinas, and lake associations have mandatory watercraft liability requirements, compelling owners to maintain liability insurance as a condition of licensing or use of facilities and recreation areas.

Sources of Watercraft Insurance

There are a number of sources of insurance coverage for watercraft owners.

- **Homeowner's insurance:** A limited amount of liability coverage for certain types of small watercraft is provided in many homeowner's[1] policies.

- **Endorsement of a homeowner's policy:** Some homeowner's policies may provide for coverage for watercraft through endorsement and payment of an additional premium.

- **Comprehensive watercraft insurance:** Such policies can provide a boat owner with higher levels of coverage, as well as protection against a broader spectrum of perils, than does a homeowner's policy. Coverage can also be provided for situations unique to watercraft ownership and use.

Watercraft Insurance - Coverage Under the Policy

In many respects, the protection provided by a comprehensive watercraft insurance policy (also known as a boat owner's policy) is similar to the coverage offered in many automobile

---

[1] Policy forms for renter's and condo owners may also provide such coverage.

insurance policies; protection is provided against a number of perils in one package. Typical coverage[1] includes the following:

- **Physical damage:** Also known as hull coverage, this coverage protects the insured against damage or loss to a covered watercraft, including trailers,[2] outboard motors, equipment, and furnishings. Insurance is typically provided on an all-risk basis, subject to certain standard exclusions. Reimbursement is generally based on actual cash value, although some insurers may offer policies using either an agreed value (face amount of insurance) or a replacement cost option.

- **Liability coverage:** This coverage is sometimes called protection and indemnity (P&I) coverage. It protects the owner against losses from legal liability arising from bodily injury or property damage caused by a watercraft accident. Coverage is normally provided up to a specific dollar amount.

- **Medical payments:** This policy provision pays medical expenses because of an injury sustained during an accident involving the insured watercraft. Coverage is usually provided up to a specific dollar amount.

- **Uninsured boater:** This coverage pays for bodily injury sustained in an incident caused by an uninsured boater. The provision usually pays up to a specified dollar limit and is normally offered as an optional coverage.

Common Policy Exclusions

A standard, comprehensive watercraft policy will specifically exclude a number of perils from coverage. In some situations, policy coverage for these excluded perils can be added through an endorsement and the payment of an additional premium. In other situations, a separate policy may be required to provide coverage. Typical policy exclusions might include the following:

- **High-risk watercraft:** Many policies exclude certain types of high-risk watercraft such as waverunners and jet skis. Special policies are available to cover such craft.

- **Nonstandard watercraft:** These include submersible or air-propelled (hovercraft) watercraft.

---

[1] The specific coverage and terms of a policy can vary from company to company and from state to state.

[2] In some policies, coverage on the trailer is optional.

- **Yachts:** Generally refers to larger vessels capable of navigating on the high seas. Such craft are normally covered under yacht policies.

- **Watercraft used for charter:** The term "charter" refers to using the insured watercraft for hire, rent, or lease.

- **High-risk activities:** Excluded high-risk activities include powerboat racing in an official race or speed contest, as well as towing individuals paragliding or parasailing. Some policies exclude water skiers towed by the insured craft from medical payments coverage.

Other Issues

While property damage and liability are coverages common to many types of property insurance, the ownership and use of watercraft present some unique situations, some of which may be covered in a comprehensive watercraft policy.

- **Wreck removal:** Coverage to pay for the removal of a wreck. For example, the Coast Guard or Army Corps of Engineers may deem a partially sunken vessel to be a hazard to navigation and order it to be removed or destroyed.

- **Salvage charges:** Refers to reasonable and necessary expenses incurred to protect a covered watercraft from a dangerous situation where loss or destruction is possible. May also cover a reward to the salvor.

- **Towing:** Some policies may provide coverage for towing a watercraft (on land or in the water) to the nearest repair site, if the craft is damaged by a covered peril.

- **Longshoremen's and harbor workers' compensation:** Provides coverage for an insured's liability, under the Federal Longshoremen's and Harbor Workers' Compensation Act, for injury to dockside workers. Coverage is statutory, with the terms of coverage prescribed by federal law. It is usually included as a part of the liability coverage in those states that require it.

- **Jones Act:** Protects the owner of the vessel from liability arising from the death of, or injury to, the captain or crew while on the water.

Watercraft Insurance

Understand the Policy

An insurance policy is a written contract between the insured and the insurance company. The protection provided by the policy typically represents a significant part of an individual's overall risk management program. Thus, it's important for an insured individual to read and understand key policy provisions such as the following:

- **What perils are covered in the policy?** A basic policy may not provide as much protection as is necessary.

- **What perils are not covered?** For an additional premium, coverage for excluded perils can often be added to a policy.

- **What are the limits of coverage?** The maximum dollar amount the insurance company will pay in the event of a covered loss.

- **What are the deductible amounts?** A deductible is a dollar amount or percentage the insured must pay before the insurance company pays its portion of the loss.

- **In the event of a loss, what are the duties of the insured?** A policy will usually list the steps that must be taken in the event of a loss.

Seek Professional Guidance

Insurance agents and brokers, insurance counselors, and other trained financial consultants can help provide answers to detailed questions about a particular policy. These professionals are also helpful in selecting the right policy and the appropriate amount of coverage.

Individual Liability Insurance

Why Individual Liability Insurance?

The risk of legal liability is a fact of modern life. It is perhaps the largest financial risk most individuals face. Common incidents, such as an automobile accident, or a neighbor's child slipping on a kitchen floor, can result in lawsuits, with damage awards of enormous size. Without liability insurance, most individuals and families could be faced with a financial disaster.

Further, state law may require liability insurance. For example, some states have compulsory auto liability insurance laws, requiring auto owners to maintain automobile liability insurance as a condition of licensing or use on public roadways. Other states require auto owners to show financial responsibility after an accident.

Sources of Individual Liability Insurance

Liability insurance is designed to cover an insured for acts of negligence that create a legal obligation to a third party. Such liability can have its source in any part of an individual's life. For many individuals, liability insurance is acquired as part of the package policies purchased to protect major assets such as a home, automobile, or watercraft. Typical[1] policies provide the following liability coverage.

- **Homeowner's[2] insurance:** Liability coverage under a homeowner's policy is provided in one of three sections:

    - **Personal liability:** These are payments the insured is legally obligated to make because of bodily injury or property damage.

    - **Medical payments to others:** These are medical expenses of injured third parties.

    - **Additional coverages:** These cover certain expenses incurred by the insured in the event of bodily injury or property damage.

---

[1] The specific coverage and terms of a policy will vary from company to company and from state to state.
[2] The liability coverage usually provided under a renter's or a condominium unit owner's policy is similar to that provided in a homeowner's policy.

- **Automobile insurance:** Liability coverage under an automobile policy is provided in one of two sections:

  - **Automobile liability:** These are payments the insured is legally obligated to make because of bodily injury or property damage due to an auto accident.

  - **Medical payments:** These are medical or funeral expenses payable because of bodily injury.

- **Watercraft liability insurance:** Liability protection under a watercraft policy is typically provided in the protection and indemnity (P&I) section. P&I includes coverage for the following:

  - **Bodily injury:** These are payments the insured is required to make for pain and suffering, disfigurement, loss of mobility, or actual medical costs.

  - **Property damage:** Covers damage or destruction of someone else's property, including loss of use. Depending on the policy, additional coverage may be available for excess medical payments, longshoremen's and harbor worker's compensation, Jones Act and damage to wharfs and piers.

A standalone, comprehensive personal liability (CPL) policy can be purchased by individuals who do not have homeowner's insurance. Liability coverage under the CPL parallels that provided in a typical homeowner's package.

Policy Exclusions

Standard policies specifically exclude liability arising from a number of activities or situations. Such exclusions limit the range of risks covered in a standard policy, allowing an insurer to provide the protection most commonly needed, at a reasonable cost. Policy coverage for these excluded risks can generally be added through an endorsement and payment of an additional premium or the purchase of a separate policy. Typical liability policy exclusions include the following:

- **Business and professional activities:** Coverage can be added for certain occupations.

- **Watercraft:** There are certain exceptions. A separate watercraft policy should be considered.

- **Aircraft:** A separate aircraft policy should be considered.

- **Other:** Excludes, among others, liability for bodily injury or property damage arising from war, communicable disease, sexual molestation or abuse, controlled substances, and workers compensation.

Personal Umbrella Excess Liability Insurance

Personal umbrella excess liability insurance is designed to provide liability coverage for situations where potential liability could exceed the limits of the protection provided in a typical homeowner's, automobile, or watercraft policy. Those who have acquired wealth, and individuals practicing certain professions, often face such risks, simply because they are seen as having the ability to pay. To meet such needs, an individual may want to consider an umbrella excess liability policy.

The term "umbrella" derives from the fact that such policies require an insured to have a base amount of liability coverage, often in the form of specified policies. In the event of a covered loss, reimbursement comes first from the base policies. Liability in excess of the limits of the base policies is then covered by the umbrella or excess policy, up to its policy limits.

Coverage under an umbrella excess liability policy has two primary goals:

- To provide larger amounts of protection than are available under other policies.
- To broaden the protection, filling in coverage gaps that may exist. Umbrella liability policies generally have fewer exclusions than other policies.

Understand the Policy

An insurance policy is a written contract between the insured and the insurance company. The protection provided by the policy typically represents a significant part of an individual's overall risk management program. Thus, it is important for an insured individual to read and understand key policy provisions such as the following.

- **What losses are covered in the policy?** A basic policy may not provide as much protection as is necessary.

- **What losses are not covered?** For an additional premium, perils or situations not covered can often be added to a policy.

- **What are the limits of coverage?** This refers to the maximum dollar amount the insurance company will pay in the event of a covered loss.

- **What are the retention amounts?** A retention is a dollar amount or percentage the insured must pay before the insurance company pays its portion of the loss.

- **In the event of a loss, what are the duties of the insured?** A policy will usually list the steps that must be taken in the event of a loss.

Seek Professional Guidance

Insurance agents and brokers, insurance counselors, and other trained financial consultants can help provide answers to detailed questions about a particular policy. These professionals are also helpful in selecting the right policy and the appropriate amount of coverage.

General Purposes of Life Insurance

Life insurance is a unique asset that can be used to solve some of life's perplexing financial problems.

Death Benefit Uses for Life Insurance

- Create an estate: Where time or other circumstances have kept the estate owner from accumulating sufficient assets to care for his or her loved ones, life insurance can create an instant estate

- Pay death taxes and other estate settlement costs: These costs can vary from a low of three to four percent to over 40 percent of the estate. Federal Estate Taxes are due nine months after death.

- Fund a business transfer: Business owners often agree to buy a deceased owner's share from his or her estate after death. Life insurance provides the ready cash to finance the transaction.

- Pay off a home mortgage: Many people would like to pass the family residence to their spouse or children free of any mortgage. Often a decreasing term policy is used, which decreases in face amount as the mortgage balance is paid down.

- Protect a business from the loss of a key employee: Key employees are difficult to attract and retain. Their untimely death may cause a severe financial strain on the business.

- Replace a charitable gift: Gifts of appreciated assets to a charitable remainder trust can provide income and estate tax benefits. Life insurance can be used to replace the value of the donated assets. Proceeds from life insurance policies can also be paid directly to a charity.

- Pay off loans: Personal or business loans can be paid off with insurance proceeds.

- Equalize inheritances: When the family business passes to children who are active in it, life insurance can give an equal amount to the other children.

- Accelerated death benefits: Federal tax law allows a "terminally ill" individual to receive the death benefits of a life insurance policy on his or her life income tax free. Such "living benefits", received prior to death, can allow a person to pay medical bills or other expenses and maintain his or her dignity by not dying destitute. If certain conditions are met, a "chronically ill" person may also receive accelerated death benefits free of federal income tax.[1]

  Existing life insurance policies should be reviewed to verify that policy provisions allow for payment of such "accelerated death" benefits.

Other Uses for Life Insurance

While life insurance products are primarily used for death benefit protection, they are also used for long-term accumulation goals.

- College fund for children or grandchildren: Cash value increases in a policy on a minor's life (or the parent's life) can be used to fund college expenses.

- Supplement retirement funds: Current insurance products provide competitive returns and are a prudent way of accumulating additional funds for retirement.

Available cash values may also serve as an "emergency reserve," if needed, or a source of loans, since life policies frequently include features permitting borrowing against these cash values[2]

---

[1] The discussion here concerns federal income tax law; state or local tax law may vary.

[2] A policy loan or withdrawal will generally reduce cash values and death benefits. If a policy lapses or is surrendered with a loan outstanding, the loan will be treated as taxable income in the current year, to the extent of gain in the policy. Policies considered to be modified endowment contracts (MECs) are subject to special rules.

Life Insurance: Glossary of Terms

Accumulation Value: Term used in Universal Life policies to describe the total of all premiums and earnings credited to the account before deductions for any expenses, loans, and surrenders.

Adjustable Life: Form of life insurance allowing the owner to change the face amount, premium amount, period of protection, or the length of the premium payment period.

Attained Age: The age of the insured on a given date.

Automatic Premium Loan: Provision in a life insurance policy authorizing the insurer to use the loan value to pay any premiums still due at the end of the grace period.

Beneficiary: Individual or entity (e.g., trust, corporation) designated to receive the proceeds of a life insurance policy upon the death of the insured.

Cash Value: Generally, the amount of cash due an owner upon surrendering a policy.

Contingent Beneficiary: Individual or legal entity designated to receive the proceeds of a life insurance policy if the primary beneficiary is deceased at the time the benefits become payable.

Contributory: Term used to describe a plan of employee coverage in which the employee pays at least part of the premium.

Cost-of-Living Rider: Designed to adjust benefits in relation to changes in the cost of living. The majority of such riders are tied to changes in the Consumer Price Index (CPI). Generally, the amount of insurance is automatically increased, without evidence of insurability, at predetermined periods for a maximum amount.

Credit Life Insurance: Group life insurance contract whereby a creditor is protected in the event of death of the insured prior to the indebtedness being paid in full.

Death Benefit: Amount stated in a policy contract as payable upon the death of the person whose life is being insured.

Decreasing Term: Form of life insurance that provides a death benefit which declines throughout the term of the contract, reaching zero at the end of the term.

Life Insurance: Glossary of Terms

Dependent Coverage: Coverage on the head of a family which is extended to his or her dependents, including only the lawful spouse and unmarried children who are not yet employed on a full-time basis. "Children" may be step, foster, adopted, or natural.

Dependent Life Insurance: Benefit that is part of a group life insurance contract, providing death protection to the eligible dependents of a covered employee.

Dividend Accumulation: Option in a life insurance policy allowing the policyholder to leave any premium dividends with the insurer to accumulate at compound interest.

Dividend Additions: Option whereby the owner can leave policy dividends with the insurer, and each dividend is used to buy a single premium life insurance policy for whatever amount it will purchase. Also called paid-up additions.

Dividend Option: Alternative ways in which an insured under a participating life insurance policy may elect to receive policy dividends.

Extended Term Insurance: Provision found in most policies which provides the option of continuing the existing amount of insurance as term insurance for as long a period of time as the contract's cash value will purchase. This is one of the nonforfeiture options available to the insured in case a premium is not paid within the grace period.

Face Amount: Amount that will be paid in the case of death or maturity of a policy.

Family Income Policy: Policy that pays an income up to a future date designated in the policy to the beneficiary after the death of the insured. The period of payment is measured from the date of the inception of the contract, and at the end of the income period the face amount of the policy is paid to the beneficiary. If the insured lives beyond the income period, only the face amount is payable in the event of his death.

Flexible Premium: Policy allowing the owner to vary the amount or timing of premiums.

Free Look: Period of time (usually 10, 20 or 30 days) during which a policyholder may examine a newly issued individual policy and surrender it in exchange for a full refund of premium if not satisfied for any reason.

Grace Period: Prescribed period, usually 30 to 31 days after the premium due date, during which an insurance contract remains in force and the premium may be paid.

Life Insurance: Glossary of Terms

Group Life Insurance: Life Insurance provided for members of a group. It is most often issued to a group of employees but may be issued to any group provided it is not formed for the purpose of buying insurance. The cost is typically lower than for individual policies because administrative expenses per life are decreased, there are certain tax advantages, and measures taken against adverse selection are effective.

Guaranteed Renewable: Contract in which the insured has the right to keep a policy in force by the timely payment of premiums for a period of time as set forth in the contract. During that period of time, the insurer has no right to make any change in any provision of the contract other than a change in the premium rate for all insureds in the same class.

Incidents of Ownership: Various rights which may be exercised under the policy contract by the policy owner. These include: (1) the right to cash in the policy, (2) to receive a loan on the cash value of the policy, and (3) to change the beneficiary.

Incontestable Clause: Clause in a policy providing that after a policy has been in effect for a given length of time (typically two or three years), the insurer shall not be able to contest the statements contained in the application.

Irrevocable Beneficiary: Beneficiary that cannot be changed without his or her consent.

Loan Value: The amount of money a policy owner can borrow using the cash value of the life insurance policy as security.

Maturity Date: Date at which the face amount of a life insurance policy becomes payable by reason of endowment.

Net Surrender Value: Amount of cash due an owner upon surrendering a policy.

Noncontributory: Plan or program of insurance, usually a group program, for which the employer or sponsor pays the entire premium.

Nonforfeiture Values: Values in a life insurance policy that by law the policy owner cannot forfeit, even if ceasing to pay the premiums. Depending on state law, these benefits may include the cash surrender value, the loan value, the paid-up insurance value, and the extended term insurance value.

Ordinary Life Policy: Life insurance policy for which premiums are paid continuously as long as the insured lives.

Life Insurance: Glossary of Terms

Permanent Life Insurance: One of three basic types of life insurance (whole life, universal life, and endowment) that remains in force until the policy matures, unless the owner fails to pay the premium and the cash value is insufficient to cover policy charges and expenses. The policy cannot be cancelled by the insurer for any reason except fraud in the application; that cancellation must occur within a period of time defined by law (usually two years). Over time, permanent insurance builds cash values which the owner can borrow against.

Policy Loan: Loan made by an insurer to a policy owner of part of or all of the cash value of the policy assigned as security for the loan.

Policy Proceeds: Amount paid on a life insurance policy at death or when the owner receives payment at surrender or maturity. This includes any dividends left on deposit and the value of any additional insurance purchased with dividends; it excludes any loans not repaid, plus unpaid interest on those loans.

Primary Beneficiary: First to receive proceeds or benefits from a policy when due.

Proceeds: (See Policy Proceeds)

Rated: Policies issued at a higher rate than standard due to impairment of the insured.

Ratings: Refers to the financial strength of an insurance company. AM Best, Standard and Poor's, and Moody's are three well-known rating services.

Renewable Term: Term insurance that may be renewed for another term without evidence of insurability.

Return of Cash Value: Provision in a life insurance policy that states that if death occurs during a certain period of years (often 20), the policy will pay an amount, in addition to the face amount, equal to the cash value of the policy as of the date of death.

Return of Premium: Rider on a life insurance policy providing that, in the event of the death of the insured within a specified period of time, the policy will pay, in addition to the face amount, an amount equal to the sum of all premiums paid.

Revocable Beneficiary: Beneficiary in a life insurance policy in which the owner reserves the right to revoke or change the beneficiary.

Secondary Beneficiary: Individual or legal entity designated to receive the proceeds of a life insurance policy if the primary beneficiary is deceased at the time the benefits become payable. (See Contingent Beneficiary)

Settlement Options: Various methods for the payment of the proceeds of a life insurance policy that may be selected in lieu of a lump sum.

Surrender: Termination of a policy.

Term Insurance: Provides life insurance coverage for a specified term of years for a specified premium. Term policies do not accumulate cash value.

Universal Life: Combination flexible premium and adjustable life policy in which the owner may modify premium payments in response to changing needs and circumstances.

Variable Life: Policy featuring level premiums allowing the owner to allocate the cash value of the policy to a wide variety of investment accounts.

Variable Universal Life: Policy combining the features of variable life insurance and universal life insurance under the same contract. Benefits are variable based upon the value of variable sub accounts; premiums and benefits are adjustable by the owner.

Waiver of Premium: Provision of a life insurance policy that continues coverage without further premium payments due to the total disability of the insured.

War Clause: Provision excluding liability of an insurer if a loss is caused by war.

Spouse Insurance

The death of a spouse is perhaps the most emotionally traumatic event humans experience. What would you do if your spouse died unexpectedly?

In over 51% of married-couple families today, both marriage partners work outside the home at least part time.[1] Consequently, the financial requirements to run the household often exceed the income of a sole spouse.

If an untimely death occurred, the inability to meet financial obligations with the remaining spouse's single income might require the hasty sale of assets or, even worse, a bank foreclosure on the family residence.

Life insurance is an excellent means of providing money when it is needed in these traumatic moments.

Some families are fortunate enough to allow either the mother or father to stay home with small children while the other earns sufficient cash to meet household and living expenses.

Obviously, the loss of a breadwinner would create a financial calamity. Couples should consider the potential cost of replacing the services of the spouse who stays at home to care for the children.

In the event of a death a surviving spouse working outside the home would face new expenditures for:

- Child care, either in the home or at a babysitter or day care center.

- Someone to take the children to the doctor, dentist, piano lessons, etc.

Perhaps the surviving parent could take time off work to fulfill these obligations, but this could result in financial loss. Most families can eliminate this potential financial emergency by acquiring a life insurance policy on each spouse.

---

[1] Source: Percent of Married Couples with both Husband and Wife in the Labor Force, United States and Puerto Rico. U.S. Census Bureau, 2013 American Community Survey, 1-Year Estimates.

Considerations in the Purchase of Life Insurance

Who Will Be the Owner of the Policy?

Life insurance proceeds are included in the estate of a deceased if he or she has any incidents of ownership in the policy. Ownership by adult children or an irrevocable life insurance trust should be considered if there is an estate tax problem.

How Much Life Insurance?

This will depend on the need it is fulfilling. Amounts needed to fund a business transfer or to pay death taxes may be readily determined.

Calculating the value of a human life to a family is more difficult. Consider these projected total earnings up to age 65 assuming a 5% annual increase including inflation.

Projected Total Earnings to Age 65

Current Age	Current Monthly Income		
	$2,000	$4,000	$8,000
25	$3,044,154	$6,088,309	$12,176,618
35	1,674,259	3,348,518	6,697,036
45	833,262	1,666,524	3,333,048
55	316,963	633,926	1,267,852

What Type of Policy Should Be Purchased?

A person trained in life insurance can explain the many different policies available and assist in selecting the one which best fits your needs.

How Should the Premium Be Paid?

Sometimes the amount of the premium can be paid from current income, while other times it may be prudent to reposition other assets so as to be able to acquire sufficient insurance protection.

Considerations in the Purchase of Life Insurance

If the insured is a business owner or executive, a corporation may assist in paying premiums. Other times it may be better to have the corporation own the policy and use the proceeds to purchase part or all of the owner's interest at death.

Insurance can also be purchased in certain qualified retirement plans.

First-to-Die Life Insurance Policies

Joint Life

As the name implies, first-to-die or joint-life insurance policies pay out the face amount when the first named insured dies. This reduces the cost of paying premiums on two separate policies, when the insurance proceeds are most needed when only the first insured dies.

The following examples illustrate how this type of policy can be effectively used.

Buy-Sell Funding

A corporation or partnership with two or more owners often experiences problems of transferring ownership to the surviving owner or owners and paying a fair cash price to the deceased owner's heirs.

This problem is usually remedied with a properly structured buy-sell agreement, which assures a fair price for the decedent's share of the business and allows the surviving business partner to retain control and ownership of the business.

Life insurance is well established as the ideal method of funding buy-sell agreements. By using a joint-life policy, the company may be able to reduce the amount of cash flow required to pay the premiums, while still guaranteeing that the funds will be available for the buy-out no matter which partner or shareholder dies first.[1]

Key Person Protection

The loss of a key employee or executive can have a devastating effect on the future of a business. The use of joint-life policies can reduce the required cash flow to insure against the loss of any one person from a selected group of key persons. Insurance proceeds can be used to find, recruit, and train replacement employees and sustain or strengthen the company's credit position.[1]

---

[1] Both buy-sell arrangements and key person protection plans are frequently funded with life insurance. Under the provisions of IRC Sec. 101(j), added by the Pension Protection Act of 2006, death proceeds from a life insurance policy owned by an employer on the life of an employee are generally includable in income, unless certain requirements are met. Professional legal and tax guidance is strongly recommended. State or local law may vary.

Working Couples

With the growing percentage of families today relying on two incomes, it is prudent to insure against the loss of either spouse. The joint-life policy should be considered as part of the solution to the loss of income from the prior death of either spouse.

Survivorship Life Insurance

Second-to-Die

The Problem—Deferred Estate Tax Buildup

For married couples, current federal estate tax law[1] allows postponement of estate taxes – through the "unlimited marital deduction" – until the death of the second spouse to die. While this provides couples with increased flexibility during lifetime, it can sometimes place a substantial tax burden on the combined estate when the surviving spouse dies.

The Survivorship Life Solution

Unlike traditional life insurance, which provides protection on the life of a single insured, survivorship life covers <u>two</u> lives, with the proceeds payable at the second death. As such, it is suited to deal with the problem discussed above.

Advantages Over Individual Coverage

- **Lower premiums:** can be more cost effective than two policies.

- Medical underwriting standards may be eased with respect to one of the insureds due to second death payouts.

Ownership Arrangements

Third party ownership (adult children or an irrevocable life insurance trust) is often desirable for persons with potential estate tax problems. The policy may sometimes be transferred out of the estate after the first insured dies. If the survivor lives three years after the gift, the full face amount should generally be out of his or her estate. Questions of ownership should be discussed with an attorney.

Other Uses for Survivorship Life

- **Key person insurance:** Useful when the employer can self insure or absorb the loss of one key individual but not two.

- **Business buyout:** Facilitates purchase of family business from aging parents. Child working in the business owns policy on parents.

- **Charitable gift asset replacement:** Provides heirs with replacement cash when assets are used to fund a charitable remainder trust.

---

[1] The discussion here concerns federal law; state or local law may differ.

Tax-Free Policy Exchanges

IRC Sec. 1035

Due to a number of factors, some newer life insurance policies may be a better buy than older, smaller policies. A tax-free exchange allows one to defer the gain on any old policies at the time they are exchanged for the new policies.

Policies Which Can Be Exchanged Tax-Free

From This ⇩	To This⇨	Type of New Contract			
		To Life Insurance	To an Endowment Contract	To a Fixed or Variable Annuity	To a Qualified Long-Term Care Contract
Life insurance		Yes	Yes	Yes	Yes
Endowment contract		No	Yes[1]	Yes	Yes
Annuity contract[2]		No	No	Yes	Yes
Qualified long-term care contract		No	No	No	Yes

Key Points

- Life policies must be on the life of same person.[3]

- Annuity contracts must be payable to the same person(s).

- When contracts are assignable, there should be a direct transfer of funds between insurance companies.[4]

- The cost basis of the old policy (including certain riders and/or rating) is carried over to the new policy.

---

[1] Provided payments begin no later than under the old contract. Endowment Contracts must meet the definition of life insurance.

[2] See Revenue Procedure 2011-38 for IRS guidance on the federal income tax treatment of partial annuity exchanges, applicable to transfers completed on or after October 24, 2011. For partial annuity exchanges completed on or after June 30, 2008 and before October 24, 2011, the guidance provided in Revenue Procedure 2008-24 generally applies.

[3] A single policy may not be exchanged for one on multiple lives, (e.g., a second-to-die policy.)

[4] Some exceptions for troubled insurers. Rev. Proc. 92-44 and 92-44A

- If cash or other property is part of the exchange, any gain will be recognized up to that amount.

- A permanent policy with an outstanding loan can be exchanged for another similar policy with the same indebtedness. If the indebtedness is reduced in the exchange, there will be income tax consequences.

- If there is a recognized gain, it is ordinary income.

Potential Problems

The early surrender of certain life insurance policies or annuity contracts may have significant, negative consequences. For example, a policy or contract owner may be required to pay a surrender charge, there may be tax penalties due, or the owner may receive less than he or she originally invested or paid into the contract.

Questions to Consider

- Determine whether the incontestability period and suicide provisions are based on the issue date of the new policy or the old one.

- Consider the rating of the new company.

- Determine whether the old policy has favorable tax status which would not transfer to the new policy.

- Determine whether the premium on the new policy will be more expensive. This may happen, for example, because of changes in health.

An experienced life insurance professional is an important guide through this process. Make certain you are medically insurable before the old policy is terminated and that there is not a period during the exchange when you have no coverage.

Modified Endowment Contracts

Life insurance policies issued on or after June 21, 1988 may be defined as "modified endowment contracts" (MECs) if the cumulative premiums paid during the first seven years (7-pay test) at any time exceed the total of the net level premiums for the same period.

As an example, assume that the net level premium for a policy is $1,000 per year and the following payments are made by two different policy owners.

Year	7-Pay Test — Cumulative Net Level Premiums	Policy Owner A — Annual Premium	Policy Owner A — Cumulative Premiums	Policy Owner B — Annual Premium	Policy Owner B — Cumulative Premiums
1	$1,000	$1,000	$1,000	$1,000	$1,000
2	2,000	500	1,500	1,000	2,000
3	3,000	1,000	2,500	1,000	3,000
4	4,000	1,500	4,000	1,500	4,500
5	5,000	1,000	5,000	500	5,000
6	6,000	1,000	6,000	1,000	6,000
7	7,000	1,000	7,000	1,000	7,000

In the policy owner A example above, even though the premium paid during the fourth year exceeds the annual net level premium of $1,000, the cumulative premiums do not exceed four times (for the four years) the net level premium; therefore, this is not a modified endowment contract.

In the policy owner B example above, however, the premiums paid in the fourth year cause the cumulative premiums paid to exceed the cumulative net level premiums allowed and thus cause this contract to become a modified endowment contract.

Additional 7-pay test periods will be required if the policy is materially changed.

Taxation of Modified Endowment Contracts

Withdrawals from modified endowment contracts (including loans) will be taxed as current income until all of the policy earnings have been taxed. There is also a 10% penalty tax if the owner is under age 59½ unless payments are due to disability or are annuity type payments.

Well-designed premium payment schedules can avoid the modified endowment contract treatment and retain the benefits which are unique to the life insurance contract.

The Need for Responsible Planning

What If You Were to Die Today?

Many individuals recognize the benefits of planning for the future. Such efforts often uncover problems and frequently provide the motivation to make needed changes. For the most part, the issues involved are positive and enjoyable (e.g., retirement, well-educated children).

However, planning for the unexpected – known as risk management – can be less pleasant. A key part of risk management is answering the question, "What if I were to die today?" Preparing for an untimely death is often referred to as "survivor benefit planning." A subset of estate planning, it addresses the need to keep one's family in their current world, financially.

Understandably, no one likes to contemplate his or her own demise. For some, death seems a distant, future event. Others are simply too "busy." Whatever the reason, delaying this part of planning can result in expensive, unintended, even tragic consequences.

Survivor Benefit Needs

The ultimate purpose of survivor benefit planning is twofold: (1) to ensure that the ongoing income needs of the survivor(s) are met, and (2) to provide for immediate lump-sum cash needs.

- **Income needs:** How much income will the survivors need, now and in the future, to cover the following:

  - **Household living expenses:** Will the family stay in the same house? Can they afford to? Do they want to? Will they have the option?

  - **Additional childcare:** Will there be a need for more help with young children?

  - **Educational expenses:** Will there be enough money for the children to go to college?

- **Lump-sum needs:** How much will the survivors need immediately and in cash? Consider the following:

  - **Final expenses:** More than the funeral, this includes unpaid medical bills, which, after a long illness, can be substantial.

  - **Estate settlement costs:** Probate expenses, attorney's fees, death taxes, etc.

  - **Mortgage payoff and debt reduction:** Will it be important to provide a paid-off house? Are there debts that should be retired?

One Final Question

If you died today, would your plan be ready?

Capital Needs Analysis Worksheet

Client Name:_____   Date:_____

What events could cause a significant reduction in your annual income?	If one of these events occurred would you want your family's lifestyle to be:
_____ _____ _____	☐ the same as it is now ☐ better than it is now ☐ lower than it is now

1. Current annual household income $_____
2. Current annual savings to all assets   (-)_____
3. Current annual spending   _____

Income available to meet spending needs:

4. Spouse income   _____
5. Social Security income   (+)_____
6. Other income   (+)_____
7. Total income available   _____
8. Additional income needed (line 3 minus line 7)   _____
9. Current savings and available capital   _____
10. Current life insurance   (+)_____
11. Total capital available   _____
12. Assumed net rate of return*   (+)_____
13. Income from assets   _____
14. Income shortfall (line 8 minus line 13)   _____
15. Additional capital required (line 14 divided by line 12) $_____

* This should be an assumed annual rate of return less an assumed inflation rate.

How Much Life Insurance?

1. Annual living expenses of survivors[1] (spouse, children, etc.)
   a. After-tax living expenses $_____
   b. Average tax rate[2] (as decimal value)   _____
   c. Tax factor (one minus line 1b)   _____
      Pre-tax annual living expenses of survivors (1a divided by 1c)   _____
2. Less: Expected pre-tax annual income
   a. Social Security benefits   _____
   b. Survivor's pension benefits   _____
   c. Survivor's earned income   _____
   d. Other income   _____
      Total expected pre-tax annual income   _____
3. Equals: Annual net living expense shortage, if any.[3] (1-2)   _____
4. Capital required to produce income to meet the annual living expense shortage
   a. Pre-tax annual rate of return   _____%
   b. Annual inflation rate   _____%
   c. Years of income required   _____yrs
   d. Multiplication factor[4]   _____
      Capital required due to shortage   (3 times 4d)   _____
5. Plus: Lump-sum expenses
   a. Final expenses and/or estate costs   _____
   b. Mortgage/other debt payoff   _____
   c. Emergency fund   _____
   d. Other fund (education, etc.)   _____
      Total lump-sum expenses   _____
6. Total capital required   (Line 4 plus line 5)   _____
7. Less: Existing capital
   a. Income producing assets   _____
   b. Life insurance   _____
      Total Present Capital   _____
8. Amount of capital to be added, if any (Line 6 minus line 7) $_____

---

[1] Consider using 70% of current family living expenses.

[2] This value should be based on the total income and payroll taxes divided by total gross income.

[3] If Line 2 is greater than Line 1, enter a zero value for Lines 3 and 4, then skip to Line 5.

[4] See tables on following pages.

How Much Life Insurance?

Multiplication Factors (for line 4d)

Years of Income	1% Pre-Tax Annual Return			2% Pre-Tax Annual Return		
	Inflation at 3.00%	Inflation at 4.00%	Inflation at 5.00%	Inflation at 3.00%	Inflation at 4.00%	Inflation at 5.00%
5	5.20	5.31	5.41	5.10	5.20	5.30
10	10.94	11.45	11.98	10.45	10.93	11.43
15	17.27	18.56	19.96	16.07	17.24	18.52
20	24.25	26.79	29.66	21.98	24.20	26.71
25	31.95	36.32	41.42	28.17	31.87	36.18
30	40.44	47.35	55.72	34.68	40.32	47.12
35	49.81	60.12	73.07	41.51	49.63	59.78
40	60.14	74.90	94.14	48.69	59.89	74.40
45	71.54	92.01	119.73	56.22	71.20	91.31

Years of Income	3% Pre-Tax Annual Return			4% Pre-Tax Annual Return		
	Inflation at 3.00%	Inflation at 4.00%	Inflation at 5.00%	Inflation at 3.00%	Inflation at 4.00%	Inflation at 5.00%
5	5.00	5.10	5.20	4.90	5.00	5.10
10	10.00	10.45	10.92	9.58	10.00	10.44
15	15.00	16.06	17.22	14.03	15.00	16.05
20	20.00	21.96	24.16	18.27	20.00	21.94
25	25.00	28.14	31.79	22.32	25.00	28.11
30	30.00	34.63	40.20	26.17	30.00	34.58
35	35.00	41.44	49.46	29.84	35.00	41.38
40	40.00	48.59	59.65	33.34	40.00	48.50
45	45.00	56.10	70.86	36.67	45.00	55.97

How Much Life Insurance?

Multiplication Factors (for line 4d)

Years of Income	5% Pre-Tax Annual Return			6% Pre-Tax Annual Return		
	Inflation at 3.00%	Inflation at 4.00%	Inflation at 5.00%	Inflation at 3.00%	Inflation at 4.00%	Inflation at 5.00%
5	4.81	4.91	5.00	4.72	4.81	4.91
10	9.18	9.58	10.00	8.82	9.19	9.59
15	13.16	14.04	15.00	12.36	13.17	14.05
20	16.76	18.29	20.00	15.44	16.79	18.31
25	20.04	22.34	25.00	18.10	20.08	22.36
30	23.02	26.20	30.00	20.40	23.07	26.24
35	25.72	29.88	35.00	22.40	25.79	29.93
40	28.17	33.39	40.00	24.13	28.26	33.45
45	30.40	36.74	45.00	25.63	30.51	36.81

Years of Income	7% Pre-Tax Annual Return			8% Pre-Tax Annual Return		
	Inflation at 3.00%	Inflation at 4.00%	Inflation at 5.00%	Inflation at 3.00%	Inflation at 4.00%	Inflation at 5.00%
5	4.64	4.73	4.82	4.56	4.64	4.73
10	8.47	8.83	9.20	8.15	8.49	8.84
15	11.64	12.39	13.19	10.99	11.67	12.41
20	14.26	15.47	16.82	13.23	14.31	15.51
25	16.43	18.15	20.12	15.00	16.49	18.20
30	18.22	20.47	23.12	16.39	18.30	20.54
35	19.70	22.48	25.86	17.49	19.79	22.57
40	20.92	24.23	28.35	18.36	21.03	24.33
45	21.93	25.75	30.61	19.04	22.06	25.87

Multiplication Factors (for line 4d)

Years of Income	9% Pre-Tax Annual Return			10% Pre-Tax Annual Return		
	Inflation at 3.00%	Inflation at 4.00%	Inflation at 5.00%	Inflation at 3.00%	Inflation at 4.00%	Inflation at 5.00%
5	4.48	4.56	4.65	4.40	4.48	4.57
10	7.85	8.17	8.50	7.57	7.87	8.18
15	10.40	11.02	11.70	9.85	10.43	11.05
20	12.31	13.28	14.35	11.50	12.36	13.32
25	13.76	15.06	16.55	12.68	13.82	15.12
30	14.84	16.47	18.37	13.53	14.93	16.55
35	15.66	17.59	19.89	14.14	15.76	17.68
40	16.28	18.47	21.14	14.58	16.39	18.58
45	16.75	19.17	22.18	14.90	16.86	19.29

Years of Income	11% Pre-Tax Annual Return			12% Pre-Tax Annual Return		
	Inflation at 3.00%	Inflation at 4.00%	Inflation at 5.00%	Inflation at 3.00%	Inflation at 4.00%	Inflation at 5.00%
5	4.33	4.41	4.49	4.26	4.33	4.41
10	7.31	7.59	7.89	7.06	7.33	7.61
15	9.36	9.89	10.46	8.90	9.39	9.92
20	10.77	11.55	12.41	10.11	10.82	11.60
25	11.74	12.75	13.89	10.91	11.80	12.81
30	12.40	13.61	15.01	11.44	12.48	13.69
35	12.86	14.24	15.85	11.78	12.95	14.33
40	13.18	14.69	16.50	12.01	13.28	14.79
45	13.40	15.01	16.98	12.16	13.50	15.12

Human Life Value

This calculator estimates a dollar value for the economic loss that would result if an individual dies before retirement. The analysis takes into account the loss of "net" earnings (subtracting taxes and personal consumption), and includes the dollar value of employee fringe benefits as well as the dollar value of the household services the individual could have provided.

Item	Value
Current annual income	$85,000
Annual rate of income increase	4.00%
Fringe benefits percentage	28.00%
Number of years until retirement	30
Uncompensated work in the home annually	$5,200
Personal consumption per month	$800
Income tax rate	30.00%
Inflation rate	4.00%
Assumed investment rate of return	6.00%
Human life value	**$2,302,289**

Types of Life Insurance Policies

In choosing the type of life insurance policy you purchase, consideration must be given to the need which is being filled, e.g., creation of an estate, payment of estate settlement costs (federal and state death taxes, last illness and burial costs, probate fees, etc.), business buy-out, key-man coverage, etc.

Decreasing Term

Level premium, decreasing coverage, no cash value: Used for financial obligations which reduce with time, e.g., mortgages or other amortized loans.

Annual Renewable Term

Increasing premium, level coverage, no cash value: Used for financial obligations which remain constant for a short or intermediate period, e.g., income during a minor's dependency.

Long-Term Level Premium Term

Level premium, level coverage, no cash value: The annual premiums are fixed for a period of time, typically 5, 10, 15 or 20 years. Used for financial obligations which remain constant for a short or intermediate period, e.g., income during a minor's dependency.

Whole Life

Level premium, level coverage, cash values: Cash value typically increases based on insurance company's general asset account portfolio performance. Used for long-term obligations, e.g., surviving spouse lifetime income needs, estate liquidity, death taxes, funding retirement needs, etc.

Single Premium Whole Life

Entire premium is paid at purchase, cash values, level coverage: Provides protection as well as serving as an asset accumulation vehicle.

Universal Life

Level or adjustable premium and coverage, cash values: Cash values may increase, based on the performance of certain assets held in the company's general account. Used for long-term obligations or sinking-fund needs: estate growth, estate liquidity, death taxes, funding retirement needs, etc.

Indexed Universal Life

Level or adjustable premium and coverage, cash values: Cash values may increase, based on the performance of an underlying stock or bond "index." The death benefit may increase or decrease (but not below a guaranteed minimum) depending on investment performance. Used for long-term obligations or sinking fund needs, estate growth, estate liquidity, paying death taxes, funding retirement needs, etc.

Variable Life and Variable Universal Life

Level or adjustable premium, level coverage, cash values: Used for long-term obligations, by those individuals who are more active investors, for estate growth, and death tax liquidity. The death benefit may increase or decrease depending on investment performance. The policy owner directs cash values to a choice of investment accounts (bond, stock, money market, etc.). However, cash values are not guaranteed.

Note: Withdrawals and loans may be available from permanent policies. Withdrawals and policy loans may reduce the death benefit and will reduce the cash value of the policy. There are different income tax consequences if they are modified endowment contracts.

Term Life Insurance

What Is Term Life Insurance?

Term life insurance, as the name suggests, provides life insurance only for a limited period of time, or term. Other types of policies, such as whole life, universal life, or variable life, are considered to be permanent insurance, and are designed to provide protection for the entire life of the insured.

Term insurance might be compared to an automobile insurance policy. While the auto policy is in force, the insured enjoys protection against loss from an auto accident. If no accident happens, no benefits are paid under the policy. At the end of the period covered by the policy, there is no refund of premiums paid. Term life insurance works in much the same way.

Term insurance thus provides only pure insurance protection and does not have the cash value feature typically found in most permanent life insurance policies. Unlike most permanent policies, in which premiums usually remain level over the life of the policy, the periodic cost of term life insurance increases as the insured becomes older. The cash-value feature found in permanent policies provides a cash build-up within the policy which allows for the level periodic premium. In later years, the premiums for a typical term life policy will far exceed those of the typical permanent policy.

Policy Variations

There are a number of different types of term insurance:

Annual renewable term: Term insurance characterized by a level death benefit, a premium that increases at each annual policy renewal, and no cash-value accumulation.

Example of Annual Renewable Term

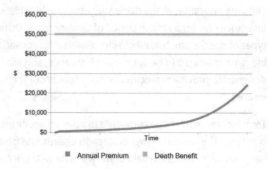

Long-term level premium term: The annual premiums are fixed for a specified period of time, typically 5, 10, 15, or 20 years. The death benefit remains constant, and there are no accumulated cash values.

Example of Long-Term Level Term

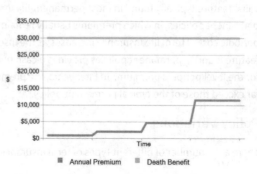

- **Decreasing term:** A policy that has a level premium, a decreasing death benefit, and no accumulation of cash values.

- **Combination policies:** In some cases, term life insurance is teamed with a permanent policy to provide the benefits of both types of policies. In both the family income policy, and the family maintenance policy, for example, a term policy with a decreasing death benefit is combined with a permanent, level benefit policy.

Common Uses of Term Insurance

Term life insurance is most useful when an insured is relatively young and the need is for temporary or short-term coverage. Some common uses of term insurance include:

- **Family protection:** To provide the funds to support a surviving spouse and/or minor children or to provide the cash for a child's college education or pay for other capital needs; to pay final bills such as medical or other estate expenses.

- **Declining needs:** In some instances, a debt, such as a mortgage, is matched with a decreasing term policy. As the debt is paid off, the policy's death benefit is reduced.

- **Business planning:** A business may use term insurance to insure a key employee, or to recruit or retain key employees through a salary continuation plan. Term insurance is also useful as a way to fund a cross-purchase buy-sell agreement, particularly where one owner is significantly younger than another.

- **Charitable gifts:** To provide funds for a gift to charity.

Optional Policy Provisions

A number of optional policy provisions, commonly referred to as riders, can be added to a basic term life policy, generally through payment of an additional premium:

- **Renewable:** This provision allows the policy to be renewed at the end of the term without the insured having to show that he or she is still insurable.

- **Convertible:** Provides the insured the option to convert a term policy to a permanent policy, usually without having to prove good health.

- **Accidental death:** Pays the beneficiaries double (in some situations triple) the face amount of the policy if the insured dies in an accident.

- **Waiver of premium:** Waives the payment of policy premiums if the insured becomes disabled and unable to work.

- **Accelerated death benefits:** An accelerated death benefits provision allows for payment of part of a policy's death benefit while an insured is still alive. Such benefits are typically payable when the insured develops a medical condition expected to lead to death within a short period of time.

Return of Premium Life Insurance

Some life insurance companies offer a variation on a base term life insurance policy known as "Return of Premium" or (ROP) life insurance. A ROP policy guarantees[1] to return to the policy owner the total premiums paid if the insured survives to the end of the term period. In some cases, this feature is part of the policy and in other cases it is added to a basic term policy through a policy rider.

- **Policy premiums:** Policy premiums are a fixed, level dollar amount, for the life of the contract. Premiums for ROP policies tend to be higher than for a term life policy without this feature.

- **Policy term:** The length of the policy term will vary depending on the insurance company. Typically, ROP policies have a longer term, for example from 15 to 35 years.

- **If the owner cancels the policy:** If the policy owner cancels or surrenders the policy before the policy term ends, there is typically no refund of the premiums paid.

- **If the insured dies:** If the insured dies before the end of the policy term, the policy will pay the face amount, less any policy loans, withdrawals, or interest due.

- **If the insured lives to the end of the policy term:** If the insured lives to the end of the policy term, the policy owner can generally surrender the policy and receive the total amount of premiums paid. In some instances, a term policy will allow the owner to convert the term insurance to a permanent policy.

---

[1] Guarantees are based on the claims-paying ability of the life insurance company issuing the policy.

Whole Life Insurance

What Is Whole Life Insurance?

Whole life insurance, sometimes called permanent insurance, or ordinary life, is designed to stay in force throughout one's lifetime. As long as the policy owner meets his or her obligations under the policy, the policy remains in force, regardless of any changes in health that may occur.

Unlike term insurance, where premium payments generally increase, as the insured gets older (the chance of death increases with age), premiums for most whole life policies remain level. A portion of each premium payment is set aside to earn interest. Over time, a whole life policy will develop cash values. The accumulated cash values form a reserve which enable the insurer to pay a policy's full death benefit, while keeping premiums level.

During life, many whole life policies have provisions to borrow a portion of the accumulated cash value. If a policy is terminated without the insured dying, there are various surrender options for the cash value available to a policy owner.

Policy Variations

There are two primary types of whole life insurance, based on the period over which the premium payments are made:

Ordinary life: An ordinary life policy assumes that premiums will be paid until the insured dies. Premiums are based on the assumption that the insured will die at a certain age, typically age 100. If an insured lives to this age, the policy pays the face amount of the death benefit.

Example of Ordinary Life

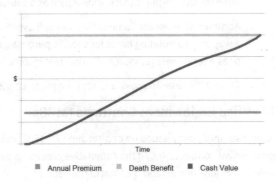

Limited-payment life: This type of whole life policy assumes that all premium payments are made over a specified, limited period, typically ranging from one to 30 years. Premiums for a limited-payment life policy are generally higher than for an ordinary life policy, because the payment period is shorter.

Example of Limited-Payment Life

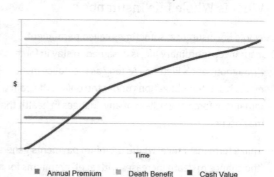

Time

■ Annual Premium   ■ Death Benefit   ■ Cash Value

Common Uses of Whole Life Insurance

Whole life policies are well suited for needs that do not diminish over time. Some commonly found uses for whole life are:

- **Family protection:** To provide funds to support a surviving spouse and/or minor children, particularly for individuals who start a family later in life; to pay final bills, such as medical or other estate expenses and federal and state death taxes.

- **Business planning:** Whole life insurance is often used for many different business purposes, such as insuring key employees, in split-dollar insurance arrangements, and funding nonqualified deferred compensation plans. Business continuation planning often involves using whole life insurance as a source of funds for buy-sell agreements.

- **Accumulation needs:** Some individuals will use the cash value feature of whole life as a way of accumulating funds for specific purposes, such as funding college education, or as a supplemental source of retirement income.

- **Charitable gifts:** To provide funds for a gift to charity.

Modified Endowment Contracts (MECs)

A life insurance policy issued on or after June 21, 1988[1] may be classified as a modified endowment contract (MEC) if the cumulative premiums paid during the first seven years (7-pay test) at any time exceed the total of the net level premiums for the same period.

---

[1] Including a policy issued before that date, but later materially changed.

If a policy is classified as a MEC, all withdrawals (including loans) will be taxed as current income, until all of the policy earnings have been taxed. There is an additional 10% penalty tax if the owner is under age 59½ at the time of withdrawal, unless the payments are due to disability or are annuity type payments.

A whole life policy can avoid treatment as a MEC through a well-designed premium payment schedule.

Additional Policy Elements

Whole life policies often have additional, useful features:

- **Policy loans:** Almost all whole policies permit the policy owner to borrow a portion of the accumulated cash value, with the insurance company charging interest on the loan. The rate charged to borrow the funds is often lower than current open market rates. A policy loan will reduce the death benefit payable if the insured dies before the loan and any interest due is repaid. A policy loan will also reduce the cash surrender value if a policy is terminated. If a policy lapses or is surrendered with a loan outstanding, the loan will be treated as taxable income for the current year, to the extent of gain in the policy.

- **Policy dividends:** Whole life contracts classified as "participating" offer the possibility of policy "dividends." Such policy dividends are not guaranteed, and represent a return to the policy owner of part of the premium paid. A dividend may be taken as cash or a policy may offer a number of other ways the dividend might be used:

  - To reduce current premium payments;

  - To buy additional, completely paid-up insurance (known as paid-up additions);

  - To be retained by the insurer, earning interest for the policyholder;

  - To purchase one-year term insurance;

  - To be added to the policy's cash value;

  - To "pay up" the policy earlier than originally scheduled.

Policy Dividends Used To Purchase Paid-Up Additions

Although policy dividends are not guaranteed, using available dividends to purchase paid-up additions can, over time, have a significant, positive impact on both the death benefit and cash value of whole life policy. The diagram illustrates how this might work, in a hypothetical life insurance policy.

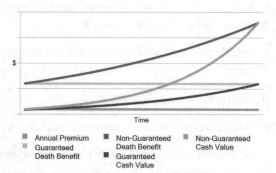

Optional Policy Provisions

A number of optional provisions, commonly referred to as riders, can be added to a basic whole life policy, generally through payment of an additional premium:

- **Waiver of premium:** Waives the payment of policy premiums if the insured becomes disabled and unable to work.

- **Accidental death:** Pays the beneficiaries double (in some situations triple) the face amount of the policy if the insured dies in an accident.

- **Spousal or family term insurance:** Allows a policy owner to purchase term insurance on a spouse or children.

- **Accelerated death benefits:** An accelerated death benefits provision allows for payment of part of a policy's death benefit while an insured is still alive. Such benefits are typically payable when the insured develops a medical condition expected to lead to death within a short period of time.

Universal Life Insurance

What Is Universal Life Insurance?

Universal life insurance contracts differ from traditional whole life policies by specifically separating and identifying the mortality, expense, and cash value parts of a policy. Dividing the policy into these three components allows the insurance company to build a higher degree of flexibility into the contract. This flexibility allows (within certain limits) the policy owner to modify the policy face amount or premium, in response to changing needs and circumstances.

A monthly charge for both the mortality element and the expense element is deducted from a policy's account balance. The remainder of the premium is allocated to the cash value element, where the funds earn interest. Unlike traditional whole life policies, complete disclosure of these internal charges against the cash value element is made to the policy owner in the form of an annual statement.

Many universal life policies have several different provisions by which the accumulated cash value can be made available to a policy owner during life, without causing the policy to lapse. If a policy is terminated without the insured dying, there are various surrender options for the cash value.

Policy Variations

There are two primary types of universal life, based on the level of death benefits:

Type I universal life: Also known as option A, type I universal policies pay a fixed, level death benefit, generally the face amount of the policy.

Example of Type I Universal Life

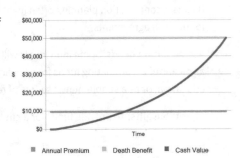

Universal Life Insurance

Type II universal life: Also known as option B, type II universal policies generally pay the face amount of the policy plus the accumulated cash values. As the cash values grow, so does the potential death benefit.

Example of Type II Universal Life

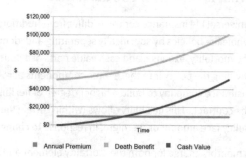

Common Uses of Universal Life

Universal life policies are useful for policy owners who expect their needs to change over time. Within certain guidelines, a universal life policy can be modified by changing the death benefit or premium payments. Some common uses are:

- **Family protection:** To provide the funds to support a surviving spouse and/or minor children, or to pay final bills such as medical or other estate expenses, as well as federal and state death taxes.

- **Business planning:** Because of its flexibility, universal life insurance is often used for many different business purposes, such as insuring key employees, in split-dollar insurance arrangements, and funding nonqualified deferred compensation plans. Business continuation planning often involves using universal life as a source of funds for buy-sell agreements.

- **Accumulation needs:** Some individuals will use the cash value feature of universal life as means of accumulating funds for specific purposes, such as funding college education, or as a supplemental source of retirement income.

- **Charitable gifts:** To provide funds for a gift to charity.

Modified Endowment Contracts (MECs)

A life insurance policy issued on or after June 21, 1988[1] may be classified as a modified endowment contract (MEC) if the cumulative premiums paid during the first seven years (7-pay test) at any time exceed the total of the net level premiums for the same period.

If a policy is classified as a MEC, all withdrawals (including loans) will be taxed as current income, until all of the policy earnings have been taxed. There is an additional 10% penalty tax if the owner is under age 59½ at the time of withdrawal, unless the payments are due to disability or are annuity type payments.

A universal life policy can avoid treatment as a MEC through a well-designed premium payment schedule. Caution must be exercised when changes in policy premium payments or death benefits are made, or when making partial withdrawals, to avoid having the policy inadvertently classified as a MEC.

Additional Policy Elements

Universal life policies have a number of additional elements to consider:

- **Surrender charges:** Most universal life policies have substantial surrender charges, if a policy is terminated. These surrender charges are generally highest in the early years of a policy, and decline over a period of time, usually from seven to 15 years.

- **Policy loans:** Universal life policies typically permit the policy owner to borrow at interest a portion of the accumulated cash value. The rate charged on the borrowed funds is often lower than current open market rates. A policy loan will reduce the death benefit payable if the insured dies before the loan is repaid; a policy loan will also reduce the cash surrender value if a policy is terminated. If the policy lapses or is surrendered with a loan outstanding, the loan will be treated as taxable income in the current year, to the extent of gain in the policy.

- **Partial withdrawals:** Most universal life policies allow a policy owner to withdraw a portion of the cash value, without terminating the policy. Such withdrawals reduce the amount of death benefit payable, and may be subject to current income tax, if the policy is classified as a MEC, or if the withdrawal exceeds cost basis for a non-MEC

---

[1] Including a policy issued before that date, but later materially changed.

policy. Some contracts allow a policy owner to put the withdrawn funds back into the policy, but the insured may have to provide evidence of insurability to restore the original death benefit.

- **Surrender options:** If a policy owner surrenders a policy, there are generally three ways in which the accumulated cash value may be received, including: (1) taking the accumulated cash value, less any surrender charges; (2) receiving a reduced amount of paid-up insurance; or (3) taking paid-up term insurance in an amount equal to the original face amount of the policy.

Optional Policy Provisions

A number of optional provisions, commonly referred to as riders, can be added to a basic universal life policy, generally through payment of an additional premium:

- **Waiver of premium:** Suspends the monthly deduction for the mortality element of the policy, if the insured becomes disabled and is unable to work.

- **Accidental death:** Pays the beneficiaries double (in some situations triple) the face amount of the policy if the insured dies in an accident.

- **Spousal or family term insurance:** Allows a policy owner to purchase term insurance on a spouse or children.

- **Accelerated death benefits:** An accelerated death benefits provision allows for payment of part of a policy's death benefit while an insured is still alive. Such benefits are typically payable when the insured develops a medical condition expected to lead to death within a short period of time.

Variable Life Insurance

What Is Variable Life Insurance?

Variable life insurance is similar to whole life in that the premium payments are level, and there is generally a minimum guaranteed death benefit. Unlike whole life policies however, variable life insurance permits the policyowner to allocate a portion of each premium payment to one or more investment options, in separate subaccounts after a deduction for expense and mortality charges.

The death benefit and cash value of a variable life policy will increase or decrease based on the performance of the investment options chosen. The death benefit, however, will not drop below an initial guaranteed amount, unless policy premiums are not paid or if loans or other withdrawals are taken from the policy. The ultimate death benefit is subject to the claims paying ability of the insurer.

Because the investment options available inside a variable life policy usually involve securities (e.g., stocks and bonds), the Securities and Exchange Commission (SEC) requires this type of policy to be accompanied by a prospectus. The prospectus provides detailed information on how the policy works, its risks, and all expenses or charges involved. The SEC also requires individuals selling variable life policies to be licensed to sell securities.

Policy Variations

There are two primary variations of variable life insurance, based on the formula used to link the amount of death benefit to the performance of the investments chosen by the policyowner. In general, if investment performance is positive, the amount of the death benefit increases; if investment performance is negative, the death benefit amount will decrease.

Example of Variable Life

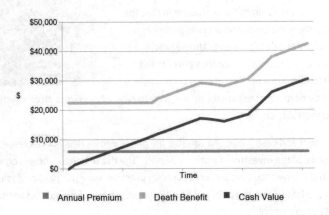

- **Corridor percentage:** Under this method, also know as the constant ratio method, the amount of the death benefit is periodically changed to equal a certain percentage of the cash value. Under current tax law, this percentage is 250% up to the insured's age 40, gradually decreasing to 100%, usually at age 95.

- **Level additions:** Also known as the net single premium approach, this method uses excess investment earnings to purchase an additional amount of single premium, paid-up insurance.

Common Uses of Variable Life

Variable life policies are well suited for use by policyowners who are comfortable with the risks and rewards of investments, and who need life insurance with the potential to provide an increasing death benefit. Some common uses are:

- **Supplement existing family protection:** As a supplement to an existing, basic life insurance plan. If the market is down when an insured dies, the variable death benefit of a variable life policy may not provide adequate funds to support a surviving spouse and/or minor children, or to pay final estate expenses.

- **Business planning:** Variable life insurance is often used for many different business purposes, such as insuring key employees, in split-dollar insurance arrangements, and funding nonqualified deferred compensation plans. Business continuation planning often involves using variable life insurance as a source of funds for buy-sell agreements.

- **Accumulation needs:** Some individuals will use the cash value feature of variable life as a way of accumulating funds for specific purposes, such as funding college education, or as a supplemental source of retirement income.

- **Charitable gifts:** To provide funds for a gift to charity.

Modified Endowment Contracts (MECs)

A life insurance policy issued on or after June 21, 1988[1] may be classified as a modified endowment contract (MEC) if the cumulative premiums paid during the first seven years (7-pay test) at any time exceed the total of the net level premiums for the same period. If a policy is classified as a MEC, all withdrawals (including loans) will be taxed as current income, until all of the policy earnings have been taxed. There is an additional 10% penalty tax if the owner is under age 59½ at the time of withdrawal, unless the payments are due to disability or are annuity type payments.

A variable life policy can avoid treatment as a MEC through a well-designed premium payment schedule.

Additional Policy Elements

Variable life policies have a number of additional elements to consider:

- **Investment options:** Most variable life policies offer a policyowner a wide range of investment options, including basic stock, bond and money market funds. Depending on the policy and insurer, other options, such as index funds, real estate funds, foreign stock funds, or zero coupon bond funds may also be offered. A policy may also include a fixed account option, in which the insurer guarantees a fixed rate of return.

---

[1] Including a policy issued before that date, but later materially changed.

- **Portfolio changes:** Many variable life policies allow a policyowner to change their investment allocation at least once a year (sometimes more frequently), usually at no charge.

- **Policy loans:** Almost all variable life policies permit the policyowner to borrow a portion of the accumulated cash value, with the insurance company charging interest on the loan. The rate charged to borrow the funds is often lower than current open market rates. A policy loan will reduce the death benefit payable if the insured dies before the loan and any interest due is repaid. A policy loan will also reduce the cash surrender value if a policy is terminated. If a policy lapses or is surrendered with a loan outstanding, the loan will be treated as taxable income in the current year, to the extent of gain in the policy.

- **Partial withdrawals:** Many variable life policies allow a policyowner to withdraw a portion of the cash value, without terminating the policy. Withdrawals may be subject to certain restrictions and/or withdrawal charges. Such withdrawals reduce the amount of death benefit payable, and may be subject to current income tax, if the policy is classified as a MEC, or if the withdrawal exceeds cost basis for a policy not classified as a MEC.

- **Policy dividends:** Variable life policies classified as participating offer the possibility of policy dividends. Dividends from a participating variable life policy are not guaranteed, and represent a return to the policyowner of a portion of the premium paid. Most participating policies offer a number of options as to how the dividends may be used.

- **Surrender charges:** Most variable life policies have substantial surrender charges, if a policy is terminated. These surrender charges are generally highest in the early years of a policy, and decline over a period of time, usually from seven to 15 years.

- **Surrender options:** If a policyowner surrenders a policy, there are generally three ways in which the accumulated cash value may be received, including: (1) taking the accumulated cash value, less any surrender charges; (2) receiving a reduced amount of paid-up insurance; or (3) taking paid-up term insurance in an amount equal to the original face amount of the policy.

Optional Policy Provisions

A number of optional provisions, commonly referred to as riders, can be added to a variable life policy, generally through payment of an additional premium:

- **Waiver of premium:** Waives the payment of policy premiums if the insured becomes disabled and unable to work.

- **Accidental death:** Pays the beneficiaries double (in some situations triple) the face amount of the policy if the insured dies in an accident.

- **Spousal or family term insurance:** Allows a policy owner to purchase term insurance on a spouse or children.

- **Accelerated death benefit:** An accelerated death benefit provision allows for payment of part of a policy's death benefit while an insured is still alive. Such benefits are typically payable when the insured develops a medical condition expected to lead to death within a short period of time.

Variable Universal Life Insurance

What Is Variable Universal Life Insurance?

A variable universal life insurance policy combines features found in both universal life policies, and variable life policies.

As with a variable life policy, a variable universal contract permits a policyowner to allocate a portion of each premium payment to one or more investment options, in separate accounts, after a deduction for expense and mortality charges. An annual statement detailing the expenses, charges, and credits allows a policyowner to track performance over time.

Following universal life policies, a variable universal contract permits the owner of a policy, within certain guidelines, to modify the policy death benefit, and change the amount and timing of premium payments, to meet changing circumstances. The ultimate death benefit is subject to the claims paying ability of the insurer.

Because the investment options available inside a variable universal life policy usually involve securities (e.g., stocks and bonds), the Securities and Exchange Commission (SEC) requires this type of policy to be accompanied by a prospectus. The prospectus provides detailed information on how the policy works, its risks, and all expenses or charges involved. The SEC also requires individuals selling variable universal life policies to be licensed to sell securities.

Policy Variations

There are two primary types of variable universal life, based on the level of death benefits:

Variable Universal Life Insurance

Type I variable universal life: Also known as option A, type I variable universal policies pay a fixed, level death benefit, generally the face amount of the policy.

Example of Type I Variable Universal Life

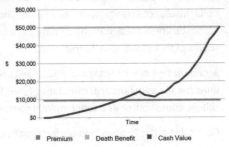

Type II variable universal life: Also known as option B, type II variable universal policies generally pay the face amount of the policy plus the accumulated cash values. As the cash values grow, so does the potential death benefit.

Example of Type II Variable Universal Life

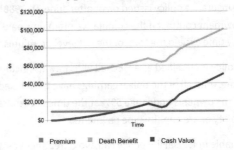

Common Uses of Variable Universal Life

Variable universal life policies are useful for policyowners who expect their needs to change over time. Within certain guidelines, the policy can be modified by changing the death benefit or premium payments. They are also well suited for use by policyowners who are comfortable with the risks and rewards of investments, or who need life insurance with the potential to provide an increasing death benefit. Some common uses are:

- **Supplement existing family protection:** As a supplement to an existing, basic life insurance plan. If the market is down when an insured dies, the variable death benefit of a variable universal life policy may not provide adequate funds to support a surviving spouse and/or minor children, or to pay final estate expenses.

- **Business planning:** Because of its flexibility, variable universal life insurance is often used for many different business purposes, such as insuring key employees, in split-dollar insurance arrangements, and funding nonqualified deferred compensation plans. Business continuation planning often involves using variable universal life as a source of funds for buy-sell agreements.

- **Accumulation needs:** Some individuals will use the investment features of variable universal life as means of accumulating funds for specific purposes, such as funding college education, or as a supplemental source of retirement income.

- **Charitable gifts:** To provide funds for a gift to charity.

Modified Endowment Contracts (MECs)

A life insurance policy issued on or after June 21, 1988[1] may be classified as a modified endowment contract if the cumulative premiums paid during the first seven years (7-pay test) at any time exceed the total of the net level premiums for the same period.

If a policy is classified as a MEC, all withdrawals (including loans) will be taxed as current income, until all of the policy earnings have been taxed. There is an additional 10% penalty tax if the owner is under age 59½ at the time of withdrawal, unless the payments are due to disability or are annuity type payments.

A variable universal life policy can avoid treatment as a MEC through a well-designed premium payment schedule. Caution must be exercised when changes in policy premium payments or death benefits are made, or when making partial withdrawals, to avoid having the policy inadvertently classified as a MEC.

Additional Policy Elements

Variable universal life policies have a number of additional elements to consider:

- **Investment options:** Most variable universal life policies offer a policyowner a wide range of investment options, including basic stock, bond and money market funds. Depending on the policy and insurer, other options, such as index funds, real estate funds, foreign stock funds, or zero coupon bond funds may also be offered. A policy may also include a fixed account option, in which the insurer guarantees a fixed rate of return.

---

[1] Including a policy issued before that date, but later materially changed.

- **Surrender charges:** Most variable universal life policies have substantial surrender charges, if a policy is terminated. These surrender charges are generally highest in the early years of a policy, and decline over a period of time, usually from seven to 15 years.

- **Policy loans:** Variable universal life policies typically permit the policyowner to borrow at interest a portion of the accumulated cash value. The rate charged on the borrowed funds is often lower than current open market rates. A policy loan will reduce the death benefit payable if the insured dies before the loan is repaid; a policy loan will also reduce the cash surrender value if a policy is terminated. If a policy lapses or is surrendered with a loan outstanding, the loan will be treated as taxable income in the current year, to the extent of gain in the policy.

- **Partial withdrawals:** Most variable universal life policies allow a policyowner to withdraw a portion of the cash value, without terminating the policy. Such withdrawals reduce the amount of death benefit payable, and may be subject to current income tax, if the policy is classified as a MEC, or if the withdrawal exceeds cost basis for a non-MEC policy. Some contracts allow a policy owner to put the withdrawn funds back into the policy, but the insured may have to provide evidence of insurability to restore the original death benefit.

- **Surrender options:** If a policyowner surrenders a policy, there are generally three ways in which the accumulated cash value may be received, including: (1) taking the accumulated cash value, less any surrender charges; (2) receiving a reduced amount of paid-up insurance, or (3) taking paid-up term insurance in an amount equal to the original face amount of the policy.

Optional Policy Provisions

A number of optional provisions, commonly referred to as riders, can be added to a basic variable universal life policy, generally through payment of an additional premium:

- **Waiver of premium:** Suspends the monthly deduction for the protection element of the policy, if the insured becomes disabled and is unable to work.

- **Accidental death:** Pays the beneficiaries double (in some situations triple) the face amount of the policy if the insured dies in an accident.

- **Spousal or family term insurance:** Allows a policy owner to purchase term insurance on a spouse or children.

- **Accelerated death benefit:** An accelerated death benefit provision allows for payment of part of a policy's death benefit while an insured is still alive. Such benefits are typically payable when the insured develops a medical condition expected to lead to death with a short period of time.

Indexed Universal Life Insurance

What is Indexed Universal Life Insurance?

Indexed universal life insurance (IUL) is a type of universal life insurance policy; it differs from a standard universal life contract in the mechanism used to credit interest to the cash value portion of the policy.

Structure of a Universal Life Policy

Unlike traditional whole life insurance, universal life policies specifically separate and identify the mortality, expense, and cash value elements of the contract. Dividing a policy into these three components allows the insurance company to build a higher degree of flexibility into the contract. Within certain limits, this flexibility allows the policy owner to modify the policy face amount[1] or premium, in response to changing needs and circumstances.

A monthly charge for both the mortality element and the expense element is deducted from a policy's account balance. The remainder of the premium is allocated to the cash value element where the funds earn interest. Complete disclosure of these internal charges against the cash value element is made to the policy owner in the form of an annual statement.

Universal life policies typically have several different provisions by which the accumulated cash value can be made available to a policy owner during life, without causing the policy to lapse. If a policy is terminated without the insured dying, there are various surrender options for the cash value.

Index Feature

In a standard universal life policy, interest is credited to the cash value portion of the policy by a method determined by the life insurance company, with most policies having a guaranteed minimum interest rate.

With an IUL policy, cash value is generally credited with a return that is the greater of the guaranteed minimum rate or the return based on a formula related to a specific market index, such as the Standard & Poor's 500 Index. If the underlying index rises sufficiently during a specific period, a greater return is credited to the cash value portion of the contract

---

[1] Evidence of insurability may be required to increase a policy's death benefit.

for that period. If the underlying index does not rise sufficiently, or even declines, the lower minimum rate is generally credited. IUL policies thus provide a way to share in gains in the underlying index, while being sheltered from index declines.

How an Index Works

Although all IUL policies share the same objective, contracts can vary greatly in their specifics. A clear understanding of the index mechanism is helpful:

- **Participation rate:** Also known as the "index rate," the "participation rate" specifies the percentage increase in the index by which a contract will grow. For example "75% of the S&P 500's increase for the calendar year" means that if the S&P 500 index increases 10% for the year, the contract would be credited with 7.5%. In some cases, this rate is subject to change by the insurance company.

- **Cap rate:** The annual maximum percentage increase allowed. For example, if the chosen market index increases 15%, a contract with a 9.0% cap rate will limit the client's increase to 9.0%. Depending on the policy, there may be no cap rate, or the cap rate may be subject to change by the insurance company.

- **Measuring the index change:** There are three primary formulas used to measure the change in an index inside of an IUL:

  - **Daily averaging:** Typically done over a one-year term, this approach compares the index value at the beginning of the term, with the daily average index value over the entire term period.

  - **Monthly averaging:** Again, typically measured over a one-year period, the monthly averaging formula compares the index value at the beginning of the term, with the index value measured on the same day each month.

  - **Point-to-Point:** Compares the index value on the first day of the term (often one year) with the value on the last day of the term; any market changes in between are ignored.

Indexed Universal Life Insurance

Policy Variations

There are two primary types of indexed universal life, based on the level of death benefits:

Type I indexed universal life:
Also known as option A, type I IUL policies pay a fixed, level death benefit, generally the face amount of the policy.

Example of Type I Indexed Universal Life

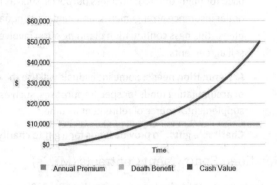

Type II indexed universal life:
Also known as option B, type II IUL policies generally pay the face amount of the policy plus the accumulated cash values. As the cash values grow, so does the potential death benefit.

Example of Type II Indexed Universal Life

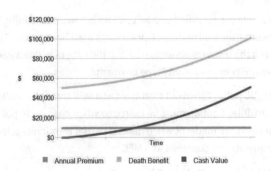

Common Uses of Indexed Universal Life

IUL policies are useful for policy owners who expect their needs to change over time. Within certain guidelines, an IUL policy can be modified by changing the death benefit or premium payments. Some common uses are:

- **Family protection:** To provide the funds to support a surviving spouse and/or minor children, or to pay final bills such as medical or other estate expenses, as well as federal and state death taxes.

- **Business planning:** Because of its flexibility, indexed universal life insurance is often used for many different business purposes, such as insuring key employees, in split-dollar insurance arrangements, and funding nonqualified deferred compensation plans. Business continuation planning often involves IUL as a source of funds for buy-sell agreements.

- **Accumulation needs:** Some individuals will use the cash value feature of IUL as means of accumulating funds for specific purposes, such as funding college education, or as a supplemental source of retirement income.

- **Charitable gifts:** To provide funds for a gift to charity.

Modified Endowment Contracts (MECs)

A life insurance policy issued on or after June 21, 1988[1] may be classified as a modified endowment contract (MEC) if the cumulative premiums paid during the first seven years (7-pay test) at any time exceed the total of the net level premiums for the same period.

If a policy is classified as a MEC, all withdrawals (including loans) will be taxed as current income, until all of the policy earnings have been taxed. There is an additional 10% penalty tax if the owner is under age 59½ at the time of withdrawal, unless the payments are due to disability or are annuity type payments.

An IUL policy can avoid treatment as a MEC through a well-designed premium payment schedule. Caution must be exercised when changes in policy premium payments or death benefits are made, or when making partial withdrawals, to avoid having the policy inadvertently classified as a MEC.

Additional Policy Elements

Indexed universal life policies have a number of additional elements to consider:

- **Surrender charges:** Most IUL policies have substantial surrender charges, if a policy is terminated. These surrender charges are generally highest in the early years of a policy, and decline over a period of time, usually from seven to 15 years.

---

[1] Including a policy issued before that date, but later materially changed.

- **Policy loans:** IUL policies typically permit the policy owner to borrow at interest a portion of the accumulated cash value. The rate charged on the borrowed funds is often lower than current open market rates. A policy loan will reduce the death benefit payable if the insured dies before the loan is repaid; a policy loan will also reduce the cash surrender value if a policy is terminated. If the policy lapses or is surrendered with a loan outstanding, the loan will be treated as taxable income in the current year, to the extent of gain in the policy.

- **Partial withdrawals:** Most IUL policies allow a policy owner to withdraw a portion of the cash value, without terminating the policy. Such withdrawals reduce the amount of death benefit payable, and may be subject to current income tax, if the policy is classified as a MEC, or if the withdrawal exceeds cost basis for a non-MEC policy. Some contracts allow a policy owner to put the withdrawn funds back into the policy, but the insured may have to provide evidence of insurability to restore the original death benefit.

- **Surrender options:** If a policy owner surrenders a policy, there are generally three ways in which the accumulated cash value may be received, including: (1) taking the accumulated cash value, less any surrender charges; (2) receiving a reduced amount of paid-up insurance; or (3) taking paid-up term insurance in an amount equal to the original face amount of the policy.

Optional Policy Provisions

A number of optional policy provisions, commonly referred to as riders, can be added to a basic indexed universal life policy, generally through payment of an additional premium. Not all riders are available from all insurance companies.

- **Waiver of premium:** Suspends the monthly deduction for the mortality element of the policy, if the insured becomes disabled and is unable to work.

- **Accidental death:** Pays the beneficiaries double (in some situations triple) the face amount of the policy if the insured dies in an accident.

- **Spousal or family term insurance:** Allows a policy owner to purchase, at the time the IUL policy is issued, term insurance on a spouse or children.

- **Accelerated death benefits:** An accelerated death benefits provision allows for payment of part of a policy's death benefit while an insured is still alive. Such benefits are typically payable when the insured develops a medical condition expected to lead to death within a short period of time.

- **Guaranteed income benefit (GIB):** If a contract owner chooses to borrow from a policy's accumulated cash value, a GIB rider assures that there will always be funds available to borrow, no matter how long the owner lives.

- **Long-term care:** Helps pay for long-term care expenses, should the insured require such care.

Seek Professional Guidance

Indexed universal life insurance policies are primarily intended to meet long-term insurance needs. Because of this, and because of the complexity of IUL contracts, the guidance of appropriate tax, legal, and other financial professionals is highly recommended.

Immediate Annuities

Immediate annuities are long-term contracts issued by a life insurance company. Typically purchased with a single, lump-sum payment, an immediate annuity can provide an income stream for a set period of time or for the rest of your life.

How Much Income Can I Receive?

The amount of income will vary, generally depending upon the following factors:

- **Amount of your purchase payment:** Generally, the larger the payment, the larger the income stream.

- **Your age:** Older individuals typically receive larger periodic payments.

- **Length of payout period selected:** A shorter payout period will usually result in a larger payment.

- **The underlying investment medium:** Usually either a fixed or variable annuity.

Funding the Annuity – Fixed or Variable

As the name implies, a "fixed" annuity pays a fixed rate of return. The insurance company invests in a portfolio of mortgages and bonds and pays out a specified rate of return. Generally, this rate is only guaranteed for a certain period of time, after which a new rate is calculated based upon then prevailing market conditions. However, most insurance companies offer a guaranteed minimum rate throughout the life of the contract.

Bear in mind that annuities are not insured by the FDIC or any other government agency. All guarantees are based upon the credit worthiness of the life insurance company.

The other primary alternative is the variable annuity, which offers the potential for higher returns in exchange for your willingness to assume a greater level of risk. A typical variable annuity contract will give you a choice among several types of investment portfolios, such as stocks or bonds, or a combination. As the markets move up and down, your annuity's value will also rise and fall. Consequently, the amount of each annuity payment will fluctuate depending upon the performance of the underlying investments.

Immediate Annuities

Variable annuities are sold by prospectus only. The prospectus contains more complete information including investment objectives, risk factors, fees, surrender charges, and any other applicable costs. Study the information in the prospectus carefully before investing.

Federal Income Taxation of Annuity Income

Because immediate annuities are purchased with after-tax dollars, the income received is prorated between ordinary income, which is taxable, and a return of principal, which is not taxable. This calculation takes into account your life expectancy and the amount of each payout. Please remember that state and local income tax law can vary. See your tax advisor for guidance.

How an Immediate Annuity Works

An immediate annuity is typically purchased with a single, lump-sum payment.

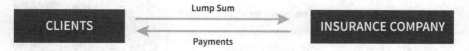

Payments and Withdrawals

- Distributions normally begin within one year from the date the annuity is established.

- Payments can be made over a fixed number of periods, or

- Payments can be made over the lifespan of one or more individuals.

- Under federal income tax law, certain withdrawals before age of 59½ may be subject to a 10% penalty tax.[1]

---

[1] State or local income tax law may differ from federal law.

Deferred Annuities

What Is a Deferred Annuity?

Life insurance is used to create an estate for an individual if he or she dies too soon. A deferred annuity, however, can provide protection against the possibility that an individual will live too long and outlive his or her accumulated assets.

The term "annuity" derives from a Latin term meaning "annual" and generally refers to any circumstance where principal and interest are liquidated through a series of regular payments made over a period of time. A "deferred" annuity is an annuity in which both the income, and any taxes due on growth inside the contract, are pushed into the future, until they are actually received by the owner.[1]

A commercial[2] deferred annuity is a special type of policy issued by an insurance company. In a typical situation, the policyowner contributes funds to the annuity. The money put into the policy is then allowed to grow for a period of time. At a future date, the policy may be "annuitized" and the accumulated funds paid out, generally through periodic payments made over either a specified period of time, or the life of an individual, or the joint lives of a couple.

Parties to an Annuity

There are four parties involved in a typical annuity:

- **Insurance company:** This is the issuer of the annuity.

- **Policyowner:** This is the individual or entity that contributes the funds. The policyowner typically has the right to terminate the annuity, to gift it to someone else, to withdraw funds from it, and to change the annuitant or beneficiary. Depending on the type of annuity, a policyowner may have other rights as well.

---

[1] Under federal law, the deferral of income tax on growth inside the policy is available only to natural persons; the tax-deferral is generally not permitted if the annuity owner is a non-natural person such as a trust or corporation.

[2] A private annuity is an agreement between individuals, usually exchanging a valuable asset (such as a business) for a lifetime income. The party promising to pay the annuity is someone who is not in the business of issuing annuities.

- **Annuitant:** This is the individual whose life is used to determine the payments during annuitization. An annuity will remain in force unless terminated by the owner, or as a result of the death of the owner, or the annuitant dies.

- **Beneficiary:** This is the individual or entity that receives any proceeds payable on the death of the annuitant or the policyowner, depending on whether the annuity is "annuitant driven" or "owner driven."

A single individual may be the policyowner, annuitant, and the beneficiary, although this is not usually recommended. More commonly, these roles are held by different individuals or entities.

Types of Deferred Annuities

There are many different ways to classify deferred annuities:

- **Method of purchase:** Annuities can be purchased with a single lump-sum of cash; such annuities are often referred to as single premium annuities. They may also be purchased with installment payments over time, either of a fixed dollar amount on a regular basis or with flexible payments.

- **When annuity payments begin:** Payments under a deferred annuity typically begin at some future time. In comparison, an "immediate" annuity, is purchased with a single premium, with annuity payments beginning one payment period (monthly, annual, etc.) later.

- **Investment options:** During the period before a policy is annuitized or completely liquidated, the funds invested by the policyowner are put to work. Depending on the type of annuity, the underlying investment vehicle will vary.

  - **Fixed annuity:** In a fixed annuity, the issuing life insurance company will guarantee a certain rate of interest, for a specified period of time, typically 1-10 years. Such annuities are useful for conservative, risk-averse individuals. The investment risk rests on the insurance company and any annuity payments are relatively predictable.

- **Variable annuity:** A buyer of a variable annuity has the option of placing the funds in the policy in a variety of investment options. The investment risk rests largely on the policyowner. Annuity payments are linked to the value of the underlying investments, which can fluctuate up or down.

- **Indexed annuity:** An indexed annuity is a type of fixed-rate annuity which combines a guaranteed minimum interest rate with a potential for greater growth, with returns being based on a formula related to a specific market index such as the Standard & Poor's 500 index. If the chosen index rises sufficiently during a specific period, a greater rate is credited to the policyowner's account for that period. Unlike variable annuities, where poor market performance can lead to decreased policy values, indexed annuities are structured to not lose value due to a declining stock market. However, because of surrender charges, an investor may lose principal value if an indexed annuity is surrendered early.

Payments from an Annuity

There are a number of ways that money may be withdrawn or received from a deferred annuity:

- **Lump-sum withdrawal:** A policyowner can withdraw all of the funds in an annuity in a single lump sum. Such a withdrawal is considered a surrender of the policy and the annuity ends. Depending on the policy and the length of time it has been in force, the insurance company may impose surrender charges, generally expressed as a percentage of the balance.

- **Partial withdrawal:** Many annuity policies allow an owner to withdraw a certain portion of the balance each year (usually 10% - 15%), without a surrender charge.

- **Partial annuitization:** Beginning in 2011, federal income tax law allows a portion of a nonqualified annuity contract, endowment, or life insurance contract to be annuitized while the balance is not annuitized, provided that the annuitization period is for 10 years or more, or is for the lives of one or more individuals.

- **Life only annuity:** Regular payments are made for as long as the annuitant lives. When the annuitant dies, payments cease and no refund is made, even if the policyowner has not recovered the initial investment.

- **Life with term certain:** Regular payments are made for the life of the annuitant, or a specified number of years. If the annuitant dies before the specified term has passed, annuity payments continue to a beneficiary for the remainder of the term.

- **Joint and survivor:** Regular payments are made over the lives of two individuals. When one dies, annuity payments (or a specified portion) continue to the survivor.

- **Refund options:** Regular payments are made over the life of the annuitant. However, if the annuitant dies before the policyowner's investment has been recovered, the balance is refunded to a named beneficiary through either a lump-sump payment or continued annuity payments.

- **Specified period:** Regular payments are made for a pre-selected number of years. If the annuitant dies before the specified period has expired, payments are continued to a named beneficiary for the remaining term.

- **Specified amount:** Payments of a set amount are paid out regularly as long as there is money in the account.

Taxation of Annuity Payments

The tax treatment of payments made from a deferred annuity will vary, depending on whether the funds used to purchase the annuity have been taxed or not,[1] and on where in the life cycle of the annuity the payments are made. In general, the following rules apply:[2]

- **Before annuitization:** Funds withdrawn from an annuity prior to annuitization are considered to be made first from interest or other growth.[3] These earnings are taxable as ordinary income. If the annuity owner is under age 59½ at the time a withdrawal is made, the earnings are also subject to a 10% federal tax penalty, unless an exception applies. If earnings are completely withdrawn and payments are then made from the owner's initial investment, the payment is treated as a tax-free recovery of basis.

---

[1] "Qualified" annuities are annuities purchased inside of a retirement plan such as a 401(k) or IRA, generally with pre-tax funds. "Nonqualified" annuities are purchased outside of an IRA or retirement plan, with money that has already been taxed. The taxation discussion here concerns nonqualified annuities.

[2] This information is based on federal law. State law may vary.

[3] Withdrawals from annuity policies entered into before August 14, 1982 were treated as first coming from principal, to the extent of premiums contributed before August 14, 1982.

- **After annuitization:** Regular annuity payments are treated as being composed of part earnings and part return of investment. The earnings portion is taxable as ordinary income. Once the owner has completely recovered his or her investment, all remaining payments are fully taxable as ordinary income. In some situations, if the owner is under age 59½ when payments are received, a 10% federal penalty tax may apply.

- **Estate taxes:** Any amount payable to a beneficiary under an annuity by reason of an owner's death is includible in the owner's gross estate. If an annuitant/owner receiving payments under a life-only annuity dies, no further payments are due and nothing is includible in his or her estate.

Other Common Annuity Provisions

There are several standard provisions commonly found in annuity policies:

- **Bailout provision:** The bailout provision applies only to fixed annuity policies. In a fixed annuity, an insurer will typically offer a guaranteed rate of interest for a specified period of time. For any subsequent time periods, a different rate of interest will usually be offered. Under the bailout provision, generally, if a renewal interest rate is more than 1% less than that offered in the previous period, the policy owner has the option of terminating the policy without paying any insurance company surrender charges. Interest or other growth withdrawn will generally be subject to current income tax and may also be subject to the 10% penalty tax if taken before age 59½.

- **Surrender charges:** Most commercial annuities do not charge a commission when an annuity is purchased. Many, however, impose a surrender charge if withdrawals in excess of a certain amount are made, or if the policy is surrendered completely. Surrender charges can range from 0% to 10% and typically decline over time.

- **Prospectus:** Variable annuities are considered by the Securities and Exchange Commission (SEC) to be a security. The SEC requires that the purchaser of a variable annuity be given a prospectus, which provides detailed information on how the annuity works, the investment options available, the risks involved, and any expenses or charges. The SEC also requires individuals selling variable annuities to be licensed to sell securities.

Certain optional provisions may be available by paying an additional charge:

- **Guaranteed death benefit:** The guaranteed death benefit provision applies only to variable annuities. If an annuitant or owner in some contracts dies before annuity payments begin, the policy will pay the named beneficiary the greater of the investment in the policy (less any withdrawals) or the policy value on the date of death.

- **Enhanced death benefit:** Some variable annuities offer an enhanced death benefit option. This feature provides that upon the death of the annuitant or owner in some contracts, the beneficiary will receive the greater of the policy's value on the date of death, or the original principal (plus any additions) compounded at 5% per year. Other enhanced death benefits include percentage increases and highest anniversary valuation.

Seek Professional Guidance

Deferred annuities are primarily intended to be long-term investments. Because of this, and because of the complexity of many annuity policies, an individual considering the purchase of a deferred annuity should carefully consider all aspects. The guidance of appropriate tax, legal, and other advisors is highly recommended.

How a Deferred Annuity Works

CLIENTS	Lump Sum or Periodic Payments →	INSURANCE COMPANY

At Withdrawal

CLIENTS	← Payments	INSURANCE COMPANY

Payments and Withdrawals

- Payments can be made over a fixed number of periods, or

- Payments can be made over the lifespan of one or more individuals.

- Under federal income tax law, certain withdrawals before age 59 ½ may be subject to a 10% penalty tax.[1]

---

[1] State or local income tax law may differ from federal law.

Variable Annuities

The term "annuity" derives from a Latin term meaning "annual" and generally refers to any circumstance where principal and interest are liquidated through a series of regular payments made over a period of time. A "deferred" annuity is an annuity in which both the income, and any taxes due on growth inside the contract, are pushed into the future, until they are actually received by the owner.[1]

A commercial,[2] tax-deferred annuity is a contract between an insurance company and a contract owner. In a typical situation, the contract owner contributes funds to the annuity. The money put into the contract is then allowed to grow for a period of time. At a future date, the contract may be annuitized and the accumulated funds paid out, generally through periodic payments made over either a specified period of time, or the life of an individual or the joint lives of a couple.

A variable annuity is a type of annuity in which the contract owner directs the overall investment strategy for the funds placed in the contract.

Fixed vs. Variable Annuities

Two primary annuity types are fixed and variable annuities. Although these annuities share many features in common, the key differences between them arise from the means used to grow the funds contributed by the contract owner.

- **Fixed annuities:** Fixed annuities are characterized by a minimum interest rate guaranteed by the issuing insurance company. Typically, a minimum annuity benefit is also guaranteed. The funds contributed to the contract by the annuity owner are placed in the insurance company's general account, and the investment risk involved rests entirely on the insurance company. With a fixed annuity, the focus is on safety of principal and stable investment returns.

---

[1] Under federal law, the deferral of income tax on growth inside the contract is available only to natural persons; the tax-deferral is generally not permitted if the annuity owner is a non-natural person such as a trust or corporation.

[2] A private annuity is an agreement between individuals, usually exchanging a valuable asset (such as a business) for a lifetime income. The party promising to pay the annuity is someone who is not in the business of issuing annuities.

- **Variable annuities:** In contrast, a variable annuity contract generally has no guarantees as to investment return or annuity benefits[1]. The funds contributed by the contract owner are placed in special, variable annuity subaccounts. Within these subaccounts, the annuity owner may choose to invest the funds in a wide variety of investment options. Annuity benefits depend upon the investment results achieved, and the investment risk rests entirely on the contract owner. With a variable annuity, the goal is to provide benefits that keep pace with inflation.

How a Variable Annuity Works

There are two distinct phases involved in the typical deferred variable annuity:

- **Accumulation:** During the accumulation phase, the contract owner contributes funds to the contract through either a single lump sum, or a series of payments. Each payment is used to purchase accumulation units in the investment subaccounts selected by the contract owner.[2] The cost of each accumulation unit is based on the market value of the investments underlying the subaccount, and the number of units outstanding.

  The number of accumulation units can vary, up or down, through additional contributions to the contract, or because of withdrawals from the contract. Any increase, or decrease, in the market price of the underlying investments is always reflected in the value of each accumulation unit. Expenses are deducted daily and are reflected in the value of each underlying unit.

- **Annuitization:** When a contract owner decides to annuitize the contract, the accumulation units are exchanged for annuity units. The number of annuity units received will depend on the price per unit, and certain insurance company assumptions regarding income, mortality and expenses. Once determined, the number of annuity units remains constant. The amount of periodic income payable is determined by multiplying the current value of each annuity unit, by the number of units. As the value of each annuity unit increases or decreases, so does the periodic income.

---

[1] Unless the contract owner selects the "Fixed Account" option.

[2] Some variable annuity contracts will deduct a portion of each payment for charges and expenses, with the remainder used to purchase accumulation units.

Common Investment Options

Depending on the insurance company and the contract, a wide variety of investment options are often available to the buyer of a variable annuity:

- **Stock:** The subaccount options which may be available can include aggressive growth, focusing on high risk/high return stocks; global and international stock, with equity investments from around the world; and specialty, emphasizing a particular industry or segment of the economy.

- **Bonds:** May include subaccounts focusing on corporate bonds; government bonds; and global or international bonds from around the world.

- **Balanced:** Includes a blend of stocks and bonds.

- **Precious metals:** Some variable contracts will offer subaccount options involving precious metals, such as gold or silver, investing either directly in the metals themselves, or through equity or debt investments in mining companies.

- **Money market:** Includes extremely high-quality short-term debt investments with an average maturity ranging from 30 – 120 days.

- **Fixed account:** In this option, the insurer guarantees a specific rate of return, for a particular period of time. Within a variable annuity contract, this is the only investment option where the investment risk rests on the insurer and not the contract owner.

Optional "Living" Benefit Riders to Variable Annuity Contracts

Many deferred variable annuity contracts offer, for an additional charge, optional "riders" to the contract which, in effect, transfer some of the market risk inherent in a variable annuity back to the issuing insurance company. These optional riders are in effect only during the accumulation phase of a deferred annuity. Once a contract has been annuitized, and regular, periodic payments have begun, the riders expire.

The specifics of how a particular rider work will vary from company to company. In general, however, they function as described below:

- **Guaranteed Minimum Income Benefit (GMIB):** Since the investment results from a variable annuity may be less than expected, the GMIB rider guarantees a minimum income to the annuitant. In order to trigger this benefit, a GMIB rider will typically require that the owner annuitize the contract.

- **Guaranteed Minimum Accumulation Benefit (GMAB):** Rather than guaranteeing a future level of income, as with the GMIB, the GMAB guarantees that the annuity's account value will be a certain dollar amount. With this rider, if the annuity's account value at the end of the guarantee period (generally seven to 10 years), is less than the guaranteed amount, the account value will be "stepped-up" to the GMAB guaranteed amount. This benefit generally does not require that the contract be annuitized.

- **Guaranteed Minimum Withdrawal Benefit (GMWB):** The GMWB rider provides that an annuity owner will be able to withdraw (without annuitizing the contract), on an annual basis, up to a specified percentage of a guaranteed or "protected" dollar amount. The annual withdrawal percentage limit typically ranges from five to seven percent of the remaining protected balance. In effect, the GMWB rider guarantees that an owner will receive back, over a period of years, the entire protected amount, even if the accumulated cash value in the annuity falls to zero. Once the entire protected amount has been withdrawn from the annuity, the contract ends, even if the owner is still alive.

- **Guaranteed Lifetime Withdrawal Benefit (GLWB):** The GLWB is similar to the GMWB in that an annuity owner is allowed to withdraw (not annuitize), on an annual basis, up to a specified percentage of a guaranteed or "protected" dollar amount. The key difference is that withdrawals under the GLWB rider continue for the owner's entire lifetime, even if total cumulative withdrawals exceed the protected dollar amount or the accumulated cash value in the annuity falls to zero.

Other Variable Annuity Contract Provisions

There are a number of key contract provisions that a buyer of a variable annuity contract should be aware of. Among these are:

- **How the contract is driven:** Some contracts are owner-driven while others are annuitant-driven. The word "driven" refers to what happens when a specific party dies or becomes disabled. With an owner-driven contract, the death of the annuitant will not terminate the contract. With an annuitant-driven contract, the death or disability of the contract owner will not result in death benefit payment, but IRC Sec. 72(s) requires payment within five years of death, unless the beneficiary is the spouse.

- **Guaranteed death benefit:** If an annuitant dies before annuity payments begin, the contract will pay the named beneficiary the greater of the investment in the contract (less any withdrawals) or the contract value on the date of death.

- **Enhanced death benefit:** Some variable annuities offer an enhanced death benefit option. This feature provides that upon the death of the annuitant, the beneficiary will receive the greater of the account's value on the date of death, or the original principal (plus any additions) compounded at a specified rate of return, for example, 5% per year. The ultimate death benefit is subject to the claims paying ability of the insurer.

- **Exchange privilege:** Allows the contract owner to periodically change the allocation of funds among the subaccounts. Such exchanges are usually allowed, often without a charge, several times a year.

- **Prospectus:** Variable annuities are considered by the Securities and Exchange Commission (SEC) to be a security. The SEC requires that the purchaser of a variable annuity be given a prospectus, which provides detailed information on how the annuity contract works, the subaccounts available, the risks, and all expenses or charges involved. The SEC also requires individuals selling variable annuities to be licensed to sell securities.

- **Contract fees and charges:** Although there is typically no commission paid when a variable annuity is purchased, variable contracts are subject to a number of fees and charges. A contract may include charges for investment management, paid to the manager of the investment subaccounts; administrative and mortality risk charges to cover the insurer's basic expenses, as well as the cost of the guaranteed death benefit provision; and surrender charges, fees imposed if withdrawals in excess of a certain amount are made, or if the contract is surrendered completely. Surrender charges can range from 0 to 10%, and typically decline over time.

Taxation of Annuity Payments

The tax treatment of payments made from an annuity will vary, depending on where in the life cycle of the annuity the payments are made. In general, the following rules apply:[1]

- **Before annuitization:** Funds withdrawn from an annuity contract prior to annuitization are considered to be made first from interest or other growth.[2] These earnings are taxable as ordinary income. If the annuity owner is under age 59½ at the time a withdrawal is made, the earnings are also generally subject to a 10% IRS penalty.[3] If earnings are completely withdrawn, and payments are then made from the owner's initial investment, the withdrawal is treated as a tax-free recovery of capital.

- **After annuitization:** Regular annuity payments are treated as being composed of part earnings, and part return of capital. The earnings portion is taxable as ordinary income. Once the owner has completely recovered his or her investment in the contract, all remaining payments are fully taxable as ordinary income.

- **Estate taxes:** Any amount payable to a beneficiary under an annuity contract by reason of an owner's death is includable in the owner's gross estate. If an annuitant/owner receiving payments under a Life Only annuity contract dies, no further payments are due, and nothing is includable in his or her estate.

---

[1] This information is based on federal law. State law may vary.

[2] For annuity contracts entered into prior to August 14, 1982, withdrawals are treated as first coming from principal.

[3] Two exceptions to the 10% penalty involve the death or disability of the contract owner or annuitant, depending on the wording of the contract.

Seek Professional Guidance

Tax-deferred annuities are primarily intended to be long-term investments. Because of this, and because of the complexity of many annuity contracts, an individual considering the purchase of a tax-deferred annuity should carefully consider all aspects before entering into the contract. The advice and counsel of appropriate tax, legal, and other advisors is highly recommended.

Indexed Annuities

The term "annuity" derives from a Latin term meaning "annual" and generally refers to any circumstance where principal and interest are liquidated through a series of regular payments made over a period of time. A tax-deferred annuity is an annuity in which taxation of interest or other growth is deferred until it is actually paid.[1]

A commercial[2] tax-deferred annuity is a contract between an insurance company and a contract owner. In a typical situation, the contract owner contributes funds to the annuity. The money put into the contract is then allowed to grow for a period of time. At a future date, the contract may be "annuitized," when the accumulated funds are paid out, generally through periodic payments made over either a specified period of time or the life of an individual or the joint lives of a couple.

An indexed annuity is a type of annuity that grows at the greater of an annual, guaranteed minimum rate or the return based on a formula related to a specific market index. Annuity contract guarantees are based on the claims-paying ability of the issuing insurance company.

Fixed vs. Indexed Annuities

Two primary annuity types are the fixed and variable annuities. (An indexed annuity is a type of fixed-rated annuity.) Although these annuities share many features in common, the primary difference between them is in the mechanism used to credit earnings to the annuity:

- **Fixed annuities:** Fixed annuities are characterized by a minimum interest rate guaranteed by the issuing insurance company. Typically, a minimum annuity benefit is also guaranteed. With a fixed annuity, the focus is on safety of principal and stable investment returns.

---

[1] Under federal law, the deferral of income tax on growth inside the contract is available only to natural persons; the tax deferral is generally not permitted if the annuity owner is a non-natural person such as a trust or corporation, unless the owner is an agent for a natural person.

[2] In comparison, a private annuity is an agreement between individuals, usually exchanging a valuable asset (such as a business) for a lifetime income. The party promising to pay the annuity is someone who is not in the business of issuing annuities.

- **Indexed annuities:** In contrast, indexed annuities (IA) are characterized by a contract return that is the greater of an annual minimum rate (typically 3%) or the return based on a formula related to a specific market index, such as the Standard & Poor's 500 index, reduced by certain expenses. If the chosen index rises sufficiently during a specific period, a greater return is credited to the contract owner's account for that period. If the market index does not rise sufficiently, or even declines, the lower minimum rate is credited. An owner is guaranteed to receive back at least all principal, if an IA contract is held for a minimum period of time, known as the penalty period. The penalty period for some indexed annuity contracts can be quite lengthy.

Understanding Indexed Annuities

Although all indexed annuities share the same objective, contracts can vary greatly. The specific structure of a contract will affect the amount and timing of growth in the contract, as well as its liquidity. Below are definitions of some common IA terminology:

- **Term:** This is the length of time the penalty period lasts and/or the time when the investor has the option to renew. The period is commonly three to seven years.

- **Participation rate:** Also known as the "index rate," the "participation rate" is the percentage increase in the index by which a contract will grow. For example, "75% of the S&P's increase for the calendar year" means that if the S&P 500 index increases 10% for the year, the contract would be credited with 7.5%. This rate is usually less than 100%. The participation rate is subject to change by the insurance company.

- **Administrative fee:** This is also known as an annual fee, spread yield, or expense load. It is a fixed charge subtracted annually by the insurer. This fee ranges from 1.0% to 2.25%.

- **Cap rate:** This is the annual maximum percentage increase allowed. For example, if the chosen market index increases 35%, a contract with a 9.0% cap rate will limit the client's increase to 9.0%. The cap rate is subject to change by the insurance company. Some contracts do not have a cap rate.

- **Floor:** This is the minimum guaranteed amount credited to the contract, typically in the three to four percent range. The investor will receive this minimum amount only if the IA is held for a specified, minimum period of time.

- **Reference (contract) value:** This is the amount the investor is entitled to, i.e., the greater of the current account value less any remaining surrender charges.

- **Anniversary date:** This is the beginning of the term used to measure the growth in a contract.

- **Index credit period:** Amounts are credited to a contract at specific points in time. The three most common period methodologies used to determine the credited amount are as follows.

  - **Annual reset:** This measures the change in the market index over a one-year period.

  - **Point-to-point:** While similar to annual reset, the period used is usually five years.

  - **Annual high watermark with look back:** While similar to point-to point, the highest annual anniversary value[1] is used to determine the gain instead, i.e., the largest number at the end of any of the five years.

- **Averaging:** Some indexed annuities will determine any increased contract value based on an average of the monthly changes in the market index, measured over a specified period.

Other Issues

Other issues to keep in mind include the following:

- **Guaranteed death benefit:** Some contracts offer, as an optional feature, a guaranteed death benefit. If an annuitant dies before annuity payments begin, the contract will pay the named beneficiary the greater of the investment in the contract (less any withdrawals) or the contract value on the date of death.

- **Contract fees and charges:** Although there is typically no commission charged when an indexed annuity is purchased, these contracts are subject to a number of fees and charges. These include administrative and mortality risk charges to cover the insurer's basic expenses as well as the cost of any guaranteed death benefit provisions. Surrender charges may also be imposed if withdrawals in excess of a certain amount are made or if the contract is surrendered. Surrender charges can range from 0 to 15% and typically decline over time. Payment of a surrender charge may result in a redemption less than the principal amount invested.

---

[1] For example, the credited amount might be the largest number at the end of any of the five years.

Taxation of Annuity Payments

The tax treatment of payments made from an annuity will vary, depending on where in the life cycle of the annuity the payments are made. In general, the following rules apply:[1]

- **Before annuitization:** Funds withdrawn from an annuity contract prior to annuitization (i.e., the beginning of regular payments) are considered to be made first from interest or other growth.[2] These earnings are taxable as ordinary income. If the annuity owner is under age 59½ at the time a withdrawal is made, the earnings are also generally subject to a 10% federal tax penalty.[3] If earnings are completely withdrawn and payments are then made from the owner's initial investment, the withdrawal is treated as a tax-free recovery of capital.

Changes to the annuity contract, including loans, collateral assignments, and ownership changes may also result in income tax consequences.

- **After annuitization:** Regular annuity payments are treated as being composed of part earnings and part return of capital. The earnings portion is taxable as ordinary income. Once the owner has completely recovered his or her investment in the contract, all remaining payments are fully taxable as ordinary income. Income amounts paid before the owner attains the age 59½ are generally subject to a 10% federal tax penalty, unless the annuitization is made for the owner's life or life expectancy.

- **Estate taxes:** Any amount payable to a beneficiary under an annuity contract by reason of an owner's death is includable in the owner's gross estate. If an annuitant/owner receiving payments under a life-only annuity contract dies, no further payments are due and nothing is includable in his or her estate.

- **Income in respect of a decedent:** Payments are still subject to income tax when received by the beneficiary. However, the beneficiary may also be eligible for a federal income tax deduction for a portion of the estate tax paid.

---

[1] Based on federal law. State law may vary.

[2] Withdrawals from annuity contracts entered into before August 14, 1982 were treated as first coming from principal, to the extent of premiums contributed before August 14, 1982.

[3] Two exceptions to the 10% penalty involve the death or disability of the contract owner.

Seek Professional Guidance

Tax-deferred annuities are primarily intended to be long-term investments. Because of this and the complexity of many annuity contracts, an individual considering the purchase of a tax-deferred annuity should carefully consider all aspects before entering into the contract. The guidance of appropriate tax, legal, and other financial professionals is highly recommended.

Combination Annuities

Combination annuities include two separate annuities; an immediate and a deferred annuity.

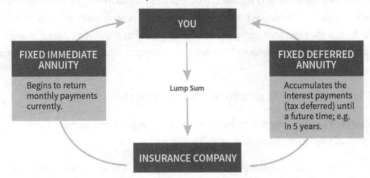

Note: Under IRC Sec. 72 (e)(12), if two annuity contracts are issued to the same person within the same calendar year, they will be treated as one contract. There is some uncertainty as to whether or not this aggregation rule applies to immediate annuities. To avoid this issue, consider two policy holders; e.g. husband and wife, or two different calendar years.

The following hypothetical example compares the combination annuity technique using a fixed rate immediate annuity and a fixed rate deferred annuity with a certificate of deposit (CD). The comparison assumes the taxpayer is in the 28% marginal income tax bracket.[1]

Interest Rates Shown Are Hypothetical	Plan One	Plan Two	
	$150,000 in a 3.5% CD	$27,795 in a 3.5% Immediate Annuity for 6 Years	$122,025 in a 3.5% Deferred Annuity Begins in 6 Years
Annual return for 6 years	$5,250	$5,168	$0
Taxes on income portion	$1,470	$141[2] (90% tax free)	$0
Net return after taxes	$3,780	$5,026	$0
Monthly return after taxes	$315	$419	$0
Amount left after 6 years	$150,000[3]	Fully paid out	$150,000[3]

Values shown in this presentation are hypothetical and not an indication of future performance.

---

[1] CDs are generally protected against a failure of the savings institution by federal deposit insurance. A fixed annuity is guaranteed by the insurance company.

[2] 90% of the annual payment is a return of principal. The balance is taxable at 28%.

[3] At the end of six years, the $150,000 in the CD may be withdrawn income tax free as a return of the investor's principal. The $150,000 in the deferred annuity will be composed of $122,025 of principal, and $27,795 of taxable earnings. Withdrawals from an annuity prior to age 59½ may be subject to a 10% penalty tax.

Taxation of Nonqualified Annuities

The term "annuity" refers to any situation where principal and interest are paid out in a series of regular payments. A "nonqualified" annuity, generally, is an annuity purchased by an individual from a life insurance company outside of an IRA or a qualified plan.[1] Many individuals purchase these annuities to provide a retirement income stream they cannot outlive.

Nonqualified annuities can be classified in a number of ways:

- **How purchased:** They can be purchased with a single, lump-sum payment, or with a series of payments made over time.

- **Underlying investment:** With a "fixed" annuity, the annuity owner's funds are placed in the insurance company's general investment account. In a "variable" annuity, these funds are placed in special investment subaccounts, as directed by the contract owner. Variable annuities are long-term investments designed for retirement. The value of the investment options chosen will fluctuate and, when redeemed, may be worth more or less than the original cost. A withdrawal charge may apply.

- **When payments begin:** An annuity can be "immediate," with payments beginning within one year of a contract being issued, or it can be "deferred," with payments beginning after an accumulation period, at a future date commonly called the "annuity starting date."

- **How long payments are made:** Payments can be made for a fixed period of time (e.g., 15 years), over the life or lives of specified individuals, or a combination of the fixed and lifetime options. (e.g., the longer of 15 years or until the annuitant[2] dies).

Unlike currently taxable investments, as long as the funds are kept **inside** the annuity, there is generally no federal income tax liability.[3] The tax "bite" is deferred until the funds are

---

[1] By way of contrast, a "private" annuity is an agreement between individuals, usually exchanging a valuable asset (such as a business) for a lifetime income. The party promising to pay the annuity is someone who is not in the business of issuing annuities.

[2] The "annuitant" is the individual whose life is used to determine how long payments will be made. Frequently the owner and the annuitant are the same individual.

[3] The discussion here concerns federal income tax law. State or local law can vary. Under federal income tax law, the deferral of tax is, with a few, narrow exceptions, not permitted if the annuity owner is a non-natural person such as a corporation or trust.

withdrawn from the contract. Depending on how and when the funds are distributed, the income and/or estate tax impact can vary.

Amounts Not Received As an Annuity – Before Annuity Starting Date

Sometimes funds are withdrawn from the contract that are not periodic annuity payments. Such distributions may take the form of cash withdrawals, dividends, loans, or a partial surrender of the contract. If funds are withdrawn from a nonqualified annuity before the annuity starting date, the annuity owner must include in income the **smaller** of:

- The amount distributed, or

- The amount by which the cash value of the contract exceeds the owner's investment in the contract. In other words, as funds are distributed the **earnings are taxed first**.

Example: Sally Smith bought a nonqualified annuity several years ago for $11,000. Before the annuity starting date, she takes a cash distribution of $6,000. At the time of the distribution, the cash value of the contract is $15,000. The distribution is allocated first to earnings, so Sally includes $4,000 ($15,000 - $11,000) in her gross income. The remaining $2,000 is received as a tax-free return of her investment.

Distributions Before Age 59½ - 10% Penalty

If funds are distributed from an annuity before the owner reaches age 59½, an additional tax of 10% may be levied on that part of a distribution that is included in gross income.

Example: If Sally had been age 58 when she took her $6,000 distribution, she would have had to pay an additional tax of $400, 10% x the $4,000 included in her gross income. The 10% penalty would not apply to the $2,000 that represented a return of her original investment.

Not all distributions before age 59½ are subject to the 10% premature distribution penalty. Federal income tax law contains a number of exceptions, [1] including distributions which are:

- Made **after** the taxpayer reaches age 59½.

---

[1] See IRC Sec. 72(q) for a complete list of the exceptions to the 10% penalty. IRS Publication 575, Pension and Annuity Income, has a "plain English" discussion of the 10% penalty and the exceptions to it.

- Made as a part of substantially equal periodic payments for the life (or life expectancy) of the taxpayer (contract owner) or the joint lives (or joint life expectancy) of the taxpayer and a designated beneficiary.

- Made because of the contract owner's total and permanent disability.

- Made because of the death of the contract holder (or primary annuitant if the holder is a non-natural person).

- Made from an immediate annuity, in which payments (made at least annually) must begin within one year of the contract's purchase date.

- Allocable to an investment in the contract before August 14, 1982.

Taxation of Annuity Payments – In General

For periodic payments made after the annuity starting date, each payment is considered to be made up of two parts:

- **Earnings** (dividends, interest, or other growth), which are currently taxable, and

- A **return of the annuity owner's invested funds**, known as the "investment in the contract," which is received income tax free. In simple terms, the investment in the contract is the total amount paid for the contract, less certain amounts received that were excluded from income.

An "exclusion ratio" is calculated which determines how much of each annuity payment is taxable, and how much is income tax free. This ratio is applied to each annuity payment until the owner has completely recovered his or her investment in the contract. Thereafter, each annuity payment is 100% taxable. The examples which follow illustrate how this works.

Fixed Annuities – Exclusion Ratio

In calculating the exclusion ratio, an estimate of the amount to be received must be made. If fixed payments are to be made for a fixed term, the calculation is relatively simple:

Example: Bill recently bought an annuity which will pay him $500 per month for 10 years, beginning when he reaches age 65. His expected return is $60,000 ($500 per month x 12 months per year x 10 years). If Bill's investment in the contract were $45,000, his exclusion ratio would be 75%, calculated as follows:

$$\frac{\text{Investment in the contract} = \$45,000}{\text{Expected return} = \ \$60,000}$$

For each $500 monthly payment, Bill would exclude $375 ($500 x 75%) from his gross income. The remaining $125 is included in his gross taxable income.

If fixed payments are to be made for the life of one or more individuals, the expected return is calculated using federal government life expectancy tables:[1]

Example: Linda, age 60, purchased an immediate annuity which was to pay her $400 per month for the rest of her life, starting on the date of purchase. Her expected return is $4,800 ($400 per month x 12 months) x the life expectancy in years from Annuity Table V (single life), which is 24.2. Thus the total expected return equals $116,160, ($4,800 x 24.2). If her investment in the contract equals $80,000, her exclusion ratio is 69%, calculated as follows:

$$\frac{\text{Investment in the contract} = \$80,000}{\text{Expected return} = \ \$116,600}$$

For each $400 monthly payment, Linda can exclude $276 ($400 x 69%) from her gross income. The remaining $124 is included in taxable income. If Linda lives more than 24.2 years, she will have completely recovered her investment in the contract, and her annuity payments from that point on will be 100% taxable.

Variable Annuities – Proportionate Amount Excluded

In a variable annuity, annuity payments are not a fixed amount; they can vary up or down as the result of fluctuating investment returns or factors such as a cost-of-living index. Because payments vary, it is not possible to calculate, as is done with a fixed payment annuity, an "expected return," in order to determine the exclusion ratio for income tax purposes.

Instead, a proportionate amount of the investment in the contract is allocated to each taxable year. In simple terms, this is calculated by dividing the investment in the contract by the projected number of payments that are to be made. If the dollar amount of annuity payments received in a particular year does not exceed the amount of investment in the

---

[1] See IRS Reg. 1.72-9.

contract allocated to that tax year, the payments are excluded from taxable income. If the total dollar amount of payments exceeds the amount of investment in the contract allocated for the year, the excess above the allocated amount is taxable.

> Example: Steven pays $20,000 for a variable annuity that will make monthly payments to him over a 10-year period. The projected number of payments is thus 120 (10 years x 12 months per year). The amount of his investment in the contract that is allocated to each monthly payment is $166.67 ($20,000 ÷ 120). If Steven's contract begins making payments to him on July 1, and he receives a total of $1,200 for the year, $1,000.02 ($166.67 x 6) will be excluded from his income. He must include the remaining $199.98 in his gross income for the year.

If a variable annuity makes payments over the life expectancy of one or more individuals, the projected number of payments is calculated using government life expectancy tables.[1]

> Example: Bob, age 65 and Alice, age 59, pay $50,000 for a variable annuity which will make annual payments to them over their joint life expectancy. According to Annuity Table VI (two lives) their joint life expectancy is 28.2 years. The amount of investment in the contract that is allocated to each annual payment is $1,773.05 ($50,000 ÷ 28.2). To the extent that any annual payment exceeds $1,773.05, the excess will be subject to taxation.

Gifting an Annuity

If a taxpayer transfers ownership of an annuity to another person, without receiving full and adequate consideration (e.g., a gift), the transaction is taxable. The transferor (the person making the gift) must include in income the excess of the contract's surrender value on the date of the transfer over the investment in the contract.

> Example: Larry gifts an annuity to his son George. On the date of the transfer, the cash surrender value of the contract was $75,000; Larry's investment in the contract was $60,000. For the year of the transfer, Larry must include in income $15,000 ($75,000 - $60,000).

These rules do not apply to transfers between spouses nor to transfers incident to a divorce.

---

[1] See IRC Reg. 1.72-9.

Taxation of Nonqualified Annuities

Exchanging an Annuity

In some situations, an annuity owner will want to exchange an existing annuity contract for a different contract. For income tax purposes, such exchanges are governed by IRC Sec. 1035. As long as certain requirements are met, these exchanges are tax-free and allow the annuity owner to roll-over any gain in the old contract to the new one.

Complete Surrender of an Annuity Contract

An amount received by a taxpayer for the complete surrender, redemption, or maturity of an annuity is taxable only to the extent that the proceeds exceed the investment in the contract.

> Example: Michael receives $95,000 for the complete surrender of an annuity contract. His investment in the contract is $75,000. In the year of surrender (regardless of when the proceeds are actually received), he must include $20,000 in gross income ($95,000 - $75,000).

Death

The tax treatment of amounts payable from an annuity because of the death of the owner/annuitant will vary, depending on when death occurs:

- **Death before annuity starting date:** Amounts payable at death are generally includable in the decedent's gross estate for estate tax purposes. If a named beneficiary receives the death benefit, the beneficiary must include in gross income the excess of the total amount received over the decedent's cost in the contract. Whether paid to the estate or a named beneficiary, amounts received in excess of the decedent's basis in the contract are income in respect of a decedent (IRD). Any estate tax attributable to the IRD generally qualifies as a Miscellaneous Itemized Deduction.

- **Death after annuity starting date:** Once regular annuity payments have begun, the tax results will depend first on how the annuity payments are to be made. If the annuity is payable for a single life only, once that life has ended there is nothing left to tax. Any unrecovered investment in the contract may be deducted on the decedent's final income tax return. Otherwise, there is neither an estate nor an income tax impact.

Taxation of Nonqualified Annuities

For annuity contracts which provide a benefit to those left behind (for example a refund annuity or payments under a joint and survivor contract), the situation is slightly different. If the decedent's estate is to receive the benefits, they are includable in his or her gross estate. If the benefits are payable to a named beneficiary, the value of those benefits is also generally includable in the decedent's gross estate. For income tax purposes, with either a refund or payments to a survivor, the income is generally taxable only when the amounts received exceed the investment in the contract:

- **Surviving spouse is the beneficiary:** If the designated beneficiary (the individual who becomes the new owner of the contract) is the surviving spouse of the deceased owner, IRC Sec. 72(s) lets the survivor "step in the shoes" of the deceased owner, with the distribution requirements applied by treating the surviving spouse as the owner.

Partial Annuitization

Federal income tax law allows a portion of a nonqualified annuity contract, endowment, or life insurance contract to be annuitized while the balance is not annuitized, provided that the annuitization period is for 10 years or more, or is for the lives of one or more individuals.

The investment in the contract is allocated on a pro-rata basis between each portion of the contract from which amounts are received as an annuity, and the portion of the contract from which amounts are not received as an annuity. This allocation is made for the purposes of applying the rules relating to the exclusion ratio and in determining the investment in the contract, the annuity starting date, and amounts not received as an annuity. A separate annuity starting date is determined with respect to each portion of the contract from which amounts are received as an annuity.

Seek Professional Guidance

Commercial, nonqualified annuities are complex investments that can be structured to meet a wide range of needs and situations. Similarly, the federal tax treatment of these investment products is also complex. The guidance of qualified tax and investment professionals is strongly recommended.

2001 Commissioners' Standard Ordinary (CSO) Mortality Table

Average Life Expectancy in Years

Age	Male	Female	Age	Male	Female	Age	Male	Female
0	76.62	80.84	26	51.57	55.43	52	27.40	30.90
1	75.69	79.88	27	50.62	54.46	53	26.52	30.01
2	74.74	78.91	28	49.68	53.49	54	25.65	29.14
3	73.76	77.93	29	48.74	52.53	55	24.79	28.27
4	72.78	76.95	30	47.79	51.56	56	23.94	27.41
5	71.80	75.96	31	46.85	50.60	57	23.10	26.57
6	70.81	74.97	32	45.90	49.63	58	22.27	25.73
7	69.83	73.99	33	44.95	48.67	59	21.45	24.90
8	68.84	73.00	34	44.00	47.71	60	20.64	24.08
9	67.86	72.02	35	43.05	46.75	61	19.85	23.27
10	66.88	71.03	36	42.11	45.80	62	19.06	22.47
11	65.89	70.05	37	41.16	44.84	63	18.29	21.68
12	64.91	69.07	38	40.21	43.89	64	17.54	20.90
13	63.93	68.08	39	39.27	42.94	65	16.80	20.12
14	62.95	67.10	40	38.33	42.00	66	16.08	19.36
15	61.98	66.13	41	37.39	41.05	67	15.37	18.60
16	61.02	65.15	42	36.46	40.11	68	14.68	17.86
17	60.07	64.17	43	35.53	39.17	69	13.99	17.12
18	59.12	63.20	44	34.61	38.23	70	13.32	16.40
19	58.17	62.23	45	33.69	37.29	71	12.66	15.69
20	57.23	61.26	46	32.78	36.36	72	12.01	14.99
21	56.29	60.28	47	31.87	35.43	73	11.39	14.31
22	55.34	59.31	48	30.97	34.51	74	10.78	13.64
23	54.40	58.34	49	30.07	33.60	75	10.18	12.98
24	53.45	57.37	50	29.18	32.69	76	9.61	12.34
25	52.51	56.40	51	28.28	31.79	77	9.05	11.71

2001 CSO Mortality Table

Average Life Expectancy in Years

Age	Male	Female	Age	Male	Female	Age	Male	Female
78	8.50	11.10	93	3.15	4.26	108	1.30	1.36
79	7.98	10.50	94	2.96	3.93	109	1.22	1.25
80	7.49	9.92	95	2.78	3.63	110	1.14	1.16
81	7.01	9.35	96	2.62	3.38	111	1.07	1.08
82	6.57	8.81	97	2.47	3.18	112	0.99	1.00
83	6.14	8.29	98	2.32	3.02	113	0.92	0.93
84	5.74	7.79	99	2.19	2.82	114	0.85	0.86
85	5.36	7.32	100	2.07	2.61	115	0.79	0.79
86	5.00	6.87	101	1.96	2.42	116	0.72	0.73
87	4.66	6.43	102	1.86	2.23	117	0.66	0.67
88	4.35	6.02	103	1.76	2.06	118	0.61	0.61
89	4.07	5.64	104	1.66	1.89	119	0.55	0.56
90	3.81	5.29	105	1.57	1.74	120	0.50	0.50
91	3.57	4.96	106	1.48	1.60			
92	3.35	4.61	107	1.39	1.47			

Note: Table based on composite (not smoker distinct) data.

Deaths per Thousand at Various Ages

2001 Commissioners' Standard Ordinary Mortality Table

Number Expected to Die Each Year

Age	Males Per 1000	Females Per 1000	Age	Males Per 1000	Females Per 1000	Age	Males Per 1000	Females Per 1000
0	0.97	0.48	21	1.00	0.48	42	1.96	1.48
1	0.56	0.35	22	1.02	0.50	43	2.15	1.59
2	0.39	0.26	23	1.03	0.50	44	2.39	1.72
3	0.27	0.20	24	1.05	0.52	45	2.65	1.87
4	0.21	0.19	25	1.07	0.54	46	2.90	2.05
5	0.21	0.18	26	1.12	0.56	47	3.17	2.27
6	0.22	0.18	27	1.17	0.60	48	3.33	2.50
7	0.22	0.21	28	1.17	0.63	49	3.52	2.78
8	0.22	0.21	29	1.15	0.66	50	3.76	3.08
9	0.23	0.21	30	1.14	0.68	51	4.06	3.41
10	0.23	0.22	31	1.13	0.73	52	4.47	3.79
11	0.27	0.23	32	1.13	0.77	53	4.93	4.20
12	0.33	0.27	33	1.15	0.82	54	5.50	4.63
13	0.39	0.30	34	1.18	0.88	55	6.17	5.10
14	0.47	0.33	35	1.21	0.97	56	6.88	5.63
15	0.61	0.35	36	1.28	1.03	57	7.64	6.19
16	0.74	0.39	37	1.34	1.11	58	8.27	6.80
17	0.87	0.41	38	1.44	1.17	59	8.99	7.39
18	0.94	0.43	39	1.54	1.23	60	9.86	8.01
19	0.98	0.46	40	1.65	1.30	61	10.94	8.68
20	1.00	0.47	41	1.79	1.38	62	12.25	9.39

Deaths per Thousand at Various Ages

2001 Commissioners' Standard Ordinary Mortality Table

Number Expected to Die Each Year

Age	Males Per 1000	Females Per 1000	Age	Males Per 1000	Females Per 1000	Age	Males Per 1000	Females Per 1000
63	13.71	10.14	83	95.51	60.81	103	417.20	349.06
64	15.24	10.96	84	105.43	67.27	104	437.56	378.61
65	16.85	11.85	85	116.57	74.45	105	459.21	410.57
66	18.47	12.82	86	128.91	80.99	106	482.22	443.33
67	20.09	13.89	87	142.35	90.79	107	506.69	476.89
68	21.85	15.07	88	156.73	101.07	108	532.69	510.65
69	23.64	16.36	89	171.88	112.02	109	560.31	545.81
70	25.77	17.81	90	187.66	121.92	110	589.64	581.77
71	28.15	19.47	91	202.44	126.85	111	620.79	616.33
72	31.32	21.30	92	217.83	136.88	112	653.84	649.85
73	34.62	23.30	93	234.04	151.64	113	688.94	680.37
74	38.08	25.50	94	251.14	170.31	114	726.18	723.39
75	41.91	27.90	95	269.17	193.66	115	765.70	763.41
76	46.08	30.53	96	285.64	215.66	116	807.61	804.93
77	50.92	33.41	97	303.18	238.48	117	852.07	850.44
78	56.56	36.58	98	321.88	242.16	118	899.23	892.44
79	63.06	40.05	99	341.85	255.23	119	949.22	935.11
80	70.14	43.86	100	363.19	275.73	120	1000.00	1000.00
81	78.19	49.11	101	380.08	297.84			
82	86.54	54.95	102	398.06	322.21			

Note: Table based on composite (not smoker distinct) data.

The Chance of Dying Before Age 65

Commissioners' 2001 Standard Ordinary Mortality Table

From a group of 1,000 persons your age, the chart illustrates the number who will still be alive at age 65. The third column shows the probability that you will not be alive at age 65.

From 1,000 Males			From 1,000 Females		
Age at Last Birthday	Number Still Alive at Age 65	Chance of Not Being Alive at Age 65	Age at Last Birthday	Number Still Alive at Age 65	Chance of Not Being Alive at Age 65
30	850	15%	30	881	12%
31	851	15%	31	882	12%
32	852	15%	32	882	12%
33	853	15%	33	883	12%
34	854	15%	34	884	12%
35	855	15%	35	884	12%
36	856	14%	36	885	12%
37	858	14%	37	886	11%
38	859	14%	38	887	11%
39	860	14%	39	888	11%
40	861	14%	40	889	11%
41	863	14%	41	890	11%
42	864	14%	42	892	11%
43	866	13%	43	893	11%
44	868	13%	44	894	11%
45	870	13%	45	896	10%
46	872	13%	46	898	10%

The Chance of Dying Before Age 65

Commissioners' 2001 Standard Ordinary Mortality Table

From 1,000 Males			From 1,000 Females		
Age at Last Birthday	Number Still Alive at Age 65	Chance of Not Being Alive at Age 65	Age at Last Birthday	Number Still Alive at Age 65	Chance of Not Being Alive at Age 65
47	875	13%	47	900	10%
48	877	12%	48	902	10%
49	880	12%	49	904	10%
50	884	12%	50	906	9%
51	887	11%	51	909	9%
52	890	11%	52	912	9%
53	894	11%	53	916	8%
54	899	10%	54	920	8%
55	904	10%	55	924	8%
56	910	9%	56	929	7%
57	916	8%	57	934	7%
58	923	8%	58	940	6%
59	931	7%	59	946	5%
60	939	6%	60	953	5%
61	948	5%	61	961	4%
62	959	4%	62	969	3%
63	971	3%	63	979	2%
64	984	2%	64	989	1%

Note: Table based on composite (not smoker distinct) data.

Insurance Company Rating Systems

A.M. Best

Grade	Interpretation
A++/A+	Superior. Very strong ability to meet obligations.
A/A-	Excellent. Strong ability to meet obligations.
B++/B+	Good. Good ability to meet obligations.
B/B-	Fair. Adequate ability to meet obligations.
C++/C+	Marginal. Reasonable ability to meet obligations.
C/C-	Weak. Currently has the ability to meet obligations.
D	Poor. Below minimum standards.
E	Under regulatory supervision.
F	In liquidation.
S	Rating Suspended – usually due to insufficient information.

Standard and Poor's

Grade	Interpretation
AAA	Extremely strong financial security. Highest safety.
AA+/AA/AA-	Very strong financial security. Highly safe.
A+/A/A-	Strong financial security. More susceptible to economic change than highly rated companies.
BBB+/BBB/BBB-	Good financial security. More vulnerable to economic changes than highly rated companies.
BB+/BB/BB-	Marginal financial security. Ability to meet obligations may not be adequate for long-term policies.
B+/B/B-	Weak financial security. An unfavorable business environment will probably reduce its ability to meet obligations.
CCC+/CCC/CCC-	Very weak. Currently able to meet obligations. Highly vulnerable to adverse economic conditions.
CC	Extremely weak. Questionable ability to meet obligations.
R	Regulatory action. Under supervision of insurance regulators.
NR	Not rated. No opinion is expressed about the firm's financial condition.

Insurance Company Rating Systems

Moody's

Grade	Interpretation
Aaa	Exceptional security. Unlikely to be affected by change.
Aa1/Aa2/Aa3	Excellent security. Lower than Aaa because long-term risks appear somewhat larger.
A1/A2/A3	Good security. Possibly susceptible to future impairment.
Baa1/Baa2/Baa3	Adequate security. Certain protective elements may be lacking.
Ba1/Ba2/Ba3	Questionable security. Ability to meet obligations may be moderate.
B1/B2/B3	Poor security. Assurance of punctual payment of obligations is small over the long run.
Caa	Very poor security. There may be elements of danger regarding the payment of obligations.
Ca	Extremely poor security. Companies are often in default.
C	Lowest security. Extremely poor prospects of offering financial security.

Fitch

Grade	Interpretation
AAA	Exceptionally strong. Unlikely to be affected by change.
AA+/AA/AA-	Very strong. Moderate risk factors. Very strong ability to meet obligations
A+/A/A-	Strong. Moderate risk factors. Strong ability to meet obligations.
BBB+/BBB/BBB-	Good. Risk factors may be somewhat high. Good ability to meet obligations.
BB+/BB/BB-	Moderately weak. Uncertain ability to meet obligations.
B+/B/B-	Weak. Poor ability to meet obligations.
CCC+/CCC/CCC- CC+/C/C-	Very weak. Insurers in any of these ratings viewed as having poor ability to meet obligations.
DDD/DD/D	Distressed. Insurers have either failed to meet obligations or are under regulatory supervision/intervention.
NR	Not rated.

Insurance Company Rating Systems

TheStreet.com Ratings, Inc.

Grade	Interpretation
A+/A/A-	Excellent financial security. Strong ability to deal with economic adversity.
B+/B/B-	Good financial security. Severe economic conditions may affect this company.
C+/C/C-	Fair financial security. Susceptible to downturns in the economy.
D+/D/D-	Weak financial security. Could impact policyholders.
E+/E	Very weak financial security. Significant risk, even in a stable economy.
F	Failed. Under supervision of state insurance commissioners.
U	Unrated.

Note: Some of the classifications of the above rating companies are broken down into more levels than illustrated. The financial strength of an insurance company is a very important factor to consider in purchasing life insurance or annuities.

Survivor Needs Analysis Data

Personal

Date   01/01/2018

Client(s) name		Date of birth	Retirement age
1) Paul	Johnson	01/01/1975	67
2) Sally	Johnson	01/01/1977	65

☑ Check if clients are married

The Dependent(s)

#	Name	Date of Birth	Dependent of...		Education Funding	
			Client One	Client Two	Portion to fund	Amount currently saved
1)	Robert	01/01/2004	☑	☑	100%	$10,000
2)	Catherine	01/01/2006	☑	☑	100%	$8,000
3)	Michael	01/01/2013	☑	☑	100%	$6,000
4)			☐	☐	%	
5)			☐	☐	%	

Education Information

#	School(s) name	Annual cost	Age when school begins	Years in school
1)	University of California: Los Angeles	$24,375	18	4
2)	University of California: Los Angeles	24,375	18	4
3)	University of California: Los Angeles	24,375	18	4

Income Needs

Provide income for ☑ Lifetime   or _____ of years.

Beginning today (choose one)

☐ Monthly amount _____ or ☑ _____ 90% of current monthly income

Survivor Needs Analysis Data

Income Needs

Beginning when the youngest child reaches age ___18___ (choose one):

    ☐ Monthly amount _____ or ☑ ___75%___ of current monthly income

Beginning at retirement (choose one):

    ☐ Monthly amount _____ or ☑ ___50%___ of current monthly income

☑ Include college funding for dependents

Income Sources

Employment income (Annual)

Paul $87,000   Sally $65,000

Monthly Social Security benefits

Paul		Sally	
☐ Spousal Benefits Only	☐ Not Eligible	☐ Spousal Benefits Only	☐ Not Eligible
☑ Based on Current Earnings		☑ Based on Current Earnings	
☐ Based on Maximum Earnings		☐ Based on Maximum Earnings	
☐ PIA Input (values below required)[1]		☐ PIA Input (values below required)[1]	
☐ Monthly Amount Input (values below required)[2]		☐ Monthly Amount Input (values below required)[2]	
Retirement $	Survivor $	Retirement $	Survivor $

---

[1] Use the Social Security benefit at the client's "Full Retirement Age" (FRA).

[2] For retirement input this is the amount to be received at Social Security Age. For survivor input this amount is the PIA

Other income sources

Name of income source	Owner	Amount	Start age	Monthly/ lump sum[2]	P/V[4] or F/V	End age	Inflated annually	Available to survivor	Income Type
1) Pension	Paul	$1,000	67	Monthly	PV	Life	4%	100%	Other
2) Pension	Paul	$500	65	Monthly	PV	Life	4%	100%	Other
3)									
4)									
5)									

Capital & Debt

Retirement plan balance

Paul $280,000

Sally $152,000

Other asset balance

Cash $3,500

Other $6,000

Life insurance benefits available

Paul $500,000

Sally $300,000

Debts to be repaid

Mortgage balance $294,000

Other debt $27,000

Assumptions

Paul mortality age	90	Assumed rate of return on education assets	6%
Sally mortality age	90	Annual Social Security benefit inflation rate	2%
Annual Inflation rate	4%	Final expenses	$5,000
Annual employment inflation rate – Paul	4%	Number of months of current income required for emergency reserves	3
Annual employment inflation rate – Sally	4%	Assumed rate of return for survivor's assets	7%
Annual education inflation rate	6%		

---

[2] Enter "M" if paid monthly or "L" if paid as one lump sum.

[4] Enter "P" if amount is present value or "F" if amount is future value.

Survivor Needs Now and Future

In the event of Paul's death

Areas of Need

There are two areas of needs that arise in the event of a death: Immediate cash needs, and income to support Sally and the children

Immediate Needs

This generally includes funds required immediately after death to establish an emergency reserve fund, pay final expenses, create a college fund, and repay outstanding debts. You would like to provide for the education of the children. The total amount required for these needs is $656,500. You currently have assets and life insurance in the amount of $965,500.

Income Needs

Income needs change over time. This analysis assumes that monthly income needs will be:
$11,400 or 90.00% of today's total income until the children reach age 18. $9,500 or 75.00% of today's total income after the children reach age 18. $6,333 or 50.00% of today's total income during retirement.

Results

According to the analysis, your immediate needs may be met with your total assets. However, your liquid assets of $527,500 are not sufficient to meet your needs. You may have to liquidate other assets at an inopportune time. All assets will be depleted by Sally's age 51.

Income Needs and Sources

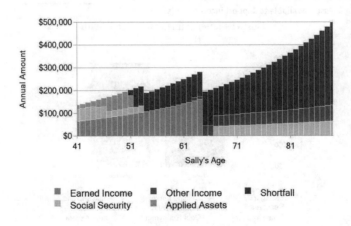

In order to provide for all needs today, you would need an additional amount of $797,043 today.

Values shown in this presentation are hypothetical and not a promise of future performance.

Survivor's Immediate Needs

In the event of Paul's death

Immediate Needs

This generally includes funds required immediately after death to establish an emergency reserve fund, pay final expenses, create a college fund, and repay outstanding debts.

Capital Needed Immediately

Emergency reserves		$38,000
Final expenses		5,000
College fund		292,500
Debt repayment		
Mortgage	$294,000	
Other debts	27,000	
Total debt repayment		321,000
Total immediate capital need		**656,500**

Capital Available

Cash	3,500	
Life insurance proceeds	500,000	
Existing college funds	24,000	
Total liquid capital		**527,500**
Amount needed from other assets		129,000
Other available assets		438,000
Additional assets required for immediate needs		0
Assets available to support income needs		**$309,000**

Funds Required Immediately Upon Death

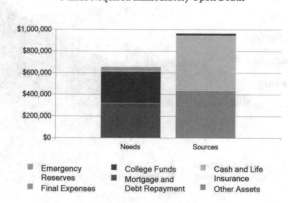

The immediate cash needs may be satisfied with current assets; however, it may not be prudent to liquidate them immediately.

Values shown in this presentation are hypothetical and not a promise of future performance.

Survivor Needs Timeline

Assumptions:

Deceased Individual:	Paul
Surviving Individual:	Sally
Rate of Return:	7.00%
Rate of Inflation:	4.00%

Analysis Results:

Total of Annual Shortfalls:	$6,752,380
Additional Capital Required:	$797,043

Age	Need	Sources				Asset Balance	Annual Shortfall
		Earned Income	Social Security	Other Income	Earnings from Assets		
					Beginning Balance	$309,000	
41	$136,800	$65,000	$53,689	$0	$21,636	$312,525	$0
42	142,272	67,600	54,763	0	21,821	314,437	0
43	147,963	70,304	55,858	0	21,886	314,523	0
44	153,881	73,116	56,975	0	21,815	312,548	0
45	160,037	76,041	49,810	0	21,270	299,633	0
46	166,438	79,082	50,806	0	20,245	283,328	0
47	173,096	82,246	25,911	0	17,966	236,356	0
48	180,019	85,536	26,430	0	14,450	182,751	0
49	187,220	88,957	26,958	0	10,449	121,895	0
50	194,709	92,515	27,497	0	5,918	53,116	0
51	202,497	96,216	28,047	0	809	0	24,309
52	210,597	100,065	28,608	0	0	0	81,925
53	219,021	104,067	29,180	0	0	0	85,774
54	189,818	108,230	0	0	0	0	81,589
55	197,411	112,559	0	0	0	0	84,852
56	205,308	117,061	0	0	0	0	88,246
57	213,520	121,744	0	0	0	0	91,776
58	222,061	126,614	0	0	0	0	95,447
59	230,943	131,678	0	0	0	0	99,265
60	240,181	136,945	0	0	0	0	103,236

Values shown in this presentation are hypothetical and not a promise of future performance.

Survivor Needs Timeline

| Age | Need | Sources | | | | Asset Balance | Annual Shortfall |
		Earned Income	Social Security	Other Income	Earnings from Assets		
61	$249,788	$142,423	$0	$0	$0	$0	$107,365
62	259,780	148,120	0	0	0	0	111,660
63	270,171	154,045	0	14,220	0	0	101,907
64	280,978	160,207	0	14,788	0	0	105,983
65	194,811	0	0	46,139	0	0	148,672
66	202,604	0	0	46,755	0	0	155,849
67	210,708	0	42,106	47,394	0	0	121,207
68	219,136	0	42,948	48,060	0	0	128,128
69	227,901	0	43,807	48,752	0	0	135,343
70	237,018	0	44,683	49,472	0	0	142,863
71	246,498	0	45,577	50,220	0	0	150,701
72	256,358	0	46,488	50,998	0	0	158,871
73	266,612	0	47,418	51,808	0	0	167,386
74	277,277	0	48,366	52,650	0	0	176,261
75	288,368	0	49,334	53,526	0	0	185,509
76	299,903	0	50,320	54,436	0	0	195,146
77	311,899	0	51,327	55,383	0	0	205,189
78	324,375	0	52,353	56,368	0	0	215,653
79	337,350	0	53,400	57,393	0	0	226,557
80	350,844	0	54,468	58,458	0	0	237,918
81	364,878	0	55,558	59,566	0	0	249,754
82	379,473	0	56,669	60,718	0	0	262,086
83	394,652	0	57,802	61,916	0	0	274,933
84	410,438	0	58,958	63,163	0	0	288,317
85	426,855	0	60,138	64,459	0	0	302,259
86	443,929	0	61,340	65,807	0	0	316,782

Values shown in this presentation are hypothetical and not a promise of future performance.

Survivor Needs Timeline

Age	Need	Sources				Asset Balance	Annual Shortfall
		Earned Income	Social Security	Other Income	Earnings from Assets		
87	$461,687	$0	$62,567	$67,209	$0	$0	$331,911
88	480,154	0	63,818	68,667	0	0	347,669
89	499,360	0	65,095	70,183	0	0	364,082

Values shown in this presentation are hypothetical and not a promise of future performance.

Survivor Analysis Detail
In the event of Paul's death

Income Objective

Age	Income Need	Annual Need (Today's Dollars)	Annual Need (Future Dollars)	Capital Value
41	90.00%	$136,800	$136,800	$1,443,406
54	75.00%	$114,000	$189,818	703,881
65	50.00%	$76,000	$194,811	627,207
			Total capital value of income need	**2,774,494**

Income Sources

Income Name	First Year's Payment	From Age	To Age[1]	COLA	Capital Value
Earned Income	$65,000	41	65	4.00%	$1,087,164
Social Security	$53,689	41	90	2.00%	457,607
Pension	$30,760	65	90	0	68,320
Pension	$14,220	63	90	4.00%	55,360
	Total capital value of income sources				**1,668,451**

Any shortfall between income objectives and income sources	1,106,043
Any shortfall due to timing of the cash flows	0
Capital required to meet income goals	1,106,043
Total immediate cash needs	656,500
Total capital required	**1,762,543**
Available capital	965,500
Additional capital needed to meet survivor goals	**$797,043**

Assumptions:

Inflation rate: 4.00%
Assumed rate of return: 7.00%

Annual Social Security benefit inflation rate: 2.00%
Mortality: 90

---

[1] The absence of a "To Age" value indicates that this income source is a lump-sum (single payment).

An Overview of Social Security Benefits

What Is Social Security?

Social Security is a system of social insurance benefits available to all covered workers in the United States. Begun in 1937, the Social Security system covers a wide range of social programs. The term "Social Security," as it is commonly used, refers to the benefits provided under one part of the system, known by its acronym, OASDI, or Old-Age, Survivors, and Disability Insurance.

OASDI benefits are funded primarily by payroll taxes paid by covered employees, employers, and self-employed individuals. Both the OASDI portion of the payroll tax, as well as that part of the tax that goes to finance hospital insurance, HI (Medicare), are provided for under the Federal Insurance Contributions Act, FICA.

Insured Status

To qualify for benefits, a worker must be either "fully" insured or "currently" insured. An insured status is acquired by earning "credits", based on the wages or self-employment income earned during a year. In 2018, an individual must earn $1,320 in covered earnings to receive one credit and $5,280 to earn the maximum of four credits for the year.

A worker generally becomes fully insured by earning 40 credits, typically by working 10 years in covered employment.[1] To be considered currently insured, a worker must have at least six credits in the last 13 calendar quarters, ending with the quarter in which he or she became entitled to benefits.

All benefits are available if a worker is fully insured. Some benefits are not available if the worker is only currently insured. Special requirements apply to disability benefits.

What Benefits Are Available?

- **Worker's benefit:** This is a monthly income for a retired or disabled worker.

- **Spouse's benefit:** Refers to monthly income for the spouse or former spouse of a retired or disabled worker.

---

[1] For those working less than 10 years, an alternative test to determine fully-insured status may apply.

- **Widow(er)'s benefit:** Refers to monthly retirement income for the surviving spouse or former spouse of a deceased worker.

- **Child's benefit:** A monthly income for the dependent child of a deceased, disabled, or retired worker. To qualify, a child must be under age 18, or 18 or 19 and a full-time elementary or high school student, or 18 or over and disabled before 22.

- **Mother's or father's benefit:** Monthly income paid to a surviving spouse who is caring for a worker's dependent child who is under age 16 or disabled before age 22. If under age 62, the spouse of a retired worker receives the same benefit.

- **Parent's benefit:** Monthly income paid to the surviving dependent parent or dependent parents of a deceased worker.

On What Is the Amount of a Social Security Benefit Based?

In general, a covered worker's benefits, and those of his or her family members, are based on the worker's earnings record. The earnings taken into account are only those reported to the Social Security Administration (SSA), up to a certain annual maximum known as the "wage base." The wage base is indexed for inflation each year and effectively places a cap on the amount of Social Security benefits a worker can receive, regardless of earnings. The wage base for 2018 is $128,400.[1]

Using a worker's earnings record, the SSA calculates a number known as the Primary Insurance Amount, or PIA. The PIA is the basic value used to determine the dollar amount of benefits available to a worker and his or her family.

What Is the Benefit Amount?

The table below summarizes the benefit amounts generally payable under OASDI in the event of a worker's death, disability, or retirement. All monthly benefit amounts are subject to reduction to meet a "family maximum" limit. Individual benefits may also be reduced if the recipient has earned income in excess of specified limits.

---

[1] The wage base for 2017 was $127,200.

An Overview of Social Security Benefits

	Death[1]	Disability[2]	Retirement[3]
Worker's benefit		100% of PIA	100% of PIA
Spouse's benefit	N/A	50% of PIA	50% of PIA
Widow(er)'s benefit	100% of PIA	N/A	N/A
Child's benefit	75% of PIA	50% of PIA	50% of PIA
Mother's or father's benefit	75% of PIA	50% of PIA	50% of PIA
Parent's benefit	82.5% of PIA[4]	N/A	N/A

Workers age 60 or older and who are not receiving Social Security benefits automatically receive a paper Social Security Statement each year, listing the worker's earnings as well as providing estimated retirement, disability, and survivors benefits.

Earnings information may also be verified by calling the SSA directly at (800) 772-1213; TTY (800) 325-0778, Monday through Friday, 7:00AM to 7:00PM. On the internet, the SSA can be found at http:www.ssa.gov/.

---

[1] Reduced widow(er)'s benefits are available at age 60.

[2] Disability benefits are subject to a very strict definition of disability. At full retirement age (FRA), disability benefits cease and retirement benefits begin.

[3] Unreduced benefits are available at FRA. For those born before 1938, FRA is age 65. For individuals born after 1937, FRA gradually increases from age 65 to age 67. For example, for baby boomers born between 1943-1954, FRA is age 66. A larger retirement benefit is available to those who continue to work past FRA.

[4] If one parent qualifies, the benefit is 82.5% of the PIA. If both parents qualify, the benefit is 75% of the PIA to each.

Who Receives Social Security Benefits?

Social Security, also known by its acronym OASDI, or "Old Age, Survivors, and Disability Insurance", pays benefits to many individuals.

Who Receives Benefits?

- **Worker's benefit:** A monthly income for a retired or disabled worker.

- **Spouse's benefit:** Monthly income for the spouse or former spouse of a retired or disabled worker.

- **Widow(er)'s benefit:** Monthly retirement income for the surviving spouse or former spouse of a deceased worker.

- **Child's benefit:** Monthly income for the dependent child of a deceased, disabled or retired worker. To receive benefits, the child must be under age 18, over age 18 and attending elementary or high school full-time, or over age 18 and disabled before age 22.

- **Mother's or father's benefit:** Monthly income paid to a surviving spouse who is caring for a worker's dependent child who is under age 16 or disabled before age 22. If under age 62, the spouse of a retired worker receives the same benefit.

- **Parent's benefit:** Monthly income paid to the surviving dependent parent or parents of a deceased worker.

Social Security and Medicare Taxes

Federal Insurance Contributions Act (FICA) taxes are deducted from an employee's paycheck each pay period. Commonly referred to as Social Security taxes, there are actually two separate taxes: the Old-Age, Survivors and Disability Insurance (OASDI) tax and the Medicare Hospital Insurance (HI) tax. For calendar 2018, OASDI applies to the first $128,400 of wages.[1] HI is 1.45% of all wages.

Social Security Taxes for Employees				
Year	OASDI Wage Base	OASDI Rate	Maximum OASDI Tax	Hospital Insurance Rate
2015	$118,500	4.2%	$4,977	1.45%
2016	118,500	6.2%	7,347	1.45%
2017	127,200	6.2%	7,886	1.45%
2018	128,400	6.2%	7,961	1.45%

Social Security Taxes for the Self-Employed				
Year	OASDI Wage Base	OASDI Rate	Maximum OASDI Tax	Hospital Insurance Rate
2015	$118,500	10.4%	$12,324	2.90%
2016	118,500	12.4%	14,694	2.90%
2017	127,200	12.4%	15,773	2.90%
2018	128,400	12.4%	15,922	2.90%

Note: Individuals with $400 or more per year in net earnings from self-employment must file IRS schedule SE with his or her income tax return.

Calculating the Social Security Tax (2018)			
Employee Portion		Self-Employed	
Covered wages	$_____	Covered wages	$_____
6.2% of 1st $128,400	$_____	12.4% of 1st $128,400	$_____
1.45% of covered wages	$_____	2.9% of covered income	$_____
Total tax	$_____	Total tax	$_____

[1] Source: Social Security Administration. The dollar amount of wages subject to OASDI is termed the "wage base." The wage base is subject to adjustment each year for changes in the national average wage.

Patient Protection and Affordable Care Act

Beginning in 2013, the Patient Protection and Affordable Care Act imposed an additional Medicare tax on certain taxpayers:

- **0.9% health insurance tax:** Taxpayers with incomes above certain thresholds pay an additional HI tax of 0.9%. For an employee, the additional 0.9% effectively increases the HI tax from 1.45% to 2.35% on income in excess of the applicable threshold. For self-employed taxpayers, the additional tax of 0.9% effectively raises the HI tax rate to 3.8% of net self-employment income in excess of the applicable threshold. For self-employed individuals, the additional 0.9% tax is <u>not</u> deductible. The thresholds are $250,000 in case of a joint return (the earnings of both spouses are considered) or a surviving spouse, $125,000 in the case of a married individual filing a separate return, and $200,000 for any other taxpayer.

Taxation of Social Security Benefits

A portion of Social Security benefits may be subject to income taxation. The following worksheet will assist in determining that tax.

1. Social Security benefits for the year $ _____
2. 50% of line 1   _____
3. Modified adjusted gross income:
   a. AGI less net Social Security benefits received   _____
   b. Tax-exempt interest and dividends received or accrued   _____
   c. Line 3a plus line 3b   _____
4. Provisional income (line 2 plus line 3c)   _____
5. Applicable "first-tier" threshold   _____
6. Line 4 less line 5 (not less than zero)   _____
7. 50% of line 6   _____
8. Amount of benefits subject to tax (smaller of line 2 or line 7)   _____

If provisional income (line 4) does not exceed the corresponding first-tier threshold (line 5), no amount is taxable. However, if provisional income exceeds the corresponding threshold, continue with the worksheet below.

9. Applicable second-tier threshold[1] $ _____
10. Line 4 minus line 9 (if less than zero then enter zero)   _____
11. 85% of line 10   _____
12. Amount taxable under first-tier (from line 8, above)   _____
13. Applicable dollar amount[1]   _____
14. Smaller of line 12 or line 13   _____
15. Line 11 plus line 14   _____
16. 85% of line 1   _____
17. Amount of benefits subject to tax (smaller of line 15 or line 16)   _____

Filing Status	First Tier Threshold (for line 5)	Second Tier Threshold (for line 9)	Applicable Dollar Amount (for line 13)
Married filing jointly	$32,000	$44,000	$6,000
Married filing separately (but lived together part of the year)	$0	$0	$0
All others	$25,000	$34,000	$4,500

Note: This is not an official IRS worksheet.

Caution: Any increase in income, such as from the sale of stock or a retirement plan distribution, may subject one to an unexpected tax on the Social Security benefits.

[1] See applicable column in table.

Taxable Portion of Social Security Benefits

Status: Married Filing Joint	
Social Security benefits received	**$10,000**
One-half of Social Security benefits received	5,000
Income (taxable income)	25,000
Tax exempt income	0
Excluded income	0
Subtotal	**30,000**
Adjustments to gross income	0
Modified AGI	**30,000**
1st tier base amount	-32,000
Excess[1]	**0**

If "Excess" is zero, none of your benefits are taxable. If "Excess" is greater than zero, the calculation continues below.

2nd tier base amount	12,000
"Excess" minus "2nd tier base amount"[1]	0
The smaller of "Excess" or "2nd tier base amount"	0
One-half of amount on previous line	0
The smaller of "One-half of Social Security benefits received" and previous line	0
85% of "Excess minus 2nd tier base amount"	0
Sum of previous two lines	0
85% of "Social Security benefits received"	8,500
Taxable benefits (lesser of previous two lines)	**0**

[1] This amount cannot be less than zero.

How Work Affects Social
Security Benefits

Monthly Social Security benefits are paid to individuals for a number of reasons, including retirement, disability, and death. If a Social Security recipient also works, some of the benefits may be reduced if the income earned exceeds certain dollar amounts.

However, the month an individual reaches "Full Retirement Age," or FRA, Social Security benefits are no longer reduced, regardless of the amount of income earned.

FRA is the age at which an individual can expect to receive 100% of his or her normal retirement benefit, without reduction for early retirement. For those born in 1937 or earlier, FRA is age 65. For those born after 1937, FRA gradually increases until it reaches age 67 for those born in 1960 or later.

Age of Social Security Benefits Recipient	Annual Exempt Amount		One Dollar of Benefits Is Lost for Every Two or Three Dollars You Earn Over the Exempt Amount
	2017	2018	
Under FRA	$16,920	$17,040	Every Two Dollars
Year FRA Reached	$44,880	$45,360	Every Three Dollars
Month FRA Reached	No Limit	No Limit	No Loss of Benefits

Example (1): An individual begins receiving Social Security benefits at age 63 in January 2018, with an entitlement of $500 per month. If the retiree works and earns $27,040 during the year, he or she would have to give up $5,000 of Social Security benefits ($1 for every $2 over the $17,040 limit), but would still receive $1,000.

Example (2): Assume an individual reaches FRA in November 2018. Also assume the individual earns $58,032 during the year, with $48,360 of this amount being received in the first 10 months of the year. The individual would give up $1,000 in benefits, $1 for every $3 earned above the $45,360 limit. Assuming a Social Security retirement benefit of $500 per month, the individual would still receive $4,000 out of $5,000 for the first 10 months of the year. Full benefits of $1,000 ($500 per month) would be received for November and December, after FRA was reached.

How Work Affects Social Security Benefits

What Counts as Earnings?

Any wages earned after retirement from work as an employee and any net earnings from self-employment count as earnings. Wages include bonuses, commissions, fees, vacation pay, pay in lieu of vacation and cash tips of $20 or more in a month.

What Doesn't Count as Earnings?

- Investment income, including stock dividends, interest from savings accounts, income from annuities, limited partnership income and rental income from real estate you own (unless you are a real estate dealer).

- Income from Social Security, pensions, other retirement pay and Veterans Administration Benefits.

- Gifts or inheritances.

- Royalties received after age 65 from patents or copyrights obtained before that year.

- If you are a retired partner, retirement payments from partnerships don't count if:

  - The payments continue for life under a written agreement which provides for payments to all partners or a class of them; and

  - You rendered no services to the partnership during the taxable year the retirement payments were received; and

  - Your share of the partnership capital was paid to you in full before the end of the partnership's taxable year and there is no obligation to you other than retirement payments.

- Income from self-employment received in a year after the year a person becomes entitled to benefits. This refers to income which is not attributable to services performed after the month of entitlement.

Benefits Withheld Restored at Full Retirement Age (FRA)

When an individual has had benefits withheld as a result of the Social Security retirement earnings test, these "lost" benefits are later restored, beginning at FRA. In the benefit re-computation at FRA, the actuarial reduction that was applied in the initial computation

How Work Affects Social Security Benefits

(because the individual applied for benefits early) is adjusted (lessened) to reflect the number of months that he or she received no or partial benefits as a result of the earnings test. A larger benefit is then paid, beginning at FRA.

For example, assume a worker claims Social Security retirement benefits at age 62. He then takes a part-time job which, over time, results in 12 months of benefits being withheld. Once the worker reaches FRA, his retirement benefit will be re-calculated, in this case as if he had first taken Social Security retirement benefits 12 months later, at age 63, rather than at age 62. This recalculation effectively "recaptures" the benefits earlier withheld.

If spousal benefits are withheld under the earnings test, they will be adjusted upward when the spouse (not the worker) attains FRA. For a spouse who has already reached FRA, there is no subsequent adjustment to benefits to take into account months for which no or a partial benefit was paid as a result of the earnings test.

Social Security Retirement Benefits

One of the original motivations for the Social Security system was the need to provide income for retired workers. Today, the retirement benefits available through Social Security provide income not only to retired workers, but to qualifying dependents as well.

Qualifying For Retirement Benefits

To qualify for Social Security retirement benefits, a worker must meet two primary requirements:

- **Fully insured:** To be "fully" insured, a worker must have earned 40 Social Security "credits," generally by working 10 years in "covered" employment.[1] In 2018, an individual must earn $1,320 in covered earnings to receive one credit and $5,280 to earn the maximum of four credits for the year.

- **Age:** Be at least age 62.

Primary Insurance Amount

In general, Social Security benefit amounts are based on the worker's lifetime earnings record. Using this earnings record, the Social Security Administration (SSA) calculates a number known as the "Primary Insurance Amount," or PIA. The PIA is the basic value used to determine the dollar amount of benefits payable.

When to Take Social Security Retirement Benefits?

Once retirement payments begin, the benefit amount generally does not change, except for annual "cost-of-living" adjustments. Thus, the decision as to when to begin to take Social Security retirement benefits is a key one. Full Social Security retirement benefits are paid at "full retirement age" (FRA). A worker who elects to receive Social Security retirement benefits at his or her FRA can expect to receive 100% of the PIA. For those born in 1937 or earlier, FRA is age 65. For those born after 1937, FRA gradually increases until it reaches age 67 for those born in 1960 and later.

---

[1] Wages or self-employment income where the earnings are subject to Social Security tax (OASDI) and the Medicare (HI) tax. For those working less than 10 years, an alternative test to determine fully-insured status may apply.

Social Security Retirement Benefits

- **Early retirement (less):** Reduced retirement benefits may begin as early as age 62. For each month (up to 36 months) that a worker is under FRA, benefits are reduced by 5/9 of 1% of the PIA. For each month in excess of 36 months, benefits are reduced an additional 5/12 of 1% of the PIA.

- **Delayed retirement (more):** A worker who delays receiving retirement benefits beyond FRA can receive a larger benefit. For each year of delay up to age 70, the benefit is increased by a specific percentage of the PIA. The amount of extra credit for each year of delay will vary depending on the year of birth. No additional credit is given for delaying receipt of benefits past age 70.

Retirement Benefits for Family Members

Other individuals may receive retirement benefits based on a worker's account:

- **Spouse's benefit:** Beginning at age 62 (or younger, if caring for a child described below), a spouse is eligible for a retirement benefit based on the worker's earnings record. The spouse's benefit is generally equal to 50% of the worker's PIA, at the spouse's FRA. Unless the spouse is caring for a child, the benefit amount is reduced if the spouse begins receiving benefits before FRA. If the spouse is entitled to a larger benefit based on his or her own work record, the larger benefit is paid.

- **Child:** A monthly retirement benefit is available to a dependent child. For this purpose, a child must be under age 18, or age 18 or 19 and a full-time elementary or high school student, or 18 or over and disabled before age 22, and unmarried. The benefit is equal to 50% of the worker's PIA.

- **Divorced spouse:** If a prior marriage lasted at least 10 years, at age 62 a divorced spouse may be entitled to retirement benefits based on the worker's record. Generally, the retirement benefit amount is 50% of the worker's PIA. The divorced spouse must not be married and benefits are reduced for early retirement.

Maximum Family Benefit

If the total benefits payable based on a retired worker's Social Security account exceed certain limits (which change each year) the individual dollar amounts for a spouse and any dependent children are proportionately reduced to bring the total within the family maximum limit.[1] Neither the worker's benefit amount nor any benefit payable to a divorced spouse is reduced because of the family maximum limit.

Federal Income Taxation of Social Security Benefits

Under federal income tax law, Social Security benefits may be subject to income tax. If one-half of Social Security benefits plus "modified adjusted gross income" (often the same as adjusted gross income) exceed a specified threshold, then a portion (up to 85%) of social security benefits is taxable. For married couples filing jointly this threshold is $32,000; for most others it is $25,000.[2] State or local income tax treatment of Social Security benefits can vary.

Reduced Benefits Because of Excess Earnings

If an individual begins receiving retirement benefits before reaching FRA, and also works, the retirement benefit will be temporarily reduced if earnings exceed certain limits. For this purpose, "earnings" generally include wages received as an employee or the net income received from self-employment. The reduction amount is calculated on a monthly basis and varies depending on the individual's current age in relation to his or her FRA.

- **Under FRA:** One dollar of benefits is lost for every two dollars earned over an annual total of $17,040 ($1,420 monthly).[3]

- **The year FRA is reached:** One dollar of benefits is lost for every three dollars earned over $45,360 ($3,780 monthly).[3]

- **At FRA:** Once FRA is reached, there is no reduction in an individual's benefit, regardless of how much is earned. Any benefits that were withheld earlier because of excess earnings are credited to the individual's account, resulting in a larger retirement benefit beginning at FRA.

- **Special rule for the first year of retirement:** A special rule applies to the first year of retirement, to benefit an individual who, before just retiring, earns more than the

---

[1] The family maximum benefit is based on a formula and ranges from 150% to 180% of the worker's benefit.

[2] The threshold is $0 for those who are married filing separately and who lived with their spouse any time during the year.

[3] 2018 values. These "exempt" amounts are subject to adjustment for inflation each calendar year.

annual limit. Under this rule, unreduced Social Security benefits are paid for any month after benefits begin that an individual does not earn more than the monthly exempt wage amount.

Verifying Social Security Records

Because Social Security benefits are based on a worker's lifetime earnings history, it is important to insure that all covered earnings are accurately listed on SSA records. There are several ways to do this:

- **Paper statements:** Workers age 60 or older and who are not receiving Social Security benefits automatically receive a paper Social Security Statement each year, listing the worker's earnings as well as providing estimated retirement, disability, and survivors benefits. A paper earnings statement may also be requested by completing Form SSA-7004, *Request for Social Security Statement*, and mailing it to the address on the form. The statement will arrive by mail in four to six weeks.

- **Online statements:** The same information previously provided on the paper statements is now available on an electronic statement. These electronic statements include a summary of a worker's earnings, as well as providing estimated retirement, disability, and survivor's benefits. To obtain a statement, an individual will need to create an account on the Social Security website at http://www.ssa.gov/myaccount. Each person who wishes to sign up must be at least age 18 and have a valid Social security number, e-mail address, and United States mailing address.

- **Telephone:** Earnings information may also be verified by calling the SSA directly at (800) 772-1213; TTY (800) 325-0778, Monday through Friday, from 7:00AM to 7:00PM.

Estimating Social Security Retirement Benefits

The Social Security administration, on its website, offers a calculator which allows an individual to estimate his or her retirement benefits, using the individual's own earnings history, taken directly from Social Security records. This calculator can be reached at: http://www.ssa.gov/planners/

Seek Professional Guidance

For many Americans, the retirement benefits provided by Social Security form an important part of their retirement income. A qualified financial professional can answer many Social Security questions. Social Security questions can also be answered by directly contacting the SSA.

When to Take Social Security Retirement Benefits

Research by the Federal government indicates that Social Security retirement benefits typically make up almost one-third of the income of Americans age 65 or older.[1] Thus, the decision as to when to begin to take Social Security retirement benefits is an important one. Once you decide to begin receiving Social Security retirement benefits, the initial benefit will generally serve as the "base" amount for the rest of your life, subject only to adjustment for increases in the cost of living.

The question is made a little easier to answer if you separate when you want to retire from when you want to begin receiving Social Security retirement benefits; these two events don't necessarily have to occur at the same time. An understanding of how your benefits are calculated, how they are taxed, and what happens if you continue to work after beginning to receive benefits, is also important.

"Full" Retirement Age – "Full" Benefits

For many years, full retirement age (FRA), the age at which "full" benefits – 100% of an individual's Primary Insurance Amount[2] (PIA) – are available was set at age 65. This is still true for those born in 1937 or earlier. However, for those born in 1938 or later, FRA gradually increases until it reaches age 67 for those born in 1960 or later.

Early Retirement – Reduced Benefits

Age 62 is generally the earliest age that someone can begin to receive Social Security retirement benefits. However, if retirement benefits begin before the "full" retirement age, the benefit paid is reduced to reflect the income that will be paid over a longer period of time. The amount of the reduction varies with the year of birth. For example, an individual born in 1937 (FRA = age 65) who began receiving benefits at age 62 had his or her retirement benefit reduced to 80% of what it would have been had they chosen to wait until FRA. However, for a worker born in 1962, for whom FRA is age 67, choosing to receive retirement benefits at age 62 results in an initial benefit reduced to 70% of what it would have been had the individual waited to age 67.

---

[1] See: "Income of the Aged Chartbook, 2014." Social Security Administration, April 2016, page 16.

[2] The PIA is calculated by the Social Security Administration based on a person's lifetime earnings record.

When to Take Social Security Retirement Benefits

Delay Retirement – A Bigger Benefit

What happens if you decide to wait and take your retirement benefits later than your FRA? You get paid for waiting, in the form of a larger retirement benefit. For each year beyond your FRA that you delay receiving retirement benefits, up to age 70, your benefit is increased by a specified percentage of the PIA. The amount of the credit for each year of delay beyond FRA will vary depending on the year of birth. For example, an individual born in 1935 who delayed receiving benefits until age 70 had his or her benefit increased by 6% for each year (five years in this case) beyond the FRA of age 65. For those born in 1943 and later, delaying retirement increases their benefit by 8% per year for each year they wait beyond their FRA.

Which Is Better? – Early or Late?

One way to answer this question is to perform a "break-even" analysis which estimates the age at which the total value of higher benefits (from delaying retirement) is greater than the total value of lower benefits (from starting retirement early).

If you expect to live longer than this break-even age you would likely benefit from delaying the start of Social Security retirement benefits. If you are in poor health, or if members of your family tend to die at relatively young ages, you will likely receive a greater benefit by beginning your benefits early.

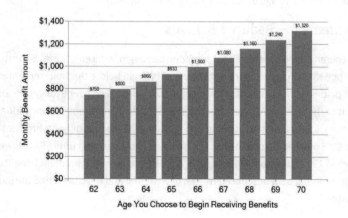

This example assumes a monthly benefit of $1,000 at a full retirement age of 66.

When to Take Social Security Retirement Benefits

Federal Income Taxation of Social Security Benefits

Under federal law, Social Security benefits may be subject to income tax. If one-half of your Social Security benefits plus your "modified adjusted gross income" (often the same as adjusted gross income) exceed certain limits, then a portion (up to 85%) of your benefits is taxable. For married couples filing jointly this threshold is $32,000; for all others it is $25,000.[1] State or local tax treatment of Social Security benefits can vary.

If You Continue Working

If you begin taking Social Security retirement benefits early and also continue working, your retirement payments will be temporarily reduced if your earnings exceed certain limits. For this purpose, "earnings" generally include wages received as an employee or the net income received from self-employment. The amount of the reduction will vary:

- **Under FRA:** One dollar of benefits is lost for every two dollars you earn over $17,040 ($1,420 monthly).[2]

- **The year you reach FRA:** One dollar of benefits is lost for every three dollars you earn over $45,360 ($3,780 monthly).[2]

Once you reach FRA there is no reduction in your retirement benefits, regardless of how much you earn.

Seek Professional Guidance

The decision as to when to take Social Security retirement benefits is an important one. A wrong decision can cost a retiree literally thousands of dollars. The guidance of financial professionals, to insure that all relevant issues are considered, is highly recommended.

---

[1] The threshold is $0 for those who are married filing separately and who lived with their spouse at any time during the year.
[2] 2018 values. These "exempt amounts" are subject to adjustment for inflation each calendar year.

Social Security Break-Even

Assumptions:

Analysis date: 1/1/2018
Date of birth: 1/1/1965
Mortality: 90
Social Security benefit rate of inflation: 2.00%

Starting at Age	Initial Annual Benefit	Total Benefit
62	$23,615	$874,972
70	$49,014	$1,190,903

At age 79 the cumulative benefits received starting at age 70 has surpassed the cumulative benefits starting at age 62.

Cumulative Social Security Benefits

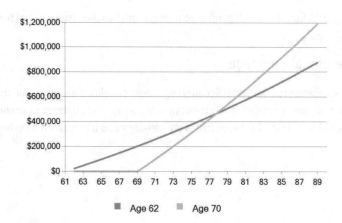

■ Age 62   ■ Age 70

The Social Security "Blackout" Period

When a worker who is covered by Social Security dies, certain monthly benefits may be available to his or her survivors. Depending on the situation, these can include:

- **Mother's or Father's benefit:** Monthly income paid to a surviving spouse who is caring for a worker's dependent child who is under age 16, or disabled before age 22.

- **Child's benefit:** A monthly income for the dependent child of a deceased, disabled, or retired worker. To qualify, a child must be under age 18, or age 18 or 19 and a full-time elementary or high school student, or 18 or over and disabled before age 22.

- **Widow(er)'s benefit:** Monthly retirement income for the surviving spouse (or former spouse) of a deceased worker.

- **Parent's benefit:** Monthly income paid to the surviving dependent parent or dependent parents of a deceased worker.

The Social Security "Blackout" Period

Social Security survivor benefits are paid only for a limited period of time. In young families with minor children, the death of one spouse leaves the surviving spouse to raise the children alone. The chart below graphs the Social Security survivor benefits typically payable in a hypothetical case in which a 26 year-old surviving spouse is left behind to raise a three year-old child.

- The surviving spouse receives a Mother's or Father's benefit until the child reaches age 16.

- The child receives a Child's benefit until reaching age 18.

- At retirement, the surviving spouse receives a Widow(er)'s benefit. The earliest age that this benefit can be paid is age 60. In this example, the survivor has chosen to receive this benefit at age 62.

The Social Security "Blackout" Period

- Between age 40, when the child reaches 18, and age 62, when the survivor begins to receive retirement benefits, no Social Security benefits are payable. This is known as the Social Security "blackout" period.

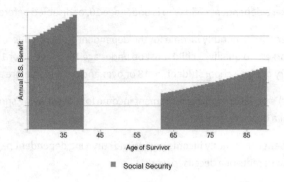

How would you cover the gap in the blackout period?

Early or Delayed Retirement's Effect on Social Security Benefits

Full retirement age (FRA) is the age at which "full" Social Security retirement benefits – 100% of an individual's Primary Insurance Amount (PIA)[1] – are available. For many years, FRA was set at age 65. Beginning with individuals born in 1938, FRA gradually increases until it reaches age 67 for those born in 1960 or later.

If an individual chooses to receive retirement benefits before his or her FRA, the benefit paid is reduced to reflect the fact that income will be paid over a longer period of time. Similarly, if an individual chooses to delay retirement benefits, the benefit is increased for each year of delay (up to age 70) beyond FRA. The table below shows the effect of early or delayed retirement on an individual's retirement benefit, depending on the year of birth.

Retirement Benefit as a Percentage of the Primary Insurance Amount at Various Ages[2]									
Year of Birth	Full Retirement Age (FRA)	Credit for each year of delayed retirement after FRA (Percent)	Benefit as a % of PIA at Age						
			62	63	64	65	66	67	70
1924	65	3	80	$86^2/_3$	$93^1/_3$	100	103	106	115
1925-1926	65	3½	80	$86^2/_3$	$93^1/_3$	100	103½	107	117½
1927-1928	65	4	80	$86^2/_3$	$93^1/_3$	100	104	108	120
1929-1930	65	4½	80	$86^2/_3$	$93^1/_3$	100	104½	109	122½
1931-1932	65	5	80	$86^2/_3$	$93^1/_3$	100	105	110	125
1933-1934	65	5½	80	$86^2/_3$	$93^1/_3$	100	105½	111	127½

[1] The PIA is calculated by the Social Security Administration based on a person's lifetime earnings record.
[2] Source: Social Security Administration.

Early or Delayed Retirement's Effect on Social Security Benefits

Retirement Benefit as a Percentage of the Primary Insurance Amount at Various Ages[1]									
		Credit for each year of delayed retirement after FRA (Percent)	Benefit as a % of PIA at Age						
Year of Birth	Full Retirement Age (FRA)		62	63	64	65	66	67	70
1935-1936	65	6	80	$86^2/_3$	$93^1/_3$	100	106	112	130
1937	65	6½	80	$86^2/_3$	$93^1/_3$	100	106½	113	132½
1938	65, 2 mos	6½	$79^1/_6$	$85^5/_9$	$92^2/_9$	$98^8/_9$	$105^5/_{12}$	$111^{11}/_{12}$	$131^5/_{12}$
1939	65, 4 mos	7	$78^1/_3$	$84^4/_9$	$91^1/_9$	$97^7/_9$	$104^2/_3$	$111^2/_3$	$132^2/_3$
1940	65, 6 mos	7	77½	$83^1/_3$	90	$96^2/_3$	103½	110½	131½
1941	65, 8 mos	7½	$76^2/_3$	$82^2/_9$	$88^8/_9$	$95^5/_9$	102½	110	132½
1942	65, 10 mos	7½	$75^5/_6$	$81^1/_9$	$87^7/_9$	$94^4/_9$	101¼	108¾	131¼
1943-1954	66	8	75	80	$86^2/_3$	$93^1/_3$	100	108	132
1955	66, 2 mos	8	$74^1/_6$	$79^1/_6$	$85^5/_9$	$92^2/_9$	$98^8/_9$	$106^2/_3$	$130^2/_3$
1956	66, 4 mos	8	$73^1/_3$	$78^1/_3$	$84^4/_9$	$91^1/_9$	$97^7/_9$	$105^1/_3$	$129^1/_3$
1957	66, 6 mos	8	72½	77½	$83^1/_3$	90	$96^2/_3$	104	128
1958	66, 8 mos	8	$71^2/_3$	$76^2/_3$	$82^2/_9$	$88^8/_9$	$95^5/_9$	$102^2/_3$	$126^2/_3$
1959	66, 10 mos	8	$70^5/_6$	$75^5/_6$	$81^1/_9$	$87^7/_9$	$94^4/_9$	$101^1/_3$	$125^1/_3$
1960 and later	67	8	70	75	80	$86^2/_3$	$93^1/_3$	100	124

[1] Source: Social Security Administration.

Social Security Survivor Benefits

While Social Security is frequently associated with retirement, it also provides benefits to qualifying survivors of deceased, insured workers.

Qualifying for Survivor Benefits

The type of survivor benefits payable by Social Security depends on whether a worker is "fully" insured or "currently" insured at the time of death.

- **Fully insured:** To be "fully" insured, a worker must have earned 40 Social Security "credits," generally by working 10 years in "covered" employment.[1] In 2018, an individual must earn $1,320 in covered earnings to receive one credit and $5,280 to earn the maximum of four credits for the year. For a fully insured worker, survivor's benefits may be payable to:

  - A spouse.

  - A divorced spouse.

  - A dependent child (or children).

  - A dependent parent (or parents).

- **Currently insured:** To be "currently" insured, a worker must have earned at least six Social Security "credits" during the 13-quarter period ending with the quarter in which death occurred. For a currently insured worker, survivor's benefits may be payable to:

  - A spouse, if caring for a dependent child.

  - A divorced spouse, if caring for a dependent child.

  - A dependent child (or children).

Primary Insurance Amount

In general, Social Security benefit amounts are based on a worker's lifetime earnings record. Using this earnings record, the Social Security Administration (SSA) calculates a number

---

[1] Wages or self-employment income where the earnings are subject to Social Security tax (OASDI) and the Medicare (HI) tax. For those working less than 10 years, an alternative test to determine fully-insured status may apply.

known as the "Primary Insurance Amount," or PIA. The PIA is the basic value used to determine the dollar amount of benefits payable.

Benefits for Surviving Family Members

The following benefits are payable to qualified surviving family members:

- **Mother's or Father's benefit:** This is a monthly benefit of 75% of the PIA, payable at any age, to a surviving spouse (or surviving divorced spouse), who is caring for a child of the deceased worker, under the age of 16 or disabled before age 22. The worker could have been either fully insured or currently insured at the time of death. The benefit ends when there are no children of the deceased worker under age 16 or disabled who are entitled to a child's benefit.

- **Child's benefit:** A monthly benefit equal to 75% of the deceased parent's PIA is available to a dependent child of the deceased worker. The worker could have been either fully insured or currently insured at the time of death. For this purpose, a child must be under age 18, or age 18 or 19 and a full-time elementary or high school student, or 18 or over and disabled before age 22, and unmarried. Generally, a child's benefit ends when the child dies, reaches age 18 and is neither disabled nor a full-time elementary or secondary student, or the child marries.

- **Widow(er)'s benefit:** This is a monthly benefit generally equal to 100% of the deceased worker's PIA, available to a surviving spouse or surviving divorced spouse. The deceased worker must have been fully insured at the time of death. A surviving spouse or surviving divorced spouse must be either (1) age 60 or over; or (2) at least age 50 but not age 60 and disabled, not entitled to a retirement benefit equal to or larger than the worker's PIA, and not married. In addition, a surviving spouse must have been married to the deceased worker for at least nine months just before the worker died, or fit one of a number of situations regarding being the parent of a child with the deceased worker. A surviving divorced spouse must have been married to the deceased worker for 10 years just before the date the divorce became final.

Social Security Survivor Benefits

- **Parent's benefit:** Provides a monthly benefit equal to 87.5% of the deceased worker's PIA if one parent qualifies or 75% of the deceased worker's PIA to each parent, if two parents qualify. The worker must have been fully insured at the time of death. Generally, to qualify a parent must be at least age 62, must not be entitled to a retirement benefit equal to or larger than the amount of the unadjusted parent's benefit after any increase to the minimum benefit, must have been receiving at least one-half of his or her support from the deceased worker, must have filed evidence with the Social Security Administration that the support requirement was met within certain time limits,[1] and must not have remarried since the insured worker's death.

- **Lump-sum payment:** A one-time, lump-sum payment of $255 may be made to the survivors of a worker who was either fully or currently insured at the time of death. Generally, the lump-sum payment is paid to a surviving spouse, living with the deceased as husband and wife, in the same household. If there is no spouse to receive the lump-sum payment, the payment is made to a child or children of the deceased. If there is more than one child, each child is entitled to an equal share of the lump sum.

Maximum Family Benefit

If the total benefits payable based on a deceased worker's Social Security account exceed certain limits (which change each year), the individual dollar amounts for all beneficiaries (except a surviving divorced spouse) are proportionately reduced to bring the total within the family maximum limit.

Federal Income Taxation of Social Security Benefits

Under federal income tax law, Social Security benefits may be subject to income tax. If one-half of Social Security benefits plus "modified adjusted gross income" (often the same as adjusted gross income) exceed a specified threshold, then a portion (up to 85%) of social security benefits is taxable. For married couples filing jointly this threshold is $32,000; for most others it is $25,000.[2] State or local income tax treatment of Social Security benefits can vary.

---

[1] Generally, within two years of the deceased worker's death.

[2] The threshold is $0 for those who are married filing separately and who lived with their spouse at any time during the year.

Reduced Benefits Because of Excess Earnings

Full retirement age (FRA) is the age at which an individual can receive "full" retirement benefits, e.g., 100% of the PIA. For those born in 1937 and earlier, FRA is age 65. For those born after 1937, FRA gradually increases until it reaches age 67 for those born in 1960 and later. If an individual begins receiving Social Security survivor's benefits before reaching FRA, and also works, the survivor's benefit will be temporarily reduced if earnings exceed certain limits. For this purpose, "earnings" generally include wages received as an employee or the net income received from self-employment. The amount of the reduction is calculated on a monthly basis and will vary depending on the individual's current age in relation to his or her FRA.

- **Under FRA:** One dollar of benefits is lost for every two dollars earned over an annual total of $17,040 ($1,420 monthly).[1]

- **The calendar year FRA is reached:** One dollar of benefits is lost for every three dollars earned over $45,360 ($3,780 monthly).[2]

- **At FRA:** Once FRA is reached, there is no reduction in an individual's benefit, regardless of how much is earned.

Verifying Social Security Records

Because Social Security benefits are based on a worker's lifetime earnings history, it is important to insure that all covered earnings are accurately listed on SSA records. There are several ways to do this:

- **Paper statements:** Workers age 60 or older and who are not receiving Social Security benefits automatically received a paper Social Security Statement each year. Listing the worker's earnings as well as providing estimated retirement, disability, and survivors benefits. A paper earnings statement may also be requested by completing Form SSA-7004, *Request for Social Security Statement*, and mailing it to the address on the form. The statement will arrive by mail in four to six weeks.

---

[1] 2018 values. These "exempt" amounts are subject to adjustment for inflation each calendar year.

- **Online statements:** The same information previously provided on the paper statements is now available on an electronic statement. These electronic statements include a summary of a worker's earnings, as well as providing estimated retirement, disability, and survivor's benefits. To obtain a statement, an individual will need to create an account on the Social Security website at http://www.ssa.gov/myaccount. Each person who wishes to sign up must be at least age 18 and have a valid Social Security number, e-mail address, and United States mailing address.

- **Telephone:** Earnings information may also be verified by calling the SSA directly at (800) 772-1213; TTY (800) 325-0778, Monday through Friday, from 7:00AM to 7:00PM.

Estimating Social Security Survivor Benefits

The Social Security Administration, on its website, offers a calculator which allows an individual to estimate his or her survivor benefits, using the individual's own earnings history, taken directly from Social Security records. This calculator can be reached at: http:www.ssa.gov/planners/

Seek Professional Guidance

The survivor benefits provided by Social Security can be an important lifeline for a family struggling to keep afloat after the death of a breadwinner. Meeting the many requirements to qualify for survivor benefits can be confusing. A trained financial professional can answer many Social Security questions. Questions can also be answered by directly contacting the SSA.

Social Security Disability Benefits

Many Americans associate the term "Social Security" primarily with retirement benefits. However, Social Security also provides benefits to workers who are severely disabled.

There is a complex maze of requirements that must be met to qualify for Social Security disability benefits, and many applicants have difficulty meeting these requirements. In 2015, for example, only 35.0% of initial Social Security disability claims were accepted.[1]

"Insured" For Disability Benefits

To be "insured" for Social Security disability benefits, a worker must generally meet two tests:[2]

- **Fully insured:** First, he or she must be "fully" insured, usually achieved by earning 40 "credits," over 10 years in "covered" employment. In 2018, an individual must earn $1,320 in covered earnings to receive one credit and $5,280 to earn the maximum of four credits for the year. For those with less than 10 years in covered employment, an alternative test applies (an absolute minimum of six quarterly credits is required), summarized in the "Duration of Work Test" table[3] shown below:

Duration of Work Test

Age Disability Occurs	Work Generally Required
Younger than age 28	1.5 years
30	2.0 years
34	3 years
38	4 years
42	5 years
44	5.5 years
46	6 years
48	6.5 years
50	7 years
52	7.5 years

[1] Annual Statistical Report on the Social Security Disability Insurance Program, 2016, October 2017. Table 61, Medical decisions at the initial adjudicative level, by year of application and program, all decisions.

[2] Certain blind individuals need only meet the "fully" insured test to qualify for disability benefits.

[3] See SSA Publication No. 05-10029, Social Security Disability Benefits, January, 2017.

Social Security Disability Benefits

Age Disability Occurs	Work Generally Required
54	8 years
56	8.5 years
58	9 years
60	9.5 years

- **20/40 rule:** A worker must have at least 20 credits during a 40-calendar quarter period (five out of 10 years) that ends with the calendar quarter the worker is determined to be disabled. Alternative tests apply to individuals disabled before age 31, summarized in the "Recent Work Test" table[1] shown on the following page.

Recent Work Test

When Disabled	Work Generally Required
In or before the quarter age 24 is reached.	1½ years of work during the three-year period ending when the disability began.
In the quarter after reaching age 24, but before the quarter age 31 is reached.	Work at least one-half of the time, beginning with the quarter after age 21 is reached, and ending with the quarter disability begins.
In the quarter age 31 is reached, or later.	Work at least five years out of the last 10 ending with the quarter disability begins.

Definition of "Disability"

A worker is "disabled" when he or she is unable to work because of a medical problem or condition that has lasted, or can be expected to last, for a continuous period of 12 months, or that will result in the worker's death. Also, a worker must be unable to engage in any "substantial gainful activity." No benefits are paid for short-term or partial disability.

---

[1] See SSA Publication No. 05-10029, Social Security Disability Benefits, January 2017.

Applying For Social Security Disability

A person who becomes disabled should apply for disability benefits as soon as possible. In addition to a mandatory five-month waiting period, the time needed to process a disability claim can be lengthy. In considering a claim, five questions will be raised:

1. **Is the individual currently working?** If the answer is "yes," or if the individual is earning more than $1,180 per month,[1] the claim will generally be denied.
2. **Is the medical problem "severe?"** The medical condition must significantly limit the individual's ability to do basic work tasks such as walking or sitting.
3. **Is the medical condition on the List of Impairments?** Certain medical problems are so severe that an individual who suffers from one of these conditions is automatically considered to be disabled.
4. **Can the worker do the work he or she did before?** Can the worker do the same job he or she held immediately before becoming disabled? If yes, the claim will be generally be denied.
5. **Can the worker do any type of work?** If yes, the claim will usually be denied.

Primary Insurance Amount

In general, Social Security benefit amounts are based on the worker's lifetime earnings record. Using this earnings record, the SSA calculates a number known as the "Primary Insurance Amount," or PIA. The PIA is the basic value used to determine the dollar amount of benefits payable to a worker and his or her qualifying dependents.

The Worker's Disability Benefit

If a worker is determined to be disabled, the benefit paid to the worker is generally 100% of his or her PIA, calculated as if the worker had reached "full retirement age" (FRA). FRA is the age at which unreduced Social Security retirement benefits are paid. This age varies with the year of birth. For those born in 1937 or earlier, FRA is age 65. For those born after 1937, FRA gradually increases until it reaches age 67 for those born in 1960 or later.

Disability payments will continue until the earliest of: (1) the worker recovers and the disability ends, or (2) the worker reaches FRA, at which point the disability benefits become retirement benefits, or (3) the worker dies.

---

[1] 2018 value. For blind individuals, this value is $1,970 per month.

Benefits for Family Members

Other individuals may receive benefits based on a disabled worker's account:

- **Spouse's benefit:** At age 62 (or younger, if caring for a child described below), a spouse is eligible for a benefit based on the worker's record. The spouse's benefit is generally equal to 50% of the worker's PIA, at the spouse's FRA. Unless the spouse is caring for a child, the benefit amount is reduced if the spouse begins receiving benefits before FRA. If the spouse is entitled to a larger benefit based on his or her own work record, the larger benefit is paid.

- **Child:** A monthly benefit is available to a dependent child. For this purpose, a child must be under age 18, or age 18 or 19 and a full-time elementary or high school student, or 18 or over and disabled before age 22, and unmarried. Generally, the benefit is equal to 50% of the worker's PIA.

- **Divorced spouse:** If a prior marriage lasted at least 10 years, at age 62 a divorced spouse may be entitled to a benefit based on the worker's record, equal to 50% of the worker's PIA. The divorced spouse must not be married and the benefit amount is reduced for early retirement.

- **Maximum family benefit:** If the total benefits payable based on a worker's Social Security account exceed certain limits (which change each year) the individual benefit amounts for a current spouse and/or child are reduced to bring the total within the family maximum limit. Neither the worker's benefit amount, nor any benefit payable to a divorced spouse, is reduced.

Federal Income Taxation of Social Security Benefits

Under federal income tax law, Social Security benefits may be subject to income tax. If one-half of Social Security benefits plus "modified adjusted gross income" (often the same as adjusted gross income) exceed a specified threshold, then a portion (up to 85%) of social security benefits is taxable. For married couples filing jointly this threshold is $32,000; for most others it is $25,000.[1] State or local income tax treatment of Social Security benefits can vary.

---

[1] The threshold is $0 for those who are married filing separately and who lived with their spouse at any time during the year.

Reduced Benefits Because of Excess Earnings

If an individual[1] begins receiving Social Security benefits before reaching FRA and also works, the benefit will be temporarily reduced if earnings exceed certain limits. For this purpose, "earnings" generally include wages received as an employee or the net income received from self-employment. The reduction amount is calculated on a monthly basis and will vary depending on the individual's current age in relation to his or her FRA.

- **Under FRA:** One dollar of benefits is lost for every two dollars earned over an annual total of $17,040 ($1,420 monthly).[2]

- **The year FRA is reached:** One dollar of benefits is lost for every three dollars earned over $45,360 ($3,780 monthly).[2]

- **At FRA:** Once FRA is reached, disability benefits become retirement benefits, and there is no reduction in an individual's benefit, regardless of how much is earned.

Verifying Social Security Records

Because Social Security benefits are based on a worker's lifetime earnings history, it is important to insure that all covered earnings are accurately listed on SSA records. There are several ways to do this:

- **Paper statements:** Workers age 60 or older and who are not receiving Social Security benefits automatically receive a paper Social Security Statement each year, listing the worker's earnings as well as providing estimated retirement, disability, and survivors benefits. A paper earnings statement may also be requested by completing Form SSA-7004, *Request for Social Security Statement*, and mailing it to the address on the form. The statement will arrive by mail in four to six weeks.

- **Online statements:** The same information previously provided on the paper statements is now available on an electronic statement. These electronic statements

---

[1] In a disability situation, this would usually apply only to a qualifying dependent; if the worker is able to work, he or she would generally no longer be considered "disabled" and disability benefits would cease.

[2] 2018 value. These "exempt" amounts are subject to adjustment for inflation each calendar year.

Social Security Disability Benefits

include a summary of a worker's earnings, as well as providing estimated retirement, disability, and survivor's benefits. To obtain a statement, an individual will need to create an account on the Social Security website at http://www.ssa.gov/myaccount. Each person who wishes to sign up must be at least age 18 and have a valid Social Security number, e-mail address, and United States mailing address.

- **Telephone:** Earnings information may also be verified by calling the SSA directly at (800) 772-1213; TTY (800) 325-0778, Monday through Friday, from 7:00AM to 7:00PM.

Estimating Social Security Disability Benefits

The Social Security Administration, on its website, offers a calculator which allows an individual to estimate his or her disability benefits, using the individual's own earnings history, taken directly from Social Security records. This calculator can be reached at: http:www.ssa.gov/planners/

Seek Professional Guidance

Applying for Social Security disability benefits can be a confusing process. Trained financial professionals can answer many Social Security disability questions. Social Security information can also be obtained by directly contacting the SSA.

Medicare Parts A and B

Consider What Medicare Does and Does Not Cover

Medicare is a health insurance program operated by the federal government. Benefits are available to qualifying individuals age 65 or older, certain disabled individuals under age 65, and those suffering from end-stage renal disease. The traditional Medicare program consists of two main parts: Part A, Hospital Insurance and Part B, Medical Insurance. There are clearly defined limits as to what Medicare will, and will not, pay.

Medicare (Part A) 2018 Hospital Insurance
Covered Services per Benefit Period

Service	Benefit	Medicare Pays	You Pay
Hospitalization: Semiprivate room and board, general nursing and miscellaneous hospital services and supplies. Includes meals, special care units, drugs, lab tests, diagnostic X-rays, medical supplies, operating and recovery room, anesthesia and rehabilitation services.	Medicare pays all covered costs for first 60 days, except the first $1,340. For the 61st through 90th days, it pays all except $335 a day. There are also 60 nonrenewable reserve days that can be used when the 90 days are past. Medicare pays all except the first $670 for each reserve day.		
Post-hospital skilled nursing facility care (in a facility approved by Medicare): You must have been in a hospital for at least three days in a row and enter the facility within 30 days after having been discharged from the hospital.	**First 20 days.**	All costs.	Nothing.
	Next 80 days.	All but $167.50	$167.50 per day
	Medicare and private insurance will not pay for most nursing home care, and you pay for custodial care.		
Home health care: Post-institutional care. You must have been in a hospital for at least three days in a row or have been in a skilled nursing facility following a hospital stay.	Pays the cost of 100 home visits, if made under a physician's treatment plan.	Full cost.	Nothing for services; 20% of approved amount for durable medical equipment.
Hospice care: May exceed the 210 days of care if recertified as terminally ill.	Two 90-day periods and one 30-day period.	All but limited costs for outpatient drugs and inpatient respite care.	Limited cost sharing for outpatient drugs and inpatient respite care.
Blood.	Blood.	All but first three pints.	For first three pints.

Medicare Parts A and B

Medicare (Part B) 2018 Medical Insurance Covered Services per Calendar Year Standard Monthly Premium: $134.00

Service	Benefit	Medicare Pays	You Pay[1]
Medical expense: Doctor's services, inpatient and outpatient medical services and supplies, physical and speech therapy, ambulance, etc.	Medicare pays for medical services in or out of hospital. Some insurance policies pay less (or nothing) for hospital outpatient medical services in a doctor's office.	80% of approved amount (after $183.00 deductible). 50% of approved charges for most outpatient mental health services.	$183.00 deductible[2] plus 20% of approved amount and limited charges above approved amount.[3] 50% of approved charges for mental health services.
Home health care[4].	Unlimited, if made under a physician's treatment plan.	Full cost.	Nothing for services; 20% of approved amount for durable medical equipment.
Outpatient hospital treatment.	Unlimited if medically necessary.	80% of approved amount (after $183.00 deductible).	$183.00 deductible[1] plus 20% of balance of approved amount.
Blood: Any blood deductibles satisfied under Part B will reduce the blood deductible requirements.	Blood.	80% of approved amount (after first three pints).	$183.00 deductible[1] plus first three pints plus 20% of balance of approved amount.

Note: If the period of hospitalization covers two calendar years, no new deductible is required for the new year. These figures are for 2018 and are subject to change each year.

---

[1] You pay for charges higher than the amount approved by Medicare unless the doctor or supplier agrees to accept Medicare's approved amount as the total charge for services rendered.

[2] Once you have had $183.00 of expense for covered services in 2018, the Part B deductible does not apply to any further covered services you receive the rest of the year.

[3] Federal law limits charges for physician services.

[4] Home health care is provided under Part B only if not covered under Part A.

Part B Premium for Certain Beneficiaries

Pursuant to one provision of the Bipartisan Budget Act of 2015, certain Medicare beneficiaries will pay a higher Part B premium in 2018. The minimum premium for those in this group will be $134.00. Individuals in this group include:

- Medicare beneficiaries not receiving Social Security benefits.

- Those who enroll in Part B for the first time in 2018.

- Those who have both Medicare and Medicaid, and Medicaid pays the Medicare premiums.

- Those whose income in 2016 exceeded certain limits. The *total* premium for those in this group will also include an income-related monthly adjustment amount. Based on their filing status and income.[1]

The table below shows the 2018 Part B premiums for these Medicare beneficiaries.

Unmarried Individuals	Married Filing Jointly	Total Monthly Premium
Equal to or less than $85,000	Equal to or less than $170,000	$134.00
$85,001 to $107,000	$170,001 to $214,000	$187.50
$107,001 to $133,500	$214,001 to $267,000	$267.90
$133,501 to $160,000	$267,001 to $320,000	$348.30
More than $160,000	More than $320,000	$428.60

Married Filing Separately	Total Monthly Premium
Equal to or less than $85,000	$134.00
More than $85,000	$428.60

[1] The measure used is modified adjusted gross income. Generally adjusted gross income plus any tax free interest or any excluded foreign earned income. An appeals process is available in case of a major life change such as the death of a spouse, divorce, or marriage.

Medicare Part C – Medicare Advantage

The original Medicare program, created in 1965, consists of Part A (hospital insurance) and Part B (medical insurance) and operates as a "fee-for-service" system. Under this program, a Medicare beneficiary can go to any physician or health facility nationwide which accepts Medicare payments.

An Alternative To Traditional Medicare

In 1997, the federal government created, as Medicare Part C, the Medicare+Choice program. This new program was designed to give Medicare beneficiaries access to a wide array of more cost-effective, private health plan choices, as an alternative to the traditional Parts A and B. In 2003, Medicare+Choice was renamed as "Medicare Advantage", as part of the Medicare Prescription Drug, Improvement, and Modernization Act.

Options Under Medicare Advantage

In general, each Medicare beneficiary is entitled to choose to receive benefits through either the original Medicare fee-for-service program under Parts A and B or through a Medicare Advantage plan. The Medicare Advantage options include:

- Health Maintenance Organizations (HMO) plans
- Preferred Provider Organization (PPO) plans
- Private Fee-for-Service (PFFS) plans
- Special Needs Plans (SNPs)
- HMO Point-of-Service (HMOPOS) plans
- Medical Savings Account (MSA) plans

Benefits Under Medicare Advantage

Medicare Advantage plans are required to provide the same benefits that are covered under the traditional fee-for-service plan, except for hospice care; original Medicare will cover the cost for hospice care. Most Medicare Advantage plans offer extra coverage, for example vision, hearing, dental, and other health and wellness programs. Most include Medicare prescription drug coverage (Part D). In addition to the Part B premium, an enrollee in a Medicare Advantage plan may have to pay an additional monthly premium.

Medicare Part C – Medicare Advantage

Medicare Advantage plans have a yearly limit on an enrollee's out-of-pocket costs for medical services. Once this limit is reached, an enrollee will pay nothing for covered services. Each plan has a different limit and the limit can change from year to year.

Making a Choice

Once a plan has been elected, that choice will remain in effect until the beneficiary changes it or the plan chosen no longer services the area in which the beneficiary resides.[1] If a beneficiary fails to make an election, he or she will remain in the traditional fee-for-service program.

- **Initial Medicare eligibility:** Beneficiaries who enroll in a Medicare Advantage plan when they first become eligible for Medicare benefits can change to the fee-for-service plan at any time during their first 12 months of enrollment. During this period they will have an extended period of guaranteed access to Medigap plans.

- **Annual enrollment:** An annual enrollment period takes place each fall, from October 15 through December 7. Elections made during this annual enrollment period take effect January 1st of the following year. As a part of the annual enrollment, Medicare beneficiaries will be provided with information about each health plan available to them. The purpose of this information is to allow Medicare beneficiaries to make informed health care choices, based on comparative data regarding quality and performance.

- **Special enrollment periods:** Special enrollment periods are available after the end of the continuous open enrollment if: (1) a plan is discontinued; (2) the Medicare beneficiary moves; (3) the plan violates its contract with Medicare; or (4) the Medicare beneficiary encounters exceptional conditions (to be specified in regulations).

---

[1] Not all Medicare Advantage options are available in all geographical areas.

Medicare Part D – Prescription Drug Coverage

Medicare Part D provides insurance coverage for prescription medications. Under this program, insurance companies and other private firms contract with Medicare (Medicare pays most of the premium) to provide prescription drug benefits to Medicare beneficiaries.

Each eligible Medicare beneficiary must select a drug plan and pay a monthly premium to receive the drug coverage. All drug plans (the choice varies by state) must provide coverage at least as good as the standard coverage specified by Medicare. Some plans may offer extra benefits such as no deductible, higher coverage limits, or cover additional drugs, in exchange for a higher monthly premium. Individuals with limited income and resources may qualify for help in paying for drug coverage.

Making a Choice

There are a number of factors to consider in making a choice about drug plans, including:

- **Initial enrollment:** A new Medicare beneficiary may enroll in a prescription drug plan during the seven-month period beginning three months before he or she turns age 65 until three months after reaching age 65. An individual who has lost "creditable coverage" (prescription drug coverage from some other source that is at least as good as the standard Medicare prescription coverage) has 63 days to select and join a Medicare prescription drug plan. An eligible beneficiary who does not enroll in a prescription drug plan within the prescribed time limits faces a penalty for late enrollment.

- **Penalty for late enrollment:** Individuals who delay joining a Medicare prescription drug plan beyond their initial eligibility face a monthly premium that will increase by at least 1% per month for each month of delay. This increased premium applies for as long as the individual is enrolled in a Medicare drug plan.

- **Changing plans:** Each year, from October 15 to December 7, a beneficiary can change to a different prescription drug plan.

Medicare Part D - Prescription Drug Coverage

- **Current prescription coverage:** Individuals who currently have prescription drug coverage from another source may not wish to enroll in a Medicare prescription drug program. In some cases the benefits provided under these other plans are better than those provided under the standard Medicare prescription drug plan.

- **Medication coverage:** Consider what medications are needed. Compare the needed medications with those covered by each plan. Each plan will have a list (termed a "formulary") showing the drugs (generic and brand-name) the plan will pay for.

- **Out-of-pocket cost:** A prescription drug plan can vary in how much it charges and how much coverage is provided. Issues such as the monthly premium, yearly deductible, any co-insurance or co-payments, and coverage limits must all be considered.

- **Pharmacy convenience:** Not all pharmacies will be contracted with all plans. Some plans will allow a beneficiary to receive prescriptions by mail.

- **Future health changes:** Even though an individual takes few or no medications now, joining a prescription drug plan now means paying the lowest possible monthly premium. Future health changes may require increased use of prescription drugs.

Standard Coverage

The standard coverage for 2018 as set by Medicare is shown in the following table:

	$405 Deductible	$406 to $3750	$3751 Until Out of Pocket Totals $5000	Above $5000 in Out of Pocket Costs
Individual Pays	$405.00	25% up to $836	$3,759	5%
Plan Pays	$0.00	75% up to $2509	$0.00	95%
Total Drug Expense	$405.00	$3,750.00	$7,509	

In 2018, once total drug spending reaches $3,750 (where the coverage gap begins), a Medicare Part D enrollee will pay 35% of the plan's cost for covered brand-name prescription drugs and 44% of the plan's cost for covered generic drugs. The amount paid by the enrollee – as well as any discount paid by the drug company – count as "out-of-pocket" spending, helping the enrollee get out of the coverage gap.

Medicare Part D - Prescription Drug Coverage

Monthly Adjustment Amount

Beginning in 2011, the Patient Protection and Affordable Care Act (PPACA) required Medicare Part D enrollees whose incomes exceed the same thresholds that apply to higher-income Part B enrollees, to pay a monthly adjustment amount. High-income enrollees will pay the regular plan premium to their Part D plan and the monthly adjustment amount to Medicare. The 2018 Part D monthly adjustment amounts are shown in the following tables:

Unmarried Individuals	Married Filing Jointly	Monthly Adjustment Amount
Equal to or less than $85,000	Equal to or less than $170,000	$0.00
$85,001 to $107,000	$170,001 to $214,000	$13.00
$107,001 to $133,500	$214,001 to $267,000	$33.60
$133,501 to $160,000	$267,001 to $320,000	$54.20
More Than $160,000	More Than $320,000	$74.80

Married Filing Separately	Monthly Adjustment Amount
Equal to or less than $85,000	$0.00
More Than $85,000	$74.80

For Those Who Currently Have Prescription Drug Coverage

Some retirees may already have prescription drug coverage. For these individuals a key step is to compare the current coverage with that provided through a Medicare plan. The benefits administrator or insurance carrier can provide additional information.

- **Coverage provided by employer or union:** If the drug coverage provided by an employer or union is, on average, at least as good as the standard Medicare coverage, the individual may choose to keep the current plan for as long as it is offered. If the plan is discontinued in the future, the individual can join a Medicare drug plan without penalty within 63 days of the coverage ending.

Medicare Part D - Prescription Drug Coverage

- **Medicare Advantage or other Medicare health plan:** Some Medicare Advantage or other Medicare health plans cover prescription drugs. If a plan does not offer prescription drug coverage, an individual may wish to switch to another Medicare Advantage or other Medicare health plan that does cover prescription drugs, or change to the original Medicare plan and join a Medicare prescription drug plan.

- **Other government insurance:** Generally, the prescription drug benefits provided by TRICARE, the Department of Veterans Affairs (VA), Federal Employee's Health Benefits Program (FEHB), or Indian Health Services are as good as the standard Medicare prescription drug plan. In most cases it will be to the individual's advantage to keep the current plan. If coverage is lost in the future, the individual can join a Medicare drug plan without penalty within 63 days of the coverage ending.

Seek Professional Guidance

The process of making decisions concerning health care insurance can be confusing and complex. The advice and counsel of trained advisers is strongly recommended. Additional information is also available from:

- **On the web:** www.medicare.gov

- **By telephone:** Contact Medicare at 1-(800) 633-4227 (TTY users: 1-(877) 486-2048)

How Medicare Prescription Drug Coverage Works

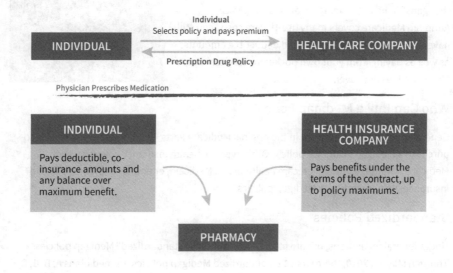

INDIVIDUAL

Individual
Selects policy and pays premium

HEALTH CARE COMPANY

Prescription Drug Policy

Physician Prescribes Medication

INDIVIDUAL

Pays deductible, co-insurance amounts and any balance over maximum benefit.

HEALTH INSURANCE COMPANY

Pays benefits under the terms of the contract, up to policy maximums.

PHARMACY

Medigap Policies

Medigap policies are supplemental health insurance policies sold by private insurers, designed to fill some of the "gaps" in health coverage provided by Medicare. Although Medicare covers many health care costs, you still have to pay certain coinsurance and deductible amounts, as well as paying from your own pocket for services that Medicare does not cover.

Who Can Buy a Medigap Policy?

Generally, you must be enrolled in the original Medicare Parts A and B before you're able to purchase a Medigap insurance policy. Other types of health insurance coverage, such as Medicare Advantage, other Medicare health plans, Medicaid, or employer-provided health insurance, do not work with Medigap policies.

Standardized Policies

Under federal regulations, private insurers can only sell "standardized" Medigap policies. Through May 31, 2010, there were 12 standardized Medigap policies, termed plans A, B, C, D, E, F, G, H, I, J, K, and L. Effective June 1, 2010, plans E, H, I, and J could no longer be sold, and plans M and N were added. Individuals who purchased a plan E, H, I, or J before June 1, 2010 may keep those plans.

The standardized policies allow you to compare "apples with apples." For example, a plan F policy will provide the same benefits, no matter which insurance company it is purchased from. However, a plan C policy will provide different coverage than a plan D policy. All Medigap policies must provide certain "core" benefits.

These standardized plans are not available to those living in Massachusetts, Minnesota, or Wisconsin; there are separate Medigap policies available for residents of these states.

Choosing a Policy

There are two primary factors to consider when choosing a Medigap policy.

- **Needed benefits:** Carefully consider what benefits you are most likely to need; you may not need the most comprehensive plan.

- **Cost:** Once you have decided which benefits you will need, shop for the policy that provides those benefits at the lowest cost.

Policy Costs Can Differ

- **Discounts:** Some insurers may offer discounts to certain classes of people, such as women, non-smokers, or married couples.

- **Medical underwriting:** An insurance company may require you to fill out a detailed questionnaire on your health. The information you provide is used to determine whether or not a policy will be issued, or what premium to charge.

- **Pre-existing conditions:** If you have a "pre-existing condition," a known health problem, before you apply for a Medigap policy, you may have to wait up to six months before that problem is covered.

- **High deductible:** There are two options for Plan F: (1) a standard option, and (2) a "high deductible" option. Choosing the high deductible option means that you must pay more of the costs before the policy begins to provide benefits. Monthly premiums for high deductible policies are typically less.

- **Medicare SELECT:** Medicare SELECT policies are sold in a few states by a few insurers. Except for emergencies, these policies require you to use pre-selected hospitals and physicians.

- **Guaranteed renewable:** Medigap policies issued after 1992 are generally guaranteed renewable. This means that as long as you pay the premiums, are honest about health issues, and the insurance company doesn't go bankrupt, the insurer can't drop your coverage. In some states, policies issued before 1992 may not be guaranteed renewable.

- **Insurer pricing methods:** The table below shows three common methods by which an insurance company will price its Medigap policies:

Pricing Method	Payment	Other Issues
Community (No-Age)	Each insured pays the same premium, regardless of age.	Premiums may increase due to inflation.
Issue-Age	Policy premium is based on your age when you purchase the policy.	Younger buyers pay lower premiums. Premiums may increase due to inflation.
Attained-Age	Premiums are based on your age each year, thus premiums increase annually.	Younger buyers pay lower premiums. Premiums can increase each year. Premiums may also increase due to inflation.

Other Resources

Professional guidance in dealing with any aspect of a Medigap policy is strongly recommended. Other available resources include:

- **Medicare:** The federal government's Centers for Medicare & Medicaid Services (CMS) has a great deal of information available on their website at www.medicare.gov. You can also reach them by phone at (800) 633-4227. TTY users should call (877) 486-2048.

- **State Health Insurance Assistance Programs:** Many states operate health insurance assistance programs designed to provide assistance and information regarding Medicare, Medigap policies, and long-term care policies.

- **State insurance department:** Each state has an insurance department that regulates the sale of all types of insurance within the state. These state agencies can provide information about Medigap policies.

Medigap Policies Compared

Medigap policies are designed to fill the "gaps" in health insurance provided under original Medicare, Parts A and B. These supplemental policies must provide standardized coverage as specified by the federal government.

The following tables compare and contrast the major components of the different policies. Not all policies are available in all states. The policies shown are not available to residents of the states of Massachusetts, Minnesota, or Wisconsin; there are separate standardized policies for residents of those states.

Medigap Plans Sold On or After June 1, 2010[1]

Plan	Core Benefits	Skilled Nursing	Part A Deductible	Part A Hospice	Part B Deductible	Part B Excess Charges	Emergency Foreign Travel	Preventive Care
A	Yes			Yes				Yes
B	Yes		Yes	Yes				Yes
C	Yes	Yes	Yes	Yes	Yes		80%	Yes
D	Yes	Yes	Yes	Yes			80%	Yes
F[2]	Yes	Yes	Yes	Yes	Yes	Yes	80%	Yes
G	Yes	Yes	Yes	Yes		Yes	80%	Yes
K[3]	Some	50%	50%	50%				Yes
L[3]	Some	75%	75%	75%				Yes
M	Yes	Yes	50%	Yes			80%	Yes
N	Yes	Yes	Yes	Yes			80%	Yes

What's included?

- **Core benefits:** Plans A-G, M and N - For Part A hospitalization, cover 100% of all copayments except that for days 1-60 of hospitalization ($1,340 in 2018), plus adding

---

[1] Through May 31, 2010, 12 standardized Medigap policies could be sold, identified as plans A, B, C, D, E, F, G,H, I, J, K, and L. Effective June 1, 2010, plans E, H, I, and J could no longer be sold, and new plans N and M were added. Individuals who purchased a plan E, H, I, or J before June 1, 2010, may keep those plans.

[2] Plan F has two options: (1) a standard option and (2) a "high deductible" option with a 2018 deductible of $2,240.00.

[3] In 2018, Plan K has an annual out-of-pocket limit of $5,240.00; Plan L has an annual out-of-pocket limit of $2,620.00.

365 lifetime days of hospital coverage after the standard benefit of 150 days is exhausted; 100% of Part B coinsurance amounts[1] after meeting the yearly deductible ($183.00 in 2018); the first three pints of blood. Plans K and L – For Part A hospitalization, cover 100% of all copayments except that for days 1-60 of hospitalization, plus adding 365 lifetime days of hospital coverage after the standard benefit of 150 days is exhausted; for Part B, Plan K pays 50% of the coinsurance amount after the annual deductible is met; Plan L pays 75% of the Part B coinsurance amount after the annual deductible is met; Plan K pays 50% of the cost of the first three pints of blood; Plan L pays 75% of the cost of the first three pints of blood.

- **Part A skilled nursing:** Plans C-G, M and N – Pay 100% of the coinsurance amount Plans C-G, M and N – Pay 100% of the coinsurance amount ($167.50 per day in 2018) for days 21-100 in a skilled nursing facility. Plans K and L – Pay the percentage shown of the coinsurance amount for days 21-100 in a skilled nursing facility.

- **Part A deductible:** Plans B-G, and N – Pay 100% of the Part A deductible ($1,340 in 2018) for the first 60 days of hospitalization. Plans K, L, and M – Pay the percentage shown of the Part A deductible for the first 60 days of hospitalization.

- **Part A hospice:** Plans A-G, M and N – Pay 100% of the Part A hospice copayment. Plans K and L – Pay the percentage shown of the Part A hospice copayment.

- **Part B deductible:** Plans C and F – Pay 100% of the annual Part B deductible ($183.00 in 2018).

- **Part B excess charges:** Plans F and G – Pay 100% of the Part B excess charges.

- **Emergency foreign travel:** Plans C-G, M and N – The insured pays a $250 deductible and then 20% of any remaining costs of emergency health care. This benefit is typically limited to a $50,000 lifetime maximum and the first 60 days of each trip.

- **Part B preventive care:** All plans – Pay 100% of the coinsurance for preventive care.

---

[1] Plan N pays 100% of the Part B coinsurance except for a co-payment of up to $20 for office visits and $50 for emergency department visits that do not result in inpatient admission.

Seek Professional Guidance

Professional guidance is strongly recommended when choosing a Medigap insurance policy. Also:

- **Medicare:** www.medicare.gov, or by phone at (800) 633-4227; TTY: (800) 486-2048.

- **State government:** Many states operate a Health Insurance Assistance Program, designed to provide information and assistance. Otherwise, the local state insurance department will often provide information about Medigap policies.

Medicaid

Medicaid is a jointly-funded, federal-state welfare program which provides medical care to individuals and families with very low resources and income. Each state administers its own program and, within guidelines set by the federal government, establishes its own rules regarding program eligibility and the type, duration, and scope of services provided.

Qualifying For Medicaid

Just being poor is no guarantee that an individual will qualify to receive Medicaid. An individual must belong to one of several specified groups as well as meet certain income and asset limitation tests.

To qualify for federal funds, states must provide care for certain, targeted populations. Included in the mandatory category are persons receiving federally assisted income maintenance payments, such as Supplemental Security Income (SSI), or Aid to Families With Dependent Children (AFDC).

A state may choose to provide healthcare services to certain "categorically needy" populations, individuals and families whose financial situation is similar to those in the mandatory group, but with different qualifying criteria. Medicaid benefits may also be offered to "medically needy" persons, those with incomes too high to qualify under any other category. Such individuals can "spend down" their excess income by incurring medical and/or remedial care expenses, reducing the excess income to a level below the maximum allowed under the state's plan.

What Medical Services Are Provided?

A wide range of services is provided to Medicaid beneficiaries. Some services are mandatory under federal rules, while others are optional. Provided services can include:

- Inpatient hospital services.

- Outpatient hospital services.

- Nursing facility services for beneficiaries age 21 and older.

- Prenatal and delivery services as well as postpartum care.

- Physicians' services and medical and surgical services of a dentist.

- Home health services for beneficiaries who are entitled to nursing facility services under the state's Medicaid plan.

- Early and periodic screening, diagnostic, and treatment (EPSDT) services for children under age 21, including vaccines.

- Payment of Medicare premiums (Part A and/or Part B) for certain needy elderly or disabled individuals.

- Long-term care (LTC).

Resource and Income Limitations

Generally, a single individual cannot have more than $2,000 in assets and still qualify for Medicaid. In this calculation, certain assets are "exempt" and are not counted:

Asset	Observation
Personal residence	Generally, with no more than $552,000 of equity. A state may raise this limit to $828,000.
Cash value life insurance	With a face value of up to $1,500.
Household goods, personal effects	Furniture, appliances, artwork, clothing, jewelry.
Automobile	One car, generally limited to a value of $4,500.
Burial funds	Generally limited to $1,500.
Burial space	Burial plot, grave marker, urn, crypt, mausoleum.
Business assets	Property employed in a trade or business, if essential to self-support.
Jointly owned residence	Exempt if other resident owners would be forced to move if property were sold.

Those applying for Medicaid must also meet certain monthly income limitations, which vary by state. These income limitations generally change from year to year.

Transferring Assets To Qualify For Medicaid

Some individuals, often those needing expensive nursing home care, will attempt to meet Medicaid's asset limitations by gifting or otherwise transferring assets to others for less than fair market value. However, such transfers can result in a delay in benefit eligibility if made within a "look-back" period of 60 months before the application date.[1]

To avoid a period of ineligibility, an individual who anticipates needing care can either (1) transfer assets more than 60 months before applying for Medicaid benefits; or, (2) keep enough assets to pay for needed care for 60 months, transfer the remainder, and not apply for Medicaid benefits until 60 months have elapsed after the last transfer.

The period of ineligibility is generally determined by dividing the value of the assets transferred by the average monthly cost of nursing home care to a private patient in the local community. Ineligibility begins on the later of: (1) the date of the gift or transfer; or, (2) the date the individual would otherwise have qualified to receive Medicaid benefits.[2]

> Example: George lives in a state where the average monthly cost of nursing home care is $6,000 per month. If he transfers property worth $120,000, he will be ineligible for Medicaid benefits for 20 months ($120,000 ÷ $6,000 = 20).

Annuities

The purchase of a commercial annuity is considered in the same light as a gift or transfer of assets for less than fair market value, unless certain requirements are met. In general, an annuity is not counted as an asset if it is: (1) irrevocable; (2) non-transferrable; (3) actuarially sound, compared to the beneficiary's life expectancy; and; (4) provides for equal payments during the annuity's term.

Additionally, there can be no payment deferral or balloon payments and the state must be named as the primary remainder beneficiary (in some cases the secondary remainder beneficiary) for the amounts paid by Medicaid for the beneficiary's care.[3]

---

[1] Under federal rules, some transfers, such as those made for the benefit of a spouse, a blind or disabled child, or a disabled individual under age 65, will not trigger a period of benefit ineligibility.

[2] Under the Deficit Reduction Act of 2005, the 60 month look-back period applies to transfers made on or after February 8, 2006. For transfers before that date, a 36 month look-back period generally applied (60 months in the case of certain trusts).

[3] Annuities purchased before February 8, 2006, the effective date of the Deficit Reduction Act of 2005, were subject to individual state rules.

Trusts

If an individual, or his or her spouse, or anyone acting on the individual's behalf, establishes a trust using at least some of the individual's funds, that trust can be considered available to the individual for determining Medicaid eligibility.

In general, payments actually made to or for the benefit of the individual are treated as income to the individual. Amounts that could be paid to or for the benefit of the individual, but are not, are treated as available resources. Amounts that could be paid to or for the benefit of the individual, but are paid to someone else, are treated as transfers for less than fair market value. Amounts that cannot, in any way, be paid to or for the benefit of the individual are also treated as transfers for less than fair market value.[1]

Certain trusts, for disabled or institutionalized individuals, are not counted as being available to the individual. These trusts must provide that the state receives any funds, up to the amount of Medicaid benefits paid on behalf of the individual, remaining in the trust when the individual dies.

Spousal Impoverishment

The high cost of nursing home care can rapidly exhaust the savings of almost anyone. Because of this, Congress has enacted laws to prevent what has been called "spousal impoverishment," which can leave the spouse who is still living at home (the "community spouse") with little or no income or resources. These provisions help ensure that the community spouse will be able to live out his or her life with independence and dignity. These spousal impoverishment rules apply when one member of a couple enters a nursing home or other medical institution and is expected to remain there for at least 30 days.

When the couple applies for Medicaid, an assessment of their combined (regardless of ownership) resources is made. The couple's home, household goods, an auto, and burial funds are not included in the accounting. The result is the couple's combined countable resources. This total is then used to determine a "Protected Resource Amount" (PRA) for the community spouse.[2] After the PRA is subtracted from the couple's combined resources, the

---

[1] Transfers from trusts for less than fair market value are subject to the same 60-month "look-back" period applicable to other transfers.

[2] The PRA may also be determined by either a court order or by a state hearing officer.

remainder is considered available to the spouse residing in the medical institution as countable resources. If the amount of countable resources is below the state's resource standard, the individual is eligible for Medicaid.

The community spouse's income is not considered available to the spouse who is in the medical facility and the two individuals are not considered a couple for income eligibility purposes. The state uses the income eligibility standard for one person rather than two. If most of the couple's income is in the name of the institutionalized spouse, and the community spouse has insufficient income in his or her own right to live on, a separate calculation is made which allocates a portion of the institutionalized spouse's income to support the community spouse and any other family members living in the household.

Estate Recovery

When a Medicaid beneficiary dies, federal law requires the states to seek recovery of amounts paid by the state for many of the services provided to Medicaid beneficiaries, unless undue hardship would result. Generally, recovery is made from property held in the beneficiary's name only. Some states may seek also recovery from a life estate, assets held in a revocable "living" trust, or jointly held assets. Assets that pass to a surviving spouse are exempt from recovery as long as that spouse is alive.

Long-Term Care Partnership

In a Long-Term Care Partnership, a state government and private health insurers work together to make available to residents of that state LTC insurance policies that are "linked" to Medicaid. If a buyer of a partnership LTC policy later faces long-term care needs that exceed the policy's limits, he or she may apply for assistance from the state's Medicaid program under more relaxed eligibility rules. In what is termed an "asset disregard," the policy owner may keep a larger amount of assets than would normally be allowed under standard Medicaid rules. These relaxed eligibility rules apply only to the amount of assets than an individual can retain; all other normal Medicaid eligibility requirements apply.

Patient Protection and Affordable Care Act (PPACA)

Beginning in 2014, PPACA expanded eligibility for Medicaid to individuals not currently eligible for Medicare (generally, individuals under age 65). This expansion embraced children, pregnant women, and adults without dependent children, with incomes up to 133% of the federal poverty level (FPL). Coverage is provided through an essential health benefits package purchased through a state's American Health Benefits Exchange.

Seek Professional Guidance

Qualifying for Medicaid services requires meeting complex legal and regulatory requirements. The guidance of trained financial professionals is highly recommended.

See the general information made available by the federal government's Centers for Medicare and Medicaid Services at: http://www.medicaid.gov/.

ABLE Account

On December 19, 2014, President Barack Obama signed into law HR 5771, the *Tax Increase Prevention Act of 2014* (TIPA 2014). In addition to extending a number of popular individual and business tax provisions, the Act also added new code section 529A to the Internal Revenue Code (IRC). This code section provides for the creation of a new type of tax-favored savings account, termed an "ABLE" (**A**chieving a **B**etter **L**ife **E**xperience) account.[1]

Overview

Individuals with disabilities face significant barriers to finding and holding employment and living independently because their access to safety-net programs such as Supplemental Security Income (SSI) and Medicaid can be lost once they establish a minimum level of savings and income.[2] ABLE accounts, similar in nature to IRC Sec. 529 plan accounts for education funding, are designed to encourage and facilitate the ability of those with significant disabilities to live and work independently, without losing the benefits of SSI or Medicaid.

Under current federal legislation, a state (or an agency or instrumentality of a state) may establish and maintain a qualified ABLE Program. In general, a qualified ABLE program must meet the following requirements:

1. Contributions may be made to an account established solely for the purpose of meeting the qualified disability expenses of the designated beneficiary of the account.
2. The program must limit a designated beneficiary to *one* account, wherever located.
3. Certain other requirements of the law. For example:

   - There must be a separate accounting for each designated beneficiary;

   - A beneficiary's ability to direct the investment of contributions to the account must be limited to no more than two times a year.

   - No interest in any portion of an account may be pledged as security for a loan.

---

[1] The discussion here concerns federal income tax law. State or local income tax law may differ.

[2] SSI has an individual resource limitation of only $2,000. In most states, qualifying for SSI also confers Medicaid eligibility. Generally, when SSI recipients have income and resources over the limit, their SSI benefits are suspended, but they remain eligible for Medicaid.

- There must be adequate safeguards to prevent aggregate contributions in excess of the limit established by the state.

A qualified ABLE program is generally exempt from federal income tax, other than the tax on unrelated business income of tax-exempt organizations.

Effect of ABLE Accounts on Federal Means-Tested Programs

An amount in an ABLE account, or any distribution from an ABLE account for qualified disability expenses, is generally disregarded for the purposes of determining eligibility for federal means-tested programs such as SSI or Medicaid. There are two exceptions to this:

- A distribution made for *housing* expenses is <u>not</u> disregarded for purposes of the SSI program.

- Any amount in excess of $100,000 is considered a "resource" for purposes of federal means-tested programs.

Generally, if a disabled individual is found to have excess resources, his or her eligibility for SSI is suspended (not terminated), but eligibility for Medicaid is unaffected.

Eligible Individual

An eligible individual is someone who became blind or disabled before reaching the age of 26. Additionally, the individual must be either (1) entitled to Social Security disability benefits or SSI, or, (2) have a physician-signed certificate of disability on file with the IRS. The certificate of disability must attest that the disabled individual is either blind or has a medically determinable physical or mental impairment which results in marked and severe functional limitations which can be expected to result in death or which has lasted or can be expected to last continually for at least 12 months.

Designated Beneficiary

A designated beneficiary of an ABLE account must be an eligible individual who is the owner of the account and who is designated at the beginning of participation in a qualified ABLE program as the beneficiary of amounts paid into the program.

Contributions

Contributions to an ABLE account are considered a completed gift of a present interest,[1] must generally be in *cash,* and are *nondeductible* for federal income tax purposes. In addition:

- On an annual basis, contributions to an ABLE account may not exceed the federal annual gift tax exclusion. For 2018 this exclusion is $15,000.[2] This limit may be exceeded in case of a rollover from a prior ABLE account. Excess contributions are subject to a 6% excise tax.

- Total overall contributions may not exceed the limit imposed on accounts under the qualified tuition program of the state maintaining the qualified ABLE program.

- Tax Cuts and Jobs Act of 2017(TCJA) – The TCJA, for 2018-2025, allows amount from 529 higher education plans to be rolled over to an ABLE account, provided that the ABLE account is owned by the beneficiary of the 529 account or a member of the beneficiary's family. Such rolled-over amounts count toward the annual limitation $15,000 in 2018) that may be contributed to an ABLE account. Any amount rolled over in excess of this limit will be included in the beneficiary's gross income.

- TCJA also included a provision to temporarily (2018-2025) increase the amount that may be contributed to an ABLE account. After the overall limitation on contributions is reached $15,000 in 2018), an ABLE account's designated beneficiary may contribute an additional amount, up the lesser of (a) the federal poverty level for a one-person household;[3] or (b) the individual's compensation for the year. TCJA also temporarily allows the designated beneficiary to claim the Saver's Credit for contributions made to his or her ABLE account.

- Contributions may be made by any person. The term "person" includes an individual, trust, estate, partnership, association, company, or corporation.

---

[1] In general, exempt from both gift tax and Generation Skipping Tax (GST).

[2] This amount is subject to adjustment for inflation in future years.

[3] For 2018, the federal poverty level for a one-person household in the continental U.S. is $12,140; for Alaska it is $15,180; and for Hawaii it is $13,960.

- If a contributor makes other gifts to a designated beneficiary, in addition to the gift to the designated beneficiary's ABLE account, the contributor's total gifts to the designated beneficiary could exceed the annual gift tax exclusion and result in a gift tax liability.

Distributions from an ABLE Account

Distributions from an ABLE account to the designated beneficiary are excluded from income to the extent that they *do not exceed* the beneficiary's qualified disability expenses.

If the amount distributed *exceeds* the beneficiary's qualified disability expenses, a portion of the distribution is included in the beneficiary's income. In calculating the taxable portion of the distribution, the difference between the qualified disability expenses and the amount distributed is reduced by an amount which bears the same ratio to the distributed amount as the qualified disability expenses bear to that amount. This follows the tax treatment of annuities, as outlined in IRC Sec. 72.

An amount includable in a beneficiary's income is also subject to an additional 10% tax.

Example: Assume that a qualified ABLE account with a balance of $100,000 (of which $50,000 consists of contributions) distributes $10,000 to a beneficiary who incurred $6,000 of qualified disability expenses. Under IRC Sec. 72, one –half of the distribution ($5,000) is includible in gross income. However, the $5,000 otherwise includable in income is reduced by $3,000 ($6,000 ÷ $10,000 x $5,000 = $3,000) to $2,000. An additional 10% tax of $200 ($2,000 x 10%) is also imposed on the distribution.[1]

Qualified Disability Expenses

Qualified disability expenses are any expenses related to the beneficiary's disability or blindness and which are made for the benefit of the designated beneficiary, including:

- Education

- Housing

- Transportation

---

[1] House Ways and Means Committee Report 113-614, November 12, 2014.

- Employment training and support

- Assistive technology and personal support services

- Health, prevention, and wellness

- Financial management and administrative services

- Legal fees

- Oversight and monitoring

- Funeral and burial expenses

- Other expenses identified in future published guidance from the IRS.

The proposed regulations provide that the term "qualified disability expenses" should be broadly construed to permit the inclusion of basic living expenses and should not be limited to expenses for items for which there is a medical necessity or which provide no benefit to others in addition to the benefit of the eligible individual.

Rollovers

Amounts in one ABLE account may be rolled over tax-free to another ABLE account for the same beneficiary.[1] However, no more than one such rollover may be made within a continuous 12 month period. Further, the funds must be deposited into the new ABLE account within 60 days of being distributed from the prior account. A tax-free rollover may also be made to another ABLE account with a different designated beneficiary if the new designated beneficiary is (1) an "eligible individual," i.e. blind or disabled before age 26, and (2) a sibling (including step-siblings and half-siblings, by either blood or adoption) of the former designated beneficiary.

In addition, the proposed regulations authorize a qualified ABLE program to allow direct program-to-program transfers to effectuate a change of qualified ABLE program or a change of designated beneficiary to another eligible individual.

---

[1] For example, if a beneficiary moves from one state to another.

Death of the Beneficiary - Transfer to State

The proposed regulations provide that upon the death of the designated beneficiary, all amounts remaining in the ABLE account are includable in the designated beneficiary's gross estate for estate tax purposes. Further, after all outstanding qualified disability expenses have been paid, any amounts remaining in the deceased beneficiary's ABLE account are subject to a claim from the state for an amount equal to the total medical assistance (Medicaid) paid for by the state. These repaid amounts are "net" of any premiums paid from the account on, by, or on behalf of the beneficiary to a Medicaid "Buy-in" program. Any funds remaining in the account after the state has been re-paid would generally be paid to the beneficiary's estate, subject to income tax on the earnings, but not subject to the 10% penalty.

Seek Professional Guidance

The ability to establish an ABLE account represents a new option for parents or guardians to provide for the needs of a disabled individual, without jeopardizing means-tested benefits such as Supplemental Security Income (SSI) or Medicare. In deciding whether or not to establish an ABLE account, and in correctly using an ABLE account if one is set up, the advice and guidance of trained, experienced financial professionals is highly recommended.

How an ABLE Account Works

An ABLE account is a tax-favored program operated by a state designed to help parents or guardians of a disabled or blind individual pay for expenses related to the disability or blindness, without losing the benefit of means-test programs such as Supplemental Security Income (SSI) or Medicaid. Annual contributions to an ABLE account generally may not exceed the federal annual gift tax exclusion. In 2018, this amount is $15,000.[1] The disability or blindness must have occurred before the individual reached age 26.

How Does It Work?

ABLE ACCOUNT

- Earnings accumulate tax-deferred.
- Amounts distributed for housing are a resource for SSI.
- Account balances above $100,000 are a resource for SSI and Medicaid.

Tax-Free Withdrawals

Taxable Withdrawals

QUALIFIED WITHDRAWALS

- Withdrawals for qualified disability expenses are generally tax-free.
- Qualified disability expenses are broadly defined; disability-related and basic living expenses are included.

NON-QUALIFIED WITHDRAWALS

- Distributed amounts in excess of qualified disability expenses are subject to tax.
- Taxable amounts calculated under IRC. Sec. 72 rules, plus a 10% penalty

---

[1] This amount is subject to adjustment for inflation in future years. Federal income tax law does not allow deductions for contributions to an ABLE account. State or local income tax law can vary widely.

The Need for Estate Planning

At a person's demise there are certain typical problems which, if not planned for, create a burden on those who are left behind.

Proper estate planning can eliminate or reduce these problems.

Financial Burdens

- Estate settlement costs are too high: These costs consist primarily of probate fees and death taxes.

  - Probate fees: These are generally paid to the executor of the estate and the attorney who assists with the probate.

  - Death taxes: Estates that exceed certain amounts may be subject to both state and federal death taxes.

- Estate assets are improperly arranged:

  - Liquidity: There are not enough liquid (cash type) assets to pay estate settlement costs.

  - Cash flow: There is not enough income to care for loved ones left behind, e.g., spouse and minor children.

Transfer of Assets

- Estate assets may be subject to probate delays and expense.

- Assets transferred to minors may be in cumbersome guardianship accounts until they attain age 18 (or 21 in some states) and are then distributed outright to the children. A court supervised guardianship may be required.

- Additional death taxes may be paid because there was no pre-death planning.

- Without planning, estate assets may not pass to the intended heirs.

Care of Minors

- Guardians: Parents can nominate a guardian for their minor children in a will.

- Asset management: If the wrong persons are chosen to manage the assets left for the minors, the assets may be lost or unnecessarily reduced.

Key Estate Planning Considerations

Although Congressional action in the last few years has effectively eliminated federal estate and gift taxes for all but the wealthiest Americans, there is still a vital need to do estate planning.

Why? There are several key reasons: (1) to be sure that all of your wishes are followed after death; (2) to plan for *state* inheritance or estate taxes, if you live (or own property) in a state which levies such a tax; and (3) to plan in advance how to pay for any estate settlement costs. Federal estate tax law may have changed, but estate planning *still* matters.

Transfer of Assets

A primary objective is to insure that your assets go to those you want to receive them.

Method	Description
Will	Considered a key element in any estate plan, a will is a legal document, prepared under state law, which names those who should receive your property. An "executor" is generally named in the will to carry out your wishes. After death, "probate" will be required, a process in which the property listed in the will is distributed to the named heirs under court supervision. Unfortunately, the probate process is frequently expensive and time-consuming, and generally makes the contents of a will a public record. If you die without a will (termed "intestate"), your property will be distributed according to state law, which may result in your assets being distributed in a manner *not* in accordance with your wishes.
Revocable Trust	Also known as a "living" trust, a revocable trust can be changed or revoked during the lifetime of the trust creator (the "grantor," "settlor," or "trustor"). Such a trust is often used as a will substitute, when the grantor transfers assets into the trust during life or at death through a "pour-over" will. A revocable trust can make settling a decedent's estate easier and less expensive than probating a will and can also provide privacy not available in probate.
Irrevocable Trust	An irrevocable trust – as the name implies – cannot be changed once it is set up. These trusts are often used in estate planning for wealthy individuals. An irrevocable trust which holds life insurance can provide the funds needed to pay death taxes and other estate settlement expenses, while keeping the life insurance proceeds outside of the taxable estate.

Key Estate Planning Considerations

Method	Description
Joint Tenancy	Assets held in joint tenancy pass automatically at the time of death to the surviving joint owner, if living. In community property states, community property with right of survivorship has the same result. How ownership of an asset is "titled" can be important.
Beneficiary Designations	Some assets, such as life insurance policies, qualified retirement plans, and IRAs allow the owner to name a "beneficiary." At death, the policy death benefit or title to the asset automatically passes to the named beneficiary or beneficiaries. In some states, "Transfer-on-Death," (TOD) and "Pay-on-Death" (POD) allow certain types of property to automatically pass to named beneficiaries upon the death of the owner. Proper beneficiary designations are essential to make sure the assets pass according to your wishes.

Planning for Estate Transfer Costs

If proper prior planning is not done, estate and inheritance taxes, legal fees, and other estate settlement expenses can significantly reduce the legacy passing to your intended heirs.

Planning for estate settlement costs: Making maximum use of non-probate transfer methods such as revocable trusts, joint tenancy, community property with right of survivorship, or named beneficiaries, can help limit estate settlement costs and avoid the delay of probate.

Planning for estate taxes:[1] If the dollar value of an estate is large enough to be subject to estate and/or inheritance taxes, these taxes can add appreciably to transfer costs. In 2018, an estate with a net value of $11,180,000[2] or less is exempt from federal estate tax. This federal estate tax threshold is also known as the "applicable exclusion amount." However, most states with an estate or inheritance tax have estate tax thresholds which are considerably lower. Thus, an estate which has no federal estate tax liability could easily be subject to state death taxes.

Under federal estate tax law there are a number of ways to shrink the taxable estate:

- **Lifetime gifts:** each individual has an annual gift tax exclusion, currently $15,000[2] per person per year, generally allowing for tax-free gifts to others.

---

[1] The discussion here primarily concerns federal law; state or local law may differ.
[2] 2018 value. This amount is subject to adjustment for inflation in future years.

Key Estate Planning Considerations

- **Marital deduction:** spouses who are both U.S. citizens can gift any amount to each other, generally with no estate or gift tax consequences. The survivor's now larger estate could face a greater estate tax problem when he or she later dies.

- **Charitable giving:** gifts to charities, during life or at death, reduce the estate size.

- **Bypass trust:** A type of trust known as a "bypass" trust allows the first-to-die of a married couple to set aside a portion of his or her assets. In years before 2011, such trusts were used in an effort not to "waste" the first-to-die's applicable exclusion amount. With the applicable exclusion amount currently set at a very high level, plus the introduction in 2011 of the "Deceased Spousal Unused Exclusion" (see below), for *federal estate tax* purposes at least, the bypass trust is less useful than before. When planning for *state death taxes*, however, often with much lower taxability thresholds, the bypass trust remains a useful estate planning tool.[1]

- **Deceased spouse unused exclusion (DSUE):** Beginning in 2011, a change in federal estate tax law provided that any portion of the applicable exclusion amount that remained unused at the death of a spouse could be held over and made available for use by the surviving spouse, in addition to the surviving spouse's own applicable exclusion amount. This "portability" opened up new planning opportunities that did not exist under prior law.

Paying estate settlement costs: While careful planning can help reduce estate settlement expenses, the planning process also needs to consider how to pay for the costs that do remain. There may be a need for funds to sustain the family until the estate is settled, to pay off debt or otherwise provide for the surviving spouse or children. An estate will often need to sell assets to raise the needed cash. While some assets are relatively liquid, others may take months or even years to be sold. Working with your investment advisor, you may need to rearrange some of your assets to provide increased liquidity to your estate. If there are currently not enough liquid assets in the estate, consider life insurance as a way to provide the needed funds.

Caring for Survivors

Your survivors – a spouse, minor children, or a disabled child of any age – must also be considered in the estate plan.

---

[1] There may also be other, *non-tax* reasons, for including a bypass trust in an estate plan.

Key Estate Planning Considerations

A guardian for dependents: In case both parents are deceased, a guardian (and one or more alternates) should be named to care for minor children or other dependents.

Asset management: Professional asset management may be necessary to insure that financial resources are not squandered.

Who Makes Medical Decisions When I Cannot?

Modern medicine can now keep someone "alive" in situations that formerly would have resulted in death. Those who do not wish to have their lives artificially prolonged by such techniques must plan ahead and put their wishes in writing:

"Living Will": Also known as a "Directive to Physicians", this document provides guidance as to the type of medical treatment to be provided or withheld and the general circumstances under which the directive applies.

Durable power of attorney for health care: Many states have laws allowing a person to appoint someone to make health care decisions for them if they become unable to do so for themselves.

Durable power of attorney for financial affairs: Allows another individual to act on your behalf with regard to financial matters in the event of incapacity.

Outside the Legal Framework

Most of the documents involved in an estate plan are legal in nature and should be prepared by an attorney. However, not all documents involved in an estate plan are legal ones:

Letter of Instructions: A "Letter of Instructions" is an informal document that can include information such as your wishes regarding disposition of your remains, contact information for key advisors and family members, the location of important documents, the description and location of assets, user names and passwords for online accounts, or notes on family history. It is used to provide, in a private manner, direction and guidance to your family or executor in settling your estate.

Ethical Will: While a legal will or a trust is used to distribute assets, an "Ethical Will" serves to transfer values and beliefs. It is a very personal expression of the writer's life and values as well as the people, events, and experiences that influenced that life. In a very real sense, an ethical will is a spiritual legacy to future generations.

Seek Professional Guidance

Although an estate plan can be as simple as a set of hand-written instructions, there are a number of situations where legal guidance is considered vital:

To create a will or trust: An experienced attorney, familiar with local law, can prepare the legal documents required to meet the needs of your individual situation.

Estate taxes: If your estate is large enough to be subject to estate tax, your attorney can suggest ways to lighten the tax burden.

Squabbling heirs: Planning may be needed to minimize potential conflicts between your heirs or beneficiaries. Such disputes can occur when siblings don't get along or there are children from more than one marriage.

Property elsewhere: If you own property in more than one state or country, there may be a need for an ancillary probate. Living trusts are often used to transfer these assets and avoid the additional probate.

In addition to your attorney, your estate planning "team" will likely include experts from other disciplines such as income tax, life insurance, trust administration, charitable giving, and investment management. The professional guidance provided by such advisors is a key part of creating and implementing a successful estate plan.

Periodic Review

Because tax law and personal lives are never static, don't just put your estate plan in a drawer and forget about it. Many financial professionals recommend a periodic estate plan review.

The Importance of
Beneficiary Designations

Some types of assets allow the owner of the asset to name a "beneficiary." If the original owner later dies, ownership of the asset passes automatically to the named beneficiary. Because beneficiary designations are easy to use, they can be a key estate planning tool. However, significant negative tax, financial, and even personal problems can arise if the "wrong" individual or entity is named as the beneficiary.

Common Named Beneficiaries

A number of individuals, entities, or organizations are commonly named as a designated beneficiary:

- **Spouse:** A married individual's spouse is perhaps the most common beneficiary designation. Assets passing to a surviving spouse generally escape federal estate tax because of the unlimited marital deduction.[1]

- **Children:** Children, as adults or minors,[2] are often named as beneficiaries. Step-children or other children adopted informally generally need to be specifically identified.

- **Other family members:** Brothers and sisters, aunts and uncles, and nieces and nephews are frequently encountered beneficiaries.

- **Estate:** In some situations, the asset owner will name his or her estate as the beneficiary.

- **Trust:** As a part of a more complex estate plan, a trust may be named as a beneficiary. The trust must exist at the time of death for the beneficiary designation to be valid.

- **Charity:** A charity may be a designated beneficiary, which can reduce the owner's taxable estate.

- **Corporation or partnership:** Buy-sell agreements, key man insurance, stock redemption, split-dollar arrangements, and salary continuation plans are all valid business reasons why a corporation or partnership may be named as a beneficiary.

---

[1] The discussion here concerns federal income and estate tax law. State or local law may vary.

[2] In many states, 18 is the "age of majority" when an individual is considered, for legal purposes, to be an "adult." In some states the age of majority is 21.

The Importance of Beneficiary Designations

General Considerations in Making Beneficiary Designations

There are a number of general issues to consider when using beneficiary designations:

- **Keep beneficiary designations current:** Divorce, the birth of a child, the death of a beneficiary, or any number of other life changes can result in the need to update a beneficiary designation. Lack of planning can result in an ex-spouse receiving retirement benefits intended to provide for others or for assets to inadvertently be paid to the estate when a named beneficiary has predeceased the owner.

- **Your estate or executor as the beneficiary:** In these situations, the transferred assets must generally go through a costly and time-consuming court-supervised process known as "probate." During probate the proceeds can be subject to the claims of creditors. In some situations there may be valid estate planning reasons for naming the estate as a beneficiary.

- **A minor as beneficiary:** In most states, a minor generally cannot legally enter into contracts or own property. If a minor is named as the beneficiary of an asset, the end result is frequently an expensive court-appointed guardianship with court supervision of the use of these funds. Once reaching his or her majority, the individual then takes control of the assets.

- **Per Capita vs. Per Stirpes:** A beneficiary designation form will generally use one of these two terms to specify how an asset will be distributed if a named beneficiary predeceases the asset owner. In a "Per Capita" distribution, generally, each survivor (a living beneficiary or a deceased beneficiary's heirs) receives an equal share. In a "Per Stirpes" distribution, generally, a deceased beneficiary's heirs divide his or her share into equal portions. Many states have modified these rules.

- **Spousal rights:** In some states, a surviving spouse may have the right to claim a portion of a decedent's estate, including part of assets that can be transferred by a beneficiary designation. In Community Property[1] states, a surviving spouse may have rights that need to be considered.

---

[1] The Community Property states are Arizona, California, Idaho, Louisiana, Nevada, New Mexico, Texas, Washington, and Wisconsin. In Alaska, spouses may opt-in to a community property arrangement.

The Importance of Beneficiary Designations

- **Common disaster:** What provision has been made for a situation in which both the asset owner and a designated beneficiary (think of spouses who travel together) die in a common disaster? This contingency is frequently addressed in an individual's will.

- **Impact on the beneficiary:** Consider how receiving an asset will impact the beneficiary's life:

  - Is the beneficiary capable of using the inheritance as the donor might wish, or will it be wasted? Is the beneficiary capable of managing the inheritance?

  - Are there income tax considerations? Assets such as deferred annuities, or retirement plans such as IRAs or 401(k) plans, have varying distribution requirements, depending on who inherits the assets. Will one beneficiary pay less income tax than another?

  - Does the intended beneficiary need the money?

  - Are there other ways, such as via a will or trust, to transfer assets to the intended beneficiary that might ultimately benefit the beneficiary more than an outright gift?

- **Conflict with other estate planning documents:** In some cases, an individual will leave contradictory instructions with regard to how his or her assets should be distributed. For example, a will may indicate that an individual's retirement plan assets are to pass to a child, while the beneficiary designation form for the retirement plan shows that the ex-wife is to receive the funds. As a general rule, the instructions contained in the beneficiary designation form will trump those contained in a will or trust.

Seek Professional Guidance

While beneficiary designations are easy to use, they should be considered to be only one part of an overall, coordinated estate plan. The guidance of experienced, trained estate, income tax, and other financial professionals is strongly recommended.

Beneficiary Audit Checklist

Client: _____   Date: _____

Document or Asset	Document Location	Firm or Service Provider	Estimated Dollar Value	Beneficiary or Beneficiaries
Will				
Trust				
Life Insurance Policy				
Qualified Retirement Plan				
Traditional IRA				
Roth IRA				
Annuity				
Nonqualified Deferred Compensation Plan				
Other 1 _____				
Other 2				
Other 3 _____				
Other 4				
Other 5 _____				
Other 6				
Other 7 _____				
Other 8				

Estate Settlement Costs Funnel

What Happens to Your Estate at Death?

At a person's demise, his or her assets are subject to a number of expenses that can significantly reduce the size of the estate left for the heirs. Proper estate planning can minimize these expenses and determine in advance how the costs that remain will be paid.

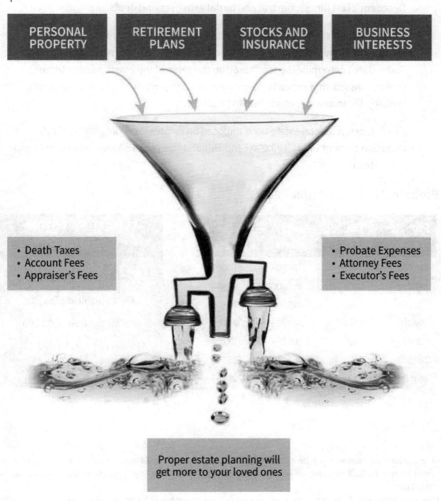

PERSONAL PROPERTY

RETIREMENT PLANS

STOCKS AND INSURANCE

BUSINESS INTERESTS

- Death Taxes
- Account Fees
- Appraiser's Fees

- Probate Expenses
- Attorney Fees
- Executor's Fees

Proper estate planning will get more to your loved ones

Estate Settlement Costs

Shortly after the death of an individual, certain costs of settling the estate must be paid in cash. Two primary goals of estate planning are to minimize these costs and decide in advance how the costs that remain will be paid.

Estate Settlement Costs

- Decedent's last illness, funeral and burial expenses and debts.

- Probate administration expenses (see below): Expenses include attorney's fees, executor's commissions, appraiser's fees, court costs, tax return preparation, etc. Some states determine the fees based on the value of the assets passing through probate. Assets that typically do not pass through probate would include: joint tenancy, life insurance, assets in living trusts, etc.

- Death taxes: A federal estate tax is imposed on estates exceeding the applicable exclusion amount of $11,180,000.[1] Individual states may also impose an inheritance or estate tax.

Probate Administration Fees[2]

Probate Assets	Fee to Each	Probate Assets	Fee to Each	TYPICAL STATUTORY FORMULA
$10,000	$400	$700,000	$17,000	4% on the 1st $100,000
40,000	1,600	750,000	18,000	
80,000	3,200	800,000	19,000	3% on the next $100,000
100,000	4,000	900,000	21,000	2% on the next $800,000
120,000	4,600	1,000,000	23,000	1% on the next $9,000,000
160,000	5,800	1,250,000	25,500	.5% on the next $15,000,000
200,000	7,000	1,500,000	28,000	

---

[1] The applicable exclusion amount is the dollar value of assets protected from federal estate tax by an individual's applicable credit amount. For 2018, the applicable exclusion amount is $11,180,000. In 2017, the applicable exclusion amount was $5,490,000.

[2] This table illustrates typical statutory attorney's fees and executor's commissions for probating an estate.

Estate Settlement Costs

Probate Assets	Fee to Each	Probate Assets	Fee to Each
$250,000	$8,000	$1,750,000	$30,500
300,000	9,000	2,000,000	33,000
350,000	10,000	2,500,000	38,000
400,000	11,000	2,750,000	40,500
450,000	12,000	3,000,000	43,000
500,000	13,000	3,500,000	48,000
550,000	14,000	4,000,000	53,000
575,000	14,500	4,500,000	58,000
600,000	15,000	5,000,000	63,000
625,000	15,500	10,000,000	113,000
650,000	16,000	15,000,000	138,000
675,000	16,500	25,000,000	TBD[1]

[1] A reasonable amount to be determined by the court.

The Federal Estate Tax

An Overview for 2018

The federal estate tax is an excise tax on the right to transfer property after death. The gross estate includes the fair market value of all assets owned by the decedent as of the date of death, including retirement plans and life insurance policies. When the taxable portion of an estate reaches $1,000,000, it enters the top estate tax bracket of 40%.

The tax applies only to taxable estates in 2018 that *exceed* the applicable exclusion amount of $11,180,000.[1]

Transfers between spouses generally qualify for the unlimited marital deduction and are free of current tax.

The estate tax return (Form 706) and any taxes due are generally payable nine months after date of death. In some situations, a portion of the taxes may be paid to the IRS in installments.

If the value of the estate assets declines during the first six months after death (which often happens if the decedent owned a business), the value (for all assets) as of six months after death may be used on the tax return.

Lifetime gifts that exceed the annual gift tax exclusion (In 2018, $15,000 per donee per year) will also reduce the estate owner's applicable credit amount.

Some transfers made during one's lifetime may be brought back into the decedent's estate. A few examples are listed below:

- Gifts of life insurance policies within three years prior to death.

- Transfer of an asset from which the donor retains an income for his or her life.

- Transfer of an asset where donor retains the right to alter or terminate the transfer.

- Assets placed in joint tenancy with another are included in the gross estate.

---

[1] The applicable exclusion amount is the dollar value of assets protected from federal estate tax by an individual's applicable credit amount. For 2018, the applicable exclusion amount is $11,180,000. In 2017, the applicable exclusion amount was $5,490,000.

How the Federal Estate Tax Works

A Simplified Illustration

1. DETERMINE THE GROSS ESTATE.

Total the fair market value of all assets the decedent owned:

- Residence, real estate.
- Business interests, stocks, bonds, retirement accounts.
- Life insurance, personal property, etc.

2. SUBTRACT THE DEDUCTIONS.

Certain items may be deducted to determine the taxable estate amount:

- Assets passing to surviving spouse.
- Debts of the decedent.
- Probate and burial expenses.
- Bequests to charities, etc.
- State death taxes.

3. CALCULATE THE TAX.

Using the taxable estate amount, calculate the federal estate tax.

Graduated tax rates are used, with the highest marginal rate in 2018 being 40%.

4. TAKE APPLICABLE CREDITS.

For assets passing to someone other than a spouse, reduce the tax by the applicable credit amount.

Other credits may apply.

5. PAY THE TAX.

After subtracting the credits, any remaining tax is due nine months after death – in cash.

Due in Cash

Federal Estate Tax Tables

Recent Federal Estate Tax Changes

The past few years have seen a parade of changes to the federal estate tax. Under the provisions of the Economic Growth and Tax Relief Reconciliation Act of 2001 (EGTRRA), the federal estate tax underwent a number of scheduled changes during the years 2002-2010. During this period, the top federal estate tax rate decreased, while the dollar amount of assets that could be transferred at death free of estate tax gradually increased. Under EGTRRA, the federal estate tax even completely disappeared for one year, 2010.

The 2010 Tax Relief Act temporarily extended many of the tax provisions of EGTRRA. Under this legislation, in 2012, a top marginal rate of 35% applied to taxable transfers in excess of $500,000, with an "applicable exclusion amount" of $5,120,000. The applicable exclusion amount is the dollar amount of assets protected from estate tax by an individual's "applicable credit amount."

The American Taxpayer Relief Act of 2012 (ATRA 2012), effective in 2013, provided for a top marginal estate tax rate of 40%, on taxable transfers in excess of $1,000,000.

Finally, the Tax Cuts and Jobs Act of 2017, (TCJA), for 2018-2025, doubled the applicable exclusion amount from $5,000,000 under prior law, to $10,000,000. Adjusted for inflation, the applicable exclusion amount for 2018 is $11,180,000, equal to an applicable credit amount of $4,417,800. Both of these values are subject to adjustment for inflation in future years. Under the TCJA, the applicable exclusion amount (and the equivalent applicable credit amount) will return to the $5,000,000 level, adjusted for inflation, in 2026.

Federal Estate Tax Table

The following table applies to the taxable estates of individuals dying in 2018. In simple terms, the "taxable" estate is a decedent's gross estate (everything he or she owned on the date of death) less transfers to a spouse, gifts to charity, and taxes and other allowable estate expenses.

Under current law, this tax rate table is not scheduled to change in future years.

Federal Estate Tax Tables

If Taxable Estate...		Tentative Tax Is...		
Is Over...	But Not Over...	Tax	Plus %	Of Excess Over...
$0	$10,000	$0	18.00%	$0
10,000	20,000	1,800	20.00%	10,000
20,000	40,000	3,800	22.00%	20,000
40,000	60,000	8,200	24.00%	40,000
60,000	80,000	13,000	26.00%	60,000
80,000	100,000	18,200	28.00%	80,000
100,000	150,000	23,800	30.00%	100,000
150,000	250,000	38,800	32.00%	150,000
250,000	500,000	70,800	34.00%	250,000
500,000	750,000	155,800	37.00%	500,000
750,000	1,000,000	248,300	39.00%	750,000
1,000,000	and up	345,800	40.00%	1,000,000

Federal Estate Tax Worksheet

Assumes Death Occurs During 2018

A. Fair market value of real estate and business property $\qquad$ $_____

B. Fair market value of investments, stocks, bonds, funds, etc. $_____

C. Fair market value of personal and other property $_____

   D. **Gross estate** (sum of items A, B and C) $_____

E. Administration expenses (funeral expenses, etc.) $_____

F. Debts of decedent $_____

G. Marital deduction (assets to spouse) $_____

H. Charitable deduction (bequests to charity) $_____

I. State death taxes $_____

   J. **Total deductions** (sum of items E through I) ($_____)

   K. **Taxable estate** (item D minus item J) $_____

L. Adjusted taxable gifts (gifts made during life) $_____

M. Estate tax base amount (sum of items K and L) $_____

   N. **Gross estate tax** (on item M from table below) $_____

O. Applicable credit (maximum of $4,417,800)[1] $_____

P. Gift taxes paid on lifetime gifts $_____

   Q. **Total credits** (sum of items O and P) ($_____)

   R. **Net federal estate tax** (item N minus item Q) $_____

---

[1] In 2018, the applicable credit may exceed $4,417,800 (up to a maximum of $8,835,600) if there is a "deceased spousal unused exclusion amount" available.

Federal Estate Tax Approximator

Assumes Death Occurs in 2018

Item Description	Value
Estimated gross estate at death	$10,000,000
Debts, probate, mortgages, etc.	-2,500,000
State death taxes	0
Net estate at death	**7,500,000**
Assets passing to spouse	-5,000,000
Assets passing to charities	-1,000,000
Taxable estate	**1,500,000**
Adjusted taxable gifts made after 1976	100,000
Adjusted taxable estate	**1,600,000**
Tentative federal estate tax	585,800
Gift taxes paid after 1976	-10,000
Applicable (unified) credit amount[1]	-2,141,800
Federal estate tax due	**0**

[1] Calculated using an annual inflation rate for the applicable exclusion amount of 0.

Valuation of Estate Assets

Assets belonging to the deceased estate owner are included in his or her estate at their fair market value on the date of death or, if the executor elects, their value six months after date of death.[1]

A Few Selected Assets

Type of Assets	How Asset Is Valued	Reference
Listed stocks and bonds (including over the counter)	The mean between highest and lowest quoted selling prices on the valuation date.	Reg. Sec. 20.2031-2(b)(1)
Mutual funds	Valued at their bid price or redemption value (i.e., the amount the fund would pay the shareholder if it redeemed the shares on the valuation date).	Regs. Secs. 20.2031-8 (b) and 25. 2512-6(b); U.S. vs. Cartwright, 411 U.S. 546 (1973)
Survivor's annuity (under a joint and survivor annuity contract)	The amount that the same insurance company would require for a single life annuity on the survivor, as of the applicable valuation date.	Reg. Sec. 20.2031-8
Close corporation stock	Fair market value is based on history and nature of business, economic outlook, book value, earning capacity, dividend paying capacity, goodwill, recent sales of stock and similar publicly traded company stock.	Rev. Rul. 59-60, 1959-1 CB 237
Real estate	Fair market value of real estate in the United States or in a foreign country.	IRC Secs. 2031, 2032A, 2033
Real estate (farm or corporate owned)	Value may be determined by actual use rather than on its highest and best use if certain conditions are met.	IRC Sec. 2032A
Mortgages and notes	The amount of the unpaid principal plus accrued interest, unless a lower value can be proven (i.e., an insolvent debtor).	Reg. Sec. 20.2031-4

---

[1] "Six months after date of death" is referred to as the "alternate valuation date." Use of the alternate valuation date election must reduce both the value of the gross estate and the federal estate tax liability. If this election is made, assets sold or distributed during the six-month period are valued at the date of sale or distribution. Under proposed regulations, generally effective for decedents dying on or after April 25, 2008, the alternate valuation date method may be elected only if the property remaining in the estate six months after the decedent's death has declined in value due to "market conditions" and not merely because of a lapse of time or other post-death event.

Valuation of Estate Assets

Type of Assets	How Asset Is Valued	Reference
Life insurance on the decedent's life	Amount receivable by the estate or by a named beneficiary, if the deceased insured had incidents of ownership in the policy.	Reg. Sec. 20.2042-1
Life insurance policy owned by decedent on the life of another person	The cost of buying another policy of the same value and same type on the same insured.	Reg. Sec. 20.2031-8
Joint tenancy with a spouse	One-half of the value of property owned jointly by spouses is included in the estate of the first spouse to die.	IRC Sec. 2040(b)
Joint tenancy with other than spouse (general rule)	Entire value of property less the original contribution of the survivor is included in the estate of the first joint tenant to die.	IRC Sec. 2040(a)

Basic Steps in the Estate Planning Process

There are basic steps to take in planning your estate. A typical program would be as follows:

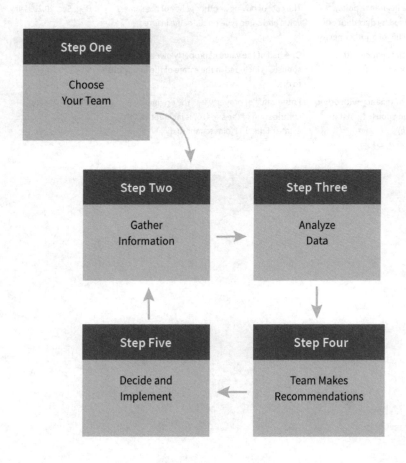

Basic Steps in the Estate Planning Process

The Basic Steps

- **Choose your team:** Choose, as needed, your attorney, tax professional, insurance professional, trust officer, planned-giving specialist or financial advisor.
- **Gather information:** A completed fact finder serves to list your goals and objectives, shows names, ages, assets and liabilities, desired heirs; goals and objectives.
- **Analyze data:** Pretend death occurred yesterday. What happens to your estate, your business, and your family? What if you die 10 years from now? Your team analyzes the data to provide you with the results.
- **Team makes recommendations:** Review the suggestions made by your team to overcome current plan shortcomings.
- **Decide and implement:** Select the plan that best fits your needs and goals. Sign essential documents (e.g. wills and trusts), purchase needed insurance, and change investments as necessary.
- **Periodic review:** Starting the cycle over. Because the world – and your assets – are constantly changing, many advisors recommend an annual planning review.

Meet the Estate Planning Team

Estate planning is a complex field that covers many areas including wills, trusts, insurance, accounting, business continuation, and estate, gift and income taxes. It would be difficult to find one person who is a trained and licensed expert in all of these areas. Most often, the needed skills and knowledge are available only by bringing together an Estate Planning Team. The various members of the team  can then work closely to preserve the estate and pass it on to the heirs with the least amount of expense and aggravation.

You Are the Captain of Your Team

Possible team members may include the following:

- Attorney.

- Tax Professional.

- Insurance Professional.

- Trust Administrator.

- Charitable Advisor.

- Financial Advisor.

Choose the Estate Planning Team

Estate planning is a complex field that covers many areas including wills, trusts, insurance, accounting, business continuation, and estate, gift, and income taxes. It would be difficult to find one person who is a trained and licensed expert in all of these areas. Most often, the needed skills and knowledge are available only by bringing together an Estate Planning Team. The various members of the team can then work closely to preserve the estate and pass it on to the heirs with the least amount of expense and aggravation. Potential members of the team may include the following.

Estate Planning Attorney

Most attorneys can draft a basic will. However, one who specializes in estate planning law will be more familiar with the various tools and techniques available to save you and your heirs thousands of dollars in taxes, probate and administration expenses.

Tax Professional

Federal and state laws require that a number of income and estate tax returns be filed shortly after your demise. Even in the simplest of situations, properly completing these tax returns can be a complex and confusing process. These returns will be even more involved if you own a business or rental real estate.

Insurance Professional

Life insurance is often utilized in estate planning solutions. Contracts differ greatly and are issued by companies with varying degrees of financial strength.

A life insurance professional will help you choose a financially strong company, the correct type of policy for your situation, and the correct amount of insurance. Determining who will be the owner of a life insurance policy is a key question. The answer can add or avoid hundreds of thousands of dollars in estate taxes.

Choose the Estate Planning Team

Trust Administrator

If you select a corporate fiduciary (a bank or trust company) as executor of your will or trustee of your trust, you should consider involving them in the development of your estate plan.

Sometimes they have important provisions which should be added to the will or trust document to help them administer the estate.

Planned-Giving Specialist

Charitable organizations often have planned-giving specialists who are well versed in methods of making lifetime gifts or bequests at the time of death, which can benefit you and your heirs.

Financial Advisor

Sometimes the life insurance professional, accountant, or other member of the estate planning team may have special training in financial planning. Other times, a person who specializes in financial planning may be part of your team. If so, he or she will often take a very active part in directing the formation of the overall estate plan.

The Captain of the Team

You are the captain of the team. The final decisions must be made by you after carefully reviewing the recommendations of the other members of your estate planning team.

How Often Should Legal Documents Be Reviewed?

Once a legal document is completed and signed, it is often carefully laid to rest in a safe deposit box or file drawer and comes out again only when a party dies or a conflict arises.

Prudent persons periodically review and update their legal documents. Just how often depends, of course, on the document and which circumstances have changed. The following list sets forth some events that may require the updating of a legal document.

Life Events

- Marriage.
- Dissolution of a marriage (divorce).
- Death of a spouse.
- Disability of a spouse or child.
- A substantial change in estate size.
- A move to another state.
- Death of executor, trustee or guardian.
- Birth or adoption.
- Serious illness of family member.
- Change in business interest.
- Retirement.
- Change in health.
- Change in insurability for life insurance.
- Acquisition of property in another state.
- Changes in tax, property or probate and trust law.
- A change in beneficiary attitudes.
- Financial responsibility of a child.

If there is any question as to the effect of a change in circumstances on your will, trust, buy-sell agreement, asset titles and beneficiary designations, etc., contact the appropriate member of your team and have it reviewed before a crisis arises.

Choosing an Attorney

Choosing an attorney is a key part of your personal financial life. Unfortunately, the process of finding the right individual can be confusing and frustrating. First of all, you need to be able to find someone who is qualified in the area of the law with which you need help. Secondly, you should be comfortable working with that person.

Always remember that your attorney works for you. Your attorney has a professional and ethical duty to put your interests first. The attorney's primary role is to provide advice and guidance; the final decision as to what action should be taken is yours.

How to Find an Attorney

Talk to people you know and ask about their experience. Another good idea is to check with the local bar association because they often have a referral program.

What Criteria Should Be Used?

In simple terms, the goal is to find the best qualified person you can afford.

On your part, you need to know exactly what it is you wish to accomplish. Do you want to set up a trust? Do you need help in settling an estate? Do you have a dispute with the IRS? Are you filing for divorce? Were you injured in an accident? Have you been charged with a crime? Do you need to draft documents and contracts for your business?

No one individual can be proficient in all areas of the law. That's why most attorneys tend to concentrate their efforts in a specific area of expertise, which can facilitate your search.

What Does Being Licensed Mean?

An individual must pass the state bar exam to practice law in a particular state. Each state is different and has its own examination. Therefore, being licensed in one state does not allow an attorney to practice law in another state. Passing a state's bar means that the individual has demonstrated that he or she possesses a minimum level of legal knowledge and is therefore authorized to represent clients before the courts of that state.

An attorney should be willing to furnish you with his or her state bar number. You can then check with the state bar to verify that the attorney is licensed. In some states, you can find out if he or she has been disciplined for past misconduct. Of course, merely being licensed is no assurance that a particular attorney is the best person to handle your case.

Interview the Attorney

Interview your attorney as you would anyone you were considering hiring for a job. Your attorney should be someone you are comfortable with and with whom you can communicate freely. Even more important, your attorney must be someone you can trust.

Experience

Ask the attorney about his or her legal background and experience. Although many state bar associations do not require an attorney to be experienced or qualified in a specific area of law to practice in that area, some states do recognize highly specialized areas of legal expertise. At a minimum, you should know if your attorney has ever handled the type of matter you need help with.

Next, you should ask about your attorney's non-law background and experience. Most attorneys have had a life outside of law school. The most important experience relating to your matter may not be law or even law related.

Large Firm vs. Individual Practitioner

Since most attorneys tend to specialize in their practice of law, they often find that they can not provide all the services a client may require. Therefore, an attorney generally has two choices: work with a large firm and refer the client to specialists within the firm; or develop a list of outside attorneys to refer clients to for matters they choose not to handle. From the client's point of view, this decision is a matter of personal choice.

- **Large firms:** Advantages: One-stop shopping, generally good in-house expertise and can usually handle a variety of concerns. Disadvantages: May lack understanding of you and your business; sometimes more expensive.

- **Individual Practitioner:** Advantages: More likely to take the time to fully understand you and your needs; generally lower hourly rates. Disadvantages: Limited expertise, may hit time constraints when doing trials. In addition, you may need to work with more than one office to handle all matters.

Items to Discuss Before Meeting with an Attorney

There are several topics that should be considered prior to meeting with the attorney who will draft a will or a trust.

Guardians for Minor Children

Who is best able to cope with the raising of your minor children? A brother, sister, or a close friend may be a better choice than a grandparent.

Factors to consider would include the ages of the proposed guardians and their children, the ages of your children and the number of them who are still minors, and the health and financial situation of all parties. Decide on alternative choices, in the event your first choice is unwilling or unable to serve. If you name a couple as guardians and one of them dies, would you want the surviving co-guardian to act as sole guardian? What if they divorce?

Executor of the Estate

If all or part of your estate passes through probate, whom do you want to handle the details of paying your debts and death taxes and distributing the remaining assets to the beneficiaries named in your will?

Living Trust

Is it important to you to avoid probate? Make a list of your assets and their approximate values, along with a list of mortgages or other debt on any property. Your attorney can give you an estimate of what it will cost your heirs to pass your estate through probate.

The living trust is frequently used to avoid or reduce probate expenses. Ask your attorney to explain the advantages and disadvantages of this type of trust.

Trustee

If you have a trust, either in your will or a separate living trust, you will need to name a trustee to manage investments, pay taxes, make distributions, etc. In the event he or she dies, you will want to provide for one or more successor trustees.

Items to Discuss Before Meeting with an Attorney

A Corporate or Individual Fiduciary

Executors and trustees are referred to as "fiduciaries" because of the higher standard of care which is required of them in managing the assets of another person. Consider the facts of your own estate relative to the list of advantages shown below.

- Advantages of a corporate fiduciary:

  - Don't die or become disabled – permanence.

  - Financially accountable for their mistakes.

  - Impartial as to the children. This may prevent the children from becoming bitter towards an individual trustee who happens to be a friend or relative and who doesn't make distributions every time the children ask for something.

  - Have investment expertise, tax and accounting abilities, and computer capabilities. Studies show that they save many dollars in the average estate.

  - Refuse loans to hard-up friends of the trustee.

  - Keep current with the constant changes in the law.

- Advantages of an individual fiduciary:

  - A relative or friend may not charge a fee.

  - A relative or friend may have a more personal interest.

  - An individual may have special expertise (i.e., running the family business).

Suggestion: Some people prefer the use of an individual and a corporate trustee, as co-trustees, to obtain the advantages of each.

Distributions to Children

If you do not want your assets distributed outright to your children in the event of your demise, they should probably be held in a trust. The trustee will take care of their needs as instructed in the trust. However, at some future time you will probably want to distribute the assets to them.

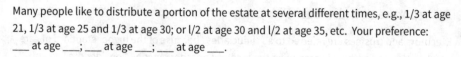

Items to Discuss Before Meeting with an Attorney

Many people like to distribute a portion of the estate at several different times, e.g., 1/3 at age 21, 1/3 at age 25 and 1/3 at age 30; or l/2 at age 30 and l/2 at age 35, etc. Your preference: ___ at age ___; ___ at age ___; ___ at age ___.

Final Heirs

In the event your children pass away prior to inheriting your estate, to whom would you want your estate to pass? For example, one could pass ½ to each spouse's side of the family (e.g., parents, brothers, sisters, etc.).

Healthcare Decisions

Who makes healthcare decisions if you are unable to do so? Consider alternative choices if your first choice is unwilling or unable to serve.

Charitable Bequests

Would you be interested in making a charitable bequest, especially if it reduced your income and death taxes?

Other Questions

Would you want your children to remain in the present house?

Is it important to reduce your death tax obligation?

Is it important that your assets pass to your heirs without the expense and delay of probate?

Advantages of a Will

Avoids Distribution Under the Law of Intestacy

The state intestacy law will pass property to certain relatives of the decedent. These laws have been drafted to be fair in the average situation, but most persons would like to choose who will receive their estate when they die.

Permits the Nomination of a Guardian for Minor Children

Without a nomination in a will, the court will appoint a guardian of the person for minor children. Relatives are not always the best choice for a guardian and consideration must be given to the financial situation of the potential guardian, as well as his or her health, age, willingness and ability to care for your children.

Waiver of the Probate Bond

In the absence of a will, the court will require a fiduciary bond to be posted by the administrator (executor) of the estate to guarantee the replacement of any funds embezzled or diverted by him. Since this additional cost must be borne by the estate, the estate owner may want to waive the bond requirement in the will. Great care should be used in selecting an executor.

Choosing the Executor

The duties of the executor of an estate can be very time consuming and frustrating, especially to a spouse who has just lost his or her loved one. In the will, a qualified individual and/or a corporate trust company can be chosen to handle these responsibilities.

Making Specific Bequests to Individuals

An individual may bequeath specific items of jewelry, heirlooms and furniture, or make cash bequests, and be certain that they will pass to the proper persons. Without a will, written or oral instructions may not be followed.

Sale of Assets During the Administration of Probate

Additional expense to the estate can generally be avoided by permitting the sale of assets without the executor having to publish a notice of sale in the newspaper. A sale of assets may be necessary in order to pay death taxes and expenses of probate.

Authorizing the Continuation of a Business

Unless the will authorizes the continuation of a business, the executor must operate it at his or her own risk. Many executors may elect not to administer the estate unless this risk is borne by the estate.

Deferring Distributions to Minors

When parents die leaving minor children, each child's share of the estate must be held in a guardianship account until he or she attains the age of 18 (or 21), at which time the entire remaining share is distributed outright. Trust provisions can be placed in the will to defer these distributions until a more mature age.

Peace of Mind

Although this advantage cannot be measured in dollars and cents, when the estate is in order an emotional load is lifted from the person who is concerned for his or her family's well being.

Types of Wills and Trusts

There are many varieties of wills and trusts to fit the needs of each individual. Only a qualified attorney should draft these documents.

A few of the more common documents are listed below.

- **Basic will:** A basic or simple will generally gives everything outright to a surviving spouse, children or other heirs.

- **Will with contingent trust:** Frequently, married couples with minor children will pass everything to their spouse, if living, and if not, to a trust for their minor children until they become more mature.

- **Pour-over will:** The so-called "pour-over" will is generally used in conjunction with a living trust. It picks up any assets that were not transferred to the trust during the person's lifetime and pours them into the trust upon death. The assets may be subject to probate administration, however.

- **Tax-saving will:** A will may be used to create a testamentary bypass trust. This trust provides lifetime benefits to the surviving spouse, without having those trust assets included in the survivor's estate at his or her subsequent death.

- **Living trust without tax planning:** Generally, the surviving spouse has full control of the principal and income of this type of trust. Its main purpose is to avoid probate. If required, the trust can also be used to manage the assets for beneficiaries who are not yet ready to inherit the assets outright, because they lack experience in financial and investment matters.

- **Bypass trust:** This type of trust allows the first spouse to die of a married couple to set aside up to $11,180,000[1] in assets for specific heirs while providing income and flexibility to the surviving spouse. The appreciation on assets in the trust can avoid estate tax.

---

[1] The applicable exclusion amount is the dollar value of assets protected from federal estate tax by an individual's applicable credit amount. For 2018, the applicable exclusion amount is $11,180,000. In 2017, the applicable exclusion amount was $5,490,000.

- **QTIP trust:** A type of trust known as a QTIP trust allows the first spouse to die to specify who will receive his or her assets after the surviving spouse dies. Use of a QTIP also permits the deferral of death taxes on the assets until the death of the surviving spouse.

  QTIP means "qualified terminable interest property." The income earned on assets in a QTIP trust must be given to the surviving spouse for his or her lifetime. After the death of the surviving spouse, however, the assets then pass to beneficiaries chosen by the first spouse to die, frequently children of a prior marriage.

  Even if there are no children of a prior marriage, some estate owners use this type of trust to prevent a subsequent spouse of the survivor from diverting or wasting estate assets. A QTIP trust can only hold certain qualifying property. For this reason, it is often used in tandem with a bypass trust.

- **Qualified domestic trust:** Transfers at death to a noncitizen spouse will not qualify for the marital deduction unless the assets pass to a qualified domestic trust (QDOT). The QDOT rules require a U.S. Trustee (unless waived by the IRS) and other measures that help ensure collection of a death tax at the surviving noncitizen spouse's later demise.

Note: Additional trusts may be used for current income tax savings or to remove life insurance from the taxable estate, but the above-described documents should generally be considered for a person's estate plan.

Various Estate Planning Arrangements

A Summary of Benefits

Benefits	No Will	Basic Will	Trust Will	Basic Living Trust	Bypass with Living Trust	Bypass, QTIP,[1] & Living Trust
1. Allows you to select:						
a. Beneficiaries of estate,	No	Yes	Yes	Yes	Yes	Yes
b. Executor of will,	No	Yes	Yes	Yes[2]	Yes[2]	Yes[2]
c. Guardians for children, and	No	Yes	Yes	Yes[2]	Yes[2]	Yes[2]
d. Trustees of trust.	No	No	Yes	Yes	Yes	Yes
2. Avoids probate costs.[3]	No	No	No	Yes	Yes	Yes
3. Provides asset management for children over age 18.	No	No	Yes	Yes	Yes	Yes
4. Protects estate owner from a conservatorship.	No	No	No	Yes	Yes	Yes
5. Designed to save death taxes for couples.	No	No	Maybe[4]	No	Yes	Yes
6. Allows the first spouse to die to determine the ultimate beneficiaries of the estate in excess of $11,180,000[5], while still deferring the death taxes.	No	No	Yes	No	No	Yes

[1] QTIP stands for qualified terminable interest property trust.

[2] Each living trust is generally accompanied by a "pour over" type of will which picks up assets not put into the trust during lifetime and transfers them after death. Executors/guardians are named in a will.

[3] If all of the assets are in the living trust, probate is not necessary. However, there will usually be some expense for legal advice or the transfer of assets not in the trust. Without a trust, probate costs may exceed 5% of the total estate.

[4] Some trust wills contain bypass trusts designed to save death taxes, while others merely manage assets.

[5] The applicable exclusion amount is the dollar value of assets protected from federal estate tax by an individual's applicable credit amount. For 2018, the applicable exclusion amount is $11,180,000. In 2017, the applicable exclusion amount was $5,490,000.

Various Estate Planning Arrangements

Brief Description of Arrangement

- **No will:** Your estate passes to heirs picked by the legislature.

- **Basic will:** Generally passes everything to your spouse, if living, otherwise to your children when they reach age 18.

- **Trust will:** May contain bypass and QTIP trusts or may pass everything to your spouse, if living, otherwise for children.

- **Basic living trust:** Designed to avoid probate and provide asset management. Used for smaller estates and single persons.

- **Bypass with living trust:** Designed to set aside assets for specific heirs while giving the surviving spouse income and flexibility. Appreciation on assets inside the trust can avoid estate tax.

- **Bypass and QTIP with living trust:** Same as the bypass with living trust, plus it gives the first spouse to die more control over who will eventually receive his or her assets after the surviving spouse dies. Also called a QTIP trust.

No Will? No Problem!

State Drawn Will in Common Law States

Last Will of Paul Procrastinator

First: I direct the Probate Judge to appoint anyone of his choosing to administer all property in my name and distribute it under the terms of this will.

Second: I direct that all of my assets be converted to cash, all of my debts paid, including taxes, probate fees, administrative fees, and attorney's fee.

Third: I direct that one-half (if I am survived by one child) or one-third (if I am survived by two or more children) of my separate property, be paid to my spouse.

Fourth: I direct that the balance of my estate be distributed outright, and in cash, in equal shares to my children. If any child be a minor, I direct that his share be held by a guardian for his benefit. The guardian may be anyone of the court's choosing.

Fifth: When each of my minor children attains age 18, I direct that his share be then paid to him outright, regardless of his financial or emotional maturity.

Sixth: In the event that my spouse does not survive me, I direct that his/her share be added to the children's shares created under Articles Fourth and Fifth

Seventh: If none of my children survive me but my spouse does, I direct that the remainder under Article Third be distributed outright in the following manner:

- One-half of my separate property to my spouse.

- The balance to my parents, if living, otherwise to my brothers and sisters or their heirs.

Eighth: If I am not survived by my spouse, children or parents, I direct the Probate Court to seek out my closest blood relatives and divide my estate among them in a way which gives an equal share to my closest relatives or their descendants.

Ninth: If no relatives are located, I direct that all of my property go to the State.

No Will? No Problem!

State Drawn Will in Community Property States

Last Will of Paul Procrastinator

First: I direct the Probate Judge to appoint anyone of his choosing to administer all property in my name and distribute it under the terms of this will.

Second: I direct that all of my assets be converted to cash, all of my debts paid, including taxes, probate fees, administrative fees, and attorney's fee.

Third: I direct that all our community property and one-half (if I am survived by one child) or one-third (if I am survived by two or more children) of my separate property, be paid to my spouse.

Fourth: I direct that the balance of my estate be distributed outright, and in cash, in equal shares to my children. If any child be a minor, I direct that his share be held by a guardian for his benefit. The guardian may be anyone of the court's choosing.

Fifth: When each of my minor children attains age 18, I direct that his share be then paid to him outright, regardless of his financial or emotional maturity.

Sixth: In the event that my spouse does not survive me, I direct that his/her share be added to the children's shares created under Articles Fourth and Fifth.

Seventh: If none of my children survive me but my spouse does, I direct that the remainder under Article Third be distributed outright in the following manner:

- One-half of my separate property and all of our community property to my spouse.
- The balance to my parents, if living, otherwise to my brothers and sisters or their heirs.

Eighth: If I am not survived by my spouse, children or parents, I direct the Probate Court to seek out my closest blood relatives and divide my estate among them in a way which gives an equal share to my closest relatives or their descendants.

Ninth: If no relatives are located, I direct that all of my property go to the State.

Note: The community property states are Arizona, California, Idaho, Louisiana, Nevada, New Mexico, Texas, Washington, and Wisconsin. In Alaska, spouses may opt-in to a community property arrangement.

Duties of an Executor

The executor of an estate is named in one's will and has many duties and responsibilities. Some of the more important tasks include:

- Find the latest will and read it.

- File a petition with the court to probate the will.

- Assemble all of the decedent's assets.

  - Take possession of safe deposit box contents.

  - Consult with banks and savings and loans in the area to find all accounts of the deceased. Also check for cash and other valuables hidden around the home.

  - Transfer all securities to his or her name (as executor) and continue to collect dividends and interest on behalf of the heirs of the deceased.

  - Find, inventory and protect household and personal effects and other personal property.

  - Collect all life insurance proceeds payable to the estate.

  - Find and inventory all real estate deeds, mortgages, leases and tax information. Provide immediate management for rental properties.

  - Arrange ancillary administration for out-of-state property.

  - Collect monies owed the deceased and check interests in estates of other deceased persons.

- Find and safeguard business interests, valuables, personal property, important papers, the residence, etc.

- Inventory all assets and arrange for appraisal of those for which it is appropriate.

- Determine liquidity needs. Assemble bookkeeping records. Review investment portfolio. Sell appropriate assets.

- Pay valid claims against the estate. Reject improper claims and defend the estate, if necessary.

- Pay state and federal taxes due.

  - File income tax returns for the decedent and the estate.

  - Determine whether the estate qualifies for special use valuation under IRC Sec. 2032A or the deferral of estate taxes under IRC Secs. 6161 or 6166.

  - If the surviving spouse is not a U.S. citizen, consider a qualified domestic trust to defer the payment of federal estate taxes.

  - File federal estate tax return and state death and/or inheritance tax return.

- Prepare statement of all receipts and disbursements. Pay attorney's fees and executor's commissions. Assist the attorney in defending the estate, if necessary.

- Distribute specific bequests and the residue; obtain tax releases and receipts as directed by the court. Establish a testamentary trust (or pour over into a living trust), where appropriate.

Steps in a Probate

An Overview

EXECUTOR/ADMINISTRATOR	Submits Will for Probate →	PROBATE COURT

1. TAKES CONTROL OF ESTATE ASSETS.

- Makes an inventory.
- Has assets appraised.
- Maintains insurance on assets.

2. NOTIFIES CREDITORS OF PROBATE.

- Sells assets, if necessary.
- Pays valid creditor's claims.
- Defends against frivolous claims.

3. PREPARES TAX RETURNS.

- Prepares final income tax return.
- Prepares federal estate tax return (if the taxable estate exceeds $11,180,000 in 2018).

4. PETITIONS COURT TO:

- Pay attorney and executor fees, and
- Distribute remaining assets to beneficiaries (or their trusts).

Avoiding Probate

The probating of a will permits a court of law to supervise the transfer of assets from the decedent to his heirs. A typical probate lasts about one year, with six months generally being a minimum time if everything proceeds according to schedule.

Because of high attorney's fees, executor's commissions and court costs, and the often-unwanted publicity and the time delay involved in probating an estate, many people attempt to avoid probate administration. Some of the methods of avoidance are listed below.

Joint Tenancy

Joint tenancy is a form of title arrangement, usually between spouses. The joint tenancy is dissolved after one tenant dies, with title passing automatically to the surviving joint tenant. There may be income tax disadvantages to this arrangement. Creditors of either joint tenant can attach the asset. It may also frustrate estate tax savings which are anticipated from carefully drafted wills and trusts.

Community Property with Rights of Survivorship

Title passes automatically to the surviving spouse with no income tax disadvantages as with joint tenancy.

Totten Trust

A Totten trust is a vehicle for passing savings accounts to heirs. Passbook accounts are held in trust for another. Typical wording would be: "John Doe, in trust for Johnny Doe."

Life Insurance

The proceeds of life insurance are rarely subject to probate administration, unless the insured's estate is the beneficiary or all of the named beneficiaries pre-decease the insured.

Lifetime Gifts

Even gifts made shortly prior to death will avoid probate. However, they may be brought back into the estate for death tax purposes. Also, gifts carry the donor's basis to the donee, whereas appreciated assets in the decedent's estate will generally get a new or stepped-up basis.

Revocable Living Trust

The revocable living trust is an effective method of avoiding probate. It has the additional advantage of providing management of the funds for the heirs for some time after the decedent's demise. Also, in the event the person setting up the living trust (also called an inter-vivos trust) becomes mentally incompetent or otherwise incapacitated, a successor trustee can take over management of the estate. Generally, this type of trust will not produce any estate tax savings.

Transfer on Death (TOD)

Many states have adopted the provisions of the Uniform TOD Security Registration Act, which permits securities and securities accounts to be registered so that ownership automatically passes to named beneficiaries at the death of the owner(s).

Transfer on Death

Many states have adopted a version of the Uniform TOD Security Registration Act. TOD is an acronym that stands for "transfer on death". The provisions of the Act permit securities and securities accounts to be registered so that ownership automatically passes to named beneficiaries upon the death of the owner or the last-to-die of multiple owners. In general, the result is a simplified, nonprobate transfer similar to pay-on-death (POD) transfers of bank accounts or Totten trusts. Assets transferred via TOD registration generally receive a full step-up in cost basis.

In the case of multiple owners, the property must be titled so that ownership will vest in the survivor of them before the asset passes to the named beneficiary. Thus, the owners may hold the property as joint tenants, as tenants by the entireties, or as "owners of community property held in survivorship form." A disadvantage of multiple ownership is that all parties must sign for any future account changes.

Beneficiary Designations

Beneficiary designations determine who receives the assets at death. The Act allows naming a contingent beneficiary to receive the assets if the beneficiary fails to survive. It also provides that "lineal descendants per stirpes[1]" may be substitute beneficiaries.

Acronyms Approved in Statute	Example of Use
TOD = transfer on death	John S. Doe TOD John S. Doe, Jr.
POD = pay on death	John S. Doe POD John S. Doe, Jr.
JT TEN = joint tenants	John S. Doe Mary B. Doe JT TEN TOD John S. Doe, Jr.
SUB BENE = substitute beneficiary	John S. Doe TOD John S. Doe, Jr. SUB BENE Peter Doe
LDPS = lineal descendants per stirpes	John S. Doe Mary B. Doe TOD John S. Doe, Jr. LDPS

Creditor and Third-Party Claims

Generally, the Act does not provide any protection against the claims of third parties such as creditors, or individuals with other interests, such as a spouse's community property interest. A creditor or other party asserting a conflicting interest can do so simply by giving notice to the registering entity (the broker-dealer). As a practical matter, this will usually block transfer of the asset until the conflict is resolved.

---

[1] "Per stirpes" is a Latin term which can be translated variously as "per branch" or "by the roots." In estate planning it refers to a common method of dividing an estate among the heirs of an estate owner.

Seek Professional Guidance

As a general rule, TOD registration as an estate planning tool is most useful in smaller estates, those without estate tax problems, or in situations involving a single estate owner with a single beneficiary. Estate owners are advised to seek the advice and counsel of a competent estate planning attorney in their state of residence before making any decisions regarding the use of TOD registration.

Holding Title

Separate Property

Property owned by either a husband or wife that is not owned by the other is called separate property. This generally includes property acquired by either spouse prior to marriage, by gift, will or inheritance, or as money damages for personal injury, and all of the rents, issues and profits thereof.

Community Property

Both real and personal property earned or accumulated during marriage through the efforts of either husband or wife living together in a community property state. Deceased spouse's will has control over one-half of the community property.

Community Property With Right of Survivorship

Both real and personal property earned or accumulated during marriage through the efforts of either husband or wife living together in a community property state. At the first death, title automatically passes to the surviving spouse by operation of law.

Joint Tenancy

Joint ownership of equal shares by two or more persons with right of survivorship. A person's last will has no effect upon such joint tenancy assets.

Tenancy by the Entirety

Joint ownership of an asset between a husband and wife (with right of survivorship) that generally cannot be terminated without the consent of both parties.

Tenancy in Common

Ownership by two or more persons who hold undivided interests without right of survivorship. Interests need not be equal and will pass under the terms of the owner's will.

Severalty

Ownership held by one person only. This can be a natural person or a legal person, such as a corporation.

Tenancy-in-Partnership

Method by which property is owned by a partnership. Specific interest in the property cannot be conveyed by one partner alone.

Custodian for a Minor

Under the Uniform Gifts to Minors Act or Uniform Transfers to Minors Act, an adult person can hold title to property for the benefit of a minor.

Trustee

The trustee of a living or testamentary trust holds legal title to property for beneficiaries, who have equitable title.

Life Estate

A use of ownership in real property that terminates upon the death of the life tenant.

Note: Advice as to how to hold title to specific assets is the practice of law. These laws vary from state to state.

Joint Tenancy

Could joint tenancy, one of the most common forms of holding title to assets, lead to an estate planning disaster for your heirs? Joint tenancy is a form of holding equal interests in an asset by two or more persons. If one joint tenant dies, his or her share generally passes automatically to the other joint tenant by right of survivorship.

Advantages of Joint Tenancy

- **Probate avoidance:** Title to assets held in joint tenancy passes automatically at the death of one joint tenant to the others. There is no need for a formal probate (unless all the joint tenants die).

- **Convenience:** Bank accounts held in joint tenancy can be withdrawn by any joint tenant. This may be an advantage if one party becomes incompetent due to an accident, a stroke, advanced age, etc.

Potential Disadvantages of Joint Tenancy

- **Loss of control:** Your will (or trust) will have no effect on joint tenancy assets, even if you change your mind as to the persons you would like to receive your share when you die. Also, the entire asset may be available to the creditors of either joint tenant.

- **Assets may not reach your children:** Quite often assets passing to a surviving joint tenant spouse end up in joint tenancy with a new spouse. The new spouse may ultimately receive all of the assets rather than your children.

  Also, if the first joint tenant to die had children of a prior marriage they can be easily cut out of any inheritance by the surviving joint tenant.

- **Potential tax problems**

  - **Gift tax:** The creation of a joint tenancy in some assets may be subject to gift taxation if the value exceeds the $15,000 annual gift tax exclusion.[1] Gifts to one's spouse are generally not taxable.

---

[1] The annual gift tax exclusion ($15,000 in 2018) is indexed for inflation in increments of $1,000.

- **Estate tax:** A bypass trust is often used to reduce estate taxes in married couple estate planning. Holding assets in joint tenancy can completely upset this type of estate tax planning, by passing assets outside the trust.

- **Income tax:** When appreciated assets are sold, a "capital gains" tax is generally paid on the difference between the cost basis and the appreciated sales price. Assets included in one's estate generally receive a new, stepped-up cost basis at the time of death, namely the value at which the assets are included in the decedent's estate. If these assets are then sold at this higher value, there is no gain, and thus no capital gains tax is due. However, assets held in joint tenancy title generally receive only a partial step-up in basis, on the <u>decedent's</u> share. IRC Sec. 1014(b)(9). If the decedent owns the asset alone or as community property, the basis of the entire asset will be stepped-up. See IRC Secs. 1014(a) and 1014(b)(6).

Note: State income tax laws should also be examined before changing the form of ownership.

Dissolving an Unwanted Joint Tenancy

After careful examination, if it is decided to dissolve a joint tenancy in real property, it is generally done by creating a new deed by which the joint tenants transfer their interests to themselves as tenants in common or community property.

It may also be possible to change title by a separate written agreement between the parties. Since the transfer of real estate is governed by the law of the state in which it is situated, local legal counsel should be sought prior to any change of title.

Note: The changing of title to assets can have very serious tax consequences and should be undertaken only after competent professional advice.

Should Appreciated Assets be held in Community Property or Joint Tenancy?

For Persons Owning Real Property or Appreciated Personal Property in Community Property States[1]

Assumptions:

> You bought land as an investment in 1988 for $40,000 (your basis).
> Today, it is worth $220,000.

Capital Gains

If you were to sell the land today for $220,000, you would incur a taxable gain on $180,000, the difference between your basis ($40,000) and your sale price ($220,000). Such profits are subject to income tax at capital gains rates.

Stepped-Up Basis

If, instead, you died and your surviving spouse then sold the land, the tax picture would be different. At the date of death, IRC Sec. 1014(b) permits the basis of a decedent's property to be stepped-up to its value as of date of death.[2]

The Surviving Spouse's Half of the Investment

If the title is in joint tenancy, the survivor's share will retain its original cost basis. In our example this would be $20,000. (See IRC Sec. 1014(b)(9).) If the title is in community property, the survivor's share will get a stepped-up basis. In our example this would be $110,000. See IRC Sec. 1014(b)(6).

---

[1] The community property states are Arizona, California, Idaho, Louisiana, Nevada, New Mexico, Texas, Washington, and Wisconsin. In Alaska, spouses may opt-in to a community property arrangement.

[2] The discussion here concerns federal income tax law. State or local income tax law may vary.

Should Appreciated Assets be held in Community Property or Joint Tenancy?

	If Joint Tenancy		If Community Property	
	Decedent	Survivor	Decedent	Survivor
Original Cost Basis	$20,000	$20,000	$20,000	$20,000
Today's Value	110,000	110,000	110,000	110,000
- Death Occurs -	-	-	-	-
Basis of Decedent's Half	110,000	-	110,000	-
Basis of Survivor's Half	-	20,000	-	110,000
Taxable Amount (capital gain if sold by survivor for $220,000)	0	90,000	0	0
Total Taxable Amount	$90,000		$0	

The result: If the land were sold shortly after death, holding title in joint tenancy could subject $90,000 to income tax, as shown above.

Revocable Living Trust

Inter-vivos Trusts

A trust is created when one person (the trustor or grantor) transfers to another person or a corporation (the trustee) a property interest to be held for the benefit of himself or others (the beneficiaries).

If the trust is created during the trustor's lifetime, rather than in his will, it is an inter-vivos or living trust. When the trustor retains the right to dissolve the trust arrangement, it is a revocable living trust.

What Are Some of the Advantages?

- Assets in the trust are not subject to probate administration. This usually saves executor's and attorney's fees. It also grants more privacy as to who gets the trust assets, when they receive them and how much they get.

- Professional management is available if the trustor becomes incompetent, disabled or wants to be free of the worries of management.

- Should the trustor (also usually the original trustee) die, or be unable to serve, a successor trustee can step in and manage the trust assets without delay or red tape.

- Annual court accountings, with their legal fees, are not required, although some states do not require annual accountings for testamentary trusts (will trusts), either.

- The trustee can collect life insurance proceeds immediately after the trustor dies and can (if permitted under the trust document) use the proceeds to care for family members without any need for court approval.

What Are Some of the Disadvantages?

- Creditors may not be cut off as quickly as they are in probated estates, e.g., four months in some states.

- A little more effort is required to transfer assets into the trust and records should be kept of transactions by the trustee.

- The attorney usually charges a higher fee to establish a living trust, as opposed to a will with a testamentary trust. There may also be ongoing administrative charges.

Note: Assets in a revocable living trust are included in one's gross estate for federal estate tax purposes.

Funding Your Revocable Living Trust

Many people have established living trusts in an effort to avoid probate administration, reduce death taxes, or provide management of assets for minor children.

A great number of these trusts are completely unfunded. In other words, title to the person's assets has never been transferred into the name of the trust. In order to avoid probate, the assets must be in the trust (the trust must be the legal owner of the assets) at the time the estate owner dies. Individuals who have established living trusts should periodically check the title of their assets to verify that they are held in the trust name.

- Savings and loan and bank accounts can be easily changed into the trust name by the institution.

- Real estate is generally transferred into the trust name by having an attorney prepare a new deed.

- Promissory notes and deeds of trust can be assigned to the trust.

- Personal effects, furniture, furnishings, clothing, jewelry and items that have no certificate of ownership can be transferred with a deed of gift or assignment of personal property.

- A stockbroker can assist you in transferring your securities.

- Certificates of limited partnership should be examined for instructions and requirements for making the transfer.

- Closely held corporation stock must be changed into the trustee's name. If there is a buy-sell agreement, it must be reviewed for any prohibition against this type of transfer. Also, if the corporation is either an S corporation or a professional corporation, special rules must be followed.

- General partnership interests can be put into the trust if the partnership agreement permits such transfers.

- Sole proprietorships require a bill of sale or an assignment of interest, which includes the goodwill of the business.

- Life insurance proceeds made payable to the living trust will be managed for the benefit of your heirs along with the other assets in the trust until such time as they are to be distributed.

- Qualified plan benefits and IRAs should be paid to the surviving spouse, if living; otherwise they may be paid to the living trust. Retirement benefits paid to a living trust will be subject to faster payout requirements unless the trust is also qualified as a designated beneficiary trust.

Note: Check with an attorney concerning all transfers to your trust. The transfer of various assets after death with an affidavit may be permitted.

Durable Power of Attorney

A power of attorney is a written document which one person (the principal) uses to empower another person (the agent or attorney-in-fact) to act on his or her behalf.

Powers Which May Be Included

NON-TAX POWERS	TAX-RELATED POWERS
• To buy, sell or lease assets • To sue on the principal's behalf • To collect from creditors • To change provisions in a living trust • To operate the principal's business	• The power to make gifts to the spouse (to equalize the estates) and to children, grandchildren, etc. (to utilize the annual gift tax exclusions) • The power to make disclaimers • The power to create living trusts to benefit the principal, spouse and heirs • The power to complete transfers to a living trust if the principal becomes incompetent • The power to join the competent spouse in signing income and gift tax returns • The power to exercise special powers of appointment

Additional Considerations

Some powers, such as the power to execute and revoke a will, can not be given to another individual. In addition, powers of attorney are usually notarized and those affecting real property may need to be recorded.

A power can be a "general" power, giving the agent all powers held by the principal; a "limited" power restricts the agent to performing only those actions specifically listed.

The document can be written to empower the agent now, or to become effective only upon the occurrence of a specific event, such as the principal's incapacity (sometimes referred to as a "springing" power). A durable power of attorney may save the often-considerable costs of a conservatorship. A conservatorship, however, has the benefit of court supervision.

Note: Significant powers may be granted under a power of attorney. Before using a preprinted form, legal advice should be obtained.

Who Makes Medical Decisions When I Cannot?

Today's advanced medical technology allows physicians to keep a person "alive" in situations that formerly would have resulted in death. Individuals who do not wish their lives to be prolonged by such artificial techniques must plan ahead and put their desires in writing.

In the now famous case of <u>Cruzan v. Dir. Mo. Dept. of Health</u>, 110 S. Ct. 2841 1990, the U.S. Supreme Court held that a state may demand clear and convincing proof of a person's wish to refuse or withdraw medical support. Ms. Cruzan was an accident victim who had not made clear her desire to have medical support withdrawn. Because of this failure, she could have been kept alive, in a vegetative state, for years, at an estimated cost of $200,000 per year.

When Should Medical Treatment Be Withheld?

As the following examples are read, one might ask, "Would I want medical support withdrawn in this situation?"

- In a coma with no hope of recovery.

- In a coma with a small likelihood of recovery with permanent brain damage.

- Afflicted with brain damage or disease, severe in nature, and a terminal illness.

- Afflicted with brain damage or disease, severe in nature, but without terminal illness.

In these situations, and others, difficult decisions must be made as to the treatment to be provided or withheld (for example, artificial respiration, medicine, food, water, etc.).

When a patient is incapable of expressing his or her wishes, some other way must be found to guide the decision making process. The "living will" and "durable power of attorney for health care" (advance health care directives) are useful in this regard.

Living Will

Most states recognize some form of what has been called a "living will", or "directive to physicians." Such a document sets down in writing a person's wishes as to the type of medical treatment to be provided, or withheld, and the general circumstances under which the directive applies.

Durable Power of Attorney for Health Care

Many states also have provision for a durable power of attorney for health care, which allows an individual to appoint another person to make health care decisions for them if they became unable to do so. The agent is generally empowered to make decisions beyond end-of-life issues, such as admission to a nursing home, consent for surgical operations, and care in the event of senility or other disability.

Advance Health Care Directives

End-of-Life Decision Making

Modern medicine can now keep a person alive in situations that, in years past, would have resulted in the individual's death. Frequently, a patient in such a condition is unable to communicate his or her wishes with regard to the type of medical care to be provided. In the absence of any other guidance, the attending physician will typically use all available means to keep the individual alive, even when death is certain, with no hope of recovery.

However, many individuals feel that once death is inevitable, life should not be artificially prolonged through the use of such technology. The decision to start or withdraw such life-sustaining support, although always difficult, can be made easier with advance planning.

The term "advance health care directives" is commonly used to describe two key documents (sometimes combined into one) designed to address these end-of-life decisions:

- Living Will.

- Durable Power of Attorney for Health Care.

Individual state law governs the use of these documents, and such legislation can vary widely. Individuals who live in more than one state may need to execute a living will and a durable power of attorney for health care for each state.

Living Will

A living will, also known as a "directive to physicians," is a written statement of the individual's health care wishes should he or she become seriously ill and unable to communicate. The document is designed to provide guidance to someone else appointed to make health care decisions for the individual, or to the attending physician if there is no health care agent. A living will might include:

- Directions as to pain medication.

- Directions as to when to provide, withhold, or withdraw artificial nutrition and hydration, and all other forms of health care, including cardiopulmonary resuscitation.

- A discussion of any religious beliefs that might impact medical treatment.

- Instructions for funeral and burial services.

Because it is impossible to foresee the future, the living will should be written in the broadest possible manner, to cover a wide range of situations.

Durable Power of Attorney for Health Care

In a durable power of attorney for health care, sometimes known as a "health care proxy," an individual (the principal) appoints another person (the agent) to make health care decisions if the principal is incapable of doing so.[1] A durable power of attorney may employ a "springing" power, which means that the power "springs" into life when the principal becomes incapacitated.[2] Additional powers granted to the agent could include:

- Access to medical records.

- Authority to transfer the principal to another facility or to another state.

- Ability to authorize a "Do Not Resuscitate" (DNR) order.

- Postmortem powers to dispose of the remains, to authorize an autopsy, or to donate all or part of the principal's body for transplant, education, or research purposes.

Other Points

- **Talk about the issues:** the individual should spend time talking with family, friends, clergy, and physician about his or her wishes in end-of-life decisions.
- **Make the documents available:** if a living will and/or a durable power of attorney exist, be sure that those involved know where to locate the documents.

---

[1] Many states have provision in their laws for the appointment of a surrogate such as a spouse, domestic partner, or other close family member to make health care decisions for the principal, in situations where no durable power of attorney for health care exists.

[2] Under the Health Insurance Portability and Accountability Act (HIPAA), a physician is prohibited from discussing a patient's medical condition without the patient's consent. Thus, if an individual becomes incapacitated, the person named as agent under a durable power of attorney for health care may not have access to the principal's health-care information. Without this information, the agent would be unable to legally establish that the principal had become incapacitated, and would not be able to trigger any "springing" power. A HIPPA authorization can be used to give the agent access to the principal's health-care information.

- **Revocation:** an individual can generally revoke a living will or durable power of attorney at any time.

Additional Resources

Non-profit organizations such as the following provide support and education on end-of-life issues:

- **National Hospice and Palliative Care Organization:** (703) 837-1500; on the internet at: www.nhpco.org

Seek Professional Guidance

The counsel and guidance of legal, religious, and medical professionals is essential to the successful preparation of advance health care directives.

Lifetime Gifts

Lifetime gifts and transfers at death are taxed using a unified tax rate schedule that has cumulatively progressive rates. Each taxable transfer, including the final transfer at death, begins in the tax bracket attained by the prior gift.

Annual Gift Tax Exclusion

Each taxpayer is allowed to transfer/gift a certain amount of assets each year, without concern for gift taxes. This "annual exclusion amount" is currently $15,000[1] per donor and a gift of this amount can be given to each of any number of donees. If husband and wife agree, they can "split" gifts and give twice this amount, $30,000, to each of any number of children, grandchildren, etc.

Marital Deduction

There is an unlimited marital deduction for gifts of separate or community property passing from one spouse to another. Transfers to spouses who are not U.S. citizens are not protected by the gift tax marital deduction, but a non-citizen spouse is entitled to a special, annual gift tax exemption if such a gift would qualify for the marital deduction if the spouse were a U.S. citizen. For 2018, this special exemption amount is $152,000.

Educational or Medical Expenses

A donor may give, free of gift tax consequences, unlimited amounts for a donee's school tuition (not books, supplies, or other expenses) or qualified medical expenses. Such gifts must be made directly to the school or health care provider, and not to the donee.

Deductibility for Income Tax Purposes

Gifts or gift taxes are not deductible for income tax purposes, unless contributed to a qualified charity.

Gift Tax Returns

These returns are filed annually, generally by April 15 of the year following the gift for amounts in excess of the annual gift tax exclusion.

---

[1] 2018 value. This amount is subject to adjustment for inflation in future years.

Capital Gains and Losses

A donee generally takes over the basis of gifted property from the donor, known as "carry-over" basis. A later sale of gifted property by the donee can result in a capital gain, a capital loss, or a situation in which there is neither a gain nor a loss.

Includability of Gifts in the Estate

Gifts made within three years of death are not considered in the computation of the taxable estate. However, if they exceed the annual gift tax exclusion, they may be added to the taxable estate as adjusted taxable gifts. This, in effect, pushes the assets remaining in the taxable estate into the higher tax brackets; however, the appreciation on the assets from date of gift until date of death is not brought into the computation.

Gifts of life insurance policies, however, are still included if made within three years of death. Certain incomplete transfers (e.g., retained life estates, revocable transfers, etc.) will also be included in the gross estate without regard to when they were made.

All taxable transfers made within three years (except gifts that qualify for the annual gift tax exclusion) will be included for determining whether an estate qualifies for an IRC Sec. 303 stock redemption, the IRC Sec. 2032A special use valuation or the IRC Sec. 6166 deferral of estate tax payment.

Advantages of Making Gifts

- Gifts put future appreciation of assets out of the estate.

- The gift tax paid reduces the taxable estate.

- Making gifts of income-producing assets may reduce current income taxes.

- Probate administration is not necessary for gifted assets.

- The donor can see the beneficiaries enjoy the assets while he or she is still living.

The Federal Gift Tax

Assumptions:

Year intended gift is made: 2018
Value of intended gift (in excess of the annual gift tax exclusion amount)[1]: $1,000,000
Total taxable gifts made in prior years: $100,000
Total applicable credit amount used in prior years: $10,000

Item Description	Value
Total current and prior taxable gifts	$1,100,000
Total gift tax computed on current and prior taxable gifts	385,800
Total gift tax computed on prior taxable gifts only	23,800
Tentative tax due on this gift (difference)	362,000
Applicable credit amount available for this gift	2,141,800
Applicable credit amount used in prior years	10,000
Remaining credit applied to this gift (no greater than tax due)	362,000
Net gift tax due	**$0**

[1] Does not include gifts to spouse or charity, or gifts of less than the annual exclusion amount ($15,000 in 2018) to any number of persons.

Annual Exclusion Gifts

Reducing the Federal Estate Tax[1]

By following a consistent program of annual lifetime gifts to children, grandchildren, etc., an estate owner can dramatically reduce his or her taxable estate. The following chart illustrates the results of such a gifting program. It assumes that the gifts are made at the beginning of each year and will grow at 5.00% annually outside the donor's estate. In 2018, a person can give up to $15,000 per year to any number of people without incurring a gift tax.

Annual Gift	Number of Years Over Which Gifts Are Made				
	5 Years	10 Years	15 Years	20 Years	25 Years
$15,000	$87,029	$198,102	$339,862	$520,789	$751,702
30,000	174,057	396,204	679,725	1,041,578	1,503,404
45,000	261,086	594,305	1,019,587	1,562,366	2,255,105
60,000	348,115	792,407	1,359,450	2,083,155	3,006,807
75,000	435,143	990,509	1,699,312	2,603,944	3,758,509
90,000	522,172	1,188,611	2,039,174	3,124,733	4,510,211
105,000	609,201	1,386,713	2,379,037	3,645,521	5,261,913
120,000	696,230	1,584,814	2,718,899	4,166,310	6,013,614
135,000	783,258	1,782,916	3,058,761	4,687,099	6,765,316
150,000	870,287	1,981,018	3,398,624	5,207,888	7,517,018

_____ x _____ % = _____

Potential amount removed from estate (See chart above.)	Estimated top estate tax bracket (See below.)	Approximate savings which could pass to your heirs

Top Federal Estate Tax Brackets

Years	Top Bracket	Applicable Exclusion Amount[2]
2015	40%	5,430,000
2016	40%	5,450,000
2017	40%	5,490,000
2018	40%	$11,180,000

Note: If some of the annual gift amounts are used to purchase life insurance outside of the estate, the potential wealth-building effect becomes very dramatic.

---

[1] The discussion here concerns federal tax law. State or local law may differ.

[2] The "applicable exclusion amount" is the dollar amount of assets protected from federal estate tax.

IRC Sec. 2503(c) Trust for Minors

Estate owners often seek to reduce the size of their estates by making gifts to their minor children or grandchildren. Because most minors cannot manage such gifts, there is a need to provide supervision for gifted assets until the donees reach adulthood.

One possible solution is to set up a trust, with minor children or grandchildren as trust beneficiaries. Because assets in a trust are typically not distributed to the beneficiaries until a future date, such gifts are usually considered to be gifts of a "future" interest.

The Gift Tax Problem

Gifts in excess of $15,000 per donor[1] to any donee are subject to a gift tax. Gifts under $15,000 may be subject to gift taxes if they are considered to be a future interest instead of a present interest[2] to the beneficiary.

IRC Sec. 2503(c) provides an exception to the general rule that gifts made in trust are gifts of a future interest. Gifts meeting the requirements of this code section qualify as gifts of a present interest, and thus qualify for the annual gift tax exclusion of $15,000.

The Requirements of IRC Sec. 2503(c)

- Principal and income may be expended for the minor by the trustee[3] before the minor reaches age 21[4].

- Any principal and income not expended will pass to the minor at age 21.

- Should the minor die prior to age 21, the trust principal and any accumulated income will be paid to the minor's estate or to whomever he or she appoints.

---

[1] Gifts meeting the requirements of IRC Sec. 2503(b) qualify for an annual gift tax exclusion of $15,000 per donee (2018). Client and spouse can combine gifts for a total of $30,000.

[2] A gift generally qualifies as a "present interest" if the recipient has an unrestricted right to use, enjoy, or possess the gift.

[3] The trustee's ability to distribute funds for the benefit of the minor(s) should not be restricted.

[4] Local state law may provide that an individual reaches his or her majority at an age younger than 21. The gift tax exclusion of IRC Sec. 2503(c), however, is based on an individual reaching age 21.

IRC Sec. 2503(c) Trust for Minors

Income Tax Issues

Trust income is taxable to the trust or, if distributed, to the minor. However, for certain children, unearned income in excess of $2,100 per year (2018) is subject to taxation (the "kiddie" tax) at the income tax rates applicable to estates and trusts.

Seek Professional Guidance

When considering gifts to minors, the advice and counsel of professional estate and income tax specialists is strongly recommended.

How an IRC Sec. 2503(c) Trust Works

A donor may seek to reduce the size of his or her estate by gifting assets to minor children or grandchildren. If the gifts are made through a trust, a trustee can manage the assets until the children reach adulthood. If the trust meets the requirements of IRC Sec. 2503(c), gifts to the trust qualify for the annual gift tax exclusion of $15,000 per year.

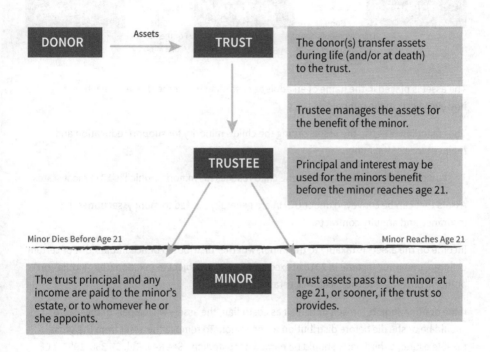

DONOR — Assets → **TRUST**

The donor(s) transfer assets during life (and/or at death) to the trust.

Trustee manages the assets for the benefit of the minor.

TRUSTEE

Principal and interest may be used for the minors benefit before the minor reaches age 21.

Minor Dies Before Age 21 — Minor Reaches Age 21

The trust principal and any income are paid to the minor's estate, or to whomever he or she appoints.

MINOR

Trust assets pass to the minor at age 21, or sooner, if the trust so provides.

Note: 2018 value. This amount is subject to adjustment for inflation in future years.

Uniform Gifts to Minors Act

The Uniform Gifts to Minors Act (UGMA) provides a simple and inexpensive method of making gifts to minors, which will qualify as a present interest for the annual gift tax exclusion of $15,000 per year for each minor.[1]

The asset is placed in the name of an adult as custodian under the UGMA. Legal title, however, vests in the minor.

The custodian is to use the assets during the child's minority for support, education and maintenance of the minor.

The custodianship terminates when the child reaches his majority, which is 18 in most states.

Assets that can be conveyed under UGMA are generally limited to money, securities, life insurance and annuity contracts.

Income on the assets is taxable to the minor, whether distributed or accumulated. For certain children, unearned income in 2018 in excess of $2,100 is subject to taxation (the "kiddie" tax) at the income tax rates applicable to estates and trusts.

If the donor appoints himself or herself as custodian, the assets will be part of the estate should he or she die before distribution to the minor. To remove the asset from the gross taxable estate, a third party should be named as custodian. See Rev. Rul. 57-366, 1957-2 CB 618; Rev. Rul. 59-357, 1959-2 CB 212.

Note: Almost all states have changed to Uniform Transfers To Minors Act (UTMA), which is more flexible as to distribution ages and assets which can be held in custodial name.

---

[1] 2018 value. This amount is subject to adjustment for inflation in future years.

Uniform Transfers to Minors Act

The Uniform Transfers to Minor's Act (UTMA) provides a simple and inexpensive method of making a gift or bequest to a minor without the expense of a trust.

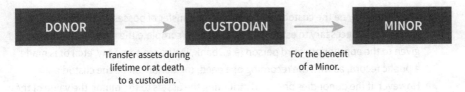

Duties of the Custodian

- Collect, hold, manage, invest and reinvest the assets.
- Deal with assets as a prudent person would.

Payments by Custodian

- Make payments to the minor (or for his or her benefit) in whatever amounts the custodian considers advisable.
- Consideration need not be made as to:
  - Another's duty or ability to support the minor, or
  - Any other income available to the minor.

Life Insurance Rules for Policies Held in Custodianship

- Life or endowment policies on the minor's life must name his or her estate as the sole beneficiary.
- The minor, his or her estate, or the custodian (as custodian for the minor) must be the irrevocable beneficiary of policies on the life of someone other than the minor.

Termination of a Custodianship

The custodianship is generally ended when the minor becomes of age (18 or 21). A few states have provisions allowing the custodianship to be extended to age 25.[1] Some states permit the donor to select any age between 18 and 21 to distribute the assets.

---

[1] If the donor specifies that the custodianship will extend past the child's reaching age 21, the transfer will not qualify as a gift of a present interest.

Further Considerations

- Both real and personal property can be transferred.

- The donor may be the custodian. Sometimes a transfer of possession and control to a third party is necessary to establish one's intent to complete the transfer. If notice is given to the appropriate third person (e.g., bank, insurance company, etc.) or is made a public record, as with the recording of a deed, the donor can be the custodian. However, if the donor dies prior to distributing the assets to the minor, the value of the assets will be included in his or her gross estate.

- A transfer may be for only one minor and only one person may act as custodian at a time. Successor custodians may be appointed. Title to the property vests in the minor and he or she is subject to income tax on the earnings or gain. For certain children, unearned income in 2018 in excess of $2,100 is subject to taxation (the "kiddie" tax) at the income tax rates applicable to estates and trusts.

- These rules may vary slightly from state to state.

How a Custodial Account Works

Gifts under the UGMA or UTMA

A custodial account provides a simple and inexpensive method of making gifts to minors.

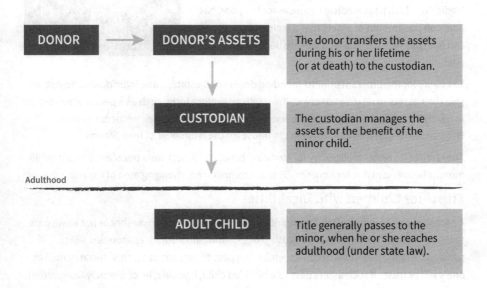

DONOR → **DONOR'S ASSETS**		The donor transfers the assets during his or her lifetime (or at death) to the custodian.
CUSTODIAN		The custodian manages the assets for the benefit of the minor child.
Adulthood		
ADULT CHILD		Title generally passes to the minor, when he or she reaches adulthood (under state law).

Special Needs Trust

To preserve the public assistance benefits of a person with a disability, such as a child with a developmental disability, etc., many people use a special needs trust.

Medicaid, which pays medical expenses for the poor, has limits on the amount of assets that a recipient can own or can earn during each year that welfare benefits are paid.

To qualify for the program prior to spending down one's estate, some individuals attempt to give their assets to relatives or invest them into an exempt form, such as a personal residence in which the spouse resides. Single persons sometimes transfer their residence to their children and retain the right to live in the house for the remainder of their lifetime.

The law denies persons eligibility for Medicaid benefits if assets were transferred less than 60 months before applying for benefits. This is a complicated, changing area of the law.

Trusts for Children with Disabilities

A parent of a child with a disability should review each asset to see whether or not it will pass to that child at time of the parent's death. For example, life insurance, annuities, IRAs, pension benefits, joint bank accounts, etc., often pass to persons other than those named in one's will or trust. If such assets pass to a disabled child, however, he or she may lose current government benefits. One must also decide whether or not to disinherit a child with a disability or use a special-needs type of trust.

Special needs trusts are generally established by the parents or other relatives of the disabled child. The trustee should have absolute discretion over how to expend the trust funds for the benefit of the disabled child:

- **Government benefits:** Government benefits should be used to meet basic needs such as food, clothing, and shelter.
- **Special needs trust:** The funds from the trust should be used for supplementary needs such as utilities, medical care, special equipment, education, job training or entertainment.

Seek Professional Guidance

Since the laws in this area are very complex and vary from state to state, experienced, knowledgeable legal counsel should be retained to draft the appropriate documents.

How a Special Needs Trust Works

Special needs trusts allow family members to provide some benefits to a disabled child without causing him or her to lose government benefits.

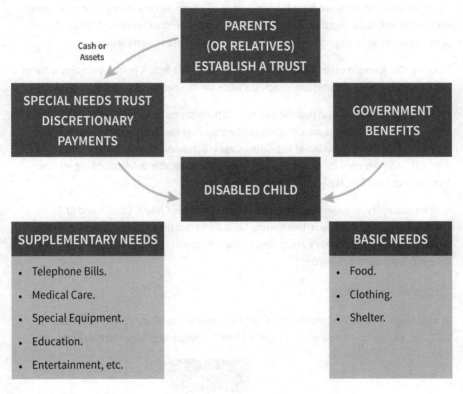

Items to Consider

- Parents can act as the trustees.
- Trust should be separate from the family trust.
- The trust may be revocable or irrevocable.
- Beneficiaries should be named to receive trust assets after the disabled child dies.
- Family members should discuss management of the trust and how it will be funded.

This is a highly specialized document and should be drafted by an attorney who is experienced in the areas of disability, government benefits, and estate planning.

Per Capita vs. Per Stirpes

Per Capita, Latin for "by the head" and *Per Stirpes*, Latin for "by the root" are terms used in estate planning to describe how an individual's assets are to be distributed at death. They are often encountered when an individual names an alternate beneficiary to receive assets such as life insurance death benefits or the funds in IRAs or other retirement plans. Such planning is needed as a primary beneficiary may predecease the estate owner.

They are also found in cases where someone dies without a will. A person who dies without a will is said to have died "intestate"; each state has laws to deal with such situations.

It's important to understand that the meaning of these terms can vary from state to state. The examples which follow are designed to illustrate how Per Capita and Per Stirpes are generally understood to operate. Individual state law, however, may lead to a different result, even if the same term is used. The guidance of a knowledgeable estate planning attorney, familiar with local law, is highly recommended.

In these examples, assume that a Parent has three children, Child X, Child Y, and Child Z. There are three grandchildren, two born to Child X and one born to Child Z. At the Parent's death, how would the Parent's assets be distributed assuming that both Child X and Child Z have predeceased the Parent?

"Simple" Per Capita

In what might be called a "simple" Per Capita distribution, the Parent's entire estate, $900,000, passes to the sole surviving child, Child Y. The grandchildren receive nothing.

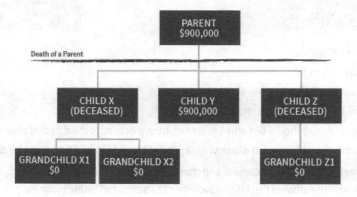

Per Capita vs. Per Stirpes

Per Capita

In another version of the Per Capita distribution, all family members who survive the Parent receive an equal share of the Parent's estate. Thus, Child Y and the grandchildren each receive $225,000 ($900,000 ÷ 4).

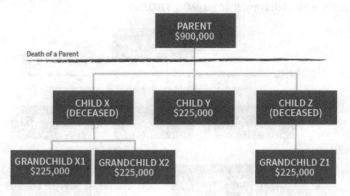

Per Capita with Representation

In a Per Capita with Representation situation, the Parent's estate of $900,000 is split three-ways, with $300,000 going to Child Y and another $300,000 passing to Child Z's survivor, Grandchild Z1. However, the children of Child X, Grandchild X1 and Grandchild X2, will split ($150,000 each) what would have been Child X's one-third portion of the Parent's estate. This type of distribution can result in unequal treatment of surviving grandchildren.

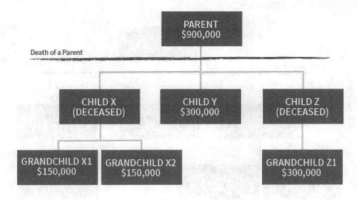

Per Capita vs. Per Stirpes

Per Capita at Each Generation

A Per Capita at Each Generation distribution usually results in a more even-handed treatment of the surviving grandchildren. In this example, the Parent's estate is again divided into three parts. Child Y receives $300,000. The remaining portion of the Parent's estate, $600,000, is divided equally, with each grandchild receiving $200,000.

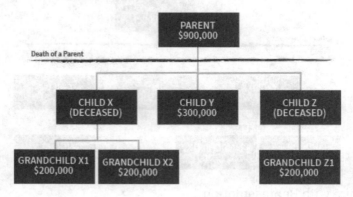

Per Stirpes

With regard to grandchildren, a Per Stirpes distribution often has the same result as a Per Capita with Representation distribution. In our example, a Per Stirpes distribution would leave $300,000 to Child Y and another $300,000 to Grandchild Z1. The children of Child X, Grandchild X1 and Grandchild X2, will split ($150,000 each) what would have been Child X's one-third portion of the Parent's estate.

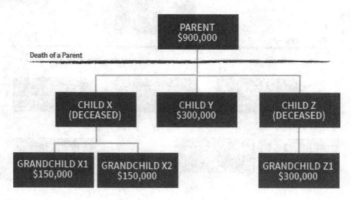

Seek Professional Guidance

Estate planning can be complex and confusing. The advice and guidance of experienced legal, tax, and financial professionals is strongly recommended.

Death Tax Reduction

The federal estate tax, which is imposed on taxable estates exceeding $11,180,000,[1] can be reduced through various techniques:

- **Lifetime gifts:** Each person can make annual gifts of $15,000[2] ($30,000 per couple, if married) to any number of donees, e.g., children or grandchildren, without incurring Federal gift tax.

- **Charitable transfers:** Bequests at death or lifetime charitable gifts can reduce the estate size and thus reduce the death tax. Charitable gifts made during life provide the added benefit of an income tax deduction. Gifts can be of a partial interest; for example, one can retain the right to income for life. Such "split-interest" gifts must be made in a trust, either a charitable lead trust or a charitable remainder trust.

- **Marital transfers:** Generally, neither lifetime gifts nor bequests at death to one's spouse are subject to death taxes. This in effect defers the tax until the surviving spouse dies. Special rules apply to non-U.S. citizen spouses.

- **Bypass trust:** This type of trust allows the first-to-die of a married couple to set aside up to $11,180,000[1] for specific heirs, while providing income and flexibility to the surviving spouse. Appreciation on assets inside the trust can avoid estate tax.

- **Deceased spouse unused applicable exclusion amount:** Any applicable exclusion amount that remains unused at the death of the first spouse to die is generally available for use by the surviving spouse, as an addition to his or her own applicable exclusion amount.

- **Estate value freezing techniques:** Corporate recapitalizations, personal holding companies and multi-tier family partnerships which previously transferred future growth of a business to a younger generation while still retaining power to control the business, have been almost eliminated.

---

[1] The applicable exclusion amount is the dollar value of assets protected from federal estate tax by an individual's applicable credit amount. For 2018, the applicable exclusion amount is $11,180,000. In 2017, the applicable exclusion amount was $5,490,000.

[2] 2018 value. This amount is subject to adjustment for inflation in future years.

- **Private annuity:** Generally, a private annuity is the sale of an asset to a younger generation in exchange for an unsecured promise to pay annual amounts for the seller's lifetime. This removes the assets from the estate; however, the payments, if accumulated, could build up over the seller's life expectancy to the size of the asset which was transferred.[1]

- **Life insurance trusts:** By transferring small amounts of the estate (equal to the insurance premium) to an irrevocable life insurance trust, an estate owner can reduce his or her current estate while creating a much larger asset outside the estate. The proceeds of the policy will not be subject to income taxes or federal estate taxes at the estate owner's demise. See IRC Sec. 101(a).

---

[1] On October 17, 2006, the IRS issued proposed regulations (NPRM REG-141901-5) on the exchange of appreciated property for an annuity contract. These proposed regulations treat the transaction as if the transferor had sold the property for cash and then used the proceeds to purchase an annuity contract. The proposed regulations are generally effective for transactions occurring after October 18, 2006.

The Marital Deduction

For both gift tax (IRC Sec. 2523) and estate tax (IRC Sec. 2056) purposes, a deduction is allowed for the value of gifts between spouses.

The deduction is unlimited; i.e., 100% of qualified transfers such as the following:

- **Outright gifts or bequests.**

- **Gifts or bequests in trust.**

  - **General power of appointment trust:** The spouse has the right to all income plus the right to determine during life and/or at death who receives the remaining principal.

  - **Revocable trust:**[1] Spouse has right to all income and to revoke or amend the trust at any time in his or her favor.

  - **Estate trust:** Income accumulates during surviving spouse's lifetime. The spouse has the right (through the use of a will) to determine at death who gets the accumulated income and principal.

  - **Qualified terminable interest property (QTIP) trust:** Spouse has the right to all income during life. No one else can benefit from the principal, but the donor (or decedent) can direct who will get the principal at the surviving spouse's later demise.

  - **Qualified domestic trust:** If the surviving spouse is not a U.S. citizen, the marital deduction will not be allowed unless the assets pass to a qualified domestic trust which meets four conditions:

    - The trust requires at least one U.S. trustee (unless waived by the IRS) who approves all distributions.

    - Spouse must have an interest which would otherwise qualify for the marital deduction if he or she were a citizen.

    - Must meet Treasury requirements designed to ensure collection of tax at surviving spouse's demise.

---

[1] At death, the trust becomes irrevocable. The surviving spouse has as much (or as little) flexibility as provided for by the grantor.

The Marital Deduction

- Executor makes irrevocable election on federal estate tax return to defer the tax.

A noncitizen spouse who becomes a U.S. citizen before the estate tax return is filed and was a resident from the decedent's death through the filing of the return is eligible for the marital deduction.

Any distributions of principal will be taxed at the same rate as if they were included in the decedent's estate.

Special Use Valuation

IRC Sec. 2032A

Valuation of Farm and Business Real Estate

For federal estate tax purposes, real estate is normally valued at its highest and best use. This can produce unfair results when valuing certain real property, such as farmland which is adjacent to highly developed and very valuable land. For this reason, Congress enacted IRC Sec. 2032A to allow certain real estate to be valued at its actual use rather than its best possible use. This special use valuation can reduce the gross estate up to $1,140,000.[1]

Requirements to Qualify for IRC Sec. 2032A

- The real property must be in the United States and must be in use for trade or business or as a farm for farming purposes on the date of the descendant's demise.

- The adjusted value[2] of the real and personal property used in the business or farming operation must be at least 50% of the adjusted value of the gross estate.

- At least 25% of the decedent's adjusted gross estate must consist of qualified real property.

- The descendant or a member of his or her family must have been a material participant in the operation of the farm or other business for at least five of the eight years preceding his or her death, disability or retirement (with Social Security benefits).

- The property must pass to a qualified heir, i.e., spouse, parents, lineal descendants or aunts and uncles and their descendants.

Valuation

If the requirements are met to qualify under IRC Sec. 2032A, the law provides two specific techniques for valuation. One is based on a special formula [IRC Sec. 2032A(e)(7)] and the other is based on a number of specified factors [Sec. 2032A(e)(8)].

---

[1] This is the value for the year 2018. This limit is subject to adjustment for inflation in future years.
[2] Adjusted value means the market value of the property less unpaid mortgages or other indebtedness against the property.

Possible Recapture

If the qualified heir disposes of the property within 10 years of the descendant's death, the law imposes an additional tax, unless the property is transferred to another qualified heir who is also a member of the descendant's family. Also, if the qualified heir does not actively manage the operation of the farm or business for more than three of any eight consecutive years, the qualified status will cease. There is a two-year grace period, immediately following the descendant's death during which the qualified heir does not need to commence use of the property.

A like-kind exchange of qualified real property for other qualified real property to be used for the same qualified use will not incur an additional estate tax.

A possible disadvantage of using the special use valuation is that the heirs receive a lower basis in property for capital gains purposes.

If a technical defect is made in filing for the election, e.g., failure to include certain required information, the executor of the descendant's estate can have a reasonable time (not exceeding 90 days) to correct the flaw. See IRC Sec. 2032A(d)(3).

The Taxpayer Relief Act of 1997 amended IRC Sec. 2032A to allow both surviving spouses and lineal descendants of the deceased to lease specially valued property on a net cash basis to certain family members. New IRC Sec. 2032A(c)(7)(E), effective for leases entered into after 12/31/76.

Deferring Payment of Federal Estate Taxes

IRC Sec. 6161 and IRC Sec. 6166

Federal estate taxes are due nine months after a person dies. Because of the hardships which this sometimes causes in estates containing nonliquid assets, Congress provided two code sections to permit deferred installment payments when certain requirements and conditions are met.

Qualification under IRC Sec. 6161 is at the discretion of the IRS for hardship situations. An estate can generally qualify under IRC Sec. 6166 if it meets all of the requirements:

	IRC Sec 6161	IRC Sec 6166
Maximum period of tax spread out.	10 years.	14 years (interest only on tax for the first four years).[1] Installment payments over a five-year period apply to certain holding companies, and lending and finance business interests.
Portion of tax affected.	Total federal estate tax.	Only tax attributable to qualifying business, less the applicable credit amount.
Interest rate.	Same as for deficiencies. Changes periodically.	2% on the portion of the tax attributable to first $1,520,000[2] of the taxable value of the business. Interest on any remainder is at 45% of the rate for deficiencies.
Requirements to qualify under each code section.	Demonstrate reasonable cause as to why tax cannot be paid when due.	• Business value is greater than 35% of the adjusted gross estate.[3] • Businesses can be combined if decedent owned 20% or more of each. • Business must be closely held: 45 or fewer shareholders/partners, or 20% or more voting ownership.

---

[1] A principal payment is due in the fifth year.

[2] 2018 value. This amount is subject to adjustment for inflation in future years.

[3] Gifts made within three years of death (in excess of the annual gift tax exclusion) are brought back into the gross estate for purposes of qualifying under IRC Sec. 6166. This prevents deathbed gifts designed to make the estate qualify for the benefits of IRC Sec. 6166.

Deferring Payment of Federal Estate Taxes

Possible Pitfalls Using Secs 6161 or 6166

- The deferred payment alternative is not available under IRC Sec. 6166 for federal estate taxes attributable to nonbusiness interests. A business owner's estate which currently qualifies for the IRC Sec. 6166 election may cease to qualify before his or her death because the nonbusiness assets appreciate faster than the business or the business may decline in value.

- The executor can be released of further liability on the unpaid tax if a bond is posted or if parties with an interest in the estate sign a special lien and agreement. However, it appears that parties with an interest would include children and grandchildren named as remaindermen in an AB type bypass trust.

- In certain situations, the IRS may require either the posting of surety bond or the granting by the executor of a special extended estate tax lien, before agreeing to installment payments under IRC Sec. 6166. See IRS Notice 2007-90, 11/13/07.

- An Internal Revenue Service lien on a business might impair the business in the raising of additional funds for expansion or in periods of financial stress.

- The benefit of the 2% rate is not available to certain holding company stock and non-readily tradable business interests. The interest rate for installment payments of estate tax attributable to such property is 45% of the rate for underpayment of tax. See IRC Secs. 6166(b)(7)(A)(iii) and 6166 (b)(8)(A)(iii).

- The tax due will be accelerated if one-half or more of an interest in the business is sold, exchanged, distributed or withdrawn. This does not apply to transfers by will or transfers involved in an IRC Sec. 303 stock redemption if the redemption proceeds are used to pay the estate tax.

- The remaining tax due will be accelerated if an installment payment of tax or interest is missed. If the delinquent payments are paid within six months, the tax will not be accelerated, but the favorable interest rate will be lost for the payment and a 5% per month penalty will be imposed. See IRC Sec. 6166(g)(3)(B).

- Neither of these sections is available for the payment of state inheritance taxes or administration expenses, unless provided by specific state laws.

Deferring Payment of Federal Estate Taxes

Life insurance proceeds are often the least expensive method of paying the estate settlement costs. Life insurance removes the risk and uncertainty that the estate may not qualify under the deferral elections or that the cash flow might not be sufficient to meet the annual obligation. Also. The proceeds are generally income tax free and can be arranged to be free of estate taxes too.

Powers of Appointment

A power of appointment may allow an estate owner to transfer to another person, e.g., spouse, child, etc., the power to decide at some future time the ultimate beneficiary of his or her estate.

This may be important when the beneficiaries are minors and the donor is not certain as to their spending habits, wealth from other sources, future needs, undesirable personal habits, etc.

The creation and exercise or non-exercise of these powers may incur certain tax liabilities and must, therefore, be carefully planned and drafted.

General Powers of Appointment

A general power of appointment is a power that permits the holder to appoint the assets to himself or herself, his or her creditors, his or her estate, or the creditors of his or her estate. Assets subject to a general power of appointment are included in the estate of the person who possesses it. If the power is released during lifetime, it may subject the assets to gift taxation. General powers of appointment created after October 21, 1942 are included in the gross estate whether exercised or permitted to lapse. See IRC Sec. 2041(a)(2). The value of the property which can be appointed is includable in the gross estate of the holder of the power.

Exception to the Rule Regarding General Powers

A person can die owning a power of appointment and not have it included in his or her estate if its use is limited by an ascertainable standard relating to the person's health, education, support or maintenance. In drafting an ascertainable standard provision, the cautious estate planner will follow the provisions set forth in the IRC Sec. 2041(b)(1)(A). Do not use words like comfort, welfare, or happiness. See Treas. Reg. Sec. 20.2041-1(c)(2).

These limited powers are sometimes called special powers of appointment and, since they are generally not subject to estate or gift taxation, can be very flexible estate planning tools.

Powers of Appointment

This type of power is often used with the AB-type bypass trust (also sometimes called an exemption or credit shelter trust). A special power of appointment is any power to appoint to persons other than the donee of the power or his or her creditors, or the donee's estate or its creditors.

Lapse of a General Power and the 5-and-5 Rule

Usually the non-exercise (or lapse) of a general power of appointment is considered to be a release of the power and hence a taxable gift. However, to the extent that the property which could have been appointed does not exceed the greater of $5,000 or 5% of the total value of the assets subject to the power, the lapse will not be a taxable transfer. See IRC Secs. 2041(b)(2) and 2514(e).

Disclaimer of a General Power of Appointment

A person who properly disclaims a power of appointment will not have the power included in his or her gross estate.

Caveat: This is a complex area of the law. The estate planner and owner must be careful to avoid unintentionally creating or exercising general powers of appointment. Also, state law should be examined for additional tax consequences.

Disclaimers

Disclaimers are a means of renouncing a gift or inheritance so that it passes to a third party without being taxed to the intended beneficiary.

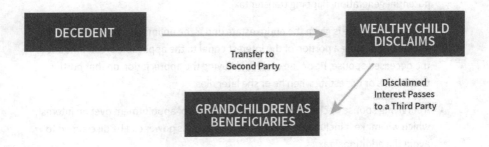

Requirements for a Successful Disclaimer

IRC Sec. 2518 sets forth the tests that must be met for a successful disclaimer:

- The refusal to accept the interest must be irrevocable and unqualified.

- It must generally[1] be made within nine months after the transfer creating the interest (i.e., death) or nine months after disclaimant's 21st birthday, if that is later.

- It must be in writing.

- The disclaimant may not have accepted any benefits from the disclaimed interest.

- Without any direction on the part of the disclaimant, the interest must pass to another person or entity (i.e., spouse, children, charity, etc.). A written transfer of an entire interest in property to the person(s) who would have received the same had it been disclaimed will be treated as an effective disclaimer provided the other listed requirements are met.

---

[1] See Reg. 25.2518-2(c)(4), as amended by TD8744 (12/31/97), for an exception to the nine-month rule for certain jointly owned property.

Situations Which May Be Improved with a Disclaimer

- A wealthy child inherits from his parents and by disclaiming the interest it will pass to his children, thus by-passing his generation for estate tax purposes (subject to potential generation-skipping transfer tax).

- A surviving spouse is given the entire estate under the unlimited marital deduction; and by disclaiming a portion of the interest equal to the applicable credit amount of the deceased spouse, he or she can avoid having the appreciation on that portion taxed in his or her estate when he or she later dies.

- A surviving spouse or child is given a general power of appointment over an interest, which will make it includable in his or her estate. This power can be disclaimed to avoid the additional tax.

Generation-Skipping Transfer Tax

Estate owners can often reduce death taxes by skipping a generation of heirs; e.g., bypass their children or give the children only a right to income for their lifetime with the remainder passing to their grandchildren.

Under prior law, when a child died under such an arrangement, the assets were not subject to federal estate tax and therefore a generation of death taxes was skipped.

In order to reduce the loss of this tax in larger estates, Congress enacted the generation-skipping transfer tax in 1976. This very complex law was repealed in 1986 but was replaced with a similar law set forth in IRC Secs. 2601-2663.

Two Common Types of Transfers

- **Generation-sharing transfers:** The transferor (e.g., grandparent) typically places assets in a trust which pays income to his or her child for life and then the remainder passes to grandchildren after the child is deceased.

- **Direct generation skip:** The transferor bypasses his or her children and gives the asset either directly to the grandchildren or a trust for their benefit.

Exempt Transfer

Each transferor has a $11,180,000[1] exemption which can be allocated between gifts made during his or her lifetime and transfers made at time of death.

Rate of Tax

Generation-skipping transfers, which exceed the exemptions shown above, will be subject to the maximum estate tax rate of 40%. This tax is in addition to the federal estate and gift tax, and is reported on IRS Forms 706GS(D), 706GS(T) or 709. See Treas. Reg. 26.2662-1.

---

[1] 2018 value. This amount is subject to adjustment for inflation in future years.

Generation-Skipping Transfer Tax

Reducing the Impact of the Generation-Skipping Transfer Tax

- Consider making full use of the annual gift tax exclusion of $15,000[1] to any number of donees, e.g., children, grandchildren, in-laws, etc.

- Encourage children or grandchildren (or trusts for their benefit) to purchase and own large life insurance policies on the parent or grandparent. At death, the insurance proceeds would not generally be subject to federal estate tax or the generation-skipping transfer tax.

Note: In order to keep the assets of an irrevocable life insurance trust from being subject to the generation-skipping transfer tax, care must be taken to see that transfers (after 3/31/88) to the trust by the insured qualify for the annual gift tax exclusion and that the insured correctly allocates part of his or her $11,180,000 exemption to each transfer.

The generation-skipping transfer tax is a very complex area of the law. Documents must be carefully drafted to avoid this tax in larger estates. For more information, examine IRS Forms 706 GS(D), (D-1) and (T) and their instructions.

---

[1] 2018 value. This amount is subject to adjustment for inflation in future years.

Dynasty Trust

A "dynasty trust" is a strategy used by the very wealthy to create a lasting financial legacy for children, grandchildren, and descendants as yet unborn. The name derives from the fact that a dynasty trust is structured to last as long as legally possible. A long "life" allows assets in the trust to grow for an extended period of years without being periodically depleted by transfer taxes, such as federal estate, gift, or generation-skipping transfer tax (GSTT)[1] as the assets pass from one generation to the next.

Because trust assets can be a tempting target, Dynasty trusts are also designed to provide protection from creditors in case of bankruptcy, a lawsuit, or divorce.

Parties to a Trust

- **Donor, grantor, or trustor:** The individual or individuals setting up the trust and contributing assets.

- **Trustee:** The individual or entity responsible for managing the trust.

- **Beneficiary:** The individual or individuals who receive the income and, ultimately, the trust assets.

Rule Against Perpetuities

At one time, all 50 states limited the legal lifespan of a trust. This "Rule Against Perpetuities" commonly limited a trust's lifespan to no more than 21 years after the death of the youngest beneficiary alive at the time a trust was created. Thus, 21 years after the death of the youngest beneficiary, the trust would terminate and trust assets would be distributed. More recently, a number of states have moved away from this rule, allowing for trusts that, theoretically at least, could run forever, or as long as there are beneficiaries alive.

General Trust Considerations

A dynasty trust involves the use of an "irrevocable" trust. Once the trust has been funded, the grantor may not change its terms or recover assets from the trust. Because the trust is irrevocable, and because a dynasty trust may last a long time, <u>very</u> careful planning is required. Factors to consider include:

---

[1] The discussion here concerns federal law. State or local law may differ.

- **When:** The trust may be set up during life or at death.

- **Trust location:** The trust should be created under the laws of a state which allows for a longer trust lifespan. It is not necessary for the grantor or the beneficiaries to live in that same state.

- **Trustee:** A corporate trustee, such as a bank or independent trust company, is often recommended.

- **Powers given to trustee and beneficiaries:** The grantor has wide flexibility in specifying the powers given to the trustee and to the beneficiaries. A grantor will want the beneficiaries to benefit from the accumulated wealth without having it included in their estates at death. "Spendthrift" provisions help provide protection against outside creditors. Since the future is unknown, trust provisions need to provide some flexibility to meet changing circumstances.

- **Income taxation:** Income distributed from the trust will be taxed to the beneficiary who receives it. If income is retained by the trust, it will be taxed to the trust itself at very high marginal tax rates. The donor could also choose to structure the trust as an "intentionally defective grantor trust" and be taxed on the income from the trust, even though he or she does not receive the income. This can allow the trust to be more valuable to future generations.

- **Trust assets:** Any type of property can be contributed to the trust, although appreciating assets are frequently chosen. Life insurance, on the life of the grantor or trust beneficiaries, can be used to leverage wealth transfer. The grantor may also contribute ownership interests in entities such as a family limited partnership or limited liability company, where valuation discounts for lack of marketability or control may apply.

Transfer Taxes

A donor may transfer assets to a dynasty trust either during life or at death. If the transfer is made during life, there may be a federal gift tax to pay. If the transfer is made at death, the transfer is subject to the federal estate tax. If trust assets or income pass to a beneficiary in a generation two or more below that of the grantor, the Generation-Skipping Transfer Tax (GSTT) also applies. The dynasty trust may be exempt from the GSTT to the extent the donor allocates his or her available GSTT exemption to the trust.

To offset these transfer taxes, each individual is allowed a certain dollar amount of assets which can be transferred to others without paying any transfer tax. In 2018, this dollar amount is equal to $11,180,000 for gift, estate, and GSTT taxes. Thus a single donor can transfer up to $11,180,000 during life or at death, to any beneficiaries, without paying any transfer tax. If both spouses of a married couple agree to combine gifts, in 2018 up to $22,360,000 may be transferred into a dynasty trust without paying any transfer taxes.

Once inside the trust, and assuming that the beneficiaries do not have powers which would cause trust assets to be included in their estates at death (and thus create a potentially taxable transfer), the assets can continue to grow without the burden of additional transfer taxes.

"Selling" Assets to the Trust

A donor may also choose to "sell" assets to a dynasty trust, typically in exchange for an installment note of equal value. Because the transfer is a <u>sale</u>, no transfer taxes apply to the transaction.

Seek Professional Guidance

Use of a dynasty trust is an estate planning technique that generally is limited to very wealthy individuals and families. Once such a trust is funded, it is irrevocable. Because of the complexity of the law surrounding such trusts, and the fact that such laws can change, the guidance of knowledgeable, experienced tax and legal professionals is highly recommended.

How a Dynasty Trust Works

A dynasty trust is used to create a financial legacy extending many years into the future.

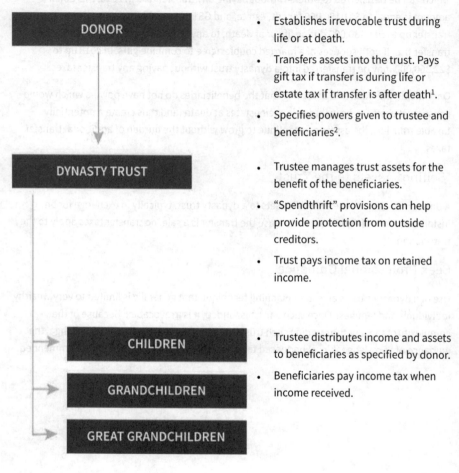

DONOR

- Establishes irrevocable trust during life or at death.
- Transfers assets into the trust. Pays gift tax if transfer is during life or estate tax if transfer is after death[1].
- Specifies powers given to trustee and beneficiaries[2].

DYNASTY TRUST

- Trustee manages trust assets for the benefit of the beneficiaries.
- "Spendthrift" provisions can help provide protection from outside creditors.
- Trust pays income tax on retained income.

CHILDREN

GRANDCHILDREN

GREAT GRANDCHILDREN

- Trustee distributes income and assets to beneficiaries as specified by donor.
- Beneficiaries pay income tax when income received.

---

[1] The discussion here concerns federal income, estate, and gift taxes. State or local law may vary widely. If assets or income pass to a beneficiary two or more generations below that of the grantor, the Generation-Skipping Transfer Tax (GSTT) also applies.

[2] Because of the complex nature of dynasty trusts, and the fact that, once established, they are irrevocable, the guidance of knowledgeable, experienced tax and legal professionals is strongly recommended.

Income in Respect of a Decedent

Under the Internal Revenue Code (IRC), a cash basis taxpayer is generally required to recognize income for federal income tax purposes when the income is actually received. If, however, a cash basis taxpayer dies after becoming entitled to an item of income, but before actually receiving it, the income may not be included on his or her final income tax return because it has not been received.

Such income is termed income in respect of a decedent (IRD).[1] In general, the ultimate recipient of the IRD (e.g., the decedent's estate or heirs) must include the IRD as taxable income for income tax purposes when received. Also, the decedent's estate must include the value of the IRD, for estate tax purposes, as property in which the decedent had an interest.[2]

The Nature of IRD

Although not defined in the IRC,[3] the regulations (Reg. 1.691(a)-1(b)) describe IRD as "those amounts to which a decedent was entitled as gross income, but which were not properly includible in computing his taxable income for the taxable year ending with the date of his death or for a previous taxable year under the method of accounting employed by the decedent." IRD also includes the following:

- All accrued income of a cash basis decedent.

- Income accrued solely by reason of the decedent's death, if the decedent reported under the accrual method.

- Income to which the decedent had a contingent claim at the time of death[4].

The regulations also specify that IRD includes income in respect of a prior decedent. If the present decedent received the right to income from a prior decedent and the amount was not properly includible in computing the present decedent's taxable income for the year ending on the date of his or her death, the amount is income in respect of the present decedent when it is paid.

---

[1] Only in very limited situations will the activities of accrual basis taxpayers generate IRD.

[2] See IRC Secs. 691(a) and 2033, respectively.

[3] State or local tax treatment of IRD may differ from federal law.

[4] The regulations do not explain the meaning of the term contingent claim. Instead, the courts must be relied upon to interpret this term.

Common Sources of IRD

Income in respect of a decedent can arise from a number of common situations. A few frequently encountered sources of IRD are listed below:

- **Wages or other employee compensation:** Such as renewal commissions or deferred compensation, earned by a cash basis decedent, but unpaid at the time of death.

- **Interest on U.S. savings bonds:** Under certain circumstances, untaxed interest on U.S. savings bonds is IRD.

- **Dividend income:** This income is created if the decedent dies between the date of record and the date of payment.

- **Rental income:** If paid after death and attributable to the period before death, rental income is IRD.

- **Distributions from qualified plans and IRAs:** These are usually considered IRD. Spousal beneficiaries of distributions from IRAs may elect to treat a decedent's IRA as his or her own and avoid having the distribution classified as IRD.

- **Partnership interests:** A decedent's share of partnership income prior to death is considered IRD.

- **S corporations:** For the estates of decedents dying after August 20, 1996, IRD can result from inheriting S corporation stock.

Deductions in Respect of a Decedent

The law allows the recipient of IRD to deduct certain expenses incurred by the decedent but not yet paid at the time of death. Such expenses are termed deductions in respect of a decedent (DRD) and are allowable as deductions for both estate and income tax purposes.[1] IRC Sec. 691(b) identifies five types of expenses and one type of credit, which qualify as DRD:

- The deduction for ordinary and necessary business expenses under IRC Sec. 162.

- The interest deduction allowed under IRC Sec. 163.

---

[1] See IRC Sec. 642(g).

- Deductible taxes under IRC Sec. 164.

- Expenses incurred for the production of income under IRC Sec. 212.

- The deduction for depletion under IRC Sec. 611.

- Foreign tax credits under IRC Sec. 27.

Income Tax Deduction for Estate Tax Paid

IRC Sec. 691(c) allows, for income tax purposes, the recipient of IRD a deduction for the federal estate tax attributable to the amount of IRD included in the decedent's estate. The amount of estate tax attributable to the IRD is determined by first calculating the estate tax due on the gross estate, which includes the IRD, and then calculating the estate tax due on the gross estate excluding the IRD.

The deduction for estate tax paid is allowed to the recipient in the year in which the IRD is actually received. For individual taxpayers, the deduction is taken as a miscellaneous itemized deduction (not subject to the 2% of AGI limitation) on Schedule A.

Federal Taxes on Income in Respect of a Decedent

Federal[1] Income and Estate Taxes

For estate tax purposes, a cash basis taxpayer who dies after becoming entitled to income, but who had not actually received it before death, is generally required to include this income in his or her taxable estate. Such income is termed income in respect of a decedent, or IRD. Common sources of IRD include earned-but-unpaid wages, untaxed interest on U. S. savings bonds and untaxed distributions from qualified plans and IRAs.

For income tax purposes, however, the decedent is not required to include the IRD on his or her final income tax return. Rather, it is the ultimate recipients of IRD (the heirs) who generally must include it as taxable income, in the year received. A recipient of IRD is allowed a deduction for the amount of estate tax attributable to the IRD included in the decedent's estate.

Assumptions:

Total taxable estate: $7,000,000

IRD assets included in taxable estate: $2,000,000

Year of death: 2018

Assumed marginal federal income tax rate: 39.60%

Annual inflation rate for the applicable exclusion amount: 0

Item	With IRD Assets	Without IRD Assets
Taxable estate	$7,000,000	$5,000,000
Federal estate tax before credits	$2,745,800	$1,945,800
Applicable (unified) credit amount	-$2,141,800	-$2,141,800
Net federal estate tax	$604,000	0
Federal estate tax with IRD assets	$604,000	
Federal estate tax without IRD assets	0	
Estate tax due to IRD assets	$604,000	
Total IRD assets	$2,000,000	
Federal estate tax on IRD assets	-$604,000	
IRD subject to federal income tax	$1,396,000	
Assumed marginal federal income tax rate	39.60%	
Federal income tax on IRD	$552,816	

[1] The discussion here concerns federal law. State or local tax treatment of IRD may differ.

Potential Combined Tax Disaster with a Child as the Beneficiary

For Qualified Plan Distributions to a Child During 2018

Through a combination of the federal estate tax and regular income tax paid by the beneficiary, the government may tax a hard-earned qualified plan fund very heavily.

Assumptions:

Qualified plan balance: $2,000,000
Beneficiary: Child

Federal estate tax bracket: 40%
Federal income tax bracket: 37.0%

Item	Amount
Beginning balance in qualified plan	$2,000,000
Federal estate tax @ 40.00%[1]	-800,000
Amount left after federal estate tax	$1,200,000
Income tax payable by the beneficiary on $1,200,000[2]	-$405,250
Amount to Child[3]	$794,750

Note: This is a hypothetical example to illustrate the potential cumulative impact of these two taxes.

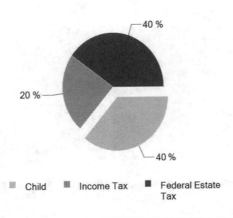

- 40 %
- 20 %
- 40 %

Child ■ Income Tax ■ Federal Estate Tax

[1] Assumes $11,180,000 exemption has been used.

[2] Assumes 2018 federal income tax rates, Single filing status, and the Standard Deduction.

[3] This calculation does not consider any state income tax.

Potential Combined Tax Disaster with a Grandchild as the Beneficiary

For Qualified Plan Distributions to a Grandchild During 2018

Through a combination of the federal estate tax, the Generation-Skipping Transfer (GST) tax and regular income tax paid by the beneficiary, the government may tax a hard-earned qualified plan fund very heavily.

Assumptions:

Qualified plan balance: $2,000,000
Beneficiary: Grandchild
Federal estate tax bracket: 40%

Generation – Skipping transfer tax rate: 40%
Federal income tax bracket: 37.0%

Item	Amount
Beginning balance in qualified plan	$2,000,000
Federal Estate Tax (FET) @ 40%[1]	-800,000
Generation-skipping transfer tax @ 40.0%	-480,000
Amount left after FET and GSTT	$720,000
Income tax payable by the beneficiary on $720,000[2]	-$227,650
Amount to Grandchild[3]	**$492,350**

Note: This is a hypothetical example to illustrate the potential cumulative impact of these three taxes.

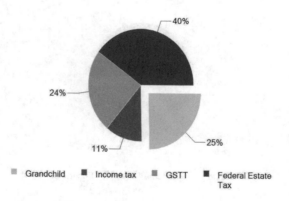

Grandchild ■ Income tax ■ GSTT ■ Federal Estate Tax

---

[1] Assumes $11,180,000 exemption has been used.

[2] Assumes 2018 federal income tax rates, Single filing status, and the Standard Deduction.

[3] This calculation does not consider any state income tax.

Effects of Skipping a Generation

The long-term effect of skipping a generation of estate taxes can be very substantial. Each estate owner has a $11,180,000[1] exemption from the generation-skipping transfer tax (GSTT). The chart below compares three possible plans for removing $11,180,000 from your estate.

Plan A: A gift of $11,180,000 to your child.

Plan B: A gift of $11,180,000 to your grandchild.

Plan C: A gift of $11,180,000 to your grandchild who pays $150,000 per year for 10 years (a total of $1,500,000) for an insurance policy on your life in the amount of $11,180,000.[2] The remaining $9,680,000 the grandchild (or a trust) retains and invests.

Comparison of Three Plans

	Plan A	Plan B	Plan C
Current gift to child[3]	$11,180,000	$0	$0
Current gift to grandchild[3]	0	11,180,000	11,180,000
Additional amount in child's estate	11,180,000	0	0
Growth for 20 years at 5%	29,663,868	0	0
Additional estate tax at child's death	11,865,547	0	0
(assumes 40% tax bracket)			
Amount passing to grandchild	17,798,321	0	0
Additional amount in grandchild's estate			
Transferred at child's death	17,798,321		
Invested at 5% for 20 years	47,224,244		
Gift to grandchild now	0	11,180,000	9,680,000
Non-insurance portion	0	78,707,074	68,147,091
Growth at 5% for 40 years			
Portion used to purchase life insurance	0	0	1,500,000
Insurance face amount	0	0	11,180,000
Growth at 5% for 30 years[4]	0	0	48,319,316
Total amount at grandchild's death	47,224,244	78,707,074	116,466,406
Federal estate tax (at 40%)	18,889,698	31,482,830	46,586,563
Net to great grandchildren	**$28,334,547**	**$47,224,244**	**$69,879,844**

Note: Assumes child or grandchild is in 40% bracket before gifts.

---

[1] 2018 value. This amount is subject to adjustment for inflation in future years.

[2] The insurance that can be purchased will vary greatly depending on age, health, etc. (Assumes 60-year old male.)

[3] A federal gift tax will be due at the time of the gift on any amount in excess of the current (2018) applicable exclusion amount of $11,180,000.

[4] Assumes the insured dies 10 years after the gift.

Transfers to Noncitizen Spouses

When a U.S. citizen dies, his or her assets are subject to federal estate taxes if they exceed the applicable exclusion amount. The applicable exclusion amount for 2018 is $11,180,000.[1]

Assets passing to a U.S. citizen spouse can generally qualify for an unlimited marital deduction that will defer any estate tax until he or she later dies. However, if the surviving spouse is not a U.S. citizen, the transfer will not qualify for the unlimited marital deduction, unless passed to a Qualified Domestic Trust (QDOT).

Transfers During Life

U.S. citizens can transfer assets of unlimited value to their citizen spouse during lifetime. If, however, the spouse is a noncitizen, any gifts in excess of $152,000 per year (2018) will be subject to federal gift tax.

Transfers at Time of Death

As noted above, transfers at the death of a U.S. citizen to a noncitizen spouse will be subject to federal estate taxes, unless the assets pass to a QDOT. The requirements for a QDOT are set forth in IRC Sec. 2056A(a) and related Treasury Regulations. The essential elements are:

- The QDOT must have at least one trustee who is an individual U.S. citizen or a domestic corporation.

- The U.S. trustee must be able to withhold taxes due on any distributions of the trust principal.

- The trust must meet the requirements set forth by the U.S. Treasury to ensure the collection of the federal estate tax.[2]

---

[1] The applicable exclusion amount is the dollar value of assets protected from federal estate tax by an individual's applicable credit amount.

[2] If the QDOT has assets exceeding $2,000,000, the U.S. trustee must be a bank, or the individual U.S. trustee must furnish a bond for 65% of the value of the QDOT assets at the transferor's demise or must furnish an irrevocable letter of credit to the U.S. government for 65% of the value. Up to $600,000 of the value of the personal residence (in the QDOT) may be excluded in determining whether the $2,000,000 threshold has been reached. See Reg. Sec. 20.2056A-2(d).

- The QDOT must also satisfy the rules which qualify interspousal transfers for the marital deduction for citizen spouses, i.e., a QTIP Trust, a general power of appointment trust or an estate trust. See IRS Letter Ruling 9021037.

- The executor of the estate must make both the QTIP trust election (if applicable) and QDOT election to qualify for the marital deduction. See IRC Sec. 2056A(b)(14) and IRS Letter Ruling 9032014.

What if Death Occurs Without a QDOT?

If the death of a U.S. citizen results in a direct transfer of assets to a noncitizen spouse, the surviving noncitizen spouse may voluntarily establish a QDOT and transfer the assets to the trust before the date on which the tax return is due, i.e., nine months after date of death. See IRC Sec. 2056(d)(2)(B) and Reg. Sec. 20.2056A-2(b)(2).

If the surviving spouse becomes a U.S. citizen before the estate tax return is due, the requirement for a QDOT disappears. Also, if citizenship is obtained after the filing of the tax return and no taxable distributions were made from the QDOT, the surviving spouse may provide the trustee with evidence of citizenship and thereby relax the requirements for a U.S. trustee, etc. See Reg. 20.2056A-10(a).

Trusts that qualify for the marital deduction, but not for the QDOT, may be reformed in court to make them meet the requirements of the Code. See IRC Sec. 2056(d)(5) and Reg. Sec. 20.2056A-4(a)(2).

Distributions from a QDOT

Distributions to a surviving noncitizen spouse of trust income (or distributions of principal on account of hardship) are not subject to the QDOT tax. However, other distributions of trust principal will be subject to federal estate taxes calculated at the marginal estate tax rate of the deceased citizen spouse.

Transfers to Noncitizen Spouses

When a U.S. resident noncitizen spouse dies, he or she is entitled to the same applicable credit amount available to U.S. citizens. In 2018, the applicable credit amount is $4,417,800, equivalent to $11,180,000 of assets. See IRC Sec. 2010. If the noncitizen spouse is a nonresident alien, at death he or she is generally entitled to an applicable exclusion amount of only $13,000, equivalent to $60,000 of assets. See IRC Sec. 2102.[1]

Special Rules for Canadian Spouses

The U.S. imposes an estate tax on the worldwide assets of its residents and citizens. Canada, however, does not impose an estate tax. Instead, capital property of a Canadian resident decedent is deemed to have been disposed of immediately before death for its full fair market value and 50% of any appreciation is subject to Canadian income tax.

The U.S. system is an estate tax system; the Canadian system is an income tax system. Because of the inconsistency of the two tax systems and the possibility of a double tax being imposed on a single asset, the U.S. and Canada have entered into a tax treaty which specifies a series of credits available to residents of one country for taxes paid to the other country.

A modification (Protocol) to the U.S. - Canada tax treaty provides for reciprocal tax credits, significantly reducing the double taxation arising from the imposition of both the U.S. federal estate tax and the Canadian income tax, upon the death of an individual.

Some highlights of this protocol include the following:

- The Protocol became effective on November 9, 1995 and was retroactively effective for deaths occurring after November 10, 1988.

- Canadian citizens and residents are allowed a larger applicable credit amount than is generally available to nonresident, alien decedents.

- Instead of a marital deduction, a credit is allowed against U.S. estate tax for property passing to a Canadian spouse.

- A credit is allowed against U.S. estate tax for income tax paid to Canada as a result of the decedent's death.

---

[1] See Estate of Barkat A. Khan v. Commissioner, TC Memo 1998-22.

- U.S. estate tax will not be imposed on most Canadian resident decedents whose estates are worth $1,200,000 (U.S. dollars) or less, unless those estates include real property or business interests located in the U.S.

- A Canadian spousal rollover is available to U.S resident decedents.

- A credit is provided against Canadian income tax for U.S. estate tax paid on property located in the U.S. or generating income from the U.S.

- Because it applied retroactively, the Protocol allowed estates in both the U.S. and Canada to file refund claims within one year of its effective date or within the ordinary statute of limitations.

Seek Professional Guidance

The United States has entered into a number of tax treaties with foreign countries. Individuals with a non-U.S. citizen spouse or individuals with property in foreign countries are advised to seek professional guidance and counsel when planning their estates.

Estate Freezing Generally

When the taxable portion of an estate reaches $1,000,000, it enters the top estate tax bracket. When 40% of each additional dollar of estate growth is earmarked for estate taxes, many estate owners look for methods of freezing the growth of their present estate. Techniques developed over the years can be classified in three categories:

- **Gifts of assets.**

  - Lifetime gifts to children of $15,000[1] or less per year are generally free of gift taxes.

  - Gifts to an irrevocable life insurance trust can create very large amounts of capital which are not subject to estate or income tax.

  - Gifts to charities can produce both income and estate tax savings.

- **Intrafamily sales of assets.**

  - An installment sale of an asset to a child in exchange for secured promissory notes will put future growth of the asset in the child's estate.

  - A private annuity is the sale of an asset for an unsecured promise to pay annual amounts for the seller's lifetime.[2]

- **Changes in business organizations.**

  - Corporate recapitalizations.

  - Personal holding company.

  - Multi-tier family partnerships.

The Revenue Reconciliation Act of 1990 repealed the so-called antifreeze provision of the IRC Sec. 2036(c) and replaced it with a new Chapter 14 entitled "Special Valuation Rules." See IRC Secs. 2701 – 2704. The purpose of this new chapter is to impose a gift tax at the time an estate-freezing transaction occurs rather than waiting until the taxpayer dies. IRC Sec. 2701 establishes a valuation rule for estate-freezing techniques involving interests in corporations and partnerships, e.g., recapitalizations.

---

[1] 2018 value. This amount is subject to adjustment for inflation in future years.

[2] On October 17, 2006, the IRS issued proposed regulations (NPRM REG-141901-5) on the exchange of appreciated property for an annuity contract. These proposed regulations treat the transaction as if the transferor had sold the property for cash and then used the proceeds to purchase an annuity contract. The proposed regulations are generally effective for transactions occurring after October 18, 2006.

Family General Partnership

Family partnerships are often used as a method of dividing business income with children in lower tax brackets and shifting future appreciation out of one's estate.

Family General Partnership

The rules set forth in IRC Sec. 704(e) deal with partnerships where capital is a material income-producing factor, as opposed to businesses which earn income by providing services.

Family members can either purchase an interest in the business or receive it by gift. If the value exceeds the annual gift tax exclusion amount, currently $15,000,[1] there may be gift taxes due. The donor parent may use his or her applicable credit amount to eliminate or reduce gift taxes on amounts exceeding the annual gift tax exclusion.

A trust for minors can be a partner if the trust is administered solely for the beneficiaries' best interests. See Treas. Reg. Sec. 1.704-1(e)(2)(vii).

Why Consider a Family Partnership?

What is the effect of shifting estate growth to a younger generation? Assume a business currently valued at $2,000,000 which has a growth potential of 10%.

	Parents Retain Ownership	Set Up a Family Partnership
Current value of business	$2,000,000	$2,000,000
Amount transferred to children	0	1,000,000
Amount remaining in the estate	2,000,000	1,000,000
Growth of business (10 years at 10%)	5,187,485	2,593,742
Federal estate tax at 40%	2,074,994	1,037,497
Potential estate tax savings		**$1,037,497**
Growth of business (20 years at 10%)	$13,455,000	$6,727,500
Federal estate tax at 40%	5,382,000	2,691,000
Potential estate tax savings		**$2,691,000**

---

[1] 2018 value. This amount is subject to adjustment for inflation in future years.

Family Partnerships Are Not for Everyone

Before proceeding with a family partnership arrangement, business owners must ask if they really want to have a child involved in their business. What effect will the reduced income have on their lifestyle? Will there be a gift tax due and payable when the transfer is made? Will the tax savings compensate for the increased complexity?

Family Limited Partnership

Family limited partnerships (FLP) can be used with business, personal or investment assets. Their traditional purpose has been to divide investment income with children in lower income tax brackets and increase the family's net spendable income.

They have also been used for long-range estate planning. Closely held businesses, along with other assets, are subject to Federal estate and generation skipping transfer taxes. These taxes can effectively prevent the transfer of a family business from one generation to the next. The FLP provides a valuable estate planning tool to lessen these tax burdens.

In recent years, such partnerships have also been employed as a method of protecting family assets from creditors.

IRC Sec. 704(e) effectively limits FLPs to business/investment activities where capital is a material income-producing factor, as contrasted with activities which earn income by providing services.

How It Works

The parents set up a FLP and transfer capital assets into the partnership. Within the partnership structure, the parents act as the general partners; the children (or grandchildren) are the limited partners.

In a limited partnership, the general partners often own only a small proportion of the partnership (for example 5%), while the limited partners own the majority interest. The general partners have complete responsibility and control of partnership activities, as well as the liability for partnership debts and losses.

The limited partners have no control or management rights. Their liability is limited to the amount of their contribution to the partnership.

One of the most attractive features of the FLP is its flexibility. Some estate planning strategies must be irrevocable in order to be effective. Once set up, these irrevocable tools cannot be changed or undone. By contrast, the FLP document can be modified to respond to changes in the family or business structure.

Family Limited Partnership

Reasons to Consider a Family Limited Partnership

There are three primary reasons for creating an FLP:

- **Income tax benefits:** Income generated by a limited partnership is often allocated according to ownership. With the limited partners (the children or grandchildren) owning the majority interest, most of the income generated could flow through to them and be taxed at their lower marginal tax rate.

- **Estate planning benefits:** When the parents contribute assets to the partnership, they are transferring asset value and shifting asset growth from themselves to a younger generation.

Consider the following hypothetical example in which a business has a current value of $200,000 and is expected to grow by 10% per year. Over time, the parents transfer 90% of the business to the children.

	Retain for Parents	Contribute to FLP
Current value	$200,000	$200,000
Amount transferred to children	$0	$180,000
Amount remaining in estate	$200,000	$20,000
Asset value in 20 years	$1,345,500	$134,550
Federal estate tax assumed at 40%	$538,200	$53,820
Potential estate tax savings	$484,380	

Often a gifted ownership interest can receive a discounted value because the interest is either a minority interest or lacks marketability. This minority interest issue should be carefully reviewed with your legal advisor:

- **Protecting assets from lawsuits:** Most state limited partnership statutes prevent the creditors of a limited partner from attaching partnership assets. While the creditors may get a charging order against the debtor's partnership interest, as a practical matter it is very difficult to collect the debt. The FLP may provide one of the most effective asset protection structures available today.

Family Limited Partnerships Are Not for Everyone

Before considering a FLP, there are a number of questions that the parent or parents must answer. Do they really want to have a child involved in their business? Will the income shared with the child affect the parents' lifestyle? Will a gift tax be due and payable when the transfer is made to the child? Will the income tax savings compensate for the increased complexity?

Additionally, legal counsel must be obtained. Because of the complexity involved, FLPs are not appropriate for every situation. The documentation for such a partnership must be carefully designed to avoid problems with both federal law and the law of the state under which the limited partnership is being created.

Installment Sale

The installment sale method allows a taxpayer to spread the profit on a sale over the entire period during which the payments are received. Each payment received is treated as part return of investment and part profit and interest. This relieves the seller of paying tax on income not yet received.

The seller must either use the installment method or elect not to use it and include all of the gain in the current year.

Imputed Interest

If no interest is charged under the terms of the agreement, the IRS imputes interest to the transaction. This means that even if the seller does not collect any interest on the transaction, the IRS will pretend that he or she does and require him or her to include the imputed interest in his or her annual income.

Depreciable Property

If the property sold has been subject to excess depreciation (i.e., greater than straight-line depreciation), any recapture of the excess depreciation must be reported in the year of the sale. Any gain in excess of the recaptured amount may be eligible for installment treatment. When the parties are related, installment sale treatment is only available for sales of depreciated property if it can be demonstrated that tax avoidance was not a principal purpose for the installment sale.

Sales to Related Parties

Any installment sale to a related party[1] who then sells (or otherwise disposes of) the property may cancel the installment reporting of the first sale unless at least two years have passed since the first sale and the property is not marketable securities. See IRC Sec. 453(e).

Sales by Dealers

Sales of real or personal property by a dealer or anyone who regularly sells property on the installment plan cannot be reported on the installment method. Neither can sales of personal property that would have to be included in business inventory if it were on hand at the end of the tax year.

---

[1] Related parties generally include one's spouse, ancestors, descendants, brothers, sisters and business entities or trusts controlled by any of them. See IRC Sec. 453(f)(1).

Advantages of Installment Sales

If installment-sale reporting is available, it has several important advantages.

- By spreading income over two or more tax years, the gain may be taxed in lower tax brackets.

- Even if no taxes are saved, if the payment can be postponed for one or more years, the deferred tax dollars can earn income until they become due.

- Potential future appreciation of the asset may be removed from the seller's estate.

- One may be able to shift high-income-producing assets to a family member in a lower tax bracket.

Notes: An installment sale of an interest in a corporation or partnership should not be regulated by the special valuation rules of IRC Sec. 2701. In some situations there may be interest due on deferred tax liabilities. See IRC Sec. 453A.

Private Annuity

A private annuity is a contract between two individuals to exchange a valuable asset for a lifetime income.

A Typical Example

PARENT (ANNUITANT)	Transfers valuable assets (usually highly appreciated). → ← An unsecured promise to pay an annual sum for lifetime of annuitant.	CHILD (PAYOR)

Formula

$$\frac{\text{Fair Market Value of Asset}}{\text{Annuity Factor for Age and Sex of Annuitant (See IRC Sec. 7520.)}} = \text{Annual Payment Necessary to Avoid Gift Tax}$$

- If the annuity payment is large enough, there will be no gift tax.
- The annuity factor is dependent upon the parent's age.
- Parent can make annual gifts to child to assist in meeting the annual payments.
- Payments to annuitant are partially income tax-free with the remainder taxed as ordinary income, but they are not deductible to the payer.[1]

Estate Planning Considerations

ADVANTAGES	DISADVANTAGES
• The asset and future appreciation may be removed from the annuitant's estate without gift tax or estate tax liability.	• Annuitant may live too long with the payer paying too much for the asset, thus increasing the size of annuitant's estate.
• The annuitant gets a lifetime income.	• Payments are not tax deductible.
• Some of the payments will be considered a return of capital and not taxable.	• If payer dies, it may be difficult to collect the payments. A life policy could guarantee funds.

[1] On 10/17/06, the IRS issued proposed regulations (NPRM REG-141901-5) on the exchange of appreciated property for an annuity contract. These proposed regulations treat the transaction as if the transferor had sold the property for cash and then used the proceeds to purchase an annuity contract. The proposed regulations were generally effective for transactions occurring after 10/18/06, with a six-month delay until 04/18/07 for certain types of transactions.

Corporate Recapitalization

Recapitalization is a reorganization of the corporation's capital structure by readjusting the amount and type of stock outstanding. Typically, the corporation issues both voting preferred stock and common stock in exchange for the owner's currently held common stock.

Prior to 1987, most of the value of the company at the time of the recapitalization was assigned to the preferred stock.

The common stock, therefore, had very little value and could be gifted to or sold to the children with very little, if any, gift tax consequence. Since the future appreciation of the business would be reflected in the common stock, the parents could transfer all of the future appreciation while still effectively retaining control of the business until their deaths.

In 1987, Congress effectively eliminated recapitalizations as an estate freezing device by enacting IRC Sec. 2036(c).

Rules Under IRC Sec. 2701

The Revenue Reconciliation Act of 1990 repealed IRC Sec. 2036(c) and enacted IRC Sec. 2701, which specifically deals with valuation in the transfer of business interests. Recapitalization freezes may be beneficial under this law if all the rules are carefully followed:

- First, the business must be valued using appraisal standards acceptable to the IRS.

- Second, the preferred stock, which the owner will retain, must be valued.

  - Some privileges are assigned a zero value, e.g., voting rights, conversion rights, etc.

  - At least 10% of the business value must be allocated to the common stock (if the family owns 50% or more of the business).

  - The value is based on the dividends which must be paid to the preferred stockholders. Higher dividends will increase the value of the preferred stock, but they also drain the working capital of the business.

- Finally, the value of the preferred stock is subtracted from the appraised value of the entire business, and the difference will be the value of the common stock.

- If dividends are missed, they will be added back into the value of the preferred stock when the owner dies. If dividends are not paid for four consecutive years, interest will accrue and will also be added onto the value of the preferred stock.

Joint Purchase of Assets

The technique of a joint purchase of certain assets by a parent and child brought some very attractive tax results; however, in most cases it has been eliminated as a family wealth-transfer technique. Here's how it might still work:

- A parent and an adult child find a qualified property. Joint purchases by family members must be limited to a personal residence or tangible property, such as artwork.[1]

- The parent purchases the life income interest and the child purchases the remainder interest. The IRS Table S gives the following percentages at an 8% rate. This rate varies from month to month as provided under IRC Sec. 7520.

Values	Age of Parent					
	50	55	60	65	70	75
Value of Remainder	18%	23%	28%	35%	42%	50%
Value of Life Income	82%	77%	72%	65%	58%	50%

Note: Numbers have been rounded to the nearest percent. See Reg. Sec. 25.2512-5.

Assume a father aged 55 wants to purchase a personal residence with his son under this type of arrangement. The father must invest 77% and the son only 23%. At the father's demise, his life income expires and the asset is not included in his estate—the entire 77% that he paid into the property, plus any appreciation, would be excluded.

Potential Problems

- The return on the child's investment may not be very high if the parent lives beyond life expectancy.

- If the parent gives the money to the child to make the initial purchase, there will be estate and gift tax problems. The IRS will likely treat the transaction as a purchase by the father with a gift of a future interest (the remainder) to the child. Future interests do not qualify for the annual gift tax exclusion. Furthermore, since the father retained a life income, the IRS may attempt to include the asset in his estate.

---

[1] Some analysts feel the IRS will include the asset in the parent's estate under IRC Sec. 2702.

How a Grantor-Retained Interest Trust Works

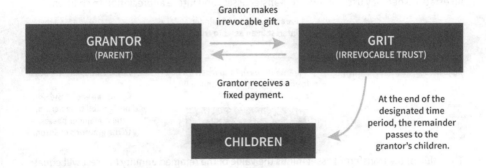

The use of the Grantor-Retained Interest Trust (GRIT) under the Revenue Reconciliation Act of 1990 is limited to those trusts which either pay the grantor a fixed payment at least annually (an annuity) or pay a fixed percentage of the trust assets as computed annually (a unitrust).

The intrafamily GRIT allowed under the prior law currently has only a limited usefulness in the areas of tangible property, e.g., art work, and personal residences which are exempt from the special valuation rules. Such a GRIT is still usable in situations involving unrelated individuals, as well as those including non-lineal descendants such as nieces, nephews and cousins.

To avoid confusion between the GRIT prior to the change in law and the type of trusts which are now permitted, we have two new forms of GRITs called GRATs and GRUTs.

The GRAT is a Grantor-Retained Annuity Trust and the GRUT is a Grantor-Retained Unitrust.

By following the new rules, senior family members may transfer assets with growth potential to junior family members with minimal payment of gift taxes.

In localities where real estate values are depressed, a personal residence GRIT may be very useful in transferring future appreciation potential to one's children.

How a Grantor-Retained Annuity Trust Works

An estate owner may use the GRAT to transfer assets and future appreciation to children.

The value of the transferred asset minus the value of the retained annuity interest will equal the value of the remainder interest that is subject to gift taxation.

Assumptions:

Value of asset placed in GRAT: $500,000

Age of grantor: 65

Type of payment: End of year

Term of payment: 10 years

Federal discount rate (changes monthly): 2.0%

Annual Payment to the Grantor	First-Year Payment as a Percentage of the Asset[2]	Value of the Retained Interest	Gift Tax Value of the Remainder Interest
$30,000	6	$269,478	$230,522
40,000	8	359,303	140,697
50,000	10	449,129	50,871
60,000	12	500,000	0

The cost of the transfer would be the gift tax on the value of the remainder interest. The gift is of a future interest and does not qualify for the annual gift tax exclusion. The gift tax on assets up to $11,180,000[3] is first offset by an individual's applicable credit amount. The tax on gifts that exceed $11,180,000 must be paid in cash in the year the gift is made.

---

[1] The payment period can be for the life of the grantor, for two or more joint lives or for a set number of years.

[2] In subsequent years the dollar amount of annual payment would remain the same but the percentage of trust assets distributed would vary.

[3] 2018 value. This amount is subject to adjustment for inflation in future years.

How a Grantor-Retained Unitrust Works

An estate owner may use the GRUT to transfer assets to his or her children.

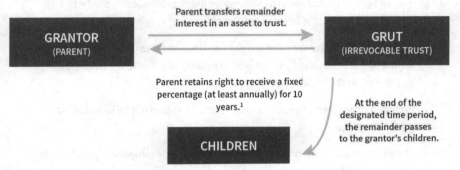

The value of the transferred asset minus the value of the retained unitrust interest will equal the value of the remainder interest that is subject to gift taxation.

For example, if the payout rate is 6%, the trustee will pay the grantor 6% of the value of the trust assets each year. If the trust assets earn more than the 6% payout, there will be a higher payment the following year.

For this reason, the GRUT is not as effective as the Grantor-Retained Annuity Trust (GRAT) in shifting asset appreciation to younger generations.

However, for persons desiring to transfer assets to children while retaining an increasing annual return of income, the GRUT should be considered.

The cost of the transfer would be the gift tax on the value of the remainder interest. The gift is of a future interest and does not qualify for the annual gift tax exclusion. The gift tax on assets up to $11,180,000[2] is first offset by the applicable credit amount. The tax on gifts which exceed $11,180,000 must be paid in cash in the year the gift is made.

---

[1] The payment period can be for the life of the grantor or a set number of years.
[2] 2018 value. This amount is subject to adjustment for inflation in future years.

Intentionally Defective Grantor Trust

An "Intentionally Defective Grantor Trust", or IDGT,[1] is an estate planning strategy used by wealthy individuals to transfer appreciating assets to others with the least possible income tax, gift tax, and estate tax burden. The strategy employs an irrevocable trust which is carefully structured to have the following attributes:

- **Income taxable to grantor:** The income from the trust is taxable to the individual setting up the trust. Trust income is otherwise taxed either to the trust itself, or, if distributed, to the trust's beneficiaries.

- **Excluded from estate:** The assets inside the IDGT should not be included in the grantor's estate.

- **Completed gifts:** Transfers to the IDGT are considered "completed" gifts for federal[2] estate and gift tax purposes.

Parties to a Trust

- **Donor, grantor, or trustor:** The individual or individuals setting up the trust and contributing assets.

- **Trustee:** The individual or entity responsible for managing the trust.

- **Beneficiary:** The individual or individuals who receive the income and, ultimately, the trust assets.

"Intentionally Defective"

The term "intentionally defective" refers to the fact that an IDGT is structured to intentionally violate the "grantor trust" rules of the Internal Revenue Code and thus cause the trust income to be taxable to the grantor during the grantor's life. The grantor trust rules were originally designed to prevent a high-bracket taxpayer from using trusts to shift income to a lower-bracket taxpayer. The "violation" occurs when the grantor or a trustee (not the grantor) who is a non-adverse party[3] retains certain powers or rights, such as:

---

[1] IDGTs are also known as "Intentionally Defective Irrevocable Trusts" or IDITs.

[2] The discussion here concerns federal tax law. State or local law may differ.

[3] Generally, a "nonadverse" party is someone who is not an "adverse" party. An adverse party is someone with a significant interest in the trust who could be negatively affected by the actions (or inaction) of either the grantor or a trustee.

- The power to control beneficial enjoyment of the trust.

- Certain administrative powers, such as the power to borrow from the trust or the power to remove assets from the trust and exchange them for assets of equal value.

- The power to revoke the trust in favor of the grantor.

- The power to use trust income to purchase life insurance on the life of the grantor and/or the grantor's spouse.

Causing the trust's income to be taxable to the grantor has several significant advantages:

- Because the grantor pays the tax on trust income, the assets inside the trust effectively grow tax free.

- The federal income tax rates applicable to trusts are extremely high, compared to the tax rates applicable to individuals. In 2018, for example, a 37.0% marginal tax rate applies when taxable trust income reaches $12,500. In comparison, for an individual taxpayer using the Single filing status, the 37.0% marginal rate only applies when taxable income reaches $500,000.

Making the Transfer – And Keeping Assets Out of the Grantor's Estate

In drafting the trust provisions, it is essential that no power or authority be retained by the grantor that might cause the assets inside the trust to be brought back into his or her estate for estate tax purposes. When the grantor transfers assets into the trust, the transfer is structured as a bona fide sale. The fact that a sale has occurred removes the assets from the donor's estate and avoids having the transfer treated as a gift, subject to federal gift tax. The sale effectively "freezes" the value of the asset and removes any future appreciation from the donor's estate.

- **Installment note:** In exchange for the assets sold to the trust, the grantor receives an installment note of equal value from the trust. The installment note may provide for regular payments of both principal and interest, or for interest-only payments with a balloon payment at the end of a specified period of time. Substantial estate tax savings can be achieved if growth in the value of trust assets exceeds the interest paid to the grantor under the installment note.

- **"Seed" money:** Prior to the sale, a grantor will frequently transfer other assets into the trust equal to between 10% - 20% of the assets to be sold. This transfer is subject to gift tax and serves to insure that the trust has sufficient income to make the projected installment payments.

- **Valuation discounts:** In some situations, the assets to be sold to the trust may first be placed in a business structure, such as a family limited partnership or limited liability company, where valuation discounts for factors such as marketability or lack of control may apply. This can allow the grantor to increase the value of the trust for the beneficiaries.

- **Capital gains:** Because the grantor and the trust are treated, for income tax purposes, as one and the same, the grantor can sell assets to the trust without recognizing any gain on the sale.

Seek Professional Guidance

An intentionally defective grantor trust is considered by many financial professionals to be a technique that should be used only after careful consideration. Although the strategy appears to be supported by case law and IRS rulings, there is no definitive statutory basis for it. Because of the inherent complexity of an IDGT, the guidance of knowledgeable tax and legal professionals is highly recommended.

How an Intentionally Defective Grantor Trust Works

An Intentionally Defective Grantor Trust (IDGT) is an estate planning strategy used to transfer appreciating assets to others with the least possible income tax, gift tax and estate tax burden.[1]

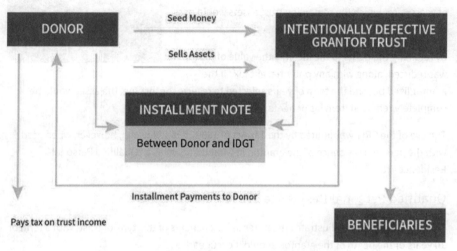

- Donor establishes IDGT and transfers "seed money" to trust. This transfer may be subject to gift tax.
- Donor then sells assets to trust in a bona-fide sale.
- Donor receives installment note from trust in exchange for the assets sold to the trust.
- IDGT makes installment payments to donor.
- Because the trust is "defective," donor pays income tax on trust income.
- At donor's death, assets in trust pass to beneficiaries.[2]

---

[1] The discussion here concerns federal income tax, gift tax, and estate tax law. State or local law may vary widely.

[2] Because of the complexity of an IDGT, the guidance of knowledgeable tax and legal professionals is highly recommended.

How a Qualified Personal Residence Trust Works

A "Grantor-Retained Income Trust", or GRIT, was a planning technique that allowed a person (the grantor) to transfer assets to a trust and then retain the income for a number of years, after which the remaining trust assets would pass to others, e.g. children, grandchildren, etc.

By retaining the rights to the income, the value of the gift was reduced, along with any potential gift tax. If the grantor lived beyond the term of years selected to receive the income, the asset would be completely removed from his or her taxable estate.

The use of the GRIT was limited by the Tax Act of 1990. It is still useful, however, when used with the personal residence of the grantor, in what is known as a "Qualified Personal Residence Trust."

Qualified Personal Residence Trust

The following example illustrates the potential tax benefits of this type of trust, with a term of 10 years or the death of the grantor, should it occur earlier:

Assumptions:

Value of residence: $500,000
Age of grantor at beginning of trust: 65
Term of the trust: 10 years
Gov't. rate for valuing remainder interest: 2.4%[1]

Value of remainder interest	$190,299
Probability of living 10 years	78.52%
Amount of taxable gift = $309,701	

---

[1] The IRC 7520 rate for November 2017; this rate is subject to change monthly.

How a Qualified Personal Residence Trust Works

Assuming the grantor lives beyond the 10-year period, he or she will have removed a $500,000 asset (plus its growth potential during the 10 years) from the taxable estate.[1]

The trust instrument should be drafted so that it is a grantor trust. This makes the trust income taxable to the grantor but also allows him or her to deduct mortgage interest and property tax payments made by the trustee.

Note: The grantor's applicable credit amount may be used to avoid paying a gift tax on the taxable portion.

---

[1] If death occurs before 10 years, the value of the trust assets is includable in the grantor's gross taxable estate.

Using Cash Value Life Insurance

Accumulating Funds to Meet Savings Goals

Saving money to reach an accumulation goal is a problem many of us face. Some goals, such as retirement or a college fund for a child, are long-term savings goals. Many of us also have shorter-term savings goals such as a vacation or a Christmas or holiday fund.

Whatever the objective, the basic problem is the same, i.e. where to put money aside to reach a particular savings goal. For many short-term goals, a savings account at a local bank or credit union is a popular choice. For college funding, Coverdell IRAs or IRC Sec. 529 plans are often used. For retirement savings, many individuals depend on Individual Retirement Accounts (IRAs) or employer-sponsored retirement plans such as an IRC Sec. 401(k) plan.

An additional option for long-term savings, one that is sometimes overlooked, is using a cash value life insurance policy.

What is Cash Value Life Insurance?

Life insurance comes in two basic variations, "term" insurance and "cash value" life insurance. Term life insurance can be compared to auto insurance. Protection is provided for a specified period of time or "term." No death benefits are paid unless the insured dies during the term the policy is in force. If the insured lives beyond the term period, the policy generally expires with nothing returned to the policy owner.

In addition to providing a death benefit, "cash value" life insurance also provides for the tax-deferred accumulation of money inside the policy. These funds can be used by the policy owner while the insured is alive to provide the resources for needs such as funding a college education, making improvements to the home, or starting a business. When the policy owner uses the cash values to meet such needs, he or she is said to have used the "living benefits" of a cash value life insurance policy.

When to Consider Cash Value Life Insurance

Using a cash value life insurance policy to reach a saving goal works best in certain situations:

- **A need for life insurance death benefit:** Apart from the need for additional savings, an individual should have a need for the death benefit that life insurance provides. For example, such a need exists when an individual has a dependent spouse or children who would suffer economically if the individual died. Someone with a large estate might need additional cash at death to pay estate and other taxes as well as final expenses.

- **Other savings aren't enough:** Because of limitations in federal tax law,[1] other accumulation vehicles might not allow enough money to be put aside to meet a particular savings goal.

- **Time frame:** Ideally, there should be at least 10 to 15 years between today and the time the money will be needed. Because of mortality expenses and other policy charges, significant cash value accumulations are generally deferred until a policy has been in force for a number of years. Additionally, federal income tax law affects the design of cash value life insurance policies as well as the taxation of cash value withdrawals in the early years a policy is in force.

- **Insurable:** The insured needs to be healthy enough to have a policy issued on his or her life.

- **An ongoing obligation:** Cash value life insurance policies tend to have a higher premium cost than comparable term life policies. Paying the premiums over a number of years represents an ongoing financial obligation, to both keep the policy in force and achieve the savings goal.

Income Tax Considerations

There are a number of income tax issues to keep in mind when considering any life insurance policy. The death benefit payable under a life insurance contract because of the death of the insured is generally received income-tax free. Federal income taxation of life insurance "living benefits" is more complicated:

- **Tax-deferred growth:** The growth of cash value inside a life insurance policy is tax-deferred.

---

[1] The discussion here concerns federal income tax law. State or local tax law may vary widely.

- **Cost recovery rule:** Amounts withdrawn from a cash-value life insurance contract are included in gross income (and become subject to tax) only when they exceed the policy owner's basis in the policy. This basis is also known as the "investment in the contract." This effectively treats withdrawals from the policy first as a non-taxable return of premium and secondly as taxable income.
- **Investment in the contract:** The total of all premiums paid less any policy dividends and any other prior tax-free distributions received.
- **Policy dividends:** Some "participating" life policies pay what are termed "dividends." Such dividends are a return of a portion of the policy owner's previously paid premiums. Policy dividends are not taxable until they exceed the owner's basis in the life insurance contract.
- **Policy loans:** Some cash value life insurance policies allow the policy owner to borrow at interest a portion of the accumulated cash value. While a policy is in force, policy loans are generally not taxable. However, if a policy is surrendered with a loan outstanding, taxable income will result to the extent that the unpaid loan amount exceeds the owner's basis in the contract.
- **Modified Endowment Contracts (MECs):** Some life insurance policies – primarily because there are large premium payments in the early years of the contract – are termed "Modified Endowment Contracts," or MECs. Under federal income tax law, distributions from a policy considered to be a MEC are treated differently than distributions from non-MEC policies. Withdrawals from a MEC (including a policy loan) will first be taxed as current income until all of the policy earnings have been taxed. If the owner is under age 59½, a 10% penalty also applies, unless the payments are due to disability or are annuity type payments. Once all policy earnings have been distributed (and taxed), any further withdrawals are treated as a non-taxable return of premium.

Accessing the Contract's Cash Values

When the time comes to use the accumulated cash values, withdrawals from the policy should be done in such a way as to avoid current income taxation (to the extent possible) and keep the policy in force.

- **Withdrawal to basis:** Initially a policy owner can take withdrawals (partial policy surrenders) until he or she has withdrawn an amount equal to the basis in the policy.

- **Switching to policy loans:** Once the basis has been withdrawn, the policy owner then begins using non-taxable policy loans. The interest payable on these policy loans is typically much less than a loan from a commercial bank or credit union.

- **A combination:** A policy owner can also use a combination of withdrawals and policy loans.

- **Caveats:** There are a number of issues that a policy owner needs to keep in mind:

  - Withdrawals reduce the death benefit available under the policy.

  - If an insured dies with a policy loan outstanding, the policy's death benefit is reduced by the amount of the loan balance.

  - Excessive use of withdrawals and policy loans can result in the policy lapsing. Such a lapse can result in unexpected, negative tax results as well as the loss of a valuable financial asset.

A Multi-function Tool

Used appropriately, cash value life insurance can serve as financial tool with multiple uses. It can be used, in conjunction with more traditional savings vehicles, as a way to accumulate funds for long-term savings goals. At the same time the policy can, if the insured dies, provide a death benefit when the funds are most needed.

Seek Professional Guidance

Determining the appropriate amount of life insurance, the best type of policy to meet the needs of an individual's specific situation, and planning when and how to access a policy's cash values can be complex and confusing. The advice and guidance of trained insurance, tax, and other financial professionals is strongly recommended.

How Are Death Taxes Paid?

Death taxes are due and payable in cash within nine months after the taxpayer's death.

Five Ways to Provide Money for Death Taxes

- **The executor may borrow the cash:** This only defers the problem, since the money will have to be repaid with interest. This includes installment payments to the government.

- **The taxpayer may pay in cash:** Rarely does a person accumulate large sums of cash. If he or she does, he or she probably will forego many profitable investment opportunities in order to keep the estate in a liquid position.

- **The taxpayer may sell stock market investments:** This may be a wise choice if the market is "up" when the stocks or bonds need to be converted to cash and the taxpayer has been investing long enough to accumulate the necessary amount.

- **The executor may liquidate other assets:** If there is not a ready market, however, the assets may be sold at a great loss.

- **The taxpayer can pay his or her estate settlement costs with life insurance.**

Advantages of Life Insurance

- The insured's beneficiaries almost always get back more than he or she paid in.

- Payment of benefit is prompt.

- There is generally no income tax on the proceeds.

- Proceeds may be free of estate tax.

- Payments can be spread out rather than paid all at once.

- It avoids many of the problems of the other four methods set forth above.

- The proceeds are generally not subject to probate.

- Life insurance provides cash for a predictable and certain need which will arise at some unpredictable moment.

Taxation of Life Insurance Proceeds

Income Taxation

Death proceeds of a life insurance policy are almost always income tax free.

Federal Estate Taxation

Proceeds of a life insurance policy will be included in your estate in two situations:

- If your estate is named as the beneficiary, or
- If you have incidents of ownership in the policy (for example, if you have the power to change beneficiaries, borrow against the cash values, surrender the policy, etc.).

Transfers Within Three Years Prior to Death

If you make a gift of a life insurance policy and then die within three years, the full face amount of the policy will be included in your gross estate for estate tax purposes.

Should You Cross-Own Policies?

Prior to 1982, married couples would frequently own the life insurance policies on each other's life. This technique often kept the insurance from being taxed when the first spouse died.

Since January 1, 1982, however, federal law has provided for an unlimited marital deduction. This means that any amount of assets transferred to one's spouse are not subject to estate or gift taxation. Therefore, any life insurance policies payable to the surviving spouse (no matter which spouse owns them) will not be taxed because of the unlimited marital deduction.[1]

The Problem

When the surviving spouse later dies, his or her estate will have been enlarged by the insurance proceeds collected at the death of the first spouse. Now there may be a substantial tax problem.[2] An irrevocable life insurance trust or ownership of the policies by children or grandchildren can remove the proceeds from the insured's estate, as well as the estate of the surviving spouse.

---

[1] The unlimited marital deduction is disallowed for surviving spouses who are not U.S. citizens.

[2] When a person dies, there is an "applicable exclusion amount" available that exempts a certain portion of an estate from federal estate tax. For married couples, any applicable exclusion amount that remains unused at the death of the first-to-die is generally available for use by the surviving spouse, as an addition to his or her own applicable exclusion amount.

Irrevocable Life Insurance Trust for a Single Person

Since estate taxes are imposed upon all the assets in the estate, many people prefer to pay the taxes by rearranging some of these assets instead of relying on their current income.

One method of achieving this goal is the irrevocable life insurance trust (ILIT). To prevent inclusion in the estate, an irrevocable trust cannot be revoked or amended by the grantor.

- **Funded irrevocable insurance trusts:** This trust has income-producing assets transferred into it, which will pay the premiums on the insurance policy from the income earned. Irrevocable life insurance trusts are typically not funded with a single, lump-sum payment because the gift taxes on the assets transferred are the same as the federal estate taxes on assets remaining in the estate. Also, if the trust is a "grantor trust" for income tax purposes, the income earned on the assets would still be included on the income tax return of the insured grantor. See IRC Sec. 677(a)(3).

- **Unfunded irrevocable insurance trusts:** Although this trust is not totally unfunded, it usually just owns an insurance policy and the grantor makes annual gifts to the trust with which the trustee can pay the premiums.

Some Areas of Concern

- **Trust is irrevocable:** This means that the grantor cannot get anything out once it is put into the trust. Some suggest that a special power of appointment in the hands of the insured's child would permit that child to appoint the trust assets back out to the insured or others. In an uncertain estate planning environment, this flexibility may be very desirable. The trustee would need to be authorized to reappoint trust assets without liability to the trust beneficiaries.

Irrevocable Life Insurance Trust for a Single Person

- **Annual gift tax exclusion may be lost:** Contributions to the trust are generally "future" interests instead of "present" interests. Future interests typically do not qualify for the $15,000 (in 2018) annual gift tax exclusion. This concern can be overcome by granting to the beneficiaries a limited power to withdraw certain sums from the trust for a short time after the grantor makes the contribution. This is sometimes referred to as a Crummey provision after the case which decided the validity of this technique [Crummey vs. U.S., 397 F.2d 82 (CA-9, 1968)]. The rules set forth in this case and subsequent rulings must be carefully followed. Crummey power holders should be actual trust beneficiaries; however, the tax court allowed contingent beneficiaries (e.g., children, grandchildren, etc.) to qualify in Est. of Maria Cristofani vs. Comm., 97 T.C. 74 (1991).[1]

- **Non-exercise of withdrawal powers:** The failure of a beneficiary to withdraw the amounts permitted under the Crummey provision will cause a lapse of that power. Lapsed amounts in excess of the specified limit[2] are generally considered to be taxable gifts from the beneficiary. However, if the beneficiary is given a limited power to appoint the amount in excess of these limits (in his or her will), the power is deemed not to lapse and therefore no gift tax is due.

  Another strategy to deal with this problem is referred to as a "hanging" power. It limits the amount which lapses each year to the larger of $5,000 or 5% of the trust assets. Any amount in excess of this limit "hangs" or carries over to later years. The IRS has, in one situation, stated its opposition to this method. See TAM 8901004.

- **Three-year rule:** If an existing life policy is gifted by the insured to an irrevocable life insurance trust and the insured dies within three years of the transfer, the policy proceeds will be included in the insured's estate. IRC Sec. 2035. On the other hand, if the trustee uses cash in the trust to purchase a new policy on the insured's life and the insured dies within the three-year period, the proceeds will generally be excluded from his or her estate. Care should be taken to make certain that the insured has no incidents of ownership in the policy or control over the trustee.

---

[1] The IRS has continued to attack the conclusion reached in the *Cristofani* case, using a substance-over-form argument. Individuals planning an irrevocable trust similar to that involved in *Cristofani* are advised to consult an attorney on the steps needed to avoid having the IRS conclude that gifts to an irrevocable trust are not gifts of a present interest.

[2] The limit is the greater of $5,000 or 5% of the value of the assets subject to the power.

Irrevocable Life Insurance Trust for a Married Couple

Since estate taxes are imposed upon all of the assets in the estate, many people prefer to pay the taxes by rearranging some of these assets instead of relying on their current income.

One method of achieving this goal is the irrevocable life insurance trust (ILIT). To prevent inclusion in the estate, an irrevocable trust cannot be revoked or amended by the grantor.

- **Funded irrevocable insurance trusts:** This trust has income-producing assets transferred into it which will pay the premiums on the insurance policy from the income earned. Irrevocable life insurance trusts are typically not funded with a single, lump-sum payment because the gift taxes on the assets transferred are the same as the federal estate taxes on assets remaining in the estate. Also, if the trust is a "grantor trust" for income tax purposes, the income earned on the assets would still be included on the income tax return of the insured grantor. See IRC Sec. 677(a)(3).
- **Unfunded irrevocable insurance trusts:** Although this trust is not totally unfunded, it usually just owns an insurance policy and the grantor makes annual gifts to the trust with which the trustee can pay the premiums.

Additional Considerations

- **Trust is irrevocable:** This means that the grantor cannot get anything out once it is put into the trust. Some suggest that a special power of appointment in the hands of the insured's child would permit that child to appoint the trust assets back out to the insured or others. In an uncertain estate planning environment, this flexibility may be very desirable. The trustee would need to be authorized to reappoint trust assets without liability to the trust beneficiaries.

- **Annual gift tax exclusion may be lost:** Contributions to the trust are generally "future" interests instead of "present" interests. Future interests typically do not qualify for the $15,000 (in 2018) annual gift tax exclusion. This concern can be overcome by granting to the beneficiaries a limited power to withdraw certain sums from the trust for a short time after the grantor makes the contribution. This is sometimes referred to as a Crummey provision after the case which decided the validity of this technique (Crummey vs. U.S., 397 F.2d 82 (CA-9, 1968)). The rules set forth in this case and subsequent rulings must be carefully followed. Crummey power holders should be actual trust beneficiaries; however, the tax court allowed annual gift tax exclusions for contingent beneficiaries (e.g., children, grandchildren, etc.) who were given withdrawal rights (Est. of Maria Cristofani vs. Comm., 97 T.C. 74 (1991)).[1]

- **Non-exercise of withdrawal powers:** The failure of a beneficiary to withdraw the amounts permitted under the Crummey provision will cause a lapse of that power. Lapsed amounts in excess of the specified limit[2] are generally considered to be taxable gifts from the beneficiary. However, if the beneficiary is given a limited power to appoint the amount in excess of these limits (e.g., in his or her will), the power is deemed not to lapse and therefore no gift tax is due.

Another strategy used to deal with this problem is referred to as a "hanging" power. It limits the amount which lapses each year to the larger of $5,000 or 5% of trust assets. Any amount in excess of this limit "hangs" or carries over to later years. The IRS has, in one situation stated its opposition to this method. See TAM 8901004.

- **Three-year rule:** If an existing life policy is gifted by the insured to an irrevocable life insurance trust and the insured dies within three years of the transfer, the policy proceeds will be included in the insured's estate. IRC Sec. 2035. On the other hand, if the trustee uses cash in the trust to purchase a new policy on the insured's life and the insured dies within the three-year period, the proceeds will generally be excluded from his or her estate. Care should be taken to make certain that the insured has no incidents of ownership in the policy or control over the trustee.

- **Second-to-die policies:** Second-to-die or survivor life policies do not pay the proceeds until both spouses are deceased, which is when the death taxes generally become due. Premiums on a single second-to-die policy are generally lower than the combined premiums on two individual policies, allowing a couple to obtain a larger face amount of insurance. If the surviving spouse will need policy proceeds to live on, however, this type of policy should generally not be used.

---

[1] The IRS has continued to attack the conclusion reached in the *Cristofani* case, using a substance-over-form argument. Individuals planning an irrevocable trust similar to that involved in *Cristofani* are advised to consult an attorney on the steps needed to avoid having the IRS conclude that gifts to an irrevocable trust are not gifts of a present interest.

[2] The limit is the greater of $5,000 or 5% of the value of the assets subject to the power.

Paying Estate Costs with Estate-Tax-Free Dollars

Since estate taxes are imposed upon the value of the assets in one's estate, many people prefer to pay for these taxes by repositioning these assets, rather than trying to solve the problem entirely from their current earnings.

The following method of systematically transferring small amounts of capital from the estate appeals to many estate owners.

Assume an estate of 16,000,000, with death occurring in 2018.

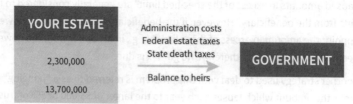

With a little planning, the entire estate may be kept intact.

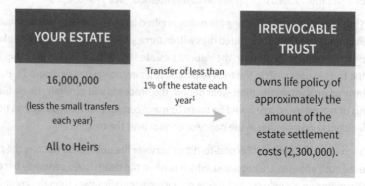

At death, this 2,300,000 can be lent to the executor to pay for the estate settlement costs or it can be used to purchase assets from the estate. The income earned by the trust assets can go to the surviving spouse and the remainder can pass to the children after his or her demise, without being taxed in his or her estate.

---

[1] Assumes approximate cost of a permanent type life insurance policy on a 50-year-old male. Actual amount will vary.

Effect of Life Insurance Transfers on Federal Estate Taxes

Assumptions:

Current net estate (less life insurance): $1,000,000
Estimated estate growth rate: 4.50%
Estimated year of death: 2020
Current life insurance inside the estate: $200,000
Amount of current life insurance available to transfer outside the estate: $200,000
Proposed new life insurance: $500,000
Annual inflation rate for the applicable exclusion amount: 0

	With Life Insurance Inside Estate	With Life Insurance Outside Estate
Potential estate size at death	$1,792,025	$1,092,025
Federal estate taxes	0	0
Savings with life insurance outside of estate		0

Payment of premiums on policies outside the estate will further reduce the estate size.

Gifts of Life Insurance Policies

Valuation (market value) of Policies

Type of Policy	Value for Gift Tax Purposes
Whole life	The interpolated terminal reserve plus unearned premium.
Whole life (paid up)	Present cost of comparable policy at present age.
New policy	The gross premium just paid.
Term policy	The interpolated terminal reserve plus unearned premium[1].

Federal Tax Status of Gifted Policies – Three Situations

Assumes husband (insured) is now deceased.

Owner/Applicant (Original Owner)	Policy Assigned To	Federal Estate Tax Status	Authority
Husband	Anyone **less than three years** prior to death.	Policy proceeds includable in the gross estate.	IRC Sec. 2035(a)
Husband	Anyone **more than three years** prior to death.	Policy proceeds generally not includable in the gross estate.	IRC Sec. 2035(a)
Wife, children or irrevocable trust	**No direct transfer** of policy ownership by the insured.	Policy proceeds generally not includable in the gross estate.	*Estate of Joseph Leder,* 90-1 USTC Para. 60,001 (10th Cir. 1989); *Estate of Eddie L. Headrick vs. Comm.,* 90-2 USTC Para. 60,049 (6th Cir. 1990); *Estate of Frank M. Perry, Sr. vs. Comm.,* 91-1 USTC Para. 60,064 (5th Cir. 1991).

Gifts of life insurance through use of an irrevocable life insurance trust (ILIT) can be an extremely effective part of your estate plan. However, every precaution should be taken in establishing and funding an ILIT if the desired tax benefits are to be realized. If there is any connection between the insured and the insurance policy, the IRS may try to establish that the trustee is merely an agent of the insured.

---

[1] This method is applicable to level premium term policies. An annual renewal term (ART) policy is valued based on the unearned premium.

Adult Children's Insurance Trust

When life insurance is owned by the insured, it is generally included in his or her gross estate (or the estate of his or her spouse). If the surviving spouse is the beneficiary, there may not be an estate tax due at the first death because of the unlimited marital deduction. However, the policy proceeds would then be part of the surviving spouse's estate to the extent they were not consumed prior to his or her demise.

In order to avoid the loss of up to 40%[1] of the insurance proceeds for additional estate taxes, many people take steps to have these proceeds excluded from their taxable estates.

Most Common Methods

The most common methods used to exclude life insurance from one's taxable estate are:

- An irrevocable life insurance trust, and
- Ownership of the policies by adult children.

Potential Problems

The irrevocable life insurance trust requires special care to make certain that the money contributed for the payment of the premiums qualifies for the annual gift tax exclusion.

In order to qualify for the annual gift tax exclusion, the gift must be a present interest. This is generally difficult to accomplish in an irrevocable trust unless the beneficiaries are given the right to withdraw the funds each time the grantor contributes to the trust. This right is sometimes called a Crummey provision. The trustee must notify the beneficiaries each time they have such a right to withdraw funds.

Also, if the contributions exceed a certain limit[2] per year per beneficiary and the beneficiary fails to withdraw the funds, the tax code states that a lapse has occurred and may subject the beneficiaries to a gift tax problem. Careful drafting of the trust can generally avoid this problem.[3]

---

[1] Under current legislation, this is the top marginal federal estate tax bracket, assuming death in 2018.

[2] The limit is the greater of $5,000 or 5% of the value of the assets subject to the power.

[3] In certain situations, the tax status of gifts to an irrevocable life insurance trust is unclear. Individuals planning an irrevocable trust are advised to consult an attorney on the steps needed to avoid having the IRS conclude that gifts to the trust are not gifts of a present interest and thus be ineligible for the annual gift tax exclusion.

Even with these inconveniences, the irrevocable life insurance trust is a very valuable estate planning tool, especially when there is a desire to provide income for a surviving spouse or the insured's children are still minors.

When children are adults, the same tax result can often be reached without the need for a trust document.

- Existing life insurance policies can be transferred to an adult child named as the owner and beneficiary. If, however, there is more than one child, there may be problems of multiple owners on the policy:

  - A gift of an existing life insurance policy to more than one owner will always be a gift of a future interest, as no single owner can exercise any right or access any policy values without the consent of all co-owners.

  - With multiple owners, the annual gift tax exclusion will not apply to the transfer of ownership nor to any premiums subsequently paid by the transferor.

- If only one child is named as owner, and two or more children are named as beneficiaries, there will be a gift tax on the portions passing to the non-owner beneficiaries at the insured's demise. As a further complication, the child named as owner could change beneficiaries at any time.

As an alternative, cash can be given to the children to purchase a new life insurance policy.

One potential problem is that some of the children may elect not to use the funds to solve estate liquidity problems by withholding the insurance proceeds from the executor.

A Possible Solution

The estate owner can encourage his or her children to set up a revocable living insurance trust with the children acting as grantors. The trustees could then apply for insurance on the estate owner's life.

After the insured's demise, the trust could be permitted to lend money to the executor of the estate or purchase assets from the estate. This procedure provides cash proceeds where they are needed most without increasing the size of the taxable estate.

The children generally follow the desires of the estate owner when they know that this trust is only part of the inheritance which they could receive.

Bypass Trust

Under federal law, each individual has an "applicable exclusion amount," a specified dollar amount of asset protected from federal estate tax. Between spouses, however, a person can pass any size estate to his or her U.S. citizen spouse[1] without concern for a federal estate tax because of the "unlimited marital deduction." For many married couples, an "I love you" will simply leaves everything to the surviving spouse.

Before 2011, however, when the surviving spouse later died, and the combined estate passed to the ultimate heirs, there was only the survivor's single applicable exclusion amount to shield the estate from federal estate tax. Using the unlimited marital deduction at the first death, in effect, <u>wasted</u> the applicable exclusion amount of the first-to-die.

To preserve the applicable exclusion amount of the first-to-die, many married couples used a "bypass" trust (also called an "exemption" or "credit shelter" trust). At the first death, the bypass trust would be funded with assets up to the applicable exclusion amount in effect for that year. A bypass trust is not subject to federal estate tax at either the first or second death, even though the assets in the trust may appreciate greatly in value.

A bypass trust is also useful in that it can be written to give the surviving spouse access to the income from the trust for life, as well as access to the trust principal, in extreme situations, for his or her health, education, support, and maintenance.

2010 and 2012 Tax Legislation

The 2010 Tax Relief Act brought a number of significant changes to federal estate tax law. One provision increased the applicable exclusion amount to $5,000,000 in 2011 and to $5,120,000 in 2012. Another section provided that any applicable exclusion amount remaining unused at the death of the first-to-die of a married couple could be carried over and used by the survivor, in addition to the surviving spouse's own applicable exclusion amount.

The American Taxpayer Relief Act of 2012 made permanent a number of the provisions in the 2010 Tax Relief Act, including the increased applicable exclusion amount and the carryover of any unused spousal applicable exclusion amount.

---

[1] If the surviving spouse is not a U.S. citizen, special rules apply.

Tax Cuts and Jobs Act of 2017

The Tax Cuts and Jobs Act of 2017 (JCTA), for 2018 – 2025, increased the base applicable exclusion amount from the $5,000,000 level set in the 2010 act, to $10,000,000.[1] Adjusted for inflation, the applicable exclusion amount for 2018 is $11,180,000. Thus, for 2018, the combined effect of all these changes is to effectively protect from federal estate tax up to $22,360,000 in assets, with or without a bypass trust.

Is the Bypass Trust Dead?

With such a large dollar amount protected from federal estate tax, many estate owners will find that a bypass trust is no longer necessary, at least from a *federal* estate tax perspective. When planning for *state* death taxes, however, which often have much lower taxability thresholds, the bypass trust may continue to be a valuable estate planning tool. Note that there may also be *non-tax* reasons for including a bypass trust in an estate plan.

Those with estates large enough to be subject to federal estate tax will likely benefit from continuing to use bypass trusts as a part of their estate plan.

Seek Professional Guidance

All estate owners are strongly advised to consult with appropriate financial, tax, and legal professionals as to the steps to take to best benefit from this changed estate planning environment.

---

[1] Under current law, in 2026, the $5,000,000 base applicable exclusion amount will again apply, adjusted for inflation.

How a Bypass Trust Works

The bypass trust is designed to make use of the applicable exclusion amount[1] of each spouse, while allowing the surviving spouse to have use of the assets of the deceased spouse. The bypass trust is generally not taxed at either death. The survivor's trust is generally taxed when the surviving spouse later dies.

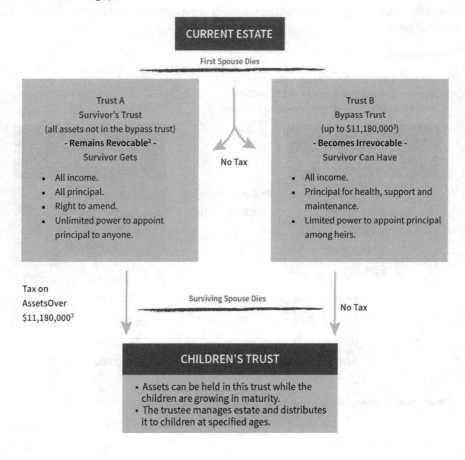

CURRENT ESTATE

First Spouse Dies

Trust A
Survivor's Trust
(all assets not in the bypass trust)
- Remains Revocable[2] -
Survivor Gets

No Tax

- All income.
- All principal.
- Right to amend.
- Unlimited power to appoint principal to anyone.

Trust B
Bypass Trust
(up to $11,180,000[3])
- Becomes Irrevocable -
Survivor Can Have

- All income.
- Principal for health, support and maintenance.
- Limited power to appoint principal among heirs.

Tax on Assets Over $11,180,000[3]

Surviving Spouse Dies

No Tax

CHILDREN'S TRUST

- Assets can be held in this trust while the children are growing in maturity.
- The trustee manages estate and distributes it to children at specified ages.

---

[1] The applicable exclusion amount is the dollar value of assets protected from federal estate tax by an individual's applicable credit amount.

[2] Trust may be irrevocable if it is a general power of appointment trust or an estate trust.

[3] For 2018, the applicable exclusion amount is $11,180,000. In 2017, the applicable exclusion amount was $5,490,000.

How An Irrevocable Life Insurance Trust Works

Any increase in the taxable estate due to additional life insurance proceeds will be taxed at one's marginal estate tax bracket, unless the policies are owned outside the estate. Brackets range from 18% to 40% on taxable estates in excess of the applicable exclusion amount of $11,180,000.[1]

Assumptions:

Your *taxable* estate at date of death: $3,000,000
Recommended new insurance amounts: $1,000,000
Potential taxable estate with new insurance: $4,000,000

If New Insurance Is Included in the Estate		If New Insurance Is Outside the Estate[2]
Portion of increased estate to the IRS **$400,000.** Portion to heirs **$600,000.**	Projected Marginal Tax Bracket **40%**[3]	All of new life insurance goes to one's beneficiaries **$1,000,000.**

Federal estate tax on	$4,000,000	=	$1,600,000
Federal estate tax on	$3,000,000	=	1,200,000
Difference		=	$400,000
Additional amount to heirs		=	**$400,000**

Note: Taxes indicated above assume full applicable credit amount is available.

---

[1] For 2018, the applicable exclusion amount is $11,180,000. In 2017, the applicable exclusion amount was $5,490,000.

[2] Typically, to keep insurance proceeds out of the estate, either adult beneficiaries or an irrevocable life insurance trust should own the policy.

[3] This is the current marginal tax bracket on a $3,000,000 taxable estate (assuming death in 2018).

How Bypass and Irrevocable Life Insurance Trusts Work

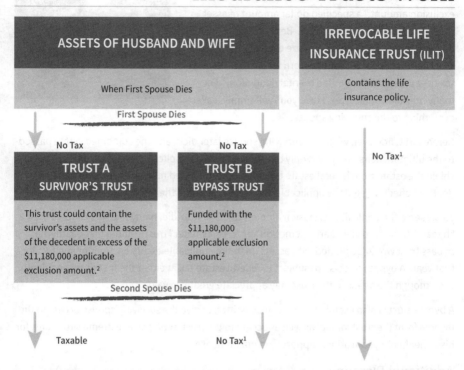

ASSETS OF HUSBAND AND WIFE	IRREVOCABLE LIFE INSURANCE TRUST (ILIT)
When First Spouse Dies	Contains the life insurance policy.

First Spouse Dies

No Tax   No Tax   No Tax[1]

TRUST A
SURVIVOR'S TRUST

This trust could contain the survivor's assets and the assets of the decedent in excess of the $11,180,000 applicable exclusion amount.[2]

TRUST B
BYPASS TRUST

Funded with the $11,180,000 applicable exclusion amount.[2]

Second Spouse Dies

Taxable   No Tax[1]

ASSETS PASS TO CHILDREN OR OTHER HEIRS

- Assets from the survivor's trust are taxable if they exceed $11,180,000 or the applicable exclusion amount at that time.[2]
- Assets from the bypass trust should not be taxable.
- Life insurance in the irrevocable life insurance trust is outside of the taxable estate.

---

[1] The tax savings from either the bypass trust or the irrevocable life insurance trust can be very substantial.

[2] The applicable exclusion amount is the dollar value of assets protected from federal estate tax by an individual's applicable credit amount. For 2018, the applicable exclusion amount is $11,180,000. In 2017, the applicable exclusion amount was $5,490,000. For married couples, any applicable exclusion amount that remains unused at the death of the first-to-die is generally available for use by the surviving spouse, as an addition to his or her own applicable exclusion amount.

Bypass and QTIP Trusts

Under federal law, each individual has an "applicable exclusion amount," a specified dollar amount of asset protected from federal estate tax. Between spouses, however, a person can pass any size estate to his or her U.S. citizen spouse[1] without concern for a federal estate tax because of the "unlimited marital deduction." For many married couples, an "I love you" will simply leaves everything to the surviving spouse.

Before 2011, however, when the surviving spouse later died, and the combined estate passed to the ultimate heirs, there was only the survivor's single applicable exclusion amount to shield the estate from federal estate tax. Using the unlimited marital deduction at the first death, in effect, <u>wasted</u> the applicable exclusion amount of the first-to-die.

To preserve the applicable exclusion amount of the first-to-die, many married couples used a "bypass" trust (also called an "exemption" or "credit shelter" trust). At the first death, the bypass trust would be funded with assets up to the applicable exclusion amount in effect for that year. A bypass trust is not subject to federal estate tax at either the first or second death, even though the assets in the trust may appreciate greatly in value.

A bypass trust is also useful in that it can be written to give the surviving spouse access to the income from the trust for life, as well as access to the trust principal, in extreme situations, for his or her health, education, support, and maintenance.

Additional Planning

Sometimes a second trust, called a "QTIP" trust, is added to the bypass trust. QTIP is an acronym for "qualified terminable interest property" trust. The QTIP allows the first spouse to die to give lifetime benefits (such as income earned on trust assets) to his or her spouse, while still retaining the right to name the persons who will ultimately receive the trust assets. Use of a QTIP recognizes that human nature is less than perfect:

---

[1] If the surviving spouse is not a U.S. citizen, special rules apply.

- **Children of a prior marriage:** In an age when divorce is common, a QTIP trust is particularly useful in protecting children of a prior marriage from being cut off by a surviving step-parent spouse.

- **Close friends:** A QTIP also reduces the possibility of the estate passing to a subsequent marriage partner or "close friend" of the surviving spouse.

Careful drafting is required to make certain the QTIP trust qualifies for the unlimited marital deduction. Special language is required if the QTIP is the beneficiary of an IRA. See Rev. Rul. 89-99, 1989-2CB 231.

2010 and 2012 Tax Legislation

The 2010 Tax Relief Act brought a number of significant changes to federal estate tax law. One provision increased the applicable exclusion amount to $5,000,000 in 2011 and to $5,120,000 in 2012. Another section provided that any applicable exclusion amount remaining unused at the death of the first-to-die of a married couple could be carried over and used by the survivor, in addition to the surviving spouse's own applicable exclusion amount.

The American Taxpayer Relief Act of 2012 made permanent a number of the provisions in the 2010 Tax Relief Act, including the increased applicable exclusion amount and the carryover of any unused spousal applicable exclusion amount.

Tax Cuts and Jobs Act of 2017

The Tax Cuts and Jobs Act of 2017 (JCTA), for 2018 – 2025, increased the base applicable exclusion amount from the $5,000,000 level set in the 2010 act, to $10,000,000.[1] Adjusted for inflation, the applicable exclusion amount for 2018 is $11,180,000. Thus, for 2018, the combined effect of all these changes is to effectively protect from federal estate tax up to $22,360,000 in assets, with or without a bypass trust.

Is the Bypass Trust Dead?

With such a large dollar amount protected from federal estate tax, many estate owners will find that a bypass trust is no longer necessary, at least from a *federal* estate tax perspective.

---

[1] Under current law, in 2026, the $5,000,000 base applicable exclusion amount will again apply, adjusted for inflation.

When planning for *state* death taxes, however, which often have much lower taxability thresholds, the bypass trust may continue to be a valuable estate planning tool. Note that there may also be *non-tax* reasons for including a bypass trust in an estate plan.

Those with estates large enough to be subject to federal estate tax will likely benefit from continuing to use bypass trusts as a part of their estate plan.

Seek Professional Guidance

All estate owners are strongly advised to consult with appropriate financial, tax, and legal professionals as to the steps to take to best benefit from this changed estate planning environment.

How Bypass and QTIP Trusts Work

The combination of bypass and QTIP trusts is designed to make use of the applicable exclusion amount[1] of each spouse, while giving the first to die the power to choose who receives his or her estate. The bypass trust is generally not taxed at either death. The survivor's and QTIP trusts are generally taxed when the surviving spouse dies.

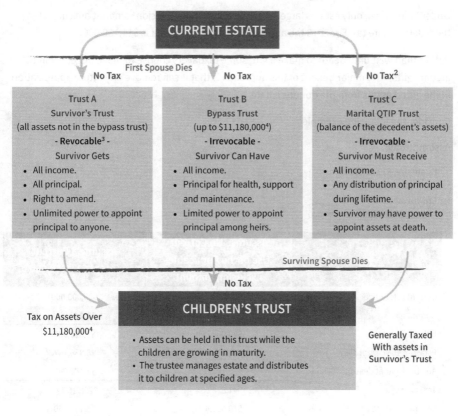

CURRENT ESTATE

First Spouse Dies

No Tax — No Tax — No Tax[2]

Trust A	Trust B	Trust C
Survivor's Trust	Bypass Trust	Marital QTIP Trust
(all assets not in the bypass trust)	(up to $11,180,000[4])	(balance of the decedent's assets)
- Revocable[3] -	- Irrevocable -	- Irrevocable -
Survivor Gets	Survivor Can Have	Survivor Must Receive
• All income.	• All income.	• All income.
• All principal.	• Principal for health, support and maintenance.	• Any distribution of principal during lifetime.
• Right to amend.	• Limited power to appoint principal among heirs.	• Survivor may have power to appoint assets at death.
• Unlimited power to appoint principal to anyone.		

Surviving Spouse Dies

No Tax

Tax on Assets Over $11,180,000[4]

CHILDREN'S TRUST

• Assets can be held in this trust while the children are growing in maturity.
• The trustee manages estate and distributes it to children at specified ages.

Generally Taxed With assets in Survivor's Trust

---

[1] The applicable exclusion amount is the dollar value of assets protected from federal estate tax by an individual's applicable credit amount.

[2] The executor may choose to have the QTIP trust taxed at the death of the first spouse, or after surviving spouse dies.

[3] Trust may be irrevocable if it is a general power of appointment trust or an estate trust.

[4] For 2018, the applicable exclusion amount is $11,180,000. In 2017, the applicable exclusion amount was $5,490,000.

Using the Applicable Exclusion Amount Today

Assets growing at about 5% per year will double in value in about 15 years. As the size of one's estate grows, so does the amount of estate tax which will one day come due.

Under federal law, only estates larger than the applicable exclusion[1] amount are subject to the federal estate tax. For 2018 the applicable exclusion amount is $11,180,000.

Rather than wait until death to make a gift, some taxpayers choose to make large, taxable lifetime gifts. The major benefit of this approach is that it can remove any future appreciation in the gifted assets from the donor's estate.

Consider the following example.

Assumptions:

Estate size: $20,000,000
Years until death: 15
Growth rate: 5%
Current gift amount: $11,180,000

	Assumes No Current Use of the Applicable Exclusion Amount	Assume a Current Gift of $11,180,000
Current estate size	$20,000,000	$20,000,000
Current gift	0	11,180,000
Balance in estate	$20,000,000	$8,820,000
Estate in 15 years at 5%	41,578,564	18,336,147
Add back gift at death	0	11,180,000
Taxable estate	$41,578,564	$29,516,147
Federal estate tax[2]	$10,611,426	$5,786,459
Potential tax savings	$4,824,967	

[1] The applicable exclusion amount is the dollar value of assets protected from federal estate tax by an individual's applicable credit amount.

[2] Calculated as though death occurs in 2033. The applicable exclusion amount ($11,180,000 in 2018) is assumed to inflate at 2.0% per year.

Deceased Spousal Unused Exclusion Amount

Under federal law, at death a person may transfer a certain amount of property without paying any federal estate tax.[1] In 2017, this "applicable exclusion amount" was $5,490,000; in 2018 it is $11,180,000.[2]

Additionally, between spouses, federal law also provides for an "unlimited marital deduction," which generally allows any amount of property to be passed to a surviving spouse without incurring federal estate tax.[3] However, unless the transferred property is consumed before the surviving spouse dies, the unlimited marital deduction simply defers the tax until the death of the surviving spouse, when it will be included in his or her estate.

Prior to passage of the 2010 Tax Relief Act, the applicable exclusion amount provision applied on a "per-person" basis. Thus, if an individual did not fully use his or her applicable exclusion amount (e.g., by leaving everything to a surviving spouse), the unused portion was effectively wasted. In this environment, estate planning (particularly for married couples) relied heavily on the use of trusts to insure that each individual's applicable exclusion amount was fully utilized.

A Permanent Benefit

For married couples, this estate planning environment was significantly changed with the passage of the 2010 Tax Relief Act.[4] Under one provision of this legislation, any applicable exclusion amount that remains unused at the death of a spouse (termed the "deceased spousal unused exclusion amount") is held over and made available for use by the surviving spouse in addition to the surviving spouse's own applicable exclusion amount. Under the 2010 Tax Relief Act, this "carry-over" was temporary and effective only for 2011 and 2012.

Under the American Taxpayer Relief Act of 2012, however, the provision was made permanent.

---

[1] The current discussion concerns federal law; state or local law may differ.

[2] Beginning in 2011, prior federal law provided for an applicable exclusion amount of $5,000,000. Adjusted for inflation, this amount would have been $5,600,000 per person in 2018. For 2018 – 2025, the Tax Cuts and Jobs Act of 2017 increased the base exemption amount to $10,000,000. Adjusted for inflation, this equals $11,180,000 per person in 2018.

[3] The unlimited marital deduction is not allowed to a surviving spouse who is not a U.S. citizen, unless certain requirements are met.

[4] This act is formally known as the Tax Relief, Unemployment Insurance Reauthorization, and Job Creation Act of 2010.

Deceased Spousal Unused Exclusion Amount

As with many other parts of federal tax law, a number of conditions and restrictions apply:

- **Election on a timely filed estate tax return:** The unused exclusion carryover is available only if the executor so chooses. The election is made by filing Form 706, United States Estate (and Generation-Skipping) Tax Return, within the time prescribed by law, (including extensions), even if Form 706 is not otherwise required to be filed.[1]

- **Use:** The deceased spousal unused exclusion amount may be used by the survivor for taxable lifetime gifts or transfers at death. The legislation does not allow a surviving spouse to utilize the unused generation skipping transfer tax exemption of a predeceased spouse.

- **Amount:** The deceased spousal unused exclusion amount is limited to the lesser of the "basic exclusion amount" or the unused applicable exclusion amount of the deceased spouse. For 2017 the basic exclusion amount was $5,490,000; in 2018, it is $11,180,000. If a surviving spouse remarries, the carryover is limited to the lesser of the basic exclusion amount or the unused applicable exclusion amount of the last such deceased spouse (even if it is zero).

Examples

The following examples[2] illustrate the application of this legislation:

Example #1: George dies in 2018, having made taxable transfers of $8,750,000 and leaving no taxable estate. An election is made on George's estate tax return to allow his wife, Susan, to use George's unused exclusion amount. At George's death, Susan has made no taxable gifts. Thereafter, Susan's applicable exclusion amount is $13,610,000, her $11,180,000 basic exclusion amount plus the $2,430,000 unused exclusion amount from George.

---

[1] See IRS Reg. 20.2010-2 for details, including information on how to avoid making the election. See also Rev. Proc. 2017-34 for details on a simplified method for certain taxpayers to obtain an extension of time to make the portability election.

[2] The applicable exclusion amount is subject to adjustment for inflation. For simplicity and ease of understanding, these examples do not assume any inflation adjustment to the applicable exclusion amount.

Deceased Spousal Unused Exclusion Amount

Example #2: Assume the same facts as Example #1, except that Susan re-marries, this time to Bob. Bob then dies, having made $10,000,000 in taxable transfers and leaving no taxable estate. An election is made on Bob's estate tax return to allow Susan to use Bob's unused exclusion amount. Although the combined unused exclusion amount from George ($2,430,000) and Bob ($1,180,000) is $3,610,000 , Susan's applicable exclusion amount is limited to $12,360,000 , the sum of her own basic applicable exclusion amount of $11,180,000 and the $1,180,000 unused applicable exclusion amount from Bob, her **last** deceased spouse.

Example #3: Assume the same basic facts as in Examples #1 and #2, except that Susan, after re-marrying, dies <u>before</u> Bob. After George's death, Susan's applicable exclusion amount is $13,610,000 , the sum of her own $11,180,000 basic exclusion amount plus the $2,430,000 unused exclusion amount from George. Susan made no taxable transfers and has a taxable estate of $9,500,000 . An election is made on Susan's estate tax return to permit Bob to use Susan's unused exclusion amount of $4,110,000 , Susan's $13,610,000 applicable exclusion amount less her $9,500,000 taxable estate. Bob's applicable exclusion amount is thus $15,290,000 , the sum of his own basic $11,180,000 applicable exclusion amount and the $4,110,000 unused exclusion amount from Susan.

Seek Professional Guidance

Because of the complex nature of estate planning, the advice and guidance of trained professionals is strongly recommended.

Estate Analysis
Data and Assumptions

January 1, 2018

Client	Years Until Death
Paul Johnson	5
Sally Johnson	10

Assets and Debt

Retirement Plans

Owner	Balance	Assumed Rate of Return
Paul	$487,000	8.00%
Sally	$239,000	8.00%

Other Assets

Jointly Held Assets	Balance	Assumed Rate of Return
Other Assets	$25,000	7.00%
Cash	$25,000	1.00%
Residence	$700,000	2.50%

Non - Jointly Held Assets	Balance	Ownership Percentage Client 1	Ownership Percentage Client 2	Assumed Rate of Return
Other Assets	$1,100,000	80.00%	20.00%	7.00%
Cash	$475,000	50.00%	50.00%	1.00%
Residence	$300,000	50.00%	50.00%	2.50%

Debt and Bequests	Amount	Ownership Percentage Client 1	Ownership Percentage Client 2
Mortgage Balance	$226,000	50.00%	50.00%
Other Debt	$62,000	50.00%	50.00%
Desired Bequest at Client 1's Death	$10,000		
Desired Bequest at Client 2's Death	$0		

Carry Forward Exclusion Amount: $0

Life Insurance

Owned by Insured

Insured	Benefit to Surviving Client	Benefit to Other
Paul	$1,000,000	$0
Sally	$500,000	$0

Not Owned by Insured

Insured	Benefit Payable to Surviving Client
Paul	$250,000
Sally	$0

Insurance to be used to illustrate an ILIT at second death

ILIT Detail	
New Insurance Premium per $1,000	$36.00
Number of Years to Pay New Premiums	20

Assumptions	
Final Expenses	$5,000
Assumed Asset Growth (Depletion) Rate Between First and Second Death	-5.00%
Annual Inflation Rate	4.00%
Annual Inflation Rate for Applicable Exclusion Amount	0.00%

Probate fees to be $2,000 plus 4.00% of the probate estate.
Administrative fees to be $5,000 plus 2.00% of the probate estate.
At first death state death taxes to be $0 plus 0.00% of the gross estate.
At second death state death taxes to be $0 plus 0.00% of the gross estate.

Estate Summary Simple Will

In the absence of a simple will, state law will pass property to certain relatives of a deceased party. The state will also appoint a guardian for minor children. The court may also require a fiduciary bond to be posted by the administrator of the estate, at a cost to the estate.

A simple will allows a person to select the executor of an estate, bequeath specific items or a specific amount to individuals or organizations, and to select the guardian for minor children.

The following illustrates the potential estate tax consequences with only a simple will in place.

At Paul's death in 2023		At Sally's death in 2028	
Gross estate	$3,795,797	Gross estate	$4,590,440
Debt	-144,000	Debt	-144,000
Taxes and fees	-111,214	Taxes and fees	-257,426
		ILIT	0
Assets to partner	3,530,583		
Amount to Others	**$10,000**	**Total to Heirs**	**$4,189,013**

At Sally's death in 2028

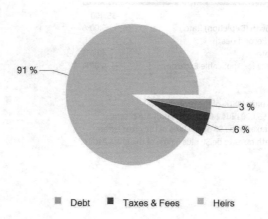

91 % — 3 % — 6 %

■ Debt   ■ Taxes & Fees   ▪ Heirs

Estate Analysis Simple Will

Paul's Estate

	Value today	Assumed annual growth rate	Value in 5 years
Assets			
Joint Ownership			
Cash	$12,500	1.00%	$13,138
Other assets	12,500	7.00%	17,532
Residence	350,000	2.50%	395,993
Non - Joint Ownership			
Retirement plans	487,000	8.00%	715,563
Cash	237,500	1.00%	249,615
Other assets	880,000	7.00%	1,234,246
Residence	150,000	2.50%	169,711
Total Assets			2,795,797
Life insurance owned by Paul			1,000,000
Gross Estate			3,795,797
Less			
Debt			144,000
Final expenses			5,000
Administration fees			38,071
Probate fees			68,143
State death taxes			0
Taxable Estate			3,540,583
Federal estate tax			0
Estate after Taxes			$3,540,583

Sally's Estate

Estate Taxes at Second Death

	Value today	Assumed annual growth rate	Value in 5 years
Assets			
Joint Ownership			
Cash	$12,500	1.00%	$13,138
Other assets	12,500	7.00%	17,532
Residence	350,000	2.50%	395,993
Non - Joint Ownership			
Retirement plans	239,000	8.00%	351,169
Cash	237,500	1.00%	249,615
Other assets	220,000	7.00%	308,561
Residence	150,000	2.50%	169,711
Total Assets Inside Estate			1,505,719
Life insurance proceeds payable to Sally			250,000
Assets from Paul's estate			3,530,583
Total Assets			5,286,302
Asset growth rate assumed after first death			-5.00%
Asset value at second death			4,090,440
Insurance owned by Sally			500,000
Gross Estate			$4,590,440

Estate Analysis Simple Will

Sally's Estate

Estate Taxes at Second Death

	Value today	Assumed annual growth rate	Value in 5 years
Less			
Debt			$144,000
Final expenses			5,000
Administration fees			86,809
Probate fees			165,618
State death taxes			0
Taxable Estate			4,189,013
Federal estate tax			0
Irrevocable life insurance trust			0
Total to Heirs			$4,189,013

Estate Summary Bypass Trust

Under current law, a person may usually pass any size estate to a spouse without incurring federal estate tax. When the surviving spouse dies, the combined estate is subject to tax. There is an applicable exclusion amount available that exempts a certain dollar amount of assets from federal estate tax. This trust is not taxed at either death and the surviving spouse can have access to the trust[1]. The amount of the exclusion and the portability of any unused exclusion, makes the use of a bypass trust unnecessary for many estate owners, at least from a federal estate tax perspective. This type of planning should be discussed with your estate attorney.

The following illustrates the use of a bypass trust.

At Paul's death in 2023		At Sally's death in 2028	
Gross estate	$3,795,797	Gross estate	$3,516,155
Debt	-144,000	Debt	-144,000
Taxes and fees	-111,214	Taxes and fees	-192,969
		ILIT	0
Assets to spouse	2,142,225	Assets to heirs	3,179,186
Amount to BT	1,388,357	BT amount to heirs	1,074,284
Amount to Others	$10,000	Total to Heirs	$4,253,470

At Sally's death in 2028

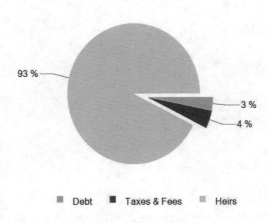

93 %

3 %

4 %

■ Debt   ■ Taxes & Fees   ■ Heirs

[1] Any applicable exclusion amount that remains unused at the death of the first-to-die is generally available for use by the surviving spouse, as an addition to his or her own applicable exclusion amount.

Estate Analysis Bypass Trust

	Value today	Assumed annual growth rate	Value in 5 years
Assets			
Joint Ownership			
Cash	$12,500	1.00%	$13,138
Other assets	12,500	7.00%	17,532
Residence	350,000	2.50%	395,993
Non - Joint Ownership			
Retirement plans	487,000	8.00%	715,563
Cash	237,500	1.00%	249,615
Other assets	880,000	7.00%	1,234,246
Residence	150,000	2.50%	169,711
Total Assets			2,795,797
Life insurance owned by Paul			1,000,000
Gross Estate			3,795,797
Less			
Debt			144,000
Final expenses			5,000
Administration fees			38,071
Probate fees			68,143
State death taxes			0
Amount to Sally			2,142,225
Taxable Estate			1,398,357
Federal estate tax			0
Amount to bypass trust			1,388,357
Estate after Taxes			**$10,000**

Estate Analysis Bypass Trust

Sally's Estate

	Value today	Assumed annual growth rate	Value in 5 years
Assets			
Joint Ownership			
Cash	$12,500	1.00%	$13,138
Other assets	12,500	7.00%	17,532
Residence	350,000	2.50%	395,993
Non - Joint Ownership			
Retirement plans	239,000	8.00%	351,169
Cash	237,500	1.00%	249,615
Other assets	220,000	7.00%	308,561
Residence	150,000	2.50%	169,711
Total Assets Inside Estate			1,505,719
Life insurance proceeds payable to Sally			250,000
Assets from Paul's estate			2,142,225
Total Assets			**3,897,944**
Asset growth rate assumed after first death			-5.00%
Asset value at second death			3,016,155
Insurance owned by Sally			500,000
Gross Estate			**3,516,155**
Less			
Debt			144,000
Final expenses			5,000
Administration fees			65,323
Probate fees			122,646
State death taxes			0
Taxable Estate			**3,179,186**
Federal estate tax			0
Irrevocable life insurance trust			0
Bypass trust amount to heirs			1,074,284
Total to Heirs			**$4,253,470**

Estate Summary Bypass and I.L.I.T.

All assets in an estate are potentially subject to estate taxation.[1] One way to have assets pass to heirs is to change ownership so that the assets are passed to the intended beneficiaries outside of the estate. A bypass trust is one way to reduce estate taxes, therefore, passing more to heirs. Life insurance trusts are another way to increase the amount of your estate that passes to your heirs. The trust is irrevocable and serves as both the owner and beneficiary of the life insurance policy. Generally the grantor makes annual gifts to the trust and the trustee pays the premiums. Certain gifts to non-spouses may be subject to gift tax.

The following illustrates the use of both a bypass (BT) and an irrevocable life insurance trust (ILIT). The ILIT is assumed to be equal to the amount of estate taxes at second death.

At Paul's death in 2023		At Sally's death in 2028	
Gross estate	$3,795,797	Gross estate	$3,516,155
Debt	-144,000	Debt	-144,000
Taxes and fees	-111,214	Taxes and fees	-192,969
		ILIT[2]	0
Assets to spouse	2,142,225	Assets to heirs	3,179,186
Amount to BT	1,388,357	BT amount to heirs	1,074,284
Amount to Others	**$10,000**	**Total to Heirs**	**$4,253,470**

At Sally's death in 2028

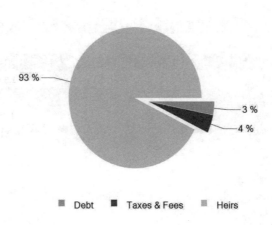

Debt ■   Taxes & Fees ■   Heirs ■

93 %
3 %
4 %

---

[1] Any applicable exclusion amount that remains unused at the death of the first-to-die is generally available for use by the surviving spouse, as an addition to his or her own applicable exclusion amount.

[2] The Life Insurance illustrated above assumes an annual premium of $0 that is payable for 10 years.

Estate Analysis Bypass and I.L.I.T.

Paul's Estate

	Value today	Assumed annual growth rate	Value in 5 years
Assets: Joint Ownership			
Cash	$12,500	1.00%	$13,138
Other assets	12,500	7.00%	17,532
Residence	350,000	2.50%	395,993
Non - Joint Ownership			
Retirement plans	487,000	8.00%	715,563
Cash	237,500	1.00%	249,615
Other assets	880,000	7.00%	1,234,246
Residence	150,000	2.50%	169,711
Total Assets			2,795,797
Life insurance owned by Paul			1,000,000
Gross Estate			3,795,797
Less: Debt			144,000
Final expenses			5,000
Administration fees			38,071
Probate fees			68,143
State death taxes			0
Amount to Sally			2,142,225
Taxable Estate			1,398,357
Federal estate tax			0
Amount to bypass trust			1,388,357
Estate after Taxes			$10,000

Estate Analysis: Bypass and I.L.I.T.

Sally's Estate

	Value today	Assumed annual growth rate	Value in 5 years
Assets: Joint Ownership			
Cash	$12,500	1.00%	$13,138
Other assets	12,500	7.00%	17,532
Residence	350,000	2.50%	395,993
Non - Joint Ownership			
Retirement plans	239,000	8.00%	351,169
Cash	237,500	1.00%	249,615
Other assets	220,000	7.00%	308,561
Residence	150,000	2.50%	169,711
Total Assets Inside Estate			1,505,719
Life insurance proceeds payable to Sally			250,000
Assets from Paul's estate			2,142,225
Total Assets			3,897,944
Asset growth rate assumed after first death			-5.00%
Asset value at second death			3,016,155
Insurance owned by Sally			500,000
Gross Estate			3,516,155
Less: Debt			144,000
Final expenses			5,000
Administration fees			65,323
Probate fees			122,646
State death taxes			0
Taxable Estate			3,179,186
Federal estate tax			0
Irrevocable life insurance trust[1]			0
Bypass trust amount to heirs			1,074,284
Total to Heirs			$4,253,470

---

[1] The Life Insurance illustrated above assumes an annual premium of $0 that is payable for 10 years. The face amount is assumed to be equal to the estate taxes at second death.

Estate Options

There are many options available that allow you to pass the maximum amount of assets to your heirs, while minimizing the amount of estate taxes that must be paid. Choosing which options are best depends upon your personal situation. Most of these options are complicated and must be established carefully.

The following illustrates the amounts that will pass to heirs using a simple will and then adding an irrevocable life insurance trust.

Amount to Heirs		
	Simple Will	ILIT[1]
At Paul's death in 2023	$10,000	$10,000
At Sally's death in 2028	4,189,013	4,189,013
Total	$4,199,013	$4,199,013

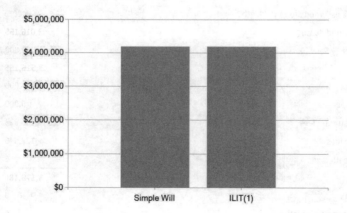

Business Owner Planning Needs

Below is a list of concerns that may be of particular interest to you, the business owner. Indicate the level of importance of each item with a check mark.

	Level of Importance		
	High	Medium	Low
Business Concerns			
Business Succession Planning			
Key Employee Planning			
Executive Benefit Planning			
Estate Concerns			
Planning Estate Distributions			
Estate Tax Planning			
Charitable Planning			
Survivorship Needs Planning			
Retirement Concerns			
Planning for Your Retirement			
Qualified Retirement Plans			
Traditional IRA/Roth IRA			
Investment Risk Analysis			
Other			
Long-term Care Planning			
Education Planning			
Disability Income Planning			
Life Insurance Planning			

Retirement and the Business Professional

Don't Put All Your Eggs in One Basket

Many entrepreneurs start or purchase a business for a number of reasons, both emotional and financial. Social status, the freedom to be your own boss, and the potential for a high income are a few of the reasons commonly cited.

For some, business ownership is also seen as a primary way to pay for retirement. If everything goes as planned, the business owner works hard and, over time, the business grows and becomes more valuable. When the owner reaches a certain age the business is sold, with the proceeds funding the retirement years.

The Realities of Business Ownership

Using the business as the sole means of achieving financial independence amounts to placing a bet that the owner will be able to sell at the right time, the right price, and under the right terms. There are several reasons why this may not happen:

- **Business failure:** Despite good intentions and hard work, businesses do fail. In 2011, for example, there were an estimated 409,040 new, small (less than 500 employees) businesses started in the United States; in the same year, an estimated 470,736 small businesses closed their doors.[1]

- **Timing of the sale:** Selling a business is a complex, often time-consuming procedure. The actual process of finding a buyer, negotiating the deal, arranging financing and finally closing the sale may extend over months or even years.

- **Proceeds:** Depending on market conditions, the amount realized may not be enough to pay for retirement. Income taxes will inevitably consume some of the proceeds. The owner may have to accept installment payments, rather than a lump sum.

- **"I am the business":** The value of a business may depend largely on the skills and/or customer relationships of a particular owner.

---

[1] Source: U.S. Small Business Administration, Office of Advocacy: "Frequently Asked Questions," March 2014. The figures shown are from March to March.

Retirement and the Business Professional

Diversification to Reduce Risk

A business owner who seeks to reduce risk will view his or her business as being simply one asset among many. In addition to the business, a diversified portfolio could include the following:

- **Qualified retirement plans:** Business income is used to fund employer-sponsored qualified plans with a current deduction for contributions and tax-deferred growth.

- **Nonqualified plans:** Nonqualified deferred compensation plans are often used to reward selected employees and serve to supplement qualified retirement plans.

- **General investment portfolio:** A business owner can develop a general investment portfolio, outside of the framework of the business.

Basic Types of Business Organizations

	Sole Proprietor	Partnership	C Corporation	S Corporation	Limited Liability Company
Creation	No written document is necessary.	Created by oral or written agreement.	Articles of Incorporation filed with state.	Articles of Incorporation filed with state.	Operating Agreement/Articles of Organization filed with state.
Life span	Expires when owner dies.	Agreement can set time. Otherwise, dissolved at death of any partner.	Continues on after shareholder's death.	Continues on after shareholder's death.	May dissolve on a member's death, retirement, bankruptcy, resignation or expulsion.
Management responsibility	Rests with sole proprietor.	Rests with partners.	Rests with board of directors who are elected by shareholders.	Rests with board of directors who are elected by shareholders.	Rests with managers or members.
Liability	Sole proprietor is personally liable for all debts.	Each partner is personally liable for all business debts or liabilities.	Liability is limited to the assets of the corporation, not shareholder's assets.	Liability is limited to the assets of the corporation, not shareholder's assets.	Liability is limited to the assets of the company, not member's assets.
Income taxes	All income and expenses are reported on tax return of sole proprietor.	Partnership prepares information return, but income is taxable to partners.[1]	Corporation pays tax on net income. Reasonable salaries are deductible to corporation and taxable to employees.	Corporation files information return, but income is taxed to shareholders.[1]	Company files information return, but income is taxed to the owners (members).[1]

[1] State law will vary: some states tax partnership, S corporations and LLC income.

Basic Types of Business Organizations

	Sole Proprietor	Partnership	C Corporation	S Corporation	Limited Liability Company
Sale or transfer during lifetime	Sole proprietor may sell or give away any asset.	A transfer will dissolve the partnership, unless remaining partner(s) agree(s) to new partner.	Stock is transferrable. Remaining shareholders may have a first right of refusal prior to a sale to an outsider.	Restricted to 100 shareholders who are resident U.S. citizens, estates and certain types of trusts.	Members may transfer interests without consent unless restricted by the operating agreement.
Sale or transfer at death	Is usually dissolved. Estate may sell or operate it.	Automatically dissolved, unless agreement to the contrary.	Stock can be transferred to heirs. Stock can also be sold or retained, unless a buy-sell agreement exists.	Estate is eligible shareholder only during estate administration. Otherwise, same as above.	Deceased's estate is an eligible shareholder. Otherwise, same as above.

Advantages and Disadvantages of Corporations

A corporation is a separate legal entity organized and operated under state law. Like a legal person, the corporation can enter contracts, own property, and hire employees. A corporation is a separate and distinct taxpayer from its owners, the shareholders.

Advantages of Incorporation

- **Limited liability:** The shareholders are not generally liable for the debts and liabilities of the corporation beyond their contributions to capital. However, lenders will usually require personal guarantees by the shareholders on loans to the corporation.

- **Continuity:** The corporation continues in existence, even if its shareholders die or sell their shares.

- **Ease of transfer:** Shares of stock can be transferred to children or other buyers to raise capital or for estate distribution purposes.

- **Centralized management:** The shareholders elect the Board of Directors, who manage the affairs of the corporation, including the election of officers.

- **Tax and fringe benefits:**
  - Tax-qualified retirement plans.
  - Medical and disability plans.
  - Group life insurance.
  - Split-dollar insurance plans.
  - Salary continuation plans.

Disadvantages of Incorporation

- Cost to establish a corporation.
- Need to observe corporate formalities.
- Double taxation of income if dividends are paid. Possible tax on excess corporate accumulated earnings.

S Corporations

Corporations that elect to be taxed as small business corporations under IRC Sec. 1362 are taxed similarly to a partnership. The corporation (as long as it qualifies for S corporation status) generally pays no tax.[1] All profits and losses flow through the corporation to the shareholders and they are taxed on the profits whether or not they are taken out of the corporation.

The S corporation is often used to spread corporate income among shareholders or family members who own the company stock (after employees receive adequate salaries).

Business losses, often incurred in the early years of a business, can be passed through to the shareholders and can be used to offset other ordinary income. Deductible losses are limited to shareholder's basis in stock including loans to the corporation.

Requirements to Elect S Corporation Treatment

- Election must be made not later than two months and 15 days after the first day of a corporation's tax year to be effective for that year.

- The number of shareholders cannot exceed 100, with all members of a family (and their estates) automatically being treated as one shareholder. The members of a family include a common ancestor, lineal descendent of the common ancestor, and the spouses, or former spouses, of such lineal descendents or common ancestor, spanning no more than six generations. See IRC Sec. 1361(c)(1).

- Each shareholder must be an individual, a decedent's estate, a bankrupt's estate or certain trusts specified in IRC Sec. 1361(c)(2), including a qualified subchapter S trust provided for by IRC Sec. 1361(d)(1).[2] Eligible shareholders also include an electing small business trust,[3] charities, and qualified pension, profit sharing and stock bonus plans,[4] and certain IRAs holding bank corporation stock.[5]

---

[1] Some states impose a tax on income or a minimum tax.

[2] A shareholder's agreement can be used to prevent stockholders from transferring S corporation stock to a nonqualifying trust.

[3] Each beneficiary of the trust is counted in determining whether the shareholder limit has been exceeded. An interest in these trusts must be acquired by gift or bequest (not purchased).

[4] See IRC Secs. 1361(b)(1)(B) and 1361(c)(6).

[5] IRC Sec. 1361(c)(2)(A)(vi).

S Corporations

- There must not be more than one class of stock, although there can be voting and nonvoting shares.

- All stockholders must consent to elect S corporation status.

Termination of the S Election[1]

- S corporation status is automatically terminated if any event occurs that would prohibit the corporation from making the election in the first place. The election terminates as of the date of the disqualifying event.

- The S election can be revoked with the consent of more than 50% of the outstanding stock held by shareholders.

- If a corporation, for three consecutive years, has both accumulated earnings and profits, as well as passive investment income exceeding 25% of its gross receipts, its election will be revoked beginning with the following tax year.

---

[1] If the election is terminated or revoked, the corporation cannot re-elect S status without IRS consent until the 5th year after the year the termination or revocation is effective.

Limited Liability Companies

The Limited Liability Company (LLC) is, for federal income tax purposes, a pass-through entity like a partnership or S corporation, but it includes the limited liability of a corporation.

	Partnership		Corporation		LLC
	General	Limited	C Type	S Type	
Personal liability for business	Yes fully liable	Only limited	Only limited	Only limited	Only limited
Participate in management	Yes	No[1]	Yes	Yes	Yes[2]
Any type or number of shareholders or members	Yes	Yes	Yes	No[3]	Yes
Avoids double taxation	Yes	Yes	No[4]	Yes	Yes

LLCs are created by statute and vary from state-to-state. The operating agreement sets forth the relationship of its members (owners) and governs how the LLC will be operated, allocation of earnings, capital contributions and distributions. The formalities found in the corporate business organization, like directors meetings, written minutes, etc., may not be required.

Federal Income Taxation of LLCs

Federal income tax law[5] provides some flexibility as to how an LLC and its members are taxed:

- **Single member LLC:** An LLC with a single member by default is "Disregarded as an entity separate from its owner...". For LLCs with a single individual member, this means that income and expenses are generally reported on the individual's personal return on Schedule C, E, or F. An LLC with a single individual member may elect to report income and expenses as a corporation. For LLCs with a single corporate member, income and expenses are typically reported on the corporation's return.

---

[1] Limited partners cannot participate in management.
[2] For a member-managed LLC. In a manager-managed LLC, members do not typically participate in management decisions.
[3] The S corporation is currently limited to 100 shareholders and there can be only one class of stock.
[4] C corporation's net income is subject to the corporate federal income tax up to 35%.
[5] See IRC Reg. 301.7701-3.

- **Multiple member LLC:** An LLC with two or more members (individual or corporate) by default reports income and expenses as a partnership. Such an LLC may elect to report income and expenses as a corporation.

State income tax law can vary and does not necessarily follow federal law.

Seek Professional Guidance

When considering an LLC, professional legal and tax guidance is strongly recommended.

Business Events Checklist

Change is a constant part of every business. In order to determine how we may best serve you, please complete the form below and return it to us at your earliest convenience.

Common Events

- ❑ Business failure/success
- ❑ Death of a family member
- ❑ Economic crisis
- ❑ Gain/loss business partner
- ❑ Health concerns

- ❑ Investment gain/loss
- ❑ Legal liability
- ❑ Legislative changes
- ❑ Loss of key employee
- ❑ Marriage or divorce

- ❑ Natural disaster
- ❑ Receipt of an inheritance
- ❑ Retirement
- ❑ Start/purchase a business
- ❑ Other:

Areas of Interest or Concern

- ❑ Business continuation
- ❑ Business expand/contract
- ❑ Business form
- ❑ Business overhead expense
- ❑ Disability planning

- ❑ Employee benefits
- ❑ Estate planning
- ❑ Executive benefits
- ❑ Health & LTC planning
- ❑ Income tax planning

- ❑ Key employee issues
- ❑ Property & Casualty planning
- ❑ Retirement planning
- ❑ Survivor benefit planning
- ❑ Other: _____

Additional Comments and Notes

_____

_____

_____

Contacting You

Name: _____   Address: _____

Telephone:_____   _____

Best time to call:_____   _____

❑   Please contact me as soon as possible   Email:_____

Employment Practices Liability Insurance

Employment Practices Liability Insurance (EPLI) began to be offered in the 1990's as one result of federal legislation such as The Americans with Disabilities Act, The Civil Rights Act of 1991, the Age Discrimination Act, and the Family Medical Leave Act. Each of these acts established new, legal rights that employees had not held in the past. These new rights sometimes provided the legal basis for an employee, former employee, or potential employee to sue an employer.

What Is It?

EPLI provides protection to an employer, including officers and directors, against claims made by employees, former employees, or potential employees relating to many types of employment-related lawsuits. Examples of some of the types of claims typically covered by an EPLI policy are:

- Sexual harassment.

- Hostile work environment.

- Discrimination (age, sex, race, religion).

- Wrongful termination as a result of downsizing, mergers, or acquisitions.

- Unfair hiring practices.

- Retaliation.

What's The Risk?

The recent economic downturn, characterized by a sharp increase in workforce reduction, has created a potentially hostile environment where the possibility of an employee lawsuit is quite high, even for firms that make every effort to comply with the law.

Statistics kept by the U.S. Equal Employment Opportunity Commission (EEOC)[1] give a rough sense of the magnitude of the risk. For FY 2014, the EEOC logged more than 88,000 new complaints.[2] While many cases are settled without going to court, in FY 2015

---

[1] The EEOC is the federal agency responsible for enforcing federal workplace discrimination laws.
[2] Source: EEOC, Charge Statistics FY1997 through FY2013.

Employment Practices Liability Insurance

the EEOC resolved 155 individual and class lawsuits, with a total monetary recovery of over $65,300,000, an average of over $421,000 in damages per case.[1]

Why Does My Business Need This?

Defending an employment practices claim, even if the claim is groundless or fraudulent, can be costly. If the employee's claim is upheld, an un-insured liability for monetary damages could be a significant threat to a company's continued existence. A business cannot rely on its general liability policy to provide protection, as nearly all standard general liability policies contain exclusions for claims resulting from employment-related practices.

Cost vs. Risk

Pricing for EPLI policies can vary widely, but is generally based on the number of employees. Because the premiums are relatively inexpensive however, the benefits of purchasing an EPLI policy typically far outweigh the cost. Small businesses may be especially vulnerable to employment related claims as they often lack formal procedures for hiring, managing, and terminating employees, or fail to implement such procedures.

In addition to the insurance protection, many policies also offer valuable loss prevention services such as online resources, access to HR consulting firms, law firms, toll free hotlines, and other specialized services, all of which can help avoid EPL lawsuits.

Understand the Policy

As with all types of insurance, it is important to understand a policy's key terms and provisions. Some of the more important issues for EPLI policies include:

- **Exclusions:** Common exclusions include intentional violations, strikes, lockouts, invasion of privacy, network security, and claims made after a business files or is placed in bankruptcy receivership, liquidation, or conservation.

- **Who picks the attorney?** If a lawsuit is filed against the insured, who chooses the attorney to defend the lawsuit? Some insurance companies permit the insured to choose an attorney, while others reserve the right to select the attorney.

---

[1] Source: EEOC, Fiscal Year 2015 Performance and Accountability Report.

- **Third party coverage:** An additional consideration is whether or not coverage is needed for vendors, independent contractors, customers, clients and other third parties. Third party liability coverage is usually available for a relatively small additional cost, but you must be sure to ask for it.

Seek Professional Guidance

Insurance agents and brokers, insurance counselors, and other trained financial consultants can help provide answers to detailed questions about a particular policy. These professionals are also helpful in selecting the right policy and the appropriative amount of coverage.

Income Tax Tables for
Estates − Trusts − Corporations

Estates and Trusts - 2018[1]

If Taxable Income Is Between...			Pay	Plus	Percent on Excess Over 1st Column
$0.00	-	2,550.00	$0.00		10.00%
2,550.00	-	9,150.00	255.00		24.00%
9,150.00	-	12,500.00	1,839.00		35.00%
12,500.00	-	and higher	3,011.50		37.00%

Corporations

The Tax Cuts and Jobs Act of 2017 made major changes to the income tax rates applicable to corporations:

- **Before 2018** – For tax years before 2018, corporate taxable income was subject to a graduated tax schedule, with marginal tax rates ranging from 15.0% to 35.0%. Personal service corporations were subject to a flat 35.0% rate on all income.

- **2018 and later** – For tax years beginning in 2018 and later, corporate taxable income, including that of personal service corporations, will be taxed at a single rate of 21.0%.

---

[1] Rates are linked to changes in inflation.

Business Continuation Analysis Data

Business Valuation

Business Owner   John   Brine

Years until retirement	15
Percentage of company owned	50%
Current life insurance benefits	$225,000
Death benefit annual rate of increase	3%

Business Name   ABC Lumber

Estimated current value	$500,000
Estimated annual growth rate	12.5%

Four Ways to Pay

Years to illustrate   10

Loan

- Interest rate   9%
- Term in years   10
- Payment frequency   ☑ Monthly   ☐ Annually

Sinking fund

- Assumed rate of return   4%
- Deposit frequency   ☐ Monthly   ☑ Annually

Life insurance

- Premium for $1,000 of death benefit $32.50
- Number of years to pay premium   10
- Premium annual increase rate   %
- Death benefit annual increase rate   %

Meet the Business Planning Team

Business planning, especially for the succession of the business, is a very complex discipline and will generally require the efforts of more than one professional.

A business planning team might consist of two or more of the following persons:

The CEO of the Team

You are the Chief Executive Officer of this team. You will make all of the final decisions after carefully reviewing the recommendations of the various members of your team.

Estate and Business Planning Attorney

Most attorneys can draft a will or establish a small corporation. However, it may be wise to choose one who emphasizes estate planning and business continuation. Your choice could mean the difference between achieving your goals and failure of the business plan.

Life Underwriter

Life insurance is very often a key element in the smooth transfer of a business to either heirs or surviving business associates. An insurance professional will be able to assist you in determining the best type of policy and the amount required to meet your goals.

Certified Public Accountant (CPA)

Almost all successful businesses require the services of a qualified accountant. The CPA designation is an indication that a person has passed rigorous examinations and has been in practice for a number of years. Some CPAs have pursued additional studies in the complex areas of business valuation methods.

Business Appraisal Expert

In the event of a disagreement with the IRS as to the value of the business interest, it would be prudent to possess a detailed appraisal by a trained and qualified expert. There are experts who specialize exclusively in this field.

Financial Professional

Sometimes the life insurance professional, accountant or other member of the business planning team may have special training in financial planning. Other times a person who specializes in financial planning may be a part of your team. This broader knowledge may help to coordinate the efforts of the team.

Types of Corporate Continuation Plans

If the owners want to keep the business in the family, but money is needed to pay estate taxes or other estate costs, a partial stock redemption under IRC Sec. 303 should be considered. If the business interest is to be passed to others, several choices are available.

Continuation Plans in Brief

- **First offer of stock to existing stockholder(s):** The stockholders agree not to sell their stock to an outsider during life or at death without first offering it to the other stockholders or the corporation at an agreed price. This plan gives no certainty to a deceased owner's heirs and will not peg the value for federal estate tax purposes.

- **Option to buy:** An agreement giving the corporation (and/or surviving stockholders) an option to purchase a deceased stockholder's shares. Since the estate is required to sell if the option is exercised, the value for federal estate tax purposes may be pegged. The heirs have no certainty since the corporation is not required to purchase the stock.

- **Cross-purchase buy-sell agreement:** A written agreement among the stockholders to purchase each other's shares at the death of an owner. The price is either stated in the agreement, set by a formula, or provides for the use of independent appraisers

- **Stock redemption plan:** Stockholders enter into an agreement with the corporation to have their estates sell their shares back to the corporation at death. The company usually carries key employee insurance policies to finance the payments for the stock.

- **Wait-and-see plan:** A written agreement among the stockholders and the corporation, generally giving the corporation an option to buy the stock. If it elects not to purchase, the surviving stockholders may buy it and, if they don't, the corporation may be required to buy the shares.

Types of Corporate Continuation Plans

Considerations in Choosing a Plan

- What is the value of the corporation and who can afford to buy it?

- How many owners are there and how old are they? What percentage of ownership does each person have?

- What is the net worth of each owner? Are the owners related?

- Are they all insurable?

- What are the individual tax brackets and the corporate tax bracket?

- Does the non-active spouse have any rights, e.g., community property interest?

Funding

Many types of corporate continuation plans are funded with life insurance. Under IRC Sec. 101(j), death proceeds from a life insurance policy owned by an employer on the life of an employee are generally includable in income. If certain regulatory requirements are met, the proceeds can be received income-tax free. State or local law may vary. Professional legal and tax guidance is strongly recommended.

Importance of a Business Continuation Plan

Competing Interests of Heirs and Surviving Owners

These interests are many and may include the following:

What Heirs of Deceased Owner Want	What Surviving Owners Want
Top dollar for their interests	Minimum cost for the interest
Prompt settlement of the estate	Prompt transfer of the business interest
Set value of business for estate tax purposes	Full control of the business - no interference from decedent's family
Relief for family from worries regarding the business and its creditors	Continuing relationship with creditors
	Retention of customers and employees

Potential Problems Without a Written Agreement

Frequent results include:

- Heated conflicts among the remaining owners and the decedent's family.
- Unhappiness on all sides, and sometimes litigation.
- Delays in settling the estate and continuing business growth.
- Loss of customers and loss of business value.
- Possible liquidation of the business which may bring less than full value.

The Solution: A Written Agreement (and Cash)

Taking the time now to see that the business will pass in an orderly manner at time of death will benefit all parties and their heirs. A written agreement can provide:

- An orderly transfer of the operation, management, and ownership of the business.
- A mutually agreeable sales price and preservation of business value.
- Mutually agreeable terms of sale.
- A value that is binding on the IRS for federal estate tax purposes.
- Stability for customers, employees, creditors and investors.

An agreement which is favorable to all parties can be more easily drafted prior to a crisis.

Commonly Asked Business
Continuation Questions

The following are commonly asked business continuation questions. Each question is followed by an answer that highlights the issues and the importance of taking action.

Question: What's the problem?

Answer: Think about the essence of a closely-held business. If it's like most firms, it has these characteristics.

- The majority stockholders actively work and manage the business and are critical to its operation.
- The majority stockholders receive most of their income from salary or bonuses.
- Stockholders have limited creditor liabilities.
- If a stockholder were to die or become permanently disabled, the legal structure of the business would survive.
- If a stockholder were to die or become permanently disabled, the personnel structure would be significantly changed.

The problem is, when a business owner dies, the business often dies too: not because anything wrong has been done but because nothing has been done, and that's wrong!

At death (or disability), no asset tends to deteriorate as quickly or as totally as a business. Often, the precipitous drop in value is staggering!

Think about it. If a friend owned a car or a home or almost any other tangible asset, one month after that friend died, the value of that car or home would be relatively the same. But if the friend owned a restaurant that didn't reopen for a month or was a doctor whose practice was closed for a month or owned a manufacturing plant which produced no goods for a month, what would the business be worth at the end of that month?

Question: Why can't leaving the business to the proper parties in a will or trust solve the problem?

Answer: Leaving the business to successors at death through will or trust provisions does not address the key problems. A disgruntled heir or a dissatisfied spouse may attack a will or trust. Often, part of the business ends up in the hands of inactive heirs who can add little to

Commonly Asked Business Continuation Questions

the business but who want income equal to working stockholders. The result is an increased probability of business failure and inevitable family discord. Most importantly, a will or trust cannot address the central problems created when a business owner dies or becomes permanently disabled.

Look at these four points, seen from the perspective of a surviving stockholder and the decedent's survivors.

Surviving Stockholder	Decedent's Survivors
Continue reasonable salaries	Pay dividends and hire family
Build and expand the business	Pay dividends and hire family
Maintain a long-term outlook	Pay dividends and hire family
Build a strong cash reserve	Pay dividends and hire family

A surviving stockholder doing his or her own job, and probably that of the deceased co-stockholder as well, would want at least the same salary as before, if not a greater salary, in recognition of the increased responsibilities. And the surviving stockholder may want profits plowed back into the business rather than being paid out as dividends.

On the other hand, the heirs of a deceased stockholder would want the corporation to pay dividends and/or hire one or more family members at the highest possible salary. Typically, lots of income will be needed to maintain the current living standard and to pay the unexpectedly high debts, taxes, and expenses that accompany death.

This is why the death or long-term disability of a stockholder almost always creates conflicting interests and dissension.

Question: What happens after a stockholder's death or disability?

Answer: When a working stockholder dies or becomes permanently disabled, there is inevitably a reorganization of the business.

The remaining stockholders generally must:

- Buy out the heirs;
- Sell out to the heirs;

Commonly Asked Business Continuation Questions

- Accept the purchasers of their stock as business associates; or
- Take the heirs into the business and share profits and decisions.

Is it possible to take one of these courses of action now? Given a choice, which course of action is realistically the most appealing?

Question: Can one be more specific about the problems and objectives of the heirs?

Answer: This can be answered by thinking about the following questions.

- If the heirs are invited to take an active part in the operation and management of the business, will they have the training, experience, ability, and willingness to carry their load and earn their salaries?
- Will all the surviving stockholders be comfortable with the new arrangement?
- If the heirs decide to trust the surviving stockholder to run the business and take care of them and remain inactive, will the dividends the firm pays be sufficient for their needs and meet their expectations?
- Will the heirs panic if business income must be re-invested back in the business rather than paid out to them as dividends?
- How will the heirs react if the surviving stockholder decides to sell stock to an outside party? Where will that leave them?
- If the heirs decide to sell their stock to an outside party, will they obtain a price they feel is fair and adequate, or will the price they need for the stock be more than a knowledgeable buyer is willing to pay?
- Do the heirs know the true value of the stock?
- Can the heirs find a buyer at a reasonable price, or at any price, if they hold only a minority interest?
- Will the surviving stockholder lose his or her job if the heirs own, and then sell, their majority interest?

Question: What are the objectives of the surviving stockholder when another stockholder dies or becomes permanently disabled?

Answer: Typically, a surviving stockholder will want to retain control. Retaining control and preventing outsiders from interfering in the management of the business and its affairs will be crucial objectives. If the business has elected S Corporation treatment (pass through of taxation), the surviving stockholder will want to be sure that election is not lost (which could easily happen if the stock falls into the wrong hands). Further, it will also be desirable to have the cash to guarantee a fair payment to buy out the deceased co-stockholder's heirs.

Question: What are the odds that death or disability could actually occur between two co-stockholders?

Answer: If either event does occur, the probability against it happening doesn't really matter, does it? But it is helpful to at least know what the actuaries know.

Probability of Death Prior to Age 65[1]

Probability of Death Prior to Age 65	Ages of Business Owners
33.7%	25/25
32.9%	30/30
31.8%	35/35
30.5%	40/40
28.7%	45/45
25.9%	50/50
21.3%	55/55
40.2%	25/30
39.3%	30/35
38.2%	35/40
36.8%	40/45
34.8%	45/50
31.5%	50/55

Note: Statistics courtesy of NumberCruncher Software, version 2007.04. June, 2008. (610.527.5216).

Question: What's the solution to all of these problems?

Answer: A legal agreement called a buy-sell agreement is often the best solution. The document, prepared by an attorney, is a legal instrument which requires the corporation (in

---

[1] The probability that one of two business owners in average physical condition will die prior to age 65 is illustrated.

the case of a stock redemption agreement) or the remaining stockholders (in the case of a cross-purchase agreement) to buy the stock of a deceased, retiring, or permanently disabled stockholder. It would require the estate of the stockholder to sell under a formula devised while both parties are alive and well.

There is even a type of buy-sell agreement that combines the flexibility of both the stock redemption and the cross purchase. This is called a wait-and-see buy-sell agreement. With it one can wait and see the best course of action, tax-wise, and then take it, even many years after the agreement is drafted.

Question: How is this agreement funded? Is there a perfect buy-sell funding mechanism?

Answer: There's no free lunch or perfect buy-sell funding vehicle. The ideal is a method that will facilitate a trouble-free transfer of the business interest and provide funds for that purchase in a manner that:

- Is relatively inexpensive;
- Is easy to administer; and
- Will not adversely affect the business or the surviving stockholder's working capital or credit position.

Since two of the most common causes of ownership termination are death and long-term disability, the financial mechanism chosen must provide ample amounts of cash, at the time needed most, whenever that occurs!

Question: What are the various funding alternatives?

Answer: There are four ways to fund a buy-sell agreement. They are using cash on hand, borrowing, making installment payments, and through life and/or disability insurance.

Here are some thoughts and questions that should be discussed with the business planning team.

- **Cash.**
  - How much cash will be required and will it be available when needed?
  - When will that cash be needed?
  - What will happen if the cash is unavailable due to an unforeseen situation?
  - Will after-tax dollars need to be kept on hand to finance the purchase?
  - Will a higher alternative rate of return have to be sacrificed in order to keep adequate cash on hand?

Commonly Asked Business Continuation Questions

- **Borrowing.**
  - Will the firm or the surviving stockholders be able to borrow money after the death or long-term disability of a stockholder/employee?
  - What rate of interest will be required and would it be deductible?
  - How serious will the cash drain impact be on corporate or personal reserves?
  - How will the borrowed funds be repaid?
- **Installment payments.**
  - Can the decedent's family afford to leave substantial sums of money at the risk of the business?
  - Where will the deceased stockholder's family obtain cash to pay taxes, debts, and other immediate estate settlement costs?
  - What rate of interest will the decedent's family want to charge on the unpaid balance? Will that interest be deductible?
  - What will the total cost be?
  - Can the business carry the extra debt and still fund company operations and future growth?
- **Insurance.**
  - Will the buyers be guaranteed that the death or disability will create sufficient cash to satisfy that need?
  - Will this method reduce or eliminate the strain on future working capital in return for relatively small, predictable annual transfer of cash to cash values?
  - Can policy cash values be used, before an insured's death, for a corporate emergency or opportunity?

It should be obvious that setting up a buy-sell agreement can be crucial to the survival of a business, as well as essential to guarantee the economic security that the business represents to family and loved ones. Such an undertaking involves a considerable amount of time, thought, and background experience in many areas, as well as teamwork and cooperation among all the members of your advisory team.

Buy-Sell Agreement

In order to guarantee a buyer for the interest in a business (particularly a minority interest which may be of very little value to one's heirs), consideration should be given to a lifetime agreement among the business owners as to how to dispose of the business.

Entity Plan

Under an entity plan the organization buys the interest of the deceased business owner. This type of arrangement is often used when there are several owners.

Cross-Purchase Plan

Under this plan each surviving owner agrees to buy the interest of any deceased owner.

An attorney should be consulted in deciding which plan is better.

Advantages of Buy-Sell Agreements

- Guarantees a buyer for an asset that probably will not pay dividends to one's heirs.

- Can establish a value for federal estate tax purposes that is binding on the IRS. See IRC Sec. 2703.

- Spells out the terms of payment and is easily funded with life insurance and disability insurance.

- Provides a smooth transition of complete ownership, management, and control to those who are going to keep the business going.

Buy-Sell Agreement

Funding a Buy-Sell Agreement

Buy-sell agreements are frequently funded with life insurance. Under the provisions of IRC Sec. 101(j), death proceeds from a life insurance policy owned by an employer on the life of an employee are generally includable in income, unless certain requirements are met. If these regulatory requirements are met, the proceeds can be received income-tax free. State or local law may vary. Professional legal and tax guidance is strongly recommended.

Buy-Sell Agreement - Partnership

At death, the disposition of a partner's interest depends upon several key factors:

- Does the partner want his/her interest sold or retained by the heirs?
- Will death costs or the needs of the heirs force the sale of the business?
- Can the remaining partners afford to buy the deceased partner's interest?
- Can the partners operate without each other?

In the absence of a continuation agreement, a partnership is dissolved at the death of a partner. The surviving partner(s) becomes the liquidation trustee, who is responsible by law for dissolving and terminating the business.

Common Problems During Dissolution

During the dissolution process, the liquidating trustee partner can expect problems:

- Creditors may become worried and may want to be paid immediately.
- Operating the business may be difficult without the deceased partner's skills.
- Debtors may not pay.
- The remaining partner may be forced to sell assets.
- Good will may be lost.
- Deceased partner's family may not understand why the income has stopped.

A Better Solution Is a Binding Buy-Sell Agreement

- **Entity plan:** Under this arrangement, the partnership purchases the deceased or withdrawing partner's interest.

Buy-Sell Agreement - Partnership

- **Cross-purchase plan:** Under this arrangement, the surviving partners purchase the deceased or withdrawing partner's interest.

Note: An attorney should be consulted in deciding which plan is better and in preparing the agreement.

A Buy-Sell Agreement Benefits All Parties

BENEFITS TO DECEASED'S FAMILY	BENEFITS TO BUYER OF SMALL BUSINESS	ADDITIONAL LIFETIME BENEFITS
• Freed of business worries. • Not forced to sell assets. • Family gets a fair price for business interest. • Estate is settled more quickly.	• The owner has full control of the business and its future earning potential. • May alleviate concerns of creditors or suppliers.	• The agreement can cover a buy out at retirement, disability or disagreement. • It produces a sense of security that heirs are protected and that the business will continue.

Funding a Buy-Sell Agreement

Buy-sell agreements are frequently funded with life insurance. Under the provisions of IRC Sec. 101(j), death proceeds from a life insurance policy owned by an employer on the life of an employee are generally includable in income, unless certain requirements are met. If these regulatory requirements are met, the proceeds can be received income-tax free. State or local law may vary. Professional legal and tax guidance is strongly recommended.

Buy-Sell Agreement - Sole Ownership

The Death of a Sole Owner

When the sole owner of a business dies, his or her executor has several choices, some of which have potential problems:

- **The executor can temporarily continue the business.**

    - The executor may be unfamiliar with the business.

    - There can be some loss in good will.

    - The executor may be liable for any business losses.

    - Creditors will typically want to be paid immediately.

    - Subsequent sale may bring less than the value determined for federal estate tax purposes.

- **The executor can close down the business.**

    - Loyal employees are out of work.

    - Family income ceases.

    - Accounts receivable may be very difficult to collect.

    - The estate may receive only minimal value for the business.

- **The business can be transferred by will to the heirs.**

    - Heirs may not have the desire or ability to run business.

    - The heirs often have conflicting interests and needs.

    - There can be some loss of good will.

    - The business may have to be sold to pay the taxes and expenses.

    - Creditors will typically want to be paid immediately.

    - Accounts receivable may be very difficult to collect.

The executor can sell the business.

- Buyers may pay only a fraction of the going-concern value.

- Creditors will typically want to be paid immediately.

- Accounts receivable may be very difficult to collect.

- Family income is eliminated.

A Better Solution

There is a better solution - a binding buy-sell agreement which benefits all parties.

- **Benefits to the deceased's family.**

  - Freed from business and creditor worries.

  - Not forced to sell assets.

  - Family gets a fair price.

  - Estate is more quickly settled.

- **Benefits to the buyer of business** (usually a key employee).

  - He or she still has a job and his or her income continues.

  - He or she owns the business and controls its future success.

Lifetime Benefits

In addition to the benefits explained above, there are also various benefits which occur during the lifetime of the owner.

- Knowing the business will continue gives employees stability.

- Knowing that he or she may someday own the business, the prospective buyer can assume more responsibility and work harder.

- Key employee can be put in charge when owner retires.

Buy-Sell Agreement - Corporation

When a stockholder dies, the disposition of his stock depends upon several key factors:

- Is the decedent a majority or minority stockholder?

- Is retention or sale of stock desired?

- Will death costs or the needs of the heirs force the sale?

- Is there a market for the stock?

Ownership Situation	Additional Considerations
Decedent was minority owner	A minority interest in a corporation has little value to an owner who is not an employee. Close corporations rarely pay dividends. Without an agreement the estate is in a poor bargaining position. Minority stockholders can cause problems.
Decedent was equal owner	Decedent's spouse or children may have a vote equal to the shareholder who is running the business.
Decedent was majority owner	Can a minority stockholder afford the buyout? Are the payments tied to the success of the business? Can a minority stockholder keep the business successful?
Decedent was sole owner	Who will buy the stock? Child? Key employee? Competitor? How will he or she pay for it if the business fails?

A Buy-Sell Agreement Brings Certainty

The best way to bring certainty to these unanswered questions is a binding buy-sell agreement which benefits all parties:

- **Benefits to the deceased's family.**

  - They receive a fair price for the stock.

  - They are free from business worries.

- **Benefits to the buyer of business.**

  - He or she has control of business and its future earning potential.

- **Price and terms.**

  - These are established prior to the crisis.

- **Additional lifetime benefits.**

  - Prospective owners work harder if the business may someday be theirs.

  - The agreement can cover a buyout at retirement, disability or disagreement.

Funding a Buy-Sell Agreement

Buy-sell agreements are frequently funded with life insurance. Under the provisions of IRC Sec. 101(j), death proceeds from a life insurance policy owned by an employer on the life of an employee are generally includable in income, unless certain requirements are met. If these regulatory requirements are met, the proceeds can be received income-tax free. State or local law may vary. Professional legal and tax guidance is strongly recommended.

Buy-Sell Agreement – Cross-Purchase vs. Stock Redemption

	Cross-Purchase Buy-Sell	Corporate Stock Redemption
Parties to the plan	A cross-purchase plan is between the shareholders themselves.	A stock redemption plan is between the corporation and the stockholders.
Income tax treatment at a later sale of stock by the surviving shareholders	Purchasing stockholders get a new basis in acquired stock, which is used to measure taxable gain at a later sale of the stock.	The surviving stockholders own a larger percentage of the outstanding shares, but their basis in the stock does not change, causing a higher capital gain at a later sale of the stock.
State laws restricting stock redemptions	Only applies to redemptions by the corporation.	State laws may require that redemptions of stock can be made only from company surplus.
Family attribution rules IRC Sec. 318	Only applies to redemptions by the corporation.	These rules may cause what appears to be a total redemption of a decedent's stock, to be treated as a taxable dividend.
Are life insurance policies available to corporate creditors?	Not generally. It is possible if the creditor is, for some reason, able to pierce the corporate veil.	The cash values and the proceeds would generally be available to the creditors of the corporation.
Who pays the premiums on insured plans?	The shareholders. If corporation pays, it must be treated as additional compensation.[1]	Corporation is the policy owner, beneficiary, and the premium payer.[1]
Are there problems when transferring the policies which the decedent owned on other shareholders?	A purchase of these policies by a surviving shareholder will create a transfer for value which may cause the proceeds to be partially subject to income taxation.	Policies are owned by the corporation. No need to make a transfer when one shareholder dies.
What if the corporation needs the proceeds?	Available only if the surviving shareholders are willing to lend the proceeds to the corporation.	Corporation has the right to collect the proceeds at date of death.

[1] Both cross-purchase and stock-redemption agreements are frequently funded with life insurance. Under the provisions of IRC Sec. 101(j), death proceeds from a life insurance policy owned by an employer on the life of an employee are generally includable in income. If certain regulatory requirements are met, the proceeds can be received income-tax free. State or local law may vary. Professional legal and tax guidance is strongly recommended.

	Cross-Purchase Buy-Sell	Corporate Stock Redemption
Which is easier to understand?	At death, there may be multiple buyers of the decedent's shares. In an insured plan this also means multiple policies on each shareholder.	Generally thought to be easier to understand. At time of death, only one buyer (the corporation) and one seller (the deceased shareholder's estate).
What's wrong with multiple insurance policies?	The plan may require many policies. The formula is: (number of shareholders) times (number of shareholders - 1). For example, if there were 5 shareholders, you would need 20 life insurance policies, i.e., 5 x (5-1)	Need only one policy for each shareholder.
Other considerations	• If a stockholder is having trouble paying the premium, he or she may allow the policy to lapse. • Insurance may cost more if the corporation is in a lower tax bracket than the individuals.	• It permits the pooling of premium obligations.[1] • No question arises as to unreasonable compensation. This often occurs when salaries are increased to pay the premiums for life insurance used to fund a cross-purchase agreement. • Life insurance proceeds are included in adjusted current earnings for purposes of the alternative minimum tax. • The voting power could be altered in an undesirable way.[2]

Wait-and-See Buy-Sell Agreement

If it seems difficult to make the decision as to which plan to use, one may consider what is called a wait-and-see buy-sell agreement.

- Stockholders and corporation agree to the following:

---

[1] When one stockholder is older and/or the majority owner and the other is younger and/or a minority owner, the insurance premiums may be vastly different.

[2] Example: Father owns 30%, son owns 30% and unrelated key man owns 40%. A combined vote of father and son controls the business. If father's stock is redeemed at his death, the unrelated key man would own a majority of the outstanding stock and control the business.

- The surviving shareholders have the option[1] to purchase the shares of the deceased shareholder, and

- The corporation has the obligation to redeem the shares to the extent they are not purchased by the shareholders.

- Funding should be as in a cross-purchase plan.

- When a shareholder dies, the survivors elect one of two options:

  - Option one.

    Collect insurance proceeds.
    Buy the shares individually.

  - Option two.

    Collect insurance proceeds.
    Lend proceeds to the corporation.
    Cause the corporation to redeem the shares.
    Corporation issues interest-bearing notes to repay loans.

- An alternative arrangement.

  - The corporation has the first option to purchase the stock at the price or formula set in the agreement.

  - If the corporation fails to exercise its option, the surviving shareholders have a second option to purchase the stock.

  - If the survivors fail to purchase the stock, or only purchase a portion of it, then the corporation is required to purchase the remainder.

---

[1] The wait-and-see plan is generally most desirable. However, if a shareholder is obligated to purchase stock and doesn't, a later purchase by the corporation would likely be a dividend.

Buy-Sell Agreement - S Corporation

Cross-Purchase

A cross-purchase buy-sell agreement would be basically the same in an S corporation as with a regular C corporation.

Stock Redemption

Because of the tax treatment of the S corporation, the stock redemption plan has a few different considerations:

- Since most income passes through to the shareholders, there is little opportunity to manipulate the corporate and individual tax brackets.

- Accumulation of funds by the S corporation would be taxed at the shareholders' top marginal tax brackets. Life insurance would lessen this problem because the premiums are often times less than the amount needed for the buyout. Applicable state insurance laws must be reviewed to make sure shareholders have an "insurable interest" in the other shareholders.

- If stock passes to too many persons in addition to the existing shareholders, currently limited to 100 persons, the S corporation election may be lost.

- A beneficiary who inherits S corporation stock (so that he or she then owns more than 50% of the shares) could possibly revoke the election, contrary to the wishes of the other shareholders.

- Life insurance proceeds may be income tax exempt to both the S corporation and individual shareholders; the basis of stock held by each shareholder is increased by his or her share of the proceeds. Income from a stock redemption may be treated as a mix of taxable dividend and capital gain, or it may be treated solely as a capital gain transaction.

Buy-Sell Agreement - S Corporation

Funding a Buy-Sell Agreement

Buy-sell agreements are frequently funded with life insurance. Under the provisions of IRC Sec. 101(j), death proceeds from a life insurance policy owned by an employer on the life of an employee are generally includable in income, unless certain requirements are met. If these regulatory requirements are met, the proceeds can be received income-tax free. State or local law may vary. Professional legal and tax guidance is strongly recommended.

Cross-Purchase Buy-Sell Agreement

A cross-purchase buy-sell agreement involves shareholders entering into an agreement with each other, rather than with the corporation, to insure an orderly disposition of their stock in the event of an untimely death or disability.

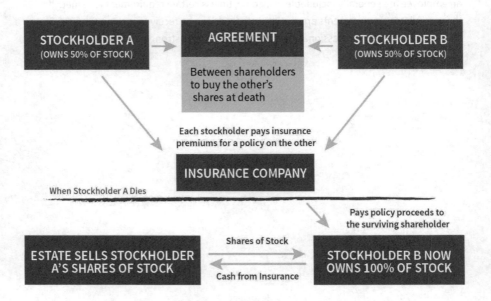

Advantages	Disadvantages
The transferred shares receive a new income tax basis equal to the price paid. This will mean a tax savings, if the stock is later sold at a higher price.	Plan is more difficult to administer if more than two or three shareholders.
No problem with state laws restricting redemptions.	Requires more policies, e.g., 12 policies for 4 shareholders, 20 policies for 5 shareholders, etc.
No problem with IRC Sec. 318 attribution rules.	Some policies may lapse if owner doesn't make the payments.
Life policies may be insulated from the corporation's creditors.	Life insurance proceeds may be taxable if the provisions of IRC Sec. 101(j) apply.

Cross-Purchase Buy-Sell Agreement with Three or More Owners

A cross-purchase buy-sell agreement involves stockholders entering into an agreement with each other, rather than the corporation, to insure an orderly disposition of their stock in the event of an untimely death or disability.

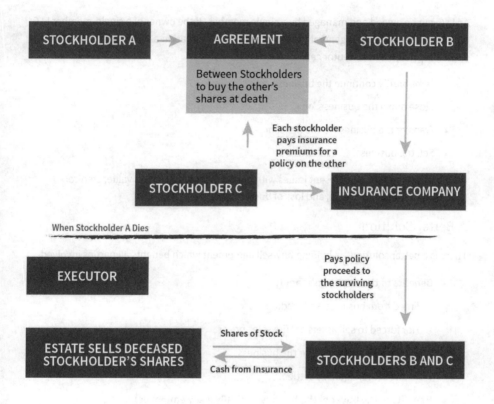

STOCKHOLDER A → AGREEMENT ← STOCKHOLDER B

Between Stockholders to buy the other's shares at death

Each stockholder pays insurance premiums for a policy on the other

STOCKHOLDER C → INSURANCE COMPANY

When Stockholder A Dies

EXECUTOR

Pays policy proceeds to the surviving stockholders

ESTATE SELLS DECEASED STOCKHOLDER'S SHARES

Shares of Stock →
← Cash from Insurance

STOCKHOLDERS B AND C

Buy-Sell Agreement – Limited Liability Company

Single-Member LLC

At death, the disposition of a member's interest in a limited liability company (LLC) depends on how the company is structured.

An LLC can be owned and managed by a single member. If the owner of a single-member LLC dies, his or her executor is generally faced with the same situation as if the decedent had been a sole proprietor. The executor can:

- Temporarily continue the business; or
- Close down the business; or
- Transfer the business to the heirs; or
- Sell the business.

Each of these options can present issues with regard to loss of business value, creditor problems, conflicts with heirs, and loss of business income.

A Better Solution

There is a better solution – a binding buy-sell agreement which benefits all parties involved.

- **Benefits to the deceased's family.**
  - Freed from business and creditor worries.
  - Not forced to sell assets at "fire sale" prices.
  - Family gets a fair price for the business.
  - Estate is more quickly settled.
- **Benefits to the buyer of the business (usually a key employee).**
  - He or she still has a job and his or her income continues.
  - He or she owns the business and controls its future success.

Buy-Sell Agreement – Limited Liability Company

- **Other advantages of buy-sell agreements.**

  - Guarantees a buyer for an asset that probably will not pay dividends to one's heirs.

  - Can establish a value for federal estate tax purposes that is binding on the IRS. IRC. Sec. 2703

  - Spells out the terms of payment. If desired, payment may be funded with life and disability insurance.[1]

  - Provides a smooth transition of complete ownership, management, and control to those who will continue the business.

---

[1] Buy-sell agreements are frequently funded with life insurance. Under the provisions of IRC Sec. 101(j), death proceeds from a life insurance policy owned by an employer on the life of an employee are generally includable in income, unless certain requirements are met. State or local income tax law may vary. Professional legal and tax guidance is strongly recommended.

Buy-Sell Agreement – Limited Liability Company

Member-Managed LLC

At death, the disposition of a member's interest in a limited liability company (LLC) depends on how the company is structured.

Like a partnership, an LLC can have two or more members. A "member-managed" LLC, as the name implies, is managed by the members themselves.

When a member of a member-managed LLC dies, the disposition of the deceased member's interest depends upon several key factors:

- Does the deceased member want his or her interest sold or retained by the heirs?

- Will death costs or the needs of the heirs force the sale of the business?

- Can the remaining members afford to buy the deceased member's interest?

- Can the members operate the business without each other?

In the absence of a continuation agreement, an LLC is dissolved at the death of a member. The surviving members become the liquidation trustees, responsible by law for dissolving and terminating the business.

Common Problems During Dissolution

If the LLC is dissolved, the liquidating trustee can expect problems:

- Creditors may become worried and may want to be paid immediately.

- Operating the business may be difficult without the deceased member's skills.

- Debtors may not pay.

- The remaining member(s) may be forced to sell assets at "fire sale" prices.

- Good will may be lost.

- The deceased member's family may not understand why the income has stopped.

Buy-Sell Agreement – Limited Liability Company

A Better Solution Is a Binding Buy-Sell Agreement[1]

- **Entity plan:** Under this arrangement, the LLC purchases the deceased or withdrawing member's interest.

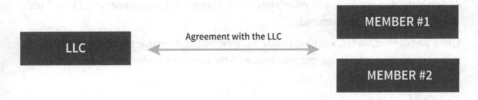

- **Cross-purchase plan:** Under this arrangement, the surviving member purchases the deceased or withdrawing member's interest.

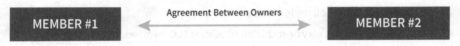

A Buy-Sell Agreement Benefits All Parties[2]

BENEFITS TO DECEASED'S FAMILY	BENEFITS TO BUYER OF BUSINESS	ADDITIONAL LIFETIME BENEFITS
• Freed of business worries. • Not forced to sell assets. • Family gets a fair price for business interest. • Estate is settled more quickly.	• The owner has full control of the business and its future earning potential. • May alleviate concerns of creditors or suppliers.	• The agreement can cover a buyout at retirement, disability, or a disagreement. • It produces a sense of security that heirs are protected and that the business will continue.

---

[1] An attorney should be consulted in deciding which plan is better and in preparing the agreement.

[2] Buy-sell agreements are frequently funded with life insurance. Under the provisions of IRC Sec. 101(j), death proceeds from a life insurance policy owned by an employer on the life of an employee are generally includable in income, unless certain requirements are met. State or local law may vary. Professional legal and tax guidance is strongly recommended.

Buy-Sell Agreement – Limited Liability Company

Manager-Managed LLC

At death, the disposition of a member's interest in a limited liability company (LLC) depends on how the company is structured.

Like a partnership, an LLC can have two or more members. A "manager-managed" LLC, is actively managed by a designated manager, with the members having only an ownership interest in the company.

Death of a Member

At the death of a <u>member</u> in a manager-managed LLC, the executor may have several choices, depending on the terms of the Operating Agreement for the LLC:

- The executor may sell the interest.
  - Potential buyers may be restricted to existing LLC members.
  - The value of the deceased member's interest may be limited by the terms of the LLC Operating Agreement or by a limited market for the interest.
  - The growth in the value of the business interest may not be realized.
  - Family income may be eliminated.
- The executor may transfer the interest to the heirs.
  - Any transfer to heirs may be restricted by the LLC Operating Agreement.
  - The heirs often have conflicting interests and needs.

Death of a Manager

If the <u>manager</u> of this type of LLC dies, the surviving members of the LLC can generally either elect a new manager to continue the business of the LLC or dissolve the LLC. Often, the deceased manager is also a member of the LLC and the deceased's membership interest must be sold or transferred as part of continuing the business of the LLC or dissolving it.

The untimely death of a manager can have a disastrous effect on the LLC:

- Creditors may become worried and may want to be paid immediately.
- Operating the business may be difficult without the deceased manager's skills.

Buy-Sell Agreement – Limited Liability Company

- Debtors may not pay.

- The remaining member(s) may be forced to sell assets at "fire sale" prices.

- Good will may be lost.

- The deceased member's family may not understand why the income has stopped.

A Better Solution Is a Binding Buy-Sell Agreement[1]

- **Entity plan:** Under this arrangement, the LLC purchases the deceased or withdrawing member's interest.

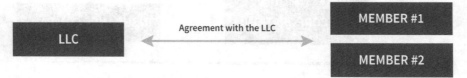

- **Cross-purchase plan:** Under this arrangement, the surviving member purchases the deceased or withdrawing member's interest.

A Buy-Sell Agreement Benefits All Parties[2]

BENEFITS TO DECEASED'S FAMILY	BENEFITS TO BUYER OF BUSINESS	ADDITIONAL LIFETIME BENEFITS
• Freed of business worries. • Not forced to sell assets. • Family gets a fair price for business interest. • Estate is settled more quickly.	• The owner has full control of the business and its future earning potential. • May alleviate concerns of creditors or suppliers.	• The agreement can cover a buy out at retirement, disability, or a disagreement. • It produces a sense of security that heirs are protected and that the business will continue.

---

[1] An attorney should be consulted in deciding which plan is better and in preparing the agreement.

[2] Buy-sell agreements are frequently funded with life insurance. Under the provisions of IRC Sec. 101(j), death proceeds from a life insurance policy owned by an employer on the life of an employee are generally includable in income, unless certain requirements are met. State or local law may vary. Professional legal and tax guidance is strongly recommended.

Stock Redemption Plan

A stock redemption plan involves shareholders entering into an agreement with the corporation to ensure an orderly disposition of their stock in the event of an untimely death.

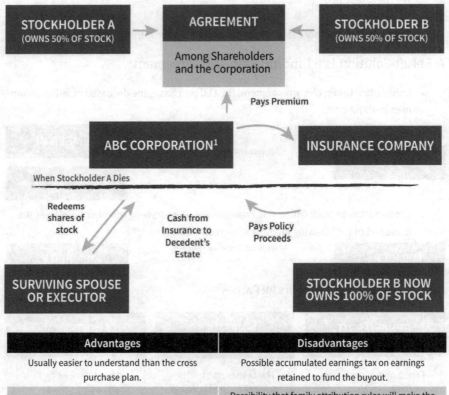

| STOCKHOLDER A (OWNS 50% OF STOCK) | AGREEMENT | STOCKHOLDER B (OWNS 50% OF STOCK) |

AGREEMENT
Among Shareholders and the Corporation

Pays Premium

ABC CORPORATION[1]   INSURANCE COMPANY

When Stockholder A Dies

Redeems shares of stock

Cash from Insurance to Decedent's Estate

Pays Policy Proceeds

SURVIVING SPOUSE OR EXECUTOR

STOCKHOLDER B NOW OWNS 100% OF STOCK

Advantages	Disadvantages
Usually easier to understand than the cross purchase plan.	Possible accumulated earnings tax on earnings retained to fund the buyout.
Fewer policies in insured plans.	Possibility that family attribution rules will make the buyout a dividend.
No questions as to unreasonable compensation.	Voting power may be altered unfavorably.
	Strict state redemption laws must be followed.
	Value of survivor's shares increase, but not basis.
	Possible increase in corporate AMT.

[1] Unless certain requirements are met, life insurance proceeds may be includable in income. See IRC Sec. 101(j).

Wait-And-See Buy-Sell Agreement

The decision as to whether a cross purchase buy-sell agreement or a stock redemption plan is better may be difficult at the time it is drafted. Many business owners use the wait-and-see approach to defer this choice until after a death occurs.

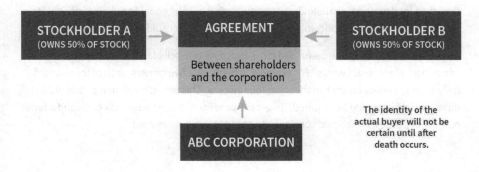

Typical Plan

- The corporation has the first option to purchase the stock at the price or formula set in the agreement.

- If the corporation fails to exercise its option, the surviving shareholders have a second option to purchase the stock.

- If they fail to purchase the stock, or only purchase a portion of it, then the corporation is required to purchase the remainder.

- If the insurance policies[1] are owned by and payable to the shareholders, the surviving shareholders may decide to lend the proceeds to the corporation after a death occurs, if they determine that a stock redemption would be most advantageous.

- When the corporation pays back the loan, it will not be considered income to the shareholder, except for interest which is paid on the loan.

- On the other hand, if a cross purchase plan is more advantageous the corporation will not exercise its first option to buy the stock.

---

[1] Unless certain requirements are met, life insurance proceeds may be includable in income. See IRC Sec. 101(j).

Trusteed Corporate Buy-Sell Agreement

One of the advantages of a cross-purchase buy-sell agreement is that each surviving stockholder gets a new income tax basis on the stock which he or she purchases from the deceased (or departing) shareholder. The new basis would be equal to the amount paid for the stock. This will reduce income taxes if the business is later sold for a higher amount.

One disadvantage to insurance-funded cross-purchase buy-sell plans becomes apparent when there are several owners. For example, if there were five owners, each of them would have to own a policy on each of the other four owners. This would mean that a total of 20 different policies would be required. To get the benefits of the increased tax basis and a fewer number of polices, one should consider a trusteed buy-sell agreement.

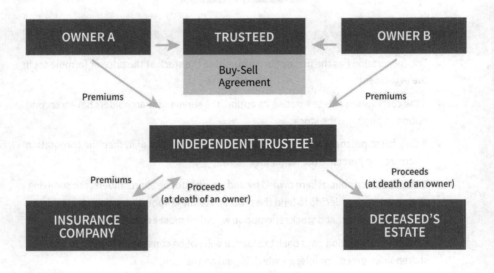

---

[1] Unless certain requirements are met, life insurance proceeds may be includable in income. See IRC Sec. 101(j).

Trusteed Corporate Buy-Sell Agreement

DURING LIFE	AT DEATH
Each owner signs an agreement with an independent trustee to do the following: • Endorse their stock certificates in blank and deliver them to the trustee. • Agree to allow the trustee to take out an insurance contract on his or her life. • Contribute funds to pay the premiums on the policies on the lives of the other owners.	• The trustee collects the insurance proceeds on the decedent's life and delivers them to his or her estate. • The trustee, under the terms of the agreement, sees that the corporation issues new shares to each of the surviving owners in exchange for the shares which belonged to the deceased owner.

Note: In situations involving three or more co-stockholders, the death of the first stockholder to die can create a "transfer for value" problem for the surviving stockholders under IRC Sec. 101(a)(2)(B).

Making Buy-Sell Agreements Acceptable to the IRS

When a business owner dies, there is a risk that the IRS will include his or her business interest in the gross estate at a value that exceeds the price at which it is actually sold to a new buyer. To reduce the possibility of such a hardship, many business owners enter into a buy-sell agreement, while they are still living.

If the new buyer happens to be the business owner's son or daughter, it is easy to imagine the parent directing his executor to sell the business to that child at a value which is far below fair market value. This would cause the estate to have a lower value and thus the government would collect a smaller federal estate tax. Therefore, buy-sell agreements between family members are generally subject to very close scrutiny by the IRS.

The government recognizes the use of buy-sell agreements to peg the value of a business for estate tax purposes, so long as there is no abuse in the area of valuing the business.

Rules for Business Valuation

The Internal Revenue Code provides these rules for business valuation in IRC Sec. 2703.

- The agreement must be a bona fide business arrangement.
- It must not be merely a device to transfer the business interest to family members[1] for less than full and adequate consideration.
- The terms of the agreement must be comparable to those found in similar arrangements entered into by persons in an arm's length transaction.

If the parties to the agreement are not related to one another and are not the natural objects of each other's bounty, they can set the value of their stock for federal estate tax purposes, with a buy-sell agreement with a formula, a fixed price or provides for independent appraisals.

If the parties to the agreement are related,[1] they must use a reasonable formula in the agreement or agree to the use of independent appraisals after death occurs in order to establish a binding value. An experienced professional business appraiser who is familiar with the industry should choose the formula.

---

[1] Family members are defined in the regulations to include one's spouse, parents of either spouse and their lineal descendants (and their spouses), and other individuals who would be the natural objects of the transferor's bounty. See Reg. Sec. 25.2701-1, 25.2701-2.

Corporate Distributions to Redeem Stock

General rule: The purchase by a corporation of its own stock is treated as a dividend taxable as ordinary income to the selling stockholder and not deductible by the corporation.

IRC Sec. 302 provides three exceptions to this rule. Redemptions which qualify are treated as a sale or exchange of stock subject to capital gain treatment.

Since the stock in the decedent's estate gets a new basis at the decedent's death (IRC Sec. 1014), a subsequent sale at that price would result in no tax.

When a Redemption Will Be Treated as a Sale

- **Is not essentially equivalent to a dividend** (IRC Sec. 302(b)(1)): This first exception to the dividend treatment of stock redemptions is perhaps the most difficult for which to qualify. The IRS must be convinced on the basis of facts and circumstances. This section should be relied upon only if the others are not available. A private ruling should be sought from the IRS.

- **Is a complete redemption of all the stockholder's interest in the corporation** (IRC Sec. 302(b)(3)): If all of stockholder's shares (voting, nonvoting, preferred and common) are redeemed, the redemption will qualify for capital gain treatment. In determining how many shares the stockholder owns, add to the shares actually owned those "constructively owned" under the IRC Sec. 318 Attribution Rules.

- **Is substantially disproportionate** (IRC Sec. 302(b)(2)): A redemption will receive capital gain treatment if immediately after the redemption the following three mathematical tests are met:

  - The stockholder owns less than 50% of the total combined voting power of all classes of stock entitled to vote.

  - The stockholder's percentage of voting stock must be less than 80% of his percentage of voting stock prior to the redemption.

  - The stockholder's percentage of common stock (voting and nonvoting) must be less than 80% of his percentage of voting stock prior to the redemption.

Corporate Distributions to Redeem Stock

Formula to Determine Number of Shares to Be Redeemed

$$\frac{(\text{number of shares owned}^{1} \quad x \quad \text{total shares outstanding})}{(5 \times \text{total shares}) \quad - \quad (4 \times \text{shares owned})} = \frac{}{\begin{array}{c}\text{Number of shares which must}\\ \text{be redeemed to qualify}\end{array}}$$

For example: 1,000 shares outstanding and B owns 600 shares

$$\frac{600 \quad x \quad 1,000}{(5 \times 1,000) \quad - \quad (4 \times 600)} = \frac{600,000}{2,600} = 230.76 \text{ shares}$$

Therefore, at least 231 shares should be redeemed to be "substantially disproportionate."

IRC Sec. 318 Attribution Rules

The attribution rules of IRC Secs. 302(c) and 318 apply to both of the following:

- Complete redemptions.

- Substantially disproportionate redemptions.

These provisions are meant to give capital gain treatment only when there is a substantial change in the ownership of the corporation. Some redemptions do not, in reality, change the control or ownership and are, therefore, treated as dividends.

The attribution rules can be divided into two groups:

- Family.

- Other entities, e.g., partnerships, estates, trusts, corporations, etc.

---

[1] Refers to shares actually and constructively owned under IRC Sec. 318.

Corporate Stock Redemption

IRC Sec. 303

IRC Sec. 303 permits a corporation to redeem a portion of a decedent's stock without it being considered a dividend and thus use corporate surplus to meet the deceased shareholder's estate settlement costs.

- The amount of stock which can be redeemed cannot exceed in value the total of federal and state death taxes (plus interest) and funeral and administration expenses. Redeemed stock can also be used to pay generation-skipping transfer tax. The amount of the stock redemption must be included in the decedent's gross estate for federal tax purposes.

- The redemption must generally occur within three years and 90 days after filing the federal estate tax return. See IRC Sec. 303(b)(1).

- In order for the stock to qualify for favorable tax treatment, the value of the stock must exceed 35% of the adjusted gross estate (gross estate less the sum of debts, losses, funeral, and administration expenses). If the decedent owns 20% or more of the value of each of two or more corporations, they can be combined to meet the 35% requirement.

- Gifts made within three years of death (exceeding the annual gift tax exclusion) are brought back into the gross estate for purposes of qualifying under Sec. 303. This is to prevent making deathbed gifts in order to qualify the remaining estate for Sec. 303.

- The Internal Revenue Code also requires that the person whose shares are redeemed must bear the burden of the federal estate taxes, the state death taxes, and administration expenses in an amount at least equal to the amount of the stock redemption. In an AB-type bypass trust, the marital or survivor's trust does not bear these expenses. Therefore, if the stock were redeemed from the marital trust, it would not qualify under Sec. 303 capital gains treatment. Likewise, if stock passes by joint tenancy to the surviving spouse and the will directs the executor to pay all death taxes and expenses of administration from the residue of the probate estate, the redemption will not qualify under Sec. 303.

- Even if the corporation has no liquid assets, the surviving spouse or adult child may lend the money to the corporation to fund a redemption. Then future corporate earnings can be paid out to the surviving spouse or child as payment of a corporate debt. The lender may receive these monies through life insurance on the life of the deceased owner.

- Care must be exercised in accumulating cash in the corporation for such a redemption. The IRS may determine it to be an unreasonable accumulation and subject to a penalty tax. A life insurance policy is an excellent method to fund the plan without accumulating large sums of cash. However, under IRC Sec. 101(j), death proceeds from a life insurance policy owned by an employer on the life of an employee are generally includable in income, unless certain requirements are met. If these regulatory requirements are met, the proceeds can be received income-tax free. State or local law may vary. Professional legal and tax guidance on this issue is strongly recommended.

Business Succession - Selling Your Business

The owner of a closely-held business faces a series of unique problems when planning to sell his or her interest in the business. Typically, an owner who would like to retire from a business can anticipate some difficulty in finding a buyer who is both willing and able to pay market value for the business, and who will be able to profitably operate the business once the retiring owner is gone. Careful planning can allow an owner to successfully make this transition, achieve a profitable sale of the business, manage the risks associated with operating the business during the transition, and reduce any potential income tax liability.

Necessary pre-sale planning includes ensuring that the business books and records are in order, all tax filings are current, any significant collections or legal issues are resolved, employee benefits are current and paid, and outstanding business debt is at a minimum. These key preparatory steps can add significant value for a potential buyer.

A Buyer for the Business

- **Employees:** Current employees, either key employees or other employees who have indicated an interest in managing the business, can be highly motivated buyers for the business.

- **Family members:** Children or other family members may be interested in purchasing the business.

- **Competitors:** Other business owners in the same field may wish to expand their operations.

- **Suppliers:** Suppliers or vendors may have an interest in the business.

- **Business broker:** An experienced business broker, one familiar with the specific industry or profession, can be helpful in finding a qualified buyer.

A "Phased-In" Transaction

If appropriate, ownership can be transferred over a period of time, allowing the new owner time to adjust to the responsibilities of management and providing for an orderly continuation of the business as the retiring owner has less and less involvement with daily business operations. The sale agreement can:

- Provide for shared ownership and control during the transition to the new ownership.
- Create an orderly transition between owners.
- Minimize potential conflicts that could disrupt successful business operations.
- Create incentives for the parties to successfully operate the business for the benefit of both.

Funding the Sale

In some instances the buyer will have the resources to pay the full purchase price, in cash. Borrowing the money, the sale of other assets, or private investors are all possible sources of funds.

Very often, however, the retiring owner will need to finance all or part of the sale and receive payments for the balance over a period of time. While this approach does entail a degree of risk, the sale can be structured as an installment sale, allowing for the deferral of reporting of both income and capital gain until the year payments are actually received.[1] An installment sale also replaces an income source that might otherwise be lost once the business is sold.

Death or Disability of the New Owner

If a retiring owner chooses to finance the sale of the business, continued payments are often dependent on the successful operation of the business by the new owner. In the event of the death or disability of the new owner, the business may fail and payments to the retired owner stop. The retiring owner can protect against these risks by requiring, as a part of the sale agreement, that life and disability insurance be purchased on the new owner, with benefits payable to the retiring owner.

Income Tax Considerations

There may be a significant income tax liability when the business is sold. Under an installment sale, the interest portion of each payment is treated as ordinary income. A sale of a business also usually involves capital gains or losses, although the tax treatment is dependent, in part, upon the form of the business entity sold:

---

[1] The discussion here concerns federal income tax law. State or local law may differ.

Business Succession - Selling Your Business

- **Sole proprietorship:** A sole proprietorship is not considered a separate entity apart from the assets of the business. The sales price is allocated among each of the individual business assets, with a resulting gain or loss reported for each asset.

- **Partnership:** An owner who sells a partnership interest generally realizes a capital gain or loss on the difference between the amount realized less the adjusted basis of the partnership interest. The sale of certain assets such as inventory may be treated as ordinary income rather than capital gain.

- **Limited liability company (LLC):** The federal government does not recognize an LLC as an entity classification for income tax purposes. An LLC must file as a sole proprietorship, a partnership, or a corporation.

- **Corporation:** An owner of a corporation can either sell his or her corporate stock or the assets of the corporation:

  - *Sale of corporate stock*: From the <u>retiring owner's</u> perspective, a sale of corporate stock is highly preferable, since the resulting capital gain or loss is realized only by the retiring owner, with, generally, no tax impact to the corporation. A portion of certain qualified Small Business Stock sales may be excluded from tax.

  - *Sale of corporate assets*: From a <u>buyer's</u> perspective, however, a sale of corporate assets is usually preferable since the buyer receives a basis in the assets equal to the purchase price. If the seller is a "C" corporation, an asset sale can result in a double tax liability; any gain is taxable to the corporation, with additional tax payable by the shareholder when the corporation is dissolved and funds distributed. If the seller is an "S" corporation, tax liability is generally paid by the shareholder, but a corporate tax may also be due if the asset sale results in any built-in gains.

Seek Professional Guidance

The successful sale of a business interest requires careful planning, sometimes well in advance of an actual transaction. The guidance of experienced tax, legal, insurance, and other financial professionals is strongly recommended.

Family Attribution

Under IRC Sec. 318(a)(1) a redeeming stockholder "constructively" owns stock directly owned by or for his spouse, children, grandchildren or parents.

Note: A stockholder is not deemed to own stock of his brothers, sisters or grandparents.

The family attribution rules can be waived if after a complete redemption the following conditions are satisfied:

- Immediately after the redemption, the redeeming stockholder can have no interest in the corporation as an officer, director or employee (creditor is all right).[1]

- The stockholder must not acquire an interest in the corporation within 10 years after the redemption except by inheritance.

- An agreement must be filed by the redeeming stockholder or his executor agreeing to notify the IRS of any stock acquisition which would violate the above rule and agreeing to maintain necessary records.

- The redeeming stockholder did not acquire the redeemed stock within 10 years before the redemption from a family member whose stock ownership would be attributed to him under the attribution rules.

- At the time of the redemption there is not a stockholder related under the attribution rules who has acquired stock from the redeeming stockholder in the prior 10 years.

Note: The last two conditions above may not apply if the IRS can be convinced tax avoidance was not a principal purpose of the transaction or that the redeeming stockholder inherited the shares.

Prohibited Interests

- Serving as custodian of stock held in an account under the Uniform Gifts to Minors Act. See Rev. Rul. 81-233, 1981-2 CB 83. However, the spouse of redeemed stockholder may act as custodian. See LR 7931043.

---

[1] A few interests the redeeming stockholder can have and not cause a loss of the waiver of family attribution rules include:
   a. Lease property from the corporation. See PLR 8328088, 4/14/83; PLR 8301035, 9/30/82; and Rev. Rul. 77-467, 1977-2 CB 92. An IRS Private Letter Ruling is applicable only to the taxpayer who requested it and may not be cited as precedent.
   b. Purchase insurance under company's health plan. See LR 8236037, 6/8/82.
   c. Continue life insurance under company group term life plan. See LR 8314018, 12/23/82.

- Acting as officer, director or employee. See IRC Sec. 302(c)(2).

- Having an interest in a trust that owns stock of the redeeming corporation. See IRC Sec. 318(a).

- Acting as an independent contractor for corporation. See Lynch, CA-9, 86-2 USTC Paragraph 9731 (1986).

Entity Attribution

In addition to the family attribution rules, the redeeming stockholder is also treated as owning a proportionate part of the stock that is actually owned by the following entities:

- A partnership in which he or she is a partner.

- An estate of which he or she is a beneficiary.

- A trust of which he or she is a beneficiary.

- A corporation in which he or she owns 50% or more of the outstanding stock.

The attribution rules are highly complex and should be dealt with only with the assistance of appropriate tax and legal advisors.

Methods of Funding a Buy-Sell Agreement

In the event of a business owner's death, there are several options to consider for funding a Buy-Sell agreement:

- **Personal funds of buyers:** Most successful business people do not keep large sums of liquid assets on hand. They have their money working in their businesses.

- **Sinking fund in the business:** Such a fund will be inadequate if death is premature and the time of need is uncertain. A corporation may develop an accumulated earnings tax problem.

- **Borrowed funds:** Loss of a key person (such as an owner) may impair the credit worthiness of the business and other partners or shareholders. Interest costs may be excessive, and the interest expense of shareholders or partners may not be deductible.

- **Installment payments to heirs by buyer:** The business may fail and the payments stop. The principal and interest payments may be too burdensome.

- **Life insurance owned by the buyer:**

  - Complete funding from policy proceeds may be available from the beginning.

  - Proceeds may be free from income tax; see IRC Sec. 101(j).

  - Cash values can be used for a buyout due to retirement or disability.

  - It is generally the most economical method.

  - Credit position is strengthened.

Who Should Own the Policy?

Improper ownership of insurance policies that are used to fund buy-sell agreements can cause serious problems for the survivors. The following hypothetical situation illustrates the proper ownership of policies:

Assumptions:

Owners: A, B and C
Ownership: 60%, 30%, 10%
Business value: $2,000,000
Funding vehicle: Life insurance

Cross-Purchase Plan				Entity Plan		
Insured	Owner, Beneficiary and Premium Payer	Amount and Number of Policies		Insured	Owner, Beneficiary and Premium Payer	Amount and Number of Policies
A (60%)	B C	$600,000 $600,000		**A** (60%)	The Business	$1,200,000
B (30%)	A C	$300,000 $300,000		**B** (30%)	The Business	$600,000
C (10%)	A B	$100,000 $100,000		**C** (10%)	The Business	$200,000

Premiums for life insurance (or disability insurance to fund a buyout) are not deductible to the individuals or to the business entity. However, the policy proceeds are generally received income-tax-free by the beneficiary. If the corporation pays the premiums on policies used by the stockholders to fund a cross-purchase plan, there will likely be constructive dividend problems. For a C corporation, policy values payable to the corporation may be subject to the corporate alternative minimum tax.

Also, under the provisions of IRC Sec. 101(j), death proceeds from a life insurance policy owned by an employer on the life of an employee are generally includable in income, unless certain requirements are met. State or local law may vary. Professional legal and tax guidance on this issue is strongly recommended.

Taxes on Premiums Paid by a Corporation

Situation	Tax Treatment of Premiums	Legal Reference
Cross-purchase buy-sell Corporation pays the premiums directly on behalf of stockholder or policyholder.	If payment is intended to be additional compensation (corporate minutes should reflect this) the corporation can deduct it and the policy owner would report additional income.	IRC Sec. 162(a)
	If payment were considered as unreasonable compensation, it would be treated as a dividend and not deducted by the corporation.	Atlas Heating & Ventilating Co. vs. Comm., 18 BTA 389
	If it were clear that the policies are to fund a cross-purchase buy-sell agreement, the premiums paid by the corporation would be treated as dividends.	Rev. Rul. 59-184, 1959-1 CB 65; Thomas F. Doran vs. Comm., 246 F2d 934 (9th Cir. 1957)
Cross-purchase buy-sell Corporation pays the premiums under a classic split-dollar agreement.	Premium payments by the corporation are generally treated as interest-bearing loans to the shareholder.[1]	Treasury Decision 9092
Stock redemption buy-sell by corporation Corporation pays the premiums directly for policies on the lives of the stockholders.	Premiums are not deductible by the corporation and not a dividend to the stockholder or policyholder.	Rev. Rul. 59-184 1959-1 CB 65; Sanders vs. Fox, 253 F2d 855 (10th Cir. 1958); and Prunier vs. Comm., 248 F2d 818 (1st Cir. 1957)

[1] Under Treasury Decision 9092 (September 11, 2003), many economic benefits of a split-dollar arrangement are currently taxable. These benefits may include: (1) value of current life insurance protection; (2) accrued cash value; (3) imputed loan interest, or (4) premium contributions from a non-policy owner. Death benefits paid to a beneficiary (other than policy owner) may be taxable. 9092 contained other split-dollar rules not addressed here and those considering split-dollar arrangements should consult legal/tax advisors. State or local law may vary.

Taxes on Premiums Paid by a Corporation

When an individual or corporation collects the proceeds of a policy by reason of the death of the insured, they are generally not subject to income taxation. See IRC Sec. 101(a).[1] For a C corporation, increases in policy values on policies owned by the corporation and death benefits payable to the corporation may be subject to the corporate alternative minimum tax.

---

[1] An exception would be a lifetime transfer of an insurance policy which violates the transfer-for-value rules of IRC Sec. 101(a)(2).

Transfers for Value

Life insurance death proceeds are typically exempt from income taxation under IRC sec. 101(a)(1). The gift of a policy during the insured's lifetime does not affect this exemption; however, the sale of a policy may subject part of the proceeds to income taxation when the insured dies. If a policy is transferred for value to a non-exempt transferee, the portion included as taxable income will be the face amount less any consideration (purchase price and subsequent premiums) paid by the transferee.

Exempt Transferees

Parties who can purchase a policy from another and are exempt transferees include the following:

- The insured.

- A partner of the insured.

- A partnership of which the insured is a partner.

- Corporation of which insured is a shareholder/officer.

- Any person where the basis is determined by reference to the transferor's basis, e.g., a gift.

Typical Violations of this Rule

- A policy owner agrees to name another person as a beneficiary in exchange for valuable consideration.

- When two persons assign policies on their own lives to each other at about the same time, the question of a transfer for valuable consideration is raised.

- A corporation changes its buy-sell agreement from a stock redemption plan to a cross purchase plan and transfers key person insurance policies to stockholders other than the insured.

- For estate planning reasons, a corporate key man life insurance policy is transferred to the insured's adult child or an irrevocable trust to keep the proceeds out of the estate. Since neither the child nor the trust is an employee, the policy is usually purchased for its current cash value.

Problem: Neither the adult child nor the trust is an exempt party. Under the transfer-for-value rule the proceeds may be out of the estate, but are partially includable as ordinary income in the year received by the beneficiary.

A better way: Have the insured purchase the policy from the corporation (the insured is an exempt party). He is now free to make a gift of the policy to the adult child or trust; however, the donor/insured must survive the 3-year contemplation of death period to avoid having the policy death benefit included in his or her estate.

Where there is a non-exempt party owning a purchased policy, it may be wise to have the insured purchase it back for its cash value and then, by a later gift, transfer it back to the non-exempt party. This will remove the taint.

Tax Cuts and Jobs Act of 2017

The Tax Cuts and Jobs Act of 2017 (TCJA), generally effective January 1, 2018, made a number of changes to federal tax law governing transfers for value:

- **Reportable policy sale** – TCJA established a new requirement to report certain information when a life insurance policy is acquired in a "reportable policy sale." A reportable policy sale refers to the acquisition of an interest in a life insurance contract, directly or indirectly, if the acquirer has no substantial family, business, or financial relationship with the insured, apart from the acquirer's interest in the life insurance contract.

- **Exempt transferees** – TCJA also mandated that the exceptions to the transfer for value rules do not apply in case of a transfer of a life insurance contract in a reportable policy sale. Thus, some part of the death benefit ultimately payable may be taxable.

- **Determination of basis** – The Act also clarified the calculation of a taxpayer's basis in a life insurance contract.

Seek Professional Guidance

Because of the complex nature of transfer for value situations, the advice and guidance of trained, experienced tax and legal professionals is strongly recommended.

Reasons to Value a Business

The following are a few of the most common reasons to value a business:

- Establish a purchase price in a buy-sell agreement.

- Determine the size of the gross estate for death tax purposes.

- Determine if the estate qualifies for tax relief provisions, such as:

  - IRC Sec. 303 stock redemption.

  - Installment payments of death taxes (IRC Sec. 6166).

  - IRC Sec. 2032A current use valuation of business-owned real estate.

- Plan for an equitable disposition of the estate among children where some are active in the business and some are not.

- Determine the value of lifetime gifts of the business.

- To develop an exit strategy when planning retirement.

Other reasons include private annuities,[1] installment sales, obtaining financing, recapitalizations, mergers, divorce settlements, charitable contributions, etc.

Fair Market Value

Treasury regulations set forth the following definition for fair market value.

"...the net amount which a willing purchaser...would pay for the interest to a willing seller, neither being under any compulsion to buy or to sell and both having reasonable knowledge of relevant facts." See Reg. Sec. 20.2031-3.

---

[1] On 10/17/06, the IRS issued proposed regulations (NPRM REG-141901-5) on the exchange of appreciated property for an annuity contract. These proposed regulations treat the transaction as if the transferor had sold the property for cash and then used the proceeds to purchase an annuity contract. These proposed regulations were generally effective for transactions occurring after 10/18/06, with a six-month delay until 04/18/07 for certain types of transactions.

Business Valuation Factors

The value of a business interest is generally based on two things:

- What the company <u>owns</u>, which is reflected on the balance sheet, and
- What the company <u>earns</u>, which is reflected in the income statement.

In valuing a business for tax purposes, the IRS is guided by the factors listed in Revenue Ruling 59-60:[1]

The Nature and History of the Business

Consideration is given to factors such as:

- Size and consistency of the growth rate.

- Stability of the business or lack thereof.

- Products, services and company assets.

- Record of sales.

- Management - especially recent changes.

- Diversity of operations.

Economic Outlook

The general economic outlook and condition of the particular industry in which the business operates will affect how a business is valued. Common questions to be considered include the following:

- Is it a growth industry?

- How competitive is this company in the industry?

- What would be the economic effect of the loss of a key employee?

---

[1] See Revenue Ruling 59-60, 1959-1 CB 237. Also see Rev. Rules. 65-192, 1965-2 CB 259; 65-193, 1965-2 C. B. 370 and 77-287, 1977-2 CB 319

Business Valuation Factors

The Book Value of the Stock

- Based on assets minus liabilities - to show liquidity position.

- Believed to be unreliable in valuing most businesses.

The Earning Capacity of the Company

This is perhaps the most significant factor:

- Earning capacity is average earnings over a five-year period multiplied by a capitalization rate.

- There is no standard table of capitalization rates.

- Capitalization rates are usually based on price-earnings ratios of similar, publicly traded companies.

The Dividend Paying Capacity

This is considered to be a primary factor:

- This does not mean dividends actually paid, but the <u>capacity</u> to pay.

- The IRS recognizes the need to retain a reasonable portion of the profits for expansion needs.

Goodwill and Other Intangible Values

- Goodwill is based on earning capacity. It represents an excess of net earnings over and above a fair return on the net tangible assets of the business.

- Other intangibles include the following:

  - Ownership of a trade or brand name.

  - Prestige and renown of the business.

  - Prolonged successful operation in a particular locality.

Prior Sales and Size of Block

- Prior sales may be meaningful if they were arms-length transactions.

- Small isolated sales or distress sales are not significant.

- Valuation of a controlling interest may carry a premium value.

- Valuation of a minority interest should include a discount.

Similar Companies

How the business performs in comparison to its competitors is another consideration. For example, the valuation may consider the market price of stocks of similar, publicly traded corporations.

- Companies must be sufficiently comparable.

- The comparative appraisal method examines price-earnings, price-book value, and price-dividend ratios of each corporation.

Weight to Be Given to Each Factor

Some factors will carry more weight than others. There is no exact mathematical formula.

A study by Standard Research Consultants[1] showed that in 74 tax cases the most frequently used factors were:

- Sale price, in 33 cases;

- Book value, in 24 cases; and

- Earning power, in 17 cases.

Earnings will typically have more importance in companies selling products and services, whereas net worth will be more important in real estate holding companies.

---

[1] Study by Standard Research Consultants, as quoted in the CLU Journal, Vol. 34, No. 2, April 1980, pp. 61-70.

Valuation Methods Explained

Since no single method can be applied in determining the value of every business, a number of approaches have developed over the years. The American Society of Appraisers has grouped these approaches into three classifications:

- Income-based.
- Market-based.
- Asset-based.

Valuation Techniques

- **Income approach:** This approach attempts to measure the stream of benefits coming into the business. The two most commonly used methods are capitalized returns and discounted future returns:

    - **Capitalized returns method:** This method examines the company's history of earnings or cash flow (either gross or net), generally over the previous five or more years. The average annual return is determined and then divided by a capitalization rate selected for the particular kind of business being valued.

    - **Discounted future returns method:** This method looks at projected future earnings of the company and then applies a discount to them to determine the current or present value of the projected income stream.

- **Market approach:** This approach is similar to that used in valuing residential real estate, wherein a house is compared to similar houses which have recently sold (after adjustments for any differences). With the market approach, a search is made for similar companies with publicly traded stock and then the selling price of its shares is adjusted to account for any differences between the two companies. Comparisons will commonly look at one or more of the following factors:

    - Price/earnings ratio.
    - Ratio of price to dividends.
    - Gross cash flow.
    - Book value.
    - Revenues.
    - Net asset value.

Valuation Methods Explained

A major problem with these methods is that it is often difficult to find similar publicly traded companies. Another problem is that comparing a closely held or privately held company with that of a publicly traded firm where the above information is readily available is often a case of comparing apples with oranges. Publicly held firms are accountable to their stockholders, where closely held or privately held firms are accountable to their owners and, as a result, are often managed entirely differently.

- **Asset based approach:** This approach is more concerned with the underlying net value of the company's tangible assets. If the business is to be continued after the owner's death, the fair market value of the assets is commonly used. If, however, the business were to be liquidated, a lower value would be used to compensate for the loss which generally occurs with the forced sale of assets:

  - **Book value:** Book value is company assets minus liabilities as shown on the balance sheet.

  - **Book value or adjusted book value:** These methods are most frequently used with companies which own many tangible assets, like a real estate holding company or with a company that has very low or negative earnings.

  - **Excess earnings method:** This method is also called Treasury method because it was developed by the Treasury Department in the 1930's. It is based on Rev. Rul. 68-609, 1968-2 CB 327 and considers both the adjusted book value and a capitalization of earnings in excess of a fair return on the company's assets.

Weighting the Methods

When several valuation methods are used, some are generally more accurate in determining the true value of the business. For example, in high asset/low income companies, more weight would probably be given to the adjusted book value than to the capitalization of earnings. Because of the influence that weighting methods have in the outcome of the business valuation, a CPA, attorney, valuation specialist or other business advisor should be consulted to arrive at the appropriate weightings.

Ownership Premium or Discount

Adjustments to the estimated value of the business are made to reflect unique circumstances which may affect its marketability. These may include location, degree of specialty required to run the business, presumed availability of buyers and other factors which could affect the sale price if offered on the open market. For example, a closely-held business is often discounted in value to reflect the control that other owners may exercise over a single owner's ability to sell his or her interest.

There are no specific rules or guidelines associated with these adjustments. Frequently they serve as a reality check to help influence the outcome of the valuations or better approximate the expectations of the valuation specialist, CPA, attorney, owners or other business advisors. As a result, the discount or premium applied to the business will usually be arrived at as a consensus of opinion among the business advisors. Particular care should be applied in selecting a rate of adjustment and, whenever possible, the rate should be provided by a valuation specialist experienced in the specific market for which the business is being valued.

Advantages and Disadvantages
of Valuation Methods

There are many different methods for valuing a business, with some better suited to a specific type of business than others. A key task of the valuation specialist is to select the most appropriate method for valuing a particular business. The method chosen should provide a reasonable estimate of value, be suitable for the intended purpose and be able to face legal challenges by the IRS or other opposing parties.

As a part of the process, a valuation specialist will often employ several different methods and average the results to arrive at a "ballpark" estimate. Because each method has strengths and weaknesses, business owners and their advisors should be familiar with the most commonly used valuation techniques.

Net Asset Value

The value is based on a sale at fair market value (FMV) of the firm's assets on a going-concern basis.

- **Strengths.**

    - Data required to perform the valuation are usually easily available.

    - Allows for adjustments (up and down) in estimating FMV.

    - Suitable for firms with heavy tangible investments, e.g., equipment and land.

    - Helpful when the firm's future is in question or where the firm has a brief or volatile earnings record.

- **Weaknesses.**

    - Can understate the value of intangible assets such as copyrights or goodwill.

    - Does not take into account future changes (up or down) in sales or income.

    - Balance sheet may not accurately reflect all assets.

Advantages and Disadvantages of Valuation Methods

Discounted Future Earnings

The value of the firm is equivalent to the capital required to produce income equal to a projected future income stream from continuing operations of the firm. The rate of return used is adjusted to take into account the level of risk assumed by a buyer in purchasing the business as a going concern.

- **Strengths.**

    - The value of the firm is based on projected future results, rather than assets.

    - Can be used with either net earnings or net cash flow.

    - Useful when future results are expected to be different (up or down) from recent history.

- **Weaknesses.**

    - May understate the value of balance sheet assets.

    - Discounts the valuation based on the level of risk. A business perceived as riskier typically receives a lower valuation than a more stable business.

    - Projections are not guarantees; unforeseen future events can cause income or earnings projections to be completely invalid.

Excess Earnings (Treasury Method)

The value of the firm is determined by adding the estimated market value of its tangible assets to the capitalized value of projected income resulting from goodwill.

- **Strengths.**

    - Takes into account both tangible and intangible assets.

    - Includes projected future values of income resulting from goodwill.

    - Is based on IRS Rev. Rul. 68-609, 1968 CB 327.

Advantages and Disadvantages of Valuation Methods

- Weaknesses.

    - Relies on estimate of period for which goodwill is expected to last, which is often difficult to assess. Projections based on this value can be unreliable.

    - May understate future revenues or value of intangible assets.

    - Though based on IRS rulings, the IRS cautions that the method can be relied on "only if there is no better basis therefore available."

Capitalization of Earnings

Value is equivalent to the capital (invested at a reasonable rate of return) required to generate an income equal to an average of the firm's recent, historical results.

- Strengths.

    - A simplified approach that arrives at an easily determined value.

    - Does not rely on projections, but on an average of results from the recent past.

    - Most useful for businesses with stable, predictable cash flows and earnings.

- Weaknesses.

    - May understate value for firms using aggressive strategies to reduce taxable income.

    - May overlook value of tangible or intangible assets.

    - Reliance on past earnings may ignore potential future growth.

Business Valuation

Revenue Ruling 59-60, 1959-1 CB 237 sets forth the factors to be considered in valuing a closely held business for death tax purposes. They are as follows:

- The history and nature of the business, i.e., the risk and the stability of the business.

- The economic outlook in general, as well as for this industry.

- The book value of the company.

- The company's earning capacity.

- The capacity to pay dividends (not its dividend paying history).

- The goodwill of the company.

- Any recent sales of company stock.

- The value of similar businesses which are publicly traded.

A Formula for Valuing Goodwill

1. Value of tangible assets $_____
2. - Liabilities   (_____)
3. = **Net value of tangible assets**   _____
4. x Industry percentage return [1]   x _____%[1]
5. = **Annual earnings attributable to assets** (line 3 x line 4)   _____
6. Average annual earnings of company[2]   _____[2]
7. **Earnings from goodwill** (line 6 minus 5)   _____
8. ÷ Capitalization rate[3]   _____%[3]
9. = **Goodwill** (line 7 ÷ line 8)   _____
10. **Goodwill plus net value of assets** (line 9 + line 3) $_____

---

[1] Industry percentage return: 8% should be used with stable, low-risk businesses and 10% with more hazardous, high-risk businesses.

[2] The average annual net earnings amount is computed on all the years of operation up to five. This should be before taxes and personal compensation to the owners.

[3] Revenue Ruling 68-609 recommends a capitalization rate of 15% for low-risk, stable businesses and 20% for hazardous, high-risk businesses.

Projected Future Growth

____Years _____% Growth $_____ x $_____ = _____

| | Current Business Value | Compound Interest Factor | Projected Business Value |

Note: This is not intended to replace a qualified appraisal.

Discount and Capitalization Rates

A Brief Explanation

Some business valuation methods attempt to compute the present value of a company based on either projected or historic earnings. These valuation methods include the discounted future earnings method, excess earnings method and capitalization of earnings method. These valuation methods rely on computed discount rates or capitalization rates to find a company's value.

While the uses of discount rates and capitalization rates in these valuation methods seem similar, there are significant differences. It is important to understand the differences and how to apply them.

What Is a Discount Rate?

There are times when a company's current or historic earnings do not fairly represent its future earnings. In these cases it may be more reasonable to rely on the company's projected earnings to compute its present value. A valuation method using a discount rate approach may be appropriate in these cases.

A discount rate is the rate of return a buyer would expect from owning a business, given an expected level of risk of ownership. The higher the risk, the higher the discount rate goes. The lower the risk and the more certain the return, the lower the discount rate.

In applying a discount rate, the higher the discount rate, the lower will be the computed value of a company. On the other hand, the lower the discount rate, the higher will be the computed value of a company.

Determining a Discount Rate

One way to determine a discount rate is to build it from available risk factors. The first factor is the risk-free rate. The 20-year Treasury bond rate as of the valuation date is generally accepted as a basic risk-free rate. This rate is readily available and is routinely published in the newspaper.

Discount and Capitalization Rates

Added to the risk-free rate is an appropriate risk factor or, in some cases, multiple risk factors. Some guidance to understanding these risk factors can be learned from referring to the Schilt's Risk Premium Table.[1]

More likely than not, a specific valuation situation will differ from the general descriptions provided in Schilt's table. For this reason, the business owner should seek the assistance of a trained valuation expert to compute an appropriate discount rate.

Schilt's Risk Premium for Discounting Projected Income Streams[2]

Category	Description	Risk Premium
1.	Includes established businesses with a strong trade position, are well financed, have depth in management, whose past earnings have been stable and whose future is highly predictable.	6 - 10%
2.	Includes established businesses in a more competitive industry that are well financed, have depth in management, have stable past earnings and whose future is fairly predictable.	11 - 15%
3.	Includes businesses in a highly-competitive industry requiring little capital to enter, no management depth and element of risk is high although past record may be good.	16 - 20%
4.	Includes small businesses that depend on the special skill(s) of one or two people and larger, established businesses that are highly cyclical. In both cases, future earnings may be expected to deviate widely from projections.	21 - 25%
5.	Includes small, one-person businesses of a personal service nature where the transferability of the income stream is in question.	26 - 30%

What Is a Capitalization Rate?

Sometimes a company's historic earnings are reasonably believed to represent the company's future earnings. This can be true of long-established businesses as well as businesses in mature industries. In these cases, a valuation method using a capitalization rate approach may be appropriate. One method for computing a capitalization rate is based

---

[1] James H. Schilt, "A Rational Approach to Capitalization Rates for Discounting the Future Income Stream of a Closely Held Company." The Financial Planner, January 1982. Reprinted with permission of James H. Schilt, ASA. (415) 986-1057.

[2] Table is intended for use with pre-tax earnings.

on the company's discount rate. Using this method, you subtract the company's growth rate from the discount rate. The following table helps to illustrate the relationship between the growth rate and capitalization rate:

Note: Assume a Discount Rate of 22%

If the company's growth rate is...	Then the company's capitalization rate will be	Growth Rate	Capitalization Rate
Less than zero	Greater than the discount rate	-2	24
Zero	equal to the discount rate	0	22
Greater than zero	less than the discount rate	+2	20

For example: If a company's discount rate is 22% and its growth rate is +2%, the capitalization rate is 20% (22%-2%=20%) using this method. If the average earnings are $50,000, the company's computed value (using the straight capitalization of earnings method) would be $250,000 ($50,000 divided by 20% equals $250,000).

The use of discount rates and capitalization rates to compute the value of a business can be very difficult and misleading. Often, important adjustments must be made to these rates to reflect unique or unusual circumstances. Business owners should rely on qualified business valuation specialists in using these rates.

Business Valuation Per Share Using The Courtroom Method

The Most Expensive Method

Title of Case	Taxpayer (Estate)	IRS	Court	% Above Estate	
				IRS	Court
Bader v. U.S.	$ 521.83	$1,250.00	$ 643.00	240	123
Baltimore National Bank v. U.S.	1,509.64	2,500.00	2,300.00	166	152
Braverman. Est. of Morris v. Comm.	2,058.25	4,000.00	2,724.92	194	132
Brush. Est. of Marjorie Gilbert v. Comm.	3.00	7.38	5.50	246	183
Burda. Est. of L.J.	3.00	20.00	5.00	667	167
Damon, Est. of Robert Hosken v. Comm.	3.00	6.00	3.75	200	125
Ewing. Est. of Anna C. v. Comm.	2,400.00	6,530.00	4,750.00	272	198
Fitts, Est. of Cora Russell v. Comm.	150.00	600.00	375.00	400	250
Garrett, Est. of Jessie Ring v. Comm.	50.39	285.65	285.65	567	567
Gessell v. Comm.	310.00	475.00	475.00	153	153
Hanscom, Meiville	50.00	100.00	100.00	200	200
Heinhold, Est. of Matthew	3.17	10.00	8.00	315	252
Huntington, Est. of Henry E.	10,638.35	16,559.67	16,100.99	156	151
Kuhn, Est. of Harold L. v. U.S.	1,290.43	1,700.00	1,355.00	132	105
Levenson, Est. of David J. v. Comm.	252.85	1,033.00	900.00	409	356
Leyman, Est. of Harry Stole v. Comm.	536.00	700.00	630.00	131	118
Louis, John J. Jr. Exr. v. U.S.	3.25	20.00	5.34	615	164
Luckenbach, Est. of Edgar F. v. Comm.	114.75	229.52	175.00	200	153
Maxcy, Est. of Hugh G. v. Comm.	7,018.68	9,358.24	7,018.68	133	100
Miller, Est. of Mary K. v. Comm.	500.00	1,150.00	860.00	230	172
Mitchell, Est. of Julian v. Comm.	700.00	980.00	800.00	140	114

Business Valuation Per Share Using The Courtroom Method

Title of Case	Taxpayer (Estate)	IRS	Court	% Above Estate	
				IRS	Court
Obermer. Nesta v. U.S.	$3,350.00	$5,921.67	$3,947.78	177	118
Reynolds. Est. of Pearl Gibbons v. Comm.	316.67	2,637.50	1,600.00	833	505
Ridgely. Est. of Mabel Lloyd v. U.S.	106.00	115.00	115.00	108	108
Righter. Est. of Jessie H. v. U.S.	424.00	1,000.00	700.00	236	165
Rothgery. Est. of Bernard Anthony v. U.S.	60.72	582.00	582.00	958	958
Russell. William E. Exr. v. U.S.	1,360.00	2,100.00	2,100.00	154	154
Schneider-Paas. Est. of A. Johannes v. Comm.	4,761.90	38,500.00	23,809.00	809	500
Snodgrass. Est. of John Milton v. U.S.	53.00	65.00	53.00	123	100
Thompson. Est. of Barbara F. v. Comm.	225.00	535.00	283.50	238	126
Tompkins. Est. of Lida R. v. Comm.	834.00	12,725.85	5,500.00	1,526	659
Wallace. Est. of Marvin R. v. U.S.	64.23	147.00	91.50	229	142
Worthen. Exr. (Stone) v. U.S.	100.00	175.00	104.00	175	104
Yeazel. Gilbert A. Exr. V. Coyle	304.11	450.00	400.00	148	132

When the IRS challenges a business valuation and the estate defends itself in court, the result can be a higher valuation and higher estate taxes. In the cases above, court valuations averaged 227% higher than the estate's. Had the estate not gone to court, IRS valuations averaged 338% higher, but court costs for attorneys, accountants, appraisers, etc., made the total costs of the court valuation and IRS valuation similar.

Time Delay in Closing Contested Estates

When the value of a business interest in an estate is challenged by the IRS, the loss to the heirs may be substantial. Part of that loss is due to the delay in getting distribution of the assets from the estate. The delay may also have a harmful effect on the morale of employees, vendors and customers.

Title of Case	Years	Months	Days
Atkins, Estate of Charles H.M. v. Comm.	3	6	4
Bader v. U.S.	7	9	24
Bendet, Estate of Louis	4	1	23
Bank of Calif. v. Comm.	6	9	15
Brush, Estate of Marjorie Gilbert v. Comm.	5	3	2
Damon, Estate of Robert Hosken v. Comm.	7	10	11
Ewing, Estate of Anna C. v. Comm.	7	6	24
Fitts, Estate of Cora Russell v. Comm.	6	7	20
Garrett, Estate of Jessie Ring v. Comm.	6	6	16
Goodall, Estate of Robert A. v. Comm.	11	7	13
Gold v. Grongquist	2	10	28
Harrison, Florence M. et al., v. Comm.	5	7	3
Heinold, Estate of Matthew I. v. Comm.	6	4	2
Houghton, Albert B. v. U.S.	8	11	25
Laird, Mary Du Pont	10	10	29
Louis, John J. Jr. Exr. v. U.S.	7	8	26
Luckenbach, Est. of Edgar F. v. Comm.	14	10	11
Maxcy, Est. of Gregg v. Comm.	8	11	21
Maxcy, Est. of Hugh G. v. Comm.	6	2	7
Miller, Est. of Mary K. v. Comm.	7	0	29
Moore, Anna H.	6	10	22
Nathan's Estate, In re	7	4	11
Patton, Estate of Walter L.	7	3	16
Perlick, Est. of Hilbert R. v. U.S.	6	11	9

Time Delay in Closing Contested Estates

Title of Case	Years	Months	Days
Reynolds, Est. of Pearl Gibbons v. Comm.	7	10	22
Ridgely, Est. of Mabel Lloyd v. U.S.	4	8	9
Righter, Est. of Jessie H. v. U.S.	9	10	25
Rothgery, Est. of Bernard Anthony v. U.S.	10	10	0
Russell, William 11E. Exr. v. U.S.	6	6	5
Schneider-Pass, Est. of Alfred Johannes v. Comm.	11	1	19
Snodgross, Est. of John Milton v. U.S.	5	5	6
Tomkins, Estate of	8	10	24
Wilber National Bank	7	2	15

Average time delay in above cases was 7½ years. A buy-sell agreement could have avoided this problem.

Odds of Disability

Insurance claims studies indicate that the odds of becoming disabled for 90 days or longer are much greater than dying during one's working years. Studies also suggest that, as the number of business owners or key employees increases, so do the odds that one of them will suffer a long-term disability.

Probability of at Least One Long-Term Disability Prior to Age 65

Age	Number of People in the Age Group					
	1	2	3	4	5	6
25	58%	82%	92%	97%	99%	99%
30	54%	79%	90%	96%	98%	99%
35	50%	75%	88%	94%	97%	98%
40	45%	70%	84%	91%	95%	97%
45	40%	64%	78%	87%	92%	95%
50	33%	55%	70%	80%	86%	91%
55	25%	43%	57%	68%	76%	82%

Note: Based on the 1985 Commissioners Individual Disability Table, most recent available.

Determining Odds of Disability Among People of Different Ages

Use the following table and worksheet to determine the risk of a long-term disability among your business owners or key employees.

	Age						
	25	30	35	40	45	50	55
Value	.42	.46	.50	.55	.60	.67	.75

Step 1: For each owner or key employee you wish to include in your analysis, choose the value from the table above that corresponds to the age closest to the actual age of the owner or key employee, and include the value in the space below.

Step 2: Multiply all of the values by each other to arrive at a single value.

_____ x _____ x _____ x _____ x _____ = _____

Step 3: Multiply the single value by 100 to convert it to a percent.

100 x _____ = _____ %

Step 4: Subtract the single value from 100% to determine the odds of long-term disability for any one of the groups of owners or key employees in your company.

100% - _____ = _____ %

Note: You can perform this analysis for any number of owners or key employees, not just the five shown in this worksheet.

Disability of a Business Owner

Many business owners have created buy-sell agreements to protect themselves and their businesses in case of an untimely death. These agreements are often funded with life insurance to ensure that the cash to purchase the business is available when needed.

Permanent disability is another threat faced by business owners. Disability of an owner can create immediate issues as to who will operate and manage the business. Often, the risk of a permanent disability is not provided for in a buy-sell agreement in spite of the fact that the probability of a long-term disability prior to age 65 is greater than the probability of death.

To provide for this risk, business owners can amend existing buy-sell agreements or create separate agreements. Special disability insurance policies can be used to fund a disability buy-sell agreement. These policies can be set up to pay a lump sum, a series of payments, or a combination of the two.

Key Elements to Consider

- **Definition of disability:** How disability is defined in the agreement is very important and should probably be tied to the definition in the disability insurance policy.

- **Elimination period:** The period of time between the first day of the disability and the trigger date, e.g., 12 months to 24 months are frequent options.

- **Trigger date:** This is the date at the end of the elimination period when the buyout begins and the insurance company begins paying on the policy.

- **Successive disability:** A disabled person may temporarily return to work but thereafter have a recurrence of the disability. In many plans, successive disability periods can be tied together to meet the elimination period.

- **Funding period:** The period over which the buyout payments are made. It can be an immediate lump sum or spread out over a period of months, or a combination of both. The funding period set in the policy should match the terms of the buy-sell agreement.

- **Recover from disability:** The recovery of a disabled person after the buyout has begun can raise several questions, among them: Does the funding stop? Can the person return to work with the same company? Lump sum settlement plans, in some cases, can remove some of the uncertainty.

- **Buy-sell agreement:** The buy-sell agreement must be in force at the time of disability in order for payments to be made from the policy.

- **Converting to individual coverage:** Sometimes the disability plan will be convertible to individual coverage if the business has no further need for the coverage, the owner needs additional individual coverage, and he or she meets certain requirements.

- **Involvement in the business:** Many insurers require that the business owner be actively involved in the business.

Tax Basics for Disability Buyouts

	Corporation		Partnership	
	Stock Redemption by the Corporation	**Cross Purchase by the Stockholders**	**Entity Buy-Sell by the Partnership**	**Cross Purchase by the Partners**
Are premiums for a disability policy to fund a buyout deductible?	No IRC Sec. 265(a)(1)	No IRC Sec. 265(a)(1)	No IRC Sec. 265(a)(1)	No IRC Sec. 265(a)(1)
Are the proceeds from a disability policy taxable income?	No IRC Sec. 104(a)(3)	No IRC Sec. 104(a)(3)	No IRC Sec. 104(a)(3)	No IRC Sec. 104(a)(3)
Are payments from the corporation or partnership to individual owner deductible to the entity?	No	N/A	No	N/A
How are benefits taxed to the individual receiving them?	If a complete redemption, it is treated as a sale or exchange. IRC Sec. 302(b)(3)	Capital gain on excess of purchase price over his or her basis in the stock. IRC Secs. 1001; 1221; 1222	Return of basis is nontaxable. Excess is generally taxed as ordinary income. IRC Sec. 736(b)	Capital gain on excess of purchase price over his or her basis in the partnership.

Disability of a Business Owner

	Corporation		Partnership	
	Stock Redemption by the Corporation	Cross Purchase by the Stockholders	Entity Buy-Sell by the Partnership	Cross Purchase by the Partners
Can the sale qualify as an installment sale to prorate the gains over the years in which payments are received?	Yes IRC Sec. 453	Yes IRC Sec. 453	Yes IRC Sec. 453	Yes IRC Sec. 453

Business Overhead Expense

Another form of disability insurance specially suited to the business owner is Business Overhead Expense (BOE). BOE policies are designed to reimburse certain business expenses of the owner while he or she is totally or partially disabled. The funds provided by the BOE policy help the business survive during the period of the owner's disability. Often, the BOE policy is the reason the owner has a business to return to after the disability. Should the disability appear permanent, the owner usually has additional time to make decisions regarding the future of the business.

Generally speaking, there are only certain types of business owners who qualify for BOE coverage. These include owners of closely held businesses, owners of small businesses and professionals with their own practices.

Some of the expenses typically covered by a BOE policy include the following:

- Legal and accounting fees.

- Utilities.

- Principal payments on debt.

- Leased equipment.

- Business insurance premiums.

- Office supplies.

- Salaries of non-owner, non-family employees.

- Professional dues.

- Business taxes.

- Rent.

- Workers compensation.

In no instance is there any payment from a BOE policy to the business owner. Instead, these funds must come from his or her own disability plan.

Business Overhead Expense

Business overhead expense (BOE) is a form of disability insurance specially suited to the business owner. BOE policies are designed to reimburse certain business expenses of the owner while he or she is totally or partially disabled. The funds provided by the BOE policy help the business survive during the period of the owner's disability. Often, the BOE policy is the reason the owner

has a business to return to after the disability. Should the disability appear permanent, the owner usually has additional time to make decisions regarding the future of the business.

Generally speaking, there are only certain types of business owners who qualify for BOE coverage. These include owners of closely held businesses, owners of small businesses and professionals with their own practices.

Some of the expenses typically covered by a BOE policy include the following:

- Legal and accounting fees.
- Utilities.
- Principal payments on debt.
- Leased equipment.
- Business insurance premiums.
- Office supplies.
- Salaries of non-owner, non-family employees.
- Professional dues.
- Business taxes.
- Rent.
- Workers compensation.

In no instance is there any payment from a BOE policy to the business owner. Instead, these funds must come from his or her own disability plan.

Disability Buy-Out Cross-Purchase Agreement

A cross-purchase buy-sell agreement involves business owners entering into an agreement with each other to assure an orderly disposition of their business interest in the event of disability.

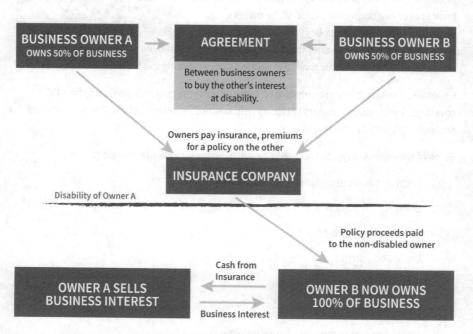

Advantages	Disadvantages
The transferred interests receive a new income tax basis equal to the price paid. This will mean a tax savings, if the interest is later sold at a higher price.	Plan is more difficult to administer if more than two or three business owners.
No problem with state laws restricting redemptions.	Requires more policies, e.g., 12 policies for 4 owners, 20 policies for 5 owners, etc.
Disability policies may be insulated from the company's creditors.	Policies may lapse if owner doesn't make the payments.

Disability Buy-Out
Stock Redemption Plan

A stock redemption plan involves stockholders entering into an agreement with the corporation to insure an orderly disposition of their stock in the event of disability.

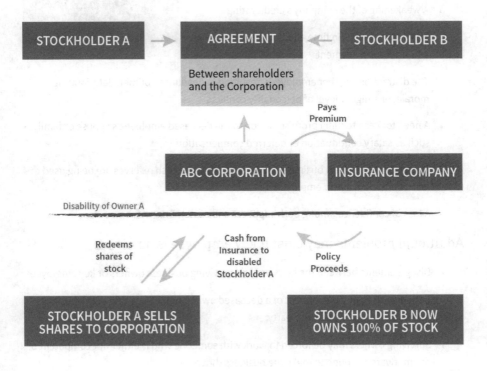

Advantages	Disadvantages
Usually easier to understand than the cross-purchase plan.	Voting power may be altered unfavorably.
Fewer policies in insured plans.	Strict state redemption laws must be followed.
No questions as to unreasonable compensation issues when agreement is properly written.	Value of non-disabled owner's shares increase but not basis.

Key Employee Insurance

The untimely death of a key employee or a business owner who is also a key employee can have a disastrous effect on a business. Some of the "costs" of such an event might include the following.

- A weakening of the company's credit rating

- The financial cost (in time and dollars) to find, hire, and train a replacement

- The distraction of other employees, resulting in deadlines not met, deteriorating morale, or a higher level of personality conflicts

- A need for cash to fulfill promises made to the deceased employee's spouse or family, such as salary continuation or deferred compensation

- The inability to seize a business opportunity, because cash reserves are being used to recruit and train a new employee

- A loss of confidence among both suppliers and customers

Additional problems may exist if key employee is an owner.

- Disagreements between the heirs and the surviving business owners or key employees

- Lack of cash to buy the interest of a deceased owner, requiring a sale of the business to an unknown, outside third party

- Surviving owners may be forced to work with someone who is either not competent or not motivated enough to make the business thrive

- The business may have to be sold to pay estate taxes

Methods of Valuing a Key Employee

There is no easy mathematical formula to determine the value of a key employee. However, over the years business owners have frequently used three different methods to estimate the worth of an employee to their company.

- **The cost of replacement method:** Totals the direct, out-of-pocket costs involved in finding, hiring and training a replacement, as well as the estimated loss-of-opportunity costs.

- **The contribution to profits method:** Estimates the impact a key employee has on the company's net profit. The firm first calculates the expected profit from a normal return on capital, e.g., the net book value of assets. Profit in excess of this normal return is assumed to result from the efforts of the key employees. An estimate is made of the percentage of profit attributable to each key employee. This percentage is then multiplied by total excess profit, to determine the dollar amount of excess profit from each key employee. This sum is then multiplied times the number of years needed to find and train a competent replacement.

- **The multiple of compensation method:** Assumes that an employee's value is accurately reflected in his or her total compensation package. The multiple that is used (for example: 2 x annual compensation), will depend on the type of business and the estimated difficulty in finding a qualified replacement. This method is perhaps the easiest way to estimate the potential loss to the firm.

Financing the Replacement
of a Key Employee

Replacing an employee – particularly a key employee – can be expensive. It is better to prepare ahead of time for this potential cost. There are a number of methods commonly used to finance the hiring and training of a new key employee:

- **Pay in cash:** However, most businesses do not keep large amounts of cash sitting idle; the money is typically working in the business. The need to raise cash quickly may result in "distress sales" of valuable assets, at a price below normal market value.

- **Establish a sinking fund:** However, dollars kept in a savings account represent lost business opportunities. For example, if each $1.00 put into a marketing campaign returns $10.00 in sales and the company has a 15% profit margin, the return on each $1.00 invested in marketing is $1.50. On an annual basis, this would be a 50% return. If the same dollar (along with the profits) were reinvested two or three times a year, with a similar increase, the ultimate return would be many times that earned in a bank account.

  Therefore, a sinking fund may be very costly when one considers the loss of business opportunities.

- **Borrow the funds:** This option assumes that the loss of a key employee does not seriously damage the firm's credit worthiness. Each dollar borrowed must be repaid, with interest. If the loan were amortized over a 10-year period, at 8% interest, for each $1,000 borrowed the company would repay a total of $1,440.

  Here, too, the business owner must take into account the "opportunity cost" of missed growth and profits, had the money used to repay the loan been invested in the company instead.

- **Life insurance policies:** Many business owners choose life insurance to protect against the loss of a key employee. The premiums are small compared to the lump sum which would have to be quickly raised, either out of earnings or by borrowing, when a death does occur.[1]

If permanent-type policies are used there will also be a cash value build up, which can be available for the business in time of need, regardless of the firm's credit worthiness.

---

[1] Under the provisions of IRC Sec. 101(j), death proceeds from a life insurance policy owned by an employer on the life of an employee are generally includable in income, unless certain requirements are met. The law was effective for contracts issued after August 17, 2006, except for contracts acquired under an IRC Sec. 1035 Exchange. State or local law may vary. Professional legal and tax guidance are strongly recommended.

Key Employee Coverage Issues

Both the IRS and the courts have long recognized that the loss of a manager, scientist, salesperson or other key individual will almost always have a serious effect on the earning power and sometimes on the very stability of a business. Although the principle applies in publicly held businesses, it is particularly true in a closely held corporation where profits are dependent on the ability, initiative, judgment or business connections of a single person or small group of owner/employees. The death or disability of a key person at the wrong time can have a dramatic impact in a smaller business.

There is no universally recognized and accepted formula for computing the economic effect of the loss of a key person. One method used in several court cases utilizes a discount approach in which a percentage discount is taken from the going concern value of the business.

Some authorities feel that if the business will survive the death of the key employee and, in time, a competent successor can be found, a discount factor of from 15% - 20% should be used. Where the business is likely to fail or be placed in serious jeopardy upon the death (or disability) of the key employee, a discount of from 20% - 45% is more appropriate. The exact discount factor should be arrived at through consultation with the officers of the company and the firm's accounting and legal advisers.

Some questions to ask in determining the factor (or range of factors) to be used include the following:

- How long will it take for a new person to reach the efficiency of the key individual?

- How much will it cost to locate and situate a replacement?

- Will the new employee demand more salary?

- How much will it cost to train the new person?

- What mistakes is a replacement likely to make during the break-in period and how much are those mistakes likely to cost the company?

- What proportion of the firm's current net profit is attributable to the key employee?

- Is the employee engaged in any projects that, if left unfinished at death or disability, would prove costly to the business? If so, how costly?

- Would a potentially profitable project have to be abandoned or would a productive department have to be closed?

- Would the employee's death result in the loss of clientele or personnel attracted to the business because of his or her personality, social contacts, unique skills, talents or managerial ability?

- What effect would the key employee's death have on the firm's credit standing?

- What proportion of the firm's actual loss is it willing to self-insure, if any?

Protecting Against the Loss
of a Key Employee

Business owners frequently use life insurance to protect their company from many of the potential problems which may otherwise damage or destroy what has taken years to build.

Life insurance is unique in that it will generally pay the pre-determined amount no matter when the death occurs.

The premiums are usually small compared to the potential death benefit. Also, if policies are used which develop cash values, they can be shown as business assets on the balance sheet, contributing to the value of the business and potentially to its borrowing power.

Borrowing against cash values may also be a lifesaving source in times of financial crisis.[1]

How Key Employee Insurance Works

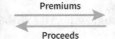

| BUSINESS | Premiums →
 ← Proceeds | LIFE INSURANCE COMPANY |

- Company owns the policy.
- Company pays the premiums.
- After death, the company collects the policy proceeds.[2]

Potential Uses for Proceeds

- Purchasing stock from the decedent's estate.

- Honoring salary continuation arrangements to surviving spouse.

- Finding, recruiting, and training a new employee.

- Paying any necessary bills and strengthening the credit position.

- Funding expansion of the business.

- Adding income-tax free corporate surplus.

---

[1] Policy loans and interest will reduce the payable death benefit of a policy. If a policy lapses or is surrendered with a loan outstanding, the loan will be treated as taxable income in the current year, to the extent of gain in the policy.

[2] Under the provisions of IRC Sec. 101(j), death proceeds from a life insurance policy owned by an employer on the life of an employee are generally includable in income, unless certain requirements are met. The law was effective for contracts issued after August 17, 2006, except for contracts acquired under an IRC Sec. 1035 Exchange. State or local law may vary. Professional legal and tax guidance is strongly recommended.

Key Employee Disability Plans

Frequently a business will retain key employee life insurance coverage. In doing so, the owners express their understanding that a business may suffer financially if a key person dies.

Often overlooked in their decision, however, is what will happen to the business if a key person is disabled. In this instance, the business may confront the same financial issues it would face if the key employee were to die. Some of these issues include the following:

- The costs to recruit a replacement.

- The costs to train a replacement.

- The opportunity costs of lost business from the disability of the key employee.

The key person disability plan will protect the business by providing funds to help cover the potential lost profits and the costs of finding and training a replacement.

Some of these plans offer a replacement benefit which will reimburse the company for some percentage of the replacement costs, up to certain limits, for the first 12 to 24 months after the key person's disability occurs.

Sometimes the key person disability plan will be convertible to individual coverage if the business has no further need for the coverage, the insured needs additional individual coverage and the insured meets certain income and, possibly, physical requirements.

Note: Key employee disability insurance has become a specialty product and providers of this important coverage are becoming more difficult to find.

Business Continuation Needs

In the event of the death of: John

The value of your business may increase over time. An annual review is an important step in verifying that your business documents and financial assets are up to date. This includes reviewing your analysis of the business needs in the event of the death of a business partner. It is vital to make sure that the funding mechanism keeps pace with the value of your business. If funds are not available to buy out the heirs of a deceased partner, it may put a severe strain on an otherwise healthy business, causing it to ultimately collapse.

	Today	5 Years	10 Years	Retirement
Estimated Value[1]	$250,000	$450,508	$811,830	$1,462,944
Insurance	225,000	260,837	302,381	350,543
Shortfall	25,000	189,671	509,449	1,112,402

John's Ownership of ABC Lumber

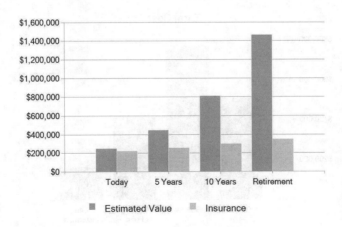

[1] These figures are approximations only. For additional information contact your business valuation consultant.

1277

Ways to Pay for Business Continuation

For: ABC Lumber

In the event of the death of: John

Assumptions:

Year to illustrate: 10
Estimated business value: $811,830

Available life insurance: $302,381
Additional funds needed: $509,449

This analysis illustrates several ways to provide for business continuation in the event of an owner's death. Whether the surviving owners or the business entity purchase the deceased owner's equity, there is a need for immediate cash. If funds are not available to buy out the heirs of a deceased owner, there may be a time-consuming legal battle that may create a strain on an otherwise healthy business, causing a risk of insolvency.

Funding Options

Funding Method	Total Dollars	Cost per Dollar
Cash	$509,449	$1.00
Loan[1]	774,418	1.52
Sinking Fund[2]	415,171	0.81
Life Insurance[3]	165,571	0.33

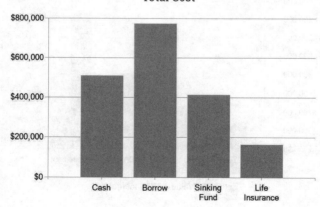

Total Cost

Values shown in this presentation are hypothetical and not a promise of future performance.

---

[1] Assumes an interest rate of 9.00% and a term of 10 years.

[2] Assumes a rate of return of 4.00% and 10 years to fund. A "sinking fund" is an account in which money is accumulated over time to pay off a debt or pay for a specific purchase.

[3] Assumes an annual premium of $16,557 and that premiums are paid for 10 years.

Qualified Deferred Compensation Plan

IRC Sec. 457

Employees (or independent contractors) of state and local governments and tax-exempt employers can elect to defer future income (and taxation) under an eligible deferred compensation plan described in IRC Sec. 457.

Eligible Deferred Compensation Plan

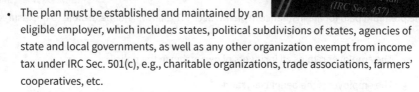

- The plan must be established and maintained by an eligible employer, which includes states, political subdivisions of states, agencies of state and local governments, as well as any other organization exempt from income tax under IRC Sec. 501(c), e.g., charitable organizations, trade associations, farmers' cooperatives, etc.

- The Small Business Job Protection Act of 1996 requires the assets of state and local government plans to be held in a trust or custodial account.

- In general, the plan cannot provide for distribution of amounts payable prior to the earlier of the participant's separation from service or attainment of age 70½, unless the participant is faced with an unforeseeable emergency. However, the plan may adopt provisions permitting in-service distribution of benefits if the total benefit is less than a specified amount, currently $5,000. Such in-service distributions may be either voluntary or involuntary and are subject to strict conditions.

- The plan must provide that the income deferred, plus assets purchased with those funds, plus the income earned on those assets remain the property of the employer. The IRS has permitted the use of a rabbi trust to prevent the employer from using the funds for other purposes. See PLR 9205002[1].

- There must be a limit of $18,500[2] of income that can be deferred in one year. For individuals who are participants in state or local government plans, and who are at least age 50, catch-up contributions of $6,000 may also be made.[1] The age 50 and over catch-up contributions are not available to participants in plans sponsored by tax-exempt organizations.

---

[1] An IRS Private Letter Ruling is applicable only to the taxpayer who requested it and may not be cited as precedent.
[2] 2018 value.

- During the three years prior to normal retirement age, other catch-up limits apply.[1]

- Plan loans can be made under the same rules that apply to qualified plans.

Excise and Penalty Taxes

The 10% penalty on early distributions from qualified and 403(b) plans does not apply to IRC Sec. 457 plans. However, the minimum distribution rules effective at age 70½ or later retirement do apply.

Life Insurance

The premium paid for life insurance in an IRC Sec. 457 plan will not be taxable to the insured if:

- The employer retains all incidents of ownership in the policy,

- The employer is the beneficiary, and

- There is no requirement to transfer the policy or its proceeds.

The death benefits paid from an IRC Sec. 457 plan to an employee's heirs are included as taxable income to those heirs under deferred compensation rules. See Treasury Reg. 1.457-10(d).

Roth 457 Plan Feature

If the employer permits, and the written plan so provides, plan participants in a 457(b) governmental plan may choose to have some or all of their salary deferral contributions treated as contributions to a designated Roth account, sometimes referred to as a "Roth 457." Unlike normal 457 contributions, which are made before-tax, Roth 457 contributions are made on an after-tax basis. If certain requirements are met, distributions from the Roth 457 are received income tax free. Contributions to a Roth 457 account are subject to the same employee elective deferral limits as the 457 plan itself.

---

[1] These other limits are two times the normal contribution limits.

Nonqualified Deferred Compensation Plan

	Employer	Key Employee
Agreement	Agrees to pay compensation for a set period after a stated date or death.	Agrees to continue service until specified date (e.g., normal retirement age). Optional: After separation, agrees not to compete and/or to provide consultation services.
Advantages	Employer retains key employee.	Employee (or heirs) receives extra retirement benefit when tax bracket may be lower.
Taxation	Benefits paid to employee (or heirs) are deductible to employer when paid or constructively received.	Benefits are taxed when payments are made or constructively received.

How It Works

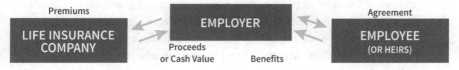

General Comments[1]

- Deferral must generally be agreed upon before the compensation is earned.

- If the plan is unfunded, the compensation is not taxable until received.

- If the plan is funded, the employee's rights must be subject to substantial risk of forfeiture and they must be nontransferable. If they are not subject to such risk or are transferable, the payments become currently taxable.

- Employer can pick and choose which employees to benefit. However, if they are not highly compensated, the plan may be subject to ERISA requirements.

- A cash value life insurance contract can be used to informally fund an agreement. It can provide the necessary funds at either death or distribution.[2]

- Nonqualified plans are not subject to the pre-age 59½ distribution penalties or the age-based mandatory distribution rules imposed on qualified plans, IRAs, etc.

---

[1] The AJCA of 2004 significantly changed nonqualified deferred compensation plan rules. If a plan fails to meet the new requirements, compensation deferred under the plan becomes currently taxable and penalties and interest apply.

[2] Under the provisions of IRC Sec. 101(j), added by the Pension Protection Act of 2006, death proceeds from a life insurance policy owned by an employer on the life of an employee are generally includable in income unless certain requirements are met. State or local law may vary. Professional legal and tax guidance is strongly recommended.

Nonqualified Deferred Compensation

Avoiding Constructive Receipt

Nonqualified deferred compensation (NQDC) plans are commonly used to provide additional benefits to selected key employees or executives. In a typical plan, an employee enters into an agreement with the employer to defer a portion of his or her compensation until a future date or event. Such plans are "nonqualified" because they do not meet the requirements of "qualified" plans under the Internal Revenue Code (IRC).[1] There are two broad categories of NQDC plans:

- **Funded:** The employer sets funds aside, beyond the reach of its general creditors, to guarantee payment of the amounts deferred. The money is deductible to the employer, and is included in the employee's gross income, in the year set aside.

- **Unfunded:** The deferred compensation is generally secured only by the employer's promise to pay. It is deductible to the employer, and is included in the employee's gross income, in the year that the funds are either actually or "constructively" received by the employee. Constructive receipt typically occurs when the employee has an unlimited right to the funds (received or not), with no "substantial risk of forfeiture."

Avoiding current taxation on deferred amounts is highly desirable as it generally results in a larger benefit when the funds are received by the employee in the future.

Avoiding Constructive Receipt – IRC Sec. 409A

The American Jobs Creation Act of 2004 (AJCA) included new IRC Sec. 409A, which added to federal income tax law a number of requirements that a NQDC plan must meet to avoid having deferred amounts treated as being constructively received in the current year. If these requirements are not met, all current and past-deferred compensation, plus any earnings, are included in the employee's gross income for the current tax year. An additional 20% tax is levied, plus an underpayment interest penalty.

IRC Sec. 409A was effective January 1, 2005 and generally applied to amounts deferred after December 31, 2004. Certain amounts deferred before January 1, 2005 are considered

---

[1] The discussion here concerns federal income tax law. State or local income tax law may differ.

"grandfathered" under the prior rules and are exempt from IRC Sec. 409A. If the plan under which these grandfathered amounts were deferred is "materially modified" on or after October 3, 2004, IRC Sec. 409A then applies to the grandfathered amounts.

In the years following passage of the AJCA, the Internal Revenue Service (IRS) issued a series of announcements on how the new law would be applied. Taxpayers were expected to comply "in good faith" with this transitional guidance. On April 10, 2007, the IRS released TD 9321, containing most of the final IRC Sec. 409A regulations.[1] These regulations, which generally apply to tax years beginning on or after January 1, 2008, required plan sponsors to conform to the final regulations no later than December 31, 2007. Notice 2007-86, issued by the IRS on October 22, 2007, generally allowed employers until December 31, 2008, to bring their plans into compliance with the statute.

Key Concepts

There are a number of key concepts involved in understanding NQDC plans:

- **Deferral of compensation:** Under the final regulations a very broad definition of "deferral of compensation" is used, "…if, under the terms of the plan and the relevant facts and circumstances, the service provider has a legally binding right during a taxable year to compensation that, pursuant to the terms of the plan, is or may be payable to (or on behalf of) the service provider in a later year."[2]

IRC Sec. 409A May Apply To:
Agreements covering a change in control
Certain incentive or bonus plans
Employment and separation agreements
Phantom or restricted stock plans
Split-dollar arrangements
Stock options/rights granted at less than Fair Market Value (FMV)
Supplemental Executive Retirement Plans (SERPS)

---

[1] At the same time, the government also released IRS Notice 2007-34, providing general guidance on the applicability of IRC Sec. 409A to split-dollar arrangements.

[2] Reg. Sec. 1.409A-1(b)(1)

- **Service provider:** The person or entity who provides services. Generally, any cash-basis taxpayer including: (1) an individual; (2) a corporation;[1] or (3) a partnership.[2]

- **Service recipient:** Any person, organization, or entity to whom services are provided.[3]

- **Substantial risk of forfeiture:** Generally, a substantial risk of forfeiture exists when receipt of the deferred compensation depends on the employee performing "substantial future services", or the "occurrence of a condition related to the compensation, and the risk of forfeiture is substantial."[3]

Exceptions and Special Situations

The final regulations exempt a number of types of compensation from IRC Sec. 409A:

- **Short-term deferrals:** Certain deferrals paid no later than 2-1/2 months after the first tax year the amounts are no longer subject to a substantial risk of forfeiture.

- **Separation pay plans:** Applicable to limited amounts of compensation, paid within a specified time period, and payable only as a result of separation from service. The final regulations carefully define the situations to which this exception applies.

- **Qualified and welfare benefit plans:** Excepted from Section 409A are many qualified pension, profit sharing, and stock bonus plans. Bona fide plans providing welfare benefits such as medical, sick leave, vacation, or disability are also excluded.

- **Stock options and stock appreciation rights:** The exercise price of the option or stock right can never be less than the FMV of the stock on the day the option or right is granted. A stock option or stock right plan may not include any deferral feature. Incentive stock options and options granted under employee stock purchase plans (statutory stock rights) are excluded from Section 409A.

- **Independent contractor:** Except for corporate directors and those providing management services, independent contractors are generally exempt from Section 409A.

---

[1] Including a C corporation, an S corporation, or a personal service corporation.

[2] For the sake of simplicity, this report uses the term "employee" for "service provider" and "employer" for "service recipient." The terms used in the final regulations are broad and intended to cover a wide range of relationships.

[3] Reg. Sec. 1.409A-1(d).

- **Educational benefits:** Covering expenses such as tuition and books paid for education for the service provider (not for family members).

- **Foreign plans:** Applicable to nonresident aliens or U.S. citizens working abroad.

Election to Defer Compensation

- **Generally:** The election must be made no later than the end of the previous tax year.

- **First year of eligibility:** The deferral election must be made within 30 days of an employee's first becoming eligible to participate in the plan.

- **Performance-based compensation:** If an employee's compensation is performance based, over a period of at least 12 months, the election to defer compensation must be made no later than six months before the end of the 12-month period.

Distributions

The timing and manner in which the deferred compensation will be paid out must be decided at the time the initial deferral election is made. Generally, distributions may be made only when one of the following events occurs:

- The employee separates from service.[1]
- Upon the employee's death or disability.
- At a specific time, or according to a fixed schedule.
- Because of a change in ownership or effective control of the employing corporation.
- Because of an unforeseeable emergency.

If a plan allows an employee to later choose to delay or change the form of payment, the new election may not be effective until 12 months after it is made. If the change relates to (1) separation from service; or (2) according to a fixed schedule or at a fixed point in time; or (3) because of a change in the service recipient's ownership, any payment made under the new election must be delayed at least five years beyond when it would have otherwise been made. Distributions made because of death, disability, or unforeseen emergency may be delayed for periods less than five years.

---

[1] Distributions to a "specified" employee may not be made until six months after the employee separates from service (or, if earlier, the date of the employee's death). A specified employee is a "key" employee, as that term is defined in IRC Sec. 416(i), of a corporation whose stock is publicly traded.

Nonqualified Deferred Compensation

Acceleration of Benefits

Under the final regulations, benefit payments may be accelerated only in certain, narrow situations, and only when done either automatically (under the terms of the plan) or upon a decision by the service recipient:

- **De minims distributions:** Amounts which do not exceed specified limits.
- **Certain legal requirements:** Such as paying required income or employment taxes, complying with a divorce decree or domestic relations order, or meeting conflict of interest or ethics standards.
- **At plan termination:** Specific requirements must be met.

Other Tax Issues

The Pension Protection Act of 2006 (PPA 2006) added two provisions to the federal income tax code which have a potentially heavy impact on NQDC plans:

- **Employer-owned life insurance contracts:** NQDC plans are sometimes funded with life insurance. Generally, amounts received under a life insurance contract paid by reason of the death of the insured are excluded from income. Under the provisions of PPA 2006, however, death proceeds from a life insurance policy owned by an employer on the life of an employee are generally includable in income, unless certain requirements are met. This law was effective for contracts issued after August 17, 2006, except for policies acquired in an IRC Sec. 1035 exchange. Until the full scope of this new legislation is clarified by the IRS, caution is advised. See IRC Sec. 101(j).

- **"At-risk" qualified plans:** Effective for funds transferred or set aside after August 17, 2006, PPA 2006 added restrictions on executive nonqualified deferred compensation at firms with under-funded qualified retirement plans. This law generally provides that during any period in which a qualified retirement plan is "at-risk", any funds set aside in a NQDC plan for high-level executives will become taxable and the 20% penalty tax and special underpayment interest penalty will apply.

Seek Professional Guidance

Given the complexities involved, and because the tax and other penalties for not meeting the requirements of the Internal Revenue Code are significant, professional guidance is strongly recommended.

Rabbi Trust

Protecting Deferred Compensation

Many employers seek to attract and retain executives and other key employees using a variety of employee benefit programs. Nonqualified[1] deferred compensation programs are one such employee benefit. In these plans, typically, compensation currently payable to an employee is "deferred" to a future point in time when the employee anticipates being in a lower marginal income-tax bracket.

In general, the compensation is deductible to the employer, and taxable to the employee, in the year the funds are received (or "constructively" received) by the employee.

From the employee's perspective, the key dilemma is balancing the value of tax deferral against the risk that the promised benefits might not be paid. In the future, when the payments are due, the employer may be either unwilling or unable to make them. If the employer sets assets aside in a manner which effectively secures future payment, the compensation is taxable to the employee in the year those funds are no longer at risk.

The "Rabbi" Trust – A Partial Answer

One partial answer to this problem is for the employer to set up a "rabbi"[2] trust in conjunction with the nonqualified deferred compensation plan. A rabbi trust is typically irrevocable and is commonly designed to hold assets to pay the future, promised benefits.

To preserve the tax-deferred nature of the arrangement, and avoid "constructive" receipt (the funds become currently taxable to the employee, received or not), assets in the trust must remain subject to the employer's creditors. The employer may not use the assets in the trust for its general business purposes and must include trust earnings in its taxable income.

Implemented correctly, the rabbi trust approach provides some protection against the employer being <u>unwilling</u> to pay the promised benefits; it provides no protection if the employer is <u>unable</u>, because of insolvency, bankruptcy, or creditor problems, to meet its obligations.

---

[1] "Nonqualified" plans do not have to meet the same strict federal tax and other legal requirements as" qualified" plans. The fact that a benefit program is "nonqualified" frequently allows an employer to favor a few, selected employees.

[2] So called because the first such arrangement approved by the IRS was established for a rabbi.

IRC Sec. 409A

The American Jobs Creation Act of 2004 included new IRC Sec. 409A, which added to federal income tax law numerous requirements that a nonqualified deferred compensation plan must meet to avoid having deferred amounts treated as being constructively received in the current year. If these requirements are not met, all current and past-deferred compensation, plus any earnings, are included in the employee's gross income for the current tax year. Further, an additional 20% tax is levied, plus an underpayment interest penalty. State or local law may differ.

While the full scope of IRC Sec. 409A is complex, several of its provisions target efforts to protect the future payment of promised benefits. These include:

- **Offshore trusts:** Use of an offshore trust, either directly or indirectly, to fund future benefits will cause the income tax penalties in IRC Sec. 409A to apply.

- **Financial "triggers":** Efforts to distribute or secure benefits in the event the employer's financial health declines, known as financial "triggers," are similarly penalized.

- **"At-risk" qualified plans:** The Pension Protection Act of 2006 added a notable restriction, aimed at firms with under-funded qualified retirement plans. Generally, for any period in which a qualified retirement plan is "at-risk," any funds set aside in a nonqualified deferred compensation plan for high-level executives will become taxable and the 20% penalty tax and special underpayment interest penalty apply.

Seek Professional Guidance

Given the complexities involved, and because the income tax penalties for not meeting the requirements of the Internal Revenue Code are significant, competent, professional guidance is strongly recommended.

Secular Trust

Protecting Deferred Compensation

Nonqualified deferred compensation plans are often used as a fringe benefit to recruit and retain key executives.

Even if funds are set aside by the employer to meet its future obligation, the company's creditors may reach the funds if there is financial difficulty.

To protect these funds, an irrevocable arrangement commonly known as a "secular" trust can be used. The employer pays the agreed-upon contributions to the trust, which invests the funds until the executive's retirement, disability, or death.

Use of a secular trust effectively shelters the funds from a number of potential threats. Unlike the popular "rabbi" trust, funds in a secular trust are not available to the company's creditors in the event of bankruptcy. Secular trust assets are also protected against a "hostile" takeover or a management decision to use the funds for other corporate purposes. For the employee, a secular trust is more secure than a rabbi trust.

General Tax Consequences

Unlike a rabbi trust, a secular trust does not provide tax deferral. In general, the income tax[1] consequences of a secular trust are as follows:

- Funds are taxable to the employee during the year they are contributed to the plan, if substantially vested.

- The contributions are deductible to the employer in the same year they are includable in the employee's income; no employer deduction is allowed for any growth or earnings inside the trust.

Many advisors feel that future tax rates will be higher; thus, paying the tax today, at lower rates, will result in a larger fund later on. One disadvantage, however, is that the employee's present tax burden increases, but his or her currently available income does not. The employer may wish to provide an additional cash bonus to pay the extra taxes.

---

[1] The discussion here concerns federal income tax law; state and/or local tax law may vary.

The possible tax advantage, combined with the separation of the funds from potential corporate creditors, makes the secular trust attractive to many executives.

Form of Trust

There are two principal forms of secular trust, the "employee-funded" secular trust and the "employer-funded" secular trust. The federal income-tax ramifications of each type of trust are quite different:

- **Employee-funded secular trust:** An employee-funded trust is generally considered to be an employee-grantor trust, with the employee taxable on both trust contributions and trust earnings each year. To the extent that contributions and earnings are currently taxed, future distributions should be received free of income tax.

- **Employer-funded secular trust:** In an employer-funded trust, the employee is taxable each year on trust contributions. In certain situations, highly-compensated employees are taxed on yearly earnings, including unrealized capital gains, municipal bond income, or even the inside build-up of life insurance. Further, because the IRS considers the trust itself to be a separately taxable entity, the earnings are taxed <u>twice</u>, once to the employee and once to the trust. To the extent that contributions and earnings have been previously taxed to the employee, distributions should be received free of income tax.

IRC Sec. 409A

The American Jobs Creation Act of 2004 included new IRC Sec. 409A, which added to federal income tax law numerous requirements that a nonqualified deferred compensation plan must meet to avoid having deferred amounts treated as being received in the current year. If these requirements are not met, all current and past-deferred compensation, plus any earnings, are included in the employee's gross income for the current tax year. Further, an additional 20% tax is levied, plus an underpayment interest penalty. State or local law may differ.

Seek Professional Guidance

Given the complexities involved, and because the income tax penalties for not meeting the requirements of the Internal Revenue Code are significant, competent, professional guidance is strongly recommended.

Split-Dollar Arrangement

The term "split-dollar arrangement" refers to a method of paying for life insurance. In a typical contract, an employer and employee agree to split the cost (premiums) and benefits (cash-value and death benefits) of a permanent life insurance policy.

The agreement between the employee and employer can take many forms. The elements commonly found in split-dollar agreements are outlined below.

Policy Ownership

There are two basic forms of policy ownership[1] for split-dollar plans.

- **Endorsement method:** The employer owns the policy but a written endorsement is added to the policy which splits the benefits between the employer and the employee.

- **Collateral assignment:** The employee owns the policy and assigns certain interests in the policy to the employer as collateral for payments made by the employer.

Splitting the Cost (premiums)

Dividing the cost of a policy can be done in any manner desired. Listed below are several typical payment arrangements:

- **Classic method.**
  - Employer pays an amount equal to the annual cash-value buildup.
  - Employee pays the balance.
- **Employer-pay-all method.**
  - Employer pays the entire premium.
  - Employee is taxed on the value of the economic benefit received.

---

[1] This report highlights split-dollar arrangements in the employer and employee context. Split-dollar arrangements are also possible between other parties, for example between a corporation and a shareholder, an employer and an independent contractor, a partnership and a partner, or a private individual and a trust.

Making the Payment

- **Employer pay all:** The employer pays the entire premium; the employee pays tax on the value of the economic benefits received.

- **Executive bonus plan:** The employer pays a bonus to the employee. From the bonus, the employee pays the economic benefit portion of the premium. The bonus payment is a deductible expense to the employer and taxable income to the employee. Some agreements provide an extra bonus amount to cover the additional tax due.

Splitting the Benefits

The employer and employee can decide to split the policy benefits in any way they wish.

- **Classic method.**

  - **Employer's share:** At death, the employer receives the greater of the cash value or the total premiums paid.

  - **Employee's share:** The employee's beneficiary receives the balance of the proceeds, e.g., the face amount less the amount repaid to the employer.

- **Employer-pay-all method.**

  - **Employer's share:** At death, the employer recovers the agreed-upon amount.

  - **Employee's share:** The employee's beneficiary receives the balance of the proceeds, e.g., the face amount less the sum paid to the employer.

A Few Uses of Split-Dollar

- **Fringe benefit:** Since the employer can pick and choose those employees who will benefit, split-dollar can be used to attract and retain key executives.

- **Estate planning:** When the estate is large enough to incur a federal estate tax (a taxable estate in excess of $11,180,000 in 2018),[1] an estate owner may consider removing life insurance from the estate. One way of reducing death taxes is the irrevocable life insurance trust.

---

[1] This is the "applicable exclusion amount", the dollar value of assets protected by from federal estate tax by an individual's applicable credit amount. In 2017, the applicable exclusion amount was $5,490,000.

- **Business continuation:** In a family-owned business there is a risk of adverse tax treatment when the corporation redeems the deceased owner's stock. See IRC Secs. 302 and 318. The proceeds of corporate owned life insurance might also create a corporate AMT problem. Under a corporate stock redemption the surviving stockholders would own stock worth more, but with an unchanged cost basis. Using a cross-purchase buy-sell agreement funded with life insurance can eliminate these problems. Differences between the owners in age and/or percentage of ownership may cause the life insurance premiums to be expensive for some stockholders. A split-dollar arrangement may assist each stockholder in purchasing enough insurance on the other stockholder(s).

- **Group term replacement:** Nondiscrimination rules can limit the amount of group term insurance available to key executives. With a split-dollar plan, executives can have increased protection now and substantial benefits at retirement.

Federal Taxation of Split-Dollar Arrangements

Split-dollar arrangements are subject to a complex web of federal income tax law[1] and regulation, including:

- **Treasury Decision 9092:** Under the final federal regulations contained in Treasury Decision 9092, issued on September 11, 2003, many of the economic benefits of a split-dollar arrangement will be treated as currently taxable. Such taxable benefits may include: (1) the value of current life insurance protection; (2) accrued cash value; (3) imputed loan interest; or (4) premium contributions from the non-owner of the policy. Depending on the relationship between the parties to a split-dollar arrangement, the economic benefits may be treated for tax purposes as compensation, dividends, a capital contribution, a gift, or "a transfer having a different tax character." Under certain circumstances, death benefits paid to a beneficiary (other than a policy owner) will be taxable income.

---

[1] The discussion here concerns federal income tax law; state or local law may vary.

- **IRC Sec. 409A – nonqualified deferred compensation:** IRC Sec. 409A concerns the federal income tax treatment of nonqualified deferred compensation agreements. Income deferred under an arrangement which does not meet the requirements of IRC Sec. 409A is generally subject to income taxation in the current year, including substantial penalties and interest. In some instances, a split-dollar arrangement may be deemed to come under the provisions of IRC Sec. 409A. See Treasury Decision 9321 and Notice 2007-34 for further details.

- **Employer-owned life insurance contracts:** Under federal law, amounts received under a life insurance contract paid by reason of the death of the insured are generally excluded from income. Under the provisions of the Pension Protection Act of 2006, however, death proceeds paid to an employer from a life policy owned by the employer on the life of an employee are generally includable in income, unless certain requirements are met. If these regulatory requirements are met, the death benefit can be received income tax free. This law was effective for contracts issued after August 17, 2006, except for policies acquired in an IRC Sec. 1035 exchange. Until the full scope of this new legislation is clarified by the IRS, caution is advised. See IRC Sec. 101(j).

Seek Professional Guidance

Split-dollar arrangements involve complex legal, tax and insurance questions. The guidance of a Certified Public Accountant (CPA), IRS Enrolled Agent (EA), or other financial professionals is strongly recommended.

Federal Taxation of Split-Dollar Arrangements

On September 11, 2003, the Treasury Department and the Internal Revenue Service (IRS) released Treasury Decision 9092, containing final regulations on the taxation of split-dollar arrangements for the purpose of federal income, employment, self-employment and gift taxes.[1] The issuance of these final regulations came after several years of regulatory review and largely follow proposed regulations issued in 2002 and 2003.

The final regulations were effective for split-dollar arrangements entered into after September 17, 2003, and to arrangements entered into before September 18, 2003, but later materially modified. Certain "grandfathering" and "safe harbor" provisions apply to arrangements entered into before September 17, 2003.

What Is a Split-Dollar Arrangement?

In general terms, a split-dollar arrangement is an agreement between two or more parties to share the benefits and/or costs of a permanent life insurance policy. Under the final regulations, it is generally any arrangement with the following elements:

- **Parties:** Includes the owner of the life insurance contract and a non-owner.

- **Premium payer:** Either party pays all or part of the premiums.

- **Premium recovery:** One of the parties paying the premiums is entitled to recover (conditionally or otherwise) all or any portion of those premiums.

- **Premium security:** Recovery of premiums paid is made from, or secured by, the proceeds of the life insurance policy.

This definition covers a range of relationships, like those between employer and employee, service recipient and service provider, corporation and shareholder, or donor and donee.

Who Owns the Policy?

The benefits of split-dollar arrangements will be taxed under one of two mutually-exclusive "regimes", depending on who owns the life insurance policy. Generally, if the employer, service recipient, corporation, or donor is the owner, the "economic benefit" regime applies.

---

[1] The rules discussed here concern federal law; state and local law may differ.

Federal Taxation of Split-Dollar Arrangements

If the employee, service provider, shareholder, or donee is the owner, the "loan" regime applies.

The "owner" is generally the person or entity named in the life insurance contract as the owner. Under a major exception to this rule, an employer, service recipient, or donor will be treated as the owner (regardless of who actually owns the contract) if, at all times, the only benefit available to an employee, service provider, or donee is the value of current life insurance protection. The final regulations include ownership attribution rules for certain compensatory split-dollar arrangements. A "non-owner" is generally any person or entity other than the contract owner who has an interest in the policy.

Economic Benefit Regime

Under the economic benefit regime, the owner of the policy is considered to be providing economic benefits to the non-owner. This regime generally applies to split-dollar agreements traditionally described as "endorsement" arrangements.

Depending on the relationship between the owner and non-owner, these economic benefits could be treated for tax purposes as compensation, dividends, a capital contribution, a gift, or "a transfer having a different tax character." The value of these benefits, reduced by any consideration paid by the non-owner to the owner, is generally measured on the last day of the non-owner's taxable year[1] and may include the following:

- **Current life insurance protection:** The value of current life insurance protection is generally calculated using an IRS-provided premium factor, published in the Internal Revenue Bulletin. Currently, this is Table 2001. If certain requirements are met, the insurer's one-year term rates may be used.

- **Cash values available to the non-owner:** Defined as cash values to which the non-owner has current[2] access, to the extent not taken into account in a prior taxable year.

- **Other:** These include the value of any other economic benefits provided to the non-owner, to the extent not taken into account in a prior taxable year.

There are a number of other tax consequences to keep in mind:

---

[1] As an alternative, the parties could agree to use the policy anniversary date.

[2] In general, these are cash values to which the non-owner has a current or future right, which are directly or indirectly accessible by the non-owner, and which are inaccessible to the owner or the owner's general creditors.

- **Non-owner payments are income to the owner:** Any amount paid by the non-owner to the owner for any economic benefit is included in the owner's gross income.

- **Investment in the contract:** In a split-dollar arrangement, only the owner of a life insurance policy may have a basis in the contract. Therefore, a non-owner has no basis in the policy until the policy (or an undivided interest) is transferred to the non-owner.

- **Amounts received under the life insurance contract:** The final regulations provide that any amount received under the life contract (other than an amount received by reason of death) and provided to the non-owner is treated as though paid by the insurance company to the owner and then by the owner to the non-owner. Death benefits paid to a beneficiary (other than the owner of the policy) are excluded from income under IRC Sec. 101(a) only to the extent such amounts are due to current life insurance protection provided to the non-owner under the agreement, the cost of which was paid by the non-owner, or which the non-owner has taken into account as an economic benefit.

Loan Regime

Under this regime, the non-owner is viewed as making an interest-bearing loan to the owner. The loan regime generally applies to "collateral assignment" arrangements.

A payment made pursuant to a split-dollar life insurance arrangement is a split-dollar loan, and the owner and non-owner are treated, respectively, as borrower and lender, if:

- **Payments:** A payment is made (directly or otherwise) from the non-owner to the owner;

- **Payment is a loan:** The payment is a loan under general federal tax principles, or a reasonable person would expect the payment to be repaid in full; and

- **Payment source:** The repayment is to be made from (or is secured by) the policy's death benefit, cash surrender value, or both.

Each premium payment under a split-dollar arrangement is a separate loan for federal tax purposes. If a split-dollar loan does not provide for an adequate rate of interest, it is considered a "below-market" loan and is recharacterized as a loan with interest at the applicable federal rate (AFR). The regulations presume a transfer by the lender to the borrower of the interest shortfall, and further presume this amount to be repaid to the lender as interest due. Other regulations with regard to forgiven interest apply.

Gift-Tax Treatment of Private Split-Dollar Arrangements

The final regulations make clear that the same general principles apply to private split-dollar arrangements. Premium payments in private split-dollar arrangement may be considered gifts or loans, with consequent federal tax results.

Sarbanes-Oxley Act of 2002

One section of the Sarbanes-Oxley Act of 2002 prohibits publicly traded companies from making certain loans to directors and executives. The final IRS split-dollar regulations leave the interpretation and administration of Sarbanes-Oxley to the Securities and Exchange Commission (SEC). In the absence of any guidance from the SEC, it remains unclear as to whether or not Sarbanes-Oxley applies to split-dollar arrangements.

IRC Sec. 409A – Nonqualified Deferred Compensation

IRC Sec. 409A concerns the federal income tax treatment of nonqualified deferred compensation arrangements. Income deferred under an arrangement which does not meet the requirements of IRC Sec. 409A is generally subject to taxation in the current year, including substantial penalties and interest. Most of the final regulations concerning IRC Sec. 409A were released in TD 9321, on April 10, 2007.

Notice 2007-34, released at the same time as the final 409A regulations, provides general guidance regarding on how IRC Sec. 409A applies to split-dollar arrangements. As explained in the notice, split-dollar arrangements which provide only death benefits are generally exempt from IRC Sec. 409A. Arrangements which provide for certain short-term (2-1/2 months) deferrals of compensation are also generally exempt.

Notice 2007-34 also listed examples of split-dollar arrangements to which IRC Sec. 409A would apply. For example, an endorsement split-dollar arrangement, taxed under the economic benefit regime, would come under IRC Sec. 409A if it includes a promise by the employer to transfer a policy's cash value to the employee at retirement. A split-dollar arrangement taxed under the loan regime would come under IRC. Sec. 409A if it provides that loan amounts can be waived, cancelled, or forgiven in the future.

Federal Taxation of Split-Dollar Arrangements

Because both the federal law and regulation are complex, caution is advised to ensure that a split-dollar arrangement does not come within the scope of IRC Sec. 409A.

Employer-Owned Life Insurance Contracts

Under federal law, amounts received under a life insurance contract paid by reason of the death of the insured are generally excluded from income. Under the provisions of the Pension Protection Act of 2006, however, death proceeds from a life policy owned by an employer on the life of an employee are generally includable in income, unless certain requirements are met. This law was effective for contracts issued after August 17, 2006, except for policies acquired in an IRC Sec. 1035 exchange. See IRC Sec. 101(j).

Seek Professional Guidance

Given the complexities involved, those considering or involved in a split-dollar arrangement are advised to seek the help of appropriate professional counselors.

Split-Dollar Arrangement

Deferred Compensation - Collateral Assignment Method

EMPLOYER	Employee assigns right to collect amounts paid after his or her death.	EMPLOYEE
Pays the portion of the premium in excess of what the employee pays.	Employer pays bonus to employee to cover costs of premiums (optional).	Pays the portion of the premium equal to the economic benefit[1] he or she receives.

INSURANCE COMPANY

Death/Retirement of Employee

AT RETIREMENT	AFTER DEATH OCCURS
• Employer borrows cash value tax free[2]. • Employer pays income to employee as retirement benefit. • Payments are tax-deductible to employer. • Payment may be grossed up to increase payment to employee.	• Employer recovers values per split-dollar agreement. • Family, beneficiaries or heirs get back policy proceeds less the amount passing to the employer. • Employer may optionally pay out income to the employee's heirs.

Note: This diagram illustrates a very basic variety of split-dollar plan which can be modified to meet the needs of both employer and employee. A separate agreement is required to address the deferred compensation aspect of this arrangement.

---

[1] Under Treasury Decision 9092, (September 11, 2003) many economic benefits of a split-dollar arrangement are currently taxable; death benefits paid to a beneficiary other than the policy owner may also be taxable. Under Treasury Decision 9321 and IRS Notice 2007-34, (April 10, 2007), some split-dollar arrangements may come under the requirements of IRC Sec. 409A concerning nonqualified deferred compensation. Those considering a split-dollar arrangement should first consult with their legal and/or tax advisors. State or local law may vary.

[2] Interest charges may apply. Loans reduce death benefits. Borrowed amounts may be taxable and subject to a 10% penalty if the policy is a MEC. For details see policy information and insurance ledger.

How Split-Dollar Collateral Assignment Works

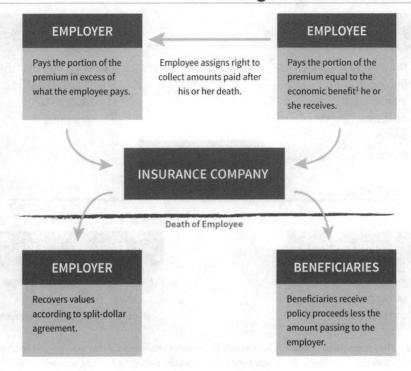

EMPLOYER

Pays the portion of the premium in excess of what the employee pays.

Employee assigns right to collect amounts paid after his or her death.

EMPLOYEE

Pays the portion of the premium equal to the economic benefit[1] he or she receives.

INSURANCE COMPANY

Death of Employee

EMPLOYER

Recovers values according to split-dollar agreement.

BENEFICIARIES

Beneficiaries receive policy proceeds less the amount passing to the employer.

Note: This diagram illustrates a very basic variety of split-dollar arrangement which can be modified to meet the needs of both employer and employee.

---

[1] Under Treasury Decision 9092, (September 11, 2003) many economic benefits of a split-dollar arrangement are currently taxable; death benefits paid to a beneficiary other than the policy owner may also be taxable. Under Treasury Decision 9321 and IRS Notice 2007-34, (April 10, 2007), some split-dollar arrangements may come under the requirements of IRC Sec. 409A concerning nonqualified deferred compensation. Those considering a split-dollar arrangement should first consult with their legal and/or tax advisors. State or local law may vary.

Split-Dollar Arrangement
Endorsement Method

EMPLOYER		EMPLOYEE
Owns policy and pays the portion of the premium in excess of what the employee pays.[1]	Employer endorses to employee the right to a part of policy proceeds and to name beneficiary	Pays the portion of the premium agreed on in the split-dollar arrangement.[2]

INSURANCE COMPANY

Death of Employee

EMPLOYER	EMPLOYEE'S HEIRS
Recovers values according to split-dollar agreement.[3]	Family, beneficiaries or heirs get back policy proceeds, less the amount passing to the employer.

Note: This diagram illustrates a very basic variety of split-dollar arrangement, in the employer and employee context. Split-dollar arrangements are also possible between other parties, for example, between a corporation and a shareholder, an employer and an independent contractor, a partnership and a partner, or a private individual and a trust. Split-dollar arrangements can be modified to meet the specific needs of the parties involved.

---

[1] Under Treasury Decision 9092, (September 11, 2003) many economic benefits of a split-dollar arrangement are currently taxable; death benefits paid to a beneficiary other than the policy owner may also be taxable. Under Treasury Decision 9321 and IRS Notice 2007-34, (April 10, 2007), some split-dollar arrangements may come under the requirements of IRC Sec. 409A concerning nonqualified deferred compensation. Those considering a split-dollar arrangement should first consult with their legal and/or tax advisors. State or local law may vary.

[2] In an employer-pay-all agreement, the employee pays nothing.

[3] Under federal law, amounts received under a life insurance contract paid by reason of the death of the insured are generally excluded from income Under the provisions of the Pension Protection Act of 2006, death proceeds from a life insurance policy owned by an employer on the life of an employee are generally includable in income, unless certain requirements are met. The law was effective for contracts issued after August 17, 2006, except for contracts acquired in an IRC Sec. 1035 exchange. Professional legal and tax guidance is strongly recommended.

Split-Dollar Arrangement Funding an Irrevocable Life Insurance Trust

Since the federal estate tax is imposed on all the assets inside an estate, many people prefer to reduce this tax by arranging to have some of their assets outside of their estate. One method of achieving this is the Irrevocable Life Insurance Trust (ILIT), a type of trust designed primarily to own life insurance policies. At death, the policy proceeds are used to provide additional dollars for estate liquidity needs. Such a trust takes maximum advantage of the gift tax laws and at the same time ensures that the proceeds of any policies inside the trust are received free of federal income and estate taxes.[1]

A split-dollar life insurance arrangement can help a key employee achieve this important estate-planning goal.

During Life

In general, the following steps would be taken:

- The employee establishes an irrevocable life insurance trust.

- The trustee of the trust obtains life insurance on the life of the employee, naming the trust as beneficiary of the policy.

- The employer and the trust enter into a split-dollar agreement, providing for a sharing of the premiums and death benefits of the policy owned by the trust. Typically the trust will pay that portion of the premium equal to the economic benefit received. The employer pays the remaining balance. As a part of the agreement, the trust assigns the policy to the employer as security for the repayment of premiums advanced.
- The employee gifts funds to the trust, to allow the trust to pay its portion of the premium. The employer may, if desired, bonus sufficient funds to the employee to cover these gifts.

---

[1] The discussion here concerns federal income and estate tax law. State or local law may vary.

Split-Dollar Arrangement Funding an ILIT

At Death

- The insurance company typically returns to the employer the amounts specified in the split-dollar agreement.

- The balance of the policy proceeds is paid directly to the trustee of the irrevocable life insurance trust. The trust (if trust provisions so provide) may then lend the funds to the employee's estate, or may use them to purchase assets from the estate. The executor would then have the cash necessary to pay the estate settlement costs without increasing the taxable estate.

- Ultimately, assets in the trust are distributed to the employee's beneficiaries.

Taxation Issues

Under Treasury Decision 9092 (September 11, 2003), many economic benefits of a split-dollar arrangement are currently taxable. Death benefits paid under a split-dollar arrangement to a beneficiary other than the policy owner may be taxable. For federal income tax purposes, split-dollar arrangements funding an irrevocable life insurance trust are generally taxed under the "loan" regime in which a non-owner (generally the business) is treated as making an interest-bearing loan to the policy owner (generally the employee). Additionally, under Treasury Decision 9321 and IRS Notice 2007-34 (April 10, 2007), some split dollar arrangements may come under the requirements of IRC Sec. 409A concerning nonqualified deferred compensation.

Because of the tax complexities involved, those considering a split-dollar arrangement should first consult with their legal and/or tax advisors. State of local income tax law may vary.

How Split-Dollar Funding A Life Insurance Trust Works

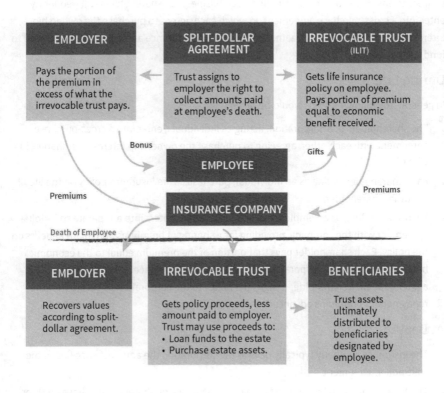

EMPLOYER

Pays the portion of the premium in excess of what the irrevocable trust pays.

SPLIT-DOLLAR AGREEMENT

Trust assigns to employer the right to collect amounts paid at employee's death.

IRREVOCABLE TRUST (ILIT)

Gets life insurance policy on employee. Pays portion of premium equal to economic benefit received.

Bonus

EMPLOYEE

Gifts

Premiums

INSURANCE COMPANY

Premiums

Death of Employee

EMPLOYER

Recovers values according to split-dollar agreement.

IRREVOCABLE TRUST

Gets policy proceeds, less amount paid to employer. Trust may use proceeds to:
• Loan funds to the estate
• Purchase estate assets.

BENEFICIARIES

Trust assets ultimately distributed to beneficiaries designated by employee.

Note: Under Treasury Decision 9092, (September 11, 2003) many economic benefits of a split-dollar arrangement are currently taxable; death benefits paid to a beneficiary other than the policy owner may also be taxable. Under Treasury Decision 9321 and IRS Notice 2007-34, (April 10, 2007), some split-dollar arrangements may come under the requirements of IRC Sec. 409A concerning nonqualified deferred compensation. Those considering a split-dollar arrangement should first consult with their legal and/or tax advisors. State or local law may vary.

Split-Dollar Arrangement Funding a Cross-Purchase Agreement

In order to ensure the orderly continuation of a business, co-shareholders will frequently enter into a cross-purchase agreement, in which each agrees to purchase the ownership interest of the other in case of death. A split-dollar life insurance arrangement can be used to fund such a need.

During Life

In general, the following steps would be taken:

- The shareholders of a corporation, acting as individuals, enter into a cross-purchase agreement with each other, agreeing to purchase the ownership interest of a shareholder who dies.
- Each shareholder, acting as an individual, purchases a life insurance policy on the life of the other shareholder.
- Each shareholder, as an employee of the corporation, enters into a separate split-dollar agreement with the company, providing for a sharing of premiums and death benefits on the policy. Each shareholder pays that portion of the premium equal to the economic benefit[1] received. The corporation pays the remaining balance. As a part of the agreement, each shareholder assigns the policy to the corporation as security for the repayment of premiums advanced.

At Death

- The insurance company typically pays to the corporation the amounts specified in the split-dollar agreement.
- The balance of the policy proceeds is paid to the surviving shareholder. These funds are used to purchase the deceased shareholder's stock from his or her estate.

---

[1] Under Treasury Decision 9092, (September 11, 2003) many economic benefits of a split-dollar arrangement are currently taxable; death benefits paid to a beneficiary other than the policy owner may also be taxable. Under Treasury Decision 9321 and IRS Notice 2007-34, (April 10, 2007), some split-dollar arrangements may come under the requirements of IRC Sec. 409A concerning nonqualified deferred compensation. Those considering a split-dollar arrangement should first consult with their legal and/or tax advisors. State or local law may vary.

How Split-Dollar Funding A Cross-Purchase Agreement Works

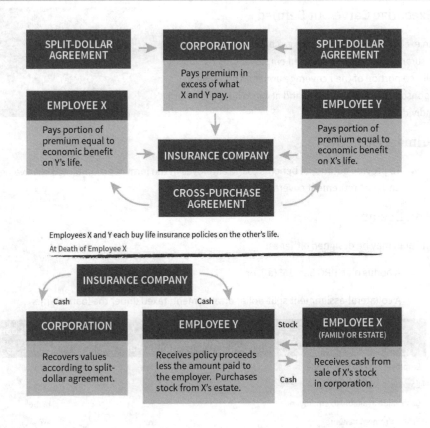

Employees X and Y each buy life insurance policies on the other's life.

At Death of Employee X

Note: Under Treasury Decision 9092, (September 11, 2003) many economic benefits of a split-dollar arrangement are currently taxable; death benefits paid to a beneficiary other than the policy owner may also be taxable. Under Treasury Decision 9321 and IRS Notice 2007-34, (April 10, 2007), some split-dollar arrangements may come under the requirements of IRC Sec. 409A concerning nonqualified deferred compensation. Those considering a split-dollar arrangement should first consult with their legal and/or tax advisors. State or local law may vary.

Executive Carve-Out Plan

An Alternative to Group Term Life Insurance

Executive Carve Out Defined

An executive "carve-out" plan is a plan which provides life insurance coverage on selected employees, by carving out all or a portion of their coverage under an employer-sponsored group term plan, and also provides them with individual policies.

Primary Objective

- To provide additional benefits to the employee in the form of accumulated cash values and post retirement coverage.

Plan Design

The plan may be designed either as:

- A bonus plan [IRC Sec. 162(a)], or

- A collateral-assignment split-dollar arrangement, taxed under the loan regime.

Advantages	IRC Sec. 162 Bonus Plans	Split-Dollar Loan Regime
Employer cost tax deductible	Yes	No
Employer cost recoverable	No	Yes
Cash value available to employee	Yes	Maybe[1]
Post retirement benefits	Yes	Yes
Employer discretion for coverage	Yes	Yes

---

[1] Subject to collateral assignment.

Executive Bonus Arrangement[1]

An executive bonus arrangement is a method of compensating selected key employees in which the employer pays the premiums of a life insurance policy covering the employee's life.

How the Plan Works

- **Life insurance policy:** The employee purchases, and is the owner of, a life insurance policy on his or her own life. The employee retains – at all times – the right to name the policy beneficiary and to receive the death benefit.

- **Employer not a beneficiary:** The employer cannot be the beneficiary, either directly or indirectly, of the insurance policy.

- **Written agreement:** A written agreement provides for payment of a "bonus" in exchange for the employee's agreement to continue working for the employer. The employer may also wish to pay a "double bonus" to help cover the employee's additional income tax liability.

- **Premium Payments:** The employer may make the premium payments directly to the life insurance company, or the payments may be included in the employee's paycheck, with the employee paying the premiums.

- **Tax treatment – employee:** The employee includes in current income – and pays tax on – the net premium paid by the employer.

- **Tax treatment – employer:** Subject to the "unreasonable compensation" rules, and as long as the employer has no interest in the policy, the additional compensation is deductible to the employer as an ordinary and necessary business expense.

Benefit to Employer	Benefit to Executive
Can reward selected key executives, with varying coverage amounts.	Executive owns the policy. If he or she changes employers, the policy is not lost.
Simple to implement, with little or no administration costs	Accumulated cash values can be used in emergencies, at retirement, or for personal investments.[2]
Premium costs are tax deductible.	Death benefit is generally received income-tax free.
Can be stopped without IRS approval or restrictions.	Proceeds may be used for estate settlement costs.

---

[1] The discussion here concerns federal income tax law. State or local income tax law may vary.

[2] A policy loan or withdrawal will generally reduce cash value and death benefits. If a policy lapses, or is surrendered with a loan outstanding, the loan will be treated as taxable income in the current year, to the extent of gain in the policy. Policies considered to be Modified Endowment Contracts (MECs) are subject to special rules.

How an Executive Bonus Arrangement Works

IRC Sec. 162

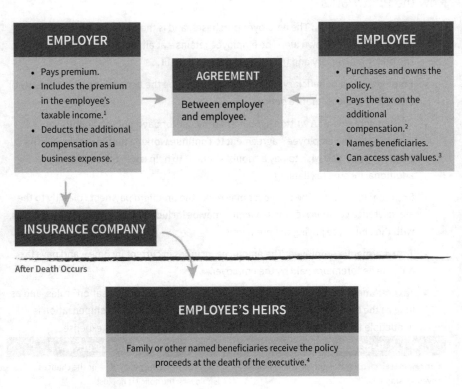

EMPLOYER

- Pays premium.
- Includes the premium in the employee's taxable income.[1]
- Deducts the additional compensation as a business expense.

AGREEMENT

Between employer and employee.

EMPLOYEE

- Purchases and owns the policy.
- Pays the tax on the additional compensation.[2]
- Names beneficiaries.
- Can access cash values.[3]

INSURANCE COMPANY

After Death Occurs

EMPLOYEE'S HEIRS

Family or other named beneficiaries receive the policy proceeds at the death of the executive.[4]

---

[1] The discussion here concerns federal income tax law. State or local law may differ.

[2] Employer may also choose to bonus the tax amounts to the employee, creating a net-no-cost scenario for the employee.

[3] A policy loan or withdrawal will generally reduce cash value and death benefits. If a policy lapses, or is surrendered with a loan outstanding, the loan will be treated as taxable income in the current year, to the extent of gain in the policy. Policies considered to be Modified Endowment Contracts (MECs) are subject to special rules.

[4] Death benefit is generally received free of income tax. See IRC Sec. 101(a).

Restricted Executive Bonus Arrangement

IRC Sec. 162[1]

A restricted executive bonus arrangement (REBA) is a method of compensating selected key employees in which the employer pays the premiums of a life insurance policy covering the employee's life.

How the Plan Works

- **Life insurance policy:** The employee purchases, and is the owner of, a life insurance policy on his or her own life. The employee retains – at all times – the right to name the policy beneficiary and to receive the death benefit.

- **Employer not a beneficiary:** The employer cannot be the beneficiary of the insurance policy.

- **Written agreement:** A written agreement provides for payment of a "bonus" in exchange for the employee's agreement to continue working for the employer. The employer may also wish to pay a "double bonus" to help cover the employee's additional income tax liability.

- **Policy endorsement:** An endorsement to the life insurance policy restricts the employee's access to certain policy benefits for a period of time. These restrictions may include the ability to assign or pledge the policy as collateral for a loan, surrender the policy, take cash withdrawals or borrow against policy cash values, or change ownership of the policy. Once the employee fulfills specific requirements, or certain events occur, the restrictive endorsement ends. These could include the employee reaching a certain age, retiring or becoming disabled, a release of the endorsement by the employer, or the employer's dissolution or bankruptcy.

- **Premium Payments:** The employer may make the premium payments to the insurance company, or they may be included in the employee's paycheck, with the employee paying the premiums.

---

[1] The discussion here concerns federal income tax law. State or local income tax law may vary.

Restricted Executive Bonus Arrangement

- **Tax treatment – employee:** The employee includes in current income – and pays tax on – the net premium paid by the employer.

- **Tax treatment – employer:** Subject to the "unreasonable compensation" rules, and as long as the employer has no interest in the policy, the additional compensation is deductible to the employer as an ordinary and necessary business expense.

Benefit to Employer	Benefit to Executive
Can reward selected key executives, with varying coverage amounts.	Executive owns the policy. If he or she changes employers, the policy is not lost.
Simple to implement, with little or no administration costs.	After restrictions end, accumulated cash values can be used in emergencies, at retirement, or for personal investments.[1]
Premium costs are tax deductible.	Death benefit is generally received income-tax free.
Plan can be terminated without IRS approval or restrictions.	Proceeds may be used for estate settlement costs.
Incentive for key employee to remain by restricting access to many policy benefits.	Access to all policy benefits once the terms of the agreement are met.

[1] A policy loan or withdrawal will generally reduce cash value and death benefits. If a policy lapses, or is surrendered with a loan outstanding, the loan will be treated as taxable income in the current year, to the extent of gain in the policy. Policies considered to be Modified Endowment Contracts (MECs) are subject to special rules.

How a Restricted Executive Bonus Arrangement Works

IRC Sec. 162

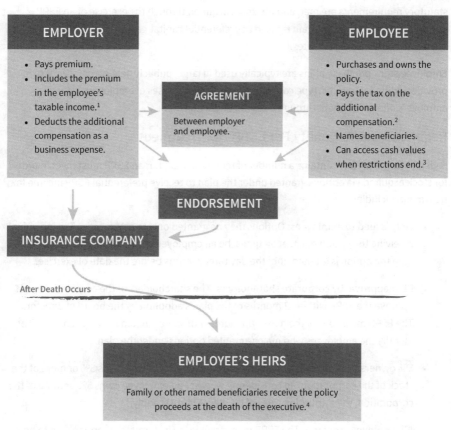

EMPLOYER

- Pays premium.
- Includes the premium in the employee's taxable income.[1]
- Deducts the additional compensation as a business expense.

AGREEMENT

Between employer and employee.

EMPLOYEE

- Purchases and owns the policy.
- Pays the tax on the additional compensation.[2]
- Names beneficiaries.
- Can access cash values when restrictions end.[3]

ENDORSEMENT

INSURANCE COMPANY

After Death Occurs

EMPLOYEE'S HEIRS

Family or other named beneficiaries receive the policy proceeds at the death of the executive.[4]

---

[1] The discussion here concerns federal income tax law. State or local law may differ.

[2] Employer may also choose to bonus the tax amounts to the employee, creating a net-no-cost scenario for the employee.

[3] A policy loan or withdrawal will general reduce cash value and death benefits. If a policy lapses, or is surrendered with a loan outstanding, the loan will be treated as taxable income in the current year, to the extent of gain in the policy. Policies considered to be Modified Endowment Contracts (MECs) are subject to special rules.

[4] Death benefit is generally received free of income tax. See IRC Sec. 101(a).

Employee Stock Purchase Plan

An "Employee Stock Purchase Plan" (ESPP) is an employee benefit program under which the employees of a corporation are granted the right to purchase shares in the employer corporation at a specified price (the "exercise" price), within a limited period of time. If all statutory requirements are met, and the stock acquired through the exercise of an ESPP option is sold at a profit, the gain is taxed at preferential capital-gains rates, rather than at higher, ordinary income tax rates.[1]

Employee stock purchase plans are typically used in large, publicly held corporations, to provide additional "equity" type compensation to broad classes of employees. Many employers offer this benefit through a payroll deduction plan.

Requirements To Qualify For ESPP Tax Treatment

Federal income tax law contains a number of requirements[2] that an ESPP must meet in order for stock acquired via options granted under the plan to receive preferential ESPP income tax treatment, including:

- **Only issued to employees:** Options may be granted only to employees. The individual receiving the option must, at all times, be an employee of the corporation from the date the option is granted until the day three months before the date of exercise.

- **Plan approval by corporate shareholders:** The shareholders of the corporation must approve the ESPP within 12 months of the plan's adoption by the board of directors. The ESPP must specify the maximum number of shares that may be issued as well as identify the employees who may be granted options under the plan.

- **5% owners:** Options may not be granted to an employee who owns 5% or more of the stock of the corporation. In considering whether an employee owns 5% or more of the corporation, the attribution rules of IRC Sec. 424(d)(1) apply.[3]

- **All employees covered:** The ESPP must provide, by its terms, that options are to be granted to all employees. However, certain classes of employees may be excluded:
  - Employees who have been employed less than two years,

---

[1] The discussion here concerns federal income tax law. State or local income tax law may differ.

[2] See IRC Sec. 423.

[3] Including stock owned by the employee's spouse, brothers or sisters, ancestors, and lineal descendants, or through a corporation, partnership, estate, or trust.

- Employees whose customary employment is 20 hours or less per week,

- Employees whose customary employment is not for more than five months in any calendar year, and

- Highly compensated employees, as defined in IRC Sec. 414(q).[1]

- **Equal rights and privileges:** The plan must provide that the same rights and privileges apply to all employees. An ESPP may limit the amount of stock that can be purchased by an employee in any one year to a uniform percentage of compensation, subject to an annual dollar maximum.

- **Option price:** The exercise price may not be less than the lesser of (1) 85% of the stock's fair market value on the date the option is granted, or (2) 85% of the stock's fair market value when the stock is purchased.

- **Option expiration:** The time period in which an option may be exercised is generally limited to 27 months. If the option price is not less than 85% of the stock's fair market value at the time the option is exercised, this time period may be up to five years.

- **Required holding period:** In order to qualify for preferential tax treatment, stock acquired under the plan must be held for the longer of (1) two years from the date the option was granted, or (2) one year from the date the stock is acquired by the employee.

- **Dollar limitation:** No more than $25,000 of employer stock may be purchased by an employee in any single calendar year.

- **Limited transferability:** The option must not be transferable by the individual to whom it is granted other than by will or the laws of descent and distribution, and it must be exercisable, during the individual's lifetime, only by such individual.

Federal Income Tax Treatment Of ESPP Options

Under an ESPP, the employee has no taxable income at the time an option is granted nor at the time an option is exercised. Similarly, the employer has no deductible business expense with regard to the option at the time of grant nor at the time of exercise. A taxable event will

---

[1] Generally, either a 5% owner or an employee who, in 2017, had compensation from the employer in excess of $120,000.

generally occur, however, when stock acquired via an ESPP option is sold or otherwise transferred. The tax treatment, for both the employee and the employer, will vary, depending on whether the stock is disposed of in a "qualifying" or a "disqualifying" transaction:

- **Qualifying disposition:** If an option qualifies as an ESPP option, and the employee holding the option exercises it, purchases the stock, and then keeps the stock long enough to meet the holding period requirements, a sale of the stock will be treated as a capital transaction. The capital gain or loss will be measured by the difference between the amount paid for the stock (the exercise price) and the amount received for the stock upon sale.

  - **Example 1:** George is an employee of X Corp. Three and one-half years ago, X Corp. granted George an ESPP option to buy 100 shares of X Corp. stock, at $10 per share. At the time of the grant, X Corp. stock was trading at $10 per share. Two years after receiving the option, George exercised it and purchased 100 shares of X Corp. stock, for a total price of $1,000. At the time he exercised the option, X Corp. stock was trading at $12 per share. However, there was no tax impact on either George or his employer in the year he exercised his option. Earlier this month, George sold his X Corp. stock for $1,500. On his income tax return for this year, George will list a long-term capital gain of $500, the difference between his basis, $1,000, and the amount received for the stock, $1,500. In this situation, X Corp. has no business deduction with regard to the option granted to George.

- **Disqualifying disposition:** A "disqualifying" disposition refers to a sale or transfer of stock acquired through exercise of an ESPP option where one or more of the statutory requirements needed to qualify for preferential income tax treatment have not been met. This can occur when the options are issued at a discount, or if the holding period requirements are not met.

Option issued at a discount: If, at the time an option is granted, the exercise price is less than 100% of the fair market value of the stock, and the employee disposes of the stock after meeting the holding period requirements, or dies while holding the shares, the employee is required to include in income as "compensation" the lesser of:

- The excess of the fair market value of the shares at the time the option was granted over the option price, or

Employee Stock Purchase Plan

- The excess of the fair market value of the shares at the time of disposition or death over the amount paid for the shares.

Any excess gain is treated as capital gain.

- **Example 2:** Sally's employer, Y Corp., grants her an option to buy 100 shares of Y Corp. stock at $20 per share at a time when the stock is trading at $22 per share. 18 months later, when the stock is trading at $23 per share, Sally exercises the option and purchases the stock. 14 months after buying the stock, Sally sells her shares for $30 per share. In the year of sale, Sally is required to include in income, as compensation, $200 ($2 per share x 100 shares), the difference between the exercise price ($20) and the fair market value on the date the option was granted ($22). The remaining gain, $800 ($8 per share x 100 shares) is treated as long-term capital gain.

Selling Price ($30 x 100 shares)	$3,000
Purchase price ($20 x 100 shares)	- 2,000
= Gain	$1,000
Amount reported as wages	-200
Amount reported as capital gain	**$ 800**

In the year of sale, Y Corp is entitled to a business deduction for the "compensation" included in Sally's income. If there were a loss on the sale, it would be a capital loss and Sally would not be required to include any compensation in income.

<u>Holding period requirement not met:</u> If the holding period requirement is not met, the amount that is required to be included in income as compensation is the amount by which the stock's fair market value exceeds the exercise price on the date the stock is purchased.

- **Example 3:** Mike's employer, Z Corp., grants him an option to buy 100 shares of Z Corp. stock at $20 per share at a time when the stock is trading at $22 per share. 12 months later, when the stock is trading at $23 per share, Mike exercises the option and purchases the stock. Six months after buying the stock, and before he fully meets the holding period requirements, Mike sells his shares for $30 per share. In the year of sale, Mike is required to include in income, as compensation, $300 ($3 per share x 100 shares), the difference between the exercise price ($20) and the fair market value on the date the shares were purchased ($23). His basis in the stock is thus $2,300. The remaining gain, $700, is treated as long-term capital gain.

Selling Price ($30 x 100 shares)	$3,000
Purchase price ($20 x 100 shares)	- 2,000
= Gain	$1,000
Amount reported as wages	-300
Amount reported as capital gain	**$ 700**

In the year of sale, Z Corp is entitled to a business deduction for the "compensation" included in Mike's income. If the stock is sold at a loss, it is a capital loss.

Seek Professional Guidance

An employee stock purchase plan represent an opportunity to benefit, on a tax-favored basis, from the long-term growth of a corporate enterprise. Given the complexities of income tax law, and the sometimes volatile nature of securities markets, the guidance of tax and investment professionals is strongly recommended.

Employer-Owned Life Insurance

There are many situations in the business world where employer ownership of a life insurance contract on the life of an employee plays a vital role in the financial life of the business. For example, employer-owned life insurance (EOLI) can help defray the often high costs involved in recruiting and training an individual to replace a "key" employee. EOLI contracts are also commonly used as a funding source for buy-sell agreements and non-qualified deferred compensation arrangements.

Generally, under federal income tax law,[1] the proceeds of a life insurance contract payable because of the death of the insured are excluded from income. However, under IRC Sec. 101(j) the proceeds of an EOLI contract are generally excluded from income only to the extent of the premiums and other amounts paid by the policyholder for the contract. Any "excess" death benefit above this amount is included in gross income.

IRC Sec. 101(j) also contains a series of rules which, if followed carefully, allow the total death benefit of an EOLI life insurance contract to be received income-tax free.

Key Definitions

- **Employer-owned life insurance contract:** A life insurance contract that is (1) owned by a person engaged in a trade or business and under which such person (or a related person) is directly or indirectly a beneficiary under the contract, and (2) which covers the life of an insured who is an employee of the "applicable policyholder" on the date the contract is issued.

- **Applicable policyholder:** Generally, the person who owns the contract. The term also includes any person who bears a relationship to the owner specified in IRC Sec. 267(b) or IRC Sec. 707(b)(1), or who is engaged in trades or businesses with the owner which are under "common control" within the meaning of IRC Sec. 52(a) or (b).

- **Insured:** An individual covered by the contract who is a U.S. citizen or resident. If the contract covers the joint lives of two individuals, the term "insured" includes both.
- **Employee:** In addition to the common law definition, the term "employee" includes an officer, director, and highly compensated employee (as defined in IRC Sec. 414(q)).

---

[1] The discussion here concerns federal income tax law. State or local law may vary.

Employer-Owned Life Insurance

Notice and Consent

<u>Before</u> the EOLI contract is issued, specific "Notice and Consent" requirements must be met:

- The employee must be notified in writing that the applicable policyholder intends to insure the employee's life and the maximum face amount for which the employee could be insured at the time the contract is issued.
- The employee must provide written consent to being insured under the contract and that the coverage may continue after the insured terminates employment.
- The employee must be informed in writing that the applicable policyholder will be the beneficiary of any proceeds payable upon the death of the employee.

Exceptions

Assuming that all of the "Notice and Consent" requirements have first been met, the proceeds from an EOLI contract paid because of the death of an employee will be received income-tax free if any of the following exceptions applies:

- **Recent employment:** If the insured was an employee any time during the 12-month period before death.

- **Executives:** If, at the time the policy was *issued*, the insured was a <u>director</u>, or a <u>highly compensated employee</u>, as defined under the rules relating to qualified retirement plans, determined without regard to the election regarding the top-paid 20 percent of employees, or a <u>highly compensated individual</u>, as defined under the rules relating to self-insured medical reimbursement plans, determined by substituting the highest-paid 35% of employees for the highest-paid 25% of employees.

- **Amounts paid to the insured's heirs:** Death proceeds are excluded from income to the extent that an amount is (1) paid to a family member[1] of the insured, to an individual who is the designated beneficiary of the insured under the contract (other than the applicable policyholder), to a trust established for the benefit of any such family member or designated beneficiary, or to the estate of the insured; or (2) is used to purchase an equity (or partnership capital or profits) interest in the applicable policyholder from such a family member, beneficiary, trust, or estate.

---

[1] A family member, as defined in IRC Sec. 267(c)(4) includes the individual's brothers and sisters, spouse, ancestors, and lineal descendants.

Transition Rule and IRC Sec.1035 Exchanges

IRC Sec. 101(j) generally applies to EOLI contracts issued after August 17, 2006. There is an exception for policies issued after that date which were acquired in an IRC Sec. 1035 exchange for a contract issued on or before that date. Any material change in the death benefit or other material change can result in the contract being treated as a new contract, and thus subject to IRC Sec. 101(j).[1]

Annual Reporting Requirement

IRC Sec. 6039I imposes both record keeping and annual reporting requirements on any employer that owns one or more EOLI contracts. IRS Form 8925 is used to make the required annual report.

Seek Professional Guidance

Given the complexities involved, and because the dollar cost of not meeting the requirements of IRC Sec. 101(j) can be high, competent professional guidance is strongly recommended.

---

[1] See IRS Notice 2009-48, Q&A14, for a description of changes to existing EOLI contracts which would not be considered "material" changes.

Executive Long-Term Care

Many employers recognize the importance of a competitive employee benefits package. Employer paid long-term care (LTC) insurance, provided to selected employees, is a tax-favored[1] benefit that can help a firm recruit and retain those key individuals who play an instrumental role in a firm's growth and success.

In General

- **Employer can discriminate:** The employer is generally free to select which employees are covered under the plan; the benefits are "carved –out" from those available to rank and file employees.

- **Spouses and other dependents:** If desired, the plan can also cover spouses and other dependents.

- **Employee owns the policy:** The employee owns the policy, making it portable.

Qualified LTC Insurance for Rank and File Employees

For federal income tax purposes, long-term care insurance comes in two types: (1) "qualified" LTC insurance, policies that meet certain requirements set by federal income tax law,[2] and (2) "non-qualified" LTC insurance. Expenditures for qualified long-term care services and premiums paid for qualified long-term care insurance are treated under the federal tax code as "amounts paid for medical care."

- **Employees – premium payments not includable in income:** The premiums paid by an employer for qualified LTC insurance for an employee are not includable in the employee's taxable income.

- **Employer – deductibility of premiums:** Employer-paid premiums for qualified long-term care insurance for employees are generally deductible by the employer.

- **Employee – deductibility of premiums:** If the employee pays the premiums, the deduction is generally limited to the amount (subject to the limits shown in the table below) that, when combined with other qualified medical expenses, exceeds 7.5% of the employee's adjusted gross income (AGI).[3]

---

[1] The discussion here concerns federal income tax law; state or local law may vary.

[2] See IRC Sec. 7702B(b).

[3] The 7.5% threshold applies to 2017 and 2018. Under current law, the threshold will increase to 10.0% for 2019 and later years.

Executive Long-Term Care

Age Before Close of Tax Year	2017 Limitation	2018 Limitation
40 or less	$410	$420
41 to 50	770	780
51 to 60	1,530	1,560
61 to 70	4,090	4,160
Over 70	5,110	5,200

- **Employees – benefits received under the policies:** Benefits received under a qualified LTC contract are generally excludable from income. The exclusion is limited to the greater of $360 per day (calendar year 2018),[1] or the total un-reimbursed LTC expenses actually incurred.

Qualified LTC Insurance – "C Corporation Owner/Employees

The federal income-tax treatment of employer-paid premiums for an owner/employee of a "C" corporation is the same as that for a rank and file employee. The employer can generally deduct the premiums paid, and the premiums are not included in the owner/employee's taxable income. Benefits received under the policy are received income-tax free, subject to the $360 per day or actual expenses incurred limitation.

Qualified LTC Insurance - Sole Proprietors & Other Owner/Employees

For a sole proprietor, a partner in a partnership, a more than 2% owner of an "S" corporation, or an owner/member of a limited liability company, the federal income tax treatment of employer-paid premiums for qualified LTC policies is somewhat different:

- **Employer – qualified LTC premiums deductible:** The employer may generally deduct the premiums for qualified LTC policies paid on behalf of owner/employees.

- **Owner/employee – premiums includable in gross income:** An owner/employee must include in his or her gross income the premiums paid by the employer for qualified LTC policies.

- **Owner/employee – premiums deductible on personal return:** The owner/employee is permitted to deduct on his or her personal income tax return, as an adjustment to gross income, the lesser of the amount paid on his or her behalf, or the age-based limitation set by federal income tax law.

---

[1] This amount was also $360 in 2017.

- **Owner/employee – benefits received under the policy:** Benefits received under the policy are generally received income-tax free, subject to the $360 per day or actual expenses incurred limitation.

Seek Professional Guidance

Employer-paid qualified LTC insurance can be a significant and highly attractive employee benefit. In considering such a benefit, the guidance of experienced financial professionals is strongly recommended.

Incentive Stock Option

An "Incentive Stock Option" (ISO) is an employee benefit though which an employee is granted the right to purchase shares in the employer corporation at a specified price (the "exercise" price), within a fixed period of time. If all statutory requirements are met, and the stock purchased with the ISO is sold at a profit, the gain is taxed at preferential capital-gains rates, rather than at higher, ordinary income tax rates.[1]

ISO plans are often used in larger, publicly held corporations to attract and retain key employees and executives.

Requirement To Qualify For ISO Tax Treatment

Federal income tax law contains a number of requirements that an employer stock-option plan must meet in order for stock acquired via options issued under the plan to receive preferential ISO income tax treatment, including:

- **Written plan:** The ISO must be issued under the terms of a written plan (on paper or in electronic form), approved by the shareholders of the corporation within 12 months of the plan's adoption by the board of directors. The plan must specify the total number of shares that may be issued via ISOs as well identify the employees, or class of employee, the plan is intended to benefit.[2]

- **Time limit on option issuance:** No options may be granted under the plan more than 10 years after the plan is adopted or approved, whichever comes first.

- **Exercise time limit:** An option may not be exercisable for more than 10 years.

- **Exercise price:** Generally, the option's exercise price must not be less than the fair market value of the stock on the date the option is granted.

- **Limited transferability:** The option must not be transferable by the individual to whom it is granted other than by will or the laws of descent and distribution, and it must be exercisable, during the individual's lifetime, only by such individual.

---

[1] The discussion here concerns federal income tax law. State or local income tax law may differ.
[2] There are no non-discrimination rules; the employer may pick and choose which employees to benefit.

- **Only issued to employees:** The individual receiving the ISO must, at all times, be an employee[1] of the granting corporation for a period extending from the date the option is granted until the day three months before the date of exercise.[2]

- **Required holding period:** Stock acquired under the terms of an ISO must be held for the longer of (1) two years from the date the option was granted, or (2) one year from the date the stock is acquired by the employee.

- **Dollar limitation:** ISO tax treatment is limited to the first $100,000 of aggregate fair market value of stock exercisable for the first time by any individual in any calendar year. Stock acquired via ISOs in excess of $100,000 is generally treated as having been acquired through a "non-statutory" stock option, with different income tax treatment.

- **10% shareholders:** An option is <u>not</u> considered to be an ISO if it is issued to an individual who owns, directly or indirectly, 10% or more of the employing corporation. This restriction does not apply if: (1) the exercise price is at least 110% of the stock's fair market value at the time the option is granted and (2) the option is exercisable for only five years after the grant date.

Federal Income Tax Treatment Of Incentive Stock Options

There is no tax impact at the time an ISO is granted to an employee. Tax issues arise when the option is exercised and when the acquired stock is later disposed of.

- **At time of exercise:** When the employee exercises the option, and purchases the stock, he or she has no income for regular income tax purposes, no employment (FICA or FUTA) taxes are due, and the employer has no business deduction. However, for Alternative Minimum Tax (AMT) purposes, the employee is generally required to recognize the difference between the exercise price and the stock's fair market value as an adjustment in computing AMT. The amount included in income as an AMT adjustment is added to the basis of the stock for computing AMT gain or loss.[3]

---

[1] Options may not be granted to non-employee directors or independent contractors.

[2] A disabled employee may exercise the option up to 12 months after terminating employment. For a deceased employee, the option may be exercised by the deceased's heirs at any time until the option expires.

[3] No AMT adjustment is required if the option is exercised, and the stock disposed of, in the same calendar year, or if the stock is disposed of in a "disqualifying" transaction.

- **Example 1:** George receives an ISO to purchase 100 shares of his employer's stock at $10 per share. George later exercises the option at a time when the stock is trading at $13 per share. On his income tax return for that year, George must include $300 as an AMT adjustment, the difference between the exercise price and the fair market value on the date he exercised the option. His basis in the stock for regular income tax purposes is $1,000; his basis in the stock for AMT purposes is $1,300.

The tax treatment applicable when stock acquired through an ISO is disposed of depends on whether it is done in a "qualifying" or a "disqualifying" transaction:

- **"Qualifying" disposition:** If a stock option qualifies as an ISO at the time of exercise, and the stock is held by the employee for the required holding period, the gain or loss on the sale of the stock is treated as a <u>capital</u> gain or loss.[1]

  - **Example 2:** Jane is granted an ISO to purchase 100 shares of her employer's stock, at $10 per share. 10 months later, she exercises the option and purchases the stock, paying $1,000 for her 100 shares. Three years after exercising the option, Jane sells the stock for $1,500. For the year of sale, Jane must recognize a long-term capital gain of $500 ($1,500 - $1,000). Her employer is not entitled to any business deduction with regard to the stock acquired through the ISO.

- **"Disqualifying" disposition:** If a stock option qualifies as an ISO at the time of exercise, but the stock is not held by the employee for the required holding period, the difference between the exercise price and the fair market value of the stock at the time of exercise is treated as compensation. Any gain above the fair market value is treated as a capital gain.

  - **Example 3:** Harry is granted an ISO to purchase 100 shares of his employer's stock, at $10 per share. 10 months later, he exercises the option and purchases the stock, paying a total of $1,000 for his 100 shares, at a time when the stock is trading at $12 per share. Six months after exercising the option, Harry sells his 100 shares for $1,500. Because he did not meet the holding period requirements, Harry must, for the year of sale, include $200 in income as compensation, the difference between what he paid for the stock and the fair market value of the shares at the time the

---

[1] The holding period for capital gain or loss purposes begins on the date the option is exercised.

option was exercised, ($1,200 - $1,000). The remaining $300 ($1,500 - $1,200) is treated as short-term capital gain. If otherwise allowable, Harry's employer is entitled to a business expense deduction for the $200 of compensation. No FICA or FUTA taxes are due and there is no withholding requirement.

Seek Professional Guidance

Incentive stock options represent an opportunity to benefit, on a tax-favored basis, from the long-term growth of a corporate enterprise. Given the complexities of income tax law, and the sometimes volatile nature of securities markets, the guidance of tax and investment professionals is strongly recommended.

Life Insurance in the Business World

Life insurance plays a number of important roles in the business world, benefiting business owners, employees, and family members.

Business Continuation

The loss of a business owner or a key employee can seriously damage a small business or even result in the business closing its doors. Advance planning can help cushion the impact of such events.

- **Death of a business owner:** If a business owner dies, a buy-sell agreement can provide a smooth transition of total ownership and control to those who will keep the business going. For a corporation, a stock-redemption agreement may be used to ease the transfer of the deceased owner's shares to the surviving shareholders. Life insurance is frequently used to fund these types of agreements.[1]

- **Key-employee insurance:** Life insurance on the life of a key employee helps to cover the costs of finding and training a replacement, as well as meeting any monetary obligations to the deceased employee's survivors.[1]

Retirement Planning

There are many ways in which life insurance is used in accumulating funds for retirement:

- **Fully-insured defined benefit retirement plan:** IRC Sec. 412(e)(3)[2] allows for the use of annuities and/or life insurance policies to fund retirement.

- **Life insurance inside qualified retirement plans:** Federal income tax law allows defined benefit retirement plans and certain types of defined contribution retirement plans to allocate a portion of the funds contributed each year to life insurance as a retirement funding vehicle.

- **Nonqualified deferred compensation:** These arrangements allow selected employees (the employer can pick and choose) to defer receipt of a portion of their compensation until a later date. These plans do not meet federal income tax requirements to be considered "qualified" plans. Life insurance can be used to informally fund such arrangements.

---

[1] Under the provisions of IRC Sec. 101(j), death proceeds from a life insurance policy owned by an employer on the life of an employee are generally includable in income, unless certain requirements are met. State or local income tax law may vary.

[2] Previously, IRC Sec. 412(i).

Life Insurance in the Business World

Estate and Survivor Financial Needs Planning

Life insurance also plays a significant role in estate and survivor needs planning:

- **Group term life insurance:** Group term life insurance can be provided to the employees of a business, with premiums generally much lower than individual term life policies. Generally, the first $50,000 of such coverage is tax-free to the employee.

- **Executive life insurance:** An employer can help fund employee-owned, individual life insurance policies for selected executives or key employees through either a "bonus" plan under IRC Sec. 162, or as a part of collateral assignment split-dollar arrangement.[1]

- **Death benefit only plan:** A Death Benefit Only (DBO) plan is a form of deferred compensation plan. In a DBO plan an employee defers a portion of his or her compensation. No benefits are payable during the employee's lifetime. At the employee's death, the deferred compensation is paid to the employee's named beneficiary, with the entire benefit being taxed as ordinary income.

Seek Professional Guidance

Correctly used, life insurance is a highly useful tool in the business world. However, careful attention must be paid to federal, state, and local law to ensure that all legal requirements are met. The guidance of knowledgeable legal, tax, employee benefit, and life insurance professionals is strongly recommended.

---

[1] "Split-dollar" arrangements are a way of paying for life insurance. In the business context, generally, an employer and an employee will agree to split the premiums and benefits of a life insurance policy.

Non-Statutory Stock Option

In general terms, a stock option is the right to purchase shares in a corporation at a specified price (the "exercise" price), within a fixed period of time. Under federal income tax law,[1] a "statutory" stock option is one that qualifies as an "incentive stock option" or that is granted under an employee stock purchase plan.

An option that does not qualify as a "statutory" stock option, and that is issued in conjunction with the performance of services, is considered a "non-statutory" stock option.[2] There are few regulatory restrictions with regard to the design of non-statutory stock option plans. A corporation can pick and choose which employees or independent contractors to benefit and the terms and conditions under which the options are granted can vary from one individual (or group of individuals) to the next. Non-statutory stock options are frequently used in larger, publicly-held corporations, as a way to attract and retain key employees and executives.

Federal Income Taxation Of Non-Statutory Stock Options

The tax treatment of non-statutory stock options generally depends on whether or not there is a "readily ascertainable fair market value" on the date the option is granted.

- **Readily ascertainable fair market value:** Generally, an option is considered to have a readily ascertainable fair market value if it is (1) traded on an established market, or (2) its fair market value can be otherwise measured with reasonable accuracy.[3] If either of these standards is met, the person receiving the option (the optionee) must include the fair market value of the option in income in the year the option is granted.

- **No readily ascertainable value:** If a stock option is not considered to have a readily ascertainable market value, there is generally no federal income tax impact until the option is exercised or otherwise transferred.

Options With A Readily Ascertainable Fair Market Value

If an option has a readily ascertainable fair market value on the date of grant, the optionee must include in income in the same year the fair market value of the option, less any amount

---

[1] The discussion here concerns federal income tax law. State or local income tax law may differ.

[2] Non-statutory stock options are also called "non-qualified" stock options.

[3] IRC Reg. 1.83-7(b)(2) lists a series of tests to determine the fair market value of the option under this alternative method.

he or she pays for the option (typically zero). The corporation treats an equivalent dollar amount as deductible "compensation," subject to FICA, FUTA, and wage withholding:

- **Example 1:** Harry is an employee of XYZ Corp. Harry was recently granted an option to buy 100 shares of XYZ stock at $10 per share. XYZ options are traded on an established market and, on the day of the grant, had a value of $15 per share. Harry must include $1,500 ($15 per share x 100 shares) in his income this year as additional compensation. XYZ Corp. is allowed a business deduction for the amount included in Harry's income; Harry's W-2 will show an additional $1,500 of compensation, less employment taxes and normal income tax withholding.

- **If the option lapses:** If an option expires without being exercised, the optionee has a capital loss on the date of expiration, generally equal to his or her basis[1] in the option. Depending on how long the option was held, the loss can be either short-term or long-term.

  - **Example 2:** Because of a prolonged stock market decline, Sally allows an option to purchase 100 shares of her employer's stock to expire. At the time the option was granted two years ago, Sally was required to include $1,000 in income as additional compensation. On her income tax return for the year the option expires, Sally may claim a $1,000 long-term capital loss.

- **Sale of the option:** If an optionee chooses to sell an option without exercising it, the transaction is treated as the sale of a capital asset, with the holding period measured from the date the option was granted to the date of sale.

  - **Example 3:** George is an independent contractor who has done consulting work for ABC Corp. Two years ago George was granted an option to purchase 100 shares of ABC Corp. stock, at $20 per share. ABC options are traded on an established market and, on the day of the grant, had a value of $10 per share. In the year the option was granted, George was required to include in income an additional $1,000 ($10 per share x 100 shares). However, because business has been slow lately, George decides to sell his option, at the current market price of $15 per share. On his income tax return for the year of the sale, George will treat the transaction as a long-term capital gain of $500, the $1,500 sales proceeds, less $1,000, his basis in the option.

---

[1] Typically, the amount included in income at the time the option was granted. If the optionee paid any additional money for the option, the extra amount would also be included in basis.

- **Exercising the option:** An optionee can also choose to exercise the option, and purchase the underlying stock. For federal income tax purposes, the stock acquired through exercise of the option is treated as a capital asset.

  - **Example 4:** Two years ago, Susan was given an option to purchase 100 shares of her employer's stock at $10 per share. At the time the option was granted, the option had a fair market value of $10 per share. On her income tax return for that year, Susan was required to include an additional $1,000 in income ($10 per share x 100 shares). This year, when the stock was trading at $25 per share, Susan exercises the option and purchases 100 shares. Susan's basis in the stock is $2,000, calculated as follows: $1,000, the amount previously included in income, plus $1,000, the cost to exercise the option this year ($10 per share x 100 shares).

  Susan's holding period in the stock begins the day after she exercises her option. If she waits more than one year before selling the stock, and then sells it for $30 per share, she will have a long-term capital gain of $1,000; the $3,000 sales proceeds, minus her basis of $2,000.

- **At death:** Because the option is taxed at grant, there is no special tax treatment if an optionee dies holding either an un-exercised option, or the underlying stock. The optionee's heirs generally take the asset at FMV on the date of death. Any subsequent sale or transfer is treated in the same manner as with any other investment property.

Options Without A Readily Ascertainable Fair Market Value

If an option does not have a readily ascertainable fair market value on the grant date, there is generally no taxable event until it is either exercised, sold, or otherwise transferred. In the tax year that the optionee recognizes income, the corporation treats an equivalent dollar amount as deductible "compensation," subject to FICA, FUTA, and wage withholding.

- **If the option lapses:** If the optionee allows the option to expire unexercised, there is generally no loss for income tax purposes.

  - **Example 5:** Five years ago, Bob was granted an option by his employer to buy 100 shares of the employer's stock at $10 per share. In that year Bob was not required to include any additional compensation in his gross income as a result of being granted the option. Since then the stock has steadily declined in value. This year the option expired, unexercised. Bob has no deductible loss as a result of the option expiration.

- **Sale of the option in an "arms-length" transaction:** If the optionee chooses to sell or otherwise dispose of the option, the income tax treatment is generally determined by whether or not the sale or disposition is in an "arms-length"[1] transaction. Such a sale will result in compensation to the optionee to the extent that the sales proceeds exceed any amount paid for the option.

  - **Example 6:** Barbara, an employee of EFG Corp., is granted an option to buy 100 shares of EFG Corp. stock at $20 per share. Barbara pays nothing for the option. Six months later, Barbara decides to sell her option to an unrelated third party in an arms-length transaction, at $25 per share. For the year of sale, Barbara must include $2,500 in gross income, the amount realized from the sale ($25 per share x 100 shares), less the price paid for the option (zero).

- **Sale of the option to a related party:** The sale or other disposition of the option to a "related party"[2] is treated as if it were done in a "non-arms-length" transaction.[3] In this situation, the optionee must include in income in the year of transfer any money or property received. When the transferee (the party purchasing the option) ultimately exercises the option, the optionee must also include in gross income the excess of the fair market value of the stock acquired by the transferee over the sum of the exercise price paid and any amount included in income at the time the option was transferred.

  - **Example 7:** Five years ago, Bill was granted an option by his employer to purchase 100 shares of the employer's stock, at $25 per share. Last year, Bill sold the option to his wife, for $10 per share, or $1,000. On last year's income tax return, Bill included $1,000 as additional compensation. This year, when the stock was trading at $50 per share, Bill's wife exercised the option and purchased the stock. Bill is required to include an additional $1,500 in gross income this year, the difference between the fair market value of the stock $5,000 ($50 per share x 100 shares) less the sum of the exercise price, $2,500 ($25 per share x 100 shares) plus the $1,000 Bill included in income last year.

---

[1] Generally, "arms length" refers to a sale or transfer to someone who is not related to the optionee.
[2] See IRS Reg. 1.83-7(a) for a definition of "related party."
[3] In some situations, non-arms-length transactions may be challenged by the IRS. See IRS Notice 2003-47.

- **Exercising the option:** At exercise, the optionee will generally recognize income to the extent that the fair market value of the stock exceeds the exercise price

  - **Example 8:** 18 months ago, Michael was granted a stock option by his employer to buy 200 shares of the employer's stock at $20 per share. This year, he purchased the stock when the shares were trading at $40 per share. On his income tax return for this year, Michael must include $4,000 as additional compensation, the difference between the market price of the stock at the time of his purchase, $8,000 ($40 per share x 200 shares) and the exercise price he paid, $4,000 ($20 per share x 200 shares).

- **Taxation at sale:** An optionee's basis in stock acquired through the exercise of a non-statutory stock option is equal to the exercise price plus the amount the optionee was required to include in income as a result of exercising the option. The optionee's holding period begins on the day after the stock is acquired.

  - **Example 9:** Continuing with Example 8, Michael's basis in his employer's stock is $8,000, the sum of the exercise price, $4,000, and the $4,000 that Michael was required to include in income as a result of exercising the option. If he holds the stock for more than a year, and then sells all 200 shares for a total sales price of $10,000, he will have, in the year of sale, a long-term capital gain of $2,000.

- **At death:** If an optionee dies holding an un-exercised stock option that was not taxed at the time of grant, any income or gain realized by the optionee's heirs by selling or otherwise disposing of the option is treated as income in respect of a decedent.

Restricted Property

If an individual receives stock or other property that has restrictions that affect its value, the individual does not include the value of the property in income until it has been "substantially vested." Property becomes substantially vested when it is:

- **Transferrable:** the owner can sell, gift, pledge or otherwise dispose of it; and

- **No substantial risk of forfeiture:** there is no good risk that the property will be taken away or lost.

In general, in the year that property becomes substantially vested, it must be included in income at its fair market value, less any amount paid for it.

Alternatively, an individual may elect, under IRC Sec. 83(b), to include the value of restricted property in income at the time of transfer. The election must be made within 30 days of receiving the property. With regard to non-statutory stock options, such an election is usually made when the amount that must be included in income is relatively low; any later appreciation would not be included in income as "compensation." The individual's basis for gain or loss would include the amount paid for it plus any amount included in income as compensation.

IRC Sec. 409A – Nonqualified Deferred Compensation

IRC Sec. 409A concerns the federal income tax treatment of nonqualified deferred compensation plans. Under such plans, an employee enters into an agreement with the employer to defer a portion of his or her compensation until a future date or event. If the requirements of IRC Sec. 409A are not met, all current and past-deferred compensation amounts, plus any earnings, are included in the employee's gross income for the current tax year. An additional 20% tax is levied, plus an underpayment interest penalty.[1]

In some situations, non-statutory stock options could be considered deferred compensation. To avoid having these options treated as "deferred compensation," the following rules must followed:[2]

- No option discount: The exercise price may never be less than the fair market value of the underlying stock on the date the option is granted.

- Taxation: The receipt, transfer, or exercise of the option must be subject to taxation under IRC Sec. 83.

- No deferral of compensation: The option may not include any feature for the deferral of compensation other than the deferral of recognition of income until the later of exercise or disposition of the option under IRC Reg. 1.83-7.

Seek Professional Guidance

Non-statutory stock options represent an opportunity to benefit, on a tax-favored basis, from the long-term growth of a corporate enterprise. However, given the complexities of income tax law, and the sometimes volatile nature of securities markets, the guidance of tax and investment professionals is strongly recommended.

---

[1] Interest is charged at the underpayment rate plus 1%.
[2] See IRS Notice 2005-1.

Considering a Charitable Gift

Charitable giving provides help to those less fortunate than ourselves.

Reasons for Making a Charitable Gift

Many persons make gifts or bequests to charitable organizations for a number of reasons. Some of the more common motivations would include the following:

- Compassion for those in need.

- Religious and spiritual commitment.

- Perpetuation of one's beliefs, values and ideals.

- Support for the arts, sciences and education.

- A desire to share one's good fortune with others.

Whatever the reasons, U.S. tax law is designed to encourage these gifts.

Different Types of Charitable Gifts

Some donors prefer to make outright gifts of cash or other valuable assets to their favorite charities. Other individuals, although they would like to make an outright gift, depend on the income from their assets for their daily needs. Often, such donors decide to wait until they die to transfer assets to a charity, through a will or trust.

However, there are methods which allow a donor to make a gift now, while still retaining an income for life. The most popular of these methods include:

- Charitable Remainder Annuity Trust

- Charitable Remainder Unitrust

- Pooled Income Fund

- Charitable Gift Annuity

Another gifting technique assigns an income interest to the charity for a period of years (or the lifetime of a person), after which the remainder passes to the donor's heirs. Gifts made in this manner involve what are known as charitable "lead" trusts.

Potential Financial Benefits of Charitable Gifts

- **Income taxes:** May provide an income tax deduction.[1] In many cases, can avoid or delay payment of capital gains tax.

- **Cash flow:** May increase personal after-tax cash flow.

- **Estate planning:** May increase the amount passing to one's heirs.

---

[1] Federal Income Tax Law. State or local income tax law may differ.

Charitable Giving Techniques

Gifts to charity during lifetime or at death will reduce the size of the gross estate. An additional benefit of lifetime gifts is that an income tax deduction is available within certain percentage limitations.

Split-Interest Gifts

If the estate owner is not willing or able to contribute the entire asset during lifetime, he or she may consider a split-interest, deferred gift.

The ownership interests in an asset can be split or divided into two parts, a stream of income payable for one or more lifetimes or a term of years (the income interest) and the principal remaining after the income term (the remainder interest).[1] In a split-interest gift, one portion is given in trust for the charity and the other portion is retained.

Charitable Remainder Plans

When the estate owner retains the right to the income but transfers his or her rights in the remainder to a trust, it is called a charitable remainder trust.

To qualify for an income tax deduction the trust must be a unitrust, an annuity trust, a pooled income fund, or a charitable gift annuity.

- **Charitable remainder unitrust:** In this type of trust the donor retains a right to a fixed percentage of the fair market value of the trust assets, with the trust assets being re-valued annually. If the value of the assets increases, so does the annual payout and vice versa.

- **Charitable remainder annuity trust:** This trust is similar to the unitrust but instead pays a fixed dollar amount each year.

- **Pooled income fund:** Assets are transferred to a common investment fund maintained by the charity. Each donor receives annually a share of the income from the fund, in proportion to the contribution made. These annual payments continue for the lifetimes of the donor and spouse. At death, the corpus of the donor's gift, together with any capital gains, passes to the charity. Payments will increase or decrease with the investment performance of the fund.

---

[1] Technically, the present value of the income share and the present value of the remainder interest.

- **Charitable gift annuity:** The donor transfers the asset directly to the charity, in exchange for the charity's agreement to pay a fixed lifetime annuity.

The amount of the income tax deduction is dependent upon the percentage of the income interest and the period over which it will be paid (usually the life of the donor and his or her spouse). This is determined from the mortality tables published by the government.

Charitable Income Trusts

The charitable income or lead trust is the reverse of the charitable remainder trust. The income interest is assigned to the charity, usually for a period of years, and then the remainder generally passes to the donor's heirs. The amount of the estate tax deduction and the amount left for the heirs will depend upon the number of years income is to be paid to the charity, the size of the annual payments, and the investment results achieved by the trustee

Charitable Income Tax Deduction

Federal income tax law allows a deduction for gifts to qualified charitable organizations, such as churches, colleges, hospitals, charitable foundations, etc. The actual amount of the deduction is dependent upon several factors:

- **Type of charity:** Does the organization benefit the general public or does it have a more limited or private purpose?

- **Type of asset:** Is the donated item cash, a capital asset with untaxed appreciation, tangible personal property, etc.?

- **Portion of asset given:** Is it a gift of the entire asset or only an interest in the asset, like a remainder interest, which will pass to the charity at some time in the future?

- **When gift is given:** Is the gift being made now or will it occur at some future date, as under the terms of a will or trust?

Income Tax Savings

The gift of an asset to a charity generally results in a federal income tax deduction,[1] which should decrease the tax due and increase net after-tax income for the year. However, charitable contributions are not always 100% deductible in the year they're made.

Limits on Annual Charitable Deduction

Federal law limits the amount that is deductible for the year in which the gift is made, based upon one's adjusted gross income (AGI). If the limit is exceeded for the year, any excess deduction can generally be carried forward for up to five years.

If combined charitable contributions for the year do not exceed 20.0% of adjusted gross income (AGI) for the year, they may all be deducted. However, if contributions exceed 20.0% of AGI, the deduction may be limited to 60.0%, 50.0%, 30.0%, or 20.0% of AGI, depending on the type of property given and the type of charitable organization receiving the gift. In no event can the deduction exceed 60.0% of the donor's AGI for the year.

---

[1] The discussion here concerns federal income tax law; state or local income tax law may vary.

Charitable Income Tax Deduction

- **60% limit:** For 2018-2025, a 60.0% of AGI limit applies to *cash* contributions to public charities, i.e. most churches, hospitals, colleges, etc. Such charities are generally termed "50.0%" organizations.

- **50.0% limit:** A 50.0% of AGI limit generally applies to *non-cash* gifts to 50.0% public charities. If the gift is of capital gain property,[1] and a deduction is taken for the <u>fair market value</u> of the property, a 30.0% of AGI limit applies. The 50.0% of AGI limit is available for gifts of capital gain property if the deduction is limited to the <u>cost basis</u> of the asset.

- **30% limit:** This limit applies to gifts "for the use" of any charitable organization and gifts (other than capital gain property) to non-50.0% type charities.

- **20% limit:** This limit applies to gifts of capital gain property to non-50.0% type charities.

- **Patents and Intellectual Property:** A donor's deduction for gifts of patents and other intellectual property is limited to the lesser of the taxpayer's basis or the fair market value of the property. An additional deduction may be available for a limited number of future years if the donee organization realizes income from the gifted property and certain requirements are met.

Income Tax Deduction for Split-Interest Gifts

Determining the federal income tax deduction for a "split-interest" gift, i.e., a charitable remainder or charitable lead trust, can be complicated. The key factors involved are:

- How long the charity must wait before it benefits; and

- How much income is paid to the beneficiaries each year; and

- The prevailing interest rates at the time of the gift (the IRC 7520 rate).

Seek Professional Guidance

The counsel and guidance of a CPA, IRS Enrolled Agent, or other qualified tax professional is strongly recommended.

---

[1] Capital gain property as used here applies to capital assets held *long-term* (at least 12 months and 1 day).

Charitable Gifts and Estate Taxation

Gifts to a charity or to a charitable remainder trust can reduce one's taxable estate by not only the value of the gift but also its potential appreciation. If the donor retains the right to the income, as in a charitable remainder trust, the estate tax savings will not be as large. However, the donor (or donors) may choose to make gifts of the income each year to children, grandchildren or to a trust on their behalf. If certain requirements are met, these gifts will qualify for the annual gift tax exclusion of $15,000[1] from each donor to as many qualified beneficiaries as there are under the terms of the trust.

The chart below illustrates the potential savings, based on a hypothetical situation.

Assumptions:

Current estate size: $15,000,000

Estate growth rate: 6.00%

Value of charitable gift: $1,000,000

Year of death: 2018

Applicable credit: $4,417,800

Years From Now	Taxable Estate		Federal Estate Tax[2]		Estate Tax Savings With Gift
	Without the Gift	With the Gift	Without the Gift	With the Gift	
Now	$15,000,000	$14,000,000	$1,528,000	$1,128,000	$400,000
5	$20,073,384	$18,735,158	$3,557,353	$3,022,063	$535,290
10	$26,862,715	$25,071,868	$6,273,086	$5,556,747	$716,339
15	$35,948,373	$33,551,815	$9,907,349	$8,948,726	$958,623
20	$48,107,032	$44,899,897	$14,770,813	$13,487,959	$1,282,854
25	$64,378,061	$60,086,190	$21,279,224	$19,562,476	$1,716,748
30	$86,152,368	$80,408,876	$29,988,947	$27,691,551	$2,297,396
35	$115,291,302	$107,605,215	$41,644,521	$38,570,086	$3,074,435

Note: If both the income from the trust and the income tax savings from the charitable deduction are given to an irrevocable trust (or to adult children) to purchase life insurance on the life of the donor, one is able to transfer a substantial amount of money to one's heirs which is not subject to either income tax or estate tax.

---

[1] 2018 value. This amount is subject to adjustment for inflation in future years.
[2] Calculated as if death occurred in 2018.

Qualified Conservation Easement

Protecting undeveloped land for the preservation of wildlife or the public enjoyment of nature can be one of the most meaningful legacies an individual can make. Few people, however, want to make an outright gift of their ranch or farm property for such purposes.

One possible solution to this dilemma involves creating a Qualified Conservation Easement, and then donating the easement to a charitable conservation organization or government agency. The easement effectively restricts future development and use of the land, while allowing a donor to retain ownership and possession. If the easement meets certain requirements, the donor can be eligible for both income and estate tax benefits.

Federal Income and Estate Tax Benefits

The tax[1] benefits of a qualified conservation easement can be substantial:

- **Income tax benefits:** If a qualified easement is donated during life, the property owner is eligible for an income tax deduction equal to the value of the easement. The deduction is limited to 50% of the donor's "contribution base" (generally, adjusted gross income, or AGI) in the year of the donation. Any excess may be carried forward and deducted for up to 15 years.[2]

  For an *individual* considered to be a "qualified farmer or rancher,"[3] the allowable deduction is generally 100% of AGI, with a 15-year carry forward of any unused deduction.[2] For a *corporate* "farmer or rancher," the deduction is limited to 100% of the excess of the corporation's taxable income over the amount of all otherwise allowable charitable contributions. Any excess may be carried forward and deducted for up to 15 years.

  No income tax deduction is allowed if an easement is donated on the owner's death.

- **Estate tax benefits:** There are two: (1) the property value for estate tax purposes will be lower; and (2) An exclusion from the taxable estate is allowed for up to 40% of the remaining property value (maximum of $500,000) in the estate. Both are available

---

[1] The discussion here concerns federal law; state and local law may differ.

[2] See IRC Sec. 170(b)(1)(E).

[3] Generally, a "qualified farmer or rancher" is a taxpayer whose gross income from the trade or business of "farming" is more than 50% of the taxpayer's gross income for the year. See IRC Sec. 2032A(e)(5).

regardless of when the easement is donated, during life or at death.

Terms and Requirements

The terms of a conservation easement are typically determined by the property owner and the organization that is to receive the easement. There are several requirements that must be met in order for the easement to be considered a "qualified" conservation easement, as shown in the following table:

Issues	Requirements
General	• A number of general requirements must be met: (1) the property must be located in the U.S. or its possessions; (2) the land must have been owned by the decedent or a member of the decedent's family at all times during the three-year period ending on the date of the decedent's death; and (3) a qualified conservation contribution of a qualified real property interest was granted by the decedent or a member of his or her family.
	• Easement must be permanent and established for at least one of the following: (1) outdoor recreation or education of the general public; (2) protection of a natural ecosystem; (3) preservation of open space for scenic enjoyment or pursuant to a governmental conservation policy that will yield a significant public benefit; or (4) preservation of a historically important land area or certified historic structure[1].
Charitable Organization	• Donation must be to a qualified charitable or governmental organization with a commitment to protect the easement's purpose.
	• Easement must contain legally enforceable restrictions that the charitable organization can (and has the resources to) enforce.

Donor's Retained Usage

The donor can retain the right to occupy and use the property, to conduct farm operations, to construct residences and related buildings, or farm buildings, all without losing tax benefits. However, the tax benefits may be reduced or lost if the donor retains the right to subdivide or develop the property, to use it for commercial purposes other than farming, or to use the land in a way that threatens the conservation purposes of the easement.

---

[1] A historically-important land area or certified historic structure is not a qualified conservation purpose for the estate exclusion under federal tax law.

Valuation of a Conservation Easement

A conservation easement is generally valued by appraising the property before and after the donation of the easement. The difference between the two appraisals is the value of the easement. A proportional amount of the donor's income tax basis will be allocated to the easement.

Impact on a Donor's Estate

The donation of a conservation easement can impact a donor's estate in several ways:

- **Reduction in estate size:** The reduction in the value of land means that the size of a donor's estate will be reduced, potentially resulting in a lower estate tax bill.

- **Estate exclusion:** Federal tax law provides that up to 40% of the post-easement value of the property, up to a maximum of $500,000, may be excluded from the taxable estate. If the easement is worth at least 30% of the original, pre-easement value of the property, the full 40% exclusion is available. If the easement is worth less than 30%, the exclusion will be reduced according to a statutory schedule.

- **No step-up in basis:** Under current law, property received by inheritance generally receives a full step-up in basis to its fair market value on the decedent's date of death. However, property excluded from the estate as a result of the donation of a qualified conservation easement does not receive a step-up in basis. Depending on the situation, there may be circumstances where it would not make sense to use this estate exclusion.

Wealth Replacement Trust

Some of the income tax savings from a conservation easement created and donated during life can be used to fund a wealth replacement trust to benefit the donor's family. A wealth replacement trust is an irrevocable life insurance trust which owns either a life insurance policy on the life of the donor or a survivorship policy on the donor and his or her spouse. If the trust is properly structured, the life insurance proceeds can be fully excluded from federal estate taxes.

Qualified Conservation Easement

Seek Professional Guidance

Estate planning for certain land owners (farmers, ranchers, and rural business owners) presents unique estate planning challenges and opportunities. The regular guidance of appropriate legal, tax, and financial professionals is strongly recommended.

Unrelated Business Taxable Income

Under federal income tax law, a charitable remainder trust which has unrelated business taxable income is subject to a 100% excise tax on such income.[1] For example, if a CRT had $50 of UBTI, the tax would be equal to $50.

What Is Unrelated Business Taxable Income?

UBTI is defined in IRC Sec. 512. Generally, it is income derived by a charity from any unrelated trade or business carried on by it and not specifically excluded by statute.

Typically, investment income or capital gains are not UBTI (unless the asset is debt financed). Revenue from an active trade or business, however, is generally considered to be UBTI.

Many limited partnerships generate UBTI and should be carefully evaluated before being considered for placement in a CRT. Further, donors should seek competent counsel when considering a donation of either an unincorporated business or property subject to participating leases.

Debt-Financed Property

Indebtedness on property can be a problem when creating a CRT. In all debt-encumbered property transfers, the donor is considered to have received proceeds from a sale in the amount of the indebtedness. The IRS rationale is that relief from debt is the same as receiving income, and is a taxable event. At best, one has taxable income (in the amount of the debt relief) with a partial, offsetting charitable deduction for the equity in the property.

In the past the IRS had indicated that the UBTI problems discussed above would apply to indebted property transfers to a CRT unless the debt was "old and cold." An exception was allowed when the debt had been placed on the property, and the donor had held the property, more than five years before transfer.

However, even this limited exception has been overruled. The IRS, in a private letter ruling,[2] completely disqualified a CRT funded with "old and cold" indebted property. The service

---

[1] The discussion here concerns federal income tax law; state or local law may differ.

[2] See PLR 9015049 dated 1/16/90. A IRS Private Letter Ruling is applicable only to the taxpayer who requested it and may not be cited as precedent.

contended that the grantor trust rules applied, i.e., the grantor is treated as the owner of the trust if income from the trust is used to discharge a legal obligation of the grantor.

To be safe, the donor should, if possible, payoff the debt or move it to other property prior to the transfer to a charitable trust. If the debt is too substantial for this, the donor may have to use a different charitable income instrument, such as a charitable gift annuity, rather than a charitable remainder trust.

Depending on the facts of the situation, the donor and/or the advisor could directly contact the charity the donor wishes to support; the charity itself may be able to offer other alternatives. For example, the charity may be in a position to buy a portion of the property from the donor. Upon completion of the sale (a taxable event to the donor), the donor would use the proceeds from the sale to pay off the debt and then gift the remaining portion of the property that he or she owns to a Charitable Remainder Trust (CRT). The resulting charitable income tax deduction from the CRT may offset, in whole or in part, any tax liability arising from the partial sale of the property to the charity.

A donor could also consider what is termed a "bargain sale" of the property to the charity. However, the tax implications of such a transaction must be carefully examined before using this approach.

Seek Professional Guidance

Given the complexities involved, the advice and guidance of competent tax and financial professionals is strongly recommended.

Charitable Remainder Annuity Trust

A Charitable Remainder Annuity Trust (CRAT) is an irrevocable trust which pays a fixed dollar amount each year to a beneficiary, such as the donor of the trust assets, his or her spouse, child, etc. This fixed dollar amount is calculated by applying the stated payout rate, e.g. 5%, 6%, etc., to the value [1] of the assets at the time they are transferred into the trust by the donor.

After the death of the income beneficiaries, or at the end of a set number of years,[2] whatever assets remain in the trust are distributed to the charities named in the trust. If additional contributions are desired in later years, new trusts must be established.

Income Tax Considerations

The charitable income tax deduction is based on the current value of the charity's right to receive the trust assets at some time in the future (a remainder interest). There are several factors in determining this value:

- First is the length of time which the charity must wait; for example, a term of years (like 10, 15, 20, etc.) or for the donor's or other person's lifetime.

- A second factor is the fixed dollar amount payable to the income beneficiaries each year and how frequently it is paid, e.g. annually, monthly, etc. Obviously, the higher the payment, the less there will be for the charity and, therefore, the smaller the charitable deduction.

- The current rate of return on investments as determined by the applicable federal (midterm) rates (AFR) is also an important factor.[3]

All of these factors are applied to government tables to determine the current value of the charitable deduction. If the charitable deduction exceeds a certain percentage of the donor's adjusted gross income for the year of the gift, that portion must be carried over into future years.

---

[1] In cases of hard to value assets like real estate, a qualified appraisal is required to support the values.

[2] If a set number of years is chosen to determine the term of the trust (instead of the lifetime(s) of one or two beneficiaries), the maximum term is 20 years.

[3] This rate is subject to change monthly.

Gift Tax Considerations

If the income from the CRAT is payable to someone other than the donor, it may be subject to federal gift taxation. If certain requirements are met, the income gift can be made to qualify for the annual gift tax exclusion of $15,000[1] per beneficiary. Also, the marital deduction will usually eliminate any gift tax on payments to the donor's spouse.

Estate Tax Considerations

The value of the interest passing to the charity is deductible from the gross estate. If there are income beneficiaries other than the donor and his or her spouse, there may be an estate tax on the value of this income interest.

Some states allow a surviving spouse to "elect" to receive a portion of the deceased spouse's estate. Such laws are designed to prevent the surviving spouse from being completely disinherited. If state law allows assets in a CRAT to be used to satisfy the surviving spouse's election, the CRAT could cease to qualify as a charitable trust under federal law. As a result, previous income tax deductions can be lost and the assets in the trust could be added back to the deceased spouse's estate. The IRS originally provided a "safe harbor" for this situation in Revenue Procedure 2005-24, with a grandfather date of June 28, 2005. In Notice 2006-15, however, the federal government extended the June 28, 2005 date until "further guidance is issued by the Internal Revenue Service."

Almost Everyone Benefits

A taxpayer can contribute an asset (often highly appreciated and low income producing) to a CRAT and receive a current income tax deduction. The trustee can sell the appreciated asset without the trust paying any capital gains tax and then reinvest the entire proceeds.

The trust will often pay out a higher rate of return than the donor previously received. This higher return, coupled with the federal charitable income tax deduction, can provide a substantial increase in cash flow. The cash payments received by the income beneficiaries are taxed under a four-tier system. Generally, ordinary income is paid first, followed by capital gain, other income, and trust principal.

---

[1] 2018 value. This amount is subject to adjustment for inflation in future years.

Charitable Remainder Annuity Trust

Thus far, the only ones to lose are the donor's heirs. To solve this problem, many taxpayers use a portion of the increased cash flow to purchase a life insurance policy (outside of the estate) to replace all or part of the value of the asset placed in the trust. This arrangement lets almost everyone benefit.

Party	Benefit
Donor (and spouse)	Increased cash flow during retirement years
Children/heirs	Same size or larger inheritance (with insurance)
Favorite charity	Receives remaining assets after donor's death
Internal Revenue Service	Receives less income and estate tax

How a Charitable Remainder Annuity Trust Works

The donor transfers an asset to the trustee of the charitable remainder annuity trust (CRAT) and receives a fixed dollar amount for each year thereafter. A current income tax deduction is also available.

When the donor or other named beneficiary dies or the trust term ends, the remaining trust assets pass to one or more designated charities.

DONOR		CRAT
• Transfers asset to CRAT. • Receives fixed dollar amount each year.[1] • Receives income tax deduction.[2]	Asset → Annual Annuity Payout ← Income Tax Deduction ←	• Trustee sells asset and reinvests for greater return. • Pays no capital gain tax on the appreciation at the time of sale. • Trustee pays fixed dollar amount yearly.

After the beneficiary is deceased, remaining trust assets pass to the charity.[3]

CHARITABLE ORGANIZATION

- Receives any assets remaining in the trust when the beneficiary is deceased.

---

[1] The annual annuity payout is taxed under a four-tier system. Generally speaking, ordinary income is paid first, followed by capital-gain, other income, and trust principal.

[2] The income tax deduction is based on a government determined applicable federal rate and may have to be spread over more than one year, if it exceeds certain percentage of income limitations.

[3] If a surviving spouse "elects" to claim a part of a deceased spouse's estate, the income and estate tax benefits of a CRAT may be lost.

Charitable Remainder Unitrust

A Charitable Remainder Unitrust (CRUT) is an irrevocable trust which pays a fixed percentage of the value of its holdings each year to a beneficiary such as the donor of the trust assets, his or her spouse, child, etc. Unlike the fixed dollar payment of a charitable remainder annuity trust, the unitrust payments will fluctuate with the changing asset balance in the trust, reflecting year-to-year investment performance.[1]

After the death of the income beneficiaries, or at the end of a set number of years (no more than 20), whatever assets remain in the trust are distributed to the charities named in the trust. Unlike a Charitable Remainder Annuity Trust (CRAT), additional contributions to a CRUT are allowed in later years, if desired.

CRUT Variations

The standard form of CRUT requires payment of the full stated percentage throughout the life of the trust, even if assets must be liquidated. Other CRUT variations include:

- **Net-Income CRUT:** A CRUT may be drafted to pay out less than the established percentage if the trust income during the year is less than the required payout percentage. This shortage can be made up in later years when the trust earns more than the required payout percentage.

- **"Flip" CRUT:** Under IRS regulations, a CRUT may begin life as a net-income trust, and, at some pre-determined future date or triggering event, permanently convert ("flip") to a standard unitrust. A "flip" CRUT is an option for an individual seeking a current income tax deduction, tax-deferred buildup and increased income at a later date.

Income Tax Considerations

The charitable income tax deduction is based on the current value of the charity's right to receive the trust assets at some time in the future. Three factors are involved:

- The length of time, which the charity must wait; for example, a term of years (like 10, 15, 20, etc.) or for the donor's or other person's lifetime.

---

[1] Assets must be revalued each year to determine the payout amount.

- The percentage rate payable to the income beneficiaries each year and how frequently it is paid, e.g., annually, monthly, etc. The higher the payout, the less there will be for the charity; and, therefore, the smaller the charitable deduction.

- The current investment return, as determined by the IRS. These are called the IRC 7520 mid-term rates.[1]

These factors are applied to government tables to determine the current value of the charitable deduction. If the charitable deduction exceeds a certain percentage of the donor's adjusted gross income in the year of the gift, the excess must be carried over to future years.

Gift Tax Considerations

If the income from the CRUT is payable to someone other than the donor, it may be subject to federal gift taxation. If certain requirements are met, the income gift can be made to qualify for the annual gift tax exclusion of $15,000[2] per beneficiary. Also, the marital deduction will usually eliminate any tax on payments to the donor's spouse.

Estate Tax Considerations

The value of the interest passing to the charity is deductible from the gross estate. If there are income beneficiaries other than the donor and his or her spouse, there may be an estate tax on the value of this income interest.

Some states allow a surviving spouse to "elect" to receive a portion of the deceased spouse's estate. Such laws are designed to prevent the surviving spouse from being completely disinherited. If state law allows assets in a CRUT to be used to satisfy the surviving spouse's election, the CRUT could cease to qualify as a charitable trust under federal law. As a result, previous income tax deductions can be lost and the assets in the trust could be added back to the deceased spouse's estate.[3]

---

[1] This rate changes monthly.

[2] 2018 value. This amount is subject to adjustment for inflation in future years.

[3] The IRS originally provided a "safe harbor" for this situation in Revenue Procedure 2005-24, with a grandfather date of June 28, 2005. In Notice 2006-15, however, the federal government extended the June 28, 2005 date until "further guidance is issued by the Internal Revenue Service."

Charitable Remainder Unitrust

Almost Everyone Benefits

A taxpayer can contribute an asset (often highly appreciated and low income producing) to a CRUT and receive a current income tax deduction. The trustee can sell the appreciated asset without the trust paying any capital gains tax and then reinvest the entire proceeds.

The trust will often pay out a higher rate of return than the donor previously received. This higher return, coupled with the federal charitable income tax deduction, can provide a substantial increase in cash flow. The cash payments received by the income beneficiaries are taxed under a four-tier system. Generally, ordinary income is paid first, followed by capital gain, other income, and trust principal.

Thus far, the only ones to lose are the donor's heirs. To solve this problem, many taxpayers use a portion of the increased cash flow to purchase a life insurance policy (outside of the estate) to replace the value of the asset placed in the trust. This arrangement lets almost everyone benefit.

Party	Benefit
Donor (and spouse)	Increased cash flow during retirement years
Children/heirs	Same size or larger inheritance (with insurance)
Favorite charity	Receives remaining assets after donor's death
Internal Revenue Service	Receives less income and estate tax

How a Charitable Remainder Unitrust Works

The donor transfers an asset to the trustee of the charitable remainder unitrust (CRUT) and receives a set percentage of the trust value for each year thereafter. A current income tax deduction is also available.

When the donor or other named beneficiary dies or the trust term ends, the remaining trust assets pass to one or more designated charities.

DONOR

- Transfers asset to CRUT.
- Receives annual payout.[1]
- Receives income tax deduction.[2]

Asset →

% of Trust Annually ←

Income Tax Deduction ←

CRUT

- Trustee sells asset and reinvests for greater return.
- Pays no capital gain tax due on the appreciation at the time of sale.
- Trustee pays a percentage of trust assets as valued each year.

After the beneficiary is deceased, remaining trust assets pass to the charity.[3]

CHARITABLE ORGANIZATION

- Receives any assets remaining in the trust when the beneficiary is deceased.

---

[1] The annual annuity payout is taxed under a four-tier system. Generally speaking, ordinary income is paid first, followed by capital-gain, other income, and trust principal.

[2] This deduction may have to be spread over more than one year, if it exceeds certain percentage of income limitations.

[3] If a surviving spouse "elects" to claim a part of a deceased spouse's estate, the income and estate tax benefits of a CRUT may be lost.

Charitable Remainder Trust Numerical Tests

Charitable remainder trusts (CRTs), including charitable remainder annuity trusts (CRATs) and charitable remainder unitrusts (CRUTs), are subject to a complex maze of law and regulation. The failure of a CRT to meet all requirements the law imposes can result in it being disqualified as a "charitable" trust, with negative income, gift, and estate tax consequences, as well as defeating the donor's charitable intent.[1]

Numerical Tests

A number of these requirements involve specific numerical tests:

- **5% probability test:** This test, which applies only to CRATs, measures the theoretical possibility that a non-charitable beneficiary might live long enough to exhaust the assets in the trust, leaving nothing for the charity.[2] Using a complicated mathematical formula, and government interest and longevity tables, the probability of exhausting the assets is calculated at the time property is transferred to the trust. If the probability of exhaustion is greater than 5%, no income or estate tax deduction is allowed.

- **5% minimum payment test:** This test concerns the minimum annual payment which must be made from a charitable remainder trust. For CRATs, federal law requires the payment to be not less than 5% of the initial fair market value of all property placed in the trust. For CRUTs, the law requires the minimum payment to be a fixed percentage, not less than 5%, of the net fair market value of the CRUT's assets, valued annually.

- **50% payout limitation test:** Federal tax law limits the annual payout from a CRAT to no more than 50% of the initial net fair market value of property in the trust. For CRUTs, annual payments are limited to no more than 50% of the net fair market value of the trust's assets, valued annually. A CRT which fails this test will be treated as a complex trust, with all income taxed to either the trust or its beneficiaries.

---

[1] The discussion here concerns federal tax law. State or local law may differ.

[2] With a CRUT, exhaustion of the trust assets is considered impossible as payments from the trust are based on a percentage of trust assets, not a fixed dollar payment.

- **10% minimum charitable benefit:** There is a minimum benefit that must ultimately pass to the charity. For CRATs, this minimum is 10% of the initial net fair market value of all property placed in the trust. For CRUTs, the remainder interest passing to the charity must be at least 10% of the net fair market value of trust property, valued as of the date the property is contributed to the trust.

Seek Professional Guidance

Because of the complexity of the law and regulations governing charitable remainder trusts, individuals considering a CRT are strongly advised to consult with an attorney, CPA, IRS enrolled agent, or other competent financial professional. Also, many charitable organizations have professionals on their staffs that can provide insight and guidance in designing and implementing charitable remainder trust planning.

Charitable Gift Annuity

When a donor transfers an asset to a charity[1] in exchange for an income for one or two lives, it is called a charitable gift annuity.

The income tax deduction from this arrangement will vary depending on the age of the donor, the payout rate and the applicable (mid-term) federal rate (AFR) (which is determined monthly).

The following charts illustrate the income tax deduction at various ages and AFRs. Each example assumes a cash gift of $100,000. The payouts vary with the age of the donor.[2]

Age 55 / 4.0% / $4,000		⇐ Recommended Payout ⇒		4.4% / $4,400 / Age 60
AFR Table Rate	Total Charitable Deduction	Income Excluded from Taxation[3]	Total Charitable Deduction	Income Excluded from Taxation[3]
1.4%	$16,284	$2,937	$20,458	$3,301
2.0%	22,694	2,712	25,823	3,078
2.4%	26,548	2,577	29,087	2,942

Age 65 / 4.7% / $4,700		⇐ Recommended Payout ⇒		5.1% / $5,100 / Age 70
AFR Table Rate	Total Charitable Deduction	Income Excluded from Taxation[3]	Total Charitable Deduction	Income Excluded from Taxation[3]
1.4%	$28,111	$3,613	$35,820	$4,037
2.0%	32,312	3,401	39,009	3,836
2.4%	34,898	3,271	40,991	3,711

[1] In most states, a charity must be licensed to grant a gift annuity.

[2] Many charities follow the suggested payout rates developed by the American Council on Gift Annuities, 1260 Winchester Parkway, Suite 205, Smyrna, GA, 30080-6546. Tel: (770) 874-3355. On the internet: http://acga-web.org/

[3] The amount shown represents that portion of the annual payment due to recovery of the donor's basis in the annuity. Once the basis has been completely recovered, all additional payments are fully taxable.

Charitable Gift Annuity

Age 75 / 5.8% / $5,800		⇐ Recommended Payout ⇒	6.8% / $6,800 / Age 80	
AFR Table Rate	Total Charitable Deduction	Income Excluded from Taxation[1]	Total Charitable Deduction	Income Excluded from Taxation[1]
1.4%	$41,861	$4,689	$47,309	$5,605
2.0%	44,262	4,495	49,080	5,418
2.4%	45,772	4,373	50,205	5,297

Note: Table calculated using ACGA "recommended" Single Life Gift Annuity rates effective January 1, 2012

[1] The amount shown represents that portion of the annual payment due to recovery of the donor's basis in the annuity. Once the basis has been completely recovered, all additional payments are fully taxable.

How a Charitable Gift Annuity Works

The donor transfers an asset to a charity and each year thereafter receives an annuity, i.e. a payment in a fixed dollar amount. The annual payment is set at the time the gift is made. A current income tax deduction is also available.

When the donor or other named beneficiary dies, the charity has no further financial obligations to pay.

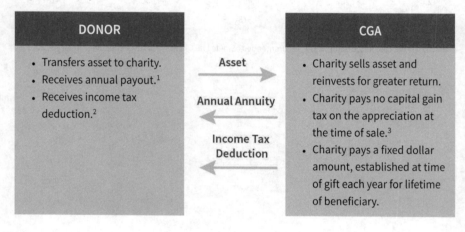

DONOR	CGA
• Transfers asset to charity. • Receives annual payout.[1] • Receives income tax deduction.[2]	• Charity sells asset and reinvests for greater return. • Charity pays no capital gain tax on the appreciation at the time of sale.[3] • Charity pays a fixed dollar amount, established at time of gift each year for lifetime of beneficiary.

Asset →

Annual Annuity ←

Income Tax Deduction ←

After the beneficiary is deceased the charity has no further obligations to pay.

---

[1] Annuity payments are part return of principal (nontaxable), part ordinary income and (if any) part capital gain. Once a donor has recovered his or her basis, the annuity payments are fully taxable.

[2] This deduction may have to be spread over more than one year if it exceeds certain percentage of income limitations.

[3] If certain requirements are met, the donor may recognize any capital gain ratably over the time period the annuity is expected to be received. Otherwise, the donor must recognize all capital gain in the year the annuity transaction is entered into.

Taxation of a Charitable Gift Annuity

Payments received from charitable gift annuities are taxed in the same manner as commercial annuities, i.e., using the annuity exclusion ratio. However, many individuals prefer the fixed, predictable income and upfront income tax deduction received when funding a gift annuity. This often gives them an advantage over payments from pooled income funds or charitable remainder trusts, from which the income may be fully taxable.

A portion of each payment from an annuity is considered to be a return of principal and is, therefore, exempt from income tax. Also, when funded with appreciated property, a portion of the payment will be taxed at capital gains rates.

Payment Allocation

The chart below illustrates the allocation of payments from a charitable gift annuity as various types of income. The examples are based on the following set of assumptions:

Amount contributed: $100,000
Age of beneficiary: 75

Payout rate: 5.8%
Applicable federal rate (AFR): 2.4%

Assuming a Cash Contribution of $100,000

Years	Annual Income	Ordinary Income	Exempt Income	Long-Term Capital Gain
1	$2,900	$713	$2,187	$0
2-12	$5,800	$1,427	$4,373	$0
13	$5,800	$1,864	$3,936	$0
Thereafter	$5,800	$5,800	$0	$0

Assuming a Stock Contribution with Basis of $50,000

Years	Annual Income	Ordinary Income	Exempt Income	Long-Term Capital Gain
1	$2,900	$713	$1,093	$1,093
2-12	$5,800	$1,427	$2,187	$2,187
13	$5,800	$1,864	$1,968	$1,968
Thereafter	$5,800	$5,800	$0	$0

Note: The donor will also receive a current income tax deduction of approximately $45,772.

Taxation of a Charitable Gift Annuity

Appreciated Capital Assets

Appreciated capital assets held long-term may be exchanged for a charitable gift annuity without taxation of the unrealized capital gain at time of transfer (much like a charitable remainder trust) unless an income beneficiary other than the donor and his or her spouse is named. In such cases, the full, unrealized gain is taxable to the donor/grantor.

Donor-Advised Funds: Where Middle-Class Americans Can Make Charitable Contributions

When it comes to charitable giving, Americans are leading the way—last year donating a record $335 billion, marking the fourth straight year of increases. And while a substantial portion of charitable dollars is doled out by High-Net-Worth individuals with the capital necessary to establish their own foundations, middle-class Americans may also make tax-deductible charitable contributions, using Donor-Advised funds (DAFs).

Just what are they? Simply put, Donor-Advised funds are charitable giving accounts, through which individuals can donate cash, securities and other assets to their pet causes, without the high costs and logistical complexities associated with traditional private foundations.

How They Work

With every Donor-Advised fund, a sponsoring organization shoulders the logistical heavy lifting, by handling all of the due diligence and record-keeping requirements. More importantly, Donor-Advised funds democratize philanthropy by aggregating multiple donors and processing high numbers of charitable transactions, thereby lowering the cost barriers to entry and making it possible for individuals with as little as $5,000 to participate in the giving process. And the reduced overhead costs allow 99% of all contributions to funnel directly into the associated charities.

Tax Benefits

There are multitudinous tax advantages to donating money through Donor-Advised funds. Unlike private foundations, DAF holders enjoy a federal income tax deduction up to 50% of adjusted gross income for cash contributions, and up to 30% of adjusted gross income for the appreciated securities they donate. And by transferring assets such as limited partnership interests to DAFs, donors avoid capital gains taxes and receive immediate fair-market-value tax deductions.

Choosing Your Sponsor

There are several different types of DAF sponsors to choose from—each with its own set of pros and cons. It's therefore critical for participants to select their sponsors wisely. Some of the different sponsor models are as follows:

- **National DAF Organizations:** Most of the approximately 30 national DAF organizations in existence are actually charitable arms of for-profit financial services institutions, such as the Vanguard Charitable Endowment Program, the Schwab Charitable Fund and the Fidelity Charitable Gift Fund. Other national DAF sponsors are non-affiliated with financial entities, including the American Endowment Foundation and the National Philanthropic Trust. In either case, national funds tend to attract wealthier donors, who rely on the sponsor's in-house talent to handle complex maneuvers, including the conversion of non-cash assets into tax-deductible gifts. National DAF organizations tend to have advanced Web platforms that let donors track data on prospective grantees, as well as fee calculators that let donors determine how much the services will cost them, before they make charitable commitments. On the downside, national organizations are typically agnostic with regards to the charities they follow, which may deter donors seeking more targeted philanthropic guidance.

- **Community Foundations:** Community foundations typically appeal to donors interested in giving to local causes, because they employ staffs more knowledgeable about local-area charity initiatives. Furthermore, donors themselves are often invited to visit the charities they support, to make sure their money is being put to proper use.

- **Public Foundations:** Public foundations typically support national and international charities that focus on a particular issue or geographic region. For this reason, public foundations personnel often have specific expertise to help DAF holders find causes near and dear to them. Case in point: the Peace Development Fund houses DAFs for donors interested in creating systemic social change throughout the Americas.

- **Other:** Other public charities, like universities and hospitals establish donor-advised funds within the walls of their respective organizations, with the mission of advancing their own charitable missions.

Disadvantages of Donor-Advised Funds

DAFs do pose some drawbacks compared to private foundation donations. Mainly, while a private foundation may accept donations in the form of illiquid assets like art, scholarships and other creative donations, Donor-Advised funds cannot always accept these assets. In addition, private foundation board members have total governance over where the money goes, while participants in Donor-Advised funds may only advise the sponsoring organization on these matters. Consequently, a sponsoring organization could theoretically ignore the donor's intent.

Conclusion

Charitable giving isn't just for the super wealthy. With more than $45 billion in assets, Donor-Advised funds account for more than 6% of all individual charitable donations. More than 100,000 charity-minded Americans are using DAFs to receive immediate tax breaks, while recommending prospective grant recipients close to their hearts.

Pooled Income Fund

A pooled income fund (PIF) is a type of fund to which more than one donor is able to make contributions.

A public charity must establish and maintain a common investment fund into which donors transfer assets while retaining a share of the annual income in proportion to his or her contribution.

The federal income tax deduction is based on the ages of the beneficiaries and the highest rate of return paid by the fund over the last three years.[1]

The frequency of payments, e.g., monthly, quarterly, etc., does not affect the tax deduction.

Pooled income funds may not invest in tax-exempt securities nor accept them as contributions. Also, neither donor nor beneficiary may serve as trustee.

Estate and Gift Taxation

If the donor causes the income to be paid to another person (like a child or a parent) there would be a taxable gift. If certain requirements are met, the income gift can be made to qualify for the annual gift tax exclusion of $15,000[2] per beneficiary.

The value of the asset passing to the PIF is removed from the donor's gross estate. Periodic payments, if received by the donor, will, however, tend to increase the estate size unless they are otherwise consumed.

After the life income beneficiaries die, the remaining assets pass to the charity.

---

[1] If the fund has been in existence for less than three years, the rate used is based on interest rates provided by the federal government.

[2] 2018 value. This amount is subject to adjustment for inflation in future years.

How a Pooled Income Fund Works

The donor transfers an asset to the trustee of the pooled income fund (PIF) and receives a proportionate share of the trust's income for each year thereafter. A current income tax deduction is also available.

When the donor or other named beneficiary dies, the remaining trust assets pass to the designated charity.

DONOR		PIF
• Transfers asset to PIF.	Asset → Annual Payment ← Income Tax Deduction ←	• Trustee sells assets and reinvests for greater return.
• Receives annual payout.		• Pays no capital gain tax due on the appreciation.
• Receives income tax deduction[1].		• Trustee pays a proportionate share of the fund's income each year for lifetime of beneficiary.

After the beneficiary is deceased, remaining trust assets pass to the charity

CHARITABLE ORGANIZATION
• Receives any assets remaining in the trust when the beneficiary is deceased.

---

[1] This deduction is based on life expectancy and the highest rate paid by the fund over the last three years. The deduction may have to be spread over more than one year, if it exceeds certain percentage of income limitations.

Charitable Lead Annuity Trust

In General

A donor may transfer assets to an irrevocable Charitable Lead Annuity Trust (CLAT). The trust then pays a fixed dollar amount to a qualified charity for either a set number of years or the lifetimes of individuals. When the trust term has ended, the remaining assets are distributed to the donor, his or her spouse, heirs or others.

The trust must pay out the same dollar amount each year, without regard to its earnings. If the trust earns more than it pays out to the charitable beneficiary, those extra earnings (or asset appreciation) will pass to the non-charitable beneficiaries (children, grandchildren, others) without additional estate or gift taxes.

Valuation of assets is required only at the time the assets are transferred to the CLAT. A new trust will be required if additional contributions are made in later years. Ideally, assets in the CLAT should have both income potential (to make the required payments to the charitable beneficiary) and growth potential (to pass long-term appreciation to the ultimate beneficiaries with a minimum of estate or gift taxes).

After the lead (or income) period has expired, if the beneficiary of the trust is other than the donor or his or her spouse, there may be a taxable gift. The gift tax would be based on the present value of the beneficiaries' right to receive the trust remainder at some future time. This calculation is dependent upon the term of the trust, the amount payable each year to the charity and the applicable federal rate (AFR) at the time of the transfer.

Planning Considerations

A donor establishing a CLAT needs to consider several key issues:

- **Income tax deduction:** If certain requirements are met, an income tax deduction is allowed for the value of the income passing to charity. With a grantor trust the donor is considered the owner of the trust (taxable on the income under the grantor trust rules) and is allowed the tax deduction, subject to certain percentage of AGI limitations. If the trust is a non-grantor trust, the trust itself is permitted an unlimited tax deduction for distributions to qualified charities. If these requirements are not met, no charitable income tax deduction is allowed to either the donor or the trust.

- **Remainder interest:** At the end of the trust term, should the assets remaining in the trust revert to the donor or pass to other individuals such as the donor's heirs?

- **Generation-Skipping Transfer Tax (GSTT):** A taxable event for GSTT purposes will occur if the individuals who ultimately receive the assets when the trust terminates are considered to be "skip'" persons, such as the donor's grandchildren or a later generation.

Estate Tax Reduction

Frequently, CLATs are set up as non-grantor trusts, with the ultimate beneficiary of the trust assets being someone other than the donor or his or her spouse. Such CLATs typically provide no income tax deduction to the donor, but do provide a means of transferring assets to children or grandchildren, with substantial valuation discounts. For example, at a 2.4% AFR, a 10-year CLAT, paying 5% annually[1] to a charity, offers a 44.5% discount from market value. The same trust, over a 15-year term, offers a 63.1% discount from market value; over 20 years a 79.5% discount from market value is achieved.

The CLAT is an excellent way for affluent individuals to meet charitable obligations, as well as make discounted, deferred transfers to heirs.

---

[1] 5% of the value of the assets, as measured at the time of the transfer into the CLAT. For example, given assets worth $1,000,000 at the time of transfer, a 5% payment would yield a fixed payment to charity of $50,000 per year, for the term of the trust.

How a Charitable Lead Annuity Trust Works

The donor transfers an asset to the trustee of a Charitable Lead Annuity Trust (CLAT). Each year thereafter, the trust pays a fixed dollar amount to selected charities. A current income tax deduction is generally allowed for the present value of the income interest paid to the charities.

At the end of the term of the trust, the remaining assets pass to the donor's heirs, spouse, or sometimes back to the donor, if living.

DONOR		CLAT		CHARITY OF CHOICE
• Transfers asset to CLAT. • Receives income tax deduction.[1]	**Asset** → **Income Tax Deduction[1]** ←	• Trustee pays fixed dollar amount each year to the selected charity for the term of the trust.	**Annual Payout** →	• Receives fixed dollar amount each year.

After the trust is terminated the remaining trust assets pass to the person or persons selected by the donor

FINAL BENEFICIARIES

These beneficiaries could be the donor, if the trust was set to last only a term of years, or it could be the donor's spouse, children, grandchildren[2], etc., which may also produce an estate tax reduction.

---

[1] The income tax deduction, allowable only to grantor trusts, is based on a government determined applicable federal rate and may have to be spread over more than one year, if it exceeds certain percentage of income limitations.

[2] Choosing grandchildren (or later descendants) to receive the assets when the trust terminates may trigger the Generation-Skipping Transfer Tax (GSTT).

Charitable Lead Unitrust

In General

A donor may transfer assets to an irrevocable Charitable Lead Unitrust (CLUT) – sometimes referred to as a charitable income unitrust. The trust then pays a fixed percentage of its assets to a qualified charity for either a set number of years or the lifetimes of individuals. When the term of the trust has ended, the remaining assets are distributed to the donor, his or her spouse, heirs or other individuals.

Valuation of assets is required every year to determine the amount of the payment for the year. Payments to charity will vary from year to year, depending upon the investment performance and expenses of the trust.

After the lead (or income) period has expired, if the beneficiary of the trust is other than the donor or his or her spouse, there may be a taxable gift. The gift tax would be based on the present value of the beneficiaries' right to receive the trust remainder at some future time. This calculation is dependent upon the term of the trust, the amount payable each year to the charity and the applicable federal rate (AFR) at the time of the transfer.

Planning Considerations

A donor establishing a CLUT needs to consider several key issues:

- **Income tax deduction:** If certain requirements are met, an income tax deduction is allowed for the value of the income passing to charity. With a grantor trust the donor is considered the owner of the trust (taxable on the income under the grantor trust rules) and is allowed the tax deduction, subject to certain percentage of AGI limitations. If the trust is a non-grantor trust, the trust itself is permitted an unlimited tax deduction for distributions to qualified charities. If these requirements are not met, no charitable income tax deduction is allowed to either the donor or the trust.

- **Remainder interest:** At the end of the trust term, should the assets remaining in the trust revert to the donor or pass to other individuals such as the donor's heirs?

- **Generation-Skipping Transfer Tax (GSTT):** A taxable event for GSTT purposes will occur if the individuals who ultimately receive the assets when the trust terminates are considered to be "skip" persons, such as the donor's grandchildren or a later generation.

Estate Tax Reduction

Frequently, CLUTs are set up as non-grantor trusts, with the ultimate beneficiary of the trust assets being someone other than the donor or his or her spouse. Such CLUTs typically provide no income deduction to the donor, but do provide a means of transferring assets to children or grandchildren, with substantial valuation discounts. For example, at a 2.0% AFR, a 10-year CLUT, paying 5% annually[1] to a charity, offers a 39.7% discount from market value. The same trust, over a 15-year term, offers a 53.1% discount from market value; over 20 years a 63.6% discount from market value is achieved.

The CLUT is an excellent way for affluent individuals to meet charitable obligations, as well as make discounted, deferred transfers to heirs.

---

[1] This amount is 5% of the value of the assets, as revalued each year.

How a Charitable Lead Unitrust Works

The donor transfers an asset to the trustee of a Charitable Lead Unitrust (CLUT). Each year thereafter, the trust pays a fixed percentage of the trust assets (revalued each year) to selected charities.

At the end of the term of the trust, the remaining assets pass to the donor's heirs, spouse or sometimes back to the donor, if living.

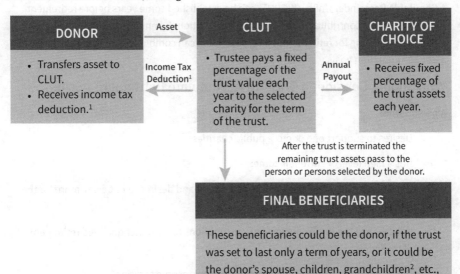

DONOR		CLUT		CHARITY OF CHOICE
• Transfers asset to CLUT. • Receives income tax deduction.[1]	Asset → ← Income Tax Deduction[1]	• Trustee pays a fixed percentage of the trust value each year to the selected charity for the term of the trust.	Annual Payout →	• Receives fixed percentage of the trust assets each year.

After the trust is terminated the remaining trust assets pass to the person or persons selected by the donor.

FINAL BENEFICIARIES

These beneficiaries could be the donor, if the trust was set to last only a term of years, or it could be the donor's spouse, children, grandchildren[2], etc., which may also produce an estate tax reduction.

---

[1] The income tax deduction, allowable only to grantor trusts, may have to be spread over more than one year if it exceeds certain percentage of income limitations.

[2] Choosing grandchildren (or later descendants) to receive the assets when the trust terminates may trigger the Generation-Skipping Transfer Tax (GSTT).

Supplementing Retirement Income with a CRUT

Another Way to Fund Retirement

In many instances, a charitable remainder trust is set up to provide cash flow during retirement, with the donor making a single, large gift to the trust. Such a trust allows an individual to combine charitable goals with retirement income planning.

A Charitable Remainder Unitrust (CRUT) can be established some years before retirement. Beyond the initial contribution, the CRUT allows additional, annual gifts to the trust. For individuals planning for retirement, this type of trust can combine charitable objectives with asset accumulation goals.

Who Should Consider a CRUT to Accumulate Retirement Assets?

A person who:

- Desires to support one or more public charities.

- Has a high level of current income;

- Has at least five to ten years before retirement and desires to put away more for the golden years;

- Has reached the maximum level of contributions to his or her qualified retirement plan; and/or

- Needs to shelter retirement funds from current income taxation.

The "Flip" CRUT – A Typical Example

- The donor establishes a CRUT with income for life or for the lives of the donor and/or spouse. Payouts are set at the annual minimum 5.0% of the net fair market value of assets or the income generated by the trust, whichever is less. The trust document specifies that the trust will convert ("flip") from its net income format to a standard form of unitrust at some pre-determined date or other triggering event. At that point, the trustee will distribute a full 5% of the trust's then value using both income and corpus if required. Prior to the "flip," the trust payout is limited to actual net income earned, up to the 5.0% payout limit.

Supplementing Retirement Income with a CRUT

- The donor makes annual gifts to the trust.

- In the early years, the trustee invests the annual gifts in capital gain assets which generate little or no current income.

- At the death of the last income beneficiary, the trust assets pass directly to the charity.

The result: Due to very small (perhaps zero) payouts in the pre-retirement years, the assets in the trust can grow much larger. When the 5.0% payments begin, the annual income can be substantially higher.

How It Works – A Hypothetical Example

Assumptions:

Married couple ages 45 and 42. First spouse dies at age 83, second spouse also dies at age 83.
Gifts of $25,000 per year (may be cash or appreciated property) are made each year for 20 years.
Net income CRUT for 20 years paying out the actual net income realized or 5.0%, whichever is less.
Trust "flips" at the end of the 20th year to a standard trust which must pay 5.0% of the trust value.
In years 1 through 20, trust assets are invested for total return; the analysis assumes 1% net income realized and paid as income with 6.0% as growth.
In years 21 through 42, trust assets are invested for total return; the analysis assumes 1.0% net income and 6.0% growth.

Pre-Retirement Period – Maximize Capital Accumulation, Minimized Income and Taxes

Year	Total Contributions to CRUT at $25,000/Year	Cumulative Deduction Allowed	Cumulative Pre-Retirement Income	CRUT Year-End Value
1	$25,000	$3,229	$32	$25,193
5	125,000	17,785	3,789	147,733
10	250,000	40,236	16,180	347,083
15	375,000	68,406	39,809	613,859
20	500,000	103,424	78,477	970,864

Supplementing Retirement Income with a CRUT

Post-Retirement ("flip") Period – Maximize Income, Charitable Legacy

Year	Total Contributions to CRUT	Current-Year Income	Cumulative Post-Retirement Income	CRUT Year-End Value
22	$500,000	$49,514	$98,057	$1,010,087
24	500,000	51,514	200,075	1,050,895
26	500,000	53,596	306,216	1,093,351
28	500,000	55,761	416,645	1,137,522
30	500,000	58,014	531,535	1,183,478
32	500,000	60,357	651,066	1,231,291
34	500,000	62,796	775,427	1,281,035
36	500,000	65,333	904,812	1,332,788
38	500,000	67,972	1,039,423	1,386,633
40	500,000	70,718	1,179,473	1,442,653
42	500,000	73,575	1,325,181	1,500,936

Total post-retirement income..$1,325,181

Charitable legacy (remainder)..................................... $1,500,936

Asset Replacement Trust

The combination of a charitable remainder trust (CRT) and an asset replacement insurance trust can greatly benefit you, your heirs and your favorite charity.

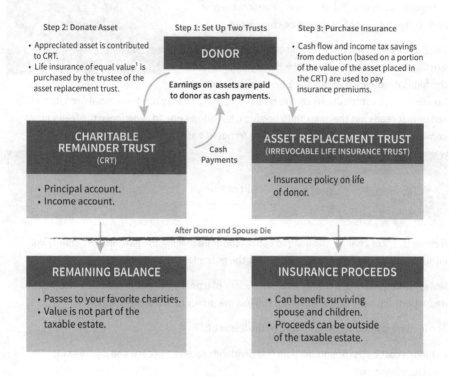

- The CRT can sell the appreciated asset without the trust paying any income tax on the capital gain. By reinvesting this larger amount, the trust can pay to the donor (and spouse, if desired) an expanded income for the rest of their lives.

- The cash payments received by the donor(s) are taxed under a four-tier system. Generally, ordinary income is paid first, followed by capital gain, other income, and trust principal.

The result: An appreciated asset has been given away which will eventually benefit a charity. Additionally, cash flow has increased for life. The value of the asset has been replaced with life insurance payable to the heirs. This combination is a true win-win-win situation.

---

[1] Where the donated asset faces a significant potential estate tax, some practitioners recommend insurance equal to the after-tax (after paying the estate tax) value of the asset rather than 100%.

Life Insurance Charitable Plan

For the individual who would like to make a substantial bequest to his or her favorite charity, but does not have sufficient assets to fulfill this desire, a charitable plan consisting of a life policy should be considered.

The policy owner (typically, the insured) can transfer an existing life insurance policy to the charity or contribute the funds necessary to purchase a new policy. Additional tax-deductible contributions can be made to help the charity pay the annual premium. This not only spreads out the amount to be given, but allows one to experience the feeling that comes from sharing with others on a more frequent basis.

YOU RECEIVE	CHARITY RECEIVES
• An income tax deduction, and	• A large sum in the future
• A feeling of satisfaction	

Gift of Policy[1]

If circumstances change, the insured can discontinue making the gifts and the charity will either continue the payments or surrender the policy for the cash values.

Note: Merely naming a charity as a beneficiary of a policy will not produce an income tax deduction, since the owner (insured) still has the power to surrender the policy.

The income tax deduction is limited to the lesser of:

- Donor's cost basis (premiums paid less dividends received in cash and policy loans outstanding); or

- The policy's value, which varies with type of policy.

    - **Ordinary life:** The interpolated terminal reserve (roughly cash value) plus any pre-paid premium.

    - **Paid-up policy:** Present cost of a comparable policy at the donor's current age.

    - **New policy:** The gross premium just paid.

    - **Term insurance:** The portion of premium that is still unearned by the insurer.

---

[1] This is generally funds to purchase a new policy and a small annual contribution to pay premiums.

Private Foundations

People give money and property to charity for a number of reasons. Among the most common are the following:

- To make a difference in the lives of others.

- The desire to help society by funding a worthy cause.

- To enjoy the income, gift, and estate tax benefits derived from charitable giving.

Despite these benefits, one concern a donor may have is the loss of control over money and property gifted to a charity. To meet this concern, a donor can create a private foundation that must distribute annually to charitable causes favored by the donor.[1]

What Is a Private Foundation?

A private foundation is a charitable organization created and funded by a donor (during life or at death) which is designed to achieve one or more specific charitable purposes. Overall management of the foundation is provided by a board of directors or trustees often selected by the donor. The directors or trustees can be paid reasonable compensation for their services.

Tax law describes a private foundation as a charitable organization exempt from income tax under IRC Sec. 501(c)(3) other than the following:

- Organizations that generally receive a substantial part of their support from the general public or from the government.

- Religious organizations.

- Educational institutions with regular learning facilities, a student body and a specific curriculum.

- Organizations devoted to promoting public safety.

In addition, a private foundation does not include any charitable organization which:

---

[1] A private foundation serves not only to distribute funds to charity, but also to transmit the donor's name and personal values to succeeding generations.

- Receives more than one-third of its support from the sum total of gifts, grants, contributions, membership fees and receipts from a permissible business or activity; and/or,

- Receives one-third or less of its support each year from the sum of gross investment income and excess unrelated business income.

Choice of Entity

A private foundation can be structured as either a corporation or a trust. There are advantages to each type of arrangement:

- A corporation may be more flexible than a trust, to meet changing circumstances. Corporations operate through a board of directors and officers.

- Trustees may be held to a higher degree of responsibility than corporate officers, with respect to liability.

- It may be easier to establish a trust. A trust can be written to allow the donor to be more specific and restrictive; an important point if a donor wants to realize a tax deduction before a tax year closes.

- The filing requirements for a trust may be simpler than for a corporation, which could reduce administrative costs.

Tax Deduction for Contributions to a Private Foundation

Contributions to a private foundation are generally deductible as follows:

- Cash contributions are generally deductible up to 30% of a donor's adjusted gross income (AGI).

- Gifts of appreciated property are generally deductible up to 20% of a donor's AGI.

- Gifts of qualified appreciated stock are fully deductible up to fair market value. The deduction for full market value of qualified appreciated stock by one donor is limited to 10% of the stock of a corporation.

- All appreciated property (other than qualified stock) contributed by a donor during the donor's lifetime is deductible only up to cost basis.

- Testamentary (at death) bequests of cash and property are fully deductible from the decedent's estate.

- Lifetime gifts of cash or appreciated property, which exceed the applicable 20% or 30% of AGI limitation, can be carried forward for up to five years.

Note: The contribution and deduction limitations described above are unique to private foundations. Gifts to public charities are treated differently under federal tax law.

Special Rules for Private Foundations

Private foundations are subject to a variety of complex tax rules that must be carefully followed to avoid additional taxation and/or penalties. Some of the most important rules include:

- **Failure to distribute income:** If a private foundation fails to distribute its annual income by the end of the year, it is subject to a tax of 30%. The tax can increase to 100% if the income is not distributed by the date the tax is assessed or by the date the IRS issues a warning (90-day letter).

- **Self dealing:** An excise tax is triggered when a disqualified person[1] engages in any of the following activities:

  - Selling, exchanging or leasing property.

  - Lending money or providing credit.

  - Furnishing goods or services.

  - Paying compensation or reimbursing expenses.

  - Transferring foundation income or assets to or for the use of a disqualified person.

  - Furnishing foundation money or property to a government official.

  A disqualified person who conducts an act of self-dealing is subject to an initial penalty tax of 10% of the amount involved and a 200% additional tax if the self-dealing isn't corrected in a timely manner. Foundation managers who knowingly participate in acts of self-dealing are subject to a tax of 5%. If foundation managers fail to correct an act, an additional penalty of 50% may be imposed.

---

[1] Under current law, a disqualified person is an individual who is a substantial contributor to a foundation, a foundation manager, certain family members, related business entities, government officials, and others who may hold a fiduciary capacity with regard to the foundation. A disqualified person can be held liable for an excise tax even if a transaction was completed at arms length.

- **Excess business holdings:** A private foundation that possesses any excess business holdings is subject to a tax of 10%.

- **Net investment income:** A private foundation is liable for an excise tax of 2% on its net investment income. This minimal tax is easily reduced to 1% by making qualified grants to public charities

- **Investment jeopardizes charitable purpose:** An excise tax of 10% is imposed if the foundation invests its income and funds in such a way that its charitable purpose is jeopardized.

- **Legislative activities:** An excise tax of 20% is imposed if funds are used for legislative activities or for engaging in propaganda. In addition, foundation managers who authorize such expenditures can be liable for an additional 5% tax.

- As an alternative, a prospective donor may wish to consider contributing to a Donor Advised Fund, a simpler and less expensive option.

Seek Professional Guidance

The rules for establishing and managing a private foundation are extensive and complex. The counsel and guidance of competent, experienced income tax and legal professionals is strongly recommended.

Supporting Organizations

Supporting organizations, like private foundations, are often established and funded by individuals or families. Unlike private foundations, however, supporting organizations are afforded many of the benefits of being a public charity, while avoiding the taxes and regulations imposed on private foundations by federal income tax law.

A supporting organization which meets the requirements of IRC Sec. 509(a)(3) is distinguished from a private foundation in that it serves public, rather than private, purposes; it is this public focus which justifies the organization's status as a nonprivate foundation.

Creating a Supporting Organization

A supporting organization is typically created as a charitable trust. Occasionally, the donor will establish the organization as a nonprofit corporation under local (state) law. At least one public charity (university, hospital, museum, etc.) should be identified in the organizing document as a recipient of the new organization's support. Frequently, the creator and his or her family serve as trustees or directors of the supporting organization, along with representatives of the charities named.

Qualification as a Supporting Organization

The following three tests must be satisfied:

- The supporting organization must operate exclusively for the benefit of one or more specified public charities.

- It must be operated, supervised, or controlled by or in connection with, one or more public charities.

- The supporting organization must not be controlled (directly or indirectly) by a disqualified person.[1]

Tax Treatment of Supporting Organizations

Generally, a supporting organization is accorded the benefits of being a public charity, including the following:

---

[1] A disqualified person is defined in IRC Sec. 4946.

- **Income tax deduction for gifts:** Gifts of cash to a supporting organization (as with a public charity) are deductible up to 50% of the donor's adjusted gross income in the year of contribution. Gifts of appreciated property held long term are deductible form the donor's taxable income at full market value, up to 30% of the donor's adjusted gross income, with a five-year carry forward of any unused deductions. Any unused deductions may be carried forward up to five years.

- **Not subject to private foundation excise taxes:** Specifically, the prohibitions against self-dealing, minimum distribution requirements, taxes on net-investment income, excess business holdings, jeopardizing investments, and prohibited expenditures do not apply to supporting organizations.

Control Issues

While many individuals focus on the tax benefits of charitable giving, other donors are concerned with the loss of control over money and property gifted to a charity. For such patrons, the private foundation is usually the preferred means of achieving philanthropic goals. The greater control found in a private foundation comes at a cost, in the form of greater tax restrictions and increased regulation.

While the creator of a supporting organization does not have the same level of control as the individual who establishes a private foundation, he or she can still have a significant voice in the organization. From a practical standpoint, the supported charities will carefully consider the opinion of the ultimate source of their support.

Family Participation

An unspoken benefit of creating a supporting organization is the opportunity for a donor to involve his or her children and/or grandchildren in directing the family's philanthropic legacy to public charities in the community. By involving a younger generation in the organization, a donor is sometimes able to convey deeply held family values, while at the same time transferring funds to charitable causes.

Private Foundation vs. Supporting Organization

	Private Foundation (non-operating)	Supporting Organization
Deductibility limitations		
Value of appreciated assets	Cost basis[1] at time of transfer	Market value at time of transfer
Deduction allowable in tax year		
Gifts of cash	Up to 30% of AGI	Up to 50% of AGI
Gifts of appreciated assets	Up to 20% of AGI	Up to 30% of AGI
Carryover of deduction	Maximum of five years	Maximum of five years
Tax restrictions excise taxes		
Tax on net investment income	Yes	No
Tax on self-dealing	Yes	No
Tax on failure to distribute income	Yes	No
Tax on excess business holdings	Yes	No
Tax on jeopardy investments	Yes	No
Tax on taxable expenditures	Yes	No

---

[1] A market value deduction is allowed for publicly traded stock under IRC Sec. 170(e)(5).

Charitable Remainder Trust
Data and Assumptions

January 1, 2018

Client

Paul Johnson
Sally Johnson

Charitable Remainder Trust Information

Donor's Name(s) for Reports:	Paul and Sally Johnson
First Income Beneficiary:	Paul Johnson
First Income Beneficiary DOB	1/15/1936
Second Income Beneficiary:	Sally Johnson
Second Income Beneficiary DOB	2/7/1938
Trust Transfer Date	3/12/2018
Charitable Beneficiary:	UC Irvine
Assets Transferred to Trust	$1,000,000
Assumed Rate of Return on Trust	5.25%
Duration of Payments	Term of Years
Trust Term	15
Annual Income Payout for CRAT	5.00%
Annual Income Payout for CRUT	6.00%
IRC Section 7520 Rate	3.20%

Wealth Replacement Trust

Life Insurance Death Benefit	$900,000
First Year Premium	$12,500

Charitable Remainder Annuity Trust

Donor: Paul and Sally Johnson

Charitable Beneficiary: UC Irvine

Income Beneficiary: Paul Johnson
                       Sally Johnson

There are many reasons for making a gift or a bequest to a charitable organization. Some of these reasons may include; compassion for those in need, religious or spiritual commitment, support for the arts, science and education. Whatever the reason, U.S. tax law is designed to encourage these gifts.

A charitable remainder annuity trust (CRAT) is an irrevocable trust which pays a fixed dollar amount each year to a beneficiary. This dollar amount is based on applying the trust percentage to the value of the assets initially transferred to the trust by the donor. The charitable entity receives the amount in the trust when the trust terminates.

This illustrates placing an asset worth $1,000,000 into this irrevocable trust. In return, you or your selected beneficiaries could receive $50,000 per year. Your potential income tax deduction would be $411,645. This arrangement will pass the 10% test.

A minimum of 10% of the property placed in the trust must be passed to the charitable beneficiary in order to comply with IRS rules.

Income Tax Deduction

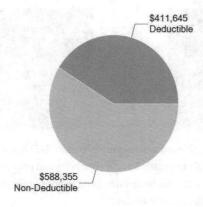

$411,645
Deductible

$588,355
Non-Deductible

Wealth Replacement Trust

Donor: Paul and Sally Johnson
Charitable beneficiary: UC Irvine

Step 2: Donate Asset

- Appreciated asset is contributed to CRAT
- Life insurance of equal value[1] is purchased by the trustee of the asset replacement trust

Step 1: Set Up Two Trusts

DONOR

Earnings on assets are paid to donor as cash payments.

Step 3: Purchase Insurance

- Cash flow and income tax savings from deduction (based on a portion of the value of the asset placed in the CRT) are used to pay insurance premiums

$1,000,000
Asset

First Year Premium
$12,500

CHARITABLE REMAINDER ANNUITY TRUST (CRAT)

- Principal account.
- Income account.

Annual Cash
Payments[2]
$50,000
(5.00 %)

WEALTH REPLACEMENT TRUST
(IRREVOCABLE LIFE INSURANCE TRUST)

- Insurance policy on life of donor.

When the Term of Years Has Passed
or Last Beneficiary Dies

REMAINING BALANCE

- Passes to your favorite charities.
- Value is not part of the taxable estate.

INSURANCE PROCEEDS
$900,000

- Can benefit surviving spouse and children.
- Proceeds can be outside of the taxable estate.

The combination of a charitable remainder annuity trust (CRAT) and a wealth replacement insurance trust can greatly benefit your heirs and your favorite charity. The insurance proceeds will pass to your designated beneficiaries upon your death. The proceeds may not be includable in your estate.

---

[1] Where the donated asset faces a significant potential estate tax, some practitioners recommend insurance equal to the after-tax (after paying the estate tax) value of the asset rather than 100%.

[2] Annual payments remain the same each year.

Charitable Remainder Unitrust

Donor: Paul and Sally Johnson
Charitable Beneficiary: UC Irvine

Income Beneficiary: Paul Johnson
Sally Johnson

There are many reasons for making a gift or a bequest to a charitable organization. Some of these reasons may include; compassion for those in need, religious or spiritual commitment, support for the arts, science and education. Whatever the reason, U.S. tax law is designed to encourage these gifts.

A charitable remainder unitrust (CRUT) is an irrevocable trust which pays a fixed percentage of the trust balance each year to one or more beneficiaries. These income beneficiaries may be the donor, the donor's spouse, the donor's children, etc. The charitable entity receives the amount left in the trust after the income beneficiaries die, or after a set number of years.

This illustrates placing an asset worth $1,000,000 into this irrevocable trust. In return, you or your beneficiaries could receive average annual payments of $55,727. Your potential income tax deduction would be $407,191. This arrangement will pass the 10% test.

A minimum of 10% of the property placed in the trust must be passed to the charitable beneficiary in order to comply with IRS rules.

Income Tax Deduction

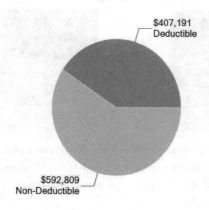

$407,191
Deductible

$592,809
Non-Deductible

Wealth Replacement Trust

Donor: Paul and Sally Johnson
Charitable beneficiary: UC Irvine

Step 2: Donate Asset

- Appreciated asset is contributed to CRUT.
- Life insurance of equal value[1] is purchased by the trustee of the asset replacement trust.

Step 1: Set Up Two Trusts

DONOR

Earnings on assets are paid to donor as cash payments.

Step 3: Purchase Insurance

- Cash flow and income tax savings from deduction (based on a portion of the value of the asset placed in the CRT) are used to pay insurance premiums.

$1,000,000
Asset

First Year Premium
$12,500

CHARITABLE REMAINDER UNITRUST (CRUT)

- Principal account.
- Income account.

Annual Cash Payments[2]
$55,727
(6.00 %)

WEALTH REPLACEMENT TRUST
(IRREVOCABLE LIFE INSURANCE TRUST)

- Insurance policy on life of donor.

When the Term of Years Has Passed
or Last Beneficiary Dies

REMAINING BALANCE

- Passes to your favorite charities.
- Value is not part of the taxable estate.

INSURANCE PROCEEDS
$900,000

- Can benefit surviving spouse and children.
- Proceeds can be outside of the taxable estate.

The combination of a charitable remainder unitrust (CRUT) and a wealth replacement insurance trust can greatly benefit your heirs and your favorite charity. The insurance proceeds will pass to your designated beneficiaries upon your death. The proceeds may not be includable in your estate.

---

[1] Where the donated asset faces a significant potential estate tax, some practitioners recommend insurance equal to the after-tax (after paying the estate tax) value of the asset rather than 100%.

[2] Annual payments will vary with the value of the trust. Assumes a rate of return on trust assets of 5.25%.

Agenda for Discussion

List Planning Objectives

Level of Importance

	High	Medium	Low
1. Getting the estate in order	_____	_____	_____
2. Probate avoidance	_____	_____	_____
3. Death tax reduction	_____	_____	_____
4. Care of children after death	_____	_____	_____
5. Transferring the business	_____	_____	_____
6. Providing sufficient cash flow	_____	_____	_____
7. Covering risk exposure	_____	_____	_____
8. Retirement planning	_____	_____	_____

Specific Areas Which Need Current Review

1. ___ Present wills and trusts
2. ___ Insurance program
3. ___ Current investments
4. ___ Fringe benefit package
5. ___ Business agreements
6. ___ Gifting program
7. ___ Disability income
8. ___ Long-term care

9. _____

10. _____

11. _____

12. _____

Agenda

Items to Be Discussed
1. Introductions
2. Review current financial status
3. List priorities
4. Discuss next steps
5. Ensure all your questions are answered

Business Owner Planning Needs

Below is a list of concerns that may be of particular interest to you, the business owner. Indicate the level of importance of each item with a check mark.

	Level of Importance		
	High	Medium	Low
Business Concerns			
Business Succession Planning			
Key Employee Planning			
Executive Benefit Planning			
Estate Concerns			
Planning Estate Distributions			
Estate Tax Planning			
Charitable Planning			
Survivorship Needs Planning			
Retirement Concerns			
Planning for Your Retirement			
Qualified Retirement Plans			
Traditional IRA/Roth IRA			
Investment Risk Analysis			
Other			
Long-term Care Planning			
Education Planning			
Disability Income Planning			
Life Insurance Planning			

Planner Input Sheet

Planner: _____

Case No.: _____

Date: _____

Client Name: _____

Date Needed: _____

Instructions for Preparation of Proposal

Place client's name in header or footer? _____

___ No

___ Yes -- _____

Place page number in lower-left corner of each page?

___ No

___ Yes -- Begin with page number _____

File numbers to be printed (in the same order they are to appear in the report) are as follows:

___,___,___,___,___,___,___,___,___,___,___,___,___,___

___,___,___,___,___,___,___,___,___,___,___,___,___,___

___,___,___,___,___,___,___,___,___,___,___,___,___,___

Remember - If it's too long it may not get read!

    ___ Add disclaimer at beginning of report.
    ___ Omit disclaimer at beginning of report.

Other Instructions:

_____

_____

_____

_____

_____

_____

Receipt for Documents

The following documents are received this ___ day of _____, 20___, for the purpose of study and analysis for _____. It is understood that this material will be treated confidentially and returned as soon as the review process is completed, or sooner if requested.

Reviewer's Signature:_____

Address:_____ Phone No:_____

Items Received

Wills

___Client   Dated_____   ___ Spouse   Dated _____

Trust agreements

Type:_____   Dated: _____

Type: _____   Dated: _____

Business agreements

Type: _____   Dated: _____

Type: _____   Dated:_____

Insurance and annuity contracts

Company	Policy No.	Company	Policy No.

Receipt for Documents

Mutual Fund, Brokerage and 401(k) Account Statements (list companies)

_____

_____

_____

Other Statements (list companies)

_____

_____

The policies and documents for which the above receipt was given have been returned to me.

Date: _____ Client Signature: _____

Planning Task List

Items for the Client to Accomplish

In order for the planning process to proceed successfully and smoothly, the following items need to be accomplished by the indicated dates.

❑ 1. _____

_____

_____   Due date: _____

❑ 2. _____

_____

_____   Due date: _____

❑ 3. _____

_____

_____   Due date: _____

❑ 4. _____

_____

_____   Due date: _____

❑ 5. _____

_____

_____   Due date: _____

❑ 6. _____

_____

_____   Due date: _____

❑ Please, call if there are questions or concerns: _____

Planning Task List

Items for the Planner to Accomplish

☐ 1. _____

_____

_____   Due date: _____

☐ 2. _____

_____

_____   Due date: _____

☐ 3. _____

_____

_____   Due date: _____

☐ 4. _____

_____

_____   Due date: _____

☐ 5. _____

_____

_____   Due date: _____

☐ 6. _____

_____

_____   Due date: _____

Action Items

If we are to be successful in implementing the steps we have agreed upon it is usually best to have a timetable. The following table shows who needs to complete the items and when they need to be completed. Working together we will finish these action items in a timely manner.

Date	Who	Action
3/12/2012	Paul	Complete Life Insurance Application
3/24/2012	Paul	Complete Physical
4/1/2012	Sally	Make first payment on policy

Goals

Reviewing your goals is an important step in making sure the action plan is on the right course. Listed below are the items that you said were important to you.

Goals to Be Accomplished
Family is taken care of if something happens to Paul
Make sure Ryan and Patty's education is paid for
Retire at age 65 with current lifestyle

Client Referral

Others Who May Appreciate Our Services

One of the key sources of future business is the thoughtful referral received from a satisfied client. Are there friends, family members, or co-workers who might benefit from our services?

Name: _____

Address: _____

City/ST/Zip: _____

Telephone: _____Work Home (circle one)

Relationship: _____

Name: _____

Address: _____

City/ST/Zip: _____

Telephone: _____Work Home (circle one)

Relationship: _____

Name: _____

Address: _____

City/ST/Zip: _____

Telephone: _____Work Home (circle one)

Relationship: _____

Name: _____

Address: _____

City/ST/Zip: _____

Telephone: _____Work Home (circle one)

Relationship: _____

Business Owner Planning Needs

Below is a list of concerns that may be of particular interest to you, the business owner. Indicate the level of importance of each item with a check mark.

	Level of Importance		
	High	Medium	Low
Business Concerns			
Business Succession Planning			
Key Employee Planning			
Executive Benefit Planning			
Estate Concerns			
Planning Estate Distributions			
Estate Tax Planning			
Charitable Planning			
Survivorship Needs Planning			
Retirement Concerns			
Planning for Your Retirement			
Qualified Retirement Plans			
Traditional IRA/Roth IRA			
Investment Risk Analysis			
Other			
Long-term Care Planning			
Education Planning			
Disability Income Planning			
Life Insurance Planning			

Divorce Checklist

A married couple functions, on many levels, as a single "unit." A divorce splits that unit apart, leaving two separate individuals with separate lives. Once the decision to divorce has been made, a number of issues need to be considered to insure a successful conclusion.

Legal and Professional Guidance

Most professionals recommend that each party to the divorce retain an attorney to advise and guide them through the divorce process. An experienced attorney, familiar with local law, can answer many questions surrounding the legal issues involved. Other individuals, such as tax or investment professionals, may also need to be involved.

- **Pre-nuptial agreement:** A pre-nuptial agreement can have a major impact on the terms of a divorce.

- **Annulment vs. divorce:** In some cases an "annulment" (cancellation of the marriage as if it had never occurred) may be possible.

- **Who's going to pay?** In most cases, divorce is expensive. The parties involved will need to determine how the expenses of the divorce will be paid.

- **Income tax issues:** Unless a divorce is final by the end of the calendar year, a couple is still considered to be married for federal income tax purposes.[1] The guidance of a CPA, IRS Enrolled Agent, or other tax professional is strongly recommended.

- **Restraining order:** If abuse or violence is present, a court restraining order may be required to insure the safety of all involved individuals.

Children

If there are minor children involved, a number of questions must be answered:

- **Custody:** Who will the child (or children) live with? One parent may have sole custody or custody may be a joint responsibility.

- **Visitation rights:** What visitation rights does the non-custodial parent have? What about the grandparents?

---

[1] The comments here reflect federal income tax law. State or local income tax law may differ.

- **Children's rights:** What rights do the children have? For example, can a child choose which parent he or she wishes to live with?

- **Child support:** Is child support needed? If so, who will pay the child support, how much, and for how long? A related issue concerns providing healthcare.[1]

- **Income tax exemption:** Who will claim the income tax exemption for the children? By default, federal income tax law grants the exemption to the custodial parent, but this may be changed if the parties agree.[2]

- **College funding:** Have provisions been made for funding college?

Division of Wealth

Dividing a couple's wealth can be one of the most contentious parts of a divorce. Separately owned assets generally remain the property of the individual owner. Jointly held assets may have to be sold and the cash proceeds divided among the spouses.

- **Earned income:** How much each spouse earns from employment outside the home can determine whether alimony might be paid, who pays it, how much, and for how long.[3]

- **Real estate:** Including the family residence, vacation homes, or investment real estate.

- **Checking and savings accounts:** Funds held in banks or credit unions.

- **Stocks and bonds:** Assets held in securities accounts.

- **Retirement accounts:** IRAs, corporate qualified retirement plans, and non-qualified deferred compensation arrangements.

- **Life insurance:** Some insurance policies develop cash values over time.

---

[1] Under federal income tax law, child support is not reportable income to the recipient and may not be deducted by the payer.

[2] The Tax Cuts and Jobs Act of 2017 temporarily suspends the deduction for personal and dependent exemptions for 2018 – 2025.

[3] Under one provision of the Tax Cuts and Jobs Act of 2017, alimony and separate maintenance payments are not deductible by the payor spouse nor are they includable in income by the recipient spouse. This change is permanent and is generally effective for any divorce or separation instrument executed after December 31, 2018. Under prior law, alimony and separate maintenance payments were deductible by the payor spouse as an adjustment to gross income and were includable in income by the recipient spouse.

- **Personal belongings:** Including clothing, furniture, and furnishings.

- **Large personal property items:** Such as autos, boats, or airplanes.

- **Hidden assets:** One spouse may attempt to hide assets from the other spouse.

- **Debts:** Dividing joint obligations are a part of the divorce process.

Moving Forward – Establishing Separate Lives

A number of steps must be taken to establish a new, separate life. Some of these are defensive in nature, while others are a normal part of establishing a separate identity.

- **Cash flow analysis:** Consider income and expenses. If an individual is not already employed outside the home, a job may be necessary. Also, additional education may be a benefit.

- **Alimony:** One spouse may be required to make cash payments to the other.

- **Where to live?** One spouse may remain in the former family residence while the other spouse must find a new home.

- **Separate finances:** Commonly encountered issues include:

  - Closing any joint credit cards, and savings and checking accounts. Separate checking and savings accounts should be opened. Separate credit cards should be obtained. Any joint securities accounts should be closed and separate accounts opened.

  - Verify individual credit reports.

  - As needed, obtain separate life, auto, and homeowner's (or renter's) insurance.

  - Change beneficiaries of life insurance policies and retirement plans.

  - Estate planning should be re-done, including a new will and/or trust.

Beneficiary Audit Checklist

Client: _____   Date: _____

Document or Asset	Document Location	Firm or Service Provider	Estimated Dollar Value	Beneficiary or Beneficiaries
Will				
Trust				
Life Insurance Policy				
Qualified Retirement Plan				
Traditional IRA				
Roth IRA				
Annuity				
Nonqualified Deferred Compensation Plan				
Other 1				
Other 2				
Other 3				
Other 4				
Other 5				
Other 6				
Other 7				
Other 8				

Financial Review Checklist

A financial review typically covers a number of topics. The review is designed to catch problems before they occur, measure progress toward established goals and make necessary adjustments in response to changed conditions.

Review Topics:

- **Cash flow management:** Is there more month than there is income? What about an emergency cash reserve? Can you easily pay your debts each month?

- **Risk management – Property and casualty:** If your home burns down, can you afford to rebuild? What about auto insurance? If you're sued, do you have liability coverage?

- **Risk management – Health, disability, and long-term care:** Becoming sick or injured, and not seeking medical care, can have life-and-death consequences. A serious disability often reduces income while increasing the need for medical and long-term care.

- **Risk management – Life insurance:** If you died today, would your loved ones be able to maintain their existing lifestyle? Or, would they have to sell the home or other assets?

- **Income tax:** Did you owe additional taxes last year? What methods are you using to keep your tax burden as low as legally possible?

- **Accumulation – General:** How much will it cost to send the kids to college? Do you have that much set aside? Are there other dreams you can't pay for out of current cash flow?

- **Accumulation – Retirement:** Can you afford to retire? Do you know how much it will cost to retire? What strategies are you following to ensure a comfortable retirement?

- **Estate planning:** If death occurred today, would your estate pass to your chosen heirs? If you haven't planned ahead, it might not. Do you have an estate tax problem?

Comments or Questions

_____

_____

_____

_____

_____

_____

_____

_____

_____

_____

_____

Life Events Checklist

Change is a constant part of every life. In order to determine how we may best serve you, please complete the form below and return it to us at your earliest convenience.

Common Life Events

- ❏ New child or grandchild
- ❏ New job or promotion
- ❏ Receipt of an inheritance
- ❏ Major investment gain/loss
- ❏ Health concerns

- ❏ Change in marital status
- ❏ Change in estate plan
- ❏ Sale or purchase of home
- ❏ Start/purchase a business
- ❏ Sold or acquired assets

- ❏ Death of family member
- ❏ New investments or insurance
- ❏ Retirement
- ❏ Gain/loss business partner
- ❏ Other: _____

Areas of Interest or Concern

- ❏ Retirement planning
- ❏ Estate planning
- ❏ Major asset purchase/lease
- ❏ Business/exec. benefits
- ❏ Pers. property/liability ins.

- ❏ Education funding
- ❏ Income tax planning
- ❏ Planning for parents
- ❏ Business continuation
- ❏ Disability income

- ❏ Investment review
- ❏ Survivor benefit planning
- ❏ Health/LTC planning
- ❏ Charitable giving
- ❏ Other: _____

Additional Comments and Notes

_____

_____

_____

Contacting You

Name:_____   Address:_____

Telephone:_____

Best time to call:_____

❏   Please contact me as soon as possible   Email:_____

Recommendations

After reviewing your situation, these are the next steps that will be needed to reach your goals.

1. Obtain $500,000 additional coverage for Paul

2. Review budget for savings

3. Increase retirement savings for Sally by $350

4. Set up college funds for Ryan and Patty

Index

C

Cafeteria plans, 119, 121, 127, 138-141
Capital asset, 221, 224, 242, 516, 700,
  1332-1333, 1341
Capital gains, 211, 221-224, 239, 242,
  244, 247-248, 260, 278, 287, 300,
  347, 363, 396-397, 404, 406, 429,
  444, 453, 527, 550, 552, 657, 687,
  702, 1055-1056, 1068, 1089, 1130,
  1229, 1232, 1290, 1338-1339, 1348,
  1351, 1356, 1363, 1365
Capital losses, 221, 243
Capitalization Rate, 1244, 1246, 1252,
  1255-1256
Cash Equivalents, 45-47, 379, 425
Cash Flow, 4, 25, 33, 37, 42-43, 317,
  362-363, 365, 482, 553, 632, 644,
  757, 794, 848, 1005, 1092, 1246,
  1250, 1338, 1351-1352, 1356, 1376,
  1379, 1390, 1392-1393, 1407, 1409
Cash Management, 2, 25-28
Certificate of Deposit (CD), 31, 915
CGA, 1362
Chapter 7, 56
Chapter 13, 56, 59
Charitable bequests, 1036
Charitable giving, 4, 19, 304, 309,
  1008, 1010, 1337, 1339-1340, 1365,
  1367, 1381, 1386, 1411
CLAT, 1370-1372
CLUT, 1373-1375
COBRA, 105, 107, 133, 136-137, 147,
  152, 301
Collectibles, 46-47, 222-223, 244,
  287, 320, 336, 365, 527, 545, 647,
  650, 812, 816, 820
College, 8-10, 13, 15, 17-18, 45, 52,
  61, 265, 282, 379, 437, 460, 474,
  548, 755-761, 767-768, 770,
  773-774, 785-800, 802, 839, 855,
  867, 870, 874, 879, 884, 890, 933,
  935-936, 1134, 1406, 1409, 1412
College funding, 8, 933, 1134, 1406
Commodities, 46-47, 238, 363-364,
  399, 414, 446
Community property, 677, 1007,
  1012, 1044, 1048, 1050, 1052,
  1055-1057, 1067, 1193
Consumer Price Index, 20, 253, 265,
  344-345, 351, 435-436, 440, 757,
  840
Contingent Deferred sales charge, 391,
  393, 395
Corporate bond, 431-433
Corporate Continuation Plans,
  1192-1193
Corporate Stock Redemption,
  1209-1210, 1229-1230, 1293
Coverdell Education Savings Account,
  760, 765, 771, 776-781, 783
CRAT, 1350-1351, 1353-1354, 1358,
  1388-1390
Credit card, 7, 9, 21, 23, 51-52, 55,
  60-63, 235, 503
Credit record, 9, 51, 55-56
Credit report, 22-23, 51, 54-55, 57-59
CRT, 237, 1348-1349, 1358-1359,
  1379, 1390, 1392
CRUT, 1354-1358, 1376-1378, 1388,
  1391-1392
Custodial account, 122, 150, 559, 760,
  767, 774, 783, 1077, 1279
Custodian, 150, 230, 523, 541, 549,
  1053, 1074-1076, 1234

D

Defined Benefit (DB), 304, 491
Defined benefit (DB) Pension Plans,
  304

Government securities, 434-439
GRAT, 1125-1127
GRIT, 1125, 1132
GRUT, 1125, 1127

H

Health care portability, 133-135
Health reimbursement arrangement
(HRA), 146, 148
Health savings account (HSA), 149,
155, 525, 543, 690
Hedge fund, 364, 446-447
Higher education savings plan,
764-769, 772
Holding title, 1052-1054, 1057
Home Ownership, 64, 66, 471
Human life value, 862
Hurricane tax relief, 313-316

I

ILIT, 1140, 1142, 1146, 1153,
1163-1164, 1168, 1171, 1303-1304
Incentive Stock Option, 1325-1328,
1331
Income in respect of a decedent, 913,
921, 1103-1106, 1335
Income Tax Deduction, 73, 281, 310,
913, 1084, 1105, 1338-1342, 1344,
1349-1351, 1353-1354, 1356-1357,
1360, 1362-1363, 1365, 1368-1373,
1375, 1380, 1386, 1389, 1391
Income tax tables, 213-218, 1189
Income taxation, 233, 361, 626, 686,
894, 947, 954, 959, 967, 973, 1100,
1135-1136, 1139, 1183, 1209,
1239-1240, 1294, 1331, 1376
Index fund, 372, 397-398

Indexes and Averages, 420-422
Individual Retirement Account (IRA),
149, 470
Inflation risk, 337-338, 361, 389, 398,
408, 430, 433, 438-440, 445, 527,
545
Inflation-protected securities, 436,
439-442
Installment sale, 1114, 1120-1121,
1232, 1265
Insurance company rating systems,
929-931
Investment advisor, 382-383, 394-396,
1008
Investment real estate, 46-47, 471,
1406
Investment risk, 73, 336-339, 372-373,
379, 405, 425, 450, 469-470, 473,
495, 552, 568, 575, 581-582, 590,
612, 617, 621, 627, 652, 658-659,
663, 672, 758-759, 762, 767, 769,
897-898, 903-905, 1175, 1395, 1404
IRA Historical Limits, 522
IRA rollover, 695-697, 716, 721, 724
IRC Sec. 72, 238, 535, 560, 609, 625,
647, 667, 693, 697, 751-752, 907,
915, 917, 922, 1001
IRC Sec. 72(t)(2)(A)(iv), 751-752
IRC Sec. 101, 173, 848, 1085, 1193,
1202, 1204, 1208-1209, 1213-1214,
1217, 1219, 1221-1225, 1230,
1236-1237, 1239-1240, 1272, 1275,
1281, 1286, 1294, 1297, 1299,
1310, 1313, 1319, 1321, 1329
IRC Sec. 103, 443
IRC Sec. 104, 233-234, 1264
IRC Sec. 104(a)(3), 233-234, 1264
IRC Sec. 105, 132, 145, 147
IRC Sec. 106, 132, 233
IRC Sec. 125, 138, 156, 622
IRC Sec. 162, 130, 1104, 1238, 1308,

Liquidity risk, 338
Load fund, 389-390, 394, 402
Loan Amortization, 84-86
Long-term care, 6, 105, 116, 127, 139,
 146, 150, 152, 158-185, 187-189,
 304, 308, 311, 461, 463, 466, 851,
 892, 988, 993, 996, 1175,
 1322-1324, 1393, 1395, 1404, 1409
Long-term level premium, 863, 866
Long-term liabilities, 46, 48-49
LTC Partnership, 175-176
Lump-sum distributions, 305, 693-695

M

Mandatory withholding, 273-274, 313,
 693, 698-699
Marital deduction, 558, 850, 1008,
 1011, 1018, 1022, 1040, 1067,
 1086-1087, 1096, 1110-1112, 1139,
 1147, 1149, 1154-1155, 1159, 1351,
 1355
Market volatility, 425-427
Marketable government bond, 437
Medicaid, 91, 104-105, 112, 116, 128,
 160, 162, 166, 170, 174-177, 204,
 462-463, 978, 986, 988, 992-999,
 1003-1004, 1078
Medical decisions, 193, 197, 466, 970,
 1009, 1062-1063
Medical reimbursement plans, 132,
 144-145, 1320
Medical Savings Account (MSA),
 156, 979
Medicare, 91, 105, 112, 116, 120-122,
 125, 127, 136, 149, 152, 159,
 166-167, 171, 175, 204, 240-241,
 250-251, 286, 462-463, 466, 475,
 603, 626, 941, 945-946, 952, 965,
 976-989, 991, 993, 996-997, 1003

Medicare Advantage, 105, 462,
 979-980, 984, 986
Medicare Part C, 979-980
Medicare Part D, 125, 981-984
Medicare Parts A and B, 976-978, 986
Medigap, 166, 463, 466, 980, 986-991
Modern Portfolio Theory, 365,
 368-371
Modified endowment contract,
 853-854, 870, 875, 879, 884, 890
Money purchase plan, 569-575, 674
Monte Carlo Simulation, 340-341
Mortgage, 35, 38, 41, 44, 46, 64-67,
 69-80, 159, 162, 211-212, 228,
 235-236, 246, 254, 257, 261, 280,
 315, 386, 428-429, 431, 437,
 452-454, 467, 471, 474, 502-507,
 527, 545, 812, 825, 838, 856, 858,
 867, 934, 936, 1133, 1162
Mortgage interest, 66, 73, 78,
 211-212, 235-236, 254, 257, 261,
 280, 452-453, 1133
Municipal bond, 242, 245, 407, 430,
 443-445, 1290
Mutual fund, 27-28, 245, 247-248,
 372, 387-397, 399-410, 419, 430,
 433, 438, 442, 445, 454, 470, 653,
 759, 1398

N

National Spending Patterns, 34
Net Asset Value (NAV), 388-389,
 395, 399, 402
Net investment income, 121, 228, 235,
 237-241, 247, 347, 1384, 1387
Net Unrealized Appreciation (NUA),
 700
Net Worth, 44-49, 73, 367, 385-386,
 447, 450, 1193, 1245

Qualified Conservation Easement,
281, 291, 294, 1344-1347
Qualified Deferred Compensation
Plan, 1279-1280
Qualified retirement plan, 73,
273-274, 308, 311-313, 432, 441,
496, 653, 668, 677, 691, 693, 696,
700, 714, 719, 791, 1014, 1286,
1288, 1376, 1408
Qualified Roth Contribution, 666-668,
693, 698
Qualified Terminable Interest Property
(QTIP), 1086

R

Rebalancing, 395, 426-427
Redemption fee, 395
Refinancing, 69-70, 78, 80, 503, 507
REIT, 248, 253, 259, 452-454
Rent with option, 70
Renting, 60, 64, 67, 807
Required Minimum Distributions
(RMD), 706
Retirement goals, 8, 461, 481, 510,
512-513, 516
Retirement Income Planning, 491-494,
497, 1376
Retirement plan distributions, 688-691
Retirement planning, 5, 19, 167, 171,
458, 462, 465-467, 1185, 1329,
1393, 1411
Revenue ruling 2002-62, 752-753
Right of Accumulation (ROA), 395
Risk analysis, 377, 1175, 1395, 1404
Risk Management, 2, 4, 17, 182, 372,
808, 810, 815, 828, 833, 836, 855,
1409

S

S Corporation, 147, 238-239, 253,
259, 1059, 1104, 1181-1183, 1197,
1212-1213, 1284
Safe Harbor 401(k), 307, 613-616
Savings Accounts, 25-26, 31-32, 47,
122, 139, 154, 156-157, 245, 337,
361, 470, 527, 544, 758-759, 764,
776-777, 791, 950, 1048, 1406-1407
Savings Bonds, 27-28, 434-435,
437-438, 760, 789, 791, 1104, 1106
Sec. 2503(c), 219, 1071-1073
Section 529 Qualified Tuition Plans,
762-763
Secular Trust, 1289-1290
SEP-IRA, 652
Separate property, 1043-1044, 1052
Series EE Bonds, 27-28, 434-435
Series HH Bonds, 28, 436
Series I Bonds, 27-28, 435
Severalty, 1053
Share class, 391, 396
SIMPLE retirement plan, 653-658
Simplified Employee Pension (SEP),
524, 645-651, 665, 689
Single life table, 714, 717-719, 750,
752
Single sum, 327, 330, 332
Social Security, 21, 57, 136, 193,
196-197, 211, 239, 242, 245, 250,
274, 284, 286, 301, 444, 460, 466,
469, 471-472, 475, 477, 483-492,
494, 508-510, 516, 532-533, 538,
560, 563, 565, 569-570, 577, 584,
590, 593, 599, 609, 629, 635, 646,
649, 651, 662, 665, 670-671,
857-858, 933-934, 940-975, 978,
999, 1088
Social Security benefit, 21, 488,
508-509, 516, 933-934, 940, 942,

T

If you like this book, imagine what the application can do for you...

The only financial planning application combining needs analysis, client education and presentation materials. It is designed to help you promote productivity, increase sales, acquire and retain clients.

Analytics. Eleven needs analysis modules – including survivor needs, college funding, retirement needs, business continuation, estate needs and more – allow you to quickly develop an analysis and recommend solutions.

Financial Content. Over 600 reports on today's financial topics help educate clients, support recommendations and build trust.

Interactive Calculators. Over 60 easy-input calculators illustrate a need and motivate clients toward a decision.

Compelling Presentations. Professional presentations can be created in minutes that include a title page, table of contents, FINRA review letters and legal disclaimers.

For a **FREE** trial call (800) 777-3162 or visit Advisys.com